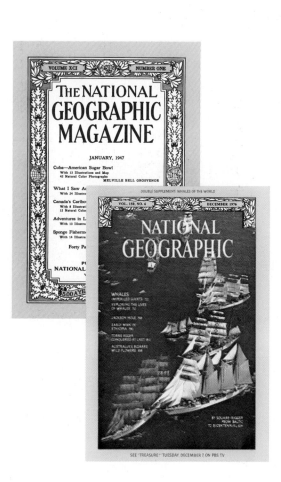

INDEX
1947-1976

NATIONAL
GEOGRAPHIC

INDEX

1947-1976

INCLUSIVE

NATIONAL GEOGRAPHIC SOCIETY

WASHINGTON, D. C.

Contents

5   Foreword by Robert E. Doyle, *President,
National Geographic Society*

6   Introduction by Gilbert M. Grosvenor, *Editor,*
NATIONAL GEOGRAPHIC MAGAZINE

14   A Picture History of National Geographic, 1947-1976

53   Expeditions and Scientific Researches of the Society,
with a preface by Melvin M. Payne, *Chairman,
Board of Trustees,* and *Chairman, Committee for
Research and Exploration*

82   Medals and Awards of the Society

88   Founders of the Society

90   Presidents and Members of the Board of Trustees

94   Geographical Distribution of Membership

97   INDEX to the NATIONAL GEOGRAPHIC 1947-1976

A publication of the National Geographic Society.

STAFF FOR THIS BOOK:

Editor: JOHN SCOFIELD

Project Editor: HOWARD E. PAINE

Text: ALLEN A. BORAIKO

Expeditions and Researches: PAUL H. OEHSER

Index: JOLENE M. BLOZIS, *Chief, Indexing Division;*
MARTHA K. HIGHTOWER, GEORGE I. BURNESTON III,
PHILIP G. GUTEKUNST, BARBARA L. KLEIN, ANNE K. McCAIN,
BRIT A. PETERSON, JESSICA C. TAYLOR, VIRGINIA
C. THOMPSON, LINDA C. CORBIN, ELLA L. SMITH

Research: ANN K. WENDT, *Chief;* FRANCES H. PARKER,
Associate Chief; CAROLYN H. ANDERSON, LESLEY
B. ROGERS, MICHAELINE A. SWEENEY

Design and Production: N. TAYLOR GREGG,
ROBERT E. PULLMAN, CHARLES C. UHL

Engraving and Printing: JOHN R. METCALFE

Printed and bound by R. R. Donnelley & Sons Company,
Crawfordsville, Indiana

OVERLEAF: CLOAKED IN SPRAY, A SOUTHERN RIGHT WHALE BREACHES
OFF PATAGONIA'S DESERT COAST. PHOTOGRAPH BY DES AND JEN BARTLETT.

Foreword

"I AM NOT A SCIENTIFIC MAN, nor can I lay claim to any special knowledge that would entitle me to be called a 'Geographer.'" Modest words like these often appear in the letters fellow National Geographic Society members write to me. It would surprise many of them to find that they are echoing the soft denial made in 1888 by Gardiner Greene Hubbard, a founder and first President of the Society.

Geographer or not, any member of the Society can come to know the world in astonishing and intimate detail. The key to this remarkable familiarity lies in this book and its companion volume, *National Geographic Index, 1888-1946*. With these comprehensive reference tools, past issues of NATIONAL GEOGRAPHIC yield a trove of authoritative information and rich images.

ROBERT S. OAKES

This volume, *National Geographic Index, 1947-1976*, contains more than 14,000 entries spanning thirty years and more than 2,000 lucid and fascinating articles. It guides you to the summit of Mount Everest and the face of the moon, directs you to intriguing facts about subjects as varied as Polynesia and plankton, and charts your course through time from ancient China to scientific breakthroughs as new as tomorrow.

Also in this volume, a special "Picture History of National Geographic, 1947-1976" recalls the phenomenal growth and change in your Society and its official journal during the past three decades. In 1947 the Society already numbered more than a million and a half members, a tremendous tribute to the late Gilbert H. Grosvenor, master builder of GEOGRAPHIC and Editor from 1899 to 1954. Working closely with him was the late John Oliver La Gorce, Editor from 1954 to 1957. Another close colleague, Thomas W. McKnew, former Secretary and now Advisory Chairman of the Board, helped encourage the Society's expansion to a worldwide membership of nearly 9 1/2 million at the end of 1976.

Outstanding editorial direction continued at NATIONAL GEOGRAPHIC under Melville Bell Grosvenor, who became Editor in 1957 and whose infectious enthusiasm inspired many Society projects: the first National Geographic globe and World Atlas, the modern Book Service and Special Publications, and an award-winning series of television specials. Now Editor Emeritus, he was succeeded in 1967 by Frederick G. Vosburgh, who ensured that accuracy, grace, and style continued to be the hallmark of GEOGRAPHIC writing.

In the introduction that follows, Gilbert M. Grosvenor, Editor since 1970, outlines the reasons for NATIONAL GEOGRAPHIC's success, among them an adherence to high editorial standards and a willingness to pioneer new processes and directions to achieve what has always been the Society's, and the magazine's, primary purpose, "the increase and diffusion of geographic knowledge."

Many of the letters I receive close with the gratifying postscript that, better than anything else, NATIONAL GEOGRAPHIC offers its readers the pleasure and excitement of having the world at their fingertips. You'll discover that the way to that pleasure and excitement is also at your fingertips—in this new *National Geographic Index, 1947-1976*.

Robert E. Doyle

PRESIDENT

Bringing the World
Into Your Home

AN INTRODUCTION BY GILBERT M. GROSVENOR

Editor, National Geographic Magazine

David Lewis and Ice Bird *enter Antarctica's Penola Strait.*

NOVEMBER 29, 1972: *The situation is not encouraging. My 32-foot steel sloop* Ice Bird *lies dismasted, wallowing uncontrollably in the wild seas of the sixtieth southern parallel, swept by zero-temperature winds and snow showers. . . . the life raft is gone.*

Aboard the battered *Ice Bird,* seaman and adventurer David Lewis ponders "what seems like a certain rendezvous with death." Six weeks and 3,600 nautical miles out from Sydney, Australia, the first singlehanded attempt to circumnavigate Antarctica's frozen perimeter nears a premature conclusion in the hurricane-force winds of the "screaming sixties", breeding ground of one-hundred-foot-high waves. Incredibly, *Ice Bird* rides out the storm to limp 2,500 miles eastward to Palmer Station, a U. S. Antarctic research base. Months of refitting make her seaworthy again, but a second dismasting cuts short

Ice Bird's odyssey for good, and on March 20, 1974, she motors into the harbor of Cape Town, South Africa, final port in an 11,000-mile voyage around two-thirds of the southernmost continent.

Published in the December 1973 and August 1975 NATIONAL GEOGRAPHICS, David Lewis's vivid and sometimes heart-stopping narrative of his Antarctic enterprise is a classic adventure story, one that illustrates what GEOGRAPHIC does best: It interprets the world to its readers through the lens of personal experience, be it the reader's own, that of the author, or that of the author's subject. Reporting from a personal perspective is an editorial tradition at NATIONAL GEOGRAPHIC. One of the keys to the magazine's outstanding success, it broadens isolated and solitary adventures like that of *Ice Bird* and her master into accounts that call up common intuition to illuminate uncommon experience. Few of us will ever suffer the unique rigors or taste the secret satisfaction of a lone voyage around the greater part of Antarctica, but in reading his story, we can grasp David Lewis's will to survive, his pride in achievement, and his hope in the face of failure. Universally familiar feelings thus sensitize us to the magnitude of another's rare accomplishment.

THERE IS MORE in the pages of NATIONAL GEOGRAPHIC than adventure and exploration, of course. Traditionally, GEOGRAPHIC has chronicled the fundamental changes that overtake and transform great civilizations and tiny tribes. This, too, it does with the human interest and sympathetic understanding of people that are hallmarks of GEOGRAPHIC reporting.

Take, for example, the pageant of "The Lost Empire of the Incas," a December 1973 article. Titling themselves "Sons of the Sun," in 1438 Inca lords embarked on a whirlwind series of conquests. By 1525 they had expanded their formerly minor agricultural state into the "Four Quarters of the World"—an imperial domain stretching 2,500 miles southward from the Equator through Ecuador and Peru to central Chile. Backbone of this realm was the Andes, a sawtooth mountain chain that provided what is for me the real highlight of this report on one of aboriginal America's greatest empires: the stunning photograph (right) of an Inca child who froze to death some five hundred years before my birth.

Seemingly asleep, a young boy about 8 or 9 years of age huddles beneath a llama-wool tunic. Perhaps drugged with some of the narcotic coca leaves found in the feathered pouch beside him, he died of exposure when entombed on Chile's 17,815-foot El Plomo peak near the southern edge of the once flourishing Inca Empire. Most probably he was left in that desolate spot as a sacrifice to the sun—a high honor in Inca eyes. Miniature idols and keepsakes surround him: the costumed silver image of an Inca goddess, llama figurines of gold and shell, and leather pouches holding his baby teeth and fingernail parings, left with the boy so that in the afterlife he would not have to search for missing parts of his body. NATIONAL GEOGRAPHIC's emphasis on human interest allows

Time rests lightly on the face of an Inca boy who froze to death in the Andes five centuries ago.

LOREN McINTYRE

this image of a long-ago child to leap five centuries and achieve its full effect on our imagination, reminding us that back of any larger-than-life civilization there lies a more intimate and immediate human dimension, one that lingers long after its mother culture has vanished.

IN ALL ITS REPORTING, NATIONAL GEOGRAPHIC demonstrates a sure instinct for the exciting and revealing, the products of which are superlative imagery and fascinating text. This is especially true of the magazine's coverage of science and natural history, traditional areas of interest for a journal whose parent society numbered no fewer than 16 scientists and naturalists among its 33 founding members.

The combination of educational value and pictorial beauty that distinguishes GEOGRAPHIC articles on science and nature is one of the most important elements in the magazine's enormous and long-standing popular appeal. These qualities of instruction and graphic attractiveness lend individual issues of NATIONAL GEOGRAPHIC enduring value as reference works on topics as varied as the how and why of our planet's climate and geology, the subtle mysteries of our universe and its physics, and the rainbow-hued creatures of the Red Sea, such as the hawkfish (right).

Technology now alters our environment more rapidly and with greater effect than ever before in history. As it does so, NATIONAL GEOGRAPHIC's science and nature coverage becomes increasingly important for readers who seek reliable information in order to form their own opinions on issues that are sometimes debated without benefit of solid fact or reasoned argument. Here is where GEOGRAPHIC, with its straightforward, lucid, and comprehensive reporting, has a special contribution to make.

One of the most recent entries in this index is "The Pipeline: Alaska's Troubled Colossus." Published in November 1976,

In undersea plaid, a hawkfish patrols a Red Sea coral reef.

DAVID DOUBILET

it proved to be one of the year's most popular articles. It deals with a controversial subject and reveals much about the character of NATIONAL GEOGRAPHIC.

Almost to the moment of publication, the pipeline story was reviewed, revised, and rewritten to keep pace with continuing construction of the mammoth Alaskan project. Such up-to-the-minute coverage is more than a hasty installment in a simple monthly accounting of change: it draws upon the basic continuity of GEOGRAPHIC reporting. When our staff began work on this piece, they were taking up a subject— our fuel resources and how to manage them—that is hardly new to NATIONAL GEOGRAPHIC: In 1904 we surveyed the "Natural-Gas, Oil, and Coal Supply of the United States"; in 1918 we discussed oil shales; and in 1920 we presented "Where the World Gets Its Oil: But Where Will Our Children Get It . . . ?" In 1972 we published "The Search for Tomorrow's Power" and followed it two years later with "Oil: The Dwindling Treasure." Since then articles on wind power and solar energy have appeared, and others on geothermal energy, nuclear power, and energy conservation are in preparation. The consistent ability of NATIONAL GEOGRAPHIC to combine continuity and topicality results, as in the pipeline story, in timely coverages backed by solid, factual reporting, which may stretch back over many decades.

AS NATIONAL GEOGRAPHIC documents the changes sweeping our world, it is constantly challenged to present the compellingly human side of a story or issue and to report at the same time without speculation or exaggeration. This difficult demand is best met by letting the facts speak for themselves, as we did in "Brazil's Kreen-Akarores: Requiem for a Tribe?", a February 1975 look at a beleaguered Indian tribe deep in the jungled Amazon Basin.

Beset by highway builders, stricken with foreign disease, and awed by a non-Indian material culture far in advance of their own, the Kreen-Akarores are nearing both tribal and personal extinction. In reporting the irreversible changes that "progress" is working on these Stone Age people, we chose to do no more than portray the fundamental humanity of their plight, believing that strong enough in itself to make the case for the survival and protection of the Kreen-Akarores. This approach yielded sad and powerful vignettes: a chief with skin so weather-hardened that at first it resisted and broke penicillin needles that could save him from the white man's influenza, and a young boy presented with a gift of fishing line that he cannot yet use because he has never seen such a thing before.

Occasionally, the task of reporting without polemicizing is best accomplished through photographs: An affecting image can go far to make a point without disturbing the factual balance of an article. This is true of the haunting portrait of famine (right) that illustrated a July 1975 survey of our world's growing population and strained food supply. Equally eloquent images have appeared in GEOGRAPHIC articles on pollution, mercury poisoning, and endangered whales, where they serve the same purpose—to educate without editorializing.

NOT LONG AGO I came across a yellowed brochure written in 1915 and intended for advertisers in the pages of NATIONAL GEOGRAPHIC. Its author was John Oliver La Gorce, Editor of the magazine from 1954 to 1957.

Sketching the character of NATIONAL GEOGRAPHIC for his readers, the future Editor summed up the matter in a single sentence: "The Geographic seems to anticipate where the world's attention is to be focused and turns its searchlight there— it presents to its readers what they want, when they want it, in a comprehensive and illuminating way. . . ." As Editor, I like to think that NATIONAL GEOGRAPHIC readers would find that simple description as fitting today as it was in 1915—only more so.

Sad-eyed and stoic, a Bengali girl endures famine in Bangladesh.

STEVE RAYMER

A Picture History of National Geographic 1947-1976

THREE GENERATIONS of readers have grown up with the unique institution known as NATIONAL GEOGRAPHIC. Often they have inherited shelves of back issues of the magazine from parents or grandparents. Just as often, they add to these carefully stored collections of the yellow-bordered journal, intending to pass them on to their own children and grandchildren.

Longtime readers of GEOGRAPHIC regard it with the loyalty they would show a member of the family. They seldom discard an issue or allow it to go unread, nor do they have the magazine bound just to place it high on some inaccessible bookshelf. And unlike some things handed down through the family and maintained only for display or out of sentiment, GEOGRAPHIC remains in constant use: by schoolchildren seeking essay topics, by parents who value it as a teaching aid or reference work, and by the entire family as a source of intriguing information not always available elsewhere and rarely in so fascinating a format.

Finally, GEOGRAPHIC fascinates as much by what it says about itself as by the endless variety and color of its contents. The following picture history forms an absorbing almanac of the magazine's evolution during three decades and demonstrates why NATIONAL GEOGRAPHIC has attracted millions of readers who call it "their" magazine.

1947

● *Aided by a Society grant, an oceanographic expedition surveys topography, geology, and marine life of the Mid-Atlantic Ridge.*

● *A joint Geographic – U. S. Army Air Forces expedition studies a solar eclipse in Brazil.*

● *A Society – Smithsonian Institution expedition finds evidence of a previously unknown preceramic culture in southern Mexico.*

1948

● *National Geographic joins with the Smithsonian Institution in Arnhem Land to survey Australia's Aboriginal culture, and in Panama to discover the first urn burials ever found between the southeastern United States and Ecuador.*

● *The Society announces discovery in Alaska of the nesting place of the bristle-thighed curlew, a mystery for 163 years.*

The face of a long-dead Olmec lives on in a colossal stone head (**below**). Discovered by a Society – Smithsonian Institution expedition, the pre-Maya sculpture appeared in a 1947 article on Mexico's ancient past.

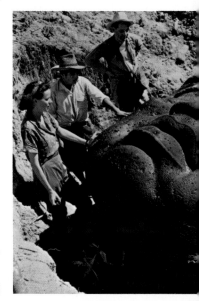

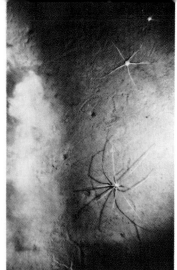

DAVID OWEN

Bottom-dwelling spider at lower right and the brittle star just above it appeared in a 1948 article on oceanographic probes along the Mid-Atlantic Ridge. Touching bottom at 5,850 feet, a camera equipped with an electronic flash raised the silt swirl at left.

U.S. NAVY, OFFICIAL PHOTOGRAPH

Winged miniature, a ruby-throated hummingbird visits a feeder of honey water in a 1947 GEOGRAPHIC photograph by Dr. Harold E. Edgerton, father of the electronic flash. Dainty wings "scull" the air in a figure-eight motion as the bird hovers above the quarter-size floor of its nest.

During the U. S. Navy Antarctic expedition of 1946-47, officer-in-charge Rear Adm. Richard E. Byrd, Jr., **(above)** takes his bearings with a sun compass on a flight near the south magnetic pole. Byrd also used the device, more reliable in polar regions than the magnetic compass, on his 1926 flight over the North Pole. The late Albert H. Bumstead, chief cartographer of the Society, invented the sun compass for Byrd's historic polar ventures.

RICHARD H. STEWART

15

1949

• *Society-backed expeditions gather data on the scarlet ibis in Venezuela and capture a specimen of Nepal's rare spiny babbler, the first such bird taken by a scientist in more than a century.*

• *The National Geographic— Palomar Observatory Sky Survey begins to map the heavens to a depth of one billion light-years for a monumental sky atlas.*

1950

• *Beginning a three-year Society-funded study, University of Miami scientists identify previously unrecognized larval fishes among plankton in the Florida Current.*

• *Jean and Franc Shor take the highroad in Afghanistan in the November 1950 issue, commencing their career as NATIONAL GEOGRAPHIC's husband-and-wife writer-photographer team.*

Daydreaming amid his characters, Charles Dickens figured in a 1949 GEOGRAPHIC devoted entirely to "The British Way."

Nepali child bride, arrayed in silk, jewels, and gold, appeared in the January 1950 issue.

First Grosvenor Medal goes to namesake Dr. Gilbert H. Grosvenor (**below**, at left) on May 19, 1949. Dr. Charles Franklin Kettering, a Trustee of the Society, presents the honor to Dr. Grosvenor on the latter's Golden Jubilee as Editor.

Victorious in his war chariot, King Ṭḥut-mosĕ III of Egypt draws his bow against Syrians at the Biblical Armageddon. The colorful painting by H. M. Herget was one of a series illustrating the Society's popular 1951 book, *Everyday Life in Ancient Times*.

Horned brow marks a placid cowfish (**lower left**) from a 1952 article on Bahamian sea life.

"I Sailed With Portugal's Captains Courageous" in 1952 highlighted this slickered Grand Banks doryman.

PAUL A. ZAHL

ALAN VILLIERS

1951

● *The Society supports an aerial and ground survey of giant gravel pictographs of Indian origin in southeast California.*

● *The magazine receives U. S. Camera's Achievement Award for its use of editorial color photography.*

1952

● *Britain's Royal Geographical Society and Cambridge University join National Geographic to sponsor geological studies on Norway's West Spitsbergen Island.*

● *A Society research grant aids astronomer Dr. George A. Van Biesbroeck of Yerkes Observatory in making star-field measurements at Khartoum, Sudan, during the February 25, 1952, total solar eclipse. His findings substantially confirm Albert Einstein's theory of relativity.*

Perilous span of worn cables and cracked branches set a stride apart carries Franc Shor of the Foreign Editorial Staff over Central Asia's Hunza River 500 feet below, an adventure described in the October 1953 GEOGRAPHIC.

Circled cross marks an ice floe directly above the North Pole at 11:29 a.m. EST on May 20, 1953. Circling the Pole in an airplane GEOGRAPHIC Editor Gilbert H. Grosvenor became the first to locate the spot by photographing it from all sides. Plotting the lines of focus on 15 photographs, he pinpointed the Pole's position. U. S. Coast and Geodetic Survey calculations and grid lines, shown on this photograph, confirmed Dr. Grosvenor's computations.

ALFRED GREGORY (C) R. G. S. AND ALPINE CLUB

1953

- *NATIONAL GEOGRAPHIC publishes the first aerials of the North Pole, the first pictures of birds of paradise displaying in the wild, and the first color pictures of living deep-sea fishes . . .*

- *. . . and joins forces with Eastman Kodak and others to produce the first color photographs and depth map of New Mexico's Carlsbad Caverns.*

- *The La Belle Award of the Photographic Society of America is presented to NATIONAL GEOGRAPHIC for outstanding contributions to the development of color photography for magazine use.*

- *With Society backing, ornithologist E. Thomas Gilliard renews studies of New Guinea bird life and Stone Age natives.*

Edmund Hillary leads as he and his Sherpa companion Tenzing Norgay labor up the southeast ridge of Mount Everest en route to the first conquest of the world's tallest peak on May 29, 1953. As a member of an unsuccessful Swiss-led assault on the 29,028-foot Himalayan giant, Norgay had passed this way the previous spring. Hillary recounted "The Conquest of the Summit" for GEOGRAPHIC readers in the July 1954 issue.

Society Trustees join Gen. George C. Marshall, standing, in honoring Dr. Gilbert H. Grosvenor, far right, at his retirement on May 5, 1954. Editor of NATIONAL GEOGRAPHIC for 55 years and President of the Society since 1920, Dr. Grosvenor was succeeded in those posts by longtime Associate Editor and Vice President Dr. John Oliver La Gorce (at far end of table).

Diver *extraordinaire,* Capt. Jacques-Yves Cousteau recounted his discovery of the remains of a 2,200-year-old Greek merchant ship in the January 1954 GEO-GRAPHIC. The Society sponsored the early work of this French aquanaut, here holding a bronze spike from the ship, which went down off Marseille.

HAROLD E. EDGERTON

1954

- *President Dwight D. Eisenhower presents the Society's gold Hubbard Medal to the British Everest expedition. Leader Sir John Hunt and climbers Sir Edmund Hillary and Tenzing Norgay receive bronze replicas as personal awards.*

- *The Society supports an archeological expedition to probe the origin of Canada's Dorset Eskimo culture.*

- *Honor Award for Distinguished Service in Journalism is given to NATIONAL GEOGRAPHIC by the University of Missouri School of Journalism.*

- *Work begins on a two-year, Society-supported study of Mars.*

ARTHUR JOHNSON

PAINTING BY W. LANGDON KIHN

Solemn-faced Shawnee, Chief Tecumseh (**above**) appeared in the Society's 1955 book, *Indians of the Americas.*

Land diver prepares to leap 78 feet from a tower of branches and vines (**left**) in a January 1955 article on New Hebrides Islanders.

"Stars and Stripes nailed to the Pole." On April 6, 1909, Robert E. Peary carried a taffeta flag made by his wife (**lower left**) to the North Pole. Caching pieces of it en route and depositing a strip at the Pole, Peary reduced the banner to a patchwork. In 1955 his widow presented the much-worn memento to the Society.

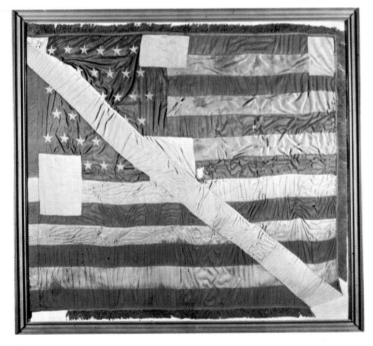

1955

• *Mrs. Robert E. Peary is awarded the Society's Special Gold Medal for contributions to her husband's Arctic explorations.*

• *Renewed Society funding enables specialists from the University of California and the Smithsonian Institution to clear the main ceremonial court of La Venta in southern Mexico. Archeological fieldwork at the ancient urban-ceremonial site establishes La Venta as a capital of Olmec civilization as long as 2,500 years ago.*

• *President and Editor Dr. John Oliver La Gorce celebrates his Golden Jubilee at NATIONAL GEOGRAPHIC and is awarded the Society's Grosvenor Medal.*

BROOKS HONEYCUTT

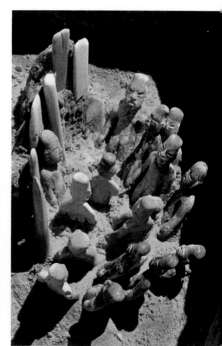

PHILIP DRUCKER

More of man's past in the Americas appeared in the pages of GEOGRAPHIC during 1956. Russell Cave in Alabama (above) yielded traces of man dating back 8,000 years. Pre-Columbian Olmec figurines of jade and serpentine (upper right), perhaps representing priests at sacrifice, came to light at La Venta, Mexico.

LUIS MARDEN

1956

• *Photography is completed for the National Geographic Society— Palomar Observatory Sky Atlas, which expands known space twenty-five times.*

• *As part of the International Geophysical Year, and with the Society's support, a shipboard geophysical observatory studies earth's magnetic field and measures cosmic-ray intensities.*

• *National Geographic Society— Smithsonian Institution excavations at Russell Cave in Alabama unearth bones, tools, and weapons indicating human occupancy of the cave from 6200 B.C. to A.D. 1650. The Society purchases the cave site for later presentation to the Federal Government as a national archeological monument.*

Fatally attractive, a bristling lionfish scouts a sponge-mantled coral shelf in the Red Sea. The venom-spined creature appeared in a 1956 GEOGRAPHIC article on marine photography.

21

LUIS MARDEN

1957

• *Grants from the Society and the Smithsonian Institution make possible field studies of Ecuador's primitive Indian tribes.*

• *The Society's modern Book Service is formally organized;* **The World in Your Garden** *inaugurates its new series.*

• *With Tulane University, the Society cosponsors excavation and restoration of Dzibilchaltun, an ancient Maya urban center in Yucatán, Mexico.*

Suns glow green in a filtered multi-exposure taken at the U. S. South Pole station by GEOGRAPHIC staff man Thomas J. Abercrombie in November 1957. First civilian photographer to reach the station, Abercrombie spent three weeks there.

In the wake of history, *Mayflower II* spans the Atlantic during a British reenactment of the original 1620 Pilgrim crossing (**left**). Longtime seaman and NATIONAL GEOGRAPHIC author Alan Villiers skippered the ship and described her voyage in the November 1957 issue.

Beached and burned on January 23, 1790, the mutiny ship *Bounty* lay undetected off Pitcairn Island in the South Pacific for 167 years until NATIONAL GEOGRAPHIC's Luis Marden (**right**) discovered her remains in Bounty Bay in January of 1957. Here Marden retrieves ship's fittings he chiseled out of limy growths that marked the line of the vessel's keel.

Newly elected President and Editor Melville Bell Grosvenor (**below,** center) with his executive staff on January 8, 1957. Seated are Dr. Thomas W. McKnew, Vice President and Secretary (left), and Robert V. Fleming, Treasurer. Standing: Melvin M. Payne, Senior Assistant Secretary (left), and Frederick G. Vosburgh, Associate Editor.

THOMAS CHRISTIAN

VOLKMAR WENTZEL

ANGELO CARUSO, JR.

"Aviation will conquer the Arctic—and the Antarctic, too." First to fly over the North Pole in 1926 and the South Pole in 1929, Trustee Adm. Richard E. Byrd died March 11, 1957.

1958

- *National Press Photographers Association (NPPA) honors Thomas J. Abercrombie of the Foreign Editorial Staff as Magazine Photographer of the Year.*

- *The Society's Hubbard Medal is presented to Dr. Paul A. Siple, scientific leader of the first group to winter at the South Pole.*

- *Society and American Museum of Natural History funding enables ornithologists to make the first color record of courting ritual among greater birds of paradise.*

- *Thomas W. McKnew is elected Executive Vice President and Secretary; Robert E. Doyle, Associate Secretary.*

- *March GEOGRAPHIC publishes the deepest undersea photographs made to this date, from 25,000 feet down in the mid-Atlantic's Romanche trench.*

Brooding cliffs in the Judaean wilderness and the sectarians they once sheltered were featured in a 1958 article. About 100 B.C. the Essenes, a Jewish religious group, retired to the cliffs at Wadi Qumran near the northwest shore of the Dead Sea. There they prepared and stored copies of the Old Testament, creating cave libraries and the famous Dead Sea scrolls. To date, copies of all Old Testament books except Esther have been found at Qumran.

Lightning erupts above lava-flanked Ilha Nova (New Island) in the Azores in a 20-minute time exposure (**below**). Rising in September 1957, the volcano sank back into the sea in October, only to reappear in November; by March 1958 it squatted as a steaming quarter-mile-wide islet at the western end of Fayal Island. The up-and-down evolution of Ilha Nova appeared in the June 1958 GEOGRAPHIC.

Atomic kaleidoscope at the tip of a platinum needle (**below**) appeared in the September 1958 article "You and the Obedient Atom." Magnified 750,000 times and supercooled, individual atoms glow as blobs of light.

ROBERT F. SISSON

24

JOHN M. ALLEGRO

JOHN C. TREVER

Best preserved of the Dead Sea manuscripts, this leather scroll contains the full 66 chapters of the messianic Book of Isaiah, a favorite Old Testament text of the Essene scribes who copied it.

W. ROBERT MOORE

Stubborn stump of bristlecone pine (**lower right**) resists time in California's White Mountains. A March 1958 article on these oldest known living things included this 4,000-year-old tree, its wood polished by wind-borne grit.

ERWIN W. MÜLLER

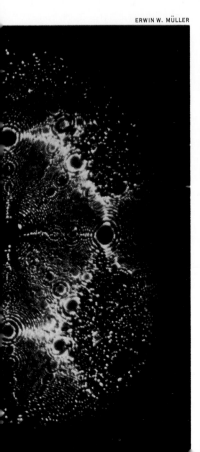

PAINTING BY HERVEY GARRETT SMITH

Polar crossings, over the ice and beneath it, were reported in the January 1959 NATIONAL GEOGRAPHIC. British Commonwealth Trans-Antarctic expedition tractors set out from Shackleton Base on the Weddell Sea in late 1957 and paused at Amundsen-Scott Station at the South Pole on January 19, 1958 *(above).*

1959

- *Hubbard Medal awarded to Sir Vivian Fuchs, leader of the British Trans-Antarctic expedition.*

- *GEOGRAPHIC's John E. Fletcher places first, J. Baylor Roberts second and third in color class in White House News Photographers Association contest.*

- *The September NATIONAL GEOGRAPHIC bears the first of a continuing series of color covers.*

- *Vice Chairman of the Board and retired Editor Dr. John Oliver La Gorce dies December 23.*

- *The Aviation/Space Writers Association's James J. Strebig Memorial Award goes to Assistant Editor Allan C. Fisher, Jr., for "Cape Canaveral's 6,000-mile Shooting Gallery" (October).*

The expedition covered 2,158 miles in all, arriving at McMurdo Sound on March 2, 1958. Painting (**facing page**) shows the atomic-powered submarine *Nautilus* passing beneath the frozen Chukchi Sea during the first Arctic transpolar voyage. *Nautilus* reached the North Pole on August 3, 1958.

Nearly complete skull of "East Africa Man" elates prehistorian Louis S. B. Leakey (**lower left**). Later supported by the Society, Dr. Leakey and his wife unearthed *Zinjanthropus boisei* in 1959 in Tanzania's Olduvai Gorge. First sign of the landmark discovery was a fossilized jaw dated at 1,750,000 years (**below**).

U. S. and Asian leaders — President Dwight D. Eisenhower and Indian Prime Minister Jawaharlal Nehru meet at the University of Delhi in December 1959 (**above**). Ike donned cap and gown at this midpoint of a 22,000-mile goodwill tour of Europe, Asia, and Africa, reported in the May 1960 GEOGRAPHIC.

Undersea butterfly, explorer Jacques-Yves Cousteau's diving saucer (**far left**) glides over a marine meadow in the Caribbean off Guadeloupe. Construction of the two-man submarine was made possible by grants from the National Geographic Society.

Pre-Columbian Peruvian grave doll (**left**) illustrated a June 1960 article on the Smithsonian Institution. The National Geographic Society and the Smithsonian have long shared a common purpose: the increase and diffusion of knowledge.

New presses, paper, and inks make up the September 1960 NATIONAL GEOGRAPHIC (**lower left**). By the beginning of 1960, rising Society membership required a monthly edition of 2 1/2 million copies of the magazine, prompting a successful eight-month printing transfer from Washington, D. C., to new presses in Chicago, Illinois.

1960

- *National Geographic scientist Barry C. Bishop joins Sir Edmund Hillary in winter high-altitude research in the Himalayas.*

- *The Society deeds Alabama's Russell Cave, occupied by man 8,000 years ago, to the National Park Service.*

- *Titles are added to the magazine's spine for easy reference, beginning with the January issue.*

- *First bound and indexed set of Geographic maps offered:* Atlas of the Fifty United States.

- *Wild Animals of North America issued by the Book Service.*

- *The Society assists in the first probe with free-diving gear of the Well of Sacrifice at Chichén Itzá, Yucatán. Thousands of artifacts are recovered.*

Abandoned to ruin and loose rock, cliff houses at Wetherill Mesa in Colorado's Mesa Verde National Park once sheltered the Anasazi—the Ancient Ones—the Pueblo culture that succumbed to a late 13th-century drought. Long House (**above**) stretches 295 feet along a canyon face; multistory apartments and storage rooms, 181 in all, conform in size and shape to the irregular rock of the mesa. The December 1961 President's Annual Message to Members pointed to archeological and restoration work at Wetherill Mesa as an example of research assisted by the Society.

1961

- *First political Geographic world globe offered to members.*

- *Robert E. Doyle elected Vice President of the Society.*

- *Staff photographer Dean Conger chosen NPPA Magazine Photographer of the Year.*

- *"Countdown for Space" in the May NATIONAL GEOGRAPHIC earns senior editorial staff member Kenneth F. Weaver the Aviation/Space Writers Association Writing Award of the Year.*

- *GEOGRAPHIC reports discovery by E. Thomas Gilliard of previously unknown New Britain birds.*

- *The Society begins its support of Jane Goodall and her studies of chimpanzee behavior at Gombe Stream National Park in western Tanzania.*

"Geography in the round": The Society's globe, with its unique plastic "thinking cap," was introduced in 1961.

Burnished by sunset, a gun battery (**left**) marks the line held by Stonewall Jackson at the first Battle of Bull Run in 1861. Stilled cannon appeared in the April 1961 Civil War Centennial issue.

DEAN CONGER

Riding *Friendship 7* through three sunsets in space, Astronaut John Glenn (**above**, left) splashed down on February 20, 1962 in time for a fourth sunset in the Atlantic. Shown aboard a recovery ship collecting gear from his capsule, the first American to orbit earth received the Society's Hubbard Medal on April 9, 1962.

New headquarters of the National Geographic Society take shape in the heart of Washington, D. C. By 1962 the Society's steadily expanding membership and

WINFIELD PARKS

THE White House

GEORGE F. MOBLEY

Pleased President and Mrs. John F. Kennedy accept presentation copies of *The White House: An Historic Guide,* requested by Mrs. Kennedy and prepared by

the Society in 1962 as a public service. On the cover is an unusual view of the Executive Mansion taken from atop an extended firetruck ladder.

1962

- *Lt. Col. John H. Glenn, Jr., carries Geographic flag on first U. S. orbital spaceflight.*

- *East African fossil discoveries earn Dr. and Mrs. Louis S. B. Leakey the Society's Hubbard Medal.*

- *The* GEOGRAPHIC *publishes more editorial color this year than any other magazine.*

- *Thomas W. McKnew becomes Vice Chairman of the Board of Trustees; Melvin M. Payne, Secretary and Executive Vice President.*

- *The Society issues* Men, Ships, and the Sea, *a history of seafaring from raft to atom-powered ship.*

services required construction of new offices. Much praised for its architectural excellence, the ten-story glass and marble building was dedicated in 1964. It houses Magazine and Society staffs, photographic laboratories, and Explorers Hall, a museum of adventure, exploration, and science. Open to the public, the hall and its changing exhibits display the results of many Society-supported expeditions. The Society's old headquarters building, at far left, continues in use.

Through time and cultures, 1962 articles carried GEOGRAPHIC readers to New Guinea (**above**); to Outer Mongolia, where Supreme Court Justice William O. Douglas watches staff photographer Dean Conger eat a mutton rib Mongol fashion (**above**); and to Turkey's seacoast for the salvage of Bronze Age relics (**right**).

KATHLEEN REVIS JUDGE

Marking 75 years of NATIONAL GEOGRAPHIC and 63 years of marriage, Gilbert H. Grosvenor and his wife, Elsie May Bell, observe the Society's Diamond Anniversary at Beinn Bhreagh, their summer home near Baddeck, Nova Scotia. Dr. Grosvenor was Editor of the Society's journal for fifty-five years; Mrs. Grosvenor created its familiar blue, brown, and green flag.

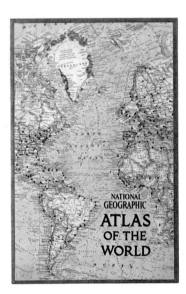

Long famous for the quality of its map supplements, the National Geographic Society in 1963 issued the first edition of its *Atlas of the World*. Revised three times, the atlas continues to be one of the most accurate, detailed, and timely volumes of its kind ever produced. More than 650,000 copies have been distributed.

1963

• *The Society celebrates the 75th anniversary of its founding in 1888.*

• *A five-year joint National Park Service — National Geographic project to excavate and study Indian cliff dwellings at Wetherill Mesa in Colorado is completed.*

• *Evidence is found at L'Anse aux Meadows in Newfoundland by a Society-funded investigation that Norsemen reached North America five centuries before Columbus.*

• *The Geographic flag is raised atop the world's highest mountain by the Society-supported American Mount Everest expedition.*

• *A National Geographic grant makes possible a National Park Service study to preserve California's coast redwoods. The survey later aided establishment of Redwood National Park.*

• *The Society's Book Service publishes* **Great Adventures With National Geographic.**

Beneath a flag at half-staff, the caisson bearing the casket of John F. Kennedy draws up at the Capitol on Sunday, November 24, 1963. A restive black gelding, riderless and with black boots

reversed in silver stirrups, suggests the fallen leader's spirit. The March 1964 NATIONAL GEOGRAPHIC carried a special tribute to the President who gave "The Last Full Measure."

White House ceremony honors the American Mount Everest expedition as President Kennedy awards the Hubbard Medal to team leader Norman Dyhrenfurth on July 8, 1963 (**lower left**). Society President Melville Bell Grosvenor and Executive Vice President Melvin M. Payne applaud at left. GEOGRAPHIC's Barry Bishop was one of six climbers to reach the summit (**below**).

"**Invite exploration . . . .**" So urges President Lyndon B. Johnson at the dedication of new Society headquarters on January 18, 1964 (**above**). Guests in Explorers Hall included Justices of the Supreme Court, Cabinet members, and Society officers.

Street boys in Sana, capital of Yemen, flick disks into the corner pockets of a carom board in a popular Yemenite game similar to

Floodlit classic, the U. S. Capitol crowns the cover of *We, the People,* second of the Society's public-service books. In 1964 the history and guide won the George Washington Honor Medal of the Freedoms Foundation.

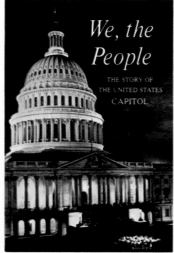

We, the People

THE STORY OF
THE UNITED STATES
CAPITOL

billiards (**facing page, lower**). The youngsters added a peaceful vignette to a March 1964 article on Yemen's civil war.

Mirrored in the eyes of mother and child (**below**), harsh life of Andean Indians was one of "The Five Worlds of Peru" in 1964.

World's tallest tree, the California coast redwood at center was reported in 1964 by GEOGRAPHIC naturalist Dr. Paul A. Zahl.

1964

- *The Society grants research funds for an ethnological study of the vanishing Ainu people of Hokkaido, Japan.*

- *Elsie May Bell Grosvenor, "first lady of National Geographic" and designer of the Society's flag, dies December 26.*

- *Reprints of 179 rare issues covering the magazine's first 20 years are offered by the Society.*

- *A new book,* Song and Garden Birds of North America, *is issued, accompanied by the Society's first recording.*

- **The Presidents of the United States,** *another Geographic public-service book, appears.*

Words of courage and resolution from Sir Winston Churchill inspired the free world. A record accompanying the August 1965 NATIONAL GEOGRAPHIC contained excerpts of Churchill's address to a joint session of Congress on December 26, 1941 (**left**), and the pageantry and sorrow of his funeral in London on January 30, 1965 (**below**). Flag-draped and topped by the Order of the Garter insignia on a black velvet cushion, the casket of "the greatest Englishman" rides a gun carriage drawn in slow march by a Royal Navy crew.

Television joined print and photographs at Geographic in 1965 with airing of the Society's first television special, "Americans on Everest." At left, President and Editor Melville Bell Grosvenor confers with executive producer Robert C. Doyle beside gear used in the 1963 American Everest ascent.

Uncommon beauty of a common egret (**right**) appeared in the Society's 1965 book *Water, Prey, and Game Birds of North America.* Records of bird songs were included with this and its companion volume, *Song and Garden Birds of North America.*

FREDERICK KENT TRUSLOW

JAMES A. MCDIVITT, NASA

- *Special Publications Division officially established.*

- *Joining with several other contributors, the National Geographic Society helps finance a project for the preparation and publication of a six-volume work on the wild flowers of the United States, under the aegis of the New York Botanical Garden.*

- *The Book Service publishes* **Wondrous World of Fishes.**

- *George Washington Honor Medal of the Freedoms Foundation is awarded the Society for its public-service books.*

Up a tree for science, chimpanzee-watcher Jane Goodall seeks a vantage point in Tanzania's Gombe Stream National Park. The photograph of the Society-supported zoologist appeared in the December 1965 magazine.

BARON HUGO VAN LAWICK

A golden tether secures slow-motion spacewalker Maj. Edward H. White II (**above**) as he floats 100 miles above earth on June 3, 1965. The first American to walk in space, White used the guidance gun in his right hand to maneuver alongside Gemini 4, reflected in his helmet visor. Exhausting the gun's compressed oxygen, White later pulled on the gold-plated tether to change his position. The cord carried oxygen and voice contact with White's partner, Maj. James A. McDivitt. In September 1965 GEOGRAPHIC published dramatic photographs of the 21-minute, 6,000-mile stroll through space.

Staff photographers collected 29 magazine awards in the 1966 "Pictures of the Year" competition. Winners included Thomas R. Smith, seated far left, who placed first in Picture Editing for the Winston Churchill articles in the August 1965 GEOGRAPHIC, which itself won an award for the year's best use of photographs in a magazine. Other winners in 1966 were, seated with Smith, Winfield Parks and William Albert Allard; standing, left to right, Albert Moldvay, David S. Boyer, W. E. Garrett, Bruce Dale, and James P. Blair.

B. ANTHONY STEWART

38

Ravaging the Renaissance heart of Florence on November 4, 1966, the flooding Arno River turns the Ponte Vecchio (Old Bridge), downstream at left, into a half-submerged weir. Palazzo Vecchio and city cathedral are at center and right. The July 1967 issue told of the disaster and the city's recovery effort.

GIANNI TORTOLI

Cavalry carrying the field, Norman knights crack Anglo-Saxon ranks at the Battle of Hastings in a panel from the Bayeux Tapestry (center). The medieval epic in cloth celebrates the Norman Conquest of England on October 14, 1066. Reproduction of the entire tapestry appeared 900 years later in the August 1966 GEOGRAPHIC.

1966

- *Dr. Gilbert H. Grosvenor, Chairman of the Board of Trustees and former Editor of NATIONAL GEOGRAPHIC and President of the Society, dies February 4. Dr. Thomas W. McKnew becomes Board Chairman.*

- *"Snowflake", the world's first-known white gorilla, is captured in Río Muni, West Africa, and becomes part of a Society-funded primate study.*

- *Funded by the Society and others, excavations uncover the classical statuary and buildings of Aphrodisias, Turkey.*

MILTON A. FORD AND VICTOR R. BOSWELL, JR.

Face-lift for a pharoah: Sandstone visage of Ramesses II swings free from a statue at Abu Simbel on the Nile (right). A 40-million-dollar international rescue effort was mounted under United Nations, Egyptian, and United States auspices to save the desert shrine, threatened by rising river waters impounded by Egypt's Aswan High Dam. The 3,200-year-old temples were sawed into blocks, marked, and then meticulously reassembled atop a plateau overlooking the new lake. The epic salvage job was reported in the May 1966 and May 1969 GEOGRAPHICS.

GEORG GERSTER

39

Portrait of planet earth, first in color from space, emerged in 1967 from the Johns Hopkins Applied Physics Laboratory. Society technicians, using the guide at top, helped correct the color.

On top of the bottom of the world, the 1966-67 American Antarctic Mountaineering expedition scaled that continent's loftiest peaks, an exploit honored by the Society's first John Oliver La Gorce Medal.

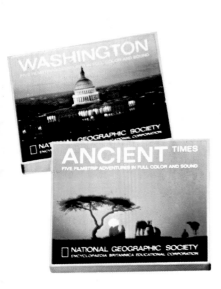

Educational filmstrips for secondary schoolchildren were the Society's new venture for 1968. Offerings ranged from "Ancient Times" and "Washington, D. C." (**above**) to "Southeast Asia."

Glowing lake mirrors twilight at the Membership Center Building, opened in 1968. The Gaithersburg, Maryland, structure, containing 400,000 square feet of space, replaced a bulging 43-year-old records facility in downtown Washington, D. C. The Membership Center houses the Cartographic Division, which produces the Society's outstanding maps, globes, and atlases. Also at the

40

1967

• **My Friends the Wild Chimpanzees,** *an account of zoologist Jane Goodall's pioneering field studies of free-roaming chimpanzees in Tanzania, is issued by the Society's Special Publications Division.*

• *Air-route pioneer and National Geographic Society Trustee Juan T. Trippe is awarded the Hubbard Medal for his lifetime of service to the art and science of aviation.*

• *Geographic's Bruce Dale is named NPPA Magazine Photographer of the Year.*

• *NATIONAL GEOGRAPHIC Director of Photography Robert E. Gilka receives the Joseph A. Sprague Memorial Award, the NPPA's highest recognition to an individual for contributions to photography.*

JAMES E. RUSSELL

Change of command at the Society and its magazine occurred again in 1967: longtime President and Editor Melville Bell Grosvenor became Chairman of the Board and Editor-in-Chief. In front of him are new Editor Frederick G. Vosburgh at his right and new President Melvin M. Payne to his left. Flanking the three are new Associate Editor Gilbert M. Grosvenor at far left and newly elected Society Secretary Robert E. Doyle.

JAMES L. STANFIELD

building, more than a thousand employees and two computers handle records and correspondence of the National Geographic Society's more than nine million members.

1968

• *NATIONAL GEOGRAPHIC Assistant Editor W. E. Garrett is named NPPA Magazine Photographer of the Year.*

• *A Society grant makes possible a behavioral and ecological study of the little-understood and possibly endangered Florida manatee.*

• *The first volume in a series of* **Research Reports** *summarizes scientific findings of Society-sponsored research projects.*

• *The Society awards its John Oliver La Gorce Medal to Harold E. Edgerton, "father" of electronic flash equipment.*

• **Man's Conquest of Space,** *a Society Special Publication, wins first prize, book category, in Aviation/Space Writers Association competition.*

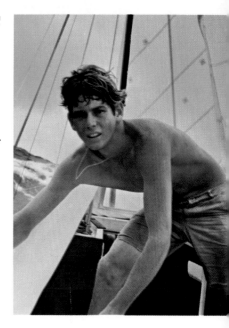

Sailor's self-portrait captures Robin Lee Graham during his lone round-the-world cruise aboard *Dove,* a feat followed in the October 1968, April 1969, and October 1970 GEOGRAPHICS.

41

Applying shadows with an air-brush, a GEOGRAPHIC relief artist portrays the moon's far side (**above**). Photograph of the crater Tsiolkovsky guides him.

Historic lunar reconnaissance: The 1968 Apollo 8 Christmas flight around the moon furnished amazing photographs for the May 1969 issue, including "earth rise" (**above**). Man first stepped on the lunar surface on July 20, 1969.

Visor of Apollo 11 Astronaut Edwin E. Aldrin (**below**) reflects fellow moon explorer Neil A. Armstrong and the lunar lander *Eagle*. Third crew member Michael Collins remained in moon orbit in the command module *Columbia*.

1969

- *Apollo 11 astronauts carry the Geographic flag to the moon.*

- *"The Music of Greece" issued as first of a series of stereo Sounds of the World recordings.*

- *The Society's Cartographic Division produces the first map to show the entire lunar surface on a single sheet.*

- **The Age of Chivalry** *issued.*

1970

- *Bringing to a close nearly 37 years of full-time service to the Society and to its journal, Vice President and Editor Frederick G. Vosburgh retires on October 1, retaining his position on the Board of Trustees. Gilbert M. Grosvenor is elected to succeed him.*

- *Hubbard Medal awarded to Apollo 11 Astronauts Neil A. Armstrong, Edwin E. Aldrin, Jr., and Michael Collins in recognition of their role in the historic moon landing of July 1969.*

Industrial river of sorrows, the Cuyahoga struggles through a Cleveland, Ohio, factory district. The sluggish, soiled waterway carries the pollution burden of steel mills, municipal sewers, chemical plants, and fertilizer runoff from upstream farms into oxygen-starved Lake Erie. The Cuyahoga's desperate condition emphasized the seriousness of "Our Ecological Crisis" in the December 1970 issue of NATIONAL GEOGRAPHIC.

Spiky pondside sentinels, cattails suggest a delicate defense against environmental abuse: heightened awareness of our world's fragile beauty. Like the grace of the mother robin stilling her nestling's hunger (**above, right**), much of earth's simple charm goes unremarked and seems beyond our perception — until we suddenly note its absence. Such thoughts led to the December 1970 portfolio: "The Fragile Beauty All About Us."

43

LILA M. BISHOP

W. E. GARRETT

MELVILLE BELL GROSVENOR

1971

• *The Society offers its first ethnic map,* **The Peoples of Mainland Southeast Asia,** *inaugurating a political and cultural map series.*

• *First photographs of snow leopards in the wild published in the November* GEOGRAPHIC.

• *National Geographic Physical Globe, one of the first to depict earth's major undersea surface features, is offered to Society members.*

• **Great Religions of the World** *issued by Society's Book Service.*

Lands and peoples of Asia appeared often in the pages of GEOGRAPHIC during 1971. Barry C. Bishop (**top**, second from right) traveled to western Nepal for a November article on life in that changing kingdom. The Society's first ethnic map (**above, left**) supplemented the March issue, which portrayed mainland southeast Asian tribespeople such as the silver-trinketed Akha woman from northern Laos (**above**).

Hunting prehistory in East Africa, anthropologist Dr. Louis S. B. Leakey (**upper right**) and his wife Mary recovered a series of spectacular fossils during 13 years of Society-aided fieldwork. He died October 1, 1972.

1972

• *The Society announces support for a joint project with the Boston Museum of Science to map a ten-mile stretch of the Grand Canyon's South Rim, the area most visited by tourists.*

• *Two new ethnic supplement maps cover the Middle East (July) and North American Indians (December).*

• *A new Geographic book,* **The Marvels of Animal Behavior,** *is added to the Society's Natural Science Library.*

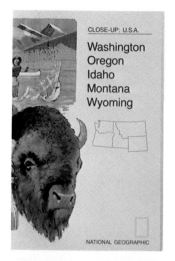

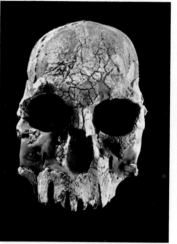

Introducing beginning readers to nature, science, and geography, in 1972 the Society combined learning and entertainment in a new series of National Geographic children's books (**above**). Created especially for ages 4 through 8, Books for Young Explorers now include 20 titles, ranging from *How Animals Hide* to *Cowboys;* over six million have been distributed.

Mapping America anew for a people eager to see their country, a new Geographic regional map series began to appear in 1973: "Close-up: U.S.A.—The Northwest" (**top center**) is designed for vacation-bound Americans.

1973

● *Mars map supplement accompanies the February issue of* NATIONAL GEOGRAPHIC.

● *A Society grant aids publication of maps of the ruins of Chan Chan, Peru, perhaps the largest prehistoric city in the Americas.*

● *The Society's Book Service focuses on America's wild regions in* **Wilderness U.S.A.**

● *Society support begins for University of Texas radio sky-mapping project.*

Many-sided man, Dr. Leonard Carmichael, shown above with an infant orangutan, died September 16, 1973. After a lifetime of achievement as author, scholar, teacher, university president, and museum director, Dr. Carmichael served the last nine years of his full life as the National Geographic Society's gracious and vigorous Vice President for Research and Exploration.

In the family tradition, Richard E. Leakey proposed in a June 1973 NATIONAL GEOGRAPHIC article that fossil skull 1470 (**bottom center**) may be evidence of the existence of early man as long ago as 2.8 million years.

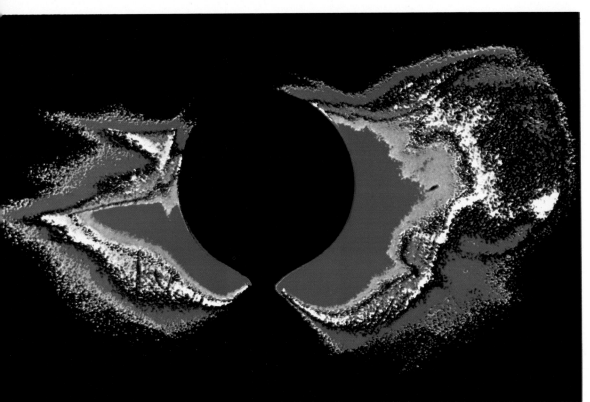

HIGH ALTITUDE OBSERVATORY AND NASA

Solar spectacle millions of miles wide, the sun's outer atmosphere, the corona, unfurls in a view color-coded to distinguish levels of brightness. A coronagraph aboard NASA's orbiting Skylab observatory masks the solar disk, indicating the vast extent of the hot gases enveloping the sun. NATIONAL GEOGRAPHIC's three-part Skylab coverage appeared in the October 1974 issue.

Diaphanous drifter on wings of latticed muscle fiber, the oceanic snail *Corolla spectabilis* seines Gulf Stream currents for food. Classed as plankton—plant and animal organisms that ride the currents—the ghostly snail is an important element in the marine food web. Gossamer geometry of *Corolla* and other free-floating life was portrayed in a 1974 article on blue-water plankton.

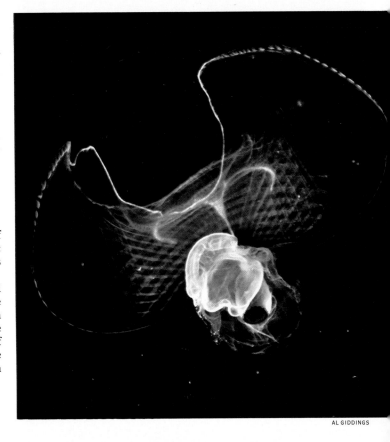

AL GIDDINGS

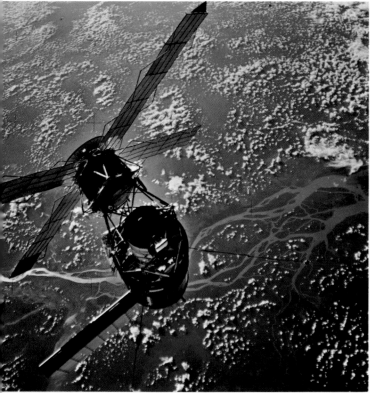

1974

- *Continuing a long tradition of support for scientific and geographic research, the Society approves its 1,000th project, which makes possible a study of canals and reservoirs at the ancient Maya urban-ceremonial center of Etzna in Campeche, Mexico.*

- *"Rare Look at North Korea" by H. Edward Kim in the August* NATIONAL GEOGRAPHIC *wins the Overseas Press Club of America Award for best reporting on Asia.*

- *Melville Bell Grosvenor, Editor-in-Chief and Chairman of the Board of Trustees, receives the Grosvenor Medal in recognition of his fifty years of outstanding service to the increase and diffusion of knowledge through* NATIONAL GEOGRAPHIC.

Exploring hometown earth from the suburbs of space, the 100-ton Skylab laboratory drifts above the cloud-flecked Amazon River Delta 270 miles below. For 5 1/2 months in 1973 and 1974, Skylab astronauts trained sensors on the planet to monitor croplands and weather and to detect hints of new fishing grounds and ore deposits. The October 1974 issue carried this lofty view.

Centuries of belief decreed earth the navel of the universe, until in 1543 astronomer Nicólaus Copernicus enthroned the sun at the center of our planetary system. Overturning tradition established by Ptolemy, a 2d-century A.D. Greek, Copernicus laid the foundations of the modern astronomy covered in the May 1974 NATIONAL GEOGRAPHIC.

Rash sea dog even on land, Francis Drake (**left**, with pistols) waits to ambush a Spanish mule train in Panama's bush in 1573. A favorite of Queen Elizabeth I, he was profiled in February 1975 by Alan Villiers, a seagoing favorite of GEOGRAPHIC readers.

Unraveling the riddle of the ancient Maya, tracing Columbus's voyages, and locating the wreck of the Civil War ironclad *Monitor* were among the GEOGRAPHIC's 1975 highlights.

Serpents and glyphs weave across the Madrid Codex (**top right**), a folding 22-foot almanac consulted by Maya priests to foretell the future.

Map (**center right**) was drafted after 1500 by Juan de la Cosa, a shipmate of Columbus on his second New World voyage in 1493-96. Green coast of a new land fills the left border of the chart, first to show mainland America.

Armor-plated wreck of the *Monitor* lies bottom up off Cape Hatteras, North Carolina, where she foundered in 1862 (**lower right**). Displaced gun turret protrudes at upper right.

A new magazine for youngsters, *World* replaced the familiar *School Bulletin* in 1975. Enthusiastic reception boosted circulation to more than 1,300,000 by mid-1976. *We Americans,* published by the Book Service for the country's Bicentennial, records 200 colorful years of U. S. history.

PAINTING BY JEAN-LEON HUENS

1975

- *"The Arab World, Inc." by John J. Putman in the October* GEOGRAPHIC *is judged "Best Magazine Reporting from Abroad" in 1975 by Overseas Press Club.*

- *Trustee Alexander Wetmore is awarded the Hubbard Medal in honor of his lifetime of contribution to ornithology.*

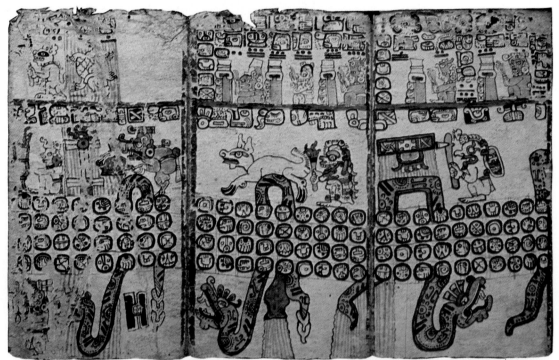

OTIS IMBODEN AND VICTOR R. BOSWELL, JR.; MUSEO DE AMÉRICA, MADRID

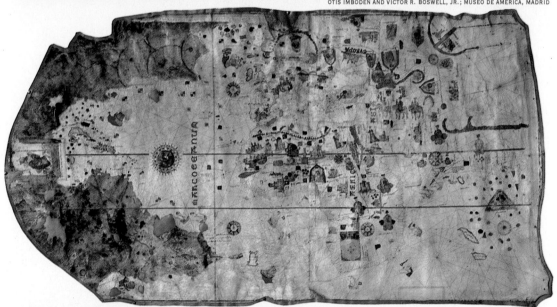

MUSEO NAVAL, MADRID

PHOTOGRAPHS BY GLEN TILLMAN, ALCOA MARINE CORPORATION; PHOTOMOSAIC BY U. S. NAVY

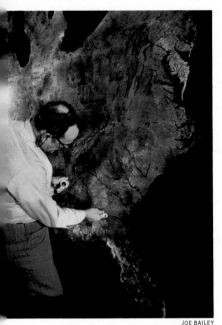

Touching up the continental United States, Tony Rossi of the General Electric Photographic Engineering Laboratory refines a billboard-size mosaic of 569 color prints made from images scanned by Landsat satellites. From this first coast-to-coast photomosaic of the 48 contiguous states came *Portrait U.S.A.,* a July 1976 map supplement.

Zeroing in on Antarctica, the Nimbus 5 satellite equipped with microwave radiation detectors produced this color-coded view of the South Polar ice cap, published in a November 1976 article on the world's changing climate. Ice sheet glows green and dark blue at center, revealing the relatively slow snow buildup of Antarctica's high summer.

Building life, geological violence and atmospheric fury fuse simple molecules into organic compounds about four billion years ago (**below**). Primitive protein chains link up with nucleic acids, and eons later a self-replicating cell appears. "Exploring the New Biology," in the September 1976 GEO-GRAPHIC, presented this theory of life's beginnings on earth.

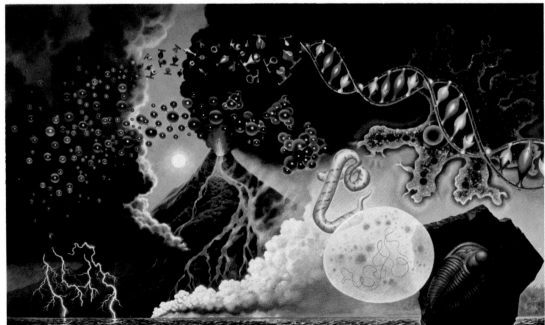

Forty-ton madonna, a mother humpback whale lazes with her calf off Maui, Hawaii. They were among "The Imperiled Giants" in the December 1976 GEOGRAPHIC.

Still-fresh wounds are reopened on the tundra as the Alaska pipeline is checked for defective welds. GEOGRAPHIC covered the oil line in November 1976.

1976

- *Robert E. Doyle elected Society President; Owen R. Anderson, Vice President and Secretary; Melvin M. Payne, Chairman of Board of Trustees.*

- *NPPA cites GEOGRAPHIC for "Best Use of Photography by a Magazine," presents its Magazine Picture Editor's Award to GEOGRAPHIC's David L. Arnold, and names staff photographer Steve Raymer Magazine Photographer of the Year.*

- *National Geographic Society membership, averaged over the year, reaches 9,350,000, an increase of 7,880,000 in the 30-year period covered by this index.*

Expeditions and Scientific Researches of the National Geographic Society

By MELVIN M. PAYNE

Chairman, Board of Trustees,
and Chairman, Committee for Research and Exploration

"UNBELIEVABLE! What a glorious, incredible sight!" In January 1976 Canadian zoologist Fred A. Urquhart stood on the flanks of central Mexico's Sierra Madre and watched countless millions of monarch butterflies stain the volcanic slopes a vibrant, quivering orange. After decades of search, and aided by the National Geographic Society through six grants from its Committee for Research and Exploration, he had located the overwintering site of the eastern population of the North American monarch. Only a simple and half-whispered "glorious, incredible sight!" caught the wonderment of the moment.

Making such moments possible for "the increase and diffusion of geographic knowledge" has always been a major aim of the National Geographic Society. Within two years of its founding in 1888, the Society endorsed geographic and geological studies in Alaska's St. Elias Mountains. While on that expedition, scientists (including two of the Society's first members) discovered Mount Logan, North America's second highest peak.

In the nearly nine decades since that 1890 expedition, the Society has aided or sponsored more than 1,300 individual researches and explorations. Some, like the 1915-1920 Mount Katmai expeditions to Alaska's Valley of Ten Thousand Smokes, have resulted in the addition of spectacular scenery to our system of national parks. Many others have fostered signal contributions to every conceivable field of geographic and scientific interest.

A sampling of projects encouraged by the Society quickly becomes a catalog of human achievement and a vivid record of the expansion of knowledge: At the ends of the earth, the Society assisted Robert E. Peary's epic 1909 "dash to the Pole" and supported two of Richard E. Byrd's historic stays at Little America in Antarctica.

Uncovering man's past in the Americas, in 1912 explorer Hiram Bingham led Society–Yale University excavations at the ruins of Machu Picchu, the lost mountaintop citadel of Peru's once great Incas. In 1938, with Society backing, Dr. Matthew W. Stirling began to uncover Mexico's pre-Columbian Olmec civilization and a stela bearing one of America's oldest written dates, equivalent to 31 B.C.

Nearly thirty years and more than 32,000 feet separate William Beebe's record-breaking 1934 bathysphere descent off Bermuda and the American Mount Everest expedition's conquest of the world's loftiest mountain in 1963. Both undertakings had Society support.

In East Africa, first the late Louis S. B. Leakey and his wife, Mary, and now their son Richard unlock the prehistoric mysteries

Fossil jaw in hand, the late Dr. Louis S. B. Leakey, at left, describes his early-man discoveries to the author.

WINFIELD PARKS

of Tanzania's Olduvai Gorge and Laetolil and Kenya's Lake Rudolf (now Lake Turkana), pushing man's history back more than three million years. Also in Tanzania, Jane Goodall observes her free-roaming friends the wild chimpanzees. In England archeologists sift the possible site of King Arthur's "Camelot." And in the United States a University of Texas radio sky survey maps the "chatter" of distant galaxies, extending our vision of the universe. All these projects receive Society aid.

Through its Committee for Research and Exploration, the Society annually approves more than one and a half million dollars in new and continuing grants to excavations, expeditions, and researches of all kinds. The following section of this index contains a list-

ing of the Society's research grants and expeditions through 1976. Concise résumés summarize the aims and results of major projects and point both interested layman and questing scholar to detailed technical monographs collected in the Society's *Research Reports,* a series now complete through 1968.* Many of these projects have also appeared in the pages of NATIONAL GEOGRAPHIC.

Describing his butterfly find to the Committee for Research and Exploration, Fred Urquhart called it "a tremendous discovery." It was indeed, and others await you in the pages that follow.

*Copies of the first nine volumes of *Research Reports* may be obtained for $5 each, postpaid, by writing to Dept. 100, National Geographic Society, Washington, D. C. 20036. Request later billing if desired.

Aeronautics and Atmospheric Science

Air-quality measurement device: development. John S. Hall. 1974

Da Vinci–Trans-America Manned Scientific Balloon Flight. Rudolf J. Engelmann. 1973

Explorer I (balloon). William E. Kepner, Albert W. Stevens, and Orvil A. Anderson. 1934

Explorer II (balloon): altitude record. Albert W. Stevens and Orvil A. Anderson. 1935. *Lifting a ton of scientific instruments and two aerial photographers,* Explorer II *reached an altitude of 13.71 miles, a record that stood unchallenged for 21 years.*

Stratosphere sampling. Bismarck, North Dakota. National Bureau of Standards. 1940-41

Anthropology

ARCHEOLOGY

North America

Agate Basin ancient Indian camp. Wyoming. Frank H. H. Roberts and William M. Bass. 1959, 1961

Arizona, central: prehistoric human adaptation in an environmental transition zone. George J. Gumerman. 1973

Baffin Island, Northwest Territories, Canada. Lorna M. McKenzie-Pollock. 1968-69

Balankanche Cave, Chichén Itzá, Mexico. E. Wyllys Andrews IV. 1959

Basket Maker occupation, Upper Grand Gulch, Utah. William D. Lipe. 1968-69

Bering Strait, Alaska. Henry B. Collins. 1936

Bison-kill site, Jones-Miller Paleo-Indian. Colorado. Dennis J. Stanford. 1973-76. *Ten thousand years old, this kill and butchering*

54

area provides a firsthand look at the daily economy of prehistoric North American Indians.

Carter's Grove, Virginia. Ivor Nöel-Hume. 1976. *Seventeenth-century settlement sites near Williamsburg add to our knowledge of the colonial South and America's early material beginnings.*

Caves and rock-shelters. Dominican Republic. Marcio Veloz Maggiolo. 1976

Chaco Canyon, New Mexico: remote-sensing analysis of prehistoric human occupations. Thomas R. Lyons. 1973

Chalcatzingo, Morelos, Mexico. David C. Grove. 1971-72

Colima, Mexico. Isabel T. Kelly. 1968, 1970

Coxcatlán, Puebla, Mexico. Richard S. Mac-Neish. 1971-73

Cuicuilco ruins, Mexico. Byron Cummings. 1924-25. *A vast ceremonial mound, sealed and preserved for many centuries by lava flows, bears impressive witness to the early beginnings of urban life among ancient Americans.*

Culture ecology, early. Mexican Gulf Coast. S. Jeffrey K. Wilkerson. 1973-75

Dorset Eskimo sites. Southampton Island, Hudson Bay. Henry B. Collins. 1954

Dry Creek, central Alaska. William R. Powers. 1976

Dzibilchaltun, Yucatán, Mexico. E. Wyllys Andrews IV. 1957-66. *Perhaps the largest and longest-inhabited site in prehistoric America, this ruined metropolis speaks eloquently of the vanished glories of Maya civilization.*

Engelbert site: Indian burials. Nichols, New York. William D. Lipe. 1968

Environmental archeology and cultural systems. Hamilton Inlet, Labrador. William W. Fitzhugh. 1971-72

Etzna: prehistoric house mounds and canals. Campeche, Mexico. Ray T. Matheny. 1974

"Exploration of Early Man Sites in Alaska" project. 1976. *The Society has joined the National Park Service in a three-year project to locate and date traces of early man in his dispersal through North America.*

Finger Lakes region, New York. Marian E. White. 1975

Gatecliff Shelter, Nevada. David H. Thomas. 1975-76

Grand Canyon, Arizona: North Rim. Douglas W. Schwartz. 1968-71

Grasshopper Pueblo habitat. Arizona. William A. Longacre. 1974

Hell Gap site. Wyoming. Cynthia and Henry T. Irwin and George A. Agogino. 1962-66

Hirundo site. Maine. David Sanger. 1972-73, 1975

Katmai National Monument, Alaska: ancient Aleut and Eskimo site. Donald E. Dummond. 1967-68

King site. Floyd County, Georgia. David J. Hally. 1973

Lahonton Lake, Nevada. Phil C. Orr. 1957

Larsen archeological site. South Dakota. William M. Bass. 1970

Lehner Paleo-Indian site. San Pedro Valley, Arizona. C. Vance Haynes and Emil W. Haury. 1973, 1975

Maya sites. Becan, Campeche, Mexico. Prentice M. Thomas, Jr. 1972-73

————Yucatán Peninsula, Mexico. E. Wyllys Andrews IV. 1968, 1970. *Dramatic artistic and scientific discoveries in the Yucatán Peninsula reflect the greatness of Maya culture at its zenith.*

Meadowcroft Rockshelter and Cross Creek Drainage. Pennsylvania. James M. Adovasio. 1976

Mississippi, southwestern. Stephen Williams. 1970, 1972

Mississippi Valley protohistoric and early 18th-century Indian-French contact period. Jeffrey P. Brain. 1974

Mummy Cave, Wyoming. Harold McCracken. 1965

Olmec sites. La Venta, Tres Zapotes, and San Lorenzo, Mexico. Philip Drucker, 1955; Robert F. Heizer, 1955, 1965-69; Matthew W. Stirling, 1938-46. *Eight successive dry-season expeditions produced a series of superlative finds illuminating Olmec culture: one of America's oldest dated works—a stela bearing a date equivalent to 31 B.C., colossal stone heads, greenstone "tiger" masks, and two ruined cities.*

Paleo-Indian quarry and living sites. Shenandoah Valley, Virginia. William M. Gardner. 1970

Port Royal, Jamaica. Edwin A. Link. 1959

Post-Hopewellian subsistence change: testing a model for. Stuart Struever. 1973

Pueblo Bonito, New Mexico. Andrew Ellicott Douglass, 1923-29; Neil M. Judd, 1920-27, 1929. *Communal dwellings in northwestern New Mexico yielded clues to the prehistory of the Southwest; tree rings in housing beams have dated their construction at A.D. 919 to 1130.*

Puerco River Valley, New Mexico: resettlement of Puebloan populations after the abandonment of Chaco Canyon. Cynthia Irwin-Williams. 1970-73

Quintana Roo: Cobá mapping project. Mexico. George E. Stuart. 1974-75

————Tancah and Tulum: murals and architecture. Mexico. Arthur G. Miller. 1972-75

Río Bec region: ecological change and cultural history. Yucatán Peninsula, Mexico. Richard E. W. Adams. 1972

Russell Cave, Jackson County, Alabama. Carl F. Miller, 1956-58. *Artifacts recovered here reveal continuous human occupancy from about 6200 B.C. to A.D. 1650. The Society bought and deeded the site to the Federal Government for preservation as a national archeological monument.*

Salts Cave, Mammoth Cave National Park, Kentucky. Patty Jo Watson. 1968-69

San Juan County, Utah. Neil M. Judd. 1923

Sandia Cave, New Mexico. George A. Agogino. 1961

Santa Rosa Island, California. Phil C. Orr. 1957

"Spanish Diggings" aboriginal flint quarries. Southeastern Wyoming. John M. Saul. 1964

Stone spheres. Jalisco, Mexico. Matthew W. Stirling. 1967-68

Tellico Reservoir, Tennessee. Jefferson Chapman. 1976

Thule culture. Northwest Hudson Bay. Charles F. Merbs. 1968-70

Towers of Hovenweep National Monu-ment. Mesa Verde, Colorado. Ray A. Williamson. 1976

Turner Farm site. North Haven, Maine. Bruce J. Bourque. 1974-75

Upper Delaware Valley Early Man Project. Charles W. McNett, Jr. 1974-76

Viking site. L'Anse aux Meadows, Newfoundland. Helge Ingstad. 1963-65. *This site has produced evidence that Norse settlers touched the North American Continent some five centuries before Columbus.*

Voyageur fur-trade materials. Minnesota-Ontario border. Robert C. Wheeler. 1963-66

Voyageurs: Fort Charlotte Underwater Project. Grand Portage National Monument, Minnesota. Robert C. Wheeler. 1975

Well of Sacrifice probe. Chichén Itzá, Mexico. William J. Folan. 1960-61. *The first exploration with modern free-diving equipment and air lift at this old Maya city's cenote brought to light jade, metal, and ceramic ornaments and figurines.*

Wetherill Mesa, Colorado. Douglas Osborne. 1958-63. *Painstaking excavation efforts co-sponsored by the Society and the National Park Service resurrected the cliffside dwellings of Indians who vanished 700 years ago.*

Xitle (volcano) and Cuicuilco (pyramid), Mexico. Robert F. Heizer. 1957

Yucatán Peninsula, Mexico: settlement patterns, pre-Columbian. Edward B. Kurjack. 1975

Central and South America

Abaj Takalik, Guatemala. John A. Graham. 1975-76. *Exploratory studies at this extensive and little-investigated group of ruins revealed chronological overlap between two ancient Middle American cultures—the Olmec and the Maya.*

Agronomy potential. Bajo de Santa Fe, El Petén, Guatemala. Bruce H. Dahlin. 1975

Architectural stones and sculpture. Peru and Bolivia. Robert F. Heizer. 1963

Ariari River Basin, Colombia: archeological chronology. John P. Marwitt. 1973-74

Chan Chan-Moche Valley Project, Peru. Carol J. Mackey and Michael E. Moseley. 1969-74. *An urban settlement on Peru's north*

coast, Chan Chan was built between the 13th and 15th centuries A.D. *and served as the capital city of the Chimu people before being conquered around 1470 by highland Incas.*

Chicama-Moche Canal Project, Peru. James S. Kus. 1968-69

Culebra, Bay of, Costa Rica. Frederick W. Lange. 1976

Cupisnique culture: Caballo Muerto complex. Peru. Thomas G. Pozorski. 1973

Ecuador Indian tribes and pre-Columbian sites. Matthew W. Stirling. 1957

Gold artifacts, pre-Columbian: catalog. Panama. Reina Torres de Arauz. 1971

Honduras cultural change (pre-Columbian Mesoamerican frontier). Paul F. Healy. 1975-76

Incas. Machu Picchu, Peru. Hiram Bingham. 1912, 1914-15. *Discovered in 1911 by explorer Hiram Bingham, Machu Picchu had been concealed from the outside world by jungle for nearly four centuries. Bingham later headed a Society–Yale University expedition to clear this lost mountaintop citadel of the Incas.*

Maya highlands, Guatemala. Robert J. Sharer. 1972-73

Maya vessels: search for evidence of seaborne contact with highland cultures of Mesoamerica. Nancy M. Farriss. 1974-75

Middle American Research Institute archeological publication. New Orleans, Louisiana. E. Wyllys Andrews IV. 1975

Monte Alto, Guatemala. Lee A. Parsons, 1968-70

—— Edwin Martin Shook. 1972

Nazca lines. Peru. Gerald S. Hawkins. 1967

—— Maria Reiche. 1974

Panama. Matthew W. Stirling. 1948-49, 1951, 1953

Prehistoric maize spread, ceramic evidence of. Peru. Mary Eubanks Dunn. 1975

Quichean civilization, central Guatemala. Kenneth L. Brown. 1976

Quiriguá, Guatemala. William R. Coe, 1974-75; Robert J. Sharer, 1976. *Long-range investigations at this site in the Maya lowlands are*

filling important gaps in our knowledge of the ancient Maya culture.

Williamsburg and Palmar Sur, Costa Rica. Matthew W. Stirling. 1964

Pacific

Huahine, Society Islands. Yosihiko H. Sinoto. 1974-75

Lau Island, Fiji. Roger C. Green. 1976

Asia

Abu Salabikh, Iraq (Sumerian city). John N. Postgate. 1976

Antiochus I: tomb. Nemrud Dagh, Turkey. Theresa Goell. 1963-64

Aphrodisias, Turkey. Kenan T. Erim. 1966-76. *As a result of this ambitious archeological project, an acropolis, a theater, a stadium, and magnificent statuary have emerged as sublime witnesses to the grandeur of the ancient Greco-Roman world.*

Bronze Age settlement. Cyprus. James R. Carpenter. 1974

Cyprus. James M. Adovasio. 1973

Jerusalem. Kathleen M. Kenyon. 1962-67

Palawan caves. Palawan Island, Philippines. Robert B. Fox. 1965-66

Radiometric dating of Paleolithic sites. Israel and Hungary. Henry P. Schwarcz. 1975

Routes through the Bakhtiari Mountains, Iran. Allen Zagarell. 1976

Samosata Mound, Turkey. Theresa Goell. 1967, 1969

Sarepta (Zarephath), Lebanon: Phoenician and Biblical city. James B. Pritchard. 1968-72. *Once a great port city that could boast of a visit by the prophet Elijah, Sarepta is now farmland harboring important Phoenician and Biblical remains.*

Shahr-i Qumis. Lost capital of Parthian Iran. John F. Hansman. 1970, 1975

Syria. Trevor F. Watkins. 1975

Tal-i Malyan, Fars, Iran. Robert H. Dyson, Jr. 1976

Tell Jemmeh, Israel. Gus W. Van Beek. 1975-76. *This site dating from the 13th century* B.C. *offers evidence of ancient trade and cul-*

tural contacts between the areas of present-day Israel and the Arabian Peninsula.

Tell Keisan, Israel. Roland DeVaux. 1971

Europe

Amber artifacts: spectroscopic provenance analysis. Curt W. Beck. 1973

Anglo-Saxon royal burial ground. Sutton Hoo, Suffolk, England. Rupert L. S. Bruce-Mitford. 1968, 1970

Apollo sanctuary. Halieis, Greece. Michael H. Jameson. 1973-74

Architecture and village layout in ancient Greece. William A. McDonald. 1971

Argolid Peninsula, Greece: postglacial environmental history. Donald R. Whitehead. 1972-73

"Camelot." South Cadbury, Somerset, England. Leslie Alcock. 1970. *Excavations of this and other sites lend credence to medieval legends of King Arthur's royal city.*

Caves of Quaternary and Holocene origin. Spain. William H. Waldren. 1971, 1973

Greece: society, culture, economy in the later Roman period. Timothy E. Gregory. 1974

Helice, Greece. Harold E. Edgerton and Peter Throckmorton. 1970-71

Ice Age Franco-Cantabrian caves: photography and analysis. Alexander Marshack. 1973

Monastery, seventh-century. Jarrow, England. Rosemary J. Cramp. 1973

Neolithic fortress site and rock paintings. Sierra de Taibilla, Spain. Michael J. Walker. 1968-70

Porto Longo Harbor, Sapienza Island, Greece. Harold E. Edgerton and Peter Throckmorton. 1970

Stonehenge, England; Callanish, Scotland. Gerald S. Hawkins. 1965

Tower of the Winds. Athens. Derek J. de Solla Price. 1964

Trade in prehistoric amber. A. Colin Renfrew and Curt W. Beck. 1975

Africa

Aten, temple of: computerized study. Karnak, Egypt. Ray W. Smith. 1968-69

Bamenda-Koumbo area, West Cameroon. Donald D. Hartle. 1967

Cave research. Mali. Johan Huizinga. 1970

Chad and Libya: archeological reconnaissance. Carleton S. Coon. 1966-67

Colossi of Memnon, Egypt. Robert F. Heizer. 1971

Engaruka, Tanzania, cultural site of early man. Hamo Sassoon. 1967

Gebel Adda, Egypt. Nicholas B. Millet. 1963-65

Iron Age settlement survey. Upper Zambezi Valley, Zambia. Joseph O. Vogel. 1976

Karamoja District, Uganda. Hamo Sassoon. 1972

Libyan Desert, Egypt: geological-anthropological survey. C. Vance Haynes. 1974-76

Megaliths of central Africa. Nicholas C. David. 1974

Mosaics of Tunisia. Margaret A. Alexander. 1973, 1976

Ngamiland, Botswana. John E. Yellen. 1973

Pyramids, cosmic-ray research in. Egypt. Luis W. Alvarez. 1968

Underwater

American Revolutionary gunboat. Lake Champlain. Philip K. Lundeberg. 1968

Battle of Lepanto shipwrecks: Greece. Spyridon Marinatos. 1971

Bermuda waters. Mendel L. Peterson. 1965-67

Byzantine shipwrecks. Turkey. George F. Bass. 1961-69, 1976. *New underwater excavation techniques allow the recovery of ship remains that shed new light on nautical architecture of the 7th through 12th centuries.*

Greek cargo ship, seventh-century. Sicilian waters. Edwin A. Link. 1962

Iron Age shipwreck. Turkey. George F. Bass. 1974-75. *An unlooted shipwreck from the seventh century B.C. promises new insight into the shipping and daily life of archaic Greece, a period little known from dry-land remains.*

Kyrenia, Cyprus. Michael L. Katzev. 1967-72. *This underwater project located and excavated a fourth-century B.C. Greek merchantman, the finest preserved ship of Greece's classical period ever found.*

Kyrenia Ship Project film documentary. Susan W. Katzev. 1975

Mediterranean Sea search. Peter Throckmorton. 1975

————— survey. George F. Bass. 1973

Monitor **search.** Cape Hatteras area, North Carolina. John J. Newton and Harold E. Edgerton. 1973-74. *The wreck of the celebrated Civil War ironclad was discovered in August 1973 by this expedition. Side-scan sonar equipment confirmed the wreck's location in 220 feet of water off Cape Hatteras.*

Porto Longo, Greece: sonar search. Peter Throckmorton. 1968-69

Portuguese frigate search. Mombasa Harbor, Kenya. Hamo Sassoon. 1975

Punic ship, third-century B.C. Sicily. Honor E. Frost. 1973

Sonar gear supplied. Eastern Mediterranean. Harold E. Edgerton. 1968

Spanish Plate Fleet research. Florida. Kip L. Wagner. 1965

ETHNOLOGY

Chewing sticks. West Africa, Egypt, and Pakistan. Memory P. Elvin-Lewis and Walter H. Lewis. 1975

North America

Aleutian survivors of the Bering land bridge. William S. Laughlin. 1972

Aleuts: Russian influence on ecology, culture, and physical anthropology. Christy G. Turner, 2d. 1972-73

Eskimo linguistics and religion. Canada. Svend Frederiksen. 1965

Hinds Cave, Val Verde County, Texas. Vaughn M. Bryant, Jr. 1975

Indian ethnobotany. California. Lowell J. Bean. 1975

Otomi Indians: resource cognition. Mexico. Kirsten J. Haring. 1973

Preceramic culture. Chiapas, Mexico. Philip Drucker. 1947

Pre-Columbian cultural change. Cozumel, Mexico. Jeremy A. Sabloff. 1971-73

Rock art, prehistoric. Nevada caves. Robert F. Heizer. 1975

Tarahumara people. Mexico. Robert A. Bye, Jr. 1972

Tlapanec Indians. Tlacoapa, Mexico. Marion Oettinger, Jr. 1971

Washo Indians: art. Nevada. Norval C. Kern, Jr. 1970

Central and South America

Afkodre **magic and religion:** Creoles. Surinam. Benjamin E. Pierce. 1971

Black Caribs. Central America. William V. Davidson. 1973-74

Chickens, black-boned: distribution and use. Middle America. Carl L. Johannessen. 1976

Copablanca Festival: ethnographic and ethnomusicological survey. Bolivia. Edwin E. Erickson. 1973

Maya salt trade. Anthony P. Andrews. 1975

Mesoamerican pottery techniques. Lewis A. Krevolin. 1972

Peasant livelihood behavior. Trinidad. Bonham C. Richardson. 1971

Prehistoric cultural development. Peruvian highlands. Clifford Evans and Betty Meggers. 1968-69

Waurá Indians. Mato Grosso, Brazil. Harald Schultz. 1961-64

Welsh colony. Patagonia. Glyn Williams. 1968-69

Pacific

Caroline Islanders: ethnohistory. Saul H. Riesenberg. 1973

Child behavior. New Hebrides. E. Richard Sorenson. 1971. *A comparative study of child-rearing behavior and its relationship to cultural organization, this project employed motion-picture filming of natives relatively untouched by European influences.*

Dani people, material culture. Netherlands New Guinea. Robert G. Gardner. 1962

Diseases and cures, native. Torres Strait Islands. George J. Simeon. 1974

Fore and Bahinemo peoples: facial expression of emotions. New Guinea. E. Richard Sorenson. 1968-69

Maori. New Zealand. William N. Fenton. 1974

New Guinea natives: religious symbolism. Wilson G. Wheatcroft. 1968-70

Polynesian dances. Cook Island. E. Richard Sorenson. 1975

Tanna Island, New Hebrides. Kalman A. Muller. 1974

Trade, migration, and marriage. New Guinea. Deborah Gewertz. 1974

Australia

Aborigines. Arnhem Land, northern Australia. Charles P. Mountford. 1948. *A comprehensive eight-month survey brought together cultural and natural history data on an aboriginal reserve the size of Maine.*

Art sanctuary. Koonalda Cave, South Australia. Christine Elvera Sharpe. 1975

Tiwi culture. Melville Island, Australia. Charles P. Mountford. 1954

Asia

Ainu of Hokkaido, Japan. M. Inez Hilger. 1965-66

Arab potters. Israel. Owen S. Rye. 1976

Bakhtiyārī tribe: role in history. Iran. Gene R. Garthwaite. 1971

Burial ritual. North Borneo. Peter A. Metcalf. 1975

Karnali Zone: cultural-ecological analysis. Western Nepal. Barry C. Bishop. 1968-69, 1971

Kenyah Dayaks: religion and social organization. Sarawak, Malaysia. Herbert L. Whittier. 1973

Kinship and marriage: hierarchy and amity. South Asia. Anthony T. Carter. 1973

Kurds. Khorasan, Iran. Robert E. Peck. 1967

Lua tribe. Northern Thailand. Peter Kunstadter. 1963-64

Man, protohistoric and early historic: interaction with environment. Isthmian Thailand. Janice Mary Stargardt. 1973

Mesolithic occupations. Cyprus. James M. Adovasio. 1972-73

Pashtoon pastoral nomadism. Afghanistan. Asen Balikci. 1972

Pastoralism in southern Sinai. Ofer Bar-Yosef. 1976

Religious centers of the Himalayas. Barbara N. Aziz. 1975

Shabakites. Northern Iraq. Sami Sáid Ahmed. 1973

Sherpa culture. Nepal and Sikkim. Luther G. Jerstad. 1965

Yazidies religious group. Middle East. Sami Sáid Ahmed. 1967

Europe

Depopulation and cultural change. Islands of western Ireland. Kevin C. Kearns. 1975

Symbol systems, Paleolithic. East Europe and the Soviet Union. Alexander Marshack. 1975-76

Africa

Afar nomadism. Ethiopia. Robert G. Gardner. 1965

Bani-Niger people: African migrants. Johan Huizinga. 1974

Fulani people: social system with their cattle. Northern Nigeria. Dale F. Lott. 1973

Kwanyama linguistic group: ethnobotany. Ovamboland, South-West Africa. Robert J. Rodin. 1972

Mandinko people: history, social structure, and ethnobotany. Pakao, southern Senegal. David M. Schaffer. 1973, 1975

Migration and communication of people of the Kisii district, Kenya. Ronald D. Garst. 1975

Ngamiland peoples: demography. Okavango River and delta, Africa. Thomas J. Larson. 1971

Rural migration: relationship to expansion of

commercial agriculture. Tanzania. Marilyn Silberfein. 1973

West African settlement geography along a linguistic and environmental transect. Reed F. Stewart. 1976

Women's role in the Pokot of Kenya. Elizabeth L. Meyerhoff. 1976

Yoruba geophagy. Nigeria. Donald E. Vermeer. 1975

PHYSICAL ANTHROPOLOGY
and
PALEOANTHROPOLOGY

African sites: Fort Ternan, Kenya; Lake Rudolf, Kenya; Olduvai Gorge, Tanzania; Omo Valley, Ethiopia. Louis S. B. Leakey, Mary Leakey, and Richard E. Leakey. 1960-68. *The Leakeys have filled major gaps in the record of early man. One of their most exciting finds was the discovery, in 1959, of* Australopithecus (Zinjanthropus) boisei, *shown by later tests to have lived 1,750,000 years ago.*

Arikara burial sites. South Dakota. T. Dale Stewart. 1971

———— Indian skeletons. North Dakota. William M. Bass. 1968-69

Calico Mountains, Mojave Desert, California. Louis S. B. Leakey, Thomas Clements, Gerald A. Smith, and Ruth D. Simpson. 1964-67

Centre for Prehistory and Palaeontology, Nairobi, Kenya. Louis S. B. Leakey. 1971

Disease, pre-Columbian American. Marvin J. Allison. 1971, 1973-74, 1976. *Analysis of diseases of mummies from graves dating as far back as A.D. 825 shows, among other things, black lung (miner's) disease and tuberculosis.*

East Africa. Louis S. B. Leakey. 1971-72.

Ecuador, coastal: demography. Douglas H. Ubelaker. 1974

Ethiopia's Upper Pliocene localities. Francis H. Brown and F. Clark Howell. 1974

Extinct fauna and early man. Mojave Desert, California. Emma Lou Davis. 1970-71

Hadar, central Afar, Ethiopia. Donald Johanson. 1975-76. *The dramatic discovery, in one small area, of skeletal remains of five to seven individual hominid specimens indicates the possibility that a prehistoric social group—perhaps a family—was caught in a mass disaster.*

Kathmandu Valley and Siwalik deposits, Nepal. Elwyn L. Simons. 1974

Laetolil beds, Tanzania. Raymonde Bonnefille. 1976

———— Mary D. Leakey. 1975-76. *Mammalian fossils found in the upper part of the Laetolil sequence have been dated as 3.35 to 3.75 million years old. Hominid remains from the same sequence bear striking similarities to material found in Ethiopia.*

Olduvai Gorge, Tanzania. Raymonde Bonnefille. 1976

———— Mary D. Leakey. 1970-75. *Continuing fieldwork at this premier archeological and paleontological site permits an ever firmer dating of fossil remains.*

Rudolf, Lake, Kenya. Richard E. Leakey. 1965-76. *Discovery at this site of skull 1470, nearly three million years old, compelled a rethinking of mankind's pedigree. It has been tentatively classified as a direct ancestor of present-day* Homo sapiens.

———— discoveries: report. F. Clark Howell. 1974

Sherpas: high-altitude adaptation and genetics. Georgio P. Morpurgo. 1976

Skeletal biology. Corinth, Greece. Henry S. Robinson. 1975

Astronomy and Astrophysics

Asteroids: Geographos and others. A. M. J. Gehrels. 1971

Astronomical alignment of Canadian Indian cairns and medicine wheels. John A. Eddy. 1975

Auroras. Carl W. Gartlein. 1938-56. *Eighteen*

Astronomy and Astrophysics

years of observations by professional and amateur astronomers produced valuable data on the brightness, color, variety, and sequence of auroras.

Beta Scorpii and companion: occultation by Jupiter. David S. Evans. 1971

Cosmic-ray monitoring. Martin A. Pomerantz. 1946-53, 1956-58, 1964

"Einstein Shift" verification. Khartoum, Sudan. George A. Van Biesbroeck. 1952. *Starfield measurements made during and after the February 25, 1952, solar eclipse substantially confirmed Einstein's theory of relativity.*

Galaxy clusters: size. Hale Observatories. Thomas W. Noonan. 1974

Geographos (asteroid 1620). Betty F. Mintz. 1968-69

—— orbit study. Samuel Herrick. 1968-69

Gravitational light-deflection effect: improved measurement. Bryce S. DeWitt. 1973

Interstellar deuterium. Jay M. Pasachoff. 1974

Kohoutek, comet, and the annular solar eclipse. Donald H. Menzel. 1973

Mars. Bloemfontein observatory, South Africa. E. C. Slipher. 1954-56. *Greenish patches and mysterious "canals" lacing the Martian surface were among the subjects of this two-year study of the red planet.*

Mars and Jupiter: spectroscopic studies. Mauna Loa, Hawaii. C. C. Kiess and C. H. Corliss. 1956-57

"Martian Pavilion," Georgetown College Observatory, presented by the Society. 1956

Planetary systems search. Arizona. A. M. J. Gehrels and Krzysztof Serkowski. 1974-76. *If successful, the search for solar-type stars with large orbiting planets can improve our estimate of the probability of life elsewhere in the universe.*

Planets, brighter. Photographic atlas prepared. E. C. Slipher and John S. Hall. 1962-63

Sky mapping, radio. James N. Douglas. 1973-75. *Radio telescopes monitor the infrared emissions of distant stars that lie beyond the range of optical telescopes.*

Sky survey, infrared photographic. Eric R. Craine. 1976

Sky survey, Palomar Observatory–National Geographic Society: photomapping. 1949-58. *A monumental sky atlas, extending to a depth of one billion light-years, resulted from this photographic survey of the heavens, which expanded the known sky 25 times.*

—— Palomar Observatory–National Geographic Society: transparent overlay map preparation. John D. Kraus. 1976

Solar corona: photography of the spectrum, polarization, and form. Donald H. Menzel. 1972

Solar corona at eclipse: spectrographic study. Donald H. Menzel. 1969

Solar eclipse. Africa. Donald H. Menzel. 1972

—— Australia. Donald H. Menzel. 1976

—— Bocaiúva, Brazil. Lyman J. Briggs. 1947. *Observations made during this Society–U. S. Army Air Forces expedition included photographs of the May 20, 1947, solar eclipse taken from 30,000 feet.*

—— Burma to the Aleutian Islands. Lyman J. Briggs. 1948

—— Canton Island, Pacific. Samuel A. Mitchell. 1937

—— Maine-New Hampshire. Albert W. Stevens and Paul A. McNally. 1932

—— Norfolk, Virginia. Simon Newcomb and Alexander Graham Bell. 1900

—— Northern Canada. Wolfgang B. Klemperer. 1963

—— Patos, Brazil. Irvine C. Gardner. 1940

—— Trans-African baseline. Jay M. Pasachoff. 1973

—— U.S.S.R. Irvine C. Gardner. 1936

—— U.S.S.R. Paul A. McNally and W. Robert Moore. 1936

Solar radiation. Mount Brukkaros, South-West Africa. Charles G. Abbot. 1925-29

Stars, peculiar early-type. Deane M. Peterson. 1974

Uranus occultation (1977). William B. Hubbard, Jr. 1976

Zodiacal light. Colorado-Nebraska border. George A. Van Biesbroeck. 1954

Biology

Animal hard parts: biological destruction of, in marine environment. Peter M. Kranz. 1973

Aquatic animals: behavior in relation to polarized light. Talbot H. Waterman. 1970-71

Biological and archeological expedition. Southeast Oceania. John E. Randall. 1969

Biological colonization of a recently formed volcanic island. Motmot, Papua New Guinea. Eldon E. Ball. 1972, 1974, 1976

Biological investigation; disease study. Bolivia. Richard G. Van Gelder. 1964

Biological studies of the northern Cordillera Vilcabamba. Peru. John W. Terborgh. 1966-68. *Much new information on biological relationships has emerged from this study of the effect of altitude upon the diversity of plant and animal species.*

Cerro Tacarcuna, Panama-Colombia border: biological exploration. Alwyn H. Gentry. 1974

Deep reefs: ecology. Western Caribbean. Walter A. Starck II. 1970

Deep-sea fauna: biology and distribution. Tropical Atlantic Ocean. Gilbert L. Voss. 1963-73. *This project included research on population dynamics, life histories and biology of species, and the physical and chemical character of ocean environments.*

Gombe National Park: establishment. Tanzania. 1968

——— support. D. N. Bryceson. 1973

Hudson Bay and Labrador: biological expedition. W. E. Clyde Todd. 1912, 1914, 1917

Natural history collection. Inner Mongolia, China. Frederick R. Wulsin. 1923-24

Netherlands Indies: collection of rare species for zoos. Sumatra. William M. Mann. 1937

Organisms from simple environments. Nicholas C. Collins. 1976

Río Camuy Cave, northwestern Puerto Rico. Russell H. Gurnee, Brother G. Nicholas, and John V. Thrailkill. 1963

Urubamba Valley, biological expedition. Peru. Frank M. Chapman. 1916

BOTANY

Algae. Australia. Ralph A. Lewin. 1976

Alpine cushion plants. George G. Spomer. 1974

Araucarian cones. Southern Argentina. Thomas N. Taylor. 1973

Asteraceae: biosystematic studies. South America. Robert Merrill King. 1973

Bahama, Turks, and Caicos Islands. William Thomas Gillis, Jr. 1973

Bali and Celebes Islands. Willem Meijer. 1976

Bamboos and bambusoid grasses: Brazil. Thomas R. Soderstrom. 1971, 1975

Bracken-fern gametophytes: comparative normal and abnormal development. Carl R. Partanen. 1971

Bromeliads. Brazilian mountains. Margaret U. Mee. 1966

Bryophytes. Southern Chile. John J. Engel. 1975

Capsicum pubescens complex: biosystematics and evolution. W. Hardy Eshbaugh. 1970-71

Chondrus crispus alga. Esther L. McCandless. 1970

Cycad *(Zamia).* Knut Norstog. 1975

Death Valley, California. Frederick V. Coville. 1931

Desert plants; *Welwitschia.* South-West Africa. Chris H. Bornman. 1968

Flax *(Linum).* Mediterranean region. Claude M. Rogers. 1971

Forest reserves in the "Green Plan." Austria. Else A. Schmidt. 1968-69

Forest types. North Cascade Range, Washington. Richard N. Mack. 1973

Forests: establishment. Celebes. Willem Meijer. 1975

Grasses: biosystematic investigation. Oaxaca and Chiapas, Mexico. Frank W. Gould. 1973

Hanging gardens. Colorado Plateau. Stanley L. Welsh. 1972

Kakabekia, microorganism with Precambrian affinities: paleobiology. Iceland. Sanford M. Siegel. 1971. *Straddling the thin line between inorganic material and living substance, the microorganism* Kakabekia *is a living fossil plant virtually identical with the earth's earliest organisms. Research on it hints at what life was like at its very beginning.*

Kokechik Bay area, Alaska. Charles M. Kirkpatrick. 1972

Kwangsi, China. G. Weidman Groff. 1937

Lepidoptera: host plants. Aldabra Atoll, Indian Ocean. Jay C. Shaffer. 1967

Lichen growths on Maya ruins. Mason E. Hale. 1975

Lichens *(Stereocaulon paschale)* as caribou fodder. K. A. Kershaw. 1976

———— (Thelotremataceae): systematics and evolution. Lesser Antilles. Mason E. Hale. 1971

———— and bryophytes. Galapagos Islands. William A. Weber. 1975

Lodgepole pine forests: biotic succession following fire. Yellowstone National Park. Dale L. Taylor. 1971

Log-fern hybrids *(Dryopteris).* Great Dismal Swamp, Virginia. Lytton J. Musselman. 1976

Madagascar. Peter Goldblatt. 1973

Mangroves: evolutionary mechanisms. Philip B. Tomlinson. 1976. *This project and the following research entry are designed to win a deeper knowledge of the breeding mechanisms of mangroves in order to draw up management policies that will halt their wholesale destruction.*

———— Old World (Indo-Pacific). Philip B. Tomlinson. 1973

———— Oriental. A. Malcolm Gill. 1968-69

Marquesas Islands. Marie-Helene Sachet. 1974

Maya Mountains, British Honduras. John D. Dwyer. 1972

Microflora: composition, variation, and ecology. Arctic Sea ice. Spencer Apollonio. 1971

Mistletoes: biogeographical affinities and chromosomal relationships. Africa. Delbert Wiens. 1971

Orchids, terrestrial: pollination. Australia. Warren P. Stoutamire. 1972-73

Phytogeographic studies. Burica Peninsula, Panama and Costa Rica. Thomas B. Croat. 1972

Plankton, blue-water. William M. Hamner. 1970

Plant collecting. Sierra de San Lazaro, Baja California. Amy Jean Gilmartin. 1968-69

Plant communities: effects of pollinating bats. Costa Rica and Arizona. Donna J. Howell. 1974

Plant succession on Soufrière of St. Vincent, Leeward Islands. John Stanley Beard. 1971

Plants and landforms. Tristan da Cunha and St. Helena Islands. Nigel M. Wace. 1975

Psilotum: classical culture, mutants, and wild occurrences. Japan. Albert S. Rouffa. 1972

Pteridophytic plants: phytogeography. Chocó, Colombia. David B. Lellinger. 1968-69

Rattan–palm collection. Asian rain forests. Jack B. Fisher. 1976

Redwoods: preservation. California. Chester C. Brown. 1963. *A National Geographic grant made possible this National Park Service survey of coast redwoods. The study eventually prompted the establishment of a new national park to preserve the giant trees.*

Sage *(Salvia).* James L. Reveal. 1974

Spore research. West Indies and northern South and Central America. Fred C. Meier. 1935

Stromatolites and algal carbonate structures of the Recent Epoch: ecology. Shark Bay, Australia. Stjepko Golubic. 1973

Subarctic plant systems and water conservation. Wayne R. Rouse. 1971

Sunflower family (Compositae): as source of fish poisons. Tod F. Stuessy. 1976

Tierra del Fuego, Argentina-Chile: study, collection, and illustration of flora. Rae Natalie P. Goodall. 1970-72. *The first fully gener-*

alized botanical collecting done in little-known Tierra del Fuego since 1764, this project aimed at the collection and description of plants native to the area before they were further disturbed by agriculture.

Wheats, cultivated: origin and ancestry. B. Lennart Johnson. 1972

Wild flowers of the United States. New York Botanical Garden. 1965. *Preparation and publication of a six-volume work on U. S. wildflowers was aided by this Society research grant.*

ECOLOGY

Camera equipment for marine biology research. Harold E. Edgerton. 1974

Dead Sea system: limnology and ecology. Joel R. Gat. 1976

Dugongs and sea turtles: exploitation. Torres Strait. Bernard Nietschmann. 1976. *The marine resource system of the strait between New Guinea and Australia contains some of the tropics' last dugongs, sea turtles, sea-grass pastures, and the human marine hunters dependent upon them.*

Ecological surveying in East Lake Rudolf, Kenya. Michael Norton-Griffiths. 1976

Everglades ecology. Everglades National Park, Florida. Frank C. Craighead, Sr. 1966, 1970

Falkland Islands: natural history and ecology. Olin S. Pettingill, Jr. 1970

Forests, semideciduous: ecology of the canopy. Panama. Pedro Galindo. 1973

Little Dunk's Bay, Great Lakes system: ecosystem. Joseph B. MacInnis and Alan R. Emery. 1970

Moose and wolf relationships. Isle Royale, Michigan. Durward L. Allen and Peter A. Jordan. 1964-65. *A complex ecological drama— the survival of an island population of moose in the face of intensive predation by timber wolves—was the substance of this project.*

New Guinea mountains. J. Linsley Gressitt. 1968-69

Papyrus swamps: effect on ecology. Lake Naivasha, Kenya. John J. Gaudet. 1971, 1973, 1975

Pollution: 70-year evaluation. Dry Tortugas, Florida. Richard H. Chesher. 1972

Protozoan communities: ecology. Lake Waiau, Hawaii. Raymond D. Dillon. 1970

Submarine limnological study. Great Lakes. Joseph B. MacInnis. 1968-69

Tidal marsh: ecosystem. Trenton, New Jersey. Dennis F. Whigham. 1974

Titicaca, Lake. Peru-Bolivia. Carl Widmer. 1972

Wildlife-habitat classification by satellite imagery. John J. Craighead. 1975

ZOOLOGY

Cave fauna. Yucatán Peninsula. Robert W. Mitchell. 1974-75

Marine organisms, complex: sensory information processing and visual behavior. Talbot H. Waterman. 1968-69, 1973-76. *Wholly new data concerning the migratory navigation of fishes are emerging from these studies of the perception of polarized light by marine vertebrates.*

Reptiles, amphibians, and insects. Ethiopia. Thomas P. Monath. 1964

Vertebrate genetic systems: comparative population cytogenetics and evolutionary roles. William P. Hall, 3d. 1971

Vertebrates: locomotion. East Africa. Charles R. Taylor. 1976

──────── Neotropical: seasonal patterns. Sinaloa, Mexico. Terry A. Vaughan. 1970

──────── populations in strip-mine areas. Frederick J. Brenner. 1971, 1973-74

Wildlife survey and collection of specimens. Nepal. S. Dillon Ripley. 1948-49

Vertebrate Zoology
HERPETOLOGY

Alligator, American: thermoregulation and ecology. Frederick R. Gehlbach. 1971

──────── thermoregulation. Clifford Ray Johnson. 1974

Amphibians. Seychelles Islands, Indian Ocean. Ronald A. Nussbaum. 1976

Amphibians and reptiles. Andes. William E. Duellman. 1974

—— Colombia. Victor H. Hutchison. 1965

Frogs: relation of activity periods to phototactic behavior. Robert G. Jaeger. 1972

—— telmatobiid; physiological ecology. Lake Titicaca, Peru-Bolivia. Victor H. Hutchison. 1973

—— and reptiles: collecting specimens. New Guinea. Richard G. Zweifel. 1968

Iguanas, land *(Conolophus pallidus* and *C. subcristatus).* Dagmar I. Werner. 1975-76. *Introduced predators threaten the survival of land iguanas native to the Galapagos Islands. This study of their life history may suggest ways to preserve these reptiles against outside environmental pressures.*

Lizards. Kalahari Desert, Africa. Raymond B. Huey. 1975

—— *(Anolis).* Bahamas and West Indies. Thomas W. Schoener. 1968-70

—— *(Anolis):* island ecology. Caribbean. George C. Gorman. 1971

—— *(Anolis limifrons):* functions and social displays. Thomas A. Jenssen. 1971

—— iguanid *(Sceloporus grammicus):* biogeography of karyotype variation. William P. Hall, 3d. 1970

Salamanders, tropical: behavioral defense mechanisms. Edmund D. Brodie, Jr. 1973, 1975

Snakes and amphibians. French Guiana. Thomas P. Monath. 1963

Toads, Yosemite *(Bufo canorus):* energetics and natural history. Martin L. Morton. 1973

Tortoises, Galapagos. James L. Patton. 1976

—— William G. Reeder. 1968-69. *Giant tortoises are in danger of extinction and exist today only on the Galapagos Islands and on Aldabra Island in the Indian Ocean. This study of the population ecology of the Galapagos colony was undertaken to provide basic facts for use in conservation efforts.*

Turtles. Africa: Roger C. Wood. 1967

—— fresh-water chelid: taxonomy, distribution, and ecology. Australia. John M. Legler. 1972, 1974, 1976

Turtles, giant leatherback: taxonomic study. Surinam. Wayne F. Frair. 1968-69

—— green. Ascension Island. Archie F. Carr. 1976

—— Pacific green. Galapagos. Craig G. MacFarland. 1975-76

—— Pacific ridley: nesting biology. David A. Hughes. 1971

—— pleurodiran: systematics, evolution, and ecology. South America. Roger C. Wood. 1970

—— sea, hawksbill: exploitation and ecology. Bernard Nietschmann. 1972

—— slider *(Pseudemys scripta).* Panama. John M. Legler. 1966

ICHTHYOLOGY

Characid, splashing *(Copeina arnoldi):* reproductive and parental behavior. Guyana. Charles O. Krekorian. 1973

Coelacanth *(Latimeria chalumnae).* Indian Ocean. Keith Stewart Thomson. 1972

Eels, garden. Red Sea. Eugenie Clark. 1971. *Scientist, diver, and underwater photographer, Eugenie Clark made use of all her talents in this ecological and behavioral study of compact colonies of Red Sea garden eels.*

Fishes. Lord Howe Island. New South Wales, Australia. Frank H. Talbot. 1972

—— collection. Río Nichare, Venezuela. James E. Böhlke. 1976

—— coral-reef. Bahamas. Raymond D. Clarke. 1974

—— coral-reef. Moluccas, Indonesia. Victor G. Springer. 1973

—— coral-reef. Solomon Islands. John E. Randall. 1973

—— electric. Walter F. Heiligenberg. 1976

—— electric, mormyriform. Peter Moller. 1975

—— electric, mormyriform. Gabon. Carl D. Hopkins. 1976

—— genetics. Atlantic and Pacific Oceans. Dennis A. Powers. 1975

—— labrid. David R. Robertson. 1975

Fishes, marine invertebrates, and algae. Southeast Oceania. John E. Randall. 1969. *Society support enabled this scientist not only to collect, photograph, and study marine specimens from the waters off Easter Island but also to conduct an onshore archeological reconnaissance.*

――――― osteoglossid. South America. Joan Dorothy Fuller. 1972

――――― pelagic. F. G. Walton Smith and Hilary B. Moore. 1953-60. *This project embraced a search for unknown larval stages of sport and food fishes in order to complete their life histories.*

――――― pelagic. North Atlantic. Frank J. Mather 3d. 1962

――――― *(Poecilia):* ethology. Mexico. Joseph S. Balsano and Ellen M. Rasch. 1976

――――― survey. Congo River's lower rapids. Tyson R. Roberts. 1972

――――― toxic-repellent effect of certain species on sharks. Red Sea. Eugenie Clark. 1972. *Toxic even when diluted, a marine poison secreted by the Red Sea sole offers clues in the search for an effective synthetic shark repellent.*

――――― tropical reef. Caribbean. Robert R. Warner. 1976

Killifish, annual: systematics, ecology, and distribution. Northern South America. Jamie E. Thomerson. 1971

Lungfish *(Clarias)* and *Tilapia.* East Africa. Geoffrey Moriaso Ole Maloiy. 1974-75

River fishes. Australia. Tim M. Berra. 1968-69

Sharks, bull: speciation. Lake Nicaragua. Jack D. Burke. 1970

――――― gray reef: social behavior and aggression. Donald R. Nelson. 1971-72

――――― reef. Rangiroa, French Polynesia. Donald R. Nelson. 1973

――――― sleeping. Mexican caves. Eugenie Clark. 1973-74.

――――― teleost symbionts. Japan. Eugenie Clark. 1975

Shore fishes. Easter Island. John E. Randall. 1968-69

Stingrays: freshwater adaptation. Thomas B. Thorson. 1974, 1976. *Most stingrays live in a marine environment, but some tolerate brackish and fresh water. How they do so was the object of this study.*

Tuna: body-temperature study. Francis G. Carey. 1967-69

MAMMALOGY

Animal tracking by satellite. Frank C. Craighead, Jr. 1970. *A dramatic advance in research technique, satellite radio tracking and biotelemetry of large mammals literally moves biology into the Space Age.*

Antelopes. East Africa. Richard Despard Estes. 1974

――――― bongo: search for. Kenya. Theodore H. Reed. 1968

――――― sable. Angola and Kenya. Richard Despard Estes. 1968-70, 1975

――――― topi. Mara Game Preserve, Tanzania. Geoffrey Moriaso Ole Maloiy. 1972

Baboons, olive: ecology and behavior. Gilgil, Kenya. Robert S. O. Harding. 1974

Bats, false vampire: social, foraging, and roosting behavior. Terry A. Vaughan. 1972

Bears, black: satellite monitoring during winter sleep. John J. Craighead. 1971

――――― brown. Alaska Peninsula. Allen W. Stokes. 1972-73

――――― grizzly: habitat survey by Landsat. John J. Craighead. 1976

――――― grizzly. Yellowstone National Park, Wyoming. Frank C. Craighead, Jr., and John J. Craighead. 1959-67

――――― polar: behavior and ecology. North Twin Island, Northwest Territories, Canada. Brian M. Knudsen. 1970-71

――――― polar: survey of dens. Svalbard, Arctic Ocean. Thor Larsen. 1971

Biotelemetry systems for wildlife research. Frank C. Craighead, Jr., and John J. Craighead. 1968-69

Bison, American: social and sexual behavior. Montana. Dale F. Lott. 1967-71

Burros, wild: social organization and commu-

nication behavior. Patricia D. Moehlman. 1970, 1972

Bushbaby, thick-tailed: ecology and behavior. South Africa. Gerald A. Doyle. 1968, 1970

Caribou telemetry tracking. Idaho. Donald R. Johnson. 1974

Cat, Iriomote *(Mayailurus iriomotensis):* ecology and conservation. Japan. Paul Leyhausen. 1973

Cetacea, cervico-spinal rete mirabile of. Merrill P. Spencer. 1974

Cheetahs. Botswana. Mark J. Owens and Delia Owens. 1974

Chimpanzees. Gombe Stream, Tanzania. Jane Goodall. 1961-71, 1976. *Spectacular new facts on chimpanzee behavior and a unique scientific record resulted from this project.*

———— communicative capacity. R. Allen Gardner and Beatrice T. Gardner. 1968-69

Deer, Key. Florida. Willard D. Klimstra. 1968-71

Dolphins, dusky. Argentina. Roger S. Payne. 1974

———— dusky and southern common. Argentina. Charles Walcott. 1975-76

———— Franciscana: life history, behavior, and acoustics. Uruguay. Robert L. Brownell, Jr. 1972-73

Dugongs. Cape York Peninsula, Australia. Paul K. Anderson. 1975

Ferrets, black-footed, and prairie dogs. Wyoming. Timothy W. Clark. 1973

Gazelles, desert. Charles R. Taylor. 1971

Gorillas, lowland: ecology. West Africa. Julie C. Webb. 1974-75

———— lowland: interrelationships with chimpanzees. Río Muni, West Africa. Arthur J. Riopelle. 1966-69

———— lowland, juvenile. Francine G. Patterson. 1976

———— mountain. Virunga Mountains, Rwanda. Dian Fossey. 1967-76. *Feeding and grooming habits, play, sexual behavior, nest building and social systems, as well as range and habitat were included in this field study highlighted by overt acceptance of the researcher by the fast-disappearing mountain gorillas.*

Gorillas, white ("Snowflake"): adolescent development. Barcelona, Spain. Arthur J. Riopelle. 1970

Guanaco. South America. William L. Franklin. 1976

Hutia, Haitian. Charles A. Woods. 1974-75

Jackals. Serengeti Plain, Tanzania. Patricia D. Moehlman. 1975-76

Jaguars. Mato Grosso, Brazil. George B. Schaller. 1976

Kobs: conventionality of territorial leks. Uganda. Helmut K. Buechner. 1971

Lemurs *(Varecia variegatus).* Madagascar and Comoro Archipelago, Indian Ocean. Ian Tattersall. 1974, 1976

Lions: ecology. Kitengela Conservation Area, Kenya. Judith Ann Rudnai. 1974

Macaques, Ceylonese. Wolfgang P. J. Dittus. 1975

———— wild bonnet. South India. Paul E. Simonds. 1975

Mammals. Chaco Boreal, Paraguay. Ralph M. Wetzel. 1973-75

———— Uintah Mountains, Utah. Gordon L. Kirkland, Jr. 1976

Mammals, large, high-altitude. Pakistan and Nepal. George B. Schaller. 1971-73. *Documenting animal life in one of the most mountainous and remote regions of southern Asia, this study resulted in a photographic "first"— published pictures of the rare, beautiful, and endangered snow leopard.*

———— Neotropical. Ralph M. Wetzel. 1968-69

———— nocturnal. Botswana. Reay H. N. Smithers. 1969

———— small: ecology on open-pit mine waste dumps. Gordon L. Kirkland, Jr. 1973

———— small: microdistribution at the coniferous-deciduous interface. Gordon L. Kirkland, Jr. 1972

———— small: speciation. Apostle Islands, Lake Superior. Richard R. Meierotto. 1970-71, 1973

———— and birds: collecting. Central Africa. Carnes Weeks and Gertrude S. Weeks. 1952

Manatees, Florida: behavior and ecology. Daniel S. Hartman. 1968. *Little understood and possibly endangered, the gentle Florida manatee and its movements, feeding, reproduction, and response to man formed the basis of this investigation.*

Marine mammals. Guadalupe and Cedros Islands, Baja California. G. Dallas Hanna and A. W. Anthony. 1922

Marsupials: evolution. South America. Larry G. Marshall. 1974

———— reproductive biology. South America. C. H. Tyndale-Biscoe. 1971

Martens: ecology. Grand Teton National Park, Wyoming. Timothy W. Clark. 1975

Mongoose, dwarf *(Helogale parvula)* and banded *(Mungos mungo):* ecology and social organization. Uganda. Jonathan P. Rood. 1973

Monkeys: red colobus and agile mangabey. Kenya. Colin P. Groves. 1972

———— rhesus: ecology and behavior. Nepal. Charles H. Southwick. 1973, 1975

———— talapoin: mating behavior. Reserved Forest of Maolmayo, Cameroon. Thelma E. Rowell. 1973

———— and lesser primates. Tigoni Primate Research Centre, Limuru, Kenya. Cynthia P. Booth. 1963

———— and loris. Ceylon. John F. Eisenberg. 1968

Nyala, mountain. Ethiopia. Leslie H. Brown. 1965

Opossum, brush-tailed *(Trichosurus vulpecula).* Ian D. Hume. 1975

Orangutans. Mount Looser Reserve, Sumatra, and Tanjung Puting Reserve, Borneo. Biruté Galdikas-Brindamour. 1971, 1973-76. *Lasting contributions to our knowledge of the orangutan have emerged from this study of their ecology and social development.*

Otters, giant Brazilian. Surinam. Nicole Duplaix-Hall. 1976

Peccaries. Peru. John W. Terborgh. 1976

Pigs, domestic and wild: cultural and ecological aspects. New Guinea. James A. Baldwin. 1973, 1976

Pika: ecological study. Western United States. Richard D. Bates. 1970-71

Primates: Neotropical. Manu National Park, Peru. John W. Terborgh. 1974-75

———— nonhuman. East Borneo. Peter S. Rodman. 1974

Raccoons, tropical: ecology and relationships. James D. Lazell, Jr. 1972

Sea lions: sonar. Thomas C. Poulter. 1970

———— Steller's. H. Dean Fisher. 1972

Seals, harbor and gray: feeding habits and population dynamics. Maine. David T. Richardson. 1972

———— Hawaiian monk *(Monachus schauinslandi).* Hawaii. G. Causey Whittow. 1976

Sheep, bighorn. Nez Perce Creek, Wyoming. E. Earl Willard. 1974-75

———— desert bighorn: environmental and physiological biology. Jack Chardon Turner. 1972

———— urial, and markhor goats. Pakistan. George B. Schaller. 1970

Shrew, golden-rumped elephant-shrew. Kenya. Galen B. Rathbun. 1971, 1974, 1976

Squirrels, Kaibab. Joseph G. Hall. 1970-71

Tenrecs. Madagascar. Edwin Gould. 1963

Whales, bowhead: population. Arctic. John R. Bockstoce. 1976

———— California gray: tracking. John E. Schultz. 1968-69

———— gray. Scammon Lagoon, Baja California. Merrill P. Spencer. 1966

———— heartbeat. Scammon Lagoon, Baja California. Paul Dudley White. 1956

———— humpback. Roger S. Payne. 1976

———— right. Charles Walcott. 1976

———— right: vocalizations and behavior. Roger S. Payne. 1971-73. *Large numbers of right whales congregate close to shore in remote bay areas on the Argentine coast. This investigation of their vocalizations and behavior seeks to shed new light on the communal urge of this endangered species.*

———— sperm: bioacoustic research. Kenneth S. Norris. 1970

Wildebeests. Ngorongoro Crater, Tanzania. Richard Despard Estes. 1963-66, 1972. *Close daily observation of wildebeest herds on the grassland and forest floor of this giant crater in East Africa has provided material for the definitive scientific work on these hoofed mammals.*

Wolverines: ecology. Northwestern Montana. Maurice G. Hornocker. 1973-75

Wolves, red, and coyotes: comparative study of vocalization. Howard McCarley. 1973

Yaks. Richard P. Palmieri. 1971, 1973

ORNITHOLOGY

Accipiters. North America. Noel F. R. Snyder. 1970-71

Albatrosses, Laysan: survival, longevity, and turnover in breeding populations. Harvey I. Fisher. 1971

Bee-eaters, African: cooperative breeding. Stephen T. Emlen. 1973-74

―――― European. Fred N. White. 1975

Bird-fossil comparative study. Trindade Island, South Atlantic Ocean. Storrs L. Olson. 1974

Birds: adaptations for tropical survival. North America. Eugene S. Morton. 1973

―――― ant-following. Brazil. Edwin O. Willis. 1974

―――― community structure. Lowland forest. David L. Pearson. 1974, 1976

―――― ecological studies. Amazon forest. Thomas E. Lovejoy III. 1971

―――― Ethiopian: library study. Emil K. Urban. 1966, 1968

―――― field studies and collecting specimens. New Guinea. Jared M. Diamond. 1965-68. *This series of ornithological expeditions furthered the classification and analysis of New Guinea's exotic bird life.*

―――― high-Andean. François Vuilleumier. 1975

―――― North American. Hudson Bay, Gulf of St. Lawrence, southern United States, Mexico, Georgia, Florida, North Dakota, New York. Arthur A. Allen. 1944-49. *Six successive seasons of bird observations from Alaska to Mexi-co were highlighted by the discovery in the Alaskan tundra of the nest and eggs of the bristle-thighed curlew on June 12, 1948. This shorebird, first described in 1785, was the only North American bird whose nesting place had not yet been located.*

Birds, piscivorous: effects of human disturbance on breeding success. Eagle Lake, California. James R. Koplin. 1971

―――― post-fire competition among hole nesters. Dale L. Taylor. 1973

―――― recolonization of exploded volcanic islands. New Guinea. Jared M. Diamond. 1972

―――― Rift Valley lakes, Ethiopia. Emil K. Urban. 1970

―――― Rio Grande do Sul, Brazil. William Belton. 1976

―――― Simen Mountains, Ethiopia. Michel Desfayes. 1970

―――― small mammals, and bat distribution. Peru. Asa C. Thoresen. 1964-65

―――― social systems. Africa. J. David Ligon. 1975

―――― songs. John R. Krebs and Malcolm L. Hunter, Jr. 1976

―――― New Guinea. E. Thomas Gilliard. 1953-54

―――― stranded on land-bridge islands. Jared M. Diamond. 1974

―――― survey. Brazil and Venezuela. Ernest G. Holt. 1929-30

―――― systematics. South America. Ned K. Johnson. 1974

―――― tropical-forest communities. James Richard Karr. 1975-76

―――― tropical Pacific islands. Jared M. Diamond. 1976

―――― UHF radiolocation system. Frank C. Craighead, Jr. 1973

―――― collection. New Britain. E. Thomas Gilliard. 1958-59. *Pioneering penetration of New Britain's rugged interior resulted in the discovery of bird species previously unknown to science.*

Birds-of-paradise study. Little Tobago, West Indies. E. Thomas Gilliard. 1958

Birds of prey: survey. South Africa. C. W. R. Knight. 1937

Bowerbirds, golden-fronted *(Amblyornis flavifrons):* search for. New Guinea. E. Thomas Gilliard. 1963. *Known only from a few specimens, capture of the golden-fronted bowerbird was the object of this expedition. Although this species was not found, important additions of other birds were made to ornithological collections.*

Brazil and Venezuela jungles: specimen collection. Orinoco headwaters. Ernest G. Holt. 1929-31

Cock-of-the-rock: dancing courtship. British Guiana. E. Thomas Gilliard. 1961

Condors: number and range; preservation. California. National Audubon Society. 1961-64

Duck, torrent: reproduction dynamics and behavior. South America. Marvin C. Cecil. 1968-70

Eagles, bald: post-fledgling activities. Thomas C. Dunstan. 1971.

—— golden. Montana. John J. Craighead. 1973. *Banding and newly developed telemetry techniques were employed in this behavioral study of a diminishing and majestic species.*

—— golden: nesting behavior. Texas. W. Grainger Hunt. 1975

Falcons, Eleanora's: territory and aggression. Morocco. Hartmut Walter. 1968-69

—— peregrine: migration. Greenland to U. S.; South America. William W. Cochran. 1975

Finches: courtship behavior. Africa. Robert B. Payne. 1971

—— Galapagos: genetic analysis of evolution patterns. Galapagos Islands. Robert I. Bowman. 1973

Flamingos: ecology and reproductive biology. Florida. M. Philip Kahl. 1972

—— global study. M. Philip Kahl. 1974. *A worldwide survey of the population dynamics of flamingos, this is the most significant study of its kind ever attempted.*

—— limnological studies of diets and distributions. Chile and Bolivia. Stuart H. Hurlbert. 1973, 1975

Flamingos, New World: population ecology. M. Philip Kahl. 1971

—— photographic study. Andros Island, Bahama Islands. John Oliver La Gorce and Louis Agassiz Fuertes. 1920

Fowl, long-tailed. Japan. Frank X. Ogasawara. 1969

Geese, cackling: breeding ecology. Yukon and Kuskokwim River Deltas, Alaska. Peter G. Mickelson. 1971-72

—— Canada: breeding biology. Yukon and Kuskokwim River Deltas, Alaska. Peter G. Mickelson. 1970

Grebes, hooded. Patagonia. Robert W. Storer. 1975

—— pied-billed. Lake Atitlán, Guatemala. Anne LaBastille. 1967-68

—— western. Gary L. Nuechterlein. 1975-76

Grouse, spruce *(Canachites canadensis).* Montana. Stanley S. Frissell. 1975

Hemipode *(Turnix sylvatica):* ecological relations, reproduction, and distribution. Andalusia, Spain. Gerald Collier. 1973

Hoatzin. British Guiana. J. Lear Grimmer. 1959-60

Hoopoes, green wood. Kenya. J. David Ligon. 1976

Hornbills, African. Fred N. White. 1976

Hummingbirds. South America. Augusto Ruschi. 1962

—— ecology. Mexico, Central America, South America. Augusto Ruschi. 1974

—— heat exchanges in nesting. Rocky Mountains. William Alexander Calder, Jr. 1972

—— rufous: utilization of time and microhabitat. William Alexander Calder, Jr. 1973, 1975

Ibises, scarlet: search for rookery. Venezuela. Paul A. Zahl. 1949

Jay, green: ecology. Colombia. Humberto Alvarez. 1974

—— Yucatán: social and reproductive biology. John William Hardy. 1973

Kiwi: olfactory sense. Bernice M. Wenzel. 1967

Oilbirds. Masakazu Konishi. 1975-76. *Undertaken in Colombia, this study concentrated on oilbird ecology, behavior, physiology, and anatomy.*

——— Venezuela. Bernice Tannenbaum. 1976

Ospreys: ecology. Connecticut River. Roger Tory Peterson and Peter Ames. 1962

——— pesticide influence on reproductive function. Flathead Lake, Montana, and northwestern California. James R. Koplin. 1968-70, 1972

Penguins, jackass. South Africa. Walter R. Siegfried. 1973, 1976

Petrels, Leach's and ashy: nocturnal orientation. Robert I. Bowman. 1971

Pheasants, mikado and Swinhoe's. Taiwan. Sheldon R. Severinghaus. 1971

Pigeons, homing: navigation analysis. Charles Walcott. 1968-69. *Aircraft tracking of homing pigeons has provided data suggesting that these birds may rely on the sun's position to orient themselves for flight.*

——— pink. Mauritius. Anthony S. Cheke. 1973

Plover, Egyptian. Thomas R. Howell. 1976

Prairie chickens and sharp-tailed grouse. North Dakota. Donald W. Sparling, Jr. 1976

Quails *(Coturnix):* calling behavior patterns. Wolfgang M. Schleidt. 1974

Raptors: tracking by satellite. Frank C. Craighead, Jr. 1976

Ruffs, male *(Philomachus pugnaz).* Julia Marian Wentworth-Shepard. 1974-75

Sea birds: ecology and reproductive behavior. Thomas R. Howell. 1969

——— ecology and tick distribution. Indian Ocean. Christopher J. Feare. 1976

——— ecology, numbers, and distribution. Aegean Sea. George E. Watson. 1966

Shorebirds, desert *(Peltohyas* and *Stiltia).* Australia. Gordon Lindsay Maclean. 1973

Storks: worldwide study of the 17 species. Asia and Africa. M. Philip Kahl. 1966-69. *This ambitious study is unprecedented in its broad and thorough treatment of the behavior, ecology, and movement of stork populations.*

Swallows, Texas cave. Charles F. Martin. 1974

Swans, mute. Chesapeake Bay. Jan G. Reese. 1976

——— whistling: migrations. Alaska breeding grounds. William J. L. Sladen. 1972-74. *Conservation of the large and beautiful whistling swan has been greatly enhanced by data gathered during years of observation of this bird as it moves from its wintering grounds in the eastern U. S. to its Alaskan summer habitat, 3,500 miles away.*

Weaverbirds, sociable: ecological role of the nest. George A. Bartholomew. 1972-73

Woodpeckers: behavior, ecology, and taxonomy. Asia. Lester L. Short. 1971

——— ivory-billed, search for. Louisiana, East Texas. John V. Dennis. 1967

Invertebrate Zoology
ENTOMOLOGY

Ants, giant Amazon. Brazil. Paul A. Zahl. 1957

Army-ant mites and leafhoppers. Paraguay. Richard J. Elzinga. 1975

Bagworms: distribution and host-tree orientation of the eggs and parasites. Herbert M. Kulman. 1970

Butterflies, Alaskan: survey. Victoria Island, Canada. Kenelm W. Philip. 1974-75

——— ecology and specimen collection. Aldabra Atoll, Indian Ocean. Jay C. Shaffer. 1967

——— equatorial alpine. Colombia. Arthur M. Shapiro. 1976

——— (Hesperiidae): systematic and distributional study. Mexico. Hugh A. Freeman. 1973-75

——— monarch: migration. Texas, Florida, California, Australia, Mexico. Fred A. Urquhart. 1968-71, 1975-76. *A dogged, decades-long search culminated in the discovery in Mexico of the overwintering site of the eastern North American monarch butterfly.*

——— Neotropical. Trinidad. William Beebe and Jocelyn Crane. 1957

Butterflies, pierid: population ecology. Ward B. Watt. 1972

Fireflies *(Pteroptyx).* Asia. Ivan Polunin. 1971

—— luminescence. Far East. John B. Buck. 1965-68

Flies (Tabanidae). Thailand. John J. S. Burton. 1968-69

—— snail-killing: Pacific Northwest. Benjamin A. Foote. 1971

Hymenoptera, stinging: phenology, mimics, and insectivorous birds. Gilbert P. Waldbauer. 1972

—— Neotropical Ichneumonidae. Charles C. Porter. 1974-75

—— systematics and zoogeography. Charles C. Porter. 1973-75

Insects (Neuroptera). South America. Lionel A. Stange. 1974-76

—— aquatic. Ecuador. Paul J. Spangler. 1975

—— aquatic: zoogeographical connections. New Caledonia. William L. Peters. 1972

—— collection. Africa. Edward S. Ross. 1957-58

—— collection. Southern Asia; Australia. Edward S. Ross. 1961-62

—— dispersal of. Ethiopia. Jørgen Birket-Smith. 1966

Insects, orthopteroid. Madeira. S. K. Gangwere. 1975

—— water balance. Namib Desert, South-West Africa. Eric B. Edney. 1973

Spiders, funnel-web builders: niche analysis. Carrizozo Malpais, New Mexico. Susan E. Riechert. 1972, 1974

Treehopper, membracid *(Umbonia crassicornis).* Florida. Thomas K. Wood. 1974

Triatominae. Central and South America. Pedro W. Wygodzinsky. 1963

Worms, railroad *(Phrixothrix):* life history. Brazil. Darwin L. Tiemann. 1968-69

MALACOLOGY

Marine invertebrates: biogeography and history. Moluccas. Joseph Rosewater and Barry R. Wilson. 1969

Marine mollusks: ecology and distribution. South Pacific. Harald A. Rehder. 1965, 1967, 1973, 1976. *Thousands of marine mollusk specimens were collected on successive expeditions to the Samoa and Fiji Islands, Cook Islands, and others in a survey of the ecology and distribution of Pacific species.*

—— shallow-water. Yucatán Peninsula, Mexico. Walter E. Vokes. 1974

Snails: heat, desiccation, and starvation. Near East. Knut Schmidt-Nielsen. 1968-69

—— high-intertidal: crab predation and shell architecture. Geerat J. Vermeij. 1974

—— land: Hispaniolan urocoptid. Fred G. Thompson. 1975

OTHER INVERTEBRATES

Brachiopod fauna, recent: marine environment. Joyce R. Richardson. 1976

Cephalopods, deep-sea: photographic record. Noel Peter Dilly. 1971, 1973

Coral reefs. Florida. Gilbert L. Voss. 1961-63. *Society grants aided this research into coral growth rates, how much fish life coral areas can sustain, and the food-chain relationship between marine plants and animals.*

—— Jamaica. Judith C. Lang. 1975

—— community structure. Lizard Island, Australia. Michel Pichon. 1976

Corals and coral-reef destruction. American Samoa. Austin E. Lamberts. 1974. *A ten-acre area of coral-reef destruction caused by herbicides was the focus of this study.*

Crabs, brachyuran. Gulf of Guinea. Raymond B. Manning. 1972

—— fiddler. Europe. Jocelyn Crane. 1959

—— hermit: ethology. Alex Henderson and Syd Radinovsky. 1971

—— tropical land. Charles L. Hogue and Donald B. Bright. 1970

Foraminifera, large calcareous: ecology. Queensland Shelf and Great Barrier Reef, Australia. Charles A. Ross. 1970

Invertebrate predation and crustacean zoo-

plankton. English Lake District. W. Gary Sprules. 1976

Lobster, spiny: mass migrations. William F. Herrnkind. 1973

Plankton: Florida Current. University of Miami Institute of Marine Sciences. 1950-52

Shrimp. Florida. Clarence P. Idyll and David A. Hughes. 1964-69

————— *Macrobrachium:* migration mechanisms. David A. Hughes. 1970

Sponges: morphological and ecological studies. Pacific reef caves. Willard D. Hartman. 1971

Squid fisheries. North Atlantic. Gilbert L. Voss. 1965

Starfish, coral-reef. Guam. Masashi Yamaguchi. 1974

————— crown-of-thorns *(Acenthaster planci):* biology and epidemiology. Walter A. Starck II. 1971. *Significant improvements in our understanding of coral-reef survival resulted from this survey of the sometimes devastating effect of crown-of-thorns starfish on corals.*

Geography

Aerial survey. Washington to Buenos Aires. Albert W. Stevens, Frederick Simpich, and Jacob Gayer. 1930

Africa: a history of exploration by Americans. James A. Casada. 1976

Agricultural development potential in a semiarid drainage basin. Central Tanzania. John W. Pawling. 1973

Alaska Peninsula and Aleutian Islands. Bernard R. Hubbard. 1934

Ancient environments and age of nonglaciated terrain. Southeastern Alaska. Ian A. Worley. 1971

Antarctic: air exploration. Lincoln Ellsworth. 1934

————— first Byrd expedition. Richard E. Byrd, Jr. 1928-30; second Byrd expedition, 1933-35. *Society grants helped Comdr. Richard E. Byrd, expedition leader, to achieve man's first flight over the South Pole. This expedition was followed by a second that explored and mapped 450,000 square miles of the southernmost continent.*

Arctic: Franz Josef Land islands (North Polar expeditions). Walter Wellman. 1898, 1906

————— MacMillan expedition. Donald B. MacMillan and Richard E. Byrd. 1925

————— survey, area north of Alaska. Robert A. Bartlett. 1924

Baseline study. Delaware Bay. William S. Gaither. 1970

Cape Horn region, South America. Amos Burg. 1934

Carlsbad Caverns, New Mexico. Willis T. Lee. 1924. *Exploration, mapping, and photographing led to Carlsbad Caverns' becoming a national park in 1930.*

China-Tibet frontier. Joseph F. Rock. 1923-30

Citröen-Haardt Trans-Asiatic Expedition. Beirut, Syria, to Peking, China. Georges-Marie Haardt. 1931. *This 7,370-mile overland exploration from the Mediterranean to the Yellow Sea was the first since the days of Marco Polo.*

Darwin Range, Santa Inés, Tierra del Fuego. E. Jack Miller and Paul H. Dix. 1964

Everest, Mount. Norman G. Dyhrenfurth and Barry C. Bishop. 1962-63. *This expedition brought not only the first American conquest of the mountain monarch but also important contributions to high-altitude research.*

Geographic education assistance. Association of American Geographers. 1962

Himalayan Mountains. Sir Edmund Hillary and Barry C. Bishop. 1960, 1962

Himalayan region, Bhutan. Pradyumna P. Karan. 1964-65

Ice caves. Canadian Cordillera. Derek C. Ford. 1973

Katmai, Mount, region, Alaska. Robert F. Griggs. 1915-20, 1930. *The Valley of Ten*

Thousand Smokes on the Alaska Peninsula was discovered, named, and explored by the Society's Katmai expeditions. The spectacular region was declared a national monument in 1918.

Land-use intensity and labor migration. St. Kitts and Nevis, Leeward Islands. Bonham C. Richardson. 1975

Landscape change. Green River area, Utah-Colorado. William L. Graf. 1976

McKinley, Mount, aerial photo survey. Bradford Washburn. 1936

Mountains and gorges, Yünnan-Szechwan, China. Joseph R. Rock. 1923, 1927, 1929

Mountains of eastern New Guinea. J. Linsley Gressitt. 1968-69

North Pole: attempt to reach. Walter Wellman. 1898

———— attempt to reach. William Ziegler, Anthony Fiala, William J. Peters. 1903

———— attempt to reach, by dirigible balloon. Walter Wellman and Henry E. Hersey. 1906-07

———— first successful effort to reach. Robert E. Peary. 1908-09

———— attempt to reach, on skis. Bjørn O. Staib. 1964

Rock, Joseph F.: biography. Stephanne B. Sutton. 1971

Reventazon and General Valleys: Quaternary river terraces. Costa Rica. Richard H. Kesel. 1974

Saharan expansion. Southern Tunisia. Ian A. Campbell. 1970

St. Elias, Mount, Alaska. Israel C. Russell. 1890-91. *First of the Society's expeditions, this undertaking included discovery of Mount Logan, Canada's highest summit, and the mapping of a 600-square-mile area.*

St. Elias Range, Alaska-Canada: Mount St. Elias-Mount Logan: aerial photography. Bradford Washburn. 1938

St. Elias Range-Yukon Territory, Canada. Bradford Washburn. 1935

Theodore Roosevelt National Memorial Park, North Dakota: feasibility study for expansion. Paul B. Kannowski. 1972

Vilcabamba Range. Plateau between the Apurímac and Urubamba Rivers, Peru. G. Brooks Baekeland and Peter R. Gimbel. 1963

Vinson Massif ascent. Sentinel Range, Ellsworth Mountains, Antarctica. Nicholas B. Clinch. 1966

West African Grain Coast: ports. William R. Stanley. 1974

CARTOGRAPHY

American Revolution: military map sources. Douglas W. Marshall. 1976

Antarctic: mapping. Lincoln Ellsworth. 1934

Chan Chan-Moche Valley site: maps published. Peru. Carol J. Mackey and Michael E. Moseley. 1973

Grand Canyon of the Colorado: mapping. Bradford Washburn. 1971-72, 1974. *No large-scale map of the canyon's South Rim, the section most visited by tourists, has ever been compiled. When completed, this extensive mapping project will remedy this surprising cartographic oversight.*

Historical map testing. Roland E. Chardon. 1976

Kennedy, Mount, and Mount Hubbard: mapping. Canada. Bradford Washburn. 1965

———— mapping. Canada. Paul Ulmer. 1966

Roads Through History: map catalog publication. Peabody Institute Library. 1965

Sikkim: physical-cultural map. Pradyumna P. Karan. 1968

Geology

'Ai (Et-Tell), Israel: soils, construction, and geologic materials. George R. Glenn. 1970

Alpine chain: geological exploration. Southern Italy. Walter Alvarez. 1975

Carboniferous deposits: statistical analysis. Fife, Scotland. Edward S. Belt. 1972

Chubb Crater, Quebec. V. Ben Meen. 1951. *Chubb Crater was proved by this study to be one of the largest known earth scars created by meteor impact.*

Glacial and floral changes, climatic history, last 140 centuries. Argentina. John H. Mercer. 1974

Hydrographic evolution, Late Glacial to Recent. Western Mediterranean. Daniel J. Stanley. 1970

Kenya, Mount: Quaternary history. East Africa. William C. Mahaney. 1976

Labrador Crater, Canada. V. Ben Meen. 1953-54

Marble Canyon Quadrangle: geology. Death Valley, California. Edward A. Johnson. 1973

Messina earthquake study. Sicily. Charles Will Wright. 1909

Recent Nile Cone history based on sediment-core analysis. Daniel J. Stanley. 1974

Salmon River, Idaho: Idaho batholith. Philip J. Shenon and John C. Reed. 1935

Saltpeter conversion and cave nitrate origins. Carol A. Hill. 1974

Sedimentation patterns, submarine. Wilmington Canyon, off Delaware. Daniel J. Stanley. 1966

Sedimentological study. Volta Delta, West Africa. John K. Adams. 1972

Sediments, internal: interrelationships with submarine lithification. Robert L. Eutsler. 1973

Skaergaard region, Greenland. Alexander R. McBirney. 1974

Submerged beach-rock pavements. Bimini, Bahamas. Mahlon M. Ball. 1971

Trondhjemites: development and the earth's early sialic crust. Fred Barker. 1972

Turbidity maximum. Westerschelde Estuary, Netherlands. Richard W. Faas. 1973

Ultramafic inclusions: origin and relationship to basalt genesis. A. William Laughlin. 1972

West Spitsbergen Island, Norway: geology and glaciology. George H. Sutton and P. C. Parks. 1952

GLACIOLOGY

Alaska: glaciers. Ralph S. Tarr and Lawrence Martin. 1909-11

—— glacier studies. Maynard M. Miller. 1961-67. *This long-term program surveyed changes in glaciers along the southern Alaska coast, with special attention to the effects of the 1964 spring earthquake.*

Alaska-British Columbia Coast Mountains: glacier differentiation. Maynard M. Miller. 1968-69

Atlin Park glaciers, British Columbia. Maynard M. Miller. 1974

Austrian Alps: glaciation chronology. Henry W. Posamentier. 1975

Baffin Island, Canada: glacial erosion. David E. Sugden. 1975

Glacier Bay, Alaska: Late Wisconsin and neoglacial history. George M. Haselton. 1975

Glaciers: presurge dynamics. Sam G. Collins. 1971

St. Elias Mountains, Alaska: glaciers. Richard L. Cameron. 1968

—— region, Alaska-Yukon Territory: glaciers. Walter A. Wood. 1964-67

MINERALOGY

Clay sediments: mineralogy and distribution. Turnagain Arm region, Alaska. Neal R. O'Brien. 1973

Fire: man's use of, to shape earths and metals. Theodore A. Wertime. 1968, 1970, 1972

Gem study. Asia. V. Ben Meen. 1964-65

Meteorite and tektite collection. Australia. Brian H. Mason and E. P. Henderson. 1963-67

Meteorite craters. Mauritania. Robert F. Fudali. 1969-70

Mineralogical research. Prince of Wales Island, Alaska. George S. Switzer. 1967

Pegmatite mineral studies. Black Hills, South Dakota. George Rapp, Jr. 1964

Tektites. Bosumtwi Crater, Ivory Coast. John Saul. 1964

PALEONTOLOGY

Algae, calcareous. North Atlantic Ocean. Walter H. Adey. 1964-65

Amphibians and reptiles: Lower Pliocene. Kansas. J. Alan Holman. 1972-73

—— Upper Miocene. Nebraska. J. Alan Holman. 1975

Biostratigraphy, Tertiary molluscan. Tierra del Fuego and Patagonia. William J. Zinsmeister. 1975

Birds, terrestrial fossils (Upper Cretaceous). Baja California. William J. Morris. 1973

Bovidae from Tanzania and Kenya. Alan W. Gentry. 1964-65

Calvert Cliffs, Maryland. Robert E. Gernant and A. Lincoln Dryden. 1968. *This world-famous paleontological area has yielded fine fossil plant and animal collections.*

Catfish. Green River Formation, Wyoming. H. Paul Buchheim and Ronald C. Surdam. 1976

Cave with scavengers. Villafranca de los Barros, Spain. Emiliano Aguirre. 1971-72

Cetacean remains, Oligocene. South Carolina. Albert E. Sanders. 1972

Coral reefs, Cretaceous. Europe and Caribbean. Anthony G. Coates. 1975

Crabs, late Cretaceous. North America. Gale A. Bishop. 1976

Desmostylia (mammalian order). Roy H. Reinhart. 1973

Dinosaurian fauna, Jurassic. Colorado. James A. Jensen. 1975. *This project has yielded part of the world's largest dinosaur; it also harbors an accumulation of fossil bones of some 15 different species of reptiles.*

Dinosaurs. Gadoufaoua, Niger Republic. Philippe Taquet. 1973

—— Morrison Formation. Western United States. Peter Dodson. 1974-75

Dry Cave: Pleistocene paleoecology. New Mexico. Arthur H. Harris. 1971

Early man and extinct animals. China Lake, California. Emma Lou Davis. 1971

Flamingos, Eocene: nesting area. Wyoming. Paul O. McGrew. 1971, 1975

Footprint castings, Oligocene. Presidio County, Texas. John A. Wilson. 1975

Foraminifera: Jurassic and Cretaceous. Pacific Ocean. Robert G. Douglas. 1970, 1974

Fossil vertebrates. Australia. Thomas H. Rich. 1975

—— terrestrial. Canadian high Arctic. Mary R. Dawson and Robert M. West. 1976

Fossils: collecting. Kenya. Vincent J. Maglio. 1968-69, 1972

—— dating, using racemization of amino acids from Africa. Jeffrey L. Bada. 1973

—— dating, using racemization of amino acids from caves. John H. Ostrom. 1970

Geomagnetic chronology of late Cenozoic South American land-mammalian ages. Larry G. Marshall. 1974, 1976

Herbivores, wild: carcasses. Kenya. Diane P. Gifford. 1976

Malagasy lemur subfossils: crania and dentitions. Ian M. Tattersall. 1969

Mammal bones. Amboseli National Park, Kenya. Anna K. Behrensmeyer. 1975-76

Mammals. James S. Mellett. 1975

—— Cretaceous. Greenwood Canyon, Montague County, Texas. Bob H. Slaughter. 1973

—— early Cretaceous. North America. Farish A. Jenkins, Jr. and A. W. Crompton. 1974-75

—— small: biologic and geologic relationships. Austria. Robert W. Wilson. 1973

—— South Dakota. Robert W. Wilson. 1965, 1974

Mammoth-kill sites. Wyoming and New Mexico. George A. Agogino. 1959-65

—— Murray Springs, Arizona. C. Vance Haynes, Jr. 1966-72. *This long-term project explored occurrences of mammoth bones with potential human associations.*

Mammoth-kill sites, Selby and Dutton, Colorado. Dennis J. Stanford. 1976

Mammoth site, late Pleistocene. South Dakota. Larry D. Agenbroad. 1975

Mammoth skeleton; man-made stone tools. Wyoming. George A. Agogino. 1960-61. *This project located and saved from destruction the skeleton of a five-ton* Mammuthus columbi *of 11,000 years ago.*

Mesozoic and Tertiary fauna. Australia and New Zealand. Thomas H. Rich. 1973, 1975

Microvertebrates, Miocene and Pliocene. South Dakota. Morton Green. 1973

Old World monkey fossils *(Cercopithecoidea)*. Mediterranean region. Eric Delson. 1971

Paleontology and archeology. Lubbock Lake site. Texas. Craig C. Black. 1973-74

Permian conodont paleoecology. Wyoming. Fred H. Behnken. 1976

Pliocene fauna. Nebraska. Michael R. Voorhies. 1965

Pliocene fossil localities. Rift Valley, Kenya. Vincent J. Maglio. 1972

Plio-Pleistocene fossils. Iran. Douglas M. Lay. 1976

Pterosaurs, giant. Texas. Douglas A. Lawson. 1975

Rhinoceros and pig fossil bones. South Dakota. Joseph P. Connolly and James D. Bump. 1940

Rocks, minerals, and fossils: collecting for conservation. Badlands, South Dakota. Robert W. Wilson. 1965, 1968-69

Salamander and frog fossils: paleogeography. Richard Dean Estes. 1973

Stanton's Cave: Pleistocene paleoclimatology. Grand Canyon, Arizona. Robert C. Euler. 1969-70

Underwater paleontology. Florida. S. David Webb. 1968-69

Vertebrates. Baja California. Theodore Downs. 1974

———— Baja California. William J. Morris. 1965-71. *Field studies and collecting for this investigation were capped by the discovery of*

the oldest Eohippus *(fossil horse) known to science.*

Vertebrates, Cenozoic. Australian Pilbara and Canning Basin areas. William D. Turnbull. 1976

———— Cenozoic. Eastern Canadian High Arctic. Mary R. Dawson and Robert M. West. 1973

———— Central America and Great American Interchange. S. David Webb. 1976

———— Jurassic and Cretaceous terrestrial. South America. José Fernando Bonaparte. 1975-76

———— late Arikarean. Nebraska. Margery C. Coombs. 1975

———— Lower Eocene. South-West Africa. John A. Van Couvering. 1975

———— Lower Triassic. Tasmania. John W. Cosgriff. 1970

———— mid-Tertiary. Charleston, South Carolina. Albert E. Sanders. 1971-72

———— Pleistocene. Lake Bonneville deposits, Utah. Wade E. Miller. 1973

———— terrestrial, present and fossil. Fernando de Noronha Island, South Atlantic. Storrs L. Olson. 1972

———— tropical South America. Bryan Patterson. 1974

STRATIGRAPHY
and PETROLOGY

Andean metamorphic rocks: petrology. Colombia and Ecuador. Tomas Feininger. 1971

Basalts: petrology and geochemistry. Snake River Plain, Idaho. William P. Leeman. 1969

Bentonite dating, Lower Paleozoic. Britain. Reuben J. Ross, Jr. 1976

Caledonides, Norwegian. William B. Size. 1976

Great Rift Valley: structural origin of the Ethiopian section. George H. Megrue and Paul A. Mohr. 1968-69

Laetolil Beds, Tanzania: stratigraphy. Richard L. Hay. 1976. *Resting ground of early-man fossils, the Laetolil Beds are 3.5 to 3.8 million*

years old. *This study will improve understanding of the deposits themselves and also add to knowledge of the fossils they contain.*

Metamorphic rocks: petrographic mapping. New Caledonia. Philippa M. Black. 1970

Miocene rocks: stratigraphy and faunas. Northwestern Nebraska. Robert M. Hunt, Jr. 1972

Olduvai Gorge, Tanzania: geological studies.

Richard L. Hay. 1962, 1968-70, 1972. *Spectacular fossil discoveries of early man by anthropologist Louis S. B. Leakey and his wife, Mary, have made Olduvai Gorge world famous. This investigation of the geology of the gorge provides an essential basis for the interpretation of the finds made by the Leakeys.*

Stuart, Mount, batholith: petrology and geochemistry. Cascade Range, Washington. Erik R. Erickson, Jr. 1971-72, 1974

Geophysics

Archeomagnetic chronology of the New World. Robert Lee DuBois. 1969-70

Joint and fracture patterns. Israel and Iceland. Amos A. Nur. 1974

OCEANOGRAPHY

Aquascope designed, built, and used in study of Chesapeake Bay. Gilbert C. Klingel. 1952-53

Bathysphere depth record set. Bermuda. William Beebe and Otis Barton. 1934. *Observations of deep-sea species never before seen by man were made during a record 3,028-foot descent.*

Calypso **expeditions.** Jacques-Yves Cousteau. 1952-67. *In 1952 the Society began cosponsorship of the oceanographic expeditions of Captain Cousteau aboard his research vessel Calypso. The French diver's investigations included Mediterranean sea life, ancient shipwrecks, the Persian Gulf, and the Atlantic continental shelf off South America.*

Freshwater streams in the sea. Cephalonia, Ionian Sea. T. Nicholas Panay. 1953

"Knee-line" depths and positions: seismic study. Mediterranean Sea. Harold E. Edgerton. 1969

Man-in-Sea project. Mediterranean Sea, off Villefranche, France. Edwin A. Link and Robert Sténuit. 1963. *This test of an underwater habitat proved that divers, once acclimated to special atmospheric conditions in a diving chamber, could live and operate at ocean depths of several hundred feet.*

Marine photographic and echo-sounding research and equipment. Harold E. Edgerton. 1950, 1952-62, 1966, 1974. *Dr. Edgerton's innovations in cameras, ultrahigh-speed lighting equipment, and echo-sounding devices have played an important role in the success of many Society research projects, especially those involving marine photography.*

Marine sediments: bioturbation. Puerto Rico. Jack Morelock. 1973

Mid-Atlantic Ridge. Maurice Ewing. 1947-48. *Extensive summer surveys of this 10,000-mile-long submerged mountain range in the Atlantic Ocean produced data on the ridge's topography, geology, and sea life.*

Mid-Atlantic Ridge Rift Valley: sonar exploration. Harold E. Edgerton. 1969

Ocean floors: global physiographical study. Bruce C. Heezen. 1970. *Society maps of the Atlantic, Indian, and Pacific Ocean floors owe much to this study's successful conversion of massive amounts of ocean-sounding data into global sea-floor physiography.*

Photographic equipment developed for underwater use. Florida. Walter A. Starck II. 1964

VOLCANOLOGY

Arenal Volcano: eruption dynamics and petrology. Costa Rica. William G. Melson. 1969

Basement rock and Tertiary volcanic correlations. Gulf of California. R. Gordon Gastil. 1972

Katmai, Mount, Alaska: examination following eruption. George C. Martin. 1912

Mont Pelée, Martinique: eruption. Robert T. Hill, Israel C. Russell, Thomas A. Jaggar. 1902

Nunivak Island: volcanic ejecta. John Sloan Dickey, Jr. 1974

Pavlof Volcano, Alaska Peninsula. Thomas A. Jaggar. 1928

Santorini Volcano: eruption date (Bronze Age). Aegean Sea. Charles J. Vitaliano. 1974. *It has been theorized that the Minoan civilization of Crete was extinguished by volcanic eruption. An exact dating of the Bronze Age eruption of Santorini will aid in determining if it was indeed responsible for the decline of Minoan culture.*

Summit Crater area: geophysical and volcanological investigation. Mount Rainier, Washington. Barry W. Prather and Maynard M. Miller. 1970-71

Tonga Islands volcanoes: survey of recent activity. William G. Melson and W. B. Bryan. 1968

Volcanic flames and fume: spectroscopy. Hawaii. Dale P. Cruikshank. 1971

Volcanic gas and petrology. Galapagos Islands. Bert E. Nordlie. 1971

Volcanic rocks. Micronesia. Fred Barker. 1976

Volcanism. Austral Islands. Rockne H. Johnson. 1971

————— late Cenozoic. Zuni Centers, New Mexico. A. William Laughlin. 1973

Volcanoes, submarine. Near Samoa. Rockne H. Johnson. 1975

Social Sciences

HISTORY

Llanos, tropical plains frontier: historical research. Northern South America. Jane M. Loy. 1973

Manuscript collections: survey. Nepal, Sikkim, and Bhutan monasteries. John F. Staal and Lewis R. Lancaster. 1973. *As the modern world encroaches upon once remote monasteries, unique manuscript collections are threatened with destruction and dispersal. Preserving, microfilming, and indexing such treasures were the aims of this survey.*

Manuscripts. St. Mpatsis Monastery, Andros Island, Aegean Sea. Antonia Tripolitis. 1968-69

Metallurgic zones described by Homer and Strabo. Northern Turkey. Theodore A. Wertime. 1970

Naval documents: cataloging and indexing. Naval Historical Foundation. 1965

Persian Royal Road Survey. Anatolia, Turkey. S. Frederick Starr. 1961. *Intended to locate, map, and photograph parts of the ancient road that once connected Susa and Persepolis, the two capitals of the Persian Empire, this survey also located portions of old Roman, Byzantine, and Seljuk routes.*

SOCIOLOGY

City street life. New York City. William H. Whyte. 1972-73. *This project, directed toward finding novel ways of solving insistent urban problems, made use of specialized motion-picture techniques to study human behavior in a city setting.*

A brooding brown bear mother keeps close watch over her cubs in Alaska's wilderness.

ALLAN L. EGBERT

Medals and Awards of the Society

T O ENCOURAGE exploration, to promote scientific advance, and to recognize outstanding service to geography, the National Geographic Society presents medals, awards, and prizes for exceptional achievement. The dozens of distinguished men and women who have received these coveted honors are listed here:

MEDALS

Nine Presidents and three Vice Presidents of the United States have presented National Geographic Society medals, beginning with Theodore Roosevelt in 1906. The Hubbard Medal, named for Gardiner Greene Hubbard, first President of the Society, is awarded for distinction in exploration, discovery, and research; the Grosvenor Medal for outstanding service to geography; the Special Gold Medal for extraordinary geographic achievement; the John Oliver La Gorce Medal for accomplishment in geographic exploration, or in the sciences, or for public service to advance international understanding.

COMDR. ROBERT E. PEARY - 1906, Hubbard Medal: Arctic explorations. 1909, Special Medal of Honor: Discovery of North Pole.

CAPT. ROALD AMUNDSEN - 1907, Hubbard Medal: Traverse of Northwest Passage. 1913, Special Gold Medal: Discovery of South Pole.

CAPT. ROBERT A. BARTLETT - 1909, Hubbard Medal: Far-north explorations with Peary's 1909 expedition.

GROVE KARL GILBERT - 1909, Hubbard Medal: Thirty years of achievements in physical geography.

SIR ERNEST H. SHACKLETON - 1910, Hubbard Medal: Antarctic explorations and farthest south, 88° 23'.

COL. GEORGE W. GOETHALS - 1914, Special Gold Medal: Directing completion of Panama Canal.

VILHJALMUR STEFANSSON - 1919, Hubbard Medal: Discoveries in Canadian Arctic.

LT. COMDR., LATER REAR ADMIRAL, RICHARD E. BYRD, JR. - 1926, Hubbard Medal: First to reach North Pole by airplane. 1930, Special Medal of Honor: First to attain South Pole by air.

FLOYD BENNETT - 1926, Special Gold Medal: Flight to North Pole with Richard E. Byrd.

COL. CHARLES A. LINDBERGH - 1927, Hubbard Medal: New York-Paris solo flight.

HUGO ECKENER - 1930, Special Medal of Honor: First global navigation of an airship.

ROY CHAPMAN ANDREWS - 1931, Hubbard Medal: Geographic discoveries in Central Asia.

AMELIA EARHART - 1932, Special Gold Medal: First solo Atlantic flight by a woman.

ANNE MORROW LINDBERGH - 1934, Hubbard Medal: Notable flights, as copilot, on Charles Lindbergh's aerial surveys.

CAPTS. ALBERT W. STEVENS AND ORVIL A. ANDERSON - 1935, Hubbard Medals: World altitude record of 72,395 feet in balloon *Explorer II*.

LINCOLN ELLSWORTH - 1936, Hubbard Medal: Extraordinary achievements in polar exploration.

THOMAS C. POULTER - 1937, Special Gold Medal: Achievements, Byrd Antarctic Expedition.

GEN. H. H. ARNOLD - 1945, Hubbard Medal: Contributions to aviation.

GILBERT H. GROSVENOR - 1949, Grosvenor Medal: Outstanding service to geography as Editor of NATIONAL GEOGRAPHIC.

COMDR. DONALD B. MacMILLAN - 1953, Hubbard Medal: Arctic explorations, 1908-52.

BRITISH EVEREST EXPEDITION - 1954, Hubbard Medal: Ascent of Mount Everest.

MRS. ROBERT E. PEARY - 1955, Special Gold Medal: Contributions to husband's polar explorations.

JOHN OLIVER LA GORCE - 1955, Grosvenor Medal: Outstanding service to the increase and diffusion of geographic knowledge, 1905-55.

PRINCE PHILIP, DUKE OF EDINBURGH - 1957, Special Gold Medal: Promoting science and better understanding among the world's peoples.

PAUL A. SIPLE - 1958, Hubbard Medal: For 30 years of Antarctic explorations, including leadership of first group to winter at the South Pole.

U. S. NAVY ANTARCTIC EXPEDITIONS - 1959, Hubbard Medal: Antarctic research and exploration, 1955-59.

SIR VIVIAN FUCHS - 1959, Hubbard Medal: Leadership of British Trans-Antarctic expedition.

CAPT. JACQUES-YVES COUSTEAU - 1961, Special Gold Medal: Undersea exploration.

DR. AND MRS. LOUIS S. B. LEAKEY - 1962, Hubbard Medal: Anthropological discoveries in East Africa.

LT. COL. JOHN H. GLENN, JR. - 1962, Hubbard Medal: Space exploration.

AMERICAN MOUNT EVEREST EXPEDITION - 1963, Hubbard Medal: Contributions to geography and high-altitude research through conquest of earth's highest peak.

AMERICAN ANTARCTIC MOUNTAINEERING EXPEDITION - 1967, John Oliver La Gorce Medal: First ascent of Antarctica's highest mountain, 1966-67.

JUAN T. TRIPPE - 1967, Hubbard Medal: Contributions to aviation.

HAROLD E. EDGERTON - 1968, John Oliver La Gorce Medal: Contributions to photographic and geophysical technology.

PHILIP VAN HORN WEEMS - 1968, John Oliver La Gorce Medal: Contributions to marine, air, and space navigation.

APOLLO 8 ASTRONAUTS COL. FRANK BORMAN, USAF, CAPT. JAMES A. LOVELL, JR., USN, AND LT. COL. WILLIAM A. ANDERS, USAF - 1969, Hubbard Medal: Space exploration; first to orbit the moon.

APOLLO 11 ASTRONAUTS NEIL A. ARMSTRONG, COL. EDWIN E. ALDRIN, JR., USAF, AND LT. COL. MICHAEL COLLINS, USAF - 1970, Hubbard Medal: Space exploration; moon landing.

MELVILLE BELL GROSVENOR - 1974, Grosvenor Medal: Outstanding service to geography.

ALEXANDER WETMORE - 1975, Hubbard Medal: Contributions to ornithology.

AWARDS
JANE M. SMITH AWARD

Jane McGrew Smith of Pittsburgh, Pennsylvania, who died in 1911, made bequests to the National Geographic Society and 14 other educational and religious institutions. A life member of the Society deeply interested in its scientific work, Miss Smith directed that her gift be used to establish an award, including life membership in the Society, in recognition of notable contributions to geography.

ALFRED H. BROOKS   1917, Geologist
HIRAM BINGHAM
                1917, Historian, explorer
HENRY PITTIER   1917, Agriculturist
GEORGE KENNAN
                1917, Authority on Russia
FRANK G. CARPENTER   1919, Journalist
WILLIAM H. DALL   1919, Naturalist
WILLIAM H. HOLMES   1919, Art curator
STEPHEN T. MATHER
                1919, Park Service Director
EDWARD W. NELSON   1919, Biologist
WALTER T. SWINGLE   1919, Plant explorer
ROBERT F. GRIGGS   1919, Botanist
O. F. COOK   1919, Plant explorer
JOSEPH STRAUSS
                1919, Rear Admiral, USN
J. B. TYRRELL   1921, Canadian explorer
HERBERT E. GREGORY   1921, Geologist
FRANK M. CHAPMAN   1921, Ornithologist
R. G. McCONNELL
                1921, Canadian explorer
DONALD B. MacMILLAN
        1921, Explorer, Lieutenant, USNR
CHARLES SHELDON   1925, Alaska explorer
ROBERT A. BARTLETT
                1925, Far-north explorer
NEIL M. JUDD   1925, Archeologist

JOSEPH F. ROCK   1925, Plant explorer

PHILIP SIDNEY SMITH   1925, Geologist

WILLIAM BROOKS CABOT
                1925, Author, engineer

KNUD RASMUSSEN
                1926, Greenland explorer

CHARLES A. LINDBERGH
        1927, Transatlantic flight pioneer

CURTIS D. WILBUR
        1929, Secretary of the Navy, retired

ANDREW E. DOUGLASS
        1929, Astronomer, dendrochronologist

HERBERT PUTNAM
                1929, Librarian of Congress

CORNELIUS A. PUGSLEY
                1929, Banker, conservationist

SIR WILFRED GRENFELL
        1930, Surgeon, missionary, author

ASHLEY C. McKINLEY
1931, Captain, USA, aerial photographer

DOUGLAS W. JOHNSON
                1931, Physiographer

ANDRÉ CITROËN 1931, French industrialist

ALBERT W. STEVENS 1931, Captain, USA,
                aerial photographer

LAURENCE M. GOULD   1931, Biologist

WILLIAM H. HOBBS   1933, Geologist

EUGENE EDWARD BUCK
        1934, President, American Society of
                Composers, Authors & Publishers

VERNON BAILEY   1934, Field naturalist

JAMES P. THOMSON
        1934, Royal Geographical Society
                of Australia

CHARLES F. MARVIN   1934, Meteorologist

W. COLEMAN NEVILS, S. J.
                1934, Classicist,
        President, Georgetown University

CLIFFORD K. BERRYMAN
        1934, Political cartoonist

LEONHARD STEJNEGER   1935, Biologist

JOSEPH P. CONNOLLY
        1935, Geologist, college president

WILLIAM R. POPE   1935, Colonel, USA

LAWRENCE J. BURPEE
        1936, Canadian commissioner

RANDOLPH P. WILLIAMS
        1936, Captain, U. S. Army Air Corps

ROGERS BIRNIE, JR.
                1936, Retired Army officer

SAMUEL S. GANNETT   1936, Geographer

HERBERT HOLLICK-KENYON
        1936, Pilot, Canadian Airways

HIS MAJESTY KING LEOPOLD
                1936, Brussels, Belgium

A. E. MURLIN
        1936, U. S. Geological Survey, retired

H. L. BALDWIN
        1936, U. S. Geological Survey, retired

ROBERT MULDROW
        1936, U. S. Geological Survey, retired

W. J. PETERS
        1936, U. S. Geological Survey, retired

PRINCE IYESATO TOKUGAWA
                1937, Tokyo, Japan

WEB HILL   1937, Merchant

STEPHEN R. CAPPS   1938, Geologist

FRANKLIN ADAMS
        1938, Authority on Latin America

GEORGE W. GODDARD
1940, Major, USAF, aerial photographer

J. FRED ESSARY   1941, Journalist

CHARLES H. DEETZ   1942, Cartographer,
        U. S. Coast & Geodetic Survey

SAMUEL WHITTEMORE BOGGS
        1943, Department of State geographer

ALEXANDER M. PATCH
                1943, Major General, USA

ELI HELMICK
        1943, Major General, USA, retired

HARRY WARNER FRANTZ   1943, Journalist

EDMUND W. STARLING
          1943, U. S. Secret Service

MRS. WILLIAM G. PADEN   1943, Author

CHRISTOVA LEITE DE CASTRO
          1944, Brazilian geographer

FRANK B. JEWETT   1945, President,
     National Academy of Sciences

FRANK M. MacFARLAND   1945, President,
     California Academy of Sciences

S. S. VISHER   1945, Geographer

SALVADOR MASSIP 1946, Cuban geographer

CHESTER W. NIMITZ   1946, Fleet Admiral,
     USN, Chief of Naval Operations

MALCOLM J. PROUDFOOT 1947, Geographer

GEOFFREY T. HELLMAN   1947, Essayist

MAURICE EWING   1947, Geologist

NICHOLAS H. DARTON   1948, Geologist

BENJAMIN R. HOFFMAN
1948, Geographical Society of Philadelphia

JOHN O'KEEFE
          1949, U. S. Army Map Service

GEORGE J. MILLER
     1949, Editor, *Journal of Geography*

EARL B. SHAW   1949, President,
     Council of Geography Teachers

MRS. ALBERT W. STEVENS
     1950, Smith life member widow

MRS. HENRY H. ARNOLD
     1950, Smith life member widow

ALBERT E. GIESECKE
     1951, Government adviser, Peru

HUGH L. DRYDEN
     1951, Director, National Advisory
          Committee for Aeronautics

HERBERT FRIEDMANN
          1951, Curator of Birds,
          U. S. National Museum

MRS. J. R. HILDEBRAND
     1951, Widow of Assistant Editor,
          NATIONAL GEOGRAPHIC

MRS. RUTH B. SHIPLEY
1951, Passport Office, Department of State

ANDREW GEORGE LATTA McNAUGHTON
     1952, General, Canadian Army, retired

MAYNARD OWEN WILLIAMS
          1953, Chief of Foreign Staff,
          NATIONAL GEOGRAPHIC

ROBERT B. ANDERSON
          1953, Secretary of the Navy

MRS. FRANKLIN L. FISHER
     1953, Widow of Illustrations Editor,
          NATIONAL GEOGRAPHIC

KENNETH H. GIBSON
     1953, Colonel, U. S. Air Force

IRA S. BOWEN   1955, Astronomer

ARDITO DESIO
     1955, Leader, K-2 Expedition

CHARLES P. MOUNTFORD
     1956, Anthropologist, Australia

SIR VIVIAN FUCHS
     1959, British geologist, explorer

ALBERT A. STANLEY
     1959, U. S. Coast & Geodetic Survey

P. V. H. WEEMS
          1959, Captain, USN, retired

EDWIN A. LINK
     1959, Inventor and undersea pioneer

SIR BRUCE INGRAM
     1959, Editor, *Illustrated London News*

ARLEIGH A. BURKE   1960, Admiral, USN,
          Chief of Naval Operations

LYNDON B. JOHNSON
1962, Vice President of the United States

DR. CALVIN H. PLIMPTON
     1964, President, Amherst College

FRANKLIN L. BURR AWARD

Mary C. Burr of Hartford, Connecticut, who died in 1930, bequeathed a fund to the National Geographic Society in memory of her father. Income from the fund is used to award cash prizes to leaders in the Society's expeditions and researches for especially meritorious work in the field of geographic science.

CAPT. ALBERT W. STEVENS
1933, 1936, Aeronaut

CAPT. ORVIL A. ANDERSON 1936, Aeronaut

CAPT. RANDOLPH P. WILLIAMS
1936, Aeronaut

DR. AND MRS. WILLIAM M. MANN
1938, Zoologists

BRADFORD WASHBURN
1939, 1965, Geographer

MATTHEW W. STIRLING
1939, 1941, 1957, Archeologist

MRS. MATTHEW W. STIRLING
1941, Archeologist

ALEXANDER WETMORE 1944, Ornithologist

THOMAS A. JAGGER 1945, Engineer

LYMAN J. BRIGGS
1945, 1954, 1962, Chairman, Committee for Research and Exploration, National Geographic Society

GEORGE VAN BIESBROECK
1947, 1948, 1953, Astronomer

EDWARD A. HALBACH, FRANCIS J. HEYDEN, S. J., CARL W. MILLER, CHARLES H. SMILEY
1948, Astronomers

ARTHUR A. ALLEN 1948, Ornithologist

CHARLES P. MOUNTFORD
1950, Anthropologist

FRANK M. SETZLER 1950, Anthropologist

HAROLD E. EDGERTON
1952, Electrical engineer

NEIL M. JUDD 1955, 1963, Archeologist

MRS. ROBERT E. PEARY
1955, Scientific collaborator

MRS. MARIE PEARY STAFFORD
1955, Scientific collaborator

ROBERT F. GRIGGS 1956, Geographer

CARL F. MILLER 1959, Archeologist

LOUIS S. B. LEAKEY AND MARY D. LEAKEY
1961, Anthropologists

JANE GOODALL 1962, 1964, Zoologist

REAR ADM. DONALD B. MacMILLAN
1963, Polar explorer

BARRY C. BISHOP
1963, Mountaineer and glaciologist

HELGE INGSTAD AND ANNE STINE INGSTAD
1964, Archeologists

RICHARD E. LEAKEY
1965, 1973, Anthropologist

NORMAN G. DYHRENFURTH
1965, Mountaineer

MAYNARD M. MILLER 1967, Glaciologist

DIAN J. FOSSEY 1973, Zoologist

KENAN T. ERIM
1973, Classical archeologist

OTHER SOCIETY AWARDS

HERBERT FRIEDMANN, WILLIAM J. MORRIS
Arnold Guyot Memorial Award, 1968, Paleontologists

ROBERT W. WILSON
Arnold Guyot Memorial Award, 1974, Paleontologist

HESLON MUKIRI GITHUA
Special National Geographic Society Award, 1968, Scientific collaborator

Meeting in Washington, D. C. — the 33 eminent

RESPONDING to an invitation to organize "a society for the increase and diffusion of geographical knowledge," the men gathered at the Cosmos Club on January 13, 1888. From this small beginning, the Society has extended its membership around the world.

Artist Stanley Meltzoff based his depiction of the meeting on individual photographs. Key at right identifies: **1** Charles J. Bell, banker; **2** Israel C. Russell, geologist; **3** Commodore George W. Melville, USN; **4** Frank Baker, anatomist; **5** W. B. Powell, educator; **6** Brig. Gen. A. W. Greely, USA, polar explorer; **7** Grove Karl Gilbert, geologist and a future President of the Society; **8** John Wesley Powell, naturalist and explorer of the Colorado River; **9** Gardiner Greene Hubbard, Boston lawyer and first President of the Society, who helped finance the telephone experiments of Alexander Graham Bell; **10** Henry Gannett, geographer and a future Society Presi-

men who founded the National Geographic Society

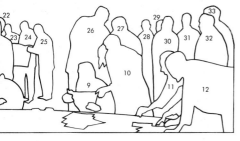

dent; **11** William H. Dall, naturalist; **12** Edward E. Hayden, meteorologist; **13** Herbert G. Ogden, topographer; **14** Arthur P. Davis, civil engineer; **15** Gilbert Thompson, topographer; **16** Marcus Baker, cartographer; **17** George Kennan, author, lecturer, and explorer of Arctic Siberia; **18** James Howard Gore, educator; **19** O. H. Tittmann, geodesist and a future President of the Society; **20** Henry W. Henshaw, naturalist; **21** George Brown Goode, naturalist and author; **22** Cleveland Abbe, meteorologist; **23** Comdr. John R. Bartlett, USN; **24** Henry Mitchell, engineer; **25** Robert Muldrow II, geologist; **26** Comdr. Winfield S. Schley, USN; **27** Capt. C. E. Dutton, USA; **28** W. D. Johnson, topographer; **29** James C. Welling, journalist and educator; **30** C. Hart Merriam, Chief, U. S. Biological Survey; **31** Capt. Rogers Birnie, Jr., USA; **32** A. H. Thompson, geographer; **33** Samuel S. Gannett, geographer.

Presidents

THIRTEEN men—explorers, inventors, geographers, and men of letters—have served as President of the National Geographic Society. They are listed below with their terms of office.

GARDINER GREENE HUBBARD
January 27, 1888—died December 11, 1897

ALEXANDER GRAHAM BELL
January 7, 1898—resigned October 1903

W J MCGEE   March 5, 1904—April 1904

GROVE KARL GILBERT   Acting President, 1904

WILLIS L. MOORE
January 27, 1905—resigned December 1909

HENRY GANNETT
January 19, 1910—died November 5, 1914

O.H. TITTMANN
January 20, 1915—resigned April 1919

JOHN E. PILLSBURY
April 16, 1919—died December 30, 1919

GILBERT H. GROSVENOR
January 21, 1920—retired May 5, 1954, becoming Chairman of the Board of Trustees. (d. 1966)

JOHN OLIVER LA GORCE
May 5, 1954—retired January 8, 1957, becoming Vice Chairman of the Board of Trustees. (d. 1959)

MELVILLE BELL GROSVENOR
January 8, 1957—retired August 1, 1967, becoming Chairman of the Board and Editor-in-Chief. On June 1, 1976, he became Chairman Emeritus of the Board.

MELVIN M. PAYNE
August 1, 1967—retired June 1, 1976, becoming Chairman of the Board of Trustees.

ROBERT E. DOYLE   June 1, 1976—

Members of the Board of Trustees

CALLED the Board of Managers until 1920, the Society's Board of Trustees numbered 27 members at the end of 1976. Past and present members are listed below with year of election to the Board and year of their death or resignation.

CLEVELAND ABBE	1888(r. 1890)
ROBERT B. ANDERSON	1960(r. 1963)
H. H. ARNOLD	1938(d. 1950)
O. P. AUSTIN	1903(d. 1933)
CYRUS C. BABB	1893(r. 1895)
MARCUS BAKER	1888(d. 1903)
J. R. BARTLETT	1888(r. 1889)
R. N. BATCHELDER	1893(r. 1894)
ALEXANDER GRAHAM BELL	1898(d. 1922)
CHARLES J. BELL	1888(d. 1929)
ROGERS BIRNIE, JR.	1888(r. 1891)
HENRY F. BLOUNT	1892(d. 1917)
FRANK BORMAN	1975-
LYMAN J. BRIGGS	1933(d. 1963)
ALFRED H. BROOKS	1905(r. 1906)
J. CARTER BROWN	1976-
WARREN E. BURGER	1974-
GEORGE K. BURGESS	1930(d. 1932)
RICHARD E. BYRD, JR.	1953(d. 1957)
LEONARD CARMICHAEL	1957(d. 1973)
THOMAS H. CARROLL	1964(d. 1964)
T. C. CHAMBERLAIN	1905(r. 1911)
COLBY M. CHESTER	1904(d. 1932)
L. O. COLBERT	1938(d. 1968)
CALVIN COOLIDGE	1929(d. 1933)
FREDERICK V. COVILLE	1897(d. 1937)
C. W. DABNEY, JR.	1895(r. 1897)
WILLIAM H. DALL	1896(r. 1899)
GEORGE DAVIDSON	1901(r. 1911)
WILLIAM M. DAVIS	1901(r. 1904)
CHARLES G. DAWES	1924(d. 1951)
DAVID T. DAY	1896(r. 1903)
CHARLES DENBY	1907(r. 1907)
ROBERT E. DOYLE	1975-
HUGH L. DRYDEN	1951(d. 1965)
JOHN JOY EDSON	1901(d. 1935)
LLOYD H. ELLIOTT	1968-
DAVID FAIRCHILD	1905(d. 1954)
FRANKLIN L. FISHER	1945(d. 1953)
ROBERT V. FLEMING	1929(d. 1967)
JOHN FOOTE	1924(d. 1931)
HENRY GANNETT	1888(d. 1914)

The Board of Trustees gathers at Society headquarters in Washington, D. C. on September 17, 1976. Seated clockwise from left: Carlisle H. Humelsine, President, The Colonial Williamsburg Foundation; Arthur B. Hanson, Society General Counsel; James H. Wakelin, Jr., former Assistant Secretary of Commerce for Science and Technology; J. Carter Brown, Director, National Gallery of Art; Melvin M. Payne, Chairman of the Board, National Geographic Society; Robert E. Doyle, Society President; Mrs. Lyndon B. Johnson; Melville Bell Grosvenor, Chairman Emeritus, and former Editor, NATIONAL GEOGRAPHIC MAGAZINE; Gen. Curtis E. LeMay, former Chief of Staff, USAF. Standing from left: Louis B. Wright, former Director, Folger Shakespeare Library; Caryl P. Haskins, former President, Carnegie Institution of Washington; Robert C. Seamans, Jr., former Administrator, Energy Research and Development Administration; Frederick G. Vosburgh, former Vice President and Editor, NATIONAL GEOGRAPHIC MAGAZINE; Lloyd H. Elliott, President, George Washington University; Gilbert M. Grosvenor, Vice President and Editor, NATIONAL GEOGRAPHIC MAGAZINE; James E. Webb, former Administrator, National Aeronautics and Space Administration; Wm. McChesney Martin, Jr., former Chairman, Federal Reserve Board; Conrad L. Wirth, former Director, National Park Service.

Not present at the September meeting (facing page, left to right): Thomas W. McKnew, Advisory Chairman of the Board; Frank Borman, President and Board Chairman, Eastern Air Lines; Warren E. Burger, United States Chief Justice; Crawford H. Greenewalt, Director, E. I. du Pont de Nemours & Company; H. Randolph Maddox, former Vice President, American Tele-

ROBERT S. OAKES

phone & Telegraph Company (died May 19, 1977); Laurance S. Rockefeller, President, Rocke-feller Brothers Fund; Juan T. Trippe, Honorary Chairman of the Board, Pan American World Airways; Alexander Wetmore, Research Associ-ate, Smithsonian Institution; Lloyd B. Wilson, Honorary Chairman of the Board, Chesapeake & Potomac Telephone Company.

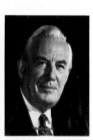

Geographical Distribution of the Society's Membership

AS OF DECEMBER 1976

United States	7,778,450
Alabama	84,385
Alaska	28,440
Arizona	99,833
Arkansas	46,639
California	1,007,810
Colorado	154,683
Connecticut	147,118
Delaware	25,785
District of Columbia	17,344
Florida	336,798
Georgia	133,659
Hawaii	45,204
Idaho	46,690
Illinois	388,178
Indiana	162,003
Iowa	101,861
Kansas	90,784
Kentucky	66,229
Louisiana	93,577
Maine	44,612
Maryland	160,821
Massachusetts	242,333
Michigan	319,630
Minnesota	179,051
Mississippi	43,621
Missouri	153,386
Montana	42,777
Nebraska	59,405
Nevada	32,211
New Hampshire	42,090
New Jersey	267,697
New Mexico	47,119
New York	528,464
North Carolina	132,114
North Dakota	23,411
Ohio	352,463
Oklahoma	92,584
Oregon	134,146
Pennsylvania	365,770
Rhode Island	33,831
South Carolina	58,432
South Dakota	24,924
Tennessee	103,163
Texas	443,053
Utah	62,320
Vermont	23,624
Virginia	184,758
Washington	213,648
West Virginia	36,159
Wisconsin	169,800
Wyoming	22,840
Possessions and territories	21,535
U. S. military and civilian personnel outside U. S.	39,638

Canada	709,597
Alberta	81,015
British Columbia	125,417
Manitoba	28,441
New Brunswick	14,097
Newfoundland	6,418
Northwest Terr.	1,605
Nova Scotia	23,180
Ontario	321,100
Prince Edward Is.	2,170
Quebec	81,491
Saskatchewan	23,253
Yukon Territory	1,410

Central and South America, Mexico	85,007
Argentina	6,694
Belize	297
Bolivia	868
Brazil	12,446
Chile	3,098
Colombia	4,313
Costa Rica	1,684
Ecuador	1,507
El Salvador	1,063
French Guiana	12
Guatemala	2,829
Guyana	342
Honduras	766
Mexico	34,759
Nicaragua	669
Panama	1,315
Paraguay	190
Peru	2,997
Surinam	255
Uruguay	821
Venezuela	8,082

Caribbean	8,611
Barbados	664
Cayman Islands	263
Cuba	13
Dominican Republic	888
Guadeloupe	84
Haiti	268
Jamaica	2,151
Leeward Islands	379
Martinique	106
Netherlands Antilles	1,418
Trinidad and Tobago	1,919
Turks Islands	16
Windward Islands	442

Atlantic Ocean	6,207
Ascension Island	7
Azores	167
Bahamas	1,868
Bermuda	2,389
Cape Verde Islands	7
Falkland Islands	24
Faeroe Islands	44
Greenland	100
Iceland	1,457
Madeira Islands	128
St. Helena	3
St. Pierre and Miquelon	13

Europe	259,151
Andorra	32
Austria	6,868
Belgium	14,086
Bulgaria	56
Czechoslovakia	2,949
Denmark	9,490
Finland	4,974

France	19,908	Egypt	633	Korea	1,263
German Democratic Republic	17	Ethiopia	321	Kuwait	873
		French Territory		Laos	13
German Federal Republic	44,187	of the Afars and the Issas	11	Lebanon	4
				Macao	24
Greece	4,768	Gabon	56	Malaysia	2,376
Hungary	4,667	Gambia	37	Mongolia	1
Ireland (Eire)	7,532	Ghana	534	Nepal	140
Italy	19,139	Guinea	4	Oman	186
Liechtenstein	111	Ivory Coast	246	Pakistan	737
Luxembourg	1,466	Kenya	1,369	Philippines	5,795
Monaco	153	Liberia	625	Qatar	145
Netherlands	30,179	Libya	585	Saudi Arabia	945
Norway	15,238	Malawi	290	Singapore	2,824
Poland	1,193	Mali	34	Sri Lanka	519
Portugal	3,487	Mauritania	8	Syria	170
Romania	774	Morocco	284	Taiwan	2,808
Spain	15,165	Mozambique	168	Thailand	2,310
Sweden	20,737	Niger	33	Turkey	3,303
Switzerland	29,043	Nigeria	1,402	United Arab Emirates	645
U.S.S.R. (see Asia)		Rhodesia	3,583	U.S.S.R.	1,412
Vatican City	14	Rwanda	72	Yemen Arab Republic	30
Yugoslavia	2,919	Senegal	112	Yemen (People's Dem.	
		Sierra Leone	139	Republic of)	10
United Kingdom	**164,770**	Somalia	12		
Channel Islands	1,306	South Africa	31,274	**Australasia**	**211,623**
England	136,814	South-West Africa	757	Australia and	
Northern Ireland	3,417	Sudan	104	Tasmania	165,612
Scotland	17,458	Tanzania	450	New Zealand	46,011
Wales	5,775	Togo	37		
		Tunisia	119	**Pacific and Indian**	
Mediterranean	**1,081**	Uganda	95	**Oceans**	**4,145**
Cyprus	340	Upper Volta	39	Comoro Islands	3
Gibraltar	99	Zaire	425	Fiji	376
Malta	642	Zambia	795	French Polynesia	277
				Gilbert Islands	50
Africa	**45,377**	**Asia**	**59,145**	Madagascar	80
Algeria	218	Afghanistan	82	Mauritius	183
Angola	47	Bahrain	334	Nauru	72
Benin	29	Bangladesh	102	New Caledonia	198
Botswana	193	Bhutan	8	New Hebrides	143
Burundi	57	Brunei	233	Papua New Guinea	2,229
Cameroon	113	Burma	106	Pitcairn Island	3
Central African		China (People's		Réunion	35
Empire	31	Republic of)	45	Ryukyu Islands	118
Chad	22	Hong Kong	3,589	Seychelles	76
Congo	14	India	7,422	Solomon Islands	127
		Indonesia	1,055	Tonga	57
		Iran	2,198	Western Samoa	118
		Iraq	196		
		Israel	7,176	**Miscellaneous**	**2,947**
		Japan	9,847		
		Jordan	219	**Grand Total**	**9,336,112**

NATIONAL
GEOGRAPHIC
INDEX 1947-1976 INCLUSIVE

This index covers issues of January 1947 through December 1976. Its companion volume covers issues of October 1888 through December 1946.

The National Geographic Society publishes semiannually for each six-issue volume of the magazine a free detailed index, available on request to members.

A

ABACO (Island), Bahama Islands:

The Loyalists. By Kent Britt. Photos by Ted Spiegel. 510-539, Apr. 1975

ABALONE:

Goggle Fishing in California Waters. By David Hellyer. Photos by Lamar Boren. 615-632, May 1949

ABBOT, J. LLOYD, Jr.: Author:

Flight Into Antarctic Darkness. Photos by David S. Boyer. 732-738, Nov. 1967

ABBOTSBURY SWANNERY, England:

The Swans of Abbotsbury. By Michael Moynihan. Photos by Barnet Saidman. 563-570, Oct. 1959

ABDUL GHAFUR: Author-Photographer:

From America to Mecca on Airborne Pilgrimage. 1-60, July 1953

ABELL, GEORGE O.: Author:

Exploring the Farthest Reaches of Space. 782-790, Dec. 1956

ABELL, SAM: Photographer:

Newfoundland Trusts in the Sea. By Gary Jennings. 112-141, Jan. 1974

Yellowstone at 100: A Walk Through the Wilderness. By Karen and Derek Craighead. 579-603, May 1972

ABERCROMBIE, THOMAS J.:

National Geographic Photographers Win Top Magazine Awards. 830-831, June 1959

Author-Photographer

Afghanistan: Crossroad of Conquerors. 297-345, Sept. 1968

Algeria: Learning to Live With Independence. 200-233, Aug. 1973

Behind the Veil of Troubled Yemen. 403-445, Mar. 1964

Cambodia: Indochina's "Neutral" Corner. 514-551, Oct. 1964

ABERCROMBIE, THOMAS J.: Author-Photographer—
Continued

Ice Fishing's Frigid Charms. 861-872, Dec. 1958

Kansai, Japan's Historic Heartland. 295-339, Mar. 1970

Morocco, Land of the Farthest West. 834-865, June 1971

Nomad in Alaska's Outback. 540-567, Apr. 1969

Saudi Arabia: Beyond the Sands of Mecca. 1-53, Jan. 1966

Switzerland, Europe's High-rise Republic. 68-113, July 1969

The Sword and the Sermon. 3-45, July 1972

Venezuela Builds on Oil. 344-387, Mar. 1963

Young-old Lebanon Lives by Trade. 479-523, Apr. 1958

Photographer

Alaska Proudly Joins the Union. By Ernest Gruening. 43-83, July 1959

Brasília, Metropolis Made to Order. By Hernane Tavares de Sá. 704-724, May 1960

Captain Smith of Jamestown. By Bradford Smith. 581-620, May 1957

Easter Island and Its Mysterious Monuments. By Howard La Fay. 90-117, Jan. 1962

Enchantress! By Theodore H. Reed. 628-641, May 1961

Man's Deepest Dive. By Jacques Piccard. 224-239, Aug. 1960

Man's First Winter at the South Pole. By Paul A. Siple. 439-478, Apr. 1958

The Mighty *Enterprise*. By Nathaniel T. Kenney. 431-448, Mar. 1963

Old-New Iran, Next Door to Russia. By Edward J. Linehan. 44-85, Jan. 1961

Underwater Archeology: Key to History's Warehouse. By George F. Bass. Photos by Thomas J. Abercrombie and Robert B. Goodman. 138-156, July 1963

You and the Obedient Atom. By Allan C. Fisher,

The wintry mass of the Hindu Kush walls in a camel train crossing the frozen Wakhan River in Afghanistan.
SABRINA AND ROLAND MICHAUD

ABERCROMBIE, THOMAS J.: Photographer—*Continued*
Jr. Photos by B. Anthony Stewart and Thomas J. Abercrombie. 303-353, Sept. 1958

ABKHAZIAN A.S.S.R., U.S.S.R.:
"Every Day Is a Gift When You Are Over 100." By Alexander Leaf. Photos by John Launois. 93-119, Jan. 1973

ABOARD the N. S. *Savannah:* World's First Nuclear Merchantman. By Alan Villiers. Photos by John E. Fletcher. 280-298, Aug. 1962

"ABOMINABLE SNOWMAN":
Wintering on the Roof of the World. By Barry C. Bishop. 503-547, Oct. 1962

ABORIGINES, Australian:
"The Alice" in Australia's Wonderland. By Alan Villiers. Photos by Jeff Carter and David Moore. 230-257, Feb. 1966
An Arnhem Land Adventure. By Donald F. Thomson. 403-430, Mar. 1948
 Arnhem Land Expedition of 1948. 430
Australia. By Alan Villiers. 309-385, Sept. 1963
 I. The West and the South. 309-345
 II. The Settled East, the Barrier Reef, the Center. 347-385
Cruise to Stone Age Arnhem Land. By Howell Walker. 417-430, Sept. 1949
Expedition to the Land of the Tiwi (Melville Island). By Charles P. Mountford. 417-440, Mar. 1956
Exploring Stone Age Arnhem Land. By Charles P. Mountford. Photos by Howell Walker. 745-782, Dec. 1949
From Spear to Hoe on Groote Eylandt. By Howell Walker. 131-142, Jan. 1953
In the Wake of Darwin's *Beagle*. By Alan Villiers. Photos by James L. Stanfield. 449-495, Oct. 1969
Queensland: Young Titan of Australia's Tropic North. By Kenneth MacLeish. Photos by Winfield Parks. 593-639, Nov. 1968
Rock Paintings of the Aborigines. By Kay and Stanley Breeden. 174-187, Feb. 1973
The Top End of Down Under. By Kenneth MacLeish. Photos by Thomas Nebbia. 145-174, Feb. 1973
Western Australia, the Big Country. By Kenneth MacLeish. Photos by James L. Stanfield. 150-187, Feb. 1975

ABRAHAM, the Friend of God. By Kenneth MacLeish. Photos by Dean Conger. 739-789, Dec. 1966

ABRAMS, AL: Author-Photographer:
Our Life on a Border Kibbutz. By Carol and Al Abrams. 364-391, Sept. 1970

ABRAMS, CAROL: Author:
Our Life on a Border Kibbutz. By Carol and Al Abrams. Photos by Al Abrams. 364-391, Sept. 1970

ABU DHABI, United Arab Emirates:
The Arab World, Inc. By John J. Putman. Photos by Winfield Parks. 494-533, Oct. 1975
Desert Sheikdoms of Arabia's Pirate Coast. By Ronald Codrai. 65-104, July 1956

ABU LATT (Island), Red Sea:
Fish Men Explore a New World Undersea. By Jacques-Yves Cousteau. 431-472, Oct. 1952

ABU SIMBEL, Egypt:
Abu Simbel's Ancient Temples Reborn. By Georg Gerster. 724-744, May 1969
Saving the Ancient Temples at Abu Simbel. By Georg Gerster. Paintings by Robert W. Nicholson. 694-742, May 1966
Threatened Treasures of the Nile. By Georg Gerster. 587-621, Oct. 1963

ABUNDANT Life in a Desert Land. By Walter Meayers Edwards. 424-436, Sept. 1973

ACADIA (Parish), Louisiana:
Cajunland, Louisiana's French-speaking Coast. By Bern Keating. Photos by Charles Harbutt and Franke Keating. 353-391, Mar. 1966

ACAPULCO, Mexico:
Mexico in Motion. By Bart McDowell. Photos by Kip Ross. 490-537, Oct. 1961
A New Riviera: Mexico's West Coast. By Nathaniel T. Kenney. Photos by Charles O'Rear. 670-699, Nov. 1973
The Two Acapulcos. By James Cerruti. Photos by Thomas Nebbia. 848-878, Dec. 1964

ACROPOLIS, Athens:
Athens: Her Golden Past Still Lights the World. By Kenneth F. Weaver. Photos by Phillip Harrington. 100-137, July 1963

ACROSS Canada by Mackenzie's Track. By Ralph Gray. 191-239, Aug. 1955

ACROSS the Alps in a Wicker Basket. By Phil Walker. 117-131, Jan. 1963

ACROSS the Frozen Desert to Byrd Station. By Paul W. Frazier. Photos by Calvin L. Larsen. 383-398, Sept. 1957

ACROSS the Potomac From Washington. By Albert W. Atwood. 1-33, Jan. 1953

ACROSS the Ridgepole of the Alps. By Walter Meayers Edwards. 410-419, Sept. 1960

ADAMS, ABIGAIL:
Patriots in Petticoats. By Lonnelle Aikman. Paintings by Louis S. Glanzman. 475-493, Oct. 1975

ADAMS, JOHN:
The Living White House. By Lonnelle Aikman. 593-643, Nov. 1966
Patriots in Petticoats. By Lonnelle Aikman. Paintings by Louis S. Glanzman. 475-493, Oct. 1975
Profiles of the Presidents: I. The Presidency and How It Grew. By Frank Freidel. 642-687, Nov. 1964

ADAMS, JOHN QUINCY:
The Living White House. By Lonnelle Aikman. 593-643, Nov. 1966
Profiles of the Presidents: I. The Presidency and How It Grew. By Frank Freidel. 642-687, Nov. 1964

ADAMS, SAMUEL:
Firebrands of the Revolution. By Eric F. Goldman. Photos by George F. Mobley. 2-27, July 1974

ADAMS FAMILY:
Literary Landmarks of Massachusetts. By William H. Nicholas. Photos by B. Anthony Stewart and John E. Fletcher. 279-310, Mar. 1950

ADDIS ABABA, Ethiopia:

Ethiopian Adventure. By Nathaniel T. Kenney. Photos by James P. Blair. 548-582, Apr. 1965

ADELAIDE, South Australia:

South Australia, Gateway to the Great Outback. By Howell Walker. Photos by Joseph J. Scherschel. 441-481, Apr. 1970

ADEN PROTECTORATE, now Democratic Yemen:

Along the Storied Incense Roads of Aden. By Hermann F. Eilts. Photos by Brian Brake. 230-254, Feb. 1957

Sailing with Sindbad's Sons. By Alan Villiers. 675-688, Nov. 1948

ADENA CULTURE. *See* Mound Builders

ADIRONDACK MOUNTAINS, New York:

My Backyard, the Adirondacks. By Anne LaBastille. Photos by David Alan Harvey. 616-639, May 1975

ADMIRAL of the Ends of the Earth. By Melville Bell Grosvenor. 36-48, July 1957

ADOBE New Mexico. By Mason Sutherland. Photos by Justin Locke. 783-830, Dec. 1949

"THE ADORATION OF THE MAGI," painting supplement. Jan. 1952

ADRIATIC REGION. *See* Trieste; Venice; Yugoslavia

ADRIFT on a Raft of Sargassum. Photos by Robert F. Sisson. 188-199, Feb. 1976

ADVENTURES in Lololand. By Rennold L. Lowy. 105-118, Jan. 1947

ADVENTURES in the Search for Man. By Louis S. B. Leakey. Photos by Hugo van Lawick. 132-152, Jan. 1963

ADVENTURES With South Africa's Black Eagles. By Jeanne Cowden. Photos by author and Arthur Bowland. 533-543, Oct. 1969

ADVENTURES with the Survey Navy. By Irving Johnson. 131-148, July 1947

ADVENTURING Along the South's Surprising Coast: Sea Islands. By James Cerruti. Photos by Thomas Nebbia and James L. Amos. 366-393, Mar. 1971

AEGEAN ISLANDS:

The Aegean Isles: Poseidon's Playground. By Gilbert M. Grosvenor. 733-781, Dec. 1958

Classical Lands of the Mediterranean, map supplement. Dec. 1949

Greece and the Aegean, Atlas series supplement. Dec. 1958

The Isles of Greece: Aegean Birthplace of Western Culture. By Melville Bell Grosvenor. Photos by Edwin Stuart Grosvenor and Winfield Parks. 147-193, Aug. 1972

On the Winds of the Dodecanese. By Jean and Franc Shor. 351-390, Mar. 1953

See also Thera

AEGEAN REGION. *See* Aegean Islands; Greece; Turkey

AEGEAN SEA:

New Tools for Undersea Archeology. By George F.

AEGEAN SEA — *Continued*

Bass. Photos by Charles R. Nicklin, Jr. 403-423, Sept. 1968

Thirty-three Centuries Under the Sea. By Peter Throckmorton. 682-703, May 1960

Underwater Archeology: Key to History's Warehouse. By George F. Bass. Photos by Thomas J. Abercrombie and Robert B. Goodman. 138-156, July 1963

AEPYORNIS (Extinct Bird):

Madagascar: Island at the End of the Earth. By Luis Marden. Photos by Albert Moldvay. 443-487, Oct. 1967

Re-creating Madagascar's Giant Extinct Bird. By Alexander Wetmore. 488-493, Oct. 1967

AERODYNAMICS. *See* Aeronautics; Wind-power Research

AERONAUTICS:

Alexander Graham Bell Museum: Tribute to Genius. By Jean Lesage. 227-256, Aug. 1956

Fact Finding for Tomorrow's Planes. By Hugh L. Dryden. Photos by Luis Marden. 757-780, Dec. 1953

Flying in the "Blowtorch" Era. By Frederick G. Vosburgh. 281-322, Sept. 1950

Happy Birthday, Otto Lilienthal! By Russell Hawkes. Photos by James Collison. 286-292, Feb. 1972

Our Air Age Speeds Ahead. By F. Barrows Colton. 249-272, Feb. 1948

Sailors of the Sky. By Gordon Young. Photos by Emory Kristof and Jack Fields. Paintings by Davis Meltzer. 49-73, Jan. 1967

See also Aviation; Balloons

AF CHAPMAN (Youth Hostel Ship):

Thumbs Up Round the North Sea's Rim. By Frances James. Photos by Erica Koch. 685-704, May 1952

AFAR TRIBE. *See* Danakil

AFGHANISTAN:

Afghanistan: Crossroad of Conquerors. By Thomas J. Abercrombie. 297-345, Sept. 1968

American Family in Afghanistan. By Rebecca Shannon Cresson. Photos by Osborne C. Cresson. 417-432, Sept. 1953

Bold Horsemen of the Steppes. By Sabrina and Roland Michaud. 634-669, Nov. 1973

In the Footsteps of Alexander the Great. By Helen and Frank Schreider. Paintings by Tom Lovell. 1-65, Jan. 1968

Sky Road East. By Tay and Lowell Thomas, Jr. 71-112, Jan. 1960

We Took the Highroad in Afghanistan. By Jean and Franc Shor. 673-706, Nov. 1950

West from the Khyber Pass. By William O. Douglas. Photos by Mercedes H. Douglas and author. 1-44, July 1958

When the President Goes Abroad (Eisenhower Tour). By Gilbert M. Grosvenor. 588-649, May 1960

Winter Caravan to the Roof of the World. By Sabrina and Roland Michaud. 435-465, Apr. 1972

AFO-A-KOM: A Sacred Symbol Comes Home. By William S. Ellis. Photos by James P. Blair. 141-148, July 1974

AFOOT in Roadless Nepal. By Toni Hagen. 361-405, Mar. 1960

AFRICA:

Adventures in the Search for Man. By Louis S. B. Leakey. Photos by Hugo van Lawick. 132-152, Jan. 1963

Africa, Atlas series supplement. Sept. 1960

Africa: Countries of the Nile, Atlas series supplement. Oct. 1963

Africa: The Winds of Freedom Stir a Continent. By Nathaniel T. Kenney. Photos by W. D. Vaughn. 303-359, Sept. 1960
    Contents: Angola; Belgian Congo (Congo Republic); Cabinda; Egypt; Ethiopia; Ghana; Kenya; Liberia; Rhodesia and Nyasaland, Federation of; South Africa

Africa and the Arabian Peninsula, map supplement. Mar. 1950

African Wildlife: Man's Threatened Legacy. By Allan C. Fisher, Jr. Photos by Thomas Nebbia. 147-187, Feb. 1972
    A Continent's Living Treasure. Paintings by Ned Seidler. 164-167

Africa's Bushman Art Treasures. By Alfred Friendly. Photos by Alex R. Willcox. 848-865, June 1963

Africa's Uncaged Elephants. Photos by Quentin Keynes. 371-382, Mar. 1951

Ambassadors of Good Will: The Peace Corps. By Sargent Shriver and Peace Corps Volunteers. 297-345, Sept. 1964
    Included: Gabon; Tanganyika

Atlantic Odyssey: Iceland to Antarctica. By Newman Bumstead. Photos by Volkmar Wentzel. 725-780, Dec. 1955

Britain Tackles the East African Bush. By W. Robert Moore. 311-352, Mar. 1950

Bushmen of the Kalahari. By Elizabeth Marshall Thomas. Photos by Laurence K. Marshall. 866-888, June 1963

Bushmen of the Kalahari (Television film). 578A-578B, Apr. 1973; 732A-732B, May 1974

Carefree People of the Cameroons. Photos by Pierre Ichac. 233-248, Feb. 1947

Exploring 1,750,000 Years Into Man's Past. By L. S. B. Leakey. Photos by Robert F. Sisson. 564-589, Oct. 1961

Face to Face With Gorillas in Central Africa. By Paul A. Zahl. 114-137, Jan. 1960

Finding the World's Earliest Man. By L. S. B. Leakey. Photos by Des Bartlett. 420-435, Sept. 1960

Flight to Adventure. By Tay and Lowell Thomas, Jr. 49-112, July 1957

Freedom Speaks French in Ouagadougou. By John Scofield. 153-203, Aug. 1966
    Contents: Cameroon; Central African Republic; Chad; Dahomey; Gambia; Guinea; Ivory Coast; Mali; Mauritania; Niger; Senegal; Togo; Upper Volta

Freedom's Progress South of the Sahara. By Howard La Fay. Photos by Joseph J. Scherschel. 603-637, Nov. 1962
    Contents: Burundi; Congo, Democratic Republic of the; Congo, People's Republic of the; Kenya; Mozambique; Rhodesia and Nyasaland, Federation of; Rwanda; South Africa; Tanganyika

How Fruit Came to America. By J. R. Magness. Paintings by Else Bostelmann. 325-377, Sept. 1951

Hunting Africa's Smallest Game (Insects). By Ed-

AFRICA—*Continued*

    ward S. Ross. 406-419, Mar. 1961

Hunting Musical Game in West Africa. By Arthur S. Alberts. 262-282, Aug. 1951

Into the Heart of Africa. By Gertrude S. Weeks. 257-263, Aug. 1956

Journey Into the Great Rift: the Northern Half. By Helen and Frank Schreider. 254-290, Aug. 1965

The Last Great Animal Kingdom. 390-409, Sept. 1960

The Leakeys of Africa: Family in Search of Prehistoric Man. By Melvin M. Payne. 194-231, Feb. 1965

Life With the King of Beasts. By George B. Schaller. 494-519, Apr. 1969

Locusts: "Teeth of the Wind." By Robert A. M. Conley. Photos by Gianni Tortoli. 202-227, Aug. 1969

Man of the Serengeti (Television film). 179A-179B, Feb. 1972

Mountains of the Moon (Ruwenzori). By Paul A. Zahl. 412-434, Mar. 1962

My Life Among Wild Chimpanzees. By Jane Goodall. Photos by Baron Hugo van Lawick and author. 272-308, Aug. 1963

My Life With Africa's Little People. By Anne Eisner Putnam. 278-302, Feb. 1960

New Discoveries Among Africa's Chimpanzees. By Baroness Jane van Lawick-Goodall. Photos by Baron Hugo van Lawick. 802-831, Dec. 1965

The Niger: River of Sorrow, River of Hope. By Georg Gerster. 152-189, Aug. 1975

Northern Africa, map supplement. Dec. 1954

Northwestern Africa, Atlas series supplement. Aug. 1966

Our Vegetable Travelers. By Victor R. Boswell. Paintings by Else Bostelmann. 145-217, Aug. 1949

The Peoples of Africa; The Heritage of Africa, map supplement. Dec. 1971

Preserving the Treasures of Olduvai Gorge. By Melvin M. Payne. Photos by Joseph J. Scherschel. 701-709, Nov. 1966

Roaming Africa's Unfenced Zoos. By W. Robert Moore. 353-380, Mar. 1950

Safari from Congo to Cairo. By Elsie May Bell Grosvenor. Photos by Gilbert Grosvenor. 721-771, Dec. 1954

Safari Through Changing Africa. By Elsie May Bell Grosvenor. Photos by Gilbert Grosvenor. 145-198, Aug. 1953

Southern Africa, Atlas series supplement. Nov. 1962

Spearing Lions with Africa's Masai. By Edgar Monsanto Queeny. 487-517, Oct. 1954

Stalking Central Africa's Wildlife. By T. Donald Carter. Paintings by Walter A. Weber. 264-286, Aug. 1956

The Sword and the Sermon (Islam). By Thomas J. Abercrombie. 3-45, July 1972

Theodore Roosevelt: a Centennial Tribute. By Bart McDowell. 572-590, Oct. 1958

When the President Goes Abroad (Eisenhower Tour). By Gilbert M. Grosvenor. 588-649, May 1960
    Included: Casablanca, Morocco; Tunis, Tunisia

Where Elephants Have Right of Way. By George

AFRICA — *Continued*

and Jinx Rodger. Photos by George Rodger. 363-389, Sept. 1960

The World in Your Garden (Flowers). By W. H. Camp. Paintings by Else Bostelmann. 1-65, July 1947

See also names of individual countries; *and* Continental Drift; Nile; Phoenicians; Rudolf, Lake; Sahara; Sinai; Suez Canal; Wildlife

AFRICANIZED HONEYBEES:

Those Fiery Brazilian Bees. By Rick Gore. Photos by Bianca Lavies. 491-501, Apr. 1976

AGA KHAN:

Weighing the Aga Khan in Diamonds. Photos by David J. Carnegie. 317-324, Mar. 1947

AGAIN — the Olympic Challenge. By Alan J. Gould. 488-513, Oct. 1964

The AGE of Sail Lives On at Mystic. By Alan Villiers. Photos by Weston Kemp. 220-239, Aug. 1968

AGELESS Splendors of Our Oldest Park: Yellowstone at 100. 604-615, May 1972

AGNEW, SPIRO T.:

First Moon Explorers (Apollo 11) Receive the Society's Hubbard Medal. 859-861, June 1970
Included: Vice President Agnew's previous presentation of medal to Apollo 8 astronauts

AGOGINO, GEORGE: Author:

Wyoming Muck Tells of Battle: Ice Age Man vs. Mammoth. By Cynthia Irwin, Henry Irwin, and George Agogino. 828-837, June 1962

AGRA, India. *See* Taj Mahal

AGRICULTURAL AND BOTANICAL EXPLORERS:

American Wild Flower Odyssey. By P. L. Ricker. 603-634, May 1953

Caught in the Assam-Tibet Earthquake. By F. Kingdon-Ward. 403-416, Mar. 1952

The Exquisite Orchids. By Luis Marden. 485-513, Apr. 1971

Nature's Gifts to Medicine. By Lonnelle Aikman. Paintings by Lloyd K. Townsend and Don Crowley. 420-440, Sept. 1974

Patent Plants Enrich Our World. By Orville H. Kneen. 357-378, Mar. 1948

Puya, the Pineapple's Andean Ancestor. By Mulford B. Foster. 463-480, Oct. 1950

Spices, the Essence of Geography. By Stuart E. Jones. 401-420, Mar. 1949

The World in Your Garden (Flowers). By W. H. Camp. Paintings by Else Bostelmann. 1-65, July 1947

The World in Your Garden. Book announced. 729-730, May 1957

AGRICULTURE:

The British Way. By Sir Evelyn Wrench. 421-541, Apr. 1949

California's Surprising Inland Delta. By Judith and Neil Morgan. Photos by Charles O'Rear. 409-430, Sept. 1976

Can the World Feed Its People? By Thomas Y. Canby. Photos by Steve Raymer. 2-31, July 1975

Erosion, Trojan Horse of Greece. By F. G. Renner. 793-812, Dec. 1947

The Family Farm Ain't What It Used To Be. By

AGRICULTURE — *Continued*

James A. Sugar. 391-411, Sept. 1974

4-H Boys and Girls Grow More Food. By Frederick Simpich. 551-582, Nov. 1948

Lanzarote, the Strangest Canary. By Stephanie Dinkins. 117-139, Jan. 1969
Included: Cinder farming

New Tricks Outwit Our Insect Enemies. By Hal Higdon. Photos by Robert F. Sisson and Emory Kristof. 380-399, Sept. 1972

Our Vegetable Travelers. By Victor R. Boswell. Paintings by Else Bostelmann. 145-217, Aug. 1949

The Revolution in American Agriculture. By Jules B. Billard. Photos by James P. Blair. 147-185, Feb. 1970
Included: Farm of the future (painting)

This Land of Ours — How Are We Using It? By Peter T. White. Photos by Emory Kristof. 20-67, July 1976

The Wasp That Plays Cupid to a Fig. By Robert F. Sisson. 690-697, Nov. 1970

What's Happening to Our Climate? By Samuel W. Matthews. 576-615, Nov. 1976
Included: The relation between climatic change and cultivation

See also Amana Colonies; Beltsville, Maryland; Cattle Raising; Coffee; Cotton and Cotton Industry; Date Raising; Fruit and Fruit Growing; Grapes and Grape Culture; Horticulture; Hutterites; Kibbutzim; Ladybugs; Maya; Pineapples and Pineapple Growing; Rice Growing; Sheep and Sheep Raising; Sugar Industry; Wheat and Wheat Growing

AGUNG, Mount, Bali, Indonesia:

Disaster in Paradise. Photos by Robert F. Sisson. 436-458, Sept. 1963
I. By Windsor P. Booth. 436-447
II. Devastated Land and Homeless People. By Samuel W. Matthews. 447-458

AHA! It Really Works! By Robert F. Sisson. 143-147, Jan. 1974

AI APAEC (Mochica Warrior-Priest):

Finding the Tomb of a Warrior-God. By William Duncan Strong. Photos by Clifford Evans, Jr. 453-482, Apr. 1947

AIARI RIVER, Brazil:

Jungle Jaunt on Amazon Headwaters. By Bernice M. Goetz. 371-388, Sept. 1952

AIKMAN, LONNELLE: Author:

Census 1960: Profile of the Nation. By Albert W. Atwood and Lonnelle Aikman. 697-714, Nov. 1959

The DAR Story. Photos by B. Anthony Stewart and John E. Fletcher. 565-598, Nov. 1951

Inside the White House. Photos by B. Anthony Stewart and Thomas Nebbia. 3-43, Jan. 1961

The Lights Are Up at Ford's Theatre. 392-401, Mar. 1970

The Living White House. 593-643, Nov. 1966

Mount Vernon Lives On. 651-682, Nov. 1953

Nature's Gifts to Medicine. Paintings by Lloyd K. Townsend and Don Crowley. 420-440, Sept. 1974

New Stars for Old Glory. 86-121, July 1959

AIKMAN, LONNELLE: Author—*Continued*

Patriots in Petticoats. Paintings by Louis S. Glanzman. 475-493, Oct. 1975

Perfume, the Business of Illusion. 531-550, Apr. 1951

Under the Dome of Freedom: The United States Capitol. Photos by George F. Mobley. 4-59, Jan. 1964

U. S. Capitol, Citadel of Democracy. 143-192, Aug. 1952

AINU (People):

Japan's "Sky People," the Vanishing Ainu. By Mary Inez Hilger. Photos by Eiji Miyazawa. 268-296, Feb. 1967

AIR Age Brings Life to Canton Island. By Howell Walker. 117-132, Jan. 1955

AIR BASES:

Alaska's Warmer Side. By Elsie May Bell Grosvenor. 737-775, June 1956
Included: Eielson Air Force Base, Ladd Air Force Base

Artists Roam the World of the U. S. Air Force. By Curtis E. LeMay. 650-673, May 1960

Flying in the "Blowtorch" Era. By Frederick G. Vosburgh. 281-322, Sept. 1950
Contents: Andrews Air Force Base, Carswell Air Force Base, Edwards Air Force Base, Eglin Air Force Base, Langley Air Force Base, Larson Air Force Base, March Air Force Base, Moffett Naval Air Station, Williams Air Force Base, Wright-Patterson Air Force Base

Okinawa, Pacific Outpost. 538-552, Apr. 1950

Our Navy in the Far East. By Arthur W. Radford. Photos by J. Baylor Roberts. 537-577, Oct. 1953

See also Canton Island; Edwards Air Force Base; Stead Air Force Base; Thule Air Base; U. S. Air Force (Of Planes and Men); U. S. Marine Corps (Here Come the Marines); U. S. Navy (Four-ocean Navy)

AIR PLANTS. *See* Bromeliads; Orchids

AIR POLLUTION:

Laboratory in a Dirty Sky. By Rudolf J. Engelmann and Vera Simons. 616-621, Nov. 1976

Mexico, the City That Founded a Nation. By Louis de la Haba. Photos by Albert Moldvay. 638-669, May 1973

Pollution, Threat to Man's Only Home. By Gordon Young. Photos by James P. Blair. 738-781, Dec. 1970

Those Successful Japanese. By Bart McDowell. Photos by Fred Ward. 323-359, Mar. 1974
Included: Air pollution in Tokyo and Yokkaichi

Venice Fights for Life. By Joseph Judge. Photos by Albert Moldvay. 591-631, Nov. 1972

What's Happening to Our Climate? By Samuel W. Matthews. 576-615, Nov. 1976

AIR RESCUE:

Air Rescue Behind Enemy Lines. By Howard Sochurek. 346-369, Sept. 1968

First American Ascent of Mount St. Elias. By Maynard M. Miller. 229-248, Feb. 1948

Seeking the Secret of the Giants. By Frank M. Setzler. Photos by Richard H. Stewart. 390-404, Sept. 1952

AIR SHOWS:

World War I Aircraft Fly Again in Rhinebeck's Rickety Rendezvous. By Harvey Arden. Photos by Howard Sochurek. 578-587, Oct. 1970

AIRBORNE UNDERSEA EXPEDITIONS:

Inflatable Ship *(Amphitrite)* Opens Era of Airborne Undersea Expeditions. By Jacques-Yves Cousteau. 142-148, July 1961

AIRCRAFT. *See* Aeronautics; Air Shows; Aircraft Carriers; Aviation; Helicopters; Jet Aircraft; U. S. Air Force

AIRCRAFT CARRIERS:

Four-ocean Navy in the Nuclear Age. By Thomas W. McKnew. 145-187, Feb. 1965

The Mighty *Enterprise*. By Nathaniel T. Kenney. Photos by Thomas J. Abercrombie. 431-448, Mar. 1963

Our Navy Explores Antarctica. By Richard E. Byrd. U. S. Navy official photos. 429-522, Oct. 1947

Our Navy in the Far East. By Arthur W. Radford. Photos by J. Baylor Roberts. 537-577, Oct. 1953

Sailors in the Sky: Fifty Years of Naval Aviation. By Patrick N. L. Bellinger. 276-296, Aug. 1961

AIRCRAFT INDUSTRY:

Flying in the "Blowtorch" Era. By Frederick G. Vosburgh. 281-322, Sept. 1950

Long Island Outgrows the Country. By Howell Walker. Photos by B. Anthony Stewart. 279-326, Mar. 1951

AIRLIFT to Berlin. 595-614, May 1949

AIRPORTS:

Newfoundland, Canada's New Province. By Andrew H. Brown. Photos by author and Robert F. Sisson. 777-812, June 1949
Included: Gander, Torbay, Harbour Grace, and other sites which were jumping-off points for early transoceanic flights

Skyway Below the Clouds. By Carl R. Markwith. Photos by Ernest J. Cottrell. 85-108, July 1949

See also Arlington County, for Washington National Airport

AJANTA, India:

India's Sculptured Temple Caves. By Volkmar Wentzel. 665-678, May 1953

AKHENATEN TEMPLE PROJECT, Egypt:

Computer Helps Scholars Re-create an Egyptian Temple. By Ray Winfield Smith. Photos by Emory Kristof. 634-655, Nov. 1970

ALABAMA:

Alabama, Dixie to a Different Tune. By Howard La Fay. Photos by Dick Durrance II. 534-569, Oct. 1975

Around the "Great Lakes of the South." By Frederick Simpich. Photos by J. Baylor Roberts. 463-491, Apr. 1948

Dixie Spins the Wheel of Industry. By William H. Nicholas. Photos by J. Baylor Roberts. 281-324, Mar. 1949

Whatever Happened to TVA? By Gordon Young. Photos by Emory Kristof. 830-863, June 1973

See also Mobile; Russell Cave

ALAMO, San Antonio, Texas:

San Antonio: "Texas, Actin' Kind of Natural." By Fred Kline. Photos by David Hiser. 524-549, Apr. 1976

ALAN VILLIERS' Tribute to Captain Cook: The Man Who Mapped the Pacific. By Alan Villiers. Photos by Gordon W. Gahan. 297-349, Sept. 1971

ÅLAND ISLANDS, Finland:

Baltic Cruise of the *Caribbee*. By Carleton Mitchell. 605-646, Nov. 1950

ALASKA:

Alaska, map supplement. June 1956

Alaska. Special Publication announced. 880-884, June 1969

Alaska! (Television film). 215A-215B, Feb. 1967

Alaska: High Roads to Adventure. Special Publication announced. 860-864, June 1976

Alaska: Rising Northern Star. By Joseph Judge. Photos by Bruce Dale. 730-767, June 1975
    Included: Alaska's land-use plan

Alaska, Seward's Icebox, Became a Treasure Chest. 766-767, June 1953

Alaska, the Big Land. By W. Robert Moore. 776-807, June 1956

Alaska Proudly Joins the Union. By Ernest Gruening. Photos by Thomas J. Abercrombie. 43-83, July 1959

Alaskan Family Robinson. By Nancy Robinson. Photos by John Metzger and Peter Robinson. 55-75, Jan. 1973

An Alaskan Family's Night of Terror (Earthquake). By Tay Pryor Thomas. 142-156, July 1964

Alaska's Automatic Lake Drains Itself (Lake George). 835-844, June 1951

Alaska's Marine Highway. By W. E. Garrett. 776-819, June 1965

Alaska's Mighty Rivers of Ice. By Maynard M. Miller. Photos by Christopher G. Knight. 194-217, Feb. 1967

Alaska's Russian Frontier: Little Diomede. Photos by Audrey and Frank Morgan. 551-562, Apr. 1951

Alaska's Warmer Side. By Elsie May Bell Grosvenor. 737-775, June 1956

Along the Yukon Trail. By Amos Burg. 395-416, Sept. 1953

Among Alaska's Brown Bears. By Allan L. Egbert and Michael H. Luque. 428-442, Sept. 1975

Bikepacking Across Alaska and Canada. By Dan Burden. 682-695, May 1973

Birds of the Alaskan Tundra. 322-327, Mar. 1972

Canada, Alaska, and Greenland, map supplement. June 1947

Caribou: Hardy Nomads of the North. By Jim Rearden. 858-878, Dec. 1974

Charting Our Sea and Air Lanes (U. S. Coast and Geodetic Survey). By Stuart E. Jones. Photos by J. Baylor Roberts. 189-209, Feb. 1957

Close-up: U.S.A., Alaska, map supplement. Text on reverse. June 1975

The Curlew's Secret. By Arthur A. Allen. 751-770, Dec. 1948

DEW Line, Sentry of the Far North. By Howard La Fay. 128-146, July 1958

Earthquake! By William P. E. Graves. 112-139, July 1964

ALASKA—*Continued*

Endeavour Sails the Inside Passage. By Amos Burg. 801-828, June 1947

"Ice Age Mammals of the Alaskan Tundra," painting supplement. Mar. 1972

John Muir's Wild America. By Harvey Arden. Photos by Dewitt Jones. 433-461, Apr. 1973

The Last U. S. Whale Hunters. By Emory Kristof. 346-353, Mar. 1973
    "Ocean mammals are to us what the buffalo was to the Plains Indian." By Lael Morgan. 354-355

Mammals of the Alaskan Tundra. 329-337, Mar. 1972

Nomads of the Far North. By Matthew W. Stirling. 471-504, Oct. 1949
    Hearty Folk Defy Arctic Storms. Paintings by W. Langdon Kihn. 479-494

Our Restless Earth (Earthquakes). By Maynard M. Miller. 140-141, July 1964

Photographing Northern Wild Flowers. By Virginia L. Wells. 809-823, June 1956

The Pipeline: Alaska's Troubled Colossus. By Bryan Hodgson. Photos by Steve Raymer. 684-717, Nov. 1976

Plants of the Alaskan Tundra. 315-321, Mar. 1972

Portrait of a Fierce and Fragile Land. By Paul A. Zahl. 303-314, Mar. 1972

Preserving America's Last Great Wilderness. By David Jeffery. 769-791, June 1975

State of Alaska, Atlas series supplement. July 1959

Timber: How Much Is Enough? By John J. Putman. Photos by Bruce Dale. 485-511, Apr. 1974

Top of the World, Atlas series supplement. Nov. 1965

The Top of the World, map supplement. Oct. 1949

Trek Across Arctic America. By Colin Irwin. 295-321, Mar. 1974

When Giant Bears Go Fishing. By Cecil E. Rhode. 195-205, Aug. 1954

See also Aleutian Islands; Diomede Islands; Fairbanks; Katmai National Monument; King Island; Mount McKinley National Park; Nikolaevsk; North Slope; Pribilof Islands; St. Elias, Mount; Yukon (River); *and Manhattan,* S.S.

ALASKA KING CRAB:

The Crab That Shakes Hands. By Clarence P. Idyll. Photos by Robert F. Sisson. 254-271, Feb. 1971

ALASKA RANGE, Alaska:

Mount McKinley Conquered by New Route. By Bradford Washburn. 219-248, Aug. 1953

ALASKAN AIR COMMAND, U. S. Air Force:

Three Months on an Arctic Ice Island. By Joseph O. Fletcher. 489-504, Apr. 1953

ALBANY, New York:

Henry Hudson's River. By Willard Price. Photos by Wayne Miller. 364-403, Mar. 1962

The Mighty Hudson. By Albert W. Atwood. Photos by B. Anthony Stewart. 1-36, July 1948

ALBATROSSES:

The Gooney Birds of Midway. By John W. Aldrich. 839-851, June 1964

ALBEMARLE COUNTY, Virginia:

Mr. Jefferson's Charlottesville. By Anne Revis.

ALBEMARLE COUNTY, Virginia—*Continued*
553-592, May 1950
See also Monticello

ALBERTA (Province), Canada:
Alberta Unearths Her Buried Treasures. By David S. Boyer. 90-119, July 1960
Canada's Heartland, the Prairie Provinces. By W. E. Garrett. 443-489, Oct. 1970
Canada's "Now" Frontier. By Robert Paul Jordan. Photos by Lowell Georgia. 480-511, Oct. 1976
Canadian Rockies, Lords of a Beckoning Land. By Alan Phillips. Photos by James L. Stanfield. 353-393, Sept. 1966
From Sun-clad Sea to Shining Mountains. By Ralph Gray. Photos by James P. Blair. 542-589, Apr. 1964
Oil, the Dwindling Treasure. By Noel Grove. Photos by Emory Kristof. 792-825, June 1974
On the Ridgepole of the Rockies. By Walter Meayers Edwards. 745-780, June 1947
Canada's Rocky Mountain Playground. 755-770
See also Bikepacking; Great Divide Trail; Waterton-Glacier International Peace Park

ALBERTS, ARTHUR S.: Author-Photographer:
Hunting Musical Game in West Africa. 262-282, Aug. 1951

ALBINO ANIMALS:
Enchantress! (White Tigress). By Theodore H. Reed. Photos by Thomas J. Abercrombie. 628-641, May 1961
Growing Up With Snowflake (Gorilla). By Arthur J. Riopelle. Photos by Michael Kuh. 491-503, Oct. 1970
"Snowflake," the World's First White Gorilla. By Arthur J. Riopelle. Photos by Paul A. Zahl. 443-448, Mar. 1967
White Tiger in My House. By Elizabeth C. Reed. Photos by Donna K. Grosvenor. 482-491, Apr. 1970

ALBUQUERQUE, New Mexico:
New Mexico: The Golden Land. By Robert Laxalt. Photos by Adam Woolfitt. 299-345, Sept. 1970

ALCOTT, LOUISA MAY:
Literary Landmarks of Massachusetts. By William H. Nicholas. Photos by B. Anthony Stewart and John E. Fletcher. 279-310, Mar. 1950

ALDANA E., GUILLERMO: Author-Photographer:
Mesa del Nayar's Strange Holy Week. 780-795, June 1971

ALDERNEY (Island), English Channel:
Britain's "French" Channel Islands. By James Cerruti. Photos by James L. Amos. 710-740, May 1971

ALDRICH, JOHN W.: Author:
The Gooney Birds of Midway. 839-851, June 1964

ALDRIN, EDWIN E., Jr.:
First Explorers on the Moon: The Incredible Story of Apollo 11. 735-797, Dec. 1969
I. Man Walks on Another World. By Neil A. Armstrong, Edwin E. Aldrin, Jr., and Michael Collins. 738-749
II. Sounds of the Space Age, From Sputnik to Lu-

ALDRIN, EDWIN E., Jr.—*Continued*
nar Landing. A record narrated by Frank Borman. 750-751
III. The Flight of Apollo 11: "One giant leap for mankind." By Kenneth F. Weaver. 752-787
First Moon Explorers (Apollo 11) Receive the Society's Hubbard Medal. 859-861, June 1970

ALEKSIUK, MICHAEL: Author:
Manitoba's Fantastic Snake Pits. Photos by Bianca Lavies. 715-723, Nov. 1975

ALEUTIAN ISLANDS, Alaska:
Exploring Aleutian Volcanoes. By G. D. Robinson. 509-528, Oct. 1948
Operation Eclipse: 1948. By William A. Kinney. 325-372, Mar. 1949
See also Atka

ALEUTIAN RANGE, Alaska:
Lonely Wonders of Katmai (National Monument). By Ernest Gruening. Photos by Winfield Parks. 800-831, June 1963

ALEUTS (People):
Atka, Rugged Home of My Aleut Friends. By Lael Morgan. 572-583, Oct. 1974
The Fur Seal Herd Comes of Age. By Victor B. Scheffer and Karl W. Kenyon. 491-512, Apr. 1952

ALEXANDER THE GREAT:
In the Footsteps of Alexander the Great. By Helen and Frank Schreider. Paintings by Tom Lovell. 1-65, Jan. 1968

ALEXANDER, HOPE: Photographer:
Friend of the Wind: The Common Tern. By Ian Nisbet. 234-247, Aug. 1973

ALEXANDER GRAHAM BELL MUSEUM, Baddeck, Nova Scotia:
Alexander Graham Bell Museum: Tribute to Genius. By Jean Lesage. 227-256, Aug. 1956
Bell Museum, Baddeck, Nova Scotia. 256, 257, 259, 261, Aug. 1959; 358-359, 361, 362, Mar. 1975
Down East to Nova Scotia. By Winfield Parks. 853-879, June 1964

ALEXANDRIA, Virginia:
Across the Potomac From Washington. By Albert W. Atwood. 1-33, Jan. 1953

ALFRED THE GREAT:
The British Way. By Sir Evelyn Wrench. 421-541, Apr. 1949

ALGAE:
Algae: the Life-givers. By Paul A. Zahl. 361-377, Mar. 1974
See also Giant Kelp; Pond Life; Salt Marshes; Sargassum; Truk Lagoon

ALGÅRD, GÖRAN: Photographer:
Iceland Tapestry. By Deena Clark. 599-630, Nov. 1951
Lapland's Reindeer Roundup. 109-116, July 1949

ALGERIA:
Algeria: Learning to Live With Independence. By Thomas J. Abercrombie. 200-233, Aug. 1973
Dry-land Fleet Sails the Sahara. By Jean du Boucher. Photos by Jonathan S. Blair. 696-725,

ALGERIA — *Continued*

Nov. 1967

France's Stepchild, Problem and Promise. By Howard La Fay. Photos by Robert F. Sisson. 768-795, June 1960

Oasis-hopping in the Sahara. By Maynard Owen Williams. 209-236, Feb. 1949

Sand in My Eyes (Motor Trip). By Jinx Rodger. 664-705, May 1958

ALGONQUIAN INDIANS:

Indian Life Before the Colonists Came. By Stuart E. Jones. Engravings by Theodore de Bry, 1590. 351-368, Sept. 1947

ALGONQUIAN LINGUISTIC STOCK:

Nomads of the Far North. By Matthew W. Stirling. 471-504, Oct. 1949
 Hearty Folk Defy Arctic Storms. Paintings by W. Langdon Kihn. 479-494

ALHAMBRA (Fortress-Palace), Granada, Spain:

Andalusia, the Spirit of Spain. By Howard La Fay. Photos by Joseph J. Scherschel. 833-857, June 1975

The Changing Face of Old Spain. By Bart McDowell. Photos by Albert Moldvay. 291-339, Mar. 1965

Speaking of Spain. By Luis Marden. 415-456, Apr. 1950

ALICE SPRINGS, Australia:

"The Alice" in Australia's Wonderland. By Alan Villiers. Photos by Jeff Carter and David Moore. 230-257, Feb. 1966

ALL-AMERICA ROSE SELECTION (AARS). *See* Portrait Rose

ALL-GIRL Team Tests the Habitat (Tektite II). By Sylvia A. Earle. Paintings by Pierre Mion. 291-296, Aug. 1971

ALL-OUT Assault on Antarctica. By Richard E. Byrd. 141-180, Aug. 1956

ALLAGASH WILDERNESS WATERWAY, Maine:

Autumn Flames Along the Allagash. By François Leydet. Photos by Farrell Grehan. 177-187, Feb. 1974

ALLARD, WILLIAM ALBERT: Author-Photographer:

Chinatown, the Gilded Ghetto (San Francisco). 627-643, Nov. 1975

Cowpunching on the Padlock Ranch. 478-499, Oct. 1973

The Hutterites, Plain People of the West. 98-125, July 1970

Two Wheels Along the Mexican Border (U. S.-Mexico). 591-635, May 1971

Yellowstone Wildlife in Winter. 637-661, Nov. 1967

Photographer

Amish Folk: Plainest of Pennsylvania's Plain People. By Richard Gehman. 227-253, Aug. 1965

Canada's Mount Kennedy: The First Ascent. By James W. Whittaker. 11-33, July 1965

Houston, Prairie Dynamo. By Stuart E. Jones. 338-377, Sept. 1967

I See America First. By Lynda Bird Johnson. 874-904, Dec. 1965

ALLARD, WILLIAM ALBERT: Photographer — *Continued*

Land of the Ancient Basques. By Robert Laxalt. 240-277, Aug. 1968

New Zealand's Cook Islands: Paradise in Search of a Future. By Maurice Shadbolt. 203-231, Aug. 1967

ALLEMAN, IRVIN E.: Artist:

Flags of the Americas. By Elizabeth W. King. 633-657, May 1949

Flags of the United Nations. By Elizabeth W. King. 213-238, Feb. 1951

ALLEN, ARTHUR A.: Author-Photographer:

The Bird's Year. 791-816, June 1951

The Curlew's Secret. 751-770, Dec. 1948

Duck Hunting With a Color Camera. 514-539, Oct. 1951

A New Light Dawns on Bird Photography. 774-790, June 1948

Sapsucker Woods, Cornell University's Exciting New Bird Sanctuary. 530-551, Apr. 1962

Sea Bird Cities Off Audubon's Labrador. 755-774, June 1948

Split Seconds in the Lives of Birds. 681-706, May 1954

Voices of the Night. 507-522, Apr. 1950

ALLEN, DAVID G.: Photographer:

The Quetzal, Fabulous Bird of Maya Land. By Anne LaBastille Bowes. 141-150, Jan. 1969

ALLEN, DURWARD L.: Author:

Wolves Versus Moose on Isle Royale. By Durward L. Allen and L. David Mech. 200-219, Feb. 1963

ALLEN, JERRY: Author:

Tom Sawyer's Town (Hannibal, Missouri). 121-140, July 1956

ALLEN, ROBERT PORTER: Author:

Our Only Native Stork, the Wood Ibis. Photos by Frederick Kent Truslow. 294-306, Feb. 1964

Roseate Spoonbills, Radiant Birds of the Gulf Coast. Photos by Frederick Kent Truslow. 274-288, Feb. 1962

Whooping Cranes Fight for Survival. Photos by Frederick Kent Truslow. 650-669, Nov. 1959

ALLIGATOR REEF, Florida:

Marvels of a Coral Realm. By Walter A. Starck II. 710-738, Nov. 1966

Photographing the Night Creatures of Alligator Reef. By Robert E. Schroeder. Photos by author and Walter A. Starck II. 128-154, Jan. 1964

ALLIGATORS:

Alligators: Dragons in Distress. By Archie Carr. Photos by Treat Davidson and Laymond Hardy. 133-148, Jan. 1967

Twilight Hope for Big Cypress. By Rick Gore. Photos by Patricia Caulfield. 251-273, Aug. 1976

See also Caymans; *and* Everglades (Region)

ALLMON, CHARLES: Author-Photographer:

Barbados, Outrider of the Antilles. 363-392, Mar. 1952

Happy-go-lucky Trinidad and Tobago. 35-75, Jan. 1953

Index 1947-1976

105

ALLMON, CHARLES: Author-Photographer—*Continued*

Shores and Sails in the South Seas (Marquesas Islands). 73-104, Jan. 1950

Photographer

Bermuda, Cradled in Warm Seas. By Beverley M. Bowie. 203-238, Feb. 1954

Martinique: A Tropical Bit of France. By Gwen Drayton Allmon. 255-283, Feb. 1959

Rubber-cushioned Liberia. By Henry S. Villard. 201-228, Feb. 1948

Spectacular Rio de Janeiro. By Hernane Tavares de Sá. 289-328, Mar. 1955

Virgin Islands: Tropical Playland, U.S.A. By John Scofield. 201-232, Feb. 1956

The *Yankee*'s Wander-world. By Irving and Electa Johnson. 1-50, Jan. 1949

ALLMON, GWEN DRAYTON: Author:

Martinique: A Tropical Bit of France. Photos by Charles Allmon. 255-283, Feb. 1959

ALLYN, RUBE: Author:

Cruising Florida's Western Waterways. Photos by Bates Littlehales. 49-76, Jan. 1955

ALONE to Antarctica. By David Lewis. Drawings by Noel Sickles. 808-821, Dec. 1973

ALONG the Post Road Today. Photos by B. Anthony Stewart. 206-233, Aug. 1962

ALONG the Storied Incense Roads of Aden. By Hermann F. Eilts. Photos by Brian Brake. 230-254, Feb. 1957

ALONG the Yangtze, Main Street of China. By W. Robert Moore. 325-356, Mar. 1948

ALONG the Yukon Trail. By Amos Burg. 395-416, Sept. 1953

ALPS (Mountains), Europe:

Across the Alps in a Wicker Basket *(Bernina)*. By Phil Walker. 117-131, Jan. 1963

Across the Ridgepole of the Alps. By Walter Meayers Edwards. 410-419, Sept. 1960
Included: Map of cableway between Chamonix, France, and La Palud, Italy

The Alps. Special Publication announced. 870-874, June 1972

The Alps—Europe's Backbone, double-sided Atlas series supplement. Sept. 1965

The Alps: Man's Own Mountains. By Ralph Gray. Photos by Walter Meayers Edwards and William Eppridge. 350-395, Sept. 1965
Included: Map of world's longest highway tunnel, Mont Blanc

The Great St. Bernard Hospice Today. By George Pickow. 49-62, Jan. 1957

Occupied Austria, Outpost of Democracy. By George W. Long. Photos by Volkmar Wentzel. 749-790, June 1951

Sheep Trek in the French Alps. By Maurice Moyal. Photos by Marcel Coen. 545-564, Apr. 1952

Soaring on Skis in the Swiss Alps. By Carolyn Bennett Patterson. Photos by Kathleen Revis. 94-121, Jan. 1961

Surprising Switzerland. By Jean and Franc Shor. 427-478, Oct. 1956

Switzerland, Europe's High-rise Republic. By Thomas J. Abercrombie. 68-113, July 1969

ALPS (Mountains), Europe—*Continued*

Switzerland Guards the Roof of Europe. By William H. Nicholas. Photos by Willard R. Culver. 205-246, Aug. 1950

See also Bavaria; Dolomites; Saint Véran; Salzkammergut; Tirol; Val d'Hérens

ALUMINUM:

Kitimat—Canada's Aluminum Titan. By David S. Boyer. 376-398, Sept. 1956

AL 'UQAYR, Saudi Arabia. *See* Gerrha

ALVIN (Research Submersible):

Project FAMOUS. 586-615, May 1975
I. Where the Earth Turns Inside Out. By J. R. Heirtzler. Photos by Emory Kristof. 586-603
II. Dive Into the Great Rift. By Robert D. Ballard. Photos by Emory Kristof. 604-615

Window on Earth's Interior. By Robert D. Ballard. Photos by Emory Kristof. 228-249, Aug. 1976

AMA, Sea Nymphs of Japan. By Luis Marden. 122-135, July 1971

AMA DABLAM (Mountain), Nepal:

Wintering on the Roof of the World. By Barry C. Bishop. 503-547, Oct. 1962

AMALFI, Italy's Divine Coast. By Luis Marden. 472-509, Oct. 1959

AMANA COLONIES, Iowa:

Iowa's Enduring Amana Colonies. By Laura Longley Babb. Photos by Steve Raymer. 863-878, Dec. 1975

AMARNATH CAVE, Kashmir:

Himalayan Pilgrimage. By Christopher Rand. 520-535, Oct. 1956

AMATEUR Gardener Creates a New Rose. By Elizabeth A. Moize. Photos by Farrell Grehan. 286-294, Aug. 1972

AMAZON BASIN INDIANS:

Amazon—The River Sea. By Loren McIntyre. 456-495, Oct. 1972

See also Cinta Larga; Erigbaagtsa; Kraho; Kreen-Akarores; Machiguenga; Suyá; Tchikao; Tukuna; Txukahameis; Waurá

AMAZON RIVER REGION, South America:

The Amazon. Photos by Loren McIntyre. 445-455, Oct. 1972

Amazon (Television film). 295A-295B, Feb. 1968

Amazon—The River Sea. By Loren McIntyre. 456-495, Oct. 1972

Exploring the Amazon. Special Publication announced. 880-884, June 1969

Giant Insects of the Amazon. By Paul A. Zahl. 632-669, May 1959

Jungle Jaunt on Amazon Headwaters. By Bernice M. Goetz. 371-388, Sept. 1952

Sea Fever. By John E. Schultz. 237-268, Feb. 1949

See also Brazil

AMBASSADORS of Good Will: The Peace Corps. By Sargent Shriver and Peace Corps Volunteers. 297-345, Sept. 1964

AMBER:

Exploring the World of Gems. By W. F. Foshag. 779-810, Dec. 1950

AMERICA:

Eight Maps of Discovery: America in the Discovery Age: the Molineaux-Wright Chart. — America Emerges: The Thirteen Original States. — Capt. John Smith's Map of Virginia. — The Opening of the American West: Burr's 1840 Map. — Captain Smith's New England. — The Pilgrims' Cape Cod. — Alaska, Seward's Icebox, Became a Treasure Chest. — George Washington's Travels, Traced on the Arrowsmith Map. 757-769, June 1953

See also Colonial America

AMERICA Enters the Modern Era. By Frank Freidel. 537-577, Oct. 1965

AMERICA Goes to the Fair. By Samuel W. Matthews. 293-333, Sept. 1954

AMERICAN and Geographic Flags Top Everest. By Melvin M. Payne. Photos by Barry C. Bishop. 157-157C, Aug. 1963

AMERICAN ANTARCTIC MOUNTAINEERING EXPEDITION:

First Conquest of Antarctica's Highest Peaks. By Nicholas B. Clinch. 836-863, June 1967

First La Gorce Medal Honors Antarctic Expedition. 864-867, June 1967

AMERICAN Family in Afghanistan. By Rebecca Shannon Cresson. Photos by Osborne C. Cresson. 417-432, Sept. 1953

The **AMERICAN** Giant Comes of Age. By Frank Freidel. 660-711, May 1965

An **AMERICAN** in Russia's Capital. By Thomas T. Hammond. Photos by Dean Conger. 297-351, Mar. 1966

An **AMERICAN** Indian's View: This Land of Ours. By N. Scott Momaday. 13-19, July 1976

The **AMERICAN** Lobster, Delectable Cannibal. By Luis Marden. Photos by David Doubilet. 462-487, Apr. 1973

AMERICAN Masters in the National Gallery. By John Walker. 295-324, Sept. 1948

An **AMERICAN** Moslem Explores the Arab Past: The Sword and the Sermon. By Thomas J. Abercrombie. 3-45, July 1972

AMERICAN MOUNT EVEREST EXPEDITION:

American and Geographic Flags Top Everest. By Melvin M. Payne. Photos by Barry C. Bishop. 157-157C, Aug. 1963

Americans on Everest (Television film). 448-452, Sept. 1965; 575, Nov. 1976

America's First Everest Expedition. 460-515, Oct. 1963

I. Six to the Summit. By Norman G. Dyhrenfurth. Photos by Barry C. Bishop. 460-473

II. How We Climbed Everest. By Barry C. Bishop. 477-507

III. The First Traverse. By Thomas F. Hornbein and William F. Unsoeld. 509-513

IV. President Kennedy Presents the Hubbard Medal. 514-515

Mount Rainier: Testing Ground for Everest. By Barry C. Bishop. 688-711, May 1963

AMERICAN MUSEUM OF NATURAL HISTORY, New York:

Expeditions

Dinosaur expedition to Texas. 710, 715, 717, May 1954

See also American Museum-Armand Denis Expedition; Edgar M. Queeny-American Museum of Natural History Expedition; Gilliard Expeditions; Weeks Expedition

Museum

Behind New York's Window on Nature: The American Museum of Natural History. By James A. Oliver. Photos by Robert F. Sisson. 220-259, Feb. 1963

Dinosaur Hall: *Brontosaurus*. 707, 719, 721, 722, May 1954

Gem collection. 786, 797, 799, 801, Dec. 1950

See also Lerner Marine Laboratory

AMERICAN MUSEUM-ARMAND DENIS EXPEDITION:

New Guinea's Rare Birds and Stone Age Men. By E. Thomas Gilliard. 421-488, Apr. 1953

AMERICAN POINT ISLAND, Minnesota:

Men, Moose, and Mink of Northwest Angle. By William H. Nicholas. 265-284, Aug. 1947

AMERICAN PRIMITIVE ART. *See* Garbisch Collection

AMERICAN Processional: History on Canvas. By John and Blanche Leeper. 173-212, Feb. 1951

AMERICAN RED CROSS:

Scenes of Postwar Finland. By La Verne Bradley. Photos by Jerry Waller. 233-264, Aug. 1947

AMERICAN REVOLUTION:

Benjamin Franklin, Philosopher of Dissent. By Alice J. Hall. Photos by Linda Bartlett. 93-123, July 1975

Firebrands of the Revolution. By Eric F. Goldman. Photos by George F. Mobley. 2-27, July 1974

From Sword to Scythe in Champlain Country. By Ethel A. Starbird. Photos by B. Anthony Stewart and Emory Kristof. 153-201, Aug. 1967

George Washington: The Man Behind the Myths. By Howard La Fay. Photos by Ted Spiegel. 90-111, July 1976

History and Beauty Blend in a Concord Iris Garden. By Robert T. Cochran, Jr. Photos by M. Woodbridge Williams. 705-719, May 1959

I'm From New Jersey. By John T. Cunningham. Photos by Volkmar Wentzel. 1-45, Jan. 1960

The Loyalists. By Kent Britt. Photos by Ted Spiegel. 510-539, Apr. 1975

Massachusetts Builds for Tomorrow. By Robert de Roos. Photos by B. Anthony Stewart. 790-843, Dec. 1966

New Stars for Old Glory. By Lonnelle Aikman. 86-121, July 1959

North Through History Aboard *White Mist*. By Melville Bell Grosvenor. Photos by Edwin Stuart Grosvenor. 1-55, July 1970

Patriots in Petticoats. By Lonnelle Aikman. Paintings by Louis S. Glanzman. 475-493, Oct. 1975

Contents: Abigail Adams, Sarah Franklin Bache, Anne Bailey, Kate Moore Barry, Martha Bell, Margaret Cochran Corbin, Lydia Darragh, Mary Katherine Goddard, Elizabeth Hager, Nancy Hart, Elizabeth Hutchinson Jackson, Dicey Langston, Sybil Ludington, Re-

AMERICAN REVOLUTION — *Continued*

becca Motte, Molly Pitcher (Mary Hays), Esther Reed, Deborah Sampson, Jane Thomas, Mercy Otis Warren, Martha Washington, Phillis Wheatley, Elizabeth Zane

Philadelphia Houses a Proud Past. By Harold Donaldson Eberlein. Photos by Thomas Nebbia. 151-191, Aug. 1960

Profiles of the Presidents: I. The Presidency and How It Grew. By Frank Freidel. 642-687, Nov. 1964

The Revolutionary War: America's Fight for Freedom. Special Publication announced. 868-875, June 1967

Thomas Jefferson: Architect of Freedom. By Mike W. Edwards. Photos by Linda Bartlett. 231-259, Feb. 1976

U. S. Capitol, Citadel of Democracy. By Lonnelle Aikman. 143-192, Aug. 1952
Included: Paintings and frescoes of the Revolution by John Trumbull and Constantino Brumidi

Washington Lives Again at Valley Forge. By Howell Walker. 197-202, Feb. 1954

See also Boston Post Roads; Daughters of the American Revolution

AMERICAN SAMOA:

Problems in Paradise. By Mary and Laurance S. Rockefeller. Photos by Thomas Nebbia. 782-793, Dec. 1974

AMERICAN Special Forces in Action in Viet Nam. By Howard Sochurek. 38-65, Jan. 1965

AMERICAN TELEPHONE AND TELEGRAPH COMPANY: Research. *See* Telstar

AMERICAN Wild Flower Odyssey. By P. L. Ricker. 603-634, May 1953

AMERICANS Afoot in Rumania. By Dan Dimancescu. Photos by Dick Durrance II and Christopher G. Knight. 810-845, June 1969

AMERICA's First Painters: Indians. By Dorothy Dunn. 349-377, Mar. 1955

AMERICA's First Undersea Park. By Charles M. Brookfield. Photos by Jerry Greenberg. 58-69, Jan. 1962

AMERICA's "Meat on the Hoof." By William H. Nicholas. 33-72, Jan. 1952

AMERICA's 6,000-mile Walk in Space. 440-447, Sept. 1965

AMERICA's Wilderness: How Much Can We Save? By Gilbert M. Grosvenor, François Leydet, and Joseph Judge. Photos by Farrell Grehan. 151-205, Feb. 1974

AMHERST, Massachusetts:

Literary Landmarks of Massachusetts. By William H. Nicholas. Photos by B. Anthony Stewart and John E. Fletcher. 279-310, Mar. 1950

AMHERST COLLEGE, Massachusetts:

Administrators of Folger Library. *See* Folger

AMIABLE Amsterdam. By William Davenport. Photos by Adam Woolfitt. 683-705, May 1974

AMID the Mighty Walls of Zion. By Lewis F. Clark. 37-70, Jan. 1954

AMISH (People):

Amish Folk: Plainest of Pennsylvania's Plain People. By Richard Gehman. Photos by William Albert Allard. 227-253, Aug. 1965

Artists Look at Pennsylvania. By John Oliver La Gorce. 37-56, July 1948

AMMAN, Jordan:

Home to the Holy Land. By Maynard Owen Williams. 707-746, Dec. 1950

AMONG Alaska's Brown Bears. By Allan L. Egbert and Michael H. Luque. 428-442, Sept. 1975

AMOS, JAMES L.: Photographer:

Atlanta, Pacesetter City of the South. By William S. Ellis. 246-281, Feb. 1969

Britain's "French" Channel Islands. By James Cerruti. 710-740, May 1971

Colorado, the Rockies' Pot of Gold. By Edward J. Linehan. 157-201, Aug. 1969

The Great Lakes: Is It Too Late? By Gordon Young. Photos by James L. Amos and Martin Rogers. 147-185, Aug. 1973

Great Smokies National Park: Solitude for Millions. By Gordon Young. 522-549, Oct. 1968

New Zealand's Bountiful South Island. By Peter Benchley. 93-123, Jan. 1972

The Original Boston: St. Botolph's Town (England). By Veronica Thomas. 382-389, Sept. 1974

San Diego, California's Plymouth Rock. By Allan C. Fisher, Jr. 114-147, July 1969

Sea Islands: Adventuring Along the South's Surprising Coast. By James Cerruti. Photos by Thomas Nebbia and James L. Amos. 366-393, Mar. 1971

Utah's Shining Oasis. By Charles McCarry. 440-473, Apr. 1975

Williamsburg, City for All Seasons. By Joseph Judge. 790-823, Dec. 1968

AMOS, WILLIAM H.: Author-Photographer:

The Living Sand. 820-833, June 1965

Teeming Life of a Pond. 274-298, Aug. 1970

AMPHIBIANS:

In the Wilds of a City Parlor. By Paul A. Zahl. 645-672, Nov. 1954

Reptiles and Amphibians (Television film). 875A-875B, Dec. 1968

Strange Animals of Australia. By David Fleay. Photos by Stanley Breeden. 388-411, Sept. 1963

See also Frogs; Salamanders; Toads

AMPHITRITE (Inflatable Ship):

Inflatable Ship Opens Era of Airborne Undersea Expeditions. By Jacques-Yves Cousteau. 142-148, July 1961

AMSTERDAM, Netherlands:

Amiable Amsterdam. By William Davenport. Photos by Adam Woolfitt. 683-705, May 1974

Mid-century Holland Builds Her Future. By Sydney Clark. 747-778, Dec. 1950

The Netherlands: Nation at War With the Sea. By Alan Villiers. Photos by Adam Woolfitt. 530-571, Apr. 1968

AMUSEMENT PARKS. *See* Disneyland; Tivoli; Walt Disney World

AN LAC, Viet Nam:

Viet Nam's Montagnards. By Howard Sochurek. 443-487, Apr. 1968

ANASAZI (Indians):

Ancient Cliff Dwellers of Mesa Verde. By Don Watson. Photos by Willard R. Culver. 349-376, Sept. 1948

Searching for Cliff Dwellers' Secrets. By Carroll A. Burroughs. 619-625, Nov. 1959

Solving the Riddles of Wetherill Mesa. By Douglas Osborne. Paintings by Peter V. Bianchi. 155-195, Feb. 1964

Your Society to Seek New Light on the Cliff Dwellers. 154-156, Jan. 1959

ANATOLIA (Region), Turkey:

Ancient Aphrodisias and Its Marble Treasures. By Kenan T. Erim. Photos by Jonathan S. Blair. 280-294, Aug. 1967

Aphrodisias, Awakened City of Ancient Art. By Kenan T. Erim. Photos by Jonathan Blair. 766-791, June 1972

Keeping House in a Cappadocian Cave. By Jonathan S. Blair. 127-146, July 1970

Peasants of Anatolia. By Alfred Marchionini. 57-72, July 1948

ANCHORAGE, Alaska:

An Alaskan Family's Night of Terror (Earthquake). By Tay Pryor Thomas. 142-156, July 1964

Earthquake! By William P. E. Graves. 112-139, July 1964

ANCIENT Aphrodisias and Its Marble Treasures. By Kenan T. Erim. Photos by Jonathan S. Blair. 280-294, Aug. 1967

ANCIENT Cliff Dwellers of Mesa Verde. By Don Watson. Photos by Willard R. Culver. 349-376, Sept. 1948

ANCIENT Mesopotamia: A Light That Did Not Fail. By E. A. Speiser. Paintings by H. M. Herget. 41-105, Jan. 1951

ANCIENT Shipwreck Yields New Facts—and a Strange Cargo. By Peter Throckmorton. Photos by Kim Hart and Joseph J. Scherschel. 282-300, Feb. 1969

ANCIENT "Skyscrapers" of the Yemen. Photos by Richard H. Sanger. 645-668, Nov. 1947

AND Now to Touch the Moon's Forbidding Face. By Kenneth F. Weaver. 633-635, May 1969

ANDALUSIA (Region), Spain:

Andalusia, the Spirit of Spain. By Howard La Fay. Photos by Joseph J. Scherschel. 833-857, June 1975

The Changing Face of Old Spain. By Bart McDowell. Photos by Albert Moldvay. 291-339, Mar. 1965

Gypsy Cave Dwellers of Andalusia. 572-582, Oct. 1957

Holy Week and the Fair in Sevilla. By Luis Marden. 499-530, Apr. 1951

Speaking of Spain. By Luis Marden. 415-456, Apr. 1950

ANDAMAN ISLANDS, India:

The Last Andaman Islanders. By Raghubir Singh. 66-91, July 1975

ANDEAN CONDORS:

The Condor, Soaring Spirit of the Andes. By Jerry McGahan. Photos by Libby McGahan. 684-709, May 1971

ANDEREGG, FRED: Photographer:

Mount Sinai's Holy Treasures (St. Catherine's Monastery). By Kurt Weitzmann. 109-127, Jan. 1964

ANDERS, WILLIAM A.:

Hubbard Medal recipient. 861, June 1970

"A Most Fantastic Voyage": The Story of Apollo 8's Rendezvous With the Moon. By Sam C. Phillips. 593-631, May 1969

ANDERSON, GEORGE W., Jr.: Author:

Our Nuclear Navy. 449-450, Mar. 1963

ANDERSON, NIKE: Author:

October Holiday on the Outer Banks. Photos by J. Baylor Roberts. 501-529, Oct. 1955

ANDERSON, RON J.: Author:

The Kiwi, New Zealand's Wonder Bird. 395-398, Sept. 1955

ANDERSON, STEWART: Author-Photographer:

The West Through Boston Eyes. 733-776, June 1949

ANDERSON, WILLIAM R.:

Submarine Through the North Pole. By William G. Lalor, Jr. Photos by John J. Krawczyk. 1-20, Jan. 1959

Author

The Arctic as a Sea Route of the Future. 21-24, Jan. 1959

ANDES (Mountains), South America:

At Home in the High Andes. By Harry Tschopik, Jr. 133-146, Jan. 1955

Avalanche! (Peru). By Bart McDowell. Photos by John E. Fletcher. 855-880, June 1962

El Sangay, Fire-breathing Giant of the Andes. By G. Edward Lewis. 117-138, Jan. 1950

In Quest of the Rarest Flamingo. By William G. Conway. Photos by Bates Littlehales. 91-105, July 1961

Parks, Plans, and People: How South America Guards Her Green Legacy. By Mary and Laurance Rockefeller. Photos by George F. Mobley. 74-119, Jan. 1967

Included: Christ of the Andes; Lake District; Moreno Glacier; Mount Aconcagua; Nahuel Huapí National Park

Peru, Homeland of the Warlike Inca. By Kip Ross. 421-462, Oct. 1950

Puya, the Pineapple's Andean Ancestor. By Mulford B. Foster. 463-480, Oct. 1950

Sky-high Bolivia. 481-496, Oct. 1950

To Torre Egger's Icy Summit. By Jim Donini. 813-823, Dec. 1976

ANDORRA:

The Enduring Pyrenees. By Robert Laxalt. Photos by Edwin Stuart Grosvenor. 794-819, Dec. 1974

ANDORRA—*Continued*

Incredible Andorra. By Lawrence L. Klingman. Photos by B. Anthony Stewart. 262-290, Aug. 1949

ANDREWS, E. WYLLYS: Author:

Dzibilchaltun: Lost City of the Maya. 91-109, Jan. 1959

ANDROS ISLAND, Bahama Islands:

Flamingos' Last Stand on Andros Island. By Paul A. Zahl. 635-652, May 1951

Probing the Deep Reefs' Hidden Realm. By Walter A. Starck II and Jo D. Starck. 867-886, Dec. 1972

See also Blue Holes

ANGEL FALLS, Venezuela:

Jungle Journey to the World's Highest Waterfall. By Ruth Robertson. 655-690, Nov. 1949

ANGKOR, Cambodia:

Angkor, Jewel of the Jungle. By W. Robert Moore. Paintings by Maurice Fiévet. 517-569, Apr. 1960

Portrait of Indochina. By W. Robert Moore and Maynard Owen Williams. Paintings by Jean Despujols. 461-490, Apr. 1951

ANGOLA, Unknown Africa. By Volkmar Wentzel. 347-383, Sept. 1961

ANIMAL BEHAVIOR:

The Marvels of Animal Behavior. Book announced. 588-590, Oct. 1972

The Mystery of Animal Behavior (Television film). 592A-592B, Oct. 1969

See also individual species

ANIMAL EYES:

Nature's Alert Eyes. By Constance P. Warner. 558-569, Apr. 1959

ANIMAL INTRODUCTION:

Florida, Noah's Ark for Exotic Newcomers. By Rick Gore. Photos by David Doubilet. 538-559, Oct. 1976

New Tricks Outwit Our Insect Enemies. By Hal Higdon. Photos by Robert F. Sisson and Emory Kristof. 380-399, Sept. 1976

See also Africanized Honeybees; Cattle Egret; Fig Wasps; Orioles; Walking Catfish

ANIMAL ORPHANAGE, Entebbe, Uganda:

Orphans of the Wild. By Bruce G. Kinloch. 683-699, Nov. 1962

ANIMAL SAFARI to British Guiana. By David Attenborough. Photos by Charles Lagus and author. 851-874, June 1957

ANIMALS:

The Animals Nobody Loved (Television film). cover announcement, Feb. 1976

Animals of East Africa. Special Publication announced. 844-849, June 1968

Animals That Build Their Homes. Children's book announced. 718-720, Nov. 1976

How Animals Hide. Children's book announced. 726-728, Nov. 1973

Tricks Animals Play. Children's book announced. 724-726, Nov. 1975

See also Amphibians; Animal Behavior; Animal

ANIMALS—*Continued*

Introduction; Birds; listing under Cephalopods; Crustaceans; Fishes; Insects; Mammals; Mollusks; Reptiles; Scorpions; Spiders; Worms; and Circus; Game Preserves; National Parks; Wildlife; Zoos

Albinos. See Albino Animals

Endangered Species:

African Wildlife: Man's Threatened Legacy. By Allan C. Fisher, Jr. Photos by Thomas Nebbia. Paintings by Ned Seidler. 147-187, Feb. 1972

India Struggles to Save Her Wildlife. By John J. Putman. Paintings by Ned Seidler. 299-343, Sept. 1976

Vanishing Wildlife of North America. Special Publication announced. 865-868, June 1973

See also Andean Condors; Bighorn Sheep; Brown Pelicans; Giant Tortoises; Gorillas; Grizzly Bears; Harp Seals; Horses, Wild; Polar Bear; Snow Leopards; Vicuñas; Whales; and Everglades

Extinct Species:

Exploring the Mind of Ice Age Man. By Alexander Marshack. 64-89, Jan. 1975

"Ice Age Mammals of the Alaskan Tundra," painting supplement. Mar. 1972

See also Aepyornis; Dinosaurs; Mammoth

Nocturnal. See Nocturnal Animals

Tagged and Monitored Animals. See Alligators; Black Bears; Caribou; Eels; Green Turtles; Grizzly Bears; Hyenas; Lobsters; Monarch Butterfly; Mountain Lions; Penguins; Polar Bear; Whistling Swans

Tool-using Species. See Chimpanzees; Egyptian Vulture; Finches (The Galapagos); Herons; Sea Otters

ANIMATION:

The Magic Worlds of Walt Disney. By Robert de Roos. Photos by Thomas Nebbia. 159-207, Aug. 1963

Animation: Mickey Mouse Explains the Art to Mr. G. O. Graphic. 168-171

ANIMISM. See Hmong; Karens

ANKARA, Turkey:

Turkey Paves the Path of Progress. By Maynard Owen Williams. 141-186, Aug. 1951

When the President Goes Abroad (Eisenhower Tour). By Gilbert M. Grosvenor. 588-649, May 1960

ANN, Cape, Massachusetts:

Windjamming Around New England. By Tom Horgan. Photos by Robert F. Sisson. 141-169, Aug. 1950

ANNAPOLIS, Maryland:

Maryland on the Half Shell. By Stuart E. Jones. Photos by Robert W. Madden. 188-229, Feb. 1972

ANTARCTIC REGIONS:

Alone to Antarctica. By David Lewis. Drawings by Noel Sickles. 808-821, Dec. 1973

Atlantic Odyssey: Iceland to Antarctica. By Newman Bumstead. Photos by Volkmar Wentzel. 725-780, Dec. 1955

Ice Bird Ends Her Lonely Odyssey. By David Lewis. 216-233, Aug. 1975

Off the Beaten Track of Empire (Prince Philip's

ANTARCTIC REGIONS – *Continued*

Tour). By Beverley M. Bowie. Photos by Michael Parker. 584-626, Nov. 1957

What's Happening to Our Climate? By Samuel W. Matthews. 576-615, Nov. 1976

See also Antarctica; South Georgia Island

ANTARCTICA:

Across the Frozen Desert to Byrd Station. By Paul W. Frazier. Photos by Calvin L. Larsen. 383-398, Sept. 1957

Admiral of the Ends of the Earth (Richard E. Byrd). By Melville Bell Grosvenor. 38-48, July 1957

All-out Assault on Antarctica. By Richard E. Byrd. 141-180, Aug. 1956

Antarctic Scientist (Paul A. Siple) Honored by The Society. 792-793, June 1958

Antarctica, Atlas series supplement. Feb. 1963

Antarctica, map supplement. Sept. 1957

Antarctica: Icy Testing Ground for Space. By Samuel W. Matthews. Photos by Robert W. Madden. 569-592, Oct. 1968

Antarctica's Nearer Side. By Samuel W. Matthews. Photos by William R. Curtsinger. 622-655, Nov. 1971

The Crossing of Antarctica. By Sir Vivian Fuchs. Photos by George Lowe. 25-47, Jan. 1959

Exploring Antarctica's Phantom Coast. By Edwin A. McDonald. Photos by W. D. Vaughn. 251-273, Feb. 1962

First Conquest of Antarctica's Highest Peaks. By Nicholas B. Clinch. 836-863, June 1967

First Flight Across the Bottom of the World. By James R. Reedy. Photos by Otis Imboden. 454-464, Mar. 1964

Flight Into Antarctic Darkness. By J. Lloyd Abbot, Jr. Photos by David S. Boyer. 732-738, Nov. 1967

Man's First Winter at the South Pole (Amundsen-Scott IGY South Pole Station). By Paul A. Siple. 439-478, Apr. 1958

New Era in the Loneliest Continent. By David M. Tyree. Photos by Albert Moldvay. 260-296, Feb. 1963
    Included: Byrd Station; McMurdo Station

Our Navy Explores Antarctica. By Richard E. Byrd. U. S. Navy official photos. 429-522, Oct. 1947

Society Honors the Conquerors of Antarctica. 589-590, Apr. 1959

Stalking Seals Under Antarctic Ice. By Carleton Ray. 54-65, Jan. 1966

This Changing Earth. By Samuel W. Matthews. 1-37, Jan. 1973

To the Men at South Pole Station. By Richard E. Byrd. 1-4, July 1957

We Are Living at the South Pole (IGY station). By Paul A. Siple. Photos by David S. Boyer. 5-35, July 1957

What We've Accomplished in Antarctica. By George J. Dufek. 527-557, Oct. 1959

Year of Discovery Opens in Antarctica. By David S. Boyer. 339-381, Sept. 1957

ANTELOPES:

Roaming Africa's Unfenced Zoos. By W. Robert Moore. 353-380, Mar. 1950
    Included: Dik-dik, Duiker, Eland, Hartebeest, Impala, Inyala, Klipspringer, Kudu, Oryx, Roan Antelope, Sable Antelope, Sitatunga, Steenbok, Tsessebe, Waterbuck, Wildebeest (Gnu)

ANTHROPOLOGY:

Adventures in the Search for Man. By Louis S. B. Leakey. Photos by Hugo van Lawick. 132-152, Jan. 1963

A Bold New Look at Our Past. The Editor. 62-63, Jan. 1975

Dr. Leakey and the Dawn of Man (Television film). 703A-703B, Nov. 1966

Ethiopia Yields First "Family" of Early Man. By Donald C. Johanson. Photos by David Brill. 790-811, Dec. 1976

Exploring 1,750,000 Years Into Man's Past. By L. S. B. Leakey. Photos by Robert F. Sisson. 564-589, Oct. 1961

Exploring the Mind of Ice Age Man. By Alexander Marshack. 64-89, Jan. 1975

Finding the World's Earliest Man *(Zinjanthropus boisei)*. By L. S. B. Leakey. Photos by Des Bartlett. 420-435, Sept. 1960

Ice Age Man, the First American. By Thomas R. Henry. Paintings by Andre Durenceau. 781-806, Dec. 1955

In Search of Man's Past at Lake Rudolf. By Richard E. Leakey. Photos by Gordon W. Gahan. 712-734, May 1970

The Leakey Tradition Lives On. By Melvin M. Payne. 143-144, Jan. 1973

The Leakeys of Africa: Family in Search of Prehistoric Man. By Melvin M. Payne. 194-231, Feb. 1965
    Included: *Homo habilis, Kenyapithecus, Proconsul, Zinjanthropus*

Lifelike Man Preserved 2,000 Years in Peat. By P. V. Glob. 419-430, Mar. 1954

Mexico's Window on the Past (National Museum). By Bart McDowell. Photos by B. Anthony Stewart. 492-519, Oct. 1968

Nomads of the World. Special Publication announced. 882-886, June 1971

Preserving the Treasures of Olduvai Gorge. By Melvin M. Payne. Photos by Joseph J. Scherschel. 701-709, Nov. 1966
    Included: *Homo erectus, Homo habilis, Kenyapithecus, Zinjanthropus*

Primitive Worlds. Special Publication announced. 865-868, June 1973

Skull 1470. By Richard E. Leakey. Photos by Bob Campbell. 819-829, June 1973

Twelve National Geographic Society Scientific Projects Under Way. 869-870, June 1954

Vanished Mystery Men of Hudson Bay. By Henry B. Collins. 669-687, Nov. 1956
    Included: Dorset Eskimos, Sadlermiuts

Vanishing Peoples of the Earth. Special Publication announced. 844-849, June 1968

Wyoming Muck Tells of Battle: Ice Age Man vs. Mammoth. By Cynthia Irwin, Henry Irwin, and George Agogino. 828-837, June 1962

See also Russell Cave, Alabama, for Stone Age; *and* Archeology; Archeomagnetism Dating; Ethnology; Potassium-Argon Dating; Radiocarbon Dating

ANTIGUA, Guatemala:

Easter Week in Indian Guatemala. By John Scofield. 406-417, Mar. 1960

Guatemala, Maya and Modern. By Louis de la Haba. Photos by Joseph J. Scherschel. 661-689, Nov. 1974

Index 1947-1976

ANTIGUA (Island), West Indies:

A Fresh Breeze Stirs the Leewards. By Carleton Mitchell. Photos by Winfield Parks. 488-537, Oct. 1966

ANTILLES, Greater. *See* Cuba; Haiti; Jamaica; Puerto Rico

ANTILLES, Lesser. *See* Barbados; Leeward Islands; Martinique; Netherlands Antilles; Tobago; Trinidad; Virgin Islands; Windward Islands

ANTI-LOCUST RESEARCH CENTRE, London:

Locusts: "Teeth of the Wind." By Robert A. M. Conley. Photos by Gianni Tortoli. 202-227, Aug. 1969

ANTIOCHUS I, King (Commagene):

Throne Above the Euphrates. By Theresa Goell. 390-405, Mar. 1961

ANTS:

At Home With the Bulldog Ant. By Robert F. Sisson. 62-75, July 1974
Face-to-Face With a World of Ants. 72-75

The Enigma of Bird Anting. By Hance Roy Ivor. 105-119, July 1956

Living Honey Jars of the Ant World. By Ross E. Hutchins. 405-411, Mar. 1962

ANTZE, PAUL: Author:

Round the World School. Photos by William Eppridge. 96-127, July 1962

APARTHEID:

The Zulus: Black Nation in a Land of Apartheid. By Joseph Judge. Photos by Dick Durrance II. 738-775, Dec. 1971

APES:

The Ape (Gibbon) With Friends in Washington. By Margaretta Burr Wells. 61-74, July 1953

Monkeys, Apes, and Man (Television film). 585A-585B, Oct. 1971

Search for the Great Apes (Television film). cover, Jan. 1976

See also Chimpanzees; Gorillas; Orangutans

APHIDS:

Following the Ladybug Home. By Kenneth S. Hagen. Photos by Robert F. Sisson. 543-553, Apr. 1970

Rose Aphids. By Treat Davidson. 851-859, June 1961

APHRODISIAS (Ancient City), Asia Minor:

Ancient Aphrodisias and Its Marble Treasures. By Kenan T. Erim. Photos by Jonathan S. Blair. 280-294, Aug. 1967

Aphrodisias, Awakened City of Ancient Art. By Kenan T. Erim. Photos by Jonathan Blair. 766-791, June 1972

APOLLO MISSIONS:

And Now to Touch the Moon's Forbidding Face. By Kenneth F. Weaver. 633-635, May 1969

Apollo 15 Explores the Mountains of the Moon. By Kenneth F. Weaver. Photos from NASA. 233-265, Feb. 1972

Apollo Missions. 289-331, Sept. 1973
I. Summing Up Mankind's Greatest Adventure. By Gilbert M. Grosvenor. 289

APOLLO MISSIONS—*Continued*

II. Exploring Taurus-Littrow. By Harrison H. Schmitt. Photos by the crew of Apollo 17. 290-307
III. Have We Solved the Mysteries of the Moon? By Kenneth F. Weaver. Paintings by William H. Bond. 309-325
IV. What Is It Like to Walk on the Moon? By David R. Scott. 326-331
V. "Teammates in Mankind's Greatest Adventure," painting supplement

Apollo 16 Brings Us Visions From Space (Photos). 856-865, Dec. 1972

The Climb Up Cone Crater (Apollo 14). By Alice J. Hall. Photos by Edgar D. Mitchell and Alan B. Shepard, Jr. 136-148, July 1971

First Explorers on the Moon: The Incredible Story of Apollo 11. 735-797, Dec. 1969
I. Man Walks on Another World. By Neil A. Armstrong, Edwin E. Aldrin, Jr., and Michael Collins. 738-749
II. Sounds of the Space Age, From Sputnik to Lunar Landing. A record narrated by Frank Borman. 750-751
III. The Flight of Apollo 11: "One giant leap for mankind." By Kenneth F. Weaver. 752-787
IV. What the Moon Rocks Tell Us. By Kenneth F. Weaver. 788-797

First Moon Explorers (Apollo 11) Receive the Society's Hubbard Medal. 859-861, June 1970
Included: Previous presentation of medal to Apollo 8 astronauts

Footprints on the Moon. By Hugh L. Dryden. Paintings by Davis Meltzer and Pierre Mion. 357-401, Mar. 1964

The Making of an Astronaut. By Robert R. Gilruth. 122-144, Jan. 1965

"A Most Fantastic Voyage": The Story of Apollo 8's Rendezvous With the Moon. By Sam C. Phillips. 593-631, May 1969

APOLLO-SOYUZ MISSION:

Apollo-Soyuz: Handclasp in Space. By Thomas Y. Canby. 183-187, Feb. 1976

APPALACHIA, U. S.:

Appalachian Valley Pilgrimage. By Catherine Bell Palmer. Photos by Justin Locke. 1-32, July 1949

The People of Cumberland Gap. By John Fetterman. Photos by Bruce Dale. 591-621, Nov. 1971

See also Cades Cove, Tennessee; West Virginia

APPALACHIAN MOUNTAINS, U. S.:

Skyline Trail from Maine to Georgia. By Andrew H. Brown. Photos by Robert F. Sisson. 219-251, Aug. 1949

See also Adirondack Mountains; Berkshires; Blue Ridge Mountains; Cumberland Country; Great Smoky Mountains; Green Mountains; White Mountains

APPALACHIAN TRAIL, U. S.:

The Appalachian Trail. Special Publication announced. 870-874, June 1972

Pack Trip Through the Smokies. By Val Hart. Photos by Robert F. Sisson. 473-502, Oct. 1952

Skyline Trail from Maine to Georgia. By Andrew H. Brown. Photos by Robert F. Sisson. 219-251, Aug. 1949

APPEL, FREDRIC C.: Author:

The Coming Revolution in Transportation. Photos by Dean Conger. 301-341, Sept. 1969

APPLE TREE:

The World of My Apple Tree. By Robert F. Sisson. 836-847, June 1972

APPLEBY FAIR, Appleby, England:

When Gypsies Gather at Appleby Fair. Photos by Bruce Dale. 848-869, June 1972

APPLIED PHYSICS LABORATORY, Johns Hopkins University. *See* DODGE Satellite

APPOMATTOX COURT HOUSE, Virginia:

Appomattox: Where Grant and Lee Made Peace With Honor a Century Ago. By Ulysses S. Grant 3rd. Photos by Bruce Dale. 435-469, Apr. 1965

AQABA, Gulf of:

The Other Side of Jordan. By Luis Marden. 790-825, Dec. 1964

The Red Sea's Gardens of Eels. By Eugenie Clark. Photos by James L. Stanfield and David Doubilet. 724-735, Nov. 1972

The Red Sea's Sharkproof Fish. By Eugenie Clark. Photos by David Doubilet. 718-727, Nov. 1974

AQUALUNG:

Fish Men Discover a 2,200-year-old Greek Ship. By Jacques-Yves Cousteau. 1-36, Jan. 1954

Fish Men Explore a New World Undersea. By Jacques-Yves Cousteau. 431-472, Oct. 1952

See also Divers and Diving

AQUARIUMS. *See* Marineland (Florida)

AQUARIUMS, Home:

In the Wilds of a City Parlor. By Paul A. Zahl. 645-672, Nov. 1954

AQUASCOPE:

One Hundred Hours Beneath the Chesapeake. By Gilbert C. Klingel. Photos by Willard R. Culver. 681-696, May 1955

AQUEDUCTS. *See* Los Angeles Aqueduct

AQUICULTURE:

Giant Kelp, Sequoias of the Sea. By Wheeler J. North. Photos by Bates Littlehales. 251-269, Aug. 1972

Shrimp Nursery: Science Explores New Ways to Farm the Sea. By Clarence P. Idyll. Photos by Robert F. Sisson. 636-659, May 1965

ARAB-ISRAELI CONFLICT:

Cairo, Troubled Capital of the Arab World. By William S. Ellis. Photos by Winfield Parks. 639-667, May 1972

Damascus, Syria's Uneasy Eden. By Robert Azzi. 512-535, Apr. 1974

Eyewitness to War in the Holy Land. By Charles Harbutt. 782-795, Dec. 1967

Israel—The Seventh Day. By Joseph Judge. Photos by Gordon W. Gahan. 816-855, Dec. 1972

New Life for the Troubled Suez Canal. By William Graves. Photos by Jonathan Blair. 792-817, June 1975

Our Life on a Border Kibbutz. By Carol and Al Abrams. Photos by Al Abrams. 364-391, Sept. 1970

ARAB NATIONS:

The Arab World. 712-732, Nov. 1958

The Arab World, Inc. By John J. Putman. Photos

ARAB NATIONS—*Continued*

by Winfield Parks. 494-533, Oct. 1975
Included: Kuwait; Oman; Saudi Arabia; United Arab Emirates

Oil, the Dwindling Treasure. By Noel Grove. Photos by Emory Kristof. 792-825, June 1974

The Peoples of the Middle East, map supplement. Text on reverse. July 1972

The Sword and the Sermon (Islam). By Thomas J. Abercrombie. 3-45, July 1972

See also Aden Protectorate; Algeria; Bahrein; Egypt; Iraq; Jordan; Kuwait; Lebanon; Morocco; Oman; Saudi Arabia; Sudan; Syria; Tunisia; United Arab Emirates; Yemen

ARABIAN PENINSULA:

Africa and the Arabian Peninsula, map supplement. Mar. 1950

In Search of Arabia's Past. By Peter Bruce Cornwall. 493-522, Apr. 1948

See also Aden Protectorate; Bahrein; Kuwait; Oman; Saudi Arabia; Yemen

ARACHNIDS. *See* Scorpions; Spiders

ARAN ISLANDS, Ireland:

The Arans, Ireland's Invincible Isles. By Veronica Thomas. Photos by Winfield Parks. 545-573, Apr. 1971

I Walked Some Irish Miles. By Dorothea Sheats. 653-678, May 1951

ARANSAS NATIONAL WILDLIFE REFUGE, Texas:

Whooping Cranes Fight for Survival. By Robert Porter Allen. Photos by Frederick Kent Truslow. 650-669, Nov. 1959

ARAUCANA CHICKENS:

Easter Egg Chickens. By Frederick G. Vosburgh. Photos by B. Anthony Stewart. 377-387, Sept. 1948

ARCHEOLOGY:

Abraham, the Friend of God. By Kenneth MacLeish. Photos by Dean Conger. 739-789, Dec. 1966

Ancient Aphrodisias and Its Marble Treasures. By Kenan T. Erim. Photos by Jonathan S. Blair. 280-294, Aug. 1967

Angkor, Jewel of the Jungle. By W. Robert Moore. Paintings by Maurice Fiévet. 517-569, Apr. 1960

Aphrodisias, Awakened City of Ancient Art. By Kenan T. Erim. Photos by Jonathan Blair. 766-791, June 1972

Arab Land Beyond the Jordan. Photos by Frank Hurley. 753-768, Dec. 1947

Archeological Map of Middle America, Land of the Feathered Serpent, map supplement. Text on reverse. Oct. 1968

An Archeologist Looks at Palestine. By Nelson Glueck. 739-752, Dec. 1947

A Bold New Look at Our Past. The Editor. 62-63, Jan. 1975

Bringing Old Testament Times to Life. By G. Ernest Wright. Paintings by Henry J. Soulen. 833-864, Dec. 1957

China Unveils Her Newest Treasures. Photos by Robert W. Madden. 848-857, Dec. 1974

Clues to America's Past. Special Publication announced. 860-864, June 1976

Computer Helps Scholars Re-create an Egyptian Temple. By Ray Winfield Smith. Photos by Emory Kristof. 634-655, Nov. 1970

Darius Carved History on Ageless Rock. By George G. Cameron. 825-844, Dec. 1950

Discovering Man's Past in the Americas. Special Publication announced. 880-884, June 1969

Exploring 1,750,000 Years Into Man's Past. By L. S. B. Leakey. Photos by Robert F. Sisson. 564-589, Oct. 1961

Exploring the Mind of Ice Age Man. By Alexander Marshack. 64-89, Jan. 1975

Finding the Tomb of a Warrior-God. By William Duncan Strong. Photos by Clifford Evans, Jr. 453-482, Apr. 1947

The Five Worlds of Peru. By Kenneth F. Weaver. Photos by Bates Littlehales. 213-265, Feb. 1964
Included: Machu Picchu; Nazca Lines; Sacsahuamán

Fresh Treasures from Egypt's Ancient Sands. By Jefferson Caffery. Photos by David S. Boyer. 611-650, Nov. 1955

The Ghosts of Jericho. By James L. Kelso. 825-844, Dec. 1951

Guatemala, Maya and Modern. By Louis de la Haba. Photos by Joseph J. Scherschel. 661-689, Nov. 1974

Hashemite Jordan, Arab Heartland. By John Scofield. 841-856, Dec. 1952
Included: 'Ammān, ancient Philadelphia; Gerasa; Jericho; Petra; Qasr 'Amra; Qasr el Kharana; *and* Copper scrolls; "Dead Sea scrolls"

The Hohokam: First Masters of the American Desert. By Emil W. Haury. Photos by Helga Teiwes. 670-695, May 1967

Hunting Prehistory in Panama Jungles. By Matthew W. Stirling. Photos by Richard H. Stewart. 271-290, Aug. 1953

In Search of Arabia's Past. By Peter Bruce Cornwall. 493-522, Apr. 1948

Iraq — Where Oil and Water Mix. By Jean and Franc Shor. 443-489, Oct. 1958
Included: Babylon; Nineveh; Ur

Jericho Gives Up Its Secrets. By Kathleen M. Kenyon and A. Douglas Tushingham. Photos by Nancy Lord. 853-870, Dec. 1953

A Lady From China's Past. Photos from *China Pictorial.* Text by Alice J. Hall. 660-681, May 1974

Last Moments of the Pompeians. By Amedeo Maiuri. Photos by Lee E. Battaglia. Paintings by Peter V. Bianchi. 651-669, Nov. 1961

The Last Thousand Years Before Christ. By G. Ernest Wright. Paintings by H. J. Soulen and Peter V. Bianchi. 812-853, Dec. 1960

The Leakeys of Africa: Family in Search of Prehistoric Man. By Melvin M. Payne. 194-231, Feb. 1965

Life Among the Wai Wai Indians. By Clifford Evans and Betty J. Meggers. 329-346, Mar. 1955

Life 8,000 Years Ago Uncovered in an Alabama Cave. By Carl F. Miller. 542-558, Oct. 1956

Lifelike Man Preserved 2,000 Years in Peat. By P.V. Glob. 419-430, Mar. 1954

Magnetic Clues Help Date the Past. By Kenneth F. Weaver. 696-701, May 1967

The Maya. 729-811, Dec. 1975
I. Children of Time. By Howard La Fay. Photos by David Alan Harvey. 729-767

II. Riddle of the Glyphs. By George E. Stuart. Photos by Otis Imboden. 768-791

III. Resurrecting the Grandeur of Tikal. By William R. Coe. 792-798

IV. A Traveler's Tale of Ancient Tikal. Paintings by Peter Spier. Text by Alice J. Hall. 799-811

The Men Who Hid the Dead Sea Scrolls. By A. Douglas Tushingham. Paintings by Peter V. Bianchi. 785-808, Dec. 1958

Mexico's Window on the Past (National Museum). By Bart McDowell. Photos by B. Anthony Stewart. 492-519, Oct. 1968

New Light on a Forgotten Past (Southeast Asia). By Wilhelm G. Solheim II. 330-339, Mar. 1971

North America Before Columbus, double-sided map supplement. Dec. 1972

On the Trail of La Venta Man. By Matthew W. Stirling. Photos by Richard H. Stewart. 137-172, Feb. 1947
Hunting Mexico's Buried Temples. 145-168

Periscope on the Etruscan Past. By Carlo M. Lerici. 337-350, Sept. 1959

The Phoenicians, Sea Lords of Antiquity. By Samuel W. Matthews. Photos by Winfield Parks. Paintings by Robert C. Magis. 149-189, Aug. 1974
Included: Excavation of the Phoenician cities of Byblos, Carthage, Kerkouane, Kition, Motya, Sarepta (Zarephath), Sidon, and Tyre; and the restoration of the Kyrenia ship and a Punic warship

"Pyramids" of the New World. By Neil Merton Judd. 105-128, Jan. 1948

Russell Cave: New Light on Stone Age Life. By Carl F. Miller. 427-437, Mar. 1958

Saving the Ancient Temples at Abu Simbel. By Georg Gerster. Paintings by Robert W. Nicholson. 694-742, May 1966

Searching for Cliff Dwellers' Secrets. By Carroll A. Burroughs. 619-625, Nov. 1959

Solving the Riddles of Wetherill Mesa. By Douglas Osborne. Paintings by Peter V. Bianchi. 155-195, Feb. 1964

Stonehenge — New Light on an Old Riddle. By Harold E. Edgerton. Paintings by Brian Hope-Taylor. 846-866, June 1960

Thera, Key to the Riddle of Minos. By Spyridon Marinatos. Photos by Otis Imboden. 702-726, May 1972

Threatened Treasures of the Nile. By Georg Gerster. 587-621, Oct. 1963
Included: Abu Simbel temples

Throne Above the Euphrates. By Theresa Goell. 390-405, Mar. 1961

The Tower of the Winds. By Derek J. de Solla Price. Paintings by Robert C. Magis. 587-596, Apr. 1967

Tutankhamun's Golden Trove. By Christiane Desroches Noblecourt. Photos by F. L. Kenett. 625-646, Oct. 1963

Twelve National Geographic Society Scientific Projects Under Way. 869-870, June 1954
Included: Eskimo ruins on Southampton and Coats Islands in Hudson Bay, Canada

20th-century Indians Preserve Customs of the Cliff Dwellers. Photos by William Belknap, Jr. 196-211, Feb. 1964
Included: Artifacts of Mesa Verde

Vanished Mystery Men of Hudson Bay. By Henry B. Collins. 669-687, Nov. 1956

ARCHEOLOGY — *Continued*

The Vikings. By Howard La Fay. Photos by Ted Spiegel. 492-541, Apr. 1970

Vinland Ruins Prove Vikings Found the New World. By Helge Ingstad. 708-734, Nov. 1964

Who Were the "Mound Builders"? By George E. Stuart. 783-801, Dec. 1972

Wyoming Muck Tells of Battle: Ice Age Man vs. Mammoth. By Cynthia Irwin, Henry Irwin, and George Agogino. 828-837, June 1962

Young-old Lebanon Lives by Trade. By Thomas J. Abercrombie. 479-523, Apr. 1958
Included: Ba'albek; Byblos; Sidon; Tyre

Your Society to Seek New Light on the Cliff Dwellers (Wetherill Mesa). 154-156, Jan. 1959

See also Chan Chan; Easter Island; Egypt; Glass, Ancient; Gravel Pictographs; Lascaux Cave; La Venta, Mexico; Machu Picchu; Mesa Verde; Mesopotamia; Panama; Petra, Jordan; Roman Empire; Scilly, Isles of; Temple Caves; Zimbabwe; *and* Anthropology; Archeology, Underwater; Potassium-Argon Dating; Radiocarbon Dating; Tree-ring Dating

ARCHEOLOGY, Underwater:

Ancient Shipwreck Yields New Facts—and a Strange Cargo. By Peter Throckmorton. Photos by Kim Hart and Joseph J. Scherschel. 282-300, Feb. 1969

Drowned Galleons Yield Spanish Gold. By Kip Wagner. Photos by Otis Imboden. 1-37, Jan. 1965

Dzibilchaltun. 91-129, Jan. 1959
I. Lost City of the Maya. By E. Wyllys Andrews. 91-109
II. Up from the Well of Time. By Luis Marden. 110-129

Exploring the Drowned City of Port Royal (Jamaica). By Marion Clayton Link. Photos by Luis Marden. 151-183, Feb. 1960

Fish Men Discover a 2,200-year-old Greek Ship. By Jacques-Yves Cousteau. 1-36, Jan. 1954

Into the Well of Sacrifice (Chichén Itzá). 540-561, Oct. 1961
I. Return to the Sacred Cenote. By Eusebio Dávalos Hurtado. 540-549
II. Treasure Hunt in the Deep Past. By Bates Littlehales. 550-561

Oldest Known Shipwreck Yields Bronze Age Cargo (Cape Gelidonya wreck). By Peter Throckmorton. 697-711, May 1962

Relics From the Rapids. By Sigurd F. Olson. Photos by David S. Boyer. 413-435, Sept. 1963

See also Aegean Sea; *Atocha; Girona;* Kyrenia Ship; *Monitor; Slot ter Hooge;* Truk Lagoon; *Vasa;* Yassi Ada

ARCHEOMAGNETISM DATING:

Magnetic Clues Help Date the Past. By Kenneth F. Weaver. 696-701, May 1967

ARCHES, Natural. *See* Arches National Monument; Canyonlands National Park, Utah; Escalante Canyon, for Grosvenor Arch *and* La Gorce Arch; Natural Bridges National Monument; Rainbow Bridge National Monument; Zion National Park

ARCHES NATIONAL MONUMENT, Utah:

Utah's Arches of Stone. By Jack Breed. 173-192, Aug. 1947

ARCHIMÈDE (Bathyscaphe):

Where the Earth Turns Inside Out (Project FAMOUS). By J. R. Heirtzler. Photos by Emory Kristof. 586-603, May 1975

ARCHITECT of Freedom: Thomas Jefferson. By Mike W. Edwards. Photos by Linda Bartlett. 231-259, Feb. 1976

ARCTIC INSTITUTE OF NORTH AMERICA: Expedition. *See* Curlews

ARCTIC OCEAN:

The Arctic as a Sea Route of the Future. By William R. Anderson. 21-24, Jan. 1959

Arctic Ocean; Arctic Ocean Floor, map supplement. Oct. 1971

Diving Beneath Arctic Ice. By Joseph B. MacInnis. Photos by William R. Curtsinger. 248-267, Aug. 1973

Life or Death for the Harp Seal. By David M. Lavigne. Photos by William R. Curtsinger. 129-142, Jan. 1976

Scientists Ride Ice Islands on Arctic Odysseys. By Lowell Thomas, Jr. Photos by Ted Spiegel. 670-691, Nov. 1965

Submarine Through the North Pole (*Nautilus*). By William G. Lalor, Jr. Photos by John J. Krawczyk. 1-20, Jan. 1959

Three Months on an Arctic Ice Island. By Joseph O. Fletcher. 489-504, Apr. 1953

Tracking Danger With the Ice Patrol. By William S. Ellis. Photos by James R. Holland. 780-793, June 1968

Up Through the Ice of the North Pole (*Skate*). By James F. Calvert. 1-41, July 1959

ARCTIC REGION:

Admiral of the Ends of the Earth (Richard E. Byrd). By Melville Bell Grosvenor. 36-48, July 1957

Banks Island: Eskimo Life on the Polar Sea. By William O. Douglas. Photos by Clyde Hare. 703-735, May 1964

Canada, Alaska, and Greenland, map supplement. June 1947

DEW Line, Sentry of the Far North. By Howard La Fay. 128-146, July 1958

Domesticating the Wild and Woolly Musk Ox. By John J. Teal, Jr. Photos by Robert W. Madden. 862-879, June 1970

Far North with "Captain Mac." By Miriam MacMillan. 465-513, Oct. 1951

First Woman Across Greenland's Ice. By Myrtle Simpson. Photos by Hugh Simpson. 264-279, Aug. 1967

Friendly Flight to Northern Europe. By Lyndon B. Johnson. Photos by Volkmar Wentzel. 268-293, Feb. 1964

I Live With the Eskimos (Canadian). By Guy Mary-Rousseliere. 188-217, Feb. 1971

Journey to the High Arctic (Television film). 590A-590B, Apr. 1971

Milestones in My Arctic Journeys. By Willie Knutsen. 543-570, Oct. 1949

Nomads of the Far North. By Matthew W. Stirling. 471-504, Oct. 1949
Hearty Folk Defy Arctic Storms. Paintings by W. Langdon Kihn. 479-494

North for Oil: *Manhattan* Makes the Historic Northwest Passage. By Bern Keating. Photos by Tomas Sennett. 374-391, Mar. 1970

North Toward the Pole on Skis. By Bjørn O. Staib. 254-281, Feb. 1965

The Peary Flag Comes to Rest. By Marie Peary Stafford. 519-532, Oct. 1954

ARCTIC REGION — *Continued*

Polar Bear: Lonely Nomad of the North. By Thor Larsen. 574-590, Apr. 1971

The Society's Hubbard Medal Awarded to Commander MacMillan. 563-564, Apr. 1953

Top of the World, Atlas series supplement. Nov. 1965

The Top of the World, map supplement. Oct. 1949

Trek Across Arctic America. By Colin Irwin. 295-321, Mar. 1974

A Visit to the Living Ice Age. By Rutherford Platt. 525-545, Apr. 1957

We Followed Peary to the Pole. By Gilbert Grosvenor and Thomas W. McKnew. 469-484, Oct. 1953

Weather From the White North. By Andrew H. Brown. Photos by John E. Fletcher. 543-572, Apr. 1955

See also Arctic Ocean; Greenland; Greenland Icecap; King Island, Alaska; Lapland; North Pole; North Slope, Alaska; Spitsbergen; *and* Caribou

ARDASTRA GARDENS, Nassau, Bahamas:

Ballerinas in Pink (Flamingos). By Carleton Mitchell. Photos by B. Anthony Stewart. 553-571, Oct. 1957

ARDEN, HARVEY: Author:

In Search of Moses. Photos by Nathan Benn. 2-37, Jan. 1976

John Muir's Wild America. Photos by Dewitt Jones. 433-461, Apr. 1973

The Pious Ones (Brooklyn's Hasidic Jews). Photos by Nathan Benn. 276-298, Aug. 1975

World War I Aircraft Fly Again in Rhinebeck's Rickety Rendezvous. Photos by Howard Sochurek. 578-587, Oct. 1970

ARGENTINA:

Argentina: Young Giant of the Far South. By Jean and Franc Shor. 297-352, Mar. 1958

Argentina Protects Its Wildlife Treasures. By William F. Conway. Photos by Des and Jen Bartlett. 290-297, Mar. 1976

Buenos Aires, Argentina's Melting-pot Metropolis. By Jules B. Billard. Photos by Winfield Parks. 662-695, Nov. 1967

Parks, Plans, and People: How South America Guards Her Green Legacy. By Mary and Laurance Rockefeller. Photos by George F. Mobley. 74-119, Jan. 1967

Which Way Now for Argentina? By Loren McIntyre. 296-333, Mar. 1975

See also Patagonia; Tierra del Fuego; Torre Egger

ARGYLL (Yawl):

Baltic Cruise of the *Caribbee*. By Carleton Mitchell. 605-646, Nov. 1950

ARIZONA:

Arizona: Booming Youngster of the West. By Robert de Roos. Photos by Robert F. Sisson. 299-343, Mar. 1963

Arizona Sheep Trek. By Francis R. Line. 457-478, Apr. 1950

Arizona's Operation Beaver Lift. By Willis Peterson. 666-680, May 1955

Arizona's Window on Wildlife (Desert Museum). By Lewis Wayne Walker. 240-250, Feb. 1958

ARIZONA — *Continued*

Desert River Through Navajo Land. By Alfred M. Bailey. Photos by author and Fred G. Brandenburg. 149-172, Aug. 1947

From Sun-clad Sea to Shining Mountains. By Ralph Gray. Photos by James P. Blair. 542-589, Apr. 1964

From Tucson to Tombstone. By Mason Sutherland. 343-384, Sept. 1953

The Hohokam: First Masters of the American Desert. By Emil W. Haury. Photos by Helga Teiwes. 670-695, May 1967

Kachinas: Masked Dancers of the Southwest. By Paul Coze. 219-236, Aug. 1957

Land of the Havasupai. By Jack Breed. 655-674, May 1948

Magnetic Clues Help Date the Past. By Kenneth F. Weaver. 696-701, May 1967

A Map Maker Looks at the United States. By Newman Bumstead. 705-748, June 1951
    Included: Grand Canyon; Hoover Dam; Lake Mead; Mount Sinyala; Painted Desert

Scorpions: Living Fossils of the Sands. By Paul A. Zahl. 436-442, Mar. 1968

Seeking the Secret of the Giants. By Frank M. Setzler. Photos by Richard H. Stewart. 390-404, Sept. 1952

Shooting Rapids in Reverse! By William Belknap, Jr. 552-565, Apr. 1962

Skyway Below the Clouds. By Carl R. Markwith. Photos by Ernest J. Cottrell. 85-108, July 1949
    Included: Douglas; Falcon Field; International Airport, Nogales; Kinsley Ranch; Mesa; Tucson

Two Wheels Along the Mexican Border. By William Albert Allard. 591-635, May 1971

See also Colorado (River); Four Corners Country; Grand Canyon; Havasu Canyon; Mazatzal Wilderness; Monument Valley; Organ Pipe Cactus National Monument; Powell, Lake; *and* Navajos

ARKANSAS:

An Ozark Family Carves a Living and a Way of Life. Photos by Bruce Dale. 124-133, July 1975

Through Ozark Hills and Hollows. By Mike W. Edwards. Photos by Bruce Dale. 656-689, Nov. 1970

ARLINGTON COUNTY, Virginia:

Across the Potomac from Washington. By Albert W. Atwood. 1-33, Jan. 1953

ARLINGTON NATIONAL CEMETERY, Virginia:

'Known but to God' (Unknown Heroes). By Beverley M. Bowie. 593-605, Nov. 1958

The Last Full Measure (Tribute to President Kennedy). By Melville Bell Grosvenor. 307-355, Mar. 1964

ARLIS II (Ice Island), Arctic Region:

North Toward the Pole on Skis. By Bjørn O. Staib. 254-281, Feb. 1965

Scientists Ride Ice Islands on Arctic Odysseys. By Lowell Thomas, Jr. Photos by Ted Spiegel. 670-691, Nov. 1965

ARLIS III (Ice Island), Arctic Region:

Scientists Ride Ice Islands on Arctic Odysseys. By Lowell Thomas, Jr. Photos by Ted Spiegel. 670-691, Nov. 1965

ARMADA. *See* Spanish Armada

ARMAGEDDON. *See* Megiddo, Israel

ARMSTRONG, NEIL A.:

First Explorers on the Moon: The Incredible Story of Apollo 11. 735-797, Dec. 1969
I. Man Walks on Another World. By Neil A. Armstrong, Edwin E. Aldrin, Jr., and Michael Collins. 738-749
II. Sounds of the Space Age, From Sputnik to Lunar Landing. A record narrated by Frank Borman. 750-751
III. The Flight of Apollo 11: "One giant leap for mankind." By Kenneth F. Weaver. 752-787

First Moon Explorers (Apollo 11) Receive the Society's Hubbard Medal. 859-861, June 1970

ARNHEM LAND, Australia:

An Arnhem Land Adventure. By Donald F. Thomson. 403-430, Mar. 1948
Arnhem Land Expedition of 1948. 430

Cruise to Stone Age Arnhem Land. By Howell Walker. 417-430, Sept. 1949

Exploring Stone Age Arnhem Land. By Charles P. Mountford. Photos by Howell Walker. 745-782, Dec. 1949

From Spear to Hoe on Groote Eylandt. By Howell Walker. 131-142, Jan. 1953

The Top End of Down Under. By Kenneth MacLeish. Photos by Thomas Nebbia. 145-174, Feb. 1973

ARNO (River), Italy:

Florence Rises From the Flood. By Joseph Judge. 1-43, July 1967

ARNOLD, DAVID L.: Photographer:

Yesterday Lingers Along the Connecticut. By Charles McCarry. 334-369, Sept. 1972

ARNOLD, HENRY H.:

Fledgling Wings of the Air Force. By Thomas W. McKnew. 266-271, Aug. 1957

Giant Effigies of the Southwest. By George C. Marshall. 389, Sept. 1952

Memorial Tribute to General of the Air Force H. H. Arnold. 400, Mar. 1950
Author

My Life in the Valley of the Moon. Photos by Willard R. Culver. 689-716, Dec. 1948

Wildlife In and Near the Valley of the Moon. Photos by Paul J. Fair. 401-414, Mar. 1950

ARNOLD, RUDY: Photographer:

Flying in the "Blowtorch" Era. By Frederick G. Vosburgh. 281-322, Sept. 1950

AROOSTOOK COUNTY, Maine, Source of Potatoes. By Howell Walker. 459-478, Oct. 1948

AROUND the "Great Lakes of the South." By Frederick Simpich. Photos by J. Baylor Roberts. 463-491, Apr. 1948

AROUND the World and the Calendar with the Geographic: The President's Annual Message. By Melville Bell Grosvenor. 832-866, Dec. 1959

"AROUND the World in Eighty Days." By Newman Bumstead. 705-750, Dec. 1951

ARRAN, Island of, Scotland:

Home to Arran, Scotland's Magic Isle. By J. Harvey Howells. 80-99, July 1965

ARROWS Speak Louder Than Words: The Last Andaman Islanders. By Raghubir Singh. 66-91, July 1975

ARROWSMITH, AARON:

Eight Maps of Discovery. 757-769, June 1953
Included: George Washington's Travels, Traced on the Arrowsmith Map

ART. *See* Cave Art; Folk Art; Greek Art; Japanese Art; Mosaics; Painting Supplements; Renaissance; Rock Paintings; Sculpture; *and* Capitol, U. S.; Corcoran Gallery of Art; Hearst San Simeon State Historical Monument; Henry E. Huntington Library and Art Gallery; Hermitage; Kunsthistorisches Museum; The Louvre; National Gallery of Art; St. Catherine's Monastery; *and* Minoan Civilization; Pre-Hispanic Culture

ART RESTORATION:

Florence Rises From the Flood. By Joseph Judge. 1-43, July 1967

Venice Fights for Life. By Joseph Judge. Photos by Albert Moldvay. 591-631, Nov. 1972
Venice's Golden Legacy. Photos by Victor R. Boswell, Jr. 609-619

ARTHUR, CHESTER A.:

Inside the White House. By Lonnelle Aikman. Photos by B. Anthony Stewart and Thomas Nebbia. 3-43, Jan. 1961

Profiles of the Presidents: III. The American Giant Comes of Age. By Frank Freidel. 660-711, May 1965

ARTISANS:

Gold, the Eternal Treasure. By Peter T. White. Photos by James L. Stanfield. 1-51, Jan. 1974
Golden Masterpieces. 29-39

Human Treasures of Japan. By William Graves. Photos by James L. Stanfield. 370-379, Sept. 1972
Contents: Ironcaster, Kabuki actor, Lacquer artist, Swordsmith, Wood sculptor

ARTISTS:

American Masters in the National Gallery. By John Walker. 295-324, Sept. 1948
Contents: George Bellows, Mary Cassatt, William Merritt Chase, John Singleton Copley, Thomas Eakins, Chester Harding, Childe Hassam, Winslow Homer, George Inness, Rembrandt Peale, John Quidor, Edward Savage, Christian Schussele, Gilbert Stuart, Thomas Sully, James Abbott McNeill Whistler

American Processional: History on Canvas. By John and Blanche Leeper. 173-212, Feb. 1951
Contents: John and Victor Audubon, George Caleb Bingham, David G. Blythe, James E. Butterworth, James H. Cafferty, Conrad Wise Chapman, John Singleton Copley, Robert Dudley, Thomas Eakins, J. G. Evans, Ambroise Louis Garneray, Henry Gilder, William Hahn, George Peter Alexander Healy, Winslow Homer, Thomas Hovenden, Frederick Kemmelmeyer, Edward Moran, Linton Park, Charles Willson Peale, Adrian Persac, Frederick Remington, C. Riess, Charles G. Rosenberg, John Searle, Dominique Serres, John Stevens, Louis Comfort Tiffany, John Trumbull, Charles F. Ulrich, Benjamin West

America's First Painters: Indians. By Dorothy Dunn. 349-377, Mar. 1955

Artists Look at Pennsylvania. By John Oliver La Gorce. 37-56, July 1948
Contents: Aaron Bohrod, Adolf Dehn, Ernest Fiene, William Gropper, Fletcher Martin, Hobson Pittman, Paul Sample

ARTISTS — *Continued*

The British Way. By Sir Evelyn Wrench. 421-541, Apr. 1949
Included: William Hogarth, Hans Holbein, Sir Edwin Landseer, Sir Joshua Reynolds, Benjamin West

Chelsea, London's Haven of Individualists. By James Cerruti. Photos by Adam Woolfitt. 28-55, Jan. 1972
Included: Sir Jacob Epstein, Anthony Gray, Walter Greaves, Edward Halliday, Augustus John, Guy Roddon, Dante Gabriel Rossetti, John Singer Sargent, William Thomson, Joseph Mallord William Turner, James McNeill Whistler

Early America Through the Eyes of Her Native Artists. By Hereward Lester Cooke, Jr. 356-389, Sept. 1962
Contents: Francis Alexander, Winthrop Chandler, James Evans, George A. Hayes, Edward Hicks, Joseph H. Hidley, H. Knight, Hyacinthe Laclotte, Linton Park, H.M.T. Powell, Charles S. Raleigh, A. Tapy, John Toole, Benjamin West, J. Wiess

Great Masters of a Brave Era in Art (Impressionist). By Hereward Lester Cooke, Jr. 661-697, May 1961
Contents: Eugene Boudin, Mary Cassatt, Paul Cézanne, Jean-Baptiste-Camille Corot, Honoré Daumier, Edgar Degas, Eugène Delacroix, Henri Fantin-Latour, Paul Gauguin, Vincent van Gogh, Édouard Manet, Claude Monet, Berthe Morisot, Camille Pissarro, Auguste Renoir, Henri Rousseau, Henri de Toulouse-Lautrec

In Quest of Beauty. By Paul Mellon. 372-385, Mar. 1967
Contents: Frédéric Bazille, Pierre Bonnard, Mary Cassatt, Paul Cézanne, Edgar Degas, Paul Gauguin, Vincent van Gogh, Édouard Manet, Claude Monet, Berthe Morisot, Pablo Picasso, Auguste Renoir, Henri Rousseau, Georges Seurat, Henri de Toulouse-Lautrec

The Kress Collection: A Gift to the Nation. By Guy Emerson. 823-865, Dec. 1961
Contents: Giovanni Bellini, Bernardo Bellotto, Abraham Van Beyeren, Paris Bordone, Canaletto (Antonio Canale), Bernardino Fungai, El Greco, Francesco Guardi, Frans Hals, Pieter de Hooch, Lorenzo Lotto, Master of the Braunschweig Diptych, The Montaione Master, Neroccio de' Landi, Piero di Cosimo, Rembrandt Van Rijn, Jusepe de Ribera, Cosimo Rosselli, Peter Paul Rubens, Jan Steen, Bernardo Strozzi, Giovanni Battista Tiepolo, Jacopo Tintoretto, Titian, Sir Anthony Van Dyck, Domenico Veneziano, Paolo Veronese, Elisabeth Vigée-Lebrun, Simon Vouet

The Louvre, France's Palace of the Arts. By Hereward Lester Cooke, Jr. 796-831, June 1971
Included: Paul Cézanne, Jean-Baptiste Chardin, Jean Clouet, Honoré Daumier, Jacques-Louis David, Eugène Delacroix, Jan van Eyck, Charles Le Brun, Édouard Manet, Andrea Mantegna, Gabriel Metsu, Michelangelo, François Perrier, Rembrandt, Hyacinthe Rigaud, Georges Seurat, Leonardo da Vinci, Jean Antoine Watteau, James Abbott McNeill Whistler

Masterpieces on Tour. By Harry A. McBride. 717-750, Dec. 1948
Contents: Hans Baldung, Alessandro Botticelli, Pieter Bruegel the Elder, Andrea del Castagno, Jean Baptiste Siméon Chardin, Albrecht Dürer, Jan Van Eyck, Frans Hals, Meindert Hobbema, Hans Holbein the Younger, Georges de La Tour, Lucas Van Leyden, Édouard Manet, Raphael, Rembrandt, Peter Paul Rubens, Jan Steen, Bernardo Strozzi, Gerard Ter Borch, Titian, Jan Vermeer, Antoine Watteau, Rogier Van der Weyden

The National Gallery After a Quarter Century. By John Walker. 348-371, Mar. 1967

ARTISTS — *Continued*

The Nation's Newest Old Masters (National Gallery of Art). By John Walker. Paintings from Kress Collection. 619-657, Nov. 1956
Contents: Nicolò dell' Abate and Denys Calvaert, Albrecht Altdorfer, Sandro Botticelli, Cima da Conegliano, François Clouet, Jacques-Louis David, Juan de Flandes, Jean-Honoré Fragonard, Orazio Gentileschi, El Greco, Lucas Van Leyden, Hans Memling, Pieter Jansz. Saenredam, St. Bartholomew Master, Jacopo Tintoretto, Titian, Juan van der Hamen y Leon, Sir Anthony Van Dyck, Paolo Veronese, Leonardo da Vinci

Our Search for British Paintings. By Franklin L. Fisher. 543-550, Apr. 1949

Under the Dome of Freedom: The United States Capitol. By Lonnelle Aikman. Photos by George F. Mobley. 4-59, Jan. 1964

U. S. Capitol, Citadel of Democracy. By Lonnelle Aikman. 143-192, Aug. 1952

Venice Fights for Life. By Joseph Judge. Photos by Albert Moldvay. 591-631, Nov. 1972
Venice's Golden Legacy. Photos by Victor R. Boswell, Jr. 609-619
Included: Giovanni Bellini, Giorgione, Giuseppe Heintz, Jacopo Tintoretto, Titian, Paolo Veronese, Andrea del Verrocchio, Leonardo da Vinci

The Vienna Treasures and Their Collectors. By John Walker. 737-776, June 1950
Contents: Michelangelo Merisi da Caravaggio, Domenico Feti, Albrecht Dürer, Francesco Guardi, Jacob Jordaens, Lorenzo Lotto, Jusepe de Ribera, Peter Paul Rubens, Jan Steen, Jacopo Tintoretto, Titian, Sir Anthony Van Dyck, Diego Rodriguez de Silva y Velázquez, Jan Vermeer, Paolo Veronese

Your National Gallery of Art After 10 Years. By John Walker. Paintings from Kress Collection. 73-103, Jan. 1952
Contents: Pieter Bruegel the Elder, Canaletto, Philippe de Champagne, Jean Baptiste Siméon Chardin, Albrecht Dürer, Benozzo Gozzoli, Jean Auguste Dominique Ingres, Giovanni Battista Piazzetta, Hubert Robert, Girolamo Romanino, Master of St. Gilles, Sebastiano del Piombo, Luca Signorelli, Sodoma, Bernardo Strozzi, Titian, Sir Anthony Van Dyck

ARTS AND CRAFTS. *See* Folk Art; Handicrafts

ARUBA (Island), Netherlands Antilles:
The Netherlands Antilles: Holland in the Caribbean. By James Cerruti. Photos by Emory Kristof. 115-146, Jan. 1970

ASCALON (Ashkelon), Israel:
An Archeologist Looks at Palestine. By Nelson Glueck. 739-752, Dec. 1947

ASCENSION ISLAND, Atlantic Ocean:
St. Helena: the Forgotten Island. By Quentin Keynes. 265-280, Aug. 1950

ASHERAH (Research Submarine):
New Tools for Undersea Archeology. By George F. Bass. Photos by Charles R. Nicklin, Jr. 403-423, Sept. 1968

ASHKELON (Ruins), Israel. *See* Ascalon

ASHUR (Ancient City):
Ancient Mesopotamia: A Light That Did Not Fail. By E. A. Speiser. Paintings by H. M. Herget. 41-105, Jan. 1951

ASIA:
Ambassadors of Good Will: The Peace Corps. By

ASIA—*Continued*

Sargent Shriver and Peace Corps Volunteers. 297-345, Sept. 1964
Included: Sarawak; Turkey

Around the World and the Calendar with the Geographic: The President's Annual Message. By Melville Bell Grosvenor. 832-866, Dec. 1959
Included: Cambodia; Hong Kong; India; Japan; Pakistan; Thailand; Viet Nam

"Around the World in Eighty Days." By Newman Bumstead. 705-750, Dec. 1951
Included: China; India; Iraq; Japan; Pakistan; Thailand; Turkey

Asia; The Peoples of Mainland Southeast Asia, map supplement. Mar. 1971

Asia and Adjacent Areas, Atlas series supplement. Dec. 1959

Asia and Adjacent Areas, map supplement. Mar. 1951

Asian Insects in Disguise. By Edward S. Ross. 433-439, Sept. 1965

Cane Bridges of Asia. Photos from Paul Popper. 243-250, Aug. 1948

The Far East, map supplement. Sept. 1952

Flight to Adventure. By Tay and Lowell Thomas, Jr. 49-112, July 1957

How Fruit Came to America. By J. R. Magness. Paintings by Else Bostelmann. 325-377, Sept. 1951

In the Footsteps of Alexander the Great. By Helen and Frank Schreider. Paintings by Tom Lovell. 1-65, Jan. 1968

The Lands and Peoples of Southeast Asia. 295-365, Mar. 1971
I. Mosaic of Cultures. By Peter T. White. Photos by W. E. Garrett. 296-329
II. New Light on a Forgotten Past. By Wilhelm G. Solheim II. 330-339
III. Pagan, on the Road to Mandalay. By W. E. Garrett. 343-365

New Guinea to Bali in *Yankee.* By Irving and Electa Johnson. 767-815, Dec. 1959
Included: Cambodia; Indonesia; Laos; Thailand

Our Navy in the Far East. By Arthur W. Radford. Photos by J. Baylor Roberts. 537-577, Oct. 1953

Our Vegetable Travelers. By Victor R. Boswell. Paintings by Else Bostelmann. 145-217, Aug. 1949

Round the World School (ISA). By Paul Antze. Photos by William Eppridge. 96-127, July 1962
Included: Hong Kong; India; Japan; Thailand

Sky Road East (Southwest Asia). By Tay and Lowell Thomas, Jr. 71-112, Jan. 1960

Southeast Asia, Atlas series supplement. May 1961

Southeast Asia, map supplement. Sept. 1955

Southeast Asia, map supplement. Dec. 1968

Southwest Asia, Atlas series supplement. May 1963

Southwest Asia, including India, Pakistan, and Northeast Africa, map supplement. June 1952

Station Wagon Odyssey: Baghdad to Istanbul. By William O. Douglas. 48-87, Jan. 1959

Viet Nam, Cambodia, Laos, and Eastern Thailand, map supplement. Text on reverse. Jan. 1965

Viet Nam, Cambodia, Laos, and Thailand, map supplement. Feb. 1967

West from the Khyber Pass. By William O. Douglas. Photos by Mercedes H. Douglas and author. 1-44, July 1958

When the President Goes Abroad (Eisenhower

ASIA—*Continued*

Tour). By Gilbert M. Grosvenor. 588-649, May 1960
Included: Afghanistan; India; Iran; Pakistan; Turkey

The World in Your Garden (Flowers). By W. H. Camp. Paintings by Else Bostelmann. 1-65, July 1947

YWCA: International Success Story. By Mary French Rockefeller. Photos by Otis Imboden. 904-933, Dec. 1963

See also individual countries; *and* Bible Lands; Himalayas; Karakoram Range; Mekong River; Pacific Fleet, U. S.; Red Sea

ASIA MINOR:

Our Vegetable Travelers. By Victor R. Boswell. Paintings by Else Bostelmann. 145-217, Aug. 1949

See also Turkey

ASIMOV, ISAAC: Author:

Five Noted Thinkers Explore the Future. 72-73, July 1976

The Next Frontier? Paintings by Pierre Mion. 76-89, July 1976

ASMAT (People):

The Asmat of New Guinea, Headhunters in Today's World. By Malcolm S. Kirk. 376-409, Mar. 1972

Netherlands New Guinea: Bone of Contention in the South Pacific. By John Scofield. 584-603, May 1962

ASPEN, Colorado:

Colorado, the Rockies' Pot of Gold. By Edward J. Linehan. Photos by James L. Amos. 157-201, Aug. 1969

A Town . . . a Mountain . . . a Way of Life. By Jill Durrance and Dick Durrance II. 788-807, Dec. 1973

ASPHALT. *See* Trinidad (Happy-Go-Lucky)

ASSAM (State), India:

Cane Bridges of Asia. Photos from Paul Popper. 243-250, Aug. 1948

Caught in the Assam-Tibet Earthquake. By F. Kingdon-Ward. 403-416, Mar. 1952

Stalking the Great Indian Rhino. By Lee Merriam Talbot. 389-398, Mar. 1957

See also Naga Hills

ASSUMPTION ISLAND, Indian Ocean:

Camera Under the Sea. By Luis Marden. 162-200, Feb. 1956

ASSYRIA (Ancient Empire):

Ancient Mesopotamia: A Light That Did Not Fail. By E. A. Speiser. Paintings by H. M. Herget. 41-105, Jan. 1951

ASTEROIDS:

Voyage to the Planets. By Kenneth F. Weaver. Paintings by Ludek Pesek. 147-193, Aug. 1970

ASTON, WILLIAM J.: Author:

Midshipmen's Cruise. By William J. Aston and Alexander G. B. Grosvenor. 711-754, June 1948

ASTROGEOLOGY. *See* Geology, Lunar; Mariner Missions (Mariner 10)

ASTRONAUTS. *See* Apollo Missions; Apollo-Soyuz Mission; Gemini Missions; Mercury Missions; Skylab Missions

ASTRONOMY:

The Amazing Universe. Special Publication announced. 870-874, June 1975

Completing the Atlas of the Universe (National Geographic Society-Palomar Observatory Sky Survey). By Ira Sprague Bowen. 185-190, Aug. 1955
  Sky Survey Plates Unlock Secrets of the Stars. 186-187

Current Scientific Projects of the National Geographic Society. 143-144, July 1953
  Included: Cosmic ray research; Sky Survey

Exploring the Farthest Reaches of Space. By George O. Abell. 782-790, Dec. 1956

First Color Portraits of the Heavens. By William C. Miller. 670-679, May 1959

First Photographs of Planets and Moon Taken with Palomar's 200-inch Telescope. By Milton L. Humason. 125-130, Jan. 1953

The Incredible Universe. By Kenneth F. Weaver. Photos by James P. Blair. 589-625, May 1974
  Pioneers in Man's Search for the Universe. Paintings by Jean-Leon Huens. Text by Thomas Y. Canby. 627-633
    Contents: Seven men who solved riddles of the cosmos: Nicolaus Copernicus, Albert Einstein, Galileo Galilei, William Herschel, Edwin Hubble, Johannes Kepler, Isaac Newton

A Map of the Heavens, map supplement. Star charts on reverse. Dec. 1957

Map of the Heavens, map supplement. Star charts on reverse. Aug. 1970

Mapping the Unknown Universe. By F. Barrows Colton. 401-420, Sept. 1950

Our Universe Unfolds New Wonders (National Geographic-Palomar Sky Survey). By Albert G. Wilson. 245-260, Feb. 1952

Sky Survey Charts the Universe. By Ira Sprague Bowen. 780-781, Dec. 1956

Split-second Time Runs Today's World. By F. Barrows Colton and Catherine Bell Palmer. 399-428, Sept. 1947

Twelve National Geographic Society Scientific Projects Under Way. 869-870, June 1954
  Included: Aurora Borealis; Cosmic rays; Mars expedition; Sky Survey; Zodiacal light observations

See also Aurora Borealis; Comets; Moon; Planets; Stars; Sun

ASTRONOMY, Ancient. *See* Calendars (The Maya); Stonehenge

ASTROPHYSICS:

The Sun. By Herbert Friedman. 713-743, Nov. 1965

ASWÂN HIGH DAM, Nile River:

Threatened Treasures of the Nile. By Georg Gerster. 587-621, Oct. 1963

Yankee Cruises the Storied Nile. By Irving and Electa Johnson. Photos by Winfield Parks. 583-633, May 1965

AT Home in the High Andes. By Harry Tschopik, Jr. 133-146, Jan. 1955

AT Home in the Sea. By Jacques-Yves Cousteau. 465-507, Apr. 1964

AT Home With Right Whales. By Roger Payne. Photos by Des and Jen Bartlett. 322-339, Mar. 1976

AT Home With the Bulldog Ant. By Robert F. Sisson. 62-75, July 1974

AT World's End in Hunza. By Jean and Franc Shor. 485-518, Oct. 1953

ATACAMA DESERT, Chile:

Chile, Republic on a Shoestring. By Gordon Young. Photos by George F. Mobley. 437-477, Oct. 1973

ATATÜRK, KEMAL:

Turkey Paves the Path of Progress. By Maynard Owen Williams. 141-186, Aug. 1951

Yankee Cruises Turkey's History-haunted Coast. By Irving and Electa Johnson. Photos by Joseph J. Scherschel. 798-845, Dec. 1969

ATEN TEMPLE. *See* Akhenaten Temple Project

ATHAPASCAN LINGUISTIC STOCK:

Nomads of the Far North. By Matthew W. Stirling. 471-504, Oct. 1949
  Hearty Folk Defy Arctic Storms. Paintings by W. Langdon Kihn. 479-494

ATHENS, Greece:

"Around the World in Eighty Days." By Newman Bumstead. 705-750, Dec. 1951

Athens: Her Golden Past Still Lights the World. By Kenneth F. Weaver. Photos by Phillip Harrington. 100-137, July 1963

Athens to Istanbul. By Jean and Franc Shor. 37-76, Jan. 1956

Erosion, Trojan Horse of Greece. By F. G. Renner. 793-812, Dec. 1947

The Tower of the Winds. By Derek J. de Solla Price. Paintings by Robert C. Magis. 587-596, Apr. 1967

War-torn Greece Looks Ahead. By Maynard Owen Williams. 711-744, Dec. 1949

ATITLÁN, Lake, Guatemala:

Guatemala Revisited. By Luis Marden. 525-564, Oct. 1947

ATKA (Island), Alaska:

Atka, Rugged Home of My Aleut Friends. By Lael Morgan. 572-583, Oct. 1974

ATKESON, RAY: Photographer:

From Sagebrush to Roses on the Columbia. By Leo A. Borah. 571-611, Nov. 1952

ATKINSON, AGNES AKIN: Author:

Br'er Possum, Hermit of the Lowlands. Photos by Charles Philip Fox. 405-418, Mar. 1953

ATLANTA, Georgia:

Atlanta, Pacesetter City of the South. By William S. Ellis. Photos by James L. Amos. 246-281, Feb. 1969

The Greener Fields of Georgia. By Howell Walker. Photos by author and B. Anthony Stewart. 287-330, Mar. 1954

ATLANTIC COAST, U. S.:

Can We Save Our Salt Marshes? By Stephen W. Hitchcock. Photos by William R. Curtsinger. 729-765, June 1972

Our Changing Atlantic Coastline. By Nathaniel T.

ATLANTIC COAST, U. S. — *Continued*

Kenney. Photos by B. Anthony Stewart. 860-887, Dec. 1962

ATLANTIC MISSILE RANGE:

Cape Canaveral's 6,000-mile Shooting Gallery. By Allan C. Fisher, Jr. Photos by Luis Marden and Thomas Nebbia. 421-471, Oct. 1959

ATLANTIC OCEAN:

Atlantic Ocean, map supplement. Dec. 1955

Atlantic Ocean; Atlantic Ocean Floor, Atlas series supplement. June 1968

Atlantic Odyssey: Iceland to Antarctica. By Newman Bumstead. Photos by Volkmar Wentzel. 725-780, Dec. 1955

Braving the Atlantic by Balloon. By Arnold Eiloart. 123-146, July 1959

By Square-rigger from Baltic to Bicentennial. By Kenneth Garrett. 824-857, Dec. 1976
  Contents: Tall-ship race from Plymouth, England to Newport, Rhode Island via Canary Islands and Bermuda

Diving Into the Blue Holes of the Bahamas. By George J. Benjamin. 347-363, Sept. 1970
  Included: Tongue of the Ocean

Exploring the Mid-Atlantic Ridge. By Maurice Ewing. 275-294, Sept. 1948

Four Years of Diving to the Bottom of the Sea (Bathyscaph). By Georges S. Houot. 715-731, May 1958

New Discoveries on the Mid-Atlantic Ridge. By Maurice Ewing. Photos by Robert F. Sisson. 611-640, Nov. 1949

Our Changing Atlantic Coastline (U. S.). By Nathaniel T. Kenney. Photos by B. Anthony Stewart. 860-887, Dec. 1962

Project FAMOUS. 586-615, May 1975
  I. Where the Earth Turns Inside Out. By J. R. Heirtzler. Photos by Emory Kristof. 586-603
  II. Dive Into the Great Rift. By Robert D. Ballard. Photos by Emory Kristof. 604-615

Search Operations. *See Thresher*

This Changing Earth. By Samuel W. Matthews. 1-37, Jan. 1973

Tracking Danger With the Ice Patrol. By William S. Ellis. Photos by James R. Holland. 780-793, June 1968

Two and a Half Miles Down. By Georges S. Houot. 80-86, July 1954

The Voyage of *Ra II*. By Thor Heyerdahl. Photos by Carlo Mauri and Georges Sourial. 44-71, Jan. 1971

See also Grand Banks; Ilha Nova; Romanche Trench; Surtsey; U. S. Coast Guard; Weather Stations; *and* Cruises and Voyages *(Finisterre; Mayflower II; Triton)*

ATLAS MOUNTAINS, Africa. *See* High Atlas

ATLASES, NGS:

United States Atlas

Atlas of the Fifty United States announced. 130-133, July 1960; 885, Dec. 1960

World Atlas

Atlas of the World announced. 889, 899-900, Dec. 1962; 832-837, June 1963
  Second edition. 819-821, June 1966; 580-581, Oct. 1967
  Third edition. 735-736, Nov. 1970

ATLASES, NGS — *Continued*

Fourth edition, with annual update. 583, Nov. 1975

Microfilmed copy placed in Time Capsule, New York World's Fair, 1964-65. 525, Apr. 1965

ATMOSPHERE:

Laboratory in a Dirty Sky. By Rudolf J. Engelmann and Vera Simons. 616-621, Nov. 1976

What's Happening to Our Climate? By Samuel W. Matthews. 576-615, Nov. 1976

See also Strato-Lab

ATOCHA:

Atocha, Tragic Treasure Galleon of the Florida Keys. By Eugene Lyon. 787-809, June 1976

Treasure! (Television film). 575, Nov. 1976; cover, Dec. 1976

ATOM:

Man's New Servant, the Friendly Atom. By F. Barrows Colton. Photos by Volkmar Wentzel. 71-90, Jan. 1954

You and the Obedient Atom. By Allan C. Fisher, Jr. 303-353, Sept. 1958

See also Cosmic Rays

The **ATOMIC** Age: Its Problems and Promises. By Frank Freidel. 66-119, Jan. 1966

ATOMIC BOMB TESTS:

Nevada Learns to Live with the Atom. By Samuel W. Matthews. 839-850, June 1953

Operation Crossroads. Photos by Joint Task Force I. Paintings by Charles Bittinger. 519-530, Apr. 1947

ATOMIC ENERGY. *See* Atom; Nuclear Energy

ATOMIC ENERGY COMMISSION (AEC). *See* Atomic Bomb Tests; South Carolina Rediscovered, for H-bomb Project

ATTENBOROUGH, DAVID: Author-Photographer:

Animal Safari to British Guiana. Photos by Charles Lagus and author. 851-874, June 1957

ATWOOD, ALBERT W.: Author:

Across the Potomac from Washington. 1-33, Jan. 1953

Census 1960: Profile of the Nation. By Albert W. Atwood and Lonnelle Aikman. 697-714, Nov. 1959

The Eternal Flame. 540-564, Oct. 1951

The Fire of Heaven: Electricity Revolutionizes the Modern World. 655-674, Nov. 1948

Gilbert Grosvenor's Golden Jubilee. 253-261, Aug. 1949

Immigrants Still Flock to Liberty's Land. 708-724, Nov. 1955

The Merrimack: River of Industry and Romance. Photos by B. Anthony Stewart. 106-140, Jan. 1951

The Mighty Hudson. Photos by B. Anthony Stewart. 1-36, July 1948

The Nation's Library (Library of Congress). 663-684, May 1950

Pittsburgh: Workshop of the Titans. 117-144, July 1949

Stately Homes of Old Virginia. 787-802, June 1953

ATWOOD, ALBERT W.: Author—*Continued*

Steel: Master of Them All. Photos by Willard R. Culver. 415-452, Apr. 1947

Today on the Delaware, Penn's Glorious River. Photos by Robert F. Sisson. 1-40, July 1952

Washington: Home of the Nation's Great. 699-738, June 1947

AUCKLAND, New Zealand:

New Zealand: Gift of the Sea. By Maurice Shadbolt. Photos by Brian Brake. 465-511, Apr. 1962

New Zealand, Pocket Wonder World. By Howell Walker. 419-460, Apr. 1952

AUDUBON, JOHN JAMES:

Blizzard of Birds: The Tortugas Terns. By Alexander Sprunt, Jr. 213-230, Feb. 1947

AUDUBON SOCIETY. *See* National Audubon Society

AURORA BOREALIS:

Unlocking Secrets of the Northern Lights. By Carl W. Gartlein. Paintings by William Crowder. 673-704, Nov. 1947

AUSTRALIA:

Australia. By Alan Villiers. 309-385, Sept. 1963
I. The West and the South. 309-345
II. The Settled East, the Barrier Reef, the Center. 347-385

Australia, Atlas series supplement. Sept. 1963

Australia, map supplement. Mar. 1948

Australia. Special Publication announced. 844-849, June 1968

Australia: The Timeless Land (Television film). 300A-300B, Feb. 1969

Australia's Amazing Bowerbirds. By Norman Chaffer. 866-873, Dec. 1961

Australia's Bizarre Wild Flowers. By Paul A. Zahl. 858-868, Dec. 1976

Captain Cook: The Man Who Mapped the Pacific. By Alan Villiers. Photos by Gordon W. Gahan. 297-349, Sept. 1971

Flight of the Platypuses. By David Fleay. 512-525, Oct. 1958

In the Wake of Darwin's *Beagle.* By Alan Villiers. Photos by James L. Stanfield. 449-495, Oct. 1969

The Making of a New Australia. By Howell Walker. 233-259, Feb. 1956

Off the Beaten Track of Empire (Prince Philip's Tour). By Beverley M. Bowie. Photos by Michael Parker. 584-626, Nov. 1957

Strange Animals of Australia. By David Fleay. Photos by Stanley Breeden. 388-411, Sept. 1963

The World in Your Garden (Flowers). By W. H. Camp. Paintings by Else Bostelmann. 1-65, July 1947

See also Alice Springs; Arnhem Land; Currumbin; Great Barrier Reef; Melbourne; Melville Island; New South Wales; Norfolk Island; Northern Territory; Queensland; South Australia; Tasmania; Victoria; Western Australia; *and* Kangaroos; Lyrebird

AUSTRALIAN NEW GUINEA:

Australian New Guinea. By John Scofield. 604-637, May 1962

Journey Into Stone Age New Guinea. By Malcolm S. Kirk. 568-592, Apr. 1969

AUSTRALIAN NEW GUINEA—*Continued*

New Guinea Festival of Faces. By Malcolm S. Kirk. 148-156, July 1969

New Guinea's Paradise of Birds. By E. Thomas Gilliard. 661-688, Nov. 1951

New Guinea's Rare Birds and Stone Age Men. By E. Thomas Gilliard. 421-488, Apr. 1953

Sheep Airlift in New Guinea. Photos by Ned Blood. 831-844, Dec. 1949

See also New Britain; Papua New Guinea

AUSTRALOPITHECUS:

Ethiopia Yields First "Family" of Early Man. By Donald C. Johanson. Photos by David Brill. 790-811, Dec. 1976

In Search of Man's Past at Lake Rudolf. By Richard E. Leakey. Photos by Gordon W. Gahan. 712-734, May 1970

AUSTRIA:

The Alps: Man's Own Mountains. By Ralph Gray. Photos by Walter Meayers Edwards and William Eppridge. 350-395, Sept. 1965

Building a New Austria. By Beverley M. Bowie. Photos by Volkmar Wentzel. 172-213, Feb. 1959

Down the Danube by Canoe. By William Slade Backer. Photos by Richard S. Durrance and Christopher G. Knight. 34-79, July 1965

Occupied Austria, Outpost of Democracy. By George W. Long. Photos by Volkmar Wentzel. 749-790, June 1951

Salzkammergut, Austria's Alpine Playground. By Beverley M. Bowie. Photos by Volkmar Wentzel. 246-275, Aug. 1960

A Stroll to Venice. By Isobel Wylie Hutchison. 378-410, Sept. 1951

Switzerland, Austria, and Northern Italy, double-sided Atlas series supplement. Sept. 1965

Tirol, Austria's Province in the Clouds. By Peter T. White. Photos by Volkmar Wentzel. 107-141, July 1961

See also Vienna

AUTOMOBILE RACE:

Rocks, Ruts, and Sand: Driving the Mexican 1000. By Michael E. Long. 569-575, Oct. 1972

AUTUMN Flames Along the Allagash. By François Leydet. Photos by Farrell Grehan. 177-187, Feb. 1974

AUVERGNE (Region), France:

Lafayette's Homeland, Auvergne. By Howell Walker. 419-436, Sept. 1957

AUYÁN-TEPUÍ (Devil Mountain), Venezuela:

Jungle Journey to the World's Highest Waterfall. By Ruth Robertson. 655-690, Nov. 1949

AVALANCHES:

Avalanche! (Peru). By Bart McDowell. Photos by John E. Fletcher. 855-880, June 1962

See also Mudslides

AVIATION:

Aviation Looks Ahead on Its 50th Birthday. By Emory S. Land. 721-739, Dec. 1953

Charting Our Sea and Air Lanes (U. S. Coast and Geodetic Survey). By Stuart E. Jones. Photos by J. Baylor Roberts. 189-209, Feb. 1957

The Coming Revolution in Transportation. By

AVIATION—*Continued*

Fredric C. Appel. Photos by Dean Conger. 301-341, Sept. 1969

Fact Finding for Tomorrow's Planes. By Hugh L. Dryden. Photos by Luis Marden. 757-780, Dec. 1953

Fifty Years of Flight. 740-756, Dec. 1953

Flying in the "Blowtorch" Era. By Frederick G. Vosburgh. 281-322, Sept. 1950

I Fly the X-15. By Joseph A. Walker. Photos by Dean Conger. 428-450, Sept. 1962

MATS: America's Long Arm of the Air. By Beverley M. Bowie. Photos by Robert F. Sisson. 283-317, Mar. 1957

National Geographic Society Honors Air Pioneer Juan Trippe. 584-586, Apr. 1968

Of Planes and Men. By Kenneth F. Weaver. Photos by Emory Kristof and Albert Moldvay. 298-349, Sept. 1965

Our Air Age Speeds Ahead. By F. Barrows Colton. 249-272, Feb. 1948

Sailors in the Sky: Fifty Years of Naval Aviation. By Patrick N. L. Bellinger. 276-296, Aug. 1961

Skyway Below the Clouds. By Carl R. Markwith. Photos by Ernest J. Cottrell. 85-108, July 1949

World War I Aircraft Fly Again in Rhinebeck's Rickety Rendezvous. By Harvey Arden. Photos by Howard Sochurek. 578-587, Oct. 1970

You and the Obedient Atom. By Allan C. Fisher, Jr. Photos by B. Anthony Stewart and Thomas J. Abercrombie. 303-353, Sept. 1958
Included: Nuclear aircraft

See also Civil Air Patrol; Helicopters; Parachute Jumps; Parachute Rigger School; U. S. Air Force; U. S. Navy

AVIATION MEDICINE:

Aviation Medicine on the Threshold of Space. By Allan C. Fisher, Jr. Photos by Luis Marden. 241-278, Aug. 1955

Our Air Age Speeds Ahead. By F. Barrows Colton. 249-272, Feb. 1948

See also Military Air Transport Service; Space Medicine; *Strato-Lab*

AWESOME Views of the Forbidding Moonscape. 233-239, Feb. 1969

The AWESOME Worlds Within a Cell. By Rick Gore. Photos by Bruce Dale. Paintings by Davis Meltzer. 355-395, Sept. 1976

AYMARÁ INDIANS:

At Home in the High Andes. By Harry Tschopik, Jr. 133-146, Jan. 1955

Flamboyant Is the Word for Bolivia. By Loren McIntyre. 153-195, Feb. 1966

The Lost Empire of the Incas. By Loren McIntyre. Art by Ned and Rosalie Seidler. 729-787, Dec. 1973

Puya, the Pineapple's Andean Ancestor. By Mulford B. Foster. 463-480, Oct. 1950

Titicaca, Abode of the Sun. By Luis Marden. Photos by Flip Schulke. 272-294, Feb. 1971

AZALEAS:

Nautical Norfolk Turns to Azaleas. By William H. Nicholas. Photos by B. Anthony Stewart. 606-614, May 1947

AZORES (Islands), Atlantic Ocean:

The Azores, Nine Islands in Search of a Future. By Don Moser. Photos by O. Louis Mazzatenta. 261-288, Feb. 1976

New Discoveries on the Mid-Atlantic Ridge. By Maurice Ewing. Photos by Robert F. Sisson. 611-640, Nov. 1949

A New Volcano Bursts from the Atlantic. By John Scofield. Photos by Robert F. Sisson. 735-757, June 1958

To Europe with a Racing Start. By Carleton Mitchell. 758-791, June 1958

AZTECS:

Archeological Map of Middle America, Land of the Feathered Serpent, map supplement. Text on reverse. Oct. 1968

Mexico, the City That Founded a Nation. By Louis de la Haba. Photos by Albert Moldvay. 638-669, May 1973

Mexico's Booming Capital. By Mason Sutherland. Photos by Justin Locke. 785-824, Dec. 1951

Mexico's Window on the Past (National Museum). By Bart McDowell. Photos by B. Anthony Stewart. 492-519, Oct. 1968

"Pyramids" of the New World. By Neil Merton Judd. 105-128, Jan. 1948

AZZI, ROBERT: Author-Photographer:

Damascus, Syria's Uneasy Eden. 512-535, Apr. 1974

Oman, Land of Frankincense and Oil. 205-229, Feb. 1973

B

B-36 (Jet Bomber):

Flying in the "Blowtorch" Era. By Frederick G. Vosburgh. 281-322, Sept. 1950

B-50. *See* Superfortresses

BAALBEK, Lebanon:

Journey Into the Great Rift: the Northern Half. By Helen and Frank Schreider. 254-290, Aug. 1965

Young-old Lebanon Lives by Trade. By Thomas J. Abercrombie. 479-523, Apr. 1958

BABB, LAURA LONGLEY: Author:

Iowa's Enduring Amana Colonies. Photos by Steve Raymer. 863-878, Dec. 1975

BABBLERS (Birds). *See* Spiny Babbler

BABCOCK, RICHARD F.: Author:

Five Noted Thinkers Explore the Future. 70-71, July 1976

BABOONS:

Life with the "Pumphouse Gang": New Insights Into Baboon Behavior. By Shirley C. Strum. Photos by Timothy W. Ransom. 672-691, May 1975

BABYLON (Ancient City):

Ancient Mesopotamia: A Light That Did Not Fail. By E. A. Speiser. Paintings by H. M. Herget. 41-105, Jan. 1951

BACK to the Historic Black Hills. By Leland D. Case. Photos by Bates Littlehales. 479-509, Oct. 1956

BACK-YARD Monsters in Color. By Paul A. Zahl. 235-260, Aug. 1952

BACKER, OLE FRIELE: Author-Photographer:

Seal Hunting Off Jan Mayen. 57-72, Jan. 1948

Photographer

Norway Cracks Her Mountain Shell. By Sydney Clark. Photos by Gilbert Grosvenor and Ole Friele Backer. 171-211, Aug. 1948

BACKER, WILLIAM SLADE: Author:

Down the Danube by Canoe. Photos by Richard S. Durrance and Christopher G. Knight. 34-79, July 1965

BACKPACK TRIPS:

Hiking the Backbone of the Rockies: Canada's Great Divide Trail. By Mike W. Edwards. Photos by Lowell Georgia. 795-817, June 1973

Mexico to Canada on the Pacific Crest Trail. By Mike W. Edwards. Photos by David Hiser. 741-779, June 1971

Yellowstone at 100: A Walk Through the Wilderness. By Karen and Derek Craighead. Photos by Sam Abell. 579-603, May 1972

BACKWOODS Japan During American Occupation. By M. A. Huberman. 491-518, Apr. 1947

BACON, EDMUND N.: Author:

Five Noted Thinkers Explore the Future. 74, July 1976

BAD Days for the Brown Pelican. By Ralph W. Schreiber. Photos by William R. Curtsinger and author. 111-123, Jan. 1975

BADDECK, Nova Scotia, Canada:

Canada's Winged Victory: the *Silver Dart*. By Gilbert M. Grosvenor. 254-267, Aug. 1959

Down East to Nova Scotia. By Winfield Parks. 853-879, June 1964

Miracle Men of the Telephone. By F. Barrows Colton. 273-316, Mar. 1947

Included: Photographs of Dr. Alexander Graham Bell and members of his family at their home in Baddeck

See also Bell Museum

BADLANDS, North Dakota:

North Dakota Comes into Its Own. By Leo A. Borah. Photos by J. Baylor Roberts. 283-322, Sept. 1951

BADLANDS, South Dakota:

Big Game Hunting (Paleontology) in the Land of Long Ago. By Joseph P. Connolly and James D. Bump. 589-605, May 1947

South Dakota Keeps Its West Wild. By Frederick Simpich. 555-588, May 1947

The West Through Boston Eyes. By Stewart Anderson. 733-776, June 1949

BAEKELAND, G. BROOKS: Author-Photographer:

By Parachute Into Peru's Lost World. Photos by author and Peter R. Gimbel. 268-296, Aug. 1964

BAFFIN ISLAND, Northwest Territories, Canada:

Far North with "Captain Mac." By Miriam Mac-Millan. 465-513, Oct. 1951

Included: Brevoort Island; Pond Inlet

I Live With the Eskimos. By Guy Mary-Rousseliere. 188-217, Feb. 1971

Milestones in My Arctic Journeys. By Willie Knutsen. 543-570, Oct. 1949

Included: Airfield at Frobisher Bay and the activities of the Arctic Search and Rescue section of the Air Force

BAGGARA (People):

With the Nuba Hillmen of Kordofan. By Robin Strachan. 249-278, Feb. 1951

BAGHDAD, Iraq:

"Around the World in Eighty Days." By Newman Bumstead. 705-750, Dec. 1951

Iraq—Where Oil and Water Mix. By Jean and Franc Shor. 443-489, Oct. 1958

Station Wagon Odyssey: Baghdad to İstanbul. By William O. Douglas. 48-87, Jan. 1959

BAHAMA ISLANDS, Atlantic Ocean:

The Bahamas, Isles of the Blue-green Sea. By Carleton Mitchell. Photos by B. Anthony Stewart. 147-203, Feb. 1958

Blue-water Plankton: Ghosts of the Gulf Stream. By William M. Hamner. 530-545, Oct. 1974

Cape Canaveral's 6,000-mile Shooting Gallery. By Allan C. Fisher, Jr. Photos by Luis Marden and Thomas Nebbia. 421-471, Oct. 1959

More of Sea Than of Land: The Bahamas. By Carleton Mitchell. Photos by James L. Stanfield. 218-267, Feb. 1967

See also Abaco; Andros Island; Bimini Islands; Great Bahama Bank; Great Inagua; Nassau

BAHREIN (Island), Persian Gulf:

In Search of Arabia's Past. By Peter Bruce Cornwall. 493-522, Apr. 1948

Troubled Waters East of Suez. By Ernest M. Eller. 483-522, Apr. 1954

BAILEY, ALFRED M.: Author-Photographer:

Desert River Through Navajo Land. Photos by author and Fred G. Brandenburg. 149-172, Aug. 1947

BAIT-FISHING ANIMALS:

Aha! It Really Works! (Heron). By Robert F. Sisson. 143-147, Jan. 1974

Something's Fishy About That Fin! (Decoy Fish). Photos by Robert J. Shallenberger and William D. Madden. 224-227, Aug. 1974

BAJA CALIFORNIA (Peninsula), Mexico:

Baja California's Rugged Outback. By Michael E. Long. 543-567, Oct. 1972

Hunting the Heartbeat of a Whale. By Paul Dudley White and Samuel W. Matthews. 49-64, July 1956

Rocks, Ruts, and Sand: Driving the Mexican 1000. By Michael E. Long. 569-575, Oct. 1972

See also Raza, Isla; Scammon Lagoon

BAJAUS (People):

Sea Gypsies of the Philippines. By Anne de Henning Singh. Photos by Raghubir Singh. 659-677, May 1976

BAKER, BETTY HAYNES: Artist:

Flags of the Americas. By Elizabeth W. King. 633-657, May 1949

Flags of the United Nations. By Elizabeth W. King. 213-238, Feb. 1951

BAKER, JOHN H.: Author:

Saving Man's Wildlife Heritage. Photos by Robert F. Sisson. 581-620, Nov. 1954

BAKHTIARI (Tribespeople):
  I Become a Bakhtiari. By Paul Edward Case. 325-358, Mar. 1947

BALD EAGLES, American:
  Eye to Eye With Eagles. By Frederick Kent Truslow. 123-148, Jan. 1961

BALEARIC ISLANDS, Mediterranean Sea:
  The Balearics Are Booming. By Jean and Franc Shor. 621-660, May 1957
  Spain's Sun-blest Pleasure Isles. By Ethel A. Starbird. Photos by James A . Sugar. 679-701, May 1976

BALI (Island), Indonesia:
  Bali by the Back Roads. By Donna K. and Gilbert M. Grosvenor. 657-697, Nov. 1969
  Bali's Sacred Mountain Blows Its Top. Photos by Robert F. Sisson. 436-458, Sept. 1963
    I. Disaster in Paradise. By Windsor P. Booth. 436-447
    II. Devastated Land and Homeless People. By Samuel W. Matthews. 447-458
  Indonesia, the Young and Troubled Island Nation. By Helen and Frank Schreider. 579-625, May 1961
  New Guinea to Bali in Yankee. By Irving and Electa Johnson. 767-815, Dec. 1959
  Republican Indonesia Tries Its Wings. By W. Robert Moore. 1-40, Jan. 1951
  This Young Giant, Indonesia. By Beverley M. Bowie. Photos by J. Baylor Roberts. 351-392, Sept. 1955
  Yankee Roams the Orient. By Irving and Electa Johnson. 327-370, Mar. 1951

The BALKANS:
  The Balkans, Atlas series supplement. Feb. 1962
  Central Europe, including the Balkan States, map supplement. Sept. 1951
  See also Bulgaria; Greece; Romania; Turkey (European); Yugoslavia

BALLARD, ROBERT D.: Author:
  Dive Into the Great Rift (Project FAMOUS). Photos by Emory Kristof. 604-615, May 1975
  Window on Earth's Interior. Photos by Emory Kristof. 228-249, Aug. 1976

BALLERINAS in Pink. By Carleton Mitchell. Photos by B. Anthony Stewart. 553-571, Oct. 1957

BALLOONS:
  Across the Alps in a Wicker Basket (Bernina). By Phil Walker. 117-131, Jan. 1963
  Braving the Atlantic by Balloon (Small World). By Arnold Eiloart. 123-146, July 1959
  Hot-air Balloons Race on Silent Winds. By William R. Berry. Photos by Don W. Jones. 392-407, Mar. 1966
  Laboratory in a Dirty Sky. By Rudolf J. Engelmann and Vera Simons. 616-621, Nov. 1976
    Contents: Project Da Vinci's manned research balloon
  The Long, Lonely Leap. By Joseph W. Kittinger, Jr. Photos by Volkmar Wentzel. 854-873, Dec. 1960
  Rockets Explore the Air Above Us. By Newman Bumstead. 562-580, Apr. 1957

BALLOONS — Continued
  To 76,000 Feet by Strato-Lab Balloon. By Malcolm D. Ross and M. Lee Lewis. 269-282, Feb. 1957
  Trailing Cosmic Rays in Canada's North. By Martin A. Pomerantz. 99-115, Jan. 1953
  We Saw the World From the Edge of Space. By Malcolm D. Ross. Photos by Walter Meayers Edwards. 671-685, Nov. 1961

BALTIC Cruise of the Caribbee. By Carleton Mitchell. 605-646, Nov. 1950

BALTIMORE, Maryland:
  Baltimore: The Hidden City. By Fred Kline. Photos by Martin Rogers. 188-215, Feb. 1975
  Chesapeake Country. By Nathaniel T. Kenney. Photos by Bates Littlehales. 370-411, Sept. 1964
  Maryland on the Half Shell. By Stuart E. Jones. Photos by Robert W. Madden. 188-229, Feb. 1972
  Spices, the Essence of Geography. By Stuart E. Jones. 401-420, Mar. 1949
    Included: McCormick and Company
  See also Sherwood Gardens; Sparrows Point

BALTISTAN (Region), Kashmir:
  Trek to Lofty Hunza — and Beyond. By Sabrina and Roland Michaud. 644-669, Nov. 1975

BALUCHISTAN:
  Pakistan, New Nation in an Old Land. By Jean and Franc Shor. 637-678, Nov. 1952

BANARAS, India:
  The Ganges, River of Faith. By John J. Putman. Photos by Raghubir Singh. 445-483, Oct. 1971

BAND, GEORGE: Photographer:
  Triumph on Everest. 1-63, July 1954
    I. Siege and Assault. By Sir John Hunt. 1-43
    II. The Conquest of the Summit. By Sir Edmund Hillary. 45-63

BANDELIER NATIONAL MONUMENT, New Mexico:
  Adobe New Mexico. By Mason Sutherland. Photos by Justin Locke. 783-830, Dec. 1949

BANDING, Bird:
  Tireless Voyager, the Whistling Swan. By William J. L. Sladen. Photos by Bianca Lavies. 134-147, July 1975

BANFF NATIONAL PARK, Alberta, Canada:
  Canadian Rockies, Lords of a Beckoning Land. By Alan Phillips. Photos by James L. Stanfield. 353-393, Sept. 1966
  Hiking the Backbone of the Rockies: Canada's Great Divide Trail. By Mike W. Edwards. Photos by Lowell Georgia. 795-817, June 1973
  On the Ridgepole of the Rockies. By Walter Meayers Edwards. 745-780, June 1947

BANGKOK, Thailand:
  "Around the World in Eighty Days." By Newman Bumstead. 705-750, Dec. 1951
  Bangkok, City of Angels. By William Graves. Photos by John Launois. 96-129, July 1973
  Hopes and Fears in Booming Thailand. By Peter T. White. Photos by Dean Conger. 76-125, July 1967
  Operation Eclipse: 1948. By William A. Kinney. 325-372, Mar. 1949

BANGKOK, Thailand—*Continued*

Scintillating Siam. By W. Robert Moore. 173-200, Feb. 1947

Thailand Bolsters Its Freedom. By W. Robert Moore. 811-849, June 1961

Yankee Roams the Orient. By Irving and Electa Johnson. 327-370, Mar. 1951

BANGLADESH, People's Republic of:

Bangladesh: Hope Nourishes a New Nation. By William S. Ellis. Photos by Dick Durrance II. 295-333, Sept. 1972

Bangladesh: The Nightmare of Famine. Photos by Steve Raymer. 33-39, July 1975

The Peaceful Mrus of Bangladesh. By Claus-Dieter Brauns. 267-286, Feb. 1973

See also former name, East Pakistan

BANKS ISLAND, Northwest Territories, Canada:

Banks Island: Eskimo Life on the Polar Sea. By William O. Douglas. Photos by Clyde Hare. 703-735, May 1964

BANTU (Tribespeople):

My Life With Africa's Little People. By Anne Eisner Putnam. 278-302, Feb. 1960

BARBADOS (Island), Lesser Antilles:

Barbados, Outrider of the Antilles. By Charles Allmon. 363-392, Mar. 1952

Robin Sails Home. By Robin Lee Graham. 504-545, Oct. 1970

BARCELONA ZOO, Barcelona, Spain:

Growing Up With Snowflake (White Gorilla). By Arthur J. Riopelle. Photos by Michael Kuh. 491-503, Oct. 1970

BAREHANDED Battle to Cleanse the Bay. By Peter T. White. Photos by Jonathan S. Blair. 866-881, June 1971

BARGES:

Inside Europe Aboard *Yankee*. By Irving and Electa Johnson. Photos by Joseph J. Scherschel. 157-195, Aug. 1964

Paris to Antwerp with the Water Gypsies. By David S. Boyer. 530-559, Oct. 1955

That Dammed Missouri River. By Gordon Young. Photos by David Hiser. 374-413, Sept. 1971

See also Rhine (River); St. Louis (New Spirit)

BARNACLES:

Friendless Squatters of the Sea. By Ethel A. Starbird. Photos by Robert F. Sisson. 623-633, Nov. 1973

BARNUM & BAILEY CIRCUS. *See* Ringling Bros. and Barnum & Bailey Circus

BARRA (Island), Scotland:

From Barra to Butt in the Hebrides. By Isobel Wylie Hutchison. 559-580, Oct. 1954

Hunting Folk Songs in the Hebrides. By Margaret Shaw Campbell. 249-272, Feb. 1947

Isles on the Edge of the Sea: Scotland's Outer Hebrides. By Kenneth MacLeish. Photos by Thomas Nebbia. 676-711, May 1970
   The Thrush on the Island of Barra. By Archibald MacLeish. 692-693

Scotland From Her Lovely Lochs and Seas. By Alan Villiers. Photos by Robert F. Sisson. 492-541, Apr. 1961

BARROW, Alaska:

Will Oil and Tundra Mix? Alaska's North Slope Hangs in the Balance. By William S. Ellis. Photos by Emory Kristof. 485-517, Oct. 1971

BARTLETT, DES: Author-Photographer:

Beavers, Nature's Aquatic Engineers. By Des and Jen Bartlett. 716-732, May 1974

Beyond the North Wind With the Snow Goose. By Des and Jen Bartlett. 822-843, Dec. 1973
   ... And Then There was Fred. ... 843-847
      Photographer

Finding the World's Earliest Man. By L. S. B. Leakey. 420-435, Sept. 1960

Patagonia. 290-339, Mar. 1976
   I. Argentina Protects Its Wildlife Treasures. By William G. Conway. 290-297
   II. Where Two Worlds Meet. 298-321
   III. At Home With Right Whales. By Roger Payne. 322-339

BARTLETT, JEN: Author-Photographer:

Beavers, Nature's Aquatic Engineers. By Des and Jen Bartlett. 716-732, May 1974

Beyond the North Wind With the Snow Goose. By Des and Jen Bartlett. 822-843, Dec. 1973
   ... And Then There was Fred. ... 843-847
      Photographer

Patagonia. 290-339, Mar. 1976
   I. Argentina Protects Its Wildlife Treasures. By William G. Conway. 290-297
   II. Where Two Worlds Meet. 298-321
   III. At Home With Right Whales. By Roger Payne. 322-339

BARTLETT, LINDA: Photographer:

Benjamin Franklin, Philosopher of Dissent. By Alice J. Hall. 93-123, July 1975

Exploring England's Canals. By Bryan Hodgson. 76-111, July 1974

Irish Ways Live On in Dingle. By Bryan Hodgson. 551-576, Apr. 1976

Mountain Voices, Mountain Days (West Virginia). By Bryan Hodgson. 118-146, July 1972

Thomas Jefferson: Architect of Freedom. By Mike W. Edwards. 231-259, Feb. 1976

BARTLETT, ROBERT A.:

Newfoundland, Canada's New Province. By Andrew H. Brown. Photos by author and Robert F. Sisson. 777-812, June 1949

BARUNTSE (Peak), Himalayas:

Beyond Everest. By Sir Edmund Hillary. 579-610, Nov. 1955

BASEL, Switzerland:

The Rhine: Europe's River of Legend. By William Graves. Photos by Bruce Dale. 449-499, Apr. 1967

BASILIQUE DE LA SAINTE MARIE MADELEINE, Vézelay, France:

Vézelay, Hill of the Pilgrims. By Melvin Hall. 229-247, Feb. 1953

BASIN REGION, Utah-Nevada. *See* Great Basin

BASKET MAKERS (Indians):

Ancient Cliff Dwellers of Mesa Verde. By Don Watson. Photos by Willard R. Culver. 349-376, Sept. 1948

BASKET MAKERS (Indians)—*Continued*

20th-century Indians Preserve Customs of the Cliff Dwellers. Photos by William Belknap, Jr. 196-211, Feb. 1964

BASQUES:

The Enduring Pyrenees. By Robert Laxalt. Photos by Edwin Stuart Grosvenor. 794-819, Dec. 1974

Land of the Ancient Basques. By Robert Laxalt. Photos by William Albert Allard. 240-277, Aug. 1968

Life in the Land of the Basques. By John E. H. Nolan. Photos by Justin Locke. 147-186, Feb. 1954

Lonely Sentinels of the American West: Basque Sheepherders. By Robert Laxalt. Photos by William Belknap, Jr. 870-888, June 1966

Pigeon Netting—Sport of Basques. Photos by Irene Burdette-Scougall. 405-416, Sept. 1949

BASS, GEORGE F.: Author:

New Tools for Undersea Archeology. Photos by Charles R. Nicklin, Jr. 403-423, Sept. 1968

Underwater Archeology: Key to History's Warehouse. Photos by Thomas J. Abercrombie and Robert B. Goodman. 138-156, July 1963

BASTAR (Region), India:

New Life for India's Villagers. By Anthony and Georgette Dickey Chapelle. 572-588, Apr. 1956

BASTOGNE, Belgium:

Belgium Comes Back. By Harvey Klemmer. Photos by Maynard Owen Williams. 575-614, May 1948

BATAVIA, Java. *See* Djakarta

BATES, MARSTON: Author-Photographer:

Ifalik, Lonely Paradise of the South Seas. 547-571, Apr. 1956

Photographer

Keeping House for a Biologist in Colombia. By Nancy Bell Fairchild Bates. 251-274, Aug. 1948

BATES, NANCY BELL FAIRCHILD: Author:

Keeping House for a Biologist in Colombia. Photos by Marston Bates. 251-274, Aug. 1948

BATHYSCAPHS:

Deep Diving off Japan. By Georges S. Houot. 138-150, Jan. 1960

Diving Through an Undersea Avalanche. By Jacques-Yves Cousteau. 538-542, Apr. 1955

Down to *Thresher* by Bathyscaph. By Donald L. Keach. 764-777, June 1964

Four Years of Diving to the Bottom of the Sea. By Georges S. Houot. 715-731, May 1958

Man's Deepest Dive *(Trieste)*. By Jacques Piccard. Photos by Thomas J. Abercrombie. 224-239, Aug. 1960

Photographing the Sea's Dark Underworld. By Harold E. Edgerton. 523-537, Apr. 1955

To the Depths of the Sea by Bathyscaphe. By Jacques-Yves Cousteau. 67-79, July 1954

Two and a Half Miles Down. By Georges S. Houot. 80-86, July 1954

See also Archimède

BATS:

Bats Aren't All Bad. By Alvin Novick. Photos by Bruce Dale. 615-637, May 1973

BATS—*Continued*

How Bats Hunt With Sound. By J. J. G. McCue. 571-578, Apr. 1961

BATTAGLIA, LEE E.: Author-Photographer:

Wedding of Two Worlds (Sikkim). 708-727, Nov. 1963

Photographer

History Revealed in Ancient Glass. By Ray Winfield Smith. Photos by B. Anthony Stewart and Lee E. Battaglia. 346-369, Sept. 1964

Last Moments of the Pompeians. By Amedeo Maiuri. Paintings by Peter V. Bianchi. 651-669, Nov. 1961

BATTLE MONUMENTS. *See* War Memorials

BATTLE OF THE BULGE:

Belgium Comes Back. By Harvey Klemmer. Photos by Maynard Owen Williams. 575-614, May 1948

Luxembourg, Survivor of Invasions. By Sydney Clark. Photos by Maynard Owen Williams. 791-810, June 1948

BATTLEFIELDS:

Battlefields of the Civil War, double-sided Atlas series supplement. Apr. 1961

Gettysburg and Vicksburg: the Battle Towns Today. By Robert Paul Jordan. Map notes by Carolyn Bennett Patterson. 4-57, July 1963
Included: Annotated maps charting course of battles

See also names of battles and wars, *as:* American Revolution; Hastings, Battle of

BATTLESHIPS:

Midshipmen's Cruise. By William J. Aston and Alexander G. B. Grosvenor. 711-754, June 1948
Included: *New Jersey; Wisconsin*

BAUMANN, J. BRUCE: Photographer:

Heart of the Bluegrass. By Charles McCarry. 634-659, May 1974

Indiana's Self-reliant Uplanders. By James Alexander Thom. 341-363, Mar. 1976

The Other Nevada. By Robert Laxalt. 733-761, June 1974

BAVARIA (State), West Germany:

Bavaria: Mod, Medieval—and Bewitching. By Gary Jennings. Photos by George F. Mobley. 409-431, Mar. 1974

See also Dinkelsbühl

"BAY OF FIRE." *See* Phosphorescent Bay

BAYEUX TAPESTRY:

900 Years Ago: the Norman Conquest. By Kenneth M. Setton. Photos by George F. Mobley. The complete Bayeux Tapestry photographed by Milton A. Ford and Victor R. Boswell, Jr. 206-251, Aug. 1966

BAYKAL, Lake, U.S.S.R.:

Siberia: Russia's Frozen Frontier. By Dean Conger. 297-345, Mar. 1967

"BE Ye Men of Valour." By Howard La Fay. 159-197, Aug. 1965

BEACH, EDWARD L.: Author:

Triton (Nuclear Submarine) Follows Magellan's

BEACH, EDWARD L.: Author—*Continued*

Wake. Photos by J. Baylor Roberts. 585-615, Nov. 1960

BEAGLE, H.M.S.:

In the Wake of Darwin's *Beagle*. By Alan Villiers. Photos by James L. Stanfield. 449-495, Oct. 1969

BEAN, ALAN L.:

Skylab, Outpost on the Frontier of Space. By Thomas Y. Canby. Photos by the nine mission astronauts. 441-469, Oct. 1974

BEAR MOUNTAIN, New York:

Skyline Trail (Appalachian Trail) from Maine to Georgia. By Andrew H. Brown. Photos by Robert F. Sisson. 219-251, Aug. 1949

BEAR RIVER MIGRATORY BIRD REFUGE, Utah:

The Dauntless Little Stilt. By Frederick Kent Truslow. 241-245, Aug. 1960

BEARD, DANIEL B.: Author:

Wildlife of Everglades National Park. Paintings by Walter A. Weber. 83-116, Jan. 1949

BEARS. *See* Black Bears; Brown Bears; Grizzly Bears; Polar Bear

La **BEAUCE** (Plain), France:

Chartres: Legacy from the Age of Faith. By Kenneth MacLeish. Photos by Dean Conger. 857-882, Dec. 1969

BEAUTY and Bounty of Southern State Trees. By William A. Dayton. Paintings by Walter A. Weber. 508-552, Oct. 1957

BEAVERS:

Arizona's Operation Beaver Lift. By Willis Peterson. 666-680, May 1955

Beavers, Nature's Aquatic Engineers. By Des and Jen Bartlett. 716-732, May 1974

The Romance of American Furs. By Wanda Burnett. 379-402, Mar. 1948

BECAUSE It Rains on Hawaii. By Frederick Simpich, Jr. 571-610, Nov. 1949

BECKER, JIM: Author:

Look What's Happened to Honolulu! Photos by Bates Littlehales. 500-531, Oct. 1969

BECKET, THOMAS À:

Canterbury Cathedral. By Kenneth MacLeish. Photos by Thomas Nebbia. 364-379, Mar. 1976

BEDI, NARESH: Photographer:

The Cobra, India's "Good Snake." By Harry Miller. 393-409, Sept. 1970

BEDI, RAJESH: Photographer:

The Cobra, India's "Good Snake." By Harry Miller. 393-409, Sept. 1970

India Struggles to Save Her Wildlife. By John J. Putman. 299-343, Sept. 1976

BEDOUIN:

Abraham, the Friend of God. By Kenneth MacLeish. Photos by Dean Conger. 739-789, Dec. 1966

Arab Land Beyond the Jordan. Photos by Frank Hurley. 753-768, Dec. 1947

Holy Land, My Country. By His Majesty King Hussein of Jordan. 784-789, Dec. 1964

BEDOUIN—*Continued*

In Search of Moses. By Harvey Arden. Photos by Nathan Benn. 2-37, Jan. 1976

Jerusalem, My Home. By Bertha Spafford Vester. 826-847, Dec. 1964

Morocco, Land of the Farthest West. By Thomas J. Abercrombie. 834-865, June 1971

The Other Side of Jordan. By Luis Marden. 790-825, Dec. 1964

Report from the Locust Wars. By Tony and Dickey Chapelle. 545-562, Apr. 1953

Saudi Arabia: Beyond the Sands of Mecca. By Thomas J. Abercrombie. 1-53, Jan. 1966

The Sword and the Sermon (Islam). By Thomas J. Abercrombie. 3-45, July 1972

BEEBE, WILLIAM: Author:

The High World of the Rain Forest. Paintings by Guy Neale. 838-855, June 1958

BEES:

Crossroads of the Insect World. By J. W. MacSwain. Photos by Edward S. Ross. 844-857, Dec. 1966

Inside the World of the Honeybee. By Treat Davidson. 188-217, Aug. 1959

Those Fiery Brazilian Bees. By Rick Gore. Photos by Bianca Lavies. 491-501, Apr. 1976

BEETLES:

Following the Ladybug Home. By Kenneth S. Hagen. Photos by Robert F. Sisson. 543-553, Apr. 1970

Larvae. *See* Glowworms; Railroad Worm

See also Fireflies

BEHIND New York's Window on Nature: The American Museum of Natural History. By James A. Oliver. Photos by Robert F. Sisson. 220-259, Feb. 1963

BEHIND the Headlines in Viet Nam. By Peter T. White. Photos by Winfield Parks. 149-189, Feb. 1967

BEHIND the Veil of Troubled Yemen. By Thomas J. Abercrombie. 403-445, Mar. 1964

BEHOLD the Computer Revolution. By Peter T. White. Photos by Bruce Dale and Emory Kristof. 593-633, Nov. 1970

BEINN BHREAGH, Cape Breton Island, Nova Scotia:

Down East to Nova Scotia. By Winfield Parks. 853-879, June 1964

BEIRUT, Lebanon:

Lebanon, Little Bible Land in the Crossfire of History. By William S. Ellis. Photos by George F. Mobley. 240-275, Feb. 1970

Young-old Lebanon Lives by Trade. By Thomas J. Abercrombie. 479-523, Apr. 1958

BELDEN, CHARLES J.: Author-Photographer:

Dinkelsbühl Rewards Its Children. 255-268, Feb. 1957

Photographer

The Palio of Siena. By Edgar Erskine Hume. 231-244, Aug. 1951

BELGIAN CONGO. *See* Zaire

BELGIUM:

Belgium Comes Back. By Harvey Klemmer. Photos by Maynard Owen Williams. 575-614, May 1948

Belgium Welcomes the World (1958 World's Fair). By Howell Walker. 795-837, June 1958

France, Belgium, and the Netherlands, Atlas series supplement. June 1960

Inside Europe Aboard *Yankee.* By Irving and Electa Johnson. Photos by Joseph J. Scherschel. 157-195, Aug. 1964

Paris to Antwerp with the Water Gypsies. By David S. Boyer. 530-559, Oct. 1955

See also Bruges

BELGRADE, Yugoslavia:

Yugoslavia, Between East and West. By George W. Long. Photos by Volkmar Wentzel. 141-172, Feb. 1951

Yugoslavia: Six Republics in One. By Robert Paul Jordan. Photos by James P. Blair. 589-633, May 1970

BELIZE (British Honduras):

Belize, the Awakening Land. By Louis de la Haba. Photos by Michael E. Long. 124-146, Jan. 1972
Included: Belize City; Belmopan

BELKNAP, WILLIAM, Jr.: Author-Photographer:

Man on the Moon in Idaho (Craters of the Moon National Monument). 505-525, Oct. 1960

Nature Carves Fantasies in Bryce Canyon. 490-511, Oct. 1958

New Mexico's Great White Sands. 113-137, July 1957

Shooting Rapids in Reverse! Jet Boats Climb the Colorado's Torrent Through the Grand Canyon. 552-565, Apr. 1962

Photographer

Lonely Sentinels of the American West: Basque Sheepherders. By Robert Laxalt. 870-888, June 1966

20th-century Indians Preserve Customs of the Cliff Dwellers. 196-211, Feb. 1964

Where Falcons Wear Air Force Blue, United States Air Force Academy. By Nathaniel T. Kenney. 845-873, June 1959

BELL, ALEXANDER GRAHAM:

Alexander Graham Bell Museum: Tribute to Genius. By Jean Lesage. 227-256, Aug. 1956

Canada's Winged Victory: the *Silver Dart.* By Gilbert M. Grosvenor. 254-267, Aug. 1959

Clarke School for the Deaf, Northampton, Massachusetts: Active for 51 years as teacher, consultant, researcher, and president of the board. 379, 385, Mar. 1955

1898: The Bells on Sable. Photos by Arthur W. McCurdy. 408-409, 416-417, Sept. 1965

Miracle Men of the Telephone. By F. Barrows Colton. 273-316, Mar. 1947

President of NGS (1898-1903). 273, Mar. 1947

The Romance of the Geographic: National Geographic Magazine Observes Its Diamond Anniversary. By Gilbert Hovey Grosvenor. 516-585, Oct. 1963

To Gilbert Grosvenor: a Monthly Monument 25 Miles High. By Frederick G. Vosburgh and the staff of the National Geographic Society. 445-

BELL, ALEXANDER GRAHAM — *Continued*
487, Oct. 1966

Washington's Historic Georgetown. By William A. Kinney. 513-544, Apr. 1953

BELL, CARL S.: Photographer:

Sky-high Bolivia. 481-496, Oct. 1950

BELL MAKING:

Mid-century Holland Builds Her Future. By Sydney Clark. 747-778, Dec. 1950

BELL MUSEUM, Baddeck, Nova Scotia:

Alexander Graham Bell Museum: Tribute to Genius. By Jean Lesage. Photos by members of the Bell and Grosvenor families. 227-256, Aug. 1956

Bell Museum, Baddeck, Nova Scotia. 256, 257, 259, 261, Aug. 1959; 358-359, 361, 362, Mar. 1975

Down East to Nova Scotia. By Winfield Parks. 853-879, June 1964

BELL RINGING (Change Ringing):

By Cotswold Lanes to Wold's End. By Melville Bell Grosvenor. 615-654, May 1948

BELL TELEPHONE COMPANY:

President, First: Gardiner Greene Hubbard. 273, Mar. 1947

BELL TELEPHONE LABORATORIES:

Miracle Men of the Telephone. By F. Barrows Colton. 273-316, Mar. 1947
Birthplace of Telephone Magic. Photos by Willard R. Culver. 289-312

New Miracles of the Telephone Age. By Robert Leslie Conly. 87-120, July 1954

Telephone a Star: the Story of Communications Satellites. By Rowe Findley. 638-651, May 1962

BELL X-1 (Rocket Ship):

Flying in the "Blowtorch" Era. By Frederick G. Vosburgh. 281-322, Sept. 1950

BELLINGER, PATRICK N. L.: Author:

Sailors in the Sky: Fifty Years of Naval Aviation. 276-296, Aug. 1961

BELTSVILLE, Maryland: Agricultural Research Center:

Beltsville Brings Science to the Farm. By Samuel W. Matthews. 199-218, Aug. 1953

BELUGAS (White Whales):

Three Whales That Flew. By Carleton Ray. Photos by W. Robert Moore. 346-359, Mar. 1962

BENCHLEY, PETER: Author:

Bermuda—Balmy, British, and Beautiful. Photos by Emory Kristof. 93-121, July 1971

Life's Tempo on Nantucket. Photos by James L. Stanfield. 810-839, June 1970

New Zealand's Bountiful South Island. Photos by James L. Amos. 93-123, Jan. 1972

The **BENDS** (Caisson Disease):

At Home in the Sea. By Jacques-Yves Cousteau. 465-507, Apr. 1964

Dzibilchaltun: Up from the Well of Time. By Luis Marden. 110-129, Jan. 1959

Fish Men Explore a New World Undersea. By Jacques-Yves Cousteau. 431-472, Oct. 1952

The **BENDS** (Caisson Disease) — *Continued*

Underwater Archeology: Key to History's Warehouse. By George F. Bass. Photos by Thomas J. Abercrombie and Robert B. Goodman. 138-156, July 1963

BENELUX NATIONS. *See* Belgium; Luxembourg; Netherlands

BENJAMIN, GEORGE J.: Author-Photographer:

Diving Into the Blue Holes of the Bahamas. 347-363, Sept. 1970

BENJAMIN FRANKLIN, Philosopher of Dissent. By Alice J. Hall. Photos by Linda Bartlett. 93-123, July 1975

BENN, NATHAN: Photographer:

Cuba's Exiles Bring New Life to Miami. By Edward J. Linehan. 68-95, July 1973

In Search of Moses. By Harvey Arden. 2-37, Jan. 1976

The Pious Ones (Brooklyn's Hasidic Jews). By Harvey Arden. 276-298, Aug. 1975

Vermont — a State of Mind and Mountains. By Ethel A. Starbird. 28-61, July 1974

BENNETT, FLOYD:

Floyd Bennett awarded Gold Medal; presentation by President Coolidge. 868, Dec. 1957

BERBERS (Tribespeople):

Trek by Mule Among Morocco's Berbers. By Victor Englebert. 850-875, June 1968

BERGEN, Norway:

Norway, Land of the Generous Sea. By Edward J. Linehan. Photos by George F. Mobley. 1-43, July 1971

Norway Cracks Her Mountain Shell. By Sydney Clark. Photos by Gilbert Grosvenor and Ole Friele Backer. 171-211, Aug. 1948

BERING SEA PEOPLE. *See* Old Bering Sea People

BERING SEA REGION. *See* King Island; Pribilof Islands

BERING STRAIT:

Alaska's Russian Frontier: Little Diomede. Photos by Audrey and Frank Morgan. 551-562, Apr. 1951

Ice Age Man, the First American. By Thomas R. Henry. Paintings by Andre Durenceau. 781-806, Dec. 1955

BERKSHIRES (Mountains), Massachusetts:

Home to the Enduring Berkshires. By Charles McCarry. Photos by Jonathan S. Blair. 196-221, Aug. 1970

Massachusetts Builds for Tomorrow. By Robert de Roos. Photos by B. Anthony Stewart. 790-843, Dec. 1966

Mountains Top Off New England. By F. Barrows Colton. Photos by Robert F. Sisson. 563-602, May 1951

BERLIN, Germany:

Airlift to Berlin. 595-614, May 1949

Berlin, Island in a Soviet Sea. By Frederick G. Vosburgh. Photos by Volkmar Wentzel. 689-704, Nov. 1951

Berlin, on Both Sides of the Wall. By Howard So-

BERLIN, Germany — *Continued*

churek. 1-47, Jan. 1970

Modern Miracle, Made in Germany. By Robert Leslie Conly. Photos by Erich Lessing. 735-791, June 1959

What I Saw Across the Rhine. By J. Frank Dobie. 57-86, Jan. 1947

BERLIN, East, East Germany:

East Germany: The Struggle to Succeed. By John J. Putman. Photos by Gordon W. Gahan. 295-329, Sept. 1974

BERLIN, West:

Life in Walled-off West Berlin. By Nathaniel T. Kenney and Volkmar Wentzel. Photos by Thomas Nebbia. 735-767, Dec. 1961

BERMUDA (Islands), Atlantic Ocean:

Bermuda — Balmy, British, and Beautiful. By Peter Benchley. Photos by Emory Kristof. 93-121, July 1971

Bermuda, Cradled in Warm Seas. By Beverley M. Bowie. Photos by Charles Allmon. 203-238, Feb. 1954

By Square-rigger from Baltic to Bicentennial. By Kenneth Garrett. 824-857, Dec. 1976
Included: Collision of tall ships in Bermuda waters

To Europe with a Racing Start. By Carleton Mitchell. 758-791, June 1958

BERN, Switzerland:

Surprising Switzerland. By Jean and Franc Shor. 427-478, Oct. 1956

Switzerland, Europe's High-rise Republic. By Thomas J. Abercrombie. 68-113, July 1969

Switzerland Guards the Roof of Europe. By William H. Nicholas. Photos by Willard R. Culver. 205-246, Aug. 1950

BERNINA (Balloon):

Across the Alps in a Wicker Basket. By Phil Walker. 117-131, Jan. 1963

BERRIES:

How Fruit Came to America. By J. R. Magness. Paintings by Else Bostelmann. 325-377, Sept. 1951

See also Cranberries

BERRY, WILLIAM R.: Author:

Hot-air Balloons Race on Silent Winds. Photos by Don W. Jones. 392-407, Mar. 1966

BESIDE the Persian Gulf. Photos by Maynard Owen Williams. 341-356, Mar. 1947

BETELGEUSE (Ketch):

Chesapeake Country. By Nathaniel T. Kenney. Photos by Bates Littlehales. 370-411, Sept. 1964

BETHLEHEM:

Hashemite Jordan, Arab Heartland. By John Scofield. 841-856, Dec. 1952

Pilgrims Follow the Christmas Star. By Maynard Owen Williams. 831-840, Dec. 1952

BETTER Days for the Navajos. By Jack Breed. Photos by Charles W. Herbert. 809-847, Dec. 1958

BEYOND Everest. By Sir Edmund Hillary. 579-610, Nov. 1955

BEYOND the Bight of Benin (Nigeria; Cameroons). By Jeannette and Maurice Fiévet. 221-253, Aug. 1959

BEYOND the North Wind With the Snow Goose. By Des and Jen Bartlett. 822-843, Dec. 1973

BHAVNANI, ENAKSHI: Author:
A Journey to "Little Tibet." Photos by Volkmar Wentzel. 603-634, May 1951

BHOTIAS (Tribespeople):
High Adventure in the Himalayas. By Thomas Weir. 193-234, Aug. 1952

BHUTAN:
Bhutan, Land of the Thunder Dragon. By Burt Kerr Todd. 713-754, Dec. 1952

Bhutan: Mountain Kingdom Between Tibet and India. By Desmond Doig. 384-415, Sept. 1961

Bhutan Crowns a New Dragon King. Photos by John Scofield. 546-571, Oct. 1974

Life Slowly Changes in Remote Bhutan. By John Scofield. 658-683, Nov. 1976

BIAMI (People):
Journey Into Stone Age New Guinea. By Malcolm S. Kirk. 568-592, Apr. 1969

BIANCHI, PETER V.: Artist:
Last Moments of the Pompeians. By Amedeo Maiuri. Photos by Lee E. Battaglia. 651-669, Nov. 1961

The Last Thousand Years Before Christ. By G. Ernest Wright. Paintings by H. J. Soulen and Peter V. Bianchi. 812-853, Dec. 1960

The Men Who Hid the Dead Sea Scrolls. By A. Douglas Tushingham. 785-808, Dec. 1958

Solving the Riddles of Wetherill Mesa. By Douglas Osborne. 155-195, Feb. 1964

BIBLE:
The British Way. By Sir Evelyn Wrench. 421-541, Apr. 1949
    Included: James I and the translation of the Bible
The Men Who Hid the Dead Sea Scrolls. By A. Douglas Tushingham. Paintings by Peter V. Bianchi. 785-808, Dec. 1958

BIBLE LANDS:
Abraham, the Friend of God. By Kenneth MacLeish. Photos by Dean Conger. 739-789, Dec. 1966

An Archeologist Looks at Palestine. By Nelson Glueck. 739-752, Dec. 1947

Bringing Old Testament Times to Life. By G. Ernest Wright. Paintings by Henry J. Soulen. 833-864, Dec. 1957

Crusader Lands Revisited. By Harold Lamb. Photos by David S. Boyer. 815-852, Dec. 1954
    Contents: Israel; Jordan; Lebanon; Syria; Turkey
Crusader Road to Jerusalem. By Franc Shor. Photos by Thomas Nebbia. 797-855, Dec. 1963
    I. Desert Ordeal of the Knights. 797-837
    II. Conquest of the Holy City. 839-855
Everyday Life in Bible Times. Book announced. 494-507, Oct. 1967

Eyewitness to War in the Holy Land. By Charles Harbutt. 782-795, Dec. 1967

Geographical Twins a World Apart. By David S. Boyer. 848-859, Dec. 1958

BIBLE LANDS — *Continued*
    Contents: Dead Sea, Sea of Galilee, Jordan River, and the caves at Qumrān compared with their counterparts in Utah
Holy Land, My Country. By His Majesty King Hussein of Jordan. 784-789, Dec. 1964

Holy Land Today, Atlas series supplement. Dec. 1963

Home to the Holy Land. By Maynard Owen Williams. 707-746, Dec. 1950

In Search of Moses. By Harvey Arden. Photos by Nathan Benn. 2-37, Jan. 1976

Israel: Land of Promise. By John Scofield. Photos by B. Anthony Stewart. 395-434, Mar. 1965

Jerusalem to Rome in the Path of St. Paul. By David S. Boyer. 707-759, Dec. 1956

Journey Into the Great Rift. By Helen and Frank Schreider. 254-290, Aug. 1965

The Land of Galilee. By Kenneth MacLeish. Photos by B. Anthony Stewart. 832-865, Dec. 1965

Lands of the Bible Today, map supplement. Dec. 1956

Lands of the Bible Today, map supplement. Dec. 1967

The Last Thousand Years Before Christ. By G. Ernest Wright. Paintings by H. J. Soulen and Peter V. Bianchi. 812-853, Dec. 1960

The Other Side of Jordan. By Luis Marden. 790-825, Dec. 1964

Pilgrims Follow the Christmas Star. By Maynard Owen Williams. 831-840, Dec. 1952

Sinai Sheds New Light on the Bible. By Henry Field. Photos by William B. and Gladys Terry. 795-815, Dec. 1948

Where Jesus Walked. By Howard La Fay. Photos by Charles Harbutt. 739-781, Dec. 1967

See also Jericho; Jerusalem; Jordan; Khirbat Qumrān; Mesopotamia; Petra, Jordan; St. Catherine's Monastery, Sinai

BICENTENNIAL, U. S.:
Benjamin Franklin, Philosopher of Dissent. By Alice J. Hall. Photos by Linda Bartlett. 93-123, July 1975

By Square-rigger from Baltic to Bicentennial (Operation Sail). By Kenneth Garrett. 824-857, Dec. 1976

Firebrands of the Revolution. By Eric F. Goldman. Photos by George F. Mobley. 2-27, July 1974

The Loyalists. By Kent Britt. Photos by Ted Spiegel. 510-539, Apr. 1975

The Nation's 200th Birthday. By Gilbert M. Grosvenor. 1, July 1974

Patriots in Petticoats. By Lonnelle Aikman. Paintings by Louis S. Glanzman. 475-493, Oct. 1975

This Land of Ours. 1-158, July 1976
    A Portfolio: "This land is your land . . ." 2-11
    A First American Views His Land. By N. Scott Momaday. 13-19
    This Land of Ours — How Are We Using It? By Peter T. White. Photos by Emory Kristof. 20-67
    Five Noted Thinkers Explore the Future. 68-75
    The Next Frontier? By Isaac Asimov. Paintings by Pierre Mion. 76-89
    George Washington: The Man Behind the Myths. By Howard La Fay. Photos by Ted Spiegel. 90-111

BICENTENNIAL, U. S.—*Continued*

Thomas Jefferson: Architect of Freedom. By Mike W. Edwards. Photos by Linda Bartlett. 231-259, Feb. 1976

BICYCLING:

Bicycles Are Back—and Booming! By Noel Grove. Photos by Michael Pfleger. 671-681, May 1973

Bikepacking Across Alaska and Canada. By Dan Burden. 682-695, May 1973

Europe Via the Hostel Route. By Joseph Nettis. 124-154, July 1955

BIG BEND NATIONAL PARK, Texas:

Big Bend: Jewel in the Texas Desert. By Nathaniel T. Kenney. Photos by James L. Stanfield. 104-133, Jan. 1968

BIG CYPRESS SWAMP, Florida:

The Imperiled Everglades. By Fred Ward. 1-27, Jan. 1972

Twilight Hope for Big Cypress. By Rick Gore. Photos by Patricia Caulfield. 251-273, Aug. 1976

BIG GAME. *See* Game Preserves; Hunting

BIG Game Hunting in the Land of Long Ago. By Joseph P. Connolly and James D. Bump. 589-605, May 1947

BIG-LIPPED PEOPLE. *See* Sara; Suyá Indians

BIG NAMBAS (Tribespeople):

Taboos and Magic Rule Namba Lives. By Kal Muller. 57-83, Jan. 1972

Yankee Roams the Orient. By Irving and Electa Johnson. 327-370, Mar. 1951

"BIG SCHMIDT" (Telescope):

Mapping the Unknown Universe. By F. Barrows Colton. 401-420, Sept. 1950

See also Sky Survey

BIG SUR (Region), California:

California's Land Apart—the Monterey Peninsula. By Mike W. Edwards. 682-703, Nov. 1972

BIG THICKET (Region), Texas:

Big Thicket of Texas. By Don Moser. Photos by Blair Pittman. 504-529, Oct. 1974

BIG TREES *(Sequoia gigantea). See* Sequoia National Park

BIGGEST Worm Farm Caters to Platypuses. By W. H. Nicholas. 269-280, Feb. 1949

BIGHORN SHEEP:

Last Stand for the Bighorn. By James K. Morgan. 383-399, Sept. 1973

BIHARIS (People):

Bangladesh: Hope Nourishes a New Nation. By William S. Ellis. Photos by Dick Durrance II. 295-333, Sept. 1972

BIKEPACKING Across Alaska and Canada. By Dan Burden. 682-695, May 1973

BIKINI (Atoll), Marshall Islands:

Operation Crossroads. Photos by Joint Task Force I. Paintings by Charles Bittinger. 519-530, Apr. 1947

BILLARD, JULES B.: Author:

Buenos Aires, Argentina's Melting-pot Metropolis.

BILLARD, JULES B.: Author—*Continued*

Photos by Winfield Parks. 662-695, Nov. 1967

Canada's Window on the Pacific: The British Columbia Coast. Photos by Ted Spiegel. 338-375, Mar. 1972

Guantánamo: Keystone in the Caribbean. Photos by W. E. Garrett and Thomas Nebbia. 420-436, Mar. 1961

Macao Clings to the Bamboo Curtain. Photos by Joseph J. Scherschel. 521-539, Apr. 1969

Montreal Greets the World (Expo 67). 600-621, May 1967

Okinawa, the Island Without a Country. Photos by Winfield Parks and David Moore. 422-448, Sept. 1969

Panama, Link Between Oceans and Continents. Photos by Bruce Dale. 402-440, Mar. 1970

The Revolution in American Agriculture. Photos by James P. Blair. 147-185, Feb. 1970

BIMINI ISLANDS, Bahama Islands:

Man-of-war Fleet Attacks Bimini. By Paul A. Zahl. 185-212, Feb. 1952

See also Lerner Marine Laboratory

BINGHAM, HIRAM:

Peru, Homeland of the Warlike Inca. By Kip Ross. 421-462, Oct. 1950

BIOCHEMISTRY:

The Awesome Worlds Within a Cell. By Rick Gore. Photos by Bruce Dale. Paintings by Davis Meltzer. 355-395, Sept. 1976

See also Bioluminescence

BIOLOGY:

Algae: the Life-givers. By Paul A. Zahl. 361-377, Mar. 1974

Antarctica's Nearer Side. By Samuel W. Matthews. Photos by William R. Curtsinger. 622-655, Nov. 1971

    Included: Laboratory studies of Antarctic land and marine life

Life in a "Dead" Sea—Great Salt Lake. By Paul A. Zahl. 252-263, Aug. 1967

The New Biology. 355-407, Sept. 1976

    I. The Awesome Worlds Within a Cell. By Rick Gore. Photos by Bruce Dale. Paintings by Davis Meltzer. 355-395

    II. The Cancer Puzzle. By Robert F. Weaver. 396-399

    III. Seven Giants Who Led the Way. Paintings by Ned Seidler. Text by Rick Gore. 401-407

        Contents: Francis Crick, Charles Darwin, Anton van Leeuwenhoek, Gregor Mendel, Thomas Hunt Morgan, Louis Pasteur, James D. Watson

See also Birds; Insects; Mammals; Marine Biology; Plants; Spiders; *and* Ecosystems

BIOLUMINESCENCE:

Fishing in the Whirlpool of Charybdis. By Paul A. Zahl. 579-618, Nov. 1953

Nature's Night Lights: Probing the Secrets of Bioluminescence. By Paul A. Zahl. 45-69, July 1971

Sailing a Sea of Fire (Phosphorescent Bay). By Paul A. Zahl. 120-129, July 1960

See also Fireflies; Hatchetfish; Railroad Worm

BIORHYTHM RESEARCH:

Six Months Alone in a Cave. By Michel Siffre. 426-435, Mar. 1975

BIRD, ROLAND T.: Author:

We Captured a 'Live' Brontosaur. 707-722, May 1954

BIRD ANTING:

The Enigma of Bird Anting. By Hance Roy Ivor. 105-119, July 1956

BIRD DOGS:

Born Hunters, the Bird Dogs. By Roland Kilbon. Paintings by Walter A. Weber. 369-398, Sept. 1947

BIRD SANCTUARIES AND ROOKERIES:

Beyond the North Wind With the Snow Goose. By Des and Jen Bartlett. 822-843, Dec. 1973
Included: De Soto, Missouri River; Sand Lake, South Dakota; Squaw Creek, Missouri

Duck Hunting with a Color Camera. By Arthur A. Allen. 514-539, Oct. 1951
Contents: Bear River Marshes, Utah; Bombay Hook, Delaware; Cayuga Lake, New York; Horseshoe Lake Island, Illinois; Lower Souris, North Dakota; Roaches Run, Virginia

New Scarlet Bird in Florida Skies. By Paul A. Zahl. 874-882, Dec. 1967
Included: Caroni Swamp Sanctuary, Trinidad; Greynolds Park Rookery, North Miami Beach

Our Only Native Stork, the Wood Ibis. By Robert Porter Allen. Photos by Frederick Kent Truslow. 294-306, Feb. 1964
Included: Bear Island Rookery; Corkscrew Swamp Sanctuary; Cuthbert Lake Rookery

The Pink Birds of Texas. By Paul A. Zahl. 641-654, Nov. 1949
Contents: Roseate spoonbills and the National Audubon Society's sanctuary system on the Texas bird islands along the Gulf of Mexico

Saving Man's Wildlife Heritage. By John H. Baker. Photos by Robert F. Sisson. 581-620, Nov. 1954
Included: The National Audubon Society's sanctuaries in Texas, Florida, and Louisiana

Sea Bird Cities Off Audubon's Labrador. By Arthur A. Allen. 755-774, June 1948
Contents: Bradore Bay Sanctuary; Fog Island Sanctuary; Mecatina Bird Sanctuary; St. Augustin Sanctuary; St. Mary Islands Sanctuary

Sea Birds of Isla Raza. By Lewis Wayne Walker. 239-248, Feb. 1951

Tireless Voyager, the Whistling Swan. By William J. L. Sladen. Photos by Bianca Lavies. 134-147, July 1975
Included: Back Bay, Virginia; Blackwater, Maryland; Eastern Neck, Maryland; Mattamuskeet, North Carolina; Pungo, North Carolina; Upper Mississippi River Wild Life and Fish Refuge, Minnesota

Wildlife of Everglades National Park. By Daniel B. Beard. Paintings by Walter A. Weber. 83-116, Jan. 1949
Included: Cuthbert Lake Rookery; East River Rookery

See also Abbotsbury Swannery, England; Aransas National Wildlife Refuge, Texas; Bear River Migratory Bird Refuge, Utah; Corkscrew Swamp, Florida; Currumbin, Australia; Everglades (Region), Florida; Las Marismas (Marshes), Spain; Little Tobago (Island), Trinidad; Red Rock Lakes National Wildlife Refuge, Montana; Sapsucker Woods, Cornell University; Wichita Mountains Wildlife Refuge, Oklahoma

BIRDS:

An Artist's Glimpses of Our Roadside Wildlife.

BIRDS — Continued

Paintings by Walter A. Weber. 16-32, July 1950
Included: Avocets, Bald eagles, Blue-winged teals, Coots, Evening grosbeaks, Fish hawks (Ospreys), Gadwalls, Holboell's grebes, Kingbirds, Magpies, Marsh hawks, Mountain chickadees, Oregon juncos, Pine grosbeaks, Prairie falcons, Pygmy owls, Ravens, Red-breasted nuthatches, Redhead ducks, Red-tailed hawks, Ring-necked pheasants, Scissor-tailed flycatchers, Shovelers, Townsend warblers, Trumpeter swans, Vermilion flycatchers

Barehanded Battle to Cleanse the Bay. By Peter T. White. Photos by Jonathan S. Blair. 866-881, June 1971
Included: Oil-crippled birds

Birds of the Alaskan Tundra. 322-327, Mar. 1972

The Bird's Year. By Arthur A. Allen. 791-816, June 1951
Contents: American bittern, Avocet, Baltimore oriole, Black-crowned night heron, Blue-headed vireo, Bronze turkey, Brown thrasher, Cardinal, Cedar waxwing, Chestnut-sided warbler, Coot, Cowbird, Eared grebe, Evening grosbeak, Gila woodpecker, Golden-fronted woodpecker, Hoary redpoll, Indigo bunting, Kentucky warbler, Least bittern, Loon, Magnolia warbler, Mourning warbler, Ovenbird, Phoebe, Puffin, Purple martin, Red-bellied woodpecker, Redpoll, Redstart, Rio Grande turkey, Ruby-throated hummingbird, Ruffed grouse, Sabine's gull, Sennett's oriole, Short-billed marsh wren, Snowy heron, Sparrow hawk, Starling, White-throated sparrow, White-winged dove, Yellow-headed blackbird

Businessman in the Bush. By Frederick Kent Truslow. 634-675, May 1970

Can We Save Our Salt Marshes? By Stephen W. Hitchcock. Photos by William R. Curtsinger. 729-765, June 1972

Corkscrew Swamp — Florida's Primeval Show Place. By Melville Bell Grosvenor. 98-113, Jan. 1958

The Curlew's Secret. By Arthur A. Allen. 751-770, Dec. 1948
Included: Alaska longspur, Alaska yellow wagtail, Baird's sandpiper, Black-bellied plover, Bristle-thighed curlew, Cackling goose, Cranes, Ducks, Emperor goose, Frigate bird, Geese, Golden plover, Hoary redpoll, Hudsonian curlew, Little brown crane, Northern phalarope, Old-squaw, Pacific godwit, Parasitic jaeger, Pectoral sandpiper, Ruddy turnstone, Sabine's gull, Savannah sparrow, Snow bunting, Spectacled eider, Tree sparrow, Varied thrush, Western sandpiper, Whistling swan, White-fronted goose, Wilson's snipe

Eden in the Outback. By Kay and Stanley Breeden. 189-203, Feb. 1973

The Enigma of Bird Anting. By Hance Roy Ivor. 105-119, July 1956

Exotic Birds in Manhattan's Bowery. By Paul A. Zahl. 77-98, Jan. 1953

Exploring Stone Age Arnhem Land. By Charles P. Mountford. Photos by Howell Walker. 745-782, Dec. 1949

Florida, Noah's Ark for Exotic Newcomers. By Rick Gore. Photos by David Doubilet. 538-559, Oct. 1976
Included: The introduction of tropical birds: budgerigar, bulbul, myna, parakeet, and parrot

The Galapagos, Eerie Cradle of New Species. By Roger Tory Peterson. Photos by Alan and Joan Root. 541-585, Apr. 1967

London's Zoo of Zoos. By Thomas Garner James. 771-786, June 1953

BIRDS—*Continued*

Lundy, Treasure Island of Birds. By P.T. Etherton. Photos by J. Allan Cash. 675-698, May 1947

Nature's Alert Eyes. By Constance P. Warner. 558-569, Apr. 1959

New Guinea's Paradise of Birds. By E. Thomas Gilliard. 661-688, Nov. 1951
Contents: Princess Stephanie bird of paradise, Ribbon-tailed bird of paradise, *Harpyopsis* eagle, *Salvadorina* duck, *Archboldia* bowerbird, *Cnemophilus macgregorii* bowerbird, and a new bowerbird named for Leonard C. Sanford

New Guinea's Rare Birds and Stone Age Men. By E. Thomas Gilliard. 421-488, Apr. 1953

A New Light Dawns on Bird Photography. By Arthur A. Allen. 774-790, June 1948
Included: Dynamics of bird flight

Peerless Nepal—A Naturalist's Paradise. By S. Dillon Ripley. Photos by Volkmar Wentzel. 1-40, Jan. 1950
Included: National Geographic Society-Yale University-Smithsonian Institution Expedition's rediscovery of the Spiny babbler and unsuccessful search for the Mountain quail; other birds noted and collected: Bush larks, Darjeeling woodpeckers, Flycatchers, Hedge sparrows, Hill partridges, Mergansers, Rose finches, Rufous-chinned laughing thrushes, Slaty-headed parakeets, Warblers, White-throated laughing thrushes, Yellow-billed blue magpies

Peru Profits from Sea Fowl. By Robert Cushman Murphy. Photos by author and Grace E. Barstow Murphy. 395-413, Mar. 1959

Pilgrimage to Holy Island and the Farnes. By John E. H. Nolan. 547-570, Oct. 1952
Included: Cormorants, Guillemots, St. Cuthbert's duck (Eider), Terns

Rare Birds Flock To Spain's Marismas. By Roger Tory Peterson. 397-425, Mar. 1958

Safari Through Changing Africa. By Elsie May Bell Grosvenor. Photos by Gilbert Grosvenor. 145-198, Aug. 1953

Saving Man's Wildlife Heritage. By John H. Baker. Photos by Robert F. Sisson. 581-620, Nov. 1954

Sea Bird Cities Off Audubon's Labrador. By Arthur A. Allen. 755-774, June 1948

Sea Birds of Isla Raza. By Lewis Wayne Walker. 239-248, Feb. 1951

Seeing Birds as Real Personalities. By Hance Roy Ivor. 523-530, Apr. 1954
Contents: Albino robins, Blue jays, Bluebirds, Cardinals, Chickadees, Cowbirds, European blackbirds, Mourning doves, Orioles, Robins, Rose-breasted grosbeaks, Thrushes, Waxwings, White doves
Bluebirds on the Wing in Color. Photos by Bernard Corby and author. 527-530

Seeking Mindanao's Strangest Creatures. By Charles Heizer Wharton. 389-408, Sept. 1948
Included: Crested serpent eagle, Hornbill, Monkey-eating eagle

Song and Garden Birds of North America. Book announced. 553-557, Oct. 1964

Split Seconds in the Lives of Birds. By Arthur A. Allen. 681-706, May 1954

Stalking Central Africa's Wildlife. By T. Donald Carter. Paintings by Walter A. Weber. 264-286, Aug. 1956

Threatened Glories of Everglades National Park. By Frederick Kent Truslow and Frederick G. Vosburgh. Photos by Frederick Kent Truslow and Otis Imboden. 508-553, Oct. 1967

BIRDS—*Continued*

Water, Prey, and Game Birds of North America. Book announced. 529-535, Oct. 1965

Where Two Worlds Meet (Patagonia). Photos by Des and Jen Bartlett. 298-321, Mar. 1976

Wildlife In and Near the Valley of the Moon. By H. H. Arnold. Photos by Paul J. Fair. 401-414, Mar. 1950

Wildlife of Everglades National Park. By Daniel B. Beard. Paintings by Walter A. Weber. 83-116, Jan. 1949

Wildlife of Mount McKinley National Park. By Adolph Murie. Paintings by Walter A. Weber. 249-270, Aug. 1953

Winged World (Television film). 877A-877B, Dec. 1967

See also Aepyornis; Albatrosses; Andean Condors; Araucana Chickens; Birds of Paradise; Black Eagles; Bowerbirds; Brown Pelicans; Cock-of-the-Rock; Cooper's Hawk; Ducks; Eagles; Egrets; Egyptian Vulture; Flamingos; Fowl; Geese; Golden Eagles; Herons; Hoatzin; Honey-Guide; Hornbills; Hummingbirds; Ibises; Kingfishers; Kites; Kiwi; Limpkin; Lorikeets; Lyrebird; Nene; Oilbirds; Orioles; Ospreys; Penguins; Pigeons; Poorwill; Puffins; Quetzal; Roseate Spoonbills; Scarlet Ibis; Snow Geese; Spiny Babbler; Stilts; Storks; Swans; Takahe; Terns; Whistling Swans; Whooping Cranes; Wood Storks; Woodpeckers; *and* Bird Sanctuaries and Rookeries

BIRDS OF PARADISE:

Feathered Dancers of Little Tobago. By E. Thomas Gilliard. Photos by Frederick Kent Truslow. 428-440, Sept. 1958

New Guinea's Paradise of Birds. By E. Thomas Gilliard. 661-688, Nov. 1951

New Guinea's Rare Birds and Stone Age Men. By E. Thomas Gilliard. 421-488, Apr. 1953

Strange Courtship of Birds of Paradise. By S. Dillon Ripley. Paintings by Walter A. Weber. 247-278, Feb. 1950

To the Land of the Head-hunters. By E. Thomas Gilliard. 437-486, Oct. 1955

BIRTHPLACE of Telephone Magic. Photos by Willard R. Culver. 289-312, Mar. 1947

BISCH, JØRGEN: Author-Photographer:

This Is the China I Saw. 591-639, Nov. 1964

BISHOP, BARRY C.:

President Kennedy Presents the Hubbard Medal. 514-515, Oct. 1963

Author

Landsat Looks at Hometown Earth. 140-147, July 1976

Author-Photographer

How We Climbed Everest. 477-507, Oct. 1963

Karnali, Roadless World of Western Nepal. By Lila M. and Barry C. Bishop. 656-689, Nov. 1971

Mount Rainier: Testing Ground for Everest. 688-711, May 1963

Wintering on the Roof of the World (Himalayas). 503-547, Oct. 1962

Photographer

American and Geographic Flags Top Everest. By Melvin M. Payne. 157-157C, Aug. 1963

Six to the Summit (Everest). By Norman G. Dyhrenfurth. 460-473, Oct. 1963

BISHOP, BARRY C.: Photographer—*Continued*

We Climbed Utah's Skyscraper Rock. By Huntley Ingalls. Photos by author and Barry C. Bishop. 705-721, Nov. 1962

BISHOP, LILA M.: Author-Photographer:

Karnali, Roadless World of Western Nepal. By Lila M. and Barry C. Bishop. 656-689, Nov. 1971

BISITUN, Mount, Iran:

Darius Carved History on Ageless Rock. By George G. Cameron. 825-844, Dec. 1950

BISMARCK ARCHIPELAGO. *See* New Britain

BISON, American:

Hays, Kansas, at the Nation's Heart. By Margaret M. Detwiler. Photos by John E. Fletcher. 461-490, Apr. 1952

Springtime Comes to Yellowstone National Park. By Paul A. Zahl. 761-779, Dec. 1956

The Wichitas: Land of the Living Prairie. By M. Woodbridge Williams. 661-697, May 1957

Yellowstone Wildlife in Winter. By William Albert Allard. 637-661, Nov. 1967

A BIT of Old Russia Takes Root in Alaska: Nikolaevsk. By Jim Rearden. Photos by Charles O'Rear. 401-425, Sept. 1972

The BITTERSWEET Waters of the Lower Colorado. By Rowe Findley. Photos by Charles O'Rear. 540-569, Oct. 1973

BITTINGER, CHARLES: Artist:

Operation Crossroads. Photos by Joint Task Force I. 519-530, Apr. 1947

BIZARRE World of the Fungi. By Paul A. Zahl. 502-527, Oct. 1965

BLACK BEARS:

Studying Wildlife by Satellite. By Frank Craighead, Jr. and John Craighead. 120-123, Jan. 1973

BLACK EAGLES:

Adventures With South Africa's Black Eagles. By Jeanne Cowden. Photos by author and Arthur Bowland. 533-543, Oct. 1969

BLACK HILLS, South Dakota:

Back to the Historic Black Hills. By Leland D. Case. Photos by Bates Littlehales. 479-509, Oct. 1956

South Dakota Keeps Its West Wild. By Frederick Simpich. 555-588, May 1947
Over Plains and Hills of South Dakota. Photos by J. Baylor Roberts. 563-586

BLACKBEARD (Island), Georgia:

Sea Islands: Adventuring Along the South's Surprising Coast. By James Cerruti. Photos by Thomas Nebbia and James L. Amos. 366-393, Mar. 1971

BLACKSTONE, WILLIAM:

The British Way. By Sir Evelyn Wrench. 421-541, Apr. 1949

BLAIR, JAMES P.: Author-Photographer:

Home to Lonely Tristan da Cunha. 60-81, Jan. 1964

BLAIR, JAMES P.—*Continued*
Photographer

Afo-A-Kom: A Sacred Symbol Comes Home. By William S. Ellis. 141-148, July 1974

Ambassadors of Good Will: The Peace Corps. By Sargent Shriver and Peace Corps Volunteers. 297-345, Sept. 1964

California, the Golden Magnet: II. Nature's North. By William Graves. Photos by James P. Blair and Jonathan S. Blair. 641-679, May 1966

California's San Andreas Fault. By Thomas Y. Canby. 38-53, Jan. 1973

Cape Cod's Circle of Seasons. By Tom Melham. 40-65, July 1975

Crystals, Magical Servants of the Space Age. By Kenneth F. Weaver. 278-296, Aug. 1968

Czechoslovakia: The Dream and the Reality. By Edward J. Linehan. 151-193, Feb. 1968

Ethiopian Adventure. By Nathaniel T. Kenney. 548-582, Apr. 1965

The Fair Reopens (New York World's Fair, 1964-1965). Text by Carolyn Bennett Patterson. 505-529, Apr. 1965

Florida Rides a Space-age Boom. By Benedict Thielen. Photos by Winfield Parks and James P. Blair. 858-903, Dec. 1963

Freedom Speaks French in Ouagadougou. By John Scofield. 153-203, Aug. 1966

From Sun-clad Sea to Shining Mountains. By Ralph Gray. 542-589, Apr. 1964

Gettysburg and Vicksburg: the Battle Towns Today. By Robert Paul Jordan. Map notes by Carolyn Bennett Patterson. 4-57, July 1963

In the Crusaders' Footsteps. By Franc Shor. Photos by Thomas Nebbia and James P. Blair. 731-789, June 1962

The Incredible Universe. By Kenneth F. Weaver. 589-625, May 1974

India's Energetic Sikhs. By John E. Frazer. 528-541, Oct. 1972

Iran: Desert Miracle. By William Graves. 2-47, Jan. 1975

The Man Who Talks to Hummingbirds. By Luis Marden. 80-99, Jan. 1963

Martha's Vineyard. By William P. E. Graves. 778-809, June 1961

New Grandeur for Flowering Washington. By Joseph Judge. 500-539, Apr. 1967

New National Park Proposed: The Spectacular North Cascades. By Nathaniel T. Kenney. 642-667, May 1968

One Man's London. By Allan C. Fisher, Jr. 743-791, June 1966

Orissa, Past and Promise in an Indian State. By Bart McDowell. 546-577, Oct. 1970

Pollution, Threat to Man's Only Home. By Gordon Young. 738-781, Dec. 1970

The Revolution in American Agriculture. By Jules B. Billard. 147-185, Feb. 1970

Rotterdam—Reborn From Ruins. By Helen Hill Miller. 526-553, Oct. 1960

Springtime of Hope in Poland. By Peter T. White. 467-501, Apr. 1972

Wild Elephant Roundup in India. By Harry Miller. Photos by author and James P. Blair. 372-385, Mar. 1969

Will Coal Be Tomorrow's "Black Gold"? By Gor-

BLAIR, JAMES P.: Photographer—*Continued*
don Young. 234-259, Aug. 1975
Yugoslavia: Six Republics in One. By Robert Paul Jordan. 589-633, May 1970

BLAIR, JONATHAN S.: Author-Photographer:
Keeping House in a Cappadocian Cave. 127-146, July 1970
Photographer
Ancient Aphrodisias and Its Marble Treasures. By Kenan T. Erim. 280-294, Aug. 1967
Aphrodisias, Awakened City of Ancient Art. By Kenan T. Erim. 766-791, June 1972
Barehanded Battle to Cleanse the Bay. By Peter T. White. 866-881, June 1971
California, the Golden Magnet: II. Nature's North. By William Graves. Photos by James P. Blair and Jonathan S. Blair. 641-679, May 1966
Cyprus Under Four Flags: A Struggle for Unity. By Kenneth MacLeish. 356-383, Mar. 1973
Dry-land Fleet Sails the Sahara. By Jean du Boucher. 696-725, Nov. 1967
Florida's Booming—and Beleaguered—Heartland. By Joseph Judge. 585-621, Nov. 1973
Home to the Enduring Berkshires. By Charles McCarry. 196-221, Aug. 1970
Madeira, Like Its Wine, Improves With Age. By Veronica Thomas. 488-513, Apr. 1973
New Life for the Troubled Suez Canal. By William Graves. 792-817, June 1975
On the Road With an Old-time Circus. By John Fetterman. 410-434, Mar. 1972
Riding the Outlaw Trail. By Robert Redford. 622-657, Nov. 1976
Sicily, Where All the Songs Are Sad. By Howard La Fay. 407-436, Mar. 1976
Stockholm, Where "Kvalitet" Is a Way of Life. By James Cerruti. Photos by Albert Moldvay and Jonathan Blair. 43-69, Jan. 1976
Yellowstone at 100: The Pitfalls of Success. By William S. Ellis. 616-631, May 1972

BLESSING OF THE FLEET:
Gloucester Blesses Its Portuguese Fleet. By Luis Marden. 75-84, July 1953

BLIGH, WILLIAM:
Huzza for Otaheite! By Luis Marden. 435-459, Apr. 1962
I Found the Bones of the *Bounty*. By Luis Marden. 725-789, Dec. 1957
Tahiti, "Finest Island in the World." By Luis Marden. 1-47, July 1962

BLIZZARD of Birds: The Tortugas Terns. By Alexander Sprunt, Jr. 213-230, Feb. 1947

BLOOD, NED: Photographer:
Sheep Airlift in New Guinea. 831-844, Dec. 1949

BLOSSOMS That Defy the Seasons. By Geneal Condon. Photos by David S. Boyer. 420-427, Sept. 1958

BLOWGUN Hunters of the South Pacific. By Jane C. Goodale. Photos by Ann Chowning. 793-817, June 1966

BLUE CRABS:
Can We Save Our Salt Marshes? By Stephen W. Hitchcock. Photos by William R. Curtsinger. 729-765, June 1972

BLUE CRABS—*Continued*
This Is My Island, Tangier (Virginia). By Harold G. Wheatley. Photos by David Alan Harvey. 700-725, Nov. 1973

BLUE-EYED Indian: A City Boy's Sojourn with Primitive Tribesmen in Central Brazil. By Harald Schultz. 65-89, July 1961

BLUE HOLES, Great Bahama Bank:
Diving Into the Blue Holes of the Bahamas. By George J. Benjamin. 347-363, Sept. 1970

BLUE RIDGE (Mountains), U. S.:
Appalachian Valley Pilgrimage. By Catherine Bell Palmer. Photos by Justin Locke. 1-32, July 1949
My Neighbors Hold to Mountain Ways. By Malcolm Ross. Photos by Flip Schulke. 856-880, June 1958
Shenandoah, I Long to Hear You. By Mike W. Edwards. Photos by Thomas Anthony DeFeo. 554-588, Apr. 1970
Skyline Trail from Maine to Georgia. By Andrew H. Brown. Photos by Robert F. Sisson. 219-251, Aug. 1949
The Virginians. By Mike W. Edwards. Photos by David Alan Harvey. 588-617, Nov. 1974

BLUE-WATER Plankton: Ghosts of the Gulf Stream. By William M. Hamner. 530-545, Oct. 1974

BLUEBIRDS:
Seeing Birds as Real Personalities. By Hance Roy Ivor. 523-530, Apr. 1954
Bluebirds on the Wing in Color. Photos by Bernard Corby and author. 527-530

BLUEGRASS (Region), Kentucky:
Heart of the Bluegrass. By Charles McCarry. Photos by J. Bruce Baumann. 634-659, May 1974

BOAT RACES:
By Square-rigger from Baltic to Bicentennial. By Kenneth Garrett. 824-857, Dec. 1976
Down East to Nova Scotia. By Winfield Parks. 853-879, June 1964
Included: Marblehead-Halifax race; Bras d'Or Lakes 15-mile race for the McCurdy Cup; Jones Trophy for Canadian yachts
To Europe with a Racing Start. By Carleton Mitchell. 758-791, June 1958
Included: Newport-to-Bermuda race
See also Yachting

BOATS:
California's Surprising Inland Delta. By Judith and Neil Morgan. Photos by Charles O'Rear. 409-430, Sept. 1976
"Delmarva," Gift of the Sea. By Catherine Bell Palmer. 367-399, Sept. 1950
Included: Chesapeake Bay boats: Bugeyes, Hampton-class sloops, Log canoes, Skipjacks
Here's New York Harbor. By Stuart E. Jones. Photos by Robert F. Sisson and David S. Boyer. 773-813, Dec. 1954
Inflatable Ship *(Amphitrite)* Opens Era of Airborne Undersea Expeditions. By Jacques-Yves Cousteau. 142-148, July 1961
The Lower Mississippi. By Willard Price. Photos by W. D. Vaughn. 681-725, Nov. 1960
On the Winds of the Dodecanese. By Jean and Franc Shor. 351-390, Mar. 1953

BOATS—*Continued*

Ships Through the Ages: A Saga of the Sea. By Alan Villiers. 494-545, Apr. 1963
Included: Small craft, precursors of the ship

Shooting Rapids in Reverse! Jet Boats Climb the Colorado's Torrent Through the Grand Canyon. By William Belknap, Jr. 552-565, Apr. 1962

The Thames Mirrors England's Varied Life. By Willard Price. Photos by Robert F. Sisson. 45-93, July 1958

Trawling the China Seas. Photos by J. Charles Thompson. 381-395, Mar. 1950
Contents: Junks, Sampans

The Upper Mississippi. By Willard Price. 651-699, Nov. 1958

Windjamming Around New England. By Tom Horgan. Photos by Robert F. Sisson. 141-169, Aug. 1950
Contents: "Brutal Beasts," Cape Cod Baby Knockabouts, Dinghies, International 210-class sloops, Lightning-class sloops

See also Barges; Canoe Trips; Coracles; Cruises and Voyages; Dhows; Dories; Dugout Canoes; Ferries; Fishing Industry; Foldboats; Hydrofoil Boats; Kayaks; Sailing Vessels; listings under Steamboats, Yachts, Yawls; *and Bounty; J. W. Westcott; River Gypsy*

BOCAIUVA, Brazil:

Eclipse Hunting in Brazil's Ranchland. By F. Barrows Colton. 285-324, Sept. 1947

BODIE ISLAND, North Carolina:

Lonely Cape Hatteras, Besieged by the Sea. By William S. Ellis. Photos by Emory Kristof. 393-421, Sept. 1969

BOLD Horsemen of the Steppes. By Sabrina and Roland Michaud. 634-669, Nov. 1973

A BOLD New Look at Our Past. The Editor. 62-63, Jan. 1975

BOLIVIA:

Amazon—The River Sea. By Loren McIntyre. 456-495, Oct. 1972

Ambassadors of Good Will: The Peace Corps. By Sargent Shriver and Peace Corps Volunteers. 297-345, Sept. 1964
Bolivia. By Edward S. Dennison. 315-319

Flamboyant Is the Word for Bolivia. By Loren McIntyre. 153-195, Feb. 1966

In Quest of the Rarest Flamingo. By William G. Conway. Photos by Bates Littlehales. 91-105, July 1961

Puya, the Pineapple's Andean Ancestor. By Mulford B. Foster. 463-480, Oct. 1950

Sky-high Bolivia. 481-496, Oct. 1950

See also Titicaca, Lake

BOMBERS:

Flying in the "Blowtorch" Era. By Frederick G. Vosburgh. 281-322, Sept. 1950

Fun Helped Them Fight. By Stuart E. Jones. 95-104, Jan. 1948

Our Air Age Speeds Ahead. By F. Barrows Colton. 249-272, Feb. 1948

BONAIRE (Island), Netherlands Antilles:

The Netherlands Antilles: Holland in the Caribbean. By James Cerruti. Photos by Emory Kristof. 115-146, Jan. 1970

BONAPARTE, NAPOLEON. *See* Napoleon I

BOND, WILLIAM H.: Artist:

Have We Solved the Mysteries of the Moon? By Kenneth F. Weaver. 309-325, Sept. 1973

"How Man Pollutes His World," painting supplement. Text notes by Gordon Young. World map on reverse. Dec. 1970

BONDAS (Tribespeople):

Orissa, Past and Promise in an Indian State. By Bart McDowell. Photos by James P. Blair. 546-577, Oct. 1970

BONIN ISLANDS, North Pacific Ocean:

The Bonins and Iwo Jima Go Back to Japan. By Paul Sampson. Photos by Joe Munroe. 128-144, July 1968

BOOBIES:

Peru Profits from Sea Fowl. By Robert Cushman Murphy. Photos by author and Grace E. Barstow Murphy. 395-413, Mar. 1959

BOOKS, NGS:

The Age of Chivalry. 544-551, Oct. 1969; 592, Oct. 1970

Alaskan Glacier Studies (1914). 196, Feb. 1967

America's Historylands, Landmarks of Liberty. 360-363, Mar. 1962

America's Wonderlands, the National Parks. 558-561, Oct. 1959; 562-563, Oct. 1961

The Book of Birds, 2 vols. (1932). 328, Sept. 1948; 576, 578, Oct. 1963; 554, Oct. 1964; 480, Oct. 1966

The Book of Dogs. 441-442, Sept. 1958
Note: The title of the revised edition (1966) is *Man's Best Friend.*

The Book of Fishes (1952). 418, Mar. 1957; 440, Mar. 1960; 563, Oct. 1961

Everyday Life in Ancient Times (1951). 766, June 1954; 563, Oct. 1961

Everyday Life in Bible Times. 494-507, Oct. 1967

Great Adventures With National Geographic. 729-733, Nov. 1963

Great Religions of the World. 587-590, Oct. 1971

Greece and Rome: Builders of Our World. 550-567, Oct. 1968; 592, Oct. 1970

Hunting Wild Life with Camera and Flashlight (1935). 296, Mar. 1952

Indians of the Americas (1955). 418, Mar. 1957; 781, June 1959

The Marvels of Animal Behavior. 588-590, Oct. 1972

Men, Ships, and the Sea. 552-555, Oct. 1962

The National Geographic Society and Its Magazine: A History (1957). 582A, Oct. 1957; 408, Sept. 1959; 880, Dec. 1964

The New America's Wonderlands. 436-438, Mar. 1975

Our Continent: A Natural History of North America. 572-574, Oct. 1976

The Renaissance: Maker of Modern Man. 588-592, Oct. 1970

Song and Garden Birds of North America. 553-557, Oct. 1964

Stalking Birds with Color Camera (1951). 437, Oct. 1955; 562-563, Oct. 1961; 532, Apr. 1962; 147, Jan. 1969

This England. 539-543, Oct. 1966

Vacationland U.S.A. 734-740, May 1970; 573, Apr. 1973

BOOKS, NGS—*Continued*

Water, Prey, and Game Birds of North America.
529-535, Oct. 1965

We Americans. 580-582, Oct. 1975

Wild Animals of North America. 554-557, Oct. 1960

Wilderness U.S.A. 582-584, Oct. 1973

Wondrous World of Fishes. 388-393, Mar. 1965

The World in Your Garden. 729-730, May 1957

The World of the American Indian. 584-586, Oct.
1974

Children's Books

First series *(Dinosaurs; Treasures in the Sea; Dogs
Working for People; Lion Cubs).* 736-738, Nov.
1972

Second series *(Honeybees; How Animals Hide;
Namu; Pandas).* 726-728, Nov. 1973

Third series *(Cats: Little Tigers in Your House;
Creepy Crawly Things: Reptiles and Amphibians;
Three Little Indians; Spiders).* 728-730, Nov.
1974

Fourth series *(The Wild Ponies of Assateague Island; A Day in the Woods; Tricks Animals Play;
Cowboys).* 724-726, Nov. 1975

Fifth series *(The Playful Dolphins; Animals that
Build their Homes; Camping Adventure; Wonders of the Desert World).* 718-720, Nov. 1976

Public Service Books

Equal Justice Under Law, Supreme Court book.
Published in cooperation with The Foundation of
the Federal Bar Association. 411, Mar. 1966;
586, Oct. 1967

George Washington—Man and Monument. Published in cooperation with the Washington National Monument Association. 586, Oct. 1967

The Living White House. Published in cooperation
with the White House Historical Association.
641, Nov. 1966; 586, Oct. 1967

We, the People, Capitol guidebook. Published in
cooperation with the United States Capitol Historical Society. 1, 2, Jan. 1964; 411, Mar. 1966;
586, Oct. 1967

The White House, guidebook. Published in cooperation with the White House Historical Association. 888-893, Dec. 1962; 1, Jan. 1964; 331,
Mar. 1964; 642, Nov. 1964; 108, Jan. 1966; 411,
Mar. 1966; 59, July 1966; 585, 586, Oct. 1967

Research Reports

1890-1954 Projects. 442, Sept. 1975

1955-1960 Projects. 444, Sept. 1972

1963 Projects. 296, Aug. 1968

1964 Projects. 300, Aug. 1969

1965 Projects. 148, July 1971

1966 Projects. 146, July 1973

1967 Projects. 148, July 1974

1968 Projects. 296, Aug. 1976

Special Publications

Alaska. 880-884, June 1969

Alaska: High Roads to Adventure. 860-864, June
1976

The Alps. 870-874, June 1972

The Amazing Universe. 870-874, June 1975

The American Cowboy in Life and Legend. 882-886,
June 1971

American Mountain People. 865-868, June 1973

America's Beginnings. 870-874, June 1974

America's Inland Waterway. 865-868, June 1973

BOOKS, NGS—*Continued*

Animals of East Africa. 844-849, June 1968

The Appalachian Trail. 870-874, June 1972

*As We Live and Breathe: The Challenge of Our En-
vironment.* 882-886, June 1971

Australia. 844-849, June 1968

The Civil War. 880-884, June 1969

Clues to America's Past. 860-864, June 1976

The Craftsman in America. 870-874, June 1975

Discovering Man's Past in the Americas. 880-884,
June 1969

Exploring Canada From Sea to Sea. 868-875, June
1967

Exploring the Amazon. 880-884, June 1969

Great American Deserts. 870-874, June 1972

Gypsies, Wanderers of the World. 880-884, June
1970

Hawaii. 880-884, June 1970

In the Footsteps of Lewis and Clark. 880-884, June
1970

The Incredible Incas and Their Timeless Land. 870-
874, June 1975

Isles of the Caribbees. 408-417, Mar. 1966

Isles of the South Pacific. 868-875, June 1967

John Muir's Wild America. 860-864, June 1976

Life in Rural America. 870-874, June 1974

The Majestic Rocky Mountains. 870-874, June
1975

Man's Conquest of Space. 844-849, June 1968

The Mighty Mississippi. 882-886, June 1971

My Friends the Wild Chimpanzees. 408-417, Mar.
1966

Nomads of the World. 882-886, June 1971

Our Country's Presidents. 408-417, Mar. 1966

The Pacific Crest Trail. 870-874, June 1974

Primitive Worlds. 865-868, June 1973

Railroads: The Great American Adventure. 860-
864, June 1976

*The Revolutionary War: America's Fight for Free-
dom.* 868-875, June 1967

The River Nile. 408-417, Mar. 1966

Those Inventive Americans. 880-884, June 1970

Undersea Treasures. 870-874, June 1974

Vanishing Peoples of the Earth. 844-849, June 1968

Vanishing Wildlife of North America. 865-868,
June 1973

The Vikings. 870-874, June 1972

World Beneath the Sea. 868-875, June 1967

See also Atlases; National Geographic Magazine:
Indexes

BOOM on San Francisco Bay. By Franc Shor. Photos
by David S. Boyer. 181-226, Aug. 1956

BOOM Time in Kuwait. By Paul Edward Case. 783-
802, Dec. 1952

The BOOMING Sport of Water Skiing. By Wilbur E.
Garrett. 700-711, Nov. 1958

BOOMS. See Dhows

BOOTH, JOHN WILKES:

The Lights Are Up at Ford's Theatre. By Lonnelle
Aikman. 392-401, Mar. 1970

BOOTH, WINDSOR P.: Author:

Disaster in Paradise (Bali). Photos by Robert F. Sisson. 436-447, Sept. 1963

BOOTHBAY HARBOR, Maine:

Seashore Summer. By Arline Strong. 436-444, Sept. 1960

BORAH, LEO A.: Author:

From Sagebrush to Roses on the Columbia. 571-611, Nov. 1952

Illinois—Healthy Heart of the Nation. Photos by B. Anthony Stewart and Willard R. Culver. 781-820, Dec. 1953

Landmarks of Literary England. Photos by Kathleen Revis. 295-350, Sept. 1955

Montana, Shining Mountain Treasureland. 693-736, June 1950

North Dakota Comes into Its Own. Photos by J. Baylor Roberts. 283-322, Sept. 1951

Ohio Makes Its Own Prosperity. Photos by B. Anthony Stewart. 435-484, Apr. 1955

BOREN, LAMAR: Photographer:

Goggle Fishing in California Waters. By David Hellyer. 615-632, May 1949

BORMAN, FRANK:

Hubbard Medal recipient. 861, June 1970

"A Most Fantastic Voyage": The Story of Apollo 8's Rendezvous With the Moon. By Sam C. Phillips. 593-631, May 1969

Sounds of the Space Age, from Sputnik to Lunar Landing. Record narrated by Frank Borman. 750-751, Dec. 1969

Space Rendezvous, Milestone on the Way to the Moon. By Kenneth F. Weaver. 539-553, Apr. 1966

BORN Hunters, the Bird Dogs. By Roland Kilbon. Paintings by Walter A. Weber. 369-398, Sept. 1947

BORNEO (Island). *See* Brunei; Sabah (North Borneo); Sarawak; Tanjung Puting Reserve

BORNHOLM (Island), Denmark:

Baltic Cruise of the *Caribbee*. By Carleton Mitchell. 605-646, Nov. 1950

2,000 Miles Through Europe's Oldest Kingdom. By Isobel Wylie Hutchison. Photos by Maynard Owen Williams. 141-180, Feb. 1949

BORTON, NAN and JAMES W.: Authors:

Ambassadors of Good Will: The Peace Corps. By Sargent Shriver and Peace Corps Volunteers. 297-345, Sept. 1964
Turkey. 331-333

BOSNIA-HERCEGOVINA (Republic), Yugoslavia:

Yugoslavia: Six Republics in One. By Robert Paul Jordan. Photos by James P. Blair. 589-633, May 1970

BOSTELMANN, ELSE: Artist:

How Fruit Came to America. By J. R. Magness. 325-377, Sept. 1951

Our Vegetable Travelers. By Victor R. Boswell. 145-217, Aug. 1949

The World in Your Garden (Flowers). By W. H. Camp. 1-65, July 1947

BOSTON, England:

The Original Boston: St. Botolph's Town. By Veronica Thomas. Photos by James L. Amos. 382-389, Sept. 1974

BOSTON, Massachusetts:

Benjamin Franklin, Philosopher of Dissent. By Alice J. Hall. Photos by Linda Bartlett. 93-123, July 1975

Firebrands of the Revolution. By Eric F. Goldman. Photos by George F. Mobley. 2-27, July 1974

Literary Landmarks of Massachusetts. By William H. Nicholas. Photos by B. Anthony Stewart and John E. Fletcher. 279-310, Mar. 1950

Massachusetts Builds for Tomorrow. By Robert de Roos. Photos by B. Anthony Stewart. 790-843, Dec. 1966

The Post Road Today. Photos by B. Anthony Stewart. 206-233, Aug. 1962

Those Proper and Other Bostonians. By Joseph Judge. Photos by Ted Spiegel. 352-381, Sept. 1974

The Wonder City That Moves by Night (Circus). By Francis Beverly Kelley. 289-324, Mar. 1948

BOSTON POST ROADS:

The Old Boston Post Roads. By Donald Barr Chidsey. 189-205, Aug. 1962

The Post Road Today. Photos by B. Anthony Stewart. 206-233, Aug. 1962

BOSWELL, VICTOR R.: Author:

Our Vegetable Travelers. Paintings by Else Bostelmann. 145-217, Aug. 1949

BOSWELL, VICTOR R., Jr.: Photographer:

The Magic Lure of Sea Shells. By Paul A. Zahl. Photos by Victor R. Boswell, Jr. and author. 386-429, Mar. 1969

900 Years Ago: the Norman Conquest. By Kenneth M. Setton. Photos by George F. Mobley. The complete Bayeux Tapestry photographed by Milton A. Ford and Victor R. Boswell, Jr. 206-251, Aug. 1966

Venice's Golden Legacy. 609-619, Nov. 1972

BOTANICAL EXPLORERS. *See* Agricultural and Botanical Explorers

BOTANICAL GARDENS. *See* Longwood Gardens; Royal Botanic Gardens

BOTTOM SCRATCHERS CLUB:

Goggle Fishing in California Waters. By David Hellyer. Photos by Lamar Boren. 615-632, May 1949

BOUCHAGE, LUC: Author:

Mysore Celebrates the Death of a Demon. Photos by Ylla. 706-711, May 1958

BOUCHER, JEAN DU: Author:

Dry-land Fleet Sails the Sahara. Photos by Jonathan S. Blair. 696-725, Nov. 1967

BOUNTY, H.M.S.:

Bounty Descendants Live on Remote Norfolk Island. By T. C. Roughley. Photos by J. Baylor Roberts. 559-584, Oct. 1960

Huzza for Otaheite! By Luis Marden. 435-459, Apr. 1962

I Found the Bones of the *Bounty*. By Luis Marden. 725-789, Dec. 1957

BOUNTY, H.M.S. (Replica):

Huzza for Otaheite! By Luis Marden. 435-459, Apr. 1962

Tahiti, "Finest Island in the World." By Luis Marden. 1-47, July 1962

BOURDILLON, TOM:

Triumph on Everest. 1-63, July 1954
I. Siege and Assault. By Sir John Hunt. 1-43
II. The Conquest of the Summit. By Sir Edmund Hillary. 45-63

BOW (River), Canada:

On the Ridgepole of the Rockies. By Walter Meayers Edwards. 745-780, June 1947

BOWDITCH, NATHANIEL:

Literary Landmarks of Massachusetts. By William H. Nicholas. Photos by B. Anthony Stewart and John E. Fletcher. 279-310, Mar. 1950

BOWEN, IRA SPRAGUE: Author:

Completing the Atlas of the Universe. 185-190, Aug. 1955
Sky Survey Plates Unlock Secrets of the Stars. 186-187

Sky Survey Charts the Universe. 780-781, Dec. 1956

BOWERBIRDS:

Australia's Amazing Bowerbirds. By Norman Chaffer. 866-873, Dec. 1961

BOWES, ANNE LaBASTILLE: Author:

The Quetzal, Fabulous Bird of Maya Land. Photos by David G. Allen. 141-150, Jan. 1969
See also LaBastille, Anne

BOWHEAD WHALES:

The Last U. S. Whale Hunters. By Emory Kristof. 346-355, Mar. 1973
"Ocean mammals are to us what the buffalo was to the Plains Indian." By Lael Morgan. 354-355

BOWIE, BEVERLEY M.:

Memorial Tribute to Beverley M. Bowie (1914-1958). 214, Feb. 1959

Author

Bermuda, Cradled in Warm Seas. Photos by Charles Allmon. 203-238, Feb. 1954

Building a New Austria. Photos by Volkmar Wentzel. 172-213, Feb. 1959

'Known but to God' (Unknown Heroes). 593-605, Nov. 1958

MATS: America's Long Arm of the Air. Photos by Robert F. Sisson. 283-317, Mar. 1957

New England, a Modern Pilgrim's Pride. 733-796, June 1955

Off the Beaten Track of Empire (Prince Philip's Tour). Photos by Michael Parker. 584-626, Nov. 1957

The Past Is Present in Greenfield Village (Henry Ford Museum). Photos by Neal P. Davis and Willard R. Culver. 96-127, July 1958

Salzkammergut, Austria's Alpine Playground. Photos by Volkmar Wentzel. 246-275, Aug. 1960

This Young Giant, Indonesia. Photos by J. Baylor Roberts. 351-392, Sept. 1955

Triumph on Everest: II. The Conquest of the Summit. By Sir Edmund Hillary. 45-63, July 1954

BOWIE, BEVERLEY M.: Author—*Continued*

Note: Sir Edmund related his personal narrative to Beverley M. Bowie.

The White Horses of Vienna. Photos by Volkmar Wentzel. 400-419, Sept. 1958

Williamsburg: Its College and Its Cinderella City. 439-486, Oct. 1954

Wisconsin, Land of the Good Life. Photos by Volkmar Wentzel. 141-187, Feb. 1957

BOWLAND, ARTHUR: Photographer:

Adventures With South Africa's Black Eagles. By Jeanne Cowden. Photos by author and Arthur Bowland. 533-543, Oct. 1969

BOY SCOUTS:

Philmont Scout Ranch Helps Boys Grow Up. By Andrew H. Brown. 399-416, Sept. 1956

Washington Lives Again at Valley Forge. By Howell Walker. 187-202, Feb. 1954
Included: Boy Scout Jamboree

BOYER, DAVID S.: Author:

Huntington Library, California Treasure House. 251-276, Feb. 1958

Micronesia: The Americanization of Eden. 702-744, May 1967

Portugal's Gem of the Ocean: Madeira. 364-394, Mar. 1959

Author-Photographer

Alberta Unearths Her Buried Treasures. 90-119, July 1960

British Columbia: Life Begins at 100. 147-189, Aug. 1958

The Canadian North: Emerging Giant. 1-43, July 1968

Geographical Twins (Holy Land and Utah) a World Apart. 848-859, Dec. 1958

The Glittering World of Rockhounds. 276-294, Feb. 1974

Jerusalem to Rome in the Path of St. Paul. 707-759, Dec. 1956

Kitimat—Canada's Aluminum Titan. 376-398, Sept. 1956

Minnesota, Where Water Is the Magic Word. Photos by author and David Brill. 200-229, Feb. 1976

Over and Under Chesapeake Bay. 593-612, Apr. 1964

Paris to Antwerp with the Water Gypsies. 530-559, Oct. 1955

Petra, Rose-red Citadel of Biblical Edom. 853-870, Dec. 1955

Powerhouse of the Northwest (Columbia River). 821-847, Dec. 1974

Rhododendron Glories of Southwest Scotland. Photos by B. Anthony Stewart and author. 641-664, May 1954

Wyoming: High, Wide, and Windy. 554-594, Apr. 1966

Year of Discovery Opens in Antarctica. 339-381, Sept. 1957

Photographer

Ambassadors of Good Will: The Peace Corps. By Sargent Shriver and Peace Corps Volunteers. 297-345, Sept. 1964

Blossoms That Defy the Seasons (Flower Preservation). By Geneal Condon. 420-427, Sept. 1958

Boom on San Francisco Bay. By Franc Shor. 181-

BOYER, DAVID S.: Photographer—*Continued*
226, Aug. 1956

Canada, My Country. By Alan Phillips. Photos by David S. Boyer and Walter Meayers Edwards. 769-819, Dec. 1961

Crusader Lands Revisited. By Harold Lamb. 815-852, Dec. 1954

Eastman of Rochester: Photographic Pioneer. By Allan C. Fisher, Jr. 423-438, Sept. 1954

Flight Into Antarctic Darkness. By J. Lloyd Abbot, Jr. 732-738, Nov. 1967

Fresh Treasures from Egypt's Ancient Sands. By Jefferson Caffery. 611-650, Nov. 1955

Here's New York Harbor. By Stuart E. Jones. Photos by Robert F. Sisson and David S. Boyer. 773-813, Dec. 1954

In the London of the New Queen. By H. V. Morton. 291-342, Sept. 1953

Lake District, Poets' Corner of England. By H. V. Morton. 511-545, Apr. 1956

London's Zoo of Zoos. By Thomas Garner James. 771-786, June 1953

Our Navy's Long Submarine Arm. By Allan C. Fisher, Jr. Photos by David S. Boyer and author. 613-636, Nov. 1952

Relics from the Rapids. By Sigurd F. Olson. 413-435, Sept. 1963

A Stroll to John o'Groat's. By Isobel Wylie Hutchison. 1-48, July 1956

We Are Living at the South Pole. By Paul A. Siple. 5-35, July 1957

BOYLE, ROBERT:
The British Way. By Sir Evelyn Wrench. 421-541, Apr. 1949

BRADFORD, ERNLE: Author:
Democracy's Fortress: Unsinkable Malta. Photos by Ted H. Funk. 852-879, June 1969

The Faeroes, Isles of Maybe. Photos by Adam Woolfitt. 410-442, Sept. 1970

BRADLEY, LA VERNE: Author:
Scenes of Postwar Finland. Photos by Jerry Waller. 233-264, Aug. 1947

BRADSTREET, ANNE:
Literary Landmarks of Massachusetts. By William H. Nicholas. Photos by B. Anthony Stewart and John E. Fletcher. 279-310, Mar. 1950

BRAGG, JOHN: Photographer:
To Torre Egger's Icy Summit. By Jim Donini. 813-823, Dec. 1976

BRAHUI (Tribespeople):
Pakistan, New Nation in an Old Land. By Jean and Franc Shor. 637-678, Nov. 1952

BRAINTREE, England. *See* New Mills

BRAKE, BRIAN: Photographer:
Along the Storied Incense Roads of Aden. By Hermann F. Eilts. 230-254, Feb. 1957

The Emperor's Private Garden: Kashmir. By Nigel Cameron. 606-647, Nov. 1958

Jerusalem, the Divided City. By John Scofield. 492-531, Apr. 1959

New Zealand: Gift of the Sea. By Maurice Shadbolt. 465-511, Apr. 1962

Peking: a Pictorial Record. 194-197, 199-223, Aug. 1960

BRAKE, BRIAN: Photographer—*Continued*
Progress and Pageantry in Changing Nigeria. By W. Robert Moore. 325-365, Sept. 1956

BRAND, VANCE D.:
Apollo-Soyuz: Handclasp in Space. By Thomas Y. Canby. 183-187, Feb. 1976

BRANDENBURG, FRED G.: Photographer:
Desert River (San Juan) Through Navajo Land. By Alfred M. Bailey. Photos by author and Fred G. Brandenburg. 149-172, Aug. 1947

BRANDING:
Cowpunching on the Padlock Ranch. By William Albert Allard. 478-499, Oct. 1973

BRAS D'OR LAKES, Nova Scotia, Canada:
Canada's Winged Victory: the *Silver Dart*. By Gilbert M. Grosvenor. 254-267, Aug. 1959

Down East to Nova Scotia. By Winfield Parks. 853-879, June 1964

BRASÍLIA, Brazil:
Brasília, Metropolis Made to Order. By Hernane Tavares de Sá. Photos by Thomas J. Abercrombie. 704-724, May 1960

Brazil, Ôba! By Peter T. White. Photos by Winfield Parks. 299-353, Sept. 1962

BRAUNS, CLAUS-DIETER: Author-Photographer:
The Peaceful Mrus of Bangladesh. 267-286, Feb. 1973

BRAVING the Atlantic by Balloon. By Arnold Eiloart. 123-146, July 1959

BRAVO (Malamute-Husky):
Antarctic Scientist Honored by The Society. 792-793, June 1958
Note: Bravo is proclaimed a VID (Very Important Dog) and is given an honorable discharge from the U. S. Navy

Man's First Winter at the South Pole. By Paul A. Siple. 439-478, Apr. 1958

BRAVO (Weather Patrol), North Atlantic:
Rugged Is the Word for Bravo. By Philip M. Swatek. 829-843, Dec. 1955

BRAZIL:
The Amazon. Photos by Loren McIntyre. 445-455, Oct. 1972

Amazon (Television film). 295A-295B, Feb. 1968

Amazon—The River Sea. By Loren McIntyre. 456-495, Oct. 1972

Blue-eyed Indian: A City Boy's Sojourn with Primitive Tribesmen in Central Brazil. By Harald Schultz. 65-89, July 1961

Brasília, Metropolis Made to Order. By Hernane Tavares de Sá. Photos by Thomas J. Abercrombie. 704-724, May 1960

Brazil, Ôba! By Peter T. White. Photos by Winfield Parks. 299-353, Sept. 1962

Brazil Protects Her Cinta Larga Indians. By W. Jesco von Puttkamer. 420-444, Sept. 1971

Brazil's Beleaguered Indians. By W. Jesco von Puttkamer. 254-283, Feb. 1975
I. Requiem for a Tribe? (Kreen-Akarores). 254-269
II. Good-bye to the Stone Age (Txukahameis). 270-283

BRAZIL — *Continued*

Brazil's Big-lipped Indians (Suyá). By Harald Schultz. 118-133, Jan. 1962

Brazil's Land of Minerals. By W. Robert Moore. 479-508, Oct. 1948

Children of the Sun and Moon (Kraho Indians). By Harald Schultz. 340-363, Mar. 1959

Drought Bedevils Brazil's Sertão. By John Wilson. Photos by Gordon W. Gahan. 704-723, Nov. 1972

Eclipse Hunting in Brazil's Ranchland. By F. Barrows Colton. Photos by Richard H. Stewart and Guy W. Starling. 285-324, Sept. 1947

Giant Insects of the Amazon. By Paul A. Zahl. 632-669, May 1959

Indians of the Amazon Darkness. By Harald Schultz. 737-758, May 1964

Jungle Jaunt on Amazon Headwaters. By Bernice M. Goetz. 371-388, Sept. 1952

The Jungle Was My Home. By Sasha Siemel. 695-712, Nov. 1952

Parks, Plans, and People: How South America Guards Her Green Legacy. By Mary and Laurance Rockefeller. Photos by George F. Mobley. 74-119, Jan. 1967

Saving Brazil's Stone Age Tribes from Extinction. By Orlando and Claudio Villas Boas. Photos by W. Jesco von Puttkamer. 424-444, Sept. 1968

Sea Fever. By John E. Schultz. 237-268, Feb. 1949

Those Fiery Brazilian Bees. By Rick Gore. Photos by Bianca Lavies. 491-501, Apr. 1976

Tukuna Maidens Come of Age. By Harald Schultz. 629-649, Nov. 1959

The Waurá: Brazilian Indians of the Hidden Xingu. By Harald Schultz. 130-152, Jan. 1966

Your Society Observes Eclipse in Brazil. 661, May 1947

See also Rio de Janeiro

BRAZILIAN BEES:

Those Fiery Brazilian Bees. By Rick Gore. Photos by Bianca Lavies. 491-501, Apr. 1976

BREADFRUIT:

Huzza for Otaheite! By Luis Marden. 435-459, Apr. 1962

Tahiti, "Finest Island in the World." By Luis Marden. 1-47, July 1962

BREAKTHROUGH in Wildlife Studies. By John Craighead. 148-158, July 1976

BRECKENFELD, GURNEY: Photographer:

Sierra High Trip. By David R. Brower. 844-868, June 1954

BREED, JACK: Author:

Better Days for the Navajos. Photos by Charles W. Herbert. 809-847, Dec. 1958

Author-Photographer

First Motor Sortie into Escalante Land. 369-404, Sept. 1949

Land of the Havasupai. 655-674, May 1948

Roaming the West's Fantastic Four Corners. 705-742, June 1952

Shooting Rapids in Dinosaur Country. Photos by author and Justin Locke. 363-390, Mar. 1954

Utah's Arches of Stone. 173-192, Aug. 1947

BREED, JACK — *Continued*

Photographer

Colorado's Friendly Topland (Rocky Mountains). By Robert M. Ormes. 187-214, Aug. 1951

Windjamming Around New England. By Tom Horgan. 141-169, Aug. 1950

BREEDEN, KAY: Author-Photographer:

Eden in the Outback. By Kay and Stanley Breeden. 189-203, Feb. 1973

Rock Paintings of the Aborigines. By Kay and Stanley Breeden. 174-187, Feb. 1973

BREEDEN, STANLEY: Author-Photographer:

Eden in the Outback. By Kay and Stanley Breeden. 189-203, Feb. 1973

Rock Paintings of the Aborigines. By Kay and Stanley Breeden. 174-187, Feb. 1973

Photographer

India Struggles to Save Her Wildlife. By John J. Putman. 299-343, Sept. 1976

Strange Animals of Australia. By David Fleay. 388-411, Sept. 1963

BR'ER Possum, Hermit of the Lowlands. By Agnes Akin Atkinson. Photos by Charles Philip Fox. 405-418, Mar. 1953

BRIDGES:

Cane Bridges of Asia. Photos from Paul Popper. 243-250, Aug. 1948

Over and Under Chesapeake Bay. By David S. Boyer. 593-612, Apr. 1964
Contents: The Chesapeake Bay Bridge-Tunnel

See also Delaware (River), for Delaware Memorial Bridge; Languedoc (Region), France, for Pont du Gard; San Francisco (City and Bay), California

BRIDGES, Natural, and Arches. *See* Arches National Monument; Canyonlands National Park; Escalante Canyon; Natural Bridges National Monument; Rainbow Bridge National Monument; Zion National Park

BRIGANTINE. *See Yankee*

BRIGGS, LYMAN J.:

Eclipse Hunting in Brazil's Ranchland. By F. Barrows Colton. Photos by Richard H. Stewart and Guy W. Starling. 285-324, Sept. 1947

Author

How Old Is It? (Radiocarbon Dating). By Lyman J. Briggs and Kenneth F. Weaver. 234-255, Aug. 1958

Uncle Sam's House of 1,000 Wonders (National Bureau of Standards). By Lyman J. Briggs and F. Barrows Colton. 755-784, Dec. 1951

When Mt. Mazama Lost Its Top: The Birth of Crater Lake. 128-133, July 1962

BRIGHT Dyes Reveal Secrets of Canada Geese. By John and Frank Craighead. 817-832, Dec. 1957

BRILL, DAVID: Photographer:

Chan Chan, Peru's Ancient City of Kings. By Michael E. Moseley and Carol J. Mackey. 318-345, Mar. 1973

Ethiopia Yields First "Family" of Early Man. By Donald C. Johanson. 790-811, Dec. 1976

Minnesota, Where Water Is the Magic Word. By David S. Boyer. Photos by author and David Brill. 200-229, Feb. 1976

BRINDAMOUR, ROD: Photographer:

Orangutans, Indonesia's "People of the Forest." By

BRINDAMOUR, ROD: Photographer—*Continued*
Biruté Galdikas-Brindamour. 444-473, Oct. 1975

BRINGING Old Testament Times to Life. By G. Ernest Wright. Paintings by Henry J. Soulen. 833-864, Dec. 1957

BRISTLE-THIGHED CURLEW:
The Curlew's Secret. By Arthur A. Allen. 751-770, Dec. 1948

BRISTLECONE PINE, Oldest Known Living Thing. By Edmund Schulman. Photos by W. Robert Moore. 355-372, Mar. 1958

BRISTOL, HORACE: Author-Photographer:
Pescadores, Wind-swept Outposts of Formosa. 265-284, Feb. 1956
Photographer
Changing Formosa, Green Island of Refuge. By Frederick Simpich, Jr. 327-364, Mar. 1957
Roaming Korea South of the Iron Curtain. By Enzo de Chetelat. 777-808, June 1950

BRITAIN Tackles the East African Bush. By W. Robert Moore. 311-352, Mar. 1950

The **BRITAIN** That Shakespeare Knew. By Louis B. Wright. Photos by Dean Conger. 613-665, May 1964

BRITAIN'S "French" Channel Islands. By James Cerruti. Photos by James L. Amos. 710-740, May 1971

BRITANNIA (Royal Yacht):
Off the Beaten Track of Empire (Prince Philip's Tour). By Beverley M. Bowie. Photos by Michael Parker. 584-626, Nov. 1957

BRITISH BROADCASTING CORPORATION (B.B.C.): Expedition:
Animal Safari to British Guiana. By David Attenborough. Photos by Charles Lagus and author. 851-874, June 1957

BRITISH Castles, History in Stone. By Norman Wilkinson. 111-129, July 1947

BRITISH COLUMBIA (Province), Canada:
Across Canada by Mackenzie's Track. By Ralph Gray. 191-239, Aug. 1955
Along the Yukon Trail. By Amos Burg. 395-416, Sept. 1953
British Columbia: Life Begins at 100. By David S. Boyer. 147-189, Aug. 1958
Canada's Window on the Pacific: The British Columbia Coast. By Jules B. Billard. Photos by Ted Spiegel. 338-375, Mar. 1972
Canadian Rockies, Lords of a Beckoning Land. By Alan Phillips. Photos by James L. Stanfield. 353-393, Sept. 1966
Endeavour Sails the Inside Passage. By Amos Burg. 801-828, June 1947
From Sun-clad Sea to Shining Mountains. By Ralph Gray. Photos by James P. Blair. 542-589, Apr. 1964
See also Columbia River; Great Divide Trail; Kitimat; *and* Bikepacking

BRITISH COMMONWEALTH OF NATIONS:
H.R.H. The Prince Philip, Duke of Edinburgh, In-

BRITISH COMMONWEALTH OF NATIONS—*Continued*
troduces to Members the Narrative of His Round-the-world Tour. 583-584, Nov. 1957
Off the Beaten Track of Empire (Prince Philip's Tour). By Beverley M. Bowie. Photos by Michael Parker. 584-626, Nov. 1957

BRITISH COMMONWEALTH TRANS-ANTARCTIC EXPEDITION:
The Crossing of Antarctica. By Sir Vivian Fuchs. Photos by George Lowe. 25-47, Jan. 1959
Man's First Winter at the South Pole. By Paul A. Siple. 439-478, Apr. 1958
Society Honors the Conquerors of Antarctica. 589-590, Apr. 1959

BRITISH EAST AFRICA. *See* present names: Kenya; Tanzania; Uganda

BRITISH GUIANA:
Animal Safari to British Guiana. By David Attenborough. Photos by Charles Lagus and author. 851-874, June 1957
Life Among the Wai Wai Indians. By Clifford Evans and Betty J. Meggers. 329-346, Mar. 1955
Strange Courtship of the (Golden) Cock-of-the-Rock. By E. Thomas Gilliard. 134-140, Jan. 1962
Strange Little World of the Hoatzin. By J. Lear Grimmer. Photos by M. Woodbridge Williams. 391-401, Sept. 1962

BRITISH HONDURAS. *See* Belize

BRITISH ISLES:
British Isles, Atlas series supplement. July 1958
The British Isles, map supplement. Apr. 1949
A Traveler's Map of the British Isles, map supplement. Text on reverse. Apr. 1974
See also Arran, Island of; Caldy; Channel Islands; Great Britain; Hebrides; Ireland, Northern; Lundy; Man, Isle of; Orkney Islands; St. Michael's Mount; Scilly, Isles of; Shetland Islands; Skomer; *and* Renaissance; Vikings

BRITISH MOUNT EVEREST EXPEDITION:
Triumph on Everest. 1-64, July 1954
I. Siege and Assault. By Sir John Hunt. 1-43
II. The Conquest of the Summit. By Sir Edmund Hillary. 45-63
III. President Eisenhower Presents the Hubbard Medal to Everest's Conquerors. 64

The **BRITISH** Way: Great Britain's Major Gifts to Freedom, Democratic Government, Science, and Society. By Sir Evelyn Wrench. Paintings from British and American artists. 421-541, Apr. 1949

BRITT, KENT: Author:
The Loyalists. Photos by Ted Spiegel. 510-539, Apr. 1975
Pennsylvania's Old-time Dutch Treat. Photos by H. Edward Kim. 564-578, Apr. 1973

BRITTANY (Region), France:
France Meets the Sea in Brittany. By Howell Walker. 470-503, Apr. 1965

BRITTON, WRIGHT: Author:
Sailing Iceland's Rugged Coasts. Photos by James A. Sugar. 228-265, Aug. 1969

BROADSTAIRS, England:

The England of Charles Dickens. By Richard W. Long. Photos by Adam Woolfitt. 443-483, Apr. 1974

> Included: Dickens Festival; "Bleak House," Dickens's summer home

BROMELIADS:

Hidden Worlds in the Heart of a Plant. By Paul A. Zahl. 389-397, Mar. 1975

Puya, the Pineapple's Andean Ancestor. By Mulford B. Foster. 463-480, Oct. 1950

BRONTOSAURS:

We Captured a 'Live' Brontosaur. By Roland T. Bird. 707-722, May 1954

BRONX ZOO. *See* New York Zoological Park

BRONZE AGE:

Oldest Known Shipwreck Yields Bronze Age Cargo. By Peter Throckmorton. 697-711, May 1962

Thirty-three Centuries Under the Sea (Shipwreck). By Peter Throckmorton. 682-703, May 1960

See also Hoabinhian Culture; Minoan Civilization

BRONZES:

China Unveils Her Newest Treasures. Photos by Robert W. Madden. 848-857, Dec. 1974

Mosaic of Cultures (Southeast Asia). By Peter T. White. Photos by W. E. Garrett. 296-329, Mar. 1971

See also Dreyfus Collection

BROOKFIELD, CHARLES M.: Author:

An Exotic New Oriole Settles in Florida. By Charles M. Brookfield and Oliver Griswold. 261-264, Feb. 1956

Key Largo Coral Reef: America's First Undersea Park. Photos by Jerry Greenberg. 58-69, Jan. 1962

BROOKLYN, New York:

Long Island Outgrows the Country. By Howell Walker. Photos by B. Anthony Stewart. 279-326, Mar. 1951

The Pious Ones (Brooklyn's Hasidic Jews). By Harvey Arden. Photos by Nathan Benn. 276-298, Aug. 1975

BROOKS, RHODA and EARLE: Authors:

Ambassadors of Good Will: The Peace Corps. By Sargent Shriver and Peace Corps Volunteers. 297-345, Sept. 1964
Ecuador. 339-345

BROWER, DAVID R.: Author:

Sierra High Trip. 844-868, June 1954

BROWER, WARD, Jr.:

Easter Egg Chickens. By Frederick G. Vosburgh. Photos by B. Anthony Stewart. 377-387, Sept. 1948

BROWN, ANDREW H.: Author:

Men Against the Hurricane. 537-560, Oct. 1950

New St. Lawrence Seaway Opens the Great Lakes to the World. 299-339, Mar. 1959

Newfoundland, Canada's New Province. Photos by Robert F. Sisson. 777-812, June 1949

Ontario, Pivot of Canada's Power. Photos by B. Anthony Stewart and Bates Littlehales. 823-852, Dec. 1953

BROWN, ANDREW H.: Author—*Continued*

Quebec's Forests, Farms, and Frontiers. 431-470, Oct. 1949

Skyline Trail from Maine to Georgia. Photos by Robert F. Sisson. 219-251, Aug. 1949

Sno-Cats Mechanize Oregon Snow Survey. Photos by John E. Fletcher. 691-710, Nov. 1949

Sweden, Quiet Workshop for the World. 451-491, Apr. 1963

Versatile Wood Waits on Man. 109-140, July 1951

Weather from the White North. Photos by John E. Fletcher. 543-572, Apr. 1955

Author-Photographer

Haunting Heart of the Everglades. Photos by author and Willard R. Culver. 145-173, Feb. 1948

Labrador Canoe Adventure. By Andrew Brown and Ralph Gray. 65-99, July 1951

Norway's Fjords Pit Men Against Mountains. 96-122, Jan. 1957

Philmont Scout Ranch Helps Boys Grow Up. 399-416, Sept. 1956

Saving Earth's Oldest Living Things (Sequoias). Photos by Raymond Moulin and author. 679-695, May 1951

Work-hard, Play-hard Michigan. 279-320, Mar. 1952

Photographer

All-out Assault on Antarctica. By Richard E. Byrd. 141-180, Aug. 1956

Native's Return to Norway. By Arnvid Nygaard. 683-691, Nov. 1953

Stop-and-Go Sail Around South Norway. By Edmond J. Moran. Photos by Randi Kjekstad Bull and Andrew H. Brown. 153-192, Aug. 1954

BROWN, JOHN:

History Awakens at Harpers Ferry. By Volkmar Wentzel. 399-416, Mar. 1957

BROWN, ROLAND W.: Author:

Fossils Lift the Veil of Time. By Harry S. Ladd and Roland W. Brown. 363-386, Mar. 1956

BROWN BEARS:

Among Alaska's Brown Bears. By Allan L. Egbert and Michael H. Luque. 428-442, Sept. 1975

When Giant Bears Go Fishing. By Cecil E. Rhode. 195-205, Aug. 1954

BROWN PELICANS:

Bad Days for the Brown Pelican. By Ralph W. Schreiber. Photos by William R. Curtsinger and author. 111-123, Jan. 1975

BRUCE, AILSA MELLON: Art Collection:

In Quest of Beauty. Text by Paul Mellon. 372-385, Mar. 1967

BRUGES, Belgium:

Belgium Comes Back. By Harvey Klemmer. Photos by Maynard Owen Williams. 575-614, May 1948

Belgium Welcomes the World (1958 World's Fair). By Howell Walker. 795-837, June 1958

Bruges, the City the Sea Forgot. By Luis Marden. 631-665, May 1955

BRUNEI (Sultanate), Borneo:

Brunei, Borneo's Abode of Peace. By Joseph Judge. Photos by Dean Conger. 207-225, Feb. 1974

In Storied Lands of Malaysia. By Maurice Shad-

BRUNEI (Sultanate), Borneo—*Continued*
bolt. Photos by Winfield Parks. 734-783, Nov. 1963

Magellan: First Voyage Around the World. By Alan Villiers. Photos by Bruce Dale. 721-753, June 1976

BRUSSELS, Belgium:
Belgium Comes Back. By Harvey Klemmer. Photos by Maynard Owen Williams. 575-614, May 1948

Belgium Welcomes the World (1958 World's Fair). By Howell Walker. 795-837, June 1958

BRY, THEODORE DE: Engravings by (1590):
Indian Life Before the Colonists Came. By Stuart E. Jones. 351-368, Sept. 1947

BRYANT, WILLIAM CULLEN:
Literary Landmarks of Massachusetts. By William H. Nicholas. Photos by B. Anthony Stewart and John E. Fletcher. 279-310, Mar. 1950

BRYCE CANYON NATIONAL PARK, Utah:
Nature Carves Fantasies in Bryce Canyon. By William Belknap, Jr. 490-511, Oct. 1958

The West Through Boston Eyes. By Stewart Anderson. 733-776, June 1949

BUCHANAN, JAMES:
The Living White House. By Lonnelle Aikman. 593-643, Nov. 1966

Profiles of the Presidents: II. A Restless Nation Moves West. By Frank Freidel. 80-121, Jan. 1965

BUCK ISLAND REEF NATIONAL MONUMENT, St. Croix, Virgin Islands:
Buck Island—Underwater Jewel. By Jerry and Idaz Greenberg. 677-683, May 1971

BUDAPEST, Hungary:
Hungary: Changing Homeland of a Tough, Romantic People. By Bart McDowell. Photos by Albert Moldvay and Joseph J. Scherschel. 443-483, Apr. 1971

BUDDHISM:
Burma, Gentle Neighbor of India and Red China. By W. Robert Moore. 153-199, Feb. 1963

Cambodia: Indochina's "Neutral" Corner. By Thomas J. Abercrombie. 514-551, Oct. 1964

The Caves of the Thousand Buddhas. By Franc and Jean Shor. 383-415, Mar. 1951

Ceylon, the Resplendent Land. By Donna K. and Gilbert M. Grosvenor. 447-497, Apr. 1966

India's Sculptured Temple Caves. By Volkmar Wentzel. 665-678, May 1953

Kunming Pilgrimage. 213-226, Feb. 1950

Little Tibet in Switzerland. By Laura Pilarski. Photos by Fred Mayer. 711-727, Nov. 1968

Report on Laos. By Peter T. White. Photos by W. E. Garrett. 241-275, Aug. 1961

Scintillating Siam. By W. Robert Moore. 173-200, Feb. 1947

Sherpaland, My Shangri-La. By Desmond Doig. 545-577, Oct. 1966

Thailand Bolsters Its Freedom. By W. Robert Moore. 811-849, June 1961

See also Lamas and Lamaism; Zen Buddhism; *and* Bhutan; Ladakh; Nepal; Sikkim; Thailand; Viet Nam

BUENAVENTURA, Colombia:
Cruising Colombia's "Ol' Man River." By Amos Burg. 615-660, May 1947

BUENOS AIRES, Argentina:
Argentina: Young Giant of the Far South. By Jean and Franc Shor. 297-352, Mar. 1958

Buenos Aires, Argentina's Melting-pot Metropolis. By Jules B. Billard. Photos by Winfield Parks. 662-695, Nov. 1967

Which Way Now for Argentina? By Loren McIntyre. 296-333, Mar. 1975

BUFFALO. *See* Bison

BUFFALO BILL. *See* Cody, William F.

BUFFALOES, Water:
Life and Death in Tana Toradja. By Pamela and Alfred Meyer. 793-815, June 1972

Marsh Dwellers of Southern Iraq. By Wilfred Thesiger. Photos by Gavin Maxwell. 205-239, Feb. 1958

The Top End of Down Under. By Kenneth MacLeish. Photos by Thomas Nebbia. 145-174, Feb. 1973

Water Dwellers in a Desert World. By Gavin Young. Photos by Nik Wheeler. 502-523, Apr. 1976

BUILDING a New Austria. By Beverley M. Bowie. Photos by Volkmar Wentzel. 172-213, Feb. 1959

BULGARIA:
Down the Danube by Canoe. By William Slade Backer. Photos by Richard S. Durrance and Christopher G. Knight. 34-79, July 1965

BULGE, Battle of the:
Belgium Comes Back. By Harvey Klemmer. Photos by Maynard Owen Williams. 575-614, May 1948

Luxembourg, Survivor of Invasions. By Sydney Clark. Photos by Maynard Owen Williams. 791-810, June 1948

BULL, RANDI KJEKSTAD: Photographer:
Stop-and-Go Sail Around South Norway. By Edmond J. Moran. Photos by Randi Kjekstad Bull and Andrew H. Brown. 153-192, Aug. 1954

BULL DERBY: Madura (Island), Java:
Postwar Journey Through Java. By Ronald Stuart Kain. 675-700, May 1948

BULLDOG ANTS:
At Home With the Bulldog Ant. By Robert F. Sisson. 62-75, July 1974
Face-to-Face With a World of Ants. 72-75

BULLFIGHTS. *See* Andalusia (Region), Spain; Camargue (Region), France; Mexico City; Portugal at the Crossroads; Tijuana, Mexico

BULLFROG Ballet Filmed in Flight. By Treat Davidson. 791-799, June 1963

BUMP, JAMES D.: Author:
Big Game Hunting in the Land of Long Ago. By Joseph P. Connolly and James D. Bump. 589-605, May 1947

BUMSTEAD, NEWMAN:
Developed further the photo-composing machine

BUMSTEAD, NEWMAN — *Continued*

invented by his father, Albert H. Bumstead. 419, Mar. 1953

Author

"Around the World in Eighty Days." 705-750, Dec. 1951

Atlantic Odyssey: Iceland to Antarctica. Photos by Volkmar Wentzel. 725-780, Dec. 1955

Children's Art Around the World. 365-387, Mar. 1957

A Map Maker Looks at the United States. 705-748, June 1951

Rockets Explore the Air Above Us. 562-580, Apr. 1957

BUNDI, India:

Feudal Splendor Lingers in Rajputana. By Volkmar Wentzel. 411-458, Oct. 1948

BUNDY, CARTER:

New Scarlet Bird in Florida Skies. By Paul A. Zahl. 874-882, Dec. 1967

BUNLAP, Pentecost Island:

Land Diving With the Pentecost Islanders. By Kal Muller. 799-817, Dec. 1970

BURDEN, DAN: Author-Photographer:

Bikepacking Across Alaska and Canada. 682-695, May 1973

BURDETT-SCOUGALL, IRENE: Photographer:

Pigeon Netting — Sport of Basques. 405-416, Sept. 1949

BUREAU OF STANDARDS. *See* National Bureau of Standards

BURG, AMOS: Author:

Endeavour Sails the Inside Passage. 801-828, June 1947

Author-Photographer

Along the Yukon Trail. 395-416, Sept. 1953

Cruising Colombia's "Ol' Man River." 615-660, May 1947

North Star Cruises Alaska's Wild West. 57-86, July 1952

BURIAL CUSTOMS:

Ancient Mesopotamia: A Light That Did Not Fail. By E. A. Speiser. Paintings by H. M. Herget. 41-105, Jan. 1951

China Unveils Her Newest Treasures. Photos by Robert W. Madden. 848-857, Dec. 1974

Fresh Treasures from Egypt's Ancient Sands. By Jefferson Caffery. Photos by David S. Boyer. 611-650, Nov. 1955

A Lady From China's Past. Photos from *China Pictorial*. Text by Alice J. Hall. 660-681, May 1974

Lifelike Man Preserved 2,000 Years in Peat. By P. V. Glob. 419-430, Mar. 1954

Periscope on the Etruscan Past. By Carlo M. Lerici. 337-350, Sept. 1959

Tutankhamun's Golden Trove. By Christiane Desroches Noblecourt. Photos by F. L. Kenett. 625-646, Oct. 1963

See also Funerals

BURIAL MOUNDS. *See* Bahrein; Ch'angsha; Indian Mounds; Ur

BURKE, ARLEIGH A.:

Hubbard Medal recipient. 589-590, Apr. 1959

BURMA:

Burma, Gentle Neighbor of India and Red China. By W. Robert Moore. 153-199, Feb. 1963

Burma's Leg Rowers and Floating Farms. Photos by W. E. Garrett. Text by David Jeffery. 826-845, June 1974

Cane Bridges of Asia. Photos from Paul Popper. 243-250, Aug. 1948

The Lands and Peoples of Southeast Asia. 295-365, Mar. 1971

I. Mosaic of Cultures. By Peter T. White. Photos by W. E. Garrett. 296-329

II. New Light on a Forgotten Past. By Wilhelm G. Solheim II. 330-339

III. Pagan, on the Road to Mandalay. By W. E. Garrett. 343-365

Operation Eclipse: 1948. By William A. Kinney. 325-372, Mar. 1949

BURNETT, WANDA: Author:

The Romance of American Furs. 379-402, Mar. 1948

BURNS, ROBERT:

Poets' Voices Linger in Scottish Shrines. By Isobel Wylie Hutchison. Photos by Kathleen Revis. 437-488, Oct. 1957

BURNS, ROBERT K., Jr.: Author-Photographer:

Saint Véran, France's Highest Village. 571-588, Apr. 1959

BURR PRIZE (Franklin L. Burr Prize):

Burr Prizes Awarded to Dr. Edgerton and Dr. Van Biesbroeck. 705-706, May 1953; 523, Apr. 1955

BURROS, Wild:

Getting to Know the Wild Burros of Death Valley. By Patricia des Roses Moehlman. Photos by Ira S. Lerner and author. 502-517, Apr. 1972

BURROUGHS, CARROLL A.: Author:

Searching for Cliff Dwellers' Secrets (Wetherill Mesa). 619-625, Nov. 1959

BUS TRIPS:

Oasis-hopping in the Sahara. By Maynard Owen Williams. 209-236, Feb. 1949

You Can't Miss America by Bus. By Howell Walker. Paintings by Walter A. Weber. 1-42, July 1950

BUSHMEN:

Africa's Bushman Art Treasures. By Alfred Friendly. Photos by Alex R. Willcox. 848-865, June 1963

Bushmen of the Kalahari. By Elizabeth Marshall Thomas. Photos by Laurence K. Marshall. 866-888, June 1963

Bushmen of the Kalahari (Television film). 578A-578B, Apr. 1973; 732A-732B, May 1974

BUSINESSMAN in the Bush. By Frederick Kent Truslow. 634-675, May 1970

BUSY Fairbanks Sets Alaska's Pace. By Bruce A. Wilson. 505-523, Oct. 1949

BUTTERFLIES:

The High World of the Rain Forest. By William Beebe. Paintings by Guy Neale. 838-855, June 1958

Keeping House for Tropical Butterflies. By Jocelyn

BUTTERFLIES—*Continued*

Crane. Photos by M. Woodbridge Williams. 193-217, Aug. 1957

See also Monarch Butterfly

BUTTRICK GARDEN, Concord, Massachusetts:

History and Beauty Blend in a Concord Iris Garden. By Robert T. Cochran, Jr. Photos by M. Woodbridge Williams. 705-719, May 1959

BUZ KASHI:

Bold Horsemen of the Steppes (Turkomans). By Sabrina and Roland Michaud. 634-669, Nov. 1973

BY Cotswold Lanes to Wold's End. By Melville Bell Grosvenor. 615-654, May 1948

BY Full-rigged Ship to Denmark's Fairyland. By Alan Villiers. Photos by Alexander Taylor and author. 809-828, Dec. 1955

BY Parachute Into Peru's Lost World. By G. Brooks Baekeland. Photos by author and Peter R. Gimbel. 268-296, Aug. 1964

BY Square-rigger from Baltic to Bicentennial. By Kenneth Garrett. 824-857, Dec. 1976

BYRD, RICHARD EVELYN:

Admiral of the Ends of the Earth. By Melville Bell Grosvenor. 36-48, July 1957

The Nation Honors Admiral Richard E. Byrd. 567-578, Apr. 1962

The Society's Hubbard Medal Awarded to Commander MacMillan. 563-564, Apr. 1953
Note: Tribute was paid to the MacMillans by Admiral Byrd.

Author

All-out Assault on Antarctica. 141-180, Aug. 1956

Our Navy Explores Antarctica. U. S. Navy official photos. 429-522, Oct. 1974

To the Men at South Pole Station. 1-4, July 1957

BYZANTINE ART:

Athens to Istanbul. By Jean and Franc Shor. 37-76, Jan. 1956

Island of Faith in the Sinai Wilderness (St. Catherine's Monastery). By George H. Forsyth. Photos by Robert F. Sisson. 82-106, Jan. 1964

Mount Sinai's Holy Treasures (St. Catherine's Monastery). By Kurt Weitzmann. Photos by Fred Anderegg. 109-127, Jan. 1964

BYZANTINE EMPIRE:

Athens to Istanbul. By Jean and Franc Shor. 37-76, Jan. 1956

A New Look at Medieval Europe. By Kenneth M. Setton. Paintings by Andre Durenceau and Birney Lettick. 799-859, Dec. 1962

Yankee Cruises Turkey's History-haunted Coast. By Irving and Electa Johnson. Photos by Joseph J. Scherschel. 798-845, Dec. 1969

C

C & O CANAL. *See* Chesapeake and Ohio Canal

CABLEWAY:

Across the Ridgepole of the Alps. By Walter Meayers Edwards. 410-419, Sept. 1960

CABOT, JOHN:

The British Way. By Sir Evelyn Wrench. 421-541, Apr. 1949

CACAO:

Happy-go-lucky Trinidad and Tobago. By Charles Allmon. 35-75, Jan. 1953

CACTI:

Abundant Life in a Desert Land. By Walter Meayers Edwards. 424-436, Sept. 1973

American Wild Flower Odyssey. By P. L. Ricker. 603-634, May 1953

CADES COVE, Tennessee:

The People of Cades Cove. By William O. Douglas. Photos by Thomas Nebbia and Otis Imboden. 60-95, July 1962

CAERNARVON CASTLE, Caernarvonshire, Wales:

The Investiture of Great Britain's Prince of Wales. By Allan C. Fisher, Jr. Photos by James L. Stanfield and Adam Woolfitt. 698-715, Nov. 1969

CAFFERY, JEFFERSON: Author:

Fresh Treasures from Egypt's Ancient Sands. Photos by David S. Boyer. 611-650, Nov. 1955

CAIRNS, ROBERT: Author:

Sunny Corsica: French Morsel in the Mediterranean. Photos by Joseph J. Scherschel. 401-423, Sept. 1973

CAIRO, Egypt:

"Around the World in Eighty Days." By Newman Bumstead. 705-750, Dec. 1951

Cairo, Troubled Capital of the Arab World. By William S. Ellis. Photos by Winfield Parks. 639-667, May 1972

Safari from Congo to Cairo. By Elsie May Bell Grosvenor. Photos by Gilbert Grosvenor. 721-771, Dec. 1954

See also Akhenaten Temple Project

CAISSON DISEASE. *See* The Bends

CAJUNLAND, Louisiana's French-speaking Coast. By Bern Keating. Photos by Charles Harbutt and Franke Keating. 353-391, Mar. 1966

CALAVERAS BIG TREES STATE PARK, California:

Saving Earth's Oldest Living Things. By Andrew H. Brown. Photos by Raymond Moulin and author. 679-695, May 1951

CALCUTTA, India:

Calcutta, India's Maligned Metropolis. By Peter T. White. Photos by Raghubir Singh. 534-563, Apr. 1973

From the Hair of Siva. By Helen and Frank Schreider. 445-503, Oct. 1960

The Ganges, River of Faith. By John J. Putman. Photos by Raghubir Singh. 445-483, Oct. 1971

CALDY, the Monks' Island (Wales). By John E. H. Nolan. 564-578, Oct. 1955

CALENDARS:

A Bold New Look at Our Past. The Editor. 62-63, Jan. 1975

Exploring the Mind of Ice Age Man. By Alexander Marshack. 64-89, Jan. 1975

The Maya: Riddle of the Glyphs. By George E. Stuart. Photos by Otis Imboden. 768-791, Dec. 1975

CALGARY, Alberta, Canada:

Canada's Heartland, the Prairie Provinces. By W. E. Garrett. 443-489, Oct. 1970

CALIFORNIA:

Bristlecone Pine, Oldest Known Living Thing. By Edmund Schulman. Photos by W. Robert Moore. 355-372, Mar. 1958

California, Horn of Plenty. By Frederick Simpich. Photos by Willard R. Culver. 553-594, May 1949

California, the Golden Magnet. By William Graves. 595-679, May 1966
I. The South. Photos by Thomas Nebbia. 595-639
II. Nature's North. Photos by James P. Blair and Jonathan S. Blair. 641-679

Californians Escape to the Desert. By Mason Sutherland. Photos by Charles W. Herbert. 675-724, Nov. 1957

California's Parched Oasis, the Owens Valley. By Judith and Neil Morgan. Photos by Jodi Cobb and Galen Rowell. 98-127, Jan. 1976

California's San Andreas Fault. By Thomas Y. Canby. Photos by James P. Blair. 38-53, Jan. 1973

California's Surprising Inland Delta. By Judith and Neil Morgan. Photos by Charles O'Rear. 409-430, Sept. 1976

California's Wonderful One (State Highway No. 1). By Frank Cameron. Photos by B. Anthony Stewart. 571-617, Nov. 1959

Close-up: U.S.A., California and Nevada, map supplement. Text on reverse. June 1974

Finding the Mt. Everest of All Living Things (Redwood Tree). By Paul A. Zahl. 10-51, July 1964

The Friendly Train Called Skunk. By Dean Jennings. Photos by B. Anthony Stewart. 720-734, May 1959

Giant Sequoias Draw Millions to California Parks. By John Michael Kauffmann. Photos by B. Anthony Stewart. 147-187, Aug. 1959

Goggle Fishing in California Waters. By David Hellyer. Photos by Lamar Boren. 615-632, May 1949

Here Come the Marines. By Frederick Simpich. 647-672, Nov. 1950
Included: San Diego; and Camps Del Mar, Pendleton, and El Toro, in southern California

How Fruit Came to America. By J. R. Magness. Paintings by Else Bostelmann. 325-377, Sept. 1951

Indians of the Far West. By Matthew W. Stirling. Paintings by W. Langdon Kihn. 175-200, Feb. 1948

John Muir's Wild America. By Harvey Arden. Photos by Dewitt Jones. 433-461, Apr. 1973

The Lure of the Changing Desert. 817-824, June 1954

The Magic Worlds of Walt Disney. By Robert de Roos. Photos by Thomas Nebbia. 159-207, Aug. 1963

A Map Maker Looks at the United States. By Newman Bumstead. 705-748, June 1951
Included: Bakersfield; Central Valley; Lake Tahoe; Los Angeles; McCloud River; Mojave Desert; Mount Shasta; Pit River; Sacramento River; San Francisco; Shasta Dam; Sierra Nevada; Tulare; Yosemite Valley

A Map of California, map supplement. June 1954

My Life in the Valley of the Moon. By H. H. Arnold. Photos by Willard R. Culver. 689-716, Dec. 1948

New Rush to Golden California. By George W. Long. 723-802, June 1954

CALIFORNIA—Continued

Northern California; Southern California, double-sided U. S. Atlas series supplement. May 1966

A Park to Save the Tallest Trees. By Melville Bell Grosvenor. 62-64, July 1966

The Revolution in American Agriculture. By Jules B. Billard. Photos by James P. Blair. 147-185, Feb. 1970

Saving Earth's Oldest Living Things. By Andrew H. Brown. Photos by Raymond Moulin and author. 679-695, May 1951
Contents: Calaveras Big Trees State Park; Giant Forest, Sequoia National Park; South Calaveras Grove

Seeking the Secret of the Giants. By Frank M. Setzler. Photos by Richard H. Stewart. 390-404, Sept. 1952
Giant Effigies of the Southwest. By George C. Marshall. 389

Shells Take You Over World Horizons. By Rutherford Platt. 33-84, July 1949

Skiing in the United States. By Kathleen Revis. 216-254, Feb. 1959

Skyway Below the Clouds. By Carl R. Markwith. Photos by Ernest J. Cottrell. 85-108, July 1949
Included: Blythe; Cahuenga Pass; Corona; Dume Point; Long Beach; Los Angeles; Palm Springs; Palos Verdes Point; Salton Sea; San Bernardino Mountains; San Gorgonio Pass; San Jacinto Mountains; Santa Monica; Santa Monica Mountains

Timber: How Much Is Enough? By John J. Putman. Photos by Bruce Dale. 485-511, Apr. 1974

Two Wheels Along the Mexican Border. By William Albert Allard. 591-635, May 1971

The West Through Boston Eyes. By Stewart Anderson. 733-776, June 1949

Wildlife In and Near the Valley of the Moon. By H. H. Arnold. Photos by Paul J. Fair. 401-414, Mar. 1950

World's Tallest Tree Discovered. By Melville Bell Grosvenor. Photos by George F. Mobley. 1-9, July 1964

See also Death Valley National Monument; Edwards Air Force Base; Henry E. Huntington Library and Art Gallery; La Jolla; Lompoc Valley; Los Angeles; Mojave Desert; Monterey Peninsula; Newport Beach; Pacific Crest Trail; Pacific Grove; Palomar Observatory; San Diego; San Francisco; Santa Barbara Islands; Sierra Nevada; Tournament of Roses; Yosemite National Park

CALIFORNIA, Baja. See Baja California

CALIFORNIA, Gulf of. See Raza, Isla

CALIFORNIA ACADEMY OF SCIENCES: Expeditions and Research:

Galapagos Scientific Project. 545, Apr. 1967

NGS grant in entomology to Dr. Edward S. Ross. 408, Mar. 1961; 15, 16, Jan. 1963; 282, Feb. 1965; 433, 437, Sept. 1965

CALIFORNIA DELTA:

California's Surprising Inland Delta. By Judith and Neil Morgan. Photos by Charles O'Rear. 409-430, Sept. 1976

The CALIFORNIA Gray Whale Comes Back. By Theodore J. Walker. 394-415, Mar. 1971

CALIFORNIA INSTITUTE OF TECHNOLOGY:

Can We Predict Quakes? By Thomas Y. Canby. 830-835, June 1976
Included: Seismological Laboratory of CIT

CALIFORNIA INSTITUTE OF TECHNOLOGY — *Continued*

Jet Propulsion Laboratory. *See* Mariner Missions; Ranger Spacecraft; Surveyor Spacecraft

Mapping the Unknown Universe. By F. Barrows Colton. 401-420, Sept. 1950

See also Sky Survey

CALIFORNIA STATE HIGHWAY NO. 1:

California's Wonderful One. By Frank Cameron. Photos by B. Anthony Stewart. 571-617, Nov. 1959

CALIFORNIA WESTERN RAILROAD:

The Friendly Train Called Skunk. By Dean Jennings. Photos by B. Anthony Stewart. 720-734, May 1959

CALVERT, JAMES F.: Author:

Up Through the Ice of the North Pole *(Skate)*. 1-41, July 1959

CALYPSO (Ship):

At Home in the Sea. By Jacques-Yves Cousteau. 465-507, Apr. 1964

Calypso Explores an Undersea Canyon (Romanche Trench). By Jacques-Yves Cousteau. Photos by Bates Littlehales. 373-396, Mar. 1958

Calypso Explores for Underwater Oil. By Jacques-Yves Cousteau. 155-184, Aug. 1955

Camera Under the Sea. By Luis Marden. 162-200, Feb. 1956

Exploring Davy Jones's Locker with *Calypso*. By Jacques-Yves Cousteau. Photos by Luis Marden. 149-161, Feb. 1956

Fish Men Discover a 2,200-year-old Greek Ship. By Jacques-Yves Cousteau. 1-36, Jan. 1954

Fish Men Explore a New World Undersea. By Jacques-Yves Cousteau. 431-472, Oct. 1952

Photographing the Sea's Dark Underworld. By Harold E. Edgerton. 523-537, Apr. 1955

CAMARACOTO INDIANS:

Jungle Journey to the World's Highest Waterfall. By Ruth Robertson. 655-690, Nov. 1949

CAMARGUE (Region), France:

The Camargue, Land of Cowboys and Gypsies. By Eugene L. Kammerman. 667-699, May 1956

France's Wild, Watery South, the Camargue. By William Davenport. 696-726, May 1973

CAMBODIA:

Angkor, Jewel of the Jungle. By W. Robert Moore. Paintings by Maurice Fiévet. 517-569, Apr. 1960

Cambodia: Indochina's "Neutral" Corner. By Thomas J. Abercrombie. 514-551, Oct. 1964

Indochina Faces the Dragon. By George W. Long. Photos by J. Baylor Roberts. 287-328, Sept. 1952

The Lands and Peoples of Southeast Asia. 295-365, Mar. 1971

  I. Mosaic of Cultures. By Peter T. White. Photos by W. E. Garrett. 296-329
  II. New Light on a Forgotten Past. By Wilhelm G. Solheim II. 330-339

The Mekong, River of Terror and Hope. By Peter T. White. Photos by W. E. Garrett. 737-787, Dec. 1968

Portrait of Indochina. By W. Robert Moore and Maynard Owen Williams. Paintings by Jean Despujols. 461-490, Apr. 1951

CAMBODIA — *Continued*

Strife-torn Indochina. By W. Robert Moore. 499-510, Oct. 1950

Viet Nam, Cambodia, Laos, and Eastern Thailand, map supplement. Text on reverse. Jan. 1965

Viet Nam, Cambodia, Laos, and Thailand, map supplement. Feb. 1967

CAMBRIDGE, Massachusetts:

Literary Landmarks of Massachusetts. By William H. Nicholas. Photos by B. Anthony Stewart and John E. Fletcher. 279-310, Mar. 1950

CAMEL CARAVANS:

I Joined a Sahara Salt Caravan. By Victor Englebert. 694-711, Nov. 1965

Winter Caravan to the Roof of the World. By Sabrina and Roland Michaud. 435-465, Apr. 1972

CAMELS:

In Search of Man's Past at Lake Rudolf. By Richard E. Leakey. Photos by Gordon W. Gahan. 712-734, May 1970

CAMERA Under the Sea. By Luis Marden. 162-200, Feb. 1956

CAMERAS. *See* Photography

CAMERON, FRANK: Author:

California's Wonderful One (State Highway No. 1). Photos by B. Anthony Stewart. 571-617, Nov. 1959

CAMERON, GEORGE G.: Author-Photographer:

Darius Carved History on Ageless Rock. 825-844, Dec. 1950

CAMERON, NIGEL: Author:

The Emperor's Private Garden: Kashmir. Photos by Brian Brake. 606-647, Nov. 1958

CAMEROON:

Afo-A-Kom: A Sacred Symbol Comes Home. By William S. Ellis. Photos by James P. Blair. 141-148, July 1974

Beyond the Bight of Benin. By Jeannette and Maurice Fiévet. 221-253, Aug. 1959

Carefree People of the Cameroons. Photos by Pierre Ichac. 233-248, Feb. 1947

Freedom Speaks French in Ouagadougou. By John Scofield. 153-203, Aug. 1966

See also Weeks Expedition

CAMOUFLAGE:

Asian Insects in Disguise. By Edward S. Ross. 433-439, Sept. 1965

How Animals Hide. Children's book announced. 726-728, Nov. 1973

See also Decoy Fish; Sargassum Fish

CAMP, W. H.: Author:

The World in Your Garden (Flowers). Paintings by Else Bostelmann. 1-65, July 1947

CAMP CARSON, Colorado:

School for Survival. By Curtis E. LeMay. 565-602, May 1953

CAMP CENTURY, Greenland:

Nuclear Power for the Polar Regions. By George J. Dufek. 712-730, May 1962

CAMP LEJEUNE MARINE BASE, North Carolina:
Here Come the Marines. By Frederick Simpich. 647-672, Nov. 1950

CAMP PENDLETON MARINE BASE, California:
Here Come the Marines. By Frederick Simpich. 647-672, Nov. 1950

CAMPBELL, MARGARET SHAW:
Author-Photographer
Hunting Folk Songs in the Hebrides. 249-272, Feb. 1947

CAMPBELL, MARJORIE WILKINS: Author:
Canada's Dynamic Heartland, Ontario. Photos by Winfield Parks. 58-97, July 1963

CAMPBELL, ROBERT M.: Photographer:
Making Friends With Mountain Gorillas. By Dian Fossey. 48-67, Jan. 1970
More Years With Mountain Gorillas. By Dian Fossey. 574-585, Oct. 1971
Skull 1470. By Richard E. Leakey. 819-829, June 1973

CAMPBELL, WILLIAM W., III: Photographer:
The President's Music Men (U. S. Marine Band). By Stuart E. Jones. 752-766, Dec. 1959

CAMPING TRIPS. See Backpack Trips; Bikepacking; Hiking; Mountain Climbing; Pack Trip; Philmont Scout Ranch

CAMPS, Summer:
Camping Adventure. Children's book announced. 718-720, Nov. 1976
In Touch With Nature. Text by Elizabeth A. Moize. Photos by Steve Raymer. 537-543, Apr. 1974
Contents: Camps near Eagle River, Wisconsin

CAN the Cooper's Hawk Survive? By Noel Snyder. Photos by author and Helen Snyder. 433-442, Mar. 1974

CAN the World Feed Its People? By Thomas Y. Canby. Photos by Steve Raymer. 2-31, July 1975

CAN We Harness the Wind? By Roger Hamilton. Photos by Emory Kristof. 812-829, Dec. 1975

CAN We Predict Quakes? By Thomas Y. Canby. 830-835, June 1976

CAN We Save Our Salt Marshes? By Stephen W. Hitchcock. Photos by William R. Curtsinger. 729-765, June 1972

CANAAN:
Abraham, the Friend of God. By Kenneth MacLeish. Photos by Dean Conger. 739-789, Dec. 1966

CANAANITES. See Phoenicians

CANADA:
Across Canada by Mackenzie's Track. By Ralph Gray. 191-239, Aug. 1955
Along the Yukon Trail. By Amos Burg. 395-416, Sept. 1953
Bikepacking Across Alaska and Canada. By Dan Burden. 682-695, May 1973
Included: Alberta; British Columbia; Yukon Territory
Canada, Atlas series supplement. Dec. 1961

CANADA—Continued
Canada, map supplement. Painting on reverse. Mar. 1972
Canada, Alaska, and Greenland, map supplement. June 1947
Canada, My Country. By Alan Phillips. Photos by David S. Boyer and Walter Meayers Edwards. 769-819, Dec. 1961
Canada Counts Its Caribou. 261-268, Aug. 1952
Canada Marks Her First Century. By Melville Bell Grosvenor. 597-599, May 1967
Canada's Caribou Eskimos (Padlermiut). By Donald B. Marsh. 87-104, Jan. 1947
Canada's Heartland, the Prairie Provinces. By W. E. Garrett. 443-489, Oct. 1970
Contents: Alberta; Manitoba; Saskatchewan
Canada's "Now" Frontier. By Robert Paul Jordan. Photos by Lowell Georgia. 480-511, Oct. 1976
Included: Oil exploration in Alberta and the Northwest Territories
Canada's Winged Victory: the Silver Dart. By Gilbert M. Grosvenor. 254-267, Aug. 1959
The Canadian North: Emerging Giant. By David S. Boyer. 1-43, July 1968
Canadian Rockies, Lords of a Beckoning Land. By Alan Phillips. Photos by James L. Stanfield. 353-393, Sept. 1966
Central Canada, Atlas series supplement. July 1963
Close-up: Canada, Maine, with the Maritime Provinces of Canada, map supplement. Text on reverse. Mar. 1975
DEW Line, Sentry of the Far North. By Howard La Fay. 128-146, July 1958
Eastern Canada, Atlas series supplement. May 1967
Exploring Canada from Sea to Sea. Special Publication announced. 868-875, June 1967
Far North with "Captain Mac." By Miriam MacMillan. 465-513, Oct. 1951
From Sun-clad Sea to Shining Mountains. By Ralph Gray. Photos by James P. Blair. 542-589, Apr. 1964
Included: Alberta; British Columbia
The Giant Tides of Fundy. By Paul A. Zahl. 153-192, Aug. 1957
The Great Lakes Region of the United States and Canada, map supplement. Dec. 1953
Hiking the Backbone of the Rockies: Canada's Great Divide Trail. By Mike W. Edwards. Photos by Lowell Georgia. 795-817, June 1973
Contents: Alberta; British Columbia
I Live With the Eskimos. By Guy Mary-Rousseliere. 188-217, Feb. 1971
The Loyalists. By Kent Britt. Photos by Ted Spiegel. 510-539, Apr. 1975
Men, Moose, and Mink of Northwest Angle. By William H. Nicholas. Photos by J. Baylor Roberts. 265-284, Aug. 1947
National Parks, Monuments and Shrines of the United States and Canada, Atlas series supplement. Text on reverse. May 1958
New Era on the Great Lakes. By Nathaniel T. Kenney. 439-490, Apr. 1959
New St. Lawrence Seaway Opens the Great Lakes to the World. By Andrew H. Brown. 299-339, Mar. 1959
Niagara Falls, Servant of Good Neighbors. Photos by Walter Meayers Edwards. 574-587, Apr. 1963

CANADA—*Continued*

Nomads of the Far North. By Matthew W. Stirling. 471-504, Oct. 1949
    Hearty Folk Defy Arctic Storms. Paintings by W. Langdon Kihn. 479-494

North for Oil: *Manhattan* Makes the Historic Northwest Passage. By Bern Keating. Photos by Tomas Sennett. 374-391, Mar. 1970

North Through History Aboard *White Mist.* By Melville Bell Grosvenor. Photos by Edwin Stuart Grosvenor. 1-55, July 1970

Northwestern United States and Neighboring Canadian Provinces, map supplement. June 1950

On the Ridgepole of the Rockies. By Walter Meayers Edwards. 745-780, June 1947
    Canada's Rocky Mountain Playground. 755-770

The Peary Flag Comes to Rest. By Marie Peary Stafford. 519-532, Oct. 1954

Playing 3,000 Golf Courses in Fourteen Lands. By Ralph A. Kennedy. 113-132, July 1952

Queen of Canada (Elizabeth II). By Phyllis Wilson. Photos by Kathleen Revis. 825-829, June 1959

Relics from the Rapids (Voyageurs). By Sigurd F. Olson. Photos by David S. Boyer. 413-435, Sept. 1963

The St. Lawrence, River Key to Canada. By Howard La Fay. Photos by John Launois. 622-667, May 1967

Trailing Cosmic Rays in Canada's North. By Martin A. Pomerantz. 99-115, Jan. 1953

Trek Across Arctic America. By Colin Irwin. 295-321, Mar. 1974

Vacationlands of the United States and Southern Canada, map supplement. Text on reverse. July 1966

We Followed Peary to the Pole. By Gilbert Grosvenor and Thomas W. McKnew. 469-484, Oct. 1953

Weather from the White North. By Andrew H. Brown. Photos by John E. Fletcher. 543-572, Apr. 1955

Western Canada, Atlas series supplement. Sept. 1966

See also names of provinces; *and* Kennedy, Mount; Northwest Territories; Resolute Bay; St. Elias, Mount; Waterton-Glacier International Peace Park; Yukon Territory

CANADA GEESE:

Bright Dyes Reveal Secrets of Canada Geese. By John and Frank Craighead. 817-832, Dec. 1957

CANAL ZONE:

Panama, Link Between Oceans and Continents. By Jules B. Billard. Photos by Bruce Dale. 402-440, Mar. 1970

CANALS:

Exploring England's Canals. By Bryan Hodgson. Photos by Linda Bartlett. 76-111, July 1974

The Imperiled Everglades. By Fred Ward. 1-27, Jan. 1972

Inside Europe Aboard *Yankee.* By Irving and Electa Johnson. Photos by Joseph J. Scherschel. 157-195, Aug. 1964

Mexico's Little Venice. By W. E. Garrett. 876-888, June 1968

North Through History Aboard *White Mist.* By Melville Bell Grosvenor. Photos by Edwin Stuart

CANALS—*Continued*

Grosvenor. 1-55, July 1970

Paris to Antwerp with the Water Gypsies. By David S. Boyer. 530-559, Oct. 1955

Twilight Hope for Big Cypress. By Rick Gore. Photos by Patricia Caulfield. 251-273, Aug. 1976

See also Chesapeake and Ohio Canal; New York State Barge Canal; Panama Canal; Suez Canal; Sweden (Baltic Cruise), for Göta Canal; *and* Amsterdam, Netherlands; Bangkok, Thailand; Bruges, Belgium; Mekong River; Venice

CANARY ISLANDS, Atlantic Ocean:

Lanzarote, the Strangest Canary. By Stephanie Dinkins. 117-139, Jan. 1969

Spain's "Fortunate Isles," the Canaries. By Jean and Franc Shor. 485-522, Apr. 1955

CANAVERAL, Cape, Florida:

Cape Canaveral's 6,000-mile Shooting Gallery. By Allan C. Fisher, Jr. Photos by Luis Marden and Thomas Nebbia. 421-471, Oct. 1959

Reaching for the Moon. By Allan C. Fisher, Jr. Photos by Luis Marden. 157-171, Feb. 1959

CANBY, THOMAS Y.: Author:

Apollo-Soyuz: Handclasp in Space. 183-187, Feb. 1976

California's San Andreas Fault. Photos by James P. Blair. 38-53, Jan. 1973

Can the World Feed Its People? Photos by Steve Raymer. 2-31, July 1975

Can We Predict Quakes? 830-835, June 1976

Pioneers in Man's Search for the Universe. Paintings by Jean-Leon Huens. 627-633, May 1974

Skylab, Outpost on the Frontier of Space. Photos by the nine mission astronauts. 441-469, Oct. 1974

CANCER RESEARCH:

The Cancer Puzzle. By Robert F. Weaver. 396-399, Sept. 1976

You and the Obedient Atom. By Allan C. Fisher, Jr. 303-353, Sept. 1958

CANE BRIDGES of Asia. Photos from Paul Popper. 243-250, Aug. 1948

CANNIBALS. *See* Asmat; Biami; Erigbaagtsa

CANOE RACE:

Winter Brings Carnival Time to Quebec. By Kathleen Revis. 69-97, Jan. 1958

CANOE TRIPS:

Across Canada by Mackenzie's Track. By Ralph Gray. 191-239, Aug. 1955

Autumn Flames Along the Allagash. By François Leydet. Photos by Farrell Grehan. 177-187, Feb. 1974

A Canoe Helps Hawaii Recapture Her Past. By Herb Kawainui Kane. Photos by David Hiser. 468-489, Apr. 1976

Down the Danube by Canoe. By William Slade Backer. Photos by Richard S. Durrance and Christopher G. Knight. 34-79, July 1965

Down the Potomac by Canoe. By Ralph Gray. Photos by Walter Meayers Edwards. 213-242, Aug. 1948

Down the Susquehanna by Canoe. By Ralph Gray. Photos by Walter Meayers Edwards. 73-120, July 1950

Hokule'a Follows the Stars to Tahiti. By David

CANOE TRIPS—*Continued*

Lewis. Photos by Nicholas deVore III. 512-537, Oct. 1976

Isles of the Pacific. 732-793, Dec. 1974
   I. The Coming of the Polynesians. By Kenneth P. Emory. 732-745
   II. The Pathfinders. Paintings by Herb Kawainui Kane. 756-769

Jungle Jaunt on Amazon Headwaters. By Bernice M. Goetz. 371-388, Sept. 1952

Jungle Journey to the World's Highest Waterfall. By Ruth Robertson. 655-690, Nov. 1949

Kayak Odyssey: From the Inland Sea to Tokyo. By Dan Dimancescu. Photos by Christopher G. Knight. 295-337, Sept. 1967

Kayaks Down the Nile. By John M. Goddard. 697-732, May 1955

Labrador Canoe Adventure. By Andrew Brown and Ralph Gray. 65-99, July 1951

Okefenokee, the Magical Swamp. By François Leydet. Photos by Farrell Grehan. 169-175, Feb. 1974

Sea Fever. By John E. Schultz. 237-268, Feb. 1949

Trek Across Arctic America. By Colin Irwin. 295-321, Mar. 1974

Voyage of the *Hokule'a* (Television film). 575, Nov. 1976

See also Voyageurs

CANOEIROS (Indians). *See* Erigbaagtsa

CANTERBURY CATHEDRAL, Canterbury, England:
Canterbury Cathedral. By Kenneth MacLeish. Photos by Thomas Nebbia. 364-379, Mar. 1976

CANTON ISLAND, Phoenix Islands, Pacific Ocean:
Air Age Brings Life to Canton Island. By Howell Walker. 117-132, Jan. 1955

CANYONLANDS NATIONAL PARK, Utah:
Canyonlands, Realm of Rock and the Far Horizon. By Rowe Findley. Photos by Walter Meayers Edwards. 71-91, July 1971

Cities of Stone in Utah's Canyonland. By W. Robert Moore. 653-677, May 1962

CANYONS. *See* Bryce Canyon National Park; Dinosaur National Monument; Escalante Canyon; Grand Canyon; Havasupai Indian Reservation; Sierra Nevada (Fabulous Sierra Nevada); Zion National Park; *and* listing under Gorges

CAODAISM:
Indochina Faces the Dragon. By George W. Long. Photos by J. Baylor Roberts. 287-328, Sept. 1952

CAPE BRETON ISLAND, Nova Scotia, Canada:
Nova Scotia, the Magnificent Anchorage. By Charles McCarry. Photos by Gordon W. Gahan. 334-363, Mar. 1975
See also Baddeck

CAPE CANAVERAL, Florida. *See* Canaveral, Cape

CAPE COD, Massachusetts:
Cape Cod, Where Sea Holds Sway Over Man and Land. By Nathaniel T. Kenney. Photos by Dean Conger. 149-187, Aug. 1962

Cape Cod's Circle of Seasons. By Tom Melham. Photos by James P. Blair. 40-65, July 1975

Captain Smith's New England . . . and the Pilgrims' Cape Cod. 764-765, June 1953

CAPE COD, Massachusetts—*Continued*
Massachusetts Builds for Tomorrow. By Robert de Roos. Photos by B. Anthony Stewart. 790-843, Dec. 1966

Windjamming Around New England. By Tom Horgan. Photos by Robert F. Sisson. 141-169, Aug. 1950

CAPE HATTERAS NATIONAL SEASHORE, North Carolina:
Lonely Cape Hatteras, Besieged by the Sea. By William S. Ellis. Photos by Emory Kristof. 392-421, Sept. 1969

CAPE OF GOOD HOPE PROVINCE, Republic of South Africa:
Safari Through Changing Africa. By Elsie May Bell Grosvenor. Photos by Gilbert Grosvenor. 145-198, Aug. 1953

CAPE TOWN, Republic of South Africa:
Africa: The Winds of Freedom Stir a Continent. By Nathaniel T. Kenney. Photos by W. D. Vaughn. 303-359, Sept. 1960

Safari Through Changing Africa. By Elsie May Bell Grosvenor. Photos by Gilbert Grosvenor. 145-198, Aug. 1953

South Africa Close-up. By Kip Ross. 641-681, Nov. 1962

CAPITOL, U. S. *See* U. S. Capitol

CAPITOL REEF NATIONAL PARK, Utah. *See* Escalante Canyon

CAPPADOCIA (Region), Turkey:
Cappadocia: Turkey's Country of Cones. Photos by Marc Riboud. 122-146, Jan. 1958

Keeping House in a Cappadocian Cave. By Jonathan S. Blair. 127-146, July 1970

CAPRI, Italy's Enchanted Rock. By Carleton Mitchell. Photos by David F. Cupp. 795-809, June 1970

CAPRON, LOUIS: Author:
Florida's Emerging Seminoles. Photos by Otis Imboden. 716-734, Nov. 1969

Florida's "Wild" Indians, the Seminole. Photos by Willard R. Culver. 819-840, Dec. 1956

CAPTAIN Cook: The Man Who Mapped the Pacific. By Alan Villiers. Photos by Gordon W. Gahan. 297-349, Sept. 1971

CAPT. John Smith's Map of Virginia. 760-761, June 1953

CAPTAIN Smith of Jamestown. By Bradford Smith. 581-620, May 1957

CAPTAIN Smith's New England . . . and the Pilgrims' Cape Cod. 764-765, June 1953

The CAPTURE of Jerusalem. By Franc Shor. Photos by Thomas Nebbia. 839-855, Dec. 1963

CAPTURING Strange Creatures in Colombia. By Marte Latham. Photos by Tor Eigeland. 682-693, May 1966

CARACAS, Venezuela:
Venezuela's Crisis of Wealth. By Noel Grove. Photos by Robert W. Madden. 175-209, Aug. 1976

CARAVAGGIO, MICHELANGELO MERISI DA:
The Vienna Treasures and Their Collectors. By John Walker. 737-776, June 1950

CARAVANS, Camel:

I Joined a Sahara Salt Caravan. By Victor Englebert. 694-711, Nov. 1965

Winter Caravan to the Roof of the World. By Sabrina and Roland Michaud. 435-465, Apr. 1972

CARAVANS, Trailer:

I See America First. By Lynda Bird Johnson. Photos by William Albert Allard. 874-904, Dec. 1965

Through Europe by Trailer Caravan. By Norma Miller. Photos by Ardean R. Miller III. 769-816, June 1957

CARBON 14. *See* Radiocarbon Dating

CARDINALS:

The Bird's Year. By Arthur A. Allen. 791-816, June 1951

CAREFREE People of the Cameroons. Photos by Pierre Ichac. 233-248, Feb. 1947

CARGO CULTS:

Change Ripples New Guinea's Sepik River. By Malcolm S. Kirk. 354-381, Sept. 1973

Tanna Awaits the Coming of John Frum. By Kal Muller. 706-715, May 1974

CARIB Cruises the West Indies. By Carleton Mitchell. 1-56, Jan. 1948

CARIBBEAN Green Turtle: Imperiled Gift of the Sea. By Archie Carr. Photos by Robert E. Schroeder. 876-890, June 1967

CARIBBEAN REGION:

Cape Canaveral's 6,000-mile Shooting Gallery. By Allan C. Fisher, Jr. Photos by Luis Marden and Thomas Nebbia. 421-471, Oct. 1959
  Included: Antigua; Dominican Republic; Mayagüez, Puerto Rico; St. Lucia

Christopher Columbus and the New World He Found. By John Scofield. Photos by Adam Woolfitt. 584-625, Nov. 1975

Countries of the Caribbean, including Mexico, Central America, and the West Indies, map supplement. Oct. 1947

Imperiled Gift of the Sea: Caribbean Green Turtle. By Archie Carr. Photos by Robert E. Schroeder. 876-890, June 1967

Isles of the Caribbees. Special Publication announced. 408-417, Mar. 1966

Robin Sails Home. By Robin Lee Graham. 504-545, Oct. 1970
  Included: Barbados; Panama; Virgin Islands

See also Barbados; Belize; Cayman Trough; Cuba; Haiti; Jamaica; Martinique; Netherlands Antilles; Puerto Rico; Tobago; Trinidad (Island); Virgin Islands; West Indies; *and* names of countries bordering the Caribbean

CARIBBEE (Yawl):

Baltic Cruise of the *Caribbee*. By Carleton Mitchell. 605-646, Nov. 1950

CARIBOU:

Canada Counts Its Caribou. 261-268, Aug. 1952

Caribou: Hardy Nomads of the North. By Jim Rearden. 858-878, Dec. 1974

Trek Across Arctic America. By Colin Irwin. 295-321, Mar. 1974

CARIBOU — *Continued*

Wildlife of Mount McKinley National Park. By Adolph Murie. Paintings by Walter A. Weber. 249-270, Aug. 1953

CARIBOU ESKIMOS. *See* Padlermiut

CARLIN GOLD MINE, Nevada:

Nevada's Mountain of Invisible Gold. By Samuel W. Matthews. Photos by David F. Cupp. 668-679, May 1968

CARLSBAD CAVERNS, New Mexico:

Carlsbad Caverns in Color. By Mason Sutherland. Photos by E. "Tex" Helm. 433-468, Oct. 1953

CARMEL, California:

California's Land Apart — the Monterey Peninsula. By Mike W. Edwards. 682-703, Nov. 1972

California's Wonderful One. By Frank Cameron. Photos by B. Anthony Stewart. 571-617, Nov. 1959

CARMICHAEL, LEONARD:

Leonard Carmichael: An Appreciation. By Melvin M. Payne. 871-874, Dec. 1973

NGS Board of Trustees member. 419, 420, 423, Mar. 1957; 592, May 1957; 834, Dec. 1959; 796-797, June 1960; 881, 883, Dec. 1960

NGS Committee for Research and Exploration: Chairman. 882, Dec. 1961; 903, Dec. 1962; 9, 136, 146, 150, Jan. 1963; 626, Oct. 1963; 582, Oct. 1967; 230, Aug. 1970

NGS Vice President for Research and Exploration. 525, Apr. 1965

Author

The Smithsonian, Magnet on the Mall. Photos by Volkmar Wentzel. 796-845, June 1960

CARNEGIE, DAVID J.: Photographer:

Weighing the Aga Khan in Diamonds. 317-324, Mar. 1947

CARNIVALS:

Belgium Comes Back. By Harvey Klemmer. Photos by Maynard Owen Williams. 575-614, May 1948
  Included: *Gilles* and other carnival groups

Carnival in San Antonio. By Mason Sutherland. Photos by J. Baylor Roberts. 813-844, Dec. 1947

Carnival in Trinidad. By Howard La Fay. Photos by Winfield Parks. 693-701, Nov. 1971

Mexico's Booming Capital. By Mason Sutherland. Photos by Justin Locke. 785-824, Dec. 1951
  Included: Tepotzotlán carnival dancers, and the Huejotzingo carnival celebration

See also Gasparilla Celebration; Mardi Gras; Rio de Janeiro; Winter Carnivals

CARNIVOROUS PLANTS:

Malaysia's Giant Flowers and Insect-trapping Plants. By Paul A. Zahl. 680-701, May 1964

Plants That Eat Insects. By Paul A. Zahl. 643-659, May 1961

CAROLINE ISLANDS, Pacific Ocean:

Micronesia: The Americanization of Eden. By David S. Boyer. 702-744, May 1967

Pacific Wards of Uncle Sam. By W. Robert Moore. 73-104, July 1948

See also Ifalik; Kapingamarangi; Truk Lagoon; Ulithi; Yap Islands

CARONI SWAMP SANCTUARY, Trinidad:
New Scarlet Bird in Florida Skies. By Paul A. Zahl. 874-882, Dec. 1967

CARPATHIAN MOUNTAINS, Europe:
Americans Afoot in Rumania. By Dan Dimancescu. Photos by Dick Durrance II and Christopher G. Knight. 810-845, June 1969

CARR, ARCHIE: Author:
Alligators: Dragons in Distress. Photos by Treat Davidson and Laymond Hardy. 133-148, Jan. 1967
Imperiled Gift of the Sea: Caribbean Green Turtle. Photos by Robert E. Schroeder. 876-890, June 1967

CARR, GERALD P.:
Skylab, Outpost on the Frontier of Space. By Thomas Y. Canby. Photos by the nine mission astronauts. 441-469, Oct. 1974

CARRAO, Río, Venezuela:
Jungle Journey to the World's Highest Waterfall. By Ruth Robertson. 655-690, Nov. 1949

CARSON, Camp, Colorado:
School for Survival. By Curtis E. LeMay. 565-602, May 1953

CARTER, JEFF: Photographer:
"The Alice" in Australia's Wonderland. By Alan Villiers. Photos by Jeff Carter and David Moore. 230-257, Feb. 1966

CARTER, T. DONALD: Author:
Stalking Central Africa's Wildlife. Paintings by Walter A. Weber. 264-286, Aug. 1956

CARTHAGE (Ancient City), North Africa:
The Phoenicians, Sea Lords of Antiquity. By Samuel W. Matthews. Photos by Winfield Parks. Paintings by Robert C. Magis. 149-189, Aug. 1974

CARTIER, JACQUES:
North Through History Aboard *White Mist.* By Melville Bell Grosvenor. Photos by Edwin Stuart Grosvenor. 1-55, July 1970

CARTOGRAPHERS:
Eight Maps of Discovery. 757-769, June 1953
See also Bumstead, Newman; Chamberlin, Wellman; NGS: Cartographic Division

CARTOGRAPHY:
How We Mapped the Moon. By David W. Cook. 240-245, Feb. 1969
Landsat Looks at Hometown Earth. By Barry C. Bishop. 140-147, July 1976
Contents: How the color photomosaic supplement *Portrait U.S.A.* was made from Landsat imagery
Remote Sensing: New Eyes to See the World. By Kenneth F. Weaver. 46-73, Jan. 1969
Science Explores the Monsoon Sea. By Samuel W. Matthews. Photos by Robert F. Sisson. 554-575, Oct. 1967
See also Globes; Inter-American Geodetic Survey; NGS: Cartographic Division; U. S. Coast and Geodetic Survey

CARTOONS:
Fun Helped Them Fight. By Stuart E. Jones. 95-104, Jan. 1948

CARTOONS—*Continued*
The Magic Worlds of Walt Disney. By Robert de Roos. Photos by Thomas Nebbia. 159-207, Aug. 1963

CASABLANCA, Morocco:
From Sea to Sahara in French Morocco. By Jean and Franc Shor. 147-188, Feb. 1955
Morocco, Land of the Farthest West. By Thomas J. Abercrombie. 834-865, June 1971

CASCADE RANGE, U. S.:
Forest Fire: The Devil's Picnic. By Stuart E. Jones and Jay Johnston. 100-127, July 1968
Mexico to Canada on the Pacific Crest Trail. By Mike W. Edwards. Photos by David Hiser. 741-779, June 1971
New National Park Proposed: The Spectacular North Cascades. By Nathaniel T. Kenney. Photos by James P. Blair. 642-667, May 1968
Sno-Cats Mechanize Oregon Snow Survey. By Andrew H. Brown. Photos by John E. Fletcher. 691-710, Nov. 1949
Washington Wilderness, the North Cascades. By Edwards Park. Photos by Kathleen Revis. 335-367, Mar. 1961
See also Rainier, Mount

CASE, LELAND D.: Author:
Back to the Historic Black Hills. Photos by Bates Littlehales. 479-509, Oct. 1956

CASE, PAUL EDWARD: Author:
Boom Time in Kuwait. 783-802, Dec. 1952
I Become a Bakhtiari. 325-358, Mar. 1947

CASH, J. ALLAN: Photographer:
From Barra to Butt in the Hebrides. By Isobel Wylie Hutchison. 559-580, Oct. 1954
Lundy, Treasure Island of Birds. By P. T. Etherton. 675-698, May 1947

CASSIDY, BUTCH:
Riding the Outlaw Trail. By Robert Redford. Photos by Jonathan Blair. 622-657, Nov. 1976

CASTE SYSTEM. *See* Hindus and Hinduism

CASTERET, NORBERT: Author:
Lascaux Cave, Cradle of World Art. Photos by Maynard Owen Williams. 771-794, Dec. 1948
Author-Photographer
Probing Ice Caves of the Pyrenees. 391-404, Mar. 1953
Included: Casteret Grotto

CASTILLO DE SAN MARCOS, St. Augustine, Florida:
St. Augustine, Nation's Oldest City, Turns 400. By Robert L. Conly. 196-229, Feb. 1966

CASTLES:
Baltic Cruise of the *Caribbee.* By Carleton Mitchell. 605-646, Nov. 1950
Included: Bohus, Hammershus, Kalmar Nyckel, Karlsten Fortress, and Stegeborg
The Britain That Shakespeare Knew. By Louis B. Wright. Photos by Dean Conger. 613-665, May 1964
Included: Baynard's, Berkeley, Cawdor, Glamis, Middleham, Tower of London, Windsor
British Castles, History in Stone. By Norman Wil-

CASTLES — *Continued*

kinson. 111-129, July 1947

Building a New Austria. By Beverley M. Bowie. Photos by Volkmar Wentzel. 172-213, Feb. 1959
Included: Bernstein, Dürnstein, Forchtenstein, Güssing, Hofburg, Raabs, Riegersburg, Rosenburg, Schönbrunn, Schreckenwald

Cyprus, Idyllic Island in a Troubled Sea. By Jean and Franc Shor. 627-664, May 1952
Included: Castle of Kyrenia, St. Hilarion Castle

Hungary: Changing Homeland of a Tough, Romantic People. By Bart McDowell. Photos by Albert Moldvay and Joseph J. Scherschel. 443-483, Apr. 1971
Included: Buda, Eger, Eszterhazg, Köszeg, Royal Palace, Siklós, Székesféhérvar

Luxembourg, the Quiet Fortress. By Robert Leslie Conly. Photos by Ted H. Funk. 69-97, July 1970
Included: Lucilinburhuc on the Bock, Vianden

Modern Miracle, Made in Germany. By Robert Leslie Conly. Photos by Erich Lessing. 735-791, June 1959
Included: Gutenfels, Heidelberg, Katz, Maus, Sababurg, Schönburg

Poets' Voices Linger in Scottish Shrines. By Isobel Wylie Hutchison. Photos by Kathleen Revis. 437-488, Oct. 1957
Included: Caerlaverock, Duart, Dunnotar, Dunvegan, Edinburgh, Glamis

Rhododendron Glories of Southwest Scotland. By David S. Boyer. Photos by B. Anthony Stewart and author. 641-664, May 1954
Included: Castle Kennedy, Culzean, Lochinch

Scotland From Her Lovely Lochs and Seas. By Alan Villiers. Photos by Robert F. Sisson. 492-541, Apr. 1961
Included: Coll, Dunvegan, Edinburgh, Inverlochy, Kisimul, Urquhart

A Stroll to John o'Groat's. By Isobel Wylie Hutchison. 1-48, July 1956
Included: Balmoral, Belmont, Edinburgh, Falkland, Girnigoe, Invercauld, Sinclair Haunt

See also Caernarvon Castle; Crusader Lands; Hearst San Simeon State Historical Monument; Lullingstone Castle, England; Rhine; St. Michael's Mount; "Scotty's Castle," Death Valley; Skye, Isle of, for Dunvegan Castle; Tirol; *and* Chateaux

CATFISH:

New Florida Resident, the Walking Catfish. By Clarence P. Idyll. Photos by Robert F. Sisson. 847-851, June 1969

CATHEDRALS. *See* Canterbury Cathedral; Chartres; Notre Dame de Paris; Ste. Cécile

CATS:

The Big Cats (Television film). 442A-442B, Mar. 1974

Cats: Little Tigers in Your House. Children's book announced. 728-730, Nov. 1974

The Cats in Our Lives. By Adolph Suehsdorf. Photos by Walter Chandoha. 508-541, Apr. 1964

See also Jaguar Hunting; Lions; Mountain Lions; Snow Leopards; Tigers

CATTLE AND CATTLE RAISING:

America's "Meat on the Hoof." By William H. Nicholas. 33-72, Jan. 1952
King Ranch, Cattle Empire in Texas. 41-64

CATTLE AND CATTLE RAISING — *Continued*

Cowpunching on the Padlock Ranch. By William Albert Allard. 478-499, Oct. 1973

4-H Boys and Girls Grow More Food. By Frederick Simpich. 551-582, Nov. 1948

South in the Sudan. By Harry Hoogstraal. 249-272, Feb. 1953
Included: Zebu cattle

See also Wichita Mountains Wildlife Refuge, for Longhorns; *and* listing under Ranches

CATTLE EGRET:

A New Bird Immigrant Arrives. By Roger Tory Peterson. 281-292, Aug. 1954

CAUCASUS. *See* Abkhazian A.S.S.R.

CAUGHT in the Assam-Tibet Earthquake. By F. Kingdon-Ward. 403-416, Mar. 1952

CAULFIELD, PATRICIA: Photographer:
Twilight Hope for Big Cypress. By Rick Gore. 251-273, Aug. 1976

CAUSSES, France. *See* Languedoc

CAVE ART:

A Bold New Look at Our Past. The Editor. 62-63, Jan. 1975

The Caves of the Thousand Buddhas (Tunhwang, China). By Franc and Jean Shor. 383-415, Mar. 1951

Exploring Stone Age Arnhem Land (Australia). By Charles P. Mountford. Photos by Howell Walker. 745-782, Dec. 1949
Included: Cave paintings of Oenpelli and Groote Eylandt

Exploring the Mind of Ice Age Man. By Alexander Marshack. 64-89, Jan. 1975

India's Sculptured Temple Caves. By Volkmar Wentzel. 665-678, May 1953

Lascaux Cave, Cradle of World Art. By Norbert Casteret. Photos by Maynard Owen Williams. 771-794, Dec. 1948
Contents: La Baume Ladrone, La Henne Morte, La Mouthe, Lascaux, Montespan, Niaux, Trois Frères, Tuc D'Audoubert, in France; and Altamira in Spain

CAVE DWELLERS:

Gypsy Cave Dwellers of Andalusia. 572-582, Oct. 1957

See also Cliff Dwellers and Dwellings; Cones and Cone Dwellers; Tarahumara Indians; Tasaday Tribe

CAVES:

Bats Aren't All Bad. By Alvin Novick. Photos by Bruce Dale. 615-637, May 1973

Birds That "See" in the Dark With Their Ears. By Edward S. Ross. 282-290, Feb. 1965

Exploring America Underground. By Charles E. Mohr. 803-837, June 1964

Life and Death in Tana Toradja. By Pamela and Alfred Meyer. 793-815, June 1972

Nature's Night Lights: Probing the Secrets of Bioluminescence. By Paul A. Zahl. 45-69, July 1971
Included: Glowworms in Waitomo Caves, New Zealand

On the Trail of La Venta Man (Mexico). By Matthew W. Stirling. 137-172, Feb. 1947
Included: Cave of Guayabal

CAVES — *Continued*

Six Months Alone in a Cave (Biorhythm Research). By Michel Siffre. 426-435, Mar. 1975

See also Amarnath Cave, Kashmir; Carlsbad Caverns, New Mexico; Caves, Underwater; Ice Caves; Khirbat Qumrān; National Parks (U. S.: Heritage); Russell Cave, Alabama; *and* Cave Art; Cave Dwellers

CAVES, Underwater:

Into the Lairs of "Sleeping" Sharks. By Eugenie Clark. Photos by David Doubilet. 570-584, Apr. 1975

See also Blue Holes

CAYMAN TROUGH, Caribbean Sea:

Window on Earth's Interior. By Robert D. Ballard. Photos by Emory Kristof. 228-249, Aug. 1976

CAYMANS:

In the Wilds of a City Parlor. By Paul A. Zahl. 645-672, Nov. 1954

CELEBES (Island). *See* Sulawesi

CELLINI, BENVENUTO:

Golden Masterpieces. 29-39, Jan. 1974

CELLS:

The Awesome Worlds Within a Cell. By Rick Gore. Photos by Bruce Dale. Paintings by Davis Meltzer. 355-395, Sept. 1976
Included: Foldout showing geography of the cell

CELLULOSE:

Versatile Wood Waits on Man. By Andrew H. Brown. 109-140, July 1951

CEMETERIES, Military. *See* Arlington National Cemetery, Virginia; War Memorials

CENOTES: Yucatán, Mexico. *See* Chichén Itzá; Dzibilchaltun

CENSUS 1960: Profile of the Nation. By Albert W. Atwood and Lonnelle Aikman. 697-714, Nov. 1959

CENTENARIANS. *See* Oldest People

CENTRAL AFRICAN REPUBLIC:

Freedom Speaks French in Ouagadougou. By John Scofield. 153-203, Aug. 1966

CENTRAL AMERICA:

Archeological Map of Middle America, Land of the Feathered Serpent, map supplement. Text on reverse. Oct. 1968

Central America; Mexico, double-sided map supplement. May 1973

Countries of the Caribbean, including Mexico, Central America, and the West Indies, map supplement. Oct. 1947

Flags of the Americas. By Elizabeth W. King. 633-657, May 1949

How Fruit Came to America. By J. R. Magness. Paintings by Else Bostelmann. 325-377, Sept. 1951

Mexico and Central America, Atlas series supplement. Oct. 1961

Mexico and Central America, map supplement. Mar. 1953

Our Vegetable Travelers. By Victor R. Boswell.

CENTRAL AMERICA — *Continued*

Paintings by Else Bostelmann. 145-217, Aug. 1949

The Quetzal, Fabulous Bird of Maya Land. By Anne LaBastille Bowes. Photos by David G. Allen. 141-150, Jan. 1969

West Indies and Central America, map supplement. Jan. 1970

See also Belize; Costa Rica; Guatemala; Panama

CENTRAL PARK: Manhattan's Big Outdoors. By Stuart E. Jones. Photos by Bates Littlehales. 781-811, Dec. 1960

"The CENTRE" (Region), Australia:

Australia. II. The Settled East, the Barrier Reef, the Center. By Alan Villiers. 347-385, Sept. 1963

See also Alice Springs

CENTURY, Camp, Greenland:

Nuclear Power for the Polar Regions. By George J. Dufek. 712-730, May 1962

CEPHALONIA (Island), Greece:

Homeward With Ulysses. By Melville Bell Grosvenor. Photos by Edwin Stuart Grosvenor. 1-39, July 1973

CEPHALOPODS. *See* Chambered Nautilus; Octopuses; Squids

CERNAN, EUGENE A.:

Exploring Taurus-Littrow. By Harrison H. Schmitt. 290-307, Sept. 1973

CERRUTI, JAMES: Author:

Britain's "French" Channel Islands. Photos by James L. Amos. 710-740, May 1971

Chelsea, London's Haven of Individualists. Photos by Adam Woolfitt. 28-55, Jan. 1972

The Cotswolds, "Noicest Parrt o'England." Photos by Adam Woolfitt. 846-869, June 1974

Edinburgh: Capital in Search of a Country. Photos by Adam Woolfitt. 274-296, Aug. 1976

Gotland: Sweden's Treasure Island. Photos by Albert Moldvay. 268-288, Aug. 1973

Jamaica Goes It Alone. Photos by Thomas Nebbia. 843-873, Dec. 1967

The Netherlands Antilles: Holland in the Caribbean. Photos by Emory Kristof. 115-146, Jan. 1970

Sea Islands: Adventuring Along the South's Surprising Coast. Photos by Thomas Nebbia and James L. Amos. 366-393, Mar. 1971

Stockholm, Where "Kvalitet" Is a Way of Life. Photos by Albert Moldvay and Jonathan Blair. 43-69, Jan. 1976

The Two Acapulcos. Photos by Thomas Nebbia. 848-878, Dec. 1964

CETACEANS. *See* Porpoises; Whales

CÉVENNES (Mountains), France:

France's Past Lives in Languedoc. By Walter Meayers Edwards. 1-43, July 1951

CEYLON, now Sri Lanka:

Ceylon, Island of the "Lion People." By Helen Trybulowski Gilles. 121-136, July 1948

Ceylon, the Resplendent Land. By Donna K. and Gilbert M. Grosvenor. 447-497, Apr. 1966

Troubled Waters East of Suez. By Ernest M. Eller. 483-522, Apr. 1954

CHAD:
Freedom Speaks French in Ouagadougou. By John Scofield. 153-203, Aug. 1966

CHAFFER, NORMAN: Author-Photographer:
Australia's Amazing Bowerbirds. 866-873, Dec. 1961

CHAGNON, NAPOLEON A.: Author-Photographer:
Yanomamo, the True People. 211-223, Aug. 1976

CHALLACOMBE, J. R.: Author:
The Fabulous Sierra Nevada. 825-843, June 1954

CHALLENGER DEEP. See Mariana Trench

The CHAMBERED NAUTILUS, Exquisite Living Fossil. Photos by Douglas Faulkner. 38-41, Jan. 1976

CHAMBERLIN, WELLMAN:
Cartographer, NGS. 431, Mar. 1948
Cartographic innovations. 488, Apr. 1956; 808, Dec. 1957; 49, July 1960; 698, May 1961; 875, Dec. 1961; 897, Dec. 1962; 95, July 1966; 243, Feb. 1967
Chamberlin Trimetric Projection. 841, June 1947; 431, Mar. 1948; 826, June 1949; 399, Mar. 1950; 417, Mar. 1952; 591, Apr. 1964
Grandson of noted explorer, Walter Wellman. 347, Mar. 1967

CHAMPA, Kingdom of:
Mosaic of Cultures. By Peter T. White. Photos by W. E. Garrett. 296-329, Mar. 1971

CHAMPLAIN, SAMUEL DE:
North (U. S. and Canada) Through History Aboard White Mist. By Melville Bell Grosvenor. Photos by Edwin Stuart Grosvenor. 1-55, July 1970

CHAMPLAIN, Lake, Canada-U. S.:
From Sword to Scythe in Champlain Country. By Ethel A. Starbird. Photos by B. Anthony Stewart and Emory Kristof. 153-201, Aug. 1967
North Through History Aboard White Mist. By Melville Bell Grosvenor. Photos by Edwin Stuart Grosvenor. 1-55, July 1970

CHAN CHAN, Peru's Ancient City of Kings. By Michael E. Moseley and Carol J. Mackey. Photos by David Brill. 318-345, Mar. 1973

CHANDOHA, WALTER: Photographer:
The Cats in Our Lives. By Adolph Suehsdorf. 508-541, Apr. 1964

CHANGCHUN, China:
In Manchuria Now. By W. Robert Moore. 389-414, Mar. 1947

CHANGE Ripples New Guinea's Sepik River. By Malcolm S. Kirk. 354-381, Sept. 1973

The CHANGING Face of Old Spain. By Bart McDowell. Photos by Albert Moldvay. 291-339, Mar. 1965

CHANGING Formosa, Green Island of Refuge. By Frederick Simpich, Jr. Photos by Horace Bristol. 327-364, Mar. 1957

CHANGING Homeland of a Tough, Romantic People: Hungary. By Bart McDowell. Photos by Albert Moldvay and Joseph J. Scherschel. 443-483, Apr. 1971

The CHANGING World of Canada's Crees. By Fred Ward. 541-569, Apr. 1975

CH'ANGSHA, Hunan Province, People's Republic of China:
A Lady From China's Past. Photos from China Pictorial. Text by Alice J. Hall. 660-681, May 1974

CHANNEL Cruise to Glorious Devon. By Alan Villiers. Photos by Bates Littlehales. 208-259, Aug. 1963

CHANNEL ISLANDS, California. See Santa Barbara Islands

CHANNEL ISLANDS, English Channel:
Britain's "French" Channel Islands. By James Cerruti. Photos by James L. Amos. 710-740, May 1971

CHAPELLE, ANTHONY: Author:
Report from the Locust Wars. By Tony and Dickey Chapelle. 545-562, Apr. 1953
Author-Photographer
New Life for India's Villagers. By Anthony and Georgette Dickey Chapelle. 572-588, Apr. 1956

CHAPELLE, DICKEY:
What Was a Woman Doing There? (Memorial Tribute). By W. E. Garrett. 270-271, Feb. 1966
Author
Report from the Locust Wars. By Tony and Dickey Chapelle. 545-562, Apr. 1953
Author-Photographer
Helicopter War in South Viet Nam. 723-754, Nov. 1962
New Life for India's Villagers. By Anthony and Georgette Dickey Chapelle. 572-588, Apr. 1956
Water War in Viet Nam. 272-296, Feb. 1966

CHARACTER Marks the Coast of Maine. By John Scofield. Photos by B. Anthony Stewart. 798-843, June 1968

CHARLES, Prince of Wales:
The Investiture of Great Britain's Prince of Wales. By Allan C. Fisher, Jr. Photos by James L. Stanfield and Adam Woolfitt. 698-715, Nov. 1969

CHARLES W. MORGAN (Whaler):
The Age of Sail Lives On at Mystic. By Alan Villiers. Photos by Weston Kemp. 220-239, Aug. 1968

CHARLESTON, South Carolina:
Patriots in Petticoats. By Lonnelle Aikman. Paintings by Louis S. Glanzman. 475-493, Oct. 1975
South Carolina Rediscovered. By Herbert Ravenel Sass. 281-321, Mar. 1953

CHARLOTTE AMALIE, Virgin Islands:
Our Virgin Islands, 50 Years Under the Flag. By Carleton Mitchell. Photos by James L. Stanfield. 67-103, Jan. 1968
Virgin Islands: Tropical Playland, U.S.A. By John Scofield. Photos by Charles Allmon. 201-232, Feb. 1956

CHARLOTTESVILLE, Virginia:
Mr. Jefferson's Charlottesville. By Anne Revis. 553-592, May 1950
See also Monticello

CHARTING Our Sea and Air Lanes. By Stuart E. Jones. Photos by J. Baylor Roberts. 189-209, Feb. 1957

CHARTRES, Cathedral of, France:

Chartres: Legacy From the Age of Faith. By Kenneth MacLeish. Photos by Dean Conger. 857-882, Dec. 1969

CHARYBDIS (Whirlpool and Legendary Monster). *See* Messina, Strait of

CHATEAUX:

France's Past Lives in Languedoc. By Walter Meayers Edwards. 1-43, July 1951
    Included: Cité (Fortress), Carcassonne; Polignac

Lafayette's Homeland, Auvergne. By Howell Walker. 419-436, Sept. 1957
    Included: Aix, Chavaniac, Du Motier, La Grange, St. Romain, Tournoël

River of Counts and Kings: The Loire. By Kenneth MacLeish. Photos by Dean Conger. 822-869, June 1966
    Included: Amboise, Angers, Arlempdes, Azay-le-Rideau, Blois, Chambord, Chaumont, Chenonceaux, Cheverny, Chinon, Gien, Langeais, Saumur, Sully, Ussé

CHATURVEDI, M. D.: Author:

The Elephant and I. 489-507, Oct. 1957

CHAUCER, GEOFFREY:

The British Way. By Sir Evelyn Wrench. 421-541, Apr. 1949

CHEESE AND CHEESE MAKING:

Deep in the Heart of "Swissconsin." By William H. Nicholas. Photos by J. Baylor Roberts. 781-800, June 1947

Helping Holland Rebuild Her Land. By Gilbert M. Grosvenor and Charles Neave. 365-413, Sept. 1954

See also Goats of Thunder Hill; Switzerland (Highrise)

CHEKIANG (Province), China:

Operation Eclipse: 1948. By William A. Kinney. 325-372, Mar. 1949

CHELLEAN CULTURE:

Exploring 1,750,000 Years Into Man's Past. By L. S. B. Leakey. Photos by Robert F. Sisson. 564-589, Oct. 1961

CHELSEA, London's Haven of Individualists. By James Cerruti. Photos by Adam Woolfitt. 28-55, Jan. 1972

CHEMICAL INDUSTRY:

Today on the Delaware, Penn's Glorious River. By Albert W. Atwood. Photos by Robert F. Sisson. 1-40, July 1952

CHEMICAL POLLUTION:

Pollution, Threat to Man's Only Home. By Gordon Young. Photos by James P. Blair. 738-781, Dec. 1970

Quicksilver and Slow Death. By John J. Putman. Photos by Robert W. Madden. 507-527, Oct. 1972

CHEMISTRY:

The British Way. By Sir Evelyn Wrench. 421-541, Apr. 1949

The Romance of American Furs. By Wanda Burnett. 379-402, Mar. 1948

CHEMISTRY—*Continued*

    Included: The plasticizing of furs, developed by Dr. José B. Calva

Uncle Sam's House of 1,000 Wonders (National Bureau of Standards). By Lyman J. Briggs and F. Barrows Colton. 755-784, Dec. 1951

See also Biochemistry; Perfume

CHEROKEE INDIANS:

Pack Trip Through the Smokies. By Val Hart. Photos by Robert F. Sisson. 473-502, Oct. 1952

See also Oklahoma, the Adventurous One

CHESAPEAKE AND OHIO CANAL:

Waterway to Washington, the C & O Canal. By Jay Johnston. 419-439, Mar. 1960

CHESAPEAKE BAY, and Region:

Chesapeake Country. By Nathaniel T. Kenney. Photos by Bates Littlehales. 370-411, Sept. 1964

"Delmarva," Gift of the Sea. By Catherine Bell Palmer. 367-399, Sept. 1950

Maryland on the Half Shell. By Stuart E. Jones. Photos by Robert W. Madden. 188-229, Feb. 1972

One Hundred Hours Beneath the Chesapeake. By Gilbert C. Klingel. Photos by Willard R. Culver. 681-696, May 1955

Round About the Nation's Capital, map supplement. Apr. 1956

Roving Maryland's Cavalier Country. By William A. Kinney. 431-470, Apr. 1954

The Sailing Oystermen of Chesapeake Bay. By Luis Marden. 798-819, Dec. 1967

This Is My Island, Tangier. By Harold G. Wheatley. Photos by David Alan Harvey. 700-725, Nov. 1973

See also Eastern Shore; Virginia (Captain Smith; History Keeps House); *and* Chesapeake Bay Bridge-Tunnel; Intracoastal Waterway

CHESAPEAKE BAY BRIDGE-TUNNEL:

Over and Under Chesapeake Bay. By David S. Boyer. 593-612, Apr. 1964

CHESSMEN Come to Life in Marostica. By Alexander Taylor. 658-668, Nov. 1956

CHESTER DALE COLLECTION:

Great Masters of a Brave Era in Art (Impressionist). By Hereward Lester Cooke, Jr. 661-697, May 1961

CHETELAT, ENZO DE: Author:

Roaming Korea South of the Iron Curtain. 777-808, June 1950

CHIANG KAI-SHEK:

Eyes on the China Coast. By George W. Long. 505-512, Apr. 1953

Taiwan: The Watchful Dragon. By Helen and Frank Schreider. 1-45, Jan. 1969

CHIAPAS (State), Mexico:

The Maya. 729-811, Dec. 1975
    I. Children of Time. By Howard La Fay. Photos by David Alan Harvey. 729-767
        Included: Bonampak; Chamula; Palenque
    II. Riddle of the Glyphs. By George E. Stuart. Photos by Otis Imboden. 768-791
        Included: Palenque; Yaxchilán

See also Piedra Parada

CHICAGO, Illinois:

The Great Lakes: Is It Too Late? By Gordon Young. Photos by James L. Amos and Martin Rogers. 147-185, Aug. 1973

Illinois—Healthy Heart of the Nation. By Leo A. Borah. Photos by B. Anthony Stewart and Willard R. Culver. 781-820, Dec. 1953

Illinois: The City and the Plain. By Robert Paul Jordan. Photos by James L. Stanfield and Joseph J. Scherschel. 745-797, June 1967

Mapping the Nation's Breadbasket. By Frederick Simpich. 831-849, June 1948

CHICHÉN ITZÁ, Yucatán, Mexico:

Into the Well of Sacrifice. 540-561, Oct. 1961
  I. Return to the Sacred Cenote. By Eusebio Dávalos Hurtado. 540-549
  II. Treasure Hunt in the Deep Past. By Bates Littlehales. 550-561

The Maya, Children of Time. By Howard La Fay. Photos by David Alan Harvey. 729-767, Dec. 1975

CHICHICASTENANGO, Guatemala:

Easter Week in Indian Guatemala. By John Scofield. 406-417, Mar. 1960

Guatemala Revisited. By Luis Marden. 525-564, Oct. 1947

CHICKENS:

Easter Egg Chickens. By Frederick G. Vosburgh. Photos by B. Anthony Stewart. 377-387, Sept. 1948

See also Onagadori

CHIDSEY, DONALD BARR: Author:

The Old Boston Post Roads. 189-205, Aug. 1962

CHIHUAHUA (State), Mexico:

The Tarahumaras: Mexico's Long Distance Runners. By James Norman. Photos by David Hiser. 702-718, May 1976

CHILDHOOD Summer on the Maine Coast. By Arline Strong. 436-444, Sept. 1960

CHILDREN:

Blue-eyed Indian: A City Boy's Sojourn with Primitive Tribesmen in Central Brazil. By Harald Schultz. 65-89, July 1961

Children's Art Around the World. By Newman Bumstead. 365-387, Mar. 1957

Dinkelsbühl Rewards Its Children. By Charles Belden. 255-268, Feb. 1957

The Family: A Mormon Shrine. 459-463, Apr. 1975

4-H Boys and Girls Grow More Food. By Frederick Simpich. 551-582, Nov. 1948

The GI and the Kids of Korea. By Robert H. Mosier. 635-664, May 1953

In Touch With Nature. Text by Elizabeth A. Moize. Photos by Steve Raymer. 537-543, Apr. 1974

Norway Cracks Her Mountain Shell. By Sydney Clark. Photos by Gilbert Grosvenor and Ole Friele Backer. 171-211, Aug. 1948

Passage to Freedom in Viet Nam. By Gertrude Samuels. 858-874, June 1955

Seashore Summer: One Mother's Recipe for Small-boy Bliss. By Arline Strong. 436-444, Sept. 1960

Uncle Sam Bends a Twig in Germany. By Frederick Simpich. Photos by J. Baylor Roberts. 529-550, Oct. 1948

CHILDREN—Continued

We Build a School for Sherpa Children. By Sir Edmund Hillary. 548-551, Oct. 1962

Zoo Animals Go to School. By Marion P. McCrane. Photos by W. E. Garrett. 694-706, Nov. 1956

See also Boy Scouts; Children's Village; Children's Zoo; Clarke School for the Deaf; Little Tibet in Switzerland; Spafford Memorial Children's Hospital

CHILDREN of the Sun and Moon. By Harald Schultz; translated from German by Curtis T. Everett. 340-363, Mar. 1959

CHILDREN'S BOOKS. See Books, NGS: Children's Books

CHILDREN'S MAGAZINES, NGS. See School Bulletin; WORLD

CHILDREN'S VILLAGE in Switzerland, Pestalozzi. Photos by Alfred Lammer. 268-282, Aug. 1959

CHILDREN'S ZOO, Regent's Park, London:

London's Zoo of Zoos. By Thomas Garner James. 771-786, June 1953

CHILE:

Atlantic Odyssey: Iceland to Antarctica. By Newman Bumstead. Photos by Volkmar Wentzel. 725-780, Dec. 1955

Chile, Republic on a Shoestring. By Gordon Young. Photos by George F. Mobley. 437-477, Oct. 1973

Chile, the Long and Narrow Land. By Kip Ross. 185-235, Feb. 1960

The Lost Empire of the Incas. By Loren McIntyre. Art by Ned and Rosalie Seidler. 729-787, Dec. 1973
  A Pictorial Chronicle of the Incas. 747-753

Parks, Plans, and People: How South America Guards Her Green Legacy. By Mary and Laurance Rockefeller. Photos by George F. Mobley. 74-119, Jan. 1967

See also Easter Island; Patagonia; Torre Egger; Valparaíso

CHILIN (Kirin), China:

In Manchuria Now. By W. Robert Moore. 389-414, Mar. 1947

CHIMOR EMPIRE:

Chan Chan, Peru's Ancient City of Kings. By Michael E. Moseley and Carol J. Mackey. Photos by David Brill. 318-345, Mar. 1973

CHIMPANZEES:

Miss Goodall and the Wild Chimpanzees (Television film). 831A-831B, Dec. 1965

My Friends the Wild Chimpanzees. Special Publication announced. 408-417, Mar. 1966

My Life Among Wild Chimpanzees. By Jane Goodall. Photos by Baron Hugo van Lawick and author. 272-308, Aug. 1963

New Discoveries Among Africa's Chimpanzees. By Baroness Jane van Lawick-Goodall. Photos by Baron Hugo van Lawick. 802-831, Dec. 1965

School for Space Monkeys. 725-729, May 1961

CHIMU (People). See Chimor Empire

CHINA (People's Republic of China):

Adventures in Lololand. By Rennold L. Lowy. 105-118, Jan. 1947

CHINA (People's Republic of China)—*Continued*

Along the Yangtze, Main Street of China. By W. Robert Moore. 325-356, Mar. 1948

The Caves of the Thousand Buddhas. By Franc and Jean Shor. 383-415, Mar. 1951

China, Atlas series supplement. Nov. 1964

China Coast and Korea, map supplement. Oct. 1953

China Unveils Her Newest Treasures. Photos by Robert W. Madden. 848-857, Dec. 1974

Eyes on the China Coast. By George W. Long. 505-512, Apr. 1953

How Fruit Came to America. By J. R. Magness. Paintings by Else Bostelmann. 325-377, Sept. 1951

How the Kazakhs Fled to Freedom. By Milton J. Clark. 621-644, Nov. 1954

In Manchuria Now. By W. Robert Moore. 389-414, Mar. 1947

A Lady From China's Past. Photos from *China Pictorial.* Text to Alice J. Hall. 660-681, May 1974

Operation Eclipse: 1948. By William A. Kinney. 325-372, Mar. 1949

Our Vegetable Travelers. By Victor R. Boswell. Paintings by Else Bostelmann. 145-217, Aug. 1949

Return to Changing China. By Audrey Topping. 801-833, Dec. 1971

This Is the China I Saw. By Jørgen Bisch. 591-639, Nov. 1964
  Included: Canton; Hangchow; Peking; Shanghai; Sian; Tatung; Yun Kang Caves

Those Outlandish Goldfish! By Paul A. Zahl. 514-533, Apr. 1973
  Included: China's 1960 postage stamp series

Trawling the China Seas. Photos by J. Charles Thompson. 381-395, Mar. 1950

The World in Your Garden (Flowers). By W. H. Camp. Paintings by Else Bostelmann. 1-65, July 1947

See also Kunming; Peking

CHINA, Republic of. *See* Taiwan

CHINATOWN, the Gilded Ghetto. By William Albert Allard. 627-643, Nov. 1975

CHINCHILLAS:

The Romance of American Furs. By Wanda Burnett. 379-402, Mar. 1948

CHIRIQUÍ (Province), Panama:

Exploring Ancient Panama by Helicopter. By Matthew W. Stirling. Photos by Richard H. Stewart. 227-246, Feb. 1950

Panama, Link Between Oceans and Continents. By Jules B. Billard. Photos by Bruce Dale. 402-440, Mar. 1970

CHISOS MOUNTAINS, Texas:

Big Bend: Jewel in the Texas Desert. By Nathaniel T. Kenney. Photos by James L. Stanfield. 104-133, Jan. 1968

CHITTAGONG HILL TRACTS, Bangladesh:

Bangladesh: Hope Nourishes a New Nation. By William S. Ellis. Photos by Dick Durrance II. 295-333, Sept. 1972

The Peaceful Mrus of Bangladesh. By Claus-Dieter Brauns. 267-286, Feb. 1973

CHLOROPHYLL:

How the Sun Gives Life to the Sea (Photosynthesis). By Paul A. Zahl. 199-225, Feb. 1961

CHOCÓ (Region), Colombia:

Capturing Strange Creatures in Colombia. By Marte Latham. Photos by Tor Eigeland. 682-693, May 1966

CHOLLA CACTUS:

Abundant Life in a Desert Land. By Walter Meayers Edwards. 424-436, Sept. 1973

CHOLO INDIANS:

Capturing Strange Creatures in Colombia. By Marte Latham. Photos by Tor Eigeland. 682-693, May 1966

CHONG, JERRY: Photographer:

Saving the Nene, World's Rarest Goose. By S. Dillon Ripley. 745-754, Nov. 1965

CHOU EN-LAI:

Return to Changing China. By Audrey Topping. 801-833, Dec. 1971

CHOWNING, ANN: Photographer:

Blowgun Hunters of the South Pacific. By Jane C. Goodale. 793-817, June 1966

CHRISTCHURCH, New Zealand:

New Zealand, Pocket Wonder World. By Howell Walker. 419-460, Apr. 1952

New Zealand's Bountiful South Island. By Peter Benchley. Photos by James L. Amos. 93-123, Jan. 1972

CHRISTIANS AND CHRISTIANITY:

Hashemite Jordan, Arab Heartland. By John Scofield. 841-856, Dec. 1952

Jerusalem to Rome in the Path of St. Paul. By David S. Boyer. 707-759, Dec. 1956

The Land of Galilee. By Kenneth MacLeish. Photos by B. Anthony Stewart. 832-865, Dec. 1965

The Other Side of Jordan. By Luis Marden. 790-825, Dec. 1964

Pilgrimage to Holy Island and the Farnes. By John E. H. Nolan. 547-570, Oct. 1952

Pilgrims Follow the Christmas Star. By Maynard Owen Williams. 831-840, Dec. 1952

Searching Out Medieval Churches in Ethiopia's Wilds. By Georg Gerster. 856-884, Dec. 1970

Vézelay, Hill of the Pilgrims. By Melvin Hall. 229-247, Feb. 1953

Where Jesus Walked. By Howard La Fay. Photos by Charles Harbutt. 739-781, Dec. 1967

See also Amana Colonies; Churches; Crusades; Great St. Bernard Hospice; Greek Orthodox Church; Holy Week; Hutterites; Moravians; Mormons; Old Believers; Popes; Shakers

CHRISTIANSØ (Island), Denmark. *See* Baltic Cruise of the *Caribbee*

CHRISTMAS:

"The Adoration of the Magi," painting supplement. Jan. 1952

Christmas in Cookie Tree Land. By Louise Parker La Gorce. Photos by B. Anthony Stewart. 844-851, Dec. 1955

Old Salem, Morning Star of Moravian Faith. By Rowe Findley. Photos by Robert W. Madden. 818-837, Dec. 1970

CHRISTMAS—*Continued*

Pilgrims Follow the Christmas Star. By Maynard Owen Williams. 831-840, Dec. 1952

Williamsburg, City for All Seasons. By Joseph Judge. Photos by James L. Amos. 790-823, Dec. 1968

CHRISTOPHER COLUMBUS and the New World He Found. By John Scofield. Photos by Adam Woolfitt. 584-625, Nov. 1975

CHUBB CRATER, Quebec, Canada:

Solving the Riddle of Chubb Crater. By V. Ben Meen. Photos by Richard H. Stewart. 1-32, Jan. 1952

CHUBUT PROVINCE, Argentina:

Patagonia. Photos by Des and Jen Bartlett. 290-339, Mar. 1976
I. Argentina Protects Its Wildlife Treasures. By William G. Conway. 290-297
II. Where Two Worlds Meet. 298-321
III. At Home With Right Whales. By Roger Payne. 322-339

CHUCKWALLA MOUNTAINS, California:

Poorwill Sleeps Away the Winter. By Edmund C. Jaeger. 273-280, Feb. 1953

CHUGACH MOUNTAINS, Alaska:

Alaska's Automatic Lake Drains Itself (Lake George). 835-844, June 1951

CHURCH, RON: Photographer:

Deepstar Explores the Ocean Floor. 110-129, Jan. 1971

CHURCH OF JESUS CHRIST OF LATTER-DAY SAINTS. *See* Mormons

CHURCH OF THE NATIVITY, Bethlehem:

Hashemite Jordan, Arab Heartland. By John Scofield. 841-856, Dec. 1952

CHURCHES:

Across the Potomac from Washington. By Albert W. Atwood. 1-33, Jan. 1953

Searching Out Medieval Churches in Ethiopia's Wilds. By Georg Gerster. 856-884, Dec. 1970

See also Basilique de la Sainte Marie Madeleine; Church of the Nativity; Cones and Cone Dwellers; France (Auvergne; Normandy); Greek Orthodox Church; Istanbul, for Byzantine churches; Jerusalem; Medieval Europe; Missions; Poland; Rome; St. Catherine's Monastery; St. Peter's; Venice; War Memorials, for chapels; Westminster Abbey; *and* listing under Cathedrals

CHURCHILL, SIR WINSTON:

The British Way. By Sir Evelyn Wrench. 421-541, Apr. 1949

Tribute to Sir Winston. 153-225, Aug. 1965
I. The Churchill I Knew. By Dwight D. Eisenhower. 153-157
II. "Be Ye Men of Valour." By Howard La Fay. 159-197
III. The Funeral of Sir Winston Churchill, with Excerpts from His Speeches. Phonograph record. 198-198B
IV. The Final Tribute. Text by Carolyn Bennett Patterson. 199-225

CHURCHILL, Canada:

Canada's Heartland, the Prairie Provinces. By W. E. Garrett. 443-489, Oct. 1970

Rockets Explore the Air Above Us. By Newman Bumstead. 562-580, Apr. 1957

Trailing Cosmic Rays in Canada's North. By Martin A. Pomerantz. 99-115, Jan. 1953

CHURCHILL DOWNS, Louisville, Kentucky:

Heart of the Bluegrass. By Charles McCarry. Photos by J. Bruce Baumann. 634-659, May 1974

CICADAS:

Rip Van Winkle of the Underground (Periodical Cicada). By Kenneth F. Weaver. 133-142, July 1953

CINDER FARMING. *See* Lanzarote

CINTA LARGA INDIANS:

Brazil Protects Her Cinta Larga Indians. By W. Jesco von Puttkamer. 420-444, Sept. 1971

CIRCUS:

On the Road With an Old-time Circus. By John Fetterman. Photos by Jonathan Blair. 410-434, Mar. 1972

The Wonder City That Moves by Night. By Francis Beverly Kelley. 289-324, Mar. 1948
Circus Action in Color. By Harold E. Edgerton. 305-308

CITÉ, Île de la, Paris:

Île de la Cité, Birthplace of Paris. By Kenneth MacLeish. Photos by Bruce Dale. 680-719, May 1968

The More Paris Changes.... By Howell Walker. Photos by Gordon W. Gahan. 64-103, July 1972

CITIES Like Worcester Make America. By Howell Walker. 189-214, Feb. 1955

CITIES of Stone in Utah's Canyonland. By W. Robert Moore. 653-677, May 1962

CITRUS FRUITS:

Florida Rides a Space-age Boom. By Benedict Thielen. Photos by Winfield Parks and James P. Blair. 858-903, Dec. 1963

How Fruit Came to America. By J. R. Magness. Paintings by Else Bostelmann. 325-377, Sept. 1951
Included: Grapefruit, Lemon, Lime, Orange

Living in a Japanese Village. By William Graves. Photos by James L. Stanfield. 668-693, May 1972

"The CITY"—London's Storied Square Mile. By Allan C. Fisher, Jr. 735-777, June 1961

CITY Astride Two Continents: Istanbul. By William S. Ellis. Photos by Winfield Parks. 501-533, Oct. 1973

CITY PLANNING. *See* Brasília; Rotterdam—Reborn; *and* Urban Renewal

The CITY They Call Red China's Showcase. By Franc Shor. 193-223, Aug. 1960

CIVIL AIR PATROL:

Minutemen of the Civil Air Patrol. By Allan C. Fisher, Jr. Photos by John E. Fletcher. 637-665, May 1956

CIVIL WAR, U. S.:

Appomattox: Where Grant and Lee Made Peace

CIVIL WAR, U. S.—*Continued*

With Honor a Century Ago. By Ulysses S. Grant 3rd. Photos by Bruce Dale. 435-469, Apr. 1965

Battlefields of the Civil War, double-sided Atlas series supplement. Apr. 1961

The Civil War. By Ulysses S. Grant 3rd. 437-449, Apr. 1961

The Civil War. Special Publication announced. 880-884, June 1969

Gettysburg and Vicksburg: the Battle Towns Today. By Robert Paul Jordan. Map notes by Carolyn Bennett Patterson. 4-57, July 1963

How We Found the *Monitor.* By John G. Newton. 48-61, Jan. 1975

Just a Hundred Years Ago. By Carl Sandburg. 1-3, July 1963

Lincoln, Man of Steel and Velvet. By Carl Sandburg. 239-241, Feb. 1960

Our Land Through Lincoln's Eyes. By Carolyn Bennett Patterson. Photos by W. D. Vaughn. 243-277, Feb. 1960

The Virginians. By Mike W. Edwards. Photos by David Alan Harvey. 588-617, Nov. 1974

Witness to a War: British Correspondent Frank Vizetelly. By Robert T. Cochran, Jr. 453-491, Apr. 1961

See also American Processional: History on Canvas; Atlanta; Harpers Ferry; Mobile; South Carolina Rediscovered

CLARK, DEENA: Author:

The Flowers That Say "Aloha." Photos by Robert B. Goodman. 121-131, Jan. 1967

Home Life in Paris Today. 43-72, July 1950

Iceland Tapestry. 599-630, Nov. 1951

La Jolla, a Gem of the California Coast. Photos by J. Baylor Roberts. 755-782, Dec. 1952

CLARK, EUGENIE: Author:

Into the Lairs of "Sleeping" Sharks. Photos by David Doubilet. 570-584, Apr. 1975

The Red Sea's Gardens of Eels. Photos by James L. Stanfield and David Doubilet. 724-735, Nov. 1972

The Red Sea's Sharkproof Fish. Photos by David Doubilet. 718-727, Nov. 1974

The Strangest Sea. Photos by David Doubilet. 338-343, Sept. 1975

CLARK, HARLAN B.: Author:

Yemen—Southern Arabia's Mountain Wonderland. 631-672, Nov. 1947

CLARK, LEWIS F.: Author:

Amid the Mighty Walls of Zion (Zion National Park). 37-70, Jan. 1954

CLARK, MILTON J.: Author-Photographer:

How the Kazakhs Fled to Freedom. 621-644, Nov. 1954

CLARK, ROBERT: Photographer:

Rafting Down the Yukon. By Keith Tryck. 830-861, Dec. 1975

CLARK, RONALD W.: Author:

Liechtenstein Thrives on Stamps. 105-112, July 1948

CLARK, SYDNEY: Author:

Luxembourg, Survivor of Invasions. Photos by Maynard Owen Williams. 791-810, June 1948

Mid-century Holland Builds Her Future. 747-778, Dec. 1950

Norway Cracks Her Mountain Shell. Photos by Gilbert Grosvenor and Ole Friele Backer. 171-211, Aug. 1948

CLARK, WILLIAM:

Following the Trail of Lewis and Clark. By Ralph Gray. 707-750, June 1953

CLARKE SCHOOL FOR THE DEAF, Northampton, Massachusetts:

Deaf Children Learn to Talk at Clarke School. By Lilian Grosvenor. Photos by Willard R. Culver. 379-397, Mar. 1955

CLASSICAL LANDS:

Classical Lands of the Mediterranean, map supplement. Dec. 1949

See also Greece; Roman Empire; Rome, Italy

CLEARWATER (River), Idaho:

Idaho Loggers Battle a River. 117-130, July 1951

CLEMENS, SAMUEL LANGHORNE. *See* Twain, Mark

CLEVELAND, GROVER:

Inside the White House. By Lonnelle Aikman. Photos by B. Anthony Stewart and Thomas Nebbia. 3-34, Jan. 1961

The Living White House. By Lonnelle Aikman. 593-643, Nov. 1966

Profiles of the Presidents: III. The American Giant Comes of Age. By Frank Freidel. 660-711, May 1965

CLIFF DWELLERS AND DWELLINGS:

Ancient Cliff Dwellers of Mesa Verde. By Don Watson. Photos by Willard R. Culver. 349-376, Sept. 1948

Cities of Stone in Utah's Canyonland. By W. Robert Moore. 653-677, May 1962

Cliff Dwellers of the Bering Sea. By Juan Muñoz. 129-146, Jan. 1954

Foxes Foretell the Future in Mali's Dogon Country. By Pamela Johnson Meyer. 431-448, Mar. 1969

Searching for Cliff Dwellers' Secrets (Wetherill Mesa). By Carroll A. Burroughs. 619-625, Nov. 1959

Solving the Riddles of Wetherill Mesa. By Douglas Osborne. Paintings by Peter V. Bianchi. 155-195, Feb. 1964

20th-century Indians Preserve Customs of the Cliff Dwellers. Photos by William Belknap, Jr. 196-211, Feb. 1964

Your Society to Seek New Light on the Cliff Dwellers. 154-156, Jan. 1959

CLIFF PAINTINGS. *See* Rock Paintings

CLIMATE:

Alaska's Mighty Rivers of Ice. By Maynard M. Miller. Photos by Christopher G. Knight. 194-217, Feb. 1967

What's Happening to Our Climate? By Samuel W. Matthews. 576-615, Nov. 1976

See also Weather

The CLIMB Up Cone Crater. By Alice J. Hall. Photos by Edgar D. Mitchell and Alan B. Shepard, Jr. 136-148, July 1971

CLIMBING Half Dome the Hard Way. By Galen Rowell. 782-791, June 1974

CLIMBING Our Northwest Glaciers. Photos by Bob and Ira Spring. 103-114, July 1953

CLINCH, NICHOLAS B.:

First La Gorce Medal Honors Antarctic Expedition. 864-867, June 1967

Author

First Conquest of Antarctica's Highest Peaks. 836-863, June 1967

A CLOCK for the Ages: Potassium-Argon. By Garniss H. Curtis. 590-592, Oct. 1961

CLOCKS AND CLOCKMAKING:

Split-second Time Runs Today's World. By F. Barrows Colton and Catherine Bell Palmer. 399-428, Sept. 1947

The Tower of the Winds. By Derek J. de Solla Price. Paintings by Robert C. Magis. 587-596, Apr. 1967

CLOUD FORMATIONS:

Historic Color Portrait of Earth From Space. By Kenneth F. Weaver. Photos by DODGE Satellite. 726-731, Nov. 1967

CLOUD Gardens in the Tetons. By Frank and John Craighead. 811-830, June 1948

CLOVE-SCENTED Zanzibar. By W. Robert Moore. 261-278, Feb. 1952

CLYDE, ROBERT, Family:

The Family: A Mormon Shrine. 459-463, Apr. 1975

COACHELLA VALLEY, California:

The Lure of the Changing Desert. 817-824, June 1954

COAL AND COAL MINING:

Coal Makes the Saar a Prize. By Franc Shor. 561-576, Apr. 1954

Illinois — Healthy Heart of the Nation. By Leo A. Borah. Photos by B. Anthony Stewart and Willard R. Culver. 781-820, Dec. 1953

In Manchuria Now. By W. Robert Moore. 389-414, Mar. 1947

Mountain Voices, Mountain Days (West Virginia). By Bryan Hodgson. Photos by Linda Bartlett. 118-146, July 1972

Pittsburgh: Workshop of the Titans. By Albert W. Atwood. 117-144, July 1949

The Search for Tomorrow's Power. By Kenneth F. Weaver. Photos by Emory Kristof. 650-681, Nov. 1972

Spitsbergen Mines Coal Again. 113-120, July 1948

This Land of Ours — How Are We Using It? By Peter T. White. Photos by Emory Kristof. 20-67, July 1976

Turnaround Time in West Virginia. By Elizabeth A. Moize. Photos by Jodi Cobb. 755-785, June 1976

Will Coal Be Tomorrow's "Black Gold"? By Gordon Young. Photos by James P. Blair. 234-259, Aug. 1975

COAST, U. S. See Atlantic Coast; Pacific Coast

COAST AND GEODETIC SURVEY. See U. S. Coast and Geodetic Survey

The COAST GUARD: Small Service With a Big Mission. By William S. Ellis. 113-139, July 1974
See also U. S. Coast Guard

COATS OF ARMS:

Flags of the Americas. By Elizabeth W. King. 633-657, May 1949
Included: Coats of arms of: Argentina; Bolivia; Brazil; Chile; Colombia; Costa Rica; Cuba; Dominican Republic; Ecuador; El Salvador; Guatemala; Haiti; Honduras; Mexico; Nicaragua; Panama; Paraguay; Peru; Uruguay; Venezuela

Flags of the United Nations. By Elizabeth W. King. 213-238, Feb. 1951
Included: Coats of arms of: Bolivia; Chile; Colombia; Costa Rica; Denmark; Dominican Republic; Ecuador; El Salvador; Greece; Guatemala; Haiti; Honduras; Iceland; Mexico; Nicaragua; Paraguay; Peru; Sweden; United Kingdom; Uruguay; Venezuela

COBB, JODI: Photographer:

California's Parched Oasis, the Owens Valley. By Judith and Neil Morgan. Photos by Jodi Cobb and Galen Rowell. 98-127, Jan. 1976

Turnaround Time in West Virginia. By Elizabeth A. Moize. 755-785, June 1976

COBRAS:

The Cobra, India's "Good Snake." By Harry Miller. Photos by author and Naresh and Rajesh Bedi. 393-409, Sept. 1970

COCHRAN, DORIS M.: Author:

Nature's Tank, the Turtle. Paintings by Walter A. Weber. 665-684, May 1952

Our Snake Friends and Foes. Paintings by Walter A. Weber. 334-364, Sept. 1954

COCHRAN, ROBERT T., Jr.: Author:

History and Beauty Blend in a Concord Iris Garden. Photos by M. Woodbridge Williams. 705-719, May 1959

Witness to a War: British Correspondent Frank Vizetelly. 453-491, Apr. 1961

COCK-OF-THE-ROCK:

Strange Courtship of the Cock-of-the-Rock. By E. Thomas Gilliard. 134-140, Jan. 1962

COCLÉ INDIAN CULTURE:

Exploring the Past in Panama. By Matthew W. Stirling. Photos by Richard H. Stewart. 373-399, Mar. 1949

COCOS (Keeling) ISLANDS, Indian Ocean:

Yankee Roams the Orient. By Irving and Electa Johnson. 327-370, Mar. 1951

COD, Cape, Massachusetts. See Cape Cod

COD FISHING:

Dory on the Banks: A Day in the Life of a Portuguese Fisherman. By James H. Pickerell. 573-583, Apr. 1968

Fishing in the Lofotens. Photos by Lennart Nilsson. 377-388, Mar. 1947

I Sailed with Portugal's Captains Courageous. By Alan Villiers. 565-596, May 1952

The Lonely Dorymen (Television film). 579A-579B, Apr. 1968

COD FISHING — *Continued*

Newfoundland, Canada's New Province. By Andrew H. Brown. Photos by Robert F. Sisson. 777-812, June 1949

CODRAI, RONALD: Author-Photographer:

Desert Sheikdoms of Arabia's Pirate Coast. 65-104, July 1956

CODY, WILLIAM F.:

Hays, Kansas, at the Nation's Heart. By Margaret M. Detwiler. Photos by John E. Fletcher. 461-490, Apr. 1952

COE, WILLIAM R.: Author:

The Maya: Resurrecting the Grandeur of Tikal. 792-798, Dec. 1975

COEN, MARCEL: Photographer:

Sheep Trek in the French Alps. By Maurice Moyal. 545-564, Apr. 1952

COFFEE:

Behind the Veil of Troubled Yemen. By Thomas J. Abercrombie. 403-445, Mar. 1964
Included: The origin of coffee drinking

See also Brazil (Brazil, Ôba!); Colombia; Costa Rica; Guatemala

COFRADÍAS. *See* Guatemala Revisited; Holy Week and the Fair in Sevilla

COLLEAGUE of the Golden Years: John Oliver La Gorce. By Gilbert Grosvenor. 440-444, Mar. 1960

COLLEGES. *See* Universities and Colleges

COLLINS, HENRY B.: Author:

Vanished Mystery Men of Hudson Bay. 669-687, Nov. 1956

COLLINS, LORENCE G.: Author-Photographer:

Finding Rare Beauty in Common Rocks. 121-129, Jan. 1966

COLLINS, MICHAEL:

First Explorers on the Moon: The Incredible Story of Apollo 11. 735-797, Dec. 1969
I. Man Walks on Another World. By Neil A. Armstrong, Edwin E. Aldrin, Jr., and Michael Collins. 738-749
II. Sounds of the Space Age, From Sputnik to Lunar Landing. A record narrated by Frank Borman. 750-751
III. The Flight of Apollo 11: "One giant leap for mankind." By Kenneth F. Weaver. 752-787
First Moon Explorers (Apollo 11) Receive the Society's Hubbard Medal. 859-861, June 1970

COLLISON, JAMES: Photographer:

Happy Birthday, Otto Lilienthal! By Russell Hawkes. 286-292, Feb. 1972

COLOMBIA:

Capturing Strange Creatures in Colombia. By Marte Latham. Photos by Tor Eigeland. 682-693, May 1966

Colombia, from Amazon to Spanish Main. By Loren McIntyre. 235-273, Aug. 1970

Cruising Colombia's "Ol' Man River." By Amos Burg. 615-660, May 1947

Jungle Jaunt on Amazon Headwaters. By Bernice M. Goetz. 371-388, Sept. 1952

Keeping House for a Biologist in Colombia. By Nancy Bell Fairchild Bates. Photos by Marston

COLOMBIA — *Continued*

Bates. 251-274, Aug. 1948

See also Andean Condors; Gems; Gold; Orchids

COLOMBO, Sri Lanka:

Ceylon, Island of the "Lion People." By Helen Trybulowski Gilles. 121-136, July 1948

Ceylon, the Resplendent Land. By Donna K. and Gilbert M. Grosvenor. 447-497, Apr. 1966

COLONIAL AMERICA:

America's Beginnings. Special Publication announced. 870-874, June 1974

Benjamin Franklin, Philosopher of Dissent. By Alice J. Hall. Photos by Linda Bartlett. 93-123, July 1975

Founders of New England. By Sir Evelyn Wrench. Photos by B. Anthony Stewart. 803-838, June 1953

Founders of Virginia. By Sir Evelyn Wrench. Photos by B. Anthony Stewart. 433-462, Apr. 1948

From Sword to Scythe in Champlain Country. By Ethel A. Starbird. Photos by B. Anthony Stewart and Emory Kristof. 153-201, Aug. 1967

Massachusetts Builds for Tomorrow. By Robert de Roos. Photos by B. Anthony Stewart. 790-843, Dec. 1966
Included: Boston; Concord; Duxbury; Plymouth; Sudbury

The St. Lawrence, River Key to Canada. By Howard La Fay. Photos by John Launois. 622-667, May 1967

Thomas Jefferson: Architect of Freedom. By Mike W. Edwards. Photos by Linda Bartlett. 231-259, Feb. 1976

See also Boston Post Roads; Concord, Massachusetts; Deerfield, Massachusetts; Jamestown, Virginia; Maryland (Roving); Philadelphia, Pennsylvania; Roanoke Island, for Lost Colony; St. Augustine, Florida; Williamsburg, Virginia

COLONIZATION:

The British Way. By Sir Evelyn Wrench. 421-541, Apr. 1949

Capt. John Smith's Map of Virginia. — Captain Smith's New England . . . and the Pilgrims' Cape Cod. 760-765, June 1953

Founders of New England. By Sir Evelyn Wrench. Photos by B. Anthony Stewart. 803-838, June 1953

Founders of Virginia. By Sir Evelyn Wrench. Photos by B. Anthony Stewart. 433-462, Apr. 1948

The Vikings. By Howard La Fay. Photos by Ted Spiegel. 492-541, Apr. 1970

See also Colonial America; Jamestown, Virginia; Mozambique, for Limpopo Colonato; Roanoke Island, for Lost Colony; St. Augustine, Florida; Vinland

COLORADO:

Colorado, the Rockies' Pot of Gold. By Edward J. Linehan. Photos by James L. Amos. 157-201, Aug. 1969

Colorado by Car and Campfire. By Kathleen Revis. 207-248, Aug. 1954

Colorado's Friendly Topland (Rocky Mountains). By Robert M. Ormes. 187-214, Aug. 1951

A Map Maker Looks at the United States. By Newman Bumstead. 705-748, June 1951
Included: Antero (peak); Arkansas River; Canon City; Colorado Springs; Denver; Grand Junction; Gun-

COLORADO — *Continued*

nison; Monarch Pass; Montrose; Ouray (peak); Pikes Peak; Pueblo; Royal Gorge; Sawatch Mountains

Oil, the Dwindling Treasure. By Noel Grove. Photos by Emory Kristof. 792-825, June 1974

Shooting Rapids in Dinosaur Country. By Jack Breed. Photos by author and Justin Locke. 363-390, Mar. 1954

Skiing in the United States. By Kathleen Revis. 216-254, Feb. 1959

Stalking the West's Wild Foods. By Euell Gibbons. Photos by David Hiser. 186-199, Aug. 1973

See also Aspen; Carson, Camp; Colorado Plateaus; Four Corners Country; Mesa Verde National Park; U. S. Air Force Academy; Wetherill Mesa

COLORADO DESERT, California:

Poorwill Sleeps Away the Winter. By Edmund C. Jaeger. 273-280, Feb. 1953

COLORADO PLATEAUS, U. S.:

Hunting Uranium Around the World. By Robert D. Nininger. Photos by Volkmar Wentzel. 533-558, Oct. 1954

COLORADO RIVER AND BASIN, U. S.:

The Bittersweet Waters of the Lower Colorado. By Rowe Findley. Photos by Charles O'Rear. 540-569, Oct. 1973

Canyonlands, Realm of Rock and the Far Horizon. By Rowe Findley. Photos by Walter Meayers Edwards. 71-91, July 1971

Colorado's Friendly Topland (Rocky Mountains). By Robert M. Ormes. 187-214, Aug. 1951

Desert River Through Navajo Land. By Alfred M. Bailey. Photos by author and Fred G. Brandenburg. 149-172, Aug. 1947

First Motor Sortie into Escalante Land. By Jack Breed. 369-404, Sept. 1949

Grand Canyon: Nature's Story of Creation. By Louis Schellbach. Photos by Justin Locke. 589-629, May 1955

Lake Powell: Waterway to Desert Wonders. By Walter Meayers Edwards. 44-75, July 1967

Retracing John Wesley Powell's Historic Voyage Down the Grand Canyon. By Joseph Judge. Photos by Walter Meayers Edwards. 668-713, May 1969

Seeking the Secret of the Giants. By Frank M. Setzler. Photos by Richard H. Stewart. 390-404, Sept. 1952
Giant Effigies of the Southwest. By George C. Marshall. 389

Shooting Rapids in Reverse! Jet Boats Climb the Colorado's Torrent Through the Grand Canyon. By William Belknap, Jr. 552-565, Apr. 1962

Three Roads to Rainbow. By Ralph Gray. 547-561, Apr. 1957

COLTON, F. BARROWS: Author:

Eclipse Hunting in Brazil's Ranchland. Photos by Richard H. Stewart and Guy W. Starling. 285-324, Sept. 1947

Lightning in Action. 809-828, June 1950

Man's New Servant, the Friendly Atom. Photos by Volkmar Wentzel. 71-90, Jan. 1954

Mapping the Unknown Universe. 401-420, Sept. 1950

Miracle Men of the Telephone. 273-316, Mar. 1947

Mountains Top Off New England. Photos by Rob-

COLTON, F. BARROWS: Author — *Continued*
ert F. Sisson. 563-602, May 1951

Our Air Age Speeds Ahead. 249-272, Feb. 1948

Our Home-town Planet, Earth. 117-139, Jan. 1952

Split-second Time Runs Today's World. By F. Barrows Colton and Catherine Bell Palmer. 399-428, Sept. 1947

Uncle Sam's House of 1,000 Wonders (National Bureau of Standards). By Lyman J. Briggs and F. Barrows Colton. 755-784, Dec. 1951

Water for the World's Growing Needs. By Herbert B. Nichols and F. Barrows Colton. 269-286, Aug. 1952

COLUMBIA, South Carolina:

South Carolina Rediscovered. By Herbert Ravenel Sass. Photos by Robert F. Sisson. 281-321, Mar. 1953

COLUMBIA RIVER AND BASIN, U. S.-Canada:

The Columbia River, Powerhouse of the Northwest. By David S. Boyer. 821-847, Dec. 1974

Following the Trail of Lewis and Clark. By Ralph Gray. 707-750, June 1953

From Sagebrush to Roses on the Columbia. By Leo A. Borah. 571-611, Nov. 1952

A Map Maker Looks at the United States. By Newman Bumstead. 705-748, June 1951

Oregon's Many Faces. By Stuart E. Jones. Photos by Bates Littlehales. 74-115, Jan. 1969

COLUMBIA UNIVERSITY: Expeditions and Research:

Archeological Expedition: Virú, Peru. 453, 454, 455, 457, 463, 466, Apr. 1947

Mid-Atlantic Ridge. 275, 279, 285, 293, Sept. 1948; 611, 636, Nov. 1949; 147, July 1950; 14, 29, Jan. 1963

COLUMBUS, CHRISTOPHER:

Christopher Columbus and the New World He Found. By John Scofield. Photos by Adam Woolfitt. 584-625, Nov. 1975

COMANCHE (Mountain), Bolivia:

Puya, the Pineapple's Andean Ancestor. By Mulford B. Foster. 463-480, Oct. 1950

COMANCHE INDIANS:

Big Bend: Jewel in the Texas Desert. By Nathaniel T. Kenney. Photos by James L. Stanfield. 104-133, Jan. 1968

COMBINES (Harvesting Machines). *See* Agriculture (The Revolution); Wheat (North With the Wheat Cutters)

COMETS:

Giant Comet (Ikeya-Seki) Grazes the Sun. By Kenneth F. Weaver. 259-261, Feb. 1966
Included: Halley's comet

How to Catch a Passing Comet (Kohoutek). By Kenneth F. Weaver. 148-150, Jan. 1974

What You Didn't See in Kohoutek. By Kenneth F. Weaver. 214-223, Aug. 1974

The COMING of the Polynesians. By Kenneth P. Emory. 732-745, Dec. 1974

The COMING Revolution in Transportation. By Fredric C. Appel. Photos by Dean Conger. 301-341, Sept. 1969

COMMAGENE (Ancient Country):

Throne Above the Euphrates. By Theresa Goell. 390-405, Mar. 1961

COMMERCE:

Behold the Computer Revolution. By Peter T. White. Photos by Bruce Dale and Emory Kristof. 593-633, Nov. 1970

COMMON TERNS:

Friend of the Wind: The Common Tern. By Ian Nisbet. Photos by Hope Alexander. 234-247, Aug. 1973

COMMONWEALTH OF NATIONS. *See* former name, British Commonwealth of Nations

COMMUNAL LIVING:

From Spear to Hoe on Groote Eylandt. By Howell Walker. 131-142, Jan. 1953

Old Salem, Morning Star of Moravian Faith. By Rowe Findley. Photos by Robert W. Madden. 818-837, Dec. 1970

Return to Changing China. By Audrey Topping. 801-833, Dec. 1971

See also Amana Colonies; Hutterites; Kibbutzim; Old Believers; Padanaram; Saint Véran; Shakers; Tasaday Tribe

COMMUNICATIONS:

The Flying Telegraph (Homing Pigeon). By Joseph F. Spears. Official U. S. Army Signal Corps photos. 531-554, Apr. 1947

Miracle Men of the Telephone. By F. Barrows Colton. 273-316, Mar. 1947

New Miracles of the Telephone Age. By Robert Leslie Conly. 87-120, July 1954

See also DEW Line; Satellites

COMMUNITY DEVELOPMENT PROGRAMS. *See* Bastar, India; *and* Peace Corps; YWCA

COMO, Lake, Italy:

Lombardy's Lakes, Blue Jewels in Italy's Crown. By Franc Shor. Photos by Joseph J. Scherschel. 58-99, July 1968

COMPUTERS:

Behold the Computer Revolution. By Peter T. White. Photos by Bruce Dale and Emory Kristof. 593-633, Nov. 1970

The Coming Revolution in Transportation. By Fredric C. Appel. Photos by Dean Conger. 301-341, Sept. 1969

Computer Helps Scholars Re-create an Egyptian Temple. By Ray Winfield Smith. Photos by Emory Kristof. 634-655, Nov. 1970

We're Doing Something About the Weather! By Walter Orr Roberts. 518-555, Apr. 1972

See also Integrated Circuits; Landsat; Space Flights and Research

CONCORD, Massachusetts:

History and Beauty Blend in a Concord Iris Garden. By Robert T. Cochran, Jr. Photos by M. Woodbridge Williams. 705-719, May 1959

Literary Landmarks of Massachusetts. By William H. Nicholas. Photos by B. Anthony Stewart and John E. Fletcher. 279-310, Mar. 1950

CONCORD, New Hampshire:

The Merrimack: River of Industry and Romance. By Albert W. Atwood. Photos by B. Anthony Stewart. 106-140, Jan. 1951

CONDON, GENEAL: Author:

Blossoms That Defy the Seasons (Flower Preservation). Photos by David S. Boyer. 420-427, Sept. 1958

The CONDOR, Soaring Spirit of the Andes. By Jerry McGahan. Photos by Libby McGahan. 684-709, May 1971

CONES AND CONE DWELLERS:

Cappadocia: Turkey's Country of Cones. Photos by Marc Riboud. 122-146, Jan. 1958

Keeping House in a Cappadocian Cave. By Jonathan S. Blair. 127-146, July 1970

CONGER, CLEMENT E.: Author-Photographer:

Portugal Is Different. 583-622, Nov. 1948

CONGER, DEAN: Author-Photographer:

Siberia: Russia's Frozen Frontier. 297-345, Mar. 1967

Photographer

Abraham, the Friend of God. By Kenneth MacLeish. 739-789, Dec. 1966

An American in Russia's Capital. By Thomas T. Hammond. 297-351, Mar. 1966

The Britain That Shakespeare Knew. By Louis B. Wright. 613-665, May 1964

Brunei, Borneo's Abode of Peace. By Joseph Judge. 207-225, Feb. 1974

Cape Cod, Where Sea Holds Sway Over Man and Land. By Nathaniel T. Kenney. 149-187, Aug. 1962

Chartres: Legacy From the Age of Faith. By Kenneth MacLeish. 857-882, Dec. 1969

The Coming Revolution in Transportation. By Fredric C. Appel. 301-341, Sept. 1969

Exploring Tomorrow With the Space Agency. By Allan C. Fisher, Jr. 48-89, July 1960

From Sea to Shining Sea: A Cross Section of the United States Along Historic Route 40. By Ralph Gray. Photos by Dean Conger and author. 1-61, July 1961

Help for Philippine Tribes in Trouble. By Kenneth MacLeish. 220-255, Aug. 1971

High-stepping Idaho. By William S. Ellis. 290-317, Mar. 1973

Hopes and Fears in Booming Thailand. By Peter T. White. 76-125, July 1967

I Fly the X-15. By Joseph A. Walker. 428-450, Sept. 1962

Java—Eden in Transition. By Kenneth MacLeish. 1-43, Jan. 1971

Journey to Outer Mongolia. By William O. Douglas. 289-345, Mar. 1962

Mr. Jefferson's Monticello. By Joseph Judge. Photos by Dean Conger and Richard S. Durrance. 426-444, Sept. 1966

The Other Yosemite. By Nathaniel T. Kenney. 762-781, June 1974

The Pilot's Story: Astronaut Shepard's Firsthand Account of His Flight. 432-444, Sept. 1961

River of Counts and Kings: The Loire. By Kenneth MacLeish. 822-869, June 1966

Siberia's Empire Road, the River Ob. By Robert Paul Jordan. 145-181, Feb. 1976

CONGO, Democratic Republic of the (formerly Belgian Congo, now Zaire):

Africa: The Winds of Freedom Stir a Continent. By

CONGO, Democratic Republic of the—*Continued*
Nathaniel T. Kenney. Photos by W. D. Vaughn. 303-359, Sept. 1960
Freedom's Progress South of the Sahara. By Howard La Fay. Photos by Joseph J. Scherschel. 603-637, Nov. 1962
My Life With Africa's Little People. By Anne Eisner Putnam. 278-302, Feb. 1960
Roaming Africa's Unfenced Zoos. By W. Robert Moore. 353-380, Mar. 1950
Safari from Congo to Cairo. By Elsie May Bell Grosvenor. Photos by Gilbert Grosvenor. 721-771, Dec. 1954
White Magic in the Belgian Congo. By W. Robert Moore. 321-362, Mar. 1952
See also National Parks (Africa); Ruwenzori; Virunga Mountains; Zaire

CONGO, People's Republic of the:
Freedom's Progress South of the Sahara. By Howard La Fay. Photos by Joseph J. Scherschel. 603-637, Nov. 1962

CONGO RIVER, Africa:
White Magic in the Belgian Congo. By W. Robert Moore. 321-362, Mar. 1952

CONGRESS, U. S. *See* U. S. Congress

CONKLIN, PAUL: Photographer:
Ambassadors of Good Will: The Peace Corps. By Sargent Shriver and Peace Corps Volunteers. 297-345, Sept. 1964

CONLEY, ROBERT A. M.: Author:
Locusts: "Teeth of the Wind." Photos by Gianni Tortoli. 202-227, Aug. 1969

CONLY, ROBERT LESLIE: Author:
Luxembourg, the Quiet Fortress. Photos by Ted H. Funk. 69-97, July 1970
Men Who Measure the Earth. Photos by John E. Fletcher. 335-362, Mar. 1956
Modern Miracle, Made in Germany. Photos by Erich Lessing. 735-791, June 1959
The Mohawks Scrape the Sky. Photos by B. Anthony Stewart. 133-142, July 1952
New Miracles of the Telephone Age. 87-120, July 1954
Northern Ireland: From Derry to Down. 232-267, Aug. 1964
Porpoises: Our Friends in the Sea. Photos by Thomas Nebbia. 396-425, Sept. 1966
St. Augustine, Nation's Oldest City, Turns 400. 196-229, Feb. 1966

CONNECTICUT:
The Age of Sail Lives On at Mystic. By Alan Villiers. Photos by Weston Kemp. 220-239, Aug. 1968
Nomad Sails Long Island Sound. By Thomas Horgan. 295-338, Sept. 1957
The Old Boston Post Roads. By Donald Barr Chidsey. 189-205, Aug. 1962
The Post Road Today. Photos by B. Anthony Stewart. 206-233, Aug. 1962
Windjamming Around New England. By Tom Horgan. Photos by Robert F. Sisson. 141-169, Aug. 1950
Included: Mystic; Stonington
See also Connecticut River and Valley; New London

CONNECTICUT RIVER AND VALLEY:
Deerfield Keeps a Truce With Time. By Bart McDowell. Photos by Robert W. Madden. 780-809, June 1969
Yesterday Lingers Along the Connecticut. By Charles McCarry. Photos by David L. Arnold. 334-369, Sept. 1972

CONNOLLY, JOSEPH P.: Author:
Big Game Hunting (Paleontology) in the Land of Long Ago (South Dakota). By Joseph P. Connolly and James D. Bump. 589-605, May 1947

CONQUEST of the Holy City. By Franc Shor. Photos by Thomas Nebbia. 839-855, Dec. 1963

CONRAD, CHARLES, Jr.:
Skylab, Outpost on the Frontier of Space. By Thomas Y. Canby. Photos by the nine mission astronauts. 441-469, Oct. 1974

CONSERVATION:
African Wildlife: Man's Threatened Legacy. By Allan C. Fisher, Jr. Photos by Thomas Nebbia. Paintings by Ned Seidler. 147-187, Feb. 1972
Can We Save Our Salt Marshes? By Stephen W. Hitchcock. Photos by William R. Curtsinger. 729-765, June 1972
Escalante Canyon—Wilderness at the Crossroads. By Jon Schneeberger. 270-285, Aug. 1972
India Struggles to Save Her Wildlife. By John J. Putman. 299-343, Sept. 1976
Jackson Hole: Good-bye to the Old Days? By François Leydet. Photos by Jonathan Wright. 768-789, Dec. 1976
John Muir's Wild America. By Harvey Arden. Photos by Dewitt Jones. 433-461, Apr. 1973
Man's Wildlife Heritage Faces Extinction. By H. R. H. The Prince Philip, Duke of Edinburgh. 700-703, Nov. 1962
Minnesota, Where Water is the Magic Word. By David S. Boyer. Photos by author and David Brill. 200-229, Feb. 1976
Parks, Plans, and People: How South America Guards Her Green Legacy. By Mary and Laurance Rockefeller. Photos by George F. Mobley. 74-119, Jan. 1967
Portrait of a Fierce and Fragile Land. By Paul A. Zahl. 303-314, Mar. 1972
Saving Man's Wildlife Heritage (National Audubon Society). By John H. Baker. Photos by Robert F. Sisson. 581-620, Nov. 1954
Shrimp Nursery: Science Explores New Ways to Farm the Sea. By Clarence P. Idyll. Photos by Robert F. Sisson. 636-659, May 1965
Threatened Glories of Everglades National Park. By Frederick Kent Truslow and Frederick G. Vosburgh. Photos by Frederick Kent Truslow and Otis Imboden. 508-553, Oct. 1967
Timber: How Much Is Enough? By John J. Putman. Photos by Bruce Dale. 485-511, Apr. 1974
Twilight Hope for Big Cypress. By Rick Gore. Photos by Patricia Caulfield. 251-273, Aug. 1976
Will Oil and Tundra Mix? Alaska's North Slope Hangs in the Balance. By William S. Ellis. Photos by Emory Kristof. 485-517, Oct. 1971
Yellowstone Wildlife in Winter. By William Albert Allard. 637-661, Nov. 1967
See also Bird Sanctuaries and Rookeries; Connecticut River and Valley; National Monuments; Na-

CONSERVATION—*Continued*

tional Parks; Netherlands, for land reclamation; Sea Islands, Georgia-South Carolina; Texas (Fabulous State); U. S. Soil Conservation Service; Wild Rivers; Willamette River and Valley; *and* listing under Wildlife Refuges; *and* names of species

CONSHELF BASES:

At Home in the Sea. By Jacques-Yves Cousteau. 465-507, Apr. 1964

Working for Weeks on the Sea Floor. By Jacques-Yves Cousteau. Photos by Philippe Cousteau and Bates Littlehales. 498-537, Apr. 1966

The World of Jacques-Yves Cousteau (Television film). 529A-529B, Apr. 1966

CONSTELLATIONS:

A Map of the Heavens, map supplement. Star charts on reverse. Dec. 1957

Map of the Heavens, map supplement. Star charts on reverse. Aug. 1970

Unlocking Secrets of the Northern Lights. By Carl W. Gartlein. Paintings by William Crowder. 673-704, Nov. 1947
    Included: Pleiades, Southern Cross, Taurus

CONSTITUTION HALL, Washington, D. C.:

The DAR Story. By Lonnelle Aikman. Photos by B. Anthony Stewart and John E. Fletcher. 565-598, Nov. 1951

Gilbert Grosvenor's Golden Jubilee. By Albert W. Atwood. 253-261, Aug. 1949

The CONTENTED Land: New Zealand's North Island. By Charles McCarry. Photos by Bates Littlehales. 190-213, Aug. 1974

CONTINENTAL DRIFT:

Project FAMOUS. 586-615, May 1975
    I. Where the Earth Turns Inside Out. By J. R. Heirtzler. Photos by Emory Kristof. 586-603
    II. Dive Into the Great Rift. By Robert D. Ballard. Photos by Emory Kristof. 604-615

Science Explores the Monsoon Sea. By Samuel W. Matthews. Photos by Robert F. Sisson. 554-575, Oct. 1967

This Changing Earth. By Samuel W. Matthews. 1-37, Jan. 1973

Window on Earth's Interior. By Robert D. Ballard. Photos by Emory Kristof. 228-249, Aug. 1976
    Contents: Cayman Trough

CONTINENTAL SHELF RESEARCH:

The Deepest Days. By Robert Sténuit. 534-547, Apr. 1965

Outpost Under the Ocean. By Edwin A. Link. Photos by Bates Littlehales. 530-533, Apr. 1965

Tomorrow on the Deep Frontier. By Edwin A. Link. 778-801, June 1964

See also Conshelf Bases

A CONTINENT'S Living Treasure. Paintings by Ned Seidler. 164-167, Feb. 1972

CONWAY, WILLIAM G.: Author:

Argentina Protects Its Wildlife Treasures. Photos by Des and Jen Bartlett. 290-297, Mar. 1976

In Quest of the Rarest Flamingo. Photos by Bates Littlehales. 91-105, July 1961

COOBER PEDY, South Australia:

Coober Pedy: Opal Capital of Australia's Outback. By Kenny Moore. Photos by Penny Tweedie. 560-571, Oct. 1976

COOK, JAMES:

The British Way. By Sir Evelyn Wrench. 421-541, Apr. 1949

Captain Cook: The Man Who Mapped the Pacific. By Alan Villiers. Photos by Gordon W. Gahan. 297-349, Sept. 1971

COOK ISLANDS, South Pacific Ocean:

New Zealand's Cook Islands: Paradise in Search of a Future. By Maurice Shadbolt. Photos by William Albert Allard. 203-231, Aug. 1967

COOKE, HEREWARD LESTER, Jr.: Author:

Early America Through the Eyes of Her Native Artists. 356-389, Sept. 1962

Great Masters of a Brave Era in Art (Impressionist). 661-697, May 1961

The Louvre, France's Palace of the Arts. 796-831, June 1971

COOKE, HOPE:

Wedding of Two Worlds. By Lee E. Battaglia. 708-727, Nov. 1963

COOKIES:

Christmas in Cookie Tree Land. By Louise Parker La Gorce. Photos by B. Anthony Stewart. 844-851, Dec. 1955

COOLIDGE, CALVIN:

Inside the White House. By Lonnelle Aikman. Photos by B. Anthony Stewart and Thomas Nebbia. 3-43, Jan. 1961

The Living White House. By Lonnelle Aikman. 593-643, Nov. 1966

Profiles of the Presidents: IV. America Enters the Modern Era. By Frank Freidel. 537-577, Oct. 1965

COOPER RIVER WATER PROJECT:

South Carolina Rediscovered. By Herbert Ravenel Sass. Photos by Robert F. Sisson. 281-321, Mar. 1953

COOPERATIVE FARMS. *See* Amana Colonies; China (Return); Groote Eylandt (From Spear to Hoe); Hutterites; Kibbutzim; Old Believers; Old Salem; Padanaram; Saint Véran

COOPER'S HAWK:

Can the Cooper's Hawk Survive? By Noel Snyder. Photos by author and Helen Snyder. 433-442, Mar. 1974

COPENHAGEN, Denmark:

"Around the World in Eighty Days." By Newman Bumstead. 705-750, Dec. 1951

Baltic Cruise of the *Caribbee*. By Carleton Mitchell. 605-646, Nov. 1950

Copenhagen, Wedded to the Sea. By Stuart E. Jones. Photos by Gilbert M. Grosvenor. 45-79, Jan. 1963

Denmark, Field of the Danes. By William Graves. Photos by Thomas Nebbia. 245-275, Feb. 1974

Friendly Flight to Northern Europe. By Lyndon B. Johnson. Photos by Volkmar Wentzel. 268-293, Feb. 1964

Thumbs Up Round the North Sea's Rim. By Fran-

COPENHAGEN, Denmark—*Continued*

ces James. Photos by Erica Koch. 685-704, May 1952

2,000 Miles Through Europe's Oldest Kingdom. By Isobel Wylie Hutchison. Photos by Maynard Owen Williams. 141-180, Feb. 1949

Under Canvas in the Atomic Age. By Alan Villiers. 49-84, July 1955

COPERNICUS, NICOLAUS:

Pioneers in Man's Search for the Universe. Paintings by Jean-Leon Huens. Text by Thomas Y. Canby. 627-633, May 1974

Voyage to the Planets. By Kenneth F. Weaver. Paintings by Ludek Pesek. 147-193, Aug. 1970

COPPER:

Ancient Mesopotamia: A Light That Did Not Fail. By E. A. Speiser. Paintings by H. M. Herget. 41-105, Jan. 1951

From Tucson to Tombstone. By Mason Sutherland. 343-384, Sept. 1953

Montana, Shining Mountain Treasureland. By Leo A. Borah. 693-736, June 1950
  Included: Anaconda Copper Mining Company

"Rockhounds" Uncover Earth's Mineral Beauty. By George S. Switzer. 631-660, Nov. 1951
  Included: Ontonagon copper boulder

See also Mines and Mining (Congo; Michigan); *and* Alaska, the Big Land

COPRA:

Copra-ship Voyage to Fiji's Outlying Islands. By Marjory C. Thomas. 121-140, July 1950

Pacific Wards of Uncle Sam. By W. Robert Moore. 73-104, July 1948

Shores and Sails in the South Seas. By Charles Allmon. 73-104, Jan. 1950

CORA INDIANS:

Mesa del Nayar's Strange Holy Week. By Guillermo Aldana E. 780-795, June 1971

CORACLES:

Wales, Land of Bards. By Alan Villiers. Photos by Thomas Nebbia. 727-769, June 1965

CORALS AND CORAL REEFS:

Fish Men Explore a New World Undersea. By Jacques-Yves Cousteau. 431-472, Oct. 1952

Fluorescent Gems from Davy Jones's Locker. By Paul A. Zahl. 260-271, Aug. 1963

Life Cycle of a Coral. By Robert F. Sisson. 780-793, June 1973

Life Springs From Death in Truk Lagoon. By Sylvia A. Earle. Photos by Al Giddings. 578-613, May 1976
  From Graveyard to Garden. 604-613

Man-of-war Fleet Attacks Bimini. By Paul A. Zahl. 185-212, Feb. 1952

Probing the Deep Reefs' Hidden Realm. By Walter A. Starck II and Jo D. Starck. 867-886, Dec. 1972

Rainbow World Beneath the Red Sea. Photos by David Doubilet. 344-365, Sept. 1975

Starfish Threaten Pacific Reefs. By James A. Sugar. 340-353, Mar. 1970

The Strangest Sea (Red Sea). By Eugenie Clark. Photos by David Doubilet. 338-343, Sept. 1975

Tektite II: Part One. Science's Window on the Sea.

CORALS AND CORAL REEFS—*Continued*

By John G. VanDerwalker. Photos by Bates Littlehales. 256-289, Aug. 1971

Unsung Beauties of Hawaii's Coral Reefs (Nudibranchs). By Paul A. Zahl. 510-525, Oct. 1959

See also Alligator Reef; Great Barrier Reef; John Pennekamp Coral Reef State Park; Key Largo Coral Reef; Sha'ab Rūmi (Roman Reef); *and* Aqaba, Gulf of; Bermuda; Buck Island; Fiji Islands; Tuamotu Archipelago

CORBY, BERNARD: Photographer:

Bluebirds on the Wing in Color. Photos by Bernard Corby and Hance Roy Ivor. 527-530, Apr. 1954

CORCA DHUIBHNE. *See* Dingle Peninsula, Ireland

CORCORAN GALLERY OF ART, Washington, D. C.:

American Processional: History on Canvas. By John and Blanche Leeper. 173-212, Feb. 1951

CORDILLERA ORIENTAL, Andes Mountains. *See* Oriental, Cordillera

CÓRDOBA, Spain:

Andalusia, the Spirit of Spain. By Howard La Fay. Photos by Joseph J. Scherschel. 833-857, June 1975

Holy Week and the Fair in Sevilla. By Luis Marden. 499-530, Apr. 1951

CORFU (Island), Greece:

Homeward With Ulysses. By Melville Bell Grosvenor. Photos by Edwin Stuart Grosvenor. 1-39, July 1973

CORK INDUSTRY:

Portugal Is Different. By Clement E. Conger. 583-622, Nov. 1948

CORKSCREW SWAMP—Florida's Primeval Show Place. By Melville Bell Grosvenor. 98-113, Jan. 1958

CORMORANTS:

Peru Profits from Sea Fowl. By Robert Cushman Murphy. Photos by author and Grace E. Barstow Murphy. 395-413, Mar. 1959

Sea Bird Cities Off Audubon's Labrador. By Arthur A. Allen. 755-774, June 1948

CORN GROWING:

The Family Farm Ain't What It Used To Be. By James A. Sugar. 391-411, Sept. 1974

CORNELL UNIVERSITY: Expeditions and Research:

Aurora borealis. 869, June 1954

Curlew Expedition in 1948 to Alaska. 751, 761, Dec. 1948

"Library of Natural Sounds." 508, 511, Apr. 1950; 545, Apr. 1962; 14, Jan. 1963

Peru Project. 246, 247, Feb. 1964

Sapsucker Woods, Cornell University's Exciting New Bird Sanctuary. By Arthur A. Allen. 530-551, Apr. 1962

CORNING MUSEUM OF GLASS, Corning, New York:

History Revealed in Ancient Glass. By Ray Winfield Smith. Photos by B. Anthony Stewart and Lee E. Battaglia. 346-369, Sept. 1964

CORNWALL, PETER BRUCE: Author:

In Search of Arabia's Past. 493-522, Apr. 1948

CORNWALL (County), England:

Cowes to Cornwall. By Alan Villiers. Photos by Robert B. Goodman. 149-201, Aug. 1961

See also St. Michael's Mount

CORONATIONS:

Bhutan Crowns a New Dragon King. Photos by John Scofield. 546-571, Oct. 1974

Coronation in Katmandu (Mahendra, King of Nepal). By E. Thomas Gilliard. Photos by Marc Riboud. 139-152, July 1957

Coronations a World Apart. By the Editor. 299, Mar. 1968

In the London of the New Queen (Elizabeth II). By H. V. Morton. 291-342, Sept. 1953

Iran's Shah Crowns Himself and His Empress. By Franc Shor. Photos by James L. Stanfield and Winfield Parks. 301-321, Mar. 1968

Silkworms in England Spin for the Queen. By John E. H. Nolan. 689-704, May 1953

South Seas' Tonga Hails a King (Taufa'ahau Tupou IV). By Melville Bell Grosvenor. Photos by Edwin Stuart Grosvenor. 322-343, Mar. 1968

CORPUS CHRISTI CELEBRATION:

Spain's "Fortunate Isles," the Canaries. By Jean and Franc Shor. 485-522, Apr. 1955

CORSICA (Island), France:

Sunny Corsica: French Morsel in the Mediterranean. By Robert Cairns. Photos by Joseph J. Scherschel. 401-423, Sept. 1973

COSMIC RAYS:

Trailing Cosmic Rays in Canada's North. By Martin A. Pomerantz. 99-115, Jan. 1953

COSMONAUTS. *See* Apollo-Soyuz Mission

COSTA DEL SOL, Spain:

Andalusia, the Spirit of Spain. By Howard La Fay. Photos by Joseph J. Scherschel. 833-857, June 1975

COSTA RICA:

Costa Rica, Free of the Volcano's Veil. By Robert de Roos. 125-152, July 1965

Nature's Living, Jumping Jewels. By Paul A. Zahl. 130-146, July 1973

See also Ostional Beach

COTSWOLD HILLS, England:

By Cotswold Lanes to Wold's End. By Melville Bell Grosvenor. 615-654, May 1948

The Cotswolds, "Noicest Parrt o'England." By James Cerruti. Photos by Adam Woolfitt. 846-869, June 1974

The Thames Mirrors England's Varied Life. By Willard Price. Photos by Robert F. Sisson. 45-93, July 1958

COTTAGE INDUSTRIES:

Domesticating the Wild and Woolly Musk Ox. By John J. Teal, Jr. Photos by Robert W. Madden. 862-879, June 1970

From Barra to Butt in the Hebrides. By Isobel Wylie Hutchison. 559-580, Oct. 1954

Isles on the Edge of the Sea: Scotland's Outer Hebrides. By Kenneth MacLeish. Photos by Thomas Nebbia. 676-711, May 1970

Mountain Voices, Mountain Days. By Bryan

COTTAGE INDUSTRIES—*Continued*

Hodgson. Photos by Linda Bartlett. 118-146, July 1972

An Ozark Family Carves a Living and a Way of Life. Photos by Bruce Dale. 124-133, July 1975

COTTON AND COTTON INDUSTRY:

Dixie Spins the Wheel of Industry. By William H. Nicholas. Photos by J. Baylor Roberts. 281-324, Mar. 1949

The Greener Fields of Georgia. By Howell Walker. Photos by author and B. Anthony Stewart. 287-330, Mar. 1954

See also Alabama, Dixie to a Different Tune; The Merrimack; South Carolina Rediscovered

COTTRELL, ERNEST J.: Photographer:

Skyway Below the Clouds. By Carl R. Markwith. 85-108, July 1949

COUGARS. *See* Mountain Lions

COUNTDOWN For Space. By Kenneth F. Weaver. 702-734, May 1961

COUSTEAU, JACQUES-YVES:

Jacques-Yves Cousteau Receives National Geographic Society Medal at White House. 146-147, July 1961

The World of Jacques-Yves Cousteau (Television film). 529A-529B, Apr. 1966

Author

At Home in the Sea. 465-507, Apr. 1964

Calypso Explores an Undersea Canyon (Romanche Trench). Photos by Bates Littlehales. 373-396, Mar. 1958

Calypso Explores for Underwater Oil. 155-184, Aug. 1955

Diving Saucer *(Denise)* Takes to the Deep. 571-586, Apr. 1960

Diving Through an Undersea Avalanche. 538-542, Apr. 1955

Exploring Davy Jones's Locker with *Calypso*. Photos by Luis Marden. 149-161, Feb. 1956

Fish Men Discover a 2,200-year-old Greek Ship. 1-36, Jan. 1954

Fish Men Explore a New World Undersea. 431-472, Oct. 1952

Inflatable Ship *(Amphitrite)* Opens Era of Airborne Undersea Expeditions. 142-148, July 1961

To the Depths of the Sea by Bathyscaphe. 67-79, July 1954

Working for Weeks on the Sea Floor. Photos by Philippe Cousteau and Bates Littlehales. 498-537, Apr. 1966

COUSTEAU, PHILIPPE: Photographer:

Working for Weeks on the Sea Floor. By Jacques-Yves Cousteau. Photos by Philippe Cousteau and Bates Littlehales. 498-537, Apr. 1966

COWBIRDS:

The Bird's Year. By Arthur A. Allen. 791-816, June 1951

COWBOYS:

The American Cowboy in Life and Legend. Special Publication announced. 882-886, June 1971

Cowboys. Children's book announced. 724-726, Nov. 1975

Cowpunching on the Padlock Ranch. By William

COWBOYS — *Continued*

Albert Allard. 478-499, Oct. 1973

See also British Columbia: Life Begins; Montana, Shining Mountain Treasureland; North Dakota Comes; San Antonio, Texas; Sonora Is Jumping; South Dakota Keeps; West (Region), U. S.; *and Gardians;* Gauchos; *and* listing under Ranches

COWDEN, JEANNE: Author-Photographer:

Adventures With South Africa's Black Eagles. Photos by author and Arthur Bowland. 533-543, Oct. 1969

COWES, Isle of Wight:

The British Way. By Sir Evelyn Wrench. 421-541, Apr. 1949

Cowes to Cornwall. By Alan Villiers. Photos by Robert B. Goodman. 149-201, Aug. 1961

COWPUNCHING on the Padlock Ranch. By William Albert Allard. 478-499, Oct. 1973

COWS. *See* Cattle and Cattle Raising

COYOTES:

The Animals Nobody Loved (Television film). cover announcement, Feb. 1976

The "Lone" Coyote Likes Family Life. By Hope Ryden. Photos by author and David Hiser. 278-294, Aug. 1974

COZE, PAUL: Author-Photographer:

Kachinas: Masked Dancers of the Southwest. 219-236, Aug. 1957

COZUMEL ISLAND, Mexico:

Probing the Deep Reefs' Hidden Realm. By Walter A. Starck II and Jo D. Starck. 867-886, Dec. 1972

CRABS:

Can We Save Our Salt Marshes? By Stephen W. Hitchcock. Photos by William R. Curtsinger. 729-765, June 1972

The Crab That Shakes Hands. By Clarence P. Idyll. Photos by Robert F. Sisson. 254-271, Feb. 1971

This Is My Island, Tangier (Virginia). By Harold G. Wheatley. Photos by David Alan Harvey. 700-725, Nov. 1973

CRAFTS. *See* Embroidery; Folk Art; Goldsmithing; Handicrafts; Weaving

CRAFTSMEN:

The Craftsman in America. Special Publication announced. 870-874, June 1975

See also Artisans

CRAIGHEAD, CHARLES: Photographer:

Sharing the Lives of Wild Golden Eagles. By John Craighead. Photos by Charles and Derek Craighead. 420-439, Sept. 1967

CRAIGHEAD, DEREK: Author:

Yellowstone at 100: A Walk Through the Wilderness. By Karen and Derek Craighead. Photos by Sam Abell. 579-603, May 1972

Photographer

Sharing the Lives of Wild Golden Eagles. By John Craighead. Photos by Charles and Derek Craighead. 420-439, Sept. 1967

CRAIGHEAD, FRANK, Jr., and JOHN:

Author-Photographers

Bright Dyes Reveal Secrets of Canada Geese. 817-832, Dec. 1957

Cloud Gardens in the Tetons. 811-830, June 1948

Knocking Out Grizzly Bears For Their Own Good. 276-291, Aug. 1960

Studying Wildlife by Satellite. 120-123, Jan. 1973

Trailing Yellowstone's Grizzlies by Radio. 252-267, Aug. 1966

We Survive on a Pacific Atoll. 73-94, Jan. 1948

White-water Adventure on Wild Rivers of Idaho. 213-239, Feb. 1970

Wildlife Adventuring in Jackson Hole. 1-36, Jan. 1956

CRAIGHEAD, JOHN: Author:

Sharing the Lives of Wild Golden Eagles. Photos by Charles and Derek Craighead. 420-439, Sept. 1967

Studying Grizzly Habitat by Satellite. 148-158, July 1976

CRAIGHEAD, KAREN: Author:

Yellowstone at 100: A Walk Through the Wilderness. By Karen and Derek Craighead. Photos by Sam Abell. 579-603, May 1972

CRANBERRIES:

The People of New Jersey's Pine Barrens. By John McPhee. Photos by William R. Curtsinger. 52-77, Jan. 1974

CRANE, JOCELYN: Author:

Keeping House for Tropical Butterflies. Photos by M. Woodbridge Williams. 193-217, Aug. 1957

CRANES (Birds). *See* Sandhill Cranes; Whooping Cranes

CRATER LAKE NATIONAL PARK, Oregon:

Crater Lake Summer. By Walter Meayers Edwards. 134-148, July 1962

When Mt. Mazama Lost Its Top: The Birth of Crater Lake. By Lyman J. Briggs. 128-133, July 1962

CRATERS OF THE MOON NATIONAL MONUMENT, Idaho:

Man on the Moon in Idaho. By William Belknap, Jr. 505-525, Oct. 1960

La CRAU (Plain), France:

Sheep Trek in the French Alps. By Maurice Moyal. Photos by Marcel Coen. 545-564, Apr. 1952

CRAYFISH. *See* Spiny Lobsters

CREE INDIANS:

The Changing World of Canada's Crees. By Fred Ward. 541-569, Apr. 1975

Nomads of the Far North. By Matthew W. Stirling. 471-504, Oct. 1949

Hearty Folk Defy Arctic Storms. Paintings by W. Langdon Kihn. 479-494

CRESSON, OSBORNE C.: Photographer:

American Family in Afghanistan. By Rebecca Shannon Cresson. 417-432, Sept. 1953

CRESSON, REBECCA SHANNON: Author:

American Family in Afghanistan. Photos by Osborne C. Cresson. 417-432, Sept. 1953

We Lived in Turbulent Tehran. 707-720, Nov. 1953

CRETAN CIVILIZATION. *See* Minoan Civilization

CRETE (Island), Greece:

The Aegean Isles: Poseidon's Playground. By Gilbert M. Grosvenor. 733-781, Dec. 1958

Crete, Cradle of Western Civilization. By Maynard Owen Williams. 693-706, Nov. 1953

War-torn Greece Looks Ahead. By Maynard Owen Williams. 711-744, Dec. 1949

CRICKETS, Nature's Expert Fiddlers. By Catherine Bell Palmer. 385-394, Sept. 1953

CRIME DETECTION:

The FBI: Public Friend Number One. By Jacob Hay. Photos by Robert F. Sisson. 860-886, June 1961

CRO-MAGNON MAN:

A Bold New Look at Our Past. The Editor. 62-63, Jan. 1975

Exploring the Mind of Ice Age Man. By Alexander Marshack. 64-89, Jan. 1975

CROATIA (Republic), Yugoslavia:

Yugoslavia: Six Republics in One. By Robert Paul Jordan. Photos by James P. Blair. 589-633, May 1970

CROCODILIANS:

Wildlife of Everglades National Park. By Daniel B. Beard. Paintings by Walter A. Weber. 83-116, Jan. 1949
    Included: Alligators; Crocodiles
See also Alligators; Caymans

CROMWELL, EATON: Photographer:

Switzerland's Enchanted Val d'Hérens. By Georgia Engelhard Cromwell. 825-848, June 1955

CROMWELL, GEORGIA ENGELHARD: Author:

Switzerland's Enchanted Val d'Hérens. 825-848, June 1955

CROMWELL, OLIVER:

The British Way. By Sir Evelyn Wrench. 421-541, Apr. 1949

CROPP, BEN: Photographer:

Diving With Sea Snakes. By Kenneth MacLeish. 565-578, Apr. 1972

CROSS, JOHN W., Jr.: Author:

Westminster, World Series of Dogdom. 91-116, Jan. 1954

The CROSSING of Antarctica. By Sir Vivian Fuchs. Photos by George Lowe. 25-47, Jan. 1959

CROSSROADS of the Insect World. By J. W. MacSwain. Photos by Edward S. Ross. 844-857, Dec. 1966

CROWDER, WILLIAM: Artist:

Unlocking Secrets of the Northern Lights. By Carl W. Gartlein. 673-704, Nov. 1947

CROWLEY, DON: Artist:

Nature's Gifts to Medicine. By Lonnelle Aikman. Paintings by Lloyd K. Townsend and Don Crowley. 420-440, Sept. 1974

CROWN JEWELS:

Questing for Gems. By George S. Switzer. 835-863, Dec. 1971

CROWN JEWELS—*Continued*
    Included: Great Britain; Iran; czarist Russia
See also Coronations (England; Iran)

CRUISE to Stone Age Arnhem Land. By Howell Walker. 417-430, Sept. 1949

CRUISES AND VOYAGES:

Adventures with the Survey Navy. By Irving Johnson. 131-148, July 1947

The Aegean Isles: Poseidon's Playground. By Gilbert M. Grosvenor. 733-781, Dec. 1958

Alone to Antarctica. By David Lewis. Drawings by Noel Sickles. 808-821, Dec. 1973

Atlantic Odyssey: Iceland to Antarctica. By Newman Bumstead. Photos by Volkmar Wentzel. 725-780, Dec. 1955

Baltic Cruise of the *Caribbee*. By Carleton Mitchell. 605-646, Nov. 1950

A Canoe Helps Hawaii Recapture Her Past. By Herb Kawainui Kane. Photos by David Hiser. 468-489, Apr. 1976

Captain Cook: The Man Who Mapped the Pacific. By Alan Villiers. Photos by Gordon W. Gahan. 297-349, Sept. 1971

Carib Cruises the West Indies. By Carleton Mitchell. 1-56, Jan. 1948

Channel Cruise to Glorious Devon. By Alan Villiers. Photos by Bates Littlehales. 208-259, Aug. 1963

Christopher Columbus and the New World He Found. By John Scofield. Photos by Adam Woolfitt. 584-625, Nov. 1975

Cowes to Cornwall. By Alan Villiers. Photos by Robert B. Goodman. 149-201, Aug. 1961

Cruising Colombia's "Ol' Man River." By Amos Burg. 615-660, May 1947

Cruising Florida's Western Waterways. By Rube Allyn. Photos by Bates Littlehales. 49-76, Jan. 1955

Cruising Japan's Inland Sea. By Willard Price. 619-650, Nov. 1953

Discoverers of the Pacific; Islands of the Pacific, double-sided map supplement. Dec. 1974

Down East to Nova Scotia. By Winfield Parks. 853-879, June 1964

Endeavour Sails the Inside Passage. By Amos Burg. 801-828, June 1947

Exploring England's Canals. By Bryan Hodgson. Photos by Linda Bartlett. 76-111, July 1974

Far North with "Captain Mac." By Miriam MacMillan. 465-513, Oct. 1951

Finisterre Sails the Windward Islands. By Carleton Mitchell. Photos by Winfield Parks. 755-801, Dec. 1965

French Riviera: Storied Playground on the Azure Coast. By Carleton Mitchell. Photos by Thomas Nebbia. 798-835, June 1967

A Fresh Breeze Stirs the Leewards. By Carleton Mitchell. Photos by Winfield Parks. 488-537, Oct. 1966

H.R.H. The Prince Philip, Duke of Edinburgh, Introduces to Members the Narrative of His Round-the-World Tour. 583-584, Nov. 1957

Hokule'a Follows the Stars to Tahiti. By David Lewis. Photos by Nicholas deVore III. 512-537, Oct. 1976

Homeward With Ulysses. By Melville Bell Grosve-

CRUISES AND VOYAGES — *Continued*

nor. Photos by Edwin Stuart Grosvenor. 1-39, July 1973

How We Sailed the New *Mayflower* to America. By Alan Villiers. 627-672, Nov. 1957

Huzza for Otaheite! (*Bounty* Voyage). By Luis Marden. 435-459, Apr. 1962

I Sailed with Portugal's Captains Courageous. By Alan Villiers. 565-596, May 1952

Ice Bird Ends Her Lonely Odyssey. By David Lewis. 216-233, Aug. 1975

Inside Europe Aboard *Yankee*. By Irving and Electa Johnson. Photos by Joseph J. Scherschel. 157-195, Aug. 1964

The Isles of Greece: Aegean Birthplace of Western Culture. By Melville Bell Grosvenor. Photos by Edwin Stuart Grosvenor and Winfield Parks. 147-193, Aug. 1972

Lost World of the Galapagos (*Yankee* Cruise). By Irving and Electa Johnson. 681-703, May 1959

Magellan: First Voyage Around the World. By Alan Villiers. Photos by Bruce Dale. 721-753, June 1976

Midshipmen's Cruise. By William J. Aston and Alexander G. B. Grosvenor. 711-754, June 1948

More of Sea Than of Land: The Bahamas. By Carleton Mitchell. Photos by James L. Stanfield. 218-267, Feb. 1967

New Guinea to Bali in *Yankee*. By Irving and Electa Johnson. 767-815, Dec. 1959

North for Oil: *Manhattan* Makes the Historic Northwest Passage. By Bern Keating. Photos by Tomas Sennett. 374-391, Mar. 1970

North Through History Aboard *White Mist*. By Melville Bell Grosvenor. Photos by Edwin Stuart Grosvenor. 1-55, July 1970

Off the Beaten Track of Empire (Prince Philip's Tour). By Beverley M. Bowie. Photos by Michael Parker. 584-626, Nov. 1957

Robin Sails Home. By Robin Lee Graham. 504-545, Oct. 1970

'Round the Horn by Submarine. By Paul C. Stimson. 129-144, Jan. 1948

Safe Landing on Sable, Isle of 500 Shipwrecks. By Melville Bell Grosvenor. 398-431, Sept. 1965

Saga of a Ship, the *Yankee* (Brigantine). By Luis Marden. 263-269, Feb. 1966

Sailing Iceland's Rugged Coasts. By Wright Britton. Photos by James A. Sugar. 228-265, Aug. 1969

Sailing with Sindbad's Sons. By Alan Villiers. 675-688, Nov. 1948

Scotland from Her Lovely Lochs and Seas. By Alan Villiers. Photos by Robert F. Sisson. 492-541, Apr. 1961

Sea Fever. By John E. Schultz. 237-268, Feb. 1949

Sir Francis Drake. By Alan Villiers. Photos by Gordon W. Gahan. 216-253, Feb. 1975

Slow Boat to Florida. By Dorothea and Stuart E. Jones. 1-65, Jan. 1958

A Teen-ager Sails the World Alone. By Robin Lee Graham. 445-491, Oct. 1968

To Europe with a Racing Start (*Finisterre*). By Carleton Mitchell. 758-791, June 1958

Trawling the China Seas. Photos by J. Charles Thompson. 381-395, Mar. 1950

Triton Follows Magellan's Wake. By Edward L. Beach. Photos by J. Baylor Roberts. 585-615, Nov. 1960

CRUISES AND VOYAGES — *Continued*

Twilight of the Arab Dhow. By Marion Kaplan. 330-351, Sept. 1974

Under Canvas in the Atomic Age. By Alan Villiers. 49-84, July 1955

The Vikings. By Howard La Fay. Photos by Ted Spiegel. 492-541, Apr. 1970

The Voyage of *Ra II*. By Thor Heyerdahl. Photos by Carlo Mauri and Georges Sourial. 44-71, Jan. 1971

White Mist Cruises to Wreck-haunted St. Pierre and Miquelon. By Melville Bell Grosvenor. 378-419, Sept. 1967

Windjamming Around New England. By Tom Horgan. Photos by Robert F. Sisson. 141-169, Aug. 1950

World-roaming Teen-ager Sails On. By Robin Lee Graham. 449-493, Apr. 1969

Yankee Cruises the Storied Nile. By Irving and Electa Johnson. Photos by Winfield Parks. 583-633, May 1965

Yankee Cruises Turkey's History-haunted Coast. By Irving and Electa Johnson. Photos by Joseph J. Scherschel. 798-845, Dec. 1969

Yankee Roams the Orient. By Irving and Electa Johnson. 327-370, Mar. 1951

The *Yankee*'s Wander-world. By Irving and Electa Johnson. 1-50, Jan. 1949

See also Boats; Canoe Trips; Ferries; Kayaks; Rivers and River Trips; Sailing Vessels; Ships; U. S. Navy

CRUSADES:

Crusader Lands Revisited. By Harold Lamb. Photos by David S. Boyer. 815-852, Dec. 1954

Crusader Road to Jerusalem. By Franc Shor. Photos by Thomas Nebbia. 797-855, Dec. 1963
I. Desert Ordeal of the Knights. 797-837
II. Conquest of the Holy City. 839-855

In the Crusaders' Footsteps. By Franc Shor. Photos by Thomas Nebbia and James P. Blair. 731-789, June 1962

CRUSTACEANS:

Diving Beneath Arctic Ice. By Joseph B. MacInnis. Photos by William R. Curtsinger. 248-267, Aug. 1973

Life in a "Dead" Sea — Great Salt Lake. By Paul A. Zahl. 252-263, Aug. 1967

Man-of-war Fleet Attacks Bimini. By Paul A. Zahl. 185-212, Feb. 1952

Photographing the Night Creatures of Alligator Reef. By Robert E. Schroeder. Photos by author and Walter A. Starck II. 128-154, Jan. 1964

See also Barnacles; Crabs; Lobsters and Lobstering; Plankton; Shrimp

CRUZEN, RICHARD H.:

Our Navy Explores Antarctica. By Richard E. Byrd. U. S. Navy official photos. 429-522, Oct. 1947

CRYSTAL RIVER, Florida:

Florida's Manatees, Mermaids in Peril. By Daniel S. Hartman. Photos by James A. Sugar. 342-353, Sept. 1969

CRYSTALS:

Crystals, Magical Servants of the Space Age. By Kenneth F. Weaver. Photos by James P. Blair. 278-296, Aug. 1968

CRYSTALS — *Continued*

The Laser's Bright Magic. By Thomas Meloy. Photos by Howard Sochurek. 858-881, Dec. 1966

See also Frost; Gems; Rocks; Snowflakes

CUBA:

Cuba — American Sugar Bowl. By Melville Bell Grosvenor. 1-56, Jan. 1947

Guantánamo: Keystone in the Caribbean. By Jules B. Billard. Photos by W. E. Garrett and Thomas Nebbia. 420-436, Mar. 1961

CUBAN REFUGEES:

Cuba's Exiles Bring New Life to Miami. By Edward J. Linehan. Photos by Nathan Benn. 63-95, July 1973

CUBEOS (Indians):

Jungle Jaunt on Amazon Headwaters. By Bernice M. Goetz. 371-388, Sept. 1952

CUEVA DE LAS LECHUZAS, Peru:

Birds That "See" in the Dark With Their Ears. By Edward S. Ross. 282-290, Feb. 1965

CULVER, WILLARD R.: Photographer:

Ancient Cliff Dwellers of Mesa Verde. By Don Watson. 349-376, Sept. 1948

Birthplace of Telephone Magic. 289-312, Mar. 1947

California, Horn of Plenty. By Frederick Simpich. 553-594, May 1949

Deaf Children Learn to Talk at Clarke School. By Lilian Grosvenor. 379-397, Mar. 1955

Dragonflies — Rainbows on the Wing. By James G. Needham. 215-229, Aug. 1951

El Morro: Story in Stone. By Edwards Park. 237-244, Aug. 1957

Florida's "Wild" Indians, the Seminole. By Louis Capron. 819-840, Dec. 1956

Haunting Heart of the Everglades. By Andrew H. Brown. Photos by author and Willard R. Culver. 145-173, Feb. 1948

History Repeats in Old Natchez. By William H. Nicholas. 181-208, Feb. 1949

Home Life in Paris Today. By Deena Clark. 43-72, July 1950

Illinois — Healthy Heart of the Nation. By Leo A. Borah. Photos by B. Anthony Stewart and Willard R. Culver. 781-820, Dec. 1953

Land of Louisiana Sugar Kings. By Harnett T. Kane. 531-567, Apr. 1958

Man's Mightiest Ally. 423-450, Apr. 1947

My Life in the Valley of the Moon. By H. H. Arnold. 689-716, Dec. 1948

New Miracles of the Telephone Age. By Robert Leslie Conly. 87-120, July 1954

One Hundred Hours Beneath the Chesapeake. By Gilbert C. Klingel. 681-696, May 1955

The Past Is Present in Greenfield Village. By Beverley M. Bowie. Photos by Neal P. Davis and Willard R. Culver. 96-127, July 1958

Rhode Island, Modern City-State. By George W. Long. 137-170, Aug. 1948

"Rockhounds" Uncover Earth's Mineral Beauty. By George S. Switzer. 631-660, Nov. 1951

Switzerland Guards the Roof of Europe. By William H. Nicholas. 205-246, Aug. 1950

Uncle Sam's House of 1,000 Wonders (National Bu-

CULVER, WILLARD R.: Photographer — *Continued*

reau of Standards). By Lyman J. Briggs and F. Barrows Colton. 755-784, Dec. 1951

U. S. Capitol, Citadel of Democracy. By Lonnelle Aikman. 143-192, Aug. 1952

Westminster, World Series of Dogdom. By John W. Cross, Jr. 91-116, Jan. 1954

CUMBERLAND (Island), Georgia:

Sea Islands: Adventuring Along the South's Surprising Coast. By James Cerruti. Photos by Thomas Nebbia and James L. Amos. 366-393, Mar. 1971

CUMBERLAND COUNTRY, Kentucky-Tennessee:

The People of Cumberland Gap. By John Fetterman. Photos by Bruce Dale. 591-621, Nov. 1971

CUMBERLAND VALLEY, Pennsylvania:

Appalachian Valley Pilgrimage. By Catherine Bell Palmer. Photos by Justin Locke. 1-32, July 1949

CUNEIFORM SCRIPT:

Darius Carved History on Ageless Rock. By George G. Cameron. 825-844, Dec. 1950

CUNNINGHAM, JOHN T.: Author:

I'm From New Jersey. Photos by Volkmar Wentzel. 1-45, Jan. 1960

Staten Island Ferry, New York's Seagoing Bus. By John T. Cunningham and Jay Johnston. Photos by W. D. Vaughn. 833-843, June 1959

CUPP, DAVID F.: Photographer:

Capri, Italy's Enchanted Rock. By Carleton Mitchell. 795-809, June 1970

Kuwait, Aladdin's Lamp of the Middle East. By John E. Frazer. 636-667, May 1969

Nevada's Mountain of Invisible Gold. By Samuel W. Matthews. 668-679, May 1968

Solving the Mystery of Mexico's Great Stone Spheres. By Matthew W. Stirling. 295-300, Aug. 1969

CURAÇAO (Island), Netherlands Antilles:

The Netherlands Antilles: Holland in the Caribbean. By James Cerruti. Photos by Emory Kristof. 115-146, Jan. 1970

CURE RIVER VALLEY, France. *See* Vézelay

CURLEWS:

The Curlew's Secret. By Arthur A. Allen. 751-770, Dec. 1948

CURLING:

Winter Brings Carnival Time to Quebec. By Kathleen Revis. 69-97, Jan. 1958

CURRENT Scientific Projects of the National Geographic Society. 143-144, July 1953

CURRENTS, Ocean. *See* Gulf Stream; Map Supplements

CURRUMBIN, Australia:

Honey Eaters of Currumbin (Lorikeets). By Paul A. Zahl. 510-519, Oct. 1956

CURTIS, GARNISS H.: Author:

A Clock for the Ages: Potassium-Argon. 590-592, Oct. 1961

CURTSINGER, WILLIAM R.: Photographer:

Antarctica's Nearer Side. By Samuel W. Matthews.

CURTSINGER, WILLIAM R.: Photographer—Continued
622-655, Nov. 1971

Bad Days for the Brown Pelican. By Ralph W. Schreiber. Photos by William R. Curtsinger and author. 111-123, Jan. 1975

Can We Save Our Salt Marshes? By Stephen W. Hitchcock. 729-765, June 1972

Diving Beneath Arctic Ice. By Joseph B. MacInnis. 248-267, Aug. 1973

Life or Death for the Harp Seal. By David M. Lavigne. 129-142, Jan. 1976

The People of New Jersey's Pine Barrens. By John McPhee. 52-77, Jan. 1974

Swimming With Patagonia's Right Whales. By Roger Payne. Photos by William R. Curtsinger and Charles R. Nicklin, Jr. 576-587, Oct. 1972

The Treasure of Porto Santo. By Robert Sténuit. Photos by author and William R. Curtsinger. 260-275, Aug. 1975

CUSCO. See Cuzco, Peru

CUSS I (Drilling Barge). See Mohole, Project

CUSTER, GEORGE A.:
I See America First. By Lynda Bird Johnson. Photos by William Albert Allard. 874-904, Dec. 1965

North Dakota Comes into Its Own. By Leo A. Borah. Photos by J. Baylor Roberts. 283-322, Sept. 1951

CUZCO (Cusco), Peru:
The Five Worlds of Peru. By Kenneth F. Weaver. Photos by Bates Littlehales. 213-265, Feb. 1964

The Lost Empire of the Incas. By Loren McIntyre. Art by Ned and Rosalie Seidler. 729-787, Dec. 1973
    Included: A pictorial chronicle of the Incas

Peru, Homeland of the Warlike Inca. By Kip Ross. 421-462, Oct. 1950

CYANA (Diving Saucer):
Where the Earth Turns Inside Out (Project FAMOUS). By J. R. Heirtzler. Photos by Emory Kristof. 586-603, May 1975

CYCLADES (Islands), Greece:
The Isles of Greece: Aegean Birthplace of Western Culture. By Melville Bell Grosvenor. Photos by Edwin Stuart Grosvenor and Winfield Parks. 147-193, Aug. 1972

See also Thera

CYPRESS GARDENS, Florida:
The Booming Sport of Water Skiing. By Wilbur E. Garrett. 700-711, Nov. 1958

CYPRESS SWAMP. See Big Cypress Swamp

CYPRUS (Island), Mediterranean Sea:
Cyprus, Geography's Stepchild. By Franc Shor. 873-884, June 1956

Cyprus, Idyllic Island in a Troubled Sea. By Jean and Franc Shor. 627-664, May 1952

Cyprus Under Four Flags: A Struggle for Unity. By Kenneth MacLeish. Photos by Jonathan Blair. 356-383, Mar. 1973

See also Kyrenia Ship

CZECHOSLOVAKIA:
Czechoslovakia: The Dream and the Reality. By Edward J. Linehan. Photos by James P. Blair.

CZECHOSLOVAKIA—Continued
151-193, Feb. 1968

Down the Danube by Canoe. By William Slade Backer. Photos by Richard S. Durrance and Christopher G. Knight. 34-79, July 1965

Poland and Czechoslovakia, Atlas series supplement. Sept. 1958

D

The DAR Story. By Lonnelle Aikman. Photos by B. Anthony Stewart and John E. Fletcher. 565-598, Nov. 1951

DNA. See Deoxyribonucleic Acid

DS-2 (Diving Saucer):
At Home in the Sea. By Jacques-Yves Cousteau. 465-507, Apr. 1964

DACCA, Bangladesh:
Bangladesh: Hope Nourishes a New Nation. By William S. Ellis. Photos by Dick Durrance II. 295-333, Sept. 1972

Bangladesh: The Nightmare of Famine. Photos by Steve Raymer. 33-39, July 1975

East Pakistan Drives Back the Jungle. By Jean and Franc Shor. 399-426, Mar. 1955

DADE COUNTY, Florida. See Miami

DAIRY CATTLE. See Cattle and Cattle Raising

DAIRY FARMS. See Family Farm; Thunder Hill Goat Farm

DAIRY INDUSTRIES. See Cheese and Cheese Making

DAK PEK, Viet Nam:
Viet Nam's Montagnards. By Howard Sochurek. 443-487, Apr. 1968

DALAI LAMA:
Little Tibet in Switzerland. By Laura Pilarski. Photos by Fred Mayer. 711-727, Nov. 1968

My Life in Forbidden Lhasa. By Heinrich Harrer. 1-48, July 1955

DALE, BRUCE: Photographer:
Alaska: Rising Northern Star. By Joseph Judge. 730-767, June 1975

Appomattox: Where Grant and Lee Made Peace With Honor a Century Ago. By Ulysses S. Grant 3rd. 435-469, Apr. 1965

The Awesome Worlds Within a Cell. By Rick Gore. Paintings by Davis Meltzer. 355-395, Sept. 1976

Bats Aren't All Bad. By Alvin Novick. 615-637, May 1973

Behold the Computer Revolution. By Peter T. White. Photos by Bruce Dale and Emory Kristof. 593-633, Nov. 1970

Freedom Speaks French in Ouagadougou. By John Scofield. 153-203, Aug. 1966

Hong Kong, Saturday's Child. By Joseph Judge. 541-573, Oct. 1971

Île de la Cité, Birthplace of Paris. By Kenneth MacLeish. 680-719, May 1968

Kenya Says Harambee! By Allan C. Fisher, Jr. 151-205, Feb. 1969

Magellan: First Voyage Around the World. By Alan Villiers. 721-753, June 1976

DALE, BRUCE: Photographer — *Continued*

The Navajos. By Ralph Looney. 740-781, Dec. 1972

An Ozark Family Carves a Living and a Way of Life. 124-133, July 1975

Panama, Link Between Oceans and Continents. By Jules B. Billard. 402-440, Mar. 1970

The People of Cumberland Gap. By John Fetterman. 591-621, Nov. 1971

The Rhine: Europe's River of Legend. By William Graves. 449-499, Apr. 1967

St. Louis: New Spirit Soars in Mid-America's Proud Old City. By Robert Paul Jordan. 605-641, Nov. 1965

Snow-mantled Stehekin: Where Solitude Is in Season. By Pat Hutson. 572-588, Apr. 1974

Southern California's Trial by Mud and Water. By Nathaniel T. Kenney. 552-573, Oct. 1969

Through Ozark Hills and Hollows. By Mike W. Edwards. 656-689, Nov. 1970

Timber: How Much Is Enough? By John J. Putman. 485-511, Apr. 1974

Washington: The City Freedom Built. By William Graves. Photos by Bruce Dale and Thomas Nebbia. 735-781, Dec. 1964

When Gypsies Gather at Appleby Fair. 848-869, June 1972

White Mist Cruises to Wreck-haunted St. Pierre and Miquelon. By Melville Bell Grosvenor. 378-419, Sept. 1967

DALE COLLECTION. *See* Chester Dale Collection

DALLAS, Texas:

The Fabulous State of Texas. By Stanley Walker. Photos by B. Anthony Stewart and Thomas Nebbia. 149-195, Feb. 1961

DALMATIA (Region), Yugoslavia:

Yugoslavia, Between East and West. By George W. Long. Photos by Volkmar Wentzel. 141-172, Feb. 1951

Yugoslavia: Six Republics in One. By Robert Paul Jordan. Photos by James P. Blair. 589-633, May 1970

Yugoslavia's Window on the Adriatic. By Gilbert M. Grosvenor. 219-247, Feb. 1962

DALRYMPLE-HAMILTON, SIR FREDERICK:

Rhododendron Glories of Southwest Scotland. By David S. Boyer. Photos by B. Anthony Stewart and author. 641-664, May 1954

DAMASCUS, Syria:

Damascus, Syria's Uneasy Eden. By Robert Azzi. 512-535, Apr. 1974

Jerusalem to Rome in the Path of St. Paul. By David S. Boyer. 707-759, Dec. 1956

The Sword and the Sermon (Islam). By Thomas J. Abercrombie. 3-45, July 1972

DAMS:

Along the Yangtze, Main Street of China. By W. Robert Moore. 325-356, Mar. 1948
Included: The proposed dam across the Yangtze

Around the "Great Lakes of the South." By Frederick Simpich. Photos by J. Baylor Roberts. 463-491, Apr. 1948
Contents: TVA system

The Bittersweet Waters of the Lower Colorado. By Rowe Findley. Photos by Charles O'Rear. 540-

DAMS — *Continued*

569, Oct. 1973

Britain Tackles the East African Bush. By W. Robert Moore. 311-352, Mar. 1950
Included: Dam for Lake Victoria, just below Owen Falls

The Canadian North: Emerging Giant. By David S. Boyer. 1-43, July 1968

Following the Trail of Lewis and Clark. By Ralph Gray. 707-750, June 1953

From Sagebrush to Roses on the Columbia. By Leo A. Borah. 571-611, Nov. 1952
Included: Dams completed and dams under construction: Albeni Falls, American Falls, Anderson Ranch, Bonneville, Chief Joseph, The Dalles, Detroit, Grand Coulee, Hungry Horse, Lookout Point, McNary, Minidoka, Palisades, Rock Island

A Map Maker Looks at the United States. By Newman Bumstead. 705-748, June 1951
Included: Grand Coulee, Hoover, Jackson Lake, Shasta

The Mekong, River of Terror and Hope. By Peter T. White. Photos by W. E. Garrett. 737-787, Dec. 1968

Powerhouse of the Northwest (Columbia River). By David S. Boyer. 821-847, Dec. 1974

That Dammed Missouri River. By Gordon Young. Photos by David Hiser. 374-413, Sept. 1971

Whatever Happened to TVA? By Gordon Young. Photos by Emory Kristof. 830-863, June 1973

See also Aswân High Dam; Powell, Lake, for Glen Canyon Dam; St. Lawrence Seaway

The **DANAKIL:** Nomads of Ethiopia's Wasteland. By Victor Englebert. 186-211, Feb. 1970

DANAKIL DEPRESSION, Ethiopia:

The Danakil: Nomads of Ethiopia's Wasteland. By Victor Englebert. 186-211, Feb. 1970

DA NANG, Viet Nam:

Behind the Headlines in Viet Nam. By Peter T. White. Photos by Winfield Parks. 149-189, Feb. 1967

DANUBE (River), Europe:

Down the Danube by Canoe. By William Slade Backer. Photos by Richard S. Durrance and Christopher G. Knight. 34-79, July 1965

DAR ES SALAAM, Tanzania:

Tanzania Marches to Its Own Drum. By Peter T. White. Photos by Emory Kristof. 474-509, Apr. 1975

Weighing the Aga Khan in Diamonds. Photos by David J. Carnegie. 317-324, Mar. 1947

DAR POMORZA:

By Square-rigger from Baltic to Bicentennial. By Kenneth Garrett. 824-857, Dec. 1976

DARIÉN GAP, Panama:

We Drove Panama's Darién Gap. By Kip Ross. 368-389, Mar. 1961

DARIUS THE GREAT, King (Persia):

Darius Carved History on Ageless Rock. By George G. Cameron. 825-844, Dec. 1950

In the Footsteps of Alexander the Great. By Helen and Frank Schreider. Paintings by Tom Lovell. 1-65, Jan. 1968

DARIUSLEUT (Sect):

The Hutterites, Plain People of the West. By William Albert Allard. 98-125, July 1970

DARLEY, JAMES M.:

Chief Cartographer, NGS. 875, Dec. 1961; 897, Dec. 1962; 108, 109, July 1964

DARWIN, CHARLES:

The British Way. By Sir Evelyn Wrench. 421-541, Apr. 1949

The Galapagos, Eerie Cradle of New Species. By Roger Tory Peterson. Photos by Alan and Joan Root. 541-585, Apr. 1967

In the Wake of Darwin's *Beagle*. By Alan Villiers. Photos by James L. Stanfield. 449-495, Oct. 1969

Lost World of the Galapagos. By Irving and Electa Johnson. 681-703, May 1959

DARWIN, Australia:

The Top End of Down Under. By Kenneth MacLeish. Photos by Thomas Nebbia. 145-174, Feb. 1973

DASARA (Festival): Mysore, India:

Mysore Celebrates the Death of a Demon. By Luc Bouchage. Photos by Ylla. 706-711, May 1958

DASSEN ISLAND, South Africa:

Oil and Penguins Don't Mix. Photos by Mike Holmes. 384-397, Mar. 1973

DATA PROCESSING, Electronic:

Behold the Computer Revolution. By Peter T. White. Photos by Bruce Dale and Emory Kristof. 593-633, Nov. 1970

Computer Helps Scholars Re-create an Egyptian Temple. By Ray Winfield Smith. Photos by Emory Kristof. 634-655, Nov. 1970

DATE LINE: United Nations, New York. By Carolyn Bennett Patterson. Photos by B. Anthony Stewart and John E. Fletcher. 305-331, Sept. 1961

DATE RAISING:

The Lure of the Changing Desert (California). 817-824, June 1954

DATING METHODS:

This Changing Earth. By Samuel W. Matthews. 1-37, Jan. 1973
    Included: Carbon 14 dating, fossil dating, paleomagnetics, potassium-argon dating, radioactive-isotope dating

What's Happening to Our Climate? By Samuel W. Matthews. 576-615, Nov. 1976
    Included: Ice-core dating, Sea-core dating, Tree-ring dating

See also Archeomagnetism Dating; Potassium-Argon Dating; Radiocarbon Dating; Tree-ring Dating

DAUFUSKIE (Island), South Carolina:

Sea Islands: Adventuring Along the South's Surprising Coast. By James Cerruti. Photos by Thomas Nebbia and James L. Amos. 366-393, Mar. 1971

DAUGHTERS OF THE AMERICAN REVOLUTION:

The DAR Story. By Lonnelle Aikman. Photos by B. Anthony Stewart and John E. Fletcher. 565-598, Nov. 1951

The **DAUNTLESS** Little Stilt. By Frederick Kent Truslow. 241-245, Aug. 1960

DÁVALOS HURTADO, EUSEBIO: Author:

Into the Well of Sacrifice. I. Return to the Sacred Cenote. 540-549, Oct. 1961

DAVENPORT, WILLIAM: Author:

Amiable Amsterdam. Photos by Adam Woolfitt. 683-705, May 1974

France's Wild, Watery South, the Camargue. 696-726, May 1973

Provence, Empire of the Sun. Photos by James A. Sugar. 692-715, May 1975

DAVIDSON, TREAT: Author-Photographer:

Bullfrog Ballet Filmed in Flight. 791-799, June 1963

Freezing the Trout's Lightning Leap. 525-530, Apr. 1958

Inside the World of the Honeybee. 188-217, Aug. 1959

Rose Aphids. 851-859, June 1961

Tree Snails, Gems of the Everglades. 372-387, Mar. 1965

Photographer

Alligators: Dragons in Distress. By Archie Carr. Photos by Treat Davidson and Laymond Hardy. 133-148, Jan. 1967

Moths That Behave Like Hummingbirds. 770-775, June 1965

DA VINCI, Project:

Laboratory in a Dirty Sky. By Rudolf J. Engelmann and Vera Simons. 616-621, Nov. 1976

DAVIS, MALCOLM: Author:

Nature's Clown, the Penguin. By David Hellyer and Malcolm Davis. 405-428, Sept. 1952

DAVIS, NEAL P.: Photographer:

The Past Is Present in Greenfield Village. By Beverley M. Bowie. Photos by Neal P. Davis and Willard R. Culver. 96-127, July 1958

DAVIS STRAIT, North America-Greenland:

I Sailed with Portugal's Captains Courageous. By Alan Villiers. 565-596, May 1952

DAVY, SIR HUMPHRY:

The British Way. By Sir Evelyn Wrench. 421-541, Apr. 1949

DAWSON, Canada:

Along the Yukon Trail. By Amos Burg. 395-416, Sept. 1953

DAYTON, WILLIAM A.: Author:

Beauty and Bounty of Southern State Trees. Paintings by Walter A. Weber. 508-552, Oct. 1957

Wealth and Wonder of Northern State Trees. Paintings by Walter A. Weber. 651-691, Nov. 1955

DEAD, Rites for the. *See* Burial Customs; Funerals

DEAD SEA, Israel-Jordan:

Abraham, the Friend of God. By Kenneth MacLeish. Photos by Dean Conger. 739-789, Dec. 1966

Geographical Twins (Holy Land and Utah) a World Apart. By David S. Boyer. 848-859, Dec. 1958

DEAD SEA SCROLLS:

The Men Who Hid the Dead Sea Scrolls. By A.

DEAD SEA SCROLLS — *Continued*

Douglas Tushingham. Paintings by Peter V. Bianchi. 785-808, Dec. 1958

The **DEADLY** Fisher. By Charles E. Lane. 388-397, Mar. 1963

DEAF, Institutes for Teaching the:

Deaf Children Learn to Talk at Clarke School. By Lilian Grosvenor. Photos by Willard R. Culver. 379-397, Mar. 1955

Washington's Historic Georgetown. By William A. Kinney. 513-544, Apr. 1953
Included: Volta Bureau

DEARBORN, Michigan. *See* Henry Ford Museum

DEATH of an Island, Tristan da Cunha. By P. J. F. Wheeler. 678-695, May 1962

DEATH VALLEY NATIONAL MONUMENT, California:

Death Valley, the Land and the Legend. By Rowe Findley. Photos by David Hiser. 69-103, Jan. 1970

Getting to Know the Wild Burros of Death Valley. By Patricia des Roses Moehlman. Photos by Ira S. Lerner and author. 502-517, Apr. 1972

The Great Mojave Desert (Television film). 294A-294B, Feb. 1971

See also Los Angeles Aqueduct

DE BRY, THEODORE. *See* Bry, Theodore de

DECEPTION ISLAND, Antarctica:

Antarctica's Nearer Side. By Samuel W. Matthews. Photos by William R. Curtsinger. 622-655, Nov. 1971

DECOY FISH:

Something's Fishy About That Fin! Photos by Robert J. Shallenberger and William D. Madden. 224-227, Aug. 1974

DEEP DIVER (Submarine):

A Taxi for the Deep Frontier. By Kenneth Mac-Leish. Photos by Bates Littlehales. 139-150, Jan. 1968

DEEP Diving off Japan. By Georges S. Houot. 138-150, Jan. 1960

DEEP in the Heart of "Swissconsin." By William H. Nicholas. Photos by J. Baylor Roberts. 781-800, June 1947

DEEP SEA DRILLING PROJECT:

This Changing Earth. By Samuel W. Matthews. 1-37, Jan. 1973

DEEP-SEA Window Into the Earth. By Robert D. Ballard. Photos by Emory Kristof. 228-249, Aug. 1976

DEEP SUBMERGENCE SYSTEMS REVIEW GROUP (DSSRG). *See* Tomorrow on the Deep Frontier

The **DEEPEST** Days. By Robert Sténuit. 534-547, Apr. 1965

DEEPSTAR Explores the Ocean Floor. Photos by Ron Church. 110-129, Jan. 1971

DEER. *See* Caribou; Reindeer

DEERFIELD, Massachusetts:

Deerfield Keeps a Truce With Time. By Bart McDowell. Photos by Robert W. Madden. 780-809, June 1969

DEERING, JAMES: Estate:

Vizcaya: An Italian Palazzo in Miami. By William H. Nicholas. Photos by Justin Locke. 595-604, Nov. 1950

DeFEO, THOMAS A.: Photographer:

Satellites Gave Warning of Midwest Floods. By Peter T. White. 574-592, Oct. 1969

Shenandoah, I Long to Hear You. By Mike W. Edwards. 554-588, Apr. 1970

DEFOE, DANIEL:

The British Way. By Sir Evelyn Wrench. 421-541, Apr. 1949

DE LA HABA, LOUIS: Author:

Belize, the Awakening Land. Photos by Michael E. Long. 124-146, Jan. 1972

Guatemala, Maya and Modern. Photos by Joseph J. Scherschel. 661-689, Nov. 1974

Mexico, the City That Founded a Nation. Photos by Albert Moldvay. 638-669, May 1973

DELAWARE:

"Delmarva," Gift of the Sea. By Catherine Bell Palmer. 367-399, Sept. 1950

Our Changing Atlantic Coastline. By Nathaniel T. Kenney. Photos by B. Anthony Stewart. 860-887, Dec. 1962
Included: Dewey Beach; Rehoboth Beach

Today on the Delaware, Penn's Glorious River. By Albert W. Atwood. Photos by Robert F. Sisson. 1-40, July 1952

See also Henlopen Dunes; Noxontown Pond

DELAWARE (River), U. S.:

Today on the Delaware, Penn's Glorious River. By Albert W. Atwood. Photos by Robert F. Sisson. 1-40, July 1952

DELHI, India:

Delhi, Capital of a New Dominion. By Phillips Talbot. 597-630, Nov. 1947

See also New Delhi

DELIGHT (Yawl):

Sailing Iceland's Rugged Coasts. By Wright Britton. Photos by James A. Sugar. 228-265, Aug. 1969

DE'LISLE, GORDON: Photographer:

Australia. By Alan Villiers. 309-385, Sept. 1963
I. The West and the South. 309-345
II. The Settled East, the Barrier Reef, the Center. 347-385

DELMARVA PENINSULA (Delaware-Maryland-Virginia):

"Delmarva," Gift of the Sea. By Catherine Bell Palmer. 367-399, Sept. 1950

DELOS (Island), Greece:

Fish Men Discover a 2,200-year-old Greek Ship. By Jacques-Yves Cousteau. 1-36, Jan. 1954

The Isles of Greece: Aegean Birthplace of Western Culture. By Melville Bell Grosvenor. Photos by Edwin Stuart Grosvenor and Winfield Parks. 147-193, Aug. 1972

DELTA, Inland. *See* California Delta

DELTA REGIONAL PRIMATE RESEARCH CENTER, Tulane University:

Director. *See* Riopelle, Arthur J.

DEMOCRACY'S Fortress: Unsinkable Malta. By Ernle Bradford. Photos by Ted H. Funk. 852-879, June 1969

DENIS, ARMAND:
New Guinea's Rare Birds and Stone Age Men. By E. Thomas Gilliard. 421-488, Apr. 1953
Note: Armand Denis was the leader of the American Museum-Armand Denis Expedition.

DENISE (Diving Saucer):
Diving Saucer Takes to the Deep. By Jacques-Yves Cousteau. 571-586, Apr. 1960
See also Amphitrite (Denise Carrier)

DENMARK:
Baltic Cruise of the Caribbee. By Carleton Mitchell. 605-646, Nov. 1950
By Full-rigged Ship to Denmark's Fairyland. By Alan Villiers. Photos by Alexander Taylor and author. 809-828, Dec. 1955
Denmark, Field of the Danes. By William Graves. Photos by Thomas Nebbia. 245-275, Feb. 1974
Friendly Flight to Northern Europe. By Lyndon B. Johnson. Photos by Volkmar Wentzel. 268-293, Feb. 1964
Lifelike Man Preserved 2,000 Years in Peat. By P. V. Glob. 419-430, Mar. 1954
Thumbs Up Round the North Sea's Rim. By Frances James. Photos by Erica Koch. 685-704, May 1952
2,000 Miles Through Europe's Oldest Kingdom. By Isobel Wylie Hutchison. Photos by Maynard Owen Williams. 141-180, Feb. 1949
Under Canvas in the Atomic Age (U. S. Coast Guard). By Alan Villiers. 49-84, July 1955
The Vikings. By Howard La Fay. Photos by Ted Spiegel. 492-541, Apr. 1970
See also Copenhagen; Faeroe Islands; Greenland

DENNISON, EDWARD S.: Author:
Ambassadors of Good Will: The Peace Corps. By Sargent Shriver and Peace Corps Volunteers. 297-345, Sept. 1964
Bolivia. 315-319

DENTON, IVAN, Family:
An Ozark Family Carves a Living and a Way of Life. Photos by Bruce Dale. 124-133, July 1975

DENVER, Colorado:
Colorado, the Rockies' Pot of Gold. By Edward J. Linehan. Photos by James L. Amos. 157-201, Aug. 1969
Colorado by Car and Campfire. By Kathleen Revis. 207-248, Aug. 1954

DEOXYRIBONUCLEIC ACID (DNA):
The Awesome Worlds Within a Cell. By Rick Gore. Photos by Bruce Dale. Paintings by Davis Meltzer. 355-395, Sept. 1976
Included: The "Language of Life" foldout showing the replication of DNA and the manufacture of RNA and proteins

DEPARTMENT OF DEFENSE GRAVITY EXPERIMENT. See DODGE Satellite

DE ROOS, ROBERT: Author:
Arizona: Booming Youngster of the West. Photos by Robert F. Sisson. 299-343, Mar. 1963
Costa Rica, Free of the Volcano's Veil. 125-152, July 1965

DE ROOS, ROBERT: Author—Continued
The Flower Seed Growers: Gardening's Color Merchants. Photos by Jack Fields. 720-738, May 1968
Los Angeles, City of the Angels. Photos by Thomas Nebbia. 451-501, Oct. 1962
The Magic Worlds of Walt Disney. Photos by Thomas Nebbia. 159-207, Aug. 1963
Massachusetts Builds for Tomorrow. Photos by B. Anthony Stewart. 790-843, Dec. 1966
New England's "Lively Experiment," Rhode Island. Photos by Fred Ward. 370-401, Sept. 1968
The Philippines, Freedom's Pacific Frontier. Photos by Ted Spiegel. 301-351, Sept. 1966

DESERT MUSEUM, Arizona:
Arizona's Window on Wildlife. By Lewis Wayne Walker. 240-250, Feb. 1958

DESERT Ordeal of the Knights (First Crusade). By Franc Shor. Photos by Thomas Nebbia. 797-837, Dec. 1963

DESERT River Through Navajo Land. By Alfred M. Bailey. Photos by author and Fred G. Brandenburg. 149-172, Aug. 1947

DESERT Sheikdoms of Arabia's Pirate Coast. By Ronald Codrai. 65-104, July 1956

DESERTS:
Abundant Life in a Desert Land. By Walter Meayers Edwards. 424-436, Sept. 1973
Great American Deserts. Special Publication announced. 870-874, June 1972
The Hohokam: First Masters of the American Desert. By Emil W. Haury. Photos by Helga Teiwes. 670-695, May 1967
In Search of Arabia's Past. By Peter Bruce Cornwall. 493-522, Apr. 1948
Lake Powell: Waterway to Desert Wonders. By Walter Meayers Edwards. 44-75, July 1967
The Lure of the Changing Desert. 817-824, June 1954
Magnetic Clues Help Date the Past. By Kenneth F. Weaver. 696-701, May 1967
Report from the Locust Wars. By Tony and Dickey Chapelle. 545-562, Apr. 1953
Scorpions: Living Fossils of the Sands. By Paul A. Zahl. 436-442, Mar. 1968
Wonders of the Desert World. Children's book announced. 718-720, Nov. 1976
See also Atacama Desert, Chile; Baja California; Chubut Province, Argentina; Colorado Desert; Coober Pedy, South Australia; Death Valley National Monument; Four Corners Country; Gobi; Great Rift Valley; Iran; Mazatzal Wilderness, Arizona; Mojave Desert; Oman; Organ Pipe Cactus National Monument; Sahara; Sinai; Sonoran Desert

DESERTS, Salt. See Danakil Depression, Ethiopia

DESIGN, Industrial:
Can We Harness the Wind? By Roger Hamilton. Photos by Emory Kristof. 812-829, Dec. 1975

DESPUJOLS, JEAN: Artist:
Portrait of Indochina. By W. Robert Moore and Maynard Owen Williams. 461-490, Apr. 1951

DETROIT, Michigan:
Work-hard, Play-hard Michigan. By Andrew H. Brown. 279-320, Mar. 1952

DETROIT (River), Michigan-Ontario:
J. W. Westcott, Postman for the Great Lakes. By Cy La Tour. 813-824, Dec. 1950

DETWILER, MARGARET M.: Author:
Hays, Kansas, at the Nation's Heart. Photos by John E. Fletcher. 461-490, Apr. 1952

DEVASTATED Land and Homeless People (Bali). By Samuel W. Matthews. Photos by Robert F. Sisson. 447-458, Sept. 1963

DEVEREUX, WALTER B.: Author:
New York Again Hails the Horse. 697-720, Nov. 1954

DEVIL DANCE:
A Journey to "Little Tibet." By Enakshi Bhavnani. Photos by Volkmar Wentzel. 603-634, May 1951
A Woman Paints the Tibetans. By Lafugie. 659-692, May 1949

DEVIL MOUNTAIN, Venezuela. See Auyán-tepuí

DEVIL'S ISLAND, Îles du Salut, French Guiana:
Yankee Roams the Orient. By Irving and Electa Johnson. 327-370, Mar. 1951

DEVONSHIRE, England:
Channel Cruise to Glorious Devon. By Alan Villiers. Photos by Bates Littlehales. 208-259, Aug. 1963

DeVORE, NICHOLAS, III: Photographer:
Hokule'a Follows the Stars to Tahiti. By David Lewis. 512-537, Oct. 1976
Should They Build a Fence Around Montana? By Mike W. Edwards. 614-657, May 1976
Growing Up in Montana. 650-657
Trek Across Arctic America. By Colin Irwin. 295-321, Mar. 1974
Wind, Wave, Star, and Bird. By David Lewis. 747-781, Dec. 1974

DEW LINE (Distant Early Warning Line), Sentry of the Far North. By Howard La Fay. 128-146, July 1958

DHAHRAN (Aẓ Ẓahrān), Saudi Arabia:
In Search of Arabia's Past. By Peter Bruce Cornwall. 493-522, Apr. 1948
Saudi Arabia: Beyond the Sands of Mecca. By Thomas J. Abercrombie. 1-53, Jan. 1966

DHANI NIVAT, Prince. See Sonakul, D.

DHOWS:
Sailing with Sindbad's Sons. By Alan Villiers. 675-688, Nov. 1948
Contents: Bayan; Sheikh Mansur; and Baggalas, Booms, Sambuks, Zarooks
Twilight of the Arab Dhow. By Marion Kaplan. 330-351, Sept. 1974

DIABLE, Île du, French Guiana. See Devil's Island

DIAMOND JUBILEE:
Weighing the Aga Khan in Diamonds. Photos by David J. Carnegie. 317-324, Mar. 1947

DIAMOND ROCK ("H.M.S. Diamond Rock"), Martinique:
Carib Cruises the West Indies. By Carleton Mitchell. 1-56, Jan. 1948

DIAMONDS:
Britain Tackles the East African Bush. By W. Robert Moore. 311-352, Mar. 1950
Included: Williamson mine in Tanganyika
Exploring the World of Gems. By W. F. Foshag. 779-810, Dec. 1950
The Jungle Was My Home. By Sasha Siemel. 695-712, Nov. 1952
The Many-sided Diamond. By George S. Switzer. 568-586, Apr. 1958
Questing for Gems. By George S. Switzer. 835-863, Dec. 1971
Weighing the Aga Khan in Diamonds. Photos by David J. Carnegie. 317-324, Mar. 1947
White Magic in the Belgian Congo. By W. Robert Moore. 321-362, Mar. 1952

DIARY of the President's Daughter: I See America First. By Lynda Bird Johnson. Photos by William Albert Allard. 874-904, Dec. 1965

DICKENS, CHARLES:
The British Way. By Sir Evelyn Wrench. 421-541, Apr. 1949
The England of Charles Dickens. By Richard W. Long. Photos by Adam Woolfitt. 443-483, Apr. 1974

DICKEY CHAPELLE Killed in Action. By W. E. Garrett. 270-271, Feb. 1966

DICKINSON, EMILY:
Literary Landmarks of Massachusetts. By William H. Nicholas. Photos by B. Anthony Stewart and John E. Fletcher. 279-310, Mar. 1950

DIETZ, ROBERT S.: Author:
The Explosive Birth of Myojin Island. 117-128, Jan. 1954

DIFFENDERFER, HOPE A.: Author:
Okinawa, the Island Rebuilt. 265-288, Feb. 1955

The DIFFIDENT Truffle, France's Gift to Gourmets. 419-426, Sept. 1956

DIKES AND LEVEES:
California's Surprising Inland Delta. By Judith and Neil Morgan. Photos by Charles O'Rear. 409-430, Sept. 1976
Included: Map showing the 1,100 miles of levees that rim the 55 islands reclaimed from marshland
Helping Holland Rebuild Her Land. By Gilbert M. Grosvenor and Charles Neave. 365-413, Sept. 1954
The Lower Mississippi. By Willard Price. Photos by W. D. Vaughn. 681-725, Nov. 1960

DIMANCESCU, DAN: Author:
Americans Afoot in Rumania. Photos by Dick Durrance II and Christopher G. Knight. 810-845, June 1969
Kayak Odyssey: From the Inland Sea to Tokyo. Photos by Christopher G. Knight. 295-337, Sept. 1967

DINGLE PENINSULA, Ireland:
Irish Ways Live On in Dingle. By Bryan Hodgson. Photos by Linda Bartlett. 551-576, Apr. 1976

DINKELSBUHL (Germany) Rewards Its Children. By Charles Belden. 255-268, Feb. 1957

DINKINS, STEPHANIE: Author-Photographer:

Lanzarote, the Strangest Canary. 117-139, Jan. 1969

DINOSAUR NATIONAL MONUMENT, Colorado-Utah:

Shooting Rapids in Dinosaur Country. By Jack Breed. Photos by author and Justin Locke. 363-390, Mar. 1954

DINOSAURS:

Dinosaurs. Children's book announced. 736-738, Nov. 1972

We Captured a 'Live' Brontosaur. By Roland T. Bird. 707-722, May 1954

See also Dinosaur National Monument

DIOMEDE ISLANDS, Bering Strait:

Alaska's Russian Frontier: Little Diomede. Photos by Audrey and Frank Morgan. 551-562, Apr. 1951

Nomad in Alaska's Outback. By Thomas J. Abercrombie. 540-567, Apr. 1969

North Star Cruises Alaska's Wild West. By Amos Burg. 57-86, July 1952

DISASTER in Paradise (Bali). 436-458, Sept. 1963
I. By Windsor P. Booth. Photos by Robert F. Sisson. 436-447
II. Devastated Land and Homeless People. By Samuel W. Matthews. Photos by Robert F. Sisson. 447-458

DISCOVERED: the Monarch's Mexican Haven. By Fred A. Urquhart. Photos by Bianca Lavies. 161-173, Aug. 1976

DISCOVERERS. *See* Explorers, Discoverers, and Navigators

DISCOVERY. *See* Exploration and Discovery

The DISCUS FISH Yields a Secret. By Gene Wolfsheimer. 675-681, May 1960

DISNEY, WALT:

The Magic Worlds of Walt Disney. By Robert de Roos. Photos by Thomas Nebbia. 159-207, Aug. 1963

Walt Disney: Genius of Laughter and Learning. By Melville Bell Grosvenor. 157D, Aug. 1963

DISNEY WORLD, Florida:

Florida's Booming—and Beleaguered—Heartland. By Joseph Judge. Photos by Jonathan Blair. 585-621, Nov. 1973

DISNEYLAND, Anaheim, California:

The Magic Worlds of Walt Disney. By Robert de Roos. Photos by Thomas Nebbia. 159-207, Aug. 1963

DISTANT EARLY WARNING LINE. *See* DEW Line

DISTRICT OF COLUMBIA. *See* Washington, D. C.

DIVE Into the Great Rift. By Robert D. Ballard. Photos by Emory Kristof. 604-615, May 1975

DIVERS, Land: New Hebrides. *See* Land Divers

DIVERS AND DIVING:

At Home in the Sea. By Jacques-Yves Cousteau. 465-507, Apr. 1964

Australia's Great Barrier Reef. Photos by Valerie

DIVERS AND DIVING—*Continued*

and Ron Taylor. 728-741, June 1973

Bermuda—Balmy, British, and Beautiful. By Peter Benchley. Photos by Emory Kristof. 93-121, July 1971
Included: Salvage diving

Blue-water Plankton: Ghosts of the Gulf Stream. By William M. Hamner. 530-545, Oct. 1974

Buck Island—Underwater Jewel. By Jerry and Idaz Greenberg. 677-683, May 1971

The Deepest Days. By Robert Sténuit. 534-547, Apr. 1965

Diving Beneath Arctic Ice. By Joseph B. MacInnis. Photos by William R. Curtsinger. 248-267, Aug. 1973

Diving Into the Blue Holes of the Bahamas. By George J. Benjamin. 347-363, Sept. 1970

Diving Through an Undersea Avalanche. By Jacques-Yves Cousteau. 538-542, Apr. 1955

Diving With Sea Snakes. By Kenneth MacLeish. Photos by Ben Cropp. 565-578, Apr. 1972

Exploring Australia's Coral Jungle. By Kenneth MacLeish. 743-779, June 1973

Goggle Fishing in California Waters. By David Hellyer. Photos by Lamar Boren. 615-632, May 1949

Ice Fishing's Frigid Charms. By Thomas J. Abercrombie. 861-872, Dec. 1958

Into the Lairs of "Sleeping" Sharks. By Eugenie Clark. Photos by David Doubilet. 570-584, Apr. 1975

Life Cycle of a Coral. By Robert F. Sisson. 780-793, June 1973

Life Springs From Death in Truk Lagoon. By Sylvia A. Earle. Photos by Al Giddings. 578-613, May 1976
From Graveyard to Garden. 604-613

Marineland, Florida's Giant Fish Bowl. By Gilbert Grosvenor La Gorce. Photos by Luis Marden. 679-694, Nov. 1952

Marvels of a Coral Realm. By Walter A. Starck II. 710-738, Nov. 1966

Mzima, Kenya's Spring of Life. By Joan and Alan Root. 350-373, Sept. 1971

On the Winds of the Dodecanese. By Jean and Franc Shor. 351-390, Mar. 1953

Outpost Under the Ocean. By Edwin A. Link. Photos by Bates Littlehales. 530-533, Apr. 1965

Photographing the Night Creatures of Alligator Reef (Florida). By Robert E. Schroeder. Photos by author and Walter A. Starck II. 128-154, Jan. 1964

Probing the Deep Reefs' Hidden Realm. By Walter A. Starck II and Jo D. Starck. 867-886, Dec. 1972

Project FAMOUS. Photos by Emory Kristof. 586-615, May 1975
I. Where the Earth Turns Inside Out. By J. R. Heirtzler. 586-603
II. Dive Into the Great Rift. By Robert D. Ballard. 604-615

Stalking Seals Under Antarctic Ice. By Carleton Ray. 54-65, Jan. 1966

A Taxi for the Deep Frontier. By Kenneth MacLeish. Photos by Bates Littlehales. 139-150, Jan. 1968

Tektite II. 256-296, Aug. 1971
I. Science's Window on the Sea. By John G. VanDerwalker. Photos by Bates Littlehales. 256-289

DIVERS AND DIVING — *Continued*

II. All-girl Team Tests the Habitat. By Sylvia A. Earle. Paintings by Pierre Mion. 291-296

Tomorrow on the Deep Frontier. By Edwin A. Link. 778-801, June 1964

Twenty Fathoms Down for Mother-of-Pearl. By Winston Williams. Photos by Bates Littlehales. 512-529, Apr. 1962

Working for Weeks on the Sea Floor. By Jacques-Yves Cousteau. Photos by Philippe Cousteau and Bates Littlehales. 498-537, Apr. 1966

World Beneath the Sea. Special Publication announced. 868-875, June 1967

The World of Jacques-Yves Cousteau (Television film). 529A-529B, Apr. 1966

See also Ama; Aquascope; Archeology, Underwater; Bathyscaphs; *Calypso* (Fish Men); *Deepstar*; Diving Cylinder; Diving Saucers; Sponge Fishing Industry; Submarines, Nuclear-powered

DIVING BELL (Rescue Compartment):

Our Navy's Long Submarine Arm. By Allan C. Fisher, Jr. 613-636, Nov. 1952

DIVING BOATS. *See* Bathyscaphs; Submersibles

DIVING CYLINDER:

The Long, Deep Dive. By Lord Kilbracken. Photos by Bates Littlehales. 718-731, May 1963

Our Man-in-Sea Project. By Edwin A. Link. 713-717, May 1963

DIVING SAUCERS:

Diving Saucer *(Denise)* Takes to the Deep. By Jacques-Yves Cousteau. 571-586, Apr. 1960

See also Cyana; DS-2

DIXIE Spins the Wheel of Industry. By William H. Nicholas. Photos by J. Baylor Roberts. 281-324, Mar. 1949

DJAKARTA (Batavia), Java:

Java — Eden in Transition. By Kenneth MacLeish. Photos by Dean Conger. 1-43, Jan. 1971

Postwar Journey Through Java. By Ronald Stuart Kain. 675-700, May 1948

DJOKJAKARTA, Java:

Postwar Journey Through Java. By Ronald Stuart Kain. 675-700, May 1948

See also Jogjakarta

A **DO-IT-YOURSELF** Gardener Creates a New All-America Rose. By Elizabeth A. Moize. Photos by Farrell Grehan. 286-294, Aug. 1972

DOBIE, J. FRANK: Author:

What I Saw Across the Rhine. 57-86, Jan. 1947

DODECANESE (Islands), Aegean Sea:

The Isles of Greece: Aegean Birthplace of Western Culture. By Melville Bell Grosvenor. Photos by Edwin Stuart Grosvenor and Winfield Parks. 147-193, Aug. 1972

On the Winds of the Dodecanese. By Jean and Franc Shor. 351-390, Mar. 1953

DODGE SATELLITE:

Historic Color Portrait of Earth From Space. By Kenneth F. Weaver. Photos by DODGE Satellite. 726-731, Nov. 1967

DODO (Bird):

Mauritius, Island of the Dodo. By Quentin Keynes. 77-104, Jan. 1956

DOG SHOWS:

Dog Mart Day in Fredericksburg. By Frederick G. Vosburgh. 817-832, June 1951

Westminster, World Series of Dogdom. By John W. Cross, Jr. 91-116, Jan. 1954

DOGON (People):

Foxes Foretell the Future in Mali's Dogon Country. By Pamela Johnson Meyer. 431-448, Mar. 1969

DOGS:

Book of Dogs. Book announced. 441-442, Sept. 1958

Note: The title of the revised edition (1966) is *Man's Best Friend.*

Born Hunters, the Bird Dogs. By Roland Kilbon. Paintings by Walter A. Weber. 369-398, Sept. 1947

Contents: American Cocker Spaniel, American Water Spaniel, Brittany Spaniel, Chesapeake Bay Retriever, Clumber Spaniel, Curly-coated Retriever, English Cocker Spaniel, English Setter, English Springer Spaniel, Flat-coated Retriever, German Short-haired Pointer, Golden Retriever, Gordon Setter, Irish Setter, Irish Water Spaniel, Labrador Retriever, Pointer, Sussex Spaniel, Weimaraner, Welsh Springer Spaniel, Wirehaired Pointing Griffon

Dogs Work for Man. By Edward J. Linehan. Paintings by Edwin Megargee and R. E. Lougheed. 190-233, Aug. 1958

Dogs Working for People. Children's book announced. 736-738, Nov. 1972

See also Bravo; Dog Shows; St. Bernard Dogs; Sled Dogs

DOIG, DESMOND: Author:

Sherpaland, My Shangri-La. 545-577, Oct. 1966

Sikkim. 398-429, Mar. 1963

Author-Photographer

Bhutan: Mountain Kingdom Between Tibet and India. 384-415, Sept. 1961

DOLLS:

The World in Dolls. By Samuel F. Pryor. Photos by Kathleen Revis. 817-831, Dec. 1959

See also Dzibilchaltun, for Temple of the Seven Dolls

DOLOMITES (Mountains), Italy:

A Stroll to Venice. By Isobel Wylie Hutchison. 378-410, Sept. 1951

Note: The author walked from Innsbruck, Austria, through the Tyrol and Dolomites, to Venice, Italy.

DOLPHINS. *See* Porpoises

DOMESTICATING the Wild and Woolly Musk Ox. By John J. Teal, Jr. Photos by Robert W. Madden. 862-879, June 1970

DOMINICA (Island), Leeward Islands, West Indies:

Finisterre Sails the Windward Islands. By Carleton Mitchell. Photos by Winfield Parks. 755-801, Dec. 1965

DONINI, JIM: Author-Photographer:

To Torre Egger's Icy Summit. 813-823, Dec. 1976

DONNELLEY, R. R., & SONS COMPANY, Chicago, Illinois:

Exploring an Epic Year: A Message from Your Society's President and Editor. By Melville Bell Grosvenor. 874-886, Dec. 1960

DOOR PENINSULA, Wisconsin:

Wisconsin's Door Peninsula. By William S. Ellis. Photos by Ted Rozumalski. 347-371, Mar. 1969

DORDOGNE (Department), France:

Exploring the Mind of Ice Age Man. By Alexander Marshack. 64-89, Jan. 1975
Included: The caves of La Roche, Lascaux, Pech-Merle, Rouffignac, and the Blanchard rock shelter
See also Lascaux Cave

DORIES:

Dory on the Banks: A Day in the Life of a Portuguese Fisherman. By James H. Pickerell. 573-583, Apr. 1968

DORSET ESKIMOS:

Vanished Mystery Men of Hudson Bay. By Henry B. Collins. 669-687, Nov. 1956

DORSETSHIRE, England. *See* Abbotsbury Swannery

DORYMEN (Portuguese Fishermen):

Dory on the Banks: A Day in the Life of a Portuguese Fisherman. By James H. Pickerell. 573-583, Apr. 1968

I Sailed with Portugal's Captains Courageous. By Alan Villiers. 565-596, May 1952

The Lonely Dorymen (Television film). 579A-579B, Apr. 1968
See also Blessing of the Fleet

DORZE (People):

Ethiopia's Artful Weavers. By Judith Olmstead. Photos by James A. Sugar. 125-141, Jan. 1973

DOTIALS (Tribespeople):

High Adventure in the Himalayas. By Thomas Weir. 193-234, Aug. 1952

DOUBILET, DAVID: Photographer:

The American Lobster, Delectable Cannibal. By Luis Marden. 462-487, Apr. 1973

Florida, Noah's Ark for Exotic Newcomers. By Rick Gore. 538-559, Oct. 1976

Into the Lairs of "Sleeping" Sharks. By Eugenie Clark. 570-584, Apr. 1975

Rainbow World Beneath the Red Sea. 344-365, Sept. 1975

The Red Sea's Gardens of Eels. By Eugenie Clark. Photos by James L. Stanfield and David Doubilet. 724-735, Nov. 1972

The Red Sea's Sharkproof Fish. By Eugenie Clark. 718-727, Nov. 1974

The Strangest Sea (Red Sea). By Eugenie Clark. 338-343, Sept. 1975

DOUGLAS, MERCEDES H.: Photographer:

Station Wagon Odyssey: Baghdad to Istanbul. By William O. Douglas. Photos by author and Mercedes H. Douglas. 48-87, Jan. 1959

West from the Khyber Pass. By William O. Douglas. Photos by Mercedes H. Douglas and author. 1-44, July 1958

DOUGLAS, WILLIAM O.: Author:

Banks Island: Eskimo Life on the Polar Sea. Photos by Clyde Hare. 703-735, May 1964

The Friendly Huts of the White Mountains. Photos by Kathleen Revis. 205-239, Aug. 1961

Journey to Outer Mongolia. Photos by Dean

DOUGLAS, WILLIAM O.: Author—*Continued*

Conger. 289-345, Mar. 1962

The People of Cades Cove. Photos by Thomas Nebbia and Otis Imboden. 60-95, July 1962
Author-Photographer

Station Wagon Odyssey: Baghdad to Istanbul. Photos by author and Mercedes H. Douglas. 48-87, Jan. 1959

West from the Khyber Pass. Photos by Mercedes H. Douglas and author. 1-44, July 1958

DOVE (Sloop):

Robin Sails Home. By Robin Lee Graham. 504-545, Oct. 1970

A Teen-ager Sails the World Alone. By Robin Lee Graham. 445-491, Oct. 1968

World-roaming Teen-ager Sails On. By Robin Lee Graham. 449-493, Apr. 1969

DOWN East Cruise. By Tom Horgan. Photos by Luis Marden. 329-369, Sept. 1952

DOWN East to Nova Scotia. By Winfield Parks. 853-879, June 1964

DOWN Mark Twain's River on a Raft. By Rex E. Hieronymus. 551-574, Apr. 1948

DOWN the Danube by Canoe. By William Slade Backer. Photos by Richard S. Durrance and Christopher G. Knight. 34-79, July 1965

DOWN the Grand Canyon 100 Years After Powell. By Joseph Judge. Photos by Walter Meayers Edwards. 668-713, May 1969

DOWN the Potomac by Canoe. By Ralph Gray. Photos by Walter Meayers Edwards. 213-242, Aug. 1948

DOWN the Susquehanna by Canoe. By Ralph Gray. Photos by Walter Meayers Edwards. 73-120, July 1950

DOWN to *Thresher* by Bathyscaph. By Donald L. Keach. 764-777, June 1964

DOYLE, ROBERT E.:

Board of Trustees member (1975). 225, Aug. 1976

President of NGS. 159, 224-226, Aug. 1976

Secretary (1967). 577, 581, 587, 590, Oct. 1967

Secretary, Assistant (1951). 225, Aug. 1976

Secretary, Associate (1958), for Membership of NGS. 225, Aug. 1976

Vice President of NGS (1961). 577, 587, Oct. 1967

DRAGON Lizards of Komodo. By James A. Kern. 872-880, Dec. 1968

DRAGONFLIES:

Dragonflies—Rainbows on the Wing. By James G. Needham. 215-229, Aug. 1951
Contents: Blue Backs, Damsons, *Didymops, Epo-nina, Erythrodiplax umbrata,* Golden Wings, *Gom-phus,* Green Darners, Green Jackets, Hoolets, *Libellula axillena, Libellula pulchella, Progomphus alachuensis,* Saddlebags, Seminoles, Sky Pilots

DRAKE, SIR FRANCIS:

The British Way. By Sir Evelyn Wrench. 421-541, Apr. 1949

Sir Francis Drake. By Alan Villiers. Photos by Gor-

DRAKE, SIR FRANCIS—*Continued*
don W. Gahan. 216-253, Feb. 1975

The World of Elizabeth I. By Louis B. Wright. Photos by Ted Spiegel. 668-709, Nov. 1968
Included: Historical map based on the Hondius Map of 1589, showing Drake's voyage around the world

DRAKENSBERG RANGE, South Africa. See Black Eagles; *and* Africa's Bushman Art Treasures

DRAMA. *See* Theater

DRESDEN, DONALD WILLIAM: Author:
Paris, Home Town of the World. Photos by Justin Locke. 767-804, June 1952

DREYFUS COLLECTION (Renaissance Bronzes):
Your National Gallery of Art After 10 Years. By John Walker. 73-103, Jan. 1952

DRILLING, Undersea. *See Glomar Challenger;* Mohole, Project

DRIVING the Mexican 1000: Rocks, Ruts, and Sand. By Michael E. Long. 569-575, Oct. 1972

DROUGHT:
Drought Bedevils Brazil's Sertão. By John Wilson. Photos by Gordon W. Gahan. 704-723, Nov. 1972

Drought Threatens the Tuareg World. By Victor Englebert. 544-571, Apr. 1974

The Imperiled Everglades. By Fred Ward. 1-27, Jan. 1972

The Niger: River of Sorrow, River of Hope. By Georg Gerster. 152-189, Aug. 1975

Oklahoma, the Adventurous One. By Robert Paul Jordan. Photos by Robert W. Madden. 149-189, Aug. 1971

The Top End of Down Under. By Kenneth MacLeish. Photos by Thomas Nebbia. 145-174, Feb. 1973

What's Happening to Our Climate? By Samuel W. Matthews. 576-615, Nov. 1976

DROWNED Galleons Yield Spanish Gold. By Kip Wagner. Photos by Otis Imboden. 1-37, Jan. 1965

DRUCKER, PHILIP: Author:
Gifts for the Jaguar God. By Philip Drucker and Robert F. Heizer. 367-375, Sept. 1956

DRUGS:
Nature's Gifts to Medicine. By Lonnelle Aikman. Paintings by Lloyd K. Townsend and Don Crowley. 420-440, Sept. 1974
See also Medicine and Health

DRUIDS. *See* Stonehenge

DRUMS to Dynamos on the Mohawk. By Frederick G. Vosburgh. Photos by B. Anthony Stewart. 67-110, July 1947

DRY-LAND Fleet Sails the Sahara. By Jean du Boucher. Photos by Jonathan S. Blair. 696-725, Nov. 1967

DRY TORTUGAS (Islands), Florida:
Blizzard of Birds: The Tortugas Terns. By Alexander Sprunt, Jr. 213-230, Feb. 1947
See also Shrimp (Shrimp Nursery)

DRYDEN, HUGH L.: Author:
Fact Finding for Tomorrow's Planes. Photos by Luis Marden. 757-780, Dec. 1953

Footprints on the Moon. Paintings by Davis Meltzer and Pierre Mion. 357-401, Mar. 1964

The International Geophysical Year: Man's Most Ambitious Study of His Environment. 285-298, Feb. 1956

DUBAI, United Arab Emirates:
The Arab World, Inc. By John J. Putman. Photos by Winfield Parks. 494-533, Oct. 1975

DUBLIN, Ireland:
Dublin's Historic Horse Show. By Maynard Owen Williams. 115-132, July 1953

The Friendly Irish. By John Scofield. Photos by James A. Sugar. 354-391, Sept. 1969

I Walked Some Irish Miles. By Dorothea Sheats. 653-678, May 1951

DU BOUCHER, JEAN: Author:
Dry-land Fleet Sails the Sahara. Photos by Jonathan S. Blair. 696-725, Nov. 1967

DUBROVNIK (Ragusa), Yugoslavia:
Yugoslavia's Window on the Adriatic. By Gilbert M. Grosvenor. 219-247, Feb. 1962

DUCK RAISING:
Long Island Outgrows the Country. By Howell Walker. Photos by B. Anthony Stewart. 279-326, Mar. 1951

DUCKBILLS. *See* Platypuses

DUCKS:
Duck Hunting with a Color Camera. By Arthur A. Allen. 514-539, Oct. 1951
Contents: Baldpates; Black Ducks; Buffleheads; Canvasbacks; Eiders; Gadwalls; Golden-eyes; Mallards; Mergansers; Muscovy Ducks; Old-squaws; Pintails; Redheads; Ringnecks; Ruddy Ducks; Scaups, Greater and Lesser; Shovellers; Teals, Blue-winged, and Cinnamon; Widgeons, European; Wood Ducks

DUFEK, GEORGE J.:
Hubbard Medal recipient. 589-590, Apr. 1959; 530, Oct. 1959

Author
Nuclear Power for the Polar Regions. 712-730, May 1962

What We've Accomplished in Antarctica. 527-557, Oct. 1959

DUGOUT CANOES:
Jungle Journey to the World's Highest Waterfall. By Ruth Robertson. 655-690, Nov. 1949

Sea Fever. By John E. Schultz. 237-268, Feb. 1949

DULUTH, Minnesota:
Minnesota Makes Ideas Pay. By Frederick G. Vosburgh. Photos by John E. Fletcher and B. Anthony Stewart. 291-336, Sept. 1949

DUMAS, FRÉDÉRIC:
Fish Men Explore a New World Undersea. By Jacques-Yves Cousteau. 431-472, Oct. 1952

DUNCAN, DAVID D.: Photographer:
Power Comes Back to Peiping. By Nelson T. Johnson and W. Robert Moore. 337-368, Sept. 1949

DUNKIRK, France:

Thumbs Up Round the North Sea's Rim. By Frances James. Photos by Erica Koch. 685-704, May 1952

DUNN, DOROTHY: Author:

America's First Painters: Indians. 349-377, Mar. 1955

DU PONT, PIERRE S.: Estate:

Wonderland in Longwood Gardens. By Edward C. Ferriday, Jr. 45-64, July 1951

DU PONT DE NEMOURS, E. I., & COMPANY, Wilmington, Delaware:

Today on the Delaware, Penn's Glorious River. By Albert W. Atwood. Photos by Robert F. Sisson. 1-40, July 1952

DURBAN, South Africa:

Safari Through Changing Africa. By Elsie May Bell Grosvenor. Photos by Gilbert Grosvenor. 145-198, Aug. 1953

DURBAR:

Progress and Pageantry in Changing Nigeria. By W. Robert Moore. 325-365, Sept. 1956

DURENCEAU, ANDRE: Artist:

Ice Age Man, the First American. By Thomas R. Henry. 781-806, Dec. 1955

A New Look at Medieval Europe. By Kenneth M. Setton. Paintings by Andre Durenceau and Birney Lettick. 799-859, Dec. 1962

DURRANCE, DICK, II: Author-Photographer:

A Town . . . a Mountain . . . a Way of Life. By Jill Durrance and Dick Durrance II. 788-807, Dec. 1973

Photographer

Alabama, Dixie to a Different Tune. By Howard La Fay. 534-569, Oct. 1975

Americans Afoot in Rumania. By Dan Dimancescu. Photos by Dick Durrance II and Christopher G. Knight. 810-845, June 1969

Bangladesh: Hope Nourishes a New Nation. By William S. Ellis. 295-333, Sept. 1972

Down the Danube by Canoe. By William Slade Backer. Photos by Richard S. Durrance and Christopher G. Knight. 34-79, July 1965

Leningrad, Russia's Window on the West. By Howard La Fay. 636-673, May 1971

Library of Congress: The Nation's Bookcase. By Fred Kline. 671-687, Nov. 1975

Mr. Jefferson's Monticello. By Joseph Judge. Photos by Dean Conger and Richard S. Durrance. 426-444, Sept. 1966

On the Track of the West's Wild Horses. By Hope Ryden. Photos by author and Dick Durrance II. 94-109, Jan. 1971

White-water Adventure on Wild Rivers of Idaho. By Frank Craighead, Jr. and John Craighead. 213-239, Feb. 1970

The Zulus: Black Nation in a Land of Apartheid. By Joseph Judge. 738-775, Dec. 1971

DURRANCE, JILL: Author-Photographer:

A Town . . . a Mountain . . . a Way of Life. By Jill Durrance and Dick Durrance II. 788-807, Dec. 1973

DUTCH EAST INDIA COMPANY: Ship. See *Slot ter Hooge*

DUTCH WEST INDIES. *See* Netherlands Antilles

DYGERT, RUTH E.: Author:

Ambassadors of Good Will: The Peace Corps. By Sargent Shriver and Peace Corps Volunteers. 297-345, Sept. 1964
Tanganyika. 321-323

DYHRENFURTH, NORMAN G.: Author:

Six to the Summit (Everest). Photos by Barry C. Bishop. 460-473, Oct. 1963

See also American Mount Everest Expedition

DYNAMIC Ontario. By Marjorie Wilkins Campbell. Photos by Winfield Parks. 58-97, July 1963

DZIBILCHALTUN, Yucatán, Mexico:

Dzibilchaltun. 91-129, Jan. 1959
I. Lost City of the Maya. By E. Wyllys Andrews. 91-109
II. Up from the Well of Time. By Luis Marden. 110-129

E

ECA. *See* Economic Cooperation Administration

EAGLE (Lunar Module). *See* Apollo Missions (Apollo 11)

EAGLE (Training Ship):

Under Canvas in the Atomic Age (U. S. Coast Guard Cadets). By Alan Villiers. 49-84, July 1955
See also Operation Sail

EAGLES:

Seeking Mindanao's Strangest Creatures. By Charles Heizer Wharton. 389-408, Sept. 1948
Included: Crested Serpent Eagle, Monkey-eating Eagle

See also Bald Eagles, American; Black Eagles; Golden Eagles

EARLE, SYLVIA A.: Author:

All-girl Team Tests the Habitat. Paintings by Pierre Mion. 291-296, Aug. 1971

Life Springs From Death in Truk Lagoon. Photos by Al Giddings. 578-603, May 1976

EARLIEST Geographics to Be Reprinted. By Melvin M. Payne. 688-689, Nov. 1964

EARLY AMERICA Through the Eyes of Her Native Artists. By Hereward Lester Cooke, Jr. 356-389, Sept. 1962

EARLY MAN. *See* Man, Prehistoric

EARTH:

Apollo 16 Brings Us Visions From Space. 856-865, Dec. 1972

The Earth From Orbit. By Paul D. Lowman, Jr. 645-671, Nov. 1966

"The Earth from Space," photo supplement. Apollo astronauts on reverse. Sept. 1973

Extraordinary Photograph Shows Earth Pole to Pole. Photos by Nimbus I. 190-193, Feb. 1965

Have We Solved the Mysteries of the Moon? By Kenneth F. Weaver. Paintings by William H. Bond. 309-325, Sept. 1973
Included: Diagrams and text comparing the moon with the earth

EARTH — *Continued*

Historic Color Portrait of Earth From Space. By Kenneth F. Weaver. Photos by DODGE Satellite. 726-731, Nov. 1967

"How Man Pollutes His World," painting supplement. Map of the World. Dec. 1970

Our Earth as a Satellite Sees It. By W. G. Stroud. 293-302, Aug. 1960

Our Home-town Planet, Earth. By F. Barrows Colton. 117-139, Jan. 1952

Pollution, Threat to Man's Only Home. By Gordon Young. Photos by James P. Blair. 738-781, Dec. 1970

Scientists Drill at Sea to Pierce Earth's Crust (Project Mohole). By Samuel W. Matthews. Photos by J. Baylor Roberts. 686-697, Nov. 1961

Seeing the Earth from 80 Miles Up. By Clyde T. Holliday. 511-528, Oct. 1950

Skylab Looks at Earth. 471-493, Oct. 1974

This Changing Earth. By Samuel W. Matthews. 1-37, Jan. 1973

The Violent Earth (Television film). 286A-286B, Feb. 1973

Voyage to the Planets. By Kenneth F. Weaver. Paintings by Ludek Pesek. 147-193, Aug. 1970

What's Happening to Our Climate? By Samuel W. Matthews. 576-615, Nov. 1976

EARTHQUAKES:

An Alaskan Family's Night of Terror. By Tay Pryor Thomas. 142-156, July 1964

California's San Andreas Fault. By Thomas Y. Canby. Photos by James P. Blair. 38-53, Jan. 1973

Can We Predict Quakes? By Thomas Y. Canby. 830-835, June 1976

Caught in the Assam-Tibet Earthquake. By F. Kingdon-Ward. 403-416, Mar. 1952

Death of an Island, Tristan da Cunha. By P. J. F. Wheeler. 678-695, May 1962

Earthquake! (Alaska, 1964). By William P. E. Graves. 112-139, July 1964

Earthquake in Guatemala. By Bart McDowell. Photos by W. E. Garrett and Robert W. Madden. 810-829, June 1976

The Night the Mountains Moved (Montana). By Samuel W. Matthews. Photos by J. Baylor Roberts. 329-359, Mar. 1960

Our Home-town Planet, Earth. By F. Barrows Colton. 117-139, Jan. 1952

Our Restless Earth. By Maynard M. Miller. 140-141, July 1964

Peru, Homeland of the Warlike Inca. By Kip Ross. 421-462, Oct. 1950
    Included: Cusco earthquake of May 21, 1950

This Changing Earth. By Samuel W. Matthews. 1-37, Jan. 1973

The Violent Earth (Television film). 286A-286B, Feb. 1973

Volcano and Earthquake Show Nature's Awesome Power. The Editor. 303, Mar. 1960

See also Port Royal, Jamaica; Skopje, Yugoslavia

EARTH'S Richest Nation—A Tiny Pacific Islet. By Mike Holmes. 344-353, Sept. 1976

EARTHWORMS:

Biggest Worm Farm Caters to Platypuses. By W. H. Nicholas. 269-280, Feb. 1949

EARTHWORMS — *Continued*

Capturing Strange Creatures in Colombia. By Marte Latham. Photos by Tor Eigeland. 682-693, May 1966

The EAST (Region), U. S.:

The Parks in Your Backyard. By Conrad L. Wirth. 647-707, Nov. 1963
    The East. 675-689

See also New England

EAST AFRICA:

East Africa's Majestic Flamingos. Photos by M. Philip Kahl. 276-294, Feb. 1970

The Leakey Tradition Lives On. By Melvin M. Payne. 143-144, Jan. 1973

See also Kenya; Tanzania; Uganda

EAST From Bali by Seagoing Jeep to Timor. By Helen and Frank Schreider. 236-279, Aug. 1962

EAST GERMANY. *See* German Democratic Republic

EAST INDIA COMPANY, Dutch. *See Slot ter Hooge*

EAST PAKISTAN:

East Pakistan Drives Back the Jungle. By Jean and Franc Shor. 399-426, Mar. 1955

Pakistan: Problems of a Two-part Land. By Bern Keating. Photos by Albert Moldvay. 1-47, Jan. 1967

See also Bangladesh

EAST ST. LOUIS, Illinois:

"Pyramids" of the New World. By Neil Merton Judd. 105-128, Jan. 1948

EASTER:

Easter Greetings From the Ukrainians. By Robert Paul Jordan. Photos by James A. Sugar. 556-563, Apr. 1972

Easter Week in Indian Guatemala. By John Scofield. 406-417, Mar. 1960

Nikolaevsk: A Bit of Old Russia Takes Root in Alaska. By Jim Rearden. Photos by Charles O'Rear. 401-425, Sept. 1972

"EASTER Egg" Chickens. By Frederick G. Vosburgh. Photos by B. Anthony Stewart. 377-387, Sept. 1948

EASTER ISLAND, Pacific Ocean:

Easter Island and Its Mysterious Monuments. By Howard La Fay. Photos by Thomas J. Abercrombie. 90-117, Jan. 1962

The *Yankee's* Wander-world. By Irving and Electa Johnson. 1-50, Jan. 1949

EASTERN MEDITERRANEAN LANDS:

Lands of the Eastern Mediterranean, Atlas series supplement. Jan. 1959

See also Cyprus; Egypt; Israel; Jerusalem; Jordan; Lebanon; Sinai; Syria; Turkey

EASTERN ORTHODOX CHURCH. *See* St. Catherine's Monastery

EASTERN SHORE, Maryland-Virginia:

Chesapeake Country. By Nathaniel T. Kenney. Photos by Bates Littlehales. 370-411, Sept. 1964

"Delmarva," Gift of the Sea. By Catherine Bell Palmer. 367-399, Sept. 1950

Maryland on the Half Shell. By Stuart E. Jones.

EASTERN SHORE, Maryland-Virginia—*Continued*

Photos by Robert W. Madden. 188-229, Feb. 1972

Roving Maryland's Cavalier Country. By William A. Kinney. 431-470, Apr. 1954

Tireless Voyager, the Whistling Swan. By William J. L. Sladen. Photos by Bianca Lavies. 134-147, July 1975

See also Chesapeake Bay (The Sailing Oystermen); Chesapeake Bay Bridge-Tunnel

EASTMAN, GEORGE:

Eastman of Rochester: Photographic Pioneer. By Allan C. Fisher, Jr. 423-438, Sept. 1954

EBERLEIN, HAROLD DONALDSON: Author:

Philadelphia Houses a Proud Past. Photos by Thomas Nebbia. 151-191, Aug. 1960

ECHOLOCATION:

Stalking Seals Under Antarctic Ice. By Carleton Ray. 54-65, Jan. 1966

See also Bats; Killer Whales; Oilbirds; Porpoises

ECLIPSES, Solar:

Burr Prizes Awarded to Dr. Edgerton and Dr. Van Biesbroeck. 705-706, May 1953; 523, Apr. 1955

Eclipse Hunting in Brazil's Ranchland. By F. Barrows Colton. Photos by Richard H. Stewart and Guy W. Starling. 285-324, Sept. 1947

Operation Eclipse: 1948. By William A. Kinney. 325-372, Mar. 1949

Contents: Eclipse observation stations in Burma; Thailand; China; Korea; Japan; Aleutian Islands

Solar Eclipse, Nature's Super Spectacular. By Donald H. Menzel and Jay M. Pasachoff. 222-233, Aug. 1970

The Solar Eclipse From a Jet. By Wolfgang B. Klemperer. 785-796, Nov. 1963

Included: Path of totality of eclipse from Hokkaido, Japan, to beyond Bar Harbor, Maine

South in the Sudan. By Harry Hoogstraal. 249-272, Feb. 1953

Included: Khartoum, 1952 eclipse site (total eclipse of the sun, February 25)

The Sun. By Herbert Friedman. 713-743, Nov. 1965

Your Society Observes Eclipse in Brazil. 661, May 1947

ECOLOGY:

African Wildlife: Man's Threatened Legacy. By Allan C. Fisher, Jr. Photos by Thomas Nebbia. Paintings by Ned Seidler. 147-187, Feb. 1972

As We Live and Breathe: The Challenge of Our Environment. Special Publication announced. 882-886, June 1971

Florida, Noah's Ark for Exotic Newcomers. By Rick Gore. Photos by David Doubilet. 538-559, Oct. 1976

The Imperiled Everglades. By Fred Ward. 1-27, Jan. 1972

Our Ecological Crisis. 737-795, Dec. 1970

I. Pollution, Threat to Man's Only Home. By Gordon Young. Photos by James P. Blair. 738-781

II. "How Man Pollutes His World," painting supplement. Map of the World.

III. The Fragile Beauty All About Us. Photos by Harry S. C. Yen. 785-795

See also Bighorn Sheep; Corals and Coral Reefs; Gi-

ECOLOGY—*Continued*

ant Kelp; Giant Tortoises; Lions; Ospreys; Tundra; Walking Catfish; Willamette River; *and* Ecosystems; Photosynthesis

ECONOMIC COOPERATION ADMINISTRATION:

Roaming Korea South of the Iron Curtain. By Enzo de Chetelat. 777-808, June 1950

War-torn Greece Looks Ahead. By Maynard Owen Williams. 711-744, Dec. 1949

With Uncle Sam and John Bull in Germany. By Frederick Simpich. 117-140, Jan. 1949

ECONOMICS:

Five Noted Thinkers Explore the Future. 68-75, July 1976

Included: Isaac Asimov, Richard F. Babcock, Edmund N. Bacon, Buckminster Fuller, Gerard Piel

ECOSYSTEMS:

Abundant Life in a Desert Land. By Walter Meayers Edwards. 424-436, Sept. 1973

Can We Save Our Salt Marshes? By Stephen W. Hitchcock. Photos by William R. Curtsinger. 729-765, June 1972

Hidden Worlds in the Heart of a Plant (Bromeliad). By Paul A. Zahl. 389-397, Mar. 1975

The Living Sand. By William H. Amos. 820-833, June 1965

Miracle of the Potholes. By Rowe Findley. Photos by Robert F. Sisson. 570-579, Oct. 1975

Mzima, Kenya's Spring of Life. By Joan and Alan Root. 350-373, Sept. 1971

Teeming Life of a Pond. By William H. Amos. 274-298, Aug. 1970

ECUADOR:

Ambassadors of Good Will: The Peace Corps. By Sargent Shriver and Peace Corps Volunteers. 297-345, Sept. 1964

Ecuador. By Rhoda and Earle Brooks. 339-345

Ecuador—Low and Lofty Land Astride the Equator. By Loren McIntyre. 259-298, Feb. 1968

El Sangay, Fire-breathing Giant of the Andes. By G. Edward Lewis. 117-138, Jan. 1950

Sea Fever. By John E. Schultz. 237-268, Feb. 1949

See also Galapagos Islands; Vilcabamba

EDDY, WILLIAM A.:

Saudi Arabia, Oil Kingdom. Photos by Maynard Owen Williams. 497-512, Apr. 1948

EDEN in the Outback. By Kay and Stanley Breeden. 189-203, Feb. 1973

EDGAR M. QUEENY-AMERICAN MUSEUM OF NATURAL HISTORY EXPEDITION:

Spearing Lions with Africa's Masai. By Edgar Monsanto Queeny. 487-517, Oct. 1954

EDGEØYA (Island), Svalbard:

Polar Bear: Lonely Nomad of the North. By Thor Larsen. 574-590, Apr. 1971

EDGERTON, GLEN E.: Author:

An Engineer's View of the Suez Canal. 123-140, Jan. 1957

EDGERTON, HAROLD E.:

Burr Prizes Awarded to Dr. Edgerton and Dr. Van Biesbroeck. 705-706, May 1953; 523, Apr. 1955;

EDGERTON, HAROLD E. — *Continued*

467, Oct. 1955; 847, June 1960
Note: Electronic flashlight for ultra-high-speed photography invented by Dr. Edgerton.

Author

Circus Action in Color. 305-308, Mar. 1948

Stonehenge — New Light on an Old Riddle. Paintings by Brian Hope-Taylor. 846-866, June 1960

Author-Photographer

Freezing the Flight of Hummingbirds. By Harold E. Edgerton, R. J. Niedrach, and Walker Van Riper. 245-261, Aug. 1951

Hummingbirds in Action. 221-232, Aug. 1947

Photographing the Sea's Dark Underworld. 523-537, Apr. 1955

Photographer

Calypso Explores an Undersea Canyon (Romanche Trench). By Jacques-Yves Cousteau. Photos by Bates Littlehales and Harold E. Edgerton. 373-396, Mar. 1958

Fish Men Discover a 2,200-year-old Greek Ship. By Jacques-Yves Cousteau. 1-36, Jan. 1954

To the Depths of the Sea by Bathyscaphe. By Jacques-Yves Cousteau. 67-79, July 1954

The Wonder City That Moves by Night (Circus). By Francis Beverly Kelley. 289-324, Mar. 1948

EDINBURGH, Scotland:

Edinburgh: Capital in Search of a Country. By James Cerruti. Photos by Adam Woolfitt. 274-296, Aug. 1976

Midshipmen's Cruise. By William J. Aston and Alexander G. B. Grosvenor. 711-754, June 1948

Poets' Voices Linger in Scottish Shrines. By Isobel Wylie Hutchison. Photos by Kathleen Revis. 437-488, Oct. 1957

EDISON, THOMAS ALVA: Laboratory and Buildings. *See* Greenfield Village

EDMONTON, Alberta, Canada:

Canada's "Now" Frontier. By Robert Paul Jordan. Photos by Lowell Georgia. 480-511, Oct. 1976

EDUCATIONAL AIDS, NGS. *See* Atlases; Books; Films and Filmstrips; Globes; Map Supplements; NGM: Indexes; Recordings; *WORLD*

EDWARDS, DUNCAN: Photographer:

Roman Life in 1,600-year-old Color Pictures (Mosaics). By Gino Vinicio Gentili. 211-229, Feb. 1957

EDWARDS, MIKE W.: Author:

California's Land Apart — the Monterey Peninsula. 682-703, Nov. 1972

Hiking the Backbone of the Rockies: Canada's Great Divide Trail. Photos by Lowell Georgia. 795-817, June 1973

Mexico to Canada on the Pacific Crest Trail. Photos by David Hiser. 741-779, June 1971

Shenandoah, I Long to Hear You. Photos by Thomas Anthony DeFeo. 554-588, Apr. 1970

Should They Build a Fence Around Montana? Photos by Nicholas deVore III. 614-649, May 1976

Thomas Jefferson: Architect of Freedom. Photos by Linda Bartlett. 231-259, Feb. 1976

Through Ozark Hills and Hollows. Photos by Bruce Dale. 656-689, Nov. 1970

The Virginians. Photos by David Alan Harvey. 588-617, Nov. 1974

EDWARDS, WALTER MEAYERS:

Author-Photographer

Abundant Life in a Desert Land. 424-436, Sept. 1973

Across the Ridgepole of the Alps. 410-419, Sept. 1960

Crater Lake Summer. 134-148, July 1962

Eternal France. 725-764, June 1960

France's Past Lives in Languedoc. 1-43, July 1951

Lake Powell: Waterway to Desert Wonders. 44-75, July 1967

On the Ridgepole of the Rockies. 745-780, June 1947
Canada's Rocky Mountain Playground. 755-770

Photographer

The Alps: Man's Own Mountains. By Ralph Gray. Photos by Walter Meayers Edwards and William Eppridge. 350-395, Sept. 1965

The Camargue, Land of Cowboys and Gypsies. By Eugene L. Kammerman. 667-699, May 1956

Canada, My Country. By Alan Phillips. Photos by David S. Boyer and Walter Meayers Edwards. 769-819, Dec. 1961

Canyonlands, Realm of Rock and the Far Horizon. By Rowe Findley. 71-91, July 1971

Down the Potomac by Canoe. By Ralph Gray. 213-242, Aug. 1948

Down the Susquehanna by Canoe. By Ralph Gray. 73-120, July 1950

Micronesia: The Americanization of Eden. By David S. Boyer. 702-744, May 1967

Retracing John Wesley Powell's Historic Voyage Down the Grand Canyon. By Joseph Judge. 668-713, May 1969

We Saw the World From the Edge of Space. By Malcolm D. Ross. 671-685, Nov. 1961

EDWARDS AIR FORCE BASE, California:

Fact Finding for Tomorrow's Planes. By Hugh L. Dryden. Photos by Luis Marden. 757-780, Dec. 1953

EELS:

Night Life in the Gulf Stream. By Paul A. Zahl. 391-418, Mar. 1954

The Red Sea's Gardens of Eels. By Eugenie Clark. Photos by James L. Stanfield and David Doubilet. 724-735, Nov. 1972

EFFIGIES, Indian. *See* Gravel Pictographs

EGBERT, ALLAN L.: Author-Photographer:

Among Alaska's Brown Bears. By Allan L. Egbert and Michael H. Luque. 428-442, Sept. 1975

EGGS:

Easter Egg Chickens. By Frederick G. Vosburgh. Photos by B. Anthony Stewart. 377-387, Sept. 1948

Easter Greetings From the Ukrainians. By Robert Paul Jordan. Photos by James A. Sugar. 556-563, Apr. 1972

See also Aepyornis; Cooper's Hawk; Ospreys; Scarlet Ibis

EGRETS:

Saving Man's Wildlife Heritage. By John H. Baker. Photos by Robert F. Sisson. 581-620, Nov. 1954

Wildlife of Everglades National Park. By Daniel B.

EGRETS—*Continued*

Beard. Paintings by Walter A. Weber. 83-116, Jan. 1949

See also Cattle Egret

EGYPT:

Abraham, the Friend of God. By Kenneth Mac-Leish. Photos by Dean Conger. 739-789, Dec. 1966

Africa: Countries of the Nile, Atlas series supplement. Oct. 1963

Africa: The Winds of Freedom Stir a Continent. By Nathaniel T. Kenney. Photos by W. D. Vaughn. 303-359, Sept. 1960

"Around the World in Eighty Days." By Newman Bumstead. 705-750, Dec. 1951
    Included: Cairo; Giza; Ismailia; Port Said; Suez Canal

Eyewitness to War in the Holy Land. By Charles Harbutt. 782-795, Dec. 1967

Fresh Treasures from Egypt's Ancient Sands. By Jefferson Caffery. Photos by David S. Boyer. 611-650, Nov. 1955

In Search of Moses. By Harvey Arden. Photos by Nathan Benn. 2-37, Jan. 1976

Island of Faith in the Sinai Wilderness (St. Catherine's Monastery). By George H. Forsyth. Photos by Robert F. Sisson. 82-106, Jan. 1964

Journey Into the Great Rift: the Northern Half. By Helen and Frank Schreider. 254-290, Aug. 1965

Kayaks Down the Nile. By John M. Goddard. 697-732, May 1955

Mount Sinai's Holy Treasures (St. Catherine's Monastery). By Kurt Weitzmann. Photos by Fred Anderegg. 109-127, Jan. 1964

Nile Valley, Land of the Pharaohs, Atlas series supplement. Text on reverse. May 1965

The River Nile. Special Publication announced. 408-417, Mar. 1966

Round the World School (ISA). By Paul Antze. Photos by William Eppridge. 96-127, July 1962

Safari from Congo to Cairo. By Elsie May Bell Grosvenor. Photos by Gilbert Grosvenor. 721-771, Dec. 1954

Sinai Sheds New Light on the Bible. By Henry Field. Photos by William B. and Gladys Terry. 795-815, Dec. 1948

Troubled Waters East of Suez. By Ernest M. Eller. 483-522, Apr. 1954

Tutankhamun's Golden Trove. By Christiane Desroches Noblecourt. Photos by F. L. Kenett. 625-646, Oct. 1963

YWCA: International Success Story. By Mary French Rockefeller. Photos by Otis Imboden. 904-933, Dec. 1963

Yankee Cruises the Storied Nile. By Irving and Electa Johnson. Photos by Winfield Parks. 583-633, May 1965

See also Abu Simbel; Akhenaten Temple Project; Cairo; Suez Canal; *and* Gold

EGYPTIAN VULTURE:

Tool-using Bird: The Egyptian Vulture. By Baroness Jane van Lawick-Goodall. Photos by Baron Hugo van Lawick. 631-641, May 1968

EIGELAND, TOR: Photographer:

Capturing Strange Creatures in Colombia. By Marte Latham. 682-693, May 1966

EIGHT Maps of Discovery. 757-769, June 1953

1898: The Bells on Sable. Photos by Arthur W. McCurdy. 408-409, 416-417, Sept. 1965

EILER, TERRY: Photographer:

Indian Shangri-La of the Grand Canyon. By Jay Johnston. 355-373, Mar. 1970

EILOART, ARNOLD: Author:

Braving the Atlantic by Balloon *(Small World).* 123-146, July 1959

EILTS, HERMANN F.: Author:

Along the Storied Incense Roads of Aden. Photos by Brian Brake. 230-254, Feb. 1957

EIRE. *See* Ireland, Republic of

EISENHOWER, DWIGHT D.:

The Eisenhower Story. By Howard La Fay. 1-39, July 1969

Inside the White House. By Lonnelle Aikman. Photos by B. Anthony Stewart and Thomas Nebbia. 3-43, Jan. 1961

The Living White House. By Lonnelle Aikman. 593-643, Nov. 1966

President Eisenhower Presents the Hubbard Medal to Everest's Conquerors (British). 64, July 1954

President Eisenhower Presents the Society's Hubbard Medal to the Conquerors of Antarctica. 589-590, Apr. 1959

President Eisenhower Presents to Prince Philip the National Geographic Society's Medal. 865-868, Dec. 1957

Profiles of the Presidents: V. The Atomic Age: Its Problems and Promises. By Frank Freidel. 66-119, Jan. 1966

When the President Goes Abroad. By Gilbert M. Grosvenor. 588-649, May 1960

World's Last Salute to a Great American. By William Graves and other members of the National Geographic staff. 40-51, July 1969
                    Author

The Churchill I Knew. 153-157, Aug. 1965

A Message From the President of the United States. 587, May 1960

EISENHOWER, MAMIE GENEVA DOUD:

The Eisenhower Story. By Howard La Fay. 1-39, July 1969
                    Author

Introduction to article, "Inside the White House." 1, Jan. 1961

EISTEDDFODS:

Wales, Land of Bards. By Alan Villiers. Photos by Thomas Nebbia. 727-769, June 1965

ELDFELL (Volcano), Heimaey, Iceland. *See* former name, Kirkjufell

ELECTRICITY:

Can We Harness the Wind? By Roger Hamilton. Photos by Emory Kristof. 812-829, Dec. 1975

The Fire of Heaven. By Albert W. Atwood. 655-674, Nov. 1948

Lightning in Action. By F. Barrows Colton. 809-828, June 1950

The Search for Tomorrow's Power. By Kenneth F. Weaver. Photos by Emory Kristof. 650-681, Nov. 1972

Solar Energy, the Ultimate Powerhouse. By John

ELECTRICITY — *Continued*

L. Wilhelm. Photos by Emory Kristof. 381-397, Mar. 1976

Uncle Sam's House of 1,000 Wonders (National Bureau of Standards). By Lyman J. Briggs and F. Barrows Colton. 755-784, Dec. 1951

Whatever Happened to TVA? By Gordon Young. Photos by Emory Kristof. 830-863, June 1973

See also Hydroelectric Power; Nuclear Energy

ELECTRON MICROGRAPHS:

At Home With the Bulldog Ant. By Robert F. Sisson. 62-75, July 1974
Face-to-Face With a World of Ants (Electron Micrographs). 72-75

ELECTRONICS:

New Miracles of the Telephone Age. By Robert Leslie Conly. 87-120, July 1954

See also Computers; DEW Line; Electron Micrographs; Infrared Radiation; Lasers; Microelectronics; Radar; Satellites; Sonar

ELEPHANT SEALS. *See* Sea Elephants

ELEPHANTS:

Africa's Uncaged Elephants. Photos by Quentin Keynes. 371-382, Mar. 1951

Bhutan, Land of the Thunder Dragon. By Burt Kerr Todd. 713-754, Dec. 1952

The Elephant and I. By M. D. Chaturvedi. 489-507, Oct. 1957

On the Road With an Old-time Circus. By John Fetterman. Photos by Jonathan Blair. 410-434, Mar. 1972

Where Elephants Have Right of Way (Africa). By George and Jinx Rodger. Photos by George Rodger. 363-389, Sept. 1960

Wild Elephant Roundup in India. By Harry Miller. Photos by author and James P. Blair. 372-385, Mar. 1969

See also Mammoth

EL HATILLO CULTURE:

Exploring the Past in Panama. By Matthew W. Stirling. Photos by Richard H. Stewart. 373-399, Mar. 1949

ELISABETHVILLE, Democratic Republic of the Congo:

White Magic in the Belgian Congo. By W. Robert Moore. 321-362, Mar. 1952

ELISOFON, ELIOT: Photographer:

Yesterday's Congo, Today's Zaire. By John J. Putman. 398-432, Mar. 1973

ELIZABETH I, Queen (England):

The British Way. By Sir Evelyn Wrench. 421-541, Apr. 1949

Founders of Virginia. By Sir Evelyn Wrench. Photos by B. Anthony Stewart. 433-462, Apr. 1948

The World of Elizabeth I. By Louis B. Wright. Photos by Ted Spiegel. 668-709, Nov. 1968

ELIZABETH II, Queen (Great Britain and Northern Ireland):

In the London of the New Queen. By H. V. Morton. 291-342, Sept. 1953

The Investiture of Great Britain's Prince of Wales. By Allan C. Fisher, Jr. Photos by James L. Stanfield and Adam Woolfitt. 698-715, Nov. 1969

ELIZABETH II — *Continued*

Queen Elizabeth Opens Parliament. By W. E. Roscher. Photos by Robert B. Goodman. 699-707, Nov. 1961

Queen of Canada. By Phyllis Wilson. Photos by Kathleen Revis. 825-829, June 1959

Silkworms in England Spin for the Queen. By John E. H. Nolan. 689-704, May 1953

ELIZABETHAN AGE:

The British Way. By Sir Evelyn Wrench. 421-541, Apr. 1949

Folger: Biggest Little Library in the World. By Joseph T. Foster. Photos by B. Anthony Stewart and John E. Fletcher. 411-424, Sept. 1951
Note: The Folger Collection, which includes the Renaissance library of Sir R. Leicester Harmsworth, forms the Western World's most valuable historical library on English civilization of the 16th and early 17th centuries.

See also Drake, Sir Francis; Elizabeth I; Shakespeare, William

ELIZALDE, MANUEL, Jr.:

First Glimpse of a Stone Age Tribe. 881-882, Dec. 1971

Help for Philippine Tribes in Trouble. By Kenneth MacLeish. Photos by Dean Conger. 220-255, Aug. 1971

The Tasadays, Stone Age Cavemen of Mindanao. By Kenneth MacLeish. Photos by John Launois. 219-249, Aug. 1972

ELK:

Jackson Hole: Good-bye to the Old Days? By François Leydet. Photos by Jonathan Wright. 768-789, Dec. 1976
Included: National Elk Refuge, Wyoming

Yellowstone Wildlife in Winter. By William Albert Allard. 637-661, Nov. 1967

ELK MOUNTAINS, Colorado:

Colorado's Friendly Topland. By Robert M. Ormes. 187-214, Aug. 1951

ELLER, ERNEST M.: Author:

Troubled Waters East of Suez. 483-522, Apr. 1954

ELLESMERE ISLAND, Canada:

Domesticating the Wild and Woolly Musk Ox. By John J. Teal, Jr. Photos by Robert W. Madden. 862-879, June 1970

Far North with "Captain Mac." By Miriam MacMillan. 465-513, Oct. 1951
Included: Cape Sabine; Fort Conger; Wade Point

North Toward the Pole on Skis. By Bjørn O. Staib. 254-281, Feb. 1965

The Peary Flag Comes to Rest. By Marie Peary Stafford. 519-532, Oct. 1954

Three Months on an Arctic Ice Island. By Joseph O. Fletcher. 489-504, Apr. 1953

We Followed Peary to the Pole. By Gilbert Grosvenor and Thomas W. McKnew. 469-484, Oct. 1953

ELLICE ISLANDS, Pacific Ocean:

Adventures with the Survey Navy. By Irving Johnson. 131-148, July 1947

ELLIS, MELVIN R.: Author:

Raccoon: Amiable Rogue in a Black Mask. 841-854, Dec. 1956

ELLIS, MELVIN R.: Author — *Continued*

Skunks Want Peace — or Else! Photos by Charles Philip Fox. 279-294, Aug. 1955

ELLIS, WILLIAM S.: Author:

Afo-A-Kom: A Sacred Symbol Comes Home. Photos by James P. Blair. 141-148, July 1974

Atlanta, Pacesetter City of the South. Photos by James L. Amos. 246-281, Feb. 1969

Bangladesh: Hope Nourishes a New Nation. Photos by Dick Durrance II. 295-333, Sept. 1972

Cairo, Troubled Capital of the Arab World. Photos by Winfield Parks. 639-667, May 1972

The Coast Guard: Small Service With a Big Mission. 113-139, July 1974

High-stepping Idaho. Photos by Dean Conger. 290-317, Mar. 1973

Istanbul, the City That Links Europe and Asia. Photos by Winfield Parks. 501-533, Oct. 1973

Lebanon, Little Bible Land in the Crossfire of History. Photos by George F. Mobley. 240-275, Feb. 1970

Lonely Cape Hatteras, Besieged by the Sea. Photos by Emory Kristof. 393-421, Sept. 1969

Romania: Maverick on a Tightrope. Photos by Winfield Parks. 688-713, Nov. 1975

Tracking Danger With the Ice Patrol. Photos by James R. Holland. 780-793, June 1968

Will Oil and Tundra Mix? Alaska's North Slope Hangs in the Balance. Photos by Emory Kristof. 485-517, Oct. 1971

Wisconsin's Door Peninsula. Photos by Ted Rozumalski. 347-371, Mar. 1969

Yellowstone at 100: The Pitfalls of Success. Photos by Jonathan Blair. 616-631, May 1972

ELLSWORTH HIGHLAND TRAVERSE:

Exploring Antarctica's Phantom Coast. By Edwin A. McDonald. Photos by W. D. Vaughn. 251-273, Feb. 1962

ELLSWORTH MOUNTAINS, Antarctica. *See* Sentinel Range

EL MORRO: Story in Stone (New Mexico). By Edwards Park. 237-244, Aug. 1957

EL SANGAY, Fire-breathing Giant of the Andes. By G. Edward Lewis. 117-138, Jan. 1950

ELSIE (Yawl):

Down East to Nova Scotia. By Winfield Parks. 853-879, June 1964

EMBROIDERY:

Madeira, Like Its Wine, Improves With Age. By Veronica Thomas. Photos by Jonathan Blair. 488-513, Apr. 1973

EMERALDS:

Questing for Gems. By George S. Switzer. 835-863, Dec. 1971

EMERSON, GILBERT: Artist:

How Man-made Satellites Can Affect Our Lives. By Joseph Kaplan. 791-810, Dec. 1957

EMERSON, GUY: Author:

The Kress Collection: A Gift to the Nation. 823-865, Dec. 1961

EMERSON, RALPH WALDO:

Literary Landmarks of Massachusetts. By William

EMERSON, RALPH WALDO — *Continued*

H. Nicholas. Photos by B. Anthony Stewart and John E. Fletcher. 279-310, Mar. 1950

EMORY, KENNETH P.: Author:

The Coming of the Polynesians. 732-745, Dec. 1974

The EMPEROR'S Private Garden: Kashmir. By Nigel Cameron. Photos by Brian Brake. 606-647, Nov. 1958

ENCHANTRESS! (White Tigress). By Theodore H. Reed. Photos by Thomas J. Abercrombie. 628-641, May 1961

ENCYCLOPAEDIA BRITANNICA EDUCATIONAL CORPORATION:

The World in Geographic Filmstrips. By Melvin M. Payne. 134-137, Jan. 1968

ENDANGERED SPECIES:

African Wildlife: Man's Threatened Legacy. By Allan C. Fisher, Jr. Photos by Thomas Nebbia. Paintings by Ned Seidler. 147-187, Feb. 1972

India Struggles to Save Her Wildlife. By John J. Putman. Paintings by Ned Seidler. 299-343, Sept. 1976

Vanishing Wildlife of North America. Special Publication announced. 865-868, June 1973

See also Andean Condors; Bighorn Sheep; Brown Pelicans; Giant Tortoises; Gorillas; Grizzly Bears; Harp Seals; Horses, Wild; Polar Bear; Snow Leopards; Vicuñas; Whales; *and* Everglades

ENDEAVOUR (Bark):

Captain Cook: The Man Who Mapped the Pacific. By Alan Villiers. Photos by Gordon W. Gahan. 297-349, Sept. 1971

ENDEAVOUR (Cutter) Sails the Inside Passage. By Amos Burg. 801-828, June 1947

The ENDURING Pyrenees. By Robert Laxalt. Photos by Edwin Stuart Grosvenor. 794-819, Dec. 1974

ENERGY RESEARCH AND DEVELOPMENT ADMINISTRATION. *See* listing under former name, Atomic Energy Commission

ENERGY SOURCES:

Can We Harness the Wind? By Roger Hamilton. Photos by Emory Kristof. 812-829, Dec. 1975

The Fire of Heaven: Electricity Revolutionizes the Modern World. By Albert W. Atwood. 655-674, Nov. 1948

Five Noted Thinkers Explore the Future. 68-75, July 1976

Included: Isaac Asimov, Richard F. Babcock, Edmund N. Bacon, Buckminster Fuller, Gerard Piel

Hunting Uranium Around the World. By Robert D. Nininger. Photos by Volkmar Wentzel. 533-558, Oct. 1954

The Search for Tomorrow's Power. By Kenneth F. Weaver. Photos by Emory Kristof. 650-681, Nov. 1972

This Land of Ours — How Are We Using It? By Peter T. White. Photos by Emory Kristof. 20-67, July 1976

See also Coal; Hydroelectric Power; Natural Gas; Nuclear Energy; Oil; Solar Energy

ENGELMANN, RUDOLF J.: Author:

Laboratory in a Dirty Sky. By Rudolf J. Engelmann and Vera Simons. 616-621, Nov. 1976

ENGINEERING:

Abu Simbel's Ancient Temples Reborn. By Georg Gerster. 724-744, May 1969

Saving the Ancient Temples at Abu Simbel. By Georg Gerster. Paintings by Robert W. Nicholson. 694-742, May 1966

Threatened Treasures of the Nile. By Georg Gerster. 587-621, Oct. 1963

See also Bridges; Dams; Tunnels; *and* St. Lawrence Seaway; Suez Canal; *and* listings under Pipelines

ENGLAND:

"Around the World in Eighty Days." By Newman Bumstead. 705-750, Dec. 1951
    Included: Canterbury; Eton; London; and Thames River

"Be Ye Men of Valour" (Churchill's Life; Funeral). By Howard La Fay. 159-197, Aug. 1965

The Britain That Shakespeare Knew. By Louis B. Wright. Photos by Dean Conger. 613-665, May 1964

British Castles, History in Stone. By Norman Wilkinson. 111-129, July 1947

British Isles, Atlas series supplement. July 1958

The British Isles, map supplement. Apr. 1949

The British Way: Great Britain's Major Gifts to Freedom, Democratic Government, Science, and Society. By Sir Evelyn Wrench. 421-541, Apr. 1949

The England of Charles Dickens. By Richard W. Long. Photos by Adam Woolfitt. 443-483, Apr. 1974

Exploring England's Canals. By Bryan Hodgson. Photos by Linda Bartlett. 76-111, July 1974

The Final Tribute (Churchill Funeral). Text by Carolyn Bennett Patterson. 199-225, Aug. 1965

Founders of New England. By Sir Evelyn Wrench. Photos by B. Anthony Stewart. 803-838, June 1953

Founders of Virginia. By Sir Evelyn Wrench. Photos by B. Anthony Stewart. 433-462, Apr. 1948

Landmarks of Literary England. By Leo A. Borah. Photos by Kathleen Revis. 295-350, Sept. 1955

Midshipmen's Cruise. By William J. Aston and Alexander G. B. Grosvenor. 711-754, June 1948

A New Look at Medieval Europe. By Kenneth M. Setton. Paintings by Andre Durenceau and Birney Lettick. 799-859, Dec. 1962

900 Years Ago: The Norman Conquest. By Kenneth M. Setton. Photos by George F. Mobley. 206-251, Aug. 1966

The Original Boston: St. Botolph's Town. By Veronica Thomas. Photos by James L. Amos. 382-389, Sept. 1974

Our Search for British Paintings. By Franklin L. Fisher. 543-550, Apr. 1949

Pilgrimage to Holy Island and the Farnes. By John E. H. Nolan. 547-570, Oct. 1952

Queen Elizabeth Opens Parliament. By W. E. Roscher. Photos by Robert B. Goodman. 699-707, Nov. 1961

Round the World School (ISA). By Paul Antze. Photos by William Eppridge. 96-127, July 1962

Shakespeare's Britain, map supplement. May 1964

Silkworms in England Spin for the Queen. By John E. H. Nolan. 689-704, May 1953

A Stroll to London. By Isobel Wylie Hutchison. Photos by B. Anthony Stewart. 171-204, Aug. 1950

ENGLAND — *Continued*

The Thames Mirrors England's Varied Life. By Willard Price. Photos by Robert F. Sisson. 45-93, July 1958

This Britain (Television film). 583, Nov. 1975; cover announcement, Dec. 1975

This England. Book announced. 539-543, Oct. 1966

Thumbs Up Round the North Sea's Rim. By Frances James. Photos by Erica Koch. 685-704, May 1952

A Traveler's Map of the British Isles, map supplement. Text on reverse. Apr. 1974

The World of Elizabeth I. By Louis B. Wright. Photos by Ted Spiegel. 668-709, Nov. 1968

See also Abbotsbury Swannery; Appleby Fair; Canterbury Cathedral; Cornwall; Cotswold Hills; Devonshire; Kew; Lake District; London; Portsmouth; Stonehenge; *and* Elizabethan Age; *Mayflower II*

ENGLEBERT, VICTOR: Author-Photographer:

The Danakil: Nomads of Ethiopia's Wasteland. 186-211, Feb. 1970

Drought Threatens the Tuareg World. 544-571, Apr. 1974

I Joined a Sahara Salt Caravan. 694-711, Nov. 1965

Trek by Mule Among Morocco's Berbers. 850-875, June 1968

ENGLISH CHANNEL:

Channel Cruise to Glorious Devon. By Alan Villiers. Photos by Bates Littlehales. 208-259, Aug. 1963

Cowes to Cornwall. By Alan Villiers. Photos by Robert B. Goodman. 149-201, Aug. 1961

See also Channel Islands; St. Michael's Mount

ENGLISH SETTLERS. *See* Founders of New England; Founders of Virginia; Roanoke Island, for Lost Colony; Williamsburg, Virginia; *and* Victoria, Kansas (19th Century)

The ENIGMA of Bird Anting. By Hance Roy Ivor. 105-119, July 1956

ENTEBBE ANIMAL REFUGE, Uganda:

Orphans of the Wild. By Bruce G. Kinloch. 683-699, Nov. 1962

ENTERPRISE (Nuclear Carrier):

The Mighty *Enterprise.* By Nathaniel T. Kenney. Photos by Thomas J. Abercrombie. 431-448, Mar. 1963

ENVIRONMENTAL CONCERNS. *See* Air Pollution; Chemical Pollution; Conservation; Ecology; Land Use; Oil Spills; Pesticide Pollution; Strip Mining; Water Pollution

EPPRIDGE, WILLIAM: Photographer:

The Alps: Man's Own Mountains. By Ralph Gray. Photos by Walter Meayers Edwards and William Eppridge. 350-395, Sept. 1965

Round the World School. By Paul Antze. 96-127, July 1962

EQUATORIAL GUINEA, Republic of. *See* Río Muni

ERIE, Lake, Canada-U. S.:

The Great Lakes: Is It Too Late? By Gordon Young. Photos by James L. Amos and Martin Rogers. 147-185, Aug. 1973

ERIGBAAGTSA (Indians):

Indians of the Amazon Darkness. By Harald Schultz. 737-758, May 1964

ERIM, KENAN T.: Author:

Ancient Aphrodisias and Its Marble Treasures. Photos by Jonathan S. Blair. 280-294, Aug. 1967

Aphrodisias, Awakened City of Ancient Art. Photos by Jonathan Blair. 766-791, June 1972

ERONGARÍCUARO, Mexico:

Lost Kingdom in Indian Mexico (Tarascan). By Justin Locke. 517-546, Oct. 1952

EROSION:

Erosion, Trojan Horse of Greece. By F. G. Renner. 793-812, Dec. 1947

Water for the World's Growing Needs. By Herbert B. Nichols and F. Barrows Colton. 269-286, Aug. 1952

See also Forests and Reforestation; Mud Slides; This Land of Ours; U. S. Soil Conservation Service

ERTAUD, JACQUES: Photographer:

Fish Men Discover a 2,200-year-old Greek Ship. By Jacques-Yves Cousteau. 1-36, Jan. 1954

Fish Men Explore a New World Undersea. By Jacques-Yves Cousteau. 431-472, Oct. 1952

ERZURUM, Turkey:

Turkey Paves the Path of Progress. By Maynard Owen Williams. 141-186, Aug. 1951

Where Turk and Russian Meet. By Ferdinand Kuhn. 743-766, June 1952

ESCALANTE CANYON, Utah:

Escalante: Utah's River of Arches. By W. Robert Moore. 399-425, Sept. 1955

Escalante Canyon — Wilderness at the Crossroads. By Jon Schneeberger. 270-285, Aug. 1972

First Motor Sortie into Escalante Land. By Jack Breed. 369-404, Sept. 1949

ESCORTING Mona Lisa to America. By Edward T. Folliard. 838-847, June 1963

ESKIMAUAN LINGUISTIC STOCK:

Nomads of the Far North. By Matthew W. Stirling. 471-504, Oct. 1949
Hearty Folk Defy Arctic Storms. Paintings by W. Langdon Kihn. 479-494

ESKIMOS:

Alaska: Rising Northern Star. By Joseph Judge. Photos by Bruce Dale. 730-767, June 1975
Included: Inupiat and Nunamiut Eskimos; also Eskimos of Nunapitchuk, Selawik, and Wainwright

Alaska Proudly Joins the Union. By Ernest Gruening. Photos by Thomas J. Abercrombie. 43-83, July 1959

Alaska's Russian Frontier: Little Diomede. Photos by Audrey and Frank Morgan. 551-562, Apr. 1951

Banks Island: Eskimo Life on the Polar Sea. By William O. Douglas. Photos by Clyde Hare. 703-735, May 1964

Canada Counts Its Caribou. 261-268, Aug. 1952

Canada's Caribou Eskimos. By Donald B. Marsh. 87-104, Jan. 1947

The Canadian North: Emerging Giant. By David S. Boyer. 1-43, July 1968

Caribou: Hardy Nomads of the North. By Jim

ESKIMOS — Continued

Rearden. 858-878, Dec. 1974

Cliff Dwellers of the Bering Sea. By Juan Muñoz. 129-146, Jan. 1954

Domesticating the Wild and Woolly Musk Ox. By John J. Teal, Jr. Photos by Robert W. Madden. 862-879, June 1970

Far North with "Captain Mac." By Miriam MacMillan. 465-513, Oct. 1951
Included: Eskimos of Baffin Island, Greenland, Labrador; Polar Eskimos

Greenland Feels the Winds of Change. By John J. Putman. Photos by George F. Mobley. 366-393, Sept. 1975
Included: Polar Eskimos of northwest Greenland, last of the true Eskimos

I Live With the Eskimos (Canadian). By Guy Mary-Rousseliere. 188-217, Feb. 1971

Indians of North America, double-sided map supplement. Dec. 1972
Included: Central Eskimos; Copper Eskimos

The Last U. S. Whale Hunters. By Emory Kristof. 346-355, Mar. 1973
"Ocean mammals are to us what the buffalo was to the Plains Indian." By Lael Morgan. 354-355

Milestones in My Arctic Journeys. By Willie Knutsen. 543-570, Oct. 1949

Nomad in Alaska's Outback. By Thomas J. Abercrombie. 540-567, Apr. 1969

Nomads of the Far North. By Matthew W. Stirling. 471-504, Oct. 1949
Hearty Folk Defy Arctic Storms. Paintings by W. Langdon Kihn. 479-494

North Star Cruises Alaska's Wild West. By Amos Burg. 57-86, July 1952

Trek Across Arctic America. By Colin Irwin. 295-321, Mar. 1974

Vanished Mystery Men of Hudson Bay. By Henry B. Collins. 669-687, Nov. 1956

A Visit to the Living Ice Age. By Rutherford Platt. 525-545, Apr. 1957

Weather from the White North. By Andrew H. Brown. Photos by John E. Fletcher. 543-572, Apr. 1955

Will Oil and Tundra Mix? Alaska's North Slope Hangs in the Balance. By William S. Ellis. Photos by Emory Kristof. 485-517, Oct. 1971

ESSENES:

The Men Who Hid the Dead Sea Scrolls. By A. Douglas Tushingham. Paintings by Peter V. Bianchi. 785-808, Dec. 1958

ESTATES AND PLANTATIONS:

Land of Louisiana Sugar Kings. By Harnett T. Kane. Photos by Willard R. Culver. 531-567, Apr. 1958

Philadelphia Houses a Proud Past. By Harold Donaldson Eberlein. Photos by Thomas Nebbia. 151-191, Aug. 1960

Rhododendron Glories of Southwest Scotland. By David S. Boyer. Photos by B. Anthony Stewart and author. 641-664, May 1954

South Carolina Rediscovered. By Herbert Ravenel Sass. Photos by Robert F. Sisson. 281-321, Mar. 1953

See also Buttrick Garden; Georgia (Greener Fields); Hearst San Simeon State Historical Monument; Henry E. Huntington Library and Art Gallery;

ESTATES AND PLANTATIONS—*Continued*
Longwood Gardens (Du Pont Estate); Maryland (Cavalier Country); Monticello; Mount Vernon; Natchez, Mississippi; Virginia (History Keeps House in Virginia; Stately Homes); Vizcaya (James Deering Estate)

ESTES, RICHARD D.: Author:
The Flamingo Eaters of Ngorongoro (Hyenas). 535-539, Oct. 1973

The ETERNAL Flame. By Albert W. Atwood. 540-564, Oct. 1951

ETERNAL France. By Walter Meayers Edwards. 725-764, June 1960

The ETERNAL Treasure, Gold. By Peter T. White. Photos by James L. Stanfield. 1-51, Jan. 1974

ETHERTON, P. T.: Author:
Lundy, Treasure Island of Birds. Photos by J. Allan Cash. 675-698, May 1947

ETHIOPIA:
Africa: The Winds of Freedom Stir a Continent. By Nathaniel T. Kenney. Photos by W. D. Vaughn. 303-359, Sept. 1960
The Danakil: Nomads of Ethiopia's Wasteland. By Victor Englebert. 186-211, Feb. 1970
Ethiopia: The Hidden Empire (Television film). 884A-884B, Dec. 1970
Ethiopia Yields First "Family" of Early Man. By Donald C. Johanson. Photos by David Brill. 790-811, Dec. 1976
Ethiopian Adventure. By Nathaniel T. Kenney. Photos by James P. Blair. 548-582, Apr. 1965
Ethiopia's Artful Weavers. By Judith Olmstead. Photos by James A. Sugar. 125-141, Jan. 1973
Locusts: "Teeth of the Wind." By Robert A. M. Conley. Photos by Gianni Tortoli. 202-227, Aug. 1969
Safari from Congo to Cairo. By Elsie May Bell Grosvenor. Photos by Gilbert Grosvenor. 721-771, Dec. 1954
Searching Out Medieval Churches in Ethiopia's Wilds. By Georg Gerster. 856-884, Dec. 1970

ETHNOLOGY:
Primitive Worlds. Special Publication announced. 865-868, June 1973
Vanishing Peoples of the Earth. Special Publication announced. 844-849, June 1968
See also Gypsies; Nomads
Africa
The Peoples of Africa, double-sided map supplement. Dec. 1971
See also Bedouin; Berbers; Bushmen; Danakil; Dogon; Lotuka; Masai; Nuba; Pygmies; Tuareg; Zululand
Americas
See Eskimos; Indians
Asia
The Peoples of Mainland Southeast Asia, double-sided map supplement. Mar. 1971
See also Ainu; Bajaus; Bakhtiari; Bedouin; Intha; Karens; Kashgais; Kazakhs; Kirghiz; Kurds; Lolos; Lua; Ma'dan; Montagnards; Mrus; Muria Gonds; Sea Dyaks; Tasadays; T'boli; Tharus; Turkomans; *and* Andaman Islands; Bhutan; Hunza; Ladakh; Naga Hills; Tibet; Wakhan

ETHNOLOGY—*Continued*
Australia
See Aborigines
Europe
See Basques; Lapland
Middle East
The Peoples of the Middle East, map supplement. Text on reverse. July 1972
Pacific Islands
Discoverers of the Pacific, double-sided map supplement. Dec. 1974
See also New Britain; New Guinea; New Hebrides
Union of Soviet Socialist Republics
Peoples of the Soviet Union, double-sided map supplement. Feb. 1976

ETRUSCANS:
Periscope on the Etruscan Past. By Carlo M. Lerici. 337-350, Sept. 1959

EUPHRATES (River), Asia:
Throne Above the Euphrates. By Theresa Goell. 390-405, Mar. 1961

EUROPE:
Across the Ridgepole of the Alps. By Walter Meayers Edwards. 410-419, Sept. 1960
The Age of Chivalry. Book announced. 544-551, Oct. 1969
The Alps—Europe's Backbone, Atlas series double-sided map supplement. Sept. 1965
The Alps: Man's Own Mountains. By Ralph Gray. Photos by Walter Meayers Edwards and William Eppridge. 350-395, Sept. 1965
"Around the World in Eighty Days." By Newman Bumstead. 705-750, Dec. 1951
Atlantic Odyssey: Iceland to Antarctica. By Newman Bumstead. Photos by Volkmar Wentzel. 725-780, Dec. 1955
Baltic Cruise of the *Caribbee.* By Carleton Mitchell. 605-646, Nov. 1950
A Bold New Look at Our Past. The Editor. 62-63, Jan. 1975
Central Europe, including the Balkan States, map supplement. Sept. 1951
Classical Lands of the Mediterranean, map supplement. Dec. 1949
Down the Danube by Canoe. By William Slade Backer. Photos by Richard S. Durrance and Christopher G. Knight. 34-79, July 1965
Europe, Atlas series supplement. June 1962
Europe, map supplement. June 1957
Europe, map supplement. June 1969
Europe and the Near East, map supplement. June 1949
Europe Via the Hostel Route. By Joseph Nettis. 124-154, July 1955
Exploring the Mind of Ice Age Man. By Alexander Marshack. 64-89, Jan. 1975
Friendly Flight to Northern Europe. By Lyndon B. Johnson. Photos by Volkmar Wentzel. 268-293, Feb. 1964
Here Rest in Honored Glory . . . (War Memorials). By Howell Walker. 739-768, June 1957
Included: The following memorial cemeteries: Brittany; Cambridge; Épinal; Normandy; Rhône; Sicily-Rome
How Fruit Came to America. By J. R. Magness.

EUROPE — *Continued*

Paintings by Else Bostelmann. 325-377, Sept. 1951

In the Crusaders' Footsteps. By Franc Shor. Photos by Thomas Nebbia and James P. Blair. 731-789, June 1962

Inside Europe Aboard *Yankee*. By Irving and Electa Johnson. Photos by Joseph J. Scherschel. 157-195, Aug. 1964

A New Look at Medieval Europe. By Kenneth M. Setton. Paintings by Andre Durenceau and Birney Lettick. 799-859, Dec. 1962

Northern Europe, map supplement. Aug. 1954

Our Vegetable Travelers. By Victor R. Boswell. Paintings by Else Bostelmann. 145-217, Aug. 1949

The Renaissance: Maker of Modern Man. Book announced. 588-590, Oct. 1970

The Rhine: Europe's River of Legend. By William Graves. Photos by Bruce Dale. 449-499, Apr. 1967

Round the World School (ISA). By Paul Antze. Photos by William Eppridge. 96-127, July 1962
    Included: Berlin; England; Greece; Italy; Paris

A Stroll to Venice. By Isobel Wylie Hutchison. 378-410, Sept. 1951
    Contents: The author's trek from Innsbruck, Austria, through the Tyrol and Dolomites, to Venice, Italy

Through Europe by Trailer Caravan. By Norma Miller. Photos by Ardean R. Miller III. 769-816, June 1957
    Included: Austria; France; Germany; Italy; Netherlands; Switzerland

Thumbs Up Round the North Sea's Rim. By Frances James. Photos by Erica Koch. 685-704, May 1952
    Included: Belgium; Denmark; England; France; Germany; Sweden

To Europe with a Racing Start *(Finisterre).* By Carleton Mitchell. 758-791, June 1958

The Vikings. By Howard La Fay. Photos by Ted Spiegel. 492-541, Apr. 1970

Western Europe, map supplement. Dec. 1950

What's Happening to Our Climate? By Samuel W. Matthews. 576-615, Nov. 1976

When the President Goes Abroad (Eisenhower Tour). By Gilbert M. Grosvenor. 588-649, May 1960
    Included: France; Greece; Italy; Spain

White Storks, Vanishing Sentinels of the Rooftops. By Roger Tory Peterson. 838-853, June 1962

The World in Your Garden (Flowers). By W. H. Camp. Paintings by Else Bostelmann. 1-65, July 1947

Yankee Sails Across Europe (Television film). 469A-469B, Apr. 1967

See also names of individual countries

EUROPE'S Shy and Spectacular Kingfisher. Photos by Carl-Johan Junge and Emil Lütken. 413-419, Sept. 1974

EVANGELINE COUNTRY, Louisiana:

Cajunland, Louisiana's French-speaking Coast. By Bern Keating. Photos by Charles Harbutt and Franke Keating. 353-391, Mar. 1966

EVANS, CHARLES:

Triumph on Everest. 1-63, July 1954
    I. Siege and Assault. By Sir John Hunt. 1-43

EVANS, CHARLES — *Continued*
    II. The Conquest of the Summit. By Sir Edmund Hillary. 45-63

EVANS, CLIFFORD: Author-Photographer:

Life Among the Wai Wai Indians. By Clifford Evans and Betty J. Meggers. 329-346, Mar. 1955
        Photographer

Finding the Tomb of a Warrior-God. By William Duncan Strong. 453-482, Apr. 1947

EVANS, RONALD E.:

Exploring Taurus-Littrow. By Harrison H. Schmitt. Photos by the crew of Apollo 17. 290-307, Sept. 1973

EVEREST, Mount, Nepal-Tibet:

American and Geographic Flags Top Everest. By Melvin M. Payne. Photos by Barry C. Bishop. 157-157C, Aug. 1963

Americans on Everest (Television film). 448-452, Sept. 1965; 575, Nov. 1976

The First Traverse. By Thomas F. Hornbein and William F. Unsoeld. 509-513, Oct. 1963

How We Climbed Everest. By Barry C. Bishop. 477-507, Oct. 1963

Six to the Summit. By Norman G. Dyhrenfurth. Photos by Barry C. Bishop. 460-473, Oct. 1963

Triumph on Everest. 1-63, July 1954
    I. Siege and Assault. By Sir John Hunt. 1-43
    II. The Conquest of the Summit. By Sir Edmund Hillary. 45-63

EVERETT, CURTIS T.:

Children of the Sun and Moon (Kraho Indians). By Harald Schultz; translated from German by Curtis T. Everett. 340-363, Mar. 1959

EVERGLADES (Region), Florida:

Businessman in the Bush. By Frederick Kent Truslow. 634-675, May 1970

Eye to Eye With Eagles. By Frederick Kent Truslow. 123-148, Jan. 1961

Florida Rides a Space-age Boom. By Benedict Thielen. Photos by Winfield Parks and James P. Blair. 858-903, Dec. 1963

Florida's Emerging Seminoles. By Louis Capron. Photos by Otis Imboden. 716-734, Nov. 1969
    Contents: Seminole and Miccosukee reservations and settlements

Florida's "Wild" Indians, the Seminole. By Louis Capron. Photos by Willard R. Culver. 819-840, Dec. 1956

Haunting Heart of the Everglades. By Andrew H. Brown. Photos by author and Willard R. Culver. 145-173, Feb. 1948

The Imperiled Everglades. By Fred Ward. 1-27, Jan. 1972

Our Only Native Stork, the Wood Ibis. By Robert Porter Allen. Photos by Frederick Kent Truslow. 294-306, Feb. 1964

Saving Man's Wildlife Heritage. By John H. Baker. Photos by Robert F. Sisson. 581-620, Nov. 1954

Shrimp Nursery: Science Explores New Ways to Farm the Sea. By Clarence P. Idyll. Photos by Robert F. Sisson. 636-659, May 1965

The Swallow-tailed Kite: Graceful Aerialist of the Everglades. 496-505, Oct. 1972

Threatened Glories of Everglades National Park. By Frederick Kent Truslow and Frederick G. Vosburgh. Photos by Frederick Kent Truslow

EVERGLADES (Region), Florida — *Continued*

and Otis Imboden. 508-553, Oct. 1967
  Included: Drainage from Lake Okeechobee in 1880, 1920, and 1967

Tree Snails, Gems of the Everglades. By Treat Davidson. 372-387, Mar. 1965

When Disaster Struck a Woodpecker's Home. By Frederick Kent Truslow. 882-884, Dec. 1966

Wildlife of Everglades National Park. By Daniel B. Beard. Paintings by Walter A. Weber. 83-116, Jan. 1949

EVERHART, WILLIAM C.: Author:

So Long, St. Louis, We're Heading West. 643-669, Nov. 1965

"EVERY Day Is a Gift When You Are Over 100." By Alexander Leaf. Photos by John Launois. 93-119, Jan. 1973

EVERYONE'S Servant, the Post Office. By Allan C. Fisher, Jr. Photos by Volkmar Wentzel. 121-152, July 1954

EVOLUTION:

The Galapagos, Eerie Cradle of New Species. By Roger Tory Peterson. Photos by Alan and Joan Root. 541-585, Apr. 1967

In the Wake of Darwin's *Beagle*. By Alan Villiers. Photos by James L. Stanfield. 449-495, Oct. 1969

EWING, MAURICE: Author:

Exploring the Mid-Atlantic Ridge. 275-294, Sept. 1948

New Discoveries on the Mid-Atlantic Ridge. Photos by Robert F. Sisson. 611-640, Nov. 1949

The EXODUS:

In Search of Moses. By Harvey Arden. Photos by Nathan Benn. 2-37, Jan. 1976
  Included: Map of Sinai Peninsula indicating two possible routes

EXOTIC Birds in Manhattan's Bowery. By Paul A. Zahl. 77-98, Jan. 1953

An EXOTIC New Oriole Settles in Florida. By Charles M. Brookfield and Oliver Griswold. 261-264, Feb. 1956

EXPEDITION to the Land of the Tiwi. By Charles P. Mountford. 417-440, Mar. 1956

EXPEDITIONS AND RESEARCH. *See* listing of NGS expeditions and scientific researches, preceding this index; *and* names of universities and laboratories

EXPÉDITIONS POLAIRES FRANÇAISES:

Wringing Secrets from Greenland's Icecap. By Paul-Émile Victor. 121-147, Jan. 1956

EXPERIMENT in International Living. By Hugh M. Hamill, Jr. 323-350, Mar. 1953

EXPLORATION AND DISCOVERY:

Arctic Ocean, double-sided map supplement. Oct. 1971
  Included: Notes on explorations from earliest searches for the Northwest Passage to present-day voyages and the finding of petroleum reserves

Eight Maps of Discovery. 757-769, June 1953

Great Adventures With National Geographic. Book announced. 729-733, Nov. 1963

Historical Map of the United States, map supplement. June 1953
  Included: A legend of exploration

EXPLORATION AND DISCOVERY — *Continued*

75 Years Exploring Earth, Sea, and Sky: National Geographic Society Observes Its Diamond Anniversary. By Melvin M. Payne. 1-43, Jan. 1963

The World of Elizabeth I. By Louis B. Wright. Photos by Ted Spiegel. 668-709, Nov. 1968

See also Antarctica; North Pole; Space Flights and Research; Speleology

EXPLORER I (Stratosphere Balloon):

NGS-U. S. Army Air Corps balloon flight (1934). 427, Apr. 1949; 14, 22-23, 24-25, Jan. 1963; 477, Oct. 1966; 578, 579, 588, Oct. 1967; 226, Aug. 1976

EXPLORER II (Stratosphere Balloon):

NGS-U. S. Army Air Corps balloon flight (1935). 562, 586, May 1947; 249, Feb. 1948; 850, June 1948; 345, Sept. 1948; 427, 525, Apr. 1949; 511, Oct. 1950; 102, Jan. 1953; 262, Aug. 1955; 707, Nov. 1955; 496, Apr. 1956; 494, 495, Oct. 1956; 269, 273-274, 276, 282, Feb. 1957; 271, 281, Aug. 1957; 807, Dec. 1957; 648, Nov. 1958; 856, Dec. 1960; 5, 14, 22, 24, 26-27, Jan. 1963; 580, Oct. 1963; 294, Sept. 1965; 477, Oct. 1966; 578, 579, 588, Oct. 1967; 849, June 1968; 226, Aug. 1976

EXPLORERS (Senior Scouts):

Philmont Scout Ranch Helps Boys Grow Up. By Andrew H. Brown. 399-416, Sept. 1956

EXPLORERS, DISCOVERERS, AND NAVIGATORS:

The British Way. By Sir Evelyn Wrench. 421-541, Apr. 1949
  Included: Cabot's Discovery of North America (1497). — Francis Drake and the Elizabethan Seamen (1588). — James Cook (1728-79). — A Very Gallant Gentleman — Lawrence Edward Grace Oates (1880-1912)

North for Oil: *Manhattan* Makes the Historic Northwest Passage. By Bern Keating. Photos by Tomas Sennett. 374-391, Mar. 1970
  Included: Roald Amundsen, John Cabot, Sir John Franklin, Henry Hudson,. Henry A. Larsen, Robert McClure, George P. Steele

North (U. S. and Canada) Through History Aboard *White Mist.* By Melville Bell Grosvenor. Photos by Edwin Stuart Grosvenor. 1-55, July 1970
  Included: Jacques Cartier, Samuel de Champlain, Henry Hudson

Our Navy Explores Antarctica. By Richard E. Byrd. U. S. Navy official photos. 429-522, Oct. 1947
  Includes, in addition to members of this expedition: Capt. James Cook, Sir James Clark Ross, Capt. Robert F. Scott, Sir Ernest Shackleton, Fabian Gottlieb von Bellingshausen, and J. Dumont D'Urville

Three Months on an Arctic Ice Island. By Joseph O. Fletcher. 489-504, Apr. 1953

Trek Across Arctic America. By Colin Irwin. 295-321, Mar. 1974
  Included: Roald Amundsen, Knud Rasmussen

See also Anderson, William R.; Beach, Edward L.; Bligh, William; Byrd, Richard Evelyn; Calvert, James F.; Columbus, Christopher; Cook, James; Cousteau, Jacques-Yves; Darwin, Charles; Drake, Sir Francis; Dufek, George J.; Eiloart, Arnold; Fuchs, Sir Vivian; Henry, Prince; Houot, Georges S.; Lalor, William G., Jr.; Lewis, M. Lee; Lewis and Clark Expedition; McDonald, Edwin A.; McDonald, Eugene F., Jr.; Mackenzie, Alexander; MacMillan, Donald Baxter; Magellan, Ferdinand; Mudie, Colin; Peary, Robert E.; Piccard, Jacques; Prather, Victor A., Jr.; Raleigh, Sir Walter; Roosevelt, Theodore;

EXPLORERS, DISCOVERERS, AND NAVIGATORS —
Continued
Ross, Malcolm D.; Siple, Paul A.; Smith, John; *and*
Agricultural and Botanical Explorers; listing under Astronauts; Basques (Life in the Land of), for
Juan Sebastián del Cano; Divers and Diving;
Founders of New England; Founders of Virginia;
Mountain Climbing; Phoenicians; Polynesians;
Vikings

EXPLORERS CLUB of New York: Expeditions:

Exploring New Britain's Land of Fire. By E.
Thomas Gilliard. 260-292, Feb. 1961

First Motor Sortie into Escalante Land. By Jack
Breed. 369-404, Sept. 1949

New Guinea's Paradise of Birds. By E. Thomas
Gilliard. 661-668, Nov. 1951
Note: The true summit of Mount Wilhelm was
reached and flag No. 128 of the Explorers Club was
unfurled.

EXPLORERS HALL, National Geographic Society:

Curator: T. Keilor Bentley. 578, Oct. 1967

Dedication of 17th Street Headquarters. 669, 670-675, 677, May 1964; 659, May 1965

Display of *Aepyornis* egg from Madagascar. 479,
487, 492-493, Oct. 1967

Display of Mount Everest Expedition equipment.
451, Sept. 1965

Displays. 741-742, Dec. 1964; 505, Oct. 1968

Emperor Haile Selassie I (Ethiopia) signs guest
book. 555, Apr. 1965

Globe, Great. 673-675, 677, 679, May 1964; 880,
Dec. 1964; 578-579, Oct. 1967

NGS flag, taken to moon and back by Apollo 11 astronauts, now on display in Explorers Hall. 859,
860, June 1970

Picturephone. 750, Dec. 1964

Presentation of Hubbard Medal to Juan T. Trippe.
584, Apr. 1968

Visitors, number of. 669, May 1964

EXPLORING Aleutian Volcanoes. By G. D. Robinson.
509-528, Oct. 1948

EXPLORING America Underground (Caves). By
Charles E. Mohr. 803-837, June 1964

EXPLORING America's Great Sand Barrier Reef. By
Eugene R. Guild. Photos by John E. Fletcher and
author. 325-350, Sept. 1947

EXPLORING an Epic Year. By Melville Bell Grosvenor. 874-886, Dec. 1960

EXPLORING Ancient Panama by Helicopter. By Matthew W. Stirling. Photos by Richard H. Stewart.
227-246, Feb. 1950

EXPLORING Antarctica's Phantom Coast. By Edwin
A. McDonald. Photos by W. D. Vaughn. 251-273, Feb. 1962

EXPLORING Australia's Coral Jungle. By Kenneth
MacLeish. 743-779, June 1973

EXPLORING Canyonlands National Park. By Rowe
Findley. Photos by Walter Meayers Edwards.
71-91, July 1971

EXPLORING Davy Jones's Locker with *Calypso*. By
Jacques-Yves Cousteau. Photos by Luis Marden.
149-161, Feb. 1956

EXPLORING England's Canals. By Bryan Hodgson.
Photos by Linda Bartlett. 76-111, July 1974

EXPLORING New Britain's Land of Fire. By E.
Thomas Gilliard. 260-292, Feb. 1961

EXPLORING 1,750,000 Years Into Man's Past. By
L. S. B. Leakey. Photos by Robert F. Sisson.
564-589, Oct. 1961

EXPLORING Ottawa. By Bruce Hutchison. 565-596,
Nov. 1947

EXPLORING Our Neighbor World, the Moon. By
Donald H. Menzel. 277-296, Feb. 1958

EXPLORING Stone Age Arnhem Land. By Charles P.
Mountford. Photos by Howell Walker. 745-782,
Dec. 1949

EXPLORING Taurus-Littrow. By Harrison H.
Schmitt. Photos by the crew of Apollo 17. 290-307, Sept. 1973

EXPLORING the Drowned City of Port Royal (Jamaica). By Marion Clayton Link. Photos by Luis
Marden. 151-183, Feb. 1960

EXPLORING the Farthest Reaches of Space. By
George O. Abell. 782-790, Dec. 1956

EXPLORING the Lives of Whales. By Victor B.
Scheffer. 752-767, Dec. 1976

EXPLORING the Mid-Atlantic Ridge. By Maurice
Ewing. 275-294, Sept. 1948

EXPLORING the Mind of Ice Age Man. By Alexander
Marshack. 64-89, Jan. 1975

EXPLORING the New Biology. 355-407, Sept. 1976
I. The Awesome Worlds Within a Cell. By Rick
Gore. Photos by Bruce Dale. Paintings by Davis Meltzer. 355-395
II. The Cancer Puzzle. By Robert F. Weaver.
396-399
III. Seven Giants Who Led the Way. Paintings
by Ned Seidler. Text by Rick Gore. 401-407

EXPLORING the Past in Panama. By Matthew W.
Stirling. Photos by Richard H. Stewart. 373-399,
Mar. 1949

EXPLORING the World of Gems. By W. F. Foshag.
779-810, Dec. 1950

EXPLORING Tomorrow With the Space Agency. By
Allan C. Fisher, Jr. Photos by Dean Conger. 48-89, July 1960

The **EXPLOSIVE** Birth of Myojin Island. By Robert S.
Dietz. 117-128, Jan. 1954

EXPO 67:

Montreal Greets the World. By Jules B. Billard.
600-621, May 1967

EXPO '70:

Kansai, Japan's Historic Heartland. By Thomas J.
Abercrombie. 295-339, Mar. 1970

EXPOSITIONS. *See* Fairs

EXQUISITE Living Fossil, the Chambered Nautilus.
Photos by Douglas Faulkner. 38-41, Jan. 1976

The **EXQUISITE** Orchids. By Luis Marden. 485-513,
Apr. 1971

EXTRAORDINARY Photograph Shows Earth ·Pole to
Pole. Photos by Nimbus I. 190-193, Feb. 1965

EXTRAORDINARY Photographs of Earth Taken by Satellite *Tiros*. By W. G. Stroud. 293-302, Aug. 1960

EXUMA CAYS, Bahama Islands:

The Bahamas, Isles of the Blue-green Sea. By Carleton Mitchell. Photos by B. Anthony Stewart. 147-203, Feb. 1958

More of Sea Than of Land: The Bahamas. By Carleton Mitchell. Photos by James L. Stanfield. 218-267, Feb. 1967

EYE to Eye With Eagles. By Frederick Kent Truslow. 123-148, Jan. 1961

EYES:

Nature's Alert Eyes (Animal Eyes). By Constance P. Warner. 558-569, Apr. 1959

EYES on the China Coast. By George W. Long. 505-512, Apr. 1953

EYEWITNESS to War in the Holy Land. By Charles Harbutt. 782-795, Dec. 1967

F

FAO. *See* United Nations Food and Agriculture Organization

The FBI: Public Friend Number One. By Jacob Hay. Photos by Robert F. Sisson. 860-886, June 1961

F.N.R.S. 3 (Bathyscaph):

Deep Diving off Japan. By Georges S. Houot. 138-150, Jan. 1960

Diving Through an Undersea Avalanche. By Jacques-Yves Cousteau. 538-542, Apr. 1955

Four Years of Diving to the Bottom of the Sea. By Georges S. Houot. 715-731, May 1958

Photographing the Sea's Dark Underworld. By Harold E. Edgerton. 523-537, Apr. 1955

To the Depths of the Sea by Bathyscaphe. By Jacques-Yves Cousteau. 67-79, July 1954

Two and a Half Miles Down. By Georges S. Houot. 80-86, July 1954

FABLED Mount of St. Michael. By Alan Villiers. Photos by Bates Littlehales. 880-898, June 1964

The FABULOUS Sierra Nevada. By J. R. Challacombe. 825-843, June 1954

The FABULOUS State of Texas. By Stanley Walker. Photos by B. Anthony Stewart and Thomas Nebbia. 149-195, Feb. 1961

FACE to Face With Gorillas in Central Africa. By Paul A. Zahl. 114-137, Jan. 1960

FACT Finding for Tomorrow's Planes. By Hugh L. Dryden. Photos by Luis Marden. 757-780, Dec. 1953

FAEROE ISLANDS, North Atlantic Ocean:

The Faeroes, Isles of Maybe. By Ernle Bradford. Photos by Adam Woolfitt. 410-422, Sept. 1970

The Last Vikings (Television film). 434A-434B, Mar. 1972

FAIR, PAUL J.: Photographer:

Wildlife In and Near the Valley of the Moon. By H. H. Arnold. 401-414, Mar. 1950

FAIRBANKS, Alaska:

Busy Fairbanks Sets Alaska's Pace. By Bruce A. Wilson. 505-523, Oct. 1949

FAIRS:

America Goes to the Fair. By Samuel W. Matthews. 293-333, Sept. 1954

Australian New Guinea. By John Scofield. 604-637, May 1962
Included: Intertribal Fair

Belgium Welcomes the World (World's Fair). By Howell Walker. 795-837, June 1958

The Fair Reopens (New York World's Fair). Photos by James P. Blair. Text by Carolyn Bennett Patterson. 505-529, Apr. 1965
Included: Visitors' guide

4-H Boys and Girls Grow More Food. By Frederick Simpich. 551-582, Nov. 1948

Holy Week and the Fair in Sevilla (Spain). By Luis Marden. 499-530, Apr. 1951

I Walked Some Irish Miles. By Dorothea Sheats. 653-678, May 1951
Included: Galway Fair; Killorglin's Puck Fair

Kansai, Japan's Historic Heartland. By Thomas J. Abercrombie. 295-339, Mar. 1970
Included: Expo '70

Montreal Greets the World. By Jules B. Billard. 600-621, May 1967
Included: Expo 67

Russia as I Saw It. By Richard M. Nixon. Photos by B. Anthony Stewart. 715-750, Dec. 1959
Included: American National Exhibition at Sokolniki Park in Moscow

Seattle Fair Looks to the 21st Century (World's Fair). By Carolyn Bennett Patterson. Photos by Thomas Nebbia. 402-427, Sept. 1962

When Gypsies Gather at Appleby Fair. Photos by Bruce Dale. 848-869, June 1972

A Woman Paints the Tibetans. By Lafugie. 659-692, May 1949
Included: Himis Fair

See also Dog Shows; Horse Shows; Pennsylvania Dutch (Folk Festival); Sing-Sing

FAIRY TERNS:

What a Place to Lay an Egg! By Thomas R. Howell. 414-419, Sept. 1971

FALCONRY:

A New Light Dawns on Bird Photography. By Arthur A. Allen. 774-790, June 1948

FALI (Tribespeople):

Carefree People of the Cameroons. Photos by Pierre Ichac. 233-248, Feb. 1947

FALKLAND ISLANDS AND DEPENDENCIES:

Off the Beaten Track of Empire (Prince Philip's Tour). By Beverley M. Bowie. Photos by Michael Parker. 584-626, Nov. 1957

People and Penguins of the Faraway Falklands. By Olin Sewall Pettingill, Jr. 387-416, Mar. 1956

'Round the Horn by Submarine. By Paul C. Stimson. 129-144, Jan. 1948

The FAMILY FARM Ain't What It Used To Be. By James A. Sugar. 391-411, Sept. 1974

FAMILY in Search of Prehistoric Man: The Leakeys of Africa. By Melvin M. Payne. 194-231, Feb. 1965

FAMILY LIFE:

The Family: a Mormon Shrine. 459-463, Apr. 1975

FAMILY LIFE—*Continued*

Growing Up in Montana. Photos by Nicholas deVore III. 650-657, May 1976

An Ozark Family Carves a Living and a Way of Life. Photos by Bruce Dale. 124-133, July 1975

FAMINE:

Bangladesh: The Nightmare of Famine. Photos by Steve Raymer. 33-39, July 1975

Can the World Feed Its People? By Thomas Y. Canby. Photos by Steve Raymer. 2-31, July 1975

Drought Bedevils Brazil's Sertão. By John Wilson. Photos by Gordon W. Gahan. 704-723, Nov. 1972

Drought Threatens the Tuareg World. By Victor Englebert. 544-571, Apr. 1974

The Niger: River of Sorrow, River of Hope. By Georg Gerster. 152-189, Aug. 1975

Report from the Locust Wars. By Tony and Dickey Chapelle. 545-562, Apr. 1953

FAMOUS (French-American Mid-Ocean Undersea Study):

Project FAMOUS—Man's First Voyages Down to the Mid-Atlantic Ridge. By J. R. Heirtzler and Robert D. Ballard. Photos by Emory Kristof. 586-615, May 1975

FANCH'ENG, People's Republic of China:

Return to Changing China. By Audrey Topping. 801-833, Dec. 1971

FAR EAST:

The Far East, map supplement. Sept. 1952

Our Navy in the Far East. By Arthur W. Radford. Photos by J. Baylor Roberts. 537-577, Oct. 1953

Pacific Fleet: Force for Peace. By Franc Shor. Photos by W.E. Garrett. 283-335, Sept. 1959

Yankee Roams the Orient. By Irving and Electa Johnson. 327-370, Mar. 1951

See also Burma; China; Hong Kong; Indonesia; Japan; Korea; Macao; Malaysia; Philippines; Quemoy; Singapore; Southeast Asia; Taiwan

FAR NORTH with "Captain Mac." By Miriam MacMillan. 465-513, Oct. 1951

FARADAY, MICHAEL:

The British Way. By Sir Evelyn Wrench. 421-541, Apr. 1949

FARMS:

The Family Farm Ain't What It Used To Be. By James A. Sugar. 391-411, Sept. 1974

Life in Rural America. Special Publication announced. 870-874, June 1974

See also Agriculture; Aquiculture; Estates and Plantations; Floating Farms; Harmony Hollow; listing under Ranches; Thunder Hill Goat Farm

FARNE ISLANDS, England:

Pilgrimage to Holy Island and the Farnes. By John E. H. Nolan. 547-570, Oct. 1952

FAULKNER, DOUGLAS: Author-Photographer:

Finned Doctors of the Deep. 867-873, Dec. 1965

Photographer

The Chambered Nautilus, Exquisite Living Fossil. 38-41, Jan. 1976

FAULTS AND FAULTING:

This Changing Earth. By Samuel W. Matthews.

FAULTS AND FAULTING—*Continued*

1-37, Jan. 1973

See also Cayman Trough; Great Rift Valley; Mariana Trench; Mid-Atlantic Rift; San Andreas Fault

FAYAL (Island), Azores:

A New Volcano Bursts From the Atlantic. By John Scofield. Photos by Robert F. Sisson. 735-757, June 1958

FEAST Day in Kapingamarangi. By W. Robert Moore. 523-537, Apr. 1950

FEATHERED Dancers of Little Tobago. By E. Thomas Gilliard. Photos by Frederick Kent Truslow. 428-440, Sept. 1958

FEDERAL BUREAU OF INVESTIGATION:

The FBI: Public Friend Number One. By Jacob Hay. Photos by Robert F. Sisson. 860-886, June 1961

FEDERAL REPUBLIC OF GERMANY. See Germany, Federal Republic of (West Germany)

FERRAR, NICHOLAS and JOHN:

Founders of Virginia. By Sir Evelyn Wrench. Photos by B. Anthony Stewart. 433-462, Apr. 1948

FERRIDAY, EDWARD C., Jr.: Author:

Wonderland in Longwood Gardens. 45-64, July 1951

FERRIES:

Alaska's Marine Highway: Ferry Route to the North. By W.E. Garrett. 776-819, June 1965

Hydrofoil Ferry "Flies" the Strait of Messina. By Gilbert Grosvenor. 493-496, Apr. 1957

Staten Island Ferry, New York's Seagoing Bus. By John T. Cunningham and Jay Johnston. Photos by W. D. Vaughn. 833-843, June 1959

FÈS, Morocco. See Fez

FESTIVALS:

Adobe New Mexico. By Mason Sutherland. Photos by Justin Locke. 783-830, Dec. 1949
Included: Fiesta time at Santa Fe and Taos

Belgium Welcomes the World. By Howell Walker. 795-837, June 1958
Included: Bayard Festival, Ath; Begonia Festival, Lochristi; Blessing of the Sea, Heist; Bruegel Festival, Wingene

Brazil's Land of Minerals. By W. Robert Moore. 479-508, Oct. 1948
Included: Holy Week

Carnival in San Antonio. By Mason Sutherland. Photos by J. Baylor Roberts. 813-844, Dec. 1947
Included: Fiesta de San Jacinto

The Cobra, India's "Good Snake." By Harry Miller. 393-409, Sept. 1970

Dinkelsbühl Rewards Its Children. By Charles Belden. 255-268, Feb. 1957

Exploring the Past in Panama. By Matthew W. Stirling. Photos by Richard H. Stewart. 373-399, Mar. 1949
Included: Fiesta in Ocú, carnival time in Parita, and a *balsería* in Tambor

Feudal Splendor Lingers in Rajputana. By Volkmar Wentzel. 411-458, Oct. 1948
Included: Gangor Festival and the wedding of the Prince of Jodhpur to the Princess of Jaisalmer

FESTIVALS — *Continued*

From Sagebrush to Roses on the Columbia. By Leo A. Borah. 571-611, Nov. 1952

From Tucson to Tombstone. By Mason Sutherland. 343-384, Sept. 1953

The Ganges, River of Faith. By John J. Putman. Photos by Raghubir Singh. 445-483, Oct. 1971
Included: Ardh Kumbh Mela, Divali, Durga Puja, Solar New Year

Happy-go-lucky Trinidad and Tobago. By Charles Allmon. 35-75, Jan. 1953

Honolulu, Mid-ocean Capital. By Frederick Simpich, Jr. Photos by B. Anthony Stewart. 577-624, May 1954

Land of the Havasupai (Indians). By Jack Breed. 655-674, May 1948

Life and Death in Tana Toradja. By Pamela and Alfred Meyer. 793-815, June 1972

Lost Kingdom in Indian Mexico (Tarascan). By Justin Locke. 517-546, Oct. 1952

Mexico's Booming Capital. By Mason Sutherland. Photos by Justin Locke. 785-824, Dec. 1951
Included: Flag Day; the festive celebration in the Zócalo, Mexico City; the *Posadas* (Lodgings), commemorating Mary and Joseph's visit to Bethlehem; Tepotzotlán's Marathon Dance; and the Huejotzingo celebration

Mysore Celebrates the Death of a Demon. By Luc Bouchage. Photos by Ylla. 706-711, May 1958

New Guinea Festival of Faces. By Malcolm S. Kirk. 148-156, July 1969

Rare Birds Flock to Spain's Marismas. By Roger Tory Peterson. 397-425, Mar. 1958
Included: Fiesta at El Rocío, Spain

Sky-high Bolivia. Photos by T. Ifor Rees and Carl S. Bell. 481-496, Oct. 1950
Included: *Alasitas,* Indian fiesta dance (La Diablada), La Paz carnival, livestock fair, Tiquina area fiesta

Sponge Fishermen of Tarpon Springs (Florida). By Jennie E. Harris. 119-136, Jan. 1947

Switzerland's Once-in-a-generation Festival (Vevey). By Jean and Franc Shor. 563-571, Oct. 1958

Vézelay, Hill of the Pilgrims (France). By Melvin Hall. 229-247, Feb. 1953

Weighing the Aga Khan in Diamonds. Photos by David J. Carnegie. 317-324, Mar. 1947

Work-hard, Play-hard Michigan. By Andrew H. Brown. 279-320, Mar. 1952

The Yankee Sailor Who Opened Japan (Commodore Perry). By Ferdinand Kuhn. 85-102, July 1953

See also Arnhem Land (Exploring Stone Age), for Balnuknuk; Aspen, Colorado, for Winterskol and Aspen Music Festival; Balearic Islands; Bavaria, for Fasching, Oberammergau Passion Play, and Wagner Festival; Berkshires, Massachusetts, for Berkshire Music Festival; Broadstairs, England, for Dickens Festival; Camargue (Region), France, for Fete of the Two St. Marys and Gypsy Festival of St. Sarah; Canary Islands, for Corpus Christi celebration; Gasparilla Celebration; Germany (Modern Miracle); Italy (Amalfi); Jerusalem; Languedoc (Region), France, for Bastille Day; Madeira; Maine (Down East Cruise), for Lobster Festival; Mardi Gras; Normandy (France); Oslo, Norway, for Constitution Day; Palio; Pennsylvania Dutch; Russell, Kansas, for Prairiesta; Switzerland (Val d'Hérens), for Cantonal Festival of Costumes; Texas (Fabulous State); Tournament of Roses; Tukuna

FESTIVALS — *Continued*

Indians, for puberty rites; Unoto; Up Helly Aa (Viking Festival); Wales, for Eisteddfods; Wisconsin ("Swissconsin"), for William Tell Pageant; *and* Carnivals; Coronations; Fairs; Religious Ceremonies and Processions; Winter Carnivals

FETTERMAN, JOHN: Author:
On the Road With an Old-time Circus. Photos by Jonathan Blair. 410-434, Mar. 1972

The People of Cumberland Gap. Photos by Bruce Dale. 591-621, Nov. 1971

FEUDAL Splendor Lingers in Rajputana. By Volkmar Wentzel. 411-458, Oct. 1948

FEZ (Fès), Morocco:
From Sea to Sahara in French Morocco. By Jean and Franc Shor. 147-188, Feb. 1955

Morocco, Land of the Farthest West. By Thomas J. Abercrombie. 834-865, June 1971

FIELD, HENRY: Author:
Sinai Sheds New Light on the Bible. Photos by William B. and Gladys Terry. 795-815, Dec. 1948

FIELDS, JACK: Photographer:
The Flower Seed Growers: Gardening's Color Merchants. By Robert de Roos. 720-738, May 1968

Micronesia: The Americanization of Eden. By David S. Boyer. 702-744, May 1967

Sailors of the Sky. By Gordon Young. Photos by Emory Kristof and Jack Fields. Paintings by Davis Meltzer. 49-73, Jan. 1967

FIESTAS. *See* Festivals

FIÉVET, JEANNETTE: Author-Illustrator:
Beyond the Bight of Benin. By Jeannette and Maurice Fiévet. 221-253, Aug. 1959

FIÉVET, MAURICE: Artist:
Angkor, Jewel of the Jungle. By W. Robert Moore. 517-569, Apr. 1960

Author-Illustrator
Beyond the Bight of Benin. By Jeannette and Maurice Fiévet. 221-253, Aug. 1959

FIFTH ARMY, U. S.:
Italy Smiles Again. By Edgar Erskine Hume. 693-732, June 1949

FIFTY Years of Flight. 740-756, Dec. 1953

FIG WASPS:
The Wasp That Plays Cupid to a Fig. By Robert F. Sisson. 690-697, Nov. 1970

FIJI ISLANDS, Pacific Ocean:
Copra-ship Voyage to Fiji's Outlying Islands. By Marjory C. Thomas. 121-140, July 1950
Included: Kava ceremony and the fire walkers of Mbengga

The Islands Called Fiji. By Luis Marden. 526-561, Oct. 1958

A Teen-ager Sails the World Alone. By Robin Lee Graham. 445-491, Oct. 1968

FILLMORE, MILLARD:
Profiles of the Presidents: II. A Restless Nation Moves West. By Frank Freidel. 80-121, Jan. 1965

FILMS AND FILMSTRIPS, NGS:
Film-strip service planned. 581, Oct. 1967

FILMS AND FILMSTRIPS, NGS — *Continued*

More than 50 films are available covering dozens of subjects in the fields of science and social studies. 583, Nov. 1975

The World in Geographic Filmstrips. By Melvin M. Payne. 134-137, Jan. 1968

See also Television Films

The **FINAL** Flight (Exploring Taurus-Littrow). By Harrison H. Schmitt. Photos by the crew of Apollo 17. 290-307, Sept. 1973

The **FINAL** Tribute (Churchill Funeral). Text by Carolyn Bennett Patterson. 199-225, Aug. 1965

FINCHES:

Exotic Birds in Manhattan's Bowery. By Paul A. Zahl. 77-98, Jan. 1953

The Galapagos, Eerie Cradle of New Species. By Roger Tory Peterson. Photos by Alan and Joan Root. 541-585, Apr. 1967

FINDING an "Extinct" New Zealand Bird. By R. V. Francis Smith. 393-401, Mar. 1952

FINDING Rare Beauty in Common Rocks. By Lorence G. Collins. 121-129, Jan. 1966

FINDING the Mt. Everest of All Living Things (Redwood Tree). By Paul A. Zahl. 10-51, July 1964

FINDING the Tomb of a Warrior-God. By William Duncan Strong. Photos by Clifford Evans, Jr. 453-482, Apr. 1947

FINDING the World's Earliest Man. By L. S. B. Leakey. Photos by Des Bartlett. 420-435, Sept. 1960

FINDLEY, ROWE: Author:

The Bittersweet Waters of the Lower Colorado. Photos by Charles O'Rear. 540-569, Oct. 1973

Canyonlands, Realm of Rock and the Far Horizon. Photos by Walter Meayers Edwards. 71-91, July 1971

Death Valley, the Land and the Legend. Photos by David Hiser. 69-103, Jan. 1970

Kansas City, Heartland U.S.A. Photos by Ted Spiegel. 112-139, July 1976

Miracle of the Potholes. Photos by Robert F. Sisson. 570-579, Oct. 1975

Old Salem, Morning Star of Moravian Faith. Photos by Robert W. Madden. 818-837, Dec. 1970

Telephone a Star: the Story of Communications Satellites. 638-651, May 1962

FINE ARTS. *See* Artists, for paintings; Sculpture; *and* listing under Art

FINISTERRE (Yawl):

The Bahamas, Isles of the Blue-green Sea. By Carleton Mitchell. Photos by B. Anthony Stewart. 147-203, Feb. 1958

Finisterre Sails the Windward Islands. By Carleton Mitchell. Photos by Winfield Parks. 755-801, Dec. 1965

A Fresh Breeze Stirs the Leewards. By Carleton Mitchell. Photos by Winfield Parks. 488-537, Oct. 1966

More of Sea Than of Land: The Bahamas. By Carleton Mitchell. Photos by James L. Stanfield. 218-267, Feb. 1967

To Europe with a Racing Start. By Carleton Mitchell. 758-791, June 1958

FINLAND:

Baltic Cruise of the *Caribbee*. By Carleton Mitchell. 605-646, Nov. 1950

Finland: Plucky Neighbor of Soviet Russia. By William Graves. Photos by George F. Mobley. 587-629, May 1968

Friendly Flight to Northern Europe. By Lyndon B. Johnson. Photos by Volkmar Wentzel. 268-293, Feb. 1964

North With Finland's Lapps. By Jean and Franc Shor. 249-280, Aug. 1954

Scenes of Postwar Finland. By La Verne Bradley. Photos by Jerry Waller. 233-264, Aug. 1947

FINNED Doctors of the Deep (Wrasses). By Douglas Faulkner. 867-873, Dec. 1965

FIRE FIGHTING:

Forest Fire: The Devil's Picnic. By Stuart E. Jones and Jay Johnston. 100-127, July 1968

The **FIRE** of Heaven: Electricity Revolutionizes the Modern World. By Albert W. Atwood. 655-674, Nov. 1948

FIRE WALKING:

Copra-ship Voyage to Fiji's Outlying Islands. By Marjory C. Thomas. 121-140, July 1950

The Islands Called Fiji. By Luis Marden. 526-561, Oct. 1958

FIREBRANDS of the Revolution. By Eric F. Goldman. Photos by George F. Mobley. 2-27, July 1974

FIREFLIES:

Nature's Night Lights: Probing the Secrets of Bioluminescence. By Paul A. Zahl. 45-69, July 1971

Torchbearers of the Twilight. By Frederick G. Vosburgh. 697-704, May 1951

Wing-borne Lamps of the Summer Night. By Paul A. Zahl. 48-59, July 1962

FIRST American Ascent of Mount St. Elias. By Maynard M. Miller. 229-248, Feb. 1948

A **FIRST** American Views His Land. By N. Scott Momaday. 13-19, July 1976

FIRST Colony in Space. By Isaac Asimov. Paintings by Pierre Mion. 76-89, July 1976

FIRST Color Photographs on the Moon's Rocky Face. By Homer E. Newell. 578-592, Oct. 1966

FIRST Color Portraits of the Heavens. By William C. Miller. 670-679, May 1959

FIRST Color Record of the Life Cycle of a Coral. By Robert F. Sisson. 780-793, June 1973

FIRST Conquest of Antarctica's Highest Peaks. By Nicholas B. Clinch. 836-863, June 1967

FIRST Crossings of the Ends of the Earth. The Editor. 1, Jan. 1959

FIRST Explorers on the Moon: The Incredible Story of Apollo 11. 735-797, Dec. 1969

FIRST Flight Across the Bottom of the World. By James R. Reedy. Photos by Otis Imboden. 454-464, Mar. 1964

FIRST Glimpse of a Stone Age Tribe. 881-882, Dec. 1971

FIRST Lady of the National Geographic (Elsie May Bell Grosvenor). By Gilbert Hovey Grosvenor. 101-121, July 1965

FIRST La Gorce Medal Honors Antarctic Expedition. 864-867, June 1967

FIRST Masters of the American Desert: The Hohokam. By Emil W. Haury. Photos by Helga Teiwes. 670-695, May 1967

FIRST Moon Explorers (Apollo 11) Receive the Society's Hubbard Medal. 859-861, June 1970

FIRST Motor Sortie into Escalante Land. By Jack Breed. 369-404, Sept. 1949

FIRST Photographs of Planets and Moon Taken With Palomar's 200-inch Telescope. By Milton L. Humason. 125-130, Jan. 1953

FIRST Photographs of Snow Leopards in the Wild. By George B. Schaller. 702-707, Nov. 1971

The FIRST Traverse (Mount Everest). By Thomas F. Hornbein and William F. Unsoeld. 509-513, Oct. 1963

FIRST Voyage Around the World (Magellan). By Alan Villiers. Photos by Bruce Dale. 721-753, June 1976

FIRST Woman Across Greenland's Ice. By Myrtle Simpson. Photos by Hugh Simpson. 264-279, Aug. 1967

FIRSTHAND Look at the Soviet Union. By Thomas T. Hammond. Photos by Erich Lessing. 352-407, Sept. 1959

FISH-BAITING ANIMALS:
Aha! It Really Works! (Heron). By Robert F. Sisson. 143-147, Jan. 1974
Something's Fishy About That Fin! (Decoy Fish). Photos by Robert J. Shallenberger and William D. Madden. 224-227, Aug. 1974

FISH FARMING. See Shrimp (Shrimp Nursery)

FISH Men Discover a 2,200-year-old Greek Ship. By Jacques-Yves Cousteau. 1-36, Jan. 1954

FISH Men Explore a New World Undersea. By Jacques-Yves Cousteau. 431-472, Oct. 1952

FISHER, ALLAN C., Jr.: Author:
African Wildlife: Man's Threatened Legacy. Photos by Thomas Nebbia. Paintings by Ned Seidler. 147-187, Feb. 1972
Australia's Pacesetter State, Victoria. Photos by Thomas Nebbia. 218-253, Feb. 1971
Aviation Medicine on the Threshold of Space. Photos by Luis Marden. 241-278, Aug. 1955
Cape Canaveral's 6,000-mile Shooting Gallery. Photos by Luis Marden and Thomas Nebbia. 421-471, Oct. 1959
"The City"—London's Storied Square Mile. 735-777, June 1961
Eastman of Rochester: Photographic Pioneer. 423-438, Sept. 1954
Everyone's Servant, the Post Office. Photos by Volkmar Wentzel. 121-152, July 1954
Exploring Tomorrow With the Space Agency. Photos by Dean Conger. 48-89, July 1960
The Investiture of Great Britain's Prince of Wales. Photos by James L. Stanfield and Adam Woolfitt. 698-715, Nov. 1969

FISHER, ALLAN C., Jr.: Author—Continued
Kenya Says Harambee! Photos by Bruce Dale. 151-205, Feb. 1969
Minutemen of the Civil Air Patrol. Photos by John E. Fletcher. 637-665, May 1956
The Nation's River. Photos by James L. Stanfield. 432-469, Oct. 1976
One Man's London. Photos by James P. Blair. 743-791, June 1966
Our Navy's Long Submarine Arm. 613-636, Nov. 1952
Reaching for the Moon. Photos by Luis Marden. 157-171, Feb. 1959
Rhodesia, a House Divided. Photos by Thomas Nebbia. 641-671, May 1975
San Diego, California's Plymouth Rock. Photos by James L. Amos. 114-147, July 1969
You and the Obedient Atom. 303-353, Sept. 1958

FISHER, FRANKLIN L.:
Memorial Tribute to Franklin L. Fisher. 692, Nov. 1953
Author
Our Search for British Paintings. 543-550, Apr. 1949

FISHER, MELVIN A.:
Atocha, Tragic Treasure Galleon of the Florida Keys. By Eugene Lyon. 787-809, June 1976

FISHER TOWERS, Utah:
We Climbed Utah's Skyscraper Rock. By Huntley Ingalls. Photos by author and Barry C. Bishop. 705-721, Nov. 1962

FISHERMEN:
Dory on the Banks: A Day in the Life of a Portuguese Fisherman. By James H. Pickerell. 573-583, Apr. 1968
Fishing in the Lofotens. Photos by Lennart Nilsson. 377-388, Mar. 1947
Gloucester Blesses Its Portuguese Fleet. By Luis Marden. 75-84, July 1953
I Sailed with Portugal's Captains Courageous. By Alan Villiers. 565-596, May 1952
The Lonely Dorymen (Television film). 579A-579B, Apr. 1968
The Sailing Oystermen of Chesapeake Bay. By Luis Marden. 798-819, Dec. 1967
Shad in the Shadow of Skyscrapers. By Dudley B. Martin. Photos by Luis Marden. 359-376, Mar. 1947
Trawling the China Seas. Photos by J. Charles Thompson. 381-395, Mar. 1950
See also Basques (Land of the Ancient; Life in the Land); Goggle Fishing; Lobsters and Lobstering; Sea Gypsies; Sponge Fishing Industry; Tuna

FISHERWOMEN:
Ama, Sea Nymphs of Japan. By Luis Marden. 122-135, July 1971

FISHES:
An Artist's Glimpses of Our Roadside Wildlife. Paintings by Walter A. Weber. 16-32, July 1950
Included: Black bass, Cutthroat trout, Eastern brook trout, Golden trout, Northern pike, Rainbow trout, Yellow perch
The Book of Fishes (1952). 418, Mar. 1957; 440, Mar. 1960; 563, Aug. 1961
Exploring Stone Age Arnhem Land. By Charles P.

FISHES — *Continued*

Mountford. Photos by Howell Walker. 745-782, Dec. 1949

Finned Doctors of the Deep (Wrasses). By Douglas Faulkner. 867-873, Dec. 1965

Fish Men Explore a New World Undersea. By Jacques-Yves Cousteau. 431-472, Oct. 1952

Fishing in the Whirlpool of Charybdis. By Paul A. Zahl. 579-618, Nov. 1953

Florida, Noah's Ark for Exotic Newcomers. By Rick Gore. Photos by David Doubilet. 538-559, Oct. 1976

I Sailed with Portugal's Captains Courageous. By Alan Villiers. 565-596, May 1952

In the Wilds of a City Parlor. By Paul A. Zahl. 645-672, Nov. 1954

Lake Sunapee's Golden Trout. Photos by Robert F. Sisson. 529-536, Oct. 1950

Man-of-war Fleet Attacks Bimini. By Paul A. Zahl. 185-212, Feb. 1952

Marineland, Florida's Giant Fish Bowl. By Gilbert Grosvenor La Gorce. Photos by Luis Marden. 679-694, Nov. 1952

Marvels of a Coral Realm. By Walter A. Starck II. 710-738, Nov. 1966

Nature's Alert Eyes. By Constance P. Warner. 558-569, Apr. 1959

Night Life in the Gulf Stream. By Paul A. Zahl. 391-418, Mar. 1954

One Hundred Hours Beneath the Chesapeake. By Gilbert C. Klingel. Photos by Willard R. Culver. 681-696, May 1955

Photographing the Night Creatures of Alligator Reef (Florida). By Robert E. Schroeder. Photos by author and Walter A. Starck II. 128-154, Jan. 1964

Rainbow World Beneath the Red Sea. Photos by David Doubilet. 344-365, Sept. 1975

The Strangest Sea (Red Sea). By Eugenie Clark. Photos by David Doubilet. 338-343, Sept. 1975

Wondrous World of Fishes. Book announced. 388-393, Mar. 1965

See also Decoy Fish; Discus Fish; Eels; Goldfish; Grunion; Hatchetfish; Herring; Menhaden; Mudskippers; Piranhas; Sailfish; Salmon; Sargassum Fish; Scorpionfish; Sea Horses; Shad; Sharks; Skates; Sole; Trout; Walking Catfish

FISHING (Industry):

Chesapeake Country. By Nathaniel T. Kenney. Photos by Bates Littlehales. 370-411, Sept. 1964

The Crab That Shakes Hands. By Clarence P. Idyll. Photos by Robert F. Sisson. 254-271, Feb. 1971

"Delmarva," Gift of the Sea. By Catherine Bell Palmer. 367-399, Sept. 1950

Down East Cruise. By Tom Horgan. Photos by Luis Marden. 329-369, Sept. 1952

Gloucester Blesses Its Portuguese Fleet. By Luis Marden. 75-84, July 1953

Golden Beaches of Portugal. By Alan Villiers. 673-696, Nov. 1954

Life's Tempo on Nantucket. By Peter Benchley. Photos by James L. Stanfield. 810-839, June 1970

Maryland on the Half Shell. By Stuart E. Jones. Photos by Robert W. Madden. 188-229, Feb. 1972

Menhaden — Uncle Sam's Top Commercial Fish.

FISHING (Industry) — *Continued*

By Leonard C. Roy. Photos by Robert F. Sisson. 813-823, June 1949

Newfoundland Trusts in the Sea. By Gary Jennings. Photos by Sam Abell. 112-141, Jan. 1974

Quicksilver and Slow Death. By John J. Putman. Photos by Robert W. Madden. 507-527, Oct. 1972

Included: Mercury contamination of fish in Japan and the United States

Shad in the Shadow of Skyscrapers. By Dudley B. Martin. Photos by Luis Marden. 359-376, Mar. 1947

Sicily the Three-Cornered. By Luis Marden. 1-48, Jan. 1955

This Is My Island, Tangier (Virginia). By Harold G. Wheatley. Photos by David Alan Harvey. 700-725, Nov. 1973

Included: Crabbing

Trawling the China Seas. Photos by J. Charles Thompson. 381-395, Mar. 1950

See also Cod Fishing; Herring; Lobsters and Lobstering; Oyster Fleet; Shrimp Fishing; Tuna

FISHING (Sport):

Goggle Fishing in California Waters. By David Hellyer. Photos by Lamar Boren. 615-632, May 1949

See also Ice Fishing; Trout Fishing

FISHING, Night (Marine Biology Studies):

Night Life in the Gulf Stream. By Paul A. Zahl. 391-418, Mar. 1954

FISHING in the Whirlpool of Charybdis. By Paul A. Zahl. 579-618, Nov. 1953

FISHING VESSELS. *See* Fishing (Industry)

FITCH, CLYDE:

Literary Landmarks of Massachusetts. By William H. Nicholas. Photos by B. Anthony Stewart and John E. Fletcher. 279-310, Mar. 1950

FITZ ROY, ROBERT:

In the Wake of Darwin's *Beagle*. By Alan Villiers. Photos by James L. Stanfield. 449-495, Oct. 1969

FIVE Noted Thinkers Explore the Future. 68-75, July 1976

The FIVE Worlds of Peru. By Kenneth F. Weaver. Photos by Bates Littlehales. 213-265, Feb. 1964

FJORDS:

Norway's Fjords Pit Men Against Mountains. By Andrew H. Brown. 96-122, Jan. 1957

FLAGS:

American and Geographic Flags Top Everest. By Melvin M. Payne. Photos by Barry C. Bishop. 157-157C, Aug. 1963

Flags of the Americas. By Elizabeth W. King. 633-657, May 1949

Contents: The Flag of the United States and the Jack. — Flags of the President, the Vice President, and Heads of Executive Departments of the United States. — Flags of the United States Armed Forces and Government Agencies. — Flags of the Latin-American Republics.

Flags of the United Nations (60 Member Countries). By Elizabeth W. King. 213-238, Feb. 1951

Flags of the United Nations (99 Member States). 332-345, Sept. 1961

FLAGS — *Continued*

New Stars for Old Glory. By Lonnelle Aikman. 86-121, July 1959

The Palio of Siena. By Edgar Erskine Hume. 231-244, Aug. 1951

Contents: The standard of Siena; ward and guild banners; also, the performances of the *giuocatori di bandiera,* skilled flag manipulators

The Peary Flag (U. S. Flag) Comes to Rest. By Marie Peary Stafford. 519-532, Oct. 1954

See also NGS: Flag

FLAMBOYANT Is the Word for Bolivia. By Loren McIntyre. 153-195, Feb. 1966

FLAMINGOS:

Ballerinas in Pink. By Carleton Mitchell. Photos by B. Anthony Stewart. 553-571, Oct. 1957

East Africa's Majestic Flamingos. By M. Philip Kahl. 276-294, Feb. 1970

Included: Greater flamingo; Lesser flamingo

The Flamingo Eaters of Ngorongoro. By Richard D. Estes. 535-539, Oct. 1973

Contents: Flamingos as hyenas' prey

Flamingos' Last Stand on Andros Island. By Paul A. Zahl. 635-652, May 1951

Freeing Flamingos From Anklets of Death. By John G. Williams. Photos by Alan Root. 934-944, Dec. 1963

In Quest of the Rarest Flamingo (James's Flamingo). By William G. Conway. Photos by Bates Littlehales. 91-105, July 1961

FLAT TOP COALFIELD, West Virginia:

Mountain Voices, Mountain Days. By Bryan Hodgson. Photos by Linda Bartlett. 118-146, July 1972

FLEA MARKET, Paris, France:

Paris Flea Market. By Franc Shor. Photos by Alexander Taylor. 318-326, Mar. 1957

FLEAY, DAVID: Author:

Strange Animals of Australia. Photos by Stanley Breeden. 388-411, Sept. 1963

Author-Photographer

Flight of the Platypuses. 512-525, Oct. 1958

FLEDGLING Wings of the Air Force. By Thomas W. McKnew. 266-271, Aug. 1957

FLEMING, SIR ALEXANDER:

The British Way. By Sir Evelyn Wrench. 421-541, Apr. 1949

FLEMING, ROBERT V.:

Memorial tribute: Robert V. Fleming, 1890-1967. By Melville Bell Grosvenor. 526-529, Apr. 1968

NGS Board of Trustees member. 706, May 1953; 81, Jan. 1957

Treasurer of NGS. 260, 261, Aug. 1949; 64, 65A-65B, 65D, July 1954; 419, 420, 421, 423, Mar. 1957

Vice President of NGS. 882, 883, Dec. 1960; 585, Oct. 1963; 672, May 1964; 589, Oct. 1967

FLETCHER, JOHN E.: Author-Photographer:

Graduation by Parachute (Parachute Rigger School). 833-846, June 1952

Photographer

Aboard the N.S. *Savannah:* World's First Nuclear

FLETCHER, JOHN E.: Photographer — *Continued*

Merchantman. By Alan Villiers. 280-298, Aug. 1962

All-out Assault on Antarctica. By Richard E. Byrd. 141-180, Aug. 1956

America Goes to the Fair. By Samuel W. Matthews. 293-333, Sept. 1954

Avalanche! (Peru). By Bart McDowell. 855-880, June 1962

Beltsville Brings Science to the Farm. By Samuel W. Matthews. 199-218, Aug. 1953

The DAR Story. By Lonnelle Aikman. Photos by B. Anthony Stewart and John E. Fletcher. 565-598, Nov. 1951

Date Line: United Nations, New York. By Carolyn Bennett Patterson. Photos by B. Anthony Stewart and John E. Fletcher. 305-331, Sept. 1961

"Delmarva," Gift of the Sea. By Catherine Bell Palmer. 367-399, Sept. 1950

Dog Mart Day in Fredericksburg. By Frederick G. Vosburgh. 817-832, June 1951

Exploring America's Great Sand Barrier Reef. By Eugene R. Guild. Photos by John E. Fletcher and author. 325-350, Sept. 1947

Exploring Ottawa. By Bruce Hutchison. 565-596, Nov. 1947

Folger: Biggest Little Library in the World. By Joseph T. Foster. Photos by B. Anthony Stewart and John E. Fletcher. 411-424, Sept. 1951

Hays, Kansas, at the Nation's Heart. By Margaret M. Detwiler. 461-490, Apr. 1952

Literary Landmarks of Massachusetts. By William H. Nicholas. Photos by B. Anthony Stewart and John E. Fletcher. 279-310, Mar. 1950

Mardi Gras in New Orleans. By Carolyn Bennett Patterson. Photos by Robert F. Sisson and John E. Fletcher. 726-732, Nov. 1960

Men Who Measure the Earth. By Robert Leslie Conly. 335-362, Mar. 1956

The Merrimack: River of Industry and Romance. By Albert W. Atwood. 106-140, Jan. 1951

Minnesota Makes Ideas Pay. By Frederick G. Vosburgh. Photos by John E. Fletcher and B. Anthony Stewart. 291-336, Sept. 1949

Minutemen of the Civil Air Patrol. By Allan C. Fisher, Jr. 637-665, May 1956

Mount Vernon Lives On. By Lonnelle Aikman. 651-682, Nov. 1953

Pittsburgh: Workshop of the Titans. By Albert W. Atwood. 117-144, July 1949

Quebec's Forests, Farms, and Frontiers. By Andrew H. Brown. 431-470, Oct. 1949

Sea to Lakes on the St. Lawrence. By George W. Long. Photos by B. Anthony Stewart and John E. Fletcher. 323-366, Sept. 1950

Sno-Cats Mechanize Oregon Snow Survey. By Andrew H. Brown. 691-710, Nov. 1949

Stately Homes of Old Virginia. By Albert W. Atwood. 787-802, June 1953

The United Nations: Capital of the Family of Man. By Adlai E. Stevenson. Photos by B. Anthony Stewart and John E. Fletcher. 297-303, Sept. 1961

Washington's Historic Georgetown. By William A. Kinney. 513-544, Apr. 1953

Weather From the White North. By Andrew H. Brown. 543-572, Apr. 1955

FLETCHER, JOSEPH O.: Author:

Three Months on an Arctic Ice Island. 489-504, Apr. 1953

FLETCHER'S ICE ISLAND, Arctic Region. *See* T-3

FLIGHT Into Antarctic Darkness. By J. Lloyd Abbot, Jr. Photos by David S. Boyer. 732-738, Nov. 1967

The **FLIGHT** of Apollo 11. By Kenneth F. Weaver. 752-787, Dec. 1969

The **FLIGHT** of *Freedom 7*. By Carmault B. Jackson, Jr. 416-431, Sept. 1961

FLIGHT of the Platypuses. By David Fleay. 512-525, Oct. 1958

FLIGHT to Adventure. By Tay and Lowell Thomas, Jr. 49-112, July 1957

FLIGHT to Adventure: Sky Road East. By Tay and Lowell Thomas, Jr. 71-112, Jan. 1960

FLIGHT to Venus and Mercury. By Kenneth F. Weaver. 858-869, June 1975

FLOATING FARMS:

Burma's Leg Rowers and Floating Farms. Photos by W. E. Garrett. Text by David Jeffery. 826-845, June 1974

FLOODS AND FLOOD CONTROL:

Alaska's Automatic Lake Drains Itself (Lake George). 835-844, June 1951

Florence Rises From the Flood. By Joseph Judge. 1-43, July 1967

The Imperiled Everglades. By Fred Ward. 1-27, Jan. 1972
Included: South Florida's canal system

The Lower Mississippi. By Willard Price. Photos by W. D. Vaughn. 681-725, Nov. 1960

The Mekong, River of Terror and Hope. By Peter T. White. Photos by W. E. Garrett. 737-787, Dec. 1968

The Netherlands: Nation at War With the Sea. By Alan Villiers. Photos by Adam Woolfitt. 530-571, Apr. 1968

Satellites Gave Warning of Midwest Floods. By Peter T. White. Photos by Thomas A. DeFeo. 574-592, Oct. 1969

Shawneetown Forsakes the Ohio. By William H. Nicholas. Photos by J. Baylor Roberts. 273-288, Feb. 1948

Southern California's Trial by Mud and Water. By Nathaniel T. Kenney. Photos by Bruce Dale. 552-573, Oct. 1969

Threatened Glories of Everglades National Park. By Frederick Kent Truslow and Frederick G. Vosburgh. Photos by Frederick Kent Truslow and Otis Imboden. 508-553, Oct. 1967

Venice Fights for Life. By Joseph Judge. Photos by Albert Moldvay. 591-631, Nov. 1972

See also Dams; Dikes and Levees; Snow Survey

FLORENCE, Italy:

Florence Rises From the Flood. By Joseph Judge. 1-43, July 1967

Italy Smiles Again. By Edgar Erskine Hume. 693-732, June 1949

The Renaissance Lives On in Tuscany. By Luis Marden. Photos by Albert Moldvay. 626-659,

FLORENCE, Italy — *Continued*
Nov. 1974

FLORES (Island), Lesser Sunda Islands:

East From Bali by Seagoing Jeep to Timor. By Helen and Frank Schreider. 236-279, Aug. 1962

FLORICULTURE:

Amateur Gardener Creates a New Rose. By Elizabeth A. Moize. Photos by Farrell Grehan. 286-294, Aug. 1972

The Exquisite Orchids. By Luis Marden. 485-513, Apr. 1971

The Flower Seed Growers: Gardening's Color Merchants. By Robert de Roos. Photos by Jack Fields. 720-738, May 1968

Patent Plants Enrich Our World. By Orville H. Kneen. 357-378, Mar. 1948

See also Longwood Gardens; Royal Botanic Gardens

FLORIDA:

American Wild Flower Odyssey. By P. L. Ricker. 603-634, May 1953

Atocha, Tragic Treasure Galleon of the Florida Keys. By Eugene Lyon. 787-809, June 1976
Included: The State of Florida's supervision of treasure trove — search, salvage, and distribution

The Booming Sport of Water Skiing. By Wilbur E. Garrett. 700-711, Nov. 1958

Close-up: U.S.A., Florida, map supplement. Text on reverse. Nov. 1973

Cruising Florida's Western Waterways. By Rube Allyn. Photos by Bates Littlehales. 49-76, Jan. 1955

Drowned Galleons Yield Spanish Gold. By Kip Wagner. Photos by Otis Imboden. 1-37, Jan. 1965

An Exotic New Oriole Settles in Florida. By Charles M. Brookfield and Oliver Griswold. 261-264, Feb. 1956

Florida, Noah's Ark for Exotic Newcomers. By Rick Gore. Photos by David Doubilet. 538-559, Oct. 1976

Florida Rides a Space-age Boom. By Benedict Thielen. Photos by Winfield Parks and James P. Blair. 858-903, Dec. 1963

Florida's Booming — and Beleaguered — Heartland. By Joseph Judge. Photos by Jonathan Blair. 585-621, Nov. 1973

Florida's Manatees, Mermaids in Peril. By Daniel S. Hartman. Photos by James A. Sugar. 342-353, Sept. 1969

How Fruit Came to America. By J. R. Magness. Paintings by Else Bostelmann. 325-377, Sept. 1951

Indian Life Before the Colonists Came. By Stuart E. Jones. Engravings by Theodore de Bry, 1590. 351-368, Sept. 1947

Limpkin, the "Crying Bird" That Haunts Florida Swamps. By Frederick Kent Truslow. 114-121, Jan. 1958

Little Horses of the Sea (Sea Horses). By Paul A. Zahl. 131-153, Jan. 1959
Included: Key Largo; Sanibel Island; Tarpon Springs

Men Against the Hurricane. By Andrew H. Brown. 537-560, Oct. 1950

St. Augustine, Nation's Oldest City, Turns 400. By Robert L. Conly. 196-229, Feb. 1966

Saving Man's Wildlife Heritage. By John H. Baker.

FLORIDA — *Continued*

Photos by Robert F. Sisson. 581-620, Nov. 1954

Shrimp Nursery: Science Explores New Ways to Farm the Sea. By Clarence P. Idyll. Photos by Robert F. Sisson. 636-659, May 1965

Slow Boat to Florida (*Tradewinds*). By Dorothea and Stuart E. Jones. 1-65, Jan. 1958

See also Big Cypress Swamp; Canaveral, Cape; Corkscrew Swamp; Crystal River; Everglades; Florida Keys; Marineland; Miami; Tampa; Tarpon Springs

FLORIDA ISLAND, Solomon Islands:

Adventures with the Survey Navy. By Irving Johnson. 131-148, July 1947

FLORIDA KEYS, Florida:

The Lower Keys, Florida's "Out Islands." By John Scofield. Photos by Emory Kristof and Bates Littlehales. 72-93, Jan. 1971

See also Alligator Reef; Dry Tortugas; John Pennekamp Coral Reef State Park; Key West; Marquesas Keys; Tarpon Key

FLOWER PRESERVATION:

Blossoms That Defy the Seasons. By Geneal Condon. Photos by David S. Boyer. 420-427, Sept. 1958

FLOWERS:

American Wild Flower Odyssey. By P. L. Ricker. 603-634, May 1953

Britain's "French" Channel Islands. By James Cerruti. Photos by James L. Amos. 710-740, May 1971

Cloud Gardens in the Tetons. By Frank and John Craighead. 811-830, June 1948

Crossroads of the Insect World. By J. W. MacSwain. Photos by Edward S. Ross. 844-857, Dec. 1966

England's Scillies, the Flowering Isles. By Alan Villiers. Photos by Bates Littlehales. 126-145, July 1967

The Flower Seed Growers: Gardening's Color Merchants. By Robert de Roos. Photos by Jack Fields. 720-738, May 1968
Included: The World of Flowers. Painting by Ned M. Seidler

The Flowers That Say "Aloha." By Deena Clark. Photos by Robert B. Goodman. 121-131, Jan. 1967

In the Gardens of Olympus (Washington). By Paul A. Zahl. 85-123, July 1955

Jerusalem, My Home. By Bertha Spafford Vester. 826-847, Dec. 1964
Included: Wild flower paintings

Malaysia's Giant Flowers and Insect-trapping Plants. By Paul A. Zahl. 680-701, May 1964

The Netherlands: Nation at War With the Sea. By Alan Villiers. Photos by Adam Woolfitt. 530-571, Apr. 1968
Included: Flower bulb industry

Patent Plants Enrich Our World. By Orville H. Kneen. Photos from U. S. Plant Patents. 357-378, Mar. 1948

Photographing Northern Wild Flowers. By Virginia L. Wells. 809-823, June 1956

Saving Man's Wildlife Heritage. By John H. Baker. Photos by Robert F. Sisson. 581-620, Nov. 1954

A Visit to the Living Ice Age. By Rutherford Platt. 525-545, Apr. 1957

FLOWERS — *Continued*

The World in Your Garden. By W. H. Camp. Paintings by Else Bostelmann. 1-65, July 1947
Contents: Abelia, African-Violet, Azalea, Bellflower, Bird-of-Paradise Flower, Blackberry-Lily, Blanket-Flower, Bleeding Heart, Blue Lace-Flower, Bottle-Brush, California Poppy, Calla, Camellia, Candytuft, Canna, Cape Marigold, Castor-Oil-Plant, Catawba Rhododendron, China Aster, Chrysanthemum, Clarkia, Clematis, Common Hyacinth, Cosmos, Crown Imperial, Crown-of-Thorns, Cup-Flower, Cypress Vine, Dahlia, Daisy, East Indian Lotus, Eucalyptus (Gum-Tree), Flamboyant (Royal) Poinciana, Flame Azalea, Forsythia, Foxglove, Frangipani, French and African Marigolds, Fringed Hibiscus, Fuchsia, Garden Verbena, Gerbera, Gladiolus, Grape-Hyacinth, Hibiscus, Hollyhock, Impatiens, Japanese Iris, Japanese Wisteria, Lobelia, Lupine, Michaelmas Daisies, Morning Glory, Nasturtium, Oleander, Oriental Poppy, Oswego Tea, Pansy (Heartsease), Pelargonium ("Geranium"), Peony, Petunia, Poinsettia, Poker-Plant, Pot Marigold, Primrose, Regal Lily, Rose, Scarlet Sage, Snakes-Head (Checkered-Lily), Snapdragon, Snowdrop, Spider Flower, Spring Crocus, Star-of-Bethlehem, Stock (Gilliflower), Strawflower, Summer Perennial Phlox, Swan River Daisy, Sweet Scabious, Tiger-Flower, Travelers-Tree, Tulip, Victoria Waterlily, Wallflower, Zinnia

The World in Your Garden. Book announced. 729-730, May 1957

See also Azaleas; Bromeliads; Flower Preservation; Gardens; Irises; Orchids; Patent Plants; Puya; Rhododendrons; Roses; Wild Flowers

FLUORESCENT Gems From Davy Jones's Locker. By Paul A. Zahl. 260-271, Aug. 1963

FLYING in the "Blowtorch" Era. By Frederick G. Vosburgh. 281-322, Sept. 1950

FLYING MAMMALS:

"Flying" Squirrels, Nature's Gliders. By Ernest P. Walker. 663-674, May 1947

Seeking Mindanao's Strangest Creatures. By Charles Heizer Wharton. 389-408, Sept. 1948

Strange Animals of Australia. By David Fleay. Photos by Stanley Breeden. 388-411, Sept. 1963

See also Bats

The **FLYING** Telegraph (Pigeons). By Joseph F. Spears. Official U. S. Army Signal Corps photos. 531-554, Apr. 1947

FOCUSING on the Tournament of Roses. By B. Anthony Stewart and J. Baylor Roberts. 805-816, June 1954

FOLDBOATS:

Squaws Along the Yukon. By Ginny Hill Wood. 245-265, Aug. 1957

FOLGER: Biggest Little Library in the World. By Joseph T. Foster. Photos by B. Anthony Stewart and John E. Fletcher. 411-424, Sept. 1951

FOLK ART:

Early America Through the Eyes of Her Native Artists. By Hereward Lester Cooke, Jr. Paintings by American primitive artists. 356-389, Sept. 1962

Easter Greetings From the Ukrainians. By Robert Paul Jordan. Photos by James A. Sugar. 556-563, Apr. 1972

Mountain Voices, Mountain Days (West Virginia). By Bryan Hodgson. Photos by Linda Bartlett. 118-146, July 1972

FOLK ART—*Continued*

An Ozark Family Carves a Living and a Way of Life. Photos by Bruce Dale. 124-133, July 1975

Pennsylvania's Old-time Dutch Treat. By Kent Britt. Photos by H. Edward Kim. 564-578, Apr. 1973

See also Embroidery; Weaving

FOLK SONGS:

Hunting Folk Songs in the Hebrides. By Margaret Shaw Campbell. 249-272, Feb. 1947

Hunting Musical Game in West Africa. By Arthur S. Alberts. 262-282, Aug. 1951

See also Ozark Plateau

FOLLIARD, EDWARD T.: Author:

Escorting Mona Lisa to America. 838-847, June 1963

FOLLOWING the Ladybug Home. By Kenneth S. Hagen. Photos by Robert F. Sisson. 543-553, Apr. 1970

FOLLOWING the Trail of Lewis and Clark. By Ralph Gray. 707-750, June 1953

FOOD:

Can the World Feed Its People? By Thomas Y. Canby. 2-31, July 1975

Erosion, Trojan Horse of Greece. By F. G. Renner. 793-812, Dec. 1947

4-H Boys and Girls Grow More Food. By Frederick Simpich. 551-582, Nov. 1948

Keeping House in London. By Frances James. 769-792, Dec. 1947

The Revolution in American Agriculture. By Jules B. Billard. Photos by James P. Blair. 147-185, Feb. 1970

School for Survival. By Curtis E. LeMay. 565-602, May 1953

Shad in the Shadow of Skyscrapers. By Dudley B. Martin. Photos by Luis Marden. 359-376, Mar. 1947

See also Cheese and Cheese Making; Fruit and Fruit Growing; Truffles; Vegetables; Wild Foods; *and* Trucks, for food transport

FOOD CHAIN:

Algae: the Life-givers. By Paul A. Zahl. 361-377, Mar. 1974

Can We Save Our Salt Marshes? By Stephen W. Hitchcock. Photos by William R. Curtsinger. 729-765, June 1972

"How Man Pollutes His World," painting supplement. Map of the World. Dec. 1970

Life Springs From Death in Truk Lagoon. By Sylvia A. Earle. Photos by Al Giddings. 578-613, May 1976

Mzima, Kenya's Spring of Life. By Joan and Alan Root. 350-373, Sept. 1971

Quicksilver and Slow Death (Mercury). By John J. Putman. Photos by Robert W. Madden. 507-527, Oct. 1972

Teeming Life of a Pond. By William H. Amos. 274-298, Aug. 1970

FOOTPRINTS on the Moon. By Hugh L. Dryden. Paintings by Davis Meltzer and Pierre Mion. 357-401, Mar. 1964

FORAGING. *See* Wild Foods

FORD, HENRY, MUSEUM, Dearborn, Michigan:

The Past Is Present in Greenfield Village. By Beverley M. Bowie. Photos by Neal P. Davis and Willard R. Culver. 96-127, July 1958

FORD, MILTON A.: Photographer:

900 Years Ago: The Norman Conquest. By Kenneth M. Setton. Photos by George F. Mobley. The complete Bayeux Tapestry photographed by Milton A. Ford and Victor R. Boswell, Jr. 206-251, Aug. 1966

FORD'S THEATRE Reborn in Memory of Lincoln. By Lonnelle Aikman. 392-401, Mar. 1970

FOREST DWELLERS. *See* Cinta Larga Indians; Kreen-Akarores; Tasaday Tribe; Txukahameis

FOREST FIRE: The Devil's Picnic. By Stuart E. Jones and Jay Johnston. 100-127, July 1968

FOREST SERVICE. *See* U. S. Forest Service

FORESTS AND REFORESTATION:

Adobe New Mexico. By Mason Sutherland. Photos by Justin Locke. 783-830, Dec. 1949
Included: Carson National Forest; Santa Fe National Forest

Backwoods Japan During American Occupation. By M. A. Huberman. 491-518, Apr. 1947

Erosion, Trojan Horse of Greece. By F. G. Renner. 793-812, Dec. 1947

The Friendly Train Called Skunk. By Dean Jennings. Photos by B. Anthony Stewart. 720-734, May 1959

From Sagebrush to Roses on the Columbia. By Leo A. Borah. 571-611, Nov. 1952

A Map Maker Looks at the United States. By Newman Bumstead. Photos by U. S. Air Force. 705-748, June 1951
Included: Rain forests, Olympic Peninsula (Washington); Gifford Pinchot National Forest (Washington); the Tillamook (Oregon) burn of 1933; and the Sierra Nevada forests

Our Green Treasury, the National Forests. By Nathaniel T. Kenney. Photos by J. Baylor Roberts. 287-324, Sept. 1956

Timber: How Much Is Enough? By John J. Putman. Photos by Bruce Dale. 485-511, Apr. 1974

See also Giant Forest; Inyo National Forest; Ituri Forest; Jackson Hole, Wyoming; Olympic National Park; Sarawak; *and* Forest Fire; Lumber Industry; National Forests; Paper and Pulp Industry; Rain Forests; Redwoods; *Sequoia gigantea*

FORMOSA. *See* Taiwan

FORMOSA STRAIT, China:

Patrolling Troubled Formosa Strait. 573-588, Apr. 1955

See also Pescadores; Quemoy; Taiwan

FORSYTH, GEORGE H.: Author:

Island of Faith in the Sinai Wilderness (St. Catherine's Monastery). Photos by Robert F. Sisson. 82-106, Jan. 1964

FORT CHURCHILL, Manitoba, Canada:

Rockets Explore the Air Above Us. By Newman Bumstead. 562-580, Apr. 1957

Trailing Cosmic Rays in Canada's North. By Martin A. Pomerantz. 99-115, Jan. 1953

FORT DE FRANCE, Martinique:

Martinique: Liberté, Egalité, and Uncertainty in the Caribbean. By Kenneth MacLeish. Photos by John Launois. 124-148, Jan. 1975

FORT JEFFERSON NATIONAL MONUMENT, Florida:

The Lower Keys, Florida's "Out Islands." By John Scofield. Photos by Emory Kristof and Bates Littlehales. 72-93, Jan. 1971

FORT TERNAN, Kenya:

Adventures in the Search for Man. By Louis S. B. Leakey. Photos by Hugo van Lawick. 132-152, Jan. 1963

FORT TICONDEROGA, New York:

From Sword to Scythe in Champlain Country. By Ethel A. Starbird. Photos by B. Anthony Stewart and Emory Kristof. 153-201, Aug. 1967

North Through History Aboard *White Mist.* By Melville Bell Grosvenor. Photos by Edwin Stuart Grosvenor. 1-55, July 1970

FORTRESSES. *See* Alhambra; Castillo de San Marcos; Castles; Kremlin; Louisbourg; St. Catherine's Monastery; St. Michael's Mount; Vizcaya (Fortress-Palace); *and* Jaisalmer; Languedoc (Region), France, for Cité; Luxembourg; Peru (The Five Worlds), for Sacsahuamán; Quebec (City)

FORTUNATE ISLANDS. *See* Canary Islands

FORTUNATE ISLES. *See* Scilly, Isles of

FORTUNE TELLING. *See* Dogon

FORTY-NINERS. *See* Golden Ghosts; *and* Death Valley National Monument

FOSFORESCÉNTE, Bahía, Puerto Rico. *See* Phosphorescent Bay

FOSHAG, W. F.: Author:

Exploring the World of Gems. 779-810, Dec. 1950

FOSSEY, DIAN: Author:

Making Friends With Mountain Gorillas. Photos by Robert M. Campbell. 48-67, Jan. 1970

More Years With Mountain Gorillas. Photos by Robert M. Campbell. 574-585, Oct. 1971

FOSSILS:

Fossils Lift the Veil of Time. By Harry S. Ladd and Roland W. Brown. 363-386, Mar. 1956

See also Evolution (In the Wake of Darwin's *Beagle*); Paleontology

FOSTER, JOSEPH T.: Author:

Folger: Biggest Little Library in the World. Photos by B. Anthony Stewart and John E. Fletcher. 411-424, Sept. 1951

FOSTER, MULFORD B.: Author-Photographer:

Puya, the Pineapple's Andean Ancestor. 463-480, Oct. 1950

FOUND at Last: the Monarch's Winter Home. By Fred A. Urquhart. Photos by Bianca Lavies. 161-173, Aug. 1976

FOUNDERS of New England. By Sir Evelyn Wrench. Photos by B. Anthony Stewart. 803-838, June 1953

FOUNDERS of Virginia. By Sir Evelyn Wrench. Photos by B. Anthony Stewart. 433-462, Apr. 1948

FOUNTAIN of Fire in Hawaii. By Frederick Simpich, Jr. Photos by Robert B. Goodman and Robert Wenkam. 303-327, Mar. 1960

FOUR CORNERS COUNTRY (Utah-Colorado-Arizona-New Mexico):

Roaming the West's Fantastic Four Corners. By Jack Breed. 705-742, June 1952

Stalking the West's Wild Foods. By Euell Gibbons. Photos by David Hiser. 186-199, Aug. 1973

See also Mesa Verde National Park; Rainbow Bridge National Monument; *and* Navajos

4-H CLUBS:

America Goes to the Fair. By Samuel W. Matthews. 293-333, Sept. 1954

4-H Boys and Girls Grow More Food. By Frederick Simpich. 551-582, Nov. 1948

FOUR-OCEAN Navy in the Nuclear Age. By Thomas W. McKnew. 145-187, Feb. 1965

A **FOUR-PART** Look at the Isles of the Pacific. 732-793, Dec. 1974

FOUR Years of Diving to the Bottom of the Sea. By Georges S. Houot. 715-731, May 1958

"1470 MAN." *See* Skull 1470

FOWL:

Scientist Studies Japan's Fantastic Long-tailed Fowl. By Frank X. Ogasawara. Photos by Eiji Miyazawa. 845-855, Dec. 1970

See also Poultry; Sea Birds

FOX, CHARLES J.:

Portrait of Gilbert H. Grosvenor. 252, 258, Aug. 1949

FOX, CHARLES PHILIP: Photographer:

Br'er Possum, Hermit of the Lowlands. By Agnes Akin Atkinson. 405-418, Mar. 1953

Skunks Want Peace—or Else! By Melvin R. Ellis. 279-294, Aug. 1955

FOXES:

Foxes Foretell the Future in Mali's Dogon Country. By Pamela Johnson Meyer. 431-448, Mar. 1969

The Romance of American Furs. By Wanda Burnett. 379-402, Mar. 1948

The **FRAGILE** Beauty All About Us. Photos by Harry S. C. Yen. 785-795, Dec. 1970

FRAGILE Nurseries of the Sea: Can We Save Our Salt Marshes? By Stephen W. Hitchcock. Photos by William R. Curtsinger. 729-765, June 1972

FRANCE:

Across the Ridgepole of the Alps. By Walter Meayers Edwards. 410-419, Sept. 1960

The Alps: Man's Own Mountains. By Ralph Gray. Photos by Walter Meayers Edwards and William Eppridge. 350-395, Sept. 1965
    Included: Mont Blanc highway tunnel, from Haute Savoie, France, to Valle d'Aosta, Italy

"Around the World in Eighty Days." By Newman Bumstead. 705-750, Dec. 1951
    Included: Avignon; Corsica; Lyon; Marseille; Mont Blanc; Montpellier; Paris

The Diffident Truffle, France's Gift to Gourmets. 419-426, Sept. 1956

The Enduring Pyrenees. By Robert Laxalt. Photos by Edwin Stuart Grosvenor. 794-819, Dec. 1974

FRANCE—*Continued*

Eternal France. By Walter Meayers Edwards. 725-764, June 1960

Exploring the Mind of Ice Age Man. By Alexander Marshack. 64-89, Jan. 1975

France, Belgium, and the Netherlands, Atlas series supplement. June 1960

France's Past Lives in Languedoc. By Walter Meayers Edwards. 1-43, July 1951

French Riviera: Storied Playground on the Azure Coast. By Carleton Mitchell. Photos by Thomas Nebbia. 798-835, June 1967

High Road in the Pyrenees. By H. V. Morton. Photos by Justin Locke. 299-334, Mar. 1956

Inside Europe Aboard *Yankee.* By Irving and Electa Johnson. Photos by Joseph J. Scherschel. 157-195, Aug. 1964

Land of the Ancient Basques. By Robert Laxalt. Photos by William Albert Allard. 240-277, Aug. 1968

Life in the Land of the Basques. By John E. H. Nolan. Photos by Justin Locke. 147-186, Feb. 1954

A New Look at Medieval Europe. By Kenneth M. Setton. Paintings by Andre Durenceau and Birney Lettick. 799-859, Dec. 1962

900 Years Ago: The Norman Conquest. By Kenneth M. Setton. Photos by George F. Mobley. 206-251, Aug. 1966

Paris to Antwerp with the Water Gypsies. By David S. Boyer. 530-559, Oct. 1955

Pigeon Netting—Sport of Basques. Photos by Irene Burdett-Scougall. 405-416, Sept. 1949

Sheep Trek in the French Alps. By Maurice Moyal. Photos by Marcel Coen. 545-564, Apr. 1952

A Traveler's Map of France, map supplement. Text on reverse. June 1971

When the President Goes Abroad (Eisenhower Tour). By Gilbert M. Grosvenor. 588-649, May 1960

See also Auvergne; Brittany; Camargue (Region); Chartres; Corsica; Ice Caves (Pyrenees); Lascaux Cave; Loire River and Valley; Martinique; Normandy; Ouessant, Ile d'; Paris; Provence; St. Pierre and Miquelon; Saint Véran; Strasbourg; Vézelay; *and* Crusades; French Impressionists

FRANKLIN, BENJAMIN:

Benjamin Franklin, Philosopher of Dissent. By Alice J. Hall. Photos by Linda Bartlett. 93-123, July 1975

FRANKLIN, WILLIAM L.: Author-Photographer:

High, Wild World of the Vicuña. 77-91, Jan. 1973

FRANKLIN L. BURR PRIZE:

Burr Prizes Awarded to Dr. Edgerton and Dr. Van Biesbroeck. 705-706, May 1953

FRANZÉN, ANDERS: Author:

Ghost From the Depths: the Warship *Vasa.* 42-57, Jan. 1962

FRASER, LAURA GARDIN:

Designer of NGS Medals: Grosvenor Medal. 255, 261, Aug. 1949; 422, Mar. 1957; 516, Oct. 1963; Hubbard Medal. 564, Apr. 1953; Special Medal of Honor. 45, July 1957

FRAZER, JOHN E.: Author:

India's Energetic Sikhs. Photos by James P. Blair. 528-541, Oct. 1972

FRAZER, JOHN E.: Author—*Continued*

Kuwait, Aladdin's Lamp of the Middle East. Photos by David F. Cupp. 636-667, May 1969

FRAZIER, PAUL W.: Author:

Across the Frozen Desert to Byrd Station. Photos by Calvin L. Larsen. 383-398, Sept. 1957

FREDERICK G. VOSBURGH Retires as Editor; Gilbert M. Grosvenor Succeeds Him. By Melvin M. Payne. 838-843, Dec. 1970

FREDERICKSBURG, Virginia:

Dog Mart Day in Fredericksburg. By Frederick G. Vosburgh. 817-832, June 1951

FREEDOM Flight from Hungary. Photos by Robert F. Sisson. 424-436, Mar. 1957

FREEDOM 7 (Spacecraft). *See* Mercury Missions

FREEDOM Speaks French in Ouagadougou. By John Scofield. 153-203, Aug. 1966

FREEDOM TRAIN Tours America. 529-542, Oct. 1949

FREEDOM'S Progress South of the Sahara. By Howard La Fay. Photos by Joseph J. Scherschel. 603-637, Nov. 1962

FREEING Flamingos From Anklets of Death. By John G. Williams. Photos by Alan Root. 934-944, Dec. 1963

FREETOWN, Sierra Leone:

The Loyalists. By Kent Britt. Photos by Ted Spiegel. 510-539, Apr. 1975

Note: Slaves of Patriot colonists, liberated by the British during the American Revolution, founded Freetown after the war.

FREEZING the Flight of Hummingbirds. By Harold E. Edgerton, R. J. Niedrach, and Walker Van Riper. 245-261, Aug. 1951

FREEZING the Trout's Lightning Leap. By Treat Davidson. 525-530, Apr. 1958

FREHSEE, RICK: Photographer:

Strange March of the Spiny Lobster. By William F. Herrnkind. Photos by Rick Frehsee and Bruce Mounier. 819-831, June 1975

FREIDEL, FRANK B., Jr.: Author:

Profiles of the Presidents.
I. The Presidency and How It Grew. 642-687, Nov. 1964
II. A Restless Nation Moves West. 80-121, Jan. 1965
III. The American Giant Comes of Age. 660-711, May 1965
IV. America Enters the Modern Era. 537-577, Oct. 1965
V. The Atomic Age: Its Problems and Promises. 66-119, Jan. 1966

FRENCH-AMERICAN MID-OCEAN UNDERSEA STUDY. *See* FAMOUS

FRENCH CANADIAN PROVINCE. *See* Quebec

FRENCH EQUATORIAL AFRICA:

Freedom Speaks French in Ouagadougou. By John Scofield. 153-203, Aug. 1966

Included: Central African Republic; Chad; Gabon

FRENCH IMPRESSIONISTS:

Great Masters of a Brave Era in Art. By Hereward

FRENCH IMPRESSIONISTS — *Continued*

Lester Cooke, Jr. 661-697, May 1961

In Quest of Beauty. Text by Paul Mellon. 372-385, Mar. 1967

FRENCH NAVY. *See F.N.R.S. 3; and* Fish Men Discover; Fish Men Explore a New World, for Undersea Research Group

FRENCH POLYNESIA. *See* Marquesas Islands; Society Islands; Tuamotu Archipelago

FRENCH RIVIERA: Storied Playground on the Azure Coast. By Carleton Mitchell. Photos by Thomas Nebbia. 798-835, June 1967

FRENCH SUDAN. *See* Mali

FRENCH WEST AFRICA:

Freedom Speaks French in Ouagadougou. By John Scofield. 153-203, Aug. 1966
Included: Dahomey; Guinea; Ivory Coast; Mali; Mauritania; Niger; Senegal
See also Mali; Mauritania; Niger; *and* Tuareg

FRESCOES. *See* Cappadocia; Cave Art; Italy (Etruscan Past); Minoan Civilization

A FRESH Breeze Stirs the Leewards. By Carleton Mitchell. Photos by Winfield Parks. 488-537, Oct. 1966

FRESH Treasures from Egypt's Ancient Sands. By Jefferson Caffery. Photos by David S. Boyer. 611-650, Nov. 1955

FRESHWATER PRESERVE, Proposed. *See* Big Cypress Swamp, Florida

FRIEDMAN, HERBERT: Author:
The Sun. 713-743, Nov. 1965

FRIEDMANN, HERBERT: Author:
Honey-Guide: The Bird That Eats Wax. Paintings by Walter A. Weber. 551-560, Apr. 1954

FRIEND of the Wind: The Common Tern. By Ian Nisbet. Photos by Hope Alexander. 234-247, Aug. 1973

FRIENDLESS Squatters of the Sea. By Ethel A. Starbird. Photos by Robert F. Sisson. 623-633, Nov. 1973

FRIENDLY, ALFRED: Author:
Africa's Bushman Art Treasures. Photos by Alex R. Willcox. 848-865, June 1963

FRIENDLY Flight to Northern Europe. By Lyndon B. Johnson. Photos by Volkmar Wentzel. 268-293, Feb. 1964

The FRIENDLY Huts of the White Mountains. By William O. Douglas. Photos by Kathleen Revis. 205-239, Aug. 1961

The FRIENDLY Irish. By John Scofield. Photos by James A. Sugar. 354-391, Sept. 1969

The FRIENDLY Isles of Tonga. By Luis Marden. 345-367, Mar. 1968

The FRIENDLY Train Called Skunk. By Dean Jennings. Photos by B. Anthony Stewart. 720-734, May 1959

FRIENDSHIP 7 (Spacecraft). *See* Mercury Missions

FROBISHER BAY, Canada. *See* Baffin Island

FROGS:

Bullfrog Ballet Filmed in Flight. By Treat Davidson. 791-799, June 1963

Capturing Strange Creatures in Colombia. By Marte Latham. Photos by Tor Eigeland. 682-693, May 1966

Eden in the Outback. By Kay and Stanley Breeden. 189-203, Feb. 1973

In Quest of the World's Largest Frog. By Paul A. Zahl. 146-152, July 1967

Nature's Living, Jumping Jewels. By Paul A. Zahl. 130-146, July 1973
Contents: Miniature tropical frogs of Costa Rica

Teeming Life of a Pond. By William H. Amos. 274-298, Aug. 1970

Voices of the Night. By Arthur A. Allen. 507-522, Apr. 1950
Contents: Anderson's tree frog, Barking tree frog, Bird-voiced tree frog, Bullfrog, Canadian toad, Carpenter frog, Common toad, Common tree toad, Green frog, Green tree frog, Leopard or Meadow frog, Oak toad, Peeper, Pickerel frog, Pygmy swamp cricket frog, Spadefoot toad, Squirrel tree frog, Western toad

FROM Amazon to Spanish Main: Colombia. By Loren McIntyre. 235-273, Aug. 1970

FROM America to Mecca on Airborne Pilgrimage. By Abdul Ghafur Sheikh. 1-60, July 1953

FROM Baltic to Bicentennial by Square Rigger. By Kenneth Garrett. 824-857, Dec. 1976

FROM Barra to Butt in the Hebrides. By Isobel Wylie Hutchison. 559-580, Oct. 1954

FROM Graveyard to Garden (Truk Lagoon). Photos by Al Giddings. 604-613, May 1976

FROM Indian Canoes to Submarines at Key West. By Frederick Simpich. Photos by J. Baylor Roberts. 41-72, Jan. 1950

FROM Sagebrush to Roses on the Columbia. By Leo A. Borah. 571-611, Nov. 1952

FROM Sea to Sahara in French Morocco. By Jean and Franc Shor. 147-188, Feb. 1955

FROM Sea to Shining Sea: A Cross Section of the United States Along Historic Route 40. By Ralph Gray. Photos by Dean Conger and author. 1-61, July 1961

FROM Spear to Hoe on Groote Eylandt. By Howell Walker. 131-142, Jan. 1953

FROM Sun-clad Sea to Shining Mountains. By Ralph Gray. Photos by James P. Blair. 542-589, Apr. 1964

FROM Sword to Scythe in Champlain Country. By Ethel A. Starbird. Photos by B. Anthony Stewart and Emory Kristof. 153-201, Aug. 1967

FROM the Bahamas to Belize: Probing the Deep Reefs' Hidden Realm. By Walter A. Starck II and Jo D. Starck. 867-886, Dec. 1972

FROM the Hair of Siva. By Helen and Frank Schreider. 445-503, Oct. 1960

FROM Tucson to Tombstone. By Mason Sutherland. 343-384, Sept. 1953

FRONTIER HISTORY, U. S.:
A Restless Nation Moves West. By Frank Freidel.

FRONTIER HISTORY, U. S. — *Continued*

Paintings from the White House Collection. 80-121, Jan. 1965

So Long, St. Louis, We're Heading West. By William C. Everhart. 643-669, Nov. 1965

See also Arizona (From Tucson to Tombstone); Hays, Kansas; Outlaw Trail

FROST, ROBERT:

Robert Frost and New England. By Archibald MacLeish. 438-467, Apr. 1976
Look of a Land Beloved. Photos by Dewitt Jones. 444-467

FROST, Nature's Icing. By Robert F. Sisson. 398-405, Mar. 1976

FRUIT AND FRUIT GROWING:

California, Horn of Plenty. By Frederick Simpich. Photos by Willard R. Culver. 553-594, May 1949

How Fruit Came to America. By J. R. Magness. Paintings by Else Bostelmann. 325-377, Sept. 1951
Contents: American Plum, Apple, Apricot, Avocado, Banana, Blackberry, Blueberry, Cherry, Cranberry, Currant, Date, Fig, Gooseberry, Grape, Grapefruit, Japanese Plum, Lemon, Lime, Mango, Olive, Orange, Papaya, Peach, Pear, Persimmon, Pineapple, Plum, Prune, Quince, Raspberry, Strawberry

Our Life on a Border Kibbutz. By Carol and Al Abrams. Photos by Al Abrams. 364-391, Sept. 1970

Our Vegetable Travelers. By Victor R. Boswell. Paintings by Else Bostelmann. 145-217, Aug. 1949
Included: Watermelon, Muskmelon

Patent Plants Enrich Our World. By Orville H. Kneen. Photos from U. S. Plant Patents. 357-378, Mar. 1948

The Wasp That Plays Cupid to a Fig. By Robert F. Sisson. 690-697, Nov. 1970

The World in Your Garden. Book announced. 729-730, May 1957

See also Breadfruit; Citrus Fruits; Date Raising; Grapes and Grape Culture; Pineapples and Pineapple Growing

FUCHS, SIR VIVIAN:

Society Honors the Conquerors of Antarctica. 589-590, Apr. 1959

Author

The Crossing of Antarctica. Photos by George Lowe. 25-47, Jan. 1959

FUEGIAN INDIANS:

In the Wake of Darwin's *Beagle*. By Alan Villiers. Photos by James L. Stanfield. 449-495, Oct. 1969

FUELS, Fossil. *See* Coal; Natural Gas; Oil

FULANI (Tribespeople):

The Niger: River of Sorrow, River of Hope. By Georg Gerster. 152-189, Aug. 1975

FULLER, BUCKMINSTER: Author:

Five Noted Thinkers Explore the Future. 72-73, July 1976

FUN Helped Them Fight (Bombing Squadrons). By Stuart E. Jones. 95-104, Jan. 1948

FUNAI. *See* listing under National Foundation for the Indian

FUNAN, Kingdom of:

Mosaic of Cultures (Southeast Asia). By Peter T. White. Photos by W. E. Garrett. 296-329, Mar. 1971
See also Angkor, for Khmers

FUNCHAL, Madeira:

Madeira, Like Its Wine, Improves With Age. By Veronica Thomas. Photos by Jonathan Blair. 488-513, Apr. 1973

FUNDY, Bay of, Canada:

The Giant Tides of Fundy. By Paul A. Zahl. 153-192, Aug. 1957

FUNERALS:

Gangtok, Cloud-wreathed Himalayan Capital. By John Scofield. 698-713, Nov. 1970
Included: The funeral of Princess Sonam Padaun

Life and Death in Tana Toradja. By Pamela and Alfred Meyer. 793-815, June 1972

New Orleans and Her River. By Joseph Judge. Photos by James L. Stanfield. 151-187, Feb. 1971
Included: Jazz funeral

See also Banaras, India, for funeral ghats; Nambas; *and* Burial Customs

FUNERALS, State. *See* Churchill, Sir Winston; Eisenhower, Dwight D.; Kennedy, John F.

FUNGI:

Bizarre World of the Fungi. By Paul A. Zahl. 502-527, Oct. 1965
See also Truffles

FUNK, TED H.: Photographer:

Democracy's Fortress: Unsinkable Malta. By Ernle Bradford. 852-879, June 1969

Luxembourg, the Quiet Fortress. By Robert Leslie Conly. 69-97, July 1970

The Manx and Their Isle of Man. By Veronica Thomas. 426-444, Sept. 1972

San Marino, Little Land of Liberty. By Donna Hamilton Shor. 233-251, Aug. 1967

FURS:

The Fur Seal Herd Comes of Age. By Victor B. Scheffer and Karl W. Kenyon. 491-512, Apr. 1952

Life or Death for the Harp Seal. By David M. Lavigne. Photos by William R. Curtsinger. 129-142, Jan. 1976

Men, Moose, and Mink of Northwest Angle. By William H. Nicholas. Photos by J. Baylor Roberts. 265-284, Aug. 1947

The Romance of American Furs. By Wanda Burnett. 379-402, Mar. 1948

FUTAGAMI JIMA (Island), Japan:

Living in a Japanese Village. By William Graves. Photos by James L. Stanfield. 668-693, May 1972

FYN (Island), Denmark:

By Full-rigged Ship to Denmark's Fairyland. By Alan Villiers. Photos by Alexander Taylor and author. 809-828, Dec. 1955

G

The **GI** and the Kids of Korea. By Robert H. Mosier. 635-664, May 1953

GABON:

Ambassadors of Good Will: The Peace Corps. By Sargent Shriver and Peace Corps Volunteers. 297-345, Sept. 1964
Gabon. By John F. Murphy, Jr. 325-329

GAELS:

The Highlands, Stronghold of Scottish Gaeldom. By Kenneth MacLeish. Photos by Winfield Parks. 398-435, Mar. 1968
Isles on the Edge of the Sea: Scotland's Outer Hebrides. By Kenneth MacLeish. Photos by Thomas Nebbia. 676-711, May 1970
Scotland's Inner Hebrides: Isles of the Western Sea. By Kenneth MacLeish. Photos by R. Stephen Uzzell III. 690-717, Nov. 1974

GAHAN, GORDON W.: Photographer:

Captain Cook: The Man Who Mapped the Pacific. By Alan Villiers. 297-349, Sept. 1971
Drought Bedevils Brazil's Sertão. By John Wilson. 704-723, Nov. 1972
East Germany: The Struggle to Succeed. By John J. Putman. 295-329, Sept. 1974
In Search of Man's Past at Lake Rudolf. By Richard E. Leakey. 712-734, May 1970
Israel—The Seventh Day. By Joseph Judge. 816-855, Dec. 1972
Maui, Where Old Hawaii Still Lives. By Kenneth F. Weaver. 514-543, Apr. 1971
The More Paris Changes. . . . By Howell Walker. 64-103, July 1972
Nova Scotia, the Magnificent Anchorage. By Charles McCarry. 334-363, Mar. 1975
Sir Francis Drake. By Alan Villiers. 216-253, Feb. 1975

GALAPAGOS ISLANDS, Pacific Ocean:

The Galapagos, Eerie Cradle of New Species. By Roger Tory Peterson. Photos by Alan and Joan Root. 541-585, Apr. 1967
Giant Tortoises: Goliaths of the Galapagos. By Craig MacFarland. Photos by author and Jan MacFarland. 632-649, Nov. 1972
Included: Española; Isabela; Pinzón; Santa Cruz
In the Wake of Darwin's Beagle. By Alan Villiers. Photos by James L. Stanfield. 449-495, Oct. 1969
Lost World of the Galapagos. By Irving and Electa Johnson. 681-703, May 1959
Robin Sails Home. By Robin Lee Graham. 504-545, Oct. 1970
The Yankee's Wander-world. By Irving and Electa Johnson. 1-50, Jan. 1949

GALDIKAS-BRINDAMOUR, BIRUTÉ: Author:

Orangutans, Indonesia's "People of the Forest." Photos by Rod Brindamour. 444-473, Oct. 1975

GALILEE (Region), Israel:

The Land of Galilee. By Kenneth MacLeish. Photos by B. Anthony Stewart. 832-865, Dec. 1965
Where Jesus Walked. By Howard La Fay. Photos by Charles Harbutt. 739-781, Dec. 1967

GALILEO GALILEI:

The Renaissance Lives On in Tuscany. By Luis Marden. Photos by Albert Moldvay. 626-659, Nov. 1974

GALLATIN COUNTY, Illinois. See Shawneetown

GALLEONS AND GALLEASSES:

Drowned Galleons Yield Spanish Gold. By Kip Wagner. Photos by Otis Imboden. 1-37, Jan. 1965
See also Atocha; Girona

GALLINAZO CULTURE:

Finding the Tomb of a Warrior-God. By William Duncan Strong. Photos by Clifford Evans, Jr. 453-482, Apr. 1947

The GAMBIA:

Freedom Speaks French in Ouagadougou. By John Scofield. 153-203, Aug. 1966

GAME FISH. See Sailfish; Salmon; Trout

GAME PRESERVES:

Roaming Africa's Unfenced Zoos. By W. Robert Moore. 353-380, Mar. 1950
Safari from Congo to Cairo. By Elsie May Bell Grosvenor. Photos by Gilbert Grosvenor. 721-771, Dec. 1954
Safari Through Changing Africa. By Elsie May Bell Grosvenor. Photos by Gilbert Grosvenor. 145-198, Aug. 1953
White Magic in the Belgian Congo. By W. Robert Moore. 321-362, Mar. 1952
See also National Parks; and listing under Wildlife Refuges

GAMES. See Highland Games; Olympic Games; Sports; and Marostica, Italy, for Chess; Pennsylvania Dutch (Folk Festival)

GANDHI, MOHANDAS KARAMCHAND:

Delhi, Capital of a New Dominion. By Phillips Talbot. Photos by Volkmar Wentzel. 597-630, Nov. 1947

GANGES (River), India-Pakistan:

From the Hair of Siva. By Helen and Frank Schreider. 445-503, Oct. 1960
The Ganges, River of Faith. By John J. Putman. Photos by Raghubir Singh. 445-483, Oct. 1971

GANGTOK, Sikkim:

Gangtok, Cloud-wreathed Himalayan Capital. By John Scofield. 689-713, Nov. 1970
Sikkim. By Desmond Doig. 398-429, Mar. 1963
Wedding of Two Worlds. By Lee E. Battaglia. 708-727, Nov. 1963

GANNETS:

Sea Bird Cities Off Audubon's Labrador. By Arthur A. Allen. 755-774, June 1948

GARBISCH COLLECTION:

Early America Through the Eyes of Her Native Artists. By Hereward Lester Cooke, Jr. Paintings by American primitive artists. 356-389, Sept. 1962

GARDENING'S Color Merchants: The Flower Seed Growers. By Robert de Roos. Photos by Jack Fields. 720-738, May 1968

GARDENS:

Nautical Norfolk Turns to Azaleas. By William H. Nicholas. Photos by B. Anthony Stewart. 606-614, May 1947
Our Vegetable Travelers. By Victor R. Boswell. Paintings by Else Bostelmann. 145-217, Aug. 1949

GARDENS — *Continued*

Rhododendron Glories of Southwest Scotland. By David S. Boyer. Photos by B. Anthony Stewart and author. 641-664, May 1954

Rose Aphids. By Treat Davidson. 851-859, June 1961

South Carolina Rediscovered. By Herbert Ravenel Sass. 281-321, Mar. 1953
    Included: Cypress Gardens; Magnolia Gardens; Middleton Gardens; Swan Lake Gardens

Tropical Gardens of Key West. By Luis Marden. 116-124, Jan. 1953

The World in Your Garden (Flowers). By W. H. Camp. Paintings by Else Bostelmann. 1-65, July 1947
    Contents: Gardens of Africa, Australia, China, Colonial America, Egypt, England, France, Greece, Holland, India, Japan, the Mediterranean region, Mexico, Persia, Rome, South America, Spain; *and* Alpine meadow gardens; Botanical gardens; Buddhist gardens; Hanging gardens; Informal gardens; Moslem gardens; Renaissance gardens; Rock gardens; Victory gardens

The World in Your Garden. Book announced. 729-730, May 1957

See also Ardastra; Buttrick Garden; Kew; Longwood Gardens; Sherwood Gardens; *and* Estates and Plantations

GARDIANS (French Cowboys):

The Camargue, Land of Cowboys and Gypsies. By Eugene L. Kammerman. 667-699, May 1956

France's Wild, Watery South, the Camargue. By William Davenport. 696-726, May 1973

GARDNER, Mount, Antarctica:

First Conquest of Antarctica's Highest Peaks. By Nicholas B. Clinch. 836-863, June 1967

GARFIELD, JAMES A.:

The Living White House. By Lonnelle Aikman. 593-643, Nov. 1966

Profiles of the Presidents: III. The American Giant Comes of Age. By Frank Freidel. 660-711, May 1965

GARRETT, KENNETH: Author-Photographer:

By Square-rigger from Baltic to Bicentennial. 824-857, Dec. 1976

GARRETT, W. E.:

National Geographic Photographers Win Top Magazine Awards. 830-831, June 1959
    Author-Photographer

Alaska's Marine Highway: Ferry Route to the North. 776-819, June 1965

The Booming Sport of Water Skiing. 700-711, Nov. 1958

Canada's Heartland, the Prairie Provinces. 443-489, Oct. 1970

The Hmong of Laos: No Place to Run. 78-111, Jan. 1974

Mexico's Little Venice. 876-888, June 1968

Mountaintop War in Remote Ladakh. 664-687, May 1963

Pagan, on the Road to Mandalay. 343-365, Mar. 1971

South to Mexico City. 145-193, Aug. 1968
    Photographer

Burma's Leg Rowers and Floating Farms. Text by David Jeffery. 826-845, June 1974

GARRETT, W. E. — *Continued*

Earthquake in Guatemala. By Bart McDowell. Photos by W. E. Garrett and Robert W. Madden. 810-829, June 1976

Guantánamo: Keystone in the Caribbean. By Jules B. Billard. Photos by W. E. Garrett and Thomas Nebbia. 420-436, Mar. 1961

Life under Shellfire on Quemoy. By Franc Shor. 415-438, Mar. 1959

The Mekong, River of Terror and Hope. By Peter T. White. 737-787, Dec. 1968

Mosaic of Cultures. By Peter T. White. 296-329, Mar. 1971

Pacific Fleet: Force for Peace. By Franc Shor. 283-335, Sept. 1959

Report on Laos. By Peter T. White. 241-275, Aug. 1961

Saigon: Eye of the Storm. By Peter T. White. 834-872, June 1965

South Viet Nam Fights the Red Tide. By Peter T. White. 445-489, Oct. 1961

White Mist Cruises to Wreck-haunted St. Pierre and Miquelon. By Melville Bell Grosvenor. 378-419, Sept. 1967

Zoo Animals Go to School. By Marion P. McCrane. 694-706, Nov. 1956

GARRIOTT, OWEN K.:

Skylab, Outpost on the Frontier of Space. By Thomas Y. Canby. Photos by the nine mission astronauts. 441-469, Oct. 1974

GARTER SNAKES:

Manitoba's Fantastic Snake Pits. By Michael Aleksiuk. Photos by Bianca Lavies. 715-723, Nov. 1975

GARTLEIN, CARL W.: Author:

Unlocking Secrets of the Northern Lights. Paintings by William Crowder. 673-704, Nov. 1947

GAS, Natural. *See* Natural Gas

GASPARILLA CELEBRATION: Tampa, Florida:

America Goes to the Fair. By Samuel W. Matthews. 293-333, Sept. 1954

GASPÉ PENINSULA, Canada:

Quebec's Forests, Farms, and Frontiers. By Andrew H. Brown. 431-470, Oct. 1949

The St. Lawrence, River Key to Canada. By Howard La Fay. Photos by John Launois. 622-667, May 1967

Sea to Lakes on the St. Lawrence. By George W. Long. Photos by B. Anthony Stewart and John E. Fletcher. 323-366, Sept. 1950

GATES, THOMAS S., Jr.:

Secretary of the Navy Thomas S. Gates, Jr. accepts Hubbard Medal for the U. S. Navy Antarctic Expeditions, 1955-1959. 589-590, Apr. 1959

GATEWAY to Westward Expansion. By William C. Everhart. 643-669, Nov. 1965

GAUCHOS:

Argentina: Young Giant of the Far South. By Jean and Franc Shor. 297-352, Mar. 1958

Brazil, Ôba! By Peter T. White. Photos by Winfield Parks. 299-353, Sept. 1962

The Purple Land of Uruguay. By Luis Marden. 623-654, Nov. 1948

GEESE:

Beyond the North Wind With the Snow Goose. By Des and Jen Bartlett. 822-843, Dec. 1973

Bright Dyes Reveal Secrets of Canada Geese. By John and Frank Craighead. 817-832, Dec. 1957

Saving the Nene, World's Rarest Goose. By S. Dillon Ripley. Photos by Jerry Chong. 745-754, Nov. 1965

GEHMAN, RICHARD: Author:

Amish Folk: Plainest of Pennsylvania's Plain People. Photos by William Albert Allard. 227-253, Aug. 1965

GEISHA:

Kansai, Japan's Historic Heartland. By Thomas J. Abercrombie. 295-339, Mar. 1970

GELIDONYA, Cape, Turkey:

Oldest Known Shipwreck Yields Bronze Age Cargo. By Peter Throckmorton. 697-711, May 1962

GEMINI MISSIONS:

America's 6,000-mile Walk in Space. 440-447, Sept. 1965

The Earth From Orbit. By Paul D. Lowman, Jr. 645-671, Nov. 1966

Footprints on the Moon. By Hugh L. Dryden. Paintings by Davis Meltzer and Pierre Mion. 357-401, Mar. 1964

The Making of an Astronaut. By Robert R. Gilruth. 122-144, Jan. 1965

Space Rendezvous, Milestone on the Way to the Moon. By Kenneth F. Weaver. 539-553, Apr. 1966

GEMS:

Brazil's Land of Minerals. By W. Robert Moore. 479-508, Oct. 1948
    Contents: Amethyst, Aquamarine, Citrine, Diamond, Emerald, Morganite, Topaz, Tourmaline
Exploring the World of Gems. By W. F. Foshag. 779-810, Dec. 1950

The Glittering World of Rockhounds. By David S. Boyer. 276-294, Feb. 1974

The Purple Land of Uruguay. By Luis Marden. 623-654, Nov. 1948
    Included: Agates, Amethysts, Quartz
Questing for Gems. By George S. Switzer. 835-863, Dec. 1971
    Included: Gem mining in Africa, Brazil, and Colombia; samplings of the Crown Jewel collections of Great Britain, Iran, and czarist Russia; the history of the Koh-i-noor, Hope, and Orloff diamonds
See also Diamonds; Lapidary Work; Opal Mining

GENERAL ELECTRIC COMPANY:

Drums to Dynamos on the Mohawk. By Frederick G. Vosburgh. Photos by B. Anthony Stewart. 67-110, July 1947

Landsat Looks at Hometown Earth. By Barry C. Bishop. 140-147, July 1976
    Note: GE's Photographic Engineering Laboratory's color-mosaic expertise was combined with Landsat imagery to produce Portrait U.S.A., first color photomosaic of the 48 contiguous states.

Studying Grizzly Habitat by Satellite. By John Craighead. 148-158, July 1976
    Included: GE Image 100 computer system, used with Landsat imagery to produce satellite-computer maps of grizzly bear habitat
See also Tektite II, for undersea equipment

GENERAL MILLS, Inc.: Research and Engineering. See Strato-Lab

The GENERAL SHERMAN: Earth's Biggest Living Thing (Sequoia). 605-608, May 1958

GENERATORS, Wind-driven:

Can We Harness the Wind? By Roger Hamilton. Photos by Emory Kristof. 812-829, Dec. 1975

GENETICS:

The Awesome Worlds Within a Cell. By Rick Gore. Photos by Bruce Dale. Paintings by Davis Meltzer. 355-395, Sept. 1976

GENEVA, Switzerland:

"Around the World in Eighty Days." By Newman Bumstead. 705-750, Dec. 1951

Switzerland, Europe's High-rise Republic. By Thomas J. Abercrombie. 68-113, July 1969

Switzerland Guards the Roof of Europe. By William H. Nicholas. Photos by Willard R. Culver. 205-246, Aug. 1950

GENOA, Italy:

Italian Riviera, Land That Winter Forgot. By Howell Walker. 743-789, June 1963

GENTILI, GINO VINICIO: Author:

Roman Life in 1,600-year-old Color Pictures (Mosaics). Photos by Duncan Edwards. 211-229, Feb. 1957

GEODETIC SURVEY. See Greenland Icecap; Inter-American Geodetic Survey; U. S. Coast and Geodetic Survey

GEODYNAMICS:

Our Home-town Planet, Earth. By F. Barrows Colton. 117-139, Jan. 1952

This Changing Earth. By Samuel W. Matthews. 1-37, Jan. 1973

See also Earthquakes; Faulting; Plate Tectonics; Volcanoes

GEOGRAPHICAL Twins a World Apart. By David S. Boyer. 848-859, Dec. 1958
    Contents: Holy Land and Utah: comparisons between the Dead Sea and Great Salt Lake; the Sea of Galilee and Utah Lake; the two Jordan Rivers; the caves at Qumrān and Black Rock Cave

GEOGRAPHOS (Asteroid). 788-790, Dec. 1956; 27, Jan. 1963; 175, 178, Aug. 1970

GEOLOGY:

Afoot in Roadless Nepal (Geological Survey). By Toni Hagen. 361-405, Mar. 1960

The Earth From Orbit. By Paul D. Lowman, Jr. 645-671, Nov. 1966

Our Continent: A Natural History of North America. Book announced. 572-574, Oct. 1976

Our Home-town Planet, Earth: Examining the Iron-hearted Globe, Science Gains New Knowledge of Earthquakes, Volcanoes, and Earth's Birth and Future. By F. Barrows Colton. 117-139, Jan. 1952

Roaming the West's Fantastic Four Corners. By Jack Breed. 705-742, June 1952

This Changing Earth. By Samuel W. Matthews. 1-37, Jan. 1973

Utah's Arches of Stone. By Jack Breed. 173-192, Aug. 1947

GEOLOGY — *Continued*

Window on Earth's Interior. By Robert D. Ballard. Photos by Emory Kristof. 228-249, Aug. 1976

Contents: Cayman Trough

See also Caves; Earthquakes; Erosion; Geology, Lunar; Geophysical Research; Minerals and Metals; Mountains; Oceanography; Oil; Plate Tectonics; Stone Spheres; Volcanoes; *and* Mohole, Project; White Sands National Monument; Yellowstone National Park; Zion National Park; *and* listing under Canyons; Craters

GEOLOGY, Lunar:

Apollo 15 Explores the Mountains of the Moon. By Kenneth F. Weaver. Photos from NASA. 233-265, Feb. 1972

Awesome Views of the Forbidding Moonscape. 233-239, Feb. 1969

The Climb Up Cone Crater. By Alice J. Hall. Photos by Edgar D. Mitchell and Alan B. Shepard, Jr. 136-148, July 1971

Exploring Taurus-Littrow. By Harrison H. Schmitt. Photos by the crew of Apollo 17. 290-307, Sept. 1973

First Explorers on the Moon: The Incredible Story of Apollo 11. 735-797, Dec. 1969

I. Man Walks on Another World. By Neil A. Armstrong, Edwin E. Aldrin, Jr., and Michael Collins. 738-749

III. The Flight of Apollo 11. By Kenneth F. Weaver. 752-787

IV. What the Moon Rocks Tell Us. By Kenneth F. Weaver. 788-791

Have We Solved the Mysteries of the Moon? By Kenneth F. Weaver. Paintings by William H. Bond. 309-325, Sept. 1973

The Moon Close Up. By Eugene M. Shoemaker. Photos by Ranger 7. 690-707, Nov. 1964

That Orbèd Maiden . . . the Moon. By Kenneth F. Weaver. 207-230, Feb. 1969

GEOLOGY, Space. *See* Mariner Missions (Mariner 10)

GEOPHYSICAL RESEARCH:

How Man-made Satellites Can Affect Our Lives. By Joseph Kaplan. 791-810, Dec. 1957

Science Explores the Monsoon Sea. By Samuel W. Matthews. Photos by Robert F. Sisson. 554-575, Oct. 1967

Scientists Ride Ice Islands on Arctic Odysseys. By Lowell Thomas, Jr. Photos by Ted Spiegel. 670-691, Nov. 1965

Three Months on an Arctic Ice Island. By Joseph O. Fletcher. 489-504, Apr. 1953

See also listing under Geodetic Survey; International Geophysical Year; listing under Meteorology; Oceanography; Plate Tectonics; Seismology; Volcanoes

GEORG STAGE (School Ship):

By Full-rigged Ship to Denmark's Fairyland. By Alan Villiers. Photos by Alexander Taylor and author. 809-828, Dec. 1955

GEORGE, Lake, Alaska:

Alaska's Automatic Lake Drains Itself. 835-844, June 1951

GEORGE WASHINGTON: The Man Behind the Myths. By Howard La Fay. Photos by Ted Spiegel. 90-111, July 1976

See also Washington, George

GEORGETOWN, Washington, D. C.:

Washington: Home of the Nation's Great. By Albert W. Atwood. 699-738, June 1947

Washington's Historic Georgetown. By William A. Kinney. 513-544, Apr. 1953

GEORGIA, LOWELL: Photographer:

Canada's "Now" Frontier. By Robert Paul Jordan. 480-511, Oct. 1976

Hiking the Backbone of the Rockies: Canada's Great Divide Trail. By Mike W. Edwards. 795-817, June 1973

Nebraska . . . the Good Life. By Robert Paul Jordan. 378-407, Mar. 1974

A River Restored: Oregon's Willamette. By Ethel A. Starbird. 816-835, June 1972

GEORGIA:

Around the "Great Lakes of the South." By Frederick Simpich. Photos by J. Baylor Roberts. 463-491, Apr. 1948

Included: Map showing TVA dams

Can We Save Our Salt Marshes? By Stephen W. Hitchcock. Photos by William R. Curtsinger. 729-765, June 1972

Dixie Spins the Wheel of Industry. By William H. Nicholas. Photos by J. Baylor Roberts. 281-324, Mar. 1949

The Greener Fields of Georgia. By Howell Walker. Photos by author and B. Anthony Stewart. 287-330, Mar. 1954

"Pyramids" of the New World. By Neil Merton Judd. 105-128, Jan. 1948

Included: Irene Mound, Mounds of Bartow County, Ocmulgee National Monument

Sea Islands: Adventuring Along the South's Surprising Coast. By James Cerruti. Photos by Thomas Nebbia and James L. Amos. 366-393, Mar. 1971

Skyway Below the Clouds. By Carl R. Markwith. Photos by Ernest J. Cottrell. 85-108, July 1949

Included: Atlanta; Stone Mountain; and the Flying "S" Ranch, at Villa Rica

See also Atlanta; Okefenokee

GEORGIAN S. S. R. *See* Abkhazian A. S. S. R.

GERMAN DEMOCRATIC REPUBLIC (East Germany):

Berlin, on Both Sides of the Wall. By Howard Sochurek. 1-47, Jan. 1970

East Germany: The Struggle to Succeed. By John J. Putman. Photos by Gordon W. Gahan. 295-329, Sept. 1974

GERMAN SETTLERS. *See* Amish; Hutterites; Pennsylvania Dutch

GERMANY:

Germany, Atlas series supplement. June 1959

Included: Postwar occupied areas of Berlin

Masterpieces on Tour (German-owned Paintings). By Harry A. McBride. 717-750, Dec. 1948

Uncle Sam Bends a Twig in Germany. By Frederick Simpich. Photos by J. Baylor Roberts. 529-550, Oct. 1948

What I Saw Across the Rhine. By J. Frank Dobie. 57-86, Jan. 1947

With Uncle Sam and John Bull in Germany. By Frederick Simpich. 117-140, Jan. 1949

See also Berlin; German Democratic Republic; Germany, Federal Republic of; *and* Crusades

GERMANY, Federal Republic of (West Germany):

The Alps: Man's Own Mountains. By Ralph Gray. Photos by Walter Meayers Edwards and William Eppridge. 350-395, Sept. 1965

"Around the World in Eighty Days." By Newman Bumstead. 705-750, Dec. 1951
Included: Darmstadt; Frankfurt; Rothenburg

Bavaria: Mod, Medieval—and Bewitching. By Gary Jennings. Photos by George F. Mobley. 409-431, Mar. 1974

Down the Danube by Canoe. By William Slade Backer. Photos by Richard S. Durrance and Christopher G. Knight. 34-79, July 1965

Modern Miracle, Made in Germany. By Robert Leslie Conly. Photos by Erich Lessing. 735-791, June 1959

The Rhine: Europe's River of Legend. By William Graves. Photos by Bruce Dale. 449-499, Apr. 1967

See also Berlin, West; Dinkelsbühl

GERRHA (Ancient City), Saudi Arabia:

In Search of Arabia's Past. By Peter Bruce Cornwall. 493-522, Apr. 1948

GERSTER, GEORG: Author-Photographer:

Abu Simbel's Ancient Temples Reborn. 724-744, May 1969

The Niger: River of Sorrow, River of Hope. 152-189, Aug. 1975

Saving the Ancient Temples at Abu Simbel. Paintings by Robert W. Nicholson. 694-742, May 1966

Searching Out Medieval Churches in Ethiopia's Wilds. 856-884, Dec. 1970

Threatened Treasures of the Nile. 587-621, Oct. 1963

GETTING to Know the Wild Burros of Death Valley. By Patricia des Roses Moehlman. Photos by Ira S. Lerner and author. 502-517, Apr. 1972

GETTYSBURG, Pennsylvania:

Gettysburg and Vicksburg: the Battle Towns Today. By Robert Paul Jordan. Map notes by Carolyn Bennett Patterson. 4-57, July 1963

GHANA:

Africa: The Winds of Freedom Stir a Continent. By Nathaniel T. Kenney. Photos by W. D. Vaughn. 303-359, Sept. 1960

See also former name, Gold Coast

GHOST From the Depths: the Warship Vasa. By Anders Franzén. 42-57, Jan. 1962

The GHOSTS of Jericho. By James L. Kelso. 825-844, Dec. 1951

GHOSTS of the Gulf Stream: Blue-water Plankton. By William M. Hamner. 530-545, Oct. 1974

GIANT AFRICAN LAND SNAILS:

Formosa—Hot Spot of the East. By Frederick G. Vosburgh. Photos by J. Baylor Roberts. 139-176, Feb. 1950

GIANT BRAZIL. By Peter T. White. Photos by Winfield Parks. 299-353, Sept. 1962

GIANT COMET Grazes the Sun. By Kenneth F. Weaver. 259-261, Feb. 1966

GIANT EARTHWORMS:

Capturing Strange Creatures in Colombia. By

GIANT EARTHWORMS—Continued

Marte Latham. Photos by Tor Eigeland. 682-693, May 1966

GIANT EFFIGIES of the Southwest. By George C. Marshall. 389, Sept. 1952

GIANT FOREST, Sequoia National Park, California:

Giant Sequoias Draw Millions to California Parks. By John Michael Kauffmann. Photos by B. Anthony Stewart. 147-187, Aug. 1959

Saving Earth's Oldest Living Things. By Andrew H. Brown. Photos by Raymond Moulin and author. 679-695, May 1951

GIANT FROGS:

In Quest of the World's Largest Frog. By Paul A. Zahl. 146-152, July 1967

GIANT INSECTS of the Amazon. By Paul A. Zahl. 632-669, May 1959

GIANT KELP, Sequoias of the Sea. By Wheeler J. North. Photos by Bates Littlehales. 251-269, Aug. 1972

GIANT SEQUOIAS Draw Millions to California Parks. By John Michael Kauffmann. Photos by B. Anthony Stewart. 147-187, Aug. 1959

The GIANT TIDES of Fundy. By Paul A. Zahl. 153-192, Aug. 1957

GIANT TORTOISES: Goliaths of the Galapagos. By Craig MacFarland. Photos by author and Jan MacFarland. 632-649, Nov. 1972

GIBBONS, EUELL: Author:

Stalking the West's Wild Foods. Photos by David Hiser. 186-199, Aug. 1973

Stalking Wild Foods on a Desert Isle. Photos by David Hiser. 47-63, July 1972

GIBBONS:

The Ape With Friends in Washington. By Margaretta Burr Wells. 61-74, July 1953

GIBRALTAR:

Gibraltar—Rock of Contention. By Howard La Fay. Photos by Bates Littlehales. 102-121, July 1966

GIBSON, EDWARD G.:

Skylab, Outpost on the Frontier of Space. By Thomas Y. Canby. Photos by the nine mission astronauts. 441-469, Oct. 1974
Author
The Sun As Never Seen Before. 494-503, Oct. 1974

GIDDINGS, AL: Photographer:

Life Springs From Death in Truk Lagoon. By Sylvia A. Earle. 578-613, May 1976
From Graveyard to Garden. 604-613

GIFTS for the Jaguar God. By Philip Drucker and Robert F. Heizer. 367-375, Sept. 1956

GILBERT, SIR WILLIAM:

The British Way. By Sir Evelyn Wrench. 421-541, Apr. 1949

GILBERT GROSVENOR Is Elected Chairman of the Board, John Oliver La Gorce Chosen President and Editor of the National Geographic Society. 65, 65A-65H, 66, July 1954

See also Grosvenor, Gilbert Hovey

GILBERT GROSVENOR'S Golden Jubilee. By Albert W. Atwood. 253-261, Aug. 1949

GILBERT H. GROSVENOR VISITOR CENTER, Russell Cave, Alabama:

Russell Cave Dedicated; New Visitor Center Named for Gilbert H. Grosvenor. 440-442, Sept. 1967

GILBERT ISLANDS, Pacific Ocean. *See* Tarawa

GILGAMESH, Epic of:

Ancient Mesopotamia: A Light That Did Not Fail. By E. A. Speiser. Paintings by H. M. Herget. 41-105, Jan. 1951

GILGIT, Kashmir:

Pakistan, New Nation in an Old Land. By Jean and Franc Shor. 637-678, Nov. 1952

GILL, WILLIAM J.: Author:

Pittsburgh, Pattern for Progress. Photos by Clyde Hare. 342-371, Mar. 1965

GILLES, HELEN TRYBULOWSKI: Author:

Ceylon, Island of the "Lion People." 121-136, July 1948

GILLIARD, E. THOMAS: Author:

Coronation in Katmandu. Photos by Marc Riboud. 139-152, July 1957

Feathered Dancers of Little Tobago. Photos by Frederick Kent Truslow. 428-440, Sept. 1958
Author-Photographer

Exploring New Britain's Land of Fire. 260-292, Feb. 1961

New Guinea's Paradise of Birds. 661-688, Nov. 1951

New Guinea's Rare Birds and Stone Age Men. 421-488, Apr. 1953

Strange Courtship of the Cock-of-the-Rock. 134-140, Jan. 1962

To the Land of the Head-hunters. 437-486, Oct. 1955

GILLIARD, MARGARET: Photographer:

New Guinea's Rare Birds and Stone Age Men. By E. Thomas Gilliard. 421-488, Apr. 1953

GILLIARD EXPEDITIONS:

Exploring New Britain's Land of Fire. By E. Thomas Gilliard. 260-292, Feb. 1961

Feathered Dancers of Little Tobago. By E. Thomas Gilliard. Photos by Frederick Kent Truslow. 428-440, Sept. 1958

New Guinea's Paradise of Birds. By E. Thomas Gilliard. 661-688, Nov. 1951

To the Land of the Head-hunters. By E. Thomas Gilliard. 437-486, Oct. 1955

See also American Museum-Armand Denis Expedition

GILMAN, RAE: Photographer:

Roaming Korea South of the Iron Curtain. By Enzo de Chetelat. 777-808, June 1950

GILRUTH, ROBERT R.: Author:

The Making of an Astronaut. 122-144, Jan. 1965

GIMBEL, PETER R.: Photographer:

By Parachute Into Peru's Lost World. By G. Brooks Baekeland. Photos by author and Peter R. Gimbel. 268-296, Aug. 1964

GIMBEL BROTHERS:

Artists Look at Pennsylvania. By John Oliver La Gorce. 37-56, July 1948

GIRONA (Armada Galleass):

Priceless Relics of the Spanish Armada. By Robert Sténuit. Photos by Bates Littlehales. 745-777, June 1969

GIZA, Pyramids of, Egypt:

Fresh Treasures from Egypt's Ancient Sands. By Jefferson Caffery. Photos by David S. Boyer. 611-650, Nov. 1955

GLACIER BAY NATIONAL MONUMENT, Alaska:

John Muir's Wild America. By Harvey Arden. Photos by Dewitt Jones. 433-461, Apr. 1973

GLACIER NATIONAL PARK, Montana:

Many-splendored Glacierland. By George W. Long. Photos by Kathleen Revis. 589-636, May 1956

Montana, Shining Mountain Treasureland. By Leo A. Borah. 693-736, June 1950

The West Through Boston Eyes. By Stewart Anderson. 733-776, June 1949

GLACIERS:

Alaska's Automatic Lake Drains Itself (Lake George). 835-844, June 1951

Avalanche! (Peru). By Bart McDowell. Photos by John E. Fletcher. 855-880, June 1962

Climbing Our Northwest Glaciers. Photos by Bob and Ira Spring. 103-114, July 1953

Far North with "Captain Mac." By Miriam MacMillan. 465-513, Oct. 1951

First American Ascent of Mount St. Elias. By Maynard M. Miller. 229-248, Feb. 1948

On the Ridgepole of the Rockies. By Walter Meayers Edwards. 745-780, June 1947
Canada's Rocky Mountain Playground. 755-770

Our Navy Explores Antarctica. By Richard E. Byrd. U. S. Navy official photos. 429-522, Oct. 1947

See also Alps; Everest, Mount; Greenland; Himalayas; Ice Ages; Ice Caves (Pyrenees); McKinley, Mount; Olympic National Park; Ruwenzori

GLACIOLOGY:

Alaska's Mighty Rivers of Ice. By Maynard M. Miller. Photos by Christopher G. Knight. 194-217, Feb. 1967

Antarctica's Nearer Side. By Samuel W. Matthews. Photos by William R. Curtsinger. 622-655, Nov. 1971
Included: Glaciological studies of Deception Island

What's Happening to Our Climate? By Samuel W. Matthews. 576-615, Nov. 1976

GLANZMAN, LOUIS S.: Artist:

Patriots in Petticoats. By Lonnelle Aikman. 475-493, Oct. 1975

GLASS, Ancient:

History Revealed in Ancient Glass. By Ray Winfield Smith. Photos by B. Anthony Stewart and Lee E. Battaglia. 346-369, Sept. 1964

GLASS, Stained:

Chartres: Legacy From the Age of Faith. By Kenneth MacLeish. Photos by Dean Conger. 857-882, Dec. 1969

GLASS Menageries of the Sea. By Paul A. Zahl. 797-822, June 1955

GLEN CANYON NATIONAL RECREATION AREA, Arizona-Utah:
Lake Powell: Waterway to Desert Wonders. By Walter Meayers Edwards. 44-75, July 1967

GLENDORA, California:
Southern California's Trial by Mud and Water. By Nathaniel T. Kenney. Photos by Bruce Dale. 552-573, Oct. 1969

GLENN, JOHN H., Jr.:
John Glenn Receives the Society's Hubbard Medal. 827, June 1962
John Glenn's Three Orbits in *Friendship 7:* A Minute-by-Minute Account of America's First Orbital Space Flight. By Robert B. Voas. 792-827, June 1962

GLIDERS. *See* Sailplanes

The GLITTERING World of Rockhounds. By David S. Boyer. 276-294, Feb. 1974

GLOB, P. V.: Author:
Lifelike Man Preserved 2,000 Years in Peat. 419-430, Mar. 1954

GLOBE, Great: Explorers Hall, NGS:
12-foot globe. 673-675, 677, 679, May 1964; 880, Dec. 1964; 578-579, Oct. 1967

GLOBES, NGS:
First. 698-701, 716, May 1961; 580, 581, Oct. 1967
Manufacturer of NGS globes. 874-875, 876-878, Dec. 1961
National Geographic Physical Globe announced. 736, Nov. 1971
Number sold (265,000). 585, Oct. 1967
16-inch globe and 12-inch globe. 897, Dec. 1962
16-inch globe presented to Mrs. Lyndon B. Johnson. 676, 679, May 1964; 584, Oct. 1967

GLOMAR CHALLENGER (Deep Sea Drilling Project Ship):
This Changing Earth. By Samuel W. Matthews. 1-37, Jan. 1973

GLOUCESTER, Massachusetts:
Gloucester Blesses Its Portuguese Fleet. By Luis Marden. 75-84, July 1953
Windjamming Around New England. By Tom Horgan. Photos by Robert F. Sisson. 141-169, Aug. 1950

GLOWWORMS (Beetle Larvae):
Nature's Night Lights: Probing the Secrets of Bioluminescence. By Paul A. Zahl. 45-69, July 1971

GLUECK, NELSON: Author:
An Archeologist Looks at Palestine. 739-752, Dec. 1947

GLYPHS:
The Maya. 729-811, Dec. 1975
I. Children of Time. By Howard La Fay. Photos by David Alan Harvey. 729-767
II. Riddle of the Glyphs. By George E. Stuart. Photos by Otis Imboden. 768-791

GOATS:
The Goats of Thunder Hill. By Elizabeth Nicholds.

GOATS—*Continued*
Photos by Robert F. Sisson. 625-640, May 1954
Sheep Trek in the French Alps. By Maurice Moyal. Photos by Marcel Coen. 545-564, Apr. 1952

GOBI (Desert), Asia:
The Caves of the Thousand Buddhas. By Franc and Jean Shor. 383-415, Mar. 1951
Journey to Outer Mongolia. By William O. Douglas. Photos by Dean Conger. 289-345, Mar. 1962

GODDARD, JOHN M.: Author:
Kayaks Down the Nile. 697-732, May 1955

GODIVA, LADY:
The British Way. By Sir Evelyn Wrench. 421-541, Apr. 1949

GODLEY, JOHN, Third Baron Kilbracken. *See* Kilbracken, Lord

GOELL, THERESA: Author-Photographer:
Throne Above the Euphrates. 390-405, Mar. 1961

GOETZ, BERNICE M.: Author-Photographer:
Jungle Jaunt on Amazon Headwaters. 371-388, Sept. 1952

GOGGLE FISHING in California Waters. By David Hellyer. Photos by Lamar Boren. 615-632, May 1949

GOLD AND GOLD MINING:
Along the Yukon Trail. By Amos Burg. 395-416, Sept. 1953
Busy Fairbanks Sets Alaska's Pace. By Bruce A. Wilson. Photos by O. C. Sweet. 505-523, Oct. 1949
Gold, the Eternal Treasure. By Peter T. White. Photos by James L. Stanfield. 1-51, Jan. 1974
Golden Masterpieces. 29-39
Golden Ghosts of the Lost Sierra. By Robert Laxalt. Photos by David Hiser. 332-353, Sept. 1973
Nevada's Mountain of Invisible Gold. By Samuel W. Matthews. Photos by David F. Cupp. 668-679, May 1968
See also Spanish Treasure

GOLD COAST, West Africa:
Hunting Musical Game in West Africa. By Arthur S. Alberts. 262-282, Aug. 1951
See also Ghana

GOLD MEDAL, NGS. *See* Special Gold Medal

GOLD Medal Awarded to Mrs. Robert E. Peary. 148, Jan. 1956

GOLDEN Beaches of Portugal. By Alan Villiers. 673-696, Nov. 1954

GOLDEN COCK-OF-THE-ROCK:
Strange Courtship of the Cock-of-the-Rock. By E. Thomas Gilliard. 134-140, Jan. 1962

GOLDEN EAGLES:
Scotland's Golden Eagles at Home. By C. Eric Palmar. 273-286, Feb. 1954
Sharing the Lives of Wild Golden Eagles. By John Craighead. Photos by Charles and Derek Craighead. 420-439, Sept. 1967

GOLDEN Ghosts of the Lost Sierra. By Robert Laxalt. Photos by David Hiser. 332-353, Sept. 1973

GOLDEN HIND (Sailing Ship):

Sir Francis Drake. By Alan Villiers. Photos by Gordon W. Gahan. 216-253, Feb. 1975

GOLDEN JUBILEES:

Gilbert Grosvenor's Golden Jubilee. By Albert W. Atwood. 253-261, Aug. 1949

La Gorce, John Oliver: Golden Jubilee. 422, 423, Mar. 1957; 442, Mar. 1960

GOLDEN TROUT:

Lake Sunapee's Golden Trout. Photos by Robert F. Sisson. 529-536, Oct. 1950

GOLDFISH:

Those Outlandish Goldfish! By Paul A. Zahl. 514-533, Apr. 1973

GOLDMAN, ERIC F.: Author:

Firebrands of the Revolution. Photos by George F. Mobley. 2-27, July 1974

GOLDSMITHING:

Gold, the Eternal Treasure. By Peter T. White. Photos by James L. Stanfield. 1-51, Jan. 1974
Golden Masterpieces. 29-39

GOLF:

California's Land Apart—the Monterey Peninsula. By Mike W. Edwards. 682-703, Nov. 1972
    Included: Cypress Point Golf Links; Monterey Peninsula Country Club; Pacific Grove Municipal Golf Links; Pebble Beach Golf Links; Spyglass Hill Golf Course
Playing 3,000 Golf Courses in Fourteen Lands. By Ralph A. Kennedy. 113-132, July 1952

GOLIATH FROGS. See Giant Frogs

GOLIATHS of the Galapagos (Giant Tortoises). By Craig MacFarland. Photos by author and Jan MacFarland. 632-649, Nov. 1972

GOMBE STREAM GAME RESERVE, Tanzania:

My Life Among Wild Chimpanzees. By Jane Goodall. Photos by Baron Hugo van Lawick and author. 272-308, Aug. 1963
New Discoveries Among Africa's Chimpanzees. By Baroness Jane van Lawick-Goodall. Photos by Baron Hugo van Lawick. 802-831, Dec. 1965

GONDS (Tribespeople). See Muria Gonds

GOOD-BYE to the Stone Age: Brazil's Txukahameis. Photos by W. Jesco von Puttkamer. 270-283, Feb. 1975

GOOD HOPE, Cape of, South Africa:

Yankee Roams the Orient. By Irving and Electa Johnson. 327-370, Mar. 1951

A GOOD Life on the Potomac. By James L. Stanfield. 470-479, Oct. 1976

GOOD-WILL Ambassadors of the U.S. Navy Win Friends in the Far East. By Franc Shor. Photos by W. E. Garrett. 283-335, Sept. 1959

GOODALE, JANE C.: Author:

Blowgun Hunters of the South Pacific. Photos by Ann Chowning. 793-817, June 1966
Photographer
Expedition to the Land of the Tiwi. By Charles P. Mountford. 417-440, Mar. 1956

GOODALL, JANE:

Miss Goodall and the Wild Chimpanzees (Television film). 831A-831B, Dec. 1965
Author-Photographer
My Life Among Wild Chimpanzees. Photos by Baron Hugo van Lawick and author. 272-308, Aug. 1963
See also Lawick-Goodall, Jane van

GOODALL, RAE NATALIE P.: Author:

Housewife at the End of the World. Photos by James L. Stanfield. 130-150, Jan. 1971

GOODMAN, ROBERT B.: Photographer:

Australia. By Alan Villiers. 309-385, Sept. 1963
Cowes to Cornwall (England). By Alan Villiers. 149-201, Aug. 1961
The Flowers That Say "Aloha." By Deena Clark. 121-131, Jan. 1967
Fountain of Fire in Hawaii. By Frederick Simpich, Jr. Photos by Robert B. Goodman and Robert Wenkam. 303-327, Mar. 1960
Queen Elizabeth Opens Parliament. By W. E. Roscher. 699-707, Nov. 1961
Underwater Archeology: Key to History's Warehouse. By George F. Bass. Photos by Thomas J. Abercrombie and Robert B. Goodman. 138-156, July 1963
Western Samoa, the Pacific's Newest Nation. By Maurice Shadbolt. 573-602, Oct. 1962

The GOONEY BIRDS of Midway. By John W. Aldrich. 839-851, June 1964

GOOSE BAY, Labrador, Newfoundland:

Milestones in My Arctic Journeys. By Willie Knutsen. 543-570, Oct. 1949
    Included: Activities of the Search and Rescue section of the Air Force

GORE, RICK: Author:

The Awesome Worlds Within a Cell. Photos by Bruce Dale. Paintings by Davis Meltzer. 355-395, Sept. 1976
Florida, Noah's Ark for Exotic Newcomers. Photos by David Doubilet. 538-559, Oct. 1976
Seven Giants Who Led the Way. Paintings by Ned Seidler. 401-407, Sept. 1976
Those Fiery Brazilian Bees. Photos by Bianca Lavies. 491-501, Apr. 1976
Twilight Hope for Big Cypress. Photos by Patricia Caulfield. 251-273, Aug. 1976

GORGES. See Asia (Cane Bridges); Dinosaur National Monument, for Green and Yampa Rivers; Languedoc (Region), France, for Gorges du Tarn; Olduvai Gorge; Yangtze (River); and listing under Canyons

GORILLAS:

Face to Face With Gorillas in Central Africa. By Paul A. Zahl. 114-137, Jan. 1960
Growing Up With Snowflake. By Arthur J. Riopelle. Photos by Michael Kuh. 491-503, Oct. 1970
Jambo—First Gorilla Raised by Its Mother in Captivity. By Ernst M. Lang. Photos by Paul Steinemann. 446-453, Mar. 1964
Making Friends With Mountain Gorillas. By Dian Fossey. Photos by Robert M. Campbell. 48-67, Jan. 1970

GORILLAS—*Continued*

More Years With Mountain Gorillas. By Dian Fossey. Photos by Robert M. Campbell. 574-585, Oct. 1971

"Snowflake," the World's First White Gorilla. By Arthur J. Riopelle. Photos by Paul A. Zahl. 443-448, Mar. 1967

GOTLAND (Island), Sweden:

Gotland: Sweden's Treasure Island. By James Cerruti. Photos by Albert Moldvay. 268-288, Aug. 1973

GOULD, ALAN J.: Author:

Again—the Olympic Challenge. 488-513, Oct. 1964

GOVERNMENT:

The British Way: Great Britain's Major Gifts to Freedom, Democratic Government, Science, and Society. By Sir Evelyn Wrench. 421-541, Apr. 1949

See also names of countries

GRADUATION by Parachute. By John E. Fletcher. 833-846, June 1952

GRAHAM, ROBIN LEE: Author-Photographer:

Robin Sails Home. 504-545, Oct. 1970

A Teen-ager Sails the World Alone. 445-491, Oct. 1968

World-roaming Teen-ager Sails On. 449-493, Apr. 1969

GRAN SABANA (Region), Venezuela:

Jungle Journey to the World's Highest Waterfall. By Ruth Robertson. 655-690, Nov. 1949

GRANADA, Spain:

Andalusia, the Spirit of Spain. By Howard La Fay. Photos by Joseph J. Scherschel. 833-857, June 1975

The Changing Face of Old Spain. By Bart McDowell. Photos by Albert Moldvay. 291-339, Mar. 1965

Speaking of Spain. By Luis Marden. 415-456, Apr. 1950

GRAND BANKS, Atlantic Ocean:

Dory on the Banks: A Day in the Life of a Portuguese Fisherman. By James H. Pickerell. 573-583, Apr. 1968

I Sailed with Portugal's Captains Courageous. By Alan Villiers. 565-596, May 1952

Newfoundland Trusts in the Sea. By Gary Jennings. Photos by Sam Abell. 112-141, Jan. 1974

GRAND CANYON, Arizona:

Grand Canyon: Nature's Story of Creation. By Louis Schellbach. Photos by Justin Locke. 589-629, May 1955

Retracing John Wesley Powell's Historic Voyage Down the Grand Canyon. By Joseph Judge. Photos by Walter Meayers Edwards. 668-713, May 1969

Shooting Rapids in Reverse! Jet Boats Climb the Colorado's Torrent Through the Grand Canyon. By William Belknap, Jr. 552-565, Apr. 1962

See also Havasupai Indian Reservation

GRAND CANYON NATIONAL PARK, Arizona:

Grand Canyon: Nature's Story of Creation. By

GRAND CANYON NATIONAL PARK, Arizona—*Continued*

Louis Schellbach. Photos by Justin Locke. 589-629, May 1955

The West Through Boston Eyes. By Stewart Anderson. 733-776, June 1949

GRAND CONGLOUÉ (Island), Mediterranean Sea:

Fish Men Discover a 2,200-year-old Greek Ship. By Jacques-Yves Cousteau. 1-36, Jan. 1954

GRAND COULEE DAM, Washington:

From Sagebrush to Roses on the Columbia. By Leo A. Borah. 571-611, Nov. 1952

Powerhouse of the Northwest (Columbia River). By David S. Boyer. 821-847, Dec. 1974

GRAND TETON NATIONAL PARK, Wyoming:

Cloud Gardens in the Tetons. By Frank and John Craighead. 811-830, June 1948

I See America First. By Lynda Bird Johnson. Photos by William Albert Allard. 874-904, Dec. 1965

Jackson Hole: Good-bye to the Old Days? By François Leydet. Photos by Jonathan Wright. 768-789, Dec. 1976

The West Through Boston Eyes. By Stewart Anderson. 733-776, June 1949

Wildlife Adventuring in Jackson Hole. By Frank and John Craighead. 1-36, Jan. 1956

Wyoming: High, Wide, and Windy. By David S. Boyer. 554-594, Apr. 1966

GRANT, ULYSSES S.:

Appomattox: Where Grant and Lee Made Peace With Honor a Century Ago. By Ulysses S. Grant 3rd. Photos by Bruce Dale. 435-469, Apr. 1965

Profiles of the Presidents: III. The American Giant Comes of Age. By Frank Freidel. 660-711, May 1965

GRANT, ULYSSES S., 3rd: Author:

Appomattox: Where Grant and Lee Made Peace With Honor a Century Ago. Photos by Bruce Dale. 435-469, Apr. 1965

The Civil War. 437-449, Apr. 1961

GRAPES AND GRAPE CULTURE:

How Fruit Came to America. By J. R. Magness. Paintings by Else Bostelmann. 325-377, Sept. 1951

My Life in the Valley of the Moon (California). By H. H. Arnold. Photos by Willard R. Culver. 689-716, Dec. 1948

GRASS-SKIRTED Yap. By W. Robert Moore. 805-830, Dec. 1952

GRASSHOPPERS:

Back-yard Monsters in Color. By Paul A. Zahl. 235-260, Aug. 1952

GRASSHOPPERS, Migratory. *See* Locusts

GRAVEL PICTOGRAPHS:

Giant Effigies of the Southwest. By George C. Marshall. 389, Sept. 1952

Seeking the Secret of the Giants. By Frank M. Setzler. Photos by Richard H. Stewart. 390-404, Sept. 1952

Included: Map of Colorado River Basin, showing sites near Blythe, Ripley, Topock; the Hâ-âk lying site near Gila River Indian Reservation

's GRAVENHAGE (The Hague), Netherlands:
Mid-century Holland Builds Her Future. By Sydney Clark. 747-778, Dec. 1950

GRAVES, WILLIAM: Author:
Bangkok, City of Angels. Photos by John Launois. 96-129, July 1973

California, the Golden Magnet. 595-679, May 1966
I. The South. Photos by Thomas Nebbia. 595-639
II. Nature's North. Photos by James P. Blair and Jonathan S. Blair. 641-679

Denmark, Field of the Danes. Photos by Thomas Nebbia. 245-275, Feb. 1974

Earthquake! (Alaska, 1964). 112-139, July 1964

Finland: Plucky Neighbor of Soviet Russia. Photos by George F. Mobley. 587-629, May 1968

Human Treasures of Japan. Photos by James L. Stanfield. 370-379, Sept. 1972

The Imperiled Giants (Whales). 722-751, Dec. 1976

Iran: Desert Miracle. Photos by James P. Blair. 2-47, Jan. 1975

Living in a Japanese Village. Photos by James L. Stanfield. 668-693, May 1972

Maine's Lobster Island, Monhegan. Photos by Kosti Ruohomaa. 285-298, Feb. 1959

Martha's Vineyard. Photos by James P. Blair. 778-809, June 1961

Mobile, Alabama's City in Motion. Photos by Joseph J. Scherschel and Robert W. Madden. 368-397, Mar. 1968

New Life for the Troubled Suez Canal. Photos by Jonathan Blair. 792-817, June 1975

The Rhine: Europe's River of Legend. Photos by Bruce Dale. 449-499, Apr. 1967

San Francisco Bay, the Westward Gate. Photos by James L. Stanfield. 593-637, Nov. 1969

Tokyo, the Peaceful Explosion. Photos by Winfield Parks. 445-487, Oct. 1964

Washington: The City Freedom Built. Photos by Bruce Dale and Thomas Nebbia. 735-781, Dec. 1964

World's Last Salute to a Great American (Dwight D. Eisenhower). By William Graves and other members of the National Geographic staff. 40-51, July 1969

GRAY, RALPH: Author:
The Alps: Man's Own Mountains. Photos by Walter Meayers Edwards and William Eppridge. 350-395, Sept. 1965

Down the Potomac by Canoe. Photos by Walter Meayers Edwards. 213-242, Aug. 1948

Down the Susquehanna by Canoe. Photos by Walter Meayers Edwards. 73-120, July 1950

From Sun-clad Sea to Shining Mountains. Photos by James P. Blair. 542-589, Apr. 1964

Rhododendron Time on Roan Mountain. 819-828, June 1957

Author-Photographer
Across Canada by Mackenzie's Track. 191-239, Aug. 1955

Following the Trail of Lewis and Clark. 707-750, June 1953

From Sea to Shining Sea: A Cross Section of the United States Along Historic Route 40. Photos by Dean Conger and author. 1-61, July 1961

Labrador Canoe Adventure. By Andrew Brown and Ralph Gray. 65-99, July 1951

GRAY, RALPH: Author-Photographer—*Continued*
Three Roads to Rainbow. 547-561, Apr. 1957

Vacation Tour Through Lincoln Land. 141-184, Feb. 1952

GRAY WHALES:
The California Gray Whale Comes Back. By Theodore J. Walker. 394-415, Mar. 1971

GREAT ANDAMANESE (Negrito Tribe):
The Last Andaman Islanders. By Raghubir Singh. 66-91, July 1975

GREAT BAHAMA BANK, Bahama Islands:
Diving Into the Blue Holes of the Bahamas. By George J. Benjamin. 347-363, Sept. 1970

Strange March of the Spiny Lobster. By William F. Herrnkind. Photos by Rick Frehsee and Bruce Mounier. 819-831, June 1975

GREAT BARRIER REEF, Australia:
Australia. II. The Settled East, the Barrier Reef, the Center. By Alan Villiers. 347-385, Sept. 1963

Australia's Great Barrier Reef. Photos by Valerie and Ron Taylor. 728-741, June 1973

Exploring Australia's Coral Jungle. By Kenneth MacLeish. 743-779, June 1973

Life Cycle of a Coral. By Robert F. Sisson. 780-793, June 1973

On Australia's Coral Ramparts. By Paul A. Zahl. 1-48, Jan. 1957

Queensland: Young Titan of Australia's Tropic North. By Kenneth MacLeish. Photos by Winfield Parks. 593-639, Nov. 1968

GREAT BASIN, U.S.:
Indians of the Far West. By Matthew W. Stirling. Paintings by W. Langdon Kihn. 175-200, Feb. 1948

See also Death Valley National Monument; Great Salt Lake; Mojave Desert

GREAT BRITAIN:
"Be Ye Men of Valour" (Churchill's Life and Funeral). By Howard La Fay. 159-197, Aug. 1965

The Britain That Shakespeare Knew. By Louis B. Wright. Photos by Dean Conger. 613-665, May 1964

British Castles, History in Stone. By Norman Wilkinson. 111-129, July 1947

British Isles, Atlas series supplement. July 1958

The British Isles, map supplement. Apr. 1949

The British Way: Great Britain's Major Gifts to Freedom, Democratic Government, Science, and Society. By Sir Evelyn Wrench. 421-541, Apr. 1949

The Final Tribute (Churchill Funeral). By Carolyn Bennett Patterson. 199-225, Aug. 1965

The Investiture of Great Britain's Prince of Wales. By Allan C. Fisher, Jr. Photos by James L. Stanfield and Adam Woolfitt. 698-715, Nov. 1969

Our Search for British Paintings. By Franklin L. Fisher. 543-550, Apr. 1949

Shakespeare's Britain, map supplement. May 1964

This Britain (Television film). 583, Nov. 1975; cover, Dec. 1975

A Traveler's Map of the British Isles, map supplement. Text on reverse. Apr. 1974

See also England; Scotland; Wales; *and* Arran, Island of; Caldy (Island); Channel Islands; Hebri-

GREAT BRITAIN—*Continued*

des; Ireland, Northern; Lundy (Island); Man, Isle of; Orkney Islands; St. Michael's Mount; Scilly, Isles of; Shetland Islands; Skomer (Island); Skye, Isle of; *and* Gems

GREAT BRITAIN II (Ketch):

By Square-rigger from Baltic to Bicentennial. By Kenneth Garrett. 824-857, Dec. 1976

GREAT DIVIDE TRAIL, Alberta-British Columbia, Canada:

Hiking the Backbone of the Rockies: Canada's Great Divide Trail. By Mike W. Edwards. Photos by Lowell Georgia. 795-817, June 1973
    Included: Banff, Jasper, Kootenay, and Yoho National Parks; Mount Assiniboine, Mount Robson, and Willmore Wilderness Provincial Parks

GREAT INAGUA (Island), Bahamas:

Carib Cruises the West Indies. By Carleton Mitchell. 1-56, Jan. 1948

GREAT LAKES, and Region, U. S.-Canada:

Close-up: U.S.A., Wisconsin, Michigan, and the Great Lakes, map supplement. Text on reverse. Aug. 1973

The Great Lakes: Is It Too Late? By Gordon Young. Photos by James L. Amos and Martin Rogers. 147-185, Aug. 1973

The Great Lakes Region of the United States and Canada, map supplement. Dec. 1953

J. W. Westcott, Postman for the Great Lakes. By Cy La Tour. 813-824, Dec. 1950

New Era on the Great Lakes. By Nathaniel T. Kenney. 439-490, Apr. 1959

New St. Lawrence Seaway Opens the Great Lakes to the World. By Andrew H. Brown. 299-339, Mar. 1959

Northeastern United States, including the Great Lakes Region, Atlas series supplement. Apr. 1959

Relics from the Rapids (Voyageurs). By Sigurd F. Olson. Photos by David S. Boyer. 413-435, Sept. 1963

See also Illinois; Indiana; Michigan; Minnesota; New York; Ohio; Ontario; Wisconsin

GREAT LAMESHUR BAY, St. John (Island), U. S. Virgin Islands. *See* Tektite II

GREAT Masters of a Brave Era in Art. By Hereward Lester Cooke, Jr. 661-697, May 1961

GREAT PLAINS, U. S. *See* Midwest

GREAT RIFT VALLEY, Africa-Asia:

Journey Into the Great Rift: the Northern Half. By Helen and Frank Schreider. 254-290, Aug. 1965

See also Aqaba, Gulf of; Danakil Depression, Ethiopia; Dead Sea; Olduvai Gorge; Red Sea; Rudolf, Lake

The GREAT ST. BERNARD HOSPICE Today. By George Pickow. 49-62, Jan. 1957

GREAT SALT LAKE, Utah:

Geographical Twins a World Apart. By David S. Boyer. 848-859, Dec. 1958
    Included: Great Salt Lake and the Dead Sea

Life in a "Dead" Sea—Great Salt Lake. By Paul A. Zahl. 252-263, Aug. 1967
    Included: Ancient inland sea, Lake Bonneville

Utah's Shining Oasis. By Charles McCarry. Photos by James L. Amos. 440-473, Apr. 1975

GREAT SAND BARRIER REEF, North Carolina-Virginia:

Exploring America's Great Sand Barrier Reef. By Eugene R. Guild. Photos by John E. Fletcher and author. 325-350, Sept. 1947

How We Found the *Monitor.* By John G. Newton. 48-61, Jan. 1975

Lonely Cape Hatteras, Besieged by the Sea. By William S. Ellis. Photos by Emory Kristof. 393-421, Sept. 1969

October Holiday on the Outer Banks. By Nike Anderson. Photos by J. Baylor Roberts. 501-529, Oct. 1955

Our Changing Atlantic Coastline. By Nathaniel T. Kenney. Photos by B. Anthony Stewart. 860-887, Dec. 1962

GREAT SMOKY MOUNTAINS, North Carolina-Tennessee:

Around the "Great Lakes of the South." By Frederick Simpich. Photos by J. Baylor Roberts. 463-491, Apr. 1948

Great Smokies National Park: Solitude for Millions. By Gordon Young. Photos by James L. Amos. 522-549, Oct. 1968

Pack Trip Through the Smokies. By Val Hart. Photos by Robert F. Sisson. 473-502, Oct. 1952

The People of Cades Cove. By William O. Douglas. Photos by Thomas Nebbia and Otis Imboden. 60-95, July 1962

Skyline Trail from Maine to Georgia. By Andrew H. Brown. Photos by Robert F. Sisson. 219-251, Aug. 1949

GREATER BIRDS OF PARADISE:

Feathered Dancers of Little Tobago. By E. Thomas Gilliard. Photos by Frederick Kent Truslow. 428-440, Sept. 1958

GRECO-ROMAN CULTURE. *See* Aphrodisias

GREECE:

The Aegean Isles: Poseidon's Playground. By Gilbert M. Grosvenor. 733-781, Dec. 1958

"Around the World in Eighty Days." By Newman Bumstead. 705-750, Dec. 1951
    Included: Athens; Corinth; Gulf of Korinthiakós; Gulf of Patraïkós; Kallithéa; Piraiévs

Athens to Istanbul. By Jean and Franc Shor. 37-76, Jan. 1956

Classical Lands of the Mediterranean, map supplement. Dec. 1949

Erosion, Trojan Horse of Greece. By F. G. Renner. 793-812, Dec. 1947

Greece and Rome: Builders of Our World. Book announced. 550-567, Oct. 1968

Greece and the Aegean, Atlas series supplement. Dec. 1958

Homeward With Ulysses (Ionian Islands). By Melville Bell Grosvenor. Photos by Edwin Stuart Grosvenor. 1-39, July 1973

In the Footsteps of Alexander the Great. By Helen and Frank Schreider. Paintings by Tom Lovell. 1-65, Jan. 1968

The Isles of Greece: Aegean Birthplace of Western Culture. By Melville Bell Grosvenor. Photos by Edwin Stuart Grosvenor and Winfield Parks. 147-193, Aug. 1972

Jerusalem to Rome in the Path of St. Paul. By David S. Boyer. 707-759, Dec. 1956

Round the World School (ISA). By Paul Antze.

GREECE—*Continued*

Photos by William Eppridge. 96-127, July 1962

War-torn Greece Looks Ahead. By Maynard Owen Williams. 711-744, Dec. 1949

When the President Goes Abroad (Eisenhower Tour). By Gilbert M. Grosvenor. 588-649, May 1960

YWCA: International Success Story. By Mary French Rockefeller. Photos by Otis Imboden. 904-933, Dec. 1963

See also Athens; Crete (Island); Dodecanese (Islands); Olympic Games; Thera (Island)

GREEK ART AND ARCHITECTURE:

Athens: Her Golden Past Still Lights the World. By Kenneth F. Weaver. Photos by Phillip Harrington. 100-137, July 1963

Athens to Istanbul. By Jean and Franc Shor. 37-76, Jan. 1956

The Tower of the Winds. By Derek J. de Solla Price. Paintings by Robert C. Magis. 587-596, Apr. 1967

GREEK ORTHODOX CHURCH:

Hashemite Jordan, Arab Heartland. By John Scofield. 841-856, Dec. 1952

Home to the Holy Land. By Maynard Owen Williams. 707-746, Dec. 1950

On the Winds of the Dodecanese. By Jean and Franc Shor. 351-390, Mar. 1953

Sponge Fishermen of Tarpon Springs. By Jennie E. Harris. 119-136, Jan. 1947

See also St. Catherine's Monastery

GREEKS:

Cyprus Under Four Flags: A Struggle for Unity. By Kenneth MacLeish. Photos by Jonathan Blair. 356-383, Mar. 1973

Sponge Fishermen of Tarpon Springs (Florida). By Jennie E. Harris. 119-136, Jan. 1947

GREELY, A. W.:

Far North with "Captain Mac." By Miriam MacMillan. 465-513, Oct. 1951
Included: Greely Arctic Expedition of 1881-1884

GREEN, RAY O., Jr.: Photographer:

The Swallow-tailed Kite: Graceful Aerialist of the Everglades. 496-505, Oct. 1972

GREEN BAY, Wisconsin:

Wisconsin's Door Peninsula. By William S. Ellis. Photos by Ted Rozumalski. 347-371, Mar. 1969

GREEN MOUNTAINS, Vermont:

Mountains Top Off New England. By F. Barrows Colton. Photos by Robert F. Sisson. 563-602, May 1951

Sugar Weather in the Green Mountains. By Stephen Greene. Photos by Robert F. Sisson. 471-482, Apr. 1954

GREEN RIVER, Wyoming-Colorado-Utah:

Shooting Rapids in Dinosaur Country. By Jack Breed. Photos by author and Justin Locke. 363-390, Mar. 1954

GREEN TURTLES:

Imperiled Gift of the Sea: Caribbean Green Turtle. By Archie Carr. Photos by Robert E. Schroeder. 876-890, June 1967

GREENBERG, IDAZ: Author-Photographer:

Buck Island—Underwater Jewel. By Jerry and Idaz Greenberg. 677-683, May 1971

GREENBERG, JERRY: Author-Photographer:

Buck Island—Underwater Jewel. By Jerry and Idaz Greenberg. 677-683, May 1971

Florida's Coral City Beneath the Sea. 70-89, Jan. 1962

Photographer

Key Largo Coral Reef: America's First Undersea Park. By Charles M. Brookfield. 58-69, Jan. 1962

Sharks: Wolves of the Sea. By Nathaniel T. Kenney. 222-257, Feb. 1968

GREENE, STEPHEN: Author:

Sugar Weather in the Green Mountains. Photos by Robert F. Sisson. 471-482, Apr. 1954

The **GREENER** Fields of Georgia. By Howell Walker. Photos by author and B. Anthony Stewart. 287-330, Mar. 1954

GREENEWALT, CRAWFORD H.:

Author-Photographer

The Hummingbirds. 658-679, Nov. 1960

The Marvelous Hummingbird Rediscovered. 98-101, July 1966

Photographing Hummingbirds in Brazil. 100-115, Jan. 1963

GREENFIELD VILLAGE, Michigan:

The Past Is Present in Greenfield Village (Henry Ford Museum). By Beverley M. Bowie. Photos by Neal P. Davis and Willard R. Culver. 96-127, July 1958

GREENHOUSES. *See* Kew (Royal Botanic Gardens); Longwood Gardens (Du Pont Estate); Scilly, Isles of; *and* Flowers (Flower Seed Growers)

GREENLAND:

Canada, Alaska, and Greenland, map supplement. June 1947

Far North with "Captain Mac." By Miriam MacMillan. 465-513, Oct. 1951
Included: Cape Morris Jesup; Cape York; Disko Island; Etah; Godhavn; Godthaab; Holsteinsborg; Jakobshavn; Nugâtsiaq; Qutdligssat; Refuge Harbor; Sioropaluk; Sukkertoppen; Thule

Greenland Feels the Winds of Change. By John J. Putman. Photos by George F. Mobley. 366-393, Sept. 1975

Greenland's "Place by the Icebergs." By Mogens Bloch Poulsen. Photos by Thomas Nebbia. 849-869, Dec. 1973

I Sailed with Portugal's Captains Courageous. By Alan Villiers. 565-596, May 1952

Milestones in My Arctic Journeys. By Willie Knutsen. 543-570, Oct. 1949

The Peary Flag Comes to Rest. By Marie Peary Stafford. 519-532, Oct. 1954

Vinland Ruins Prove Vikings Found the New World. By Helge Ingstad. 708-734, Nov. 1964

A Visit to the Living Ice Age. By Rutherford Platt. 525-545, Apr. 1957

We Followed Peary to the Pole. By Gilbert Grosvenor and Thomas W. McKnew. 469-484, Oct. 1953

What's Happening to Our Climate? By Samuel W. Matthews. 576-615, Nov. 1976

GREENLAND—*Continued*

See also Greenland Icecap; Thule Air Base; *and* Vikings

GREENLAND ICECAP:

First Woman Across Greenland's Ice. By Myrtle Simpson. Photos by Hugh Simpson. 264-279, Aug. 1967

Nuclear Power for the Polar Regions. By George J. Dufek. 712-730, May 1962

Wringing Secrets from Greenland's Icecap. By Paul-Emile Victor. 121-147, Jan. 1956

GREGORY, ALFRED: Photographer:

Triumph on Everest. 1-63, July 1954
I. Siege and Assault. By Sir John Hunt. 1-43
II. The Conquest of the Summit. By Sir Edmund Hillary. 45-63

GREHAN, FARRELL: Photographer:

Amateur Gardener Creates a New Rose. By Elizabeth A. Moize. 286-294, Aug. 1972

Autumn Flames Along the Allagash. By François Leydet. 177-187, Feb. 1974

The Mazatzal's Harsh but Lovely Land Between. By François Leydet. 161-167, Feb. 1974

Okefenokee, the Magical Swamp. By François Leydet. 169-175, Feb. 1974

The Olympics: Northwest Majesty. By François Leydet. 188-197, Feb. 1974

GRENADA (Island), West Indies:

Carib Cruises the West Indies. By Carleton Mitchell. 1-56, Jan. 1948

Finisterre Sails the Windward Islands. By Carleton Mitchell. Photos by Winfield Parks. 755-801, Dec. 1965

The GRENADINES (Islands), West Indies:

Finisterre Sails the Windward Islands. By Carleton Mitchell. Photos by Winfield Parks. 755-801, Dec. 1965

GREYNOLDS PARK, North Miami Beach, Florida:

New Scarlet Bird in Florida Skies. By Paul A. Zahl. 874-882, Dec. 1967

GRIFFIN, EDWARD I.: Author:

Making Friends With a Killer Whale. 418-446, Mar. 1966

GRIMMER, J. LEAR: Author:

Strange Little World of the Hoatzin. Photos by M. Woodbridge Williams. 391-401, Sept. 1962

GRISWOLD, OLIVER: Author:

An Exotic New Oriole Settles in Florida. By Charles M. Brookfield and Oliver Griswold. 261-264, Feb. 1956

GRIZZLY BEARS:

Grizzly! (Television film). 639A-639B, Nov. 1967

Knocking Out Grizzly Bears For Their Own Good. By Frank and John Craighead. 276-291, Aug. 1960

Studying Grizzly Habitat by Satellite. By John Craighead. 148-158, July 1976

Trailing Yellowstone's Grizzlies by Radio. By Frank Craighead, Jr. and John Craighead. 252-267, Aug. 1966

GROOTE EYLANDT (Island), Australia:

Exploring Stone Age Arnhem Land. By Charles P.

GROOTE EYLANDT (Island), Australia—*Continued*

Mountford. Photos by Howell Walker. 745-782, Dec. 1949

From Spear to Hoe on Groote Eylandt. By Howell Walker. 131-142, Jan. 1953

GROSVENOR, ALEXANDER G. B.: Author:

Midshipmen's Cruise. By William J. Aston and Alexander G. B. Grosvenor. 711-754, June 1948

GROSVENOR, ANNE REVIS. *See* Revis, Anne, for article by

GROSVENOR, DONNA KERKAM:

Author-Photographer

Bali by the Back Roads. By Donna K. and Gilbert M. Grosvenor. 657-697, Nov. 1969

Ceylon, the Resplendent Land. By Donna K. and Gilbert M. Grosvenor. 447-497, Apr. 1966

Miniature Monaco. By Gilbert M. and Donna Kerkam Grosvenor. 546-573, Apr. 1963

Photographer

What's Black and White and Loved All Over? By Theodore H. Reed. 803-815, Dec. 1972

White Tiger in My House. By Elizabeth C. Reed. 482-491, Apr. 1970

GROSVENOR, EDWIN AUGUSTUS:

Literary Landmarks of Massachusetts. By William H. Nicholas. Photos by B. Anthony Stewart and John E. Fletcher. 279-310, Mar. 1950

GROSVENOR, EDWIN STUART: Photographer:

The Enduring Pyrenees. By Robert Laxalt. 794-819, Dec. 1974

Homeward With Ulysses. By Melville Bell Grosvenor. 1-39, July 1973

The Isles of Greece: Aegean Birthplace of Western Culture. By Melville Bell Grosvenor. Photos by Edwin Stuart Grosvenor and Winfield Parks. 147-193, Aug. 1972

North Through History Aboard *White Mist.* By Melville Bell Grosvenor. 1-55, July 1970

South Seas' Tonga Hails a King. By Melville Bell Grosvenor. 322-343, Mar. 1968

GROSVENOR, ELSIE MAY BELL:

First Lady of the National Geographic. By Gilbert Hovey Grosvenor. 101-121, July 1965

To Gilbert Grosvenor: a Monthly Monument 25 Miles High. By Frederick G. Vosburgh and the staff of the National Geographic Society. 445-487, Oct. 1966

Author

Alaska's Warmer Side. 737-775, June 1956

Safari from Congo to Cairo. Photos by Gilbert Grosvenor. 721-771, Dec. 1954

Safari Through Changing Africa. Photos by Gilbert Grosvenor. 145-198, Aug. 1953

GROSVENOR, GILBERT HOVEY:

Board of Trustees, Chairman (1954-1966). 65, 65B, 65D, July 1954; 445, 464, 485, Oct. 1966

Editor (1899-1954). 65, 65B, July 1954; 459, 518, 529, 560, 561, 581, Oct. 1963; 445, Oct. 1966

Gilbert Grosvenor's Golden Jubilee. By Albert W. Atwood. 253-261, Aug. 1949

Grosvenor Medal Presented to Dr. Grosvenor by Charles F. Kettering. 253-255, 260, 261, Aug. 1949; 65G, July 1954; 449, 481, Oct. 1966

GROSVENOR, GILBERT HOVEY—*Continued*

President of NGS (1920-1954). 65, 65B, July 1954

Russell Cave Dedicated; New Visitor Center Named for Gilbert H. Grosvenor. 440-442, Sept. 1967

To Gilbert Grosvenor: a Monthly Monument 25 Miles High. By Frederick G. Vosburgh and the staff of the National Geographic Society. 445-487, Oct. 1966

The two-volume *Book of Birds*, edited by Gilbert H. Grosvenor and Alexander Wetmore. 328, Sept. 1948; 576, 578, Oct. 1963; 554, Oct. 1964; 480, Oct. 1966

Author

First Lady of the National Geographic (Elsie May Bell Grosvenor). 101-121, July 1965

Hydrofoil Ferry "Flies" the Strait of Messina. 493-496, Apr. 1957

The National Geographic Society and Its Magazine: A History. Publication announced. 582A, Oct. 1957; 880, Dec. 1964

The Romance of the Geographic: National Geographic Magazine Observes Its Diamond Anniversary. 516-585, Oct. 1963

Author-Photographer

We Followed Peary to the Pole. By Gilbert Grosvenor and Thomas W. McKnew. 469-484, Oct. 1953

Photographer

Alaska's Warmer Side. By Elsie May Bell Grosvenor. 737-775, June 1956

Alexander Graham Bell Museum: Tribute to Genius. By Jean Lesage. 227-256, Aug. 1956

Norway Cracks Her Mountain Shell. By Sydney Clark. Photos by Gilbert Grosvenor and Ole Friele Backer. 171-211, Aug. 1948

Safari from Congo to Cairo. By Elsie May Bell Grosvenor. 721-771, Dec. 1954

Safari Through Changing Africa. By Elsie May Bell Grosvenor. 145-198, Aug. 1953

Turkey Paves the Path of Progress. By Maynard Owen Williams. 141-186, Aug. 1951

GROSVENOR, MRS. GILBERT HOVEY. *See* Grosvenor, Elsie May Bell

GROSVENOR, GILBERT M.:

Associate Editor (1967-1970). 576, 583, 584, 586-588, Oct. 1967; 843, Dec. 1970; 226, Aug. 1976

Board of Trustees, member (1966-   ). 485, Oct. 1966; 584, 588, Oct. 1967; 843, Dec. 1970; 226, Aug. 1976

Editor (1970-   ). 838-843, Dec. 1970; 226, Aug. 1976

Vice President of NGS (1967-   ). 576, 584, 587, 588, Oct. 1967; 843, Dec. 1970

Author-Photographer

The Aegean Isles: Poseidon's Playground. 733-781, Dec. 1958

Bali by the Back Roads. By Donna K. and Gilbert M. Grosvenor. 657-697, Nov. 1969

Canada's Winged Victory: the *Silver Dart*. 254-267, Aug. 1959

Ceylon, the Resplendent Land. By Donna K. and Gilbert M. Grosvenor. 447-497, Apr. 1966

Helping Holland Rebuild Her Land. By Gilbert M. Grosvenor and Charles Neave. 365-413, Sept. 1954

Miniature Monaco. By Gilbert M. and Donna Kerkam Grosvenor. 546-573, Apr. 1963

GROSVENOR, GILBERT M.—*Continued*

When the President Goes Abroad (Eisenhower Tour). 588-649, May 1960

Yugoslavia's Window on the Adriatic. 219-247, Feb. 1962

Photographer

Copenhagen, Wedded to the Sea. By Stuart E. Jones. 45-79, Jan. 1963

Italian Riviera, Land That Winter Forgot. By Howell Walker. 743-789, June 1963

The Leakeys of Africa: Family in Search of Prehistoric Man. By Melvin M. Payne. 194-231, Feb. 1965

GROSVENOR, MRS. GILBERT M. *See* Grosvenor, Donna Kerkam

GROSVENOR, LILIAN: Author:

Deaf Children Learn to Talk at Clarke School. Photos by Willard R. Culver. 379-397, Mar. 1955

GROSVENOR, MELVILLE BELL:

Board of Trustees, Chairman (1967-1976). 576-577, 584-589, Oct. 1967; 442, Sept. 1970

Board of Trustees, Chairman Emeritus (1976-   ). 225, 226, Aug. 1976

Board of Trustees, member (1945-1967). 65, 65B, 65D, July 1954; 835, Dec. 1959; 882, 883, Dec. 1960; 583, 584, Oct. 1967

Editor (1957-1967). 419-423, Mar. 1957

Editor-in-Chief (1967-   ). 576-577, 584, 586, 589, Oct. 1967; 225, 226, Aug. 1976

President of NGS (1957-1967). 419-423, Mar. 1957

Author

Admiral of the Ends of the Earth (Richard E. Byrd). 36-48, July 1957

Homeward With Ulysses. Photos by Edwin Stuart Grosvenor. 1-39, July 1973

The Isles of Greece: Aegean Birthplace of Western Culture. Photos by Edwin Stuart Grosvenor and Winfield Parks. 147-193, Aug. 1972

The Last Full Measure (Tribute to President Kennedy). 307-355, Mar. 1964

The Nation Honors Admiral Richard E. Byrd (Byrd Memorial Dedication). 567-578, Apr. 1962

National Geographic Society Presents Russell Cave to the American People. 438, Mar. 1958

North Through History Aboard *White Mist*. Photos by Edwin Stuart Grosvenor. 1-55, July 1970

Our Society Welcomes Its 3,000,000th Member. 579-582, Apr. 1962

A Park to Save the Tallest Trees. 62-64, July 1966

Robert V. Fleming, 1890-1967. 526-529, Apr. 1968

Safe Landing on Sable, Isle of 500 Shipwrecks. 398-431, Sept. 1965

South Seas' Tonga Hails a King. Photos by Edwin Stuart Grosvenor. 322-343, Mar. 1968

White Mist Cruises to Wreck-haunted St. Pierre and Miquelon. 378-419, Sept. 1967

World's Tallest Tree Discovered. Photos by George F. Mobley. 1-9, July 1964

Author-Photographer

Around the World and the Calendar with the Geographic: The President's Annual Message. 832-866, Dec. 1959

By Cotswold Lanes to Wold's End. 615-654, May 1948

Corkscrew Swamp—Florida's Primeval Show

GROSVENOR, MELVILLE BELL—*Continued*
Place. 98-113, Jan. 1958
Cuba—American Sugar Bowl. 1-56, Jan. 1947
Photographer
The Leakeys of Africa: Family in Search of Prehistoric Man. By Melvin M. Payne. 194-231, Feb. 1965

GROSVENOR, MRS. MELVILLE BELL. *See* Revis, Anne, for article

GROSVENOR ARCH, Utah. *See* Escalante Canyon

GROSVENOR MEDAL:
Designed by Laura Gardin Fraser. 255, 261, Aug. 1949; 422, Mar. 1957; 516, Oct. 1963
Recipients
Grosvenor, Gilbert H.:
First Grosvenor Medal recipient. 253, 254, 255, 260, 261, Aug. 1949; 65G, July 1954; 449, 481, Oct. 1966
Gilbert Grosvenor's Golden Jubilee. By Albert W. Atwood. 253-261, Aug. 1949
La Gorce, John Oliver:
John Oliver La Gorce Is Elected Vice-Chairman of the Board, Melville Bell Grosvenor President and Editor of the National Geographic Society. 419-423, Mar. 1957
Presentation of medal by Gilbert H. Grosvenor. 422, 423, 442, Mar. 1960; 449, Oct. 1966

GROTTOES:
Probing Ice Caves of the Pyrenees. By Norbert Casteret. 391-404, Mar. 1953
Included: Casteret Grotto
See also Caves

GROUNDNUT SCHEME: East Africa:
Britain Tackles the East African Bush. By W. Robert Moore. 311-352, Mar. 1950

GROVE, NOEL: Author:
Bicycles Are Back—and Booming! Photos by Michael Pfleger. 671-681, May 1973
Mark Twain: Mirror of America. Photos by James L. Stanfield. 300-337, Sept. 1975
North With the Wheat Cutters. Photos by James A. Sugar. 194-217, Aug. 1972
Oil, the Dwindling Treasure. Photos by Emory Kristof. 792-825, June 1974
Venezuela's Crisis of Wealth. Photos by Robert W. Madden. 175-209, Aug. 1976
A Village Fights for Its Life. 40-67, July 1973

GROWING Pains Beset Puerto Rico. By William H. Nicholas. Photos by Justin Locke. 419-460, Apr. 1951

GROWING Up in Montana. Photos by Nicholas deVore III. 650-657, May 1976

GROWING Up With Snowflake (White Gorilla). By Arthur J. Riopelle. Photos by Michael Kuh. 491-503, Oct. 1970

GRUENING, ERNEST: Author:
Alaska Proudly Joins the Union. Photos by Thomas J. Abercrombie. 43-83, July 1959
Lonely Wonders of Katmai. Photos by Winfield Parks. 800-831, June 1963

GRUNION, the Fish That Spawns on Land. By Clarence P. Idyll. Photos by Robert F. Sisson. 714-723, May 1969

GUADALAJARA, Mexico:
The Most Mexican City, Guadalajara. By Bart McDowell. Photos by Volkmar Wentzel. 412-441, Mar. 1967

GUADELOUPE (Island), West Indies:
A Fresh Breeze Stirs the Leewards. By Carleton Mitchell. Photos by Winfield Parks. 488-537, Oct. 1966

GUAM (Island), Pacific Ocean:
Magellan: First Voyage Around the World. By Alan Villiers. Photos by Bruce Dale. 721-753, June 1976
Starfish Threaten Pacific Reefs. By James A. Sugar. 340-353, Mar. 1970
See also Pacific Fleet

GUANA (Island), Virgin Islands:
Carib Cruises the West Indies. By Carleton Mitchell. 1-56, Jan. 1948

GUANAJUATO, Mexico:
Experiment in International Living. By Hugh M. Hamill, Jr. 323-350, Mar. 1953

GUAÑAPE CULTURE:
Finding the Tomb of a Warrior-God. By William Duncan Strong. Photos by Clifford Evans, Jr. 453-482, Apr. 1947

GUANO AND GUANO INDUSTRY:
Peru Profits from Sea Fowl. By Robert Cushman Murphy. Photos by author and Grace E. Barstow Murphy. 395-413, Mar. 1959

GUANTÁNAMO: Keystone in the Caribbean. By Jules B. Billard. Photos by W. E. Garrett and Thomas Nebbia. 420-436, Mar. 1961

GUATEMALA:
Earthquake in Guatemala. By Bart McDowell. Photos by W. E. Garrett and Robert W. Madden. 810-829, June 1976
Easter Week in Indian Guatemala. By John Scofield. 406-417, Mar. 1960
Guatemala, Maya and Modern. By Louis de la Haba. Photos by Joseph J. Scherschel. 661-689, Nov. 1974
Guatemala Revisited. By Luis Marden. 525-564, Oct. 1947
The Maya. 729-811, Dec. 1975
I. Children of Time. By Howard La Fay. Photos by David Alan Harvey. 729-767
II. Riddle of the Glyphs. By George E. Stuart. Photos by Otis Imboden. 768-791
III. Resurrecting the Grandeur of Tikal. By William R. Coe. 792-798
IV. A Traveler's Tale of Ancient Tikal. Paintings by Peter Spier. Text by Alice J. Hall. 799-811
The Quetzal, Fabulous Bird of Maya Land. By Anne LaBastille Bowes. Photos by David G. Allen. 141-150, Jan. 1969

GUAYAQUIL, Ecuador:
Ecuador—Low and Lofty Land Astride the Equator. By Loren McIntyre. 259-298, Feb. 1968

GUAYMAS, Mexico:
Tracking America's Man in Orbit. By Kenneth F. Weaver. Photos by Robert F. Sisson. 184-217, Feb. 1962

GUAYMI INDIANS:

Exploring the Past in Panama. By Matthew W. Stirling. Photos by Richard H. Stewart. 373-399, Mar. 1949

GUERNSEY (Island), English Channel:

Britain's "French" Channel Islands. By James Cerruti. Photos by James L. Amos. 710-740, May 1971

GUIDED MISSILES:

Cape Canaveral's 6,000-mile Shooting Gallery. By Allan C. Fisher, Jr. Photos by Luis Marden and Thomas Nebbia. 421-471, Oct. 1959

Our Air Age Speeds Ahead. By F. Barrows Colton. 249-272, Feb. 1948

Seeing the Earth from 80 Miles Up. By Clyde T. Holliday. 511-528, Oct. 1950

See also Nike

GUILD, EUGENE R.: Author-Photographer:

Exploring America's Great Sand Barrier Reef. Photos by John E. Fletcher and author. 325-350, Sept. 1947

GUINEA:

Freedom Speaks French in Ouagadougou. By John Scofield. 153-203, Aug. 1966

GUINEA, Gulf of:

Calypso Explores an Undersea Canyon. By Jacques-Yves Cousteau. Photos by Bates Littlehales. 373-396, Mar. 1958
    Included: Islands: Annobón; Príncipe; São Tomé

GUINEY, LOUISE IMOGEN:

Literary Landmarks of Massachusetts. By William H. Nicholas. Photos by B. Anthony Stewart and John E. Fletcher. 279-310, Mar. 1950

GULF COAST, U. S.:

Cajunland, Louisiana's French-speaking Coast. By Bern Keating. Photos by Charles Harbutt and Franke Keating. 353-391, Mar. 1966

Cruising Florida's Western Waterways. By Rube Allyn. Photos by Bates Littlehales. 49-76, Jan. 1955

Louisiana Trades with the World. By Frederick Simpich. Photos by J. Baylor Roberts. 705-738, Dec. 1947

The Lower Mississippi. By Willard Price. Photos by W. D. Vaughn. 681-725, Nov. 1960

Oil, the Dwindling Treasure. By Noel Grove. Photos by Emory Kristof. 792-825, June 1974
    Included: Plans for superports in Alabama, Louisiana, and Texas

The Pink Birds of Texas. By Paul A. Zahl. 641-654, Nov. 1949

Roseate Spoonbills, Radiant Birds of the Gulf Coast. By Robert Porter Allen. Photos by Frederick Kent Truslow. 274-288, Feb. 1962

See also Houston; Key West; Mobile

GULF OF CALIFORNIA. *See* Raza, Isla

GULF STREAM:

Blue-water Plankton: Ghosts of the Gulf Stream. By William M. Hamner. 530-545, Oct. 1974

Night Life in the Gulf Stream. By Paul A. Zahl. 391-418, Mar. 1954

Strange Babies of the Sea (Plankton). By Hilary B.

GULF STREAM — *Continued*

Moore. Paintings by Craig Phillips and Jacqueline Hutton. 41-56, July 1952

GULL ISLAND, Quebec, Canada:

Sea Bird Cities Off Audubon's Labrador. By Arthur A. Allen. 755-774, June 1948

GULLERS, KARL W.: Photographer:

Viking Festival in the Shetlands. 853-862, Dec. 1954

GULLS:

Sea Bird Cities Off Audubon's Labrador. By Arthur A. Allen. 755-774, June 1948
    Included: Black-backed Gull, Herring Gull, Ring-billed Gull

Sea Birds of Isla Raza. By Lewis Wayne Walker. 239-248, Feb. 1951
    Included: Heermann's Gulls, Yellow-footed Gulls

GUNBOATS, Ironclad:

How We Found the *Monitor*. By John G. Newton. 48-61, Jan. 1975

GUT, Silkworm:

Spain's Silkworm Gut. By Luis Marden. 100-108, July 1951

GUTHRIE, RUSSELL D.: Author:

Re-creating a Vanished World. 294-301, Mar. 1972

GUTMANN, JOHN: Photographer:

Kunming Pilgrimage. 213-226, Feb. 1950

GUYANA. *See* former name, British Guiana

GYANGTSE, Tibet:

A Woman Paints the Tibetans. By Lafugie. 659-692, May 1949

GYPSIES:

The Camargue, Land of Cowboys and Gypsies. By Eugene L. Kammerman. 667-699, May 1956

France's Wild, Watery South, the Camargue. By William Davenport. 696-726, May 1973

Gypsies, Wanderers of the World. Special Publication announced. 880-884, June 1970

Gypsy Cave Dwellers of Andalusia (Spain). 572-582, Oct. 1957

Hungary: Changing Homeland of a Tough, Romantic People. By Bart McDowell. Photos by Albert Moldvay and Joseph J. Scherschel. 443-483, Apr. 1971

Speaking of Spain. By Luis Marden. 415-456, Apr. 1950

When Gypsies Gather at Appleby Fair. Photos by Bruce Dale. 848-869, June 1972

GYPSY MOTH:

New Tricks Outwit Our Insect Enemies. By Hal Higdon. Photos by Robert F. Sisson and Emory Kristof. 380-399, Sept. 1972

H

HD-4:

Hydrofoil boat, *HD-4,* designed by Alexander Graham Bell. 493, 495, 496, Apr. 1957; 257, 264, Aug. 1959; 554-555, Oct. 1963

H.R.H. The Prince Philip, Duke of Edinburgh, Introduces to Members the Narrative of His Round-

H.R.H. The Prince Philip, Duke of Edinburgh — *Continued*
the-World Tour. 583-584, Nov. 1957
See also Philip, H.R.H. The Prince

HA ON (Kibbutz), Israel:
Our Life on a Border Kibbutz. By Carol and Al Abrams. Photos by Al Abrams. 364-391, Sept. 1970

HÂ-ÂK VÂ-ÂK (Hâ-âk Lying Site), Arizona:
Seeking the Secret of the Giants. By Frank M. Setzler. Photos by Richard H. Stewart. 390-404, Sept. 1952

HABER, HEINZ: Author:
Space Satellites, Tools of Earth Research. Paintings by William N. Palmstrom. 487-509, Apr. 1956

HADAR, Ethiopia:
Ethiopia Yields First "Family" of Early Man. By Donald C. Johanson. Photos by David Brill. 790-811, Dec. 1976

HADJ (Moslem Pilgrimage to Mecca):
From America to Mecca on Airborne Pilgrimage. By Abdul Ghafur. 1-60, July 1953
Saudi Arabia: Beyond the Sands of Mecca. By Thomas J. Abercrombie. 1-53, Jan. 1966
The Sword and the Sermon. By Thomas J. Abercrombie. 3-45, July 1972

HAGEN, KENNETH S.: Author:
Following the Ladybug Home. Photos by Robert F. Sisson. 543-553, Apr. 1970

HAGEN, TONI: Author-Photographer:
Afoot in Roadless Nepal. 361-405, Mar. 1960

HAGERSTOWN VALLEY, Maryland:
Appalachian Valley Pilgrimage. By Catherine Bell Palmer. Photos by Justin Locke. 1-32, July 1949

The **HAGUE** ('s Gravenhage), Netherlands:
Mid-century Holland Builds Her Future. By Sydney Clark. 747-778, Dec. 1950
The Netherlands: Nation at War With the Sea. By Alan Villiers. Photos by Adam Woolfitt. 530-571, Apr. 1968

HAIFA, Israel:
An Archeologist Looks at Palestine. By Nelson Glueck. 739-752, Dec. 1947

HAILE SELASSIE I, Emperor (Ethiopia):
Ethiopian Adventure. By Nathaniel T. Kenney. Photos by James P. Blair. 548-582, Apr. 1965

HAITI, Republic of:
Haiti: Beyond Mountains, More Mountains. By Carolyn Bennett Patterson. Photos by Thomas Nebbia. 70-97, Jan. 1976
Haiti — West Africa in the West Indies. By John Scofield. 226-259, Feb. 1961

HAKLUYT, RICHARD:
Founders of Virginia. By Sir Evelyn Wrench. Photos by B. Anthony Stewart. 433-462, Apr. 1948

HALE, SARAH JOSEPHA:
Literary Landmarks of Massachusetts. By William H. Nicholas. Photos by B. Anthony Stewart and John E. Fletcher. 279-310, Mar. 1950

HALEAKALA NATIONAL PARK, Hawaii:
Maui, Where Old Hawaii Still Lives. By Kenneth F. Weaver. Photos by Gordon W. Gahan. 514-543, Apr. 1971

HALF DOME (Massif), Yosemite National Park, California:
Climbing Half Dome the Hard Way. By Galen Rowell. 782-791, June 1974

HALIFAX RACE (Marblehead-Halifax Yacht Race):
Down East to Nova Scotia. By Winfield Parks. 853-879, June 1964

HALL, ALICE J.: Author:
Benjamin Franklin, Philosopher of Dissent. Photos by Linda Bartlett. 93-123, July 1975
The Climb Up Cone Crater. Photos by Edgar D. Mitchell and Alan B. Shepard, Jr. 136-148, July 1971
A Lady From China's Past. Photos from *China Pictorial.* 660-681, May 1974
A Traveler's Tale of Ancient Tikal. Paintings by Peter Spier. 799-811, Dec. 1975

HALL, MELVIN: Author-Photographer:
Vézelay, Hill of the Pilgrims. 229-247, Feb. 1953

HALL, ROSS: Photographer:
Idaho Loggers Battle a River. 117-130, July 1951

HALLSTROM, E. J. L.:
Sheep Airlift in New Guinea. Photos by Ned Blood. 831-844, Dec. 1949

HAMI, Sinkiang:
The Caves of the Thousand Buddhas. By Franc and Jean Shor. 383-415, Mar. 1951

HAMILL, HUGH M., Jr.: Author-Photographer:
Experiment in International Living. 323-350, Mar. 1953

HAMILTON, ROGER: Author:
Can We Harness the Wind? Photos by Emory Kristof. 812-829, Dec. 1975

HAMILTON (River), Labrador, Newfoundland:
Labrador Canoe Adventure. By Andrew Brown and Ralph Gray. 65-99, July 1951

HAMMARSKJÖLD, DAG: Author-Photographer:
A New Look at Everest. 87-93, Jan. 1961

HAMMOND, THOMAS T.: Author:
An American in Russia's Capital. Photos by Dean Conger. 297-351, Mar. 1966
Firsthand Look at the Soviet Union. Photos by Erich Lessing. 352-407, Sept. 1959

HAMMURABI, King (Babylon):
Ancient Mesopotamia: A Light That Did Not Fail. By E. A. Speiser. Paintings by H. M. Herget. 41-105, Jan. 1951

HAMNER, WILLIAM M.: Author:
Blue-water Plankton: Ghosts of the Gulf Stream. 530-545, Oct. 1974

HAN DYNASTY TOMBS:
China Unveils Her Newest Treasures. Photos by Robert W. Madden. 848-857, Dec. 1974

HAN DYNASTY TOMBS—*Continued*

A Lady From China's Past. Photos from *China Pictorial*. Text by Alice J. Hall. 660-681, May 1974

HANDCLASP in Space: Apollo-Soyuz. By Thomas Y. Canby. 183-187, Feb. 1976

HANDICRAFTS:

The Craftsman in America. Special Publication announced. 870-874, June 1975

Human Treasures of Japan. By William Graves. Photos by James L. Stanfield. 370-379, Sept. 1972

Kyoto and Nara: Keepers of Japan's Past. By Charles McCarry. Photos by George F. Mobley. 836-851, June 1976

The Past Is Present in Greenfield Village. By Beverley M. Bowie. Photos by Neal P. Davis and Willard R. Culver. 96-127, July 1958

Williamsburg, City for All Seasons. By Joseph Judge. Photos by James L. Amos. 790-823, Dec. 1968

Williamsburg: Its College and Its Cinderella City. By Beverley M. Bowie. 439-486, Oct. 1954

See also Folk Art; *and* specific crafts

HANG GLIDERS:

Happy Birthday, Otto Lilienthal! By Russell Hawkes. Photos by James Collison. 286-292, Feb. 1972

HANKOW, China:

Along the Yangtze, Main Street of China. By W. Robert Moore. 325-356, Mar. 1948

HANNIBAL, Missouri:

Mark Twain: Mirror of America. By Noel Grove. Photos by James L. Stanfield. 300-337, Sept. 1975

Tom Sawyer's Town. By Jerry Allen. 121-140, July 1956

The West Through Boston Eyes. By Stewart Anderson. 733-776, June 1949

HAPPY Birthday, Otto Lilienthal! By Russell Hawkes. Photos by James Collison. 286-292, Feb. 1972

HAPPY-GO-LUCKY Trinidad and Tobago. By Charles Allmon. 35-75, Jan. 1953

HAPSBURGS (Rulers). *See* The Vienna Treasures and Their Collectors

HARBERTON, Estancia, Tierra del Fuego:

Housewife at the End of the World. By Rae Natalie P. Goodall. Photos by James L. Stanfield. 130-150, Jan. 1971

HARBIN, China:

In Manchuria Now. By W. Robert Moore. 389-414, Mar. 1947

HARBUTT, CHARLES: Author-Photographer:

Eyewitness to War in the Holy Land. 782-795, Dec. 1967

Photographer

Cajunland, Louisiana's French-speaking Coast. By Bern Keating. Photos by Charles Harbutt and Franke Keating. 353-391, Mar. 1966

Today Along the Natchez Trace, Pathway Through History. By Bern Keating. 641-667, Nov. 1968

Where Jesus Walked. By Howard La Fay. 739-781, Dec. 1967

HARDING, WARREN GAMALIEL:

The Living White House. By Lonnelle Aikman. 593-643, Nov. 1966

Profiles of the Presidents: IV. America Enters the Modern Era. By Frank Freidel. 537-577, Oct. 1965

HARDY, LAYMOND: Photographer:

Alligators: Dragons in Distress. By Archie Carr. Photos by Treat Davidson and Laymond Hardy. 133-148, Jan. 1967

HARE, CLYDE: Photographer:

Banks Island: Eskimo Life on the Polar Sea. By William O. Douglas. 703-735, May 1964

Pittsburgh, Pattern for Progress. By William J. Gill. 342-371, Mar. 1965

HARGRAVE, THOMAS J.: Author-Photographer:

Photographing a Volcano in Action. 561-563, Oct. 1955

HARMONY HOLLOW (Farm), Virginia:

The World of My Apple Tree. By Robert F. Sisson. 836-847, June 1972

HARMSWORTH, SIR LEICESTER: Renaissance Library:

Folger: Biggest Little Library in the World. By Joseph T. Foster. Photos by B. Anthony Stewart and John E. Fletcher. 411-424, Sept. 1951

HAROLD II, King (England):

900 Years Ago: the Norman Conquest. By Kenneth M. Setton. Photos by George F. Mobley. 206-251, Aug. 1966

HARP SEALS:

Life or Death for the Harp Seal. By David M. Lavigne. Photos by William R. Curtsinger. 129-142, Jan. 1976

HARPERS FERRY, West Virginia:

History Awakens at Harpers Ferry. By Volkmar Wentzel. 399-416, Mar. 1957

HARRER, HEINRICH: Author-Photographer:

My Life in Forbidden Lhasa. 1-48, July 1955

HARRINGTON, PHILLIP: Photographer:

Athens: Her Golden Past Still Lights the World. By Kenneth F. Weaver. 100-137, July 1963

HARRIS, JENNIE E.: Author:

Sponge Fishermen of Tarpon Springs. 119-136, Jan. 1947

HARRISON, BENJAMIN:

Profiles of the Presidents: III. The American Giant Comes of Age. By Frank Freidel. 660-711, May 1965

HARRISON, WILLIAM HENRY:

Profiles of the Presidents: II. A Restless Nation Moves West. By Frank Freidel. 80-121, Jan. 1965

HART, KIM: Photographer:

Ancient Shipwreck Yields New Facts—and a Strange Cargo. By Peter Throckmorton. Photos by Kim Hart and Joseph J. Scherschel. 282-300, Feb. 1969

HART, VAL: Author:

Pack Trip Through the Smokies. Photos by Robert F. Sisson. 473-502, Oct. 1952

HART DYKE, ZOË, LADY:

Silkworms in England Spin for the Queen. By John E. H. Nolan. 689-704, May 1953

HARTMAN, DANIEL S.: Author:

Florida's Manatees, Mermaids in Peril. Photos by James A. Sugar. 342-353, Sept. 1969

HARTZOG, GEORGE B., Jr.: Author:

The Next 100 Years: A Master Plan for Yellowstone. 632-637, May 1972

Parkscape, U.S.A.: Tomorrow in Our National Parks. 48-93, July 1966

HARVESTING:

North With the Wheat Cutters. By Noel Grove. Photos by James A. Sugar. 194-217, Aug. 1972

HARVEY, DAVID ALAN: Photographer:

The Maya, Children of Time. By Howard La Fay. 729-767, Dec. 1975

My Backyard, the Adirondacks. By Anne LaBastille. 616-639, May 1975

This Is My Island, Tangier. By Harold G. Wheatley. 700-725, Nov. 1973

The Virginians. By Mike W. Edwards. 588-617, Nov. 1974

HARVEY, WILLIAM:

The British Way. By Sir Evelyn Wrench. 421-541, Apr. 1949

HASHEMITE Jordan, Arab Heartland. By John Scofield. 841-856, Dec. 1952

HASIDIC JEWS:

The Pious Ones (Brooklyn's Hasidic Jews). By Harvey Arden. Photos by Nathan Benn. 276-298, Aug. 1975

HASTINGS, Battle of (1066):

900 Years Ago: The Norman Conquest. By Kenneth M. Setton. Photos by George F. Mobley. 206-251, Aug. 1966

HATCH RIVER EXPEDITIONS:

Shooting Rapids in Dinosaur Country. By Jack Breed. Photos by author and Justin Locke. 363-390, Mar. 1954

HATCHETFISH, Torchbearers of the Deep. By Paul A. Zahl. 713-714, May 1958

HATTERAS, Cape, North Carolina:

Exploring America's Great Sand Barrier Reef. By Eugene R. Guild. Photos by John E. Fletcher and author. 325-350, Sept. 1947

How We Found the *Monitor*. By John G. Newton. 48-61, Jan. 1975

Contents: Search in two expeditions for the wreck of the first ironclad gunboat, lost off Cape Hatteras during the Civil War

Lonely Cape Hatteras, Besieged by the Sea. By William S. Ellis. Photos by Emory Kristof. 393-421, Sept. 1969

October Holiday on the Outer Banks. By Nike Anderson. Photos by J. Baylor Roberts. 501-529, Oct. 1955

HAUN, DECLAN: Photographer:

Quebec: French City in an Anglo-Saxon World. By Kenneth MacLeish. Photos by James L. Stanfield and Declan Haun. 416-442, Mar. 1971

HAUNTING Heart of the Everglades. By Andrew H. Brown. Photos by author and Willard R. Culver. 145-173, Feb. 1948

HAURY, EMIL W.: Author:

The Hohokam: First Masters of the American Desert. Photos by Helga Teiwes. 670-695, May 1967

HAVANA (Habana), Cuba:

Cuba—American Sugar Bowl. By Melville Bell Grosvenor. 1-56, Jan. 1947

HAVASUPAI INDIAN RESERVATION, Grand Canyon, Arizona:

Indian Shangri-La of the Grand Canyon. By Jay Johnston. Photos by Terry Eiler. 355-373, Mar. 1970

Land of the Havasupai. By Jack Breed. 655-674, May 1948

HAVE Excavations on the Island of Thera Solved the Riddle of the Minoans? By Spyridon Marinatos. Photos by Otis Imboden. 702-726, May 1972

HAVE We Solved the Mysteries of the Moon? By Kenneth F. Weaver. Paintings by William H. Bond. 309-325, Sept. 1973

HAWAII:

Because It Rains on Hawaii. By Frederick Simpich, Jr. 571-610, Nov. 1949

A Canoe Helps Hawaii Recapture Her Past. By Herb Kawainui Kane. Photos by David Hiser. 468-489, Apr. 1976

Captain Cook: The Man Who Mapped the Pacific. By Alan Villiers. Photos by Gordon W. Gahan. 297-349, Sept. 1971

Close-up: U.S.A., Hawaii, map supplement. Text on reverse. Apr. 1976

The Flowers That Say "Aloha." By Deena Clark. Photos by Robert B. Goodman. 121-131, Jan. 1967

Hawaii, Atlas series supplement. July 1960

Hawaii. Special Publication announced. 880-884, June 1970

Hawaii, Island of Fire and Flowers. By Gordon Young. Photos by Robert W. Madden. 399-425, Mar. 1975

Hawaii, U.S.A. By Frederick Simpich, Jr. Photos by Thomas Nebbia. 1-45, July 1960

Hokule'a Follows the Stars to Tahiti. By David Lewis. Photos by Nicholas deVore III. 512-537, Oct. 1976

Isles of the Pacific. 732-793, Dec. 1974

Saving the Nene, World's Rarest Goose. By S. Dillon Ripley. Photos by Jerry Chong. 745-754, Nov. 1965

Unsung Beauties of Hawaii's Coral Reefs (Nudibranchs). By Paul A. Zahl. 510-525, Oct. 1959

YWCA: International Success Story. By Mary French Rockefeller. Photos by Otis Imboden. 904-933, Dec. 1963

See also Honolulu; Maui

HAWAII VOLCANOES NATIONAL PARK, Hawaii:

Fountain of Fire in Hawaii (Kilauea Iki Crater). By Frederick Simpich, Jr. Photos by Robert B. Goodman and Robert Wenkam. 303-327, Mar. 1960

Hawaii, Island of Fire and Flowers. By Gordon

HAWAII VOLCANOES NATIONAL PARK—*Continued*

Young. Photos by Robert W. Madden. 399-425, Mar. 1975

Photographing a Volcano in Action. By Thomas J. Hargrave. 561-563, Oct. 1955

Volcanic Fires of the 50th State: Hawaii National Park. By Paul A. Zahl. 793-823, June 1959

HAWKES, RUSSELL: Author:

Happy Birthday, Otto Lilienthal! Photos by James Collison. 286-292, Feb. 1972

HAWKS:

Can the Cooper's Hawk Survive? By Noel Snyder. Photos by author and Helen Snyder. 433-442, Mar. 1974

A New Light Dawns on Bird Photography. By Arthur A. Allen. 774-790, June 1948
  Included: Cooper's hawk, Peregrine falcon, Red-tailed hawk, Sparrow hawk; and Falconry

HAWTHORNE, NATHANIEL:

Literary Landmarks of Massachusetts. By William H. Nicholas. Photos by B. Anthony Stewart and John E. Fletcher. 279-310, Mar. 1950

HAY, JACOB: Author:

The FBI: Public Friend Number One. Photos by Robert F. Sisson. 860-886, June 1961

HAYDEN, CARL: Author:

The Nation's Capitol Revealed as Never Before. 1-3, Jan. 1964

HAYDON, Mount, Alaska:

First American Ascent of Mount St. Elias. By Maynard M. Miller. 229-248, Feb. 1948

HAYES, RUTHERFORD B.:

Profiles of the Presidents: III. The American Giant Comes of Age. By Frank Freidel. 660-711, May 1965

HAYS, Kansas, at the Nation's Heart. By Margaret M. Detwiler. Photos by John E. Fletcher. 461-490, Apr. 1952

HEADHUNTERS:

Roaming India's Naga Hills. By S. Dillon Ripley. 247-264, Feb. 1955
  Included: Angami, Kalyo Kengyu, and Rengma tribes

To the Land of the Head-hunters (New Guinea). By E. Thomas Gilliard. 437-486, Oct. 1955
  Included: Sepik River tribes of Gaikarobi, Iatmul, Kanganaram, Malingai, and Telefolmin

See also Asmat; Iban

HEARST SAN SIMEON STATE HISTORICAL MONUMENT, California:

California's Wonderful One (State Highway No. 1). By Frank Cameron. Photos by B. Anthony Stewart. 571-617, Nov. 1959

HEART of the Bluegrass. By Charles McCarry. Photos by J. Bruce Baumann. 634-659, May 1974

HEART RESEARCH:

Hunting the Heartbeat of a Whale. By Paul Dudley White and Samuel W. Matthews. 49-64, July 1956

Making Friends With a Killer Whale ("Namu"). By Edward I. Griffin. 418-446, Mar. 1966

HEARTY Folk Defy Arctic Storms. Paintings by W. Langdon Kihn. 479-494, Oct. 1949

HEAVENS:

A Map of the Heavens, map supplement. Star charts on reverse. Dec. 1957

Map of the Heavens, map supplement. Star charts on reverse. Aug. 1970

HEBREWS:

Abraham, the Friend of God. By Kenneth MacLeish. Photos by Dean Conger. 739-789, Dec. 1966

Bringing Old Testament Times to Life. By G. Ernest Wright. Paintings by Henry J. Soulen. 833-864, Dec. 1957

The Last Thousand Years Before Christ. By G. Ernest Wright. Paintings by H. J. Soulen and Peter V. Bianchi. 812-853, Dec. 1960

See also Moses

HEBRIDES (Islands), Scotland:

Scotland From Her Lovely Lochs and Seas. By Alan Villiers. Photos by Robert F. Sisson. 492-541, Apr. 1961

See also Inner Hebrides; Outer Hebrides

HEIMAEY (Island), Westmann Islands, Iceland:

A Village Fights for Its Life. By Noel Grove. 40-67, July 1973

HEIRTZLER, JAMES R.: Author:

Where the Earth Turns Inside Out. Photos by Emory Kristof. 586-603, May 1975

HEIZER, ROBERT F.: Author:

Gifts for the Jaguar God. By Philip Drucker and Robert F. Heizer. 367-375, Sept. 1956

HELICOPTERS:

Air Rescue Behind Enemy Lines (North Viet Nam). By Howard Sochurek. 346-369, Sept. 1968

Aviation Looks Ahead on Its 50th Birthday. By Emory S. Land. 721-739, Dec. 1953

Everyone's Servant, the Post Office. By Allan C. Fisher, Jr. Photos by Volkmar Wentzel. 121-152, July 1954

Exploring Ancient Panama by Helicopter. By Matthew W. Stirling. Photos by Richard H. Stewart. 227-246, Feb. 1950

Flying in the "Blowtorch" Era. By Frederick G. Vosburgh. 281-322, Sept. 1950

Helicopter War in South Viet Nam. By Dickey Chapelle. 723-754, Nov. 1962

The Incredible Helicopter. By Peter T. White. 533-557, Apr. 1959

Our Air Age Speeds Ahead. By F. Barrows Colton. 249-272, Feb. 1948

HELLYER, DAVID: Author:

Goggle Fishing in California Waters. Photos by Lamar Boren. 615-632, May 1949

Nature's Clown, the Penguin. By David Hellyer and Malcolm Davis. 405-428, Sept. 1952

HELM, ENNIS CREED ("Tex"): Photographer:

Carlsbad Caverns in Color. By Mason Sutherland. 433-468, Oct. 1953

HELP for Philippine Tribes in Trouble. By Kenneth MacLeish. Photos by Dean Conger. 220-255, Aug. 1971

HELPING Holland Rebuild Her Land. By Gilbert M. Grosvenor and Charles Neave. 365-413, Sept. 1954

HELSINKI, Finland:

Baltic Cruise of the *Caribbee*. By Carleton Mitchell. 605-646, Nov. 1950

Finland: Plucky Neighbor of Soviet Russia. By William Graves. Photos by George F. Mobley. 587-629, May 1968

HENLOPEN DUNES, Delaware:

The Living Sand. By William H. Amos. 820-833, June 1965

HENRY VIII, King (England):

The British Way. By Sir Evelyn Wrench. 421-541, Apr. 1949

HENRY, Prince, the Navigator:

Prince Henry, the Explorer Who Stayed Home. By Alan Villiers. Photos by Thomas Nebbia. 616-656, Nov. 1960

HENRY, PATRICK:

Firebrands of the Revolution. By Eric F. Goldman. Photos by George F. Mobley. 2-27, July 1974

HENRY, THOMAS R.: Author:

Ice Age Man, the First American. Paintings by Andre Durenceau. 781-806, Dec. 1955

The Smithsonian Institution. 325-348, Sept. 1948

HENRY, Cape, Virginia:

Exploring America's Great Sand Barrier Reef. By Eugene R. Guild. Photos by John E. Fletcher and author. 325-350, Sept. 1947

HENRY E. HUNTINGTON LIBRARY AND ART GALLERY, San Marino, California:

Huntington Library, California Treasure House. By David S. Boyer. 251-276, Feb. 1958

HENRY FORD MUSEUM, Dearborn, Michigan:

The Past Is Present in Greenfield Village. By Beverley M. Bowie. Photos by Neal P. Davis and Willard R. Culver. 96-127, July 1958

HENRY HUDSON'S River. By Willard Price. Photos by Wayne Miller. 364-403, Mar. 1962

HERALDRY. See Coats of Arms

HERBAL MEDICINE:

Karnali, Roadless World of Western Nepal. By Lila M. and Barry C. Bishop. 656-689, Nov. 1971

Nature's Gifts to Medicine. By Lonnelle Aikman. Paintings by Lloyd K. Townsend and Don Crowley. 420-440, Sept. 1974

The People of Cumberland Gap. By John Fetterman. Photos by Bruce Dale. 591-621, Nov. 1971

HERBERT, CHARLES W.: Photographer:

Better Days for the Navajos. By Jack Breed. 809-847, Dec. 1958

Californians Escape to the Desert. By Mason Sutherland. 675-724, Nov. 1957

Sonora Is Jumping. By Mason Sutherland. 215-246, Feb. 1955

HERBS. See Bromeliads; Herbal Medicine; and Kew

HERE Come the Marines. By Frederick Simpich. 647-672, Nov. 1950

HERE Rest in Honored Glory . . . (War Memorials). By Howell Walker. 739-768, June 1957

HÉRENS, Val d', Switzerland:

Switzerland's Enchanted Val d'Hérens. By Georgia Engelhard Cromwell. 825-848, June 1955

HERE'S New York Harbor. By Stuart E. Jones. Photos by Robert F. Sisson and David S. Boyer. 773-813, Dec. 1954

HERGET, H. M.: Artist:

Ancient Mesopotamia: A Light That Did Not Fail. By E. A. Speiser. 41-105, Jan. 1951
How the Herget Paintings Were Composed. 57

HERITAGE of Beauty and History (U. S. National Parks). By Conrad L. Wirth. 587-661, May 1958

HERM (Island), English Channel:

Britain's "French" Channel Islands. By James Cerruti. Photos by James L. Amos. 710-740, May 1971

HERMES, R. C.: Photographer:

The Solemn, Sociable Puffins. By R. M. Lockley. 414-422, Sept. 1954

HERMITAGE (State Museum), Leningrad, U.S.S.R.:

Leningrad, Russia's Window on the West. By Howard La Fay. Photos by Dick Durrance II. 636-673, May 1971

HERO (Research Vessel):

Antarctica's Nearer Side. By Samuel W. Matthews. Photos by William R. Curtsinger. 622-655, Nov. 1971

HEROD THE GREAT, King (Judea):

The Ghosts of Jericho. By James L. Kelso. 825-844, Dec. 1951

HERONS:

Aha! It Really Works! By Robert F. Sisson. 143-147, Jan. 1974
Contents: Green heron that fishes with bait

Wildlife of Everglades National Park. By Daniel B. Beard. Paintings by Walter A. Weber. 83-116, Jan. 1949

HERRING:

Scenes of Postwar Finland. By La Verne Bradley. Photos by Jerry Waller. 233-264, Aug. 1947
See also Menhaden

HERRNKIND, WILLIAM F.: Author:

Strange March of the Spiny Lobster. Photos by Rick Frehsee and Bruce Mounier. 819-831, June 1975

HEYDEN, FRANCIS J.:

Eclipse Hunting in Brazil's Ranchland. By F. Barrows Colton. Photos by Richard H. Stewart and Guy W. Starling. 285-324, Sept. 1947

HEYERDAHL, THOR: Author:

The Voyage of *Ra II*. Photos by Carlo Mauri and Georges Sourial. 44-71, Jan. 1971

HIBERNATION. See Grizzly Bears; Poorwill

HIDDEN Worlds in the Heart of a Plant (Bromeliad). By Paul A. Zahl. 389-397, Mar. 1975

HIEROGLYPHS:

Computer Helps Scholars Re-create an Egyptian Temple. By Ray Winfield Smith. Photos by Emory Kristof. 634-655, Nov. 1970
See also Glyphs, for Maya glyphs

HIERONYMUS, REX E.: Author:

Down Mark Twain's River on a Raft. 551-574, Apr. 1948

HIGAONON TRIBE:

Help for Philippine Tribes in Trouble. By Kenneth MacLeish. Photos by Dean Conger. 220-255, Aug. 1971

HIGDON, HAL: Author:

New Tricks Outwit Our Insect Enemies. Photos by Robert F. Sisson and Emory Kristof. 380-399, Sept. 1972

HIGH, Wild World of the Vicuña. By William L. Franklin. 77-91, Jan. 1973

HIGH Adventure in the Himalayas. By Thomas Weir. 193-234, Aug. 1952

HIGH ATLAS (Mountains), Africa:

Morocco, Land of the Farthest West. By Thomas J. Abercrombie. 834-865, June 1971

Trek by Mule Among Morocco's Berbers. By Victor Englebert. 850-875, June 1968

HIGH Road in the Pyrenees. By H. V. Morton. Photos by Justin Locke. 299-334, Mar. 1956

HIGH-STEPPING Idaho. By William S. Ellis. Photos by Dean Conger. 290-317, Mar. 1973

HIGH Trail Through the Canadian Rockies. By Mike W. Edwards. Photos by Lowell Georgia. 795-817, June 1973

The **HIGH** World of the Rain Forest. By William Beebe. Paintings by Guy Neale. 838-855, June 1958

HIGHLAND GAMES:

Over the Sea to Scotland's Skye. By Robert J. Reynolds. 87-112, July 1952

The **HIGHLANDS**, Stronghold of Scottish Gaeldom. By Kenneth MacLeish. Photos by Winfield Parks. 398-435, Mar. 1968

HIGHWAYS AND ROADS:

Amalfi, Italy's Divine Coast. By Luis Marden. 472-509, Oct. 1959

California's Wonderful One (State Highway No. 1). By Frank Cameron. Photos by B. Anthony Stewart. 571-617, Nov. 1959

From Sea to Shining Sea: A Cross Section of the United States Along Historic Route 40. By Ralph Gray. Photos by Dean Conger and author. 1-61, July 1961

From Sun-clad Sea to Shining Mountains. By Ralph Gray. Photos by James P. Blair. 542-589, Apr. 1964

Contents: "International 89": Mexico's West Coast Highway; U. S. 89; Canada's Coleman-Kananaskis Road and Banff-Jasper Highway

The Old Boston Post Roads. By Donald Barr Chidsey. 189-205, Aug. 1962

Our Growing Interstate Highway System. By Robert Paul Jordan. 195-219, Feb. 1968

The Post Road Today. Photos by B. Anthony Stewart. 206-233, Aug. 1962

Trucks Race the Clock From Coast to Coast. By James A. Sugar. 226-243, Feb. 1974

See also Natchez Trace; New York State Thruway; Pan American Highway

HIKING:

Afoot in Roadless Nepal. By Toni Hagen. 361-405, Mar. 1960

Americans Afoot in Rumania. By Dan Dimancescu. Photos by Dick Durrance II and Christopher G. Knight. 810-845, June 1969

The Friendly Huts of the White Mountains. By William O. Douglas. Photos by Kathleen Revis. 205-239, Aug. 1961

Hiking the Backbone of the Rockies: Canada's Great Divide Trail. By Mike W. Edwards. Photos by Lowell Georgia. 795-817, June 1973

Karnali, Roadless World of Western Nepal. By Lila M. and Barry C. Bishop. 656-689, Nov. 1971

Mexico to Canada on the Pacific Crest Trail. By Mike W. Edwards. Photos by David Hiser. 741-779, June 1971

Pack Trip Through the Smokies. By Val Hart. Photos by Robert F. Sisson. 473-502, Oct. 1952

Sierra High Trip. By David R. Brower. 844-868, June 1954

Skyline Trail from Maine to Georgia. By Andrew H. Brown. Photos by Robert F. Sisson. 219-251, Aug. 1949

Thumbs Up Round the North Sea's Rim. By Frances James. Photos by Erica Koch. 685-704, May 1952

Yellowstone at 100: A Walk Through the Wilderness. By Karen and Derek Craighead. Photos by Sam Abell. 579-603, May 1972

See also Pilgrimages; Walking Tours

HILDEBRAND, JESSE RICHARDSON:

Memorial Tribute to Jesse Richardson Hildebrand. 104, Jan. 1952

HILGER, MARY INEZ: Author:

Japan's "Sky People," the Vanishing Ainu. Photos by Eiji Miyazawa. 268-296, Feb. 1967

HILLARY, SIR EDMUND:

The Crossing of Antarctica. By Sir Vivian Fuchs. Photos by George Lowe. 25-47, Jan. 1959

President Eisenhower Presents the Hubbard Medal to Everest's Conquerors. 64, July 1954

Triumph on Everest. 1-63, July 1954

Author

Beyond Everest. 579-610, Nov. 1955

The Conquest of the Summit. 45-63, July 1954

We Build a School for Sherpa Children. 548-551, Oct. 1962

HILO, Hawaii:

Hawaii, Island of Fire and Flowers. By Gordon Young. Photos by Robert W. Madden. 399-425, Mar. 1975

HILTON HEAD (Island), South Carolina:

Sea Islands: Adventuring Along the South's Surprising Coast. By James Cerruti. Photos by Thomas Nebbia and James L. Amos. 366-393, Mar. 1971

HIMALAYAS (Mountains), Asia:

American and Geographic Flags Top Everest. By Melvin M. Payne. Photos by Barry C. Bishop. 157-157C, Aug. 1963

Americans on Everest (Television film). 448-452, Sept. 1965; 575, Nov. 1976

Beyond Everest. By Sir Edmund Hillary. 579-610, Nov. 1955

HIMALAYAS (Mountains), Asia—*Continued*

Caught in the Assam-Tibet Earthquake. By F. Kingdon-Ward. 403-416, Mar. 1952

The First Traverse. By Thomas F. Hornbein and William F. Unsoeld. 509-513, Oct. 1963

High Adventure in the Himalayas. By Thomas Weir. 193-234, Aug. 1952

Himalayan Pilgrimage. By Christopher Rand. 520-535, Oct. 1956

How We Climbed Everest. By Barry C. Bishop. 477-507, Oct. 1963

A New Look at Everest. By Dag Hammarskjöld. 87-93, Jan. 1961

Six to the Summit. By Norman G. Dyhrenfurth. Photos by Barry C. Bishop. 460-473, Oct. 1963

Triumph on Everest. 1-63, July 1954
  I. Siege and Assault. By Sir John Hunt. 1-43
  II. The Conquest of the Summit. By Sir Edmund Hillary. 45-63

Wintering on the Roof of the World. By Barry C. Bishop. 503-547, Oct. 1962
  Slow Death Threatens Man in the Thin Air of 19,000 Feet. 530-531

A Woman Paints the Tibetans. By Lafugie. 659-692, May 1949

See also Bhutan; Kashmir; Ladakh; Mustang; Nepal; Sikkim

HIMIS MONASTERY, Ladakh:

A Journey to "Little Tibet." By Enakshi Bhavnani. Photos by Volkmar Wentzel. 603-634, May 1951

A Woman Paints the Tibetans. By Lafugie. 659-692, May 1949

HINDUS AND HINDUISM:

Bangladesh: Hope Nourishes a New Nation. By William S. Ellis. Photos by Dick Durrance II. 295-333, Sept. 1972

The Cobra, India's "Good Snake." By Harry Miller. 393-409, Sept. 1970

Delhi, Capital of a New Dominion. By Phillips Talbot. 597-630, Nov. 1947

From the Hair of Siva. By Helen and Frank Schreider. 445-503, Oct. 1960

The Ganges, River of Faith. By John J. Putman. Photos by Raghubir Singh. 445-483, Oct. 1971

Himalayan Pilgrimage. By Christopher Rand. 520-535, Oct. 1956

The Idyllic Vale of Kashmir. By Volkmar Wentzel. 523-550, Apr. 1948

India in Crisis. By John Scofield. 599-661, May 1963

India's Sculptured Temple Caves. By Volkmar Wentzel. 665-678, May 1953

Karnali, Roadless World of Western Nepal. By Lila M. and Barry C. Bishop. 656-689, Nov. 1971

The Lands and Peoples of Southeast Asia. 295-365, Mar. 1971

Orissa, Past and Promise in an Indian State. By Bart McDowell. Photos by James P. Blair. 546-577, Oct. 1970

Royal Wedding at Jaisalmer. By Marilyn Silverstone. 66-79, Jan. 1965

HIPPOPOTAMUSES:

Mzima, Kenya's Spring of Life. Photos by Joan and Alan Root. 350-373, Sept. 1971

HISER, DAVID: Photographer:

A Canoe Helps Hawaii Recapture Her Past. By Herb Kawainui Kane. 468-489, Apr. 1976

Death Valley, the Land and the Legend. By Rowe Findley. 69-103, Jan. 1970

Golden Ghosts of the Lost Sierra. By Robert Laxalt. 332-353, Sept. 1973

The "Lone" Coyote Likes Family Life. By Hope Ryden. Photos by author and David Hiser. 278-294, Aug. 1974

Mexico to Canada on the Pacific Crest Trail. By Mike W. Edwards. 741-779, June 1971

San Antonio: "Texas, Actin' Kind of Natural." By Fred Kline. 524-549, Apr. 1976

Stalking the West's Wild Foods. By Euell Gibbons. 186-199, Aug. 1973

Stalking Wild Foods on a Desert Isle. By Euell Gibbons. 47-63, July 1972

The Tarahumaras: Mexico's Long Distance Runners. By James Norman. 702-718, May 1976

That Dammed Missouri River. By Gordon Young. 374-413, Sept. 1971

HISPANIOLA (Island), West Indies:

Christopher Columbus and the New World He Found. By John Scofield. Photos by Adam Woolfitt. 584-625, Nov. 1975

See also Haiti

HISTORIC Color Portrait of Earth From Space. By Kenneth F. Weaver. Photos by DODGE Satellite. 726-731, Nov. 1967

HISTORY, Ancient. *See* Alexander the Great; Aphrodisias; Archeology; Bible Lands; Commagene; Egypt; Greece; Mesopotamia; Roman Empire; Thera; *and* names of ancient peoples, *as:* Essenes; Etruscans; Phoenicians

HISTORY, Medieval. *See* Byzantine Empire; Medieval Europe; *and* Crusades; Norman Conquest

HISTORY, U. S.:

American Processional: History on Canvas. By John and Blanche Leeper. 173-212, Feb. 1951

America's Beginnings. Special Publication announced. 870-874, June 1974

America's Historylands, Landmarks of Liberty. Book announced. 360-363, Mar. 1962

Clues to America's Past. Special Publication announced. 860-864, June 1976

Early America Through the Eyes of Her Native Artists. By Hereward Lester Cooke, Jr. 356-389, Sept. 1962

Following the Trail of Lewis and Clark. By Ralph Gray. 707-750, June 1953

From Sea to Shining Sea: A Cross Section of the United States Along Historic Route 40. By Ralph Gray. Photos by Dean Conger and author. 1-61, July 1961

Historical Map of the United States, map supplement. June 1953

In the Footsteps of Lewis and Clark. Special Publication announced. 880-884, June 1970

New Stars for Old Glory. By Lonnelle Aikman. 86-121, July 1959

North Through History Aboard *White Mist.* By Melville Bell Grosvenor. Photos by Edwin Stuart Grosvenor. 1-55, July 1970

Our Country's Presidents. Special Publication announced. 408-417, Mar. 1966

HISTORY, U. S. — *Continued*

Profiles of the Presidents. By Frank Freidel.
I. The Presidency and How It Grew. 642-687, Nov. 1964
II. A Restless Nation Moves West. 80-121, Jan. 1965
III. The American Giant Comes of Age. 660-711, May 1965
IV. America Enters the Modern Era. 537-577, Oct. 1965
V. The Atomic Age: Its Problems and Promises. 66-119, Jan. 1966

Shrines of Each Patriot's Devotion. By Frederick G. Vosburgh. 51-82, Jan. 1949

So Long, St. Louis, We're Heading West. By William C. Everhart. 643-669, Nov. 1965

Today Along the Natchez Trace, Pathway Through History. By Bern Keating. Photos by Charles Harbutt. 641-667, Nov. 1968

The Virginians. By Mike W. Edwards. Photos by David Alan Harvey. 588-617, Nov. 1974

We Americans. Book announced. 580-582, Oct. 1975

See also America; Bicentennial; Colonial America; Founders of New England; Founders of Virginia; *and* American Revolution; Civil War, U. S.; World War II; *also* U. S. Capitol; White House; *and* names of presidents, the states, and historical cities and sites, *as:* Boston; Concord; Deerfield; Harpers Ferry; Jamestown; Mystic Seaport; Natchez; Philadelphia; Roanoke Island; St. Augustine; Williamsburg

HISTORY and Beauty Blend in a Concord Iris Garden. By Robert T. Cochran, Jr. Photos by M. Woodbridge Williams. 705-719, May 1959

HISTORY Awakens at Harpers Ferry. By Volkmar Wentzel. 399-416, Mar. 1957

HISTORY Keeps House in Virginia. By Howell Walker. 441-484, Apr. 1956

HISTORY Repeats in Old Natchez. By William H. Nicholas. Photos by Willard R. Culver. 181-208, Feb. 1949

HISTORY Revealed in Ancient Glass. By Ray Winfield Smith. Photos by B. Anthony Stewart and Lee E. Battaglia. 346-369, Sept. 1964

HISTORY Written in the Skies (U. S. Air Force). 273-294, Aug. 1957

HITCHCOCK, STEPHEN W.: Author:
Can We Save Our Salt Marshes? Photos by William R. Curtsinger. 729-765, June 1972

HLUHLUWE GAME RESERVE, South Africa:
Roaming Africa's Unfenced Zoos. By W. Robert Moore. 353-380, Mar. 1950
Safari Through Changing Africa. By Elsie May Bell Grosvenor. Photos by Gilbert Grosvenor. 145-198, Aug. 1953

The **HMONG** of Laos: No Place to Run. By W. E. Garrett. 78-111, Jan. 1974

HOABINHIAN CULTURE:
New Light on a Forgotten Past (Southeast Asia). By Wilhelm G. Solheim II. 330-339, Mar. 1971

HOATZIN:
Strange Little World of the Hoatzin. By J. Lear Grimmer. Photos by M. Woodbridge Williams. 391-401, Sept. 1962

HODGE, JOHN R.: Author:
With the U. S. Army in Korea. 829-840, June 1947

HODGSON, BRYAN: Author:
Exploring England's Canals. Photos by Linda Bartlett. 76-111, July 1974
Irish Ways Live On in Dingle. Photos by Linda Bartlett. 551-576, Apr. 1976
Mountain Voices, Mountain Days. Photos by Linda Bartlett. 118-146, July 1972
The Pipeline: Alaska's Troubled Colossus. Photos by Steve Raymer. 684-717, Nov. 1976

HOGARTH, WILLIAM:
The British Way. By Sir Evelyn Wrench. 421-541, Apr. 1949

HOGS AND HOG RAISING:
America's "Meat on the Hoof." By William H. Nicholas. 33-72, Jan. 1952
The Diffident Truffle, France's Gift to Gourmets. 419-426, Sept. 1956
    Included: Truffle-hunting sows
The Family Farm Ain't What It Used To Be. By James A. Sugar. 391-411, Sept. 1974

HOHOKAM INDIANS:
The Hohokam: First Masters of the American Desert. By Emil W. Haury. Photos by Helga Teiwes. 670-695, May 1967
Magnetic Clues Help Date the Past. By Kenneth F. Weaver. 696-701, May 1967

HOKKAIDŌ (Island), Japan:
Japan's "Sky People," the Vanishing Ainu. By Mary Inez Hilger. Photos by Eiji Miyazawa. 268-296, Feb. 1967
Snow Festival in Japan's Far North. By Eiji Miyazawa. 824-833, Dec. 1968

HOKULE'A (Voyaging Canoe):
A Canoe Helps Hawaii Recapture Her Past. By Herb Kawainui Kane. Photos by David Hiser. 468-489, Apr. 1976
Hokule'a Follows the Stars to Tahiti. By David Lewis. Photos by Nicholas deVore III. 512-537, Oct. 1976
Voyage of the *Hokule'a* (Television film). 575, Nov. 1976

HOLIDAYS. *See* Christmas; Easter; Memorial Day Ceremonies; New Year Celebrations; *and* Festivals

HOLLAND, JAMES R.: Photographer:
Tracking Danger With the Ice Patrol. By William S. Ellis. 780-793, June 1968

HOLLAND. *See* Netherlands

HOLLAND, Michigan:
Work-hard, Play-hard Michigan. By Andrew H. Brown. 279-320, Mar. 1952

HOLLAND in the Caribbean: The Netherlands Antilles. By James Cerruti. Photos by Emory Kristof. 115-146, Jan. 1970

HOLLIDAY, CLYDE T.: Author:
Seeing the Earth From 80 Miles Up. 511-528, Oct. 1950

HOLMES, MIKE: Author-Photographer:
Nauru, the World's Richest Nation. 344-353, Sept. 1976

HOLMES, MIKE; Photographer—*Continued*
Oil and Penguins Don't Mix. 384-397, Mar. 1973

HOLY ISLAND (Lindisfarne), England:
Pilgrimage to Holy Island and the Farnes. By John E. H. Nolan. 547-570, Oct. 1952

HOLY LAND. *See* Bible Lands

HOLY Land, My Country. By His Majesty King Hussein of Jordan. 784-789, Dec. 1964

HOLY WEEK:
Andalusia, the Spirit of Spain. By Howard La Fay. Photos by Joseph J. Scherschel. 833-857, June 1975

Easter Week in Indian Guatemala. By John Scofield. 406-417, Mar. 1960

Guatemala, Maya and Modern. By Louis de la Haba. Photos by Joseph J. Scherschel. 661-689, Nov. 1974

Holy Week and the Fair in Sevilla (Spain). By Luis Marden. 499-530, Apr. 1951

Mesa del Nayar's Strange Holy Week. By Guillermo Aldana E. 780-795, June 1971

HOME Life in Paris Today. By Deena Clark. 43-72, July 1950

HOME to Arran, Scotland's Magic Isle. By J. Harvey Howells. 80-99, July 1965

HOME to Lonely Tristan da Cunha. By James P. Blair. 60-81, Jan. 1964

HOME to the Enduring Berkshires. By Charles McCarry. Photos by Jonathan S. Blair. 196-221, Aug. 1970

HOME to the Holy Land. By Maynard Owen Williams. 707-746, Dec. 1950

HOMER:
Homeward With Ulysses. By Melville Bell Grosvenor. Photos by Edwin Stuart Grosvenor. 1-39, July 1973

HOMESTEADING:
Alaskan Family Robinson. By Nancy Robinson. Photos by John Metzger and Peter Robinson. 55-75, Jan. 1973

HOMEWARD With Ulysses. By Melville Bell Grosvenor. Photos by Edwin Stuart Grosvenor. 1-39, July 1973

HONDURAS, British. *See* Belize

HONEY ANTS:
Living Honey Jars of the Ant World. By Ross E. Hutchins. 405-411, Mar. 1962

HONEY EATERS of Currumbin (Lorikeets). By Paul A. Zahl. 510-519, Oct. 1956

HONEY-GUIDE: The Bird That Eats Wax. By Herbert Friedmann. Paintings by Walter A. Weber. 551-560, Apr. 1954

HONEYBEES:
Honeybees. Children's book announced. 726-728, Nov. 1973

Inside the World of the Honeybee. By Treat Davidson. 188-217, Aug. 1959

Those Fiery Brazilian Bees. By Rick Gore. Photos

HONEYBEES—*Continued*
by Bianca Lavies. 491-501, Apr. 1976

HONEYCUTT, BROOKS; Photographer:
Life 8,000 Years Ago Uncovered in an Alabama Cave. By Carl F. Miller. 542-558, Oct. 1956

HONG KONG:
Eyes on the China Coast. By George W. Long. 505-512, Apr. 1953

Hong Kong, Saturday's Child. By Joseph Judge. Photos by Bruce Dale. 541-573, Oct. 1971

Hong Kong Hangs On. By George W. Long. Photos by J. Baylor Roberts. 239-272, Feb. 1954

Hong Kong Has Many Faces. By John Scofield. 1-41, Jan. 1962

Hong Kong Restored. 483-490, Apr. 1947

Round the World School (ISA). By Paul Antze. Photos by William Eppridge. 96-127, July 1962

Those Outlandish Goldfish! By Paul A. Zahl. 514-533, Apr. 1973

Trawling the China Seas. Photos by J. Charles Thompson. 381-395, Mar. 1950

YWCA: International Success Story. By Mary French Rockefeller. Photos by Otis Imboden. 904-933, Dec. 1963

See also Pacific Fleet, U. S.

HONOLULU, Oahu, Hawaii:
Because It Rains on Hawaii. By Frederick Simpich, Jr. 571-610, Nov. 1949

Honolulu, Mid-ocean Capital. By Frederick Simpich, Jr. Photos by B. Anthony Stewart. 577-624, May 1954

Look What's Happened to Honolulu! By Jim Becker. Photos by Bates Littlehales. 500-531, Oct. 1969

HONSHU (Island), Japan:
Backwoods Japan During American Occupation. By M. A. Huberman. 491-518, Apr. 1947

Kayak Odyssey: From the Inland Sea to Tokyo. By Dan Dimancescu. Photos by Christopher G. Knight. 295-337, Sept. 1967

HOOGSTRAAL, HARRY; Author:
South in the Sudan. 249-272, Feb. 1953

Yemen Opens the Door to Progress. 213-244, Feb. 1952

HOOVER, HERBERT:
The Living White House. By Lonnelle Aikman. 593-643, Nov. 1966

Profiles of the Presidents: IV. America Enters the Modern Era. By Frank Freidel. 537-577, Oct. 1965

HOPE DIAMOND:
Questing for Gems. By George S. Switzer. 835-863, Dec. 1971

HOPE for Big Cypress Swamp. By Rick Gore. Photos by Patricia Caulfield. 251-273, Aug. 1976

HOPE-TAYLOR, BRIAN; Artist:
Stonehenge—New Light on an Old Riddle. By Harold E. Edgerton. 846-866, June 1960

HOPEH (Province), China. *See* Peking

HOPES and Fears in Booming Thailand. By Peter T. White. Photos by Dean Conger. 76-125, July 1967

HOPES and Worries Along the Columbia River, Powerhouse of the Northwest. By David S. Boyer. 821-847, Dec. 1974

HOPEWELL CULTURE. *See* Mound Builders

HOPI INDIANS. *See* Kachinas

HORGAN, THOMAS: Author:
Down East Cruise (Maine). Photos by Luis Marden. 329-369, Sept. 1952
Nomad Sails Long Island Sound. 295-338, Sept. 1957
Windjamming Around New England. Photos by Robert F. Sisson. 141-169, Aug. 1950

HORN, Cape, South America:
'Round the Horn by Submarine. By Paul C. Stimson. 129-144, Jan. 1948

HORNBEIN, THOMAS F.: Author:
The First Traverse. By Thomas F. Hornbein and William F. Unsoeld. 509-513, Oct. 1963
See also American Mount Everest Expedition

HORNBILLS, African Red-billed:
Inside a Hornbill's Walled-up Nest. Photos by Joan and Alan Root. 846-855, Dec. 1969

HORNOCKER, MAURICE G.: Author-Photographer:
Stalking the Mountain Lion—to Save Him. 638-655, Nov. 1969

HORROR Strikes on Good Friday (Alaska Earthquake). By William P. E. Graves. 112-139, July 1964

HORSE FAIRS. *See* Appleby Fair

HORSE RACES:
Heart of the Bluegrass (Kentucky). By Charles McCarry. Photos by J. Bruce Baumann. 634-659, May 1974
The Palio of Siena (Italy). By Edgar Erskine Hume. 231-244, Aug. 1951

HORSE SHOWS:
Dublin's Historic Horse Show. By Maynard Owen Williams. 115-132, July 1953
New York Again Hails the Horse (National Horse Show). By Walter B. Devereux. 697-720, Nov. 1954

HORSEMEN. *See* Cowboys; Kazakhs; Turkomans

HORSES:
Heart of the Bluegrass (Kentucky). By Charles McCarry. Photos by J. Bruce Baumann. 634-659, May 1974
Contents: Thoroughbred racehorses
King Ranch, Cattle Empire in Texas. 41-64, Jan. 1952
The White Horses of Vienna. By Beverley M. Bowie. Photos by Volkmar Wentzel. 401-419, Sept. 1958

HORSES, Wild:
The Animals Nobody Loved (Television film). cover announcement, Feb. 1976
On the Track of the West's Wild Horses. By Hope Ryden. Photos by author and Dick Durrance II. 94-109, Jan. 1971
Safe Landing on Sable, Isle of 500 Shipwrecks. By Melville Bell Grosvenor. 398-431, Sept. 1965

HORSES, Wild—*Continued*
The Wild Ponies of Assateague Island. Children's book announced. 724-726, Nov. 1975

HORSTMAN, ROBERT and NINA: Authors:
Our Friend From the Sea (Seal). Photos by Robert F. Sisson. 728-736, Nov. 1968

HORTICULTURE:
England's Scillies, the Flowering Isles. By Alan Villiers. Photos by Bates Littlehales. 126-145, July 1967
The Flower Seed Growers: Gardening's Color Merchants. By Robert de Roos. Photos by Jack Fields. 720-738, May 1968
The Netherlands: Nation at War With the Sea. By Alan Villiers. Photos by Adam Woolfitt. 530-571, Apr. 1968
Patent Plants Enrich Our World. By Orville H. Kneen. Photos from U. S. Plant Patents. 357-378, Mar. 1948
See also Flowers; Fruit and Fruit Growing; Vegetables; *and* Gardens

HOSTELS:
Europe Via the Hostel Route. By Joseph Nettis. 124-154, July 1955
Lake District, Poets' Corner of England. By H. V. Morton. Photos by David S. Boyer. 511-545, Apr. 1956
Thumbs Up Round the North Sea's Rim. By Frances James. Photos by Erica Koch. 685-704, May 1952

HOT-AIR Balloons Race on Silent Winds. By William R. Berry. Photos by Don W. Jones. 392-407, Mar. 1966

HOUOT, GEORGES S.: Author:
Deep Diving off Japan. 138-150, Jan. 1960
Two and a Half Miles Down. 80-86, July 1954
Author-Photographer
Four Years of Diving to the Bottom of the Sea. 715-731, May 1958
See also F.N.R.S. 3, for dives

HOUSES:
History Keeps House in Virginia. By Howell Walker. 441-484, Apr. 1956
History Repeats in Old Natchez. By William H. Nicholas. Photos by Willard R. Culver. 181-208, Feb. 1949
Inside the White House. By Lonnelle Aikman. Photos by B. Anthony Stewart and Thomas Nebbia. 3-43, Jan. 1961
Land of Louisiana Sugar Kings. By Harnett T. Kane. Photos by Willard R. Culver. 531-567, Apr. 1958
Land of the Pilgrims' Pride. By George W. Long. Photos by Robert F. Sisson. 193-219, Aug. 1947
Literary Landmarks of Massachusetts. By William H. Nicholas. Photos by B. Anthony Stewart and John E. Fletcher. 279-310, Mar. 1950
The Living White House. By Lonnelle Aikman. 593-643, Nov. 1966
Mr. Jefferson's Charlottesville. By Anne Revis. 553-592, May 1950
Philadelphia Houses a Proud Past. By Harold Donaldson Eberlein. Photos by Thomas Nebbia. 151-191, Aug. 1960

HOUSES—*Continued*

Rhododendron Glories of Southwest Scotland. By David S. Boyer. Photos by B. Anthony Stewart and author. 641-664, May 1954

Roving Maryland's Cavalier Country. By William A. Kinney. 431-470, Apr. 1954

Stately Homes of Old Virginia. By Albert W. Atwood. 787-802, June 1953

Vacation Tour Through Lincoln Land. By Ralph Gray. 141-184, Feb. 1952

Washington: Home of the Nation's Great. By Albert W. Atwood. 699-738, June 1947
    Contents: Ashburton House, Blair House, Clara Barton Home, Decatur House, Laird-Dunlop House, Madison Houses, Petersen House, Surratt House, Tayloe House, Tudor Place, The White House

See also Hearst San Simeon State Historical Monument; Henry E. Huntington Library and Art Gallery; Henry Ford Museum; Monticello; Mount Vernon

HOUSES, Underwater. *See* Conshelf Bases; Link Igloo; SPID; Tektite II

HOUSEWIFE at the End of the World. By Rae Natalie P. Goodall. Photos by James L. Stanfield. 130-150, Jan. 1971

HOUSTON, Texas:

Houston, Prairie Dynamo. By Stuart E. Jones. Photos by William Albert Allard. 338-377, Sept. 1967

HOW Bats Hunt With Sound. By J. J. G. McCue. 571-578, Apr. 1961

HOW Fruit Came to America. By J. R. Magness. Paintings by Else Bostelmann. 325-377, Sept. 1951

HOW Man-made Satellites Can Affect Our Lives. By Joseph Kaplan. 791-810, Dec. 1957

HOW Old Is It? By Lyman J. Briggs and Kenneth F. Weaver. 234-255, Aug. 1958

HOW One of the Society's Maps Saved a Precious Cargo. 844, June 1947

HOW the Decoy Fish Catches Its Dinner. Photos by Robert J. Shallenberger and William D. Madden. 224-227, Aug. 1974

HOW the Kazakhs Fled to Freedom. By Milton J. Clark. 621-644, Nov. 1954

HOW the Sun Gives Life to the Sea. By Paul A. Zahl. 199-225, Feb. 1961

HOW to Catch a Passing Comet. By Kenneth F. Weaver. 148-150, Jan. 1974

HOW to End a War: Grant and Lee at Appomattox. By Ulysses S. Grant 3rd. Photos by Bruce Dale. 435-469, Apr. 1965

HOW We Climbed Everest. By Barry C. Bishop. 477-507, Oct. 1963

HOW We Found the *Monitor*. By John G. Newton. 48-61, Jan. 1975

HOW We Plan to Put Men on the Moon. By Hugh L. Dryden. Paintings by Davis Meltzer and Pierre Mion. 357-401, Mar. 1964

HOW We Sailed the New *Mayflower* to America. By Alan Villiers. 627-672, Nov. 1957

HOWE, JULIA WARD:

Literary Landmarks of Massachusetts. By William H. Nicholas. Photos by B. Anthony Stewart and John E. Fletcher. 279-310, Mar. 1950

HOWELL, THOMAS R.: Author:

What a Place to Lay an Egg! 414-419, Sept. 1971

HOWELLS, J. HARVEY: Author:

Home to Arran, Scotland's Magic Isle. 80-99, July 1965

HOXIE BROS. GIGANTIC 3-RING CIRCUS:

On the Road With an Old-time Circus. By John Fetterman. Photos by Jonathan Blair. 410-434, Mar. 1972

HSINKING, Manchuria. *See* Changchun

HUACA DE LA CRUZ, Virú Valley, Peru:

Finding the Tomb of a Warrior-God. By William Duncan Strong. Photos by Clifford Evans, Jr. 453-482, Apr. 1947

HUASCARÁN NEVADO (Peak), Peru:

Avalanche! By Bart McDowell. Photos by John E. Fletcher. 855-880, June 1962

HUBBARD, GARDINER GREENE:

Clarke School for the Deaf. 382, 385, 386, 387, Mar. 1955

First President of National Geographic Society and of Bell Telephone Company. 273, Mar. 1947; 517, 522, Oct. 1963; 1, 101, 103, 113, July 1965; 456, 458, Oct. 1966; 584, Apr. 1968

A founder of the NGS. 387, Mar. 1955; 3, Jan. 1963; 459, Oct. 1963; 456, Oct. 1966

HUBBARD MEDAL:

Medal designed by Laura Gardin Fraser; both sides shown. 564, Apr. 1953

Recipients

American Mount Everest Expedition: Medal presented to Norman G. Dyhrenfurth, leader of the expedition, with 21 gold-plated bronze replicas to individual members. 514-515, Oct. 1963; 1B, Jan. 1964; 331, Mar. 1964; 15, July 1965

Apollo 8 and Apollo 11 astronauts. 859-861, June 1970

Arnold, Henry H. 868, Dec. 1957; 583, Oct. 1963; 584, Apr. 1968

Bartlett, Robert A. 787, June 1949; 470, Oct. 1953

British Mount Everest Expedition: Medal presented to Sir John Hunt, with bronze replicas to Sir John, Sir Edmund Hillary, and Tenzing Norgay (in India). 64, July 1954; 846, June 1955; 867-868, Dec. 1957; 98, Jan. 1966; 584, Apr. 1968

Byrd, Richard E. 250, Feb. 1948; 65H, July 1954; 38, 39, July 1957; 868, Dec. 1957; 574, 576, Apr. 1962; 556, Oct. 1963; 571, Oct. 1965; 584, Apr. 1968

Ellsworth, Lincoln. 868, Dec. 1957; 583, Oct. 1963; 689, Nov. 1964; 847, June 1967; 584, Apr. 1968

Fuchs, Sir Vivian. 589-590, Apr. 1959

Glenn, John H., Jr. 827, June 1962; 904, 905, 906, Dec. 1962; 29, Jan. 1963; 584, Apr. 1968

Leakey, Dr. and Mrs. Louis S. B. 903, 905, Dec. 1962; 197, 231, Feb. 1965

Lindbergh, Anne Morrow. 562, Oct. 1963

Lindbergh, Charles A. 868, Dec. 1957; 563, Oct. 1963; 584, 586, Apr. 1968

HUBBARD MEDAL—*Continued*

MacMillan, Donald Baxter. 563-564, Apr. 1953

Peary, Robert E. 867, Dec. 1957; 589, Apr. 1959; 905, Dec. 1962; 514, Oct. 1963; 584, Apr. 1968

Shackleton, Sir Ernest H. 868, Dec. 1957

Siple, Paul A. 792-793, June 1958

Trippe, Juan. 584-586, Apr. 1968

U. S. Navy Antarctic Expeditions of 1955-1959: Medal presented to Secretary of the Navy Thomas S. Gates, Jr., with gold duplicates to Adm. Arleigh A. Burke and Rear Adm. George Dufek. 589-590, Apr. 1959; 530, Oct. 1959

Wetmore, Alexander. 151, Aug. 1975

HUBERMAN, M. A.: Author:

Backwoods Japan During American Occupation. 491-518, Apr. 1947

HUDSON, HENRY:

Henry Hudson's River. By Willard Price. Photos by Wayne Miller. 364-403, Mar. 1962

North Through History Aboard *White Mist*. By Melville Bell Grosvenor. Photos by Edwin Stuart Grosvenor. 1-55, July 1970

HUDSON (River), New York:

Henry Hudson's River. By Willard Price. Photos by Wayne Miller. 364-403, Mar. 1962

Here's New York Harbor. By Stuart E. Jones. Photos by Robert F. Sisson and David S. Boyer. 773-813, Dec. 1954

The Mighty Hudson. By Albert W. Atwood. Photos by B. Anthony Stewart. 1-36, July 1948

North Through History Aboard *White Mist*. By Melville Bell Grosvenor. Photos by Edwin Stuart Grosvenor. 1-55, July 1970

Shad in the Shadow of Skyscrapers. By Dudley B. Martin. Photos by Luis Marden. 359-376, Mar. 1947

See also Operation Sail

HUDSON BAY, Canada:

Trailing Cosmic Rays in Canada's North. By Martin A. Pomerantz. 99-115, Jan. 1953

See also Igloolik; James Bay; McConnell River Region; Southampton Island

HUE, Viet Nam:

Behind the Headlines in Viet Nam. By Peter T. White. Photos by Winfield Parks. 149-189, Feb. 1967

Portrait of Indochina. By W. Robert Moore and Maynard Owen Williams. Paintings by Jean Despujols. 461-490, Apr. 1951

HUENS, JEAN-LEON: Artist:

Pioneers in Man's Search for the Universe. By Thomas Y. Canby. 627-633, May 1974

Sir Francis Drake. By Alan Villiers. Photos by Gordon W. Gahan. 216-253, Feb. 1975

HUMAN BODY:

The Incredible Machine (Television film). 299, Sept. 1975; cover announcement, Oct. 1975; 583, Nov. 1975; 575, Nov. 1976

See also Medicine and Health

HUMAN Treasures of Japan. By William Graves. Photos by James L. Stanfield. 370-379, Sept. 1972

HUMASON, MILTON L.: Author:

First Photographs of Planets and Moon Taken with

HUMASON, MILTON L.: Author—*Continued*

Palomar's 200-inch Telescope. 125-130, Jan. 1953

HUMBOLDT REDWOODS STATE PARK, California. *See* Redwood Trees (Finding the Mt. Everest of All Living Things; World's Tallest Tree)

HUME, EDGAR ERSKINE: Author:

Italy Smiles Again. 693-732, June 1949

The Palio of Siena. 231-244, Aug. 1951

HUMMINGBIRDS:

Freezing the Flight of Hummingbirds. By Harold E. Edgerton, R. J. Niedrach, and Walker Van Riper. 245-261, Aug. 1951

The Hummingbirds. By Crawford H. Greenewalt. 658-679, Nov. 1960

Hummingbirds in Action. By Harold E. Edgerton. 221-232, Aug. 1947

The Man Who Talks to Hummingbirds (Augusto Ruschi). By Luis Marden. Photos by James Blair. 80-99, Jan. 1963

The Marvelous Hummingbird Rediscovered. By Crawford H. Greenewalt. 98-101, July 1966

Photographing Hummingbirds in Brazil. By Crawford H. Greenewalt. 100-115, Jan. 1963

HUNAN PROVINCE, People's Republic of China. *See* Ch'angsha

HUNGARIANS:

Freedom Flight from Hungary. Photos by Robert F. Sisson. 424-436, Mar. 1957

HUNGARY:

Down the Danube by Canoe. By William Slade Backer. Photos by Richard S. Durrance and Christopher G. Knight. 34-79, July 1965

Hungary: Changing Homeland of a Tough, Romantic People. By Bart McDowell. Photos by Albert Moldvay and Joseph J. Scherschel. 443-483, Apr. 1971

HUNT, SIR JOHN:

President Eisenhower Presents the Hubbard Medal to Everest's Conquerors. 64, July 1954

Triumph on Everest. 1-63, July 1954

Siege and Assault. By Sir John Hunt. 1-43

HUNTER, WILLIAM and JOHN:

The British Way. By Sir Evelyn Wrench. 421-541, Apr. 1949

HUNTING:

Cliff Dwellers of the Bering Sea. By Juan Muñoz. 129-146, Jan. 1954
Included: Seal and walrus hunting

Nomad in Alaska's Outback. By Thomas J. Abercrombie. 540-567, Apr. 1969
Included: Walrus hunting

We Dwelt in Kashgai Tents (Iran). By Jean and Franc Shor. 805-832, June 1952

See also Falconry; Jaguar Hunting; Lions (Spearing Lions); Sealing; Whaling; *and* Bird Dogs

HUNTING Africa's Smallest Game (Insects). By Edward S. Ross. 406-419, Mar. 1961

HUNTING Folk Songs in the Hebrides. By Margaret Shaw Campbell. 249-272, Feb. 1947

HUNTING Mexico's Buried Temples. Photos by Richard H. Stewart. 145-168, Feb. 1947

HUNTING Musical Game in West Africa. By Arthur S. Alberts. 262-282, Aug. 1951

HUNTING Prehistory in Panama Jungles. By Matthew W. Stirling. Photos by Richard H. Stewart. 271-290, Aug. 1953

HUNTING the Heartbeat of a Whale. By Paul Dudley White and Samuel W. Matthews. 49-64, July 1956

HUNTING Uranium Around the World. By Robert D. Nininger. Photos by Volkmar Wentzel. 533-558, Oct. 1954

HUNTINGTON, HENRY E., LIBRARY AND ART GALLERY, San Marino, California:
Huntington Library, California Treasure House. By David S. Boyer. 251-276, Feb. 1958

HUNZA:
At World's End in Hunza. By Jean and Franc Shor. 485-518, Oct. 1953

"Every Day Is a Gift When You Are Over 100." By Alexander Leaf. Photos by John Launois. 93-119, Jan. 1973

Sky Road East. By Tay and Lowell Thomas, Jr. 71-112, Jan. 1960

Trek to Lofty Hunza—and Beyond. By Sabrina and Roland Michaud. 644-669, Nov. 1975

HUPEH (Province), China. See Hankow

HURLEY, FRANK: Photographer:
Arab Land Beyond the Jordan. 753-768, Dec. 1947

HURON, Lake, Canada-U. S.:
The Great Lakes: Is It Too Late? By Gordon Young. Photos by James L. Amos and Martin Rogers. 147-185, Aug. 1973

HURRICANES:
Cajunland, Louisiana's French-speaking Coast. By Bern Keating. Photos by Charles Harbutt and Franke Keating. 353-391, Mar. 1966
Included: Hurricane Audrey (1957); Hurricane Betsy (1965)

Men Against the Hurricane. By Andrew H. Brown. 537-560, Oct. 1950

We're Doing Something About the Weather! By Walter Orr Roberts. 518-555, Apr. 1972

HURTADO, EUSEBIO DÁVALOS. See Dávalos Hurtado, Eusebio

HUSSEIN, King (Jordan):
The Other Side of Jordan. By Luis Marden. 790-825, Dec. 1964
Author
Holy Land, My Country. 784-789, Dec. 1964

HUTCHINS, ROSS E.: Author-Photographer:
Living Honey Jars of the Ant World. 405-411, Mar. 1962

HUTCHISON, BRUCE: Author:
Exploring Ottawa. 565-596, Nov. 1947

HUTCHISON, ISOBEL WYLIE: Author:
From Barra to Butt in the Hebrides. 559-580, Oct. 1954

HUTCHISON, ISOBEL WYLIE: Author—*Continued*
Poets' Voices Linger in Scottish Shrines. Photos by Kathleen Revis. 437-488, Oct. 1957

Shetland and Orkney, Britain's Far North. 519-536, Oct. 1953

A Stroll to John o'Groat's. 1-48, July 1956

A Stroll to London. Photos by B. Anthony Stewart. 171-204, Aug. 1950

A Stroll to Venice. 378-410, Sept. 1951

2,000 Miles Through Europe's Oldest Kingdom. Photos by Maynard Owen Williams. 141-180, Feb. 1949

HUTSON, PAT: Author:
Snow-mantled Stehekin: Where Solitude Is in Season. Photos by Bruce Dale. 572-588, Apr. 1974

The HUTTERITES, Plain People of the West. By William Albert Allard. 98-125, July 1970

HUTTON, JACQUELINE: Artist:
Strange Babies of the Sea. By Hilary B. Moore. Paintings by Craig Phillips and Jacqueline Hutton. 41-56, July 1952

HUZZA for Otaheite! By Luis Marden. 435-459, Apr. 1962

HYBRIDS:
Amateur Gardener Creates a New Rose. By Elizabeth A. Moize. Photos by Farrell Grehan. 286-294, Aug. 1972

The Exquisite Orchids. By Luis Marden. 485-513, Apr. 1971

See also Africanized Honeybees

HYDROELECTRIC POWER:
The Fire of Heaven. By Albert W. Atwood. 655-674, Nov. 1948

New St. Lawrence Seaway Opens the Great Lakes to the World. By Andrew H. Brown. 299-339, Mar. 1959

Niagara Falls, Servant of Good Neighbors. Photos by Walter Meayers Edwards. 574-587, Apr. 1963

Powerhouse of the Northwest (Columbia River). By David S. Boyer. 821-847, Dec. 1974

See also Cooper River Water Project; Kemano Power Development

HYDROFOIL BOATS:
Hydrofoil, *HD-4*, designed by Alexander Graham Bell. 493, 495, 496, Apr. 1957; 257, 264, Aug. 1959; 554-555, Oct. 1963

Hydrofoil Ferry "Flies" the Strait of Messina. By Gilbert Grosvenor. 493-496, Apr. 1957
Contents: *Arrow of the Sun, HD-4*

HYENAS:
The Flamingo Eaters of Ngorongoro. By Richard D. Estes. 535-539, Oct. 1973

Hyenas, the Hunters Nobody Knows. By Hans Kruuk. Photos by Baron Hugo van Lawick. 44-57, July 1968

I

IC. *See* Integrated Circuits

IGY. *See* International Geophysical Year

ISA. *See* International School of America

I BECOME a Bakhtiari. By Paul Edward Case. 325-358, Mar. 1947

I FLY the X-15. By Joseph A. Walker. Photos by Dean Conger. 428-450, Sept. 1962

I FOUND the Bones of the *Bounty*. By Luis Marden. 725-789, Dec. 1957

I JOINED a Sahara Salt Caravan. By Victor Englebert. 694-711, Nov. 1965

I LIVE With the Eskimos. By Guy Mary-Rousseliere. 188-217, Feb. 1971

I SAILED with Portugal's Captains Courageous. By Alan Villiers. 565-596, May 1952

I SEE America First. By Lynda Bird Johnson. Photos by William Albert Allard. 874-904, Dec. 1965

I WALKED Some Irish Miles. By Dorothea Sheats. 653-678, May 1951

IBAN (People):
Brunei, Borneo's Abode of Peace. By Joseph Judge. Photos by Dean Conger. 207-225, Feb. 1974

In Storied Lands of Malaysia. By Maurice Shadbolt. Photos by Winfield Parks. 734-783, Nov. 1963

Jungle Journeys in Sarawak. By Hedda Morrison. 710-736, May 1956

IBERIAN PENINSULA:
Spain and Portugal, Atlas series supplement. Mar. 1965

See also Gibraltar; Portugal; Spain

IBISES:
New Scarlet Bird in Florida Skies. By Paul A. Zahl. 874-882, Dec. 1967

Search for the Scarlet Ibis in Venezuela. By Paul A. Zahl. 633-661, May 1950

Wildlife of Everglades National Park. By Daniel B. Beard. Paintings by Walter A. Weber. 83-116, Jan. 1949

See also Wood Storks

IBIZA (Island), Balearics:
Spain's Sun-blest Pleasure Isles. By Ethel A. Starbird. Photos by James A. Sugar. 679-701, May 1976

ICE AGE MAN:
A Bold New Look at Our Past. The Editor. 62-63, Jan. 1975

Exploring the Mind of Ice Age Man. By Alexander Marshack. 64-89, Jan. 1975

Ice Age Man, the First American. By Thomas R. Henry. Paintings by Andre Durenceau. 781-806, Dec. 1955

Wyoming Muck Tells of Battle: Ice Age Man vs. Mammoth. By Cynthia Irwin, Henry Irwin, and George Agogino. 828-837, June 1962

ICE AGES:
"Ice Age Mammals of the Alaskan Tundra," painting supplement. Map of Canada. Mar. 1972

A Visit to the Living Ice Age. By Rutherford Platt. 525-545, Apr. 1957

What's Happening to Our Climate? By Samuel W. Matthews. 576-615, Nov. 1976

ICE BIRD (Sloop):
Alone to Antarctica. By David Lewis. Drawings by

ICE BIRD (Sloop)—*Continued*
Noel Sickles. 808-821, Dec. 1973

Ice Bird Ends Her Lonely Odyssey. By David Lewis. 216-233, Aug. 1975

ICE CAVES:
Probing Ice Caves of the Pyrenees. By Norbert Casteret. 391-404, Mar. 1953

ICE-CORE DATING:
What's Happening to Our Climate? By Samuel W. Matthews. 576-615, Nov. 1976

ICE FISHING:
Ice Fishing's Frigid Charms. By Thomas J. Abercrombie. 861-872, Dec. 1958

ICE ISLANDS:
North Toward the Pole on Skis. By Bjørn O. Staib. 254-281, Feb. 1965

Scientists Ride Ice Islands on Arctic Odysseys. By Lowell Thomas, Jr. Photos by Ted Spiegel. 670-691, Nov. 1965

See also T-3

ICE SCULPTURE:
Snow Festival in Japan's Far North. Photos by Eiji Miyazawa. 824-833, Dec. 1968

ICEBERGS:
Far North with "Captain Mac." By Miriam MacMillan. 465-513, Oct. 1951

Our Navy Explores Antarctica. By Richard E. Byrd. U. S. Navy official photos. 429-522, Oct. 1947

Tracking Danger with the Ice Patrol. By William S. Ellis. Photos by James R. Holland. 780-793, June 1968

ICEBREAKERS:
North for Oil: *Manhattan* Makes the Historic Northwest Passage. By Bern Keating. Photos by Tomas Sennett. 374-391, Mar. 1970

Our Navy Explores Antarctica. By Richard E. Byrd. U. S. Navy official photos. 429-522, Oct. 1947

Sea to Lakes on the St. Lawrence. By George W. Long. Photos by B. Anthony Stewart and John E. Fletcher. 323-366, Sept. 1950

ICELAND:
"Around the World in Eighty Days." By Newman Bumstead. 705-750, Dec. 1951
Included: Hekla Volcano; Reykjavík; Vatna Jökull

Atlantic Odyssey: Iceland to Antarctica. By Newman Bumstead. Photos by Volkmar Wentzel. 725-780, Dec. 1955

Friendly Flight to Northern Europe. By Lyndon B. Johnson. Photos by Volkmar Wentzel. 268-293, Feb. 1964

Iceland Tapestry. By Deena Clark. 599-630, Nov. 1951

Sailing Iceland's Rugged Coasts. By Wright Britton. Photos by James A. Sugar. 228-265, Aug. 1969

This Changing Earth. By Samuel W. Matthews. 1-37, Jan. 1973

See also Heimaey; Surtsey; *and* Vikings

ICHAC, PIERRE: Photographer:
Carefree People of the Cameroons. 233-248, Feb. 1947

ICONS:

Mount Sinai's Holy Treasures (St. Catherine's Monastery). By Kurt Weitzmann. Photos by Fred Anderegg. 109-127, Jan. 1964

IDAHO:

Following the Trail of Lewis and Clark. By Ralph Gray. 707-750, June 1953

Forest Fire: The Devil's Picnic. By Stuart E. Jones and Jay Johnston. 100-127, July 1968
  Included: Blazes in Kaniksu National Forest and Nezperce National Forest

High-stepping Idaho. By William S. Ellis. Photos by Dean Conger. 290-317, Mar. 1973

Idaho Loggers Battle a River. 117-130, July 1951

Man on the Moon in Idaho. By William Belknap, Jr. 505-525, Oct. 1960

A Map Maker Looks at the United States. By Newman Bumstead. 705-748, June 1951
  Included: Coeur d'Alene; Lewiston; Pleasant Valley Rapids; Pocatello; Seven Devils country; Snake River; Weiser

White-water Adventure on Wild Rivers of Idaho. By Frank Craighead, Jr. and John Craighead. 213-239, Feb. 1970

See also Morgan Creek

IDYLL, CLARENCE P.: Author:

The Crab That Shakes Hands. Photos by Robert F. Sisson. 254-271, Feb. 1971

Grunion, the Fish That Spawns on Land. Photos by Robert F. Sisson. 714-723, May 1969

The Incredible Salmon. Photos by Robert F. Sisson. Paintings by Walter A. Weber. 195-219, Aug. 1968

New Florida Resident, the Walking Catfish. Photos by Robert F. Sisson. 847-851, June 1969

Shrimp Nursery: Science Explores New Ways to Farm the Sea. Photos by Robert F. Sisson. 636-659, May 1965

Shrimpers Strike Gold in the Gulf. Photos by Robert F. Sisson. 699-707, May 1957

The **IDYLLIC** Vale of Kashmir. By Volkmar Wentzel. 523-550, Apr. 1948

IFALIK, Lonely Paradise of the South Seas. By Marston Bates. 547-571, Apr. 1956

IGLOOLIK, Northwest Territories, Canada:

I Live With the Eskimos. By Guy Mary-Rousseliere. 188-217, Feb. 1971

IGUANAS:

The Galapagos, Eerie Cradle of New Species. By Roger Tory Peterson. Photos by Alan and Joan Root. 541-585, Apr. 1967

In the Wilds of a City Parlor. By Paul A. Zahl. 645-672, Nov. 1954

Lost World of the Galapagos. By Irving and Electa Johnson. 681-703, May 1959

IKEYA-SEKI COMET:

Giant Comet Grazes the Sun. By Kenneth F. Weaver. 259-261, Feb. 1966

ÎLE DE LA CITÉ, Birthplace of Paris. By Kenneth MacLeish. Photos by Bruce Dale. 680-719, May 1968

ILHA NOVA, Azores:

A New Volcano Bursts from the Atlantic. By John

ILHA NOVA, Azores—*Continued*

Scofield. Photos by Robert F. Sisson. 735-757, June 1958

ILLINOIS:

Following the Trail of Lewis and Clark. By Ralph Gray. 707-750, June 1953

Illinois—Healthy Heart of the Nation. By Leo A. Borah. Photos by B. Anthony Stewart and Willard R. Culver. 781-820, Dec. 1953

Illinois: The City and the Plain. By Robert Paul Jordan. Photos by James L. Stanfield and Joseph J. Scherschel. 745-797, June 1967

Mapping the Nation's Breadbasket. By Frederick Simpich. 831-849, June 1948

The Upper Mississippi. By Willard Price. 651-699, Nov. 1958

Vacation Tour Through Lincoln Land. By Ralph Gray. 141-184, Feb. 1952

Who Were the "Mound Builders"? By George E. Stuart. 783-801, Dec. 1972

See also Cairo; East St. Louis; Shawneetown

ILLINOIS (River), Illinois:

Down Mark Twain's River on a Raft. By Rex E. Hieronymus. 551-574, Apr. 1948
  Included: Illinois River; Mississippi River

ILLUSTRATED LONDON NEWS:

Witness to a War (U. S. Civil War): British Correspondent Frank Vizetelly. By Robert T. Cochran, Jr. 453-491, Apr. 1961

ILULÍSSAT, Greenland. *See* Jakobshavn

I'M From New Jersey. By John T. Cunningham. Photos by Volkmar Wentzel. 1-45, Jan. 1960

IMBODEN, OTIS: Photographer:

Drowned Galleons Yield Spanish Gold. By Kip Wagner. 1-37, Jan. 1965

First Flight Across the Bottom of the World. By James R. Reedy. 454-464, Mar. 1964

Florida's Emerging Seminoles. By Louis Capron. 716-734, Nov. 1969

The Maya: Riddle of the Glyphs. By George E. Stuart. 768-791, Dec. 1975

The People of Cades Cove. By William O. Douglas. Photos by Thomas Nebbia and Otis Imboden. 60-95, July 1962

Thera, Key to the Riddle of Minos. By Spyridon Marinatos. 702-726, May 1972

Threatened Glories of Everglades National Park. By Frederick Kent Truslow and Frederick G. Vosburgh. Photos by Frederick Kent Truslow and Otis Imboden. 508-553, Oct. 1967

YWCA: International Success Story. By Mary French Rockefeller. 904-933, Dec. 1963

IMMIGRANTS:

Australia

Coober Pedy: Opal Capital of Australia's Outback. By Kenny Moore. Photos by Penny Tweedie. 560-571, Oct. 1976

The Making of a New Australia. By Howell Walker. 233-259, Feb. 1956

South Australia, Gateway to the Great Outback. By Howell Walker. Photos by Joseph J. Scherschel. 441-481, Apr. 1970

Israel

Israel—The Seventh Day. By Joseph Judge. Photos by Gordon W. Gahan. 816-855, Dec. 1972

IMMIGRANTS — *Continued*

Our Life on a Border Kibbutz. By Carol and Al Abrams. Photos by Al Abrams. 364-391, Sept. 1970

United States

Chinatown, the Gilded Ghetto. By William Albert Allard. 627-643, Nov. 1975

Cuba's Exiles Bring New Life to Miami. By Edward J. Linehan. Photos by Nathan Benn. 68-95, July 1973

Immigrants Still Flock to Liberty's Land. By Albert W. Atwood. 708-724, Nov. 1955

New England's "Little Portugal." By O. Louis Mazzatenta. 90-109, Jan. 1975

See also Hutterites; Moravians; Old Believers (Russians); Swiss Colonists; Ukrainians

The IMPERILED Everglades. By Fred Ward. 1-27, Jan. 1972

The IMPERILED Giants. By William Graves. 722-751, Dec. 1976

IMPERILED Gift of the Sea: Caribbean Green Turtle. By Archie Carr. Photos by Robert E. Schroeder. 876-890, June 1967

IMPERILED Phantom of Asian Peaks: First Photographs of Snow Leopards in the Wild. By George B. Schaller. 702-707, Nov. 1971

IMPRESSIONIST ART. *See* French Impressionists

IMPRINTING. *See* Snow Geese

IN Manchuria Now. By W. Robert Moore. 389-414, Mar. 1947

IN Quest of Beauty. Text by Paul Mellon. 372-385, Mar. 1967

IN Quest of the Rarest Flamingo. By William G. Conway. Photos by Bates Littlehales. 91-105, July 1961

IN Quest of the World's Largest Frog. By Paul A. Zahl. 146-152, July 1967

IN Search of Arabia's Past. By Peter Bruce Cornwall. 493-522, Apr. 1948

IN Search of Man's Past at Lake Rudolf. By Richard E. Leakey. Photos by Gordon W. Gahan. 712-734, May 1970

IN Search of Moses. By Harvey Arden. Photos by Nathan Benn. 2-37, Jan. 1976

IN Storied Lands of Malaysia. By Maurice Shadbolt. Photos by Winfield Parks. 734-783, Nov. 1963

IN the Crusaders' Footsteps. By Franc Shor. Photos by Thomas Nebbia and James P. Blair. 731-789, June 1962

IN the Footsteps of Alexander the Great. By Helen and Frank Schreider. Paintings by Tom Lovell. 1-65, Jan. 1968

IN the Gardens of Olympus. By Paul A. Zahl. 85-123, July 1955

IN the London of the New Queen. By H. V. Morton. 291-342, Sept. 1953

IN the Wake of Darwin's *Beagle.* By Alan Villiers. Photos by James L. Stanfield. 449-495, Oct. 1969

IN the Wilds of a City Parlor. By Paul A. Zahl. 645-672, Nov. 1954

IN Touch With Nature. Text by Elizabeth A. Moize. Photos by Steve Raymer. 537-543, Apr. 1974

INCAS:

The Five Worlds of Peru. By Kenneth F. Weaver. Photos by Bates Littlehales. 213-265, Feb. 1964

Flamboyant is the Word for Bolivia. By Loren McIntyre. 153-193, Feb. 1966

The Incredible Incas and Their Timeless Land. Special Publication announced. 870-874, June 1975

The Lost Empire of the Incas. By Loren McIntyre. Art by Ned and Rosalie Seidler. 729-787, Dec. 1973

A pictorial chronicle of the Incas. 747-753

Peru, Homeland of the Warlike Inca. By Kip Ross. 421-462, Oct. 1950

Titicaca, Abode of the Sun. By Luis Marden. Photos by Flip Schulke. 272-294, Feb. 1971

INCREDIBLE Andorra. By Lawrence L. Klingman. Photos by B. Anthony Stewart. 262-290, Aug. 1949

The INCREDIBLE Helicopter. By Peter T. White. 533-557, Apr. 1959

The INCREDIBLE Kangaroo. By David H. Johnson. 487-500, Oct. 1955

INCREDIBLE Photograph Shows Earth From Pole to Pole. Photos by Nimbus I. 190-193, Feb. 1965

The INCREDIBLE Salmon. By Clarence P. Idyll. Photos by Robert F. Sisson. Paintings by Walter A. Weber. 195-219, Aug. 1968

The INCREDIBLE Universe. By Kenneth F. Weaver. Photos by James P. Blair. 589-625, May 1974

INDIA:

Around the World and the Calendar with the Geographic. By Melville Bell Grosvenor. 832-866, Dec. 1959

"Around the World in Eighty Days." By Newman Bumstead. 705-750, Dec. 1951
Included: Agra; Calcutta; Delhi

Calcutta, India's Maligned Metropolis. By Peter T. White. Photos by Raghubir Singh. 534-563, Apr. 1973

Can the World Feed Its People? By Thomas Y. Canby. Photos by Steve Raymer. 2-31, July 1975

The Cobra, India's "Good Snake." By Harry Miller. 393-409, Sept. 1970

Delhi, Capital of a New Dominion. By Phillips Talbot. 597-630, Nov. 1947

The Elephant and I. By M. D. Chaturvedi. 489-507, Oct. 1957

Enchantress! (White Tigress). By Theodore H. Reed. Photos by Thomas J. Abercrombie. 628-641, May 1961

Feudal Splendor Lingers in Rajputana. By Volkmar Wentzel. 411-458, Oct. 1948

From the Hair of Siva (Ganges River). By Helen and Frank Schreider. 445-503, Oct. 1960

The Ganges, River of Faith. By John J. Putman. Photos by Raghubir Singh. 445-483, Oct. 1971

High Adventure in the Himalayas. By Thomas Weir. 193-234, Aug. 1952

How Fruit Came to America. By J. R. Magness. Paintings by Else Bostelmann. 325-377, Sept. 1951

INDIA—*Continued*

India in Crisis. By John Scofield. 599-661, May 1963

India Struggles to Save Her Wildlife. By John J. Putman. Paintings by Ned Seidler. 299-343, Sept. 1976

India's Energetic Sikhs. By John E. Frazer. Photos by James P. Blair. 528-541, Oct. 1972

India's Sculptured Temple Caves. By Volkmar Wentzel. 665-678, May 1953

Mountaintop War in Remote Ladakh. By W. E. Garrett. 664-687, May 1963

Mysore Celebrates the Death of a Demon. By Luc Bouchage. Photos by Ylla. 706-711, May 1958

Nature's Gifts to Medicine. By Lonnelle Aikman. Paintings by Lloyd K. Townsend and Don Crowley. 420-440, Sept. 1974

New Life for India's Villagers (Bastar). By Anthony and Georgette Dickey Chapelle. 572-588, Apr. 1956

Orissa, Past and Promise in an Indian State. By Bart McDowell. Photos by James P. Blair. 546-577, Oct. 1970

Our Vegetable Travelers. By Victor R. Boswell. Paintings by Else Bostelmann. 145-217, Aug. 1949

Roaming India's Naga Hills. By S. Dillon Ripley. 247-264, Feb. 1955

Round the World School. By Paul Antze. Photos by William Eppridge. 96-127, July 1962

Royal Wedding at Jaisalmer. By Marilyn Silverstone. 66-79, Jan. 1965

Southwest Asia, including India, Pakistan, and Northeast Africa, map supplement. June 1952

Troubled Waters East of Suez. By Ernest M. Eller. 483-522, Apr. 1954

When the President Goes Abroad (Eisenhower). By Gilbert M. Grosvenor. 588-649, May 1960

Wild Elephant Roundup in India. By Harry Miller. Photos by author and James P. Blair. 372-385, Mar. 1969

YWCA: International Success Story. By Mary French Rockefeller. Photos by Otis Imboden. 904-933, Dec. 1963

See also Andaman Islands; Assam; Kashmir; Sikkim

INDIAN MOUNDS:

Exploring Ancient Panama by Helicopter. By Matthew W. Stirling. Photos by Richard H. Stewart. 227-246, Feb. 1950

Exploring the Past in Panama. By Matthew W. Stirling. Photos by Richard H. Stewart. 373-399, Mar. 1949

"Pyramids" of the New World. By Neil Merton Judd. 105-128, Jan. 1948

Who Were the "Mound Builders"? By George E. Stuart. 783-801, Dec. 1972

INDIAN OCEAN:

Calypso Explores for Underwater Oil. By Jacques-Yves Cousteau. 155-184, Aug. 1955

Camera Under the Sea. By Luis Marden. 162-200, Feb. 1956

Exploring Davy Jones's Locker with *Calypso*. By Jacques-Yves Cousteau. Photos by Luis Marden. 149-161, Feb. 1956

Indian Ocean Floor, map supplement. Oct. 1967

INDIAN OCEAN—*Continued*

Science Explores the Monsoon Sea. By Samuel W. Matthews. Photos by Robert F. Sisson. 554-575, Oct. 1967

Yankee Roams the Orient. By Irving and Electa Johnson. 327-370, Mar. 1951

See also Andaman Islands; Ceylon; Madagascar; Maldives; Seychelles (Islands); Zanzibar; *and* Dhows

INDIAN Shangri-La of the Grand Canyon. By Jay Johnston. Photos by Terry Eiler. 355-373, Mar. 1970

INDIANA:

Indiana's Self-reliant Uplanders. By James Alexander Thom. Photos by J. Bruce Baumann. 341-363, Mar. 1976

Mapping the Nation's Breadbasket. By Frederick Simpich. 831-849, June 1948

So Much Happens Along the Ohio River. By Frederick Simpich. Photos by Justin Locke. 177-212, Feb. 1950

Vacation Tour Through Lincoln Land. By Ralph Gray. 141-184, Feb. 1952

INDIANS OF CENTRAL AMERICA:

Archeological Map of Middle America, Land of the Feathered Serpent, map supplement. Text on reverse. Oct. 1968

Christopher Columbus and the New World He Found. By John Scofield. Photos by Adam Woolfitt. 584-625, Nov. 1975

Easter Week in Indian Guatemala. By John Scofield. 406-417, Mar. 1960

Exploring Ancient Panama by Helicopter. By Matthew W. Stirling. Photos by Richard H. Stewart. 227-246, Feb. 1950

Exploring the Past in Panama. By Matthew W. Stirling. Photos by Richard H. Stewart. 373-399, Mar. 1949

Included: Guaymi Indians, Coclé Indian culture, and pottery from the El Hatillo and Monagrillo sites

Guatemala, Maya and Modern. By Louis de la Haba. Photos by Joseph J. Scherschel. 661-689, Nov. 1974

Guatemala Revisited. By Luis Marden. 525-564, Oct. 1947

Hunting Prehistory in Panama Jungles. By Matthew W. Stirling. Photos by Richard H. Stewart. 271-290, Aug. 1953

The Maya. 729-811, Dec. 1975

We Drove Panama's Darién Gap. By Kip Ross. 368-389, Mar. 1961

Included: Chocós, Cuna

INDIANS OF NORTH AMERICA:

Alaska: Rising Northern Star. By Joseph Judge. Photos by Bruce Dale. 730-767, June 1975

Included: Ahtena, Athapaskan, Haida, and Tlingit Indians; also Indians of Nulato

America's First Painters. By Dorothy Dunn. 349-377, Mar. 1955

Contents: The art of the Apaches, Navajos, Pueblo, Sioux, Woodland and Plains tribes

Amid the Mighty Walls of Zion. By Lewis F. Clark. Photos by Justin Locke and author. 37-70, Jan. 1954

Contents: Basket Makers, Paiutes, Pueblo

Arizona: Booming Youngster of the West. By Robert de Roos. Photos by Robert F. Sisson. 299-343, Mar. 1963

INDIANS OF NORTH AMERICA—*Continued*

Canada's Heartland, the Prairie Provinces. By W. E. Garrett. 443-489, Oct. 1970
Included: Chipewyans, Crees

Canada's Window on the Pacific: The British Columbia Coast. By Jules B. Billard. Photos by Ted Spiegel. 338-375, Mar. 1972
Included: Haida, Kwakiutl, Tsimshian

The Canadian North: Emerging Giant. By David S. Boyer. 1-43, July 1968

A First American Views His Land. By N. Scott Momaday. 13-19, July 1976

Following the Trail of Lewis and Clark. By Ralph Gray. 707-750, June 1953
Included: Arikara, Blackfeet, Flathead, Mandan, Minnetaree, Oto, Shoshoni, Sioux, Teton Sioux

From Tucson to Tombstone. By Mason Sutherland. 343-384, Sept. 1953
Included: Apaches, Hopi, Papagos; the San Carlos Apache, and the San Xavier Indian Reservations

Grand Canyon: Nature's Story of Creation. By Louis Schellbach. Photos by Justin Locke. 589-629, May 1955
Included: Havasupai, Hopi, Navajos

Hays, Kansas, at the Nation's Heart. By Margaret M. Detwiler. Photos by John E. Fletcher. 461-490, Apr. 1952
Included: Cheyennes, Comanches, Kaws, Pawnees, Pueblo

Ice Age Man, the First American. By Thomas R. Henry. Paintings by Andre Durenceau. 781-806, Dec. 1955

Indian Life Before the Colonists Came. By Stuart E. Jones. Engravings by Theodore de Bry, 1590. 351-368, Sept. 1947

Indians of North America; North America Before Columbus, double-sided map supplement. Dec. 1972

Indians of the Far West. By Matthew W. Stirling. Paintings by W. Langdon Kihn. 175-200, Feb. 1948
Contents: Cahuilla, Cayuse, Chemehuevi, Chumash, Costanoan, Dalles, Diegueño, Flatheads, Gabrieleño, Hidatsa, Hupa, Kamia, Klamath, Klikitat, Maidu, Miwok, Modoc, Mohave, Mono, Nez Percé, Paiute, Palus, Pomo, Shasta, Shoshoni, Tenino, Umatilla, Ute, Walla Walla, Wanapum, Wappo, Wintun, Yakima, Yokut, Yuki, Yuma, Yurok

Kachinas: Masked Dancers of the Southwest. By Paul Coze. 219-236, Aug. 1957

Life 8,000 Years Ago Uncovered in an Alabama Cave. By Carl F. Miller. Photos by Brooks Honeycutt. 542-558, Oct. 1956

Men, Moose, and Mink of Northwest Angle. By William H. Nicholas. Photos by J. Baylor Roberts. 265-284, Aug. 1947
Included: Chippewa, Sioux

Mexico, the City That Founded a Nation. By Louis de la Haba. Photos by Albert Moldvay. 638-669, May 1973

Mexico in Motion. By Bart McDowell. Photos by Kip Ross. 490-537, Oct. 1961

Mexico's Booming Capital. By Mason Sutherland. Photos by Justin Locke. 785-824, Dec. 1951

Mexico's Window on the Past (National Museum). By Bart McDowell. Photos by B. Anthony Stewart. 492-519, Oct. 1968
Included: Aztecs, Maya, Mixtecs, Olmecs, Teotihuacanos, Toltecs, Zapotecs

Nature's Gifts to Medicine. By Lonnelle Aikman. Paintings by Lloyd K. Townsend and Don Crow

INDIANS OF NORTH AMERICA—*Continued*

ley. 420-440, Sept. 1974

The New Indians (Television film). 575, Nov. 1976

New Mexico: The Golden Land. By Robert Laxalt. Photos by Adam Woolfitt. 299-345, Sept. 1970
Included: Apache, Navajo, Pueblo (Santa Clara, Taos, Zuni)

Nomads of the Far North. By Matthew W. Stirling. 471-504, Oct. 1949
Hearty Folk Defy Arctic Storms. Paintings by W. Langdon Kihn. 479-494
Contents: Algonquian and Athapascan linguistic stocks: Chipewyan, Cree, Kutchin, Micmac, Montagnais, Naskapi, Yellowknife

North Dakota Comes into Its Own. By Leo A. Borah. Photos by J. Baylor Roberts. 283-322, Sept. 1951

Oklahoma, the Adventurous One. By Robert Paul Jordan. Photos by Robert W. Madden. 149-189, Aug. 1971
Included: Cherokees, Cheyennes, Choctaws, Creek-Seminoles, Quapaws, Shawnee-Peoria

On the Trail of La Venta Man. By Matthew W. Stirling. Photos by Richard H. Stewart. 137-172, Feb. 1947
Hunting Mexico's Buried Temples. 145-168

Seeking the Secret of the Giants. By Frank M. Setzler. Photos by Richard H. Stewart. 390-404, Sept. 1952
Included: Maricopa, Pima, Yuma

So Long, St. Louis, We're Heading West. By William C. Everhart. 643-669, Nov. 1965

South to Mexico City. By W. E. Garrett. 145-193, Aug. 1968
Included: Pre-Columbian civilizations; present-day Tarahumara and Tarascan Indians

That Dammed Missouri River. By Gordon Young. Photos by David Hiser. 374-413, Sept. 1971
Included: The Arikaras, Hidatsas, and Mandans of Fort Berthold Indian Reservation; also Sioux of Standing Rock Reservation

Three Little Indians. Children's book announced. 728-730, Nov. 1974

20th-century Indians Preserve Customs of the Cliff Dwellers. Photos by William Belknap, Jr. 196-211, Feb. 1964

Will Oil and Tundra Mix? Alaska's North Slope Hangs in the Balance. By William S. Ellis. Photos by Emory Kristof. 485-517, Oct. 1971
Included: Athapascan Indians of Arctic Village

The World of the American Indian. Book announced. 584-586, Oct. 1974

Wyoming Muck Tells of Battle: Ice Age Man vs. Mammoth. By Cynthia Irwin, Henry Irwin, and George Agogino. 828-837, June 1962

See also Anasazi; Aztecs; Comanche; Cora; Crees; Havasupai; Hohokam; Maya; Menominees; Miccosukees; Mohawks; Mound Builders; Navajos; Pueblo; Seminoles; Sioux; Stoney; Tarahumara; Tarascans; Tlingit

INDIANS OF SOUTH AMERICA:

Amazon—The River Sea. By Loren McIntyre. 456-495, Oct. 1972
Included: Achual, Aguaruna, Auca, Kamayurá, Karajá, Kraho, Kréen-Akaróre, Kuikúro, Machiguenga, Shipibo, Txukahamẽi, Waiká, Waurá, Xavante

Animal Safari to British Guiana. By David Attenborough. Photos by Charles Lagus and author. 851-874, June 1957
Included: Acawai, Macushí

Blue-eyed Indian: A City Boy's Sojourn with Primi-

INDIANS OF SOUTH AMERICA—*Continued*

tive Tribesmen in Central Brazil. By Harald Schultz. 65-89, July 1961

Brazil, Ôba! By Peter T. White. Photos by Winfield Parks. 299-353, Sept. 1962
Included: Kashinaua, Pacaás Novos

Colombia, from Amazon to Spanish Main. By Loren McIntyre. 235-273, Aug. 1970
Included: Arhuaco, Chibcha, Guajiro, Kogi, Tucano

Cruising Colombia's "Ol' Man River." By Amos Burg. 615-660, May 1947

Ecuador—Low and Lofty Land Astride the Equator. By Loren McIntyre. 259-298, Feb. 1968
Included: Auca, Cayapa, Cofán, Colorado, Inca, Jivaro, Secoya

The Five Worlds of Peru. By Kenneth F. Weaver. Photos by Bates Littlehales. 213-265, Feb. 1964
Included: Aymará, Huanchaco, Inca, Shapra, Shipibo, Uru

Flamboyant Is the Word for Bolivia. By Loren McIntyre. 153-195, Feb. 1966
Included: Aymará, Inca

Giant Insects of the Amazon. By Paul A. Zahl. 632-669, May 1959
Included: Galibi, Paricura

High, Wild World of the Vicuña. By William L. Franklin. 77-91, Jan. 1973
Included: Indians of the Inca nation; present-day Indians

In the Wake of Darwin's *Beagle*. By Alan Villiers. Photos by James L. Stanfield. 449-495, Oct. 1969
Included: Indians of the Tierra del Fuego region

Jungle Jaunt on Amazon Headwaters. By Bernice M. Goetz. 371-388, Sept. 1952

The Lost Empire of the Incas. By Loren McIntyre. Art by Ned and Rosalie Seidler. 729-787, Dec. 1973
A pictorial chronicle of the Incas. 747-753
Included: Present-day Aymaras; Quechuas

Puya, the Pineapple's Andean Ancestor. By Mulford B. Foster. 463-480, Oct. 1950
Included: Aymarás, Quechuas, Sibundoys

Seeking the Truth About the Feared Piranha. By Paul A. Zahl. 715-733, Nov. 1970
Included: Karajá, Maká

Sky-high Bolivia. Photos by T. Ifor Rees and Carl S. Bell. 481-496, Oct. 1950

Titicaca, Abode of the Sun. By Luis Marden. Photos by Flip Schulke. 272-294, Feb. 1971
Included: Aymarás, Incas, Quechuas, Urus

See also Aymará; Camaracoto; Chimor Empire; Cholo; Cinta Larga; Erigbaagtsa; Incas; Kraho; Kreen-Akarores; Machiguenga; Mochica Culture; Motilones; Quechuas; Suyá; Tchikao; Tukuna; Txukahameis; Wai Wai; Waurá; Yanomamo

INDIO (River), Panama:

Hunting Prehistory in Panama Jungles. By Matthew W. Stirling. Photos by Richard H. Stewart. 271-290, Aug. 1953

INDOCHINA:

Indochina Faces the Dragon. By George W. Long. Photos by J. Baylor Roberts. 287-328, Sept. 1952

The Lands and Peoples of Southeast Asia. 295-365, Mar. 1971
I. Mosaic of Cultures. By Peter T. White. Photos by W. E. Garrett. 296-329
II. New Light on a Forgotten Past. By Wilhelm G. Solheim II. 330-339

INDOCHINA—*Continued*

III. Pagan, on the Road to Mandalay. By W. E. Garrett. 343-365

Portrait of Indochina. By W. Robert Moore and Maynard Owen Williams. Paintings by Jean Despujols. 461-490, Apr. 1951

Strife-torn Indochina. By W. Robert Moore. 499-510, Oct. 1950

War and Quiet on the Laos Frontier. By W. Robert Moore. 665-680, May 1954

See also Cambodia; Laos; Viet Nam

INDONESIA:

East From Bali by Seagoing Jeep to Timor. By Helen and Frank Schreider. 236-279, Aug. 1962

Indonesia, the Young and Troubled Island Nation. By Helen and Frank Schreider. 579-625, May 1961

New Guinea to Bali in *Yankee*. By Irving and Electa Johnson. 767-815, Dec. 1959

Republican Indonesia Tries Its Wings. By W. Robert Moore. 1-40, Jan. 1951

This Young Giant, Indonesia. By Beverley M. Bowie. Photos by J. Baylor Roberts. 351-392, Sept. 1955

See also Bali; Java; Lesser Sunda Islands; Moluccas; Sulawesi; Tanjung Puting Reserve

INDUSTRIAL MUSEUMS. *See* Corning Museum of Glass; John Woodman Higgins Armory

INDUSTRIES:

Barehanded Battle to Cleanse the Bay: San Francisco's Tragic Oil Spill Triggers Spontaneous Cooperation Between Industry and Concerned Citizens. By Peter T. White. Photos by Jonathan S. Blair. 866-881, June 1971

Behold the Computer Revolution. By Peter T. White. Photos by Bruce Dale and Emory Kristof. 593-633, Nov. 1970

Crystals, Magical Servants of the Space Age. By Kenneth F. Weaver. Photos by James P. Blair. 278-296, Aug. 1968

Kitimat—Canada's Aluminum Titan. By David S. Boyer. 376-398, Sept. 1956

Man's New Servant, the Friendly Atom. By F. Barrows Colton. Photos by Volkmar Wentzel. 71-90, Jan. 1954

Pollution, Threat to Man's Only Home. By Gordon Young. Photos by James P. Blair. 738-781, Dec. 1970

A River Restored: Oregon's Willamette. By Ethel A. Starbird. Photos by Lowell J. Georgia. 816-835, June 1972

Those Successful Japanese. By Bart McDowell. Photos by Fred Ward. 323-359, Mar. 1974

Water for the World's Growing Needs. By Herbert B. Nichols and F. Barrows Colton. 269-286, Aug. 1952

Will Oil and Tundra Mix? Alaska's North Slope Hangs in the Balance. By William S. Ellis. Photos by Emory Kristof. 485-517, Oct. 1971

Yesterday Lingers Along the Connecticut. By Charles McCarry. Photos by David L. Arnold. 334-369, Sept. 1972

You and the Obedient Atom. By Allan C. Fisher, Jr. Photos by B. Anthony Stewart and Thomas J. Abercrombie. 303-353, Sept. 1958

See also specific types of industry

INFLATABLE Ship Opens Era of Airborne Undersea Expeditions. By Jacques-Yves Cousteau. 142-148, July 1961

INFRARED RADIATION:

Remote Sensing: New Eyes to See the World. By Kenneth F. Weaver. 46-73, Jan. 1969

See also Photography, Infrared

INGALLS, HUNTLEY: Author-Photographer:

We Climbed Utah's Skyscraper Rock. Photos by author and Barry C. Bishop. 705-721, Nov. 1962

INGSTAD, HELGE: Author:

Vinland Ruins Prove Vikings Found the New World. 708-734, Nov. 1964

INISHEER; INISHMAAN; INISHMORE (Islands), Ireland:

The Arans, Ireland's Invincible Isles. By Veronica Thomas. Photos by Winfield Parks. 545-573, Apr. 1971

INLAND SEA, Japan:

Cruising Japan's Inland Sea. By Willard Price. 619-650, Nov. 1953

Kayak Odyssey: From the Inland Sea to Tokyo. By Dan Dimancescu. Photos by Christopher G. Knight. 295-337, Sept. 1967

Living in a Japanese Village. By William Graves. Photos by James L. Stanfield. 668-693, May 1972

INLAND WATERWAYS. *See* Canals; Inside Passage; Intracoastal Waterway, Atlantic; Rivers; St. Lawrence Seaway

INLE (Lake), Burma:

Burma's Leg Rowers and Floating Farms. Photos by W. E. Garrett. Text by David Jeffery. 826-845, June 1974

INNER HEBRIDES (Islands), Scotland:

Scotland From Her Lovely Lochs and Seas. By Alan Villiers. Photos by Robert F. Sisson. 492-541, Apr. 1961

Scotland's Inner Hebrides: Isles of the Western Sea. By Kenneth MacLeish. Photos by R. Stephen Uzzell III. 690-717, Nov. 1974

See also Skye

INNSBRUCK, Austria:

Occupied Austria, Outpost of Democracy. By George W. Long. Photos by Volkmar Wentzel. 749-790, June 1951

A Stroll to Venice. By Isobel Wylie Hutchison. 378-410, Sept. 1951

Tirol, Austria's Province in the Clouds. By Peter T. White. Photos by Volkmar Wentzel. 107-141, July 1961

INSECT CONTROL:

Beltsville Brings Science to the Farm. By Samuel W. Matthews. 199-218, Aug. 1953

Man's New Servant, the Friendly Atom. By F. Barrows Colton. Photos by Volkmar Wentzel. 71-90, Jan. 1954

Included: Insects tagged with radioisotopes, easily identified; sterilizing of screwworm fly; experiments on effectiveness of insect poisons

New Tricks Outwit Our Insect Enemies. By Hal Higdon. Photos by Robert F. Sisson and Emory Kristof. 380-399, Sept. 1972

The Revolution in American Agriculture. By Jules

INSECT CONTROL — *Continued*

B. Billard. Photos by James P. Blair. 147-185, Feb. 1970

See also Ladybugs; Locusts; Spiders (What's So Special)

INSECT-TRAPPING PLANTS. *See* Carnivorous Plants

INSECTICIDE POLLUTION. *See* Chemical Pollution

INSECTS:

Asian Insects in Disguise. By Edward S. Ross. 433-439, Sept. 1965

Back-yard Monsters in Color. By Paul A. Zahl. 235-260, Aug. 1952

Contents: Black widow spider, Blister beetle, Broad-neck root borer, Bumblebee, Carpenter ant, Caterpillar, Cecropia moth, Colorado potato beetle, Housefly, Japanese beetle, Lacewing, Ladybird beetle, Locust, Long-horned grasshopper, Mosquito, Paper wasp, Parasitic fly, Polyphemus moth, Praying mantis, Queen butterfly, Scarab beetle, Scavenger beetle, Short-horned grasshopper, Soldier beetle, Sphinx moth, Sulphur butterfly, Tussock moth

Crossroads of the Insect World. By J. W. MacSwain. Photos by Edward S. Ross. 844-857, Dec. 1966

Included: African katydid, Ambush bug, Bee fly, Blister beetle, *Ceratina* bee, Crab spider, Gnat, Halictine bee, *Hesperapis* bee, Honeybee, Malaysian mantis, *Megachile* bee, *Phyciodes* butterfly, Scarab beetle, Skipper, Syrphid fly

The Exquisite Orchids. By Luis Marden. 485-513, Apr. 1971

Included: Pollination by insects

Giant Insects of the Amazon. By Paul A. Zahl. 632-669, May 1959

The Hidden World (Television film). 853A-853B, Dec. 1966

The High World of the Rain Forest. By William Beebe. Paintings by Guy Neale. 838-855, June 1958

Included: Ant lion, Beetles, Butterflies, Caterpillars, Flies, Grasshoppers, Praying mantises, Spiders, Tree hoppers

Hunting Africa's Smallest Game. By Edward S. Ross. 406-419, Mar. 1961

The Living Sand. By William H. Amos. 820-833, June 1965

Included: Ant lion, Digger wasp, Sand locust, Tiger beetle, Velvet ant (Wingless wasp), Yellow-banded wasp

Malaysia's Giant Flowers and Insect-trapping Plants. By Paul A. Zahl. 680-701, May 1964

Miracle of the Potholes. By Rowe Findley. Photos by Robert F. Sisson. 570-579, Oct. 1975

Nature's Alert Eyes. By Constance P. Warner. 558-569, Apr. 1959

Included: Horsefly, Praying mantis

Nature's Night Lights: Probing the Secrets of Bioluminescence. By Paul A. Zahl. 45-69, July 1971

Nature's Year in Pleasant Valley. By Paul A. Zahl. 488-525, Apr. 1968

Plants That Eat Insects. By Paul A. Zahl. 643-659, May 1961

Teeming Life of a Pond. By William H. Amos. 274-298, Aug. 1970

See also Ants; Aphids; Bird Anting; Butterflies; Cicadas; Crickets; Dragonflies; Fireflies; Honeybees; Ladybugs; Locusts; Mantis; Moths; Railroad Worm; Wasps

INSIDE a Hornbill's Walled-up Nest. Photos by Joan and Alan Root. 846-855, Dec. 1969

INSIDE Europe Aboard *Yankee*. By Irving and Electa Johnson. Photos by Joseph J. Scherschel. 157-195, Aug. 1964

INSIDE PASSAGE (Washington-British Columbia-Alaska):

Alaska's Marine Highway: Ferry Route to the North. By W. E. Garrett. 776-819, June 1965

Alaska's Warmer Side. By Elsie May Bell Grosvenor. 737-775, June 1956

Endeavour Sails the Inside Passage. By Amos Burg. 801-828, June 1947

Making Friends With a Killer Whale. By Edward I. Griffin. 418-446, Mar. 1966

INSIDE the White House. By Lonnelle Aikman. Photos by B. Anthony Stewart and Thomas Nebbia. 3-43, Jan. 1961

INSIDE the World of the Honeybee. By Treat Davidson. 188-217, Aug. 1959

INTEGRATED CIRCUITS:

Crystals, Magical Servants of the Space Age. By Kenneth F. Weaver. Photos by James P. Blair. 278-296, Aug. 1968

INTER-AMERICAN GEODETIC SURVEY (IAGS):

Expedition to Amazon source. 445, 459, 460, Oct. 1972

Men Who Measure the Earth. By Robert Leslie Conly. Photos by John E. Fletcher. 335-362, Mar. 1956

INTER-AMERICAN HIGHWAY. *See* Pan American Highway

INTERNATIONAL GEOPHYSICAL YEAR (IGY):

The International Geophysical Year. By Hugh L. Dryden. 285-298, Feb. 1956

Man's First Winter at the South Pole. By Paul A. Siple. 439-478, Apr. 1958

To the Men at South Pole Station. By Richard E. Byrd. 1-4, July 1957

We Are Living at the South Pole. By Paul A. Siple. Photos by David S. Boyer. 5-35, July 1957

Year of Discovery Opens in Antarctica. By David S. Boyer. 339-381, Sept. 1957

See also Expéditions Polaires Françaises; Operation Deep Freeze; Rockets Explore the Air; Satellites (How Man-made Satellites Can Affect Our Lives; Space Satellites)

INTERNATIONAL ICE PATROL:

Tracking Danger With the Ice Patrol. By William S. Ellis. Photos by James R. Holland. 780-793, June 1968

INTERNATIONAL INDIAN OCEAN EXPEDITION:

Science Explores the Monsoon Sea. By Samuel W. Matthews. Photos by Robert F. Sisson. 554-575, Oct. 1967

INTERNATIONAL PARK. *See* Waterton-Glacier International Peace Park

INTERNATIONAL SCHOOL OF AMERICA (ISA):

Round the World School. By Paul Antze. Photos by William Eppridge. 96-127, July 1962

INTERSTATE HIGHWAY SYSTEM:

Our Growing Interstate Highway System. By Rob-

INTERSTATE HIGHWAY SYSTEM — *Continued*

ert Paul Jordan. 195-219, Feb. 1968

Trucks Race the Clock From Coast to Coast. By James A. Sugar. 226-243, Feb. 1974

INTERSTATE PARK. *See* Palisades Interstate Park

INTHA (People):

Burma's Leg Rowers and Floating Farms. Photos by W. E. Garrett. Text by David Jeffery. 826-845, June 1974

INTO the Heart of Africa. By Gertrude S. Weeks. 257-263, Aug. 1956

INTO the Lairs of "Sleeping" Sharks. By Eugenie Clark. Photos by David Doubilet. 570-584, Apr. 1975

INTO the Well of Sacrifice (Chichén Itzá). By Eusebio Dávalos Hurtado and Bates Littlehales. Photos by Bates Littlehales. 540-561, Oct. 1961

INTRACOASTAL WATERWAY, Atlantic Coast, U. S.:

America's Inland Waterway. Special Publication announced. 865-868, June 1973

Slow Boat to Florida. By Dorothea and Stuart E. Jones. 1-65, Jan. 1958

See also Florida Keys; Sea Islands

INVENTORS AND INVENTIONS:

Alexander Graham Bell Museum: Tribute to Genius. By Jean Lesage. 227-256, Aug. 1956

Behold the Computer Revolution. By Peter T. White. Photos by Bruce Dale and Emory Kristof. 593-633, Nov. 1970

The British Way: Great Britain's Major Gifts to Freedom, Democratic Government, Science, and Society. By Sir Evelyn Wrench. 421-541, Apr. 1949

Cities Like Worcester Make America. By Howell Walker. 189-214, Feb. 1955

Included: Bigelow's power carpet loom; Blanchard's lathe; Goddard's liquid-fueled rocket; Hawes's envelope-folding machine; Howe's sewing machine; piano wire; the steam calliope; Whitney's cotton gin

Miracle Men of the Telephone. By F. Barrows Colton. 273-316, Mar. 1947

Those Inventive Americans. Special Publication announced. 880-884, June 1970

Yesterday Lingers Along the Connecticut. By Charles McCarry. Photos by David L. Arnold. 334-369, Sept. 1972

Included: Samuel Colt (six-shooter); John C. Garand (M-1 rifle); Samuel Morey (steamboat); James F. Tasker (bridges); Eli Whitney (interchangeable parts)

See also Bell, Alexander Graham; Ford, Henry, Museum; Franklin, Benjamin; Jefferson, Thomas; Wright, Orville and Wilbur; *and* NGS: Inventions

The INVESTITURE of Great Britain's Prince of Wales. By Allan C. Fisher, Jr. Photos by James L. Stanfield and Adam Woolfitt. 698-715, Nov. 1969

INYO NATIONAL FOREST, California:

Bristlecone Pine, Oldest Known Living Thing. By Edmund Schulman. Photos by W. Robert Moore. 355-372, Mar. 1958

IONIAN ISLANDS, Greece:

Homeward With Ulysses. By Melville Bell Grosvenor. Photos by Edwin Stuart Grosvenor. 1-39, July 1973

IONOSPHERE:

Unlocking Secrets of the Northern Lights. By Carl W. Gartlein. Paintings by William Crowder. 673-704, Nov. 1947

IOS (Island), Greece:

The Isles of Greece: Aegean Birthplace of Western Culture. By Melville Bell Grosvenor. Photos by Edwin Stuart Grosvenor and Winfield Parks. 147-193, Aug. 1972

IOWA:

The Family Farm Ain't What It Used To Be. By James A. Sugar. 391-411, Sept. 1974

Following the Trail of Lewis and Clark. By Ralph Gray. 707-750, June 1953

Iowa's Enduring Amana Colonies. By Laura Longley Babb. Photos by Steve Raymer. 863-878, Dec. 1975

Mapping the Nation's Breadbasket. By Frederick Simpich. 831-849, June 1948

IRAN:

Coronations a World Apart. By the Editor. 299, Mar. 1968

Darius Carved History on Ageless Rock. By George G. Cameron. 825-844, Dec. 1950

I Become a Bakhtiari. By Paul Edward Case. 325-358, Mar. 1947
    Beside the Persian Gulf. Photos by Maynard Owen Williams. 341-356

In the Footsteps of Alexander the Great. By Helen and Frank Schreider. Paintings by Tom Lovell. 1-65, Jan. 1968

Iran: Desert Miracle. By William Graves. Photos by James P. Blair. 2-47, Jan. 1975

Iran's Shah Crowns Himself and His Empress. By Franc Shor. Photos by James L. Stanfield and Winfield Parks. 301-321, Mar. 1968

Journey Into Troubled Iran. By George W. Long. Photos by J. Baylor Roberts. 425-464, Oct. 1951

Oil, the Dwindling Treasure. By Noel Grove. Photos by Emory Kristof. 792-825, June 1974

Old-new Iran, Next Door to Russia. By Edward J. Linehan. Photos by Thomas J. Abercrombie. 44-85, Jan. 1961

Our Vegetable Travelers. By Victor R. Boswell. Paintings by Else Bostelmann. 145-217, Aug. 1949

Questing for Gems. By George S. Switzer. 835-863, Dec. 1971

Sky Road East. By Tay and Lowell Thomas, Jr. 71-112, Jan. 1960

Station Wagon Odyssey: Baghdad to Istanbul. By William O. Douglas. 48-87, Jan. 1959

Troubled Waters East of Suez. By Ernest M. Eller. 483-522, Apr. 1954

We Dwelt in Kashgai Tents. By Jean and Franc Shor. 805-832, June 1952

We Lived in Turbulent Tehran. By Rebecca Shannon Cresson. 707-720, Nov. 1953

West from the Khyber Pass. By William O. Douglas. Photos by Mercedes H. Douglas and author. 1-44, July 1958

When the President Goes Abroad (Eisenhower). By Gilbert M. Grosvenor. 588-649, May 1960

IRAQ:

Abraham, the Friend of God. By Kenneth MacLeish. Photos by Dean Conger. 739-789, Dec. 1966

IRAQ — Continued

Ancient Mesopotamia: A Light That Did Not Fail. By E. A. Speiser. Paintings by H. M. Herget. 41-105, Jan. 1951

"Around the World in Eighty Days." By Newman Bumstead. 705-750, Dec. 1951
    Included: Baghdad; Basra; Tigris River

Beside the Persian Gulf. Photos by Maynard Owen Williams. 341-356, Mar. 1947
    Included: Port near Basra

Iraq — Where Oil and Water Mix. By Jean and Franc Shor. 443-489, Oct. 1958

The Kurds of Iraq: "We Who Face Death." By LeRoy Woodson, Jr. 364-387, Mar. 1975

Marsh Dwellers of Southern Iraq. By Wilfred Thesiger. Photos by Gavin Maxwell. 205-239, Feb. 1958

Report from the Locust Wars. By Tony and Dickey Chapelle. 545-562, Apr. 1953

Station Wagon Odyssey: Baghdad to Istanbul. By William O. Douglas. 48-87, Jan. 1959

Troubled Waters East of Suez. By Ernest M. Eller. 483-522, Apr. 1954

Water Dwellers in a Desert World. By Gavin Young. Photos by Nik Wheeler. 502-523, Apr. 1976

West from the Khyber Pass. By William O. Douglas. Photos by Mercedes H. Douglas and author. 1-44, July 1958

IRAZÚ (Volcano), Costa Rica:

Costa Rica, Free of the Volcano's Veil. By Robert de Roos. 125-152, July 1965

IRELAND, Northern:

Ireland's Rugged Coast Yields Priceless Relics of the Spanish Armada. By Robert Sténuit. Photos by Bates Littlehales. 745-777, June 1969

The Magic Road Round Ireland. By H. V. Morton. Photos by Robert F. Sisson. 293-333, Mar. 1961

Northern Ireland: From Derry to Down. By Robert L. Conly. 232-267, Aug. 1964

IRELAND, Republic of:

The Arans, Ireland's Invincible Isles. By Veronica Thomas. Photos by Winfield Parks. 545-573, Apr. 1971

British Isles, Atlas series supplement. July 1958

The British Isles, map supplement. Apr. 1949

Dublin's Historic Horse Show. By Maynard Owen Williams. 115-132, July 1953

The Friendly Irish. By John Scofield. Photos by James A. Sugar. 354-391, Sept. 1969

I Walked Some Irish Miles. By Dorothea Sheats. 653-678, May 1951

Irish Ways Live On in Dingle. By Bryan Hodgson. Photos by Linda Bartlett. 551-576, Apr. 1976
    Included: Efforts to preserve Gaelic language and literature

The Magic Road Round Ireland. By H. V. Morton. Photos by Robert F. Sisson. 293-333, Mar. 1961

Playing 3,000 Golf Courses in Fourteen Lands. By Ralph A. Kennedy. 113-132, July 1952

A Traveler's Map of the British Isles, map supplement. Text on reverse. Apr. 1974

IRIAN. See former name, Netherlands New Guinea

IRISES:

History and Beauty Blend in a Concord Iris Garden

IRISES — *Continued*

(Buttrick). By Robert T. Cochran, Jr. Photos by M. Woodbridge Williams. 705-719, May 1959

IROQUOIS CONFEDERACY. *See* Mohawks

IRRIGATION:

Behind the Veil of Troubled Yemen. By Thomas J. Abercrombie. 403-445, Mar. 1964

Californians Escape to the Desert. By Mason Sutherland. Photos by Charles W. Herbert. 675-724, Nov. 1957

Erosion, Trojan Horse of Greece. By F. G. Renner. 793-812, Dec. 1947

From Sagebrush to Roses on the Columbia. By Leo A. Borah. 571-611, Nov. 1952

The Hohokam: First Masters of the American Desert. By Emil W. Haury. Photos by Helga Teiwes. 670-695, May 1967

I Become a Bakhtiari. By Paul Edward Case. 325-358, Mar. 1947

North Dakota Comes into Its Own. By Leo A. Borah. Photos by J. Baylor Roberts. 283-322, Sept. 1951

Sand in My Eyes. By Jinx Rodger. Photos by George Rodger. 664-705, May 1958

Two Wheels Along the Mexican Border. By William Albert Allard. 591-635, May 1971

Water for the World's Growing Needs. By Herbert B. Nichols and F. Barrows Colton. 269-286, Aug. 1952

Western Australia, the Big Country. By Kenneth MacLeish. Photos by James L. Stanfield. 150-187, Feb. 1973

IRWIN, COLIN: Author-Photographer:

Trek Across Arctic America. 295-321, Mar. 1974

IRWIN, CYNTHIA and HENRY: Authors:

Wyoming Muck Tells of Battle: Ice Age Man vs. Mammoth. By Cynthia Irwin, Henry Irwin, and George Agogino. 828-837, June 1962

IRWIN, JAMES B.:

Apollo 15 Explores the Mountains of the Moon. By Kenneth F. Weaver. Photos from NASA. 233-265, Feb. 1972

What Is It Like to Walk on the Moon? By David R. Scott. 326-331, Sept. 1973

ISBJORN (Ketch):

Wind, Wave, Star, and Bird. By David Lewis. Photos by Nicholas deVore III. 747-781, Dec. 1974

ISCHIA, Island of the Unexpected. By Dorothea and Stuart E. Jones. 531-550, Apr. 1954

ISLA RAZA, Gulf of California. *See* Raza, Isla

ISLAM:

The Arab World, Inc. By John J. Putman. Photos by Winfield Parks. 494-533, Oct. 1975

Saudi Arabia: Beyond the Sands of Mecca. By Thomas J. Abercrombie. 1-53, Jan. 1966

The Sword and the Sermon. By Thomas J. Abercrombie. 3-45, July 1972

See also Moslems

ISLAND of Faith in the Sinai Wilderness. By George H. Forsyth. Photos by Robert F. Sisson. 82-106, Jan. 1964

ISLANDS, Formation of:

This Changing Earth. By Samuel W. Matthews. 1-37, Jan. 1973

See also the volcanic islands: Ilha Nova; Myojin; Surtsey

The ISLANDS Called Fiji. By Luis Marden. 526-561, Oct. 1958

ISLE OF MAN. *See* Man, Isle of

ISLE ROYALE, Michigan:

Wolves Versus Moose on Isle Royale. By Durward L. Allen and L. David Mech. 200-219, Feb. 1963

The ISLES of Greece: Aegean Birthplace of Western Culture. By Melville Bell Grosvenor. Photos by Edwin Stuart Grosvenor and Winfield Parks. 147-193, Aug. 1972

The ISLES of the Pacific. By Kenneth P. Emory, David Lewis, Mary and Laurance S. Rockefeller. Photos by Nicholas deVore III and Thomas Nebbia. Paintings by Herb Kawainui Kane. 732-793, Dec. 1974

ISLES of the Western Sea: Scotland's Inner Hebrides. By Kenneth MacLeish. Photos by R. Stephen Uzzell III. 690-717, Nov. 1974

ISLES on the Edge of the Sea: Scotland's Outer Hebrides. By Kenneth MacLeish. Photos by Thomas Nebbia. 676-711, May 1970

ISMAILI (Moslems):

Weighing the Aga Khan in Diamonds. Photos by David J. Carnegie. 317-324, Mar. 1947

ISRAEL:

Abraham, the Friend of God. By Kenneth MacLeish. Photos by Dean Conger. 739-789, Dec. 1966

Included: Abraham in Canaan; Beersheba; Gerar; Uru Salem (Jerusalem)

An Archeologist Looks at Palestine. By Nelson Glueck. 739-752, Dec. 1947

Eyewitness to War in the Holy Land. By Charles Harbutt. 782-795, Dec. 1967

Holy Land Today, Atlas series supplement. Dec. 1963

Home to the Holy Land. By Maynard Owen Williams. 707-746, Dec. 1950

Israel: Land of Promise. By John Scofield. Photos by B. Anthony Stewart. 395-434, Mar. 1965

Israel — The Seventh Day. By Joseph Judge. Photos by Gordon W. Gahan. 816-855, Dec. 1972

The Land of Galilee. By Kenneth MacLeish. Photos by B. Anthony Stewart. 832-865, Dec. 1965

Lands of the Bible Today, map supplement. Dec. 1956

Lands of the Bible Today, map supplement. Dec. 1967

New Life for the Troubled Suez Canal. By William Graves. Photos by Jonathan Blair. 792-817, June 1975

Included: The cross-canal fighting between Egypt and Israel, 1967-1973; Egypt's 1973 attack on Israel's Sinai fortifications, with photographs of the remains of those fortifications

Our Life on a Border Kibbutz. By Carol and Al Abrams. Photos by Al Abrams. 364-391, Sept. 1970

ISRAEL — *Continued*

Pilgrims Follow the Christmas Star. By Maynard Owen Williams. 831-840, Dec. 1952

Where Jesus Walked. By Howard La Fay. Photos by Charles Harbutt. 739-781, Dec. 1967

See also Jerusalem

ISRAELITES:

Bringing Old Testament Times to Life. By G. Ernest Wright. Paintings by Henry J. Soulen. 833-864, Dec. 1957

In Search of Moses. By Harvey Arden. Photos by Nathan Benn. 2-37, Jan. 1976

The Last Thousand Years Before Christ. By G. Ernest Wright. Paintings by H. J. Soulen and Peter V. Bianchi. 812-853, Dec. 1960

ISTANBUL, Turkey:

"Around the World in Eighty Days." By Newman Bumstead. 705-750, Dec. 1951

Athens to Istanbul. By Jean and Franc Shor. 37-76, Jan. 1956

Istanbul, the City That Links Europe and Asia. By William S. Ellis. Photos by Winfield Parks. 501-533, Oct. 1973

A New Look at Medieval Europe. By Kenneth M. Setton. Paintings by Andre Durenceau and Birney Lettick. 799-859, Dec. 1962
    Included: Constantinople

Robert College, Turkish Gateway to the Future. By Franc Shor. 399-418, Sept. 1957

Turkey Paves the Path of Progress. By Maynard Owen Williams. 141-186, Aug. 1951

ITALIAN RIVIERA, Land That Winter Forgot. By Howell Walker. 743-789, June 1963

See also Portofino

ITALY:

Across the Alps in a Wicker Basket *(Bernina)*. By Phil Walker. 117-131, Jan. 1963

Across the Ridgepole of the Alps. By Walter Meayers Edwards. 410-419, Sept. 1960

The Alps: Man's Own Mountains. By Ralph Gray. Photos by Walter Meayers Edwards and William Eppridge. 350-395, Sept. 1965

Amalfi, Italy's Divine Coast. By Luis Marden. 472-509, Oct. 1959

Ancient Shipwreck Yields New Facts—and a Strange Cargo. By Peter Throckmorton. Photos by Kim Hart and Joseph J. Scherschel. 282-300, Feb. 1969

"Around the World in Eighty Days." By Newman Bumstead. 705-750, Dec. 1951
    Included: Anzio; Elba; Genoa; Larderello Valley; La Spezia; Otranto; Pisa; Rome; Turin; Vesuvius

Fishing in the Whirlpool of Charybdis. By Paul A. Zahl. 579-618, Nov. 1953

Hydrofoil Ferry "Flies" the Strait of Messina. By Gilbert Grosvenor. 493-496, Apr. 1957

Italian Riviera, Land That Winter Forgot. By Howell Walker. 743-789, June 1963

Italy, Atlas series supplement. Nov. 1961

Italy Smiles Again. By Edgar Erskine Hume. 693-732, June 1949

Lombardy's Lakes, Blue Jewels in Italy's Crown. By Franc Shor. Photos by Joseph J. Scherschel. 58-99, July 1968

A New Look at Medieval Europe. By Kenneth M. Setton. Paintings by Andre Durenceau and Bir-

ITALY — *Continued*

ney Lettick. 799-859, Dec. 1962

Periscope on the Etruscan Past. By Carlo M. Lerici. 337-350, Sept. 1959

Round the World School (ISA). By Paul Antze. Photos by William Eppridge. 96-127, July 1962

A Stroll to Venice. By Isobel Wylie Hutchison. 378-410, Sept. 1951

A Traveler's Map of Italy, map supplement. Text on reverse. June 1970

United Italy Marks Its 100th Year. By Nathaniel T. Kenney. 593-647, Nov. 1961

When the President Goes Abroad. By Gilbert M. Grosvenor. 588-649, May 1960

See also Florence; Marostica; Pompeii; Portofino; Rome; Siena; Trieste; Tuscany; Venice; *and* islands: Capri; Ischia; Sicily

ITHACA (Island), Greece:

Homeward With Ulysses. By Melville Bell Grosvenor. Photos by Edwin Stuart Grosvenor. 1-39, July 1973

ITURI FOREST, Zaire:

My Life With Africa's Little People. By Anne Eisner Putnam. 278-302, Feb. 1960

IVIZA (Island), Spain. *See* Ibiza

IVOR, HANCE ROY: Author:

The Enigma of Bird Anting. 105-119, July 1956

Author-Photographer

Seeing Birds as Real Personalities. 523-530, Apr. 1954
    Bluebirds on the Wing in Color. Photos by Bernard Corby and author. 527-530

IVORY COAST, Republic of:

Freedom Speaks French in Ouagadougou. By John Scofield. 153-203, Aug. 1966

IWO JIMA (Island), Volcano Islands:

Adventures with the Survey Navy. By Irving Johnson. 131-148, July 1947

The Bonins and Iwo Jima Go Back to Japan. By Paul Sampson. Photos by Joe Munroe. 128-144, July 1968

J

J. W. WESTCOTT, Postman for the Great Lakes. By Cy La Tour. 813-824, Dec. 1950

JACKSON, ANDREW:

Inside the White House. By Lonnelle Aikman. Photos by B. Anthony Stewart and Thomas Nebbia. 3-43, Jan. 1961

The Living White House. By Lonnelle Aikman. 593-643, Nov. 1966

Profiles of the Presidents: II. A Restless Nation Moves West. By Frank Freidel. 80-121, Jan. 1965

Today Along the Natchez Trace, Pathway Through History. By Bern Keating. Photos by Charles Harbutt. 641-667, Nov. 1968

JACKSON, CARMAULT B., Jr.: Author:

The Flight of *Freedom 7.* 416-431, Sept. 1961

JACKSON HOLE, Wyoming:

I See America First. By Lynda Bird Johnson. Photos by William Albert Allard. 874-904, Dec. 1965

JACKSON HOLE, Wyoming—*Continued*

Jackson Hole: Good-bye to the Old Days? By François Leydet. Photos by Jonathan Wright. 768-789, Dec. 1976

Wildlife Adventuring in Jackson Hole. By Frank and John Craighead. 1-36, Jan. 1956

Wyoming: High, Wide, and Windy. By David S. Boyer. 554-594, Apr. 1966

JACOBS, FENNO: Photographer:

Mid-century Holland Builds Her Future. By Sydney Clark. 747-778, Dec. 1950

JACQUES-YVES COUSTEAU Receives National Geographic Society Medal at White House. 146-147, July 1961

See also Cousteau, Jacques-Yves

JADE:

China Unveils Her Newest Treasures. By Robert W. Madden. 848-857, Dec. 1974

Exploring the World of Gems. By W. F. Foshag. 779-810, Dec. 1950

JAEGER, EDMUND C.: Author:

Poorwill Sleeps Away the Winter. 273-280, Feb. 1953

JAFFA. *See* Tel Aviv-Jaffa

JAGANNATH FESTIVAL:

Orissa, Past and Promise in an Indian State. By Bart McDowell. Photos by James P. Blair. 546-577, Oct. 1970

JAGUAR GOD:

Gifts for the Jaguar God. By Philip Drucker and Robert F. Heizer. 367-375, Sept. 1956

JAGUAR HUNTING:

The Jungle Was My Home. By Sasha Siemel. 695-712, Nov. 1952

JAINS (Religious Sect):

India's Sculptured Temple Caves. By Volkmar Wentzel. 665-678, May 1953

JAIPUR, India:

Feudal Splendor Lingers in Rajputana. By Volkmar Wentzel. 411-458, Oct. 1948

JAISALMER, India:

Feudal Splendor Lingers in Rajputana. By Volkmar Wentzel. 411-458, Oct. 1948

Royal Wedding at Jaisalmer. By Marilyn Silverstone. 66-79, Jan. 1965

JAKARTA, Indonesia. *See* Djakarta

JAKOBSHAVN, Greenland:

Greenland's "Place by the Icebergs." By Mogens Bloch Poulsen. Photos by Thomas Nebbia. 849-869, Dec. 1973

JALISCO (State), Mexico:

The Most Mexican City, Guadalajara. By Bart McDowell. Photos by Volkmar Wentzel. 412-441, Mar. 1967

See also Stone Spheres

JAMAICA (Island), West Indies:

Exploring the Drowned City of Port Royal. By Marion Clayton Link. Photos by Luis Marden. 151-183, Feb. 1960

JAMAICA (Island), West Indies—*Continued*

Jamaica—Hub of the Caribbean. By W. Robert Moore. 333-362, Mar. 1954

Jamaica Goes It Alone. By James Cerruti. Photos by Thomas Nebbia. 843-873, Dec. 1967

Wing-borne Lamps of the Summer Night (Fireflies). By Paul A. Zahl. 48-59, July 1962

JAMBO—First Gorilla Raised by Its Mother in Captivity. By Ernst M. Lang. Photos by Paul Steinemann. 446-453, Mar. 1964

JAMES I, King (England, Scotland, and Ireland):

The British Way. By Sir Evelyn Wrench. 421-541, Apr. 1949
    Included: Translation of the Bible

JAMES, FRANCES: Author:

Keeping House in London. 769-792, Dec. 1947

Thumbs Up Round the North Sea's Rim. Photos by Erica Koch. 685-704, May 1952

JAMES, THOMAS GARNER: Author:

Kew: The Commoners' Royal Garden. Photos by B. Anthony Stewart. 479-506, Apr. 1950

London's Zoo of Zoos. 771-786, June 1953

Portsmouth, Britannia's Sally Port. Photos by B. Anthony Stewart. 513-544, Apr. 1952

JAMES (River), Virginia:

Stately Homes of Old Virginia. By Albert W. Atwood. 787-802, June 1953

JAMES BAY, Quebec, Canada:

The Changing World of Canada's Crees. By Fred Ward. 541-569, Apr. 1975

JAMESTOWN, Virginia:

Captain Smith of Jamestown. By Bradford Smith. 581-620, May 1957

JAMMU AND KASHMIR. *See* former name, Kashmir

JAN MAYEN (Island), Norwegian Sea:

Seal Hunting Off Jan Mayen. By Ole Friele Backer. 57-72, Jan. 1948

JANE M. SMITH AWARD:

Ingram, Sir Bruce. 474, Apr. 1961

Johnson, Lyndon B.: Vice President Johnson Accepts the Society's Jane Smith Award. 906, Dec. 1962; 113, Jan. 1966; 468, Oct. 1966

JANITZIO (Island), Lake Pátzcuaro, Mexico. *See* Pátzcuaro

JAPAN:

Ama, Sea Nymphs of Japan. By Luis Marden. 122-135, July 1971

Around the World and the Calendar with the Geographic: The President's Annual Message. By Melville Bell Grosvenor. 832-866, Dec. 1959

Backwoods Japan During American Occupation. By M. A. Huberman. 491-518, Apr. 1947

The Bonins and Iwo Jima Go Back to Japan. By Paul Sampson. Photos by Joe Munroe. 128-144, July 1968

Cruising Japan's Inland Sea. By Willard Price. 619-650, Nov. 1953

Human Treasures of Japan. By William Graves. Photos by James L. Stanfield. 370-379, Sept. 1972
    Contents: Ryujo Hori, doll maker; Gonroku Mat-

JAPAN — *Continued*

suda, lacquer artist; Tesshi Nagano, ironcaster; Utae-mon Nakamura, Kabuki actor; Sadaichi Tsukiyama, samurai swordsmith

Japan, the Exquisite Enigma. By Franc Shor. Photos by John Launois. 733-777, Dec. 1960

Japan and Korea, Atlas series supplement. Dec. 1960

Japan Tries Freedom's Road. By Frederick G. Vosburgh. Photos by J. Baylor Roberts. 593-632, May 1950

Japan's "Sky People," the Vanishing Ainu. By Mary Inez Hilger. Photos by Eiji Miyazawa. 268-296, Feb. 1967

Kansai, Japan's Historic Heartland. By Thomas J. Abercrombie. 295-339, Mar. 1970
   Included: Expo '70

Kayak Odyssey: From the Inland Sea to Tokyo. By Dan Dimancescu. Photos by Christopher G. Knight. 295-337, Sept. 1967

Kyoto and Nara: Keepers of Japan's Past. By Charles McCarry. Photos by George F. Mobley. 836-851, June 1976
   Kyoto Says Happy New Year. 852-859

Nature's Night Lights: Probing the Secrets of Bioluminescence. By Paul A. Zahl. 45-69, July 1971

Oil, the Dwindling Treasure. By Noel Grove. Photos by Emory Kristof. 792-825, June 1974

Operation Eclipse: 1948. By William A. Kinney. 325-372, Mar. 1949

Our Navy in the Far East. By Arthur W. Radford. Photos by J. Baylor Roberts. 537-577, Oct. 1953

Our Vegetable Travelers. By Victor R. Boswell. Paintings by Else Bostelmann. 145-217, Aug. 1949

Round the World School (ISA). By Paul Antze. Photos by William Eppridge. 96-127, July 1962

Snow Festival in Japan's Far North. By Eiji Miyazawa. 824-833, Dec. 1968

Those Successful Japanese. By Bart McDowell. Photos by Fred Ward. 323-359, Mar. 1974

The World in Your Garden (Flowers). By W. H. Camp. Paintings by Else Bostelmann. 1-65, July 1947

YWCA: International Success Story. By Mary French Rockefeller. Photos by Otis Imboden. 904-933, Dec. 1963

The Yankee Sailor Who Opened Japan (Commodore Perry). By Ferdinand Kuhn. 85-102, July 1953

See also Futagami Jima; Japan Trench; Myojin Island; Tokyo; *and* Mercury (Metallic Element); Onagadori; Shrimp (Shrimp Nursery)

JAPAN TRENCH, Pacific Ocean:

Deep Diving off Japan. By Georges S. Houot. 138-150, Jan. 1960

JAPANESE ART:

Human Treasures of Japan. By William Graves. Photos by James L. Stanfield. 370-379, Sept. 1972
   Included: Ironcasting, Kabuki, Lacquer working, Swordsmithing, Wood sculpture

Kyoto and Nara: Keepers of Japan's Past. By Charles McCarry. Photos by George F. Mobley. 836-851, June 1976

JARAWAS (Negrito Tribe):

The Last Andaman Islanders. By Raghubir Singh. 66-91, July 1975

JARCHÉ, JAMES: Photographer:

In the London of the New Queen. By H. V. Morton. 291-342, Sept. 1953

JAVA (Island), Indonesia:

Java — Eden in Transition. By Kenneth MacLeish. Photos by Dean Conger. 1-43, Jan. 1971

Postwar Journey Through Java. By Ronald Stuart Kain. 675-700, May 1948

JAVAHÉ INDIANS:

Blue-eyed Indian: A city boy's sojourn with primitive tribesmen in central Brazil. By Harald Schultz. 65-89, July 1961

JEEP, Amphibious. *See Tortuga II*

JEFFERSON, THOMAS:

Inside the White House. By Lonnelle Aikman. Photos by B. Anthony Stewart and Thomas Nebbia. 3-43, Jan. 1961

The Living White House. By Lonnelle Aikman. 593-643, Nov. 1966

Mr. Jefferson's Charlottesville. By Anne Revis. 553-592, May 1950

Mr. Jefferson's Monticello. By Joseph Judge. Photos by Dean Conger and Richard S. Durrance. 426-444, Sept. 1966

Profiles of the Presidents: I. The Presidency and How It Grew. By Frank Freidel. 642-687, Nov. 1964

Thomas Jefferson: Architect of Freedom. By Mike W. Edwards. Photos by Linda Bartlett. 231-259, Feb. 1976

JEFFERY, DAVID: Author:

Burma's Leg Rowers and Floating Farms. Photos by W. E. Garrett. 826-845, June 1974

Preserving America's Last Great Wilderness (Alaska). 769-791, June 1975

JEH (Tribe):

Viet Nam's Montagnards. By Howard Sochurek. 443-487, Apr. 1968

JEKYLL ISLAND, Georgia:

Sea Islands: Adventuring Along the South's Surprising Coast. By James Cerruti. Photos by Thomas Nebbia and James L. Amos. 366-393, Mar. 1971

JELLYFISHES:

Glass Menageries of the Sea. By Paul A. Zahl. 797-822, June 1955

See also Portuguese Man-of-War

JENNER, EDWARD:

The British Way. By Sir Evelyn Wrench. 421-541, Apr. 1949

JENNINGS, DEAN: Author:

The Friendly Train Called Skunk. Photos by B. Anthony Stewart. 720-734, May 1959

JENNINGS, GARY: Author:

Bavaria: Mod, Medieval — and Bewitching. Photos by George F. Mobley. 409-431, Mar. 1974

Newfoundland Trusts in the Sea. Photos by Sam Abell. 112-141, Jan. 1974

JERICHO, Jordan:

The Ghosts of Jericho. By James L. Kelso. 825-844, Dec. 1951

JERICHO, Jordan—*Continued*

Hashemite Jordan, Arab Heartland. By John Scofield. 841-856, Dec. 1952

Jericho Gives Up Its Secrets. By Kathleen M. Kenyon and A. Douglas Tushingham. Photos by Nancy Lord. 853-870, Dec. 1953

JERSEY (Island), English Channel:

Britain's "French" Channel Islands. By James Cerruti. Photos by James L. Amos. 710-740, May 1971

JERSTAD, LUTHER G.:

American and Geographic Flags Top Everest. By Melvin M. Payne. Photos by Barry C. Bishop. 157-157C, Aug. 1963

See also American Mount Everest Expedition

JERUSALEM:

An Archeologist Looks at Palestine. By Nelson Glueck. 739-752, Dec. 1947

Conquest of the Holy City (First Crusade). By Franc Shor. Photos by Thomas Nebbia. 839-855, Dec. 1963

Crusader Lands Revisited. By Harold Lamb. Photos by David S. Boyer. 815-852, Dec. 1954

Eyewitness to War in the Holy Land. By Charles Harbutt. 782-795, Dec. 1967

Hashemite Jordan, Arab Heartland. By John Scofield. 841-856, Dec. 1952

Holy Land, My Country. By His Majesty King Hussein of Jordan. 784-789, Dec. 1964

Home to the Holy Land. By Maynard Owen Williams. 707-746, Dec. 1950

Jerusalem, My Home. By Bertha Spafford Vester. 826-847, Dec. 1964

Jerusalem, the Divided City. By John Scofield. Photos by Brian Brake. 492-531, Apr. 1959

Jerusalem to Rome in the Path of St. Paul. By David S. Boyer. 707-759, Dec. 1956

The Other Side of Jordan. By Luis Marden. 790-825, Dec. 1964

Pilgrims Follow the Christmas Star. By Maynard Owen Williams. 831-840, Dec. 1952

Reunited Jerusalem Faces Its Problems. By Kenneth MacLeish. Photos by Ted Spiegel. 835-871, Dec. 1968

Where Jesus Walked. By Howard La Fay. Photos by Charles Harbutt. 739-781, Dec. 1967

YWCA: International Success Story. By Mary French Rockefeller. Photos by Otis Imboden. 904-933, Dec. 1963

JESUS:

The Land of Galilee. By Kenneth MacLeish. Photos by B. Anthony Stewart. 832-865, Dec. 1965

Where Jesus Walked. By Howard La Fay. Photos by Charles Harbutt. 739-781, Dec. 1967

JET AIRCRAFT:

Aviation Looks Ahead on Its 50th Birthday. By Emory S. Land. 721-739, Dec. 1953

Fact Finding for Tomorrow's Planes. By Hugh L. Dryden. Photos by Luis Marden. 757-780, Dec. 1953

Flying in the "Blowtorch" Era. By Frederick G. Vosburgh. 281-322, Sept. 1950

Of Planes and Men. By Kenneth F. Weaver. Photos by Emory Kristof and Albert Moldvay. 298-349, Sept. 1965

JET AIRCRAFT—*Continued*

Our Air Age Speeds Ahead. By F. Barrows Colton. 249-272, Feb. 1948

The Solar Eclipse From a Jet. By Wolfgang B. Klemperer. 785-796, Nov. 1963

JET BOATS:

Shooting Rapids in Reverse! Jet Boats Climb the Colorado's Torrent Through the Grand Canyon. By William Belknap, Jr. 552-565, Apr. 1962

JET PROPULSION LABORATORY, California Institute of Technology. *See* Mariner Missions; Ranger Spacecraft; Surveyor Spacecraft

JET SUBMARINES. *See* DS-2; Denise

JETHOU (Island), English Channel:

Britain's "French" Channel Islands. By James Cerruti. Photos by James L. Amos. 710-740, May 1971

JEWELRY. *See* Gems; Gold

JHELUM (River), Kashmir-Pakistan:

The Idyllic Vale of Kashmir. By Volkmar Wentzel. 523-550, Apr. 1948

JODHPUR, India:

Feudal Splendor Lingers in Rajputana. By Volkmar Wentzel. 411-458, Oct. 1948

JOGJAKARTA, Java:

Java—Eden in Transition. By Kenneth Macleish. Photos by Dean Conger. 1-43, Jan. 1971

See also former name, Djokjakarta

JOHANSON, DONALD C.: Author:

Ethiopia Yields First "Family" of Early Man. Photos by David Brill. 790-811, Dec. 1976

JOHN ELLIOTT PILLSBURY (Research Vessel):

Squids: Jet-powered Torpedoes of the Deep. By Gilbert L. Voss. Photos by Robert F. Sisson. 386-411, Mar. 1967

JOHN F. KENNEDY: The Last Full Measure. By Melville Bell Grosvenor. 307-355, Mar. 1964

See also Kennedy, John F.

JOHN FRUM CULT:

Tanna Awaits the Coming of John Frum. By Kal Muller. 706-715, May 1974

JOHN GLENN Receives the Society's Hubbard Medal. 827, June 1962

JOHN GLENN'S Three Orbits in *Friendship 7*. By Robert B. Voas. 792-827, June 1962

JOHN MUIR'S Wild America. By Harvey Arden. Photos by Dewitt Jones. 433-461, Apr. 1973

JOHN OLIVER LA GORCE Is Elected Vice-Chairman of the Board, Melville Bell Grosvenor President and Editor of the National Geographic Society. 419-423, Mar. 1957

See also La Gorce, John Oliver

JOHN PENNEKAMP CORAL REEF STATE PARK, Florida:

Florida's Coral City Beneath the Sea. By Jerry Greenberg. 70-89, Jan. 1962

Key Largo Coral Reef: America's First Undersea Park. By Charles M. Brookfield. Photos by Jerry Greenberg. 58-69, Jan. 1962

JOHN PENNEKAMP CORAL REEF STATE PARK, Florida—*Continued*

The Lower Keys, Florida's "Out Islands." By John Scofield. Photos by Emory Kristof and Bates Littlehales. 72-93, Jan. 1971

JOHN WOODMAN HIGGINS ARMORY:

Cities Like Worcester Make America. By Howell Walker. 189-214, Feb. 1955

JOHNS HOPKINS APPLIED PHYSICS LABORATORY. *See* DODGE Satellite

JOHNS HOPKINS UNIVERSITY: Research:

Torchbearers of the Twilight (Fireflies). By Frederick G. Vosburgh. 697-704, May 1951
    Contents: The experiments of Dr. William D. McElroy with cold light, such as that of fireflies

JOHNS ISLAND, South Carolina:

Sea Islands: Adventuring Along the South's Surprising Coast. By James Cerruti. Photos by Thomas Nebbia and James L. Amos. 366-393, Mar. 1971

JOHNSON, ANDREW:

The Living White House. By Lonnelle Aikman. 593-643, Nov. 1966

Profiles of the Presidents: III. The American Giant Comes of Age. By Frank Freidel. 660-711, May 1965

JOHNSON, DAVID H.: Author:

The Incredible Kangaroo. 487-500, Oct. 1955

JOHNSON, IRVING and ELECTA:

Windjamming Around New England. By Tom Horgan. Photos by Robert F. Sisson. 141-169, Aug. 1950
    Contains information about Irving Johnson and his brigantine, *Yankee*

Author-Photographers

Adventures with the Survey Navy. 131-148, July 1947

Inside Europe Aboard *Yankee* (Ketch). Photos by Irving Johnson and Joseph J. Scherschel. 157-195, Aug. 1964

Lost World of the Galapagos. 681-703, May 1959

New Guinea to Bali in *Yankee* (Brigantine). 767-815, Dec. 1959

Saga of a Ship, the *Yankee* (Brigantine). By Luis Marden. 263-269, Feb. 1966

South Seas' Incredible Land Divers (New Hebrides Islanders). Photos by Arthur Johnson and Irving Johnson. 77-92, Jan. 1955

Yankee (Ketch) Cruises the Storied Nile. Photos by Winfield Parks. 583-633, May 1965

Yankee (Ketch) Cruises Turkey's History-haunted Coast. Photos by Joseph J. Scherschel. 798-845, Dec. 1969

Yankee (Brigantine) Roams the Orient. 327-370, Mar. 1951

The *Yankee*'s (Brigantine) Wander-world. 1-50, Jan. 1949

JOHNSON, LYNDA BIRD: Author:

I See America First. Photos by William Albert Allard. 874-904, Dec. 1965

JOHNSON, LYNDON B.:

The Living White House. By Lonnelle Aikman. 593-643, Nov. 1966

JOHNSON, LYNDON B.—*Continued*

President Johnson Dedicates the Society's New Headquarters. 669-679, May 1964

Profiles of the Presidents: V. The Atomic Age: Its Problems and Promises. By Frank Freidel. 66-119, Jan. 1966

Vice President Johnson Accepts the Society's Jane M. Smith Award. 906, Dec. 1962

Vice President Lyndon B. Johnson presents the Hubbard Medal to John H. Glenn, Jr. 827, June 1962

Author

Friendly Flight to Northern Europe. Photos by Volkmar Wentzel. 268-293, Feb. 1964

JOHNSON, NELSON T.: Author:

Power Comes Back to Peiping. By Nelson T. Johnson and W. Robert Moore. 337-368, Sept. 1949

JOHNSTON, JAY: Author:

Forest Fire: The Devil's Picnic. By Stuart E. Jones and Jay Johnston. 100-127, July 1968

Indian Shangri-La of the Grand Canyon. Photos by Terry Eiler. 355-373, Mar. 1970

Staten Island Ferry, New York's Seagoing Bus. By John T. Cunningham and Jay Johnston. Photos by W. D. Vaughn. 833-843, June 1959

Waterway to Washington, the C & O Canal. 419-439, Mar. 1960

JOINT HURRICANE WARNING CENTER, Miami, Florida:

Men Against the Hurricane. By Andrew H. Brown. 537-560, Oct. 1950

JOINT OCEANOGRAPHIC INSTITUTIONS FOR DEEP EARTH SAMPLING (JOIDES). *See* Deep Sea Drilling Project

JOINT TASK FORCE I. *See* Operation Crossroads

JONES, DEWITT: Photographer:

John Muir's Wild America. By Harvey Arden. 433-461, Apr. 1973

Look of a Land Beloved (New England). 444-467, Apr. 1976

JONES, DON W.: Photographer:

Hot-air Balloons Race on Silent Winds. By William R. Berry. 392-407, Mar. 1966

JONES, DOROTHEA SHEATS: Author:

Pennsylvania Avenue, Route of Presidents. By Dorothea and Stuart E. Jones. Photos by Volkmar Wentzel. 63-95, Jan. 1957

Slow Boat to Florida (*Tradewinds*). By Dorothea and Stuart E. Jones. 1-65, Jan. 1958

Author-Photographer

Ischia, Island of the Unexpected. By Dorothea and Stuart E. Jones. 531-550, Apr. 1954

See also Sheats, Dorothea

JONES, LILIAN GROSVENOR. *See* Grosvenor, Lilian

JONES, STUART E.: Author:

Central Park: Manhattan's Big Outdoors. Photos by Bates Littlehales. 781-811, Dec. 1960

Charting Our Sea and Air Lanes (U. S. Coast and Geodetic Survey). Photos by J. Baylor Roberts. 189-209, Feb. 1957

Copenhagen, Wedded to the Sea. Photos by Gilbert M. Grosvenor. 45-79, Jan. 1963

JONES, STUART E.: Author—*Continued*

Forest Fire: The Devil's Picnic. By Stuart E. Jones and Jay Johnston. 100-127, July 1968

Fun Helped Them Fight. 95-104, Jan. 1948

Here's New York Harbor. Photos by Robert F. Sisson and David S. Boyer. 773-813, Dec. 1954

Houston, Prairie Dynamo. Photos by William Albert Allard. 338-377, Sept. 1967

Indian Life Before the Colonists Came. Engravings by Theodore de Bry, 1590. 351-368, Sept. 1947

Maryland on the Half Shell. Photos by Robert W. Madden. 188-229, Feb. 1972

Oregon's Many Faces. Photos by Bates Littlehales. 74-115, Jan. 1969

Pennsylvania Avenue, Route of Presidents. By Dorothea and Stuart E. Jones. Photos by Volkmar Wentzel. 63-95, Jan. 1957

The President's Music Men (Marine Band). Photos by William W. Campbell III. 752-766, Dec. 1959

Slow Boat to Florida (*Tradewinds*). By Dorothea and Stuart E. Jones. 1-65, Jan. 1958

Spices, the Essence of Geography. 401-420, Mar. 1949

When in Rome. . . . Photos by Winfield Parks. 741-789, June 1970

Author-Photographer

Ischia, Island of the Unexpected. By Dorothea and Stuart E. Jones. 531-550, Apr. 1954

JONES, MRS. STUART E. *See* Jones, Dorothea Sheats

JORDAN, ROBERT PAUL: Author:

Canada's "Now" Frontier. Photos by Lowell Georgia. 480-511, Oct. 1976

Easter Greetings From the Ukrainians. Photos by James A. Sugar. 556-563, Apr. 1972

Gettysburg and Vicksburg: the Battle Towns Today. Map notes by Carolyn Bennett Patterson. 4-57, July 1963

Illinois: The City and the Plain. Photos by James L. Stanfield and Joseph J. Scherschel. 745-797, June 1967

Nebraska . . . the Good Life. Photos by Lowell Georgia. 378-407, Mar. 1974

Oklahoma, the Adventurous One. Photos by Robert W. Madden. 149-189, Aug. 1971

Our Growing Interstate Highway System. 195-219, Feb. 1968

St. Louis: New Spirit Soars in Mid-America's Proud Old City. Photos by Bruce Dale. 605-641, Nov. 1965

Siberia's Empire Road, the River Ob. Photos by Dean Conger. 145-181, Feb. 1976

Yugoslavia: Six Republics in One. Photos by James P. Blair. 589-633, May 1970

JORDAN:

Abraham, the Friend of God. By Kenneth MacLeish. Photos by Dean Conger. 739-789, Dec. 1966

Arab Land Beyond the Jordan. Photos by Frank Hurley. 753-768, Dec. 1947

Hashemite Jordan, Arab Heartland. By John Scofield. 841-856, Dec. 1952

Holy Land, My Country. By His Majesty King Hussein of Jordan. 784-789, Dec. 1964

Home to the Holy Land. By Maynard Owen Williams. 707-746, Dec. 1950

JORDAN—*Continued*

Jerusalem, My Home. By Bertha Spafford Vester. 826-847, Dec. 1964

Journey Into the Great Rift: the Northern Half. By Helen and Frank Schreider. 254-290, Aug. 1965

The Other Side of Jordan. By Luis Marden. 790-825, Dec. 1964

Pilgrims Follow the Christmas Star. By Maynard Owen Williams. 831-840, Dec. 1952

Where Jesus Walked. By Howard La Fay. Photos by Charles Harbutt. 739-781, Dec. 1967

See also Arab-Israeli Conflict; Jericho; Jerusalem; Khirbat Qumrān; Petra

JORDAN (River), Israel-Jordan:

Geographical Twins a World Apart. By David S. Boyer. 848-859, Dec. 1958
Included: A comparison of the Jordan River in the Holy Land with the Jordan River in Utah

JORDAN (River), Utah. *See* article, *preceding*

JOSEPH CONRAD: (Training Ship):

The Age of Sail Lives On at Mystic. By Alan Villiers. Photos by Weston Kemp. 220-239, Aug. 1968

JOURNEY Into Stone Age New Guinea. By Malcolm S. Kirk. 568-592, Apr. 1969

JOURNEY Into the Great Rift: the Northern Half. By Helen and Frank Schreider. 254-290, Aug. 1965

JOURNEY Into Troubled Iran. By George W. Long. Photos by J. Baylor Roberts. 425-464, Oct. 1951

A JOURNEY to "Little Tibet" (Ladakh). By Enakshi Bhavnani. Photos by Volkmar Wentzel. 603-634, May 1951

JOURNEY to Mars. By Kenneth F. Weaver. Paintings by Ludek Pesek. 231-263, Feb. 1973

JOURNEY to Outer Mongolia. By William O. Douglas. Photos by Dean Conger. 289-345, Mar. 1962

JUBILEES. *See* Grosvenor, Gilbert H.: Golden Jubilee; La Gorce, John Oliver: Golden Anniversary; *and* Diamond Jubilee (Aga Khan)

JUDAISM:

Abraham, the Friend of God. By Kenneth MacLeish. Photos by Dean Conger. 739-789, Dec. 1966

Bringing Old Testament Times to Life. By G. Ernest Wright. Paintings by Henry J. Soulen. 833-864, Dec. 1957

In Search of Moses. By Harvey Arden. Photos by Nathan Benn. 2-37, Jan. 1976

The Last Thousand Years Before Christ. By G. Ernest Wright. Paintings by H. J. Soulen and Peter V. Bianchi. 812-853, Dec. 1960

The Pious Ones (Brooklyn's Hasidic Jews). By Harvey Arden. Photos by Nathan Benn. 276-298, Aug. 1975

See also Israel; Jerusalem; *and* Essenes

JUDD, NEIL MERTON: Author:

"Pyramids" of the New World. 105-128, Jan. 1948

JUDGE, JOSEPH: Author:

Alaska: Rising Northern Star. Photos by Bruce Dale. 730-767, June 1975

Brunei, Borneo's Abode of Peace. Photos by Dean

JUDGE, JOSEPH: Author—*Continued*

Conger. 207-225, Feb. 1974

Florence Rises From the Flood. 1-43, July 1967

Florida's Booming—and Beleaguered—Heartland. Photos by Jonathan Blair. 585-621, Nov. 1973

Hong Kong, Saturday's Child. Photos by Bruce Dale. 541-573, Oct. 1971

Israel—The Seventh Day. Photos by Gordon W. Gahan. 816-855, Dec. 1972

Mr. Jefferson's Monticello. Photos by Dean Conger and Richard S. Durrance. 426-444, Sept. 1966

New Grandeur for Flowering Washington. Photos by James P. Blair. 500-539, Apr. 1967

New Orleans and Her River. Photos by James L. Stanfield. 151-187, Feb. 1971

Retracing John Wesley Powell's Historic Voyage Down the Grand Canyon. Photos by Walter Meayers Edwards. 668-713, May 1969

Those Proper and Other Bostonians. Photos by Ted Spiegel. 352-381, Sept. 1974

Venice Fights for Life. Photos by Albert Moldvay. 591-631, Nov. 1972

Williamsburg, City for All Seasons. Photos by James L. Amos. 790-823, Dec. 1968

Wind River Range: Many-treasured Splendor. 198-205, Feb. 1974

The Zulus: Black Nation in a Land of Apartheid. Photos by Dick Durrance II. 738-775, Dec. 1971

JUDGE, KATHLEEN REVIS. *See* Revis, Kathleen

JUDITH RIVER BASIN, Montana. *See* Spring Creek Hutterite Colony

JUMP, World's Highest:

The Long, Lonely Leap (Parachute Jump). By Joseph W. Kittinger, Jr. Photos by Volkmar Wentzel. 854-873, Dec. 1960

JUNEAU, Alaska:

Endeavour Sails the Inside Passage. By Amos Burg. 801-828, June 1947

JUNEAU ICEFIELD, Alaska:

Alaska's Mighty Rivers of Ice. By Maynard M. Miller. Photos by Christopher G. Knight. 194-217, Feb. 1967

JUNGE, CARL-JOHAN: Photographer:

The Shy and Spectacular Kingfisher. Photos by Carl-Johan Junge and Emil Lütken. 413-419, Sept. 1974

JUNGFRAU (Peak), Switzerland:

Switzerland Guards the Roof of Europe. By William H. Nicholas. Photos by Willard R. Culver. 205-246, Aug. 1950

JUNGLE Jaunt on Amazon Headwaters. By Bernice M. Goetz. 371-388, Sept. 1952

JUNGLE Journey to the World's Highest Waterfall. By Ruth Robertson. 655-690, Nov. 1949

JUNGLE Journeys in Sarawak. By Hedda Morrison. 710-736, May 1956

The JUNGLE Was My Home. By Sasha Siemel. 695-712, Nov. 1952

JUNKS (Boats):

Hong Kong, Saturday's Child. By Joseph Judge. Photos by Bruce Dale. 541-573, Oct. 1971

Return to Changing China. By Audrey Topping. 801-833, Dec. 1971

Trawling the China Seas. Photos by J. Charles Thompson. 381-395, Mar. 1950

Water War in Viet Nam. By Dickey Chapelle. 272-296, Feb. 1966

JUPITER (Planet):

Mystery Shrouds the Biggest Planet. By Kenneth F. Weaver. 285-294, Feb. 1975

Voyage to the Planets. By Kenneth F. Weaver. Paintings by Ludek Pesek. 147-193, Aug. 1970

JURUENA (River), Brazil:

Indians of the Amazon Darkness. By Harald Schultz. 737-758, May 1964

JUST a Hundred Years Ago (U. S. Civil War). By Carl Sandburg. 1-3, July 1963

JUTLAND (Peninsula), Denmark:

2,000 Miles Through Europe's Oldest Kingdom. By Isobel Wylie Hutchison. Photos by Maynard Owen Williams. 141-180, Feb. 1949

JUTLAND, Battle of (May 31, 1916):

The British Way. By Sir Evelyn Wrench. 421-541, Apr. 1949

K

KABUKI:

Human Treasures of Japan. By William Graves. Photos by James L. Stanfield. 370-379, Sept. 1972

Kansai, Japan's Historic Heartland. By Thomas J. Abercrombie. 295-339, Mar. 1970

KACHINAS: Masked Dancers of the Southwest. By Paul Coze. 219-236, Aug. 1957

KADAYAN (People):

Brunei, Borneo's Abode of Peace. By Joseph Judge. Photos by Dean Conger. 207-225, Feb. 1974

KAFIRS (Tribespeople):

In the Footsteps of Alexander the Great. By Helen and Frank Schreider. Paintings by Tom Lovell. 1-65, Jan. 1968

KAHL, M. PHILIP: Author-Photographer:

East Africa's Majestic Flamingos. 276-294, Feb. 1970

KAIN, RONALD STUART: Author:

Postwar Journey Through Java. 675-700, May 1948

KALAHARI BUSHMEN:

Africa's Bushman Art Treasures. By Alfred Friendly. Photos by Alex R. Willcox. 848-865, June 1963

Bushmen of the Kalahari. By Elizabeth Marshall Thomas. 866-888, June 1963

Bushmen of the Kalahari (Television film). 578A-578B, Apr. 1973; 732A-732B, May 1974

KALAVRYTA, Greece:

Erosion, Trojan Horse of Greece. By F. G. Renner. 793-812, Dec. 1947

KALIMNOS (Island), Greece:

The Isles of Greece: Aegean Birthplace of Western Culture. By Melville Bell Grosvenor. Photos by Edwin Stuart Grosvenor and Winfield Parks. 147-193, Aug. 1972

KALTENTHALER, HENRY: Photographer:

New Guinea's Rare Birds and Stone Age Men. By E. Thomas Gilliard. 421-488, Apr. 1953

KAMMERMAN, EUGENE L.: Author:

The Camargue, Land of Cowboys and Gypsies. 667-699, May 1956

KANDY, Sri Lanka:

Ceylon, Island of the "Lion People." By Helen Trybulowski Gilles. 121-136, July 1948

Ceylon, the Resplendent Land. By Donna K. and Gilbert M. Grosvenor. 447-497, Apr. 1966

KANE, HARNETT T.: Author:

Land of Louisiana Sugar Kings. Photos by Willard R. Culver. 531-567, Apr. 1958

New Orleans: Jambalaya on the Levee. Photos by Justin Locke. 143-184, Feb. 1953

Rome: Eternal City with a Modern Air. Photos by B. Anthony Stewart. 437-491, Apr. 1957

Trieste—Side Door to Europe. 824-857, June 1956

KANE, HERB KAWAINUI: Artist:

The Pathfinders. 756-769, Dec. 1974

Author

A Canoe Helps Hawaii Recapture Her Past. Photos by David Hiser. 468-489, Apr. 1976

KANGAROOS:

The Incredible Kangaroo. By David H. Johnson. 487-500, Oct. 1955

Strange Animals of Australia. By David Fleay. Photos by Stanley Breeden. 388-411, Sept. 1963

KANSAI, Japan's Historic Heartland, Hosts Expo '70. By Thomas J. Abercrombie. 295-339, Mar. 1970

KANSAS:

Following the Trail of Lewis and Clark. By Ralph Gray. 707-750, June 1953

Hays, Kansas, at the Nation's Heart. By Margaret M. Detwiler. Photos by John E. Fletcher. 461-490, Apr. 1952

Mapping the Nation's Breadbasket. By Frederick Simpich. 831-849, June 1948

Skyway Below the Clouds. By Carl R. Markwith. Photos by Ernest J. Cottrell. 85-108, July 1949
    Included: Pittsburg and Wichita

See also Missouri (River)

KANSAS CITY, Missouri:

Kansas City, Heartland U.S.A. By Rowe Findley. Photos by Ted Spiegel. 112-139, July 1976

KANSU (Province), China:

The Caves of the Thousand Buddhas. By Franc and Jean Shor. 383-415, Mar. 1951
    Contents: Ansi; Kiuchuan (Suchow); Yumen; and the Tunhwang Caves

KAPINGAMARANGI (Atoll), Caroline Islands:

Feast Day in Kapingamarangi. By W. Robert Moore. 523-537, Apr. 1950

KAPLAN, JOSEPH: Author:

How Man-made Satellites Can Affect Our Lives.

KAPLAN, JOSEPH: Author—Continued

Paintings by Gilbert Emerson. 791-810, Dec. 1957

KAPLAN, MARION: Author-Photographer:

Twilight of the Arab Dhow. 330-351, Sept. 1974

KAPSIKI (Tribespeople):

Carefree People of the Cameroons. Photos by Pierre Ichac. 233-248, Feb. 1947

KARAKORAM RANGE, Central Asia. See Hunza

KARAMOJONG (Tribespeople):

Uganda, Africa's Uneasy Heartland. By Howard La Fay. Photos by George F. Mobley. 708-735, Nov. 1971

KARENS (Tribespeople):

Spirits of Change Capture the Karens. By Peter Kunstadter. 267-285, Feb. 1972

KARNAK, Egypt. See Akhenaten Temple Project

KARNALI (River), Nepal:

Peerless Nepal—A Naturalist's Paradise. By S. Dillon Ripley. Photos by Volkmar Wentzel. 1-40, Jan. 1950

KARNALI ZONE, Nepal:

Karnali, Roadless World of Western Nepal. By Lila M. and Barry C. Bishop. 656-689, Nov. 1971

KARNATKA (State), India. See former name, Mysore

KASHGAIS (Nomads):

Journey into Troubled Iran. By George W. Long. Photos by J. Baylor Roberts. 425-464, Oct. 1951

We Dwelt in Kashgai Tents. By Jean and Franc Shor. 805-832, June 1952

KASHMIR:

The Emperor's Private Garden: Kashmir. By Nigel Cameron. Photos by Brian Brake. 606-647, Nov. 1958

Himalayan Pilgrimage. By Christopher Rand. 520-535, Oct. 1956

How the Kazakhs Fled to Freedom. By Milton J. Clark. 621-644, Nov. 1954

The Idyllic Vale of Kashmir. By Volkmar Wentzel. 523-550, Apr. 1948

A Journey to "Little Tibet." By Enakshi Bhavnani. Photos by Volkmar Wentzel. 603-634, May 1951

Mountaintop War in Remote Ladakh. By W. E. Garrett. 664-687, May 1963

A Woman Paints the Tibetans. By Lafugie. 659-692, May 1949

See also Gilgit; Hunza

KATAHDIN, Mount, Maine:

Mountains Top Off New England. By F. Barrows Colton. Photos by Robert F. Sisson. 563-602, May 1951

Skyline Trail from Maine to Georgia. By Andrew H. Brown. Photos by Robert F. Sisson. 219-251, Aug. 1949

KATMAI NATIONAL MONUMENT, Alaska:

Lonely Wonders of Katmai. By Ernest Gruening. Photos by Winfield Parks. 800-831, June 1963

KATMANDU, Nepal:

Coronation in Katmandu. By E. Thomas Gilliard. Photos by Marc Riboud. 139-152, July 1957

KATMANDU, Nepal — *Continued*

Peerless Nepal — A Naturalist's Paradise. By S. Dillon Ripley. Photos by Volkmar Wentzel. 1-40, Jan. 1950

KATZEV, MICHAEL L.: Author:

Last Harbor for the Oldest Ship. By Susan W. and Michael L. Katzev. 618-625, Nov. 1974

Resurrecting the Oldest Known Greek Ship. Photos by Bates Littlehales. 841-857, June 1970

KATZEV, SUSAN W.: Author:

Last Harbor for the Oldest Ship. By Susan W. and Michael L. Katzev. 618-625, Nov. 1974

KAUFFMANN, JOHN MICHAEL: Author:

Giant Sequoias Draw Millions to California Parks. Photos by B. Anthony Stewart. 147-187, Aug. 1959

KAULONG (People):

Blowgun Hunters of the South Pacific. By Jane C. Goodale. Photos by Ann Chowning. 793-817, June 1966

KAYAKS:

Kayak Odyssey: From the Inland Sea to Tokyo. By Dan Dimancescu. Photos by Christopher G. Knight. 295-337, Sept. 1967

Kayaks Down the Nile. By John M. Goddard. 697-732, May 1955

White-water Adventure on Wild Rivers of Idaho. By Frank Craighead, Jr. and John Craighead. 213-239, Feb. 1970

KAZAKHS (Tribespeople):

How the Kazakhs Fled to Freedom. By Milton J. Clark. 621-644, Nov. 1954

KAZIRANGA WILD LIFE SANCTUARY, Assam, India:

Stalking the Great Indian Rhino. By Lee Merriam Talbot. 389-398, Mar. 1957

KEA (Island), Greece:

The Isles of Greece: Aegean Birthplace of Western Culture. By Melville Bell Grosvenor. Photos by Edwin Stuart Grosvenor and Winfield Parks. 147-193, Aug. 1972

KEACH, DONALD L.: Author:

Down to *Thresher* by Bathyscaph. 764-777, June 1964

KEATING, BERN: Author:

Cajunland, Louisiana's French-speaking Coast. Photos by Charles Harbutt and Franke Keating. 353-391, Mar. 1966

North for Oil: *Manhattan* Makes the Historic Northwest Passage. Photos by Tomas Sennett. 374-391, Mar. 1970

Pakistan: Problems of a Two-part Land. Photos by Albert Moldvay. 1-47, Jan. 1967

Today Along the Natchez Trace, Pathway Through History. Photos by Charles Harbutt. 641-667, Nov. 1968

KEATING, FRANKE: Photographer:

Cajunland, Louisiana's French-speaking Coast. By Bern Keating. Photos by Charles Harbutt and Franke Keating. 353-391, Mar. 1966

KEELING ISLANDS, Indian Ocean. *See* Cocos Islands

KEEPING House for a Biologist in Colombia. By Nancy Bell Fairchild Bates. Photos by Marston Bates. 251-274, Aug. 1948

KEEPING House for Tropical Butterflies. By Jocelyn Crane. Photos by M. Woodbridge Williams. 193-217, Aug. 1957

KEEPING House in a Cappadocian Cave. By Jonathan S. Blair. 127-146, July 1970

KEEPING House in London. By Frances James. 769-792, Dec. 1947

KEIJO, Korea. *See* Seoul

KEKOPEY RANCH, Kenya:

Life With the "Pumphouse Gang": New Insights Into Baboon Behavior. By Shirley C. Strum. Photos by Timothy W. Ransom. 672-691, May 1975

KELLEY, FRANCIS BEVERLY: Author:

The Wonder City That Moves by Night. 289-324, Mar. 1948

KELP:

Giant Kelp, Sequoias of the Sea. By Wheeler J. North. Photos by Bates Littlehales. 251-269, Aug. 1972

KELSO, JAMES L.: Author-Photographer:

The Ghosts of Jericho. 825-844, Dec. 1951

KEMANO POWER DEVELOPMENT:

Kitimat — Canada's Aluminum Titan. By David S. Boyer. 376-398, Sept. 1956

KEMP, WESTON: Photographer:

The Age of Sail Lives On at Mystic. By Alan Villiers. 220-239, Aug. 1968

KENETT, F. L.: Photographer:

Tutankhamun's Golden Trove. By Christiane Desroches Noblecourt. 625-646, Oct. 1963

KENNEDY, JACQUELINE BOUVIER:

Inside the White House. By Lonnelle Aikman. Photos by B. Anthony Stewart and Thomas Nebbia. 3-43, Jan. 1961

The Last Full Measure. By Melville Bell Grosvenor. 307-355, Mar. 1964

The Living White House. By Lonnelle Aikman. 593-643, Nov. 1966

The White House (guidebook) presented to President and Mrs. John F. Kennedy. 888-889, 892, Dec. 1962

KENNEDY, JOHN F.:

Distinguished Flying Cross awarded posthumously to Victor A. Prather, Jr. 684, 685, Nov. 1961

Inside the White House. By Lonnelle Aikman. Photos by B. Anthony Stewart and Thomas Nebbia. 3-43, Jan. 1961

Jacques-Yves Cousteau Receives National Geographic Society Medal at White House. 146-147, July 1961

The Last Full Measure. By Melville Bell Grosvenor. 307-355, Mar. 1964

The Living White House. By Lonnelle Aikman. 593-643, Nov. 1966

President Kennedy Presents the Hubbard Medal (American Mount Everest Expedition). 514-515, Oct. 1963

KENNEDY, JOHN F. — *Continued*

Profiles of the Presidents: V. The Atomic Age: Its Problems and Promises. By Frank Freidel. 66-119, Jan. 1966

To the Memory of Our Beloved President, Friend to All Mankind. 1A-1B, Jan. 1964

White House News Photographers Association's first-place award presented to Robert F. Sisson. 880, Dec. 1961

The White House (guidebook) presented to President and Mrs. John F. Kennedy. 888-889, 892, Dec. 1962

KENNEDY, JOHN F., SPACE CENTER, Florida:

Cape Canaveral's 6,000-mile Shooting Gallery. By Allan C. Fisher, Jr. Photos by Luis Marden and Thomas Nebbia. 421-471, Oct. 1959

"A Most Fantastic Voyage": The Story of Apollo 8's Rendezvous With the Moon. By Sam C. Phillips. 593-631, May 1969

Reaching for the Moon. By Allan C. Fisher, Jr. Photos by Luis Marden. 157-171, Feb. 1959

KENNEDY, MRS. JOHN F. *See* Kennedy, Jacqueline Bouvier

KENNEDY, RALPH A.: Author:

Playing 3,000 Golf Courses in Fourteen Lands. 113-132, July 1952

KENNEDY, ROBERT F.: Author:

Canada's Mount Kennedy. II. A Peak Worthy of the President. 5-9, July 1965

KENNEDY, Mount, Canada:

Canada's Mount Kennedy. 1-33, July 1965
I. The Discovery. By Bradford Washburn. 1-3
II. A Peak Worthy of the President. By Robert F. Kennedy. 5-9
III. The First Ascent. By James W. Whittaker. Photos by William Albert Allard. 11-33

The Massif of Mount Hubbard, Mount Alverstone, and Mount Kennedy. Map announced. 736, Nov. 1968

KENNEY, NATHANIEL T.: Author:

Africa: The Winds of Freedom Stir a Continent. Photos by W. D. Vaughn. 303-359, Sept. 1960

Big Bend: Jewel in the Texas Desert. Photos by James L. Stanfield. 104-133, Jan. 1968

Cape Cod, Where Sea Holds Sway Over Man and Land. Photos by Dean Conger. 149-187, Aug. 1962

Chesapeake Country. Photos by Bates Littlehales. 370-411, Sept. 1964

Ethiopian Adventure. Photos by James P. Blair. 548-582, Apr. 1965

Kings Point: Maker of Mariners. Photos by Volkmar Wentzel. 693-706, Nov. 1955

Life in Walled-off West Berlin. By Nathaniel T. Kenney and Volkmar Wentzel. Photos by Thomas Nebbia. 735-767, Dec. 1961

Maytime Miracle in Sherwood Gardens. 700-709, May 1956

The Mighty *Enterprise*. Photos by Thomas J. Abercrombie. 431-448, Mar. 1963

New Era on the Great Lakes. 439-490, Apr. 1959

New National Park Proposed: The Spectacular North Cascades. Photos by James P. Blair. 642-667, May 1968

A New Riviera: Mexico's West Coast. Photos by

KENNEY, NATHANIEL T.: Author — *Continued*

Charles O'Rear. 670-699, Nov. 1973

The Other Yosemite. Photos by Dean Conger. 762-781, June 1974

Our Changing Atlantic Coastline. Photos by B. Anthony Stewart. 860-887, Dec. 1962

Our Green Treasury, the National Forests. Photos by J. Baylor Roberts. 287-324, Sept. 1956

Sharks: Wolves of the Sea. 222-257, Feb. 1968

Southern California's Trial by Mud and Water. Photos by Bruce Dale. 552-573, Oct. 1969

United Italy Marks Its 100th Year. 593-647, Nov. 1961

Where Falcons Wear Air Force Blue, United States Air Force Academy. Photos by William Belknap, Jr. 845-873, June 1959

KENTUCKY:

Around the "Great Lakes of the South." By Frederick Simpich. Photos by J. Baylor Roberts. 463-491, Apr. 1948

Heart of the Bluegrass. By Charles McCarry. Photos by J. Bruce Baumann. 634-659, May 1974

The People of Cumberland Gap. By John Fetterman. Photos by Bruce Dale. 591-621, Nov. 1971

So Much Happens Along the Ohio River. By Frederick Simpich. Photos by Justin Locke. 177-212, Feb. 1950

Vacation Tour Through Lincoln Land. By Ralph Gray. 141-184, Feb. 1952

Whatever Happened to TVA? By Gordon Young. Photos by Emory Kristof. 830-863, June 1973

KENYA:

Adventures in the Search for Man. By Louis S. B. Leakey. Photos by Hugo van Lawick. 132-152, Jan. 1963

Africa's Uncaged Elephants. Photos by Quentin Keynes. 371-382, Mar. 1951

Britain Tackles the East African Bush. By W. Robert Moore. 311-352, Mar. 1950

East Africa's Majestic Flamingos. By M. Philip Kahl. 276-294, Feb. 1970

Freeing Flamingos From Anklets of Death (Lake Magadi). By John G. Williams. Photos by Alan Root. 934-944, Dec. 1963

Kenya Says *Harambee!* By Allan C. Fisher, Jr. Photos by Bruce Dale. 151-205, Feb. 1969

The Leakeys of Africa: Family in Search of Prehistoric Man. By Melvin M. Payne. 194-231, Feb. 1965

A New Look at Kenya's "Treetops." By Quentin Keynes. 536-541, Oct. 1956

Roaming Africa's Unfenced Zoos. By W. Robert Moore. 353-380, Mar. 1950
Included: "Treetops Hotel," near Mount Kenya

Spearing Lions with Africa's Masai. By Edgar Monsanto Queeny. 487-517, Oct. 1954

Where Elephants Have Right of Way. By George and Jinx Rodger. Photos by George Rodger. 363-389, Sept. 1960

See also Mzima Springs; Rudolf, Lake; Tsavo National Park; *and* Baboons; Dhows; YWCA

KENYON, KARL W.: Author:

Return of the Sea Otter. Photos by James A. Mattison, Jr. 520-539, Oct. 1971

KENYON, KARL W. — *Continued*
Author-Photographer
The Fur Seal Herd Comes of Age. By Victor B. Scheffer and Karl W. Kenyon. 491-512, Apr. 1952

KENYON, KATHLEEN M.: Author:
Jericho Gives Up Its Secrets. By Kathleen M. Kenyon and A. Douglas Tushingham. Photos by Nancy Lord. 853-870, Dec. 1953

KERN, JAMES A.: Author-Photographer:
Dragon Lizards of Komodo. 872-880, Dec. 1968

KERRY, County, Ireland. *See* Dingle Peninsula

KERTEZI, Greece:
Erosion, Trojan Horse of Greece. By F. G. Renner. 793-812, Dec. 1947

KERWIN, JOSEPH P.:
Skylab, Outpost on the Frontier of Space. By Thomas Y. Canby. Photos by the nine mission astronauts. 441-469, Oct. 1974

KETCHES. *See Betelgeuse; Carib; Great Britain II; Nomad; Tectona; Tradewinds; Yankee*

KEW: The Commoners' Royal Garden. By Thomas Garner James. Photos by B. Anthony Stewart. 479-506, Apr. 1950

KEY LARGO CORAL REEF, Florida:
Florida's Coral City Beneath the Sea. By Jerry Greenberg. 70-89, Jan. 1962
Key Largo Coral Reef: America's First Undersea Park. By Charles M. Brookfield. Photos by Jerry Greenberg. 58-69, Jan. 1962

KEY WEST, Florida:
From Indian Canoes to Submarines at Key West. By Frederick Simpich. Photos by J. Baylor Roberts. 41-72, Jan. 1950
The Lower Keys, Florida's "Out Islands." By John Scofield. Photos by Emory Kristof and Bates Littlehales. 72-93, Jan. 1971
Our Navy's Long Submarine Arm. By Allan C. Fisher, Jr. 613-636, Nov. 1952
Tropical Gardens of Key West. By Luis Marden. 116-124, Jan. 1953
See also Shrimp Fishing (Shrimpers)

KEYNES, QUENTIN: Author-Photographer:
Mauritius, Island of the Dodo. 77-104, Jan. 1956
A New Look at Kenya's "Treetops." 536-541, Oct. 1956
St. Helena: the Forgotten Island. 265-280, Aug. 1950
Seychelles, Tropic Isles of Eden. 670-695, Nov. 1959
Photographer
Africa's Uncaged Elephants. 371-382, Mar. 1951

KHIRBAT QUMRĀN, Jordan:
The Men Who Hid the Dead Sea Scrolls. By A. Douglas Tushingham. Paintings by Peter V. Bianchi. 785-808, Dec. 1958

KHMER REPUBLIC. *See* Cambodia

KHMERS:
Angkor: Jewel of the Jungle. By W. Robert Moore. Paintings by Maurice Fiévet. 517-569, Apr. 1960

KIBBUTZIM:
Israel: Land of Promise. By John Scofield. Photos by B. Anthony Stewart. 395-434, Mar. 1965
The Land of Galilee. By Kenneth MacLeish. Photos by B. Anthony Stewart. 832-865, Dec. 1965
Our Life on a Border Kibbutz. By Carol and Al Abrams. Photos by Al Abrams. 364-391, Sept. 1970

KIHN, W. LANGDON: Artist:
Hearty Folk Defy Arctic Storms. 479-494, Oct. 1949
Indians of the Far West. By Matthew W. Stirling. 175-200, Feb. 1948

KILAUEA VOLCANO, Hawaii:
Fountain of Fire in Hawaii. By Frederick Simpich, Jr. Photos by Robert B. Goodman and Robert Wenkam. 303-327, Mar. 1960
Hawaii, Island of Fire and Flowers. By Gordon Young. Photos by Robert W. Madden. 399-425, Mar. 1975
Photographing a Volcano in Action. By Thomas J. Hargrave. 561-563, Oct. 1955
Volcanic Fires of the 50th State: Hawaii National Park. By Paul A. Zahl. 793-823, June 1959

KILBON, ROLAND: Author:
Born Hunters, the Bird Dogs. Paintings by Walter A. Weber. 369-398, Sept. 1947

KILBRACKEN, LORD (John Godley, Third Baron Kilbracken): Author:
The Long, Deep Dive. Photos by Bates Littlehales. 718-731, May 1963

KILLARNEY, Lakes of, Ireland:
Dublin's Historic Horse Show. By Maynard Owen Williams. 115-132, July 1953

KILLER BEES. *See* Africanized Honeybees

KILLER WHALES:
Making Friends With a Killer Whale. By Edward I. Griffin. 418-446, Mar. 1966
Namu. Children's book announced. 726-728, Nov. 1973
Where Two Worlds Meet (Patagonia). Photos by Des and Jen Bartlett. 298-321, Mar. 1976

KIM, H. EDWARD: Author-Photographer:
Rare Look at North Korea. 252-277, Aug. 1974
Photographer
Pennsylvania's Old-time Dutch Treat. By Kent Britt. 564-578, Apr. 1973
South Korea: What Next? By Peter T. White. 394-427, Sept. 1975

KIMBERLEY (Region), Australia:
Western Australia, the Big Country. By Kenneth MacLeish. Photos by James L. Stanfield. 150-187, Feb. 1975

KINDERZECHE (Festival):
Dinkelsbühl (Germany) Rewards Its Children. By Charles Belden. 255-268, Feb. 1957

KING, ELIZABETH W.: Author:
Flags of the Americas. 633-657, May 1949
Flags of the United Nations. 213-238, Feb. 1951

KING CRABS:
The Crab That Shakes Hands. By Clarence P. Idyll. Photos by Robert F. Sisson. 254-271, Feb. 1971

Index 1947-1976

261

KING ISLAND, Alaska:

Cliff Dwellers of the Bering Sea. By Juan Muñoz. 129-146, Jan. 1954

North Star Cruises Alaska's Wild West. By Amos Burg. 57-86, July 1952

KING RANCH, Texas:

America's "Meat on the Hoof." By William H. Nicholas. 33-72, Jan. 1952
King Ranch, Cattle Empire in Texas. 41-64

KINGDON-WARD, F.: Author-Photographer:

Caught in the Assam-Tibet Earthquake. 403-416, Mar. 1952

KINGFISHERS:

The Shy and Spectacular Kingfisher (European). Photos by Carl-Johan Junge and Emil Lütken. 413-419, Sept. 1974

KINGS CANYON NATIONAL PARK, California:

Giant Sequoias Draw Millions to California Parks. By John Michael Kauffmann. Photos by B. Anthony Stewart. 147-187, Aug. 1959

KINGS POINT, New York: U. S. Merchant Marine Academy:

Kings Point: Maker of Mariners. By Nathaniel T. Kenney. Photos by Volkmar Wentzel. 693-706, Nov. 1955

KINGSTON, Massachusetts:

Land of the Pilgrims' Pride. By George W. Long. Photos by Robert F. Sisson. 193-219, Aug. 1947

KINGSTON, Ontario, Canada:

Sea to Lakes on the St. Lawrence. By George W. Long. Photos by B. Anthony Stewart and John E. Fletcher. 323-366, Sept. 1950

KINLOCH, BRUCE G.: Author-Photographer:

Orphans of the Wild. 683-699, Nov. 1962

KINNEY, WILLIAM A.: Author:

Operation Eclipse: 1948. 325-372, Mar. 1949

Roving Maryland's Cavalier Country. 431-470, Apr. 1954

Washington's Historic Georgetown. 513-544, Apr. 1953

KIRGHIZ (People):

We Took the Highroad in Afghanistan. By Jean and Franc Shor. 673-706, Nov. 1950

Winter Caravan to the Roof of the World. By Sabrina and Roland Michaud. 435-465, Apr. 1972

KIRIN (Chilin), Manchuria:

In Manchuria Now. By W. Robert Moore. 389-414, Mar. 1947

KIRK, MALCOLM S.: Author-Photographer:

The Asmat of New Guinea, Headhunters in Today's World. 376-409, Mar. 1972

Change Ripples New Guinea's Sepik River. 354-381, Sept. 1973

Journey Into Stone Age New Guinea. 568-592, Apr. 1969

New Guinea Festival of Faces. 148-156, July 1969

KIRKJUFELL (Volcano), Heimaey, Iceland:

A Village Fights for Its Life. By Noel Grove. 40-67, July 1973

KITES:

Alexander Graham Bell Museum: Tribute to Genius. By Jean Lesage. 227-256, Aug. 1956

Miracle Men of the Telephone. By F. Barrows Colton. 273-316, Mar. 1947
Included: Illustrations of Alexander Graham Bell's multicelled and tetrahedral kites

KITES (Birds):

The Swallow-tailed Kite: Graceful Aerialist of the Everglades. Photos by Ray O. Green, Jr., Norman D. Reed, and Myron H. Wright, Jr. 496-505, Oct. 1972

KITIMAT—Canada's Aluminum Titan. By David S. Boyer. 376-398, Sept. 1956

KITTINGER, JOSEPH W., Jr.: Author:

The Long, Lonely Leap. Photos by Volkmar Wentzel. 854-873, Dec. 1960

The KIWI, New Zealand's Wonder Bird. By Ron J. Anderson. 395-398, Sept. 1955

KLEMMER, HARVEY: Author:

Belgium Comes Back. Photos by Maynard Owen Williams. 575-614, May 1948

KLEMPERER, WOLFGANG B.: Author:

The Solar Eclipse From a Jet. 785-796, Nov. 1963

KLINE, FRED: Author:

Baltimore: The Hidden City. Photos by Martin Rogers. 188-215, Feb. 1975

Library of Congress: The Nation's Bookcase. Photos by Dick Durrance II. 671-687, Nov. 1975

San Antonio: "Texas, Actin' Kind of Natural." Photos by David Hiser. 524-549, Apr. 1976

KLINGEL, GILBERT C.: Author:

One Hundred Hours Beneath the Chesapeake. Photos by Willard R. Culver. 681-696, May 1955

KLINGMAN, LAWRENCE L.: Author:

Incredible Andorra. Photos by B. Anthony Stewart. 262-290, Aug. 1949

KNEEN, ORVILLE H.: Author:

Patent Plants Enrich Our World. 357-378, Mar. 1948

KNIGHT, CHRISTOPHER G.: Photographer:

Alaska's Mighty Rivers of Ice. By Maynard M. Miller. 194-217, Feb. 1967

Americans Afoot in Rumania. By Dan Dimancescu. Photos by Dick Durrance II and Christopher G. Knight. 810-845, June 1969

Down the Danube by Canoe. By William Slade Backer. Photos by Richard S. Durrance and Christopher G. Knight. 34-79, July 1965

Kayak Odyssey: From the Inland Sea to Tokyo. By Dan Dimancescu. 295-337, Sept. 1967

KNIK GLACIER AND RIVER, Alaska:

Alaska's Automatic Lake Drains Itself (Lake George). 835-844, June 1951

KNOCKING Out Grizzly Bears for Their Own Good. By Frank and John Craighead. 276-291, Aug. 1960

'KNOWN but to God' (Unknown Heroes). By Beverley M. Bowie. 593-605, Nov. 1958

KNUDSEN, DON C.: Photographer:

Alaska's Automatic Lake Drains Itself (Lake

KNUDSEN, DON C.: Photographer—*Continued*
George). 835-844, June 1951

KNUTSEN, WILLIE: Author:
Milestones in My Arctic Journeys. 543-570, Oct. 1949

KOBLICK, IAN:
Tektite II. 256-296, Aug. 1971
I. Science's Window on the Sea. By John G. VanDerwalker. Photos by Bates Littlehales. 256-289

KOCH, ERICA: Photographer:
Thumbs Up Round the North Sea's Rim. By Frances James. 685-704, May 1952

KOFFLER, CAMILLA (Ylla): Photographer:
Mysore Celebrates the Death of a Demon. By Luc Bouchage. 706-711, May 1958

KØGE, Denmark:
2,000 Miles Through Europe's Oldest Kingdom. By Isobel Wylie Hutchison. Photos by Maynard Owen Williams. 141-180, Feb. 1949

KOH-I-NOOR (Diamond):
Questing for Gems. By George S. Switzer. 835-863, Dec. 1971

KOHOUTEK (Comet):
How to Catch a Passing Comet. By Kenneth F. Weaver. 148-150, Jan. 1974
What You Didn't See in Kohoutek. By Kenneth F. Weaver. 214-223, Aug. 1974

KOM, Kingdom of, Cameroon:
Afo-A-Kom: A Sacred Symbol Comes Home. By William S. Ellis. Photos by James P. Blair. 141-148, July 1974

KOMODO DRAGONS:
Dragon Lizards of Komodo. By James A. Kern. 872-880, Dec. 1968

KORDOFAN (Province), Sudan:
With the Nuba Hillmen of Kordofan. By Robin Strachan. 249-278, Feb. 1951

KOREA:
Japan and Korea, Atlas series supplement. Dec. 1960

KOREA, North:
Rare Look at North Korea. By H. Edward Kim. 252-277, Aug. 1974

KOREA, South:
Operation Eclipse: 1948. By William A. Kinney. 325-372, Mar. 1949
Roaming Korea South of the Iron Curtain. By Enzo de Chetelat. 777-808, June 1950
South Korea: Success Story in Asia. By Howard Sochurek. 301-345, Mar. 1969
South Korea: What Next? By Peter T. White. Photos by H. Edward Kim. 394-427, Sept. 1975
With the U. S. Army in Korea. By John R. Hodge. 829-840, June 1947
YWCA: International Success Story. By Mary French Rockefeller. Photos by Otis Imboden. 904-933, Dec. 1963

KOREAN WAR:
The GI and the Kids of Korea. By Robert H. Mosier. 635-664, May 1953

KOREAN WAR—*Continued*
Our Navy in the Far East. By Arthur W. Radford. Photos by J. Baylor Roberts. 537-577, Oct. 1953
South Korea: Success Story in Asia. By Howard Sochurek. 301-345, Mar. 1969
Included: Truce talks; border skirmishes

KORNBLAU, GERALD: Photographer:
The GI and the Kids of Korea. By Robert H. Mosier. 635-664, May 1953

KORONGO (Tribespeople):
With the Nuba Hillmen of Kordofan. By Robin Strachan. Photos by George Rodger. 249-278, Feb. 1951

KOS (Island), Greece:
The Isles of Greece: Aegean Birthplace of Western Culture. By Melville Bell Grosvenor. Photos by Edwin Stuart Grosvenor and Winfield Parks. 147-193, Aug. 1972

KRAHO INDIANS:
Children of the Sun and Moon. By Harald Schultz; translated from German by Curtis T. Everett. 340-363, Mar. 1959

KRAWCZYK, JOHN J.: Photographer:
Submarine Through the North Pole. By William G. Lalor, Jr. 1-20, Jan. 1959

KREEN-AKARORES (Indians):
Brazil's Kreen-Akarores: Requiem for a Tribe? By W. Jesco von Puttkamer. 254-269, Feb. 1975

KREMLIN, Moscow, U.S.S.R.:
An American in Russia's Capital. By Thomas T. Hammond. Photos by Dean Conger. 297-351, Mar. 1966

KRESS COLLECTION:
The Kress Collection: A Gift to the Nation. By Guy Emerson. 823-865, Dec. 1961
The Nation's Newest Old Masters (National Gallery of Art). By John Walker. 619-657, Nov. 1956
Your National Gallery of Art After 10 Years. By John Walker. 73-103, Jan. 1952

KRISTOF, EMORY:
Designed shutterless camera. 492, Apr. 1975
Author-Photographer
The Last U. S. Whale Hunters. 346-353, Mar. 1973
Photographer
Behold the Computer Revolution. By Peter T. White. Photos by Bruce Dale and Emory Kristof. 593-633, Nov. 1970
Bermuda—Balmy, British, and Beautiful. By Peter Benchley. 93-121, July 1971
Can We Harness the Wind? By Roger Hamilton. 812-829, Dec. 1975
Computer Helps Scholars Re-create an Egyptian Temple. By Ray Winfield Smith. 634-655, Nov. 1970
From Sword to Scythe in Champlain Country. By Ethel A. Starbird. Photos by B. Anthony Stewart and Emory Kristof. 153-201, Aug. 1967
Lonely Cape Hatteras, Besieged by the Sea. By William S. Ellis. 393-421, Sept. 1969
The Lower Keys, Florida's "Out Islands." By John Scofield. Photos by Emory Kristof and Bates Littlehales. 72-93, Jan. 1971
The Netherlands Antilles: Holland in the Caribbe-

KRISTOF, EMORY — *Continued*
an. By James Cerruti. 115-146, Jan. 1970

New Tricks Outwit Our Insect Enemies. By Hal Higdon. Photos by Robert F. Sisson and Emory Kristof. 380-399, Sept. 1972

Of Planes and Men. By Kenneth F. Weaver. Photos by Emory Kristof and Albert Moldvay. 298-349, Sept. 1965

Oil, the Dwindling Treasure. By Noel Grove. 792-825, June 1974

Project FAMOUS. 586-615, May 1975
I. Where the Earth Turns Inside Out. By J. R. Heirtzler. 586-603
II. Dive Into the Great Rift. By Robert D. Ballard. 604-615

Sailors of the Sky. By Gordon Young. Photos by Emory Kristof and Jack Fields. Paintings by Davis Meltzer. 49-73, Jan. 1967

The Search for Tomorrow's Power. By Kenneth F. Weaver. 650-681, Nov. 1972

Solar Energy, the Ultimate Powerhouse. By John L. Wilhelm. 381-397, Mar. 1976

Tanzania Marches to Its Own Drum. By Peter T. White. 474-509, Apr. 1975

This Land of Ours — How Are We Using It? By Peter T. White. 20-67, July 1976

Whatever Happened to TVA? By Gordon Young. 830-863, June 1973

Will Oil and Tundra Mix? Alaska's North Slope Hangs in the Balance. By William S. Ellis. 485-517, Oct. 1971

Window on Earth's Interior. By Robert D. Ballard. 228-249, Aug. 1976

KRUGER NATIONAL PARK, South Africa:
Safari Through Changing Africa. By Elsie May Bell Grosvenor. Photos by Gilbert Grosvenor. 145-198, Aug. 1953

KRUNG THEP, Thailand. *See* Bangkok

KRUUK, HANS: Author:
Hyenas, the Hunters Nobody Knows. Photos by Baron Hugo van Lawick. 44-57, July 1968

KUBASOV, VALERIY:
Apollo-Soyuz: Handclasp in Space. By Thomas Y. Canby. 183-187, Feb. 1976

KUH, MICHAEL: Photographer:
Growing Up With Snowflake. By Arthur J. Riopelle. 491-503, Oct. 1970

KUHN, DELIA: Author:
Poland Opens Her Doors. By Delia and Ferdinand Kuhn. Photos by Erich Lessing. 354-398, Sept. 1958

KUHN, FERDINAND: Author:
Poland Opens Her Doors. By Delia and Ferdinand Kuhn. Photos by Erich Lessing. 354-398, Sept. 1958

Where Turk and Russian Meet. 743-766, June 1952

The Yankee Sailor Who Opened Japan. 85-102, July 1953

KUNMING, Yunnan, China:
Kunming Pilgrimage. 213-226, Feb. 1950

KUNSTADTER, PETER: Author-Photographer:
Living With Thailand's Gentle Lua. 122-152, July 1966

KUNSTADTER, PETER: Author-Photographer — *Continued*
Spirits of Change Capture the Karens. 267-285, Feb. 1972

KUNSTHISTORISCHES MUSEUM, Vienna, Austria:
The Vienna Treasures and Their Collectors. By John Walker. 737-776, June 1950

KUNTZ, ROBERT E.: Photographer:
Yemen Opens the Door to Progress. By Harry Hoogstraal. 213-244, Feb. 1952

KURDISTAN (Region), Asia:
The Kurds of Iraq: "We Who Face Death." By LeRoy Woodson, Jr. 364-387, Mar. 1975
See also Tepe Gawra

KURDS (People):
Iraq — Where Oil and Water Mix. By Jean and Franc Shor. 443-489, Oct. 1958

The Kurds of Iraq: "We Who Face Death." By LeRoy Woodson, Jr. 364-387, Mar. 1975

KUTZTOWN, Pennsylvania:
Pennsylvania Dutch Folk Festival. By Maynard Owen Williams. 503-516, Oct. 1952

Pennsylvania's Old-time Dutch Treat. By Kent Britt. Photos by H. Edward Kim. 564-578, Apr. 1973

KUUSAMO, Finland:
Scenes of Postwar Finland. By La Verne Bradley. Photos by Jerry Waller. 233-264, Aug. 1947

KUWAIT:
The Arab World, Inc. By John J. Putman. Photos by Winfield Parks. 494-533, Oct. 1975

Boom Time in Kuwait. By Paul Edward Case. 783-802, Dec. 1952

Kuwait, Aladdin's Lamp of the Middle East. By John E. Frazer. Photos by David F. Cupp. 636-667, May 1969

Oil, the Dwindling Treasure. By Noel Grove. Photos by Emory Kristof. 792-825, June 1974

KWAJALEIN (Atoll), Marshall Islands:
Adventures with the Survey Navy. By Irving Johnson. 131-148, July 1947

We Survive on a Pacific Atoll. By John and Frank Craighead. 73-94, Jan. 1948

KWAKIUTL INDIANS:
Canada's Window on the Pacific: The British Columbia Coast. By Jules B. Billard. Photos by Ted Spiegel. 338-375, Mar. 1972

KYOTO, Japan:
Kansai, Japan's Historic Heartland. By Thomas J. Abercrombie. 295-339, Mar. 1970

Kyoto and Nara: Keepers of Japan's Past. By Charles McCarry. Photos by George F. Mobley. 836-851, June 1976
Kyoto Says Happy New Year. 852-859

KYRENIA SHIP:
Last Harbor for the Oldest Ship. By Susan W. and Michael L. Katzev. 618-625, Nov. 1974

Resurrecting the Oldest Known Greek Ship. By Michael L. Katzev. Photos by Bates Littlehales. 841-857, June 1970

KYUSHU (Island), Japan:

Backwoods Japan During American Occupation. By M. A. Huberman. 491-518, Apr. 1947

L

L-5 (Space Colony, A.D. 2026):

The Next Frontier? By Isaac Asimov. Paintings by Pierre Mion. 76-89, July 1976

L. S. B. LEAKEY FOUNDATION:

Contributions invited; address given. 144, Jan. 1973

Early-man research in Ethiopia sponsored. 805, Dec. 1976

LaBASTILLE, ANNE: Author:

My Backyard, the Adirondacks. Photos by David Alan Harvey. 616-639, May 1975

See also Bowes, Anne LaBastille

LA BEAUCE (Plain), France:

Chartres: Legacy From the Age of Faith. By Kenneth MacLeish. Photos by Dean Conger. 857-882, Dec. 1969

LABORATORY in a Dirty Sky. By Rudolf J. Engelmann and Vera Simons. 616-621, Nov. 1976

LABRADOR (Region), Newfoundland:

Far North with "Captain Mac." By Miriam MacMillan. 465-513, Oct. 1951

Labrador Canoe Adventure. By Andrew Brown and Ralph Gray. 65-99, July 1951

Milestones in My Arctic Journeys. By Willie Knutsen. 543-570, Oct. 1949

Included: Activities of the Search and Rescue section of the Air Force at Goose Bay

Newfoundland, Canada's New Province. By Andrew H. Brown. Photos by author and Robert F. Sisson. 777-812, June 1949

School for Survival. By Curtis E. LeMay. 565-602, May 1953

LACQUER WARE:

Human Treasures of Japan. By William Graves. Photos by James L. Stanfield. 370-379, Sept. 1972

A Lady From China's Past. Photos from China Pictorial. Text by Alice J. Hall. 660-681, May 1974

LA CRAU (Plain), France:

Sheep Trek in the French Alps. By Maurice Moyal. Photos by Marcel Coen. 545-564, Apr. 1952

LADAKH (District), Jammu and Kashmir:

A Journey to "Little Tibet." By Enakshi Bhavnani. Photos by Volkmar Wentzel. 603-634, May 1951

Mountaintop War in Remote Ladakh. By W. E. Garrett. 664-687, May 1963

A Woman Paints the Tibetans. By Lafugie. 659-692, May 1949

LADD, HARRY S.: Author:

Fossils Lift the Veil of Time. By Harry S. Ladd and Roland W. Brown. 363-386, Mar. 1956

A LADY From China's Past. Photos from China Pictorial. Text by Alice J. Hall. 660-681, May 1974

LADYBUGS:

Following the Ladybug Home. By Kenneth S. Ha-

LADYBUGS — Continued

gen. Photos by Robert F. Sisson. 543-553, Apr. 1970

New Tricks Outwit Our Insect Enemies. By Hal Higdon. Photos by Robert F. Sisson and Emory Kristof. 380-399, Sept. 1972

LA FAY, HOWARD: Author:

Alabama, Dixie to a Different Tune. Photos by Dick Durrance II. 534-569, Oct. 1975

Algeria: France's Stepchild, Problem and Promise. Photos by Robert F. Sisson. 768-795, June 1960

Andalusia, the Spirit of Spain. Photos by Joseph J. Scherschel. 833-857, June 1975

"Be Ye Men of Valour" (Churchill's Life and Funeral). 159-197, Aug. 1965

Carnival in Trinidad. Photos by Winfield Parks. 693-701, Nov. 1971

DEW Line, Sentry of the Far North. 128-146, July 1958

Easter Island and Its Mysterious Monuments. Photos by Thomas J. Abercrombie. 90-117, Jan. 1962

The Eisenhower Story. 1-39, July 1969

Freedom's Progress South of the Sahara. Photos by Joseph J. Scherschel. 603-637, Nov. 1962

George Washington: The Man Behind the Myths. Photos by Ted Spiegel. 90-111, July 1976

Gibraltar — Rock of Contention. Photos by Bates Littlehales. 102-121, July 1966

Leningrad, Russia's Window on the West. Photos by Dick Durrance II. 636-673, May 1971

The Maya, Children of Time. Photos by David Alan Harvey. 729-767, Dec. 1975

Portugal at the Crossroads. Photos by Volkmar Wentzel. 453-501, Oct. 1965

The St. Lawrence, River Key to Canada. Photos by John Launois. 622-667, May 1967

Sicily, Where All the Songs Are Sad. Photos by Jonathan Blair. 407-436, Mar. 1976

Uganda, Africa's Uneasy Heartland. Photos by George F. Mobley. 708-735, Nov. 1971

The Vikings. Photos by Ted Spiegel. 492-541, Apr. 1970

Where Jesus Walked. Photos by Charles Harbutt. 739-781, Dec. 1967

LAFAYETTE, Marquis de:

Lafayette's Homeland, Auvergne. By Howell Walker. 419-436, Sept. 1957

LAFUGIE, Madame: Author-Artist:

A Woman Paints the Tibetans. 659-692, May 1949

LA GORCE, GILBERT GROSVENOR:

NGM advertising director. 442, 444, Mar. 1960

Author

Marineland, Florida's Giant Fish Bowl. Photos by Luis Marden. 679-694, Nov. 1952

LA GORCE, JOHN OLIVER:

Board of Trustees, Vice Chairman. 419-423, Mar. 1957; 98, Jan. 1966

Colleague of the Golden Years: John Oliver La Gorce (Memorial Tribute). By Gilbert Grosvenor. 440-444, Mar. 1960

Editor (1954-1957). 65, 65D, July 1954; 441, 442, 444, Mar. 1960; 46-47, 67, July 1967

Editor, Assistant. 418, Mar. 1957

Editor, Associate. 65, 65C, July 1954; 418, Mar.

LA GORCE, JOHN OLIVER—*Continued*

1957; 441, 443, Mar. 1960

Golden Anniversary with the Society. 422, 423, Mar. 1957; 442, Mar. 1960

Grosvenor Medal recipient. 422, 423, Mar. 1957

President of NGS (1954-1957). 65, 65D, July 1954; 418, 419, 423, Mar. 1957; 440-444, Mar. 1960

Vice President of NGS. 255, 260, 261, Aug. 1949; 65, 65C, July 1954; 441, 443, Mar. 1960

Author

Artists Look at Pennsylvania. 37-56, July 1948

LA GORCE, LOUISE PARKER: Author:

Christmas in Cookie Tree Land. Photos by B. Anthony Stewart. 844-851, Dec. 1955

LA GORCE MEDAL:

First La Gorce Medal Honors Antarctic Expedition. 864-867, June 1967
    Note: Melvin M. Payne guided the design of the medal, which was executed by Peter V. Bianchi and Howard E. Paine.

LAGUS, CHARLES: Photographer:

Animal Safari to British Guiana. By David Attenborough. Photos by Charles Lagus and author. 851-874, June 1957

LAHEY, CARLOTTA GONZALES: Artist:

Flags of the Americas. By Elizabeth W. King. 633-657, May 1949

Flags of the United Nations. By Elizabeth W. King. 213-238, Feb. 1951

LAIRD, NORMAN: Photographer:

Nature's Clown, the Penguin. By David Hellyer and Malcolm Davis. 405-428, Sept. 1952

LA JOLLA, California:

Goggle Fishing in California Waters. By David Hellyer. Photos by Lamar Boren. 615-632, May 1949

La Jolla, a Gem of the California Coast. By Deena Clark. Photos by J. Baylor Roberts. 755-782, Dec. 1952

LAKE CHARLES, Louisiana:

Louisiana Trades With the World. By Frederick Simpich. Photos by J. Baylor Roberts. 705-738, Dec. 1947

LAKE DISTRICT, Poets' Corner of England. By H. V. Morton. Photos by David S. Boyer. 511-545, Apr. 1956

LAKE OF THE WOODS, U. S.-Canada:

Men, Moose, and Mink of Northwest Angle. By William H. Nicholas. Photos by J. Baylor Roberts. 265-284, Aug. 1947

LAKE Sunapee's Golden Trout (New Hampshire). Photos by Robert F. Sisson. 529-536, Oct. 1950

LAKEHURST, New Jersey. *See* Parachute Rigger School

LAKES:

Alaska's Automatic Lake Drains Itself (Lake George). 835-844, June 1951

Around the "Great Lakes of the South." By Frederick Simpich. Photos by J. Baylor Roberts. 463-491, Apr. 1948

Geographical Twins a World Apart. By David S.

LAKES—*Continued*

Boyer. 848-859, Dec. 1958
    Contents: Holy Land and Utah: comparisons between the Dead Sea and Great Salt Lake; the Sea of Galilee and Utah Lake

Italy Smiles Again. By Edgar Erskine Hume. 693-732, June 1949
    Included: Como, Garda, Maggiore

Labrador Canoe Adventure. By Andrew Brown and Ralph Gray. 65-99, July 1951
    Included: Dyke, Forget-me-not, Gabbro, Grand, Jacopie, Lake E, Lake Melville, Sandgirt, Winokapau

Lake District, Poets' Corner of England. By H. V. Morton. Photos by David S. Boyer. 511-545, Apr. 1956

Lombardy's Lakes, Blue Jewels in Italy's Crown. By Franc Shor. Photos by Joseph J. Scherschel. 58-99, July 1968
    Included: Como, Garda, Maggiore

A Map Maker Looks at the United States. By Newman Bumstead. Photos by U. S. Air Force. 705-748, June 1951
    Included: Chelan, Crater, Diamond, Franklin Delano Roosevelt, Jackson, Kachess, Mead, Michigan, Tahoe, Utah

The Night the Mountains Moved (Montana's 1959 Earthquake). By Samuel W. Matthews. Photos by J. Baylor Roberts. 329-359, Mar. 1960
    Included: Hebgen Lake, Earthquake Lake

When Mt. Mazama Lost Its Top: The Birth of Crater Lake. By Lyman J. Briggs. 128-133, July 1962

See also by name

LALIBALA, Ethiopia:

Searching Out Medieval Churches in Ethiopia's Wilds. By Georg Gerster. 856-884, Dec. 1970

LALOR, WILLIAM G., Jr.: Author:

Submarine Through the North Pole. Photos by John J. Krawczyk. 1-20, Jan. 1959

LAMAS AND LAMAISM:

Bhutan, Land of the Thunder Dragon. By Burt Kerr Todd. 713-754, Dec. 1952

Bhutan Crowns a New Dragon King. By John Scofield. 546-571, Oct. 1974

Gangtok, Cloud-wreathed Himalayan Capital. By John Scofield. 698-713, Nov. 1970

A Journey to "Little Tibet" (Ladakh). By Enakshi Bhavnani. Photos by Volkmar Wentzel. 603-634, May 1951
    Included: Yellow Hat lamas and Red lamas

My Life in Forbidden Lhasa. By Heinrich Harrer. 1-48, July 1955

Sikkim. By Desmond Doig. 398-429, Mar. 1963

A Woman Paints the Tibetans. By Lafugie. 659-692, May 1949

LAMB, HAROLD: Author:

Crusader Lands Revisited. Photos by David S. Boyer. 815-852, Dec. 1954

LAMMER, ALFRED: Photographer:

Children's Village in Switzerland, Pestalozzi. 268-282, Aug. 1959

LAMPREYS. *See* Sea Lampreys

LANCASTER COUNTY, Pennsylvania:

Amish Folk: Plainest of Pennsylvania's Plain Peo-

LANCASTER COUNTY, Pennsylvania — *Continued*
ple. By Richard Gehman. Photos by William Albert Allard. 227-253, Aug. 1965

Artists Look at Pennsylvania. By John Oliver La Gorce. 37-56, July 1948

LAND, EMORY S.: Author:
Aviation Looks Ahead on Its 50th Birthday. 721-739, Dec. 1953

A LAND Apart — the Monterey Peninsula (California). By Mike W. Edwards. 682-703, Nov. 1972

LAND DIVERS:
Land Diving With the Pentecost Islanders. By Kal Muller. 799-817, Dec. 1970

South Seas' Incredible Land Divers. By Irving and Electa Johnson. 77-92, Jan. 1955

The LAND of Galilee. By Kenneth MacLeish. Photos by B. Anthony Stewart. 832-865, Dec. 1965

LAND of Louisiana Sugar Kings. By Harnett T. Kane. Photos by Willard R. Culver. 531-567, Apr. 1958

LAND of the Ancient Basques. By Robert Laxalt. Photos by William Albert Allard. 240-277, Aug. 1968

LAND of the Havasupai. By Jack Breed. 655-674, May 1948

LAND of the Pilgrims' Pride. By George W. Long. Photos by Robert F. Sisson. 193-219, Aug. 1947

LAND SNAILS. *See* Giant African Land Snails

LAND USE:
A First American Views His Land. By N. Scott Momaday. 13-19, July 1976

Five Noted Thinkers Explore the Future. 68-75, July 1976
Included: The ideas of Isaac Asimov, Richard F. Babcock, Edmund N. Bacon, Buckminster Fuller, Gerard Piel

This Land of Ours — How Are We Using It? By Peter T. White. Photos by Emory Kristof. 20-67, July 1976
Included: Maps: Land use, 1776 and 1976; megalopolises, from weather satellite, reflecting energy use; population density, 1776, 1876, 1976; transportation routes, 1776, 1876, 1976

See also Agriculture; Forests and Reforestation; Interstate Highway System; National Parks; Strip Mining

LAND YACHTS:
Dry-land Fleet Sails the Sahara. By Jean du Boucher. Photos by Jonathan S. Blair. 696-725, Nov. 1967

Wind Raiders of the Sahara (Television film). 436A-436B, Sept. 1973

LANDMARKS of Literary England. By Leo A. Borah. Photos by Kathleen Revis. 295-350, Sept. 1955

The LANDS and Peoples of Southeast Asia. By Peter T. White, Wilhelm G. Solheim II, and W. E. Garrett. Photos by W. E. Garrett. 295-365, Mar. 1971

LANDSAT (Satellites):
Landsat Looks at Hometown Earth. By Barry C. Bishop. 140-147, July 1976

Studying Grizzly Habitat by Satellite. By John Craighead. 148-158, July 1976

LANDSEER, EDWIN:
The British Way. By Sir Evelyn Wrench. 421-541, Apr. 1949

LANDSLIDES. *See* Avalanches; Mudslides

LANE, CHARLES E.: Author:
The Deadly Fisher. 388-397, Mar. 1963
Photographer
X-Rays Reveal the Inner Beauty of Shells. By Hilary B. Moore. 427-434, Mar. 1955

LANG, ERNST M.: Author:
Jambo — First Gorilla Raised by Its Mother in Captivity. Photos by Paul Steinemann. 446-453, Mar. 1964

LANGUEDOC (Region), France:
France's Past Lives in Languedoc. By Walter Meayers Edwards. 1-43, July 1951

LANKA. *See* former name, Ceylon

L'ANSE AU MEADOW, Newfoundland:
Vinland Ruins Prove Vikings Found the New World. By Helge Ingstad. 708-734, Nov. 1964

LANZAROTE, the Strangest Canary. By Stephanie Dinkins. 117-139, Jan. 1969

LAOS:
The Hmong of Laos: No Place to Run. By W. E. Garrett. 78-111, Jan. 1974

The Lands and Peoples of Southeast Asia. 295-365, Mar. 1971
I. Mosaic of Cultures. By Peter T. White. Photos by W. E. Garrett. 296-329
II. New Light on a Forgotten Past. By Wilhelm G. Solheim II. 330-339

Little Laos, Next Door to Red China. By Elizabeth Perazic. 46-69, Jan. 1960

The Mekong, River of Terror and Hope. By Peter T. White. Photos by W. E. Garrett. 737-787, Dec. 1968

Report on Laos. By Peter T. White. Photos by W. E. Garrett. 241-275, Aug. 1961

Viet Nam, Cambodia, Laos, and Eastern Thailand, map supplement. Text on reverse. Jan. 1965

Viet Nam, Cambodia, Laos, and Thailand, map supplement. Feb. 1967

War and Quiet on the Laos Frontier. By W. Robert Moore. 665-680, May 1954

LA PAZ, Baja California, Mexico:
Baja California's Rugged Outback. By Michael E. Long. 543-567, Oct. 1972

Rocks, Ruts, and Sand: Driving the Mexican 1000. By Michael E. Long. 569-575, Oct. 1972

LA PAZ, Bolivia:
Flamboyant Is the Word for Bolivia. By Loren McIntyre. 153-195, Feb. 1965

Sky-high Bolivia. 481-496, Oct. 1950

LAPIDARY WORK:
The Glittering World of Rockhounds. By David S. Boyer. 276-294, Feb. 1974

My Neighbors Hold to Mountain Ways. By Malcolm Ross. Photos by Flip Schulke. 856-880, June 1958

"Rockhounds" Uncover Earth's Mineral Beauty. By George S. Switzer. 631-660, Nov. 1951

LA PITA, Panama:

Exploring Ancient Panama by Helicopter. By Matthew W. Stirling. Photos by Richard H. Stewart. 227-246, Feb. 1950

LAPLAND:

Friendly Flight to Northern Europe. By Lyndon B. Johnson. Photos by Volkmar Wentzel. 268-293, Feb. 1964

Lapland's Reindeer Roundup. 109-116, July 1949

North with Finland's Lapps. By Jean and Franc Shor. 249-280, Aug. 1954

Norway, Land of the Generous Sea. By Edward J. Linehan. Photos by George F. Mobley. 1-43, July 1971

LARSEN, CALVIN L.: Photographer:

Across the Frozen Desert to Byrd Station. By Paul W. Frazier. 383-398, Sept. 1957

LARSEN, THOR: Author-Photographer:

Polar Bear: Lonely Nomad of the North. 574-590, Apr. 1971

LASCAUX CAVE, Cradle of World Art (France). By Norbert Casteret. Photos by Maynard Owen Williams. 771-794, Dec. 1948

LASERS:

The Laser's Bright Magic. By Thomas Meloy. Photos by Howard Sochurek. 858-881, Dec. 1966

LAS MARISMAS (Marshes), Spain:

Rare Birds Flock to Spain's Marismas. By Roger Tory Peterson. 397-425, Mar. 1958

The **LAST** Andaman Islanders. By Raghubir Singh. 66-91, July 1975

The **LAST** Full Measure. By Melville Bell Grosvenor. 307-355, Mar. 1964

The **LAST** Great Animal Kingdom: A Portfolio of Africa's Vanishing Wildlife. 390-409, Sept. 1960

LAST Harbor for the Oldest Ship. By Susan W. and Michael L. Katzev. 618-625, Nov. 1974

LAST Moments of the Pompeians. By Amedeo Maiuri. Photos by Lee E. Battaglia. Paintings by Peter V. Bianchi. 651-669, Nov. 1961

LAST of the Cape Horners (*Pamir*). By Alan Villiers. 701-710, May 1948

LAST Stand for the Bighorn. By James K. Morgan. 383-399, Sept. 1973

The **LAST** Thousand Years Before Christ. By G. Ernest Wright. Paintings by H. J. Soulen and Peter V. Bianchi. 812-853, Dec. 1960

The **LAST** U. S. Whale Hunters. By Emory Kristof. 346-353, Mar. 1973

LAS VEGAS, Nevada:

The Other Nevada. By Robert Laxalt. Photos by J. Bruce Baumann. 733-761, June 1974

LATHAM, MARTE: Author:

Capturing Strange Creatures in Colombia. Photos by Tor Eigeland. 682-693, May 1966

LA TOUR, CY: Author-Photographer:

J. W. Westcott, Postman for the Great Lakes. 813-824, Dec. 1950

LAUNOIS, JOHN: Photographer:

Bangkok, City of Angels. By William Graves. 96-129, July 1973

"Every Day Is a Gift When You Are Over 100." By Alexander Leaf. 93-119, Jan. 1973

Japan, the Exquisite Enigma. By Franc Shor. 733-777, Dec. 1960

Martinique: Liberté, Egalité, and Uncertainty in the Caribbean. By Kenneth MacLeish. 124-148, Jan. 1975

The St. Lawrence, River Key to Canada. By Howard La Fay. 622-667, May 1967

The Tasadays, Stone Age Cavemen of Mindanao. By Kenneth MacLeish. 219-249, Aug. 1972

Vienna, City of Song. By Peter T. White. 739-779, June 1968

LA VENTA, Mexico:

Gifts for the Jaguar God. By Philip Drucker and Robert F. Heizer. 367-375, Sept. 1956

On the Trail of La Venta Man. By Matthew W. Stirling. Photos by Richard H. Stewart. 137-172, Feb. 1947

Hunting Mexico's Buried Temples. 145-168

LAVIES, BIANCA: Photographer:

Found at Last: the Monarch's Winter Home. By Fred A. Urquhart. 161-173, Aug. 1976

Manitoba's Fantastic Snake Pits. By Michael Aleksiuk. 715-723, Nov. 1975

Those Fiery Brazilian Bees. By Rick Gore. 491-501, Apr. 1976

Tireless Voyager, the Whistling Swan. By William J. L. Sladen. 134-147, July 1975

LAVIGNE, DAVID M.: Author:

Life or Death for the Harp Seal. Photos by William R. Curtsinger. 129-142, Jan. 1976

LAW:

Ancient Mesopotamia: A Light That Did Not Fail. By E. A. Speiser. Paintings by H. M. Herget. 41-105, Jan. 1951

Included: The Law Protects Zealously the Institution of Marriage. — Justice Catches Up With a Corrupt Magistrate

The British Way. By Sir Evelyn Wrench. 421-541, Apr. 1949

Included: Jury System (1066-1086); Magna Carta (1215); The Mother of Parliaments (1295); William Blackstone (1723-1780)

LAW ENFORCEMENT:

The FBI: Public Friend Number One. By Jacob Hay. Photos by Robert F. Sisson. 860-886, June 1961

LAWA (People). *See* Lua

LAWICK, HUGO VAN: Photographer:

Adventures in the Search for Man. By Louis S. B. Leakey. 132-152, Jan. 1963

Hyenas, the Hunters Nobody Knows. By Hans Kruuk. 44-57, July 1968

The Leakeys of Africa: Family in Search of Prehistoric Man. By Melvin M. Payne. 194-231, Feb. 1965

My Life Among Wild Chimpanzees. By Jane Goodall. Photos by Baron Hugo van Lawick and author. 272-308, Aug. 1963

New Discoveries Among Africa's Chimpanzees. By

LAWICK, HUGO VAN: Photographer — *Continued*

Baroness Jane van Lawick-Goodall. 802-831, Dec. 1965

Tool-using Bird: The Egyptian Vulture. By Baroness Jane van Lawick-Goodall. 631-641, May 1968

LAWICK-GOODALL, JANE VAN: Author:

New Discoveries Among Africa's Chimpanzees. Photos by Baron Hugo van Lawick. 802-831, Dec. 1965

Tool-using Bird: The Egyptian Vulture. Photos by Baron Hugo van Lawick. 631-641, May 1968

See also Goodall, Jane

LAWRENCE, Massachusetts:

The Merrimack: River of Industry and Romance. By Albert W. Atwood. Photos by B. Anthony Stewart. 106-140, Jan. 1951

LAXALT, ROBERT: Author:

The Enduring Pyrenees. Photos by Edwin Stuart Grosvenor. 794-819, Dec. 1974

Golden Ghosts of the Lost Sierra. Photos by David Hiser. 332-353, Sept. 1973

Land of the Ancient Basques. Photos by William Albert Allard. 240-277, Aug. 1968

Lonely Sentinels of the American West: Basque Sheepherders. Photos by William Belknap, Jr. 870-888, June 1966

New Mexico: The Golden Land. Photos by Adam Woolfitt. 299-345, Sept. 1970

The Other Nevada. Photos by J. Bruce Baumann. 733-761, June 1974

LAYKAWKEY (Village), Thailand:

Spirits of Change Capture the Karens. By Peter Kunstadter. 267-285, Feb. 1972

LEAF, ALEXANDER: Author:

"Every Day Is a Gift When You Are Over 100." Photos by John Launois. 93-119, Jan. 1973

LEAKEY, LOUIS S. B.:

Dr. Leakey and the Dawn of Man (Television film). 703A-703B, Nov. 1966

The Leakey Tradition Lives On. By Melvin M. Payne. 143-144, Jan. 1973

The Leakeys of Africa: Family in Search of Prehistoric Man. By Melvin M. Payne. 194-231, Feb. 1965

Preserving the Treasures of Olduvai Gorge. By Melvin M. Payne. Photos by Joseph J. Scherschel. 701-709, Nov. 1966

Author

Adventures in the Search for Man. Photos by Hugo van Lawick. 132-152, Jan. 1963

Exploring 1,750,000 Years Into Man's Past. Photos by Robert F. Sisson. 564-589, Oct. 1961

Finding the World's Earliest Man. Photos by Des Bartlett. 420-435, Sept. 1960

LEAKEY, RICHARD E.: Author:

In Search of Man's Past at Lake Rudolf. Photos by Gordon W. Gahan. 712-734, May 1970

Skull 1470. Photos by Bob Campbell. 819-829, June 1973

LEAKEY FAMILY:

The Leakeys of Africa: Family in Search of Prehistoric Man. By Melvin M. Payne. 194-231, Feb. 1965

LEBANON:

Journey Into the Great Rift: The Northern Half. By Helen and Frank Schreider. 254-290, Aug. 1965

Lebanon, Little Bible Land in the Crossfire of History. By William S. Ellis. Photos by George F. Mobley. 240-275, Feb. 1970

The Phoenicians, Sea Lords of Antiquity. By Samuel W. Matthews. Photos by Winfield Parks. Paintings by Robert C. Magis. 149-189, Aug. 1974

Troubled Waters East of Suez. By Ernest M. Eller. 483-522, Apr. 1954

YWCA: International Success Story. By Mary French Rockefeller. Photos by Otis Imboden. 904-933, Dec. 1963

Young-old Lebanon Lives by Trade. By Thomas J. Abercrombie. 479-523, Apr. 1958

LEE, ROBERT E.:

Appomattox: Where Grant and Lee Made Peace With Honor a Century Ago. By Ulysses S. Grant 3rd. Photos by Bruce Dale. 435-469, Apr. 1965

LEEPER, JOHN and BLANCHE: Authors:

American Processional: History on Canvas. 173-212, Feb. 1951

LEEWARD ISLANDS, West Indies:

Carib Cruises the West Indies. By Carleton Mitchell. 1-56, Jan. 1948

A Fresh Breeze Stirs the Leewards. By Carleton Mitchell. Photos by Winfield Parks. 488-537, Oct. 1966

LEGACY From the Age of Faith, Chartres. By Kenneth MacLeish. Photos by Dean Conger. 857-882, Dec. 1969

LEGENDS. *See* Gilgamesh, Epic of; Hâ-âk Vâ-âk; Marostica, Italy, for Chess Game (Living Pieces); Messina, Strait of, for Charybdis; St. Michael's Mount; Stonehenge

LEH, Ladakh (District), Jammu and Kashmir:

A Journey to "Little Tibet." By Enakshi Bhavnani. Photos by Volkmar Wentzel. 603-634, May 1951

A Woman Paints the Tibetans. By Lafugie. 659-692, May 1949

LEIS:

The Flowers That Say "Aloha." By Deena Clark. Photos by Robert B. Goodman. 121-131, Jan. 1967

LEM (Lunar Excursion Module). *See* Apollo Missions

LeMAY, CURTIS E.: Author:

Artists Roam the World of the U. S. Air Force. 650-673, May 1960

School for Survival. 565-602, May 1953

U. S. Air Force: Power for Peace. 291-297, Sept. 1965

LE MOYNE DE MORGUES, JACQUES:

Indian Life Before the Colonists Came. By Stuart E. Jones. Engravings by Theodore de Bry, 1590. 351-368, Sept. 1947

Included: The artist, Jacques le Moyne de Morgues, and reproductions of his paintings from De Bry's engravings

LEMURS, Flying:

Seeking Mindanao's Strangest Creatures. By Charles Heizer Wharton. 389-408, Sept. 1948

LENDOMBWEY. *See* Malekula (Island)

LENINGRAD, U.S.S.R.:

Leningrad, Russia's Window on the West. By Howard La Fay. Photos by Dick Durrance II. 636-673, May 1971

LEONARD CARMICHAEL: An Appreciation. By Melvin M. Payne. 871-874, Dec. 1973
See also Carmichael, Leonard C.

LEONOV, ALEKSEY A.:

Apollo-Soyuz: Handclasp in Space. By Thomas Y. Canby. 183-187, Feb. 1976

LEOPARDS. *See* Snow Leopards

LERICI, CARLO M.: Author:

Periscope on the Etruscan Past. 337-350, Sept. 1959

LERNER, IRA S.: Photographer:

Getting to Know the Wild Burros of Death Valley. By Patricia des Roses Moehlman. Photos by Ira S. Lerner and author. 502-517, Apr. 1972

LERNER MARINE LABORATORY, Bahama Islands:

The Bahamas, Isles of the Blue-green Sea. By Carleton Mitchell. Photos by B. Anthony Stewart. 147-203, Feb. 1958

Man-of-War Fleet Attacks Bimini. By Paul A. Zahl. 185-212, Feb. 1952

LERWICK, Shetland Islands. *See* Up Helly Aa

LESAGE, JEAN: Author:

Alexander Graham Bell Museum: Tribute to Genius. 227-256, Aug. 1956

LESBOS (Island), Greece:

The Isles of Greece: Aegean Birthplace of Western Culture. By Melville Bell Grosvenor. Photos by Edwin Stuart Grosvenor and Winfield Parks. 147-193, Aug. 1972

LESSER SUNDA ISLANDS:

Dragon Lizards of Komodo. By James A. Kern. 872-880, Dec. 1968

East From Bali by Seagoing Jeep to Timor. By Helen and Frank Schreider. 236-279, Aug. 1962
See also Bali

LESSING, ERICH: Photographer:

Firsthand Look at the Soviet Union. By Thomas T. Hammond. 352-407, Sept. 1959

Modern Miracle, Made in Germany. By Robert Leslie Conly. 735-791, June 1959

Poland Opens Her Doors. By Delia and Ferdinand Kuhn. 354-398, Sept. 1958

LESSON and Challenge. By James H. Wakelin, Jr. 759-763, June 1964

LETHBRIDGE, JOHN:

The Treasure of Porto Santo. By Robert Sténuit. Photos by author and William R. Curtsinger. 260-275, Aug. 1975

LETTICK, BIRNEY: Artist:

A New Look at Medieval Europe. By Kenneth M. Setton. Paintings by Andre Durenceau and Birney Lettick. 799-859, Dec. 1962

LEVEES. *See* Dikes and Levees

LEVKAS (Island), Greece:

Homeward With Ulysses (Ionian Islands). By Mel-

LEVKAS (Island), Greece—*Continued*
ville Bell Grosvenor. Photos by Edwin Stuart Grosvenor. 1-39, July 1973

LEWIS, DAVID: Author:

Alone to Antarctica. Drawings by Noel Sickles. 808-821, Dec. 1973

Hokule'a Follows the Stars to Tahiti. Photos by Nicholas deVore III. 512-537, Oct. 1976

Wind, Wave, Star, and Bird. Photos by Nicholas deVore III. 747-781, Dec. 1974

Author-Photographer

Ice Bird Ends Her Lonely Odyssey. 216-233, Aug. 1975

LEWIS, G. EDWARD: Author-Photographer:

El Sangay, Fire-breathing Giant of the Andes. 117-138, Jan. 1950

LEWIS, LEWIS: Author-Photographer:

New Life for the "Loneliest Isle" (Tristan da Cunha). 105-116, Jan. 1950

LEWIS, M. LEE: Author:

To 76,000 Feet by *Strato-Lab* Balloon. By Malcolm D. Ross and M. Lee Lewis. 269-282, Feb. 1957

LEWIS, Isle of, Scotland:

Isles on the Edge of the Sea: Scotland's Outer Hebrides. By Kenneth MacLeish. Photos by Thomas Nebbia. 676-711, May 1970

LEWIS AND CLARK EXPEDITION:

Following the Trail of Lewis and Clark. By Ralph Gray. 707-750, June 1953

In the Footsteps of Lewis and Clark. Special Publication announced. 880-884, June 1970

So Long, St. Louis, We're Heading West. By William C. Everhart. 643-669, Nov. 1965

LEXINGTON, Kentucky:

Heart of the Bluegrass. By Charles McCarry. Photos by J. Bruce Baumann. 634-659, May 1974

LEYDET, FRANÇOIS: Author:

Autumn Flames Along the Allagash. Photos by Farrell Grehan. 177-187, Feb. 1974

Jackson Hole: Good-bye to the Old Days? Photos by Jonathan Wright. 768-789, Dec. 1974

The Mazatzal's Harsh but Lovely Land Between. Photos by Farrell Grehan. 161-167, Feb. 1974

Okefenokee, the Magical Swamp. Photos by Farrell Grehan. 169-175, Feb. 1974

The Olympics: Northwest Majesty. Photos by Farrell Grehan. 188-197, Feb. 1974

LHASA, Tibet:

My Life in Forbidden Lhasa. By Heinrich Harrer. 1-48, July 1955

LIBBY, ERNEST L.: Author-Photographer:

Miracle of the Mermaid's Purse (Skate). 413-420, Sept. 1957

LIBERIA:

Africa: The Winds of Freedom Stir a Continent. By Nathaniel T. Kenney. Photos by W. D. Vaughn. 303-359, Sept. 1960

Rubber-cushioned Liberia. By Henry S. Villard. Photos by Charles W. Allmon. 201-228, Feb. 1948

LIBRARIES:

The DAR Story. By Lonnelle Aikman. Photos by B. Anthony Stewart and John E. Fletcher. 565-598, Nov. 1951
    Included: Genealogical Library

Florence Rises From the Flood. By Joseph Judge. 1-43, July 1967
    Included: Biblioteca Nazionale Centrale, Gabinetto Vieusseux

Literary Landmarks of Massachusetts. By William H. Nicholas. Photos by B. Anthony Stewart and John E. Fletcher. 279-310, Mar. 1950
    Included: Adams Library, The Athenaeum, Boston College Library, Boston Public Library, Converse Memorial Library, Houghton Library, Lamont Library

Miami's Expanding Horizons. By William H. Nicholas. 561-594, Nov. 1950
    Included: Brett Memorial Library, Miami Memorial Library, Montgomery Museum and Library, State Library, University of Miami Library

See also Folger; Henry E. Huntington Library and Art Gallery; Library of Congress

LIBRARY OF CONGRESS, Washington, D. C.:

Library of Congress: The Nation's Bookcase. By Fred Kline. Photos by Dick Durrance II. 671-687, Nov. 1975

The Nation's Library. By Albert W. Atwood. 663-684, May 1950

LIECHTENSTEIN Thrives on Stamps. By Ronald W. Clark. 105-112, July 1948

LIFE Among the Wai Wai Indians. By Clifford Evans and Betty J. Meggers. 329-346, Mar. 1955

LIFE and Death in Tana Toradja. By Pamela and Alfred Meyer. 793-815, June 1972

LIFE Ashore Beckons the Sea Gypsies. By Anne de Henning Singh. Photos by Raghubir Singh. 659-677, May 1976

LIFE Cycle of a Coral. By Robert F. Sisson. 780-793, June 1973

LIFE 8,000 Years Ago Uncovered in an Alabama Cave. By Carl F. Miller. 542-558, Oct. 1956

LIFE in a "Dead" Sea—Great Salt Lake. By Paul A. Zahl. 252-263, Aug. 1967

LIFE in the Enduring Pyrenees. By Robert Laxalt. Photos by Edwin Stuart Grosvenor. 794-819, Dec. 1974

LIFE in the Land of the Basques. By John E. H. Nolan. Photos by Justin Locke. 147-186, Feb. 1954

LIFE in Walled-off West Berlin. By Nathaniel T. Kenney and Volkmar Wentzel. Photos by Thomas Nebbia. 735-767, Dec. 1961

LIFE or Death for the Harp Seal. By David M. Lavigne. Photos by William R. Curtsinger. 129-142, Jan. 1976

LIFE Slowly Changes in Remote Bhutan. By John Scofield. 658-683, Nov. 1976

LIFE Springs From Death in Truk Lagoon. By Sylvia A. Earle. Photos by Al Giddings. 578-613, May 1976

LIFE under Shellfire on Quemoy. By Franc Shor. Photos by Wilbur E. Garrett. 415-438, Mar. 1959

LIFE with the King of Beasts. By George B. Schaller. 494-519, Apr. 1969

LIFE with the "Pumphouse Gang": New Insights Into Baboon Behavior. By Shirley C. Strum. Photos by Timothy W. Ransom. 672-691, May 1975

LIFELIKE Man Preserved 2,000 Years in Peat. By P. V. Glob. 419-430, Mar. 1954

LIFE'S Tempo on Nantucket. By Peter Benchley. Photos by James L. Stanfield. 810-839, June 1970

LIGHTHOUSES. *See* Devonshire, England, for Eddystone; Farne Islands, for Longstone Islet; Maine (Down East Cruise), for Boon Island, Neddick, Petit Manan Island, Portland Head, Seguin, Two Bush Island, West Quoddy Head; Outer Banks, for Cape Hatteras Light

LIGHTNING in Action. By F. Barrows Colton. 809-828, June 1950

The **LIGHTS** Are Up at Ford's Theatre. By Lonnelle Aikman. 392-401, Mar. 1970

LIGUUS FASCIATUS (Snail):

Tree Snails, Gems of the Everglades. By Treat Davidson. 372-387, Mar. 1965

LILIENTHAL, OTTO:

Happy Birthday, Otto Lilienthal! By Russell Hawkes. Photos by James Collison. 286-292, Feb. 1972

LIMESTONE SINKS:

Manitoba's Fantastic Snake Pits. By Michael Aleksiuk. Photos by Bianca Lavies. 715-723, Nov. 1975

LIMNOLOGY. *See* Mzima Springs; Pond Life

LIMPKIN, the "Crying Bird" That Haunts Florida Swamps. By Frederick Kent Truslow. 114-121, Jan. 1958

LINCOLN, ABRAHAM:

Inside the White House. By Lonnelle Aikman. Photos by B. Anthony Stewart and Thomas Nebbia. 3-43, Jan. 1961

The Lights Are Up at Ford's Theatre. By Lonnelle Aikman. 392-401, Mar. 1970

Lincoln, Man of Steel and Velvet. By Carl Sandburg. 239-241, Feb. 1960

The Living White House. By Lonnelle Aikman. 593-643, Nov. 1966

Our Land Through Lincoln's Eyes. By Carolyn Bennett Patterson. Photos by W. D. Vaughn. 243-277, Feb. 1960

Profiles of the Presidents: III. The American Giant Comes of Age. By Frank Freidel. 660-711, May 1965

Vacation Tour Through Lincoln Land. By Ralph Gray. 141-184, Feb. 1952

Washington: Home of the Nation's Great. By Albert W. Atwood. 699-738, June 1947

LINCOLN, Nebraska:

The West Through Boston Eyes. By Stewart Anderson. 733-776, June 1949

LINDBERGH, JON:

The Deepest Days. By Robert Sténuit. 534-547, Apr. 1965

Outpost Under the Ocean. By Edwin A. Link. Photos by Bates Littlehales. 530-533, Apr. 1965

LINDISFARNE (Island), England:
Pilgrimage to Holy Island and the Farnes. By John E. H. Nolan. 547-570, Oct. 1952

LINE, FRANCIS R.: Author-Photographer:
Arizona Sheep Trek. 457-478, Apr. 1950

LINEHAN, EDWARD J.: Author:
Colorado, the Rockies' Pot of Gold. Photos by James L. Amos. 157-201, Aug. 1969
Cuba's Exiles Bring New Life to Miami. Photos by Nathan Benn. 68-95, July 1973
Czechoslovakia: The Dream and the Reality. Photos by James P. Blair. 151-193, Feb. 1968
Dogs Work for Man. Paintings by Edwin Megargee and R. E. Lougheed. 190-233, Aug. 1958
Norway, Land of the Generous Sea. Photos by George F. Mobley. 1-43, July 1971
Old-new Iran, Next Door to Russia. Photos by Thomas J. Abercrombie. 44-85, Jan. 1961

LINK, EDWIN A.:
Exploring the Drowned City of Port Royal. By Marion Clayton Link. Photos by Luis Marden. 151-183, Feb. 1960
Author
Our Man-in-Sea Project. 713-717, May 1963
Outpost Under the Ocean. Photos by Bates Littlehales. 530-533, Apr. 1965
Tomorrow on the Deep Frontier. 778-801, June 1964

LINK, MARION CLAYTON: Author:
Exploring the Drowned City of Port Royal. Photos by Luis Marden. 151-183, Feb. 1960

LINK IGLOO:
Tomorrow on the Deep Frontier. By Edwin A. Link. 778-801, June 1964

LIONS:
Life with the King of Beasts. By George B. Schaller. 494-519, Apr. 1969
Lion Cubs. Children's book announced. 736-738, Nov. 1972
Spearing Lions with Africa's Masai. By Edgar Monsanto Queeny. 487-517, Oct. 1954

LIPAS (Sailing Craft):
Sea Gypsies of the Philippines. By Anne de Henning Singh. Photos by Raghubir Singh. 659-677, May 1976

LIPIZZANERS:
The White Horses of Vienna. By Beverley M. Bowie. Photos by Volkmar Wentzel. 401-419, Sept. 1958

LISBON, Portugal:
Portugal at the Crossroads. By Howard La Fay. Photos by Volkmar Wentzel. 453-501, Oct. 1965
Portugal Is Different. By Clement E. Conger. 583-622, Nov. 1948

LISTER, JOSEPH, LORD:
The British Way. By Sir Evelyn Wrench. 421-541, Apr. 1949

LITERATURE:
The Britain That Shakespeare Knew. By Louis B. Wright. Photos by Dean Conger. 613-665, May 1964

LITERATURE — *Continued*
The British Way. By Sir Evelyn Wrench. 421-541, Apr. 1949
Included: Geoffrey Chaucer, William Shakespeare, James I and the Translation of the Bible, John Milton, Daniel Defoe, Some British Poets, Charles Dickens
Chelsea, London's Haven of Individualists. By James Cerruti. Photos by Adam Woolfitt. 28-55, Jan. 1972
Included: Thomas Carlyle, George Eliot, George Meredith, R. J. Minney, Sir Thomas More, Tom Pocock, Dante Gabriel Rossetti, Jonathan Swift, Algernon Charles Swinburne, Mark Twain
The England of Charles Dickens. By Richard W. Long. Photos by Adam Woolfitt. 443-483, Apr. 1974
A First American Views His Land. By N. Scott Momaday. 13-19, July 1976
The Fragile Beauty All About Us. By Harry S. C. Yen. 785-795, Dec. 1970
Included: Chinese poetry, 6th century B.C.-A.D. 1269
Lake District, Poets' Corner of England. By H. V. Morton. Photos by David S. Boyer. 511-545, Apr. 1956
Landmarks of Literary England. By Leo A. Borah. Photos by Kathleen Revis. 295-350, Sept. 1955
Literary Landmarks of Massachusetts. By William H. Nicholas. Photos by B. Anthony Stewart and John E. Fletcher. 279-310, Mar. 1950
Contents: Adams family, Alcott family, Nathaniel Bowditch, Anne Bradstreet, William Cullen Bryant, Dana family, Emily Dickinson, Ralph Waldo Emerson, Clyde Fitch, Louise Imogen Guiney, Sarah Josepha Hale, Nathaniel Hawthorne, Julia Ward Howe, Henry Wadsworth Longfellow, James Russell Lowell, Herman Melville, John Boyle O'Reilly, Harriet Beecher Stowe, Henry David Thoreau, Noah Webster, John Greenleaf Whittier
Mark Twain: Mirror of America. By Noel Grove. Photos by James L. Stanfield. 300-337, Sept. 1975
Poets' Voices Linger in Scottish Shrines. By Isobel Wylie Hutchison. Photos by Kathleen Revis. 437-488, Oct. 1957
Contents: Sir James Barrie, James Boswell, John Buchan, Robert Burns, Lord Byron, Thomas Carlyle, Sir Arthur Conan Doyle, James Hogg, Violet Jacob, Samuel Johnson, Allan Ramsay, Sir Walter Scott, William Shakespeare, Adam Smith, Tobias Smollett, Robert Louis Stevenson, William Wordsworth
Robert Frost and New England. By Archibald MacLeish. 438-467, Apr. 1976
Look of a Land Beloved. Photos by Dewitt Jones. 444-467
A Stroll to John o' Groat's. By Isobel Wylie Hutchison. 1-48, July 1956
Included: Sir James Barrie, Michael Bruce, Thomas Carlyle, William Shakespeare, Adam Smith, Robert Louis Stevenson
A Stroll to London. By Isobel Wylie Hutchison. Photos by B. Anthony Stewart. 171-204, Aug. 1950
Included: James Boswell, Brontë sisters, Thomas Carlyle, Charles Dickens, George Eliot, Samuel Johnson, Sir Walter Scott, William Shakespeare, William Wordsworth
See also Elizabethan Age; Gilgamesh, Epic of; *Odyssey; Ramayana*

LITTLE AMERICA, Antarctica:
Admiral of the Ends of the Earth (Richard E. Byrd).

LITTLE AMERICA, Antarctica—*Continued*

By Melville Bell Grosvenor. 36-48, July 1957

All-out Assault on Antarctica. By Richard E. Byrd. 141-180, Aug. 1956

Our Navy Explores Antarctica. By Richard E. Byrd. U. S. Navy official photos. 429-522, Oct. 1947

LITTLE ANDAMAN ISLAND, India:

The Last Andaman Islanders. By Raghubir Singh. 66-91, July 1975

LITTLE FALLS, New York:

Drums to Dynamos on the Mohawk. By Frederick G. Vosburgh. Photos by B. Anthony Stewart. 67-110, July 1947

LITTLE Horses of the Sea. By Paul A. Zahl. 131-153, Jan. 1959

LITTLE Laos, Next Door to Red China. By Elizabeth Perazic. 46-69, Jan. 1960

LITTLE Tibet in Switzerland. By Laura Pilarski. Photos by Fred Mayer. 711-727, Nov. 1968

LITTLE TOBAGO (Island), West Indies:

Feathered Dancers of Little Tobago. By E. Thomas Gilliard. Photos by Frederick Kent Truslow. 428-440, Sept. 1958
Contents: Greater Birds of Paradise

LITTLEHALES, BATES:

Designed OceanEye camera housing. 262, 271, 277, Aug. 1971

Author-Photographer

Into the Well of Sacrifice. II. Treasure Hunt in the Deep Past. 550-561, Oct. 1961

Photographer

Back to the Historic Black Hills. By Leland D. Case. 479-509, Oct. 1956

Calypso Explores an Undersea Canyon. By Jacques-Yves Cousteau. 373-396, Mar. 1958

Central Park: Manhattan's Big Outdoors. By Stuart E. Jones. 781-811, Dec. 1960

Channel Cruise to Glorious Devon. By Alan Villiers. 208-259, Aug. 1963

Chesapeake Country. By Nathaniel T. Kenney. 370-411, Sept. 1964

Cruising Florida's Western Waterways. By Rube Allyn. 49-76, Jan. 1955

England's Scillies, the Flowering Isles. By Alan Villiers. 126-145, July 1967

Fabled Mount of St. Michael. By Alan Villiers. 880-898, June 1964

The Five Worlds of Peru. By Kenneth F. Weaver. 213-265, Feb. 1964

Gettysburg and Vicksburg: the Battle Towns Today. By Robert Paul Jordan. Map notes by Carolyn Bennett Patterson. 4-57, July 1963

Giant Kelp, Sequoias of the Sea. By Wheeler J. North. 251-269, Aug. 1972

Gibraltar—Rock of Contention. By Howard La Fay. 102-121, July 1966

In Quest of the Rarest Flamingo. By William G. Conway. 91-105, July 1961

The Long, Deep Dive. By Lord Kilbracken. 718-731, May 1963

Look What's Happened to Honolulu! By Jim Becker. 500-531, Oct. 1969

The Lower Keys, Florida's "Out Islands." By John

LITTLEHALES, BATES—*Continued*

Scofield. Photos by Emory Kristof and Bates Littlehales. 72-93, Jan. 1971

New England, a Modern Pilgrim's Pride. By Beverley M. Bowie. 733-796, June 1955

New Zealand's North Island: The Contented Land. By Charles McCarry. 190-213, Aug. 1974

Nomad Sails Long Island Sound. By Thomas Horgan. 295-338, Sept. 1957

Off Santa Barbara: California's Ranches in the Sea. By Earl Warren, Jr. 257-283, Aug. 1958

Ohio Makes Its Own Prosperity. By Leo A. Borah. Photos by B. Anthony Stewart and Bates Littlehales. 435-484, Apr. 1955

Ontario, Pivot of Canada's Power. By Andrew H. Brown. Photos by B. Anthony Stewart and Bates Littlehales. 823-852, Dec. 1953

Oregon's Many Faces. By Stuart E. Jones. 74-115, Jan. 1969

Outpost Under the Ocean. By Edwin A. Link. 530-533, Apr. 1965

Priceless Relics of the Spanish Armada. By Robert Sténuit. 745-777, June 1969

Resurrecting the Oldest Known Greek Ship. By Michael L. Katzev. 841-857, June 1970

Science's Window on the Sea. By John G. VanDerwalker. 256-289, Aug. 1971

A Taxi for the Deep Frontier. By Kenneth MacLeish. 139-150, Jan. 1968

Twenty Fathoms Down for Mother-of-Pearl. By Winston Williams. 512-529, Apr. 1962

Working for Weeks on the Sea Floor. By Jacques-Yves Cousteau. Photos by Philippe Cousteau and Bates Littlehales. 498-537, Apr. 1966

LIVESTOCK:

America Goes to the Fair. By Samuel W. Matthews. 293-333, Sept. 1954

Beltsville Brings Science to the Farm. By Samuel W. Matthews. 199-218, Aug. 1953

Carnival in San Antonio. By Mason Sutherland. Photos by J. Baylor Roberts. 813-844, Dec. 1947

4-H Boys and Girls Grow More Food. By Frederick Simpich. 551-582, Nov. 1948

See also Bull Derby; Cattle and Cattle Raising; Goats; Horses; Musk Oxen; Sheep and Sheep Raising

LIVING Honey Jars of the Ant World. By Ross E. Hutchins. 405-411, Mar. 1962

LIVING in a Japanese Village (Futagami Jima). By William Graves. Photos by James L. Stanfield. 668-693, May 1972

The LIVING Sand. By William H. Amos. 820-833, June 1965

The LIVING White House. By Lonnelle Aikman. 593-643, Nov. 1966

LIVING With Thailand's Gentle Lua. By Peter Kunstadter. 122-152, July 1966

LIZARDS:

In the Wilds of a City Parlor. By Paul A. Zahl. 645-672, Nov. 1954

The Lure of the Changing Desert. 817-824, June 1954

See also Komodo Dragons

LIZARRIETA, Col de, Pyrenees Mountains:

Pigeon Netting — Sport of Basques. Photos by Irene Burdett-Scougall. 405-416, Sept. 1949

LOBSTERS AND LOBSTERING:

The American Lobster, Delectable Cannibal. By Luis Marden. Photos by David Doubilet. 462-487, Apr. 1973

Maine's Lobster Island, Monhegan. By William P. E. Graves. Photos by Kosti Ruohomaa. 285-298, Feb. 1959

Martha's Vineyard. By William P. E. Graves. Photos by James P. Blair. 778-809, June 1961

See also Spiny Lobsters

LOCKE, JUSTIN: Author-Photographer:

Lost Kingdom in Indian Mexico. 517-546, Oct. 1952

Photographer

Adobe New Mexico. By Mason Sutherland. 783-830, Dec. 1949

Amid the Mighty Walls of Zion. By Lewis F. Clark. 37-70, Jan. 1954

Appalachian Valley Pilgrimage. By Catherine Bell Palmer. 1-32, July 1949

Grand Canyon: Nature's Story of Creation. By Louis Schellbach. 589-629, May 1955

Growing Pains Beset Puerto Rico. By William H. Nicholas. 419-460, Apr. 1951

High Road in the Pyrenees. By H. V. Morton. 299-334, Mar. 1956

Life in the Land of the Basques. By John E. H. Nolan. 147-186, Feb. 1954

Mexico's Booming Capital. By Mason Sutherland. 785-824, Dec. 1951

Miami's Expanding Horizons. By William H. Nicholas. 561-594, Nov. 1950

New Orleans: Jambalaya on the Levee. By Harnett T. Kane. 143-184, Feb. 1953

Paris, Home Town of the World. By Donald William Dresden. 767-804, June 1952

Shooting Rapids in Dinosaur Country. By Jack Breed. Photos by author and Justin Locke. 363-390, Mar. 1954

The Smithsonian Institution. By Thomas R. Henry. 325-348, Sept. 1948

So Much Happens Along the Ohio River. By Frederick Simpich. 177-212, Feb. 1950

Vizcaya: An Italian Palazzo in Miami. By William H. Nicholas. 595-604, Nov. 1950

LOCKLEY, R. M.: Author:

The Solemn, Sociable Puffins. 414-422, Sept. 1954

LOCUSTS:

Locusts: "Teeth of the Wind." By Robert A. M. Conley. Photos by Gianni Tortoli. 202-227, Aug. 1969

Report from the Locust Wars. By Tony and Dickey Chapelle. 545-562, Apr. 1953

LOCUSTS, 17-year:

Rip Van Winkle of the Underground. By Kenneth F. Weaver. 133-142, July 1953

LOFOTEN (Islands), Norway:

Fishing in the Lofotens. Photos by Lennart Nilsson. 377-388, Mar. 1947

LOGGERS:

Idaho Loggers Battle a River. 117-130, July 1951

LOIRE RIVER AND VALLEY, France:

River of Counts and Kings: The Loire. By Kenneth MacLeish. Photos by Dean Conger. 822-869, June 1966

LOLOS (Tribespeople):

Adventures in Lololand. By Rennold L. Lowy. 105-118, Jan. 1947

LOMBARDY'S Lakes, Blue Jewels in Italy's Crown. By Franc Shor. Photos by Joseph J. Scherschel. 58-99, July 1968

LOMPOC VALLEY, California:

The Flower Seed Growers: Gardening's Color Merchants. By Robert de Roos. Photos by Jack Fields. 720-738, May 1968

LONDON, England:

"Around the World in Eighty Days." By Newman Bumstead. 705-750, Dec. 1951

"Be Ye Men of Valour" (Churchill's Life; Funeral). By Howard La Fay. 159-197, Aug. 1965

Benjamin Franklin, Philosopher of Dissent. By Alice J. Hall. Photos by Linda Bartlett. 93-123, July 1975

The Britain That Shakespeare Knew. By Louis B. Wright. Photos by Dean Conger. 613-665, May 1964

The British Way. By Sir Evelyn Wrench. 421-541, Apr. 1949

Chelsea, London's Haven of Individualists. By James Cerruti. Photos by Adam Woolfitt. 28-55, Jan. 1972

"The City" — London's Storied Square Mile. By Allan C. Fisher, Jr. 735-777, June 1961

The England of Charles Dickens. By Richard W. Long. Photos by Adam Woolfitt. 443-483, Apr. 1974

The Final Tribute (Churchill's Funeral). Text by Carolyn Bennett Patterson. 199-225, Aug. 1965

Founders of New England. By Sir Evelyn Wrench. Photos by B. Anthony Stewart. 803-838, June 1953

Founders of Virginia. By Sir Evelyn Wrench. Photos by B. Anthony Stewart. 433-462, Apr. 1948

In the London of the New Queen. By H. V. Morton. 291-342, Sept. 1953

Keeping House in London. By Frances James. 769-792, Dec. 1947

Landmarks of Literary England. By Leo A. Borah. Photos by Kathleen Revis. 295-350, Sept. 1955

London's Zoo of Zoos. By Thomas Garner James. 771-786, June 1953

One Man's London. By Allan C. Fisher, Jr. Photos by James P. Blair. 743-791, June 1966

Queen Elizabeth Opens Parliament. By W. E. Roscher. Photos by Robert B. Goodman. 699-707, Nov. 1961

A Stroll to London. By Isobel Wylie Hutchison. Photos by B. Anthony Stewart. 171-204, Aug. 1950

The Thames Mirrors England's Varied Life. By Willard Price. Photos by Robert F. Sisson. 45-93, July 1958

The World of Elizabeth I. By Louis B. Wright. Photos by Ted Spiegel. 668-709, Nov. 1968

LONDON, England—*Continued*
See also Kew; Royal Academy of Arts

The "LONE" Coyote Likes Family Life. By Hope Ryden. Photos by author and David Hiser. 278-294, Aug. 1974

LONE Sailor Completes His Globe-girdling Voyage. By Robin Lee Graham. 504-545, Oct. 1970

LONELY Cape Hatteras, Besieged by the Sea. By William S. Ellis. Photos by Emory Kristof. 393-421, Sept. 1969

LONELY Sentinels of the American West: Basque Sheepherders. By Robert Laxalt. Photos by William Belknap, Jr. 870-888, June 1966

LONELY Wonders of Katmai. By Ernest Gruening. Photos by Winfield Parks. 800-831, June 1963

LONG, GEORGE W.:
Memorial Tribute to George W. Long (1913-1958). 215, Feb. 1959
Author
Eyes on the China Coast. 505-512, Apr. 1953
Hong Kong Hangs On. Photos by J. Baylor Roberts. 239-272, Feb. 1954
Indochina Faces the Dragon. Photos by J. Baylor Roberts. 287-328, Sept. 1952
Journey Into Troubled Iran. Photos by J. Baylor Roberts. 425-464, Oct. 1951
Land of the Pilgrims' Pride. Photos by Robert F. Sisson. 193-219, Aug. 1947
Macau, a Hole in the Bamboo Curtain. Photos by J. Baylor Roberts. 679-688, May 1953
Malaya Meets Its Emergency. Photos by J. Baylor Roberts. 185-228, Feb. 1953
Many-splendored Glacierland. Photos by Kathleen Revis. 589-636, May 1956
New Rush to Golden California. 723-802, June 1954
Occupied Austria, Outpost of Democracy. Photos by Volkmar Wentzel. 749-790, June 1951
Rhode Island, Modern City-State. Photos by Willard R. Culver. 137-170, Aug. 1948
Sea to Lakes on the St. Lawrence. Photos by B. Anthony Stewart and John E. Fletcher. 323-366, Sept. 1950
Yugoslavia, Between East and West. Photos by Volkmar Wentzel. 141-172, Feb. 1951

LONG, MICHAEL E.: Author:
Rocks, Ruts, and Sand: Driving the Mexican 1000. 569-575, Oct. 1972
Author-Photographer
Baja California's Rugged Outback. 543-567, Oct. 1972
Photographer
Belize, the Awakening Land. By Louis de la Haba. 124-146, Jan. 1972

LONG, RICHARD W.: Author:
The England of Charles Dickens. Photos by Adam Woolfitt. 443-483, Apr. 1974

The LONG, Deep Dive. By Lord Kilbracken. Photos by Bates Littlehales. 718-731, May 1963

The LONG, Lonely Leap. By Joseph W. Kittinger, Jr. Photos by Volkmar Wentzel. 854-873, Dec. 1960

LONG Distance Runners: Mexico's Tarahumaras. By James Norman. Photos by David Hiser. 702-718, May 1976

LONG ISLAND, New York:
Long Island Outgrows the Country. By Howell Walker. Photos by B. Anthony Stewart. 279-326, Mar. 1951
See also Kings Point (Merchant Marine Academy)

LONG ISLAND SOUND, Connecticut-New York:
Nomad Sails Long Island Sound. By Thomas Horgan. 295-338, Sept. 1957

A LONG Life, a Good Life on the Potomac. By James L. Stanfield. 470-479, Oct. 1976

LONGEVITY:
"Every Day Is a Gift When You Are Over 100." By Alexander Leaf. Photos by John Launois. 93-119, Jan. 1973

LONGFELLOW, HENRY WADSWORTH:
Literary Landmarks of Massachusetts. By William H. Nicholas. Photos by B. Anthony Stewart and John E. Fletcher. 279-310, Mar. 1950

LONGHORNS (Cattle). *See* Wichita Mountains Wildlife Refuge

LONGSHIPS:
The Vikings. By Howard La Fay. Photos by Ted Spiegel. 492-541, Apr. 1970

LONGWOOD GARDENS, Kennett Square, Pennsylvania:
Wonderland in Longwood Gardens. By Edward C. Ferriday, Jr. 45-64, July 1951

A LOOK at Alaska's Tundra. By Russell D. Guthrie and Paul A. Zahl. 294-337, Mar. 1972

LOOK of a Land Beloved. Photos by Dewitt Jones. 444-467, Apr. 1976

LOOK What's Happened to Honolulu! By Jim Becker. Photos by Bates Littlehales. 500-531, Oct. 1969

LOONEY, RALPH: Author:
The Navajos. Photos by Bruce Dale. 740-781, Dec. 1972

LORD, NANCY: Photographer:
Jericho Gives Up Its Secrets. By Kathleen M. Kenyon and A. Douglas Tushingham. 853-870, Dec. 1953

LORIKEETS:
Honey Eaters of Currumbin. By Paul A. Zahl. 510-519, Oct. 1956

LOS ALAMOS, New Mexico:
Adobe New Mexico. By Mason Sutherland. Photos by Justin Locke. 783-830, Dec. 1949

LOS ALAMOS SCIENTIFIC LABORATORY, New Mexico:
The Search for Tomorrow's Power. By Kenneth F. Weaver. Photos by Emory Kristof. 650-681, Nov. 1972

LOS ANGELES, California:
California, the Golden Magnet. 595-679, May 1966
I. The South. By William Graves. Photos by Thomas Nebbia. 595-639
Los Angeles, City of the Angels. By Robert de Roos.

LOS ANGELES, California—*Continued*
Photos by Thomas Nebbia. 451-501, Oct. 1962
New Rush to Golden California. By George W. Long. 723-802, June 1954
See also Los Angeles Basin

LOS ANGELES AQUEDUCT:
California's Parched Oasis, the Owens Valley. By Judith and Neil Morgan. Photos by Jodi Cobb and Galen Rowell. 98-127, Jan. 1976

LOS ANGELES BASIN, California:
Southern California's Trial by Mud and Water. By Nathaniel T. Kenney. Photos by Bruce Dale. 552-573, Oct. 1969

LOST COLONY. *See* Roanoke Island, North Carolina

The LOST Empire of the Incas. By Loren McIntyre. Art by Ned and Rosalie Seidler. 729-787, Dec. 1973

LOST Kingdom in Indian Mexico By Justin Locke. 517-546, Oct. 1952

The LOST SIERRA, California:
Golden Ghosts of the Lost Sierra. By Robert Laxalt. Photos by David Hiser. 332-353, Sept. 1973

LOST World of the Galapagos. By Irving and Electa Johnson. 681-703, May 1959

LOTUKA (Tribespeople):
South in the Sudan. By Harry Hoogstraal. 249-272, Feb. 1953

LOUDER, MAX:
North With the Wheat Cutters. By Noel Grove. Photos by James A. Sugar. 194-217, Aug. 1972

LOUGHEED, R. E.: Artist:
Dogs Work for Man. By Edward J. Linehan. Paintings by Edwin Megargee and R. E. Lougheed. 190-233, Aug. 1958

LOUISBOURG (Fortress), Nova Scotia:
Nova Scotia, the Magnificent Anchorage. By Charles McCarry. Photos by Gordon W. Gahan. 334-363, Mar. 1975
The St. Lawrence, River Key to Canada. By Howard La Fay. Photos by John Launois. 622-667, May 1967

LOUISE, Lake, Canada:
Canadian Rockies, Lords of a Beckoning Land. By Alan Phillips. Photos by James L. Stanfield. 353-393, Sept. 1966

LOUISIADE ARCHIPELAGO, Pacific Ocean:
Adventures with the Survey Navy. By Irving Johnson. 131-148, July 1947

LOUISIANA:
Cajunland, Louisiana's French-speaking Coast. By Bern Keating. Photos by Charles Harbutt and Franke Keating. 353-391, Mar. 1966
Land of Louisiana Sugar Kings. By Harnett T. Kane. Photos by Willard R. Culver. 531-567, Apr. 1958
Louisiana Trades with the World. By Frederick Simpich. Photos by J. Baylor Roberts. 705-738, Dec. 1947
The Lower Mississippi. By Willard Price. Photos by W. D. Vaughn. 681-725, Nov. 1960
Skyway Below the Clouds. By Carl R. Markwith. Photos by Ernest J. Cottrell. 85-108, July 1949

LOUISIANA—*Continued*
Included: Monroe; Shreveport; Shreveport Municipal Airport
See also New Orleans

LOUSMA, JACK R.:
Skylab, Outpost on the Frontier of Space. By Thomas Y. Canby. Photos by the nine mission astronauts. 441-469, Oct. 1974

The LOUVRE, Paris:
The Louvre, France's Palace of the Arts. By Hereward Lester Cooke, Jr. 796-831, June 1971

LOVELL, JAMES A., Jr.:
Hubbard Medal recipient. 861, June 1970
"A Most Fantastic Voyage": The Story of Apollo 8's Rendezvous With the Moon. By Sam C. Phillips. 593-631, May 1969
Space Rendezvous, Milestone on the Way to the Moon. By Kenneth F. Weaver. 539-553, Apr. 1966

LOVELL, TOM: Artist:
In the Footsteps of Alexander the Great. By Helen and Frank Schreider. 1-65, Jan. 1968

LOW COUNTRIES, Europe:
France, Belgium, and the Netherlands, Atlas series supplement. June 1960
See also Belgium; Luxembourg; Netherlands

LOWE, GEORGE: Photographer:
The Crossing of Antarctica. By Sir Vivian Fuchs. 25-47, Jan. 1959
Triumph on Everest. 1-63, July 1954
I. Siege and Assault. By Sir John Hunt. 1-43
II. The Conquest of the Summit. By Sir Edmund Hillary. 45-63

LOWELL, JAMES RUSSELL:
Literary Landmarks of Massachusetts. By William H. Nicholas. Photos by B. Anthony Stewart and John E. Fletcher. 279-310, Mar. 1950

LOWELL, Massachusetts:
The Merrimack: River of Industry and Romance. By Albert W. Atwood. Photos by B. Anthony Stewart. 106-140, Jan. 1951

LOWELL OBSERVATORY: Expedition:
New Light on the Changing Face of Mars. By E. C. Slipher. 427-436, Sept. 1955

LOWER CALIFORNIA. *See* Baja California

The LOWER Keys, Florida's "Out Islands." By John Scofield. Photos by Emory Kristof and Bates Littlehales. 72-93, Jan. 1971

The LOWER Mississippi. By Willard Price. Photos by W. D. Vaughn. 681-725, Nov. 1960

LOWER SLAUGHTER, England:
By Cotswold Lanes to Wold's End. By Melville Bell Grosvenor. 615-654, May 1948

LOWER SOURIS NATIONAL WILDLIFE REFUGE, North Dakota:
Duck Hunting with a Color Camera. By Arthur A. Allen. 514-539, Oct. 1951

LOWMAN, PAUL D., Jr.: Author:
The Earth From Orbit. 645-671, Nov. 1966

LOWREY, PERRY:

Jungle Journey to the World's Highest Waterfall. By Ruth Robertson. 655-690, Nov. 1949

LOWY, RENNOLD L.: Author-Photographer:

Adventures in Lololand. 105-118, Jan. 1947

The **LOYALISTS** (Tories): Americans With a Difference. By Kent Britt. Photos by Ted Spiegel. 510-539, Apr. 1975

LUA (People):

Living With Thailand's Gentle Lua. By Peter Kunstadter. 122-152, July 1966

LUBUMBASHI, Zaire. See former name, Elisabethville, Democratic Republic of the Congo

LUCERNE, Switzerland:

Switzerland Guards the Roof of Europe. By William H. Nicholas. Photos by Willard R. Culver. 205-246, Aug. 1950

LUHIT (River), China-India:

Caught in the Assam-Tibet Earthquake. By F. Kingdon-Ward. 403-416, Mar. 1952

LULLINGSTONE CASTLE, England:

Silkworms in England Spin for the Queen. By John E. H. Nolan. 689-704, May 1953

LUMBER INDUSTRY:

Backwoods Japan During American Occupation. By M. A. Huberman. 491-518, Apr. 1947

Beauty and Bounty of Southern State Trees. By William A. Dayton. Paintings by Walter A. Weber. 508-552, Oct. 1957

Canada's Dynamic Heartland, Ontario. By Marjorie Wilkins Campbell. Photos by Winfield Parks. 58-97, July 1963

Canada's Window on the Pacific: The British Columbia Coast. By Jules B. Billard. Photos by Ted Spiegel. 338-375, Mar. 1972

From Sagebrush to Roses on the Columbia. By Leo A. Borah. 571-611, Nov. 1952

Louisiana Trades With the World. By Frederick Simpich. Photos by J. Baylor Roberts. 705-738, Dec. 1947

Ontario, Pivot of Canada's Power. By Andrew H. Brown. Photos by B. Anthony Stewart and Bates Littlehales. 823-852, Dec. 1953

Timber: How Much Is Enough? By John J. Putman. Photos by Bruce Dale. 485-511, Apr. 1974

Versatile Wood Waits on Man. By Andrew H. Brown. 109-140, July 1951

Idaho Loggers Battle a River. 117-130

Wealth and Wonder of Northern State Trees. By William A. Dayton. Paintings by Walter A. Weber. 651-691, Nov. 1955

LUMINESCENCE. See Bioluminescence; and Fluorescent Gems

LUNAR RESEARCH:

And Now to Touch the Moon's Forbidding Face. By Kenneth F. Weaver. 633-635, May 1969

Awesome Views of the Forbidding Moonscape. 233-239, Feb. 1969

Contents: Photos by Lunar Orbiter 2, 4, 5

What the Moon Rocks Tell Us. By Kenneth F. Weaver. 788-791, Dec. 1969

Included: Lunar Receiving Laboratory at the

LUNAR RESEARCH — *Continued*

Manned Spacecraft Center in Houston, Texas

See also Apollo Missions; Ranger Spacecraft; Surveyor Spacecraft; *and* Moon

LUNDY (Island), England:

Lundy, Treasure Island of Birds. By P. T. Etherton. Photos by J. Allan Cash. 675-698, May 1947

LUQUE, MICHAEL H.: Author-Photographer:

Among Alaska's Brown Bears. By Allan L. Egbert and Michael H. Luque. 428-442, Sept. 1975

The **LURE** of the Changing Desert. 817-824, June 1954

LÜTKEN, EMIL: Photographer:

The Shy and Spectacular Kingfisher. Photos by Carl-Johan Junge and Emil Lütken. 413-419, Sept. 1974

LUXEMBOURG:

Luxembourg, Survivor of Invasions. By Sydney Clark. Photos by Maynard Owen Williams. 791-810, June 1948

Luxembourg, the Quiet Fortress. By Robert Leslie Conly. Photos by Ted H. Funk. 69-97, July 1970

LUZ, HORST: Photographer:

Proud Primitives, the Nuba People. By Oskar Luz. 673-699, Nov. 1966

LUZ, OSKAR: Author:

Proud Primitives, the Nuba People. Photos by Horst Luz. 673-699, Nov. 1966

LYON, EUGENE: Author:

Atocha, Tragic Treasure Galleon of the Florida Keys. 787-809, June 1976

LYREBIRD, Australia's Meistersinger. By L. H. Smith. 849-857, June 1955

M

MACAO:

Eyes on the China Coast. By George W. Long. 505-512, Apr. 1953

Macao Clings to the Bamboo Curtain. By Jules B. Billard. Photos by Joseph J. Scherschel. 521-539, Apr. 1969

Macau, a Hole in the Bamboo Curtain. By George W. Long. Photos by J. Baylor Roberts. 679-688, May 1953

MacARTHUR, DOUGLAS:

Japan Tries Freedom's Road. By Frederick G. Vosburgh. Photos by J. Baylor Roberts. 593-632, May 1950

McBAIN, DONALD: Photographer:

Beltsville Brings Science to the Farm. By Samuel W. Matthews. 199-218, Aug. 1953

Stately Homes of Old Virginia. By Albert W. Atwood. 787-802, June 1953

The Wild Animals in My Life. By William M. Mann. 497-524, Apr. 1957

Williamsburg: Its College and Its Cinderella City. By Beverley M. Bowie. 439-486, Oct. 1954

McBRIDE, HARRY A.: Author:

Masterpieces on Tour. 717-750, Dec. 1948

McCARRY, CHARLES: Author:

Heart of the Bluegrass. Photos by J. Bruce Baumann. 634-659, May 1974

Home to the Enduring Berkshires. Photos by Jonathan S. Blair. 196-221, Aug. 1970

Kyoto and Nara: Keepers of Japan's Past. Photos by George F. Mobley. 836-851, June 1976

New Zealand's North Island: The Contented Land. Photos by Bates Littlehales. 190-213, Aug. 1974

Nova Scotia, the Magnificent Anchorage. Photos by Gordon W. Gahan. 334-363, Mar. 1975

Utah's Shining Oasis. Photos by James L. Amos. 440-473, Apr. 1975

Yesterday Lingers Along the Connecticut. Photos by David L. Arnold. 334-369, Sept. 1972

McCLELLAN-KERR ARKANSAS RIVER NAVIGATION SYSTEM:

Oklahoma, the Adventurous One. By Robert Paul Jordan. Photos by Robert W. Madden. 149-189, Aug. 1971

McCONNELL RIVER REGION, Canada:

Beyond the North Wind With the Snow Goose. By Des and Jen Bartlett. 822-843, Dec. 1973
. . . And Then There Was Fred. . . . 843-847

McCRANE, MARION P.: Author:

Zoo Animals Go to School. Photos by W. E. Garrett. 694-706, Nov. 1956

McCUE, J. J. G.: Author:

How Bats Hunt With Sound. 571-578, Apr. 1961

McCURDY, ARTHUR W.: Photographer:

1898: The Bells on Sable. 408-409, 416-417, Sept. 1965

McDADE, MATT C.: Author:

New York State's New Main Street. 567-618, Nov. 1956

McDIVITT, JAMES A.:

America's 6,000-mile Walk in Space. 440-447, Sept. 1965

McDONALD, EDWIN A.: Author:

Exploring Antarctica's Phantom Coast. Photos by W. D. Vaughn. 251-273, Feb. 1962

McDONALD, EUGENE F., Jr.:

The Society's Hubbard Medal Awarded to Commander MacMillan. 563-564, Apr. 1953
Note: Lieutenant Commander McDonald, present at the ceremony, was a member of the 1925 National Geographic Society — United States Navy MacMillan Arctic Expedition.

McDOWELL, BART: Author:

Avalanche! Photos by John E. Fletcher. 855-880, June 1962

The Changing Face of Old Spain. Photos by Albert Moldvay. 291-339, Mar. 1965

Deerfield Keeps a Truce With Time. Photos by Robert W. Madden. 780-809, June 1969

Earthquake in Guatemala. Photos by W. E. Garrett and Robert W. Madden. 810-829, June 1976

Hungary: Changing Homeland of a Tough, Romantic People. Photos by Albert Moldvay and Joseph J. Scherschel. 443-483, Apr. 1971

Mexico in Motion. Photos by Kip Ross. 490-537, Oct. 1961

McDOWELL, BART: Author — *Continued*

Mexico's Window on the Past. Photos by B. Anthony Stewart. 492-519, Oct. 1968

The Most Mexican City, Guadalajara. Photos by Volkmar Wentzel. 412-441, Mar. 1967

Orissa, Past and Promise in an Indian State. Photos by James P. Blair. 546-577, Oct. 1970

Puerto Rico's Seven-league Bootstraps. Photos by B. Anthony Stewart. 755-793, Dec. 1962

Theodore Roosevelt: a Centennial Tribute. 572-590, Oct. 1958

Those Successful Japanese. Photos by Fred Ward. 323-359, Mar. 1974

MACEDONIA (Republic), Yugoslavia:

Yugoslavia: Six Republics in One. By Robert Paul Jordan. Photos by James P. Blair. 589-633, May 1970

McELROY, WILLIAM D.:

Torchbearers of the Twilight (Fireflies). By Frederick G. Vosburgh. 697-704, May 1951

MacFARLAND, CRAIG: Author-Photographer:

Giant Tortoises: Goliaths of the Galapagos. Photos by author and Jan MacFarland. 632-649, Nov. 1972

MacFARLAND, JAN: Photographer:

Giant Tortoises: Goliaths of the Galapagos. By Craig MacFarland. Photos by author and Jan MacFarland. 632-649, Nov. 1972

McGAHAN, JERRY: Author:

The Condor, Soaring Spirit of the Andes. Photos by Libby McGahan. 684-709, May 1971

McGAHAN, LIBBY: Photographer:

The Condor, Soaring Spirit of the Andes. By Jerry McGahan. 684-709, May 1971

MACHIGUENGA INDIANS:

Amazon — The River Sea. By Loren McIntyre. 456-495, Oct. 1972

By Parachute Into Peru's Lost World. By G. Brooks Baekeland. Photos by author and Peter R. Gimbel. 268-296, Aug. 1964

MACHU PICCHU, Peru:

The Five Worlds of Peru. By Kenneth F. Weaver. Photos by Bates Littlehales. 213-265, Feb. 1964

Peru, Homeland of the Warlike Inca. By Kip Ross. 421-462, Oct. 1950
Contents: National Geographic Society — Yale University expeditions

MacINNIS, JOSEPH B.: Author:

Diving Beneath Arctic Ice. Photos by William R. Curtsinger. 248-267, Aug. 1973

McINTYRE, LOREN:

Editorial on writer-photographers. 295, Mar. 1975
Author-Photographer

Amazon — The River Sea. 456-495, Oct. 1972

Colombia, from Amazon to Spanish Main. 235-273, Aug. 1970

Ecuador — Low and Lofty Land Astride the Equator. 259-298, Feb. 1968

Flamboyant Is the Word for Bolivia. 153-195, Feb. 1966

The Lost Empire of the Incas. Art by Ned and Rosalie Seidler. 729-787, Dec. 1973

McINTYRE, LOREN—*Continued*

Which Way Now for Argentina? 296-333, Mar. 1975

Photographer

The Amazon. 445-455, Oct. 1972

Mystery of the Ancient Nazca Lines. 716-728, May 1975

MACKENZIE, ALEXANDER:

Across Canada by Mackenzie's Track. By Ralph Gray. 191-239, Aug. 1955

MACKEY, CAROL J.: Author:

Chan Chan, Peru's Ancient City of Kings. By Michael E. Moseley and Carol J. Mackey. Photos by David Brill. 318-345, Mar. 1973

McKINLEY, WILLIAM:

Inside the White House. By Lonnelle Aikman. Photos by B. Anthony Stewart and Thomas Nebbia. 3-43, Jan. 1961

The Living White House. By Lonnelle Aikman. 593-643, Nov. 1966

Profiles of the Presidents: III. The American Giant Comes of Age. By Frank Freidel. 660-711, May 1965

McKINLEY, Mount, Alaska:

Mount McKinley Conquered by New Route. By Bradford Washburn. 219-248, Aug. 1953

McKNEW, THOMAS W.:

Achievements and awards. 582, Apr. 1962; 588, 590, Oct. 1967

Anniversary, twenty-fifth, with the Society: Board of Trustees dinner. 423, Mar. 1957

Board of Trustees, Advisory Chairman. 576, 579, 588, 590, Oct. 1967; 529, Apr. 1968; 861, June 1970; 227, Aug. 1976

Board of Trustees, Chairman. 484, Oct. 1966; 588, Oct. 1967

Board of Trustees, Vice Chairman. 579, 582, Apr. 1962; 583, 626, Oct. 1963; 484, Oct. 1966

Building Committee, Chairman. 673, May 1964; 588, Oct. 1967

Life Trustee. 588, Oct. 1967

National Geographic Society Trustees Elect Key Executives. 576-590, Oct. 1967

Secretary. 586, May 1947; 835, 836, Dec. 1959; 588, Oct. 1967

Vice President of NGS. 419, 420, 421, 423, Mar. 1957; 866, 867, Dec. 1957; 793, June 1958

Vice President, Executive, of NGS. 834, 835, 836, Dec. 1959; 882, 883, Dec. 1960; 881, Dec. 1961; 579, 580, 582, Apr. 1962; 588, Oct. 1967

Author

Fledgling Wings of the Air Force. 266-271, Aug. 1957

Four-ocean Navy in the Nuclear Age. 145-187, Feb. 1965

We Followed Peary to the Pole. By Gilbert Grosvenor and Thomas W. McKnew. 469-484, Oct. 1953

MacLEISH, ARCHIBALD: Author:

Robert Frost and New England. 438-444, Apr. 1976

The Thrush on the Island of Barra. 692-693, May 1970

MacLEISH, KENNETH: Author:

Abraham, the Friend of God. Photos by Dean Conger. 739-789, Dec. 1966

Canterbury Cathedral. Photos by Thomas Nebbia. 364-379, Mar. 1976

Chartres: Legacy From the Age of Faith. Photos by Dean Conger. 857-882, Dec. 1969

Cyprus Under Four Flags: A Struggle for Unity. Photos by Jonathan Blair. 356-383, Mar. 1973

Diving With Sea Snakes. Photos by Ben Cropp. 565-578, Apr. 1972

Exploring Australia's Coral Jungle. 743-779, June 1973

Help for Philippine Tribes in Trouble. Photos by Dean Conger. 220-255, Aug. 1971

The Highlands, Stronghold of Scottish Gaeldom. Photos by Winfield Parks. 398-435, Mar. 1968

Île de la Cité, Birthplace of Paris. Photos by Bruce Dale. 680-719, May 1968

Isles on the Edge of the Sea: Scotland's Outer Hebrides. Photos by Thomas Nebbia. 676-711, May 1970

Java—Eden in Transition. Photos by Dean Conger. 1-43, Jan. 1971

The Land of Galilee. Photos by B. Anthony Stewart. 832-865, Dec. 1965

Martinique: Liberté, Egalité, and Uncertainty in the Caribbean. Photos by John Launois. 124-148, Jan. 1975

Quebec: French City in an Anglo-Saxon World. Photos by James L. Stanfield and Declan Haun. 416-442, Mar. 1971

Queensland: Young Titan of Australia's Tropic North. Photos by Winfield Parks. 593-639, Nov. 1968

Reunited Jerusalem Faces Its Problems. Photos by Ted Spiegel. 835-871, Dec. 1968

River of Counts and Kings: The Loire. Photos by Dean Conger. 822-869, June 1966

Scotland's Inner Hebrides: Isles of the Western Sea. Photos by R. Stephen Uzzell III. 690-717, Nov. 1974

Singapore, Reluctant Nation. Photos by Winfield Parks. 269-300, Aug. 1966

The Tasadays, Stone Age Cavemen of Mindanao. Photos by John Launois. 219-249, Aug. 1972

A Taxi for the Deep Frontier. Photos by Bates Littlehales. 139-150, Jan. 1968

The Top End of Down Under. Photos by Thomas Nebbia. 145-174, Feb. 1973

Western Australia, the Big Country. Photos by James L. Stanfield. 150-187, Feb. 1975

MacLEOD CLAN:

Over the Sea to Scotland's Skye. By Robert J. Reynolds. 87-112, July 1952

MacMILLAN, DONALD BAXTER:

Far North with "Captain Mac." By Miriam MacMillan. 465-513, Oct. 1951

The Society's Hubbard Medal Awarded to Commander MacMillan. 563-564, Apr. 1953

A Visit to the Living Ice Age. By Rutherford Platt. 525-545, Apr. 1957
Included: MacMillan's route in the *Bowdoin*

MacMILLAN, MIRIAM: Author:

Far North with "Captain Mac." 465-513, Oct. 1951

McMURDO STATION, Antarctica:

First Flight Across the Bottom of the World. By James R. Reedy. Photos by Otis Imboden. 454-464, Mar. 1964

Flight Into Antarctic Darkness. By J. Lloyd Abbot, Jr. Photos by David S. Boyer. 732-738, Nov. 1967

MacNEIL, NORMAN M.: Photographer:

Square-rigger in a Tempest *(Pamir)*. 703-710, May 1948

McNEIL RIVER STATE GAME SANCTUARY, Alaska:

Among Alaska's Brown Bears. By Allan L. Egbert and Michael H. Luque. 428-442, Sept. 1975

McPHEE, JOHN: Author:

The People of New Jersey's Pine Barrens. Photos by William R. Curtsinger. 52-77, Jan. 1974

MACQUARIE ISLAND, South Pacific Ocean:

Nature's Clown, the Penguin. By David Hellyer and Malcolm Davis. 405-428, Sept. 1952

MacSWAIN, J. W.: Author:

Crossroads of the Insect World. Photos by Edward S. Ross. 844-857, Dec. 1966

MADAGASCAR:

Madagascar: Island at the End of the Earth. By Luis Marden. Photos by Albert Moldvay. 443-487, Oct. 1967

Re-creating Madagascar's Giant Extinct Bird. By Alexander Wetmore. 488-493, Oct. 1967

The World in Your Garden. By W. H. Camp. Paintings by Else Bostelmann. 1-65, July 1947

MA'DAN (Tribespeople):

Marsh Dwellers of Southern Iraq. By Wilfred Thesiger. Photos by Gavin Maxwell. 205-239, Feb. 1958

Water Dwellers in a Desert World. By Gavin Young. Photos by Nik Wheeler. 502-523, Apr. 1976

MADDEN, ROBERT W.: Photographer:

Antarctica: Icy Testing Ground for Space. By Samuel W. Matthews. 569-592, Oct. 1968

China Unveils Her Newest Treasures. 848-857, Dec. 1974

Deerfield Keeps a Truce With Time. By Bart McDowell. 780-809, June 1969

Domesticating the Wild and Woolly Musk Ox. By John J. Teal, Jr. 862-879, June 1970

Earthquake in Guatemala. By Bart McDowell. Photos by W. E. Garrett and Robert W. Madden. 810-829, June 1976

Hawaii, Island of Fire and Flowers. By Gordon Young. 399-425, Mar. 1975

Maryland on the Half Shell. By Stuart E. Jones. 188-229, Feb. 1972

Mobile, Alabama's City in Motion. By William Graves. Photos by Joseph J. Scherschel and Robert W. Madden. 368-397, Mar. 1968

Oklahoma, the Adventurous One. By Robert Paul Jordan. 149-189, Aug. 1971

Old Salem, Morning Star of Moravian Faith. By Rowe Findley. 818-837, Dec. 1970

Quicksilver and Slow Death. By John J. Putman. 507-527, Oct. 1972

Toronto: Canada's Dowager Learns to Swing. By Ethel A. Starbird. 190-215, Aug. 1975

MADDEN, ROBERT W.: Photographer—*Continued*

Venezuela's Crisis of Wealth. By Noel Grove. 175-209, Aug. 1976

MADDEN, WILLIAM D.: Photographer:

Something's Fishy About That Fin! Photos by Robert J. Shallenberger and William D. Madden. 224-227, Aug. 1974

MADEIRA ISLANDS, Atlantic Ocean:

Madeira, Like Its Wine, Improves With Age. By Veronica Thomas. Photos by Jonathan Blair. 488-513, Apr. 1973

Portugal's Gem of the Ocean: Madeira. By David S. Boyer. 364-394, Mar. 1959

The Treasure of Porto Santo. By Robert Sténuit. Photos by author and William R. Curtsinger. 260-275, Aug. 1975

MADISON, DOLLEY:

Inside the White House. By Lonnelle Aikman. Photos by B. Anthony Stewart and Thomas Nebbia. 3-43, Jan. 1961

The Living White House. By Lonnelle Aikman. 593-643, Nov. 1966

MADISON, JAMES:

Profiles of the Presidents: I. The Presidency and How It Grew. By Frank Freidel. 642-687, Nov. 1964

MADOERA (Island), Java. *See* Madura

MADRID, Spain:

"Around the World in Eighty Days." By Newman Bumstead. 705-750, Dec. 1951

The Changing Face of Old Spain. By Bart McDowell. Photos by Albert Moldvay. 291-339, Mar. 1965

Speaking of Spain. By Luis Marden. 415-456, Apr. 1950

MADRID CODEX:

The Maya. 729-811, Dec. 1975

MADURA (Island), Indonesia:

Postwar Journey Through Java. By Ronald Stuart Kain. 675-700, May 1948

MAGDALENA (River), Colombia:

Cruising Colombia's "Ol' Man River." By Amos Burg. 615-660, May 1947

MAGELLAN, FERDINAND:

Magellan: First Voyage Around the World. By Alan Villiers. Photos by Bruce Dale. 721-753, June 1976

Included: Strait of Magellan, discovered October 21, 1520

Triton Follows Magellan's Wake. By Edward L. Beach. Photos by J. Baylor Roberts. 585-615, Nov. 1960

The **MAGIC** Lure of Sea Shells. By Paul A. Zahl. Photos by Victor R. Boswell, Jr. and author. 386-429, Mar. 1969

The **MAGIC** Road Round Ireland. By H. V. Morton. Photos by Robert F. Sisson. 293-333, Mar. 1961

The **MAGIC** Worlds of Walt Disney. By Robert de Roos. Photos by Thomas Nebbia. 159-207, Aug. 1963

MAGIS, ROBERT C.: Artist:

The Phoenicians, Sea Lords of Antiquity. By Samuel W. Matthews. Photos by Winfield Parks. 149-189, Aug. 1974

The Tower of the Winds. By Derek J. de Solla Price. 587-596, Apr. 1967

MAGNA CARTA:

The British Way. By Sir Evelyn Wrench. 421-541, Apr. 1949

MAGNESS, J. R.: Author:

How Fruit Came to America. Paintings by Else Bostelmann. 325-377, Sept. 1951

MAGNETIC Clues Help Date the Past. By Kenneth F. Weaver. 696-701, May 1967

MAGNETIC STORMS:

The Sun. By Herbert Friedman. 713-743, Nov. 1965

Unlocking Secrets of the Northern Lights. By Carl W. Gartlein. Paintings by William Crowder. 673-704, Nov. 1947

MAGNETISM DATING METHOD:

Magnetic Clues Help Date the Past. By Kenneth F. Weaver. 696-701, May 1967

MAH JONG (Yawl):

The Aegean Isles: Poseidon's Playground. By Gilbert M. Grosvenor. 733-781, Dec. 1958

MAHARASHTRA (State), India. See Shirala

MAHENDRA, King (Nepal):

Coronation in Katmandu. By E. Thomas Gilliard. Photos by Marc Riboud. 139-152, July 1957

MAIL. See Mail Boat; Postal Service; and Boston Post Roads; Natchez Trace; and West (So Long, St. Louis)

MAIL BOAT:

J. W. Westcott, Postman for the Great Lakes. By Cy La Tour. 813-824, Dec. 1950

MAINE:

The American Lobster, Delectable Cannibal. By Luis Marden. Photos by David Doubilet. 462-487, Apr. 1973

Aroostook County, Maine, Source of Potatoes. By Howell Walker. 459-478, Oct. 1948

Can We Save Our Salt Marshes? By Stephen W. Hitchcock. Photos by William R. Curtsinger. 729-765, June 1972

Character Marks the Coast of Maine. By John Scofield. Photos by B. Anthony Stewart. 798-843, June 1968

Close-up: U.S.A., Maine, with the Maritime Provinces of Canada, map supplement. Text on reverse. Mar. 1975

Down East Cruise (Nomad). By Tom Horgan. Photos by Luis Marden. 329-369, Sept. 1952

Mountains Top Off New England. By F. Barrows Colton. Photos by Robert F. Sisson. 563-602, May 1951

Seashore Summer: One Mother's Recipe for Smallboy Bliss. By Arline Strong. 436-444, Sept. 1960

Skyline Trail from Maine to Georgia. By Andrew H. Brown. Photos by Robert F. Sisson. 219-251, Aug. 1949

Stalking Wild Foods on a Desert Isle. By Euell Gib-

MAINE — Continued

bons. Photos by David Hiser. 47-63, July 1972

See also Allagash Wilderness Waterway; Monhegan Island

MAIURI, AMEDEO: Author:

Last Moments of the Pompeians. Photos by Lee E. Battaglia. Paintings by Peter V. Bianchi. 651-669, Nov. 1961

MAJORCA (Island), Balearic Islands:

The Balearics Are Booming. By Jean and Franc Shor. 621-660, May 1957

Spain's Sun-blest Pleasure Isles. By Ethel A. Starbird. Photos by James A. Sugar. 679-701, May 1976

MAKAT, Lake, Tanzania:

The Flamingo Eaters of Ngorongoro (Hyenas). By Richard D. Estes. 535-539, Oct. 1973

MAKING Friends With a Killer Whale. By Edward I. Griffin. 418-446, Mar. 1966

MAKING Friends With Mountain Gorillas. By Dian Fossey. Photos by Robert M. Campbell. 48-67, Jan. 1970

The MAKING of a New Australia. By Howell Walker. 233-259, Feb. 1956

The MAKING of a West Pointer. By Howell Walker. 597-626, May 1952

The MAKING of an Astronaut. By Robert R. Gilruth. 122-144, Jan. 1965

MAKKAH, Saudi Arabia. See Mecca

MALACOLOGY. See Mollusks

MALAGASY REPUBLIC. See Madagascar

MALAYA:

In Storied Lands of Malaysia. By Maurice Shadbolt. Photos by Winfield Parks. 734-783, Nov. 1963

Malaya Meets Its Emergency. By George W. Long. Photos by J. Baylor Roberts. 185-228, Feb. 1953

MALAYS:

Brunei, Borneo's Abode of Peace. By Joseph Judge. Photos by Dean Conger. 207-225, Feb. 1974

Help for Philippine Tribes in Trouble. By Kenneth MacLeish. Photos by Dean Conger. 220-255, Aug. 1971

Contents: The Higaonon, Mansaka, T'boli, and Ubo tribes of Malay stock (Southern Mongoloids) on Mindanao

Singapore, Reluctant Nation. By Kenneth MacLeish. Photos by Winfield Parks. 269-300, Aug. 1966

MALAYSIA:

Asian Insects in Disguise. By Edward S. Ross. 433-439, Sept. 1965

In Storied Lands of Malaysia. By Maurice Shadbolt. Photos by Winfield Parks. 734-783, Nov. 1963

Malaysia's Giant Flowers and Insect-trapping Plants. By Paul A. Zahl. 680-701, May 1964

MALDIVES, Indian Ocean:

The Marvelous Maldive Islands. By Alan Villiers. 829-849, June 1957

MALEKULA (Island), New Hebrides:
Taboos and Magic Rule Namba Lives. By Kal Muller. 57-83, Jan. 1972

MALI:
Foxes Foretell the Future in Mali's Dogon Country. By Pamela Johnson Meyer. 431-448, Mar. 1969
Freedom Speaks French in Ouagadougou. By John Scofield. 153-203, Aug. 1966
The Niger: River of Sorrow, River of Hope. By Georg Gerster. 152-189, Aug. 1975

The MALIGNED Coyote. By Hope Ryden. Photos by author and David Hiser. 278-294, Aug. 1974

MALLE, LOUIS: Photographer:
Calypso Explores for Underwater Oil. By Jacques-Yves Cousteau. 155-184, Aug. 1955

MALLORCA (Island), Balearic Islands. See Majorca

MALTA:
Democracy's Fortress: Unsinkable Malta. By Ernle Bradford. Photos by Ted H. Funk. 852-879, June 1969

MAMMALS:
African Wildlife: Man's Threatened Legacy. By Allan C. Fisher, Jr. Photos by Thomas Nebbia. 147-187, Feb. 1972
A Continent's Living Treasure. Paintings by Ned Seidler. 164-167
An Artist's Glimpses of Our Roadside Wildlife. Paintings by Walter A. Weber. 16-32, July 1950
Contents: Abert's Squirrel, Badgers, Black Bears, Coyotes, Moose, Pronghorn Antelopes, Skunks, Virginia Deer
Exploring the Mind of Ice Age Man. By Alexander Marshack. 64-89, Jan. 1975
Included: Mammals of the Ice Age as depicted in the art of Cro-Magnon man
"Ice Age Mammals of the Alaskan Tundra," painting supplement. Map of Canada. Mar. 1972
London's Zoo of Zoos. By Thomas Garner James. 771-786, June 1953
Mammals of the Alaskan Tundra. 329-337, Mar. 1972
Orphans of the Wild. By Bruce G. Kinloch. 683-699, Nov. 1962
Portrait of a Fierce and Fragile Land. By Paul A. Zahl. 303-314, Mar. 1972
Roaming Africa's Unfenced Zoos. By W. Robert Moore. 353-380, Mar. 1950
Contents: Antelopes, Buffaloes, Elephants, Gazelles, Giraffes, Gorillas, Hippopotamuses, Leopards, Lions, Okapi, Rhinoceroses, Wart Hogs, Zebras
The Romance of American Furs. By Wanda Burnett. 379-402, Mar. 1948
Contents: Beaver, Chinchillas, Foxes, Minks, Muskrats, Seals
Seeking Mindanao's Strangest Creatures. By Charles Heizer Wharton. 389-408, Sept. 1948
Contents: Cloud Rat, Flying Lemur, Tarsier, Tree Shrew
The Wild Animals in My Life. By William M. Mann. 497-524, Apr. 1957
Contents: Animals of the National Zoological Park
Wild Animals of North America. Book announced. 554-557, Oct. 1960
Wildlife In and Near the Valley of the Moon. By H. H. Arnold. Photos by Paul J. Fair. 401-414, Mar. 1950

MAMMALS—Continued
Contents: Deer, Elk, Ground Squirrels, Raccoons
Wildlife of Everglades National Park. By Daniel B. Beard. Paintings by Walter A. Weber. 83-116, Jan. 1949
Contents: Bobcat, Manatee, Marsh Rabbit, Otter, Porpoise, Puma, Raccoon
Wolves Versus Moose on Isle Royale. By Durward L. Allen and L. David Mech. 200-219, Feb. 1963
The Wonder City That Moves by Night. By Francis Beverly Kelley. 289-324, Mar. 1948
Zoo Animals Go to School. By Marion P. McCrane. Photos by W. E. Garrett. 694-706, Nov. 1956
See also names of individual species; and Paleontology

MAMMOTH:
Wyoming Muck Tells of Battle: Ice Age Man vs. Mammoth. By Cynthia Irwin, Henry Irwin, and George Agogino. 828-837, June 1962

MAN, Isle of, Irish Sea:
The Manx and Their Isle of Man. By Veronica Thomas. Photos by Ted H. Funk. 426-444, Sept. 1972

MAN, Prehistoric:
Adventures in the Search for Man (Kenyapithecus wickeri). By Louis S. B. Leakey. Photos by Hugo van Lawick. 132-152, Jan. 1963
A Bold New Look at Our Past. The Editor. 62-63, Jan. 1975
Ethiopia Yields First "Family" of Early Man. By Donald C. Johanson. Photos by David Brill. 790-811, Dec. 1976
Exploring 1,750,000 Years Into Man's Past. By L. S. B. Leakey. Photos by Robert F. Sisson. 564-589, Oct. 1961
Exploring the Mind of Ice Age Man. By Alexander Marshack. 64-89, Jan. 1975
Finding the World's Earliest Man (Zinjanthropus boisei). By L. S. B. Leakey. Photos by Des Bartlett. 420-435, Sept. 1960
Ice Age Man, the First American. By Thomas R. Henry. Paintings by Andre Durenceau. 781-806, Dec. 1955
In Search of Man's Past at Lake Rudolf. By Richard E. Leakey. Photos by Gordon W. Gahan. 712-734, May 1970
The Leakey Tradition Lives On. By Melvin M. Payne. 143-144, Jan. 1973
The Leakeys of Africa: Family in Search of Prehistoric Man. By Melvin M. Payne. 194-231, Feb. 1965
Included: Homo habilis, Kenyapithecus, Proconsul, Zinjanthropus
Lifelike Man Preserved 2,000 Years in Peat. By P. V. Glob. 419-430, Mar. 1954
Preserving the Treasures of Olduvai Gorge. By Melvin M. Payne. Photos by Joseph J. Scherschel. 701-709, Nov. 1966
Included: Homo erectus, Homo habilis, Kenyapithecus, Zinjanthropus
Skull 1470. By Richard E. Leakey. Photos by Bob Campbell. 819-829, June 1973
Vanished Mystery Men of Hudson Bay. By Henry B. Collins. 669-687, Nov. 1956
Included: Dorset Eskimos, Sadlermiuts
Wyoming Muck Tells of Battle: Ice Age Man vs. Mammoth. By Cynthia Irwin, Henry Irwin, and George Agogino. 828-837, June 1962

The MAN Behind the Myths: George Washington. By Howard La Fay. Photos by Ted Spiegel. 90-111, July 1976

MAN-IN-SEA PROJECT:

The Deepest Days. By Robert Sténuit. 534-547, Apr. 1965

The Long, Deep Dive. By Lord Kilbracken. Photos by Bates Littlehales. 718-731, May 1963

Our Man-in-Sea Project. By Edwin A. Link. 713-717, May 1963

Outpost Under the Ocean. By Edwin A. Link. Photos by Bates Littlehales. 530-533, Apr. 1965

A Taxi for the Deep Frontier. By Kenneth MacLeish. Photos by Bates Littlehales. 139-150, Jan. 1968

MAN-OF-WAR:

The Deadly Fisher. By Charles E. Lane. 388-397, Mar. 1963

Man-of-war Fleet Attacks Bimini. By Paul A. Zahl. 185-212, Feb. 1952

MAN on the Moon in Idaho. By William Belknap, Jr. 505-525, Oct. 1960

MAN Versus Nature. The Editor. 555, Oct. 1969

MAN Walks on Another World. By Neil A. Armstrong, Edwin E. Aldrin, Jr., and Michael Collins. 738-749, Dec. 1969

The MAN Who Talks to Hummingbirds. By Luis Marden. Photos by James Blair. 80-99, Jan. 1963

MANATEES:

Florida's Manatees, Mermaids in Peril. By Daniel S. Hartman. Photos by James A. Sugar. 342-353, Sept. 1969

Guatemala Revisited. By Luis Marden. 525-564, Oct. 1947

MANAUS, Brazil:

Sea Fever. By John E. Schultz. 237-268, Feb. 1949

MANCHURIA:

In Manchuria Now. By W. Robert Moore. 389-414, Mar. 1947

MANDINGOS (Tribespeople):

Rubber-cushioned Liberia. By Henry S. Villard. Photos by Charles W. Allmon. 201-228, Feb. 1948

MANHATTAN, New York City:

Tourist Manhattan; Greater New York, double-sided U. S. Atlas series supplement. July 1964

The World in New York City. By Peter T. White. 52-107, July 1964

See also Central Park

MANHATTAN, S.S. (Tanker):

North for Oil: Manhattan Makes the Historic Northwest Passage. By Bern Keating. Photos by Tomas Sennett. 374-391, Mar. 1970

MANITOBA (Province), Canada:

Across Canada by Mackenzie's Track. By Ralph Gray. 191-239, Aug. 1955

Canada's Heartland, the Prairie Provinces. By W. E. Garrett. 443-489, Oct. 1970

Manitoba's Fantastic Snake Pits. By Michael Aleksiuk. Photos by Bianca Lavies. 715-723, Nov. 1975

See also Churchill

MANKATO, Minnesota:

Satellites Gave Warning of Midwest Floods. By Peter T. White. Photos by Thomas A. DeFeo. 574-592, Oct. 1969

MANN, WILLIAM M.: Author:

The Wild Animals in My Life. 497-524, Apr. 1957

MANNED SPACECRAFT CENTER, Houston, Texas:

First Explorers on the Moon: The Incredible Story of Apollo 11. 735-797, Dec. 1969

I. Man Walks on Another World. By Neil A. Armstrong, Edwin E. Aldrin, Jr., and Michael Collins. 738-749

III. The Flight of Apollo 11: "One giant leap for mankind." By Kenneth F. Weaver. 752-787

IV. What the Moon Rocks Tell Us. By Kenneth F. Weaver. 788-791

Houston, Prairie Dynamo. By Stuart E. Jones. Photos by William Albert Allard. 338-377, Sept. 1967

"A Most Fantastic Voyage": The Story of Apollo 8's Rendezvous With the Moon. By Sam C. Phillips. 593-631, May 1969

MAN'S Deepest Dive. By Jacques Piccard. Photos by Thomas J. Abercrombie. 224-239, Aug. 1960

MAN'S First Winter at the South Pole. By Paul A. Siple. 439-478, Apr. 1958

MAN'S Mightiest Ally. Photos by Willard R. Culver. 423-450, Apr. 1947

MAN'S New Servant, the Friendly Atom. By F. Barrows Colton. Photos by Volkmar Wentzel. 71-90, Jan. 1954

MAN'S Own Mountains, the Alps. By Ralph Gray. Photos by Walter Meayers Edwards and William Eppridge. 350-395, Sept. 1965

MAN'S Wildlife Heritage Faces Extinction. By H. R. H. The Prince Philip, Duke of Edinburgh. 700-703, Nov. 1962

MANSAKA TRIBE:

Help for Philippine Tribes in Trouble. By Kenneth MacLeish. Photos by Dean Conger. 220-255, Aug. 1971

MANSFIELD, Mount, Vermont:

Mountains Top Off New England. By F. Barrows Colton. Photos by Robert F. Sisson. 563-602, May 1951

MANTIS:

Praying Mantis. Photos by John G. Pitkin. 685-692, May 1950

MANUSCRIPTS, Medieval. See Henry E. Huntington Library and Art Gallery; Medieval Europe; St. Catherine's Monastery

The MANX and Their Isle of Man. By Veronica Thomas. Photos by Ted H. Funk. 426-444, Sept. 1972

The MANY-SIDED Diamond. By George S. Switzer. 568-586, Apr. 1958

MANY-SPLENDORED Glacierland. By George W. Long. Photos by Kathleen Revis. 589-636, May 1956

MAO TSE-TUNG:

Return to Changing China. By Audrey Topping. 801-833, Dec. 1971

MAORIS:

New Zealand: Gift of the Sea. By Maurice Shadbolt. Photos by Brian Brake. 465-511, Apr. 1962

New Zealand, Pocket Wonder World. By Howell
Walker. 419-460, Apr. 1952

New Zealand's Cook Islands: Paradise in Search of
a Future. By Maurice Shadbolt. Photos by William Albert Allard. 203-231, Aug. 1967

New Zealand's North Island: The Contented Land.
By Charles McCarry. Photos by Bates Littlehales. 190-213, Aug. 1974

A MAP Maker Looks at the United States. By Newman Bumstead. 705-748, June 1951

MAP MAKING. *See* Cartography

MAP SUPPLEMENTS:

Africa

Africa. Atlas series. Sept. 1960

Africa: Countries of the Nile. Atlas series. Oct. 1963

Africa and the Arabian Peninsula. Mar. 1950

The Heritage of Africa; The Peoples of Africa. Dec.
1971

Nile Valley, Land of the Pharaohs. Atlas series.
Text on reverse. May 1965

Northern Africa. Dec. 1954

Northwestern Africa. Atlas series. Aug. 1966

Southern Africa. Atlas series. Nov. 1962

Antarctica

Antarctica. Sept. 1957

Antarctica. Atlas series. Feb. 1963

Arctic

The Top of the World. Oct. 1949

Top of the World. Atlas series. Nov. 1965

Arctic Ocean

Arctic Ocean; Arctic Ocean Floor. Oct. 1971

Asia

Asia; The Peoples of Mainland Southeast Asia.
Mar. 1971

Asia and Adjacent Areas. Mar. 1951

Asia and Adjacent Areas. Atlas series. Dec. 1959

China. Atlas series. Nov. 1964

China Coast and Korea. Oct. 1953

The Far East. Sept. 1952

Japan and Korea. Atlas series. Dec. 1960

Southeast Asia. Sept. 1955

Southeast Asia. Dec. 1968

Southeast Asia. Atlas series. May 1961

Southwest Asia. Atlas series. May 1963

*Southwest Asia, including India, Pakistan, and
Northeast Africa*. June 1952

Viet Nam, Cambodia, Laos, and Eastern Thailand.
Text on reverse. Jan. 1965

Viet Nam, Cambodia, Laos, and Thailand. Feb.
1967

See also Union of Soviet Socialist Republics

Atlantic Ocean

Atlantic Ocean. Dec. 1955

Atlantic Ocean; Atlantic Ocean Floor. Atlas series.
June 1968

Australia

Australia. Mar. 1948

Australia. Atlas series. Sept. 1963

Bible Lands

Holy Land Today. Atlas series. Dec. 1963

MAP SUPPLEMENTS — *Continued*

Lands of the Bible Today. Dec. 1956

Lands of the Bible Today. Dec. 1967

Lands of the Eastern Mediterranean. Atlas series.
Jan. 1959

Canada

Canada. Atlas series. Dec. 1961

Canada. Text on reverse. Mar. 1972

Canada, Alaska, and Greenland. June 1947

Central Canada. Atlas series. July 1963

Eastern Canada. Atlas series. May 1967

*The Great Lakes Region of the United States and
Canada*. Dec. 1953

Maine, with the Maritime Provinces of Canada.
Close-up series. Text on reverse. Mar. 1975

*National Parks, Monuments and Shrines of the
United States and Canada*. Atlas series. Text on
reverse. May 1958

*Vacationlands of the United States and Southern
Canada*. Text on reverse. July 1966

Western Canada. Atlas series. Sept. 1966

Caribbean

*Countries of the Caribbean, including Mexico, Cen-
tral America, and the West Indies*. Oct. 1947

Florida, with Puerto Rico and the Virgin Islands.
Close-up series. Text on reverse. Nov. 1973

West Indies. Mar. 1954

West Indies. Atlas series. Dec. 1962

West Indies and Central America. Jan. 1970

Central America

*Archeological Map of Middle America, Land of the
Feathered Serpent*. Text on reverse. Oct. 1968

Central America; Mexico. May 1973

*Countries of the Caribbean, including Mexico, Cen-
tral America, and the West Indies*. Oct. 1947

Mexico and Central America. Mar. 1953

Mexico and Central America. Atlas series. Oct.
1961

West Indies and Central America. Jan. 1970

Ethnic Maps

Discoverers of the Pacific, double sided. Dec. 1974

Indians of North America, double sided. Dec. 1972

The Peoples of Africa, double sided. Dec. 1971

The Peoples of Mainland Southeast Asia, double
sided. Mar. 1971

The Peoples of the Middle East. Text on reverse.
July 1972

Peoples of the Soviet Union, double sided. Feb.
1976

Europe

The Balkans. Atlas series. Feb. 1962

Central Europe, including the Balkan States. Sept.
1951

Classical Lands of the Mediterranean. Dec. 1949

Europe. June 1957

Europe. June 1969

Europe. Atlas series. June 1962

Europe and the Near East. June 1949

France:

France, Belgium, and the Netherlands. Atlas series. June 1960

A Traveler's Map of France. Text on reverse.
June 1971

MAP SUPPLEMENTS — *Continued*

Germany. Atlas series. June 1959

Great Britain:

The British Isles. Apr. 1949

British Isles. Atlas series. July 1958

Shakespeare's Britain. May 1964

A Traveler's Map of the British Isles. Text on reverse. Apr. 1974

Greece and the Aegean. Atlas series. Dec. 1958

Italy:

Italy. Atlas series. Nov. 1961

A Traveler's Map of Italy. Text on reverse. June 1970

Northern Europe. Aug. 1954

Poland and Czechoslovakia. Atlas series. Sept. 1958

Scandinavia. Atlas series. Apr. 1963

Spain and Portugal. Atlas series. Mar. 1965

Switzerland, Austria, and Northern Italy; The Alps — Europe's Backbone. Atlas series. Sept. 1965

Western Europe. Dec. 1950

See also Union of Soviet Socialist Republics

Greenland

Canada, Alaska, and Greenland. June 1947

Heavens

A Map of the Heavens. Star charts on reverse. Dec. 1957

Map of the Heavens. Star charts on reverse. Aug. 1970

Indian Ocean

Indian Ocean Floor. Oct. 1967

Mars

The Red Planet Mars. Text on reverse. Feb. 1973

Mediterranean

Classical Lands of the Mediterranean. Dec. 1949

Lands of the Eastern Mediterranean. Atlas series. Jan. 1959

Mexico

Archeological Map of Middle America, Land of the Feathered Serpent. Text on reverse. Oct. 1968

Countries of the Caribbean, including Mexico, Central America, and the West Indies. Oct. 1947

Mexico; Central America. May 1973

Mexico and Central America. Mar. 1953

Mexico and Central America. Atlas series. Oct. 1961

Middle America

Archeological Map of Middle America, Land of the Feathered Serpent. Text on reverse. Oct. 1968

Middle East and Near East

Europe and the Near East. June 1949

Holy Land Today. Atlas series. Dec. 1963

Lands of the Bible Today. Dec. 1956

Lands of the Bible Today. Dec. 1967

Lands of the Eastern Mediterranean. Atlas series. Jan. 1959

The Peoples of the Middle East. Text on reverse. July 1972

Moon

The Earth's Moon. Feb. 1969

North America

North America. Mar. 1952

MAP SUPPLEMENTS — *Continued*

North America. Atlas series. Apr. 1964

North America Before Columbus; Indians of North America. Dec. 1972

See also Canada; Mexico; United States

Pacific Ocean

Islands of the Pacific; Discoverers of the Pacific. Dec. 1974

Pacific Ocean. Dec. 1952

Pacific Ocean; Pacific Islands. Atlas series. Apr. 1962

Pacific Ocean; Pacific Ocean Floor. Oct. 1969

Skies

A Map of the Heavens. Star charts on reverse. Dec. 1957; Aug. 1970

South America

Eastern South America. Mar. 1955

Eastern South America. Atlas series. Sept. 1962

Northwestern South America. Atlas series. Feb. 1964

South America. Oct. 1950

South America. Atlas series. Feb. 1960

South America. Text on reverse. Oct. 1972

Southern South America. Atlas series. Mar. 1958

Union of Soviet Socialist Republics

Eastern Soviet Union. Atlas series. Mar. 1967

Soviet Union; Peoples of the Soviet Union. Feb. 1976

Union of Soviet Socialist Republics. Dec. 1960

Western Soviet Union. Atlas series. Sept. 1959

United States

Alaska:

Alaska. June 1956

Alaska. Close-up series. Text on reverse. June 1975

Canada, Alaska, and Greenland. June 1947

State of Alaska. Atlas series. July 1959

Battlefields of the Civil War; Cockpit of the Civil War. Atlas series. Apr. 1961

California:

California and Nevada. Close-up series. Text on reverse. June 1974

A Map of California. June 1954

Northern California; Southern California. U. S. Atlas series. May 1966

Florida, with U. S. Virgin Islands and Puerto Rico and text on reverse. Close-up series. Nov. 1973

The Great Lakes: Wisconsin, Michigan, and the Great Lakes. Close-up series. Text on reverse. Aug. 1973

The Great Lakes Region of the United States and Canada. Dec. 1953

Hawaii:

Hawaii. Atlas series. July 1960

Hawaii. Close-up series. Text on reverse. Apr. 1976

Historical Map of the United States. June 1953

Maine, with the Maritime Provinces of Canada. Close-up series. Text on reverse. Mar. 1975

The Mid-Atlantic States. Close-up series. Text on reverse. Oct. 1976

National Parks, Monuments and Shrines of the United States and Canada. Atlas series. Text on reverse. May 1958

MAP SUPPLEMENTS—*Continued*

New England:

New England. June 1955

Western New England. Close-up series. Text on reverse. July 1975

New York City: *Greater New York; Tourist Manhattan.* U. S. Atlas series. July 1964

The North Central States. Close-up series. Text on reverse. Mar. 1974

North Central United States. June 1948

North Central United States. Atlas series. Nov. 1958

Northeastern United States, including the Great Lakes Region. Atlas series. Apr. 1959

The Northwest. Close-up series. Text on reverse. Mar. 1973

Northwestern United States. Atlas series. Apr. 1960

Northwestern United States and Neighboring Canadian Provinces. June 1950

Portrait U.S.A., first color photomosaic of the 48 contiguous United States from Landsat satellite imagery; *The United States.* July 1976

The South Central States. Close-up series. Text on reverse. Oct. 1974

South Central United States. Dec. 1947

South Central United States. Atlas series. Feb. 1961

The Southeast. Close-up series. Text on reverse. Oct. 1975

Southeastern United States. Feb. 1947

Southeastern United States. Atlas series. Jan. 1958

Southwestern United States. Dec. 1948

Southwestern United States. Atlas series. Nov. 1959

The United States. Sept. 1956

The United States. Feb. 1968

The United States. Atlas series. July 1961

The United States; Portrait U.S.A. (photomosaic). July 1976

United States: Washington to Boston. Atlas series. Aug. 1962

The United States of America. June 1951

Vacationlands of the United States and Southern Canada. Text on reverse. July 1966

Washington, D. C.:

A Pocket Map of Central Washington; A Pocket Map of Suburban Washington. Sept. 1948

Round About the Nation's Capital. Apr. 1956

Tourist Washington; Suburban Washington. U. S. Atlas series. Dec. 1964

World

The Political World; The Physical World. Nov. 1975

The World. Mar. 1957

The World. Feb. 1965

The World. Atlas series. Nov. 1960

The World. Text on reverse. Dec. 1970

World: *The Great Whales: Migration and Range.* Text on reverse. Dec. 1976

The World Map. Dec. 1951

MAPLE SUGAR AND SYRUP:

Sugar Weather in the Green Mountains. By Stephen Greene. Photos by Robert F. Sisson. 471-482, Apr. 1954

MAPPING the Nation's Breadbasket. By Frederick Simpich. 831-849, June 1948

MAPPING the Unknown Universe. By F. Barrows Colton. 401-420, Sept. 1950

MARBLE:

Mountains Top Off New England. By F. Barrows Colton. Photos by Robert F. Sisson. 563-602, May 1951

MARBLE CANYON NATIONAL MONUMENT, Arizona:

Retracing John Wesley Powell's Historic Voyage Down the Grand Canyon. By Joseph Judge. Photos by Walter Meayers Edwards. 668-713, May 1969

MARBLEHEAD, Massachusetts:

Windjamming Around New England. By Tom Horgan. Photos by Robert F. Sisson. 141-169, Aug. 1950

MARBLEHEAD-HALIFAX RACE:

Down East to Nova Scotia. By Winfield Parks. 853-879, June 1964

MARBORÉ (Massif), France-Spain:

Probing Ice Caves of the Pyrenees. By Norbert Casteret. 391-404, Mar. 1953

MARCHIONINI, ALFRED: Author-Photographer:

Peasants of Anatolia. 57-72, July 1948

MARDEN, LUIS: Author:

The American Lobster, Delectable Cannibal. Photos by David Doubilet. 462-487, Apr. 1973

The Exquisite Orchids. 485-513, Apr. 1971

Included: The newly discovered *Epistephium mardeni*

Guatemala Revisited. 525-564, Oct. 1947

Madagascar: Island at the End of the Earth. Photos by Albert Moldvay. 443-487, Oct. 1967

The Man Who Talks to Hummingbirds. Photos by James Blair. 80-99, Jan. 1963

The Renaissance Lives On In Tuscany. Photos by Albert Moldvay. 626-659, Nov. 1974

Saga of a Ship, the *Yankee* (Brigantine). 263-269, Feb. 1966

The Sailing Oystermen of Chesapeake Bay. 798-819, Dec. 1967

Titicaca, Abode of the Sun. Photos by Flip Schulke. 272-294, Feb. 1971

Author-Photographer

Ama, Sea Nymphs of Japan. 122-135, July 1971

Amalfi, Italy's Divine Coast. 472-509, Oct. 1959

Bruges, the City the Sea Forgot. 631-665, May 1955

Camera Under the Sea. 162-200, Feb. 1956

Dzibilchaltun: Up from the Well of Time. 110-129, Jan. 1959

The Friendly Isles of Tonga. 345-367, Mar. 1968

Gloucester Blesses Its Portuguese Fleet. 75-84, July 1953

Holy Week and the Fair in Sevilla. 499-530, Apr. 1951

Huzza for Otaheite! (*Bounty* Voyage). 435-459, Apr. 1962

I Found the Bones of the *Bounty.* 725-789, Dec. 1957

The Islands Called Fiji. 526-561, Oct. 1958

The Other Side of Jordan. 790-825, Dec. 1964

The Purple Land of Uruguay. 623-654, Nov. 1948

MARDEN, LUIS: Author-Photographer — *Continued*
Sicily the Three-cornered. 1-48, Jan. 1955
Spain's Silkworm Gut. 100-108, July 1951
Speaking of Spain. 415-456, Apr. 1950
Tahiti, "Finest Island in the World." 1-47, July 1962
Tropical Gardens of Key West. 116-124, Jan. 1953

Photographer
Aviation Looks Ahead on Its 50th Birthday. By Emory S. Land. 721-739, Dec. 1953
Aviation Medicine on the Threshold of Space. By Allan C. Fisher, Jr. 241-278, Aug. 1955
Cape Canaveral's 6,000-mile Shooting Gallery. By Allan C. Fisher, Jr. Photos by Luis Marden and Thomas Nebbia. 421-471, Oct. 1959
Down East Cruise *(Nomad)*. By Tom Horgan. 329-369, Sept. 1952
Exploring Davy Jones's Locker with *Calypso*. By Jacques-Yves Cousteau. 149-161, Feb. 1956
Exploring the Drowned City of Port Royal. By Marion Clayton Link. 151-183, Feb. 1960
Fact Finding for Tomorrow's Planes. By Hugh L. Dryden. 757-780, Dec. 1953
Hydrofoil Ferry "Flies" the Strait of Messina. By Gilbert Grosvenor. 493-496, Apr. 1957
Marineland, Florida's Giant Fish Bowl. By Gilbert Grosvenor La Gorce. 679-694, Nov. 1952
Reaching for the Moon (Rockets). By Allan C. Fisher, Jr. 157-171, Feb. 1959
Shad in the Shadow of Skyscrapers. By Dudley B. Martin. 359-376, Mar. 1947

MARDI GRAS:
Mardi Gras in New Orleans. By Carolyn Bennett Patterson. Photos by Robert F. Sisson and John E. Fletcher. 726-732, Nov. 1960
Mobile, Alabama's City in Motion. By William Graves. Photos by Joseph J. Scherschel and Robert W. Madden. 368-397, Mar. 1968
New Orleans: Jambalaya on the Levee. By Harnett T. Kane. Photos by Justin Locke. 143-184, Feb. 1953
New Orleans and Her River. By Joseph Judge. Photos by James L. Stanfield. 151-187, Feb. 1971

MARE IMBRIUM, Moon:
Have We Solved the Mysteries of the Moon? By Kenneth F. Weaver. Paintings by William H. Bond. 309-325, Sept. 1973

MARIANA ISLANDS, Pacific Ocean:
Pacific Wards of Uncle Sam. By W. Robert Moore. 73-104, July 1948

MARIANA TRENCH, Pacific Ocean:
Man's Deepest Dive (Challenger Deep). By Jacques Piccard. Photos by Thomas J. Abercrombie. 224-239, Aug. 1960

MARINATOS, SPYRIDON: Author:
Thera, Key to the Riddle of Minos. Photos by Otis Imboden. 702-726, May 1972

MARINE BAND, U. S.:
The President's Music Men. By Stuart E. Jones. Photos by William W. Campbell III. 752-766, Dec. 1959

MARINE BIOLOGY:
Adrift on a Raft of Sargassum. Photos by Robert F.

MARINE BIOLOGY — *Continued*
Sisson. 188-199, Feb. 1976
Antarctica's Nearer Side. By Samuel W. Matthews. Photos by William R. Curtsinger. 622-655, Nov. 1971
At Home in the Sea. By Jacques-Yves Cousteau. 465-507, Apr. 1964
Calypso Explores an Undersea Canyon (Romanche Trench). By Jacques-Yves Cousteau. Photos by Bates Littlehales. 373-396, Mar. 1958
Camera Under the Sea. By Luis Marden. 162-200, Feb. 1956
Deep Diving off Japan. By Georges S. Houot. 138-150, Jan. 1960
Deepstar Explores the Ocean Floor. Photos by Ron Church. 110-129, Jan. 1971
Diving Beneath Arctic Ice. By Joseph B. MacInnis. Photos by William R. Curtsinger. 248-267, Aug. 1973
Diving Saucer Takes to the Deep. By Jacques-Yves Cousteau. 571-586, Apr. 1960
Exploring Davy Jones's Locker with *Calypso*. By Jacques-Yves Cousteau. Photos by Luis Marden. 149-161, Feb. 1956
Fishing in the Whirlpool of Charybdis. By Paul A. Zahl. 579-618, Nov. 1953
Four Years of Diving to the Bottom of the Sea. By Georges S. Houot. 715-731, May 1958
Glass Menageries of the Sea. By Paul A. Zahl. 797-822, June 1955
Hatchetfish, Torchbearers of the Deep. By Paul A. Zahl. 713-714, May 1958
How the Sun Gives Life to the Sea. By Paul A. Zahl. 199-225, Feb. 1961
Miami's Expanding Horizons. By William H. Nicholas. 561-594, Nov. 1950
Included: University of Miami marine biology study and National Geographic Society — University of Miami long-range program to study plankton
Nature's Night Lights: Probing the Secrets of Bioluminescence. By Paul A. Zahl. 45-69, July 1971
Night Life in the Gulf Stream. By Paul A. Zahl. 391-418, Mar. 1954
One Hundred Hours Beneath the Chesapeake. By Gilbert C. Klingel. Photos by Willard R. Culver. 681-696, May 1955
Oregon's Sidewalk on the Sea. By Paul A. Zahl. 708-734, Nov. 1961
Patagonia. Photos by Des and Jen Bartlett. 290-339, Mar. 1976
I. Argentina Protects Its Wildlife Treasures. By William G. Conway. 290-297
II. Where Two Worlds Meet. 298-321
III. At Home With Right Whales. By Roger Payne. 322-339
Photographing the Sea's Dark Underworld. By Harold E. Edgerton. 523-537, Apr. 1955
Sailing a Sea of Fire (Phosphorescent Bay, Puerto Rico). By Paul A. Zahl. 120-129, July 1960
Strange Babies of the Sea (Plankton). By Hilary B. Moore. Paintings by Craig Phillips and Jacqueline Hutton. 41-56, July 1952
Tektite II. 256-296, Aug. 1971
I. Science's Window on the Sea. By John G. VanDerwalker. Photos by Bates Littlehales. 256-289
II. All-girl Team Tests the Habitat. By Sylvia A. Earle. Paintings by Pierre Mion. 291-296

MARINE BIOLOGY—*Continued*

To the Depths of the Sea by Bathyscaphe. By Jacques-Yves Cousteau. 67-79, July 1954

Two and a Half Miles Down. By Georges S. Houot. 80-86, July 1954

See also Corals and Coral Reefs

MARINE GARDENS. *See* Ras Muhammad

MARINE RESEARCH. *See* Airborne Undersea Expeditions; Marine Biology; Oceanography

MARINELAND, Florida's Giant Fish Bowl. By Gilbert Grosvenor La Gorce. Photos by Luis Marden. 679-694, Nov. 1952

MARINER MISSIONS:

Journey to Mars (Mariner 9). By Kenneth F. Weaver. Paintings by Ludek Pesek. 231-263, Feb. 1973

Mariner Scans a Lifeless Venus (Mariner 2). By Frank Sartwell. Paintings by Davis Meltzer. 733-742, May 1963

Mariner Unveils Venus and Mercury (Mariner 10). By Kenneth F. Weaver. 858-869, June 1975

Voyage to the Planets. By Kenneth F. Weaver. Paintings by Ludek Pesek. 147-193, Aug. 1970
Included: Mariner 2, Mariner 4, Mariner 5, Mariner 6, Mariner 7

MARINES, U. S. *See* U. S. Marine Corps

Las MARISMAS (Marshes), Spain:

Rare Birds Flock to Spain's Marismas. By Roger Tory Peterson. 397-425, Mar. 1958

MARITIME ALPS, Europe:

Sheep Trek in the French Alps. By Maurice Moyal. Photos by Marcel Coen. 545-564, Apr. 1952

MARITIME PROVINCES, Canada:

Close-up: Canada, Maine, with the Maritime Provinces of Canada, map supplement. Text on reverse. Mar. 1975

See also New Brunswick; Nova Scotia

MARK TWAIN: Mirror of America. By Noel Grove. Photos by James L. Stanfield. 300-337, Sept. 1975

See also Twain, Mark

MARKETS AND STORES:

Keeping House in London. By Frances James. 769-792, Dec. 1947

Paris Flea Market. By Franc Shor. Photos by Alexander Taylor. 318-326, Mar. 1957

MARKWITH, CARL R.: Author:

Skyway Below the Clouds. Photos by Ernest J. Cottrell. 85-108, July 1949

MAROSTICA, Italy:

Chessmen Come to Life in Marostica. By Alexander Taylor. 658-668, Nov. 1956

MARQUESAS ISLANDS, Pacific Ocean:

Shores and Sails in the South Seas. By Charles Allmon. 73-104, Jan. 1950
Included: Fatu Hiva; Fatu Huku; Hiva Oa; Nuku Hiva; Tahuata; Ua Huka; Ua Pu

MARQUESAS KEYS, Florida:

Atocha, Tragic Treasure Galleon of the Florida Keys. By Eugene Lyon. 787-809, June 1976

MARS (Planet):

Journey to Mars. By Kenneth F. Weaver. Paintings by Ludek Pesek. 231-263, Feb. 1973

Mars: A New World to Explore. By Carl Sagan. 821-841, Dec. 1967

New Light on the Changing Face of Mars. By E. C. Slipher. 427-436, Sept. 1955

The Red Planet Mars; "The Dusty Face of Mars," map-and-painting supplement. Feb. 1973

The Search for Life on Mars. By Kenneth F. Weaver. 264-265, Feb. 1973

Voyage to the Planets. By Kenneth F. Weaver. Paintings by Ludek Pesek. 147-193, Aug. 1970

MARS RESEARCH EXPEDITION: South Africa:

New Light on the Changing Face of Mars. By E. C. Slipher. 427-436, Sept. 1955

MARSEILLE, France:

French Riviera: Storied Playground on the Azure Coast. By Carleton Mitchell. Photos by Thomas Nebbia. 798-835, June 1967

Provence, Empire of the Sun. By William Davenport. Photos by James A. Sugar. 692-715, May 1975

MARSH, DONALD B.: Author-Photographer:

Canada's Caribou Eskimos. 87-104, Jan. 1947

MARSH ARABS. *See* Ma'dan

MARSH DWELLERS of Southern Iraq. By Wilfred Thesiger. Photos by Gavin Maxwell. 205-239, Feb. 1958

MARSHACK, ALEXANDER:

A Bold New Look at Our Past. The Editor. 62-63, Jan. 1975

Author

Exploring the Mind of Ice Age Man. 64-89, Jan. 1975

MARSHALL, GEORGE C.:

Tribute to General George C. Marshall. 113, Jan. 1960

Author

Giant Effigies of the Southwest. 389, Sept. 1952

Our War Memorials Abroad: A Faith Kept. 731-737, June 1957

MARSHALL, LAURENCE K.: Photographer:

Bushmen of the Kalahari. By Elizabeth Marshall Thomas. 866-888, June 1963

MARSHALL ISLANDS, Pacific Ocean:

Pacific Wards of Uncle Sam. By W. Robert Moore. 73-104, July 1948

See also Bikini; Kwajalein

MARSHALL KALAHARI EXPEDITIONS:

Bushmen of the Kalahari. By Elizabeth Marshall Thomas. Photos by Laurence K. Marshall. 866-888, June 1963

MARSHES. *See* Abbotsbury Swannery; Everglades; Iraq (Marsh Dwellers; Water Dwellers); Las Marismas; Salt Marshes

MARSHFIELD, Massachusetts:

Land of the Pilgrims' Pride. By George W. Long. Photos by Robert F. Sisson. 193-219, Aug. 1947

MARSUPIALS:

Eden in the Outback. By Kay and Stanley Breeden. 189-203, Feb. 1973

Strange Animals of Australia. By David Fleay. Photos by Stanley Breeden. 388-411, Sept. 1963

See also Kangaroos; Opossums

MARTHA'S VINEYARD, Massachusetts:

Martha's Vineyard. By William P. E. Graves. Photos by James P. Blair. 778-809, June 1961

Windjamming Around New England. By Tom Horgan. Photos by Robert F. Sisson. 141-169, Aug. 1950

MARTIN, DUDLEY B.: Author:

Shad in the Shadow of Skyscrapers. Photos by Luis Marden. 359-376, Mar. 1947

MARTINIQUE (Island), West Indies:

Carib Cruises the West Indies. By Carleton Mitchell. 1-56, Jan. 1948

Finisterre Sails the Windward Islands. By Carleton Mitchell. Photos by Winfield Parks. 755-801, Dec. 1965

Martinique: A Tropical Bit of France. By Gwen Drayton Allmon. Photos by Charles Allmon. 255-283, Feb. 1959

Martinique: Liberté, Egalité, and Uncertainty in the Caribbean. By Kenneth MacLeish. Photos by John Launois. 124-148, Jan. 1975

The **MARVELOUS HUMMINGBIRD** Rediscovered. By Crawford H. Greenewalt. 98-101, July 1966

The **MARVELOUS** Maldive Islands. By Alan Villiers. 829-849, June 1957

MARVELS of a Coral Realm. By Walter A. Starck II. 710-738, Nov. 1966

MARY-ROUSSELIERE, GUY: Author-Photographer:

I Live With the Eskimos. 188-217, Feb. 1971

MARYLAND:

Appalachian Valley Pilgrimage. By Catherine Bell Palmer. Photos by Justin Locke. 1-32, July 1949

Chesapeake Country. By Nathaniel T. Kenney. Photos by Bates Littlehales. 370-411, Sept. 1964

"Delmarva," Gift of the Sea. By Catherine Bell Palmer. 367-399, Sept. 1950

Down the Potomac by Canoe. By Ralph Gray. Photos by Walter Meayers Edwards. 213-242, Aug. 1948

Down the Susquehanna by Canoe. By Ralph Gray. Photos by Walter Meayers Edwards. 73-120, July 1950

Maryland on the Half Shell. By Stuart E. Jones. Photos by Robert W. Madden. 188-229, Feb. 1972

The Nation's River. By Allan C. Fisher, Jr. Photos by James L. Stanfield. 432-469, Oct. 1976

Nature's Year in Pleasant Valley. By Paul A. Zahl. 488-525, Apr. 1968

Roving Maryland's Cavalier Country. By William A. Kinney. 431-470, Apr. 1954

The Sailing Oystermen of Chesapeake Bay. By Luis Marden. 798-819, Dec. 1967

Skyway Below the Clouds. By Carl R. Markwith. Photos by Ernest J. Cottrell. 85-108, July 1949
Included: Hyde Field, near Clinton

Waterway to Washington, the C & O Canal. By Jay Johnston. 419-439, Mar. 1960

See also Baltimore; Beltsville; Eastern Shore

MASAI (Tribespeople):

Man of the Serengeti (Television film). 179A-179B, Feb. 1972

Preserving the Treasures of Olduvai Gorge. By Melvin M. Payne. Photos by Joseph J. Scherschel. 701-709, Nov. 1966

Spearing Lions with Africa's Masai. By Edgar Monsanto Queeny. 487-517, Oct. 1954

MASCARENE ISLANDS, Indian Ocean. *See* Mauritius

MASQAT. *See* Muscat and Oman

MASSACHUSETTS:

The American Lobster, Delectable Cannibal. By Luis Marden. Photos by David Doubilet. 462-487, Apr. 1973

Captain Smith's New England . . . and the Pilgrims' Cape Cod. 765, June 1953

Down East Cruise. By Tom Horgan. Photos by Luis Marden. 329-369, Sept. 1952

Founders of New England. By Sir Evelyn Wrench. Photos by B. Anthony Stewart. 803-838, June 1953

How Fruit Came to America. By J. R. Magness. Paintings by Else Bostelmann. 325-377, Sept. 1951

Land of the Pilgrims' Pride. By George W. Long. Photos by Robert F. Sisson. 193-219, Aug. 1947

Literary Landmarks of Massachusetts. By William H. Nicholas. Photos by B. Anthony Stewart and John E. Fletcher. 279-310, Mar. 1950

Massachusetts Builds for Tomorrow. By Robert de Roos. Photos by B. Anthony Stewart. 790-843, Dec. 1966

The Merrimack: River of Industry and Romance. By Albert W. Atwood. Photos by B. Anthony Stewart. 106-140, Jan. 1951

Mountains Top Off New England. By F. Barrows Colton. Photos by Robert F. Sisson. 563-602, May 1951

New England's "Little Portugal." By O. Louis Mazzatenta. 90-109, Jan. 1975

The Old Boston Post Roads. By Donald Barr Chidsey. 189-205, Aug. 1962

Patriots in Petticoats. By Lonnelle Aikman. Paintings by Louis S. Glanzman. 475-493, Oct. 1975

The Post Road Today. Photos by B. Anthony Stewart. 206-233, Aug. 1962

Shrines of Each Patriot's Devotion. By Frederick G. Vosburgh. 51-82, Jan. 1949

Windjamming Around New England. By Tom Horgan. Photos by Robert F. Sisson. 141-169, Aug. 1950
Contents: Beverly; Cape Ann; Cape Cod; Gloucester; Hyannis; Marblehead; Martha's Vineyard; Nantucket; Provincetown; Rockport; Salem; Woods Hole

See also Berkshires; Boston; Buttrick Garden; Cape Cod; Deerfield; Gloucester; Martha's Vineyard; Nantucket; Worcester; *and* Clarke School for the Deaf

MASSANUTTEN MOUNTAIN, Virginia:

Appalachian Valley Pilgrimage. By Catherine Bell Palmer. Photos by Justin Locke. 1-32, July 1949

A **MASTER** Plan for Yellowstone: The Next 100 Years. By George B. Hartzog, Jr. 632-637, May 1972

MASTERPIECES on Tour. By Harry A. McBride. 717-750, Dec. 1948

MATHEMATICIANS. *See* Bowditch, Nathaniel; Newton, Isaac

MATO GROSSO (State), Brazil:
Indians of the Amazon Darkness. By Harald Schultz. 737-758, May 1964

The Jungle Was My Home. By Sasha Siemel. 695-712, Nov. 1952

See also Cinta Larga Indians; Kreen-Akarores; Txukahameis

MATS: America's Long Arm of the Air. By Beverley M. Bowie. Photos by Robert F. Sisson. 283-317, Mar. 1957

MATTERNES, JAY H.: Artist:
"Ice Age Mammals of the Alaskan Tundra," painting supplement. Map of Canada. Mar. 1972

Skull 1470. By Richard E. Leakey. Photos by Bob Campbell. 819-829, June 1973

MATTHEWS, SAMUEL W.: Author:
America Goes to the Fair. 293-333, Sept. 1954

Antarctica: Icy Testing Ground for Space. Photos by Robert W. Madden. 569-592, Oct. 1968

Antarctica's Nearer Side. Photos by William R. Curtsinger. 622-655, Nov. 1971

Bali's Sacred Mountain Blows Its Top. 436-458, Sept. 1963
II. Devastated Land and Homeless People. Photos by Robert F. Sisson. 447-458

Beltsville Brings Science to the Farm. 199-218, Aug. 1953

Hunting the Heartbeat of a Whale. By Paul Dudley White and Samuel W. Matthews. 49-64, July 1956

Nevada Learns to Live With the Atom. 839-850, June 1953

Nevada's Mountain of Invisible Gold. Photos by David F. Cupp. 668-679, May 1968

The Night the Mountains Moved (Montana's 1959 Earthquake). Photos by J. Baylor Roberts. 329-359, Mar. 1960

The Phoenicians, Sea Lords of Antiquity. Photos by Winfield Parks. Paintings by Robert C. Magis. 149-189, Aug. 1974

Science Explores the Monsoon Sea. Photos by Robert F. Sisson. 554-575, Oct. 1967

Scientists Drill at Sea to Pierce Earth's Crust (Project Mohole). Photos by J. Baylor Roberts. 686-697, Nov. 1961

This Changing Earth. 1-37, Jan. 1973

What's Happening to Our Climate? 576-615, Nov. 1976

MATTISON, JAMES A., Jr.: Photographer:
Return of the Sea Otter. By Karl W. Kenyon. 520-539, Oct. 1971

MAUI (Island), Hawaii:
Maui, Where Old Hawaii Still Lives. By Kenneth F. Weaver. Photos by Gordon W. Gahan. 514-543, Apr. 1971

MAURI, CARLO: Photographer:
The Voyage of *Ra II*. By Thor Heyerdahl. Photos by Carlo Mauri and Georges Sourial. 44-71, Jan. 1971

MAURITANIA:
Dry-land Fleet Sails the Sahara. By Jean du

MAURITANIA—*Continued*
Boucher. Photos by Jonathan S. Blair. 696-725, Nov. 1967

Freedom Speaks French in Ouagadougou. By John Scofield. 153-203, Aug. 1966

MAURITIUS, Island of the Dodo. By Quentin Keynes. 77-104, Jan. 1956

MAXWELL, GAVIN: Photographer:
Marsh Dwellers of Southern Iraq. By Wilfred Thesiger. 205-239, Feb. 1958

MAYA (Indians):
Dzibilchaltun. 91-129, Jan. 1959
I. Lost City of the Maya. By E. Wyllys Andrews. 91-109
II. Up From the Well of Time. By Luis Marden. 110-129

Guatemala, Maya and Modern. By Louis de la Haba. Photos by Joseph J. Scherschel. 661-689, Nov. 1974

Into the Well of Sacrifice (Chichén Itzá). 540-561, Oct. 1961
I. Return to the Sacred Cenote. By Eusebio Dávalos Hurtado. 540-549
II. Treasure Hunt in the Deep Past. By Bates Littlehales. 550-561

The Maya. 729-811, Dec. 1975
I. Children of Time. By Howard La Fay. Photos by David Alan Harvey. 729-767
II. Riddle of the Glyphs. By George E. Stuart. Photos by Otis Imboden. 768-791
III. Resurrecting the Grandeur of Tikal. By William R. Coe. 792-798
IV. A Traveler's Tale of Ancient Tikal. Paintings by Peter Spier. Text by Alice J. Hall. 799-811

"Pyramids" of the New World. By Neil Merton Judd. 105-128, Jan. 1948

MAYER, FRED: Photographer:
Little Tibet in Switzerland. By Laura Pilarski. 711-727, Nov. 1968

MAYFLOWER (Ship):
Founders of New England. By Sir Evelyn Wrench. Photos by B. Anthony Stewart. 803-838, June 1953

MAYFLOWER II (Ship):
How We Sailed the New *Mayflower* to America. By Alan Villiers. 627-672, Nov. 1957

"Mayflower II," painting supplement. Nov. 1957

We're Coming Over on the *Mayflower*. By Alan Villiers. 708-728, May 1957

MAYTIME Miracle in Sherwood Gardens. By Nathaniel T. Kenney. 700-709, May 1956

MAZAMA, Mount, Oregon:
Crater Lake Summer. By Walter Meayers Edwards. 134-148, July 1962

When Mt. Mazama Lost Its Top: The Birth of Crater Lake. By Lyman J. Briggs. 128-133, July 1962

MAZATZAL WILDERNESS, Arizona:
The Mazatzal's Harsh but Lovely Land Between. By François Leydet. Photos by Farrell Grehan. 161-167, Feb. 1974

MAZZATENTA, O. LOUIS: Author-Photographer:
New England's "Little Portugal." 90-109, Jan. 1975

MAZZATENTA, O. LOUIS — *Continued*
Photographer

The Azores, Nine Islands in Search of a Future. By Don Moser. 261-288, Feb. 1976

MEANCO (Raft):

Down Mark Twain's River on a Raft. By Rex E. Hieronymus. 551-574, Apr. 1948

MEAT INDUSTRY:

America's "Meat on the Hoof." By William H. Nicholas. 33-72, Jan. 1952

MECCA, Saudi Arabia:

From America to Mecca on Airborne Pilgrimage. By Abdul Ghafur. 1-60, July 1953

Saudi Arabia: Beyond the Sands of Mecca. By Thomas J. Abercrombie. 1-53, Jan. 1966

The Sword and the Sermon. By Thomas J. Abercrombie. 3-45, July 1972

MECH, L. DAVID: Author:

Wolves Versus Moose on Isle Royale. By Durward L. Allen and L. David Mech. 200-219, Feb. 1963

MEDALS. *See* Grosvenor Medal; Hubbard Medal; La Gorce Medal; Special Gold Medal

MEDELLÍN, Colombia:

Cruising Colombia's "Ol' Man River." By Amos Burg. 615-660, May 1947

MEDICINE AND HEALTH:

America's "Meat on the Hoof." By William H. Nicholas. 33-72, Jan. 1952
Included: Pharmaceuticals from glandular by-products — insulin, liver extract, thyroid, adrenocorticotrophic hormone (ACTH), epinephrine (suprarenalin)

Ancient Mesopotamia: A Light That Did Not Fail. By E. A. Speiser. Paintings by H. M. Herget. 41-105, Jan. 1951
Included: Medicine Teams Up With Religion and Magic

Beltsville Brings Science to the Farm. By Samuel W. Matthews. 199-218, Aug. 1953
Included: Antibiotics, hormones

The British Way. By Sir Evelyn Wrench. 421-541, Apr. 1949
Included: William Harvey, William Hunter, John Hunter, Edward Jenner, Florence Nightingale, Lord Lister, Sir Alexander Fleming

Exploring Ancient Panama by Helicopter. By Matthew W. Stirling. Photos by Richard H. Stewart. 227-246, Feb. 1950
Included: Gorgas Memorial Laboratory; yellow fever outbreak in Utivé and control measures taken

First Woman Across Greenland's Ice. By Myrtle Simpson. Photos by Hugh Simpson. 264-279, Aug. 1967
Included: Study of the adrenal glands to learn the effects of stress on human beings

Keeping House for a Biologist in Colombia. By Nancy Bell Fairchild Bates. Photos by Marston Bates. 251-274, Aug. 1948
Included: Rockefeller Foundation laboratory; malaria and yellow fever research

Man's New Servant, the Friendly Atom. By F. Barrows Colton. Photos by Volkmar Wentzel. 71-90, Jan. 1954

Minnesota, Where Water Is the Magic Word. By David S. Boyer. Photos by author and David Brill. 200-229, Feb. 1976

MEDICINE AND HEALTH — *Continued*
Included: Mayo Clinic; University of Minnesota

Nature's Gifts to Medicine. By Lonnelle Aikman. Paintings by Lloyd K. Townsend and Don Crowley. 420-440, Sept. 1974

The New Biology. 355-407, Sept. 1976
I. The Awesome Worlds Within a Cell. By Rick Gore. Photos by Bruce Dale. Paintings by Davis Meltzer. 355-395
II. The Cancer Puzzle. By Robert F. Weaver. 396-399
III. Seven Giants Who Led the Way. Paintings by Ned Seidler. Text by Rick Gore. 401-407

Our Navy's Long Submarine Arm. By Allan C. Fisher, Jr. 613-636, Nov. 1952
Included: Research in night vision, color discernment, hearing, the physiological effects of air pressures, psychological factors in submarine life, the development of physical standards for personnel, and the psychological effect of color and color combinations in submarines

Safari Through Changing Africa. By Elsie May Bell Grosvenor. Photos by Gilbert Grosvenor. 145-198, Aug. 1953
Included: The fight against malaria, tick fever, and trypanosomiasis (sleeping sickness)

Six Months Alone in a Cave. By Michel Siffre. 426-435, Mar. 1975
Included: Biorhythm research

South in the Sudan. By Harry Hoogstraal. 249-272, Feb. 1953

White Magic in the Belgian Congo. By W. Robert Moore. 321-362, Mar. 1952

Wintering on the Roof of the World (Himalayas). By Barry C. Bishop. 503-547, Oct. 1962
Slow Death Threatens Man in the Thin Air of 19,000 Feet. 530-531

With the Nuba Hillmen of Kordofan. By Robin Strachan. 249-278, Feb. 1951
Included: Blackwater fever, cerebrospinal meningitis, jaundice, and control measures taken

Working for Weeks on the Sea Floor. By Jacques-Yves Cousteau. Photos by Philippe Cousteau and Bates Littlehales. 498-537, Apr. 1966

Yemen Opens the Door to Progress. By Harry Hoogstraal. 213-244, Feb. 1952

You and the Obedient Atom. By Allan C. Fisher, Jr. Photos by B. Anthony Stewart and Thomas J. Abercrombie. 303-353, Sept. 1958

See also Aviation Medicine; The Bends; Coal and Coal Mining, for black lung; Cook, James, for discoveries made in the relationship of diet and scurvy; Heart Research; Longevity; Man-in-Sea Project; Mercury (Metallic Element), for mercury poisoning; Peace Corps; Space Medicine; *and* Japan (Those Successful), for effects of pollution

MEDIEVAL EUROPE:

The Age of Chivalry. Book announced. 544-551, Oct. 1969

Canterbury Cathedral. By Kenneth MacLeish. Photos by Thomas Nebbia. 364-379, Mar. 1976

Chartres: Legacy From the Age of Faith. By Kenneth MacLeish. Photos by Dean Conger. 857-882, Dec. 1969

A New Look at Medieval Europe. By Kenneth M. Setton. Paintings by Andre Durenceau and Birney Lettick. 799-859, Dec. 1962

900 Years Ago: the Norman Conquest. By Kenneth M. Setton. Photos by George F. Mobley. 206-251, Aug. 1966

MEDIEVAL EUROPE—*Continued*

The Vikings. By Howard La Fay. Photos by Ted Spiegel. 492-541, Apr. 1970

See also Crusades

MEDITERRANEAN REGION:

Classical Lands of the Mediterranean, map supplement. Dec. 1949

How Fruit Came to America. By J. R. Magness. Paintings by Else Bostelmann. 325-377, Sept. 1951

Lands of the Eastern Mediterranean. Atlas series supplement. Jan. 1959

Our Vegetable Travelers. By Victor R. Boswell. Paintings by Else Bostelmann. 145-217, Aug. 1949

The Phoenicians, Sea Lords of Antiquity. By Samuel W. Matthews. Photos by Winfield Parks. Paintings by Robert C. Magis. 149-189, Aug. 1974

The World in Your Garden. By W. H. Camp. Paintings by Else Bostelmann. 1-65, July 1947

See also Balearic Islands; Bible Lands; Crete; Cyprus; Ischia; Riviera; Sicily; *and* names of countries bordering the Mediterranean

MEDITERRANEAN SEA:

Ancient Shipwreck Yields New Facts—and a Strange Cargo. By Peter Throckmorton. Photos by Kim Hart and Joseph J. Scherschel. 282-300, Feb. 1969

Diving Through an Undersea Avalanche. By Jacques-Yves Cousteau. 538-542, Apr. 1955

Fish Men Discover a 2,200-year-old Greek Ship. By Jacques-Yves Cousteau. 1-36, Jan. 1954

Fish Men Explore a New World Undersea. By Jacques-Yves Cousteau. 431-472, Oct. 1952

Four Years of Diving to the Bottom of the Sea. By Georges S. Houot. 715-731, May 1958

New Tools for Undersea Archeology. By George F. Bass. Photos by Charles R. Nicklin, Jr. 403-423, Sept. 1968

Oldest Known Shipwreck Yields Bronze Age Cargo. By Peter Throckmorton. 697-711, May 1962

Photographing the Sea's Dark Underworld. By Harold E. Edgerton. 523-537, Apr. 1955

Thirty-three Centuries Under the Sea (Shipwreck). By Peter Throckmorton. 682-703, May 1960

To the Depths of the Sea by Bathyscaphe. By Jacques-Yves Cousteau. 67-79, July 1954

Two and a Half Miles Down. By Georges S. Houot. 80-86, July 1954

Underwater Archeology: Key to History's Warehouse. By George F. Bass. Photos by Thomas J. Abercrombie and Robert B. Goodman. 138-156, July 1963

Working for Weeks on the Sea Floor. By Jacques-Yves Cousteau. Photos by Philippe Cousteau and Bates Littlehales. 498-537, Apr. 1966

Yankee Cruises Turkey's History-haunted Coast. By Irving and Electa Johnson. Photos by Joseph J. Scherschel. 798-845, Dec. 1969

MEEN, V. BEN: Author:

Solving the Riddle of Chubb Crater (Quebec). Photos by Richard H. Stewart. 1-32, Jan. 1952

MEGALOPOLIS, U.S.A.:

Washington to Boston, Atlas series supplement. Aug. 1962

MEGARGEE, EDWIN: Artist:

Dogs Work for Man. By Edward J. Linehan. Paintings by Edwin Megargee and R. E. Lougheed. 190-233, Aug. 1958

MEGGERS, BETTY J.: Author-Photographer:

Life Among the Wai Wai Indians. By Clifford Evans and Betty J. Meggers. 329-346, Mar. 1955

MEGIDDO (Armageddon), Israel:

An Archeologist Looks at Palestine. By Nelson Glueck. 739-752, Dec. 1947

Bringing Old Testament Times to Life. By G. Ernest Wright. Paintings by Henry J. Soulen. 833-864, Dec. 1957

MEKONG (River), Southeast Asia:

The Mekong, River of Terror and Hope. By Peter T. White. Photos by W. E. Garrett. 737-787, Dec. 1968

Water War in Viet Nam. By Dickey Chapelle. 272-296, Feb. 1966

MELANESIA:

Yankee Roams the Orient. By Irving and Electa Johnson. 327-370, Mar. 1951

See also Fiji Islands; Louisiade Archipelago; Malekula; New Britain; New Caledonia; New Guinea; Pentecost Island; Solomon Islands; Tanna

MELBOURNE, Australia:

Australia's Pacesetter State, Victoria. By Allan C. Fisher, Jr. Photos by Thomas Nebbia. 218-253, Feb. 1971

Sports-minded Melbourne, Host to the Olympics. 688-693, Nov. 1956

MELHAM, TOM: Author:

Cape Cod's Circle of Seasons. Photos by James P. Blair. 40-65, July 1975

MELLON, ANDREW:

The National Gallery After a Quarter Century. By John Walker. 348-371, Mar. 1967

MELLON, MR. and MRS. PAUL: Art Collection:

In Quest of Beauty. Text by Paul Mellon. 372-385, Mar. 1967

MELLON FAMILY:

Pittsburgh, Pattern for Progress. By William J. Gill. Photos by Clyde Hare. 342-371, Mar. 1965

Pittsburgh: Workshop of the Titans. By Albert W. Atwood. 117-144, July 1949

MELOY, THOMAS: Author:

The Laser's Bright Magic. Photos by Howard Sochurek. 858-881, Dec. 1966

MELTZER, DAVIS: Artist:

The Awesome Worlds Within a Cell. By Rick Gore. Photos by Bruce Dale. 355-395, Sept. 1976

Footprints on the Moon. By Hugh L. Dryden. Paintings by Davis Meltzer and Pierre Mion. 357-401, Mar. 1964

The Incredible Universe. By Kenneth F. Weaver. Photos by James P. Blair. 589-625, May 1974

Mariner Scans a Lifeless Venus. By Frank Sartwell. 733-742, May 1963

Project FAMOUS. 586-615, May 1975

Sailors of the Sky. By Gordon Young. Photos by Emory Kristof and Jack Fields. 49-73, Jan. 1967

MELVILLE, HERMAN:

Literary Landmarks of Massachusetts. By William H. Nicholas. Photos by B. Anthony Stewart and John E. Fletcher. 279-310, Mar. 1950

MELVILLE ISLAND, Australia:

Expedition to the Land of the Tiwi. By Charles P. Mountford. 417-440, Mar. 1956

MEMORIAL DAY CEREMONIES:

'Known but to God' (Unknown Heroes). By Beverley M. Bowie. 593-605, Nov. 1958

MEMORIAL TRIBUTES:

Arnold, H. H.: 1886-1950. 400, Mar. 1950

Bowie, Beverley M.: 1914-1958. 214, Feb. 1959

Carmichael, Leonard: An Appreciation. By Melvin M. Payne. 871-874, Dec. 1973

Chapelle, Dickey: What Was a Woman Doing There? By W. E. Garrett. 270-271, Feb. 1966

Churchill, Winston:
"Be Ye Men of Valour." By Howard La Fay. 159-197, Aug. 1965
The Churchill I Knew. By Dwight D. Eisenhower. 153-157, Aug. 1965
The Final Tribute. Text by Carolyn Bennett Patterson. 199-225, Aug. 1965

Eisenhower, Dwight D.: World's Last Salute to a Great American. By William Graves and other members of the National Geographic staff. 40-51, July 1969

Fleming, Robert V.: 1890-1967. By Melville Bell Grosvenor. 526-529, Apr. 1968

Grosvenor, Elsie May Bell: First Lady of the National Geographic. By Gilbert Hovey Grosvenor. 101-121, July 1965

Grosvenor, Gilbert Hovey: To Gilbert Grosvenor: a Monthly Monument 25 Miles High. By Frederick G. Vosburgh and the staff of the National Geographic Society. 445-487, Oct. 1966

Hildebrand, Jesse Richardson: 1888-1951. 104, Jan. 1952

Kennedy, John F.:
The Last Full Measure. By Melville Bell Grosvenor. 307-355, Mar. 1964
To the Memory of Our Beloved President, Friend to All Mankind. 1A-1B, Jan. 1964

La Gorce, John Oliver: Colleague of the Golden Years. By Gilbert Grosvenor. 440-444, Mar. 1960

Leakey, Louis S. B.: The Leakey Tradition Lives On. By Melvin M. Payne. 143-144, Jan. 1973

Long, George W.: 1913-1958. 215, Feb. 1959

Marshall, George C.: 1880-1959. 113, Jan. 1960

MEMORIALS. *See* Monuments and Memorials; Shrines; War Memorials

MEN, Moose, and Mink of Northwest Angle. By William H. Nicholas. Photos by J. Baylor Roberts. 265-284, Aug. 1947

MEN Against the Hurricane. By Andrew H. Brown. 537-560, Oct. 1950

The **MEN** Who Hid the Dead Sea Scrolls. By A. Douglas Tushingham. Paintings by Peter V. Bianchi. 785-808, Dec. 1958

MEN Who Measure the Earth. By Robert Leslie Conly. Photos by John E. Fletcher. 335-362, Mar. 1956

MENEN, AUBREY: Author:

St. Peter's, Rome's Church of Popes. Photos by Albert Moldvay. 865-879, Dec. 1971

MENÉNDEZ DE AVILÉS, DON PEDRO:

St. Augustine, Nation's Oldest City, Turns 400. By Robert L. Conly. 196-229, Feb. 1966

MENHADEN — Uncle Sam's Top Commercial Fish. By Leonard C. Roy. Photos by Robert F. Sisson. 813-823, June 1949

MENNONITES (People):

Amish Folk: Plainest of Pennsylvania's Plain People. By Richard Gehman. Photos by William Albert Allard. 227-253, Aug. 1965

Artists Look at Pennsylvania. By John Oliver La Gorce. 37-56, July 1948

MENOMINEES (Indians):

Wisconsin's Menominees: Indians on a Seesaw. By Patricia Raymer. Photos by Steve Raymer. 228-251, Aug. 1974

MENZEL, DONALD H.:

Devised Star Charts. 811, Dec. 1957

Author

Exploring Our Neighbor World, the Moon. 277-296, Feb. 1958

Solar Eclipse, Nature's Super Spectacular. By Donald H. Menzel and Jay M. Pasachoff. 222-233, Aug. 1970

MEO (Tribespeople). *See* Hmong

MERCHANT MARINE ACADEMY. *See* U. S. Merchant Marine Academy

MERCHANT MARINE TRAINING SHIPS. *See Dar Pomorza; Georg Stage; Joseph Conrad; and* U. S. Merchant Marine Academy

MERCHANTMAN, Nuclear. *See Savannah,* N.S.

MERCURY (Metallic Element):

Quicksilver and Slow Death. By John J. Putman. Photos by Robert W. Madden. 507-527, Oct. 1972

MERCURY (Planet):

Mariner Unveils Venus and Mercury. By Kenneth F. Weaver. 858-869, June 1975
Included: First geological maps of Mercury

Voyage to the Planets. By Kenneth F. Weaver. Paintings by Ludek Pesek. 147-193, Aug. 1970

MERCURY MISSIONS:

Countdown for Space. By Kenneth F. Weaver. 702-734, May 1961

The Earth From Orbit. By Paul D. Lowman, Jr. 645-671, Nov. 1966

Exploring Tomorrow With the Space Agency. By Allan C. Fisher, Jr. Photos by Dean Conger. 48-89, July 1960

The Flight of *Freedom 7.* By Carmault B. Jackson, Jr. 416-431, Sept. 1961

John Glenn Receives the Society's Hubbard Medal. 827, June 1962

John Glenn's Three Orbits in *Friendship 7:* A Minute-by-Minute Account of America's First Orbital Space Flight. By Robert B. Voas. 792-827, June 1962

The Pilot's Story. By Alan B. Shepard, Jr. Photos by Dean Conger. 432-444, Sept. 1961

MERCURY MISSIONS — *Continued*

Tracking America's Man in Orbit. By Kenneth F. Weaver. Photos by Robert F. Sisson. 184-217, Feb. 1962

MERMAID'S PURSE:

Miracle of the Mermaid's Purse. By Ernest L. Libby. 413-420, Sept. 1959

The MERRIMACK: River of Industry and Romance. By Albert W. Atwood. Photos by B. Anthony Stewart. 106-140, Jan. 1951

MESA DEL NAYAR, Mexico:

Mesa del Nayar's Strange Holy Week. By Guillermo Aldana E. 780-795, June 1971

MESA VERDE NATIONAL PARK, Colorado:

Ancient Cliff Dwellers of Mesa Verde. By Don Watson. Photos by Willard R. Culver. 349-376, Sept. 1948

I See America First. By Lynda Bird Johnson. Photos by William Albert Allard. 874-904, Dec. 1965

Searching for Cliff Dwellers' Secrets. By Carroll A. Burroughs. 619-625, Nov. 1959

Solving the Riddles of Wetherill Mesa. By Douglas Osborne. Paintings by Peter V. Bianchi. 155-195, Feb. 1964

20th-century Indians Preserve Customs of the Cliff Dwellers. Photos by William Belknap, Jr. 196-211, Feb. 1964

Your Society to Seek New Light on the Cliff Dwellers. 154-156, Jan. 1959

MESOPOTAMIA:

Abraham, the Friend of God. By Kenneth MacLeish. Photos by Dean Conger. 739-789, Dec. 1966

Ancient Mesopotamia: A Light That Did Not Fail. By E. A. Speiser. Paintings by H. M. Herget. 41-105, Jan. 1951

See also Euphrates (River)

A MESSAGE From the President of the United States. By Dwight D. Eisenhower. 587, May 1960

MESSINA, Strait of, Italy-Sicily:

Fishing in the Whirlpool of Charybdis. By Paul A. Zahl. 579-618, Nov. 1953

Hydrofoil Ferry "Flies" the Strait of Messina. By Gilbert Grosvenor. 493-496, Apr. 1957

METALS. *See* Minerals and Metals

METALWORK:

Priceless Relics of the Spanish Armada. By Robert Sténuit. Photos by Bates Littlehales. 745-777, June 1969

See also Bronzes; Goldsmithing; Silversmiths; Spanish Treasure

METASEQUOIA (Ancient Tree):

Kew: The Commoners' Royal Garden. By Thomas Garner James. Photos by B. Anthony Stewart. 479-506, Apr. 1950

METEORITES:

Have We Solved the Mysteries of the Moon? By Kenneth F. Weaver. Paintings by William H. Bond. 309-325, Sept. 1973

"Rockhounds" Uncover Earth's Mineral Beauty. By George S. Switzer. 631-660, Nov. 1951

METEORITES — *Continued*

See also Apollo Missions (Apollo 15); Chubb Crater

METEOROLOGY. *See* Climate; Weather; Weather Satellites; Weather Stations and Research

METROPOLIS Made to Order: Brasília. By Hernane Tavares de Sá. Photos by Thomas J. Abercrombie. 704-724, May 1960

METZGER, JOHN: Photographer:

Alaskan Family Robinson. By Nancy Robinson. Photos by John Metzger and Peter Robinson. 55-75, Jan. 1973

MEUSE (River), France-Belgium:

Paris to Antwerp With the Water Gypsies. By David S. Boyer. 530-559, Oct. 1955

MEXCALTITÁN, Mexico:

Mexico's Little Venice. By W. E. Garrett. 876-888, June 1968

MEXICO:

Archeological Map of Middle America, Land of the Feathered Serpent, map supplement. Text on reverse. Oct. 1968

Dzibilchaltun. 91-129, Jan. 1959
I. Lost City of the Maya. By E. Wyllys Andrews. 91-109
II. Up From the Well of Time. By Luis Marden. 110-129

Experiment in International Living. By Hugh M. Hamill, Jr. 323-350, Mar. 1953

From Sun-clad Sea to Shining Mountains. By Ralph Gray. Photos by James P. Blair. 542-589, Apr. 1964

Gifts for the Jaguar God. By Philip Drucker and Robert F. Heizer. 367-375, Sept. 1956

How Fruit Came to America. By J. R. Magness. Paintings by Else Bostelmann. 325-377, Sept. 1951

Hunting the Heartbeat of a Whale. By Paul Dudley White and Samuel W. Matthews. 49-64, July 1956

Into the Well of Sacrifice (Chichén Itzá). 540-561, Oct. 1961
I. Return to the Sacred Cenote. By Eusebio Dávalos Hurtado. 540-549
II. Treasure Hunt in the Deep Past. By Bates Littlehales. 550-561

Lost Kingdom in Indian Mexico. By Justin Locke. 517-546, Oct. 1952

The Maya. 729-811, Dec. 1975
I. Children of Time. By Howard La Fay. Photos by David Alan Harvey. 729-767
Included: Archeological sites: Becan; Bonampak; Chichén Itzá; Dzibilchaltún; Jaina Island; Palenque; Tancah; Tulum; Uxmal; and present-day Maya
II. Riddle of the Glyphs. By George E. Stuart. Photos by Otis Imboden. 768-791
Included: Cobá; Kohunlich; Palenque; Tancah; Yaxchilán

Mexico; Central America, double-sided map supplement. May 1973

Mexico and Central America, Atlas series supplement. Oct. 1961

Mexico and Central America, map supplement. Mar. 1953

Mexico in Motion. By Bart McDowell. Photos by Kip Ross. 490-537, Oct. 1961

Mexico's Little Venice. By W. E. Garrett. 876-888, June 1968

MEXICO — *Continued*

Mexico's Window on the Past (National Museum). By Bart McDowell. Photos by B. Anthony Stewart. 492-519, Oct. 1968

A New Riviera: Mexico's West Coast. By Nathaniel T. Kenney. Photos by Charles O'Rear. 670-699, Nov. 1973

On the Trail of La Venta Man. By Matthew W. Stirling. Photos by Richard H. Stewart. 137-172, Feb. 1947
  Hunting Mexico's Buried Temples. 145-168

"Pyramids" of the New World. By Neil Merton Judd. 105-128, Jan. 1948
  Contents: Chichén Itzá, Cholula, Cuicuilco, Mexico City, Monte Albán, San Lorenzo, Tenayuca, Tenochtitlán, Teotihuacán, Texcoco, Tlaltelolco, Uxmal

Rocks, Ruts, and Sand: Driving the Mexican 1000. By Michael E. Long. 569-575, Oct. 1972

Shells Take You Over World Horizons. By Rutherford Platt. 33-84, July 1949

Skyway Below the Clouds. By Carl R. Markwith. Photos by Ernest J. Cottrell. 85-108, July 1949
  Included: Ciudad Juárez, Hermosillo

Solving the Mystery of Mexico's Great Stone Spheres. By Matthew W. Stirling. Photos by David F. Cupp. 295-300, Aug. 1969

South to Mexico City. By W. E. Garrett. 145-193, Aug. 1968

Two Wheels Along the Mexican Border. By William Albert Allard. 591-635, May 1971

The World in Your Garden (Flowers). By W. H. Camp. Paintings by Else Bostelmann. 1-65, July 1947

See also Acapulco; Baja California; Cozumel Island; Guadalajara; Mesa del Nayar; Mexico City; Miahuatlán; Mujeres, Isla; Raza, Isla; Sierra Madre Occidental; Sonora (State)

MEXICO, Gulf of:

Shrimp Nursery: Science Explores New Ways to Farm the Sea. By Clarence P. Idyll. Photos by Robert F. Sisson. 636-659, May 1965

Shrimpers Strike Gold in the Gulf. By Clarence P. Idyll. Photos by Robert F. Sisson. 699-707, May 1957

See also Dry Tortugas; Gulf Coast, U. S.; Key West

MEXICO, Valley of:

Mexico's Window on the Past. By Bart McDowell. Photos by B. Anthony Stewart. 492-519, Oct. 1968

MEXICO CITY, Mexico:

Mexico, the City That Founded a Nation. By Louis de la Haba. Photos by Albert Moldvay. 638-669, May 1973

Mexico in Motion. By Bart McDowell. Photos by Kip Ross. 490-537, Oct. 1961

Mexico's Booming Capital. By Mason Sutherland. Photos by Justin Locke. 785-824, Dec. 1951

Mexico's Window on the Past (National Museum). By Bart McDowell. Photos by B. Anthony Stewart. 492-519, Oct. 1968

South to Mexico City. By W. E. Garrett. 145-193, Aug. 1968

MEXICO to Canada on the Pacific Crest Trail. By Mike W. Edwards. Photos by David Hiser. 741-779, June 1971

MEYER, ALFRED: Author:

Life and Death in Tana Toradja. By Pamela and Alfred Meyer. 793-815, June 1972

MEYER, CARL:

Amateur Gardener Creates a New Rose. By Elizabeth A. Moize. Photos by Farrell Grehan. 286-294, Aug. 1972

MEYER, PAMELA JOHNSON: Author:

Life and Death in Tana Toradja. By Pamela and Alfred Meyer. 793-815, June 1972
  Author-Photographer

Foxes Foretell the Future in Mali's Dogon Country. 431-448, Mar. 1969

MIAHUATLÁN, Mexico:

Solar Eclipse, Nature's Super Spectacular. By Donald H. Menzel and Jay M. Pasachoff. 222-233, Aug. 1970

MIAMI, Florida:

Cuba's Exiles Bring New Life to Miami. By Edward J. Linehan. Photos by Nathan Benn. 68-95, July 1973

Florida Rides a Space-age Boom. By Benedict Thielen. Photos by Winfield Parks and James P. Blair. 858-903, Dec. 1963

Men Against the Hurricane. By Andrew H. Brown. 537-560, Oct. 1950

Miami's Expanding Horizons. By William H. Nicholas. 561-594, Nov. 1950

See also Vizcaya (Palace)

MIAMI SEAQUARIUM, Miami, Florida:

Aha! It Really Works! (Bait-fishing Heron). By Robert F. Sisson. 143-147, Jan. 1974

MIAO TRIBE. *See* Hmong

MICARD, GASTON, COUNT:

Milestones in My Arctic Journeys. By Willie Knutsen. 543-570, Oct. 1949

MICCOSUKEES (Indians):

Florida's Emerging Seminoles. By Louis Capron. Photos by Otis Imboden. 716-734, Nov. 1969

Threatened Glories of Everglades National Park. By Frederick Kent Truslow and Frederick G. Vosburgh. Photos by Frederick Kent Truslow and Otis Imboden. 508-553, Oct. 1967

MICHAUD, SABRINA and ROLAND:
  Author-Photographers

Bold Horsemen of the Steppes (Turkomans). 634-669, Nov. 1973

Trek to Lofty Hunza—and Beyond. 644-669, Nov. 1975

Winter Caravan to the Roof of the World. 435-465, Apr. 1972

MICHELANGELO:

Florence Rises From the Flood. By Joseph Judge. 1-43, July 1967

The Renaissance Lives On in Tuscany. By Luis Marden. Photos by Albert Moldvay. 626-659, Nov. 1974

Rome: Eternal City With a Modern Air. By Harnett T. Kane. Photos by B. Anthony Stewart. 437-491, Apr. 1957
  Included: St. Peter's Dome and the Sistine Chapel

St. Peter's, Rome's Church of Popes. By Aubrey Menen. Photos by Albert Moldvay. 865-879, Dec. 1971

The Vienna Treasures and Their Collectors. By John Walker. 737-776, June 1950

MICHELANGELO—*Continued*
When in Rome. . . . By Stuart E. Jones. Photos by Winfield Parks. 741-789, June 1970
Included: Sistine Chapel, Vatican

MICHIGAN:
Close-up: U.S.A., Wisconsin, Michigan, and the Great Lakes, map supplement. Text on reverse. Aug. 1973
The Great Lakes: Is It Too Late? By Gordon Young. Photos by James L. Amos and Martin Rogers. 147-185, Aug. 1973
Ice Fishing's Frigid Charms. By Thomas J. Abercrombie. 861-872, Dec. 1958
The Past Is Present in Greenfield Village (Henry Ford Museum). By Beverley M. Bowie. Photos by Neal P. Davis and Willard R. Culver. 96-127, July 1958
Work-hard, Play-hard Michigan. By Andrew H. Brown. 279-320, Mar. 1952
See also Isle Royale

MICHIGAN, Lake, U. S.:
Wisconsin's Door Peninsula. By William S. Ellis. Photos by Ted Rozumalski. 347-371, Mar. 1969
Work-hard, Play-hard Michigan. By Andrew H. Brown. 279-320, Mar. 1952

MICHIGAN STATE UNIVERSITY. *See* Summer Institute of Glaciological and Arctic Sciences

MICMAC INDIANS:
Nomads of the Far North. By Matthew W. Stirling. Paintings by W. Langdon Kihn. 471-504, Oct. 1949

MICROBIOLOGY:
The Awesome Worlds Within a Cell. By Rick Gore. Photos by Bruce Dale. Paintings by Davis Meltzer. 355-395, Sept. 1976

MICROELECTRONICS:
Crystals, Magical Servants of the Space Age. By Kenneth F. Weaver. Photos by James P. Blair. 278-296, Aug. 1968

MICRONESIA:
Feast Day in Kapingamarangi. By W. Robert Moore. 523-537, Apr. 1950
Note: The natives of Kapingamarangi and Nukuoro are Polynesian and differ in language and customs from those of the other island groups in Micronesia.
Micronesia: The Americanization of Eden. By David S. Boyer. 702-744, May 1967
Pacific Wards of Uncle Sam. By W. Robert Moore. 73-104, July 1948
Contents: Trust Territory of Pacific Islands
See also Bikini; Ifalik; Kwajalein; Nauru; Truk Lagoon; Ulithi; Yap Islands

MICROSCOPIC STUDIES:
A Bold New Look at Our Past. The Editor. 62-63, Jan. 1975
Exploring the Mind of Ice Age Man. By Alexander Marshack. 64-89, Jan. 1975
Finding Rare Beauty in Common Rocks. By Lorence G. Collins. 121-129, Jan. 1966
Life in a "Dead" Sea—Great Salt Lake. By Paul A. Zahl. 252-263, Aug. 1967
See also Microbiology; Photography, Microscope

MICROWAVE RADIO RELAY:
New Miracles of the Telephone Age. By Robert Leslie Conly. 87-120, July 1954

MID-ATLANTIC RIDGE:
Exploring the Mid-Atlantic Ridge. By Maurice Ewing. 275-294, Sept. 1948
New Discoveries on the Mid-Atlantic Ridge. By Maurice Ewing. Photos by Robert F. Sisson. 611-640, Nov. 1949

MID-ATLANTIC RIFT:
Project FAMOUS. Photos by Emory Kristof. 586-615, May 1975
I. Where the Earth Turns Inside Out. By J. R. Heirtzler. 586-603
II. Dive Into the Great Rift. By Robert D. Ballard. 604-615

MID-ATLANTIC STATES:
Close-up: U.S.A., The Mid-Atlantic States, map supplement. Text on reverse. Oct. 1976

MID-CENTURY Holland Builds Her Future. By Sydney Clark. 747-778, Dec. 1950

MIDDLE AGES. *See* Byzantine Empire; Medieval Europe; *and* Crusades

MIDDLE AMERICA:
Archeological Map of Middle America, Land of the Feathered Serpent, map supplement. Text on reverse. Oct. 1968
See also Central America; Mexico; *and* Aztecs; Maya

MIDDLE EAST AND NEAR EAST:
Europe and the Near East, map supplement. June 1949
Eyewitness to War in the Holy Land. By Charles Harbutt. 782-795, Dec. 1967
Journey Into the Great Rift: the Northern Half. By Helen and Frank Schreider. 254-290, Aug. 1965
Lands of the Eastern Mediterranean, Atlas series supplement. Jan. 1959
Our Vegetable Travelers. By Victor R. Boswell. Paintings by Else Bostelmann. 145-217, Aug. 1949
The Peoples of the Middle East, map supplement. Text on reverse. July 1972
Sailing with Sindbad's Sons. By Alan Villiers. 675-688, Nov. 1948
Troubled Waters East of Suez. By Ernest M. Eller. 483-522, Apr. 1954
Twilight of the Arab Dhow. By Marion Kaplan. 330-351, Sept. 1974
See also Arab Nations; Bible Lands; Crusades; Cyprus; Iran; Israel; Kurdistan; Red Sea; Sinai; Trucial Coast; Turkey

MIDDLE FORK SALMON (River), Idaho:
White-water Adventure on Wild Rivers of Idaho. By Frank Craighead, Jr. and John Craighead. 213-239, Feb. 1970
Wild River (Television film). 239A-239B, Feb. 1970

MIDDLE ISLAND, Quebec, Canada. *See* St. Mary Islands Sanctuary

MIDDLE MISSISSIPPI CULTURE. *See* Russell Cave, Alabama

The MIDLANDS, England:
Exploring England's Canals. By Bryan Hodgson. Photos by Linda Bartlett. 76-111, July 1974

MIDNIGHT CAVE, Del Rio, Texas:

Six Months Alone in a Cave (Biorhythm Research). By Michel Siffre. 426-435, Mar. 1975

MID-OCEANIC RIFT SYSTEM:

Project FAMOUS. Photos by Emory Kristof. 586-615, May 1975
I. Where the Earth Turns Inside Out. By J. R. Heirtzler. 586-603
II. Dive Into the Great Rift. By Robert D. Ballard. 604-615

This Changing Earth. By Samuel W. Matthews. 1-37, Jan. 1973

MIDSHIPMEN'S Cruise. By William J. Aston and Alexander G. B. Grosvenor. 711-754, June 1948

MIDWAY ISLANDS, Pacific Ocean:

The Gooney Birds of Midway. By John W. Aldrich. 839-851, June 1964

What a Place to Lay an Egg! By Thomas R. Howell. 414-419, Sept. 1971

MIDWEST (Region), U. S.:

Mapping the Nation's Breadbasket. By Frederick Simpich. 831-849, June 1948

North With the Wheat Cutters. By Noel Grove. Photos by James A. Sugar. 194-217, Aug. 1972

The Parks in Your Backyard. By Conrad L. Wirth. 647-707, Nov. 1963
The Midlands. 691-697

Satellites Gave Warning of Midwest Floods. By Peter T. White. Photos by Thomas A. DeFeo. 574-592, Oct. 1969

That Dammed Missouri River. By Gordon Young. Photos by David Hiser. 374-413, Sept. 1971

See also Great Lakes; North Central States

MIGHT Makes Right Among Alaska's Brown Bears. By Allan L. Egbert and Michael H. Luque. 428-442, Sept. 1975

The MIGHTY *Enterprise*. By Nathaniel T. Kenney. Photos by Thomas J. Abercrombie. 431-448, Mar. 1963

The MIGHTY Hudson. By Albert W. Atwood. Photos by B. Anthony Stewart. 1-36, July 1948

MIKONOS, Aegean Islands:

The Isles of Greece: Aegean Birthplace of Western Culture. By Melville Bell Grosvenor. Photos by Edwin Stuart Grosvenor and Winfield Parks. 147-193, Aug. 1972

MILAN, Italy:

Italy Smiles Again. By Edgar Erskine Hume. 693-732, June 1949

MILESTONES in My Arctic Journeys. By Willie Knutsen. 543-570, Oct. 1949

MILITARY ACADEMY. See U. S. Military Academy

MILITARY AIR TRANSPORT SERVICE:

MATS: America's Long Arm of the Air. By Beverley M. Bowie. Photos by Robert F. Sisson. 283-317, Mar. 1957

MILITARY AIRLIFT COMMAND. See 3rd Aerospace Rescue and Recovery Group

MILK:

Deep in the Heart of "Swissconsin." By William H. Nicholas. Photos by J. Baylor Roberts. 781-800, June 1947

MILK — *Continued*

See also Thunder Hill Goat Farm

MILLER, ARDEAN R., III: Photographer:

Through Europe by Trailer Caravan. By Norma Miller. 769-816, June 1957

MILLER, CARL F.: Author:

Life 8,000 Years Ago Uncovered in an Alabama Cave. 542-558, Oct. 1956

Russell Cave: New Light on Stone Age Life. 427-437, Mar. 1958

MILLER, HARRY: Author-Photographer:

The Cobra, India's "Good Snake." 393-409, Sept. 1970

Wild Elephant Roundup in India. Photos by author and James P. Blair. 372-385, Mar. 1969

MILLER, HELEN HILL: Author:

Rotterdam — Reborn From Ruins. Photos by James Blair. 526-553, Oct. 1960

MILLER, MAYNARD M.: Author:

Alaska's Mighty Rivers of Ice. Photos by Christopher G. Knight. 194-217, Feb. 1967

Our Restless Earth. 140-141, July 1964
Author-Photographer
First American Ascent of Mount St. Elias. 229-248, Feb. 1948

MILLER, NORMA: Author:

Through Europe by Trailer Caravan. Photos by Ardean R. Miller III. 769-816, June 1957

MILLER, WAYNE: Photographer:

Henry Hudson's River. By Willard Price. 364-403, Mar. 1962

MILLER, WILLIAM C.: Author-Photographer:

First Color Portraits of the Heavens. 670-679, May 1959

MILLS, Silk:

Silkworms in England Spin for the Queen. By John E. H. Nolan. 689-704, May 1953

MILOS (Island), Aegean Islands:

The Isles of Greece: Aegean Birthplace of Western Culture. By Melville Bell Grosvenor. Photos by Edwin Stuart Grosvenor and Winfield Parks. 147-193, Aug. 1972

MILTON, JOHN:

The British Way. By Sir Evelyn Wrench. 421-541, Apr. 1949

MIN YUEN:

Malaya Meets Its Emergency. By George W. Long. Photos by J. Baylor Roberts and author. 185-228, Feb. 1953

MINAS GERAIS (State), Brazil:

Brazil's Land of Minerals. By W. Robert Moore. 479-508, Oct. 1948

See also Bocaiuva

MINDANAO (Island), Philippines:

First Glimpse of a Stone Age Tribe. 881-882, Dec. 1971

Help for Philippine Tribes in Trouble. By Kenneth MacLeish. Photos by Dean Conger. 220-255, Aug. 1971

MINDANAO (Island), Philippines—*Continued*

The Last Tribes of Mindanao (Television film). 882A-882B, Dec. 1971; 227, Aug. 1972

Seeking Mindanao's Strangest Creatures. By Charles Heizer Wharton. 389-408, Sept. 1948

The Tasadays, Stone Age Cavemen of Mindanao. By Kenneth MacLeish. Photos by John Launois. 219-249, Aug. 1972

MINERALS AND METALS:

Brazil's Land of Minerals. By W. Robert Moore. 479-508, Oct. 1948
  Contents: Bauxite, Beryls, Diamonds, Gold, Iron Ore, Iron Pyrites, Manganese, Mica, Quartz

The Canadian North: Emerging Giant. By David S. Boyer. 1-43, July 1968
  Included: Asbestos, Copper, Gold, Iron, Lead, Nickel, Silver, Uranium, Zinc

Colorado, the Rockies' Pot of Gold. By Edward J. Linehan. Photos by James L. Amos. 157-201, Aug. 1969
  Included: Gold, Lead, Molybdenum, Silver

Exploring the World of Gems. By W. F. Foshag. 779-810, Dec. 1950

Finding Rare Beauty in Common Rocks. By Lorence G. Collins. 121-129, Jan. 1966

The Glittering World of Rockhounds. By David S. Boyer. 276-294, Feb. 1974

In Manchuria Now. By W. Robert Moore. 389-414, Mar. 1947
  Included: Aluminum, Coal, Copper, Gold, Iron, Lead, Magnesite, Molybdenum, Uranium, Zinc

Questing for Gems. By George S. Switzer. 835-863, Dec. 1971

"Rockhounds" Uncover Earth's Mineral Beauty. By George S. Switzer. 631-660, Nov. 1951

Sonora Is Jumping. By Mason Sutherland. 215-246, Feb. 1955
  Included: Cobalt, Copper, Gold, Graphite, Lead, Silver, Tungsten

See also Aluminum; Copper; Diamonds; Gold; Mercury; Phosphate; Uranium

MINES AND MINING:

Brazil's Land of Minerals. By W. Robert Moore. 479-508, Oct. 1948
  Included: Historic mines of Mariana; Ouro Prêto; Sabará; São João del Rei

The Canadian North: Emerging Giant. By David S. Boyer. 1-43, July 1968
  Included: Asbestos, Copper, Gold, Iron, Lead, Nickel, Silver, Uranium, and Zinc mines

Colorado by Car and Campfire. By Kathleen Revis. 207-248, Aug. 1954
  Included: Blackhawk mines; Camp Bird Mine; Climax Mine; Leadville mines; Placer mines near Ute Pass; Smuggler Mine

From Tucson to Tombstone. By Mason Sutherland. 343-384, Sept. 1953
  Included: The Mary G, Morenci open pit, Pearce mines, Tombstone mines

In Manchuria Now. By W. Robert Moore. 389-414, Mar. 1947
  Included: Open-pit coal mine of Fushun; Coal reserves, in general; and the following: Aluminum, Copper, Gold, Iron, Lead, Magnesite, Molybdenum, Shale, Uranium, Zinc

Minnesota Makes Ideas Pay. By Frederick G. Vosburgh. Photos by John E. Fletcher and B. Anthony Stewart. 291-336, Sept. 1949
  Included: Cuyuna, Mesabi, and Vermilion iron

MINES AND MINING—*Continued*

ranges; the Mountain Iron, Embarrass (mine in a lake), and Hull-Rust-Mahoning (Hibbing open-pit) mines; and research on the smelting of taconite and carbonate slate

Montana, Shining Mountain Treasureland. By Leo A. Borah. 693-736, June 1950
  Included: Coal, Copper, Gold, Quartz, Silver, Zinc

Newfoundland, Canada's New Province. By Andrew H. Brown. Photos by author and Robert F. Sisson. 777-812, June 1949
  Included: Undersea iron mines and the lead-zinc-copper mine at Buchans

Questing for Gems. By George S. Switzer. 835-863, Dec. 1971
  Included: Mines in Africa; Asia; Australia

Should They Build a Fence Around Montana? By Mike W. Edwards. Photos by Nicholas deVore III. 614-649, May 1976
  Included: Coal and Copper mines

White Magic in the Belgian Congo. By W. Robert Moore. 321-362, Mar. 1952
  Included: Cobalt, Copper, Diamond, Gold, Tin, and Uranium mines

Work-hard, Play-hard Michigan. By Andrew H. Brown. 279-320, Mar. 1952
  Included: Calumet and Hecla Consolidated Copper mines, Mather Iron Mine, Salt mines

See also Coal and Coal Mining; Copper; Diamonds; Gold and Gold Mining; Mercury (Metallic Element); Opal Mining; Phosphate; Prospectors; Salt Mines; Tin and Tin Mining; Uranium

MINIATURE Monaco. By Gilbert M. and Donna Kerkam Grosvenor. 546-573, Apr. 1963

MINK:

Men, Moose, and Mink of Northwest Angle (Minnesota). By William H. Nicholas. Photos by J. Baylor Roberts. 265-284, Aug. 1947

The Romance of American Furs. By Wanda Burnett. 379-402, Mar. 1948

MINNESOTA:

Easter Greetings From the Ukrainians. By Robert Paul Jordan. Photos by James A. Sugar. 556-563, Apr. 1972

I See America First. By Lynda Bird Johnson. Photos by William Albert Allard. 874-904, Dec. 1965

Ice Fishing's Frigid Charms. By Thomas J. Abercrombie. 861-872, Dec. 1958

Mapping the Nation's Breadbasket. By Frederick Simpich. 831-849, June 1948

Men, Moose, and Mink of Northwest Angle. By William H. Nicholas. Photos by J. Baylor Roberts. 265-284, Aug. 1947

Minnesota, Where Water Is the Magic Word. By David S. Boyer. Photos by author and David Brill. 200-229, Feb. 1976

Minnesota Makes Ideas Pay. By Frederick G. Vosburgh. Photos by John E. Fletcher and B. Anthony Stewart. 291-336, Sept. 1949

Relics From the Rapids (Voyageurs). By Sigurd F. Olson. Photos by David S. Boyer. 413-435, Sept. 1963

The Upper Mississippi. By Willard Price. 651-699, Nov. 1958

See also Mankato

MINNESOTA RIVER, Minnesota:

Satellites Gave Warning of Midwest Floods. By Peter T. White. Photos by Thomas A. DeFeo. 574-592, Oct. 1969

MINOAN CIVILIZATION:

Thera, Key to the Riddle of Minos. By Spyridon Marinatos. Photos by Otis Imboden. 702-726, May 1972

MINOT, North Dakota:

North Dakota Comes into Its Own. By Leo A. Borah. Photos by J. Baylor Roberts. 283-322, Sept. 1951

Satellites Gave Warning of Midwest Floods. By Peter T. White. Photos by Thomas A. DeFeo. 574-592, Oct. 1969

MINUTEMEN of the Civil Air Patrol. By Allan C. Fisher, Jr. Photos by John E. Fletcher. 637-665, May 1956

MION, PIERRE: Artist:

Footprints on the Moon. By Hugh L. Dryden. Paintings by Davis Meltzer and Pierre Mion. 357-401, Mar. 1964

The Next Frontier? By Isaac Asimov. 76-89, July 1976

Robots to the Moon. By Frank Sartwell. 557-571, Oct. 1962

"Teammates in Mankind's Greatest Adventure" (Apollo Astronauts), painting supplement. Sept. 1973

Tektite II. 256-296, Aug. 1971
  I. Science's Window on the Sea. By John G. VanDerwalker. Photos by Bates Littlehales. 256-289
  II. All-girl Team Tests the Habitat. By Sylvia A. Earle. 291-296

MIQUELON. *See* St. Pierre and Miquelon

MIRACLE Men of the Telephone. By F. Barrows Colton. 273-316, Mar. 1947

MIRACLE of the Mermaid's Purse. By Ernest L. Libby. 413-420, Sept. 1959

MIRACLE of the Potholes. By Rowe Findley. Photos by Robert F. Sisson. 570-579, Oct. 1975

MISHMI HILLS, Assam, India:

Caught in the Assam-Tibet Earthquake. By F. Kingdon-Ward. 403-416, Mar. 1952

MISSILE RANGE. *See* Atlantic Missile Range

MISSILES. *See* Guided Missiles; Rockets

The **MISSION** Called 66: Today in Our National Parks. By Conrad L. Wirth. 7-47, July 1966

MISSIONARIES. *See* Mary-Rousseliere, Guy

MISSIONS:

Carnival in San Antonio. By Mason Sutherland. Photos by J. Baylor Roberts. 813-844, Dec. 1947
  Included: Espada, Mission Concepción, San José, San Juan Capistrano, and the Alamo

Cruise to Stone Age Arnhem Land. By Howell Walker. 417-430, Sept. 1949
  Included: Mission stations: Croker Island, Elcho Island, Milingimbi Island, South Goulburn Island, and Yirrkala

Far North with "Captain Mac." By Miriam MacMillan. 465-513, Oct. 1951
  Included: Catholic, Church of England, and Moravian missions

From Tucson to Tombstone. By Mason Sutherland. 343-384, Sept. 1953

MISSIONS — *Continued*

I Live With the Eskimos (Canadian). By Guy Mary-Rousseliere. 188-217, Feb. 1971

See also California, the Golden Magnet; Mesa del Nayar, Mexico; San Diego (California's Plymouth Rock); Sonora (State), Mexico

MISSISSIPPI:

Dixie Spins the Wheel of Industry. By William H. Nicholas. Photos by J. Baylor Roberts. 281-324, Mar. 1949

The Lower Mississippi. By Willard Price. Photos by W. D. Vaughn. 681-725, Nov. 1960

Skyway Below the Clouds. By Carl R. Markwith. Photos by Ernest J. Cottrell. 85-108, July 1949
  Included: East Jackson Airport; Hawkins Field, Jackson; Vicksburg

Today Along the Natchez Trace, Pathway Through History. By Bern Keating. Photos by Charles Harbutt. 641-667, Nov. 1968

See also Natchez; Vicksburg

MISSISSIPPI (River), U. S.:

Down Mark Twain's River on a Raft. By Rex E. Hieronymus. 551-574, Apr. 1948

Gettysburg and Vicksburg: the Battle Towns Today. By Robert Paul Jordan. Map notes by Carolyn Bennett Patterson. 4-57, July 1963

Land of Louisiana Sugar Kings. By Harnett T. Kane. Photos by Willard R. Culver. 531-567, Apr. 1958

The Lower Mississippi. By Willard Price. Photos by W. D. Vaughn. 681-725, Nov. 1960

Mark Twain: Mirror of America. By Noel Grove. Photos by James L. Stanfield. 300-337, Sept. 1975

The Mighty Mississippi. Special Publication announced. 882-886, June 1971

New Orleans: Jambalaya on the Levee. By Harnett T. Kane. Photos by Justin Locke. 143-184, Feb. 1953

New Orleans and Her River. By Joseph Judge. Photos by James L. Stanfield. 151-187, Feb. 1971

St. Louis: New Spirit Soars in Mid-America's Proud Old City. By Robert Paul Jordan. Photos by Bruce Dale. 605-641, Nov. 1965

The Upper Mississippi. By Willard Price. 651-699, Nov. 1958

See also Hannibal, Missouri

MISSISSIPPI VALLEY, U. S.:

"Pyramids" of the New World. By Neil Merton Judd. 105-128, Jan. 1948

MISSISSIPPIAN CULTURE:

Who Were the "Mound Builders"? By George E. Stuart. 783-801, Dec. 1972

See also Russell Cave, Alabama

MISSOURI:

Following the Trail of Lewis and Clark. By Ralph Gray. 707-750, June 1953

Mapping the Nation's Breadbasket. By Frederick Simpich. 831-849, June 1948

Skyway Below the Clouds. By Carl R. Markwith. Photos by Ernest J. Cottrell. 85-108, July 1949
  Included: The Ozarks; St. Louis; Springfield

Through Ozark Hills and Hollows. By Mike W. Edwards. Photos by Bruce Dale. 656-689, Nov. 1970

MISSOURI — *Continued*

The Upper Mississippi. By Willard Price. 651-699, Nov. 1958

See also Hannibal; Kansas City; St. Louis

MISSOURI (River), U. S.:

Following the Trail of Lewis and Clark. By Ralph Gray. 707-750, June 1953

So Long, St. Louis, We're Heading West. By William C. Everhart. 643-669, Nov. 1965

That Dammed Missouri River. By Gordon Young. Photos by David Hiser. 374-413, Sept. 1971

MR. JEFFERSON'S Charlottesville. By Anne Revis. 553-592, May 1950

MR. JEFFERSON'S Monticello. By Joseph Judge. Photos by Dean Conger and Richard S. Durrance. 426-444, Sept. 1966

MITCHELL, CARLETON: Author:

The Bahamas, Isles of the Blue-green Sea. Photos by B. Anthony Stewart. 147-203, Feb. 1958

Ballerinas in Pink. Photos by B. Anthony Stewart. 553-571, Oct. 1957

Capri, Italy's Enchanted Rock. Photos by David F. Cupp. 795-809, June 1970

Finisterre Sails the Windward Islands. Photos by Winfield Parks. 755-801, Dec. 1965

French Riviera: Storied Playground on the Azure Coast. Photos by Thomas Nebbia. 798-835, June 1967

A Fresh Breeze Stirs the Leewards. Photos by Winfield Parks. 488-537, Oct. 1966

More of Sea Than of Land: The Bahamas. Photos by James L. Stanfield. 218-267, Feb. 1967

Our Virgin Islands, 50 Years Under the Flag. Photos by James L. Stanfield. 67-103, Jan. 1968

Time Turns Back in Picture-book Portofino. Photos by Winfield Parks. 232-253, Feb. 1965

To Europe with a Racing Start *(Finisterre)*. 758-791, June 1958

Author-Photographer

Baltic Cruise of the *Caribbee*. 605-646, Nov. 1950

Carib Cruises the West Indies. 1-56, Jan. 1948

MITCHELL, EDGAR D.: Photographer:

The Climb Up Cone Crater. By Alice J. Hall. Photos by Edgar D. Mitchell and Alan B. Shepard, Jr. 136-148, July 1971

MIURA RANCH, Spain:

Holy Week and the Fair in Sevilla. By Luis Marden. 499-530, Apr. 1951

MIYAZAWA, EIJI: Photographer:

Japan's "Sky People," the Vanishing Ainu. By Mary Inez Hilger. 268-296, Feb. 1967

Scientist Studies Japan's Fantastic Long-tailed Fowl. By Frank X. Ogasawara. 845-855, Dec. 1970

Snow Festival in Japan's Far North. 824-833, Dec. 1968

MNONG TRIBE:

Viet Nam's Montagnards. By Howard Sochurek. 443-487, Apr. 1968

MOBILE, Alabama:

Mobile, Alabama's City in Motion. By William Graves. Photos by Joseph J. Scherschel and Robert W. Madden. 368-397, Mar. 1968

MOBLEY, GEORGE F.: Photographer:

Bavaria: Mod, Medieval — and Bewitching. By Gary Jennings. 409-431, Mar. 1974

Chile, Republic on a Shoestring. By Gordon Young. 437-477, Oct. 1973

Finland: Plucky Neighbor of Soviet Russia. By William Graves. 587-629, May 1968

Firebrands of the Revolution. By Eric F. Goldman. 2-27, July 1974

Greenland Feels the Winds of Change. By John J. Putman. 366-393, Sept. 1975

Kyoto and Nara: Keepers of Japan's Past. By Charles McCarry. 836-859, June 1976
  Kyoto Says Happy New Year. 852-859

Lebanon, Little Bible Land in the Crossfire of History. By William S. Ellis. 240-275, Feb. 1970

900 Years Ago: the Norman Conquest. By Kenneth M. Setton. 206-251, Aug. 1966

Norway, Land of the Generous Sea. By Edward J. Linehan. 1-43, July 1971

Parks, Plans, and People: How South America Guards Her Green Legacy. By Mary and Laurance Rockefeller. 74-119, Jan. 1967

Uganda, Africa's Uneasy Heartland. By Howard La Fay. 708-735, Nov. 1971

Under the Dome of Freedom: The United States Capitol. By Lonnelle Aikman. 4-59, Jan. 1964

World's Tallest Tree Discovered. By Melville Bell Grosvenor. 1-9, July 1964

MOCHICA CULTURE:

Finding the Tomb of a Warrior-God. By William Duncan Strong. Photos by Clifford Evans, Jr. 453-482, Apr. 1947

MODERN Miracle, Made in Germany. By Robert Leslie Conly. Photos by Erich Lessing. 735-791, June 1959

MOEHLMAN, PATRICIA DES ROSES:
Author-Photographer

Getting to Know the Wild Burros of Death Valley. Photos by Ira S. Lerner and author. 502-517, Apr. 1972

MOHAMMAD REZA PAHLAVI, Shah (Iran):

Coronations a World Apart. By the Editor. 299, Mar. 1968

Iran: Desert Miracle. By William Graves. Photos by James P. Blair. 2-47, Jan. 1975

Iran's Shah Crowns Himself and His Empress. By Franc Shor. Photos by James L. Stanfield and Winfield Parks. 301-321, Mar. 1968

MOHAMMED (Prophet):

From America to Mecca on Airborne Pilgrimage. By Abdul Ghafur. 1-60, July 1953

The Sword and the Sermon. By Thomas J. Abercrombie. 3-45, July 1972

MOHAWK (River and Valley), New York:

Drums to Dynamos on the Mohawk. By Frederick G. Vosburgh. Photos by B. Anthony Stewart. 67-110, July 1947

See also New York State Thruway

MOHAWKS (Indians):

Drums to Dynamos on the Mohawk. By Frederick G. Vosburgh. Photos by B. Anthony Stewart. 67-110, July 1947

The Mohawks Scrape the Sky (High-iron Workers).

MOHAWKS (Indians)—*Continued*

By Robert L. Conly. Photos by B. Anthony Stewart. 133-142, July 1952

MOHOLE, Project:

Scientists Drill at Sea to Pierce Earth's Crust. By Samuel W. Matthews. Photos by J. Baylor Roberts. 686-697, Nov. 1961

MOHR, CHARLES E.: Author:

Exploring America Underground. 803-837, June 1964

MOIZE, ELIZABETH A.: Author:

Amateur Gardener Creates a New Rose. Photos by Farrell Grehan. 286-294, Aug. 1972

In Touch With Nature. Photos by Steve Raymer. 537-543, Apr. 1974

Turnaround Time in West Virginia. Photos by Jodi Cobb. 755-785, June 1976

MOJAVE DESERT, California:

Californians Escape to the Desert. By Mason Sutherland. Photos by Charles W. Herbert. 675-724, Nov. 1957

The Great Mojave Desert (Television film). 294A-294B, Feb. 1971

The Lure of the Changing Desert. 817-824, June 1954

See also Los Angeles Aqueduct

MOLDVAY, ALBERT: Photographer:

The Changing Face of Old Spain. By Bart McDowell. 291-339, Mar. 1965

Gotland: Sweden's Treasure Island. By James Cerruti. 268-288, Aug. 1973

Hungary: Changing Homeland of a Tough, Romantic People. By Bart McDowell. Photos by Albert Moldvay and Joseph J. Scherschel. 443-483, Apr. 1971

Italian Riviera, Land That Winter Forgot. By Howell Walker. 743-789, June 1963

Madagascar: Island at the End of the Earth. By Luis Marden. 443-487, Oct. 1967

Mexico, the City That Founded a Nation. By Louis de la Haba. 638-669, May 1973

New Era in the Loneliest Continent. By David M. Tyree. 260-296, Feb. 1963

Of Planes and Men. By Kenneth F. Weaver. Photos by Emory Kristof and Albert Moldvay. 298-349, Sept. 1965

Pakistan: Problems of a Two-part Land. By Bern Keating. 1-47, Jan. 1967

The Renaissance Lives On in Tuscany. By Luis Marden. 626-659, Nov. 1974

St. Peter's, Rome's Church of Popes. By Aubrey Menen. 865-879, Dec. 1971

Stockholm, Where "Kvalitet" Is a Way of Life. By James Cerruti. Photos by Albert Moldvay and Jonathan Blair. 43-69, Jan. 1976

Venice Fights for Life. By Joseph Judge. 591-631, Nov. 1972

MOLECULAR BIOLOGY:

The Awesome Worlds Within a Cell. By Rick Gore. Photos by Bruce Dale. Paintings by Davis Meltzer. 355-395, Sept. 1976

MOLENAAR, CORNELIUS and DEE: Photographers:

First American Ascent of Mount St. Elias. By Maynard M. Miller. 229-248, Feb. 1948

MOLLUSKS:

The Magic Lure of Sea Shells. By Paul A. Zahl. Photos by Victor R. Boswell, Jr. and author. 386-429, Mar. 1969

Man-of-war Fleet Attacks Bimini. By Paul A. Zahl. 185-212, Feb. 1952
Included: Sea hares

Shells Take You Over World Horizons. By Rutherford Platt. 33-84, July 1949

X-Rays Reveal the Inner Beauty of Shells. By Hilary B. Moore. 427-434, Mar. 1955

See also Abalone; Chambered Nautilus; Mother-of-Pearl; Nudibranchs; Octopuses; Oyster Fleet; Shipworms; Snails; Squids

MOLUCCAS (Islands), Indonesia:

Magellan: First Voyage Around the World. By Alan Villiers. Photos by Bruce Dale. 721-753, June 1976

Shells Take You Over World Horizons. By Rutherford Platt. 33-84, July 1949

Spices, the Essence of Geography. By Stuart E. Jones. 401-420, Mar. 1949

See also Ternate

MOMADAY, N. SCOTT: Author:

A First American Views His Land. 13-19, July 1976

"MONA LISA" (Leonardo da Vinci):

Escorting Mona Lisa to America. By Edward T. Folliard. 838-847, June 1963

MONACO:

Miniature Monaco. By Gilbert M. and Donna Kerkam Grosvenor. 546-573, Apr. 1963

MONARCH BUTTERFLY:

Found at Last: the Monarch's Winter Home. By Fred A. Urquhart. Photos by Bianca Lavies. 161-173, Aug. 1976

Mystery of the Monarch Butterfly. By Paul A. Zahl. 588-598, Apr. 1963

MONASTERIES:

An Archeologist Looks at Palestine. By Nelson Glueck. 739-752, Dec. 1947
Included: St. Saba, St. George, Mount of Temptation

India's Sculptured Temple Caves. By Volkmar Wentzel. 665-678, May 1953

A Journey to "Little Tibet." By Enakshi Bhavnani. Photos by Volkmar Wentzel. 603-634, May 1951
Included: Himis, Lamayuru, Leh, Phayang, and Pituk monasteries

Searching Out Medieval Churches in Ethiopia's Wilds. By Georg Gerster. 856-884, Dec. 1970

A Woman Paints the Tibetans. By Lafugie. 659-692, May 1949
Included: Alchi, Dongse, Gyangtse, Himis, and Sumur monasteries

See also Great St. Bernard Hospice; Rumtek Monastery; St. Catherine's Monastery

MONGOLIAN PEOPLE'S REPUBLIC:

Journey to Outer Mongolia. By William O. Douglas. Photos by Dean Conger. 289-345, Mar. 1962

MONGOLOIDS, Southern (Malays):

Help for Philippine Tribes in Trouble. By Kenneth MacLeish. Photos by Dean Conger. 220-255, Aug. 1971

Mosaic of Cultures. By Peter T. White. Photos by W. E. Garrett. 296-329, Mar. 1971

MONHEGAN ISLAND, Maine:
  Maine's Lobster Island, Monhegan. By William
  P. E. Graves. Photos by Kosti Ruohomaa. 285-
  298, Feb. 1959

MONITOR (Civil War Gunboat):
  How We Found the *Monitor*. By John G. Newton.
  48-61, Jan. 1975

MONITOR LIZARDS. *See* Komodo Dragons

MONKEY-EATING EAGLES:
  Seeking Mindanao's Strangest Creatures. By
  Charles Heizer Wharton. 389-408, Sept. 1948

MONKEYS:
  Keeping House for a Biologist in Colombia. By
  Nancy Bell Fairchild Bates. Photos by Marston
  Bates. 251-272, Aug. 1948
    Included: Cebus, Douroucouli, Howler, Marmoset,
    Rhesus, Saimiri, Socay, Spider, Woolly
  London's Zoo of Zoos. By Thomas Garner James.
  771-786, June 1953
  Monkeys, Apes, and Man (Television film). 585A-
  585B, Oct. 1971
  Portraits of My Monkey Friends. By Ernest P.
  Walker. 105-119, Jan. 1956
  School for Space Monkeys. 725-729, May 1961
  See also Baboons

MONOLITHS. *See* Easter Island; Stonehenge

MONONGAHELA (River), Pennsylvania:
  Pittsburgh, Pattern for Progress. By William J.
  Gill. Photos by Clyde Hare. 342-371, Mar. 1965
  Pittsburgh: Workshop of the Titans. By Albert W.
  Atwood. 117-144, July 1949

MONROE, JAMES:
  Inside the White House. By Lonnelle Aikman. Photos by B. Anthony Stewart and Thomas Nebbia.
  3-43, Jan. 1961
  The Living White House. By Lonnelle Aikman.
  593-643, Nov. 1966
  Profiles of the Presidents: I. The Presidency and
  How It Grew. By Frank Freidel. 642-687, Nov.
  1964

MONSOONS:
  Science Explores the Monsoon Sea. By Samuel W.
  Matthews. Photos by Robert F. Sisson. 554-575,
  Oct. 1967

MONTAGNARDS (Vietnamese Mountain People):
  American Special Forces in Action in Viet Nam. By
  Howard Sochurek. 38-65, Jan. 1965
  Viet Nam's Montagnards. By Howard Sochurek.
  443-487, Apr. 1968

MONTANA:
  Following the Trail of Lewis and Clark. By Ralph
  Gray. 707-750, June 1953
  From Sun-clad Sea to Shining Mountains. By
  Ralph Gray. Photos by James P. Blair. 542-589,
  Apr. 1964
  Montana, Shining Mountain Treasureland. By Leo
  A. Borah. 693-736, June 1950
  The Night the Mountains Moved (1959 Earth-
  quake). By Samuel W. Matthews. Photos by J.
  Baylor Roberts. 329-359, Mar. 1960
  Sharing the Lives of Wild Golden Eagles. By John
  Craighead. Photos by Charles and Derek Craig-
  head. 420-439, Sept. 1967

MONTANA — *Continued*
  Should They Build a Fence Around Montana? By
  Mike W. Edwards. Photos by Nicholas deVore
  III. 614-657, May 1976
    Growing Up in Montana. 650-657
  See also Glacier National Park; Padlock Ranch;
  Pryor Mountain Wild Horse Range; Red Rock
  Lakes National Wildlife Refuge; Scapegoat Wil-
  derness; Surprise Creek Hutterite Colony

MONTENEGRO (Republic), Yugoslavia:
  Yugoslavia: Six Republics in One. By Robert Paul
  Jordan. Photos by James P. Blair. 589-633, May
  1970

MONTEREY PENINSULA, California:
  California's Land Apart — the Monterey Peninsula.
  By Mike W. Edwards. 682-703, Nov. 1972
  California's Wonderful One (State Highway No. 1).
  By Frank Cameron. Photos by B. Anthony Stew-
  art. 571-617, Nov. 1959

MONTEVIDEO, Uruguay:
  The Purple Land of Uruguay. By Luis Marden.
  623-654, Nov. 1948
  'Round the Horn by Submarine. By Paul C. Stimson. 129-144, Jan. 1948

MONTICELLO (Estate), Virginia:
  Mr. Jefferson's Charlottesville. By Anne Revis.
  553-592, May 1950
  Mr. Jefferson's Monticello. By Joseph Judge. Pho-
  tos by Dean Conger and Richard S. Durrance.
  426-444, Sept. 1966
  Thomas Jefferson: Architect of Freedom. By Mike
  W. Edwards. Photos by Linda Bartlett. 231-259,
  Feb. 1976

MONTREAL, Canada:
  Canada, My Country. By Alan Phillips. Photos by
  David S. Boyer and Walter Meayers Edwards.
  769-819, Dec. 1961
  Montreal Greets the World (Expo 67). By Jules B.
  Billard. 600-621, May 1967
  Quebec's Forests, Farms, and Frontiers. By An-
  drew H. Brown. 431-470, Oct. 1949
  Sea to Lakes on the St. Lawrence. By George W.
  Long. Photos by B. Anthony Stewart and John
  E. Fletcher. 323-366, Sept. 1950

MONUMENT VALLEY, Arizona-Utah:
  Better Days for the Navajos. By Jack Breed. Photos
  by Charles W. Herbert. 809-847, Dec. 1958
  I See America First. By Lynda Bird Johnson. Photos by William Albert Allard. 874-904, Dec. 1965

MONUMENTS, National. *See* National Monuments

MONUMENTS AND MEMORIALS:
  Gettysburg and Vicksburg: the Battle Towns To-
  day. By Robert Paul Jordan. Map notes by Caro-
  lyn Bennett Patterson. 4-57, July 1963
  Literary Landmarks of Massachusetts. By William
  H. Nicholas. Photos by B. Anthony Stewart and
  John E. Fletcher. 279-310, Mar. 1950
    Included: Memorials to: John Adams, Peter Bulke-
    ley, Mary Baker Eddy, Clyde Fitch, Benjamin Frank-
    lin, Louise Imogen Guiney, Henry David Thoreau
  The Nation Honors Admiral Richard E. Byrd. 567-
  578, Apr. 1962
  Paris: Vibrant Heart of France. 285-302, Aug. 1958

MONUMENTS AND MEMORIALS — *Continued*

Pennsylvania Avenue, Route of Presidents. By Dorothea and Stuart E. Jones. Photos by Volkmar Wentzel. 63-95, Jan. 1957

Shrines of Each Patriot's Devotion (United States). By Frederick G. Vosburgh. 51-82, Jan. 1949

Vacation Tour Through Lincoln Land. By Ralph Gray. 141-184, Feb. 1952

Washington: Home of the Nation's Great. By Albert W. Atwood. 699-738, June 1947
Our Magnificent Capital City. Photos by B. Anthony Stewart. 715-738

The Washington National Monument Society. By Charles Warren. 739-744, June 1947

See also Arlington National Cemetery, Virginia; Bell Museum; Harpers Ferry, West Virginia; Mount Vernon, Virginia; Shrines; War Memorials

MOON:

And Now to Touch the Moon's Forbidding Face. By Kenneth F. Weaver. 633-635, May 1969

Awesome Views of the Forbidding Moonscape. 233-239, Feb. 1969

The Earth's Moon, map supplement. Feb. 1969

Exploring Our Neighbor World, the Moon. By Donald H. Menzel. 277-296, Feb. 1958

First Explorers on the Moon. 735-797, Dec. 1969

First Photographs of Planets and Moon Taken with Palomar's 200-inch Telescope. By Milton L. Humason. 125-130, Jan. 1953

Footprints on the Moon. By Hugh L. Dryden. Paintings by Davis Meltzer and Pierre Mion. 357-401, Mar. 1964

Have We Solved the Mysteries of the Moon? By Kenneth F. Weaver. Paintings by William H. Bond. 309-325, Sept. 1973

The Moon Close Up. By Eugene M. Shoemaker. Photos by Ranger 7. 690-707, Nov. 1964

Reaching for the Moon. By Allan C. Fisher, Jr. Photos by Luis Marden. 157-171, Feb. 1959

Robots to the Moon. By Frank Sartwell. Paintings by Pierre Mion. 557-571, Oct. 1962

Surveyor: Candid Camera on the Moon. By Homer E. Newell. 578-592, Oct. 1966

That Orbèd Maiden . . . the Moon. By Kenneth F. Weaver. 207-230, Feb. 1969

What Is It Like to Walk on the Moon? (Apollo 15). By David R. Scott. 326-331, Sept. 1973

See also Apollo Missions

MOON ROCKS:

What the Moon Rocks Tell Us. By Kenneth F. Weaver. 788-791, Dec. 1969

See also Geology, Lunar

MOONQUAKES:

Have We Solved the Mysteries of the Moon? By Kenneth F. Weaver. Paintings by William H. Bond. 309-325, Sept. 1973

MOORE, DAVID: Photographer:

"The Alice" in Australia's Wonderland. By Alan Villiers. Photos by Jeff Carter and David Moore. 230-257, Feb. 1966

New South Wales, the State That Cradled Australia. By Howell Walker. 591-635, Nov. 1967

Okinawa, the Island Without a Country. By Jules B. Billard. Photos by Winfield Parks and David Moore. 422-448, Sept. 1969

MOORE, HILARY B.: Author:

Strange Babies of the Sea (Plankton). Paintings by Craig Phillips and Jacqueline Hutton. 41-56, July 1952

X-Rays Reveal the Inner Beauty of Shells. 427-434, Mar. 1955

MOORE, KENNY: Author:

Coober Pedy: Opal Capital of Australia's Outback. Photos by Penny Tweedie. 560-571, Oct. 1976

MOORE, W. ROBERT: Author:

Portrait of Indochina. By W. Robert Moore and Maynard Owen Williams. Paintings by Jean Despujols. 461-490, Apr. 1951

Power Comes Back to Peiping. By Nelson T. Johnson and W. Robert Moore. 337-368, Sept. 1949

The Spotlight Swings to Suez. 105-115, Jan. 1952

Author-Photographer

Alaska, the Big Land. 776-807, June 1956

Along the Yangtze, Main Street of China. 325-356, Mar. 1948

Angkor, Jewel of the Jungle. Paintings by Maurice Fiévet. 517-569, Apr. 1960

Brazil's Land of Minerals. 479-508, Oct. 1948

Britain Tackles the East African Bush. 311-352, Mar. 1950

Burma, Gentle Neighbor of India and Red China. 153-199, Feb. 1963

Cities of Stone in Utah's Canyonland. 653-677, May 1962

Clove-scented Zanzibar. 261-278, Feb. 1952

Escalante: Utah's River of Arches. 399-425, Sept. 1955

Feast Day in Kapingamarangi. 523-537, Apr. 1950

Grass-skirted Yap. 805-830, Dec. 1952

In Manchuria Now. 389-414, Mar. 1947

Jamaica — Hub of the Caribbean. 333-362, Mar. 1954

Pacific Wards of Uncle Sam. 73-104, July 1948

Progress and Pageantry in Changing Nigeria. 325-365, Sept. 1956

Republican Indonesia Tries Its Wings. 1-40, Jan. 1951

Roaming Africa's Unfenced Zoos. 353-380, Mar. 1950

Scintillating Siam. 173-200, Feb. 1947

Strife-torn Indochina. 499-510, Oct. 1950

Thailand Bolsters Its Freedom. 811-849, June 1961

War and Quiet on the Laos Frontier. 665-680, May 1954

White Magic in the Belgian Congo. 321-362, Mar. 1952

Photographer

Alaska's Warmer Side. By Elsie May Bell Grosvenor. 737-775, June 1956

Because It Rains on Hawaii. By Frederick Simpich, Jr. 571-610, Nov. 1949

Bristlecone Pine, Oldest Known Living Thing. By Edmund Schulman. 355-372, Mar. 1958

Operation Eclipse: 1948. By William A. Kinney. 325-372, Mar. 1949

Pageantry of the Siamese Stage. By D. Sonakul. 201-212, Feb. 1947

South in the Sudan. By Harry Hoogstraal. 249-272, Feb. 1953

MOORE, W. ROBERT: Photographer — *Continued*
Three Whales That Flew. By Carleton Ray. 346-359, Mar. 1962

MOOREA (Island), Society Islands:
Tahiti, "Finest Island in the World." By Luis Marden. 1-47, July 1962

MOORS (People):
Portugal at the Crossroads. By Howard La Fay. Photos by Volkmar Wentzel. 453-501, Oct. 1965
Portugal Is Different. By Clement E. Conger. 583-622, Nov. 1948
See also Alhambra

MOOSE:
Men, Moose, and Mink of Northwest Angle (Minnesota). By William H. Nicholas. Photos by J. Baylor Roberts. 265-284, Aug. 1947
Wolves Versus Moose on Isle Royale. By Durward L. Allen and L. David Mech. 200-219, Feb. 1963

MORAN, EDMOND J.: Author:
Stop-and-Go Sail Around South Norway. Photos by Randi Kjekstad Bull and Andrew H. Brown. 153-192, Aug. 1954

MORAVIANS:
Far North with "Captain Mac." By Miriam MacMillan. 465-513, Oct. 1951
Old Salem, Morning Star of Moravian Faith. By Rowe Findley. Photos by Robert W. Madden. 818-837, Dec. 1970

MORE of Sea Than of Land: The Bahamas. By Carleton Mitchell. Photos by James L. Stanfield. 218-267, Feb. 1967

The MORE Paris Changes. . . . By Howell Walker. Photos by Gordon W. Gahan. 64-103, July 1972

MORE Years With Mountain Gorillas. By Dian Fossey. Photos by Robert M. Campbell. 574-585, Oct. 1971

MORGAN, AUDREY and FRANK: Photographers:
Alaska's Russian Frontier: Little Diomede. 551-562, Apr. 1951

MORGAN, JAMES K.: Author-Photographer:
Last Stand for the Bighorn. 383-399, Sept. 1973

MORGAN, JUDITH and NEIL: Authors:
California's Parched Oasis, the Owens Valley. Photos by Jodi Cobb and Galen Rowell. 98-127, Jan. 1976
California's Surprising Inland Delta. Photos by Charles O'Rear. 409-430, Sept. 1976

MORGAN, LAEL: Author-Photographer:
Atka, Rugged Home of My Aleut Friends. 572-583, Oct. 1974
"Ocean Mammals Are to Us What the Buffalo Was to the Plains Indian." 354-355, Mar. 1973

MORGAN CREEK, Idaho:
Last Stand for the Bighorn. By James K. Morgan. 383-399, Sept. 1973

MORMONS:
Amid the Mighty Walls of Zion. By Lewis F. Clark. 37-70, Jan. 1954
First Motor Sortie into Escalante Land. By Jack

MORMONS — *Continued*
Breed. 369-404, Sept. 1949
Roaming the West's Fantastic Four Corners. By Jack Breed. 705-742, June 1952
Utah's Shining Oasis. By Charles McCarry. Photos by James L. Amos. 440-473, Apr. 1975
The Family: A Mormon Shrine. 459-463

MOROCCO:
From Sea to Sahara in French Morocco. By Jean and Franc Shor. 147-188, Feb. 1955
Morocco, Land of the Farthest West. By Thomas J. Abercrombie. 834-865, June 1971
Trek by Mule Among Morocco's Berbers. By Victor Englebert. 850-875, June 1968
When the President Goes Abroad (Eisenhower). By Gilbert M. Grosvenor. 588-649, May 1960

MORRIS, JOE ALEX: Author:
Venice, City of Twilight Splendor. Photos by John Scofield. 543-569, Apr. 1961

MORRISON, HEDDA: Author-Photographer:
Jungle Journeys in Sarawak. 710-736, May 1956

MORRISTOWN, New Jersey:
Shrines of Each Patriot's Devotion. By Frederick G. Vosburgh. 51-82, Jan. 1949

MORTON, H. V.: Author:
High Road in the Pyrenees. Photos by Justin Locke. 299-334, Mar. 1956
In the London of the New Queen. 291-342, Sept. 1953
Lake District, Poets' Corner of England. Photos by David S. Boyer. 511-545, Apr. 1956
The Magic Road Round Ireland. Photos by Robert F. Sisson. 293-333, Mar. 1961

MOSAIC of Cultures (Southeast Asia). By Peter T. White. Photos by W. E. Garrett. 296-329, Mar. 1971

MOSAICS:
Here Rest in Honored Glory. . . . By Howell Walker. 739-768, June 1957
Mount Sinai's Holy Treasures (St. Catherine's Monastery). By Kurt Weitzmann. Photos by Fred Anderegg. 109-127, Jan. 1964
Roman Life in 1,600-year-old Color Pictures. By Gino Vinicio Gentili. Photos by Duncan Edwards. 211-229, Feb. 1957

MOSCOW, U.S.S.R.:
An American in Russia's Capital. By Thomas T. Hammond. Photos by Dean Conger. 297-351, Mar. 1966

MOSELEY, MICHAEL E.: Author:
Chan Chan, Peru's Ancient City of Kings. By Michael E. Moseley and Carol J. Mackey. Photos by David Brill. 318-345, Mar. 1973

MOSER, DON: Author:
The Azores, Nine Islands in Search of a Future. Photos by O. Louis Mazzatenta. 261-288, Feb. 1976
Big Thicket of Texas. Photos by Blair Pittman. 504-529, Oct. 1974

MOSES:
In Search of Moses. By Harvey Arden. Photos by Nathan Benn. 2-37, Jan. 1976

MOSES, Lake, Washington:
From Sagebrush to Roses on the Columbia. By Leo A. Borah. 571-611, Nov. 1952

MOSIER, ROBERT H.: Author-Photographer:
The GI and the Kids of Korea. 635-664, May 1953

MOSLEMS:
Abraham, the Friend of God. By Kenneth MacLeish. Photos by Dean Conger. 739-789, Dec. 1966
Afghanistan: Crossroad of Conquerors. By Thomas J. Abercrombie. 297-345, Sept. 1968
Crusader Lands Revisited. By Harold Lamb. Photos by David S. Boyer. 815-852, Dec. 1954
Delhi, Capital of a New Dominion. By Phillips Talbot. 597-630, Nov. 1947
From America to Mecca on Airborne Pilgrimage. By Abdul Ghafur. 1-60, July 1953
Holy Land, My Country. By His Majesty King Hussein of Jordan. 784-789, Dec. 1964
The Idyllic Vale of Kashmir. By Volkmar Wentzel. 523-550, Apr. 1948
Jerusalem, My Home. By Bertha Spafford Vester. 826-847, Dec. 1964
Jerusalem, the Divided City. By John Scofield. Photos by Brian Brake. 492-531, Apr. 1959
The Other Side of Jordan. By Luis Marden. 790-825, Dec. 1964
Reunited Jerusalem Faces Its Problems. By Kenneth MacLeish. Photos by Ted Spiegel. 835-871, Dec. 1968
Saudi Arabia: Beyond the Sands of Mecca. By Thomas J. Abercrombie. 1-53, Jan. 1966
Station Wagon Odyssey: Baghdad to Istanbul. By William O. Douglas. 48-87, Jan. 1959
The Sword and the Sermon. By Thomas J. Abercrombie. 3-45, July 1972
West From the Khyber Pass. By William O. Douglas. Photos by Mercedes H. Douglas and author. 1-44, July 1958
See also Berbers; Ismaili; Kazakhs; Ma'dan; Moors; Mozabites; Sikhs; Tuareg; Turkomans

MOSQUES:
From America to Mecca on Airborne Pilgrimage. By Abdul Ghafur. 1-60, July 1953
Included: The Kaaba, in the courtyard of the Great Mosque, Mecca; Masjid-al-Nabi (Mosque of the Prophet), in Medina; a mosque in Kuba; and Husain's tomb in Karbala
Journey Into Troubled Iran. By George W. Long. Photos by J. Baylor Roberts. 425-464, Oct. 1951
Included: Masjid-i-Shah (King's Mosque), Masjid Sheik Lutf Ullah, and the mosque at Qum
Turkey Paves the Path of Progress. By Maynard Owen Williams. 141-186, Aug. 1951
Included: Beyazit, Blue Mosque, Eyüp Ansari, Suleiman the Magnificent, Yeni Cami (New Mosque), Yeşil Cami (Green Mosque)

MOSQUITOES:
Exploring Ancient Panama by Helicopter. By Matthew W. Stirling. Photos by Richard H. Stewart. 227-246, Feb. 1950
Included: Aedes aegypti and Haemagogus mosquitoes
Keeping House for a Biologist in Colombia. By Nancy Bell Fairchild Bates. Photos by Marston Bates. 251-274, Aug. 1948
Included: Anopheles and Haemagogus mosquitoes

"A MOST Fantastic Voyage": The Story of Apollo 8's Rendezvous With the Moon. By Sam C. Phillips. 593-631, May 1969

The MOST Mexican City, Guadalajara. By Bart McDowell. Photos by Volkmar Wentzel. 412-441, Mar. 1967

MOTAGUA FAULT, Guatemala:
Earthquake in Guatemala. By Bart McDowell. Photos by W. E. Garrett and Robert W. Madden. 810-829, June 1976

MOTHER-OF-PEARL:
Twenty Fathoms Down for Mother-of-Pearl. By Winston Williams. Photos by Bates Littlehales. 512-529, Apr. 1962
See also Abalone

MOTHS:
Moths That Behave Like Hummingbirds. Photos by Treat Davidson. 770-775, June 1965

MOTILONES (Indians):
Venezuela Builds on Oil. By Thomas J. Abercrombie. 344-387, Mar. 1963

MOTORCYCLE RACES:
The Manx and Their Isle of Man. By Veronica Thomas. Photos by Ted H. Funk. 426-444, Sept. 1972
Included: International Tourist Trophy Races ("T.T."); Manx Grand Prix

MOTORCYCLE TRIPS:
Two Wheels Along the Mexican Border. By William Albert Allard. 591-635, May 1971

MOULIN, RAYMOND: Photographer:
Saving Earth's Oldest Living Things. By Andrew H. Brown. Photos by Raymond Moulin and author. 679-695, May 1951

MOUND BUILDERS (Ancient Indians):
"Pyramids" of the New World. By Neil Merton Judd. 105-128, Jan. 1948
Who Were the "Mound Builders"? By George E. Stuart. 783-801, Dec. 1972

MOUNDS. See Jericho, Jordan (The Ghosts of Jericho; Jericho Gives Up Its Secrets); La Venta, Mexico; Panama (Exploring Ancient Panama; Exploring the Past); Tepe Gawra

MOUNIER, BRUCE: Photographer:
Strange March of the Spiny Lobster. By William F. Herrnkind. Photos by Rick Frehsee and Bruce Mounier. 819-831, June 1975

MOUNT KENNEDY YUKON EXPEDITION:
Canada's Mount Kennedy. 1-33, July 1965
I. The Discovery. By Bradford Washburn. 1-3
II. A Peak Worthy of the President. By Robert F. Kennedy. 5-9
III. The First Ascent. By James W. Whittaker. Photos by William Albert Allard. 11-33

MOUNT McKINLEY NATIONAL PARK, Alaska:
Mount McKinley Conquered by New Route. By Bradford Washburn. 219-248, Aug. 1953
Wildlife of Mount McKinley National Park. By Adolph Murie. Paintings by Walter A. Weber. 249-270, Aug. 1953

MOUNT RAINIER NATIONAL PARK, Washington. See Pacific Crest Trail; Rainier, Mount

MOUNT RUSHMORE NATIONAL MEMORIAL. *See* Rushmore, Mount

MOUNT SINAI EXPEDITIONS:

Island of Faith in the Sinai Wilderness (St. Catherine's Monastery). By George H. Forsyth. Photos by Robert F. Sisson. 82-106, Jan. 1964
  Sponsors: University of Michigan, Princeton University, University of Alexandria

Mount Sinai's Holy Treasures (St. Catherine's Monastery). By Kurt Weitzmann. Photos by Fred Anderegg. 109-127, Jan. 1964

Sinai Sheds New Light on the Bible. By Henry Field. Photos by William B. and Gladys Terry. 795-815, Dec. 1948
  Sponsor: University of California African Expedition

MOUNT VERNON, Virginia:

Mount Vernon Lives On. By Lonnelle Aikman. 651-682, Nov. 1953

MOUNTAIN CLIMBING:

American and Geographic Flags Top Everest. By Melvin M. Payne. Photos by Barry C. Bishop. 157-157C, Aug. 1963

Beyond Everest. By Sir Edmund Hillary. 579-610, Nov. 1955

Canada's Mount Kennedy. 1-33, July 1965
  I. The Discovery. By Bradford Washburn. 1-3
  II. A Peak Worthy of the President. By Robert F. Kennedy. 5-9
  III. The First Ascent. By James W. Whittaker. Photos by William Albert Allard. 11-33

Climbing Our Northwest Glaciers. Photos by Bob and Ira Spring. 103-114, July 1953

Cloud Gardens in the Tetons. By Frank and John Craighead. 811-830, June 1948

Colorado by Car and Campfire. By Kathleen Revis. 207-248, Aug. 1954

Colorado's Friendly Topland (Rocky Mountains). By Robert M. Ormes. 187-214, Aug. 1951

El Sangay, Fire-breathing Giant of the Andes. By G. Edward Lewis. 117-138, Jan. 1950

The Fabulous Sierra Nevada. By J. R. Challacombe. 825-843, June 1954

First American Ascent of Mount St. Elias. By Maynard M. Miller. 229-248, Feb. 1948

First Conquest of Antarctica's Highest Peaks. By Nicholas B. Clinch. 836-863, June 1967

The First Traverse (Everest). By Thomas F. Hornbein and William F. Unsoeld. 509-513, Oct. 1963

High Adventure in the Himalayas. By Thomas Weir. 193-234, Aug. 1952

How We Climbed Everest. By Barry C. Bishop. 477-507, Oct. 1963

Mount McKinley Conquered by New Route. By Bradford Washburn. 219-248, Aug. 1953

Mount Rainier: Testing Ground for Everest. By Barry C. Bishop. 688-711, May 1963

New Guinea's Paradise of Birds. By E. Thomas Gilliard. 661-688, Nov. 1951
  Note: The true summit of Mount Wilhelm is reached.

Sierra High Trip. By David R. Brower. 844-868, June 1954

Six to the Summit (Everest). By Norman G. Dyhrenfurth. Photos by Barry C. Bishop. 460-473, Oct. 1963

Skyline Trail from Maine to Georgia. By Andrew H. Brown. Photos by Robert F. Sisson. 219-251, Aug. 1949

MOUNTAIN CLIMBING—*Continued*

Switzerland's Enchanted Val d'Hérens. By Georgia Engelhard Cromwell. 825-848, June 1955

To Torre Egger's Icy Summit. By Jim Donini. 813-823, Dec. 1976

Triumph on Everest. 1-63, July 1954
  I. Siege and Assault. By Sir John Hunt. 1-43
  II. The Conquest of the Summit. By Sir Edmund Hillary. 45-63

Wintering on the Roof of the World (Himalayas). By Barry C. Bishop. 503-547, Oct. 1962

See also Outward Bound School; Rock Climbing

MOUNTAIN LIONS:

Stalking the Mountain Lion—to Save Him. By Maurice G. Hornocker. 638-655, Nov. 1969

MOUNTAIN PEOPLE, American:

American Mountain People. Special Publication announced. 865-868, June 1973

See also Adirondack Mountains; Blue Ridge; Cades Cove; Cumberland Country; Ozark Plateau; West Virginia

MOUNTAIN VILLAGE, Alaska:

The Curlew's Secret. By Arthur A. Allen. 751-770, Dec. 1948

MOUNTAIN Voices, Mountain Days. By Bryan Hodgson. Photos by Linda Bartlett. 118-146, July 1972

MOUNTAINBURG, Arkansas:

An Ozark Family Carves a Living and a Way of Life. Photos by Bruce Dale. 124-133, July 1975

MOUNTAINS:

Afoot in Roadless Nepal. By Toni Hagen. 361-405, Mar. 1960
  Contents: Himalaya, Mahabharat, and Siwalik Ranges

A Map Maker Looks at the United States. By Newman Bumstead. 705-748, June 1951
  Included: Big Hole, Blue, Cascades, Olympics, Rockies, Sawatch, Sierra Nevada, Tetons, Wasatch, Wenatchee

Mountains Top Off New England. By F. Barrows Colton. Photos by Robert F. Sisson. 563-602, May 1951
  Contents: Berkshires, Green Mountains, White Mountains

New Guinea's Paradise of Birds. By E. Thomas Gilliard. 661-688, Nov. 1951
  Included: Bismarck Mountains (including the climbing of Mount Wilhelm); Hagen Range; Kubor Range

New Zealand, Pocket Wonder World. By Howell Walker. 419-460, Apr. 1952

The Night the Mountains Moved (Montana's 1959 Earthquake). By Samuel W. Matthews. Photos by J. Baylor Roberts. 329-359, Mar. 1960

Our Navy Explores Antarctica. By Richard E. Byrd. U. S. Navy official photos. 429-522, Oct. 1947

Preserving America's Last Great Wilderness (Alaska). Text by David Jeffery. 769-791, June 1975
  Included: Aniakchak Caldera; Brooks Range; Katmai; McKinley; Wrangell

Skyline Trail from Maine to Georgia. By Andrew H. Brown. Photos by Robert F. Sisson. 219-251, Aug. 1949

This Changing Earth. By Samuel W. Matthews. 1-37, Jan. 1973

See also names of specific mountain ranges

MOUNTAINS, Lunar. *See* Apollo Missions (Apollo 15)

MOUNTAINS, Submarine. *See* Ocean Floors

MOUNTAINS of the Moon (Ruwenzori). By Paul A. Zahl. 412-434, Mar. 1962

MOUNTAINTOP War in Remote Ladakh. By W. E. Garrett. 664-687, May 1963

MOUNTFORD, CHARLES P.: Author:
Expedition to the Land of the Tiwi. 417-440, Mar. 1956
Exploring Stone Age Arnhem Land. Photos by Howell Walker. 745-782, Dec. 1949

MOUSE RIVER, Canada-U. S.:
Satellites Gave Warning of Midwest Floods. By Peter T. White. Photos by Thomas A. DeFeo. 574-592, Oct. 1969

MOYAL, MAURICE: Author:
Sheep Trek in the French Alps. Photos by Marcel Coen. 545-564, Apr. 1952

MOYNIHAN, MICHAEL: Author:
The Swans of Abbotsbury. Photos by Barnet Saidman. 563-570, Oct. 1959

MOZABITES:
Oasis-hopping in the Sahara. By Maynard Owen Williams. 209-236, Feb. 1949

MOZAMBIQUE:
Mozambique: Land of the Good People. By Volkmar Wentzel. 197-231, Aug. 1964
Safari Through Changing Africa. By Elsie May Bell Grosvenor. Photos by Gilbert Grosvenor. 145-198, Aug. 1953

MRU TRIBE:
The Peaceful Mrus of Bangladesh. By Claus-Dieter Brauns. 267-286, Feb. 1973

MUDIE, COLIN:
Braving the Atlantic by Balloon *(Small World)*. By Arnold Eiloart. 123-146, July 1959

MUDSKIPPERS:
Who Says Fish Can't Climb Trees? By Ivan Polunin. 85-91, Jan. 1972

MUDSLIDES:
Southern California's Trial by Mud and Water. By Nathaniel T. Kenney. Photos by Bruce Dale. 552-573, Oct. 1969

MUIR, JOHN:
John Muir's Wild America. By Harvey Arden. Photos by Dewitt Jones. 433-461, Apr. 1973
John Muir's Wild America. Special Publication announced. 860-864, June 1976

MUJERES, Isla, Mexico:
Into the Lairs of "Sleeping" Sharks. By Eugenie Clark. Photos by David Doubilet. 570-584, Apr. 1975

MUKDEN, China. *See* Shenyang

MULES:
Trek by Mule Among Morocco's Berbers. By Victor Englebert. 850-875, June 1968

MULLER, KAL: Author-Photographer:
Land Diving With the Pentecost Islanders. 799-817, Dec. 1970
Taboos and Magic Rule Namba Lives. 57-83, Jan. 1972
Tanna Awaits the Coming of John Frum. 706-715, May 1974

MUMMIES:
Ancient Cliff Dwellers of Mesa Verde. By Don Watson. Photos by Willard R. Culver. 349-376, Sept. 1948
Contents: Mummification by natural dehydration; the famous mummy "Esther"
A Lady From China's Past. Photos from *China Pictorial.* Text by Alice J. Hall. 660-681, May 1974
Lifelike Man Preserved 2,000 Years in Peat. By P. V. Glob. 419-430, Mar. 1954
See also Tutankhamun

MUNICH, Germany:
Bavaria: Mod, Medieval—and Bewitching. By Gary Jennings. Photos by George F. Mobley. 409-431, Mar. 1974

MUÑOZ, JUAN: Author-Photographer:
Cliff Dwellers of the Bering Sea. 129-146, Jan. 1954

MUNROE, JOE: Photographer:
The Bonins and Iwo Jima Go Back to Japan. By Paul Sampson. 128-144, July 1968

MURCHISON MOUNTAINS, New Zealand:
Finding an "Extinct" New Zealand Bird. By R. V. Francis Smith. 393-401, Mar. 1952

MURCIA, Spain:
Spain's Silkworm Gut. By Luis Marden. 100-108, July 1951

MURIA GONDS (Tribespeople):
New Life for India's Villagers. By Anthony and Georgette Dickey Chapelle. 572-588, Apr. 1956

MURIE, ADOLPH: Author:
Wildlife of Mount McKinley National Park. Paintings by Walter A. Weber. 249-270, Aug. 1953

MUROC DRY LAKE, California:
Flying in the "Blowtorch" Era. By Frederick G. Vosburgh. 281-322, Sept. 1950

MURPHY, GRACE E. BARSTOW: Photographer:
Peru Profits from Sea Fowl. By Robert Cushman Murphy. Photos by author and Grace E. Barstow Murphy. 395-413, Mar. 1959

MURPHY, JOHN F., Jr.: Author:
Ambassadors of Good Will: The Peace Corps. By Sargent Shriver and Peace Corps Volunteers. 297-345, Sept. 1964
Gabon. 325-329

MURPHY, ROBERT CUSHMAN: Author-Photographer:
Peru Profits from Sea Fowl. Photos by author and Grace E. Barstow Murphy. 395-413, Mar. 1959

MURRES:
Sea Bird Cities Off Audubon's Labrador. By Arthur A. Allen. 755-774, June 1948

MURUNG (People):
Bangladesh: Hope Nourishes a New Nation. By William S. Ellis. Photos by Dick Durrance II. 295-333, Sept. 1972

MÚSA, Gebel (Mountain), Egypt. *See* Sinai, Mount

MUSCAT AND OMAN:
Troubled Waters East of Suez. By Ernest M. Eller. 483-522, Apr. 1954
See also Oman

MUSEUM OF SCIENCE, Boston, Massachusetts: Expeditions. *See* Mount Kennedy Yukon Expedition

MUSEUMS:
The DAR Story. By Lonnelle Aikman. Photos by B. Anthony Stewart and John E. Fletcher. 565-598, Nov. 1951
> Included: Exhibits of early Americana

Florence Rises From the Flood. By Joseph Judge. 1-43, July 1967
> Included: Archeological Museum, Bardini Museum, Bargello Museum, Horne Museum, Institute and Museum of the History of Science, Uffizi

See also American Museum of Natural History; Bell Museum; Corning Museum of Glass; Desert Museum; Eastman, George, for Eastman House; Explorers Hall, NGS; Hearst San Simeon State Historical Monument; Henry E. Huntington Library and Art Gallery; Henry Ford Museum; Hermitage; Kunsthistorisches Museum; Louvre; National Gallery of Art; National Museum of Anthropology, Mexico City; Smithsonian Institution; *and* Mystic Seaport, for Maritime Museum; New York (The World in New York City); Worcester, Massachusetts, for arms and armor

MUSHROOMS:
Bizarre World of the Fungi. By Paul A. Zahl. 502-527, Oct. 1965

MUSIC AND MUSICIANS:
The British Way. By Sir Evelyn Wrench. 421-541, Apr. 1949
> Included: Sir William Gilbert and Sir Arthur Sullivan

Carnival in Trinidad. By Howard La Fay. Photos by Winfield Parks. 693-701, Nov. 1971

Hunting Musical Game in West Africa. By Arthur S. Alberts. 262-282, Aug. 1951

Miami's Expanding Horizons. By William H. Nicholas. 561-594, Nov. 1950
> Included: Barry College Department of Music, Miami Civic Music Association, Opera Guild of Miami, Philharmonic Society of Greater Miami, University of Miami School of Music

Old Salem, Morning Star of Moravian Faith. By Rowe Findley. Photos by Robert W. Madden. 818-837, Dec. 1970
> Included: Music of the Moravians

The President's Music Men (Marine Band). By Stuart E. Jones. Photos by William W. Campbell III. 752-766, Dec. 1959

Utah's Shining Oasis. By Charles McCarry. Photos by James L. Amos. 440-473, Apr. 1976
> Included: Ballet West, Mormon Tabernacle Choir, Utah Symphony Orchestra

Vienna, City of Song. By Peter T. White. Photos by John Launois. 739-779, June 1968

See also Recordings, NGS; Songs; *and* Austria (Building a New Austria); Berkshires, for Berkshire Music Festival; China (A Lady From); Hungary; Library of Congress; New Orleans, Louisiana, for jazz; Ozark Plateau, for folk music

MUSK OXEN:
Domesticating the Wild and Woolly Musk Ox. By

MUSK OXEN — *Continued*
John J. Teal, Jr. Photos by Robert W. Madden. 862-879, June 1970

MUSKRATS:
The Romance of American Furs. By Wanda Burnett. 379-402, Mar. 1948

MUSTANG, Remote Realm in Nepal. By Michel Peissel. 579-604, Oct. 1965

MUTATIONS. *See* Albino Animals; Goldfish; Onagadori

MY Backyard, the Adirondacks. By Anne LaBastille. Photos by David Alan Harvey. 616-639, May 1975

MY Life Among Wild Chimpanzees. By Jane Goodall. Photos by Baron Hugo van Lawick and author. 272-308, Aug. 1963

MY Life in Forbidden Lhasa. By Heinrich Harrer. 1-48, July 1955

MY Life in the Valley of the Moon. By H. H. Arnold. Photos by Willard R. Culver. 689-716, Dec. 1948

MY Life With Africa's Little People. By Anne Eisner Putnam. 278-302, Feb. 1960

MY Neighbors Hold to Mountain Ways. By Malcolm Ross. Photos by Flip Schulke. 856-880, June 1958

MYCOLOGY:
Bizarre World of the Fungi. By Paul A. Zahl. 502-527, Oct. 1965

MYOJIN ISLAND (Volcano), Pacific Ocean:
The Explosive Birth of Myojin Island. By Robert S. Dietz. 117-128, Jan. 1954

MYSORE (State), India:
Mysore Celebrates the Death of a Demon. By Luc Bouchage. Photos by Ylla. 706-711, May 1958
Wild Elephant Roundup in India. By Harry Miller. Photos by author and James P. Blair. 372-385, Mar. 1969

MYSTERY of the Ancient Nazca Lines. Photos by Loren McIntyre. 716-728, May 1975

MYSTERY of the Monarch Butterfly. By Paul A. Zahl. 588-598, Apr. 1963

MYSTERY Shrouds the Biggest Planet (Jupiter). By Kenneth F. Weaver. 285-294, Feb. 1975

MYSTIC SEAPORT, Connecticut:
The Age of Sail Lives On at Mystic. By Alan Villiers. Photos by Weston Kemp. 220-239, Aug. 1968

MZABIS (People). *See* Mozabites

MZIMA SPRINGS, Tsavo National Park, Kenya:
Mzima, Kenya's Spring of Life. By Joan and Alan Root. 350-373, Sept. 1971

N

NAGA HILLS, India-Burma:
Roaming India's Naga Hills. By S. Dillon Ripley. 247-264, Feb. 1955

NAHA, Okinawa:
Okinawa, the Island Without a Country. By Jules

NAHA, Okinawa—*Continued*

B. Billard. Photos by Winfield Parks and David Moore. 422-448, Sept. 1969

NAIROBI, Kenya:

Kenya Says *Harambee!* By Allan C. Fisher, Jr. Photos by Bruce Dale. 151-205, Feb. 1969

NAMBAS (People):

Taboos and Magic Rule Namba Lives. By Kal Muller. 57-83, Jan. 1972

NAMGYAL, PALDEN THONDUP (Maharaja of Sikkim):

Wedding of Two Worlds. By Lee E. Battaglia. 708-727, Nov. 1963

NAMU (Killer Whale):

Making Friends With a Killer Whale. By Edward I. Griffin. 418-446, Mar. 1966

Namu. Children's book announced. 726-728, Nov. 1973

NANKING, China:

Along the Yangtze, Main Street of China. By W. Robert Moore. 325-356, Mar. 1948

NANTUCKET (Island), Massachusetts:

Life's Tempo on Nantucket. By Peter Benchley. Photos by James L. Stanfield. 810-839, June 1970

Windjamming Around New England. By Tom Horgan. Photos by Robert F. Sisson. 141-169, Aug. 1950

NAPLES, Italy:

Italy Smiles Again. By Edgar Erskine Hume. 693-732, June 1949

NAPO (River), Peru:

Sea Fever. By John E. Schultz. 237-268, Feb. 1949

NAPOLEON I:

St. Helena: the Forgotten Island. By Quentin Keynes. 265-280, Aug. 1950

Sunny Corsica: French Morsel in the Mediterranean. By Robert Cairns. Photos by Joseph J. Scherschel. 401-423, Sept. 1973

NARA, Japan:

Kyoto and Nara: Keepers of Japan's Past. By Charles McCarry. Photos by George F. Mobley. 836-851, June 1976

NASA. *See* National Aeronautics and Space Administration

NASSAU, New Providence (Island), Bahamas:

The Bahamas, Isles of the Blue-green Sea. By Carleton Mitchell. Photos by B. Anthony Stewart. 147-203, Feb. 1958

Ballerinas in Pink. By Carleton Mitchell. Photos by B. Anthony Stewart. 553-571, Oct. 1957

More of Sea Than of Land: The Bahamas. By Carleton Mitchell. Photos by James L. Stanfield. 218-267, Feb. 1967

NASSER, Lake, Egypt. *See* Aswân High Dam

NATAL (Province), Republic of South Africa:

The Zulus: Black Nation in a Land of Apartheid. By Joseph Judge. Photos by Dick Durrance II. 738-775, Dec. 1971

NATCHEZ, Mississippi:

History Repeats in Old Natchez. By William H. Ni-

NATCHEZ, Mississippi—*Continued*

cholas. Photos by Willard R. Culver. 181-208, Feb. 1949

NATCHEZ TRACE:

Today Along the Natchez Trace, Pathway Through History. By Bern Keating. Photos by Charles Harbutt. 641-667, Nov. 1968

The NATION Honors Admiral Richard E. Byrd. 567-578, Apr. 1962

NATIONAL ADVISORY COMMITTEE FOR AERONAUTICS: United States:

Fact Finding for Tomorrow's Planes. By Hugh L. Dryden. Photos by Luis Marden. 757-780, Dec. 1953

NATIONAL AERONAUTICS AND SPACE ADMINISTRATION (NASA): United States:

America's 6,000-mile Walk in Space. 440-447, Sept. 1965

Countdown for Space (Project Mercury). By Kenneth F. Weaver. 702-734, May 1961

Exploring Tomorrow With the Space Agency. By Allan C. Fisher, Jr. Photos by Dean Conger. 48-89, July 1960

First Explorers on the Moon: The Incredible Story of Apollo 11. 735-797, Dec. 1969

I. Man Walks on Another World. By Neil A. Armstrong, Edwin E. Aldrin, Jr., and Michael Collins. 738-749

II. Sounds of the Space Age, From Sputnik to Lunar Landing. A record narrated by Frank Borman. 750-751

III. The Flight of Apollo 11: "One giant leap for mankind." By Kenneth F. Weaver. 752-787

IV. What the Moon Rocks Tell Us. By Kenneth F. Weaver. 788-791

V. Next Steps in Space. By Thomas O. Paine. 793-797

The Flight of *Freedom 7.* By Carmault B. Jackson, Jr. 417-431, Sept. 1961

Footprints on the Moon. By Hugh L. Dryden. Paintings by Davis Meltzer and Pierre Mion. 357-401, Mar. 1964

John Glenn's Three Orbits in *Friendship 7:* A Minute-by-Minute Account of America's First Orbital Space Flight. By Robert B. Voas. 792-827, June 1962

The Making of an Astronaut. By Robert R. Gilruth. 122-144, Jan. 1965

The Pilot's Story: Astronaut Shepard's Firsthand Account of His Flight. Photos by Dean Conger. 432-444, Sept. 1961

Space Rendezvous, Milestone on the Way to the Moon. By Kenneth F. Weaver. 539-553, Apr. 1966

Surveyor: Candid Camera on the Moon. By Homer E. Newell. 578-592, Oct. 1966

Tracking America's Man in Orbit. By Kenneth F. Weaver. Photos by Robert F. Sisson. 184-217, Feb. 1962

See also Kennedy, John F., Space Center; Manned Spacecraft Center; Rockets; Satellites; Space Flights and Research; Wind-power Research

NATIONAL AUDUBON SOCIETY: United States:

Corkscrew Swamp—Florida's Primeval Show Place. By Melville Bell Grosvenor. 98-113, Jan. 1958

NATIONAL AUDUBON SOCIETY: United States—
Continued

The Pink Birds of Texas. By Paul A. Zahl. 641-654, Nov. 1949

Saving Man's Wildlife Heritage. By John H. Baker. Photos by Robert F. Sisson. 581-620, Nov. 1954

NATIONAL BUREAU OF STANDARDS, Washington, D. C.:

Split-second Time Runs Today's World. By F. Barrows Colton and Catherine Bell Palmer. 399-428, Sept. 1947

Uncle Sam's House of 1,000 Wonders. By Lyman J. Briggs and F. Barrows Colton. 755-784, Dec. 1951

NATIONAL CIVIL WAR CENTENNIAL COMMISSION: United States:

The Civil War. By Ulysses S. Grant 3rd. 437-449, Apr. 1961

NATIONAL ELK REFUGE, Wyoming:

Jackson Hole: Good-bye to the Old Days? By François Leydet. Photos by Jonathan Wright. 768-789, Dec. 1976

NATIONAL FORESTS: United States:

Adobe New Mexico. By Mason Sutherland. Photos by Justin Locke. 783-830, Dec. 1949
Included: Carson, Santa Fe

Forest Fire: The Devil's Picnic. By Stuart E. Jones and Jay Johnston. 100-127, July 1968
Included: Deschutes, Kaniksu, Nezperce, Ochoco, Snoqualmie, Wallowa-Whitman, Willamette

Mexico to Canada on the Pacific Crest Trail. By Mike W. Edwards. Photos by David Hiser. 741-779, June 1971
Included: Deschutes, Gifford Pinchot, Inyo, San Bernardino, Shasta Sierra, Trinity, Wenatchee, Willamette

Our Green Treasury, the National Forests. By Nathaniel T. Kenney. Photos by J. Baylor Roberts. 287-324, Sept. 1956
Included: Angeles, Beaverhead, Bitterroot, Carson, Coconino, Coronado, Flathead, Gifford Pinchot, Inyo, Kisatchie, Lolo, Mount Hood, Ocala, Osceola, Ottawa, Payette, Pisgah, Priest River Experimental Forest, Sequoia, Siuslaw, Superior; and the U. S. Forest Service

Timber: How Much Is Enough? By John J. Putman. Photos by Bruce Dale. 485-511, Apr. 1974
Included: Monongahela, Tongass, Willamette, and the U. S. Forest Service

Washington Wilderness, the North Cascades. By Edwards Park. Photos by Kathleen Revis. 335-367, Mar. 1961
Included: Mt. Baker, Okanogan, Wenatchee

White-water Adventure on Wild Rivers of Idaho. By Frank Craighead, Jr. and John Craighead. 213-239, Feb. 1970
Included: Bitterroot, Boise, Challis, Nezperce, Payette, Salmon

See also Florida (Florida's Booming), for Ocala National Forest; Inyo National Forest

NATIONAL FOUNDATION FOR THE INDIAN (FUNAI): Brazil. See Cinta Larga Indians; Kreen-Akarores; Txukahameis

NATIONAL GALLERY OF ART, Washington, D. C.:

American Masters in the National Gallery. By John Walker. 295-324, Sept. 1948

In Quest of Beauty. Text by Paul Mellon. French Impressionist paintings from the collections of Mr. and Mrs. Paul Mellon and Mrs. Ailsa Mellon

NATIONAL GALLERY OF ART, Washington, D. C.—
Continued
Bruce. 372-385, Mar. 1967

The Kress Collection: A Gift to the Nation. By Guy Emerson. 823-865, Dec. 1961

The National Gallery After a Quarter Century. By John Walker. 348-371, Mar. 1967

The Nation's Newest Old Masters. By John Walker. Paintings from Kress Collection. 619-657, Nov. 1956

The Vienna Treasures and Their Collectors. By John Walker. 737-776, June 1950

Washington: Home of the Nation's Great. By Albert W. Atwood. 699-738, June 1947

Your National Gallery of Art After 10 Years. By John Walker. Paintings from Kress Collection. 73-103, Jan. 1952

See also Chester Dale Collection; and Masterpieces; "Mona Lisa"

NATIONAL GEOGRAPHIC ATLAS OF THE WORLD. See Atlases, NGS: World Atlas

NATIONAL GEOGRAPHIC ATLAS SERIES MAPS. See Map Supplements

NATIONAL GEOGRAPHIC MAGAZINE (NGM):

Atlases. See Atlases, NGS

Awards Received:

Freedoms Foundation awards received by editor and two staff writers. 190, Feb. 1954

La Belle Award Received by Franklin L. Fisher on behalf of the Society for outstanding contributions to the development of color photography in magazine illustration. 692, Nov. 1953

National Geographic Photographers Win Top Magazine Awards. 830-831, June 1959

Photographers amass national awards. 878, 880-881, Dec. 1961; 898, 901, Dec. 1962

U. S. Camera Achievement Award medal (1951). 481, Oct. 1966

University of Missouri's Honor Award for Distinguished Service in Journalism (1954). 539, Oct. 1963

Editor. Gilbert Hovey Grosvenor (1899-1954); John Oliver La Gorce (1954-1957); Melville Bell Grosvenor (1957-1967); Frederick G. Vosburgh (1967-1970); Gilbert M. Grosvenor (1970-   )

Editor, Associate. See Scofield, John; Shor, Franc

Editor-in-Chief. See Grosvenor, Melville Bell

Editorial, first regular. 587, Nov. 1974

Editorial Policy. 587, Nov. 1974

History:

First Lady of the National Geographic (Elsie May Bell Grosvenor). By Gilbert Hovey Grosvenor. 101-121, July 1965

The National Geographic Society and Its Magazine: A History. By Gilbert H. Grosvenor. 582a, Oct. 1957; 880, Dec. 1964

National Geographic Society Trustees Elect Key Executives. 576-590, Oct. 1967

The Romance of the Geographic: National Geographic Magazine Observes Its Diamond Anniversary. By Gilbert Hovey Grosvenor. 516-585, Oct. 1963

75 Years Exploring Earth, Sea, and Sky: National Geographic Society Observes Its Diamond Anniversary. By Melvin M. Payne. 1-43, Jan. 1963

To Gilbert Grosvenor: A Monthly Monument 25

NATIONAL GEOGRAPHIC MAGAZINE (NGM)—
Continued

Miles High. By Frederick G. Vosburgh and the staff of the National Geographic Society. 445-487, Oct. 1966

Indexes:

Cumulative Index, Volume I. 879, 880, Dec. 1964; 738, May 1968; 442, Sept. 1970

Cumulative Index, Volume II. 879-880, Dec. 1964; 580, 581, Oct. 1967; 442, Sept. 1970

Six-Months Index. 576, Apr. 1976; 571, Oct. 1976

Issues, Early:

First issue (October 1888). 1, Jan. 1963; 459, 517-518, Oct. 1963; 688-689, Nov. 1964; 587, Nov. 1974

Flag issues. October 1917; September 1934

Maps:

Number of maps (30,000,000) sent out each year. 679, May 1964

See also Map Supplements

Offices. *See* NGS: Buildings

Paintings. *See* Painting Supplements

Photographers:

Editorial. 295, Mar. 1975; 439, Apr. 1975

See also NGM: Awards Received; NGM: Photographs, Notable; *and* names of individual photographers

Photographs, Notable:

Autochromes: NGM's first published Autochrome (1914). 299, Sept. 1975; A never-before-published Autochrome of Mark Twain made in 1908. 299, 301, Sept. 1975

Award-winning photos. 830-831, June 1959; 898, 901, Dec. 1962

Doe and Twin Fawns. Flashlight photo by George Shiras, 3d. 297, Mar. 1952; 527, Oct. 1963

First aerial photographs of the North Pole, published in October 1953. 478, 479, Oct. 1953; 10, Jan. 1959; 580, Oct. 1963; 485, Oct. 1966

First color cover of the magazine (the American flag) appeared in July 1959. 581, 585, Oct. 1967

First color series, hand-colored ("Scenes in Korea and China"), published in November 1910. 692, Nov. 1953; 65C, July 1954; 538-539, 574-575, Oct. 1963; 465, Oct. 1966

First natural-color series ("The Land of the Best"), published in April 1916; Ted Shawn and Ruth St. Denis are shown. 576, May 1951; 550, 575-576, Oct. 1963; 466-467, Oct. 1966

First photographic series: Eleven pages of pictures of the Forbidden City (Lhasa, Tibet), published in January 1905. 65, 65C, 65F, July 1954; 524-525, 565, Oct. 1963; 462-464, Oct. 1966

First successful natural-color photographs of life beneath the sea were made in 1926 and appeared in the January 1927 issue. 162, 180, Feb. 1956; 581, Oct. 1963; 135, Jan. 1964; 462, Oct. 1966; 92, Jan. 1971

First use, extensive, of photographs: Gilbert H. Grosvenor's policy. 421, Mar. 1957; 574, Oct. 1963

First use of High Speed Ektachrome film. 864, Dec. 1959

Number of color photographs made by NGM photographers (7,500,000). 149, July 1975

See also NGM: Awards Received; *and* Photography

Printing:

Beck Engraving Company, Philadelphia. 31, July 1952

NATIONAL GEOGRAPHIC MAGAZINE (NGM)—
Continued

Corinth, Mississippi, gravure facility. 224, 226, Aug. 1976

Judd & Detweiler, Inc., Washington, D. C. 559, Oct. 1951; 561, Oct. 1963

Linofilm typesetting technique and high-speed web presses introduced. 836, Dec. 1959; 584, 588, Oct. 1967

McClure, Phillips & Company, New York. 559, 561, Oct. 1963

R. R. Donnelley & Sons, Chicago. 874-886, Dec. 1960; 878, 879, Dec. 1961; 582, Apr. 1962; 897, Dec. 1962; 772, June 1967; 529, Apr. 1968

Recordings:

Recorded edition of NGM loaned by Library of Congress to the visually handicapped. 681, Nov. 1975

See also Recordings, NGS

Reprints:

The Last Full Measure (Tribute to President Kennedy). By Melville Bell Grosvenor. 355, Mar. 1964

The National Geographic Society and Its Magazine. By Gilbert H. Grosvenor. 880, Dec. 1964

Reprinting Brings Earliest Geographics to Life. By Melvin M. Payne. 688-689, Nov. 1964

Supplements. *See* Map Supplements; Painting Supplements; Photo Supplements

Writers:

Editorial. 295, Mar. 1975; 439, Apr. 1975

NATIONAL GEOGRAPHIC SOCIETY (NGS):

Atlases. *See* Atlases, NGS

Awards Presented:

General Thomas D. White Space Trophy for 1973 presented to astronaut Henry W. Hartsfield, Jr., capsule communicator for Skylab I. 452, Oct. 1974

Jane M. Smith Award recipients: Ingram, Sir Bruce. 474, Apr. 1961; Johnson, Lyndon B. 906, Dec. 1962; 113, Jan. 1966; 468, Oct. 1966

Tenzing Norkey presented with cash award and replica of the Hubbard Medal given to the British Mount Everest Expedition. 846, June 1955

See also Grosvenor Medal; Hubbard Medal; La Gorce Medal; Special Gold Medal; *and* NGS: Franklin L. Burr Prize; *and* list preceding this index

Awards Received:

Citation of Honor: Air Force Association's bronze plaque presented to the Society for providing cartographic aid to airmen during World War II. 846, Dec. 1949

See also NGM: Awards Received; NGS: Television

Board of Trustees:

Chairman. *See* Grosvenor, Gilbert Hovey; Grosvenor, Melville Bell; McKnew, Thomas W.; Payne, Melvin M.

Chairman, Advisory. *See* McKnew, Thomas W.

Chairman Emeritus. *See* Grosvenor, Melville Bell

Group Portraits. 65A-65B, July 1954; 834-835, Dec. 1959; 113, Jan. 1960; 883, Dec. 1960; 553, Oct. 1965; 484-485, Oct. 1966; 588-589, Oct. 1967; 226-227, Aug. 1976

Vice Chairman. *See* La Gorce, John Oliver; McKnew, Thomas W.

Book Service:

Began in 1954. 897, Dec. 1962; 585-586, Oct. 1967

NATIONAL GEOGRAPHIC SOCIETY (NGS)—*Continued*

See also Books, NGS, for list of titles

Buildings:

Headquarters: 17th Street Building and Explorers Hall

Architect and building contractors. 669, 670, 673, 679, May 1964

Dedication: President Johnson Dedicates the Society's New Headquarters. 669-679, May 1964

Services housed. 668, 679, May 1964

Hubbard Memorial Hall

First headquarters of the Society. 273, Mar. 1947; 65, July 1954; 564, Oct. 1963

Laying of cornerstone, April 26, 1902. 420, Mar. 1957

Mural and paintings by N. C. Wyeth. 38, July 1948; 105, July 1965

Membership Center Building

Gaithersburg, Maryland. 581, 585, 590, Oct. 1967; 209, Feb. 1972; 225, Aug. 1976

16th Street Building

History. 410, Sept. 1948; 91, Jan. 1957; 669, May 1964; 588, Oct. 1967

Burr, Franklin L., Prize. See NGS: Franklin L. Burr Prize

Cartographic Division:

Awarded U. S. Air Force Association's citation of honor for cartographic aid during World War II. 846, Dec. 1949

Chamberlin Trimetric Projection. 841, June 1947; 826, June 1949; 399, Mar. 1950; 417, Mar. 1952; 591, Apr. 1964

Established in 1915. 576, Oct. 1963; 463, Oct. 1966; 585, Oct. 1967

First color photomosaic of the United States produced by teaming Landsat imagery and the General Electric Company's color-mosaic expertise with the Society's map program. 140-147, July 1976

First known use of Two Point Equidistant Projection in mapping Asia. 418, Mar. 1951; 751, Dec. 1959

First use of Transverse Mercator Projection for mapping a long airplane flight in 1921. 524, Oct. 1947

Mapping the moon. 240-245, Feb. 1969

See also Atlases, NGS; Globes, NGS; Map Supplements; Satellite Finder

Committee for Research and Exploration:

Chairman

Briggs, Lyman J. 326, 332, 355, Mar. 1949; 101, 108, 122, Jan. 1959

Carmichael, Leonard C. 867, June 1967; 872, 873, Dec. 1973

Payne, Melvin M. 159, 225, Aug. 1976

Vice Chairman

Payne, Melvin M. 198, Feb. 1965

Wetmore, Alexander. 705, June 1947; 881-882, Dec. 1967

Dues: Use of funds. 566, Oct. 1963; 679, May 1964; 880, Dec. 1964; 102, 105, July 1965; 587, Oct. 1967

Educational Services. See Atlases; Books; Films and Filmstrips; Globes; Map Supplements; Recordings; WORLD

NATIONAL GEOGRAPHIC SOCIETY (NGS)—*Continued*

Employees: Number of. 253, 261, Aug. 1949; 443, Mar. 1960; 585, Oct. 1963; 678, 679, May 1964; 102, 108, 112-113, 118, July 1965; 459, Oct. 1966; 208, Feb. 1972

Expeditions and Research:

Amount spent annually. 586, Oct. 1967

First NGS expedition: Mount St. Elias Expedition of 1890. 248, Feb. 1948; 743, June 1956; 880, Dec. 1964; 802, June 1965; 13, July 1965

See also Books, NGS: Research Reports; NGS: Committee for Research and Exploration; *and* list preceding this index

Explorers Hall. See NGS: Buildings

Films. See NGS: Television and Educational Films

Filmstrips:

The World in Geographic Filmstrips. By Melvin M. Payne. 134-137, Jan. 1968

Flag, NGS:

Designed by Elsie May Bell Grosvenor. 637, May 1949; 145, Aug. 1953; 459, 516, 557, 564, Oct. 1963; 100, 101, 116, 118, July 1965

Founders and Founding:

33 eminent men met at the Cosmos Club, January 13, 1888. 387, Mar. 1955; 807, 830, June 1960; 1-3, Jan. 1963; 518, 573-574, Oct. 1963; 880, Dec. 1964

Franklin L. Burr Prize: Recipients:

Edgerton, Harold E. 705-706, May 1953; 523, Apr. 1955; 467, Oct. 1955; 847, June 1960

Van Biesbroeck, George. 705-706, May 1953

See also list preceding this index

Globes. See Globe, Great; Globes, NGS

Grants:

Amount of annual grants. 889, 893, 899, Dec. 1962; 571, Oct. 1963; 163, Feb. 1964; 582, 586, Oct. 1967; 148, July 1971; 873, Dec. 1973; 226, Aug. 1976

Number of, in 1967. 582, Oct. 1967

See also NGS: Expeditions and Research; NGS: Land Grants; *and* list preceding this index

Headquarters. See NGS: Buildings

History:

First Lady of the National Geographic (Elsie May Bell Grosvenor). By Gilbert Hovey Grosvenor. 101-121, July 1965

First transcontinental telephone conversation (January 25, 1915). 58, Jan. 1958

First voice voyages via telephone taken to the four corners of the United States by 800 NGS members (January 7, 1916). 278, Mar. 1947

Frederick G. Vosburgh Retires as Editor; Gilbert M. Grosvenor Succeeds Him. By Melvin M. Payne. 838-843, Dec. 1970

The National Geographic Society and Its Magazine: A History. By Gilbert H. Grosvenor. 582a, Oct. 1957; 880, Dec. 1964

National Geographic Society Trustees Elect Key Executives. 576-590, Oct. 1967

On the Geographic's 75th Birthday—Our Best to You. Introduction to anniversary issue. By Melville Bell Grosvenor. 459, Oct. 1963

Robert V. Fleming, 1890-1967. By Melville Bell Grosvenor. 526-529, Apr. 1968

The Romance of the Geographic: National Geographic Magazine Observes Its Diamond Anni-

NATIONAL GEOGRAPHIC SOCIETY (NGS)—
Continued

versary. By Gilbert Hovey Grosvenor. 516-585, Oct. 1963

75 Years Exploring Earth, Sea, and Sky: National Geographic Society Observes Its Diamond Anniversary. By Melvin M. Payne. 1-43, Jan. 1963

To Gilbert Grosvenor: A Monthly Monument 25 Miles High. By Frederick G. Vosburgh and the staff of the National Geographic Society. 445-487, Oct. 1966

Trustees Elect New Society Officers. 224-227, Aug. 1976

See also introduction to this index

Illustrations Library:

Franklin L. Fisher's contribution. 692, Nov. 1953

World's largest library of color transparencies. 136, Jan. 1968; 149, July 1975

Indexes. *See* NGM: Indexes

Inventions:

Chamberlin Trimetric Projection. 841, June 1947; 826, June 1949; 399, Mar. 1950; 417, Mar. 1952; 591, Apr. 1964

Compass, Sun, invented by Albert H. Bumstead. 442, Oct. 1947; 469, Oct. 1953; 754, Dec. 1953; 160, Aug. 1956; 38, July 1957; 22, Jan. 1963

"Geometer," used with NGS globes. 698-701, May 1961; 875, Dec. 1961; 897, Dec. 1962

OceanEye camera housing, designed by Bates Littlehales. 271, 277, Aug. 1971

Photo-composing machine, invented by Albert H. Bumstead and further developed by his son, Newman Bumstead. 419, Mar. 1953

Satellite finder. 808, 809, Dec. 1957

Jane M. Smith Award. *See* NGS: Awards Presented; *and* list preceding this index

Land Grants:

Russell Cave, Alabama, presented to the people of the United States. 438, Mar. 1958; 614, May 1958; 36, Jan. 1963; 808, June 1964; 440, Sept. 1967; 851, June 1973

Sequoia National Park, California: The NGS and its members helped preserve 2,239 acres of *Sequoia gigantea.* 679, 680, May 1951; 792, 794, June 1954; 552, Oct. 1957; 597, 614, May 1958; 162, 176, Aug. 1959; 38, Jan. 1963; 545, Oct. 1963; 107, July 1965; 627, 630, May 1966; 1, 2, July 1966

Shenandoah National Park, Virginia, increased by gift of 1,000 acres in 1926. 18, July 1949; 40, Jan. 1963

Lectures:

Annual series of lectures has been given in Constitution Hall since 1933. 565, 573, Nov. 1951

Chairman of Lecture Committee. 843, Dec. 1970

First lecture (1888). 113, July 1965

Lecturers

Arnold, H. H. 400, Mar. 1950

British Mount Everest Expedition members. 64, July 1954

Byrd, Richard E. 42, 44, July 1957

Fechtler, William H. 614-615, Nov. 1952

Foster, John W. 549, Oct. 1963

Leakey, Louis S. B. 194-195, Feb. 1965

MacMillan, Donald B. 563, Apr. 1953

Peary, Mrs. Robert E. 531, Oct. 1954

Roosevelt, Theodore. 587, Oct. 1958; 542, 585,

NATIONAL GEOGRAPHIC SOCIETY (NGS)—
Continued

Oct. 1963; 732, Nov. 1963; 468, Oct. 1966

Taft, William Howard. 585, Oct. 1963; 549, Oct. 1965

Map Cases:

Churchill, Winston, presented NGS map case by Franklin D. Roosevelt. 576, Oct. 1963; 275, Feb. 1964; 468, Oct. 1966

Eisenhower, Dwight D., during World War II, used NGS maps in a map rack made especially for him. 737, June 1947; 583, Oct. 1963

Johnson, Lyndon B., presents map cases to rulers of Scandinavian countries. 274, 276, Feb. 1964

Roosevelt, Franklin D., presented with map case. 576, Oct. 1963; 275, Feb. 1964

Truman, Harry S., presented with map case. 850, June 1948

Maps. *See* Map Supplements

Medals. *See* Grosvenor Medal; Hubbard Medal; La Gorce Medal; Special Gold Medal; *and* list preceding this index

Media Diversification. 227, Aug. 1976

Members and Membership:

Number of charter members (205). 689, Nov. 1964

Number of members (more than 9 million). 226, Aug. 1976

Membership Center Building. *See* NGS: Buildings

Museum. *See* NGS: Buildings: Explorers Hall

News Features. Sent to 2,500 editors of press, radio, and television. 836, Dec. 1959

Photographic Laboratories. 308, Mar. 1948; 436, Apr. 1953; 540, 575, 581, Oct. 1963; 193, Feb. 1967; 729, Nov. 1967; 785, Dec. 1970; 244, Feb. 1973; 237, 247, Aug. 1976

Chief: Edwin L. Wisherd. 431, Apr. 1953; 567, Apr. 1959; 864, Dec. 1959; 644, 675, May 1970

Photographic Library. *See* NGS: Illustrations Library

Photography. *See* NGM: Awards Received; NGM: Photographs, Notable; *and* Photography; *and* names of individual photographers

President. Gardiner Greene Hubbard (1888-1897); Alexander Graham Bell (1898-1903); Gilbert Hovey Grosvenor (1920-1954); John Oliver La Gorce (1954-1957); Melville Bell Grosvenor (1957-1967); Melvin M. Payne (1967-1976); Robert E. Doyle (1976-   )

Public Service Publications:

Equal Justice Under Law (The U. S. Supreme Court). Published in cooperation with The Foundation of the Federal Bar Association. 411, Mar. 1966; 586, Oct. 1967

G. Washington, Man and Monument. Published in cooperation with the Washington National Monument Association. 586, Oct. 1967

The Living White House. Published in cooperation with the White House Historical Association. 641, Nov. 1966; 586, Oct. 1967

We, the People (U. S. Capitol guidebook). Published in cooperation with the United States Capitol Historical Society. 1-2, Jan. 1964; 411, Mar. 1966; 586, Oct. 1967

The White House (guidebook). Published in cooperation with the White House Historical Association. 888-893, Dec. 1962; 1, Jan. 1964; 331, Mar. 1964; 642, Nov. 1964; 108, Jan. 1966; 411, Mar. 1966; 59, July 1966; 585, 586, Oct. 1967

NATIONAL GEOGRAPHIC SOCIETY (NGS)—
Continued

Publications. See Atlases; Books; National Geographic Magazine; NGM: Indexes; NGS: News Features; School Bulletin; WORLD

Purpose of the Society. 65, July 1954; 459, 581, Oct. 1963; 677, May 1964; 880, Dec. 1964; 466, Oct. 1966

Recordings. See Recordings, NGS

Research. See NGS: Expeditions and Research; and list preceding this index

Research Reports. See Books, NGS

Seal:

The Seal of the National Geographic Society appears on one side of the Hubbard Medal. 564, Apr. 1953

Secretary:

Anderson, Owen R. (1976-   ). 225, Aug. 1976

Austin, O. P. (1904-1932). 565, 573, Oct. 1963

Doyle, Robert E. (1967-1976). 577, 581, 587, 590, Oct. 1967

McKnew, Thomas W. (1932-1962). 586, May 1947; 635, May 1949; 254, 256, 257, Aug. 1949; 413, Sept. 1951

Payne, Melvin M. (1962-1967). 582, Apr. 1962; 1, Jan. 1964; 672, May 1964; 442, Sept. 1967

Smith, Jane M., Award. See NGS: Awards Presented; and list preceding this index

Special Publications:

Adventure, science, history, exploration spring to life in your Society's new program of Special Publications. By Melville Bell Grosvenor. 408-417, Mar. 1966

Chief: Robert L. Breeden. 411, Mar. 1966; 884, June 1970

Editorial Director: Gilbert M. Grosvenor. 843, Dec. 1970

Number of copies distributed (nearly 8 million). 865, June 1973

See also Books, NGS, for titles

Supplements. See Map Supplements; Painting Supplements; Photo Supplements

Television and Educational Films:

Awards won:

Emmy Awards. 731, Dec. 1974

George Foster Peabody Award. 587, Oct. 1967

Chief: Robert C. Doyle. 449-451, Sept. 1965; 586, 587, Oct. 1967

Number of subjects available. 583, Nov. 1975

See also Television Films, for titles

Treasurer:

Fleming, Robert V. (1935-1967). 672, May 1964; 589, Oct. 1967

Trustees. See NGS: Board of Trustees

Vice President:

Beers, Thomas M. 582, Apr. 1962; 28, July 1970

Carmichael, Leonard C. 582, 589, Oct. 1967; 861, June 1970; 588, Oct. 1972; 143, Jan. 1973; 871, 873, Dec. 1973

Doyle, Robert E. 577, 587, Oct. 1967

Fleming, Robert V. 882, 883, Dec. 1960; 585, Oct. 1963; 672, May 1964; 589, Oct. 1967

Grosvenor, Gilbert M. 576, 584, 587, 588, Oct. 1967; 136, Jan. 1968; 843, Dec. 1970

Grosvenor, Melville Bell. 65, 65D, 66, July 1954; 419, Mar. 1957

NATIONAL GEOGRAPHIC SOCIETY (NGS)—
Continued

La Gorce, John Oliver. 255, 257, 258, 260, 261, Aug. 1949; 418, Mar. 1957; 441, 443, Mar. 1960; 866, June 1967

McKnew, Thomas W. 793, June 1958

Payne, Melvin M. 175, Feb. 1960

Vosburgh, Frederick G. 585, Oct. 1963; 861, June 1970; 838, Dec. 1970

Vice President, Executive:

McKnew, Thomas W. 882, 883, Dec. 1960; 579, Apr. 1962; 148, Feb. 1965; 588, Oct. 1967

Payne, Melvin M. 582, Apr. 1962; 865, June 1967; 583, Oct. 1967

Vice President for Research and Exploration:

Carmichael, Leonard C. 525, Apr. 1965; 864, June 1967; 441, 442, Sept. 1967; 582, 586, Oct. 1967

NATIONAL GEOGRAPHIC WORLD (Magazine for Young Readers):

The School Bulletin is retired after 56 years; replaced by WORLD. 229, Sept. 1975

Start the World, I Want to Get On! 148-150, July 1975

NATIONAL INSTITUTES OF HEALTH, Bethesda, Maryland:

Capturing Strange Creatures in Colombia. By Marte Latham. Photos by Tor Eigeland. 682-693, May 1966

NATIONAL MILITARY PARKS: United States:

Gettysburg and Vicksburg: the Battle Towns Today. By Robert Paul Jordan. Map notes by Carolyn Bennett Patterson. 4-57, July 1963

Heritage of Beauty and History. By Conrad L. Wirth. 587-661, May 1958
    Included: Antietam, Chickamauga, Gettysburg, Kings Mountain, Shiloh, Vicksburg, Yorktown

NATIONAL MONUMENTS:

Italy

Time Turns Back in Picture-book Portofino. By Carleton Mitchell. Photos by Winfield Parks. 232-253, Feb. 1965

United States

Alaska: Rising Northern Star. By Joseph Judge. Photos by Bruce Dale. 730-767, June 1975
    Included: Katmai; and proposed monuments: Aniakchak Caldera, Cape Krusenstern, Harding Icefield-Kenai Fjords, Kobuk

Alaska's Warmer Side. By Elsie May Bell Grosvenor. 737-775, June 1956
    Included: Katmai National Monument, in which is located the Valley of Ten Thousand Smokes

Blizzard of Birds: The Tortugas Terns. By Alexander Sprunt, Jr. 213-230, Feb. 1947
    Included: Fort Jefferson

Heritage of Beauty and History. By Conrad L. Wirth. 587-661, May 1958
    Included: Aztec Ruins, Bandelier, Castillo de San Marcos, Cedar Breaks, Custer Battlefield, Death Valley, Devils Tower, Dinosaur, Edison Laboratory, El Morro, Fort Frederica, Fort Laramie, Fort McHenry, Fort Sumter, Great Sand Dunes, Harpers Ferry, Katmai, Lava Beds, Organ Pipe Cactus, Petrified Forest, Rainbow Bridge, Russell Cave, Saguaro, Scotts Bluff, Tuzigoot, Walnut Canyon

The Mission Called 66: Today in Our National

NATIONAL MONUMENTS — *Continued*

Parks. By Conrad L. Wirth. 7-47, July 1966
Included: Death Valley, Dinosaur, Rainbow Bridge

National Parks, Monuments and Shrines of the United States and Canada. Atlas series supplement. Text on reverse. May 1958

Parkscape, U.S.A.: Tomorrow in Our National Parks. By George B. Hartzog, Jr. 48-93, July 1966
Included: Buck Island Reef, Chesapeake and Ohio Canal, Glacier Bay, Katmai, Muir Woods, Organ Pipe Cactus, Statue of Liberty

Preserving America's Last Great Wilderness (Alaska). By David Jeffery. 769-791, June 1975
Included: Katmai; *and* proposed monuments: Aniakchak Caldera, Cape Krusenstern, Harding Icefield-Kenai Fjords, Kobuk

Shrines of Each Patriot's Devotion. By Frederick G. Vosburgh. 51-82, Jan. 1949
Contents: Ackia Battleground, Andrew Johnson, Big Hole, Cabrillo, Custer Battlefield, El Morro, Father Millet Cross, Fort Matanzas, Fort Pulaski, Fort Vancouver, George Washington Birthplace, Homestead, Lava Beds, Perry's Victory and International Peace Memorial, Pipe Spring, Scotts Bluff, Statue of Liberty, Verendrye

Today and Tomorrow in Our National Parks. By Melville Bell Grosvenor. 1-5, July 1966
Included: Glacier Bay National Monument

Utah's Arches of Stone. By Jack Breed. 173-192, Aug. 1947
Contents: Arches National Monument

See also Arizona (From Tucson to Tombstone); Bandelier National Monument; Buck Island Reef National Monument; Castillo de San Marcos; Chesapeake and Ohio Canal; Craters of the Moon National Monument; Death Valley National Monument; Dinosaur National Monument; El Morro; Fort Jefferson National Monument; Glacier Bay National Monument; Harpers Ferry; Katmai National Monument; Marble Canyon National Monument; Natural Bridges National Monument; Organ Pipe Cactus National Monument; Rainbow Bridge National Monument; Russell Cave; Santa Barbara Islands, for Channel Islands National Monument; White Sands National Monument; *and* Custer, George A., for Custer Battlefield National Monument

NATIONAL MUSEUM: United States. *See* Smithsonian Institution

NATIONAL MUSEUM OF ANTHROPOLOGY, Mexico City:

Mexico's Window on the Past. By Bart McDowell. Photos by B. Anthony Stewart. 492-519, Oct. 1968

NATIONAL MUSEUM OF CANADA: Expeditions:

Vanished Mystery Men of Hudson Bay. By Henry B. Collins. 669-687, Nov. 1956

NATIONAL OCEANIC AND ATMOSPHERIC ADMINISTRATION (NOAA):

This Changing Earth. By Samuel W. Matthews. 1-37, Jan. 1973

We're Doing Something About the Weather! By Walter Orr Roberts. 518-555, Apr. 1972

NATIONAL OCEANOGRAPHIC PROGRAM: United States:

Thresher: Lesson and Challenge. By James H. Wakelin, Jr. 759-763, June 1964

NATIONAL OCEANOGRAPHIC PROGRAM: United States — *Continued*
Included: Interagency Committee on Oceanography, Federal Council for Science and Technology, TENOC

NATIONAL OUTDOOR LEADERSHIP SCHOOL:

Wind River Range: Many-treasured Splendor. By Joseph Judge. 198-205, Feb. 1974

NATIONAL PARK SERVICE: United States:

Expeditions and Research. *See* Isle Royale; Wetherill Mesa; *and* Tree Snails

Heritage of Beauty and History. By Conrad L. Wirth. 587-661, May 1958
Contents: *National Battlefield Parks:* Manassas; *National Battlefield Sites:* Antietam; *National Historic Sites:* Adams Mansion, Fort Raleigh; *National Historical Parks:* Appomattox Court House, Colonial, Cumberland Gap, Independence, Morristown, Saratoga; *National Memorials:* House Where Lincoln Died, Lincoln Memorial, Mount Rushmore, Washington Monument, Wright Brothers; *National Military Parks:* Antietam, Chickamauga, Gettysburg, Kings Mountain, Shiloh, Vicksburg; *National Monuments:* Aztec Ruins, Bandelier, Castillo de San Marcos, Cedar Breaks, Custer Battlefield, Death Valley, Devils Tower, Dinosaur, Edison Laboratory, El Morro, Fort Frederica, Fort Laramie, Fort McHenry, Fort Sumter, Great Sand Dunes, Harpers Ferry, Katmai, Lava Beds, Organ Pipe Cactus, Petrified Forest, Rainbow Bridge, Russell Cave, Saguaro, Scotts Bluff, Tuzigoot, Walnut Canyon; *National Parks:* Acadia, Big Bend, Bryce Canyon, Carlsbad Caverns, Crater Lake, Everglades, Glacier, Grand Canyon, Grand Teton, Great Smoky Mountains, Hawaii, Kings Canyon, Lassen Volcanic, Mammoth Cave, Mesa Verde, Mount McKinley, Mount Rainier, Olympic, Rocky Mountain, Sequoia, Shenandoah, Virgin Islands, Wind Cave, Yellowstone, Yosemite, Zion

The Mission Called 66: Today in Our National Parks. By Conrad L. Wirth. 7-47, July 1966
Included: Achievements of Mission 66, ten-year program of National Park Service for improvement and expansion of national parks, 1956-1966

The Next 100 Years: A Master Plan for Yellowstone. By George B. Hartzog, Jr. 632-637, May 1972

Parkscape, U. S. A.: Tomorrow in Our National Parks. By George B. Hartzog, Jr. 48-93, July 1966
Included: Future program of National Park Service

Shrines of Each Patriot's Devotion. By Frederick G. Vosburgh. 51-82, Jan. 1949

Today and Tomorrow in Our National Parks. By Melville Bell Grosvenor. 1-5, July 1966
Included: Golden anniversary of National Park Service; history of founding in 1916; plans for the future

Yellowstone at 100: The Pitfalls of Success. By William S. Ellis. Photos by Jonathan Blair. 616-631, May 1972

NATIONAL PARKS:

Africa

African Wildlife: Man's Threatened Legacy. By Allan C. Fisher, Jr. Photos by Thomas Nebbia. Paintings by Ned Seidler. 147-187, Feb. 1972
Included: Albert National Park, Zaire; Etosha National Park, South-West Africa; Gorongosa National Park, Mozambique; Kidepo Valley National Park, Uganda; Kruger National Park, South Africa; Lake Manyara National Park, Tanzania; Mountain Zebra National Park, South Africa; Murchison Falls National Park, Uganda; Nairobi National Park, Kenya; Serengeti National Park, Tanzania; Tsavo National Park,

NATIONAL PARKS — *Continued*

    Kenya; Volcanoes National Park, Rwanda; Wankie National Park, Rhodesia

The Last Great Animal Kingdom. 390-409, Sept. 1960
    Included: Albert National Park, Congo; Amboseli National Reserve, Kenya; Kruger National Park, South Africa; Serengeti National Park, Tanganyika

Roaming Africa's Unfenced Zoos. By W. Robert Moore. 353-380, Mar. 1950
    Included: Hluhluwe Game Reserve, South Africa; Kruger National Park, South Africa; Nairobi National Park, Kenya; Parc National Albert, Congo; Umfolozi Reserve, South Africa

Uganda, Africa's Uneasy Heartland. By Howard La Fay. Photos by George F. Mobley. 708-735, Nov. 1971
    Included: Kidepo Valley National Park, Murchison Falls National Park, Queen Elizabeth National Park

Where Elephants Have Right of Way. By George and Jinx Rodger. 363-389, Sept. 1960
    Included: Amboseli National Reserve, Kenya; Murchison Falls National Park, Uganda; Nairobi Royal National Park, Kenya; Ngong National Reserve, Kenya; Queen Elizabeth National Park, Uganda; Tsavo Royal National Park, Kenya

White Magic in the Belgian Congo. By W. Robert Moore. 321-362, Mar. 1952

See also Kruger National Park, South Africa; Serengeti National Park, Tanzania; Tsavo National-al Park, Kenya

    Asia

India Struggles to Save Her Wildlife. By John J. Putman. 299-343, Sept. 1976
    Included: Borivli National Park, Corbett National Park, Kanha National Park, Kaziranga National Park

    Canada

Bikepacking Across Alaska and Canada. By Dan Burden. 682-695, May 1973
    Included: Jasper

Canada's Heartland, the Prairie Provinces. By W. E. Garrett. 443-489, Oct. 1970
    Included: Banff, Elk Island, Jasper, Wood Buffalo

Canadian Rockies, Lords of a Beckoning Land. By Alan Phillips. Photos by James L. Stanfield. 353-393, Sept. 1966
    Included: Banff, Jasper, Kootenay, Mount Robson, Waterton Lakes, Yoho

Hiking the Backbone of the Rockies: Canada's Great Divide Trail. By Mike W. Edwards. Photos by Lowell Georgia. 795-817, June 1973
    Included: Banff, Jasper, Kootenay, Yoho

On the Ridgepole of the Rockies. By Walter Meayers Edwards. 745-780, June 1947
    Canada's Rocky Mountain Playground. 755-770
    Included: Banff, Jasper

See also Waterton-Glacier International Peace Park, for Waterton Lakes National Park

    Central America

Guatemala. *See* Tikal

    South America

Parks, Plans, and People: How South America Guards Her Green Legacy. By Mary and Laurance Rockefeller. Photos by George F. Mobley. 74-119, Jan. 1967
    Included: Cabo Polonio, Iguaçu, Los Glaciares, Nahuel Huapí, Robinson Crusoe Island, Tierra del Fuego, Torres del Paine

NATIONAL PARKS — *Continued*

See also Xingu National Park, Brazil

    United States

Alaska: Rising Northern Star. By Joseph Judge. Photos by Bruce Dale. 730-767, June 1975
    Included: Mount McKinley, Sitka; *and* proposed parks: Gates of the Arctic, Lake Clark, Wrangell-St. Elias

America's Wonderlands. Book announced. 558-561, Oct. 1959; 562-563, Oct. 1961

America's Wonderlands: The National Parks (Television film). 549A-549B, Oct. 1968

The Fabulous Sierra Nevada. By J. R. Challacombe. 825-843, June 1954
    Included: Kings Canyon, Sequoia, Yosemite

From Sun-clad Sea to Shining Mountains. By Ralph Gray. Photos by James P. Blair. 542-589, Apr. 1964
    Included: Parks and scenic wonders along highway, "International 89," from Sonora, Mexico, through western United States, to British Columbia, Canada

Giant Sequoias Draw Millions to California Parks. By John Michael Kauffmann. Photos by B. Anthony Stewart. 147-187, Aug. 1959
    Included: Kings Canyon, Sequoia

Heritage of Beauty and History. By Conrad L. Wirth. 587-661, May 1958
    Included: Acadia, Big Bend, Bryce Canyon, Carlsbad Caverns, Crater Lake, Everglades, Glacier, Grand Canyon, Grand Teton, Great Smoky Mountains, Hawaii, Kings Canyon, Lassen Volcanic, Mammoth Cave, Mesa Verde, Mount McKinley, Mount Rainier, Olympic, Rocky Mountain, Sequoia, Shenandoah, Virgin Islands, Wind Cave, Yellowstone, Yosemite, Zion

I See America First. By Lynda Bird Johnson. Photos by William Albert Allard. 874-904, Dec. 1965
    Included: Grand Teton, Mesa Verde, Monument Valley, Yellowstone

John Muir's Wild America. By Harvey Arden. Photos by Dewitt Jones. 433-461, Apr. 1973
    Included: Petrified Forest, Sequoia, Yosemite

Mexico to Canada on the Pacific Crest Trail. By Mike W. Edwards. Photos by David Hiser. 741-779, June 1971
    Included: Crater Lake, Lassen Volcanic, Mount Rainier, Sequoia, Yosemite

The Mission Called 66: Today in Our National Parks. By Conrad L. Wirth. 7-47, July 1966
    Included: Acadia, Bryce Canyon, Crater Lake, Everglades, Grand Canyon, Grand Teton, Mesa Verde, Mount Rainier, Sequoia, Shenandoah, Yellowstone, Yosemite

National Parks, Monuments and Shrines of the United States and Canada. Atlas series supplement. Text on reverse. May 1958

The New America's Wonderlands. Book announced. 436-438, Mar. 1975

New Rush to Golden California. By George W. Long. 723-802, June 1954
    Included: Kings Canyon, Lassen Volcanic, Sequoia, Yosemite

Parkscape, U.S.A.: Tomorrow in Our National Parks. By George B. Hartzog, Jr. 48-93, July 1966
    Included: Canyonlands, Everglades, Great Smoky Mountains, Haleakala, Mount McKinley, North Cascades (Proposed), Redwood (Proposed), Shenandoah, Virgin Islands; *and* National Capital Parks (Washington, D. C.)

Preserving America's Last Great Wilderness (Alaska). By David Jeffery. 769-791, June 1975

NATIONAL PARKS — *Continued*

    Included: Proposed parks: Gates of the Arctic, Katmai additional acreage, Lake Clark, Mount McKinley

Sierra High Trip. By David R. Brower. 844-868, June 1954

    Included: Kings Canyon, Sequoia

Skyline Trail from Maine to Georgia. By Andrew H. Brown. Photos by Robert F. Sisson. 219-251, Aug. 1949

    Included: Great Smoky Mountains, Shenandoah

Today and Tomorrow in Our National Parks. By Melville Bell Grosvenor. 1-5, July 1966

    Included: Kings Canyon, Mount McKinley, Sequoia

Vacationland U.S.A. Book announced. 734-740, May 1970

Vacationlands of the United States and Southern Canada, map supplement. Text on reverse. July 1966

The West Through Boston Eyes. By Stewart Anderson. 733-776, June 1949

    Included: Bryce Canyon, Crater Lake, Glacier, Grand Canyon, Grand Teton, Yellowstone, Yosemite, Zion

Wilderness U.S.A. Book announced. 582-584, Oct. 1973

Wyoming: High, Wide, and Windy. By David S. Boyer. 554-594, Apr. 1966

    Included: Grand Teton, Yellowstone

See also Big Bend National Park; Bryce Canyon National Park; Canyonlands National Park; Carlsbad Caverns; Crater Lake National Park; Everglades; Glacier National Park; Grand Canyon National Park; Grand Teton National Park; Great Smoky Mountains; Haleakala National Park; Hawaii Volcanoes National Park; Isle Royale; Mesa Verde National Park; Mount McKinley National Park; Mount Rainier National Park; North Cascades National Park; Olympic National Park; Redwoods; Sequoia National Park; Shenandoah National Park; Yellowstone National Park; Yosemite National Park; Zion National Park

NATIONAL PRESERVES: Proposed. *See* Big Cypress Swamp, Florida; Big Thicket, Texas

NATIONAL RECREATION AREA. *See* Glen Canyon

NATIONAL SCENIC TRAILS: United States. *See* Appalachian Trail; Pacific Crest Trail

NATIONAL SCIENCE FOUNDATION: United States:

    Animal Studies: Alaskan Brown Bear 433, Sept. 1975; Andean Condor 686, May 1971; Baboon 674, May 1975; Coral Reef 710, 712, Nov. 1966; Fiddler Crab 16, Jan. 1963; Galapagos Tortoise 639, Nov. 1972; Garden Eel 727, Nov. 1974; Green Turtle 879, 880, June 1967; Grizzly Bear 255, Aug. 1966; Lions 496, Apr. 1969; Moose and Wolves of Isle Royale 202, Feb. 1963; Porpoises 403, Sept. 1966; Salmon 205, Aug. 1968; Wild Burro 506, Apr. 1972

    Antarctic Research. *See* International Geophysical Year; U. S. Antarctic Research Program

    Anthropology: Ethiopia 805, Dec. 1976; Karnali Zone, Nepal 662, Nov. 1971; New Britain Tribes 795, June 1966; Polynesians 736, Dec. 1974; Skull 1470 829, June 1973

    Archeology: Chan Chan 320, Mar. 1973; Dzibilchaltun 99, Jan. 1959; *Monitor* search 49, Jan. 1975; Snaketown 675, 682, May 1967; Yassi Ada wrecks 404, Sept. 1968

    Bristlecone Pine 361, Mar. 1958

    Eclipse Expedition 224, Aug. 1970

NATIONAL SCIENCE FOUNDATION: United States— *Continued*

    Education: Science projects in Pittsburgh high schools 365, 368, Mar. 1965

    Programs supported: Cayman Expedition 230, Aug. 1976; International Biological Program (Tundra ecosystems) 305, Mar. 1972; Summer Institute of Glaciological and Arctic Sciences 796, June 1965; 201, Feb. 1967; University Corporation for Atmospheric Research 523, Apr. 1972

    See also American Mount Everest Expedition; Deep Sea Drilling Project; FAMOUS; Mohole, Project

NATIONAL SEASHORES: United States. *See* Cape Cod; Cape Hatteras National Seashore

NATIONAL WEATHER SERVICE: United States:

    We're Doing Something About the Weather! By Walter Orr Roberts. 518-555, Apr. 1972

    See also former name, U. S. Weather Bureau

NATIONAL WILDLIFE REFUGES: United States:

    Alaska: Rising Northern Star. By Joseph Judge. Photos by Bruce Dale. 730-767, June 1975

        Included: Map showing existing and proposed refuges

    Beyond the North Wind With the Snow Goose. By Des and Jen Bartlett. 822-843, Dec. 1973

        Included: De Soto, Missouri River; Sand Lake, South Dakota; Squaw Creek, Missouri

    Preserving America's Last Great Wilderness (Alaska). By David Jeffery. 769-791, June 1975

    Tireless Voyager, the Whistling Swan. By William J. L. Sladen. Photos by Bianca Lavies. 134-147, July 1975

        Included: Back Bay, Virginia; Blackwater, Maryland; Eastern Neck, Maryland; Mattamuskeet, North Carolina; Pungo, North Carolina; Upper Mississippi River Wild Life and Fish Refuge

    See also Okefenokee Swamp

NATIONAL ZOOLOGICAL PARK, Washington, D. C.:

    The Ape with Friends in Washington. By Margaretta Burr Wells. 61-74, July 1953

    Director: Theodore H. Reed. 630, May 1961; 875, Dec. 1968; 482, 484, 485, 487, Apr. 1970; 164, Feb. 1972; 803, 807, Dec. 1972

    Director, Acting: Theodore H. Reed. 524, Apr. 1957

    Enchantress! By Theodore H. Reed. Photos by Thomas J. Abercrombie. 628-641, May 1961

    Portraits of My Monkey Friends. By Ernest P. Walker. 105-119, Jan. 1956

    What's Black and White and Loved All Over? By Theodore H. Reed. Photos by Donna K. Grosvenor. 803-815, Dec. 1972

    White Tiger in My House. By Elizabeth C. Reed. Photos by Donna K. Grosvenor. 482-491, Apr. 1970

    The Wild Animals in My Life. By William M. Mann. 497-524, Apr. 1957

NATIONALIST CHINA. *See* Pescadores; Quemoy; Taiwan

The NATION'S Bookcase: Library of Congress. By Fred Kline. Photos by Dick Durrance II. 671-687, Nov. 1975

The NATION'S Capitol Revealed as Never Before. By Carl Hayden. 1-3, Jan. 1964

The NATION'S Library. By Albert W. Atwood. 663-684, May 1950

The NATION'S Newest Old Masters. By John Walker. Paintings from Kress Collection. 619-657, Nov. 1956

The NATION'S River. By Allan C. Fisher, Jr. Photos by James L. Stanfield. 432-469, Oct. 1976

The NATION'S 200th Birthday. By Gilbert M. Grosvenor. 1, July 1974

NATIVE AMERICANS. *See* Aleuts; Eskimos; Indians of North America

NATIVE'S Return to Norway. By Arnvid Nygaard. Photos by Andrew H. Brown. 683-691, Nov. 1953

NATRON, Lake, Tanzania:
East Africa's Majestic Flamingos. By M. Philip Kahl. 276-294, Feb. 1970

NATURAL ARCHES AND BRIDGES. *See* Arches National Monument; Canyonlands National Park; Escalante Canyon, for Grosvenor Arch *and* La Gorce Arch; Natural Bridges National Monument; Rainbow Bridge National Monument; Zion National Park

NATURAL BRIDGES NATIONAL MONUMENT, Utah:
Roaming the West's Fantastic Four Corners. By Jack Breed. 705-742, June 1952

NATURAL GAS:
Alberta Unearths Her Buried Treasures. By David S. Boyer. 90-119, July 1960
Canada's "Now" Frontier. By Robert Paul Jordan. Photos by Lowell Georgia. 480-511, Oct. 1976
Included: Map showing oil pipeline, proposed gas pipeline, and tar sands
The Eternal Flame. By Albert W. Atwood. 540-564, Oct. 1951
The Pipeline: Alaska's Troubled Colossus. By Bryan Hodgson. Photos by Steve Raymer. 684-717, Nov. 1976
Included: Diagram, Anatomy of the pipeline; map showing potential and producing oil and gas areas
Turnaround Time in West Virginia. By Elizabeth A. Moize. Photos by Jodi Cobb. 755-785, June 1976

NATURAL HISTORY:
In the Wake of Darwin's *Beagle*. By Alan Villiers. Photos by James L. Stanfield. 449-495, Oct. 1969
Our Continent: A Natural History of North America. Book announced. 572-574, Oct. 1976
See also Nature Study; *and* Biology; Geology; Marine Biology; Paleontology; Plants

NATURAL RESOURCES:
This Land of Ours—How Are We Using It? By Peter T. White. Photos by Emory Kristof. 20-67, July 1976
See also Energy Sources; Lumber Industry; Minerals and Metals; Water Supply

A NATURALIST in Penguin Land. By Niall Rankin. 93-116, Jan. 1955

NATURE Carves Fantasies in Bryce Canyon (Utah). By William Belknap, Jr. 490-511, Oct. 1958

NATURE STUDY:
Animals that Build their Homes. Children's book announced. 718-720, Nov. 1976
Buck Island—Underwater Jewel. By Jerry and Idaz Greenberg. 677-683, May 1971

NATURE STUDY—*Continued*
Businessman in the Bush. By Frederick Kent Truslow. 634-675, May 1970
A Day in the Woods. Children's book announced. 724-726, Nov. 1975
The Fragile Beauty All About Us. Photos by Harry S. C. Yen. 785-795, Dec. 1970
Frost, Nature's Icing. By Robert F. Sisson. 398-405, Mar. 1976
In the Gardens of Olympus. By Paul A. Zahl. 85-123, July 1955
In the Wilds of a City Parlor. By Paul A. Zahl. 645-672, Nov. 1954
In Touch With Nature. Text by Elizabeth A. Moize. Photos by Steve Raymer. 537-543, Apr. 1974
Nature's Year in Pleasant Valley. By Paul A. Zahl. 488-525, Apr. 1968
Photographing Northern Wild Flowers. By Virginia L. Wells. 809-823, June 1956
Snowflakes to Keep. By Robert F. Sisson. 104-111, Jan. 1970
Teeming Life of a Pond. By William H. Amos. 274-298, Aug. 1970
Tricks Animals Play. Children's book announced. 724-726, Nov. 1975
The World of My Apple Tree. By Robert F. Sisson. 836-847, June 1972
See also the natural sciences; *and* listing under Animals

NATURE'S Alert Eyes. By Constance P. Warner. 558-569, Apr. 1959

NATURE'S Aquatic Engineers, Beavers. By Des and Jen Bartlett. 716-732, May 1974

NATURE'S Clown, the Penguin. By David Hellyer and Malcolm Davis. 405-428, Sept. 1952

NATURE'S Gifts to Medicine. By Lonnelle Aikman. Paintings by Lloyd K. Townsend and Don Crowley. 420-440, Sept. 1974

NATURE'S Living, Jumping Jewels. By Paul A. Zahl. 130-146, July 1973

NATURE'S Night Lights: Probing the Secrets of Bioluminescence. By Paul A. Zahl. 45-69, July 1971

NATURE'S Tank, the Turtle. By Doris M. Cochran. Paintings by Walter A. Weber. 665-684, May 1952

NATURE'S Toy Train, the Railroad Worm. By Darwin L. Tiemann. Photos by Robert F. Sisson. 56-67, July 1970

NATURE'S Year in Pleasant Valley. By Paul A. Zahl. 488-525, Apr. 1968

NAURU, the World's Richest Nation. By Mike Holmes. 344-353, Sept. 1976

NAUTICAL Norfolk Turns to Azaleas. By William H. Nicholas. Photos by B. Anthony Stewart. 606-614, May 1947

NAUTILUS (Nuclear-powered Submarine):
The Arctic as a Sea Route of the Future. By William R. Anderson. 21-24, Jan. 1959
Submarine Through the North Pole. By William G. Lalor, Jr. Photos by John J. Krawczyk. 1-20, Jan. 1959

NAUTILUS, Chambered:

The Chambered Nautilus, Exquisite Living Fossil. Photos by Douglas Faulkner. 38-41, Jan. 1976

Shells Take You Over World Horizons. By Rutherford Platt. 33-84, July 1949

NAVAJOS (Indians):

Better Days for the Navajos. By Jack Breed. Photos by Charles W. Herbert. 809-847, Dec. 1958

Desert River (San Juan) Through Navajo Land. By Alfred M. Bailey. Photos by author and Fred G. Brandenburg. 149-172, Aug. 1947

The Navajos. By Ralph Looney. Photos by Bruce Dale. 740-781, Dec. 1972

NAVAL AIR TECHNICAL TRAINING UNIT. See Parachute Rigger School

NAVAL BASES:

Four-ocean Navy in the Nuclear Age. By Thomas W. McKnew. 145-187, Feb. 1965

Our Navy in the Far East. By Arthur W. Radford. Photos by J. Baylor Roberts. 537-577, Oct. 1953

See also Guantánamo (Cuba); Honolulu, Hawaii, for Pearl Harbor; Key West, Florida; Portsmouth (England); San Diego, California

NAVIGATION:

Charting Our Sea and Air Lanes. By Stuart E. Jones. Photos by J. Baylor Roberts. 189-209, Feb. 1957

See also Hokule‘a; Mayflower II; Radar; Sonar; Submarines, Nuclear-powered; and Graham, Robin Lee; Henry, Prince, the Navigator; Lewis, David; Schultz, John E.; Vikings

NAVIGATION, Flight:

Our Air Age Speeds Ahead. By F. Barrows Colton. 249-272, Feb. 1948

Skyway Below the Clouds. By Carl R. Markwith. Photos by Ernest J. Cottrell. 85-108, July 1949

See also Balloons

NAVIGATORS. See Explorers, Discoverers, and Navigators

NAVY. See U. S. Navy; and listing under French Navy

NAVY HURRICANE WEATHER CENTRAL, Miami, Florida:

Men Against the Hurricane. By Andrew H. Brown. 537-560, Oct. 1950

NAWANG GOMBU (Sherpa):

American and Geographic Flags Top Everest. By Melvin M. Payne. Photos by Barry C. Bishop. 157-157C, Aug. 1963

See also American Mount Everest Expedition

NAXOS (Island), Greece:

The Isles of Greece: Aegean Birthplace of Western Culture. By Melville Bell Grosvenor. Photos by Edwin Stuart Grosvenor and Winfield Parks. 147-193, Aug. 1972

NAYARIT (State), Mexico. See Mesa del Nayar

NAZARÉ, Portugal:

Portugal Is Different. By Clement E. Conger. 583-622, Nov. 1948

NAZARENOS (Penitents):

Holy Week and the Fair in Sevilla. By Luis Marden. 499-530, Apr. 1951

NAZARETH, Israel:

The Land of Galilee. By Kenneth MacLeish. Photos by B. Anthony Stewart. 832-865, Dec. 1965

Where Jesus Walked. By Howard La Fay. Photos by Charles Harbutt. 739-781, Dec. 1967

NAZCA LINES (Figure Tracings):

Mystery of the Ancient Nazca Lines. By Loren McIntyre. 716-728, May 1975

NEALE, GUY: Artist:

The High World of the Rain Forest. By William Beebe. 838-855, June 1958

NEAR EAST. See Middle East and Near East

NEAVE, CHARLES: Author-Photographer:

Helping Holland Rebuild Her Land. By Gilbert M. Grosvenor and Charles Neave. 365-413, Sept. 1954

NEBBIA, THOMAS:

National Geographic Photographers Win Top Magazine Awards. 830-831, June 1959

Photographer

African Wildlife: Man's Threatened Legacy. By Allan C. Fisher, Jr. Paintings by Ned Seidler. 147-187, Feb. 1972

Australia's Pacesetter State, Victoria. By Allan C. Fisher, Jr. 218-253, Feb. 1971

California, the Golden Magnet: I. The South. By William Graves. 595-639, May 1966

Canterbury Cathedral. By Kenneth MacLeish. 364-379, Mar. 1976

Cape Canaveral's 6,000-mile Shooting Gallery. By Allan C. Fisher, Jr. Photos by Luis Marden and Thomas Nebbia. 421-471, Oct. 1959

Crusader Road to Jerusalem. By Franc Shor. 797-855, Dec. 1963

Denmark, Field of the Danes. By William Graves. 245-275, Feb. 1974

The Fabulous State of Texas. By Stanley Walker. Photos by B. Anthony Stewart and Thomas Nebbia. 149-195, Feb. 1961

French Riviera: Storied Playground on the Azure Coast. By Carleton Mitchell. 798-835, June 1967

Greenland's "Place by the Icebergs." By Mogens Bloch Poulsen. 849-869, Dec. 1973

Guantánamo: Keystone in the Caribbean. By Jules B. Billard. Photos by W. E. Garrett and Thomas Nebbia. 420-436, Mar. 1961

Haiti: Beyond Mountains, More Mountains. By Carolyn Bennett Patterson. 70-97, Jan. 1976

Hawaii, U.S.A. By Frederick Simpich, Jr. 1-45, July 1960

In the Crusaders' Footsteps. By Franc Shor. Photos by Thomas Nebbia and James P. Blair. 731-789, June 1962

Inside the White House. By Lonnelle Aikman. Photos by B. Anthony Stewart and Thomas Nebbia. 3-43, Jan. 1961

Isles on the Edge of the Sea: Scotland's Outer Hebrides. By Kenneth MacLeish. 676-711, May 1970

Jamaica Goes It Alone. By James Cerruti. 843-873, Dec. 1967

Life in Walled-off West Berlin. By Nathaniel T. Kenney and Volkmar Wentzel. 735-767, Dec. 1961

Los Angeles, City of the Angels. By Robert de Roos. 451-501, Oct. 1962

NEBBIA, THOMAS: Photographer—*Continued*

The Magic Worlds of Walt Disney. By Robert de Roos. 159-207, Aug. 1963

The People of Cades Cove. By William O. Douglas. Photos by Thomas Nebbia and Otis Imboden. 60-95, July 1962

Philadelphia Houses a Proud Past. By Harold Donaldson Eberlein. 151-191, Aug. 1960

Porpoises: Our Friends in the Sea. By Robert Leslie Conly. 396-425, Sept. 1966

Prince Henry, the Explorer Who Stayed Home. By Alan Villiers. 616-656, Nov. 1960

Problems in Paradise. By Mary and Laurance S. Rockefeller. 782-793, Dec. 1974

Rhodesia, a House Divided. By Allan C. Fisher, Jr. 641-671, May 1975

Sea Islands: Adventuring Along the South's Surprising Coast. By James Cerruti. Photos by Thomas Nebbia and James L. Amos. 366-393, Mar. 1971

Seattle Fair Looks to the 21st Century. By Carolyn Bennett Patterson. 402-427, Sept. 1962

Sweden, Quiet Workshop for the World. By Andrew H. Brown. Photos by Winfield Parks and Thomas Nebbia. 451-491, Apr. 1963

The Top End of Down Under. By Kenneth MacLeish. 145-174, Feb. 1973

The Two Acapulcos. By James Cerruti. 848-878, Dec. 1964

Wales, Land of Bards. By Alan Villiers. 727-769, June 1965

Washington: The City Freedom Built. By William Graves. Photos by Bruce Dale and Thomas Nebbia. 735-781, Dec. 1964

NEBRASKA:

Following the Trail of Lewis and Clark. By Ralph Gray. 707-750, June 1953

Nebraska . . . the Good Life. By Robert Paul Jordan. Photos by Lowell Georgia. 378-407, Mar. 1974

NEEDHAM, JAMES G.: Author:

Dragonflies—Rainbows on the Wing. 215-229, Aug. 1951

NEEDLEWORK. *See* Bayeux Tapestry; Embroidery

NEFERTITI, Queen (Egypt):

Computer Helps Scholars Re-create an Egyptian Temple. By Ray Winfield Smith. Photos by Emory Kristof. 634-655, Nov. 1970

NEGRITOS (People):

The Last Andaman Islanders. By Raghubir Singh. 66-91, July 1975

NELLIS AIR FORCE BASE, Nevada. *See* Nevada Wild Horse Range

NELSON, HORATIO, LORD:

The British Way. By Sir Evelyn Wrench. 421-541, Apr. 1949

Portsmouth, Britannia's Sally Port. By Thomas Garner James. Photos by B. Anthony Stewart. 513-544, Apr. 1952

NEMRUD DAGH (Mountain), Turkey:

Throne Above the Euphrates. By Theresa Goell. 390-405, Mar. 1961

NENE:

Saving the Nene, World's Rarest Goose. By S. Dillon Ripley. Photos by Jerry Chong. 745-754, Nov. 1965

NEPAL:

Afoot in Roadless Nepal (Geological Survey). By Toni Hagen. 361-405, Mar. 1960

Karnali, Roadless World of Western Nepal. By Lila M. and Barry C. Bishop. 656-689, Nov. 1971

Mustang, Remote Realm in Nepal. By Michel Peissel. 579-604, Oct. 1965

Peerless Nepal—A Naturalist's Paradise. By S. Dillon Ripley. Photos by Volkmar Wentzel. 1-40, Jan. 1950

Sherpaland, My Shangri-La. By Desmond Doig. 545-577, Oct. 1966

We Build a School for Sherpa Children. By Sir Edmund Hillary. 548-551, Oct. 1962

Wintering on the Roof of the World. By Barry C. Bishop. 503-547, Oct. 1962

See also Everest, Mount; Katmandu

NEPALESE:

Gangtok, Cloud-wreathed Himalayan Capital. By John Scofield. 698-713, Nov. 1970

NEPENTHES (Pitcher Plants):

Malaysia's Giant Flowers and Insect-trapping Plants. By Paul A. Zahl. 680-701, May 1964

NEPTUNE (Planet):

Voyage to the Planets. By Kenneth F. Weaver. Paintings by Ludek Pesek. 147-193, Aug. 1970

NETHERLANDS:

"Around the World in Eighty Days." By Newman Bumstead. 705-750, Dec. 1951
Included: Amsterdam, Edam, The Hague, Hook of Holland, Leiden, Noordwijk ann Zee, Rotterdam, Zuider Zee

France, Belgium, and the Netherlands, Atlas series supplement. June 1960

Helping Holland Rebuild Her Land. By Gilbert M. Grosvenor and Charles Neave. 365-413, Sept. 1954

Holland Against the Sea (Television film). 588A-588B, Apr. 1970

Inside Europe Aboard *Yankee.* By Irving and Electa Johnson. Photos by Joseph J. Scherschel. 157-195, Aug. 1964

Mid-century Holland Builds Her Future. By Sydney Clark. 747-778, Dec. 1950

The Netherlands: Nation at War With the Sea. By Alan Villiers. Photos by Adam Woolfitt. 530-571, Apr. 1968

Oil, the Dwindling Treasure. By Noel Grove. Photos by Emory Kristof. 792-825, June 1974

Under Canvas in the Atomic Age. By Alan Villiers. 49-84, July 1955
Included: Amsterdam, Hilversum, Marken Island, Spakenburg, Volendam

See also Amsterdam; Rotterdam

NETHERLANDS ANTILLES:

A Fresh Breeze Stirs the Leewards. By Carleton Mitchell. Photos by Winfield Parks. 488-537, Oct. 1966

The Netherlands Antilles: Holland in the Caribbean. By James Cerruti. Photos by Emory Kristof. 115-146, Jan. 1970

NETHERLANDS NEW GUINEA:

The Asmat of New Guinea, Headhunters in Today's World. By Malcolm S. Kirk. 376-409, Mar. 1972

Netherlands New Guinea. By John Scofield. 584-603, May 1962

Strange Courtship of Birds of Paradise. By S. Dillon Ripley. Paintings by Walter A. Weber. 247-278, Feb. 1950

NETTIS, JOSEPH: Author-Photographer:

Europe Via the Hostel Route. 124-154, July 1955

NEVADA:

Close-up: U.S.A., California and Nevada, map supplement. Text on reverse. June 1974

Lonely Sentinels of the American West: Basque Sheepherders. By Robert Laxalt. Photos by William Belknap, Jr. 870-888, June 1966

A Map Maker Looks at the United States. By Newman Bumstead. 705-748, June 1951
    Included: Carson City; Hoover Dam; Las Vegas; Mead, Lake; Reno; Tahoe, Lake

Nevada Learns to Live with the Atom. By Samuel W. Matthews. 839-850, June 1953

Nevada's Mountain of Invisible Gold. By Samuel W. Matthews. Photos by David F. Cupp. 668-679, May 1968

The Other Nevada. By Robert Laxalt. Photos by J. Bruce Baumann. 733-761, June 1974

The West Through Boston Eyes. By Stewart Anderson. 733-776, June 1949

See also Nevada Wild Horse Range; Stead Air Force Base

NEVADA WILD HORSE RANGE, Nevada:

On the Track of the West's Wild Horses. By Hope Ryden. Photos by author and Dick Durrance II. 94-109, Jan. 1971

NEVIS (Island), West Indies:

A Fresh Breeze Stirs the Leewards. By Carleton Mitchell. Photos by Winfield Parks. 488-537, Oct. 1966

NEW BEDFORD, Massachusetts:

New England's "Little Portugal." By O. Louis Mazzatenta. 90-109, Jan. 1975

The **NEW** Biology. 355-407, Sept. 1976
    I. The Awesome Worlds Within a Cell. By Rick Gore. Photos by Bruce Dale. Paintings by Davis Meltzer. 355-395
    II. The Cancer Puzzle. By Robert F. Weaver. 396-399
    III. Seven Giants Who Led the Way. Paintings by Ned Seidler. Text by Rick Gore. 401-407

A **NEW** Bird Immigrant Arrives. By Roger Tory Peterson. 281-292, Aug. 1954

A **NEW** *Bounty* Sails to Tahiti. By Luis Marden. 435-459, Apr. 1962

NEW BRITAIN (Island), Bismarck Archipelago:

Blowgun Hunters of the South Pacific. By Jane C. Goodale. Photos by Ann Chowning. 793-817, June 1966

Exploring New Britain's Land of Fire. By E. Thomas Gilliard. 260-292, Feb. 1961

NEW BRUNSWICK (Province), Canada:

The Loyalists. By Kent Britt. Photos by Ted Spie-

NEW BRUNSWICK (Province), Canada—*Continued*
gel. 510-539, Apr. 1975

See also Fundy, Bay of

NEW CALEDONIA (Island), Pacific Ocean:

Problems in Paradise. By Mary and Laurance S. Rockefeller. Photos by Thomas Nebbia. 782-793, Dec. 1974

Shells Take You Over World Horizons. By Rutherford Platt. 33-84, July 1949

NEW DELHI, India:

Delhi, Capital of a New Dominion. By Phillips Talbot. 597-630, Nov. 1947

India in Crisis. By John Scofield. 599-661, May 1963

When the President Goes Abroad (Eisenhower Tour). By Gilbert M. Grosvenor. 588-649, May 1960

NEW Discoveries Among Africa's Chimpanzees. By Baroness Jane van Lawick-Goodall. Photos by Baron Hugo van Lawick. 802-831, Dec. 1965

NEW Discoveries on the Mid-Atlantic Ridge. By Maurice Ewing. Photos by Robert F. Sisson. 611-640, Nov. 1949

NEW Energy from an Old Source: the Wind. By Roger Hamilton. Photos by Emory Kristof. 812-829, Dec. 1975

NEW ENGLAND:

Captain Smith of Jamestown. By Bradford Smith. 581-620, May 1957
    Included: Exploration and mapping of Maine and Massachusetts

Captain Smith's New England . . . and the Pilgrims' Cape Cod. — George Washington's Travels, Traced on the Arrowsmith Map. 765, 768, 769, June 1953

Close-up: U.S.A., Western New England, map supplement. Text on reverse. July 1975

Founders of New England. By Sir Evelyn Wrench. Photos by B. Anthony Stewart. 803-838, June 1953

The Merrimack: River of Industry and Romance. By Albert W. Atwood. Photos by B. Anthony Stewart. 106-140, Jan. 1951

Mountains Top Off New England. By F. Barrows Colton. Photos by Robert F. Sisson. 563-602, May 1951

New England, map supplement. June 1955

New England, a Modern Pilgrim's Pride. By Beverley M. Bowie. 733-796, June 1955

New England's "Little Portugal." By O. Louis Mazzatenta. 90-109, Jan. 1975

The Old Boston Post Roads. By Donald Barr Chidsey. 189-205, Aug. 1962

The Post Road Today. Photos by B. Anthony Stewart. 206-233, Aug. 1962

Robert Frost and New England. By Archibald MacLeish. 438-467, Apr. 1976
    Look of a Land Beloved. Photos by Dewitt Jones. 444-467

Shells Take You Over World Horizons. By Rutherford Platt. 33-84, July 1949

Skiing in the United States. By Kathleen Revis. 216-254, Feb. 1959

Skyline Trail from Maine to Georgia. By Andrew

NEW ENGLAND — *Continued*

H. Brown. Photos by Robert F. Sisson. 219-251, Aug. 1949

Windjamming Around New England. By Tom Horgan. Photos by Robert F. Sisson. 141-169, Aug. 1950

Yesterday Lingers Along the Connecticut. By Charles McCarry. Photos by David L. Arnold. 334-369, Sept. 1972
Included: Connecticut; Massachusetts; New Hampshire; Vermont

See also Connecticut; Maine; Massachusetts; New Hampshire; Rhode Island; Vermont

NEW Era in the Loneliest Continent. By David M. Tyree. Photos by Albert Moldvay. 260-296, Feb. 1963

NEW Era on the Great Lakes. By Nathaniel T. Kenney. 439-490, Apr. 1959

NEW Florida Resident, the Walking Catfish. By Clarence P. Idyll. Photos by Robert F. Sisson. 847-851, June 1969

NEW Grandeur for Flowering Washington. By Joseph Judge. Photos by James P. Blair. 500-539, Apr. 1967

NEW GUINEA:

The Asmat of New Guinea, Headhunters in Today's World. By Malcolm S. Kirk. 376-409, Mar. 1972

Australian New Guinea. By John Scofield. 604-637, May 1962

Change Ripples New Guinea's Sepik River. By Malcolm S. Kirk. 354-381, Sept. 1973

Journey Into Stone Age New Guinea. By Malcolm S. Kirk. 568-592, Apr. 1969

Netherlands New Guinea. By John Scofield. 584-603, May 1962

New Guinea. The Editor. 583, May 1962

New Guinea Festival of Faces. By Malcolm S. Kirk. 148-156, July 1969

New Guinea to Bali in *Yankee*. By Irving and Electa Johnson. 767-815, Dec. 1959

New Guinea's Paradise of Birds. By E. Thomas Gilliard. 661-688, Nov. 1951

New Guinea's Rare Birds and Stone Age Men. By E. Thomas Gilliard. 421-488, Apr. 1953

Off the Beaten Track of Empire (Prince Philip's Tour). By Beverley M. Bowie. Photos by Michael Parker. 584-626, Nov. 1957

Sheep Airlift in New Guinea. Photos by Ned Blood. 831-844, Dec. 1949
Contents: The Hallstrom Trust's Nondugl Sheep Station in Australian New Guinea

Strange Courtship of Birds of Paradise. By S. Dillon Ripley. Paintings by Walter A. Weber. 247-278, Feb. 1950

To the Land of the Head-hunters. By E. Thomas Gilliard. 437-486, Oct. 1955

Yankee Roams the Orient. By Irving and Electa Johnson. 327-370, Mar. 1951

NEW HAMPSHIRE:

Down East Cruise. By Tom Horgan. Photos by Luis Marden. 329-369, Sept. 1952
Included: Gosport Harbor; Portsmouth

The Friendly Huts of the White Mountains. By William O. Douglas. Photos by Kathleen Revis.

NEW HAMPSHIRE — *Continued*

205-239, Aug. 1961

Lake Sunapee's Golden Trout. Photos by Robert F. Sisson. 529-536, Oct. 1950

The Merrimack: River of Industry and Romance. By Albert W. Atwood. Photos by B. Anthony Stewart. 106-140, Jan. 1951

Mountains Top Off New England. By F. Barrows Colton. Photos by Robert F. Sisson. 563-602, May 1951

Robert Frost and New England. By Archibald MacLeish. 438-467, Apr. 1976
Look of a Land Beloved. Photos by Dewitt Jones. 444-467

Skiing in the United States. By Kathleen Revis. 216-254, Feb. 1959

Skyline Trail from Maine to Georgia. By Andrew H. Brown. Photos by Robert F. Sisson. 219-251, Aug. 1949

See also Maple Sugar and Syrup

NEW HEBRIDES (Islands), Pacific Ocean:

Yankee Roams the Orient. By Irving and Electa Johnson. 327-370, Mar. 1951

See also Malekula; Pentecost Island; Tanna

NEW JERSEY:

Can We Save Our Salt Marshes? By Stephen W. Hitchcock. Photos by William R. Curtsinger. 729-765, June 1972

Here's New York Harbor. By Stuart E. Jones. Photos by Robert F. Sisson and David S. Boyer. 773-813, Dec. 1954

I'm From New Jersey. By John T. Cunningham. Photos by Volkmar Wentzel. 1-45, Jan. 1960

Our Changing Atlantic Coastline. By Nathaniel T. Kenney. Photos by B. Anthony Stewart. 860-887, Dec. 1962
Included: Atlantic City; Brigantine; Harvey Cedars, Long Beach Island

Shad in the Shadow of Skyscrapers. By Dudley B. Martin. Photos by Luis Marden. 359-376, Mar. 1947

Today on the Delaware, Penn's Glorious River. By Albert W. Atwood. Photos by Robert F. Sisson. 1-40, July 1952

See also Bell Telephone Laboratories; Morristown; Parachute Rigger School, Lakehurst; Pine Barrens; *and* Perfume, for Delawanna

NEW Knowledge of Earth From Astronauts' Photographs. By Paul D. Lowman, Jr. 645-671, Nov. 1966

NEW Life for India's Villagers. By Anthony and Georgette Dickey Chapelle. 572-588, Apr. 1956

NEW Life for the "Loneliest Isle" (Tristan da Cunha). By Lewis Lewis. 105-116, Jan. 1950

NEW Life for the Troubled Suez Canal. By William Graves. Photos by Jonathan Blair. 792-817, June 1975

A NEW Light Dawns on Bird Photography. By Arthur A. Allen. 774-790, June 1948

NEW Light on a Forgotten Past. By Wilhelm G. Solheim II. 330-339, Mar. 1971

NEW Light on an Old Riddle: Stonehenge. By Harold E. Edgerton. Paintings by Brian Hope-Taylor. 846-866, June 1960

NEW Light on the Changing Face of Mars. By E. C. Slipher. 427-436, Sept. 1955

NEW LONDON, Connecticut:
Our Navy's Long Submarine Arm. By Allan C. Fisher, Jr. 613-636, Nov. 1952

A NEW Look at Everest. By Dag Hammarskjöld. 87-93, Jan. 1961

A NEW Look at Kenya's "Treetops." By Quentin Keynes. 536-541, Oct. 1956

A NEW Look at Medieval Europe. By Kenneth M. Setton. Paintings by Andre Durenceau and Birney Lettick. 799-859, Dec. 1962

NEW MEXICO:
Adobe New Mexico. By Mason Sutherland. Photos by Justin Locke. 783-830, Dec. 1949
A Map Maker Looks at the United States. By Newman Bumstead. 705-748, June 1951
    Included: Acoma, San Ildefonso, Santa Fe
New Mexico: The Golden Land. By Robert Laxalt. Photos by Adam Woolfitt. 299-345, Sept. 1970
New Mexico's Great White Sands. By William Belknap, Jr. 113-137, July 1957
20th-century Indians Preserve Customs of the Cliff Dwellers. Photos by William Belknap, Jr. 196-211, Feb. 1964
    Included: Acoma, Jemez, Santa Ana, Santo Domingo, and Zia pueblos
See also Carlsbad Caverns; El Morro; Los Alamos Scientific Laboratory; Navajos; Parachute Jumps (The Long, Lonely Leap); Philmont Scout Ranch; Rockets (Rockets Explore the Air), for Holloman Air Development Center; White Sands Proving Ground; *and* Mercury (Metallic Element); Uranium (Hunting Uranium)

NEW MILLS, Braintree, England:
Silkworms in England Spin for the Queen. By John E. H. Nolan. 689-704, May 1953

NEW Miracles of the Telephone Age. By Robert Leslie Conly. 87-120, July 1954

NEW National Park Proposed: The Spectacular North Cascades. By Nathaniel T. Kenney. Photos by James P. Blair. 642-667, May 1968

NEW ORLEANS, Louisiana:
Louisiana Trades with the World. By Frederick Simpich. Photos by J. Baylor Roberts. 705-738, Dec. 1947
Mardi Gras in New Orleans. By Carolyn Bennett Patterson. Photos by Robert F. Sisson and John E. Fletcher. 726-732, Nov. 1960
New Orleans: Jambalaya on the Levee. By Harnett T. Kane. Photos by Justin Locke. 143-184, Feb. 1953
New Orleans and Her River. By Joseph Judge. Photos by James L. Stanfield. 151-187, Feb. 1971

NEW PROVIDENCE ISLAND, Bahamas. *See* Nassau

A NEW Riviera: Mexico's West Coast. By Nathaniel T. Kenney. Photos by Charles O'Rear. 670-699, Nov. 1973

NEW Rush to Golden California. By George W. Long. 723-802, June 1954

NEW St. Lawrence Seaway Opens the Great Lakes to the World. By Andrew H. Brown. 299-339, Mar. 1959

NEW SALEM, Illinois:
Vacation Tour Through Lincoln Land. By Ralph Gray. 141-184, Feb. 1952

NEW Scarlet Bird in Florida Skies. By Paul A. Zahl. 874-882, Dec. 1967

NEW SOUTH WALES (State), Australia:
New South Wales, the State That Cradled Australia. By Howell Walker. Photos by David Moore. 591-635, Nov. 1967

NEW Stars for Old Glory. By Lonnelle Aikman. 86-121, July 1959

NEW Tools for Undersea Archeology. By George F. Bass. Photos by Charles R. Nicklin, Jr. 403-423, Sept. 1968

The NEW Toronto. By Ethel A. Starbird. Photos by Robert W. Madden. 190-215, Aug. 1975

NEW Tricks Outwit Our Insect Enemies. By Hal Higdon. Photos by Robert F. Sisson and Emory Kristof. 380-399, Sept. 1972

A NEW Volcano Bursts from the Atlantic. By John Scofield. Photos by Robert F. Sisson. 735-757, June 1958

NEW WORLD. *See* America; Explorers, Discoverers, and Navigators; Pre-Columbian Civilization; Pre-Hispanic Culture; Vinland

NEW YEAR CELEBRATIONS:
Focusing on the Tournament of Roses. By B. Anthony Stewart and J. Baylor Roberts. 805-816, June 1954
Kyoto Says Happy New Year. Photos by George F. Mobley. 852-859, June 1976

NEW YORK:
Down the Susquehanna by Canoe. By Ralph Gray. Photos by Walter Meayers Edwards. 73-120, July 1950
Drums to Dynamos on the Mohawk. By Frederick G. Vosburgh. Photos by B. Anthony Stewart. 67-110, July 1947
Duck Hunting with a Color Camera. By Arthur A. Allen. 514-539, Oct. 1951
From Sword to Scythe in Champlain Country. By Ethel A. Starbird. Photos by B. Anthony Stewart and Emory Kristof. 153-201, Aug. 1967
Henry Hudson's River. By Willard Price. Photos by Wayne Miller. 364-403, Mar. 1962
The Mighty Hudson. By Albert W. Atwood. Photos by B. Anthony Stewart. 1-36, July 1948
New York State's New Main Street (Thruway). By Matt C. McDade. 567-618, Nov. 1956
Niagara Falls, Servant of Good Neighbors. Photos by Walter Meayers Edwards. 574-587, Apr. 1963
Nomad Sails Long Island Sound. By Thomas Horgan. 295-338, Sept. 1957
North Through History Aboard *White Mist*. By Melville Bell Grosvenor. Photos by Edwin Stuart Grosvenor. 1-55, July 1970
Sapsucker Woods, Cornell University's Exciting New Bird Sanctuary. By Arthur A. Allen. 530-551, Apr. 1962
Shrines of Each Patriot's Devotion. By Frederick G. Vosburgh. 51-82, Jan. 1949
Skyline Trail from Maine to Georgia. By Andrew H. Brown. Photos by Robert F. Sisson. 219-251, Aug. 1949

NEW YORK—*Continued*

Today on the Delaware, Penn's Glorious River. By Albert W. Atwood. Photos by Robert F. Sisson. 1-40, July 1952

See also Adirondack Mountains; Long Island; New York (City); Rochester; *and* Old Rhinebeck Aerodrome; Thunder Hill Goat Farm; U. S. Merchant Marine Academy; U. S. Military Academy

NEW YORK (City), New York:

The Fair Reopens (World's Fair, 1964-1965). Photos by James P. Blair. Text by Carolyn Bennett Patterson. 505-529, Apr. 1965

Greater New York; Tourist Manhattan, double-sided U. S. Atlas series supplement. July 1964

Here's New York Harbor. By Stuart E. Jones. Photos by Robert F. Sisson and David S. Boyer. 773-813, Dec. 1954

Immigrants Still Flock to Liberty's Land. By Albert W. Atwood. 708-724, Nov. 1955

In the Wilds of a City Parlor. By Paul A. Zahl. 645-672, Nov. 1954

The Mohawks Scrape the Sky. By Robert L. Conly. Photos by B. Anthony Stewart. 133-142, July 1952

Contents: Brooklyn's steel-working Mohawk Indians

New York Again Hails the Horse (National Horse Show). By Walter B. Devereux. 697-720, Nov. 1954

The Romance of American Furs. By Wanda Burnett. 379-402, Mar. 1948

Shad in the Shadow of Skyscrapers. By Dudley B. Martin. Photos by Luis Marden. 359-376, Mar. 1947

Staten Island Ferry, New York's Seagoing Bus. By John T. Cunningham and Jay Johnston. Photos by W. D. Vaughn. 833-843, June 1959

The World in New York City. By Peter T. White. 52-107, July 1964

See also American Museum of Natural History; Bell Telephone Laboratories; Brooklyn; Central Park; New York Aquarium; New York Zoological Park; United Nations; Westminster Kennel Club Dog Show

NEW YORK AQUARIUM, Coney Island, New York:

Three Whales That Flew (Transportation by Aircraft). By Carleton Ray. Photos by W. Robert Moore. 346-359, Mar. 1962

NEW YORK STATE BARGE CANAL:

Drums to Dynamos on the Mohawk. By Frederick G. Vosburgh. Photos by B. Anthony Stewart. 67-110, July 1947

NEW YORK STATE THRUWAY:

New York State's New Main Street. By Matt C. McDade. 567-618, Nov. 1956

NEW YORK ZOOLOGICAL PARK, New York:

Biggest Worm Farm Caters to Platypuses. By W. H. Nicholas. 269-280, Feb. 1949

Flight of the Platypuses (Transportation by Aircraft). By David Fleay. 512-525, Oct. 1958

Zoo Animals Go to School. By Marion P. McCrane. Photos by W. E. Garrett. 694-706, Nov. 1956

NEW YORK ZOOLOGICAL SOCIETY:

Animal Studies: James's Flamingo 91, 93, July 1961; Lion 496, Apr. 1969; Mountain Lion 647, Nov. 1969; Orangutan 449, Oct. 1975; Patago-

NEW YORK ZOOLOGICAL SOCIETY—*Continued*

nian Wildlife 297, Mar. 1976; Right Whale 578, 581, 584, Oct. 1972; 328, 329, Mar. 1976; Snow Leopard 706, Nov. 1971; Weddell Seal 56, Jan. 1966

Field Station, Trinidad:

Keeping House for Tropical Butterflies. By Jocelyn Crane. Photos by M. Woodbridge Williams. 193-217, Aug. 1957

Vilcabamba Expedition:

By Parachute Into Peru's Lost World. By G. Brooks Baekeland. Photos by author and Peter R. Gimbel. 268-296, Aug. 1964

NEW ZEALAND:

Captain Cook: The Man Who Mapped the Pacific. By Alan Villiers. Photos by Gordon W. Gahan. 297-349, Sept. 1971

Finding an "Extinct" New Zealand Bird. By R. V. Francis Smith. 393-401, Mar. 1952

First Flight Across the Bottom of the World (Cape Town to Christchurch). By James R. Reedy. Photos by Otis Imboden. 454-464, Mar. 1964

In the Wake of Darwin's *Beagle.* By Alan Villiers. Photos by James L. Stanfield. 449-495, Oct. 1969

The Kiwi, New Zealand's Wonder Bird. By Ron J. Anderson. 395-398, Sept. 1955

New Zealand: Gift of the Sea. By Maurice Shadbolt. Photos by Brian Brake. 465-511, Apr. 1962

New Zealand, Pocket Wonder World. By Howell Walker. 419-460, Apr. 1952

New Zealand's Bountiful South Island. By Peter Benchley. Photos by James L. Amos. 93-123, Jan. 1972

New Zealand's Cook Islands: Paradise in Search of a Future. By Maurice Shadbolt. Photos by William Albert Allard. 203-231, Aug. 1967

New Zealand's North Island: The Contented Land. By Charles McCarry. Photos by Bates Littlehales. 190-213, Aug. 1974

See also Waitomo Caves

NEWELL, HOMER E.: Author:

Surveyor: Candid Camera on the Moon. 578-592, Oct. 1966

NEWFOUNDLAND (Province), Canada:

Atlantic Odyssey: Iceland to Antarctica. By Newman Bumstead. Photos by Volkmar Wentzel. 725-780, Dec. 1955

I Sailed with Portugal's Captains Courageous. By Alan Villiers. 565-596, May 1952

Newfoundland, Canada's New Province. By Andrew H. Brown. Photos by author and Robert F. Sisson. 777-812, June 1949

Newfoundland Trusts in the Sea. By Gary Jennings. Photos by Sam Abell. 112-141, Jan. 1974

Vinland Ruins Prove Vikings Found the New World. By Helge Ingstad. 708-734, Nov. 1964

See also Labrador

NEWPORT, Rhode Island:

By Square-rigger from Baltic to Bicentennial. By Kenneth Garrett. 824-857, Dec. 1976

Note: Newport served as host to tall and small ships from 27 nations July 1-4, 1976.

New England's "Lively Experiment," Rhode Island. By Robert de Roos. Photos by Fred Ward. 370-401, Sept. 1968

Rhode Island, Modern City-State. By George W.

NEWPORT, Rhode Island—*Continued*

Long. Photos by Willard R. Culver. 137-170, Aug. 1948

Windjamming Around New England. By Tom Horgan. Photos by Robert F. Sisson. 141-169, Aug. 1950

NEWPORT BEACH, California:

Happy Birthday, Otto Lilienthal! By Russell Hawkes. Photos by James Collison. 286-292, Feb. 1972

NEWTON, ISAAC:

The British Way. By Sir Evelyn Wrench. 421-541, Apr. 1949

NEWTON, JOHN G.: Author:

How We Found the *Monitor*. 48-61, Jan. 1975

The NEXT Frontier? By Isaac Asimov. Paintings by Pierre Mion. 76-89, July 1976

The NEXT 100 Years: A Master Plan for Yellowstone. By George B. Hartzog, Jr. 632-637, May 1972

NEXT Steps in Space. By Thomas O. Paine. 793-797, Dec. 1969

NGORONGORO CRATER, Tanzania:

The Flamingo Eaters of Ngorongoro (Hyenas). By Richard D. Estes. 535-539, Oct. 1973

Hyenas, the Hunters Nobody Knows. By Hans Kruuk. Photos by Baron Hugo van Lawick. 44-57, July 1968

Tool-using Bird: The Egyptian Vulture. By Baroness Jane van Lawick-Goodall. Photos by Baron Hugo van Lawick. 631-641, May 1968

NIAGARA FALLS, Canada-U. S.:

The Great Lakes: Is It Too Late? By Gordon Young. Photos by James L. Amos and Martin Rogers. 147-185, Aug. 1973

Niagara Falls, Servant of Good Neighbors. Photos by Walter Meayers Edwards. 574-587, Apr. 1963

NICHOLAS, WILLIAM H.: Author:

America's "Meat on the Hoof." 33-72, Jan. 1952

Biggest Worm Farm Caters to Platypuses. 269-280, Feb. 1949

Deep in the Heart of "Swissconsin." Photos by J. Baylor Roberts. 781-800, June 1947

Dixie Spins the Wheel of Industry. Photos by J. Baylor Roberts. 281-324, Mar. 1949

Growing Pains Beset Puerto Rico. Photos by Justin Locke. 419-460, Apr. 1951

History Repeats in Old Natchez. Photos by Willard R. Culver. 181-208, Feb. 1949

Literary Landmarks of Massachusetts. Photos by B. Anthony Stewart and John E. Fletcher. 279-310, Mar. 1950

Men, Moose, and Mink of Northwest Angle. Photos by J. Baylor Roberts. 265-284, Aug. 1947

Miami's Expanding Horizons. 561-594, Nov. 1950

Nautical Norfolk Turns to Azaleas. Photos by B. Anthony Stewart. 606-614, May 1947

Shawneetown Forsakes the Ohio. Photos by J. Baylor Roberts. 273-288, Feb. 1948

Switzerland Guards the Roof of Europe. Photos by Willard R. Culver. 205-246, Aug. 1950

Vizcaya: An Italian Palazzo in Miami. Photos by Justin Locke. 595-604, Nov. 1950

NICHOLDS, ELIZABETH: Author:

The Goats of Thunder Hill. Photos by Robert F. Sisson. 625-640, May 1954

NICHOLS, HERBERT B.: Author:

Water for the World's Growing Needs. By Herbert B. Nichols and F. Barrows Colton. 269-286, Aug. 1952

NICHOLSON, ROBERT W.: Artist:

Saving the Ancient Temples at Abu Simbel. By Georg Gerster. 694-742, May 1966

NICKLIN, CHARLES R., Jr.: Photographer:

New Tools for Undersea Archeology. By George F. Bass. 403-423, Sept. 1968

Swimming With Patagonia's Right Whales. By Roger Payne. Photos by William R. Curtsinger and Charles R. Nicklin, Jr. 576-587, Oct. 1972

NICOSIA, Cyprus:

Cyprus Under Four Flags: A Struggle for Unity. By Kenneth MacLeish. Photos by Jonathan Blair. 356-383, Mar. 1973

NIEDRACH, R. J.: Author-Photographer:

Freezing the Flight of Hummingbirds. By Harold E. Edgerton, R. J. Niedrach, and Walker Van Riper. 245-261, Aug. 1951

NIGER, Republic of:

Drought Threatens the Tuareg World. By Victor Englebert. 544-571, Apr. 1974

Freedom Speaks French in Ouagadougou. By John Scofield. 153-203, Aug. 1966

I Joined a Sahara Salt Caravan. By Victor Englebert. 694-711, Nov. 1965

NIGER RIVER, West Africa:

The Niger: River of Sorrow, River of Hope. By Georg Gerster. 152-189, Aug. 1975

NIGERIA:

Beyond the Bight of Benin. By Jeannette and Maurice Fiévet. 221-253, Aug. 1959

The Niger: River of Sorrow, River of Hope. By Georg Gerster. 152-189, Aug. 1975

Progress and Pageantry in Changing Nigeria. By W. Robert Moore. 325-365, Sept. 1956

Safari Through Changing Africa. By Elsie May Bell Grosvenor. Photos by Gilbert Grosvenor. 145-198, Aug. 1953

NIGHT Life in the Gulf Stream. By Paul A. Zahl. 391-418, Mar. 1954

NIGHT of Terror (Alaska Earthquake). By Tay Pryor Thomas. 142-156, July 1964

The NIGHT the Mountains Moved. By Samuel W. Matthews. Photos by J. Baylor Roberts. 329-359, Mar. 1960

NIGHTINGALE, FLORENCE:

The British Way. By Sir Evelyn Wrench. 421-541, Apr. 1949

The NIGHTMARE of Famine. Photos by Steve Raymer. 33-39, July 1975

NIKE (Guided Missile):

New Miracles of the Telephone Age. By Robert Leslie Conly. 87-120, July 1954

NIKOLAEVSK: A Bit of Old Russia Takes Root in Alaska. By Jim Rearden. Photos by Charles O'Rear. 401-425, Sept. 1972

NILE (River and Valley), Africa:

Abu Simbel's Ancient Temples Reborn. By Georg Gerster. 724-744, May 1969

Africa: Countries of the Nile, Atlas series supplement. Oct. 1963

Kayaks Down the Nile. By John M. Goddard. 697-732, May 1955

Nile Valley, Land of the Pharaohs, Atlas series supplement. Text on reverse. May 1965

The River Nile. Special Publication announced. 408-417, Mar. 1966

Safari from Congo to Cairo. By Elsie May Bell Grosvenor. Photos by Gilbert Grosvenor. 721-771, Dec. 1954

Saving the Ancient Temples at Abu Simbel. By Georg Gerster. Paintings by Robert W. Nicholson. 694-742, May 1966

South in the Sudan. By Harry Hoogstraal. 249-272, Feb. 1953

Threatened Treasures of the Nile. By Georg Gerster. 587-621, Oct. 1963

Yankee Cruises the Storied Nile. By Irving and Electa Johnson. Photos by Winfield Parks. 583-633, May 1965

NILSSON, LENNART: Photographer:

Fishing in the Lofotens. 377-388, Mar. 1947

NIMBUS (Weather Satellite):

Extraordinary Photograph Shows Earth Pole to Pole. Photos by Nimbus I. 190-193, Feb. 1965

Studying Wildlife by Satellite. By Frank Craighead, Jr. and John Craighead. 120-123, Jan. 1973

NIMITZ, CHESTER W.:

How One of The Society's Maps (Pacific Ocean) Saved a Precious Cargo. 844, June 1947

NIÑA (Schooner). *See* Marblehead-Halifax Race

900 Years Ago: the Norman Conquest. By Kenneth M. Setton. Photos by George F. Mobley. 206-251, Aug. 1966

NINEVEH (Ancient City):

Ancient Mesopotamia: A Light That Did Not Fail. By E. A. Speiser. Paintings by H. M. Herget. 41-105, Jan. 1951

NININGER, ROBERT D.: Author:

Hunting Uranium Around the World. Photos by Volkmar Wentzel. 533-558, Oct. 1954

NISBET, IAN: Author:

Friend of the Wind: The Common Tern. Photos by Hope Alexander. 234-247, Aug. 1973

NIXON, RICHARD M.: Author:

Russia as I Saw It. Photos by B. Anthony Stewart. 715-750, Dec. 1959

NO Place to Run: The Hmong of Laos. By W. E. Garrett. 78-111, Jan. 1974

NOBLECOURT, CHRISTIANE DESROCHES: Author:

Tutankhamun's Golden Trove. Photos by F. L. Kenett. 625-646, Oct. 1963

NOCTURNAL ANIMALS:

Strange Creatures of the Night (Television film). 144A-144B, Jan. 1973

See also Bats; Frogs; Hyenas; Oilbirds; Phalangers; Salamanders; Tarsiers

"NOICEST Parrt o'England"—the Cotswolds. By James Cerruti. Photos by Adam Woolfitt. 846-869, June 1974

NOLAN, JOHN E. H.: Author:

Life in the Land of the Basques. Photos by Justin Locke. 147-186, Feb. 1954

Pilgrimage to Holy Island and the Farnes. 547-570, Oct. 1952

Silkworms in England Spin for the Queen. 689-704, May 1953

Author-Photographer

Caldy, the Monks' Island. 564-578, Oct. 1955

NOMAD (Ketch):

Down East Cruise. By Tom Horgan. Photos by Luis Marden. 329-369, Sept. 1952

Nomad Sails Long Island Sound. By Thomas Horgan. 295-338, Sept. 1957

Windjamming Around New England. By Tom Horgan. Photos by Robert F. Sisson. 141-169, Aug. 1950

NOMAD in Alaska's Outback. By Thomas J. Abercrombie. 540-567, Apr. 1969

NOMADS:

Abraham, the Friend of God. By Kenneth MacLeish. Photos by Dean Conger. 739-789, Dec. 1966

Afghanistan: Crossroad of Conquerors. By Thomas J. Abercrombie. 297-345, Sept. 1968

The Danakil: Nomads of Ethiopia's Wasteland. By Victor Englebert. 186-211, Feb. 1970

Journey Into Troubled Iran. By George W. Long. Photos by J. Baylor Roberts. 425-464, Oct. 1951
Included: Bakhtiari, Kashgais, Kurds, Lurs

Nomads of the Far North (Indians and Eskimos). By Matthew W. Stirling. Paintings by W. Langdon Kihn. 471-504, Oct. 1949

Nomads of the World. Special Publication announced. 882-886, June 1971

Saudi Arabia: Beyond the Sands of Mecca. By Thomas J. Abercrombie. 1-53, Jan. 1966

We Dwelt in Kashgai Tents. By Jean and Franc Shor. 805-832, June 1952

See also Aborigines, Australian; Bakhtiari; Bedouin; Brahui; Bushmen; Eskimos (I Live With . . .); Gypsies; Ice Age Man; Kazakhs; Kirghiz; Lapland, for Lapps; Masai; Tuareg; Turkomans

NONDUGL, Wahgi Valley, New Guinea:

New Guinea's Paradise of Birds. By E. Thomas Gilliard. 661-688, Nov. 1951

Sheep Airlift in New Guinea. Photos by Ned Blood. 831-844, Dec. 1949

NORFOLK, Virginia:

Chesapeake Country. By Nathaniel T. Kenney. Photos by Bates Littlehales. 370-411, Sept. 1964

NORFOLK GARDENS, Norfolk, Virginia:

Nautical Norfolk Turns to Azaleas. By William H. Nicholas. Photos by B. Anthony Stewart. 606-614, May 1947

NORFOLK ISLAND, South Pacific:

Bounty Descendants Live on Remote Norfolk Island. By T. C. Roughley. Photos by J. Baylor Roberts. 559-584, Oct. 1960

NORKEY, TENZING. *See* Tenzing Norgay

NORMAN, JAMES: Author:

The Tarahumaras: Mexico's Long Distance Runners. Photos by David Hiser. 702-718, May 1976

NORMAN CONQUEST:

The British Way. By Sir Evelyn Wrench. 421-541, Apr. 1949

900 Years Ago: the Norman Conquest. By Kenneth M. Setton. Photos by George F. Mobley. 206-251, Aug. 1966

NORMANDY, France:

Normandy Blossoms Anew. By Howell Walker. 591-631, May 1959

The Vikings. By Howard La Fay. Photos by Ted Spiegel. 492-541, Apr. 1970

NORSEMEN. *See* Vikings

NORTH, WHEELER J.: Author:

Giant Kelp, Sequoias of the Sea. Photos by Bates Littlehales. 251-269, Aug. 1972

NORTH AFRICA. *See* Algeria; Morocco; Tunisia; *and* Carthage

NORTH AMERICA:

America in the Discovery Age: the Molineaux-Wright Chart. 757, June 1953

Clues to America's Past. Special Publication announced. 860-864, June 1976

How Fruit Came to America. By J. R. Magness. Paintings by Else Bostelmann. 325-377, Sept. 1951

Indians of North America; North America Before Columbus, double-sided map supplement. Dec. 1972

North America, Atlas series supplement. Apr. 1964

North America, map supplement. Mar. 1952

Our Continent: A Natural History of North America. Book announced. 572-574, Oct. 1976

Our Vegetable Travelers. By Victor R. Boswell. Paintings by Else Bostelmann. 145-217, Aug. 1949

The World in Your Garden (Flowers). By W. H. Camp. Paintings by Else Bostelmann. 1-65, July 1947

See also Canada; Central America; Greenland; Mexico; United States

NORTH AMERICAN AIR DEFENSE COMMAND (NORAD). *See* U. S. Air Force (Of Planes and Men)

NORTH BIMINI ISLAND, Bahama Islands. *See* Lerner Marine Laboratory

NORTH BORNEO. *See* Sabah

NORTH CALAVERAS GROVE (Sequoias), California. *See* Calaveras Big Trees State Park

NORTH CAROLINA:

Around the "Great Lakes of the South." By Frederick Simpich. Photos by J. Baylor Roberts. 463-491, Apr. 1948

NORTH CAROLINA—*Continued*

Dixie Spins the Wheel of Industry. By William H. Nicholas. Photos by J. Baylor Roberts. 281-324, Mar. 1949

Exploring America's Great Sand Barrier Reef. By Eugene R. Guild. Photos by John E. Fletcher and author. 325-350, Sept. 1947

Great Smokies National Park: Solitude for Millions. By Gordon Young. Photos by James L. Amos. 522-549, Oct. 1968

Here Come the Marines. By Frederick Simpich. 647-672, Nov. 1950
Included: Cherry Point Air Station and Camp Lejeune

Indian Life Before the Colonists Came. By Stuart E. Jones. Engravings by Theodore de Bry, 1590. 351-368, Sept. 1947

Menhaden—Uncle Sam's Top Commercial Fish. By Leonard C. Roy. Photos by Robert F. Sisson. 813-823, June 1949
Included: Morehead City-Beaufort area on Bogue Sound

My Neighbors Hold to Mountain Ways (Blue Ridge). By Malcolm Ross. Photos by Flip Schulke. 856-880, June 1958

North Carolina, Dixie Dynamo. By Malcolm Ross. Photos by B. Anthony Stewart. 141-183, Feb. 1962

Our Changing Atlantic Coastline. By Nathaniel T. Kenney. Photos by B. Anthony Stewart. 860-887, Dec. 1962
Included: Bodie Island; Hatteras Island; Wash Woods

Pack Trip Through the Smokies. By Val Hart. Photos by Robert F. Sisson. 473-502, Oct. 1952

Skyway Below the Clouds. By Carl R. Markwith. Photos by Ernest J. Cottrell. 85-108, July 1949
Included: Charlotte; High Rock Lake

See also Old Salem; Outer Banks; Roan Mountain

NORTH CASCADES NATIONAL PARK, Washington:

New National Park Proposed: The Spectacular North Cascades. By Nathaniel T. Kenney. Photos by James P. Blair. 642-667, May 1968

NORTH CENTRAL UNITED STATES:

Close-up: U.S.A., The North Central States, map supplement. Text on reverse. Mar. 1974

A Map Maker Looks at the United States. By Newman Bumstead. 705-748, June 1951
Included: Illinois: Chicago and Rock Island; Indiana: South Bend and Gary; Iowa: Davenport and Muscatine; Lake Michigan

Mapping the Nation's Breadbasket. By Frederick Simpich. 831-849, June 1948

North Central United States, Atlas series supplement. Nov. 1958

North Central United States, map supplement. June 1948

See also names of individual states

NORTH DAKOTA:

Duck Hunting with a Color Camera. By Arthur A. Allen. 514-539, Oct. 1951

Following the Trail of Lewis and Clark. By Ralph Gray. 707-750, June 1953

North Dakota Comes into Its Own. By Leo A. Borah. Photos by J. Baylor Roberts. 283-322, Sept. 1951

See also Minot

NORTH for Oil: *Manhattan* Makes the Historic Northwest Passage. By Bern Keating. Photos by Tomas Sennett. 374-391, Mar. 1970

NORTH ISLAND, New Zealand:

New Zealand's North Island: The Contented Land. By Charles McCarry. Photos by Bates Littlehales. 190-213, Aug. 1974

See also Waitomo Caves

NORTH KOREA. *See* Korea, North

NORTH MANKATO, Minnesota:

Satellites Gave Warning of Midwest Floods. By Peter T. White. Photos by Thomas A. DeFeo. 574-592, Oct. 1969

NORTH POLE:

North Toward the Pole on Skis. By Bjørn O. Staib. 254-281, Feb. 1965

The Peary Flag Comes to Rest. By Marie Peary Stafford. 519-532, Oct. 1954

Submarine Through the North Pole *(Nautilus)*. By William G. Lalor, Jr. Photos by John J. Krawczyk. 1-20, Jan. 1959

Up Through the Ice of the North Pole *(Skate)*. By James F. Calvert. 1-41, July 1959

We Followed Peary to the Pole. By Gilbert Grosvenor and Thomas W. McKnew. 469-484, Oct. 1953

NORTH SEA:

Oil, the Dwindling Treasure. By Noel Grove. Photos by Emory Kristof. 792-825, June 1974

Pilgrimage to Holy Island and the Farnes. By John E. H. Nolan. 547-570, Oct. 1952

Thumbs Up Round the North Sea's Rim. By Frances James. Photos by Erica Koch. 685-704, May 1952

NORTH SLOPE, Alaska:

Alaska: Rising Northern Star. By Joseph Judge. Photos by Bruce Dale. 730-767, June 1975

Oil, the Dwindling Treasure. By Noel Grove. Photos by Emory Kristof. 792-825, June 1974

The Pipeline: Alaska's Troubled Colossus. By Bryan Hodgson. Photos by Steve Raymer. 684-717, Nov. 1976
Included: Diagram, Anatomy of the pipeline; map showing potential and producing oil and gas areas

Will Oil and Tundra Mix? Alaska's North Slope Hangs in the Balance. By William S. Ellis. Photos by Emory Kristof. 485-517, Oct. 1971

NORTH STAR Cruises Alaska's Wild West. By Amos Burg. 57-86, July 1952

NORTH Through History Aboard *White Mist*. By Melville Bell Grosvenor. Photos by Edwin Stuart Grosvenor. 1-55, July 1970

NORTH Toward the Pole on Skis. By Bjørn O. Staib. 254-281, Feb. 1965

NORTH UIST (Island), Scotland:

Isles on the Edge of the Sea: Scotland's Outer Hebrides. By Kenneth MacLeish. Photos by Thomas Nebbia. 676-711, May 1970

NORTH VIET NAM:

Air Rescue Behind Enemy Lines. By Howard Sochurek. 346-369, Sept. 1968

NORTH With Finland's Lapps. By Jean and Franc Shor. 249-280, Aug. 1954

NORTH With the Snow Goose. By Des and Jen Bartlett. 822-843, Dec. 1973

NORTH With the Wheat Cutters. By Noel Grove. Photos by James A. Sugar. 194-217, Aug. 1972

NORTHAMPTON, Massachusetts. *See* Clarke School for the Deaf

NORTH-EAST NEW GUINEA:

To the Land of the Head-hunters. By E. Thomas Gilliard. 437-486, Oct. 1955

See also Papua New Guinea

NORTHERN IRELAND. *See* Ireland, Northern

NORTHERN LIGHTS. *See* Aurora Borealis

NORTHERN TERRITORY, Australia:

Eden in the Outback. By Kay and Stanley Breeden. 189-203, Feb. 1973

Rock Paintings of the Aborigines. By Kay and Stanley Breeden. 174-187, Feb. 1973

The Top End of Down Under. By Kenneth MacLeish. Photos by Thomas Nebbia. 145-174, Feb. 1973

NORTHWEST (Region), U. S.:

Climbing Our Northwest Glaciers. Photos by Bob and Ira Spring. 103-114, July 1953

Close-up: U.S.A., The Northwest, map supplement. Text on reverse. Mar. 1973

Forest Fire: The Devil's Picnic. By Stuart E. Jones and Jay Johnston. 100-127, July 1968
Included: Worst blazes of 1967 in Northwest

A Map Maker Looks at the United States. By Newman Bumstead. 705-748, June 1951

Mexico to Canada on the Pacific Crest Trail. By Mike W. Edwards. Photos by David Hiser. 741-779, June 1971

Northwestern United States, Atlas series supplement. Apr. 1960

Northwestern United States, map supplement. June 1950

See also names of individual states

NORTHWEST ANGLE, Minnesota:

Men, Moose, and Mink of Northwest Angle. By William H. Nicholas. Photos by J. Baylor Roberts. 265-284, Aug. 1947

NORTHWEST PASSAGE:

North for Oil: *Manhattan* Makes the Historic Northwest Passage. By Bern Keating. Photos by Tomas Sennett. 374-391, Mar. 1970

Trek Across Arctic America. By Colin Irwin. 295-321, Mar. 1974

NORTHWEST TERRITORIES, Canada:

Across Canada by Mackenzie's Track. By Ralph Gray. 191-239, Aug. 1955

Banks Island: Eskimo Life on the Polar Sea. By William O. Douglas. Photos by Clyde Hare. 703-735, May 1964
Included: Inuvik; Sachs Harbour, Banks Island

Canada's Caribou Eskimos (Padlermiut). By Donald B. Marsh. 87-104, Jan. 1947

Canada's "Now" Frontier. By Robert Paul Jordan. Photos by Lowell Georgia. 480-511, Oct. 1976

The Canadian North: Emerging Giant. By David

NORTHWEST TERRITORIES, Canada—*Continued*

S. Boyer. 1-43, July 1968

Far North with "Captain Mac." By Miriam Mac-
Millan. 465-513, Oct. 1951
Included: Baffin Island, Ellesmere Island

I Live With the Eskimos. By Guy Mary-
Rousseliere. 188-217, Feb. 1971

Milestones in My Arctic Journeys. By Willie Knutsen. 543-570, Oct. 1949

See also Ellesmere Island; Northwest Passage;
Southampton Island

NORTHWIND (Coast Guard Icebreaker):

Our Navy Explores Antarctica. By Richard E.
Byrd. U. S. Navy official photos. 429-522, Oct.
1947

NORWAY:

"Around the World in Eighty Days." By Newman
Bumstead. 705-750, Dec. 1951
Included: Bergen, Frognerseteren, Hardanger Fjord,
Holmenkollen, Oslo, Oslo Fjord

Baltic Cruise of the *Caribbee*. By Carleton Mitchell.
605-646, Nov. 1950

Friendly Flight to Northern Europe. By Lyndon B.
Johnson. Photos by Volkmar Wentzel. 268-293,
Feb. 1964

Midshipmen's Cruise. By William J. Aston and
Alexander G. B. Grosvenor. 711-754, June 1948

Native's Return to Norway (Mandal). By Arnvid
Nygaard. Photos by Andrew H. Brown. 683-691,
Nov. 1953

Norway, Land of the Generous Sea. By Edward J.
Linehan. Photos by George F. Mobley. 1-43, July
1971

Norway Cracks Her Mountain Shell. By Sydney
Clark. Photos by Gilbert Grosvenor and Ole
Friele Backer. 171-211, Aug. 1948

Norway's Fjords Pit Men Against Mountains. By
Andrew H. Brown. 96-122, Jan. 1957

Stop-and-Go Sail Around South Norway. By Edmond J. Moran. Photos by Randi Kjekstad Bull
and Andrew H. Brown. 153-192, Aug. 1954

Unlocking Secrets of the Northern Lights. By Carl
W. Gartlein. Paintings by William Crowder.
673-704, Nov. 1947

The Vikings. By Howard La Fay. Photos by Ted
Spiegel. 492-541, Apr. 1970

See also Jan Mayen (Island); Lofoten (Islands);
Svalbard (Archipelago)

NORWEGIAN SEA:

Seal Hunting Off Jan Mayen. By Ole Friele Backer.
57-72, Jan. 1948

NORWEGIANS:

The Last Vikings (Television film). 434A-434B,
Mar. 1972

NOTRE DAME DE CHARTRES (Cathedral). *See*
Chartres

NOTRE DAME DE PARIS (Cathedral):

Île de la Cité, Birthplace of Paris. By Kenneth Mac-
Leish. Photos by Bruce Dale. 680-719, May 1968

NOVA SCOTIA (Province), Canada:

Canada, My Country. By Alan Phillips. Photos by
David S. Boyer and Walter Meayers Edwards.
769-819, Dec. 1961

Canada's Winged Victory: the *Silver Dart*. By Gil-

NOVA SCOTIA (Province), Canada—*Continued*

bert M. Grosvenor. 254-267, Aug. 1959

Down East to Nova Scotia. By Winfield Parks. 853-
879, June 1964
Included: Baddeck, Boulaceet (Maskell's Harbour),
Bras d'Or Lakes, Cape George Harbour, Halifax, Lis-
comb, Lunenburg, Peggy's Cove, St. Peters Canal

Far North with "Captain Mac." By Miriam Mac-
Millan. 465-513, Oct. 1951
Included: Big Harbour (Port Bevis), Cape Breton Is-
land, Cape Canso, Cape Sable, Halifax, Sydney

The Giant Tides of Fundy. By Paul A. Zahl. 153-
192, Aug. 1957

The Loyalists. By Kent Britt. Photos by Ted Spiegel. 510-539, Apr. 1975
Included: Tories, American colonists who remained
loyal to the British Empire and moved to Canada during
and after the Revolution; their descendants today

Nova Scotia, the Magnificent Anchorage. By
Charles McCarry. Photos by Gordon W. Gahan.
334-363, Mar. 1975

See also Baddeck; Sable Island

NOVICK, ALVIN: Author:

Bats Aren't All Bad. Photos by Bruce Dale. 615-
637, May 1973

NOVOSIBIRSK, U.S.S.R.:

Siberia's Empire Road, the River Ob. By Robert
Paul Jordan. Photos by Dean Conger. 145-181,
Feb. 1976

NOXONTOWN POND, Delaware:

Teeming Life of a Pond. By William H. Amos. 274-
298, Aug. 1970

NUBA (Tribespeople):

Proud Primitives, the Nuba People. By Oskar Luz.
Photos by Horst Luz. 673-699, Nov. 1966
Contents: Masakin Qisar, Masakin Tiwal

With the Nuba Hillmen of Kordofan. By Robin
Strachan. 249-278, Feb. 1951
Contents: Fungor, Kau, Koalib, and Korongo

NUBIA (Region), Africa:

Threatened Treasures of the Nile. By Georg Gerster. 587-621, Oct. 1963

See also Abu Simbel

NUCLEAR ENERGY:

Four-ocean Navy in the Nuclear Age. By Thomas
W. McKnew. 145-187, Feb. 1965

Man's New Servant, the Friendly Atom. By F. Barrows Colton. Photos by Volkmar Wentzel. 71-90,
Jan. 1954

New Era in the Loneliest Continent (Antarctica).
By David M. Tyree. Photos by Albert Moldvay.
260-296, Feb. 1963

Nuclear Power for the Polar Regions (Camp Century). By George J. Dufek. 712-730, May 1962

Our Nuclear Navy. By George W. Anderson, Jr.
449-450, Mar. 1963

Powerhouse of the Northwest (Columbia River). By
David S. Boyer. 821-847, Dec. 1974

The Search for Tomorrow's Power. By Kenneth F.
Weaver. Photos by Emory Kristof. 650-681,
Nov. 1972

Uncle Sam's House of 1,000 Wonders. By Lyman J.
Briggs and F. Barrows Colton. 755-784, Dec.
1951

NUCLEAR ENERGY — *Continued*

Whatever Happened to TVA? By Gordon Young. Photos by Emory Kristof. 830-863, June 1973

You and the Obedient Atom. By Allan C. Fisher, Jr. 303-353, Sept. 1958

See also Atomic Bomb Tests; Cosmic Rays; *and Enterprise; Savannah*, N. S.; Submarines, Nuclear-powered

NUCLEAR REGULATORY COMMISSION. *See* listing under former name, Atomic Energy Commission

NUCLEAR WEAPONS:

Profiles of the Presidents: V. The Atomic Age: Its Problems and Promises. By Frank Freidel. 66-119, Jan. 1966

South Carolina Rediscovered. By Herbert Ravenel Sass. Photos by Robert F. Sisson. 281-321, Mar. 1953

Included: Savannah River Plant of the Atomic Energy Commission which produces H-bombs

See also Atomic Bomb Tests; U. S. Air Force (Of Planes and Men); U. S. Navy (Four-ocean Navy in the Nuclear Age)

NUCLEIC ACIDS:

The Awesome Worlds Within a Cell. By Rick Gore. Photos by Bruce Dale. Paintings by Davis Meltzer. 355-395, Sept. 1976

NUDIBRANCHS (Sea Slugs):

Unsung Beauties of Hawaii's Coral Reefs. By Paul A. Zahl. 510-525, Oct. 1959

NUESTRA SEÑORA DE ATOCHA (Galleon):

Atocha, Tragic Treasure Galleon of the Florida Keys. By Eugene Lyon. 787-809, June 1976

Treasure! (Television film). 575, Nov. 1976; cover, Dec. 1976

NUNGS (Tribespeople):

Cane Bridges of Asia. Photos from Paul Popper. 243-250, Aug. 1948

NYGAARD, ARNVID: Author:

Native's Return to Norway. Photos by Andrew H. Brown. 683-691, Nov. 1953

O

OAHU (Island), Hawaii. *See* Honolulu

OAK RIDGE, Tennessee:

Man's New Servant, the Friendly Atom. By F. Barrows Colton. Photos by Volkmar Wentzel. 71-90, Jan. 1954

Whatever Happened to TVA? By Gordon Young. Photos by Emory Kristof. 830-863, June 1973

OASIS-HOPPING in the Sahara. By Maynard Owen Williams. 209-236, Feb. 1949

OATES, LAWRENCE EDWARD GRACE:

The British Way. By Sir Evelyn Wrench. 421-541, Apr. 1949

OB (River), U.S.S.R.:

Siberia's Empire Road, the River Ob. By Robert Paul Jordan. Photos by Dean Conger. 145-181, Feb. 1976

OBSERVATORIES, Astronomical:

Georgetown University. *See* Georgetown, Wash-

OBSERVATORIES, Astronomical — *Continued*

ington, D. C.

Lamont-Hussey: South Africa. *See* South Africa (New Light on the Changing Face of Mars)

Lowell: Arizona. *See* Lowell Observatory

Naval Observatory. *See* U. S. Naval Observatory

Palomar: California. *See* Palomar Observatory

OCCUPIED Austria, Outpost of Democracy. By George W. Long. Photos by Volkmar Wentzel. 749-790, June 1951

OCEAN FARMING. *See* Aquiculture

OCEAN FLOORS:

Arctic Ocean Floor, double-sided map supplement. Oct. 1971

Atlantic Ocean Floor, double-sided Atlas series supplement. June 1968

Indian Ocean Floor, map supplement. Oct. 1967

Pacific Ocean Floor, double-sided map supplement. Oct. 1969

This Changing Earth. By Samuel W. Matthews. 1-37, Jan. 1973

"OCEAN mammals are to us what the buffalo was to the Plains Indian." By Lael Morgan. 354-355, Mar. 1973

OCEANAUTS:

Working for Weeks on the Sea Floor. By Jacques-Yves Cousteau. Photos by Philippe Cousteau and Bates Littlehales. 498-537, Apr. 1966

See also Underwater Living

OCEANIA. *See* South Sea Islands

OCEANOGRAPHY:

At Home in the Sea (Underwater Lodge). By Jacques-Yves Cousteau. 465-507, Apr. 1964

Calypso Explores an Undersea Canyon (Romanche Trench). By Jacques-Yves Cousteau. Photos by Bates Littlehales. 373-396, Mar. 1958

Deep Diving off Japan (Japan Trench). By Georges S. Houot. 138-150, Jan. 1960

The Deepest Days. By Robert Sténuit. 534-547, Apr. 1965

Deepstar Explores the Ocean Floor. Photos by Ron Church. 110-129, Jan. 1971

Exploring the Mid-Atlantic Ridge. By Maurice Ewing. 275-294, Sept. 1948

Fish Men Explore a New World Undersea. By Jacques-Yves Cousteau. 431-472, Oct. 1952

Man's Deepest Dive (Challenger Deep in the Mariana Trench). By Jacques Piccard. Photos by Thomas J. Abercrombie. 224-239, Aug. 1960

New Discoveries on the Mid-Atlantic Ridge. By Maurice Ewing. Photos by Robert F. Sisson. 611-640, Nov. 1949

Outpost Under the Ocean. By Edwin A. Link. Photos by Bates Littlehales. 530-533, Apr. 1965

Project FAMOUS. Photos by Emory Kristof. 586-615, May 1975

I. Where the Earth Turns Inside Out. By J. R. Heirtzler. 586-603

II. Dive Into the Great Rift. By Robert D. Ballard. 604-615

Science Explores the Monsoon Sea. By Samuel W. Matthews. Photos by Robert F. Sisson. 554-575, Oct. 1967

Scientists Ride Ice Islands on Arctic Odysseys. By

OCEANOGRAPHY—*Continued*

Lowell Thomas, Jr. Photos by Ted Spiegel. 670-691, Nov. 1965

Stalking Seals Under Antarctic Ice. By Carleton Ray. 54-65, Jan. 1966

Tektite II. 256-296, Aug. 1971
I. Science's Window on the Sea. By John G. Van-Derwalker. Photos by Bates Littlehales. 256-289
II. All-girl Team Tests the Habitat. By Sylvia A. Earle. Paintings by Pierre Mion. 291-296

This Changing Earth. By Samuel W. Matthews. 1-37, Jan. 1973

Three Months on an Arctic Ice Island. By Joseph O. Fletcher. 489-504, Apr. 1953

Tomorrow on the Deep Frontier. By Edwin A. Link. 778-801, June 1964

Twelve National Geographic Society Scientific Projects Under Way. 869-870, June 1954
Included: *Calypso* oceanographic expedition, off Madagascar; French Navy's bathyscaphe dives

What's Happening to Our Climate? By Samuel W. Matthews. 576-615, Nov. 1976

Window on Earth's Interior. By Robert D. Ballard. Photos by Emory Kristof. 228-249, Aug. 1976
Contents: Cayman Trough

Working for Weeks on the Sea Floor. By Jacques-Yves Cousteau. Photos by Philippe Cousteau and Bates Littlehales. 498-537, Apr. 1966

See also Airborne Undersea Expeditions; Antarctica (Antarctica's Nearer Side); Bathyscaphs; Ilha Nova (Volcanic Island); Marine Biology; Myojin Island (Volcano); National Oceanographic Program; Research Vessels; Scripps Institution of Oceanography; Tides and Tidal Bores

OCEANS. *See* Arctic Ocean; Atlantic Ocean; Indian Ocean; Pacific Ocean

OCTOBER Holiday on the Outer Banks. By Nike Anderson. Photos by J. Baylor Roberts. 501-529, Oct. 1955

OCTOPUSES:

Fish Men Explore a New World Undersea. By Jacques-Yves Cousteau. 431-472, Oct. 1952

Shy Monster, the Octopus. By Gilbert L. Voss. Photos by Robert F. Sisson. 776-799, Dec. 1971

ODENSE, Denmark:

2,000 Miles Through Europe's Oldest Kingdom. By Isobel Wylie Hutchison. Photos by Maynard Owen Williams. 141-180, Feb. 1949

ODYSSEY (Homer):

Homeward With Ulysses. By Melville Bell Grosvenor. Photos by Edwin Stuart Grosvenor. 1-39, July 1973

OEHSER, PAUL: Editor:

Research Reports (NGS). 442, Sept. 1975; 296, Aug. 1976

OF Planes and Men. By Kenneth F. Weaver. Photos by Emory Kristof and Albert Moldvay. 298-349, Sept. 1965

OFF Santa Barbara: California's Ranches in the Sea. By Earl Warren, Jr. Photos by Bates Littlehales. 257-283, Aug. 1958

OFF the Beaten Track of Empire. By Beverley M. Bowie. Photos by Michael Parker. 584-626, Nov. 1957

OFFICE OF NAVAL RESEARCH (ONR):

To 76,000 Feet by *Strato-Lab* Balloon. By Malcolm D. Ross and M. Lee Lewis. 269-282, Feb. 1957

OFFICE OF SCIENTIFIC RESEARCH AND DEVELOPMENT (OSRD):

Voices of the Night. By Arthur A. Allen. 507-522, Apr. 1950
Included: OSRD's project on jungle acoustics

OGASAWARA, FRANK X.: Author:

Scientist Studies Japan's Fantastic Long-tailed Fowl. Photos by Eiji Miyazawa. 845-855, Dec. 1970

OHIO:

Ohio Makes Its Own Prosperity. By Leo A. Borah. Photos by B. Anthony Stewart. 435-484, Apr. 1955

Skyway Below the Clouds. By Carl R. Markwith. Photos by Ernest J. Cottrell. 85-108, July 1949
Included: Dayton, Wright Field, and Zanesville

So Much Happens Along the Ohio River. By Frederick Simpich. Photos by Justin Locke. 177-212, Feb. 1950

OHIO (River), U. S.:

Shawneetown Forsakes the Ohio. By William H. Nicholas. Photos by J. Baylor Roberts. 273-288, Feb. 1948

So Much Happens Along the Ohio River. By Frederick Simpich. Photos by Justin Locke. 177-212, Feb. 1950

OHIO VALLEY, Ohio-West Virginia:

Who Were the "Mound Builders"? By George E. Stuart. 783-801, Dec. 1972

OIL:

Alberta Unearths Her Buried Treasures. By David S. Boyer. 90-119, July 1960

The Arab World, Inc. By John J. Putman. Photos by Winfield Parks. 494-533, Oct. 1975

Boom Time in Kuwait. By Paul Edward Case. 783-802, Dec. 1952

Calypso Explores for Underwater Oil. By Jacques-Yves Cousteau. 155-184, Aug. 1955

Canada's "Now" Frontier. By Robert Paul Jordan. Photos by Lowell Georgia. 480-511, Oct. 1976
Included: Map showing oil pipeline, proposed gas pipeline, and tar sands

The Canadian North: Emerging Giant. By David S. Boyer. 1-43, July 1968

The Fabulous State of Texas. By Stanley Walker. Photos by B. Anthony Stewart and Thomas Nebbia. 149-195, Feb. 1961

Happy-go-lucky Trinidad and Tobago. By Charles Allmon. 35-75, Jan. 1953

Houston, Prairie Dynamo. By Stuart E. Jones. Photos by William Albert Allard. 338-377, Sept. 1967

Iran: Desert Miracle. By William Graves. Photos by James P. Blair. 2-47, Jan. 1975

Iraq—Where Oil and Water Mix. By Jean and Franc Shor. 443-489, Oct. 1958

Journey into Troubled Iran. By George W. Long. Photos by J. Baylor Roberts. 425-464, Oct. 1951

Kuwait, Aladdin's Lamp of the Middle East. By John E. Frazer. Photos by David F. Cupp. 636-667, May 1969

OIL — *Continued*

Louisiana Trades with the World. By Frederick Simpich. Photos by J. Baylor Roberts. 705-738, Dec. 1947

Oil, the Dwindling Treasure. By Noel Grove. Photos by Emory Kristof. 792-825, June 1974

Oklahoma, the Adventurous One. By Robert Paul Jordan. Photos by Robert W. Madden. 149-189, Aug. 1971

Oman, Land of Frankincense and Oil. By Robert Azzi. 205-229, Feb. 1973

Sand in My Eyes (Algerian Sahara). By Jinx Rodger. 664-705, May 1958

Saudi Arabia: Beyond the Sands of Mecca. By Thomas J. Abercrombie. 1-53, Jan. 1966

Saudi Arabia, Oil Kingdom. Photos by Maynard Owen Williams. 497-512, Apr. 1948

Siberia's Empire Road, the River Ob. By Robert Paul Jordan. Photos by Dean Conger. 145-181, Feb. 1976

This Young Giant, Indonesia. By Beverley M. Bowie. Photos by J. Baylor Roberts. 351-392, Sept. 1955

Troubled Waters East of Suez. By Ernest M. Eller. 483-522, Apr. 1954

Venezuela Builds on Oil. By Thomas J. Abercrombie. 344-387, Mar. 1963

Venezuela's Crisis of Wealth. By Noel Grove. Photos by Robert W. Madden. 175-209, Aug. 1976

See also North Slope, Alaska; *and* Conshelf Bases, for underwater oil wellhead experiment; Tankers

OIL and Penguins Don't Mix. Photos by Mike Holmes. 384-397, Mar. 1973

OIL SPILLS:

Barehanded Battle to Cleanse the Bay. By Peter T. White. Photos by Jonathan S. Blair. 866-881, June 1971

Oil and Penguins Don't Mix. Photos by Mike Holmes. 384-397, Mar. 1973

OILBIRDS:

Birds That "See" in the Dark with Their Ears. By Edward S. Ross. 282-290, Feb. 1965

OKEECHOBEE, Lake, Florida:

The Imperiled Everglades. By Fred Ward. 1-27, Jan. 1972

OKEFENOKEE SWAMP, Florida-Georgia:

Okefenokee, the Magical Swamp. By François Leydet. Photos by Farrell Grehan. 169-175, Feb. 1974

OKINAWA (Island), Ryukyu Islands:

Okinawa, Pacific Outpost. 538-552, Apr. 1950

Okinawa, the Island Rebuilt. By Hope A. Diffenderfer. 265-288, Feb. 1955

Okinawa, the Island Without a Country. By Jules B. Billard. Photos by Winfield Parks and David Moore. 422-448, Sept. 1969

OKLAHOMA:

North With the Wheat Cutters. By Noel Grove. Photos by James A. Sugar. 194-217, Aug. 1972

Oklahoma, the Adventurous One. By Robert Paul Jordan. Photos by Robert W. Madden. 149-189, Aug. 1971

Skyway Below the Clouds. By Carl R. Markwith. Photos by Ernest J. Cottrell. 85-108, July 1949

OKLAHOMA — *Continued*

Included: Monkey Island Airport, Lake O' The Cherokees; Oklahoma City; Tulsa

The Wichitas: Land of the Living Prairie. By M. Woodbridge Williams. 661-697, May 1957

See also Mound Builders (Who Were)

ÖLAND (Island), Sweden:

Baltic Cruise of the *Caribbee*. By Carleton Mitchell. 605-646, Nov. 1950

OLD BELIEVERS:

Nikolaevsk: A Bit of Old Russia Takes Root in Alaska. By Jim Rearden. Photos by Charles O'Rear. 401-425, Sept. 1972

OLD BERING SEA PEOPLE:

Nomads of the Far North. By Matthew W. Stirling. Paintings by W. Langdon Kihn. 471-504, Oct. 1949

OLD Big Strong: The Lower Mississippi. By Willard Price. Photos by W. D. Vaughn. 681-725, Nov. 1960

The OLD Boston Post Roads. By Donald Barr Chidsey. 189-205, Aug. 1962

OLD-NEW Iran, Next Door to Russia. By Edward J. Linehan. Photos by Thomas J. Abercrombie. 44-85, Jan. 1961

OLD RHINEBECK AERODROME, Rhinebeck, New York:

World War I Aircraft Fly Again in Rhinebeck's Rickety Rendezvous. By Harvey Arden. Photos by Howard Sochurek. 578-587, Oct. 1970

OLD SALEM, North Carolina:

Old Salem, Morning Star of Moravian Faith. By Rowe Findley. Photos by Robert W. Madden. 818-837, Dec. 1970

OLD Whaling Days Still Flavor Life on Sea-swept Martha's Vineyard. By William P. E. Graves. Photos by James P. Blair. 778-809, June 1961

OLDEST Known Shipwreck Yields Bronze Age Cargo. By Peter Throckmorton. 697-711, May 1962

OLDEST PEOPLE:

"Every Day Is a Gift When You Are Over 100." By Alexander Leaf. Photos by John Launois. 93-119, Jan. 1973

OLDUVAI GORGE, Tanzania:

Adventures in the Search for Man. By Louis S. B. Leakey. Photos by Hugo van Lawick. 132-152, Jan. 1963

Dr. Leakey and the Dawn of Man (Television film). 703A-703B, Nov. 1966

Exploring 1,750,000 Years Into Man's Past. By L. S. B. Leakey. Photos by Robert F. Sisson. 564-589, Oct. 1961

Finding the World's Earliest Man (*Zinjanthropus boisei*). By L. S. B. Leakey. Photos by Des Bartlett. 420-435, Sept. 1960

The Leakey Tradition Lives On. By Melvin M. Payne. 143-144, Jan. 1973

The Leakeys of Africa: Family in Search of Prehistoric Man. By Melvin M. Payne. 194-231, Feb. 1965

Preserving the Treasures of Olduvai Gorge. By Melvin M. Payne. Photos by Joseph J. Scherschel. 701-709, Nov. 1966

OLIVER, JAMES A.: Author:
Behind New York's Window on Nature: The American Museum of Natural History. Photos by Robert F. Sisson. 220-259, Feb. 1963

OLIVES AND OLIVE OIL INDUSTRY:
How Fruit Came to America. By J. R. Magness. Paintings by Else Bostelmann. 325-377, Sept. 1951
Speaking of Spain. By Luis Marden. 415-456, Apr. 1950

OLMECS (Indians):
Gifts for the Jaguar God. By Philip Drucker and Robert F. Heizer. 367-375, Sept. 1956
On the Trail of La Venta Man. By Matthew W. Stirling. Photos by Richard H. Stewart. 137-172, Feb. 1947

OLMSTEAD, JUDITH: Author:
Ethiopia's Artful Weavers. Photos by James A. Sugar. 125-141, Jan. 1973

OLSON, SIGURD F.: Author:
Relics from the Rapids (Voyageurs). Photos by David S. Boyer. 413-435, Sept. 1963

OLYMPIC GAMES:
Again — the Olympic Challenge. By Alan J. Gould. 488-513, Oct. 1964
Sports-minded Melbourne, Host to the Olympics. 688-693, Nov. 1956
Tokyo, the Peaceful Explosion. By William Graves. Photos by Winfield Parks. 445-487, Oct. 1964

OLYMPIC MOUNTAINS, Washington:
A Map Maker Looks at the United States. By Newman Bumstead. 705-748, June 1951

OLYMPIC NATIONAL PARK, Washington:
In the Gardens of Olympus. By Paul A. Zahl. 85-123, July 1955
The Olympics: Northwest Majesty. By François Leydet. Photos by Farrell Grehan. 188-197, Feb. 1974

OLYMPIC PENINSULA, Washington. See Olympic National Park

OMAHA, Nebraska:
Nebraska . . . the Good Life. By Robert Paul Jordan. Photos by Lowell Georgia. 378-407, Mar. 1974

OMAN:
The Arab World, Inc. By John J. Putman. Photos by Winfield Parks. 494-533, Oct. 1975
Oman, Land of Frankincense and Oil. By Robert Azzi. 205-229, Feb. 1973
See also Muscat and Oman; and Dhows

ON a Peaceful Good Friday, Alaskans Feel the Dread Earthquake! By William P. E. Graves. 112-139, July 1964

ON Australia's Coral Ramparts. By Paul A. Zahl. 1-48, Jan. 1957

ON the Geographic's 75th Birthday — Our Best to You. By Melville Bell Grosvenor. 459, Oct. 1963

ON the Ridgepole of the Rockies. By Walter Meayers Edwards. 745-780, June 1947

ON the Road With an Old-time Circus. By John Fetterman. Photos by Jonathan Blair. 410-434, Mar. 1972

ON the Track of the West's Wild Horses. By Hope Ryden. Photos by author and Dick Durrance II. 94-109, Jan. 1971

ON the Trail of La Venta Man. By Matthew W. Stirling. Photos by Richard H. Stewart. 137-172, Feb. 1947

ON the Winds of the Dodecanese. By Jean and Franc Shor. 351-390, Mar. 1953

ONAGADORI (Long-tailed Fowl):
Scientist Studies Japan's Fantastic Long-tailed Fowl. By Frank X. Ogasawara. Photos by Eiji Miyazawa. 845-855, Dec. 1970

ONE Hundred Hours Beneath the Chesapeake. By Gilbert C. Klingel. Photos by Willard R. Culver. 681-696, May 1955

ONE Man's London. By Allan C. Fisher, Jr. Photos by James P. Blair. 743-791, June 1966

ONE Strange Night on Turtle Beach. By Paul A. Zahl. 570-581, Oct. 1973

ONELLI, LUIGI: Photographer:
Italy Smiles Again. By Edgar Erskine Hume. 693-732, June 1949

ONGES (Negrito Tribe):
The Last Andaman Islanders. By Raghubir Singh. 66-91, July 1975

ONTARIO (Province), Canada:
Across Canada by Mackenzie's Track. By Ralph Gray. 191-239, Aug. 1955
Canada, My Country. By Alan Phillips. Photos by David S. Boyer and Walter Meayers Edwards. 769-819, Dec. 1961
Canada's Dynamic Heartland, Ontario. By Marjorie Wilkins Campbell. Photos by Winfield Parks. 58-97, July 1963
The Great Lakes: Is It Too Late? By Gordon Young. Photos by James L. Amos and Martin Rogers. 147-185, Aug. 1973
Ontario, Pivot of Canada's Power. By Andrew H. Brown. Photos by B. Anthony Stewart and Bates Littlehales. 823-852, Dec. 1953
Relics from the Rapids (Voyageurs). By Sigurd F. Olson. Photos by David S. Boyer. 413-435, Sept. 1963
See also Kingston; Niagara Falls; Ottawa; St. Lawrence Seaway; Toronto

ONTARIO, Lake, Canada-U. S.:
The Great Lakes: Is It Too Late? By Gordon Young. Photos by James L. Amos and Martin Rogers. 147-185, Aug. 1973

OPAL MINING:
Coober Pedy: Opal Capital of Australia's Outback. By Kenny Moore. Photos by Penny Tweedie. 560-571, Oct. 1976
South Australia, Gateway to the Great Outback. By Howell Walker. Photos by Joseph J. Scherschel. 441-481, Apr. 1970

OPEC. See Organization of Petroleum Exporting Countries

The OPENING of the American West: Burr's 1840 Map. 762-763, June 1953

OPERATION CROSSROADS (Atomic Bomb Tests).
Photos by Joint Task Force I. Paintings by
Charles Bittinger. 519-530, Apr. 1947

OPERATION DEEP FREEZE:

Across the Frozen Desert to Byrd Station. By Paul
W. Frazier. Photos by Calvin L. Larsen. 383-
398, Sept. 1957

All-out Assault on Antarctica. By Richard E. Byrd.
141-180, Aug. 1956

Antarctica: Icy Testing Ground for Space. By Samuel W. Matthews. Photos by Robert W. Madden.
569-592, Oct. 1968

Flight Into Antarctic Darkness. By J. Lloyd Abbot,
Jr. Photos by David S. Boyer. 732-738, Nov.
1967

Man's First Winter at the South Pole. By Paul A. Siple. 439-478, Apr. 1958

New Era in the Loneliest Continent. By David M.
Tyree. Photos by Albert Moldvay. 260-296, Feb.
1963

We Are Living at the South Pole. By Paul A. Siple.
Photos by David S. Boyer. 5-35, July 1957

What We've Accomplished in Antarctica. By
George J. Dufek. 527-557, Oct. 1959

Year of Discovery Opens in Antarctica. By David
S. Boyer. 339-381, Sept. 1957

OPERATION ECLIPSE: 1948. By William A. Kinney.
325-372, Mar. 1949

OPERATION HIGHJUMP:

Our Navy Explores Antarctica. By Richard E.
Byrd. U. S. Navy official photos. 429-522, Oct.
1947

OPERATION SAIL:

By Square-rigger from Baltic to Bicentennial. By
Kenneth Garrett. 824-857, Dec. 1976

OPIUM:

The Hmong of Laos: No Place to Run. By W. E.
Garrett. 78-111, Jan. 1974

Nature's Gifts to Medicine. By Lonnelle Aikman.
Paintings by Lloyd K. Townsend and Don Crowley. 420-440, Sept. 1974

Spirits of Change Capture the Karens. By Peter
Kunstadter. 267-285, Feb. 1972

OPOSSUMS:

Br'er Possum, Hermit of the Lowlands. By Agnes
Akin Atkinson. Photos by Charles Philip Fox.
405-418, Mar. 1953

See also Possums (Phalangers)

OPTICS. *See* Lasers; Photography, Microscope; Telescopes; *and* Newton, Isaac, for his spectrum
experiments

ORANGES AND ORANGE GROWING:

Florida Rides a Space-age Boom. By Benedict
Thielen. Photos by Winfield Parks and James P.
Blair. 858-903, Dec. 1963

How Fruit Came to America. By J. R. Magness.
Paintings by Else Bostelmann. 325-377, Sept.
1951

ORANGUTANS:

Orangutans, Indonesia's "People of the Forest." By
Biruté Galdikas-Brindamour. Photos by Rod
Brindamour. 444-473, Oct. 1975

Search for the Great Apes (Television film). cover,
Jan. 1976

ORCHIDS:

The Exquisite Orchids. By Luis Marden. 485-513,
Apr. 1971

Hawaii, Island of Fire and Flowers. By Gordon
Young. Photos by Robert W. Madden. 399-425,
Mar. 1975

O'REAR, CHARLES: Photographer:

The Bittersweet Waters of the Lower Colorado. By
Rowe Findley. 540-569, Oct. 1973

California's Surprising Inland Delta. By Judith and
Neil Morgan. 409-430, Sept. 1976

A New Riviera: Mexico's West Coast. By Nathaniel
T. Kenney. 670-699, Nov. 1973

Nikolaevsk: A Bit of Old Russia Takes Root in
Alaska. By Jim Rearden. 401-425, Sept. 1972

OREGON:

Following the Trail of Lewis and Clark. By Ralph
Gray. 707-750, June 1953

Forest Fire: The Devil's Picnic. By Stuart E. Jones
and Jay Johnston. 100-127, July 1968
Included: Big Lake Airstrip blaze in Willamette National Forest; Ochoco National Forest; Wallowa-Whitman National Forest

From Sagebrush to Roses on the Columbia. By Leo
A. Borah. 571-611, Nov. 1952

A Map Maker Looks at the United States. By Newman Bumstead. 705-748, June 1951
Included: Albany, Astoria, Blue Mountains, Corval-
lis, Crater Lake, Diamond Lake, Eugene, Hells Canyon, Mount Hood, Oregon City, Portland, Rush Creek,
Salem, Vanport City, Willamette Valley

Oregon's Many Faces. By Stuart E. Jones. Photos
by Bates Littlehales. 74-115, Jan. 1969

Oregon's Sidewalk on the Sea. By Paul A. Zahl.
708-734, Nov. 1961

Powerhouse of the Northwest (Columbia River). By
David S. Boyer. 821-847, Dec. 1974

A River Restored: Oregon's Willamette. By Ethel
A. Starbird. Photos by Lowell J. Georgia. 816-
835, June 1972

Sno-Cats Mechanize Oregon Snow Survey. By Andrew H. Brown. Photos by John E. Fletcher.
691-710, Nov. 1949

Timber: How Much Is Enough? By John J. Putman. Photos by Bruce Dale. 485-511, Apr. 1974

The West Through Boston Eyes. By Stewart An-
derson. 733-776, June 1949
Included: Columbia River, Crater Lake, Klamath
Falls

See also Crater Lake National Park

OREGON TERRITORY:

The Opening of the American West: Burr's 1840
Map. 762-763, June 1953

O'REILLY, JOHN BOYLE:

Literary Landmarks of Massachusetts. By William
H. Nicholas. Photos by B. Anthony Stewart and
John E. Fletcher. 279-310, Mar. 1950

ORGAN PIPE CACTUS NATIONAL MONUMENT,
Arizona:

Abundant Life in a Desert Land. By Walter
Meayers Edwards. 424-436, Sept. 1973

**ORGANIZATION OF PETROLEUM EXPORTING
COUNTRIES (OPEC):**

The Arab World, Inc. By John J. Putman. Photos
by Winfield Parks. 494-533, Oct. 1975

ORIENTAL, Cordillera, Andes Mountains:
El Sangay, Fire-breathing Giant of the Andes. By G. Edward Lewis. 117-138, Jan. 1950

The ORIGINAL Boston: St. Botolph's Town. By Veronica Thomas. Photos by James L. Amos. 382-389, Sept. 1974

ORIOLES:
An Exotic New Oriole (Spotted-breasted) Settles in Florida. By Charles M. Brookfield and Oliver Griswold. 261-264, Feb. 1956

ORISSA (State), India:
Orissa, Past and Promise in an Indian State. By Bart McDowell. Photos by James P. Blair. 546-577, Oct. 1970

ORKNEY ISLANDS, Scotland:
Shetland and Orkney, Britain's Far North. By Isobel Wylie Hutchison. 519-536, Oct. 1953

ORLANDO, Florida:
Florida's Booming—and Beleaguered—Heartland. By Joseph Judge. Photos by Jonathan Blair. 585-621, Nov. 1973

ORMES, ROBERT M.: Author:
Colorado's Friendly Topland. 187-214, Aug. 1951

ORNITHOLOGY. See Birds

ORPHANS of the Wild. By Bruce G. Kinloch. 683-699, Nov. 1962

OSAKA, Japan:
Kansai, Japan's Historic Heartland. By Thomas J. Abercrombie. 295-339, Mar. 1970

OSBORNE, DOUGLAS: Author:
Solving the Riddles of Wetherill Mesa. Paintings by Peter V. Bianchi. 155-195, Feb. 1964

OSLO, Norway:
"Around the World in Eighty Days." By Newman Bumstead. 705-750, Dec. 1951
Baltic Cruise of the *Caribbee*. By Carleton Mitchell. 605-646, Nov. 1950
Norway, Land of the Generous Sea. By Edward J. Linehan. Photos by George F. Mobley. 1-43, July 1971
Norway Cracks Her Mountain Shell. By Sydney Clark. Photos by Gilbert Grosvenor and Ole Friele Backer. 171-211, Aug. 1948
Stop-and-Go Sail Around South Norway. By Edmond J. Moran. Photos by Randi Kjekstad Bull and Andrew H. Brown. 153-192, Aug. 1954
The Vikings. By Howard La Fay. Photos by Ted Spiegel. 492-541, Apr. 1970

OSPREYS:
The Osprey, Endangered World Citizen. By Roger Tory Peterson. Photos by Frederick Kent Truslow. 53-67, July 1969

OSSABAW (Island), Georgia:
Sea Islands: Adventuring Along the South's Surprising Coast. By James Cerruti. Photos by Thomas Nebbia and James L. Amos. 366-393, Mar. 1971

OSTEND, Belgium:
Belgium Comes Back. By Harvey Klemmer. Photos by Maynard Owen Williams. 575-614, May 1948

OSTIONAL BEACH, Costa Rica:
One Strange Night on Turtle Beach. By Paul A. Zahl. 570-581, Oct. 1973

OSTROFF, EUGENE: Photographer:
Vanished Mystery Men of Hudson Bay. By Henry B. Collins. 669-687, Nov. 1956

OTAHEITE. See Tahiti

The OTHER Nevada. By Robert Laxalt. Photos by J. Bruce Baumann. 733-761, June 1974

The OTHER Side of Jordan. By Luis Marden. 790-825, Dec. 1964

The OTHER Yosemite. By Nathaniel T. Kenney. Photos by Dean Conger. 762-781, June 1974

OTSEGO COUNTY, New York. See Thunder Hill Goat Farm

OTTAWA, Ontario, Canada:
Exploring Ottawa. By Bruce Hutchison. 565-596, Nov. 1947
Queen of Canada (Elizabeth II). By Phyllis Wilson. Photos by Kathleen Revis. 825-829, June 1959

OTTERS:
Return of the Sea Otter. By Karl W. Kenyon. Photos by James A. Mattison, Jr. 520-539, Oct. 1971

OUAGADOUGOU, Upper Volta:
Freedom Speaks French in Ouagadougou. By John Scofield. 153-203, Aug. 1966

OUESSANT, Ile d', France:
Atlantic Odyssey: Iceland to Antarctica. By Newman Bumstead. Photos by Volkmar Wentzel. 725-780, Dec. 1955

OUR Air Age Speeds Ahead. By F. Barrows Colton. 249-272, Feb. 1948

OUR Best to You—On the Geographic's 75th Birthday. By Melville Bell Grosvenor. 459, Oct. 1963

OUR Changing Atlantic Coastline. By Nathaniel T. Kenney. Photos by B. Anthony Stewart. 860-887, Dec. 1962

OUR Earth as a Satellite Sees It. By W. G. Stroud. 293-302, Aug. 1960

OUR Ecological Crisis. By Gordon Young. Photos by James P. Blair and Harry S. C. Yen. 737-795, Dec. 1970

OUR Friend From the Sea. By Robert and Nina Horstman. Photos by Robert F. Sisson. 728-736, Nov. 1968

OUR Green Treasury, the National Forests. By Nathaniel T. Kenney. Photos by J. Baylor Roberts. 287-324, Sept. 1956

OUR Growing Interstate Highway System. By Robert Paul Jordan. 195-219, Feb. 1968

OUR Home-town Planet, Earth. By F. Barrows Colton. 117-139, Jan. 1952

OUR Land Through Lincoln's Eyes. By Carolyn Bennett Patterson. Photos by W. D. Vaughn. 243-277, Feb. 1960

OUR Last Great Wilderness. By David Jeffery. 769-791, June 1975

OUR Life-giving Star, the Sun. By Herbert Friedman. 713-743, Nov. 1965

OUR Life on a Border Kibbutz. By Carol and Al Abrams. Photos by Al Abrams. 364-391, Sept. 1970

OUR Magnificent Capital City. Photos by B. Anthony Stewart. 715-738, June 1947

OUR Man-in-Sea Project. By Edwin A. Link. 713-717, May 1963

OUR Navy Explores Antarctica. By Richard E. Byrd. U. S. Navy official photos. 429-522, Oct. 1947

OUR Navy in the Far East. By Arthur W. Radford. Photos by J. Baylor Roberts. 537-577, Oct. 1953

OUR Navy's Long Submarine Arm. By Allan C. Fisher, Jr. 613-636, Nov. 1952

OUR Nuclear Navy. By George W. Anderson, Jr. 449-450, Mar. 1963

OUR Only Native Stork, the Wood Ibis. By Robert Porter Allen. Photos by Frederick Kent Truslow. 294-306, Feb. 1964

OUR Restless Earth. By Maynard M. Miller. 140-141, July 1964

OUR Search for British Paintings. By Franklin L. Fisher. 543-550, Apr. 1949

OUR Snake Friends and Foes. By Doris M. Cochran. Paintings by Walter A. Weber. 334-364, Sept. 1954

OUR Society Welcomes Its 3,000,000th Member. By Melville Bell Grosvenor. 579-582, Apr. 1962

OUR Society's 75 Years Exploring Earth, Sea, and Sky. By Melvin M. Payne. 1-43, Jan. 1963

OUR Universe Unfolds New Wonders. By Albert G. Wilson. 245-260, Feb. 1952

OUR Vegetable Travelers. By Victor R. Boswell. Paintings by Else Bostelmann. 145-217, Aug. 1949

OUR Virgin Islands, 50 Years Under the Flag. By Carleton Mitchell. Photos by James L. Stanfield. 67-103, Jan. 1968

OUR War Memorials Abroad: A Faith Kept. By George C. Marshall. 731-737, June 1957

OURO PRÊTO, Minas Gerais, Brazil:
Brazil's Land of Minerals. By W. Robert Moore. 479-508, Oct. 1948

OUTER BANKS, North Carolina:
Exploring America's Great Sand Barrier Reef. By Eugene R. Guild. Photos by John E. Fletcher and author. 325-350, Sept. 1947
How We Found the *Monitor*. By John G. Newton. 48-61, Jan. 1975
Note: *Monitor* was lost off the Outer Banks during the Civil War.
Lonely Cape Hatteras, Besieged by the Sea. By William S. Ellis. Photos by Emory Kristof. 393-421, Sept. 1969
October Holiday on the Outer Banks. By Nike Anderson. Photos by J. Baylor Roberts. 501-529, Oct. 1955
Our Changing Atlantic Coastline. By Nathaniel T. Kenney. Photos by B. Anthony Stewart. 860-887, Dec. 1962

OUTER HEBRIDES (Islands), Scotland:
From Barra to Butt in the Hebrides. By Isobel Wylie Hutchison. 559-580, Oct. 1954
Hunting Folk Songs in the Hebrides. By Margaret Shaw Campbell. 249-272, Feb. 1947
Isles on the Edge of the Sea. By Kenneth MacLeish. Photos by Thomas Nebbia. 676-711, May 1970
Scotland From Her Lovely Lochs and Seas. By Alan Villiers. Photos by Robert F. Sisson. 492-541, Apr. 1961

OUTER MONGOLIA. *See* Mongolian People's Republic

OUTLAW TRAIL, U. S. West:
Riding the Outlaw Trail. By Robert Redford. Photos by Jonathan Blair. 622-657, Nov. 1976

OUTPOST Under the Ocean. By Edwin A. Link. Photos by Bates Littlehales. 530-533, Apr. 1965

OUTWARD BOUND SCHOOL:
Journey to the Outer Limits (Television film). 150A-150B, Jan. 1974

OVER and Under Chesapeake Bay. By David S. Boyer. 593-612, Apr. 1964

OVER Plains and Hills of South Dakota. Photos by J. Baylor Roberts. 563-586, May 1947

OVER the Sea to Scotland's Skye. By Robert J. Reynolds. 87-112, July 1952

OWENS VALLEY, California:
California's Parched Oasis, the Owens Valley. By Judith and Neil Morgan. Photos by Jodi Cobb and Galen Rowell. 98-127, Jan. 1976

OYSTER FLEET:
The Sailing Oystermen of Chesapeake Bay. By Luis Marden. 798-819, Dec. 1967

OYSTERS:
"Delmarva," Gift of the Sea. By Catherine Bell Palmer. 367-399, Sept. 1950

OZARK PLATEAU, Arkansas-Missouri:
An Ozark Family Carves a Living and a Way of Life. Photos by Bruce Dale. 124-133, July 1975
Through Ozark Hills and Hollows. By Mike W. Edwards. Photos by Bruce Dale. 656-689, Nov. 1970

P

PA PAE, Thailand:
Living With Thailand's Gentle Lua. By Peter Kunstadter. 122-152, July 1966

PACIFIC COAST, U. S.:
California's Land Apart—the Monterey Peninsula. By Mike W. Edwards. 682-703, Nov. 1972
California's Wonderful One (State Highway No. 1). By Frank Cameron. Photos by B. Anthony Stewart. 571-617, Nov. 1959
Oregon's Sidewalk on the Sea. By Paul A. Zahl. 708-734, Nov. 1961

PACIFIC CREST TRAIL, U. S.:
Mexico to Canada on the Pacific Crest Trail. By Mike W. Edwards. Photos by David Hiser. 741-779, June 1971

PACIFIC CREST TRAIL, U. S. — *Continued*

The Pacific Crest Trail. Special Publication announced. 870-874, June 1974

PACIFIC FLEET, U. S.:

Our Navy in the Far East. By Arthur W. Radford. Photos by J. Baylor Roberts. 537-577, Oct. 1953

Pacific Fleet: Force for Peace. By Franc Shor. Photos by W. E. Garrett. 283-335, Sept. 1959

PACIFIC GROVE, California:

Mystery of the Monarch Butterfly. By Paul A. Zahl. 588-598, Apr. 1963

PACIFIC ISLANDS:

Adventures with the Survey Navy. By Irving Johnson. 131-148, July 1947
  Contents: Deboyne Lagoon, Louisiade Archipelago; Florida Island, Solomon Islands; Funafuti, Ellice Islands; Guadalcanal, Solomon Islands; Iwo Jima, Volcano Islands; Kwajalein, Marshall Islands; Nukufetau, Ellice Islands; Tarawa, Gilbert Islands; Ulithi, Caroline Islands; Uvéa, Wallis Islands

The Bonins and Iwo Jima Go Back to Japan. By Paul Sampson. Photos by Joe Munroe. 128-144, July 1968

Captain Cook: The Man Who Mapped the Pacific. By Alan Villiers. Photos by Gordon W. Gahan. 297-349, Sept. 1971

Islands of the Pacific; Discoverers of the Pacific, double-sided map supplement. Dec. 1974

Isles of the Pacific. 732-793, Dec. 1974
  I. The Coming of the Polynesians. By Kenneth P. Emory. 732-745
  II. Wind, Wave, Star, and Bird. By David Lewis. Photos by Nicholas deVore III. 747-781
  III. The Pathfinders. Paintings by Herb Kawainui Kane. 756-769
  IV. Problems in Paradise. By Mary and Laurance S. Rockefeller. Photos by Thomas Nebbia. 782-793

Isles of the South Pacific. Special Publication announced. 868-875, June 1967

Micronesia: The Americanization of Eden. By David S. Boyer. 702-744, May 1967

New Guinea to Bali in *Yankee.* By Irving and Electa Johnson. 767-815, Dec. 1959

Our Navy in the Far East. By Arthur W. Radford. Photos by J. Baylor Roberts. 537-577, Oct. 1953

Pacific Ocean, map supplement. Dec. 1952

Pacific Ocean; New Zealand, New Guinea and the Principal Islands of the Pacific, double-sided Atlas series supplement. Apr. 1962

Pacific Wards of Uncle Sam. By W. Robert Moore. 73-104, July 1948

Polynesian Adventure (Television film). 592A-592B, Apr. 1969

Shells Take You Over World Horizons. By Rutherford Platt. 33-84, July 1949

A Teen-ager Sails the World Alone. By Robin Lee Graham. 445-491, Oct. 1968

The Voyage of the Brigantine *Yankee* (Television film). 265A-265B, Feb. 1966

Yankee Roams the Orient. By Irving and Electa Johnson. 327-370, Mar. 1951
  Included: New Guinea; New Hebrides; Solomon Islands; Trobriand Islands

The *Yankee's* Wander-world. By Irving and Electa Johnson. 1-50, Jan. 1949

See also Bikini; Canton Island; Cook Islands; Eas-

PACIFIC ISLANDS — *Continued*

ter Island; Fiji Islands; Galapagos Islands; Guam; Hawaii; Ifalik; Kapingamarangi; Kwajalein; Malekula; Marquesas Islands; Midway Islands; Mindanao; Myojin Island; Nauru; New Britain; New Guinea; New Hebrides; New Zealand; Norfolk Island; Okinawa; Pentecost Island; Philippines; Pitcairn Island; Samoa; Tahiti; Taiwan; Tanna; Tonga; Truk Lagoon; Tuamotu Archipelago; Yap Islands

PACIFIC MAP Played Providential Role: How One of the Society's Maps Saved a Precious Cargo. 844, June 1947

PACIFIC NORTHWEST. *See* Northwest (Region), U. S.

PACIFIC OCEAN:

Adventures with the Survey Navy. By Irving Johnson. 131-148, July 1947

Deep Diving off Japan. By Georges S. Houot. 138-150, Jan. 1960

How One of the Society's Maps (Pacific Ocean) Saved a Precious Cargo. 844, June 1947

Islands of the Pacific; Discoverers of the Pacific, double-sided map supplement. Dec. 1974

Magellan: First Voyage Around the World. By Alan Villiers. Photos by Bruce Dale. 721-753, June 1976

Man's Deepest Dive (Mariana Trench). By Jacques Piccard. Photos by Thomas J. Abercrombie. 224-239, Aug. 1960

Pacific Ocean, double-sided Atlas series supplement. Apr. 1962

Pacific Ocean, map supplement. Dec. 1952

Pacific Ocean; Pacific Ocean Floor, double-sided map supplement. Oct. 1969

Scientists Drill at Sea to Pierce Earth's Crust (Project Mohole). By Samuel W. Matthews. Photos by J. Baylor Roberts. 686-697, Nov. 1961

See also Pacific Fleet, U. S.; Pacific Islands; *and Hokule'a; Triton*

PACIFIC RIDLEY TURTLES:

One Strange Night on Turtle Beach. By Paul A. Zahl. 570-581, Oct. 1973

PACK TRIP Through the Smokies. By Val Hart. Photos by Robert F. Sisson. 473-502, Oct. 1952

PADANARAM (Communal Village), Indiana:

Indiana's Self-reliant Uplanders. By James Alexander Thom. Photos by J. Bruce Baumann. 341-363, Mar. 1976

PADLERMIUT (Eskimos):

Canada's Caribou Eskimos. By Donald B. Marsh. 87-104, Jan. 1947

PADLOCK RANCH, Montana-Wyoming:

Cowpunching on the Padlock Ranch. By William Albert Allard. 478-499, Oct. 1973

PAGAN, Burma:

Pagan, on the Road to Mandalay. By W. E. Garrett. 343-365, Mar. 1971

PAGEANTRY of the Siamese Stage. By D. Sonakul. Photos by W. Robert Moore. 201-212, Feb. 1947

PAGODAS:

Pagan, on the Road to Mandalay. By W. E. Garrett. 343-365, Mar. 1971

PAHLAVI, MOHAMMAD REZA. *See* Mohammad Reza Pahlavi

PAINE, THOMAS:

Firebrands of the Revolution. By Eric F. Goldman. Photos by George F. Mobley. 2-27, July 1974

PAINE, THOMAS O.: Author:

Next Steps in Space. 793-797, Dec. 1969

PAINTERS. *See* Artists

PAINTING SUPPLEMENTS:

"The Adoration of the Magi," a reproduction of the tondo by Fra Angelico and Fra Filippo Lippi. Jan. 1952

"The Dusty Face of Mars." Double-sided supplement. Feb. 1973

"How Man Pollutes His World." Map on reverse. Dec. 1970

"Ice Age Mammals of the Alaskan Tundra." Map of Canada on reverse. Mar. 1972

"Mayflower II." Nov. 1957

"Teammates in Mankind's Greatest Adventure" (Apollo Astronauts). Double-sided supplement. Sept. 1973

"Whales of the World." Map on reverse. Dec. 1976

PAKISTAN:

"Around the World in Eighty Days." By Newman Bumstead. 705-750, Dec. 1951
    Included: Karachi, Khyber Pass, Kohat Pass, Peshawar, Swat (State)

Imperiled Phantom of Asian Peaks: First Photographs of Snow Leopards in the Wild. By George B. Schaller. 702-707, Nov. 1971

In the Footsteps of Alexander the Great. By Helen and Frank Schreider. Paintings by Tom Lovell. 1-65, Jan. 1968

Pakistan, New Nation in an Old Land. By Jean and Franc Shor. 637-678, Nov. 1952

Pakistan: Problems of a Two-part Land. By Bern Keating. Photos by Albert Moldvay. 1-47, Jan. 1967

Sky Road East. By Tay and Lowell Thomas, Jr. 71-112, Jan. 1960

Troubled Waters East of Suez. By Ernest M. Eller. 483-522, Apr. 1954

When the President Goes Abroad (Eisenhower Tour). By Gilbert M. Grosvenor. 588-649, May 1960

See also Hunza

PAKISTAN, East:

East Pakistan Drives Back the Jungle. By Jean and Franc Shor. 399-426, Mar. 1955

See also Bangladesh

PALEN, COLE:

World War I Aircraft Fly Again in Rhinebeck's Rickety Rendezvous. By Harvey Arden. Photos by Howard Sochurek. 578-587, Oct. 1970

PALEONTOLOGY:

Adventures in the Search for Man. By Louis S. B. Leakey. Photos by Hugo van Lawick. 132-152, Jan. 1963
    Included: *Kenyapithecus wickeri; and* fossil remains of a giant rhinoceros, giant baboon, and antelope

Big Game Hunting in the Land of Long Ago (South Dakota). By Joseph P. Connolly and James D. Bump. 589-605, May 1947

PALEONTOLOGY — *Continued*

Ethiopia Yields First "Family" of Early Man. By Donald C. Johanson. Photos by David Brill. 790-811, Dec. 1976
    Contents: *Australopithecus, Homo*

Exploring 1,750,000 Years Into Man's Past. By L. S. B. Leakey. Photos by Robert F. Sisson. 564-589, Oct. 1961
    Included: Dinotherium, giant porcupine, saber-toothed tiger, and swamp antelope

Finding the World's Earliest Man. By L. S. B. Leakey. Photos by Des Bartlett. 420-435, Sept. 1960
    Included: *Afrochoerus* (prehistoric pig), *Pelorovis* (giant sheep), *Proconsul africanus* (primitive ape), *Simopithecus jonathani* (giant baboon), *Sivatherium* (short-necked giraffe), *Zinjanthropus boisei* (early man)

Fossils Lift the Veil of Time. By Harry S. Ladd and Roland W. Brown. 363-386, Mar. 1956

In Search of Man's Past at Lake Rudolf. By Richard E. Leakey. Photos by Gordon W. Gahan. 712-734, May 1970

The Leakey Tradition Lives On. By Melvin M. Payne. 143-144, Jan. 1973

The Leakeys of Africa: Family in Search of Prehistoric Man. By Melvin M. Payne. 194-231, Feb. 1965
    Included: *Kenyapithecus, Proconsul, Zinjanthropus; and* the discovery of *Homo habilis; also,* bantam rhinoceros jaw, rodent and bird bones

Preserving the Treasures of Olduvai Gorge. By Melvin M. Payne. Photos by Joseph J. Scherschel. 701-709, Nov. 1966
    Included: *Homo erectus, Homo habilis, Kenyapithecus,* Maiko Gully "George," *Zinjanthropus; and* the broken molar of a dinotherium; the tooth and bones of an extinct elephant

Re-creating a Vanished World. By Russell D. Guthrie. 294-301, Mar. 1972

Skull 1470. By Richard E. Leakey. Photos by Bob Campbell. 819-829, June 1973

A Visit to the Living Ice Age. By Rutherford Platt. 525-545, Apr. 1957

See also Aepyornis; Brontosaurs; *and* American Museum of Natural History; Dinosaur National Monument; Smithsonian Institution

PALERMO, Sicily:

Sicily, Where All the Songs Are Sad. By Howard La Fay. Photos by Jonathan Blair. 407-436, Mar. 1976

PALESTINE. *See* Bible Lands; Israel; Jordan

PALIO (Horse Race), Siena, Italy:

The Palio of Siena. By Edgar Erskine Hume. 231-244, Aug. 1951

The Renaissance Lives On in Tuscany. By Luis Marden. Photos by Albert Moldvay. 626-659, Nov. 1974

PALISADES, New York-New Jersey:

The Mighty Hudson. By Albert W. Atwood. Photos by B. Anthony Stewart. 1-36, July 1948

PALISADES INTERSTATE PARK, New York-New Jersey:

Skyline Trail from Maine to Georgia. By Andrew H. Brown. Photos by Robert F. Sisson. 219-251, Aug. 1949

PALM SPRINGS, California:

Californians Escape to the Desert. By Mason Suth-

PALM SPRINGS, California—*Continued*
erland. Photos by Charles W. Herbert. 675-724, Nov. 1957

PALMAR, C. ERIC: Author-Photographer:
Scotland's Golden Eagles at Home. 273-286, Feb. 1954

PALMER, ALFRED MONROE:
Yemen—Southern Arabia's Mountain Wonderland. By Harlan B. Clark. 631-672, Nov. 1947

PALMER, CATHERINE BELL: Author:
Appalachian Valley Pilgrimage. 1-32, July 1949
Crickets, Nature's Expert Fiddlers. 385-394, Sept. 1953
"Delmarva," Gift of the Sea. 367-399, Sept. 1950
Split-second Time Runs Today's World. By F. Barrows Colton and Catherine Bell Palmer. 399-428, Sept. 1947

PALMSTROM, WILLIAM N.: Artist:
Space Satellites, Tools of Earth Research. By Heinz Haber. 487-509, Apr. 1956

PALOMAR OBSERVATORY, California:
Mapping the Unknown Universe. By F. Barrows Colton. 401-420, Sept. 1950
See also Sky Survey

PAMIR (Ship):
Last of the Cape Horners. By Alan Villiers. 701-710, May 1948
Square-rigger in a Tempest. 703-710

PAMIRS (Mountains), Central Asia:
We Took the Highroad in Afghanistan. By Jean and Franc Shor. 673-706, Nov. 1950
Winter Caravan to the Roof of the World. By Sabrina and Roland Michaud. 435-465, Apr. 1972

PAMPA GALERAS NATIONAL VICUÑA RESERVE, Peru:
High, Wild World of th Vicuña. By William L. Franklin. 77-91, Jan. 1973

PAMPAS (Grasslands):
High, Wild World of the Vicuña. By William L. Franklin. 77-91, Jan. 1973

PAN AMERICAN HIGHWAY:
We Drove Panama's Darién Gap. By Kip Ross. 368-389, Mar. 1961

PANAMA:
Exploring Ancient Panama by Helicopter. By Matthew W. Stirling. Photos by Richard H. Stewart. 227-246, Feb. 1950
Included: Archeological sites in provinces of Chiriquí and Veraguas
Exploring the Past in Panama. By Matthew W. Stirling. Photos by Richard H. Stewart. 373-399, Mar. 1949
Included: Azuero Peninsula, Tambor region
Hunting Prehistory in Panama Jungles. By Matthew W. Stirling. Photos by Richard H. Stewart. 271-290, Aug. 1953
Panama, Link Between Oceans and Continents. By Jules B. Billard. Photos by Bruce Dale. 402-440, Mar. 1970
Robin Sails Home. By Robin Lee Graham. 504-545, Oct. 1970
We Drove Panama's Darién Gap. By Kip Ross. 368-389, Mar. 1961

PANAMA CANAL:
Panama, Link Between Oceans and Continents. By Jules B. Billard. Photos by Bruce Dale. 402-440, Mar. 1970

PANAMIN. *See* Presidential Arm for National Minorities (Philippines)

PANAMINT RANGE, California:
Getting to Know the Wild Burros of Death Valley. By Patricia des Roses Moehlman. Photos by Ira S. Lerner and author. 502-517, Apr. 1972

PANDAS, Giant:
Pandas. Children's book announced. 726-728, Nov. 1973
What's Black and White and Loved All Over? By Theodore H. Reed. Photos by Donna K. Grosvenor. 803-815, Dec. 1972

PANTHERS. *See* Mountain Lions

PAPER AND PULP INDUSTRY:
Dixie Spins the Wheel of Industry. By William H. Nicholas. Photos by J. Baylor Roberts. 281-324, Mar. 1949
From Sagebrush to Roses on the Columbia. By Leo A. Borah. 571-611, Nov. 1952
A River Restored: Oregon's Willamette. By Ethel A. Starbird. Photos by Lowell Georgia. 816-835, June 1972
Timber: How Much Is Enough? By John J. Putman. Photos by Bruce Dale. 485-511, Apr. 1974
Versatile Wood Waits on Man. By Andrew H. Brown. 109-140, July 1951

PAPUA NEW GUINEA:
Change Ripples New Guinea's Sepik River. By Malcolm S. Kirk. 354-381, Sept. 1973
See also former name, Australian New Guinea; *and* New Britain

PAPYRUS SHIP. *See* Ra II

PARACHUTE JUMPS:
Graduation by Parachute. By John E. Fletcher. 833-846, June 1952
The Long, Lonely Leap. By Joseph W. Kittinger, Jr. Photos by Volkmar Wentzel. 854-873, Dec. 1960
See also Para-Explorers

PARACHUTE RIGGER SCHOOL, Lakehurst, New Jersey:
Graduation by Parachute. By John E. Fletcher. 833-846, June 1952

PARA-EXPLORERS Challenge Peru's Unknown Vilcabamba. By G. Brooks Baekeland. Photos by author and Peter R. Gimbel. 268-296, Aug. 1964

PARAGUAY (River), South America:
The Jungle Was My Home. By Sasha Siemel. 695-712, Nov. 1952

PARÍCUTIN (Volcano), Mexico:
Lost Kingdom in Indian Mexico. By Justin Locke. 517-546, Oct. 1952

PARIS, France:
Home Life in Paris Today. By Deena Clark. 43-72, July 1950
Île de la Cité, Birthplace of Paris. By Kenneth Mac-

PARIS, France—*Continued*

Leish. Photos by Bruce Dale. 680-719, May 1968

The Louvre, France's Palace of the Arts. By Hereward Lester Cooke, Jr. 796-831, June 1971

The More Paris Changes. . . . By Howell Walker. Photos by Gordon W. Gahan. 64-103, July 1972

Paris, Home Town of the World. By Donald William Dresden. Photos by Justin Locke. 767-804, June 1952

Paris: Vibrant Heart of France. 285-302, Aug. 1958

Paris Flea Market. By Franc Shor. Photos by Alexander Taylor. 318-326, Mar. 1957

Paris to Antwerp with the Water Gypsies. By David S. Boyer. 530-559, Oct. 1955

Round the World School (ISA). By Paul Antze. Photos by William Eppridge. 96-127, July 1962

PARITA, Panama:

Exploring the Past in Panama. By Matthew W. Stirling. Photos by Richard H. Stewart. 373-399, Mar. 1949

PARK, EDWARDS: Author:

El Morro: Story in Stone (New Mexico). 237-244, Aug. 1957

Washington Wilderness, the North Cascades. Photos by Kathleen Revis. 355-367, Mar. 1961

A PARK to Save the Tallest Trees. By Melville Bell Grosvenor. 62-64, July 1966

PARKER, MICHAEL: Photographer:

Off the Beaten Track of Empire (Prince Philip's Tour). By Beverley M. Bowie. 584-626, Nov. 1957

PARKS, WINFIELD: Author:

Down East to Nova Scotia. 853-879, June 1964

Photographer

The Arab World, Inc. By John J. Putman. 494-533, Oct. 1975

The Arans, Ireland's Invincible Isles. By Veronica Thomas. 545-573, Apr. 1971

Behind the Headlines in Viet Nam. By Peter T. White. 149-189, Feb. 1967

Brazil, Ôba! By Peter T. White. 299-353, Sept. 1962

Buenos Aires, Argentina's Melting-pot Metropolis. By Jules B. Billard. 662-695, Nov. 1967

Cairo, Troubled Capital of the Arab World. By William S. Ellis. 639-667, May 1972

Canada's Dynamic Heartland, Ontario. By Marjorie Wilkins Campbell. 58-97, July 1963

Carnival in Trinidad. By Howard La Fay. 693-701, Nov. 1971

Finisterre Sails the Windward Islands. By Carleton Mitchell. 755-801, Dec. 1965

Florida Rides a Space-age Boom. By Benedict Thielen. Photos by Winfield Parks and James P. Blair. 858-903, Dec. 1963

A Fresh Breeze Stirs the Leewards. By Carleton Mitchell. 488-537, Oct. 1966

The Highlands, Stronghold of Scottish Gaeldom. By Kenneth MacLeish. 398-435, Mar. 1968

In Storied Lands of Malaysia. By Maurice Shadbolt. 734-783, Nov. 1963

Iran's Shah Crowns Himself and His Empress. By Franc Shor. Photos by James L. Stanfield and Winfield Parks. 301-321, Mar. 1968

PARKS, WINFIELD: Photographer—*Continued*

The Isles of Greece: Aegean Birthplace of Western Culture. By Melville Bell Grosvenor. Photos by Edwin Stuart Grosvenor and Winfield Parks. 147-193, Aug. 1972

Istanbul, the City That Links Europe and Asia. By William S. Ellis. 501-533, Oct. 1973

Lonely Wonders of Katmai. By Ernest Gruening. 800-831, June 1963

Okinawa, the Island Without a Country. By Jules B. Billard. Photos by Winfield Parks and David Moore. 422-448, Sept. 1969

The Phoenicians, Sea Lords of Antiquity. By Samuel W. Matthews. Paintings by Robert C. Magis. 149-189, Aug. 1974

Queensland: Young Titan of Australia's Tropic North. By Kenneth MacLeish. 593-639, Nov. 1968

Romania: Maverick on a Tightrope. By William S. Ellis. 688-713, Nov. 1975

Singapore, Reluctant Nation. By Kenneth MacLeish. 269-300, Aug. 1966

Time Turns Back in Picture-book Portofino. By Carleton Mitchell. 232-253, Feb. 1965

Tokyo, the Peaceful Explosion. By William Graves. 445-487, Oct. 1964

When in Rome. . . . By Stuart E. Jones. 741-789, June 1970

Yankee Cruises the Storied Nile. By Irving and Electa Johnson. 583-633, May 1965

PARKS:

Parks, Plans, and People: How South America Guards Her Green Legacy. By Mary and Laurance Rockefeller. Photos by George F. Mobley. 74-119, Jan. 1967

The Parks in Your Backyard (U. S.). By Conrad L. Wirth. 647-707, Nov. 1963

See also Longwood Gardens; National Parks; State Parks; Waterton-Glacier International Peace Park

PARKSCAPE, U.S.A.: Tomorrow in Our National Parks. By George B. Hartzog, Jr. 48-93, July 1966

PARROTS. *See* Lorikeets

PASACHOFF, JAY M.: Author:

Solar Eclipse, Nature's Super Spectacular. By Donald H. Menzel and Jay M. Pasachoff. 222-233, Aug. 1970

PASADENA, California. *See* Tournament of Roses

PASSAGE to Freedom in Viet Nam. By Gertrude Samuels. 858-874, June 1955

PASSION PLAY:

Mesa del Nayar's Strange Holy Week. By Guillermo Aldana E. 780-795, June 1971

The PAST Is Present in Greenfield Village. By Beverley M. Bowie. Photos by Neal P. Davis and Willard R. Culver. 96-127, July 1958

PATAGONIA (Region), Argentina-Chile:

Magellan: First Voyage Around the World. By Alan Villiers. Photos by Bruce Dale. 721-753, June 1976

Included: Discovery and naming of Patagonia in 1520

Patagonia. Photos by Des and Jen Bartlett. 290-

PATAGONIA (Region), Argentina-Chile—*Continued*
339, Mar. 1976
I. Argentina Protects Its Wildlife Treasures. By
William G. Conway. 290-297
II. Where Two Worlds Meet. 298-321
III. At Home With Right Whales. By Roger
Payne. 322-339
Swimming With Patagonia's Right Whales. By
Roger Payne. Photos by William R. Curtsinger
and Charles R. Nicklin, Jr. 576-587, Oct. 1972

PATENTS:
Patent Plants Enrich Our World. By Orville H.
Kneen. Photos from U. S. Plant Patents. 357-
378, Mar. 1948

The **PATHFINDERS**. Paintings by Herb Kawainui
Kane. 756-769, Dec. 1974

PATHWAY Through History: Today Along the Natchez Trace. By Bern Keating. Photos by Charles
Harbutt. 641-667, Nov. 1968

PATMOS (Island), Greece:
The Isles of Greece: Aegean Birthplace of Western
Culture. By Melville Bell Grosvenor. Photos by
Edwin Stuart Grosvenor and Winfield Parks.
147-193, Aug. 1972

PATRIOTS in Petticoats. By Lonnelle Aikman. Paintings by Louis S. Glanzman. 475-493, Oct. 1975

PATROLLING Troubled Formosa Strait. 573-588,
Apr. 1955

PATTERSON, CAROLYN BENNETT: Author:
Date Line: United Nations, New York. Photos by
B. Anthony Stewart and John E. Fletcher. 305-
331, Sept. 1961
The Fair Reopens (New York World's Fair, 1964-
1965). Photos by James P. Blair. 505-529, Apr.
1965
The Final Tribute (Churchill Funeral). 199-225,
Aug. 1965
Gettysburg and Vicksburg: the Battle Towns To-
day. By Robert Paul Jordan. Map notes by Caro-
lyn Bennett Patterson. 4-57, July 1963
Haiti: Beyond Mountains, More Mountains. Pho-
tos by Thomas Nebbia. 70-97, Jan. 1976
Mardi Gras in New Orleans. Photos by Robert F.
Sisson and John E. Fletcher. 726-732, Nov. 1960
Our Land Through Lincoln's Eyes. Photos by
W. D. Vaughn. 243-277, Feb. 1960
Seattle Fair Looks to the 21st Century. Photos by
Thomas Nebbia. 402-427, Sept. 1962
Soaring on Skis in the Swiss Alps. Photos by Kath-
leen Revis. 94-121, Jan. 1961

PATTON, GEORGE S., Jr.:
Luxembourg, Survivor of Invasions. By Sydney
Clark. Photos by Maynard Owen Williams. 791-
810, June 1948

PÁTZCUARO (City and Lake), Mexico:
Lost Kingdom in Indian Mexico. By Justin Locke.
517-546, Oct. 1952

PAUL, Saint:
Jerusalem to Rome in the Path of St. Paul. By David
S. Boyer. 707-759, Dec. 1956

PAXOS (Island), Greece:
Homeward With Ulysses. By Melville Bell Grosve-
nor. Photos by Edwin Stuart Grosvenor. 1-39,
July 1973

PAYNE, MELVIN M.:
Board of Trustees, Chairman. 159, 225, 226, 227,
Aug. 1976
Committee for Research and Exploration. 433,
Mar. 1958; 827, Dec. 1965; 872-873, Dec. 1973;
Chairman. 159, 225, Aug. 1976; Secretary. 155,
Jan. 1959; 4, Jan. 1963; Vice Chairman. 198,
Feb. 1965
Peak named for. 285, Aug. 1964
President of NGS (1967-1976). 577, 583, 586, 589,
590, Oct. 1967; 843, Dec. 1970; 159, 225-227,
Aug. 1976
Secretary. 4, Jan. 1963; 1, Jan. 1964; 485, Oct. 1966
Secretary, Assistant. 297, Sept. 1947
Secretary, Associate. 834, Dec. 1959; 883, Dec.
1960
Secretary, Senior Assistant. 420, 423, Mar. 1957;
867, Dec. 1957
Vice President of NGS. 108, 155, Jan. 1959; 834,
Dec. 1959; 175, Feb. 1960; 883, Dec. 1960; 485,
486, Oct. 1966
Vice President, Executive, of NGS. 579, 582, Apr.
1962; 4, Jan. 1963; 1, Jan. 1964; 689, Nov. 1964;
865, 867, June 1967; 583, 590, Oct. 1967
Author
American and Geographic Flags Top Everest. Pho-
tos by Barry C. Bishop. 157-157C, Aug. 1963
Frederick G. Vosburgh Retires as Editor; Gilbert
M. Grosvenor Succeeds Him. 838-843, Dec. 1970
The Leakey Tradition Lives On. 143-144, Jan. 1973
The Leakeys of Africa: Family in Search of Prehis-
toric Man. 194-231, Feb. 1965
Leonard Carmichael: An Appreciation. 871-874,
Dec. 1973
Preserving the Treasures of Olduvai Gorge. Photos
by Joseph J. Scherschel. 701-709, Nov. 1966
Reprinting Brings Earliest Geographics to Life.
688-689, Nov. 1964
75 Years Exploring Earth, Sea, and Sky: National
Geographic Society Observes Its Diamond Anni-
versary. 1-43, Jan. 1963
The World in Geographic Filmstrips. 134-137, Jan.
1968

PAYNE, ROGER: Author:
At Home With Right Whales. Photos by Des and
Jen Bartlett. 322-339, Mar. 1976
Swimming With Patagonia's Right Whales. Photos
by William R. Curtsinger and Charles R. Nick-
lin, Jr. 576-587, Oct. 1972

PEACE CORPS:
Ambassadors of Good Will. By Sargent Shriver and
Peace Corps Volunteers. 297-345, Sept. 1964
Contents: Bolivia, Ecuador, Gabon, Sarawak, Tan-
ganyika, Turkey

PEACE PARK. *See* Waterton-Glacier International
Peace Park

The **PEACEFUL** Mrus of Bangladesh. By Claus-Dieter Brauns. 267-286, Feb. 1973

PEANUTS. *See* Groundnut Scheme

PEARL INDUSTRY:
Desert Sheikdoms of Arabia's Pirate Coast. By
Ronald Codrai. 65-104, July 1956
Exploring the World of Gems. By W. F. Foshag.
779-810, Dec. 1950

PEARL INDUSTRY — *Continued*

The Philippines, Freedom's Pacific Frontier. By Robert de Roos. Photos by Ted Spiegel. 301-351, Sept. 1966

PEARY, JOSEPHINE D.:

Gold Medal Awarded to Mrs. Robert E. Peary. 148, Jan. 1956

Lecture by (1895). 531, Oct. 1954

PEARY, ROBERT E.:

Far North with "Captain Mac." By Miriam MacMillan. 465-513, Oct. 1951
    Included: Battle Harbour, Labrador, where Peary gave his first interview to the press after discovery of the Pole; Eskimo friends and helpers

The Peary Flag Comes to Rest. By Marie Peary Stafford. 519-532, Oct. 1954

Three Months on an Arctic Ice Island. By Joseph O. Fletcher. 489-504, Apr. 1953
    Included: Peary's description of the Ellesmere Island ice shelf and the Arctic "whiteout"

We Followed Peary to the Pole. By Gilbert Grosvenor and Thomas W. McKnew. 469-484, Oct. 1953

The PEARY FLAG Comes to Rest. By Marie Peary Stafford. 519-532, Oct. 1954

PEASANTS of Anatolia. By Alfred Marchionini. 57-72, July 1948

PEAT-BOG BURIALS. *See* Tollund Man

PEAT SOIL:

California's Surprising Inland Delta. By Judith and Neil Morgan. Photos by Charles O'Rear. 409-430, Sept. 1976

PEERLESS Nepal — A Naturalist's Paradise. By S. Dillon Ripley. Photos by Volkmar Wentzel. 1-40, Jan. 1950

PEISSEL, MICHEL: Author-Photographer:

Mustang, Remote Realm in Nepal. 579-604, Oct. 1965

PEKING, China:

The City They Call Red China's Showcase. By Franc Shor. 193-223, Aug. 1960
    Peking: a Pictorial Record. By Brian Brake. 194-197, 199-223

Power Comes Back to Peiping. By Nelson T. Johnson and W. Robert Moore. 337-368, Sept. 1949

Return to Changing China. By Audrey Topping. 801-833, Dec. 1971

This Is the China I Saw. By Jørgen Bisch. 591-639, Nov. 1964

PELICANS. *See* Brown Pelican

PELLY BAY, Northwest Territories, Canada:

I Live With the Eskimos. By Guy Mary-Rousseliere. 188-217, Feb. 1971

PENGUINS:

Antarctica's Nearer Side. By Samuel W. Matthews. Photos by William R. Curtsinger. 622-655, Nov. 1971

A Naturalist in Penguin Land. By Niall Rankin. 93-116, Jan. 1955

Nature's Clown, the Penguin. By David Hellyer and Malcolm Davis. 405-428, Sept. 1952

Oil and Penguins Don't Mix. Photos by Mike

PENGUINS — *Continued*

Holmes. 384-397, Mar. 1973
    Included: Jackass penguins

People and Penguins of the Faraway Falklands. By Olin Sewall Pettingill, Jr. 387-416, Mar. 1956

PENITENTES (Religious Group). *See* New Mexico (Adobe; The Golden Land)

PENITENTS. *See* Guatemala (Easter Week); Sevilla, Spain (Holy Week)

PENNINE CHAIN (Mountains), England:

A Stroll to London. By Isobel Wylie Hutchison. Photos by B. Anthony Stewart. 171-204, Aug. 1950

PENNSYLVANIA:

Amish Folk: Plainest of Pennsylvania's Plain People. By Richard Gehman. Photos by William Albert Allard. 227-253, Aug. 1965

Appalachian Valley Pilgrimage. By Catherine Bell Palmer. Photos by Justin Locke. 1-32, July 1949

Artists Look at Pennsylvania. By John Oliver La Gorce. 37-56, July 1948

Down the Susquehanna by Canoe. By Ralph Gray. Photos by Walter Meayers Edwards. 73-120, July 1950

Gettysburg and Vicksburg: the Battle Towns Today. By Robert Paul Jordan. Map notes by Carolyn Bennett Patterson. 4-57, July 1963

Shrines of Each Patriot's Devotion. By Frederick G. Vosburgh. 51-82, Jan. 1949

Today on the Delaware, Penn's Glorious River. By Albert W. Atwood. Photos by Robert F. Sisson. 1-40, July 1952

See also Kutztown; Longwood Gardens; Philadelphia; Pittsburgh; Valley Forge

PENNSYLVANIA AVENUE, Washington, D. C.:

New Grandeur for Flowering Washington. By Joseph Judge. Photos by James P. Blair. 500-539, Apr. 1967

Pennsylvania Avenue, Route of Presidents. By Dorothea and Stuart E. Jones. Photos by Volkmar Wentzel. 63-95, Jan. 1957

PENNSYLVANIA DUTCH (People):

Pennsylvania Dutch Folk Festival. By Maynard Owen Williams. 503-516, Oct. 1952

Pennsylvania's Old-time Dutch Treat. By Kent Britt. Photos by H. Edward Kim. 564-578, Apr. 1973

See also Amish

PENNSYLVANIA'S Amish Folk. By Richard Gehman. Photos by William Albert Allard. 227-253, Aug. 1965

PENSAR (Island), Finland:

Scenes of Postwar Finland. By La Verne Bradley. Photos by Jerry Waller. 233-264, Aug. 1947

PENTECOST ISLAND, New Hebrides:

Land Diving With the Pentecost Islanders. By Kal Muller. 799-817, Dec. 1970

South Seas' Incredible Land Divers. By Irving and Electa Johnson. 77-92, Jan. 1955

PEOPLE and Penguins of the Faraway Falklands. By Olin Sewall Pettingill, Jr. 387-416, Mar. 1956

The **PEOPLE** of Cades Cove. By William O. Douglas. Photos by Thomas Nebbia and Otis Imboden. 60-95, July 1962

The **PEOPLE** of Cumberland Gap. By John Fetterman. Photos by Bruce Dale. 591-621, Nov. 1971

The **PEOPLE** of New Jersey's Pine Barrens. By John McPhee. Photos by William R. Curtsinger. 52-77, Jan. 1974

PEOPLE'S REPUBLIC OF CHINA. *See* China (People's Republic of)

PERAZIC, ELIZABETH: Author:
Little Laos, Next Door to Red China. 46-69, Jan. 1960

PERFUME, the Business of Illusion. By Lonnelle Aikman. 531-550, Apr. 1951

PERISCOPE on the Etruscan Past. By Carlo M. Lerici. 337-350, Sept. 1959

PERÓN, JUAN DOMINGO:
Which Way Now for Argentina? By Loren McIntyre. 296-333, Mar. 1975

PERRY, MATTHEW CALBRAITH:
The Yankee Sailor Who Opened Japan. By Ferdinand Kuhn. 85-102, July 1953

PERSEPOLIS (Ruins), Iran:
In the Footsteps of Alexander the Great. By Helen and Frank Schreider. Paintings by Tom Lovell. 1-65, Jan. 1968
Iran: Desert Miracle. By William Graves. Photos by James P. Blair. 2-47, Jan. 1975
Journey Into Troubled Iran. By George W. Long. Photos by J. Baylor Roberts. 425-464, Oct. 1951

PERSIAN EMPIRE:
In the Footsteps of Alexander the Great. By Helen and Frank Schreider. Paintings by Tom Lovell. 1-65, Jan. 1968
The Sword and the Sermon. By Thomas J. Abercrombie. 3-45, July 1972
Included: Conquest of the Persian Empire by Arab Moslems; the adoption of Persian arts and sciences by the conquerors

PERSIAN GULF:
The Arab World, Inc. By John J. Putman. Photos by Winfield Parks. 494-533, Oct. 1975
Beside the Persian Gulf. Photos by Maynard Owen Williams. 341-356, Mar. 1947
Boom Time in Kuwait. By Paul Edward Case. 783-802, Dec. 1952
Calypso Explores for Underwater Oil. By Jacques-Yves Cousteau. 155-184, Aug. 1955
In Search of Arabia's Past. By Peter Bruce Cornwall. 493-522, Apr. 1948
Saudi Arabia, Oil Kingdom. Photos by Maynard Owen Williams. 497-512
Troubled Waters East of Suez. By Ernest M. Eller. 483-522, Apr. 1954
See also Dhows

PERTH, Australia:
Western Australia, the Big Country. By Kenneth MacLeish. Photos by James L. Stanfield. 150-187, Feb. 1975

PERU:
The Amazon. Photos by Loren McIntyre. 445-455,

PERU — *Continued*
Oct. 1972
Amazon — The River Sea. By Loren McIntyre. 456-495, Oct. 1972
At Home in the High Andes. By Harry Tschopik, Jr. 133-146, Jan. 1955
Avalanche! By Bart McDowell. Photos by John E. Fletcher. 855-880, June 1962
Birds That "See" in the Dark With Their Ears. By Edward S. Ross. 282-290, Feb. 1965
By Parachute Into Peru's Lost World. By G. Brooks Baekeland. Photos by author and Peter R. Gimbel. 268-296, Aug. 1964
Included: Apurímac River, Cordillera Vilcabamba, Lake Parodi, Urubamba River
Chan Chan, Peru's Ancient City of Kings. By Michael E. Moseley and Carol J. Mackey. Photos by David Brill. 318-345, Mar. 1973
Finding the Tomb of a Warrior-God. By William Duncan Strong. Photos by Clifford Evans, Jr. 453-482, Apr. 1947
The Five Worlds of Peru. By Kenneth F. Weaver. Photos by Bates Littlehales. 213-265, Feb. 1964
The Lost Empire of the Incas. By Loren McIntyre. Art by Ned and Rosalie Seidler. 729-787, Dec. 1973
A Pictorial Chronicle of the Incas. 747-753
The Marvelous Hummingbird Rediscovered. By Crawford H. Greenewalt. 98-101, July 1966
Parks, Plans, and People: How South America Guards Her Green Legacy. By Mary and Laurance Rockefeller. Photos by George F. Mobley. 74-119, Jan. 1967
Peru, Homeland of the Warlike Inca. By Kip Ross. 421-462, Oct. 1950
Peru Profits from Sea Fowl. By Robert Cushman Murphy. Photos by author and Grace E. Barstow Murphy. 395-413, Mar. 1959
Sea Fever. By John E. Schultz. 237-268, Feb. 1949
Titicaca, Abode of the Sun. By Luis Marden. Photos by Flip Schulke. 272-294, Feb. 1971
See also Condor; Vicuñas; *and* Nazca Lines

PESCADORES (Islands), Taiwan:
Pescadores, Wind-swept Outposts of Formosa. By Horace Bristol, Sr. 265-284, Feb. 1956
See also Formosa Strait

PESEK, LUDEK: Artist:
Journey to Mars. By Kenneth F. Weaver. 231-263, Feb. 1973; Supplement, Feb. 1973
Voyage to the Planets. By Kenneth F. Weaver. 147-193, Aug. 1970

PESH MERGAS. *See* Kurds

PESTALOZZI, Switzerland:
Children's Village in Switzerland, Pestalozzi. Photos by Alfred Lammer. 268-282, Aug. 1959

PESTICIDE POLLUTION:
Can the Cooper's Hawk Survive? By Noel Snyder. Photos by author and Helen Snyder. 433-442, Mar. 1974
The Osprey, Endangered World Citizen. By Roger Tory Peterson. Photos by Frederick Kent Truslow. 53-67, July 1969
Pollution, Threat to Man's Only Home. By Gordon Young. Photos by James P. Blair. 738-781, Dec. 1970

PESTICIDE POLLUTION — *Continued*

Quicksilver and Slow Death (Mercury). By John J. Putman. Photos by Robert W. Madden. 507-527, Oct. 1972

PETÉN, Department of the, Guatemala. *See* Tikal

PETER, Saint:

St. Peter's, Rome's Church of Popes. By Aubrey Menen. Photos by Albert Moldvay. 865-879, Dec. 1971

PETERSON, ERNST: Photographer:

Montana, Shining Mountain Treasureland. By Leo A. Borah. 693-736, June 1950

PETERSON, ROGER TORY: Author:

The Galapagos, Eerie Cradle of New Species. Photos by Alan and Joan Root. 541-585, Apr. 1967

A New Bird Immigrant Arrives (Cattle Egret). 281-292, Aug. 1954

The Osprey, Endangered World Citizen. Photos by Frederick Kent Truslow. 53-67, July 1969
Author-Photographer

Rare Birds Flock to Spain's Marismas. 397-425, Mar. 1958

White Storks, Vanishing Sentinels of the Rooftops. 838-853, June 1962

PETERSON, WILLIS: Author-Photographer:

Arizona's Operation Beaver Lift. 666-680, May 1955

PETRA, Jordan:

Arab Land Beyond the Jordan. Photos by Frank Hurley. 753-768, Dec. 1947

Petra, Rose-red Citadel of Biblical Edom. By David S. Boyer. 853-870, Dec. 1955

PETROGRAPHY:

Finding Rare Beauty in Common Rocks. By Lorence G. Collins. 121-129, Jan. 1966

PETROLEUM. *See* Oil

PETSAMO REGION:

Scenes of Postwar Finland. By La Verne Bradley. Photos by Jerry Waller. 233-264, Aug. 1947

PETTINGILL, OLIN SEWALL, Jr.:
Author-Photographer

People and Penguins of the Faraway Falklands. 387-416, Mar. 1956

PEYTON, CAROLINAS:

A Long Life, a Good Life on the Potomac. By James L. Stanfield. 470-479, Oct. 1976

PFLEGER, MICHAEL: Photographer:

Bicycles Are Back — and Booming! By Noel Grove. 671-681, May 1973

PHALANGERS:

Strange Animals of Australia. By David Fleay. Photos by Stanley Breeden. 388-411, Sept. 1963

"PHANTOM COAST," Antarctica:

Exploring Antarctica's Phantom Coast. By Edwin A. McDonald. Photos by W. D. Vaughn. 251-273, Feb. 1962

PHILADELPHIA, Pennsylvania:

Artists Look at Pennsylvania. By John Oliver La Gorce. 37-56, July 1948

PHILADELPHIA, Pennsylvania — *Continued*

Benjamin Franklin, Philosopher of Dissent. By Alice J. Hall. Photos by Linda Bartlett. 93-123, July 1975

Philadelphia Houses a Proud Past. By Harold Donaldson Eberlein. Photos by Thomas Nebbia. 151-191, Aug. 1960

PHILIP, H.R.H. The Prince, Duke of Edinburgh:

Off the Beaten Track of Empire. By Beverley M. Bowie. Photos by Michael Parker. 584-626, Nov. 1957

President Eisenhower Presents to Prince Philip the National Geographic Society's Medal. 865-868, Dec. 1957
Author

H. R. H. The Prince Philip, Duke of Edinburgh, Introduces to Members the Narrative of His Round-the-world Tour. 583-584, Nov. 1957

Man's Wildlife Heritage Faces Extinction. 700-703, Nov. 1962

PHILIPPINES, Republic of the:

Magellan: First Voyage Around the World. By Alan Villiers. Photos by Bruce Dale. 721-753, June 1976
Note: Magellan was killed in a battle with natives at Mactan Island.

The Philippines, Freedom's Pacific Frontier. By Robert de Roos. Photos by Ted Spiegel. 301-351, Sept. 1966

Sea Gypsies of the Philippines. By Anne de Henning Singh. Photos by Raghubir Singh. 659-677, May 1976

See also Mindanao (Island); *and* YWCA

PHILLIPS, ALAN: Author:

Canada, My Country. Photos by David S. Boyer and Walter Meayers Edwards. 769-819, Dec. 1961

Canadian Rockies, Lords of a Beckoning Land. Photos by James L. Stanfield. 353-393, Sept. 1966

PHILLIPS, CRAIG: Artist:

Solving Life Secrets of the Sailfish. By Gilbert Voss. Photos by B. Anthony Stewart. 859-872, June 1956

Strange Babies of the Sea. By Hilary B. Moore. Paintings by Craig Phillips and Jacqueline Hutton. 41-56, July 1952

PHILLIPS, SAM C.: Author:

"A Most Fantastic Voyage": The Story of Apollo 8's Rendezvous With the Moon. 593-631, May 1969

PHILMONT SCOUT RANCH Helps Boys Grow Up. By Andrew H. Brown. 399-416, Sept. 1956

PHILOSOPHER of Dissent, Benj. Franklin. By Alice J. Hall. Photos by Linda Bartlett. 93-123, July 1975

The **PHOENICIANS,** Sea Lords of Antiquity. By Samuel W. Matthews. Photos by Winfield Parks. Paintings by Robert C. Magis. 149-189, Aug. 1974

PHOENIX ISLANDS. *See* Canton Island

PHOSPHATE:

Nauru, the World's Richest Nation. By Mike Holmes. 344-353, Sept. 1976

PHOSPHORESCENT BAY, Puerto Rico:

Sailing a Sea of Fire. By Paul A. Zahl. 120-129, July 1960

PHOTO SUPPLEMENTS:

"The Earth From Space," double-sided supplement. Photo by Harrison H. Schmitt. Sept. 1973

"Portrait U.S.A.," first color photomosaic of the 48 contiguous United States from Landsat satellite imagery. Map on reverse. July 1976

PHOTOGRAPHING a Volcano in Action. By Thomas J. Hargrave. 561-563, Oct. 1955

PHOTOGRAPHING Hummingbirds in Brazil. By Crawford H. Greenewalt. 100-115, Jan. 1963

PHOTOGRAPHING Northern Wild Flowers. By Virginia L. Wells. 809-823, June 1956

PHOTOGRAPHING the Night Creatures of Alligator Reef. By Robert E. Schroeder. Photos by author and Walter A. Starck II. 128-154, Jan. 1964

PHOTOGRAPHING the Sea's Dark Underworld. By Harold E. Edgerton. 523-537, Apr. 1955

PHOTOGRAPHY:

Eastman of Rochester: Photographic Pioneer. By Allan C. Fisher, Jr. 423-438, Sept. 1954

National Geographic Photographers Win Top Magazine Awards. 830-831, June 1959

The Romance of the Geographic: National Geographic Magazine Observes Its Diamond Anniversary. By Gilbert Hovey Grosvenor. 516-585, Oct. 1963

See also NGM: Photographs, Notable

PHOTOGRAPHY, Astronomical:

First Color Portraits of the Heavens. By William C. Miller. 670-679, May 1959

First Photographs of Planets and Moon Taken With Palomar's 200-inch Telescope. By Milton L. Humason. 125-130, Jan. 1953

See also Sky Survey

PHOTOGRAPHY, Infrared:

Remote Sensing: New Eyes to See the World. By Kenneth F. Weaver. 46-73, Jan. 1969

Skylab Looks at Earth. 471-493, Oct. 1974

PHOTOGRAPHY, Microscope:

At Home With the Bulldog Ant. By Robert F. Sisson. 62-75, July 1974

Face-to-Face With a World of Ants (electron micrographs). 72-75

Finding Rare Beauty in Common Rocks. By Lorence G. Collins. 121-129, Jan. 1966

Snowflakes to Keep. By Robert F. Sisson. 104-111, Jan. 1970

See also Crystals; Photosynthesis

PHOTOGRAPHY, Space:

"The Earth From Space," double-sided supplement. Photo by Harrison H. Schmitt. Sept. 1973

Extraordinary Photograph Shows Earth Pole to Pole. Photos by Nimbus I. 190-193, Feb. 1965

Historic Color Portrait of Earth From Space. By Kenneth F. Weaver. Photos by DODGE Satellite. 726-731, Nov. 1967

Our Earth as a Satellite Sees It. By W. G. Stroud. 293-302, Aug. 1960

A Satellite Makes a Coast-to-Coast Picture. . . .

PHOTOGRAPHY, Space—Continued

By Barry C. Bishop. 140-147, July 1976
Contents: The Landsat Portrait of the United States

Surveyor: Candid Camera on the Moon. By Homer E. Newell. 578-592, Oct. 1966

PHOTOGRAPHY, Underwater:

Camera Under the Sea. By Luis Marden. 162-200, Feb. 1956

Current Scientific Projects of the National Geographic Society. 143-144, July 1953
Included: "Aquascope"; Hand-held electronic flash equipment

Photographing the Night Creatures of Alligator Reef. By Robert E. Schroeder. Photos by author and Walter A. Starck II. 128-154, Jan. 1964

Photographing the Sea's Dark Underworld. By Harold E. Edgerton. 523-537, Apr. 1955

Where the Earth Turns Inside Out (Project FAMOUS). By J. R. Heirtzler. Photos by Emory Kristof. 586-603, May 1975
Included: LIBEC (LIght BEhind Camera)

PHOTOGRAPHY, X-Ray:

Re-creating Madagascar's Giant Extinct Bird. By Alexander Wetmore. 488-493, Oct. 1967

X-Rays Reveal the Inner Beauty of Shells. By Hilary B. Moore. 427-434, Mar. 1955

PHOTOMAPPING. See Archeology (Periscope on the Etruscan Past); Inter-American Geodetic Survey; Landsat; U. S. Coast and Geodetic Survey

PHOTOSYNTHESIS:

How the Sun Gives Life to the Sea. By Paul A. Zahl. 199-225, Feb. 1961

PHYSICS:

The British Way. By Sir Evelyn Wrench. 421-541, Apr. 1949

The Search for Tomorrow's Power. By Kenneth F. Weaver. Photos by Emory Kristof. 650-681, Nov. 1972
Included: Electromagnets, Fission, Fusion, Magnetohydrodynamics, Nuclear reactors

See also Electricity; Nuclear Energy; listing under Optics; and National Bureau of Standards

PIAZZA ARMERINA, Sicily:

Roman Life in 1,600-year-old Color Pictures. By Gino Vinicio Gentili. Photos by Duncan Edwards. 211-229, Feb. 1957

PICCARD, JACQUES: Author:

Man's Deepest Dive. Photos by Thomas J. Abercrombie. 224-239, Aug. 1960

PICKERELL, JAMES H.: Author-Photographer:

Dory on the Banks: A Day in the Life of a Portuguese Fisherman. 573-583, Apr. 1968

PICKOW, GEORGE: Author-Photographer:

The Great St. Bernard Hospice Today. 49-62, Jan. 1957

PICTOGRAPHS (Indian Effigies). See Gravel Pictographs; Nazca Lines

A PICTORIAL Chronicle of the Incas. Paintings by Ned Seidler and drawings by Rosalie Seidler. 747-753, Dec. 1973

PICTORIAL SUPPLEMENTS. See Painting Supplements; Photo Supplements

PICTURE-BOOK Portofino. By Carleton Mitchell. Photos by Winfield Parks. 232-253, Feb. 1965

PIED-À-TERRE (Motorboat):
French Riviera: Storied Playground on the Azure Coast. By Carleton Mitchell. Photos by Thomas Nebbia. 798-835, June 1967

PIEDRA PARADA, Chiapas, Mexico:
On the Trail of La Venta Man. By Matthew W. Stirling. Photos by Richard H. Stewart. 137-172, Feb. 1947
Hunting Mexico's Buried Temples. 145-168

PIEL, GERARD: Author:
Five Noted Thinkers Explore the Future. 70-71, July 1976

PIERCE, FRANKLIN:
Profiles of the Presidents: II. A Restless Nation Moves West. By Frank Freidel. 80-121, Jan. 1965

PIGEON NETTING:
Land of the Ancient Basques. By Robert Laxalt. Photos by William Albert Allard. 240-277, Aug. 1968
Pigeon Netting—Sport of Basques. Photos by Irene Burdett-Scougall. 405-416, Sept. 1949

PIGEONS:
The Flying Telegraph. By Joseph F. Spears. Official U. S. Army Signal Corps photos. 531-554, Apr. 1947

PIGS. See Hogs and Hog Raising

PILARSKI, LAURA: Author:
Little Tibet in Switzerland. Photos by Fred Mayer. 711-727, Nov. 1968

PILGRIMAGES:
Himalayan Pilgrimage. By Christopher Rand. 520-535, Oct. 1956
India's Sculptured Temple Caves. By Volkmar Wentzel. 665-678, May 1953
Kunming Pilgrimage. 213-226, Feb. 1950
Pilgrims Follow the Christmas Star. By Maynard Owen Williams. 831-840, Dec. 1952
See also Hadj; and Canterbury Cathedral; Ethiopia (Searching); Ganges; Holy Island; Jerusalem (Home to; Where Jesus Walked); Vézelay

PILGRIMS:
Founders of New England. By Sir Evelyn Wrench. Photos by B. Anthony Stewart. 803-838, June 1953

The PILOT'S Story. By Alan B. Shepard, Jr. Photos by Dean Conger. 432-444, Sept. 1961

PINE BARRENS (Region), New Jersey:
The People of New Jersey's Pine Barrens. By John McPhee. Photos by William R. Curtsinger. 52-77, Jan. 1974

PINEAPPLES AND PINEAPPLE GROWING:
Because It Rains on Hawaii. By Frederick Simpich, Jr. 571-610, Nov. 1949
Hawaii, U.S.A. By Frederick Simpich, Jr. Photos by Thomas Nebbia. 1-45, July 1960
How Fruit Came to America. By J. R. Magness. Paintings by Else Bostelmann. 325-377, Sept. 1951
See also Puya

The PINK Birds of Texas. By Paul A. Zahl. 641-654, Nov. 1949

PINKIANG, China. See Harbin

PIONEER PROBES:
Mystery Shrouds the Biggest Planet (Jupiter). By Kenneth F. Weaver. 285-294, Feb. 1975
Included: Pioneer 10, Pioneer 11
Reaching for the Moon. By Allan C. Fisher, Jr. Photos by Luis Marden. 157-171, Feb. 1959
Included: Pioneer I, Pioneer II, Pioneer III
Voyage to the Planets. By Kenneth F. Weaver. Paintings by Ludek Pesek. 147-193, Aug. 1970
Included: A Pioneer model; and plans for a future Pioneer F and Pioneer G

PIONEERS Head North to Canada's "Now" Frontier. By Robert Paul Jordan. Photos by Lowell Georgia. 480-511, Oct. 1976

PIONEERS in Man's Search for the Universe. Paintings by Jean-Leon Huens. Text by Thomas Y. Canby. 627-633, May 1974

The PIOUS Ones (Brooklyn's Hasidic Jews). By Harvey Arden. Photos by Nathan Benn. 276-298, Aug. 1975

PIPELINES, Natural Gas. See Natural Gas (Canada's; The Pipeline)

PIPELINES, Oil. See North Slope, Alaska; Trans-Andean Pipeline

PIRACY:
The Vikings. By Howard La Fay. Photos by Ted Spiegel. 492-541, Apr. 1970

PIRANHAS:
Seeking the Truth About the Feared Piranha. By Paul A. Zahl. 715-733, Nov. 1970

PISA, Italy:
The Renaissance Lives On in Tuscany. By Luis Marden. Photos by Albert Moldvay. 626-659, Nov. 1974

PITCAIRN ISLAND, South Pacific Ocean:
I Found the Bones of the Bounty. By Luis Marden. 725-789, Dec. 1957
The Yankee's Wander-world. By Irving and Electa Johnson. 1-50, Jan. 1949

The PITFALLS of Success: Yellowstone at 100. By William S. Ellis. Photos by Jonathan Blair. 616-631, May 1972

PITKIN, JOHN G.: Photographer:
Praying Mantis. 685-692, May 1950

PITTMAN, BLAIR: Photographer:
Big Thicket of Texas. By Don Moser. 504-529, Oct. 1974

PITTSBURGH, Pennsylvania:
Artists Look at Pennsylvania. By John Oliver La Gorce. 37-56, July 1948
Pittsburgh, Pattern for Progress. By William J. Gill. Photos by Clyde Hare. 342-371, Mar. 1965
Pittsburgh: Workshop of the Titans. By Albert W. Atwood. 117-144, July 1949
So Much Happens Along the Ohio River. By Frederick Simpich. Photos by Justin Locke. 177-212, Feb. 1950

"PLAIN PEOPLE." *See* Amish; Hutterites; Mennonites

PLAINEST of Pennsylvania's Plain People: Amish Folk. By Richard Gehman. Photos by William Albert Allard. 227-253, Aug. 1965

PLANETS:

First Photographs of Planets and Moon Taken with Palomar's 200-inch Telescope. By Milton L. Humason. 125-130, Jan. 1953

Voyage to the Planets. By Kenneth F. Weaver. Paintings by Ludek Pesek. 147-193, Aug. 1970

See also Earth; Jupiter; Mars; Mercury; Venus

PLANKTON:

Blue-water Plankton: Ghosts of the Gulf Stream. By William M. Hamner. 530-545, Oct. 1974

How the Sun Gives Life to the Sea (Photosynthesis). By Paul A. Zahl. 199-225, Feb. 1961

Night Life in the Gulf Stream. By Paul A. Zahl. 391-418, Mar. 1954

Sailing a Sea of Fire. By Paul A. Zahl. 120-129, July 1960

Strange Babies of the Sea. By Hilary B. Moore. Paintings by Craig Phillips and Jacqueline Hutton. 41-56, July 1952

Teeming Life of a Pond. By William H. Amos. 274-298, Aug. 1970

PLANT EXPLORERS. *See* Agricultural and Botanical Explorers

PLANTATIONS. *See* Estates and Plantations

PLANTS:

Abundant Life in a Desert Land. By Walter Meayers Edwards. 424-436, Sept. 1973

Florida, Noah's Ark for Exotic Newcomers. By Rick Gore. Photos by David Doubilet. 538-559, Oct. 1976

In the Wilds of a City Parlor. By Paul A. Zahl. 645-672, Nov. 1954

Kew: The Commoners' Royal Garden. By Thomas Garner James. Photos by B. Anthony Stewart. 479-506, Apr. 1950

Malaysia's Giant Flowers and Insect-trapping Plants. By Paul A. Zahl. 680-701, May 1964

Mountains of the Moon (Ruwenzori). By Paul A. Zahl. 412-434, Mar. 1962
     Included: Groundsels, Lichens, Lobelias

Nature's Gifts to Medicine. By Lonnelle Aikman. Paintings by Lloyd K. Townsend and Don Crowley. 420-440, Sept. 1974

Nature's Year in Pleasant Valley. By Paul A. Zahl. 488-525, Apr. 1968

Patent Plants Enrich Our World. By Orville H. Kneen. Photos from U.S. Plant Patents. 357-378, Mar. 1948

Plants of the Alaskan Tundra. 315-321, Mar. 1972

Plants That Eat Insects. By Paul A. Zahl. 643-659, May 1961

Stalking the West's Wild Foods. By Euell Gibbons. Photos by David Hiser. 186-199, Aug. 1973

Stalking Wild Foods on a Desert Isle. By Euell Gibbons. Photos by David Hiser. 47-63, July 1972

A Visit to the Living Ice Age (Far North). By Rutherford Platt. 525-545, Apr. 1957

See also Agriculture; Flowers; Fruit and Fruit Growing; Gardens; Trees; Vegetables

PLAQUEMINES PARISH, Louisiana:

New Orleans and Her River. By Joseph Judge. Photos by James L. Stanfield. 151-187, Feb. 1971

PLATE TECTONICS:

Project FAMOUS. Photos by Emory Kristof. 586-615, May 1975
     I. Where the Earth Turns Inside Out. By J. R. Heirtzler. 586-603
     II. Dive Into the Great Rift. By Robert D. Ballard. 604-615

Science Explores the Monsoon Sea. By Samuel W. Matthews. Photos by Robert F. Sisson. 554-575, Oct. 1967

This Changing Earth. By Samuel W. Matthews. 1-37, Jan. 1973

Window on Earth's Interior. By Robert D. Ballard. Photos by Emory Kristof. 228-249, Aug. 1976

PLATT, RUTHERFORD: Author-Photographer:

Shells Take You Over World Horizons. 33-84, July 1949

A Visit to the Living Ice Age. 525-545, Apr. 1957

PLATYPUSES:

Biggest Worm Farm Caters to Platypuses. By W. H. Nicholas. 269-280, Feb. 1949

Flight of the Platypuses. By David Fleay. 512-525, Oct. 1958

PLAYING 3,000 Golf Courses in Fourteen Lands. By Ralph A. Kennedy. 113-132, July 1952

PLEASANT VALLEY, Maryland:

Nature's Year in Pleasant Valley. By Paul A. Zahl. 488-525, Apr. 1968

PLEISTOCENE EPOCH:

In Search of Man's Past at Lake Rudolf. By Richard E. Leakey. Photos by Gordon W. Gahan. 712-734, May 1970

See also Ice Ages

PLUMMETING Missile of Turquoise, the Shy and Spectacular Kingfisher. Photos by Carl-Johan Junge and Emil Lütken. 413-419, Sept. 1974

PLUTO (Planet):

Voyage to the Planets. By Kenneth F. Weaver. Paintings by Ludek Pesek. 147-193, Aug. 1970

PLYWOOD:

Versatile Wood Waits on Man. By Andrew H. Brown. 109-140, July 1951

POETS:

The British Way. By Sir Evelyn Wrench. 421-541, Apr. 1949

Lake District, Poets' Corner of England. By H. V. Morton. Photos by David S. Boyer. 511-545, Apr. 1956
     Included: Samuel Taylor Coleridge, Ralph Waldo Emerson, Thomas Gray, John Keats, Percy Bysshe Shelley, Robert Southey, Alfred, Lord Tennyson, William Wordsworth

Poets' Voices Linger in Scottish Shrines. By Isobel Wylie Hutchison. Photos by Kathleen Revis. 437-488, Oct. 1957
     Included: William E. Aytoun, John Barbour, Harold Boulton, Robert Burns, Lord Byron, William Douglas, James Hogg, Violet Jacob, Marjory Kennedy-Fraser, Andrew Lang, Allan Ramsay, Sir Walter Scott, William Shakespeare, Alexander Smith, Robert Louis Stevenson

See also Frost, Robert; MacLeish, Archibald; Momaday, N. Scott

POGUE, WILLIAM R.:

Skylab, Outpost on the Frontier of Space. By Thomas Y. Canby. Photos by the nine mission astronauts. 441-469, Oct. 1974

POLAND:

Poland and Czechoslovakia, Atlas series supplement. Sept. 1958

Poland Opens Her Doors. By Delia and Ferdinand Kuhn. Photos by Erich Lessing. 354-398, Sept. 1958

Springtime of Hope in Poland. By Peter T. White. Photos by James P. Blair. 467-501, Apr. 1972

POLAR BEAR: Lonely Nomad of the North. By Thor Larsen. 574-590, Apr. 1971

POLAR REGIONS:

Nuclear Power for the Polar Regions. By George J. Dufek. 712-730, May 1962

See also Antarctic Regions; Antarctica; Arctic Ocean; Arctic Region; Greenland Icecap; North Pole; South Pole

POLK, JAMES K.:

Profiles of the Presidents: II. A Restless Nation Moves West. By Frank Freidel. 80-121, Jan. 1965

POLLINATION. *See* Bees; Fig Wasps; Flowers (Crossroads; Flower Seed Growers); Orchids; Roses

POLLUTION:

As We Live and Breathe: The Challenge of Our Environment. Special Publication announced. 882-886, June 1971

"How Man Pollutes His World," painting supplement. Map on reverse. Dec. 1970

Pollution, Threat to Man's Only Home. By Gordon Young. Photos by James P. Blair. 738-781, Dec. 1970

Problems in Paradise. By Mary and Laurance S. Rockefeller. Photos by Thomas Nebbia. 782-793, Dec. 1974

Quicksilver and Slow Death (Mercury). By John J. Putman. Photos by Robert W. Madden. 507-527, Oct. 1972

Those Successful Japanese. By Bart McDowell. Photos by Fred Ward. 323-359, Mar. 1974

Venice Fights for Life. By Joseph Judge. Photos by Albert Moldvay. 591-631, Nov. 1972

Water for the World's Growing Needs. By Herbert B. Nichols and F. Barrows Colton. 269-286, Aug. 1952

See also Air Pollution; Oil Spills; Pesticide Pollution; Water Pollution

POLUNIN, IVAN: Author-Photographer:

Who Says Fish Can't Climb Trees? 85-91, Jan. 1972

POLYNESIA:

A Canoe Helps Hawaii Recapture Her Past. By Herb Kawainui Kane. Photos by David Hiser. 468-489, Apr. 1976

Contents: Proposed voyage by *Hokule'a* to Raiatea and Tahiti

Captain Cook: The Man Who Mapped the Pacific. By Alan Villiers. Photos by Gordon W. Gahan. 297-349, Sept. 1971

Hokule'a Follows the Stars to Tahiti. By David Lewis. Photos by Nicholas deVore III. 512-537, Oct. 1976

POLYNESIA — *Continued*

Islands of the Pacific; Discoverers of the Pacific, double-sided map supplement. Dec. 1974

Isles of the Pacific. 732-793, Dec. 1974
I. The Coming of the Polynesians. By Kenneth P. Emory. 732-745
II. Wind, Wave, Star, and Bird. By David Lewis. Photos by Nicholas deVore III. 747-781
III. The Pathfinders. Paintings by Herb Kawainui Kane. 756-769
IV. Problems in Paradise. By Mary and Laurance S. Rockefeller. Photos by Thomas Nebbia. 782-793

Polynesian Adventure (Television film). 592A-592B, Apr. 1969

Yankee Roams the Orient. By Irving and Electa Johnson. 327-370, Mar. 1951
Included: Tikopia and the Stewart Islands, two Polynesian outposts in Melanesia

See also Canton Island; Cook Islands; Easter Island; Ellice Islands; Hawaii; Marquesas Islands; New Zealand; Pitcairn Island; Samoa; Society Islands; Tahiti; Tonga; Tuamotu Archipelago; Uvéa

POLYNESIAN CANOE. *See Hokule'a*

POLYNESIANS:

Feast Day in Kapingamarangi. By W. Robert Moore. 523-537, Apr. 1950

POMERANTZ, MARTIN A.: Author:

Trailing Cosmic Rays in Canada's North. 99-115, Jan. 1953

POMPEII, Italy:

Last Moments of the Pompeians. By Amedeo Maiuri. Photos by Lee E. Battaglia. Paintings by Peter V. Bianchi. 651-669, Nov. 1961

PONCE, ROJAS: Artist:

Finding the Tomb of a Warrior-God. By William Duncan Strong. Photos by Clifford Evans, Jr. 453-482, Apr. 1947

POND INLET, Baffin Island, Canada:

I Live With the Eskimos. By Guy Mary-Rousselière. 188-217, Feb. 1971

POND LIFE:

Teeming Life of a Pond. By William H. Amos. 274-298, Aug. 1970

PONIES:

The Wild Ponies of Assateague Island. Children's book announced. 724-726, Nov. 1975

See also Devonshire, for Dartmoor ponies; Sable Island, for wild ponies; Shetland Islands, for Shetland ponies

PONTING, HERBERT G.: Photographer:

Nature's Clown, the Penguin. By David Hellyer and Malcolm Davis. 405-428, Sept. 1952
Included: Photos taken on the second Scott Antarctic expedition (1911)

POOR Little Rich Land — Formosa. By Frederick G. Vosburgh. Photos by J. Baylor Roberts. 139-176, Feb. 1950

POORWILL Sleeps Away the Winter. By Edmund C. Jaeger. 273-280, Feb. 1953

POPES:

St. Peter's, Rome's Church of Popes. By Aubrey

POPES — *Continued*

Menen. Photos by Albert Moldvay. 865-879, Dec. 1971

Included: John XXIII, Julius II, Paul VI, Pius XII, and Saint Peter

POPPER, PAUL: Photographer:

Cane Bridges of Asia. 243-250, Aug. 1948

POPULATION:

Census 1960: Profile of the Nation. By Albert W. Atwood and Lonnelle Aikman. 697-714, Nov. 1959

PORCUPINES, Rambling Pincushions. By Donald A. Spencer. 247-264, Aug. 1950

PORPOISES:

Marineland, Florida's Giant Fish Bowl. By Gilbert Grosvenor La Gorce. Photos by Luis Marden. 679-694, Nov. 1952

The Playful Dolphins. Children's book announced. 718-720, Nov. 1976

Porpoises: Our Friends in the Sea. By Robert Leslie Conly. Photos by Thomas Nebbia. 396-425, Sept. 1966

PORT AU PRINCE, Haiti:

Haiti: Beyond Mountains, More Mountains. By Carolyn Bennett Patterson. Photos by Thomas Nebbia. 70-97, Jan. 1976

PORT ROYAL, Jamaica:

Exploring the Drowned City of Port Royal. By Marion Clayton Link. Photos by Luis Marden. 151-183, Feb. 1960

PORT ROYAL SOUND, South Carolina:

Sea Islands: Adventuring Along the South's Surprising Coast. By James Cerruti. Photos by Thomas Nebbia and James L. Amos. 366-393, Mar. 1971

PORTLAND, Oregon:

Powerhouse of the Northwest (Columbia River). By David S. Boyer. 821-847, Dec. 1974

A River Restored: Oregon's Willamette. By Ethel A. Starbird. Photos by Lowell J. Georgia. 816-835, June 1972

PORTO SANTO (Island), Atlantic Ocean:

Madeira, Like Its Wine, Improves With Age. By Veronica Thomas. Photos by Jonathan Blair. 488-513, Apr. 1973

The Treasure of Porto Santo. By Robert Sténuit. Photos by author and William R. Curtsinger. 260-275, Aug. 1975

PORTOFINO, Italy:

Time Turns Back in Picture-book Portofino. By Carleton Mitchell. Photos by Winfield Parks. 232-253, Feb. 1965

PORTRAIT of a Fierce and Fragile Land (Alaskan Tundra). By Paul A. Zahl. 303-314, Mar. 1972

PORTRAIT of Indochina. By W. Robert Moore and Maynard Owen Williams. Paintings by Jean Despujols. 461-490, Apr. 1951

PORTRAIT ROSE (All-America Rose Selection):

Amateur Gardener Creates a New Rose. By Elizabeth A. Moize. Photos by Farrell Grehan. 286-294, Aug. 1972

PORTRAIT U.S.A., Landsat photomosaic. July 1976

PORTRAITS of My Monkey Friends. By Ernest P. Walker. 105-119, Jan. 1956

PORTSMOUTH, Britannia's Sally Port. By Thomas Garner James. Photos by B. Anthony Stewart. 513-544, Apr. 1952

PORTUGAL:

Golden Beaches of Portugal. By Alan Villiers. 673-696, Nov. 1954

Portugal at the Crossroads. By Howard La Fay. Photos by Volkmar Wentzel. 453-501, Oct. 1965

Portugal Is Different. By Clement E. Conger. 583-622, Nov. 1948

Prince Henry, the Explorer Who Stayed Home. By Alan Villiers. Photos by Thomas Nebbia. 616-656, Nov. 1960

Spain and Portugal, Atlas series supplement. Mar. 1965

See also Azores (Islands); Macao; Madeira Islands

PORTUGUESE:

Macao Clings to the Bamboo Curtain. By Jules B. Billard. Photos by Joseph J. Scherschel. 521-539, Apr. 1969

Macau, a Hole in the Bamboo Curtain. By George W. Long. Photos by J. Baylor Roberts. 679-688, May 1953

New England's "Little Portugal." By O. Louis Mazzatenta. 90-109, Jan. 1975

PORTUGUESE FISHING FLEET:

Dory on the Banks: A Day in the Life of a Portuguese Fisherman. By James H. Pickerell. 573-583, Apr. 1968

Gloucester Blesses Its Portuguese Fleet. By Luis Marden. 75-84, July 1953

I Sailed with Portugal's Captains Courageous. By Alan Villiers. 565-596, May 1952

The Lonely Dorymen (Television film). 579A-579B, Apr. 1968

PORTUGUESE MAN-OF-WAR:

The Deadly Fisher. By Charles E. Lane. 388-397, Mar. 1963

Man-of-war Fleet Attacks Bimini. By Paul A. Zahl. 185-212, Feb. 1952

POSSUMS (American). *See* Opossums

POSSUMS (Phalangers):

Strange Animals of Australia. By David Fleay. Photos by Stanley Breeden. 388-411, Sept. 1963

POST ROADS, U. S.:

The Old Boston Post Roads. By Donald Barr Chidsey. 189-205, Aug. 1962

The Post Road Today. Photos by B. Anthony Stewart. 206-233, Aug. 1962

POSTAGE STAMPS:

Liechtenstein Thrives on Stamps. By Ronald W. Clark. 105-112, July 1948

POSTAL SERVICE, U. S.:

Everyone's Servant, the Post Office. By Allan C. Fisher, Jr. Photos by Volkmar Wentzel. 121-152, July 1954

See also J. W. Westcott (Mail Boat); Post Roads

POSTERS. *See* Painting Supplements; Photo Supplements

POSTWAR Journey Through Java. By Ronald Stuart Kain. 675-700, May 1948

POSTWAR RECOVERY:

Airlift to Berlin. 595-614, May 1949

Backwoods Japan During American Occupation. By M. A. Huberman. 491-518, Apr. 1947

Belgium Comes Back. By Harvey Klemmer. Photos by Maynard Owen Williams. 575-614, May 1948

Berlin, Island in a Soviet Sea. By Frederick G. Vosburgh. Photos by Volkmar Wentzel. 689-704, Nov. 1951

Italy Smiles Again. By Edgar Erskine Hume. 693-732, June 1949

Japan Tries Freedom's Road. By Frederick G. Vosburgh. Photos by J. Baylor Roberts. 593-632, May 1950

Keeping House in London. By Frances James. 769-792, Dec. 1947

Luxembourg, Survivor of Invasions. By Sydney Clark. Photos by Maynard Owen Williams. 791-810, June 1948

Mid-century Holland Builds Her Future. By Sydney Clark. 747-778, Dec. 1950

Occupied Austria, Outpost of Democracy. By George W. Long. Photos by Volkmar Wentzel. 749-790, June 1951

Okinawa, Pacific Outpost. 538-552, Apr. 1950

Pacific Wards of Uncle Sam. By W. Robert Moore. 73-104, July 1948

Scenes of Postwar Finland. By La Verne Bradley. Photos by Jerry Waller. 233-264, Aug. 1947

Turkey Paves the Path of Progress. By Maynard Owen Williams. 141-186, Aug. 1951

Uncle Sam Bends a Twig in Germany. By Frederick Simpich. Photos by J. Baylor Roberts. 529-550, Oct. 1948

War-torn Greece Looks Ahead. By Maynard Owen Williams. 711-744, Dec. 1949

What I Saw Across the Rhine. By J. Frank Dobie. 57-86, Jan. 1947

With the U. S. Army in Korea. By John R. Hodge. 829-840, June 1947

With Uncle Sam and John Bull in Germany. By Frederick Simpich. 117-140, Jan. 1949

POTALA (Palace), Lhasa, Tibet:

My Life in Forbidden Lhasa. By Heinrich Harrer. 1-48, July 1955

POTASSIUM-ARGON DATING:

A Clock for the Ages: Potassium-Argon. By Garniss H. Curtis. 590-592, Oct. 1961

POTATOES AND POTATO GROWING:

Aroostook County, Maine, Source of Potatoes. By Howell Walker. 459-478, Oct. 1948

Our Vegetable Travelers. By Victor R. Boswell. Paintings by Else Bostelmann. 145-217, Aug. 1949

POTHOLES, Desert:

Miracle of the Potholes. By Rowe Findley. Photos by Robert F. Sisson. 570-579, Oct. 1975

POTOMAC (River), U. S.:

Across the Potomac from Washington. By Albert

POTOMAC (River), U. S. — *Continued*

W. Atwood. 1-33, Jan. 1953

Down the Potomac by Canoe. By Ralph Gray. Photos by Walter Meayers Edwards. 213-242, Aug. 1948

The Nation's River. By Allan C. Fisher, Jr. Photos by James L. Stanfield. 432-479, Oct. 1976

A Good Life on the Potomac. 470-479

New Grandeur for Flowering Washington. By Joseph Judge. Photos by James P. Blair. 500-539, Apr. 1967

Waterway to Washington, the C & O Canal. By Jay Johnston. 419-439, Mar. 1960

See also Harpers Ferry

POUCH COVE, Newfoundland:

Newfoundland, Canada's New Province. By Andrew H. Brown. Photos by author and Robert F. Sisson. 777-812, June 1949

POULSEN, MOGENS BLOCH: Author:

Greenland's "Place by the Icebergs." Photos by Thomas Nebbia. 849-869, Dec. 1973

POULTRY:

"Delmarva," Gift of the Sea. By Catherine Bell Palmer. 367-399, Sept. 1950

Easter Egg Chickens. By Frederick G. Vosburgh. Photos by B. Anthony Stewart. 377-387, Sept. 1948

Long Island Outgrows the Country. By Howell Walker. Photos by B. Anthony Stewart. 279-326, Mar. 1951

Included: Duck raising

POWELL, JOHN WESLEY:

Retracing John Wesley Powell's Historic Voyage Down the Grand Canyon. By Joseph Judge. Photos by Walter Meayers Edwards. 668-713, May 1969

POWELL, Lake, Arizona-Utah:

Lake Powell: Waterway to Desert Wonders. By Walter Meayers Edwards. 44-75, July 1967

POWER. *See* Energy Sources

POWER Comes Back to Peiping. By Nelson T. Johnson and W. Robert Moore. 337-368, Sept. 1949

POWERHOUSE of the Northwest (Columbia River). By David S. Boyer. 821-847, Dec. 1974

PRAGUE, Czechoslovakia:

Czechoslovakia: The Dream and the Reality. By Edward J. Linehan. Photos by James P. Blair. 151-193, Feb. 1968

PRAIRIE PROVINCES, Canada:

Canada's Heartland, the Prairie Provinces. By W. E. Garrett. 443-489, Oct. 1970

Contents: Alberta, Manitoba, Saskatchewan

PRATHER, VICTOR A., Jr.:

We Saw the World From the Edge of Space. By Malcolm D. Ross. Ground photos by Walter Meayers Edwards. 671-685, Nov. 1961

PRAYING MANTIS:

Praying Mantis. Photos by John G. Pitkin. 685-692, May 1950

PRE-COLUMBIAN CIVILIZATION: U. S. Southwest:

The Hohokam: First Masters of the American Desert. By Emil W. Haury. Photos by Helga Teiwes. 670-695, May 1967

PRE-COLUMBIAN CIVILIZATION: U. S. Southwest —
Continued
Magnetic Clues Help Date the Past. By Kenneth F.
Weaver. 696-701, May 1967
See also Anasazi; Mound Builders

PRE-HISPANIC CULTURE:
Mexico
Mexico's Window on the Past (National Museum).
By Bart McDowell. Photos by B. Anthony Stew-
art. 492-519, Oct. 1968
"Pyramids" of the New World. By Neil Merton
Judd. 105-128, Jan. 1948
See also Aztecs; Maya; Olmecs
South America
Chan Chan, Peru's Ancient City of Kings. By Mi-
chael E. Moseley and Carol J. Mackey. Photos by
David Brill. 318-345, Mar. 1973
Gold, the Eternal Treasure. By Peter T. White.
Photos by James L. Stanfield. 1-51, Jan. 1974
Golden Masterpieces. 29-39
See also Incas; *and* Nazca Lines

PREHISTORY. *See* Anthropology; Archeology; Paleontology; *and* Lascaux Cave; Russell Cave, Alabama; *and* Dating Methods

PRELUDE to Gettysburg. Map notes by Carolyn Bennett Patterson. 14-21, July 1963

PRELUDE to Vicksburg. Map notes by Carolyn Bennett Patterson. 42-45, July 1963

PRESERVING America's Last Great Wilderness (Alaska). Text by David Jeffery. 769-791, June 1975

PRESERVING the Treasures of Olduvai Gorge. By
Melvin M. Payne. Photos by Joseph J. Scherschel. 701-709, Nov. 1966

The PRESIDENCY and How It Grew. By Frank Freidel. 642-687, Nov. 1964

PRESIDENT Eisenhower Presents the Hubbard Medal to Everest's Conquerors. 64, July 1954

PRESIDENT Eisenhower Presents the Society's Hubbard Medal to the Conquerors of Antarctica. 589-
590, Apr. 1959

PRESIDENT Eisenhower Presents to Prince Philip the
National Geographic Society's Medal. 865-868,
Dec. 1957

PRESIDENT Johnson Dedicates the Society's New
Headquarters. 669-679, May 1964

PRESIDENT Kennedy Presents the Hubbard Medal
(American Mount Everest Expedition). 514-515,
Oct. 1963

PRESIDENTIAL ARM FOR NATIONAL MINORITIES
(Panamin): Philippines:
First Glimpse of a Stone Age Tribe. 881-882, Dec.
1971
Help for Philippine Tribes in Trouble. By Kenneth
MacLeish. Photos by Dean Conger. 220-255,
Aug. 1971
The Tasadays, Stone Age Cavemen of Mindanao.
By Kenneth MacLeish. Photos by John Launois.
219-249, Aug. 1972

PRESIDENTS, U. S.:
Inside the White House. By Lonnelle Aikman. Pho-

PRESIDENTS, U. S. — *Continued*
tos by B. Anthony Stewart and Thomas Nebbia.
3-43, Jan. 1961
The Living White House. By Lonnelle Aikman.
593-643, Nov. 1966
Our Country's Presidents. Special Publication an-
nounced. 408-417, Mar. 1966
Profiles of the Presidents. By Frank Freidel.
I. The Presidency and How It Grew. 642-687,
Nov. 1964
Contents: George Washington, John Adams,
Thomas Jefferson, James Madison, James Monroe,
John Quincy Adams
II. A Restless Nation Moves West. 80-121, Jan.
1965
Contents: Andrew Jackson, Martin Van Buren,
William Henry Harrison, John Tyler, James K. Polk,
Zachary Taylor, Millard Fillmore, Franklin Pierce,
James Buchanan
III. The American Giant Comes of Age. 660-711,
May 1965
Contents: Abraham Lincoln, Andrew Johnson,
Ulysses S. Grant, Rutherford B. Hayes, James A.
Garfield, Chester A. Arthur, Grover Cleveland, Ben-
jamin Harrison, William McKinley
IV. America Enters the Modern Era. 537-577,
Oct. 1965
Contents: Theodore Roosevelt, William Howard
Taft, Woodrow Wilson, Warren G. Harding, Calvin
Coolidge, Herbert Hoover
V. The Atomic Age: Its Problems and Promises.
66-119, Jan. 1966
Contents: Franklin D. Roosevelt, Harry S Tru-
man, Dwight D. Eisenhower, John F. Kennedy, Lyn-
don B. Johnson
See also Adams, John; Eisenhower, Dwight D.;
Jackson, Andrew; Jefferson, Thomas; John-
son, Lyndon B.; Kennedy, John F.; Lincoln,
Abraham; Roosevelt, Theodore; Washington,
George

The PRESIDENT'S Music Men (U. S. Marine Band).
By Stuart E. Jones. Photos by William W. Campbell III. 752-766, Dec. 1959

PRIBILOF ISLANDS, Bering Sea:
The Fur Seal Herd Comes of Age. By Victor B.
Scheffer and Karl W. Kenyon. 491-512, Apr.
1952

PRICE, DEREK J. DE SOLLA: Author:
The Tower of the Winds. Paintings by Robert C.
Magis. 587-596, Apr. 1967

PRICE, EDWIN C., Jr.: Author:
Ambassadors of Good Will: The Peace Corps. By
Sargent Shriver and Peace Corps Volunteers.
297-345, Sept. 1964
Sarawak. 334-337

PRICE, WILLARD: Author:
Cruising Japan's Inland Sea. 619-650, Nov. 1953
Henry Hudson's River. Photos by Wayne Miller.
364-403, Mar. 1962
The Lower Mississippi. Photos by W. D. Vaughn.
681-725, Nov. 1960
The Thames Mirrors England's Varied Life. Photos
by Robert F. Sisson. 45-93, July 1958
The Upper Mississippi. 651-699, Nov. 1958

PRICELESS Relics of the Spanish Armada. By Robert
Sténuit. Photos by Bates Littlehales. 745-777,
June 1969

PRIMATES. *See* Baboons; Chimpanzees; Gibbons; Gorillas; Monkeys; Orangutans; Tarsiers; *and* Man, Prehistoric

PRIMITIVE PEOPLES:

Primitive Worlds. Special Publication announced. 865-868, June 1973

Vanishing Peoples of the Earth. Special Publication announced. 844-849, June 1968

See also names of specific tribes; *and* place of habitation, *as* Amazon Basin; New Guinea

PRINCE HENRY, the Explorer Who Stayed Home. By Alan Villiers. Photos by Thomas Nebbia. 616-656, Nov. 1960

PRINCE OF WALES:

The Investiture of Great Britain's Prince of Wales. By Allan C. Fisher, Jr. Photos by James L. Stanfield and Adam Woolfitt. 698-715, Nov. 1969

PRINCETON UNIVERSITY: Expeditions and Research. *See* Mount Sinai Expeditions (St. Catherine's Monastery)

PROBING Ice Caves of the Pyrenees. By Norbert Casteret. 391-404, Mar. 1953

PROBING the Deep Reefs' Hidden Realm. By Walter A. Starck II and Jo D. Starck. 867-886, Dec. 1972

PROBLEMS in Paradise. By Mary and Laurance S. Rockefeller. Photos by Thomas Nebbia. 782-793, Dec. 1974

PROBLEMS of a Two-part Land: Pakistan. By Bern Keating. Photos by Albert Moldvay. 1-47, Jan. 1967

PROFILES of the Presidents. By Frank Freidel.
I. The Presidency and How It Grew. 642-687, Nov. 1964
II. A Restless Nation Moves West. 80-121, Jan. 1965
III. The American Giant Comes of Age. 660-711, May 1965
IV. America Enters the Modern Era. 537-577, Oct. 1965
V. The Atomic Age: Its Problems and Promises. 66-119, Jan. 1966

PROGRESS and Pageantry in Changing Nigeria. By W. Robert Moore. 325-365, Sept. 1956

PROJECT APOLLO. *See* Apollo Missions

PROJECT DA VINCI. *See* Da Vinci, Project

PROJECT FAMOUS. *See* FAMOUS, Project

PROJECT GEMINI. *See* Gemini Missions

PROJECT MERCURY. *See* Mercury Missions

PROJECT MOHOLE. *See* Mohole, Project

PROSPECTORS:

Coober Pedy: Opal Capital of Australia's Outback. By Kenny Moore. Photos by Penny Tweedie. 560-571, Oct. 1976

See also Death Valley National Monument; *and* Gold and Gold Mining

PROUD Primitives, the Nuba People. By Oskar Luz. Photos by Horst Luz. 673-699, Nov. 1966

PROVENCE (Region), France:

Provence, Empire of the Sun. By William Daven-

PROVENCE (Region), France—*Continued*
port. Photos by James A. Sugar. 692-715, May 1975

PROVINCETOWN, Massachusetts:

Cape Cod, Where Sea Holds Sway Over Man and Land. By Nathaniel T. Kenney. Photos by Dean Conger. 149-187, Aug. 1962

Cape Cod's Circle of Seasons. By Tom Melham. Photos by James P. Blair. 40-65, July 1975

PRUDHOE BAY AREA, Alaska:

Will Oil and Tundra Mix? Alaska's North Slope Hangs in the Balance. By William S. Ellis. Photos by Emory Kristof. 485-517, Oct. 1971

PRYOR, PAUL: Photographer:

Exploring the World of Gems. By W. F. Foshag. 779-810, Dec. 1950

PRYOR, SAMUEL F.: Author:

The World in Dolls. Photos by Kathleen Revis. 817-831, Dec. 1959

PRYOR MOUNTAIN WILD HORSE RANGE, Montana-Wyoming:

On the Track of the West's Wild Horses. By Hope Ryden. Photos by author and Dick Durrance II. 94-109, Jan. 1971

PUBLIC HEALTH SERVICE, U. S. *See* U. S. Public Health Service

PUEBLO INDIANS:

Adobe New Mexico. By Mason Sutherland. Photos by Justin Locke. 783-830, Dec. 1949

Ancient Cliff Dwellers of Mesa Verde. By Don Watson. Photos by Willard R. Culver. 349-376, Sept. 1948
Included: Present-day Pueblo Indians

El Morro: Story in Stone. By Edwards Park. Photos by Willard R. Culver. 237-244, Aug. 1957

Kachinas: Masked Dancers of the Southwest. By Paul Coze. 219-236, Aug. 1957

20th-century Indians Preserve Customs of the Cliff Dwellers. Photos by William Belknap, Jr. 196-211, Feb. 1964

PUERTO RICO:

Growing Pains Beset Puerto Rico. By William H. Nicholas. Photos by Justin Locke. 419-460, Apr. 1951

Puerto Rico's Seven-league Bootstraps. By Bart McDowell. Photos by B. Anthony Stewart. 755-793, Dec. 1962

Sailing a Sea of Fire. By Paul A. Zahl. 120-129, July 1960

PUFFINS:

Lundy, Treasure Island of Birds. By P. T. Etherton. Photos by J. Allan Cash. 675-698, May 1947

The Solemn, Sociable Puffins. By R. M. Lockley. 414-422, Sept. 1954

PUGET SOUND AREA, Washington:

Making Friends With a Killer Whale. By Edward I. Griffin. 418-446, Mar. 1966

PULPWOOD INDUSTRY. *See* Paper and Pulp Industry

PUMAS. *See* Mountain Lions

PUNAN (People):

Brunei, Borneo's Abode of Peace. By Joseph Judge.

PUNAN (People)—*Continued*
  Photos by Dean Conger. 207-225, Feb. 1974

PUNJAB, East, India:
  India's Energetic Sikhs. By John E. Frazer. Photos by James P. Blair. 528-541, Oct. 1972

PUNJAB, West, Pakistan:
  Pakistan, New Nation in an Old Land. By Jean and Franc Shor. 637-678, Nov. 1952
  Pakistan: Problems of a Two-part Land. By Bern Keating. Photos by Albert Moldvay. 1-47, Jan. 1967

PURI, India:
  Orissa, Past and Promise in an Indian State. By Bart McDowell. Photos by James P. Blair. 546-577, Oct. 1970

PURITANS:
  Founders of New England. By Sir Evelyn Wrench. Photos by B. Anthony Stewart. 803-838, June 1953

The PURPLE Land of Uruguay. By Luis Marden. 623-654, Nov. 1948

PUTMAN, JOHN J.: Author:
  The Arab World, Inc. Photos by Winfield Parks. 494-533, Oct. 1975
  East Germany: The Struggle to Succeed. Photos by Gordon W. Gahan. 295-329, Sept. 1974
  The Ganges, River of Faith. Photos by Raghubir Singh. 445-483, Oct. 1971
  Greenland Feels the Winds of Change. Photos by George F. Mobley. 366-393, Sept. 1975
  India Struggles to Save Her Wildlife. 299-343, Sept. 1976
  Quicksilver and Slow Death (Mercury). Photos by Robert W. Madden. 507-527, Oct. 1972
  Timber: How Much Is Enough? Photos by Bruce Dale. 485-511, Apr. 1974
  Yesterday's Congo, Today's Zaire. Photos by Eliot Elisofon. 398-432, Mar. 1973

PUTNAM, ANNE EISNER: Author:
  My Life With Africa's Little People. 278-302, Feb. 1960

PUTTKAMER, W. JESCO VON: Author-Photographer:
  Brazil Protects Her Cinta Larga Indians. 420-444, Sept. 1971
  Brazil's Beleaguered Indians. 254-283, Feb. 1975
    I. Requiem for a Tribe? (Kreen-Akarores). 254-269
    II. Good-bye to the Stone Age (Txukahameis). 270-283
                    Photographer
  Saving Brazil's Stone Age Tribes From Extinction. By Orlando and Claudio Villas Boas. 424-444, Sept. 1968

PUYA, the Pineapple's Andean Ancestor. By Mulford B. Foster. 463-480, Oct. 1950

PYGMIES:
  My Life With Africa's Little People. By Anne Eisner Putnam. 278-302, Feb. 1960
  Yesterday's Congo, Today's Zaire. By John J. Putman. Photos by Eliot Elisofon. 398-432, Mar. 1973

PYONGYANG, North Korea:
  Rare Look at North Korea. By H. Edward Kim. 252-277, Aug. 1974

"PYRAMIDS" of the New World. By Neil Merton Judd. 105-128, Jan. 1948

PYRENEES (Mountains), France-Spain:
  The Enduring Pyrenees. By Robert Laxalt. Photos by Edwin Stuart Grosvenor. 794-819, Dec. 1974
  High Road in the Pyrenees. By H. V. Morton. Photos by Justin Locke. 299-334, Mar. 1956
  Incredible Andorra. By Lawrence L. Klingman. Photos by B. Anthony Stewart. 262-290, Aug. 1949
  Land of the Ancient Basques. By Robert Laxalt. Photos by William Albert Allard. 240-277, Aug. 1968
  Life in the Land of the Basques. By John E. H. Nolan. Photos by Justin Locke. 147-186, Feb. 1954
  Pigeon Netting—Sport of Basques. Photos by Irene Burdett-Scougall. 405-416, Sept. 1949
  Probing Ice Caves of the Pyrenees. By Norbert Casteret. 391-404, Mar. 1953

Q

QATIF, Saudi Arabia:
  In Search of Arabia's Past. By Peter Bruce Cornwall. 493-522, Apr. 1948

QIVIUT (Wool):
  Domesticating the Wild and Woolly Musk Ox. By John J. Teal, Jr. Photos by Robert W. Madden. 862-879, June 1970

QOMUL. *See* Hami, Sinkiang

QUEBEC (Province), Canada:
  Canada, My Country. By Alan Phillips. Photos by David S. Boyer and Walter Meayers Edwards. 769-819, Dec. 1961
  North Through History Aboard *White Mist*. By Melville Bell Grosvenor. Photos by Edwin Stuart Grosvenor. 1-55, July 1970
  Quebec's Forests, Farms, and Frontiers. By Andrew H. Brown. 431-470, Oct. 1949
  The St. Lawrence, River Key to Canada. By Howard La Fay. Photos by John Launois. 622-667, May 1967
  Sea Bird Cities Off Audubon's Labrador. By Arthur A. Allen. 755-774, June 1948
  Sea to Lakes on the St. Lawrence. By George W. Long. Photos by B. Anthony Stewart and John E. Fletcher. 323-366, Sept. 1950
  See also James Bay; Montreal; Quebec (City); St. Lawrence Seaway; *and* Chubb Crater

QUEBEC (City), Quebec, Canada:
  Quebec: French City in an Anglo-Saxon World. By Kenneth MacLeish. Photos by James L. Stanfield and Declan Haun. 416-442, Mar. 1971
  The St. Lawrence, River Key to Canada. By Howard La Fay. Photos by John Launois. 622-667, May 1967
  Winter Brings Carnival Time to Quebec. By Kathleen Revis. 69-97, Jan. 1958

QUECHUAS (Indians):
  Ambassadors of Good Will: The Peace Corps. By Sargent Shriver and Peace Corps Volunteers. 297-345, Sept. 1964
    Bolivia. By Edward S. Dennison. 315-319
  Peru, Homeland of the Warlike Inca. By Kip Ross. 421-462, Oct. 1950

QUEEN CHARLOTTE ISLANDS, British Columbia, Canada:

Canada's Window on the Pacific: The British Columbia Coast. By Jules B. Billard. Photos by Ted Spiegel. 338-375, Mar. 1972

QUEEN ELIZABETH Opens Parliament. By W. E. Roscher. Photos by Robert B. Goodman. 699-707, Nov. 1961

QUEEN ELIZABETH'S Favorite Sea Dog: Sir Francis Drake. By Alan Villiers. Photos by Gordon W. Gahan. 216-253, Feb. 1975

QUEEN of Canada. By Phyllis Wilson. Photos by Kathleen Revis. 825-829, June 1959

QUEENSLAND (State), Australia:

Queensland: Young Titan of Australia's Tropic North. By Kenneth MacLeish. Photos by Winfield Parks. 593-639, Nov. 1968

See also Great Barrier Reef

QUEENY, EDGAR MONSANTO: Author:

Spearing Lions with Africa's Masai. 487-517, Oct. 1954

QUEMOY (Islands), China:

Life under Shellfire on Quemoy. By Franc Shor. Photos by Wilbur E. Garrett. 415-438, Mar. 1959

QUESTING for Gems. By George S. Switzer. 835-863, Dec. 1971

The **QUETZAL**, Fabulous Bird of Maya Land. By Anne LaBastille Bowes. Photos by David G. Allen. 141-150, Jan. 1969

QUEZALTENANGO, Guatemala:

Guatemala Revisited. By Luis Marden. 525-564, Oct. 1947

QUICKSILVER and Slow Death. By John J. Putman. Photos by Robert W. Madden. 507-527, Oct. 1972

QUITO, Ecuador:

Ecuador—Low and Lofty Land Astride the Equator. By Loren McIntyre. 259-298, Feb. 1968

QUMRĀN. *See* Khirbat Qumrān, Jordan

R

RNA. *See* Ribonucleic Acid

RA II (Papyrus Ship):

The Voyage of *Ra II*. By Thor Heyerdahl. Photos by Carlo Mauri and Georges Sourial. 44-71, Jan. 1971

RACCOONS:

Raccoon: Amiable Rogue in a Black Mask. By Melvin R. Ellis. 841-854, Dec. 1956

RACES. *See* Automobile Race; Boat Races; Bull Derby; Horse Races; Hot-air Balloons; Land Yachts; Motorcycle Races; Olympic Games; Tall-Ships Race

RADAR:

Miracle Men of the Telephone. By F. Barrows Colton. 273-316, Mar. 1947
    Birthplace of Telephone Magic. Photos by Willard R. Culver. 289-312

Our Air Age Speeds Ahead. By F. Barrows Colton.

RADAR—*Continued*

249-272, Feb. 1948

See also DEW Line; Remote Sensing

RADFORD, ARTHUR W.: Author:

Our Navy in the Far East. Photos by J. Baylor Roberts. 537-577, Oct. 1953

RADIATION:

The Incredible Universe. By Kenneth F. Weaver. Photos by James P. Blair. 584-625, May 1974

Remote Sensing: New Eyes to See the World. By Kenneth F. Weaver. 46-73, Jan. 1969
    Included: Cosmic Rays, Gamma Rays, Infrared Radiation, Microwaves, Radar and Sonar, Ultraviolet Rays

See also Solar Energy

RADIO:

Miracle Men of the Telephone. By F. Barrows Colton. 273-316, Mar. 1947
    Birthplace of Telephone Magic. Photos by Willard R. Culver. 289-312

Our Air Age Speeds Ahead. By F. Barrows Colton. 249-272, Feb. 1948

Uncle Sam's House of 1,000 Wonders (National Bureau of Standards). By Lyman J. Briggs and F. Barrows Colton. 755-784, Dec. 1951

Unlocking Secrets of the Northern Lights. By Carl W. Gartlein. Paintings by William Crowder. 673-704, Nov. 1947

See also Microwave Radio Relay

RADIOACTIVITY:

Man's New Servant, the Friendly Atom. By F. Barrows Colton. Photos by Volkmar Wentzel. 71-90, Jan. 1954

Uncle Sam's House of 1,000 Wonders (National Bureau of Standards). By Lyman J. Briggs and F. Barrows Colton. 755-784, Dec. 1951

You and the Obedient Atom. By Allan C. Fisher, Jr. 303-353, Sept. 1958

See also Potassium-Argon Dating; Radiocarbon Dating

RADIOCARBON (Carbon-14) **DATING**:

How Old Is It? By Lyman J. Briggs and Kenneth F. Weaver. 234-255, Aug. 1958

RADIOTELEMETRY:

Antarctica's Nearer Side. By Samuel W. Matthews. Photos by William R. Curtsinger. 622-655, Nov. 1971
    Included: Radio-telemetering of penguins

Studying Wildlife by Satellite. By Frank Craighead, Jr., and John Craighead. 120-123, Jan. 1973

See also Bighorn Sheep; Grizzly Bears; Salmon (the Incredible); Whistling Swan

RAFFLESIA (Flower):

Malaysia's Giant Flowers and Insect-trapping Plants. By Paul A. Zahl. 680-701, May 1964

RAFTS:

Down Mark Twain's River on a Raft. By Rex E. Hieronymus. 551-574, Apr. 1948

Rafting Down the Yukon. By Keith Tryck. Photos by Robert Clark. 830-861, Dec. 1975

Retracing John Wesley Powell's Historic Voyage Down the Grand Canyon. By Joseph Judge. Pho-

RAFTS — *Continued*

tos by Walter Meayers Edwards. 668-713, May 1969

White-water Adventure on Wild Rivers of Idaho. By Frank Craighead, Jr., and John Craighead. 213-239, Feb. 1970

RAILROAD WORM:

Nature's Toy Train, the Railroad Worm. By Darwin L. Tiemann. Photos by Robert F. Sisson. 56-67, July 1970

RAILROADS:

Railroads: The Great American Adventure. Special Publication announced. 860-864, June 1976

Slow Train Through Viet Nam's War. By Howard Sochurek. 412-444, Sept. 1964

See also California Western Railroad; Southern Railway System

RAILS (Birds). *See* Takahe

RAIN FORESTS:

The High World of the Rain Forest (Trinidad). By William Beebe. Paintings by Guy Neale. 838-855, June 1958

See also Ituri Forest; Olympic National Park; Ruwenzori

RAINBOW BRIDGE NATIONAL MONUMENT, Utah:

Desert River Through Navajo Land. By Alfred M. Bailey. Photos by author and Fred G. Brandenburg. 149-172, Aug. 1947

Three Roads to Rainbow. By Ralph Gray. 547-561, Apr. 1957

RAINBOW World Beneath the Red Sea. By David Doubilet. 344-365, Sept. 1975

RAINIER, Mount, Washington:

Climbing Our Northwest Glaciers. Photos by Bob and Ira Spring. 103-114, July 1953

Mount Rainier: Testing Ground for Everest. By Barry C. Bishop. 688-711, May 1963

RAJASTHAN (State), India. *See* Jaisalmer; Jodhpur

RALEIGH, SIR WALTER:

Founders of Virginia. By Sir Evelyn Wrench. Photos by B. Anthony Stewart. 433-462, Apr. 1948

RAMAYANA (Epic):

Pageantry of the Siamese Stage. By D. Sonakul. Photos by W. Robert Moore. 201-212, Feb. 1947

RAMESSES II (Pharaoh):

Abu Simbel's Ancient Temples Reborn. By Georg Gerster. 724-744, May 1969

In Search of Moses. By Harvey Arden. Photos by Nathan Benn. 2-37, Jan. 1976

Saving the Ancient Temples at Abu Simbel. By Georg Gerster. Paintings by Robert W. Nicholson. 694-742, May 1966

Threatened Treasures of the Nile. By Georg Gerster. 587-621, Oct. 1963

RAMSAY, SIR WILLIAM:

The British Way. By Sir Evelyn Wrench. 421-541, Apr. 1949

RANCHES. *See* Camargue, for *manades;* Harberton, Estancia; Hutterites, for colony ranches; King Ranch; Miura Ranch; Padlock Ranch; Philmont Scout Ranch; *and* Cattle and Cattle Raising; Sheep and Sheep Raising

RAND, CHRISTOPHER: Author:

Himalayan Pilgrimage. 520-535, Oct. 1956

RANGER SPACECRAFT:

The Moon Close Up. By Eugene M. Shoemaker. Photos by Ranger 7. 690-707, Nov. 1964

Robots to the Moon. By Frank Sartwell. Paintings by Pierre Mion. 557-571, Oct. 1962

RANKIN, NIALL: Author-Photographer:

A Naturalist in Penguin Land. 93-116, Jan. 1955

RANSOM, TIMOTHY W.: Photographer:

Life with the "Pumphouse Gang": New Insights Into Baboon Behavior. By Shirley C. Strum. 672-691, May 1975

RAPA (Island), Pacific Ocean:

The *Yankee's* Wander-world. By Irving and Electa Johnson. 1-50, Jan. 1949

RAPIDS. *See* Colorado (River); Hamilton (River); San Juan (River); Wild Rivers; Yampa (River); *and* Voyageurs

RARE Birds Flock to Spain's Marismas. By Roger Tory Peterson. 397-425, Mar. 1958

RARE Look at North Korea. By H. Edward Kim. 252-277, Aug. 1974

RAROTONGA (Island), Cook Islands:

New Zealand's Cook Islands: Paradise in Search of a Future. By Maurice Shadbolt. Photos by William Albert Allard. 203-231, Aug. 1967

RAS MUHAMMAD, Sinai Peninsula:

The Red Sea's Sharkproof Fish. By Eugenie Clark. Photos by David Doubilet. 718-727, Nov. 1974

The Strangest Sea. By Eugenie Clark. Photos by David Doubilet. 338-365, Sept. 1975

Rainbow World Beneath the Red Sea. 344-365

RATELS:

Honey-Guide: The Bird That Eats Wax. By Herbert Friedmann. Paintings by Walter A. Weber. 551-560, Apr. 1954

RATIONING:

Keeping House in London. By Frances James. 769-792, Dec. 1947

RAY, CARLETON: Author:

Three Whales That Flew. Photos by W. Robert Moore. 346-359, Mar. 1962

Author-Photographer

Stalking Seals Under Antarctic Ice. 54-65, Jan. 1966

RAYLEIGH, LORD (John William Strutt):

The British Way. By Sir Evelyn Wrench. 421-541, Apr. 1949

RAYMER, PATRICIA: Author:

Wisconsin's Menominees: Indians on a Seesaw. Photos by Steve Raymer. 228-251, Aug. 1974

RAYMER, STEVE: Photographer:

Bangladesh: The Nightmare of Famine. 33-39, July 1975

Can the World Feed Its People? By Thomas Y. Canby. 2-31, July 1975

In Touch With Nature. Text by Elizabeth A. Moize. 537-543, Apr. 1974

RAYMER, STEVE: Photographer—*Continued*

Iowa's Enduring Amana Colonies. By Laura Longley Babb. 863-878, Dec. 1975

The Pipeline: Alaska's Troubled Colossus. By Bryan Hodgson. 684-717, Nov. 1976

Wisconsin's Menominees: Indians on a Seesaw. By Patricia Raymer. 228-251, Aug. 1974

RAZA, Isla, Gulf of California:

Sea Birds of Isla Raza. By Lewis Wayne Walker. 239-248, Feb. 1951

REACHING for the Moon. By Allan C. Fisher, Jr. Photos by Luis Marden. 157-171, Feb. 1959

REARDEN, JIM: Author:

Nikolaevsk: A Bit of Old Russia Takes Root in Alaska. Photos by Charles O'Rear. 401-425, Sept. 1972

Author-Photographer

Caribou: Hardy Nomads of the North. 858-878, Dec. 1974

RECLAMATION:

California's Surprising Inland Delta. By Judith and Neil Morgan. Photos by Charles O'Rear. 409-430, Sept. 1976

Holland Against the Sea (Television film). 588A-588B, Apr. 1970

The Netherlands: Nation at War With the Sea. By Alan Villiers. Photos by Adam Woolfitt. 530-571, Apr. 1968

See also Recycling

RECORDINGS, NGS:

"Bird Songs of Garden, Woodland, and Meadow," record supplement to book, *Song and Garden Birds of North America*. 554, 557, Oct. 1964

"Bird Sounds of Marsh, Upland, and Shore," record supplement to book, *Water, Prey, and Game Birds of North America*. 529, 530, 533, 534, 535, Oct. 1965

"The Funeral of Sir Winston Churchill, with Excerpts from His Speeches," record supplement. 198A-198B, Aug. 1965; 580, 581, Oct. 1967

"Sounds of the Space Age, from Sputnik to Lunar Landing," record supplement narrated by Frank Borman. 750A-750B, Dec. 1969

"Sounds of the World" series. 701, Nov. 1971; 475, Apr. 1976

RE-CREATING Madagascar's Giant Extinct Bird. By Alexander Wetmore. 488-493, Oct. 1967

RECYCLING (Waste Utilization):

Pollution, Threat to Man's Only Home. By Gordon Young. Photos by James P. Blair. 738-781, Dec. 1970

RED CROSS:

Scenes of Postwar Finland. By La Verne Bradley. Photos by Jerry Waller. 233-264, Aug. 1947
Included: American Red Cross, Finnish Red Cross

RED ROCK LAKES NATIONAL WILDLIFE REFUGE, Montana:

Return of the Trumpeter (Swan). By Frederick Kent Truslow. 134-150, July 1960

RED SEA:

At Home in the Sea (Underwater Lodge). By Jacques-Yves Cousteau. 465-507, Apr. 1964

RED SEA—*Continued*

Calypso Explores for Underwater Oil. By Jacques-Yves Cousteau. 155-184, Aug. 1955

Camera Under the Sea. By Luis Marden. 162-200, Feb. 1956

Exploring Davy Jones's Locker with *Calypso*. By Jacques-Yves Cousteau. Photos by Luis Marden. 149-161, Feb. 1956

Fish Men Explore a New World Undersea. By Jacques-Yves Cousteau. 431-472, Oct. 1952

The Red Sea's Gardens of Eels. By Eugenie Clark. Photos by James L. Stanfield and David Doubilet. 724-735, Nov. 1972

The Red Sea's Sharkproof Fish. By Eugenie Clark. Photos by David Doubilet. 718-727, Nov. 1974

The Strangest Sea. By Eugenie Clark. Photos by David Doubilet. 338-365, Sept. 1975
Rainbow World Beneath the Red Sea. 344-365

REDFORD, ROBERT: Author:

Riding the Outlaw Trail. Photos by Jonathan Blair. 622-657, Nov. 1976

REDWOODS:

Finding the Mt. Everest of All Living Things. By Paul A. Zahl. 10-51, July 1964

A Park to Save the Tallest Trees. By Melville Bell Grosvenor. 62-64, July 1966

World's Tallest Tree Discovered. By Melville Bell Grosvenor. Photos by George F. Mobley. 1-9, July 1964

REED, ELIZABETH C.: Author:

White Tiger in My House. Photos by Donna K. Grosvenor. 482-491, Apr. 1970

REED, NORMAN D.: Photographer:

The Swallow-tailed Kite: Graceful Aerialist of the Everglades. 496-505, Oct. 1972

REED, THEODORE H.: Author:

Enchantress! (White Tigress). Photos by Thomas J. Abercrombie. 628-641, May 1961

What's Black and White and Loved All Over? Photos by Donna K. Grosvenor. 803-815, Dec. 1972

REED SHIPS. *See Ra II*

REEDY, JAMES R.: Author:

First Flight Across the Bottom of the World (Cape Town to Christchurch). Photos by Otis Imboden. 454-464, Mar. 1964

REEF SHARKS:

Into the Lairs of "Sleeping" Sharks. By Eugenie Clark. Photos by David Doubilet. 570-584, Apr. 1975

REEFS. *See* Corals and Coral Reefs; Great Bahama Bank; Great Sand Barrier Reef

REFORESTATION. *See* Forests and Reforestation

REFUGEES:

Bangladesh: The Nightmare of Famine. By Steve Raymer. 33-39, July 1975

Freedom Flight from Hungary. By Robert F. Sisson. 424-436, Mar. 1957

Hong Kong Has Many Faces. By John Scofield. 1-41, Jan. 1962

Little Tibet in Switzerland. By Laura Pilarski. Photos by Fred Mayer. 711-727, Nov. 1968

`REFUGEES — *Continued*

The Mekong, River of Terror and Hope. By Peter T. White. Photos by W. E. Garrett. 737-787, Dec. 1968

Passage to Freedom in Viet Nam. By Gertrude Samuels. 858-874, June 1955

See also Cuban Refugees; Hmong; Kazakhs; *and* Berlin; Cyprus; Hong Kong Hangs On; Jerusalem; Jordan; Korea; Mali; Suez Canal; Taiwan; Viet Nam

REFUGES. *See* Animal Orphanage; Bird Sanctuaries and Rookeries; Game Preserves; National Parks; *and* listing under Wildlife Refuges

REGATTAS. *See* Yachting

REICHE, MARIA:

Mystery of the Ancient Nazca Lines. By Loren McIntyre. 716-728, May 1975

Note: Maria Reiche has photographed and charted the markings for more than 25 years.

REINDEER:

Lapland's Reindeer Roundup. 109-116, July 1949

North with Finland's Lapps. By Jean and Franc Shor. 249-280, Aug. 1954

See also Caribou

REKHI, JOGINDER SINGH: Author-Photographer: A Sikh Discovers America. 558-590, Oct. 1964

RELICS From the Rapids. By Sigurd F. Olson. Photos by David S. Boyer. 413-435, Sept. 1963

RELIGIONS AND RELIGIOUS GROUPS:

Abraham, the Friend of God. By Kenneth MacLeish. Photos by Dean Conger. 739-789, Dec. 1966

The British Way. By Sir Evelyn Wrench. 421-541, Apr. 1949

Included: James I and the Translation of the Bible. — The Pilgrim Fathers. — Cromwell. — John Wesley

From the Hair of Siva (Ganges River, India). By Helen and Frank Schreider. 445-503, Oct. 1960

Included: Buddhists, Hindus, Moslems, Sikhs

Great Religions of the World. Book announced. 587-590, Oct. 1971

Included in book: Buddhism, Christianity, Hinduism, Islam, Judaism

Jerusalem to Rome in the Path of St. Paul. By David S. Boyer. 707-759, Dec. 1956

The Lands and Peoples of Southeast Asia. 295-365, Mar. 1971

Included: Animism, Buddhism, Cao Daism, Hinduism

Station Wagon Odyssey: Baghdad to Istanbul. By William O. Douglas. 48-87, Jan. 1959

Included: Bahais, Mandaeans, Moslems, Yazidis

See also Amish; Buddhism; Caldy (Island), for Cistercians; Caodaism; Cargo Cults; Christians and Christianity; Essenes; Greek Orthodox Church; Hashemite Jordan, for Trappists; Hindus; Islam; Jains; Judaism; Lamas and Lamaism; Maya; Mennonites; Mormons; Puritans; Samaritans; Shakers; Shintoism; Sikhs; Voodooism

RELIGIOUS CEREMONIES AND PROCESSIONS:

Bali by the Back Roads. By Donna K. and Gilbert M. Grosvenor. 657-697, Nov. 1969

Belgium Comes Back. By Harvey Klemmer. Photos by Maynard Owen Williams. 575-614, May 1948

Included: Ostend's Blessing of the Sea, and ceremo-

RELIGIOUS CEREMONIES AND PROCESSIONS — *Continued*

nies and processions honoring patron saints

Belgium Welcomes the World. By Howell Walker. 795-837, June 1958

Included: Blessing of the Sea ceremony at Heist

The Cobra, India's "Good Snake." By Harry Miller. 393-409, Sept. 1970

The Condor, Soaring Spirit of the Andes. By Jerry McGahan. Photos by Libby McGahan. 684-709, May 1971

Disaster in Paradise. 436-458, Sept. 1963
I. By Windsor P. Booth. Photos by Robert F. Sisson. 436-447
II. Devastated Land and Homeless People. By Samuel W. Matthews. Photos by Robert F. Sisson. 447-458

Foxes Foretell the Future in Mali's Dogon Country. By Pamela Johnson Meyer. 431-448, Mar. 1969

From America to Mecca on Airborne Pilgrimage. By Abdul Ghafur. 1-60, July 1953

The Ganges, River of Faith. By John J. Putman. Photos by Raghubir Singh. 445-483, Oct. 1971

Guatemala Revisited. By Luis Marden. 525-564, Oct. 1947

Included: Indians' Two-way Religion. — Marimbas for Saints. — The Lord of the Burning Place

Home to the Holy Land. By Maynard Owen Williams. 707-746, Dec. 1950

Included: Abyssinian parade, Greek and Armenian Washing-of-the-Feet ceremonies, Holy Fire ceremony, Palm Sunday procession, Protestant service at the Garden Tomb

Kachinas: Masked Dancers of the Southwest. By Paul Coze. 219-236, Aug. 1957

Included: Bean Dance, Snake Dance

Mexico's Booming Capital. By Mason Sutherland. Photos by Justin Locke. 785-824, Dec. 1951

Included: The *Posadas* (Lodgings) commemorating Mary and Joseph's visit to Bethlehem; Blessing of the Animals on St. Anthony's Day

Orissa, Past and Promise in an Indian State. By Bart McDowell. Photos by James P. Blair. 546-577, Oct. 1970

Included: Jagannath Festival, Shivaratri

The Palio of Siena. By Edgar Erskine Hume. 231-244, Aug. 1951

Note: Siena's celebrated horse race honoring the Virgin is held on July 2, the feast day of the Visitation and also of the Madonna of Provenzano, and again in August, during the feast of the Assumption.

Sponge Fishermen of Tarpon Springs. By Jennie E. Harris. 119-136, Jan. 1947

Included: "Feast of Lights" of the Eastern Orthodox Church celebrating the baptism of Christ with blessing of the waters and diving for the cross

Weighing the Aga Khan in Diamonds. Photos by David J. Carnegie. 317-324, Mar. 1947

See also Blessing of the Fleet; Brittany, for *pardons;* Bruges, the City the Sea Forgot, for Play of the Holy Blood; Camargue, Land of Cowboys, for Fete of the Two St. Marys *and* Gypsy Festival of St. Sarah; Cambodia; Canary Islands, for Corpus Christi celebration; Ceylon; Coronations; Dasara (Festival), India; Festivals; Funerals; Holy Week; Indonesia; Italy (Amalfi); Jerusalem; Jordan (Sacred Shrines); Madeira Islands; Mexico (South to Mexico City), for Day of the Dead; Mustang; Peru; Pilgrimages; Sonora (State), Mexico; Spain (The Changing Face); Taiwan: The Watchful Dragon, for Taoist temple festival; Trucial Coast, for Sufi ceremony; Vézelay; Weddings

REMOTE SENSING: New Eyes to See the World. By Kenneth F. Weaver. 46-73, Jan. 1969

RENAISSANCE:

The Renaissance: Maker of Modern Man. Book announced. 588-592, Oct. 1970

The Renaissance Lives On in Tuscany. By Luis Marden. Photos by Albert Moldvay. 626-659, Nov. 1974

See also Dreyfus Collection (Renaissance Bronzes); Florence, for Renaissance art; Folger (Library), for Renaissance literature; Loire River, for Renaissance architecture

RENNER, F. G.: Author:

Erosion, Trojan Horse of Greece. 793-812, Dec. 1947

REPORT from the Locust Wars. By Tony and Dickey Chapelle. 545-562, Apr. 1953

REPORT on Laos. By Peter T. White. Photos by W. E. Garrett. 241-275, Aug. 1961

REPRINTING Brings Earliest Geographics to Life. By Melvin M. Payne. 688-689, Nov. 1964

REPTILES:

Creepy Crawly Things: Reptiles and Amphibians. Children's book announced. 728-730, Nov. 1974

London's Zoo of Zoos. By Thomas Garner James. 771-786, June 1953

The Lure of the Changing Desert. 817-824, June 1954

Reptiles and Amphibians (Television film). 875A-875B, Dec. 1968

Zoo Animals Go to School. By Marion P. McCrane. Photos by W. E. Garrett. 694-706, Nov. 1956

See also Alligators; Caymans; Crocodilians; Dinosaurs; Iguanas; Komodo Dragons; Lizards; Snakes; Tortoises; Turtles

REPUBLICAN Indonesia Tries Its Wings. By W. Robert Moore. 1-40, Jan. 1951

REQUIEM for a Tribe? Brazil's Kreen-Akarores. By W. Jesco von Puttkamer. 254-269, Feb. 1975

REQUIEM SHARKS:

Into the Lairs of "Sleeping" Sharks. By Eugenie Clark. Photos by David Doubilet. 570-584, Apr. 1975

RESCUE CRAFT:

Tomorrow on the Deep Frontier. By Edwin A. Link. 778-801, June 1964

See also Helicopters

RESCUE WORK. *See* Air Rescue; Civil Air Patrol; Diving Bell; Great St. Bernard Hospice; Guatemala (Earthquake); Military Air Transport Service; School for Survival; U. S. Air Force (Artists Roam); U. S. Coast Guard

RESEARCH REPORTS, NGS:

Research Reports. Compiled and edited by Paul H. Oehser. *1890-1954 Projects*. 442, Sept. 1975; *1955-1960 Projects*. 444, Sept. 1972; *1963 Projects*. 296, Aug. 1968; *1964 Projects*. 300, Aug. 1969; *1965 Projects*. 148, July 1971; *1966 Projects*. 146, July 1973; *1967 Projects*. 148, July 1974; *1968 Projects*. 296, Aug. 1976

RESEARCH VESSELS:

Antarctica's Nearer Side. By Samuel W. Matthews.

RESEARCH VESSELS—*Continued*

Photos by William R. Curtsinger. 622-655, Nov. 1971

Included: *Alpha Helix, Bransfield, Endurance, Hero, Professor Viese*

How We Found the *Monitor*. By John G. Newton. 48-61, Jan. 1975

Included: *Alcoa Seaprobe, Eastward*

Project FAMOUS. Photos by Emory Kristof. 586-615, May 1975

I. Where the Earth Turns Inside Out. By J. R. Heirtzler. 586-603

II. Dive Into the Great Rift. By Robert D. Ballard. 604-615

Included: *Glomar Challenger; Knorr*, R.V.; *Mizar*, U.S.N.S.; *and* submersibles *Alvin; Archimède; Cyana; Lulu*

Science Explores the Monsoon Sea. By Samuel W. Matthews. Photos by Robert F. Sisson. 554-575, Oct. 1967

Thresher: Lesson and Challenge. By James H. Wakelin, Jr. 759-763, June 1964

Included: *Atlantis II, Conrad, Gilliss*

See also Alvin; Asherah; Calypso; Deepstar; Glomar Challenger; John Elliott Pillsbury; Sea Diver

RESOLUTE BAY, Canada:

Diving Beneath Arctic Ice. By Joseph B. MacInnis. Photos by William R. Curtsinger. 248-267, Aug. 1973

RESOLUTION (Sloop):

Captain Cook: The Man Who Mapped the Pacific. By Alan Villiers. Photos by Gordon W. Gahan. 297-349, Sept. 1971

A RESTLESS Nation Moves West. By Frank Freidel. 80-121, Jan. 1965

RESURRECTING the Grandeur of Tikal. By William R. Coe. 792-798, Dec. 1975

RESURRECTING the Oldest Known Greek Ship. By Michael L. Katzev. Photos by Bates Littlehales. 841-857, June 1970

RETRACING John Wesley Powell's Historic Voyage Down the Grand Canyon. By Joseph Judge. Photos by Walter Meayers Edwards. 668-713, May 1969

THE RETURN OF DOVE (Sloop):

Robin Sails Home. By Robin Lee Graham. 504-545, Oct. 1970

RETURN of the Sea Otter. By Karl W. Kenyon. Photos by James A. Mattison, Jr. 520-539, Oct. 1971

RETURN of the Trumpeter. By Frederick Kent Truslow. 134-150, July 1960

RETURN to Changing China. By Audrey Topping. 801-833, Dec. 1971

RETURN to Lonely Tristan da Cunha. By James P. Blair. 60-81, Jan. 1964

REUNITED Jerusalem Faces Its Problems. By Kenneth MacLeish. Photos by Ted Spiegel. 835-871, Dec. 1968

REVIS, ANNE: Author:

Mr. Jefferson's Charlottesville. 553-592, May 1950

REVIS, KATHLEEN: Author-Photographer:

Colorado by Car and Campfire. 207-248, Aug. 1954

Skiing in the United States. 216-254, Feb. 1959

REVIS, KATHLEEN: Author-Photographer — *Continued*

Winter Brings Carnival Time to Quebec. 69-97, Jan. 1958

Photographer

The Friendly Huts of the White Mountains. By William O. Douglas. 205-239, Aug. 1961

Landmarks of Literary England. By Leo A. Borah. 295-350, Sept. 1955

Many-splendored Glacierland. By George W. Long. 589-636, May 1956

Poets' Voices Linger in Scottish Shrines. By Isobel Wylie Hutchison. 437-488, Oct. 1957

Queen of Canada (Elizabeth II). By Phyllis Wilson. 825-829, June 1959

Soaring on Skis in the Swiss Alps. By Carolyn Bennett Patterson. 94-121, Jan. 1961

Washington Wilderness, the North Cascades. By Edwards Park. 335-367, Mar. 1961

Westminster, World Series of Dogdom. By John W. Cross, Jr. 91-116, Jan. 1954

The World in Dolls. By Samuel F. Pryor. 817-831, Dec. 1959

REVOLUTION, American. *See* American Revolution

The REVOLUTION in American Agriculture. By Jules B. Billard. Photos by James P. Blair. 147-185, Feb. 1970

REVOLUTIONARY View of the 48 (Contiguous) States. By Barry C. Bishop. 140-147, July 1976

REWATI (White Tiger):

White Tiger in My House. By Elizabeth C. Reed. Photos by Donna K. Grosvenor. 482-491, Apr. 1970

REYNOLDS, ROBERT J.: Author-Photographer:

Over the Sea to Scotland's Skye. 87-112, July 1952

RHINE (River), Europe:

The Rhine: Europe's River of Legend. By William Graves. Photos by Bruce Dale. 449-499, Apr. 1967

RHINEBECK, New York. *See* Old Rhinebeck Aerodrome

RHINOCEROSES:

Stalking the Great Indian Rhino. By Lee Merriam Talbot. 389-398, Mar. 1957

Where Elephants Have Right of Way. By George and Jinx Rodger. 363-389, Sept. 1960

Included: Black Rhinoceros, White Rhinoceros

RHODE, CECIL E.: Author-Photographer:

When Giant Bears Go Fishing. 195-205, Aug. 1954

RHODE ISLAND:

New England's "Little Portugal." By O. Louis Mazzatenta. 90-109, Jan. 1975

New England's "Lively Experiment," Rhode Island. By Robert de Roos. Photos by Fred Ward. 370-401, Sept. 1968

Rhode Island, Modern City-State. By George W. Long. Photos by Willard R. Culver. 137-170, Aug. 1948

See also Newport

RHODE ISLAND (Sidewheeler):

How We Found the *Monitor*. By John G. Newton. 48-61, Jan. 1975

RHODE ISLAND (Sidewheeler) — *Continued*

Note: A search area was established for the *Monitor* based on the log of *Rhode Island*, which had the *Monitor* in tow.

RHODES, CECIL:

The British Way. By Sir Evelyn Wrench. 421-541, Apr. 1949

RHODES (Island), Greece:

The Isles of Greece: Aegean Birthplace of Western Culture. By Melville Bell Grosvenor. Photos by Edwin Stuart Grosvenor and Winfield Parks. 147-193, Aug. 1972

On the Winds of the Dodecanese. By Jean and Franc Shor. 351-390, Mar. 1953

RHODESIA:

Africa: The Winds of Freedom Stir a Continent. By Nathaniel T. Kenney. Photos by W. D. Vaughn. 303-359, Sept. 1960

Freedom's Progress South of the Sahara. By Howard La Fay. Photos by Joseph J. Scherschel. 603-637, Nov. 1962

Rhodesia, a House Divided. By Allan C. Fisher, Jr. Photos by Thomas Nebbia. 641-671, May 1975

Safari Through Changing Africa. By Elsie May Bell Grosvenor. Photos by Gilbert Grosvenor. 145-198, Aug. 1953

RHODODENDRONS:

Pack Trip Through the Smokies. By Val Hart. Photos by Robert F. Sisson. 473-502, Oct. 1952

Rhododendron Glories of Southwest Scotland. By David S. Boyer. Photos by B. Anthony Stewart and author. 641-664, May 1954

Rhododendron Time on Roan Mountain. By Ralph Gray. 819-828, June 1957

See also Azaleas

RHÔNE RIVER DELTA, France. *See* Camargue

RIBONUCLEIC ACID (RNA):

The Awesome Worlds Within a Cell. By Rick Gore. Photos by Bruce Dale. Paintings by Davis Meltzer. 355-395, Sept. 1976

Included: The Language of Life, foldout showing replication of DNA and manufacture of RNA and proteins

RIBOUD, MARC: Photographer:

Cappadocia: Turkey's Country of Cones. 122-146, Jan. 1958

Coronation in Katmandu. By E. Thomas Gilliard. 139-152, July 1957

RICE GROWING:

Backwoods Japan During American Occupation. By M. A. Huberman. 491-518, Apr. 1947

Bangladesh: Hope Nourishes a New Nation. By William S. Ellis. Photos by Dick Durrance II. 295-333, Sept. 1972

Spirits of Change Capture the Karens. By Peter Kunstadter. 267-285, Feb. 1972

RICHARD THE LIONHEART:

The British Way. By Sir Evelyn Wrench. 421-541, Apr. 1949

RICHELIEU (River), Canada:

North Through History Aboard *White Mist*. By Melville Bell Grosvenor. Photos by Edwin Stuart Grosvenor. 1-55, July 1970

RICKER, P. L.: Author-Photographer:
American Wild Flower Odyssey. 603-634, May 1953

RIDDLE of the Glyphs. By George E. Stuart. Photos by Otis Imboden. 768-791, Dec. 1975

RIDING SCHOOL. *See* Spanish Riding School

RIDING the Outlaw Trail. By Robert Redford. Photos by Jonathan Blair. 622-657, Nov. 1976

RIDLEY TURTLES. *See* Pacific Ridley Turtles

RIFLE BIRDS. *See* Birds of Paradise

RIFTS, Ocean. *See* Mid-Atlantic Rift

RIGHT WHALES:
At Home With Right Whales. By Roger Payne. Photos by Des and Jen Bartlett. 322-339, Mar. 1976
Swimming With Patagonia's Right Whales. By Roger Payne. Photos by William R. Curtsinger and Charles R. Nicklin, Jr. 576-587, Oct. 1972

RINGLING BROS. AND BARNUM & BAILEY CIRCUS:
The Wonder City That Moves by Night. By Francis Beverly Kelley. 289-324, Mar. 1948

RIO DE JANEIRO, Brazil:
Brazil, Ôba! By Peter T. White. Photos by Winfield Parks. 299-353, Sept. 1962
Spectacular Rio de Janeiro. By Hernane Tavares de Sá. Photos by Charles Allmon. 289-328, Mar. 1955

RIO GRANDE (River), U. S.-Mexico:
Two Wheels Along the Mexican Border. By William Albert Allard. 591-635, May 1971
See also Big Bend National Park

RÍO INDIO (Town and River), Panama:
Hunting Prehistory in Panama Jungles. By Matthew W. Stirling. Photos by Richard H. Stewart. 271-290, Aug. 1953

RÍO MUNI (Spanish Province), Africa:
In Quest of the World's Largest Frog. By Paul A. Zahl. 146-152, July 1967
"Snowflake," the World's First White Gorilla. By Arthur J. Riopelle. Photos by Paul A. Zahl. 443-448, Mar. 1967

RIOPELLE, ARTHUR J.: Author:
Growing Up With Snowflake. Photos by Michael Kuh. 491-503, Oct. 1970
"Snowflake," the World's First White Gorilla. Photos by Paul A. Zahl. 443-448, Mar. 1967

RIP VAN WINKLE of the Underground. By Kenneth F. Weaver. 133-142, July 1953

RIPLEY, S. DILLON: Author:
Peerless Nepal — A Naturalist's Paradise. Photos by Volkmar Wentzel. 1-40, Jan. 1950
Saving the Nene, World's Rarest Goose. Photos by Jerry Chong. 745-754, Nov. 1965
Strange Courtship of Birds of Paradise. Paintings by Walter A. Weber. 247-278, Feb. 1950
Author-Photographer
Roaming India's Naga Hills. 247-264, Feb. 1955

RIPLEY, California:
Seeking the Secret of the Giants. By Frank M.

RIPLEY, California—*Continued*
Setzler. Photos by Richard H. Stewart. 390-404, Sept. 1952

RIVER GYPSY (Houseboat):
The Jungle Was My Home. By Sasha Siemel. 695-712, Nov. 1952

RIVER PRESERVATION. *See* Wild Rivers: Preservation

RIVERS AND RIVER TRIPS:
The Coast Guard: Small Service With a Big Mission. By William S. Ellis. 113-139, July 1974
Cruising Florida's Western Waterways. By Rube Allyn. Photos by Bates Littlehales. 49-76, Jan. 1955
Contents: Chassahowitzka, Crystal, Homosassa, Suwannee, Weekiwachee, Withlacoochee
Desert River Through Navajo Land. By Alfred M. Bailey. Photos by author and Fred G. Brandenburg. 149-172, Aug. 1947
Contents: A 200-mile journey down the swift San Juan and Colorado Rivers, from Mexican Hat, Utah, to Lees Ferry, Arizona
Following the Trail of Lewis and Clark. By Ralph Gray. 707-750, June 1953
From Sagebrush to Roses on the Columbia. By Leo A. Borah. 571-611, Nov. 1952
Contents: Columbia River and Basin, Willamette River and Valley, Yakima River region
Geographical Twins a World Apart. By David S. Boyer. 848-859, Dec. 1958
Included: A comparison of the Jordan River in the Holy Land with its namesake in Utah
Hunting Prehistory in Panama Jungles. By Matthew W. Stirling. Photos by Richard H. Stewart. 271-290, Aug. 1953
Included: Cascaja, Coclé del Norte, Coclecito, Indio
Inside Europe Aboard *Yankee*. By Irving and Electa Johnson. Photos by Joseph J. Scherschel. 157-195, Aug. 1964
Jungle Jaunt on Amazon Headwaters. By Bernice M. Goetz. 371-388, Sept. 1952
Contents: Aiari, Querari, Vaupés
Jungle Journey to the World's Highest Waterfall. By Ruth Robertson. 655-690, Nov. 1949
Included: Acanán, Carrao, and Churún Rivers
The Jungle Was My Home. By Sasha Siemel. 695-712, Nov. 1952
Included: Cara Cara, Miranda, Paraguay, Paraguay-mirim (Estuary)
Labrador Canoe Adventure. By Andrew Brown and Ralph Gray. 65-99, July 1951
Contents: Ashuanipi, Atikonak, Hamilton, Unknown
A Map Maker Looks at the United States. By Newman Bumstead. 705-748, June 1951
Included: Arkansas, Chicago, Colorado, Columbia, Dosewallips, Duckabush, East (New York), Elwha, Gunnison, McCloud, Mississippi, Niagara, Pit, Potomac, Rock, Sacramento, Snake, Spokane
New St. Lawrence Seaway Opens the Great Lakes to the World. By Andrew H. Brown. 299-339, Mar. 1959
North Through History Aboard *White Mist*. By Melville Bell Grosvenor. Photos by Edwin Stuart Grosvenor. 1-55, July 1970
Included: Hudson, Richelieu, Saguenay, St. Lawrence
Oklahoma, the Adventurous One. By Robert Paul Jordan. Photos by Robert W. Madden. 149-189, Aug. 1971

RIVERS AND RIVER TRIPS — *Continued*

Included: McClellan-Kerr Arkansas River Navigation System

Paris to Antwerp with the Water Gypsies. By David S. Boyer. 530-559, Oct. 1955
Contents: Aisne, Meuse, Oise

Pittsburgh, Pattern for Progress. By William J. Gill. Photos by Clyde Hare. 342-371, Mar. 1965
Included: Allegheny, Monongahela, Ohio

Pittsburgh: Workshop of the Titans. By Albert W. Atwood. 117-144, July 1949
Included: Allegheny, Monongahela, Ohio

Pollution, Threat to Man's Only Home. By Gordon Young. Photos by James P. Blair. 738-781, Dec. 1970
Included: Cuyahoga, Nile, Potomac, Rhine

Probing Ice Caves of the Pyrenees. By Norbert Casteret. 391-404, Mar. 1953

Relics from the Rapids. By Sigurd F. Olson. Photos by David S. Boyer. 413-435, Sept. 1963
Included: Wild waters of the Minnesota-Ontario border

Sea Fever. By John E. Schultz. 237-268, Feb. 1949
Contents: The author's journey on the Napo and Amazon, with detail of the tidal flood, or bore, of the latter

Shooting Rapids in Dinosaur Country. By Jack Breed. Photos by author and Justin Locke. 363-390, Mar. 1954
Contents: Yampa and Green River gorges

Skylab Looks at Earth. 471-493, Oct. 1974
Included: Drainage patterns and configurations for the Amazon, Atchafalaya, Colorado, Mississippi, Ohio, Salween, Uncompahgre, and White Rivers

Whatever Happened to TVA? By Gordon Young. Photos by Emory Kristof. 830-863, June 1973

White-water Adventure on Wild Rivers of Idaho. By Frank Craighead, Jr., and John Craighead. 213-239, Feb. 1970
Included: Middle Fork Salmon, Salmon, and rivers protected or proposed for protection under the Wild and Scenic Rivers Act of 1968

Wild River (Television film). 239A-239B, Feb. 1970
Included: Hudson, Middle Fork Salmon, Potomac, Salmon

See also Allagash; Amazon; Arno; Bow; Clearwater; Colorado; Columbia; Congo; Connecticut; Danube; Delaware; Detroit; Escalante Canyon, for Escalante; Euphrates; Ganges; Hudson; James; Jhelum; Juruena; Knik; Loire; Magdalena; Mekong; Merrimack; Mississippi; Missouri; Mohawk; Niger; Nile; Ob; Ohio; Potomac; Rhine; Rio Grande; St. Lawrence; Sepik; Snake; Susquehanna; Thames; Virgin; Volga; Willamette; Yangtze; Yukon

RIVIERA (Region), Mediterranean:

French Riviera: Storied Playground on the Azure Coast. By Carleton Mitchell. Photos by Thomas Nebbia. 798-835, June 1967

Italian Riviera, Land That Winter Forgot. By Howell Walker. 743-789, June 1963

See also Monaco; Portofino

ROADS. *See* Highways and Roads

ROAMING Africa's Unfenced Zoos. By W. Robert Moore. 353-380, Mar. 1950

ROAMING India's Naga Hills. By S. Dillon Ripley. 247-264, Feb. 1955

ROAMING Korea South of the Iron Curtain. By Enzo de Chetelat. 777-808, June 1950

ROAMING the West's Fantastic Four Corners. By Jack Breed. 705-742, June 1952

ROAN MOUNTAIN, Tennessee-North Carolina:

Rhododendron Time on Roan Mountain. By Ralph Gray. 819-828, June 1957

ROANOKE ISLAND, North Carolina:

Exploring America's Great Sand Barrier Reef. By Eugene R. Guild. Photos by John E. Fletcher and author. 325-350, Sept. 1947

Indian Life Before the Colonists Came. By Stuart E. Jones. Engravings by Theodore de Bry, 1590. 351-368, Sept. 1947

Lonely Cape Hatteras, Besieged by the Sea. By William S. Ellis. Photos by Emory Kristof. 393-421, Sept. 1969

October Holiday on the Outer Banks. By Nike Anderson. Photos by J. Baylor Roberts. 501-529, Oct. 1955

ROBERT COLLEGE, Turkish Gateway to the Future. By Franc Shor. 399-418, Sept. 1957

ROBERT FROST and New England. By Archibald MacLeish. 438-444, Apr. 1976

ROBERT REDFORD Rides the Outlaw Trail. By Robert Redford. Photos by Jonathan Blair. 622-657, Nov. 1976

ROBERT V. FLEMING, 1890-1967. By Melville Bell Grosvenor. 526-529, Apr. 1968

ROBERTS, J. BAYLOR: Author-Photographer:

Focusing on the Tournament of Roses. By B. Anthony Stewart and J. Baylor Roberts. 805-816, June 1954

Photographer

Across Canada by Mackenzie's Track. By Ralph Gray. 191-239, Aug. 1955

America Goes to the Fair. By Samuel W. Matthews. 293-333, Sept. 1954

Around the "Great Lakes of the South." By Frederick Simpich. 463-491, Apr. 1948

"Around the World in Eighty Days." By Newman Bumstead. 705-750, Dec. 1951

Bounty Descendants Live on Remote Norfolk Island. By T. C. Roughley. 559-584, Oct. 1960

Carnival in San Antonio. By Mason Sutherland. 813-844, Dec. 1947

Charting Our Sea and Air Lanes. By Stuart E. Jones. 189-209, Feb. 1957

Cruising Japan's Inland Sea. By Willard Price. 619-650, Nov. 1953

Deep in the Heart of "Swissconsin." By William H. Nicholas. 781-800, June 1947

Dixie Spins the Wheel of Industry. By William H. Nicholas. 281-324, Mar. 1949

Dog Mart Day in Fredericksburg. By Frederick G. Vosburgh. 817-832, June 1951

Formosa — Hot Spot of the East. By Frederick G. Vosburgh. 139-176, Feb. 1950

From Indian Canoes to Submarines at Key West. By Frederick Simpich. 41-72, Jan. 1950

Heritage of Beauty and History. By Conrad L. Wirth. 587-661, May 1958

Hong Kong Hangs On. By George W. Long. 239-272, Feb. 1954

ROBERTS, J. BAYLOR: Photographer—*Continued*

Hunting the Heartbeat of a Whale. By Paul Dudley White and Samuel W. Matthews. 49-64, July 1956

Indochina Faces the Dragon. By George W. Long. 287-328, Sept. 1952

Iraq—Where Oil and Water Mix. By Jean and Franc Shor. 443-489, Oct. 1958

Japan Tries Freedom's Road. By Frederick G. Vosburgh. 593-632, May 1950

Journey Into Troubled Iran. By George W. Long. 425-464, Oct. 1951

La Jolla, a Gem of the California Coast. By Deena Clark. 755-782, Dec. 1952

Louisiana Trades with the World. By Frederick Simpich. 705-738, Dec. 1947

Macau, a Hole in the Bamboo Curtain. By George W. Long. 679-688, May 1953

Malaya Meets Its Emergency. By George W. Long. 185-228, Feb. 1953

Men, Moose, and Mink of Northwest Angle. By William H. Nicholas. 265-284, Aug. 1947

New Rush to Golden California. By George W. Long. 723-802, June 1954

The Night the Mountains Moved. By Samuel W. Matthews. 329-359, Mar. 1960

North Dakota Comes into Its Own. By Leo A. Borah. 283-322, Sept. 1951

October Holiday on the Outer Banks. By Nike Anderson. 501-529, Oct. 1955

Our Green Treasury, the National Forests. By Nathaniel T. Kenney. 287-324, Sept. 1956

Our Navy in the Far East. By Arthur W. Radford. 537-577, Oct. 1953

Over Plains and Hills of South Dakota. 563-586, May 1947

Pittsburgh: Workshop of the Titans. By Albert W. Atwood. 117-144, July 1949

Saving Man's Wildlife Heritage. By John H. Baker. 581-620, Nov. 1954

Scientists Drill at Sea to Pierce Earth's Crust (Project Mohole). By Samuel W. Matthews. 686-697, Nov. 1961

Seeing the Earth from 80 Miles Up. By Clyde T. Holliday. 511-528, Oct. 1950

Shawneetown Forsakes the Ohio. By William H. Nicholas. 273-288, Feb. 1948

Slow Boat to Florida. By Dorothea and Stuart E. Jones. 1-65, Jan. 1958

This Young Giant, Indonesia. By Beverley M. Bowie. 351-392, Sept. 1955

Triton Follows Magellan's Wake. By Edward L. Beach. 585-615, Nov. 1960

Uncle Sam Bends a Twig in Germany. By Frederick Simpich. 529-550, Oct. 1948

The Wonder City That Moves by Night. By Francis Beverly Kelley. 289-324, Mar. 1948

ROBERTS, WALTER ORR: Author:

We're Doing Something About the Weather! 518-555, Apr. 1972

ROBERTSON, RUTH: Author-Photographer:

Jungle Journey to the World's Highest Waterfall. 655-690, Nov. 1949

ROBIN Sails Home. By Robin Lee Graham. 504-545, Oct. 1970

ROBINSON, ANNE GROSVENOR: Author:

Seattle, City of Two Voices. Photos by B. Anthony Stewart. 494-513, Apr. 1960

ROBINSON, G. D.: Author:

Exploring Aleutian Volcanoes. 509-528, Oct. 1948

ROBINSON, NANCY: Author:

Alaskan Family Robinson. Photos by John Metzger and Peter Robinson. 55-75, Jan. 1973

ROBINSON, PETER: Photographer:

Alaskan Family Robinson. By Nancy Robinson. Photos by John Metzger and Peter Robinson. 55-75, Jan. 1973

ROBOTS to the Moon. By Frank Sartwell. Paintings by Pierre Mion. 557-571, Oct. 1962

ROCHESTER, New York:

Eastman of Rochester: Photographic Pioneer. By Allan C. Fisher, Jr. 423-438, Sept. 1954

ROCK CARVINGS:

The Caves of the Thousand Buddhas. By Franc and Jean Shor. 383-415, Mar. 1951

Darius Carved History on Ageless Rock. By George G. Cameron. 825-844, Dec. 1950

India's Sculptured Temple Caves. By Volkmar Wentzel. 665-678, May 1953

Searching Out Medieval Churches in Ethiopia's Wilds. By Georg Gerster. 856-884, Dec. 1970

See also Cappadocia; Petra

ROCK CLIMBING:

Climbing Half Dome the Hard Way. By Galen Rowell. 782-791, June 1974

We Climbed Utah's Skyscraper Rock. By Huntley Ingalls. Photos by author and Barry C. Bishop. 705-721, Nov. 1962

ROCK PAINTINGS:

Rock Paintings of the Aborigines. By Kay and Stanley Breeden. 174-187, Feb. 1973

Searching Out Medieval Churches in Ethiopia's Wilds. By Georg Gerster. 856-884, Dec. 1970

ROCKEFELLER, LAURANCE S.:

Board of Trustees, member. 647, 655, May 1958; 5, 46, 55, July 1966; 531, 533, Oct. 1966; 80, Jan. 1967; 588, Oct. 1967; 542, Apr. 1971; 227, Aug. 1976

Author

Parks, Plans, and People: How South America Guards Her Green Legacy. By Mary and Laurance Rockefeller. Photos by George F. Mobley. 74-119, Jan. 1967

Problems in Paradise. By Mary and Laurance S. Rockefeller. Photos by Thomas Nebbia. 782-793, Dec. 1974

ROCKEFELLER, MARY FRENCH: Author:

Parks, Plans, and People: How South America Guards Her Green Legacy. By Mary and Laurance Rockefeller. Photos by George F. Mobley. 74-119, Jan. 1967

Problems in Paradise. By Mary and Laurance S. Rockefeller. Photos by Thomas Nebbia. 782-793, Dec. 1974

YWCA: International Success Story. Photos by Otis Imboden. 904-933, Dec. 1963

ROCKEFELLER FOUNDATION:

Yellow fever research in Colombia. 626, May 1947; 251, 254, 258, 261, 265, 266, 268, 269, 273, Aug. 1948

ROCKET PLANES:

Flying in the "Blowtorch" Era. By Frederick G. Vosburgh. 281-322, Sept. 1950

See also X-15

ROCKETS:

Aviation Medicine on the Threshold of Space. By Allan C. Fisher, Jr. Photos by Luis Marden. 241-278, Aug. 1955

Cape Canaveral's 6,000-mile Shooting Gallery. By Allan C. Fisher, Jr. Photos by Luis Marden and Thomas Nebbia. 421-471, Oct. 1959

Exploring Tomorrow With the Space Agency. By Allan C. Fisher, Jr. Photos by Dean Conger. 48-89, July 1960

Our Air Age Speeds Ahead. By F. Barrows Colton. 249-272, Feb. 1948

Reaching for the Moon. By Allan C. Fisher, Jr. Photos by Luis Marden. 157-171, Feb. 1959

Robots to the Moon. By Frank Sartwell. Paintings by Pierre Mion. 557-571, Oct. 1962

Rockets Explore the Air Above Us. By Newman Bumstead. 562-580, Apr. 1957

Seeing the Earth from 80 Miles Up. By Clyde T. Holliday. 511-528, Oct. 1950

Space Satellites, Tools of Earth Research. By Heinz Haber. Paintings by William N. Palmstrom. 487-509, Apr. 1956

See also Apollo Missions; Gemini Missions; Mercury Missions; Nike

The **ROCKIES'** Pot of Gold, Colorado. By Edward J. Linehan. Photos by James L. Amos. 157-201, Aug. 1969

ROCKS:

Finding Rare Beauty in Common Rocks. By Lorence G. Collins. 121-129, Jan. 1966

The Glittering World of Rockhounds. By David S. Boyer. 276-294, Feb. 1974

"Rockhounds" Uncover Earth's Mineral Beauty. By George S. Switzer. 631-660, Nov. 1951

See also Geology, Lunar

ROCKS, Ruts, and Sand: Driving the Mexican 1000. By Michael E. Long. 569-575, Oct. 1972

ROCKY MOUNTAINS, Canada-U. S.:

Bikepacking Across Alaska and Canada. By Dan Burden. 682-695, May 1973

Canadian Rockies, Lords of a Beckoning Land. By Alan Phillips. Photos by James L. Stanfield. 353-393, Sept. 1966

Colorado, the Rockies' Pot of Gold. By Edward J. Linehan. Photos by James L. Amos. 157-201, Aug. 1969

Colorado by Car and Campfire. By Kathleen Revis. 207-248, Aug. 1954
Included: Longs Peak, Pikes Peak

Colorado's Friendly Topland. By Robert M. Ormes. 187-214, Aug. 1951
Contents: Elk Mountains, Front Range, Mosquito Range, Park Range, Pikes Peak, San Juan Mountains, San Miguel Mountains, Sangre de Cristo Mountains, Sawatch Mountains

Hiking the Backbone of the Rockies: Canada's

ROCKY MOUNTAINS, Canada-U. S. *—Continued*

Great Divide Trail. By Mike W. Edwards. Photos by Lowell Georgia. 795-817, June 1973

Last Stand for the Bighorn. By James K. Morgan. 383-399, Sept. 1973

The Majestic Rocky Mountains. Special Publication announced. 870-874, June 1975

The Night the Mountains Moved (Montana's 1959 Earthquake). By Samuel W. Matthews. Photos by J. Baylor Roberts. 329-359, Mar. 1960

On the Ridgepole of the Rockies. By Walter Meayers Edwards. 745-780, June 1947
Canada's Rocky Mountain Playground. 755-770

See also Aspen, Colorado; Glacier National Park; Kennedy, Mount; Teton Range; Wasatch Front

RODENTS:

In the Wilds of a City Parlor. By Paul A. Zahl. 645-672, Nov. 1954

See also Beavers; Porcupines; Squirrels

RODGER, GEORGE: Author-Photographer:

Where Elephants Have Right of Way. By George and Jinx Rodger. 363-389, Sept. 1960

Photographer

Boom Time in Kuwait. By Paul Edward Case. 783-802, Dec. 1952

Sand in My Eyes. By Jinx Rodger. 664-705, May 1958

With the Nuba Hillmen of Kordofan. By Robin Strachan. 249-278, Feb. 1951

RODGER, JINX: Author:

Sand in My Eyes. 664-705, May 1958

Where Elephants Have Right of Way. By George and Jinx Rodger. Photos by George Rodger. 363-389, Sept. 1960

ROGERS, MARTIN: Photographer:

Baltimore: The Hidden City. By Fred Kline. 188-215, Feb. 1975

The Great Lakes: Is It Too Late? By Gordon Young. Photos by James L. Amos and Martin Rogers. 147-185, Aug. 1973

ROLAND, ARTHUR (Pseudonym). *See* Kilbon, Roland

ROMAN EMPIRE:

Classical Lands of the Mediterranean, map supplement. Dec. 1949

Greece and Rome: Builders of Our World. Book announced. 550-567, Oct. 1968

A New Look at Medieval Europe. By Kenneth M. Setton. Paintings by Andre Durenceau and Birney Lettick. 799-859, Dec. 1962

Roman Life in 1,600-year-old Color Pictures. By Gino Vinicio Gentili. Photos by Duncan Edwards. 211-229, Feb. 1957

ROMAN RUINS. *See* Camargue; England (The British Way; A Stroll to London); Languedoc; Turkey (Aphrodisias; *Yankee* Cruises)

The **ROMANCE** of American Furs. By Wanda Burnett. 379-402, Mar. 1948

The **ROMANCE** of the Geographic: National Geographic Magazine Observes Its Diamond Anniversary. By Gilbert Hovey Grosvenor. 516-585, Oct. 1963

ROMANCHE TRENCH, Atlantic Ocean:

Calypso Explores an Undersea Canyon. By Jacques-Yves Cousteau. Photos by Bates Littlehales. 373-396, Mar. 1958

ROMANIA:

Americans Afoot in Rumania. By Dan Dimancescu. Photos by Dick Durrance II and Christopher G. Knight. 810-845, June 1969

The Balkans, Atlas series supplement. Feb. 1962

Down the Danube by Canoe. By William Slade Backer. Photos by Richard S. Durrance and Christopher G. Knight. 34-79, July 1965

Romania: Maverick on a Tightrope. By William S. Ellis. Photos by Winfield Parks. 688-713, Nov. 1975

ROMANIES. *See* Gypsies

ROME, Italy:

Italy Smiles Again. By Edgar Erskine Hume. 693-732, June 1949

Jerusalem to Rome in the Path of St. Paul. By David S. Boyer. 707-759, Dec. 1956

Rome: Eternal City with a Modern Air. By Harnett T. Kane. Photos by B. Anthony Stewart. 437-491, Apr. 1957

St. Peter's, Rome's Church of Popes. By Aubrey Menen. Photos by Albert Moldvay. 865-879, Dec. 1971

A Traveler's Map of Italy, map supplement. Text on reverse. June 1970

When in Rome. . . . By Stuart E. Jones. Photos by Winfield Parks. 741-789, June 1970

RONNING, CHESTER:

Return to Changing China. By Audrey Topping. 801-833, Dec. 1971

ROOKERIES. *See* Bird Sanctuaries and Rookeries; Pribilof Islands, for Polovina Seal Rookery

ROOSEVELT, FRANKLIN D.:

Inside the White House. By Lonnelle Aikman. Photos by B. Anthony Stewart and Thomas Nebbia. 3-43, Jan. 1961

The Living White House. By Lonnelle Aikman. 593-643, Nov. 1966

Profiles of the Presidents: V. The Atomic Age: Its Problems and Promises. By Frank Freidel. 66-119, Jan. 1966

ROOSEVELT, THEODORE:

Inside the White House. By Lonnelle Aikman. Photos by B. Anthony Stewart and Thomas Nebbia. 3-43, Jan. 1961

The Living White House. By Lonnelle Aikman. 593-643, Nov. 1966

North Dakota Comes into Its Own. By Leo A. Borah. Photos by J. Baylor Roberts. 283-322, Sept. 1951

Included: Roosevelt's log cabin, now a museum on the State Capitol grounds

Profiles of the Presidents: IV. America Enters the Modern Era. By Frank Freidel. 537-577, Oct. 1965

Theodore Roosevelt: a Centennial Tribute. By Bart McDowell. 572-590, Oct. 1958

ROOT, ALAN: Photographer:

Freeing Flamingos From Anklets of Death. By John G. Williams. 934-944, Dec. 1963

ROOT, ALAN: Photographer—*Continued*

The Galapagos, Eerie Cradle of New Species. By Roger Tory Peterson. Photos by Alan and Joan Root. 541-585, Apr. 1967

Inside a Hornbill's Walled-up Nest. By Joan and Alan Root. 846-855, Dec. 1969

Mzima, Kenya's Spring of Life. By Joan and Alan Root. 350-373, Sept. 1971

ROOT, JOAN: Photographer:

The Galapagos, Eerie Cradle of New Species. By Roger Tory Peterson. Photos by Alan and Joan Root. 541-585, Apr. 1967

Inside a Hornbill's Walled-up Nest. By Joan and Alan Root. 846-855, Dec. 1969

Mzima, Kenya's Spring of Life. By Joan and Alan Root. 350-373, Sept. 1971

ROSCHER, W. E.: Author:

Queen Elizabeth Opens Parliament. Photos by Robert B. Goodman. 699-707, Nov. 1961

ROSE APHIDS. By Treat Davidson. 851-859, June 1961

ROSEATE SPOONBILLS:

The Pink Birds of Texas. By Paul A. Zahl. 641-654, Nov. 1949

Roseate Spoonbills, Radiant Birds of the Gulf Coast. By Robert Porter Allen. Photos by Frederick Kent Truslow. 274-288, Feb. 1962

Saving Man's Wildlife Heritage. By John H. Baker. Photos by Robert F. Sisson. 581-620, Nov. 1954

ROSENSTIEL SCHOOL OF MARINE SCIENCE. *See* University of Miami: Marine Research

ROSES:

Amateur Gardener Creates a New Rose (Portrait). By Elizabeth A. Moize. Photos by Farrell Grehan. 286-294, Aug. 1972

Patent Plants Enrich Our World. By Orville H. Kneen. Photos from U. S. Plant Patents. 357-378, Mar. 1948

See also Tournament of Roses

ROSIER CREEK, Virginia:

A Good Life on the Potomac. By James L. Stanfield. 470-479, Oct. 1976

ROSS, EDWARD S.: Author:

Hunting Africa's Smallest Game. 406-419, Mar. 1961

Author-Photographer

Asian Insects in Disguise. 433-439, Sept. 1965

Birds That "See" in the Dark With Their Ears. 282-290, Feb. 1965

Photographer

Crossroads of the Insect World. By J. W. MacSwain. 844-857, Dec. 1966

ROSS, KIP: Author-Photographer:

Chile, the Long and Narrow Land. 185-235, Feb. 1960

Peru, Homeland of the Warlike Inca. 421-462, Oct. 1950

South Africa Close-up. 641-681, Nov. 1962

We Drove Panama's Darién Gap. 368-389, Mar. 1961

Photographer

Mexico in Motion. By Bart McDowell. 490-537, Oct. 1961

ROSS, MALCOLM D.: Author:

My Neighbors Hold to Mountain Ways. Photos by Flip Schulke. 856-880, June 1958

North Carolina, Dixie Dynamo. Photos by B. Anthony Stewart. 141-183, Feb. 1962

To 76,000 Feet by *Strato-Lab* Balloon. By Malcolm D. Ross and M. Lee Lewis. 269-282, Feb. 1957

We Saw the World From the Edge of Space. Ground photos by Walter Meayers Edwards. 671-685, Nov. 1961

ROTH, TOM and TOMMY:

Down Mark Twain's River on a Raft. By Rex E. Hieronymus. 551-574, Apr. 1948

ROTTERDAM, Netherlands:

Rotterdam—Reborn From Ruins. By Helen Hill Miller. Photos by James Blair. 526-553, Oct. 1960

ROUGHEST Road Race: the Mexican 1000. By Michael E. Long. 569-575, Oct. 1972

ROUGHLEY, T. C.: Author:

Bounty Descendants Live on Remote Norfolk Island. Photos by J. Baylor Roberts. 559-584, Oct. 1960

ROUMANIA. *See* Romania

The ROUND Earth on Flat Paper. By Wellman Chamberlin. 399, Mar. 1950

'ROUND the Horn by Submarine. By Paul C. Stimson. 129-144, Jan. 1948

ROUND THE WORLD SCHOOL. By Paul Antze. Photos by William Eppridge. 96-127, July 1962

ROUNDUP. *See* Cattle and Cattle Raising; Elephants (Wild Elephant Roundup); Reindeer

ROVER (Lunar Vehicle):

Apollo 15 Explores the Mountains of the Moon. By Kenneth F. Weaver. Photos from NASA. 233-265, Feb. 1972

Detailed diagram of Rover. 148, July 1971

Exploring Taurus-Littrow. By Harrison H. Schmitt. Photos by the crew of Apollo 17. 290-307, Sept. 1973

What Is It Like to Walk on the Moon? By David R. Scott. 326-331, Sept. 1973

ROVING Maryland's Cavalier Country. By William A. Kinney. 431-470, Apr. 1954

ROWELL, GALEN: Author-Photographer:

Climbing Half Dome the Hard Way. 782-791, June 1974

Photographer

California's Parched Oasis, the Owens Valley. By Judith and Neil Morgan. Photos by Jodi Cobb and Galen Rowell. 98-127, Jan. 1976

ROY, LEONARD C.: Author:

Menhaden—Uncle Sam's Top Commercial Fish. Photos by Robert F. Sisson. 813-823, June 1949

ROYAL ACADEMY OF ARTS, London:

Our Search for British Paintings. By Franklin L. Fisher. 543-550, Apr. 1949

ROYAL AIR FORCE (RAF). *See* Airlift to Berlin

ROYAL BOTANIC GARDENS, England:

Kew: The Commoners' Royal Garden. By Thomas

ROYAL BOTANIC GARDENS, England—*Continued*

Garner James. Photos by B. Anthony Stewart. 479-506, Apr. 1950

ROYAL GEOGRAPHICAL SOCIETY: Expeditions. *See* British Mount Everest Expedition

ROYAL ONTARIO MUSEUM OF GEOLOGY AND MINERALOGY, Canada: Expeditions. *See* Chubb Crater

ROYAL Wedding at Jaisalmer. By Marilyn Silverstone. 66-79, Jan. 1965

ROZUMALSKI, TED: Photographer:

Wisconsin's Door Peninsula. By William S. Ellis. 347-371, Mar. 1969

RUBBER-CUSHIONED Liberia. By Henry S. Villard. Photos by Charles W. Allmon. 201-228, Feb. 1948

RUBIES:

Questing for Gems. By George S. Switzer. 835-863, Dec. 1971

See also Lasers

RUDOLF, Lake, and Region, Kenya:

In Search of Man's Past at Lake Rudolf. By Richard E. Leakey. Photos by Gordon W. Gahan. 712-734, May 1970

Skull 1470. By Richard E. Leakey. Photos by Bob Campbell. 819-829, June 1973

RUGGED Is the Word for Bravo (Weather Station). By Phillip M. Swatek. 829-843, Dec. 1955

RUGS AND RUG MAKING:

Journey into Troubled Iran. By George W. Long. Photos by J. Baylor Roberts. 425-464, Oct. 1951

See also Afghanistan: Crossroad; Kashmir (Idyllic Vale); *and* Kashgais; Navajos; Turkomans

RUHR (Region), Germany:

With Uncle Sam and John Bull in Germany. By Frederick Simpich. 117-140, Jan. 1949

RUINS. *See* Archeology; listing under Roman Ruins; names of ancient countries; *and* the following: Angkor; Aphrodisias; Ascalon; Athens: Her Golden Past; Jericho; Machu Picchu; Megiddo (Armageddon); Morocco; Pagan; Persepolis; Petra; Stonehenge; Zimbabwe

RUMANIA. *See* Romania

RUMTEK MONASTERY, Sikkim:

Gangtok, Cloud-wreathed Himalayan Capital. By John Scofield. 698-713, Nov. 1970

RUOHOMAA, KOSTI: Photographer:

Maine's Lobster Island, Monhegan. By William P. E. Graves. 285-298, Feb. 1959

RUPERT HOUSE, Quebec, Canada:

The Changing World of Canada's Crees. By Fred Ward. 541-569, Apr. 1975

RUSCHI, AUGUSTO:

The Man Who Talks to Hummingbirds. By Luis Marden. Photos by James Blair. 80-99, Jan. 1963

RUSHMORE, Mount, South Dakota:

Back to the Historic Black Hills. By Leland D. Case. Photos by Bates Littlehales. 479-509, Oct. 1956

RUSHMORE, Mount, South Dakota—*Continued*
South Dakota Keeps Its West Wild. By Frederick Simpich. 555-588, May 1947

RUSSELL, Kansas:
Hays, Kansas, at the Nation's Heart. By Margaret M. Detwiler. Photos by John E. Fletcher. 461-490, Apr. 1952

RUSSELL CAVE, Alabama:
Life 8,000 Years Ago Uncovered in an Alabama Cave. By Carl F. Miller. 542-558, Oct. 1956
National Geographic Society Presents Russell Cave to the American People. By Melville Bell Grosvenor. 438, Mar. 1958
Russell Cave: New Light on Stone Age Life. By Carl F. Miller. 427-437, Mar. 1958
Russell Cave Dedicated; New Visitor Center Named for Gilbert H. Grosvenor. 440-442, Sept. 1967

RUSSIA. *See* Union of Soviet Socialist Republics

RUSSIANS:
Nikolaevsk: A Bit of Old Russia Takes Root in Alaska. By Jim Rearden. Photos by Charles O'Rear. 401-425, Sept. 1972

RUSSIA'S Mighty River Road, the Volga. By Howard Sochurek. 579-613, May 1973

RUSSIA'S Window on the West: Leningrad. By Howard La Fay. Photos by Dick Durrance II. 636-673, May 1971

RUTHERFORD, ERNEST, LORD:
The British Way. By Sir Evelyn Wrench. 421-541, Apr. 1949

RUWENZORI (Mountains of the Moon), Africa:
Mountains of the Moon. By Paul A. Zahl. 412-434, Mar. 1962

RWANDA. *See* Virunga Mountains

RYDEN, HOPE: Author-Photographer:
The "Lone" Coyote Likes Family Life. Photos by author and David Hiser. 278-294, Aug. 1974
On the Track of the West's Wild Horses. Photos by author and Dick Durrance II. 94-109, Jan. 1971

RYUKYU ISLANDS. *See* Okinawa

S

SÁ, HERNANE TAVARES DE: Author:
Brasília, Metropolis Made to Order. Photos by Thomas J. Abercrombie. 704-724, May 1960
Spectacular Rio de Janeiro. Photos by Charles Allmon. 289-328, Mar. 1955

SAAR:
Coal Makes the Saar a Prize. By Franc Shor. 561-576, Apr. 1954

SAARINEN, EERO:
St. Louis: New Spirit Soars in Mid-America's Proud Old City. By Robert Paul Jordan. Photos by Bruce Dale. 605-641, Nov. 1965
Included: The Gateway Arch, designed by Saarinen

SABA (Island), West Indies:
A Fresh Breeze Stirs the Leewards. By Carleton Mitchell. Photos by Winfield Parks. 488-537, Oct. 1966

SABA (Island), West Indies—*Continued*
The Netherlands Antilles: Holland in the Caribbean. By James Cerruti. Photos by Emory Kristof. 115-146, Jan. 1970

SABAH (North Borneo):
In Storied Lands of Malaysia. By Maurice Shadbolt. Photos by Winfield Parks. 734-783, Nov. 1963
Malaysia's Giant Flowers and Insect-trapping Plants. By Paul A. Zahl. 680-701, May 1964

SABLE ISLAND, Nova Scotia:
Safe Landing on Sable, Isle of 500 Shipwrecks. By Melville Bell Grosvenor. 398-431, Sept. 1965
Included: Maps, 1766 to 1964, indicating eastward shift of the island; map of known shipwreck sites 1898: The Bells on Sable. Photos by Arthur W. McCurdy. 408-409, 416-417

SACRAMENTO, California:
California, Horn of Plenty. By Frederick Simpich. Photos by Willard R. Culver. 553-594, May 1949
California, the Golden Magnet. By William Graves. 595-679, May 1966
II. Nature's North. Photos by James P. Blair and Jonathan S. Blair. 641-679
New Rush to Golden California. By George W. Long. 723-802, June 1954

A SACRED Symbol Comes Home: Afo-A-Kom. By William S. Ellis. Photos by James P. Blair. 141-148, July 1974

SADLERMIUTS (Eskimos):
Vanished Mystery Men of Hudson Bay. By Henry B. Collins. 669-687, Nov. 1956

SAFARI from Congo to Cairo. By Elsie May Bell Grosvenor. Photos by Gilbert Grosvenor. 721-771, Dec. 1954

SAFARI Through Changing Africa. By Elsie May Bell Grosvenor. Photos by Gilbert Grosvenor. 145-198, Aug. 1953

SAFE Landing on Sable, Isle of 500 Shipwrecks. By Melville Bell Grosvenor. 398-431, Sept. 1965

SAGA of a Ship, the *Yankee* (Brigantine). By Luis Marden. 263-269, Feb. 1966

SAGAN, CARL: Author:
Mars: a New World to Explore. 821-841, Dec. 1967

SAGUARO (Cactus):
Abundant Life in a Desert Land. By Walter Meayers Edwards. 424-436, Sept. 1973

SAGUENAY RIVER REGION, Canada:
North Through History Aboard *White Mist*. By Melville Bell Grosvenor. Photos by Edwin Stuart Grosvenor. 1-55, July 1970
Quebec's Forests, Farms, and Frontiers. By Andrew H. Brown. 431-470, Oct. 1949
Sea to Lakes on the St. Lawrence. By George W. Long. Photos by B. Anthony Stewart and John E. Fletcher. 323-366, Sept. 1950

SAHARA (Desert), Africa:
Algeria: France's Stepchild, Problem and Promise. By Howard La Fay. Photos by Robert F. Sisson. 768-795, June 1960
Algeria: Learning to Live With Independence. By Thomas J. Abercrombie. 200-233, Aug. 1973

SAHARA (Desert), Africa—*Continued*

Drought Threatens the Tuareg World. By Victor Englebert. 544-571, Apr. 1974

Dry-land Fleet Sails the Sahara. By Jean du Boucher. Photos by Jonathan S. Blair. 696-725, Nov. 1967

Freedom Speaks French in Ouagadougou. By John Scofield. 153-203, Aug. 1966

I Joined a Sahara Salt Caravan. By Victor Englebert. 694-711, Nov. 1965

Oasis-hopping in the Sahara. By Maynard Owen Williams. 209-236, Feb. 1949

Sand in My Eyes. By Jinx Rodger. 664-705, May 1958

The Sword and the Sermon. By Thomas J. Abercrombie. 3-45, July 1972

Wind Raiders of the Sahara (Television film). 436A-436B, Sept. 1973

SAHEL (Sub Sahara), Africa:

Drought Threatens the Tuareg World. By Victor Englebert. 544-571, Apr. 1974

The Niger: River of Sorrow, River of Hope. By Georg Gerster. 152-189, Aug. 1975

SAIDMAN, BARNET: Photographer:

The Swans of Abbotsbury (Dorsetshire, England). By Michael Moynihan. 563-570, Oct. 1959

SAIGON, Viet Nam:

Indochina Faces the Dragon. By George W. Long. Photos by J. Baylor Roberts. 287-328, Sept. 1952

Portrait of Indochina. By W. Robert Moore and Maynard Owen Williams. Paintings by Jean Despujols. 461-490, Apr. 1951

Saigon: Eye of the Storm. By Peter T. White. Photos by W. E. Garrett. 834-872, June 1965

Slow Train Through Viet Nam's War. By Howard Sochurek. 412-444, Sept. 1964

South Viet Nam Fights the Red Tide. By Peter T. White. Photos by W. E. Garrett. 445-489, Oct. 1961

SAILFISH:

Solving Life Secrets of the Sailfish. By Gilbert Voss. Photos by B. Anthony Stewart. Paintings by Craig Phillips. 859-872, June 1956

SAILING. *See* Cruises and Voyages; Sailing Vessels; Yachting

SAILING a Sea of Fire. By Paul A. Zahl. 120-129, July 1960

SAILING CARS:

Dry-land Fleet Sails the Sahara. By Jean du Boucher. Photos by Jonathan S. Blair. 696-725, Nov. 1967

Wind Raiders of the Sahara (Television film). 436A-436B, Sept. 1973

SAILING Iceland's Rugged Coasts. By Wright Britton. Photos by James A. Sugar. 228-265, Aug. 1969

The SAILING Oystermen of Chesapeake Bay. By Luis Marden. 798-819, Dec. 1967

SAILING VESSELS:

The Age of Sail Lives On at Mystic. By Alan Villiers. Photos by Weston Kemp. 220-239, Aug. 1968

SAILING VESSELS—*Continued*

Included: *Alice, Charles W. Morgan, Joseph Conrad, L. A. Dunton*

By Square-rigger from Baltic to Bicentennial. By Kenneth Garrett. 824-857, Dec. 1976
Included: The tall-ships race

Last of the Cape Horners *(Pamir)*. By Alan Villiers. 701-710, May 1948
Contents: *Abraham Rydberg, Archibald Russell, Grace Harwar, Kjøbenhavn, Kommodore Johnsen, Lawhill, Moshulu, Padua, Pamir, Parma, Passat, Pommern, Viking*
Square-rigger in a Tempest *(Pamir)*. 703-710

Life's Tempo on Nantucket. By Peter Benchley. Photos by James L. Stanfield. 810-839, June 1970

The Sailing Oystermen of Chesapeake Bay. By Luis Marden. 798-819, Dec. 1967

Windjamming Around New England. By Tom Horgan. Photos by Robert F. Sisson. 141-169, Aug. 1950
Included: *Abigail Chandler, Bluenose, Bolero, Bowdoin, Charles W. Morgan, Daniel I. Tenny, Fiddlers' Green, Gertrude L. Thebaud, Great Republic, Hannah, Hero, Joseph Conrad, Lagoda, Malabar XIII, Manxman, Nomad, Regina M., Telegraph, Wanderer, Yankee*

See also Dhows; Fishing (Industry); Galleons; Junks; *Lipas;* Longships; Square-riggers; Training Ships; listing under Yachts; *and Beagle,* H.M.S.; *Bounty; Dove; Endeavour; Girona; Hokule'a; Ice Bird; Isbjorn; Mayflower II; Ra II*

SAILING with Sindbad's Sons. By Alan Villiers. 675-688, Nov. 1948

The SAILOR Who Gave Us the New World: Christopher Columbus. By John Scofield. Photos by Adam Woolfitt. 584-625, Nov. 1975

SAILORS in the Sky: Fifty Years of Naval Aviation. By Patrick N. L. Bellinger. 276-296, Aug. 1961

SAILPLANES:

Sailors of the Sky. By Gordon Young. Photos by Emory Kristof and Jack Fields. Paintings by Davis Meltzer. 49-73, Jan. 1967

ST. AUBYN, SIR FRANCIS CECIL. *See* St. Levan, Baron

ST. AUGUSTINE, Florida:

St. Augustine, Nation's Oldest City, Turns 400. By Robert L. Conly. 196-229, Feb. 1966

ST. BERNARD DOGS:

The Great St. Bernard Hospice Today. By George Pickow. 49-62, Jan. 1957

ST. BERNARD HOSPICE, Switzerland:

The Great St. Bernard Hospice Today. By George Pickow. 49-62, Jan. 1957

ST. BOTOLPH'S Town: the Original Boston. By Veronica Thomas. Photos by James L. Amos. 382-389, Sept. 1974

ST. CATHERINES (Island), Georgia:

Sea Islands: Adventuring Along the South's Surprising Coast. By James Cerruti. Photos by Thomas Nebbia and James L. Amos. 366-393, Mar. 1971

ST. CATHERINE'S MONASTERY, Sinai (Peninsula):

Island of Faith in the Sinai Wilderness. By George H. Forsyth. Photos by Robert F. Sisson. 82-106,

ST. CATHERINE'S MONASTERY, Sinai (Peninsula)—
Continued
Jan. 1964

Mount Sinai's Holy Treasures. By Kurt Weitzmann. Photos by Fred Anderegg. 109-127, Jan. 1964

Sinai Sheds New Light on the Bible. By Henry Field. Photos by William B. and Gladys Terry. 795-815, Dec. 1948

ST. CHRISTOPHER (Island), West Indies:

A Fresh Breeze Stirs the Leewards. By Carleton Mitchell. Photos by Winfield Parks. 488-537, Oct. 1966

ST. ELIAS, Mount, Alaska-Canada:

First American Ascent of Mount St. Elias. By Maynard M. Miller. 229-248, Feb. 1948

ST. EUSTATIUS (Island). *See* Sint Eustatius

ST. HELENA (Island), Atlantic Ocean:

St. Helena: the Forgotten Island. By Quentin Keynes. 265-280, Aug. 1950

ST. JOHN (Island), U. S. Virgin Islands:

Tektite II (Sea and Space Research Project). 256-296, Aug. 1971

ST. JOHN'S, Newfoundland:

Newfoundland, Canada's New Province. By Andrew H. Brown. Photos by author and Robert F. Sisson. 777-812, June 1949

Newfoundland Trusts in the Sea. By Gary Jennings. Photos by Sam Abell. 112-141, Jan. 1974

ST. KITTS (Island). *See* St. Christopher

ST. LAWRENCE (River), Canada-U. S.:

North Through History Aboard *White Mist*. By Melville Bell Grosvenor. Photos by Edwin Stuart Grosvenor. 1-55, July 1970

Quebec's Forests, Farms, and Frontiers. By Andrew H. Brown. 431-470, Oct. 1949

The St. Lawrence, River Key to Canada. By Howard La Fay. Photos by John Launois. 622-667, May 1967

Sea to Lakes on the St. Lawrence. By George W. Long. Photos by B. Anthony Stewart and John E. Fletcher. 323-366, Sept. 1950

See also Montreal; Quebec (City)

ST. LAWRENCE, Gulf of, Canada:

Sea Bird Cities Off Audubon's Labrador. By Arthur A. Allen. 755-774, June 1948

ST. LAWRENCE SEAWAY, Canada-U. S.:

New St. Lawrence Seaway Opens the Great Lakes to the World. By Andrew H. Brown. 299-339, Mar. 1959

ST. LEVAN, BARON and BARONESS:

Fabled Mount of St. Michael. By Alan Villiers. Photos by Bates Littlehales. 880-898, June 1964

ST. LOUIS, Île, Paris, France:

Île de la Cité, Birthplace of Paris. By Kenneth MacLeish. Photos by Bruce Dale. 680-719, May 1968

The More Paris Changes. . . . By Howell Walker. Photos by Gordon W. Gahan. 64-103, July 1972

ST. LOUIS, Missouri:

"Pyramids" of the New World. By Neil Merton

ST. LOUIS, Missouri—*Continued*

Judd. 105-128, Jan. 1948
  Included: "The Mound City"

St. Louis: New Spirit Soars in Mid-America's Proud Old City. By Robert Paul Jordan. Photos by Bruce Dale. 605-641, Nov. 1965

So Long, St. Louis, We're Heading West. By William C. Everhart. 643-669, Nov. 1965

ST. LUCIA (Island), West Indies:

Finisterre Sails the Windward Islands. By Carleton Mitchell. Photos by Winfield Parks. 755-801, Dec. 1965

ST. MARY ISLANDS SANCTUARY, Quebec, Canada:

Sea Bird Cities Off Audubon's Labrador. By Arthur A. Allen. 755-774, June 1948
  Contents: Birds on Cliff, Harbour, and Middle Islands

ST. MARYS, West Virginia:

So Much Happens Along the Ohio River. By Frederick Simpich. Photos by Justin Locke. 177-212, Feb. 1950

ST. MICHAEL'S MOUNT, England:

Fabled Mount of St. Michael. By Alan Villiers. Photos by Bates Littlehales. 880-898, June 1964

ST. PAUL (Apostle). *See* Paul, Saint

ST. PAUL, Minnesota:

Minnesota, Where Water Is the Magic Word. By David S. Boyer. Photos by author and David Brill. 200-229, Feb. 1976

Minnesota Makes Ideas Pay. By Frederick G. Vosburgh. Photos by John E. Fletcher and B. Anthony Stewart. 291-336, Sept. 1949

The Upper Mississippi. By Willard Price. 651-699, Nov. 1958

ST. PETER'S (Basilica), Vatican City:

Rome: Eternal City with a Modern Air. By Harnett T. Kane. Photos by B. Anthony Stewart. 437-491, Apr. 1957

St. Peter's, Rome's Church of Popes. By Aubrey Menen. Photos by Albert Moldvay. 865-879, Dec. 1971

When in Rome. . . . By Stuart E. Jones. Photos by Winfield Parks. 741-789, June 1970

ST. PIERRE, Martinique:

Martinique: A Tropical Bit of France. By Gwen Drayton Allmon. Photos by Charles Allmon. 255-283, Feb. 1959

ST. PIERRE AND MIQUELON (Archipelago), North Atlantic Ocean:

White Mist Cruises to Wreck-haunted St. Pierre and Miquelon. By Melville Bell Grosvenor. 378-419, Sept. 1967

ST. SIMONS (Island), Georgia:

Sea Islands: Adventuring Along the South's Surprising Coast. By James Cerruti. Photos by Thomas Nebbia and James L. Amos. 366-393, Mar. 1971

ST. THOMAS, Virgin Islands:

A Fresh Breeze Stirs the Leewards. By Carleton Mitchell. Photos by Winfield Parks. 488-537, Oct. 1966

Virgin Islands: Tropical Playland, U.S.A. By John Scofield. Photos by Charles Allmon. 201-232, Feb. 1956

SAINT VÉRAN, France's Highest Village. By Robert K. Burns, Jr. 571-588, Apr. 1959

ST. VINCENT (Island), West Indies:

Finisterre Sails the Windward Islands. By Carleton Mitchell. Photos by Winfield Parks. 755-801, Dec. 1965

STE. CÉCILE, Cathedral of, Albi, France:

France's Past Lives in Languedoc. By Walter Meayers Edwards. 1-43, July 1951

SALAMANDERS:

In the Wilds of a City Parlor. By Paul A. Zahl. 645-672, Nov. 1954

The Shadowy World of Salamanders. By Paul A. Zahl. 104-117, July 1972

SALEM, Massachusetts:

Literary Landmarks of Massachusetts. By William H. Nicholas. Photos by B. Anthony Stewart and John E. Fletcher. 279-310, Mar. 1950

SALERNO, Gulf of:

Amalfi, Italy's Divine Coast. By Luis Marden. 472-509, Oct. 1959

SALERNO, Italy:

Italy Smiles Again. By Edgar Erskine Hume. 693-732, June 1949

SALISBURY, Rhodesia:

Rhodesia, a House Divided. By Allan C. Fisher, Jr. Photos by Thomas Nebbia. 641-671, May 1975

SALMON:

The Columbia River, Powerhouse of the Northwest. By David S. Boyer. 821-847, Dec. 1974

Endeavour Sails the Inside Passage. By Amos Burg. 801-828, June 1947

The Incredible Salmon. By Clarence P. Idyll. Photos by Robert F. Sisson. Paintings by Walter A. Weber. 195-219, Aug. 1968

Life portraits of a famous family: Pacific salmon. 214-216

A River Restored: Oregon's Willamette. By Ethel A. Starbird. Photos by Lowell J. Georgia. 816-835, June 1972

When Giant Bears Go Fishing. By Cecil E. Rhode. 195-205, Aug. 1954

SALMON (River), Idaho:

White-water Adventure on Wild Rivers of Idaho. By Frank Craighead, Jr. and John Craighead. 213-239, Feb. 1970

Wild River (Television film). 239A-239B, Feb. 1970

See also Morgan Creek

SALT:

I Joined a Sahara Salt Caravan. By Victor Englebert. 694-711, Nov. 1965

See also Danakil Depression; Dead Sea; Great Salt Lake; Salzkammergut

SALT LAKE CITY, Utah:

Utah's Shining Oasis. By Charles McCarry. Photos by James L. Amos. 440-473, Apr. 1975

SALT MARSHES:

Can We Save Our Salt Marshes? By Stephen W. Hitchcock. Photos by William R. Curtsinger. 729-765, June 1972

Sea Islands: Adventuring Along the South's Sur-

SALT MARSHES—*Continued*

prising Coast. By James Cerruti. Photos by Thomas Nebbia and James L. Amos. 366-393, Mar. 1971

SALT MINES:

Salzkammergut, Austria's Alpine Playground. By Beverley M. Bowie. Photos by Volkmar Wentzel. 246-275, Aug. 1960

SALUT, Îles du, French Guiana. *See* Devil's Island

SALVAGE:

New Life for the Troubled Suez Canal. By William Graves. Photos by Jonathan Blair. 792-817, June 1975

See also Kyrenia Ship; *Monitor; Slot ter Hooge; Thresher; Vasa;* Yassi Ada; *and* Spanish Treasure

SALZBURG, Austria:

Occupied Austria, Outpost of Democracy. By George W. Long. Photos by Volkmar Wentzel. 749-790, June 1951

SALZKAMMERGUT, Austria's Alpine Playground. By Beverley M. Bowie. Photos by Volkmar Wentzel. 246-275, Aug. 1960

SAMARITANS:

Hashemite Jordan, Arab Heartland. By John Scofield. 841-856, Dec. 1952

SAMOA:

Problems in Paradise. By Mary and Laurance S. Rockefeller. Photos by Thomas Nebbia. 782-793, Dec. 1974

A Teen-ager Sails the World Alone. By Robin Lee Graham. 445-491, Oct. 1968

Western Samoa, the Pacific's Newest Nation. By Maurice Shadbolt. Photos by Robert B. Goodman. 573-602, Oct. 1962

SAMPSON, PAUL: Author:

The Bonins and Iwo Jima Go Back to Japan. Photos by Joe Munroe. 128-144, July 1968

SAMUELS, GERTRUDE: Author:

Passage to Freedom in Viet Nam. 858-874, June 1955

SAN ANDREAS FAULT, California:

California's San Andreas Fault. By Thomas Y. Canby. Photos by James P. Blair. 38-53, Jan. 1973

SAN ANTONIO, Texas:

Carnival in San Antonio. By Mason Sutherland. Photos by J. Baylor Roberts. 813-844, Dec. 1947

The Fabulous State of Texas. By Stanley Walker. Photos by B. Anthony Stewart and Thomas Nebbia. 149-195, Feb. 1961

San Antonio: "Texas, Actin' Kind of Natural." By Fred Kline. Photos by David Hiser. 524-549, Apr. 1976

SAN DIEGO, California:

California, Horn of Plenty. By Frederick Simpich. Photos by Willard R. Culver. 553-594, May 1949

California, the Golden Magnet. By William Graves. 595-679, May 1966

I. The South. Photos by Thomas Nebbia. 595-639

New Rush to Golden California. By George W. Long. 723-802, June 1954

SAN DIEGO, California—*Continued*

San Diego, California's Plymouth Rock. By Allan C. Fisher, Jr. Photos by James L. Amos. 114-147, July 1969

SAN FRANCISCO (City and Bay), California:

Barehanded Battle to Cleanse the Bay. By Peter T. White. Photos by Jonathan S. Blair. 866-881, June 1971

Boom on San Francisco Bay. By Franc Shor. Photos by David S. Boyer. 181-226, Aug. 1956

California, Horn of Plenty. By Frederick Simpich. Photos by Willard R. Culver. 553-594, May 1949

California, the Golden Magnet. By William Graves. 595-679, May 1966
II. Nature's North. Photos by James P. Blair and Jonathan S. Blair. 641-679

Chinatown, the Gilded Ghetto. By William Albert Allard. 627-643, Nov. 1975

New Rush to Golden California. By George W. Long. 723-802, June 1954

Northern California; Southern California, double-sided U. S. Atlas series supplement. May 1966

San Francisco Bay, the Westward Gate. By William Graves. Photos by James L. Stanfield. 593-637, Nov. 1969

This Changing Earth. By Samuel W. Matthews. 1-37, Jan. 1973
Included: 1906 earthquake

SAN JACINTO WEEK (Fiesta):

Carnival in San Antonio. By Mason Sutherland. Photos by J. Baylor Roberts. 813-844, Dec. 1947

SAN JUAN, Puerto Rico:

Growing Pains Beset Puerto Rico. By William H. Nicholas. Photos by Justin Locke. 419-460, Apr. 1951

Puerto Rico's Seven-league Bootstraps. By Bart McDowell. Photos by B. Anthony Stewart. 755-793, Dec. 1962

SAN JUAN (River), U. S.:

Desert River Through Navajo Land. By Alfred M. Bailey. Photos by author and Fred G. Brandenburg. 149-172, Aug. 1947
See also Powell, Lake

SAN JUAN MOUNTAINS, Colorado-New Mexico:

Colorado's Friendly Topland. By Robert M. Ormes. 187-214, Aug. 1951

SAN LORENZO, Veracruz, Mexico:

On the Trail of La Venta Man. By Matthew W. Stirling. Photos by Richard H. Stewart. 137-172, Feb. 1947
Hunting Mexico's Buried Temples. 145-168

SAN MARCOS, Castillo de, St. Augustine, Florida. *See* Castillo de San Marcos

SAN MARINO (Republic):

San Marino, Little Land of Liberty. By Donna Hamilton Shor. Photos by Ted H. Funk. 233-251, Aug. 1967

United Italy Marks Its 100th Year. By Nathaniel T. Kenney. 593-647, Nov. 1961

SAN MARINO, California. *See* Henry E. Huntington Library and Art Gallery

SAN MIGUEL MOUNTAINS, Colorado:

Colorado's Friendly Topland. By Robert M. Ormes. 187-214, Aug. 1951

SAN SIMEON, California. *See* Hearst San Simeon State Historical Monument

SANCTUARIES. *See* Bird Sanctuaries and Rookeries; Pribilof Islands, for Polovina Seal Rookery; *and* listing under Wildlife Refuges

SAND DUNES:

The Living Sand. By William H. Amos. 820-833, June 1965

SAND in My Eyes. By Jinx Rodger. 664-705, May 1958

SAND YACHTS:

Dry-land Fleet Sails the Sahara. By Jean du Boucher. Photos by Jonathan S. Blair. 696-725, Nov. 1967

Wind Raiders of the Sahara (Television film). 436A-436B, Sept. 1973

SANDBURG, CARL: Author:

Just a Hundred Years Ago (U. S. Civil War). 1-3, July 1963

Lincoln, Man of Steel and Velvet. 239-241, Feb. 1960

SANDHILL CRANES:

Beyond the North Wind With the Snow Goose. By Des and Jen Bartlett. 822-843, Dec. 1973
. . . And Then There Was Fred. . . . 843-847

SANDYS, SIR EDWIN:

Founders of Virginia. By Sir Evelyn Wrench. Photos by B. Anthony Stewart. 433-462, Apr. 1948

SANGER, RICHARD H.: Photographer:

Ancient "Skyscrapers" of the Yemen. 645-668, Nov. 1947

SANTA BARBARA ISLANDS, California:

Off Santa Barbara: California's Ranches in the Sea. By Earl Warren, Jr. Photos by Bates Littlehales. 257-283, Aug. 1958

SANTA FE, New Mexico:

Adobe New Mexico. By Mason Sutherland. Photos by Justin Locke. 783-830, Dec. 1949

New Mexico: The Golden Land. By Robert Laxalt. Photos by Adam Woolfitt. 299-345, Sept. 1970

SANTANDER, Spain:

Under Canvas in the Atomic Age (United States Coast Guard Cadets). By Alan Villiers. 49-84, July 1955

SANTIAGO, Chile:

Chile, Republic on a Shoestring. By Gordon Young. Photos by George F. Mobley. 437-477, Oct. 1973

Chile, the Long and Narrow Land. By Kip Ross. 185-235, Feb. 1960

SANTIAGO ATITLÁN, Guatemala:

Guatemala, Maya and Modern. By Louis de la Haba. Photos by Joseph J. Scherschel. 661-689, Nov. 1974

Guatemala Revisited. By Luis Marden. 525-564, Oct. 1947

SANTORIN. *See* Thera

SAPELO (Island), Georgia:

Sea Islands: Adventuring Along the South's Surprising Coast. By James Cerruti. Photos by Thomas Nebbia and James L. Amos. 366-393, Mar. 1971

SAPPORO, Japan:

Snow Festival in Japan's Far North. By Eiji Miyazawa. 824-833, Dec. 1968

SAPSUCKER WOODS, Cornell University's Exciting New Bird Sanctuary. By Arthur A. Allen. 530-551, Apr. 1962

SARA (Tribespeople):

Into the Heart of Africa. By Gertrude S. Weeks. 257-263, Aug. 1956

SARAWAK:

Ambassadors of Good Will: The Peace Corps. By Sargent Shriver and Peace Corps Volunteers. 297-345, Sept. 1964
    Sarawak. By Edwin C. Price, Jr. 334-337

In Storied Lands of Malaysia. By Maurice Shadbolt. Photos by Winfield Parks. 734-783, Nov. 1963

Jungle Journeys in Sarawak. By Hedda Morrison. 710-736, May 1956

SARCOPHAGI:

Ancient Shipwreck Yields New Facts—and a Strange Cargo. By Peter Throckmorton. Photos by Kim Hart and Joseph J. Scherschel. 282-300, Feb. 1969

Fresh Treasures from Egypt's Ancient Sands. By Jefferson Caffery. Photos by David S. Boyer. 611-650, Nov. 1955

SARGASSO SEA:

Night Life in the Gulf Stream. By Paul A. Zahl. 391-418, Mar. 1954

SARGASSUM:

Adrift on a Raft of Sargassum. Photos by Robert F. Sisson. 188-199, Feb. 1976

SARGASSUM FISH:

Adrift on a Raft of Sargassum. Photos by Robert F. Sisson. 188-199, Feb. 1976

SARGON II, King (Assyria):

Ancient Mesopotamia: A Light That Did Not Fail. By E. A. Speiser. Paintings by H. M. Herget. 41-105, Jan. 1951

SARK (Island), English Channel:

Britain's "French" Channel Islands. By James Cerruti. Photos by James L. Amos. 710-740, May 1971

SARTWELL, FRANK: Author:

Mariner Scans a Lifeless Venus. Paintings by Davis Meltzer. 733-742, May 1963

Robots to the Moon. Paintings by Pierre Mion. 557-571, Oct. 1962

SASKATCHEWAN (Province), Canada:

Canada's Heartland, the Prairie Provinces. By W. E. Garrett. 443-489, Oct. 1970

The Canadian North: Emerging Giant. By David S. Boyer. 1-43, July 1968

Hunting Uranium Around the World. By Robert D. Nininger. Photos by Volkmar Wentzel. 533-558, Oct. 1954

SASS, HERBERT RAVENEL: Author:

South Carolina Rediscovered. Photos by Robert F. Sisson. 281-321, Mar. 1953

SATELLITE FINDER:

The National Geographic Society Satellite Finder (Map overlay). 808-809, Dec. 1957

SATELLITES:

How Man-made Satellites Can Affect Our Lives. By Joseph Kaplan. 791-810, Dec. 1957

The Next Frontier? By Isaac Asimov. Paintings by Pierre Mion. 76-89, July 1976

Satellites Gave Warning of Midwest Floods. By Peter T. White. Photos by Thomas A. DeFeo. 574-592, Oct. 1969

Space Satellites, Tools of Earth Research. By Heinz Haber. Paintings by William N. Palmstrom. 487-509, Apr. 1956

Telephone a Star: the Story of Communications Satellites. By Rowe Findley. 638-651, May 1962

See also DODGE; Landsat; Mariner Missions; Nimbus

SATMAR HASIDIM. *See* Hasidic Jews

SATURN (Planet):

Voyage to the Planets. By Kenneth F. Weaver. Paintings by Ludek Pesek. 147-193, Aug. 1970

SATURN V (Rocket):

First Explorers on the Moon: The Incredible Story of Apollo 11. 735-797, Dec. 1969
    III. The Flight of Apollo 11: "One giant leap for mankind." By Kenneth F. Weaver. 752-787
    V. Next Steps in Space. By Thomas O. Paine. 793-797

"A Most Fantastic Voyage": The Story of Apollo 8's Rendezvous With the Moon. By Sam C. Phillips. 593-631, May 1969

SAUDI ARABIA:

Africa and the Arabian Peninsula, map supplement. Mar. 1950

The Arab World. 712-732, Nov. 1958

The Arab World, Inc. By John J. Putman. Photos by Winfield Parks. 494-533, Oct. 1975

From America to Mecca on Airborne Pilgrimage. By Abdul Ghafur. 1-60, July 1953

In Search of Arabia's Past. By Peter Bruce Cornwall. 493-522, Apr. 1948
    Saudi Arabia, Oil Kingdom. Photos by Maynard Owen Williams. 497-512

Oil, the Dwindling Treasure. By Noel Grove. Photos by Emory Kristof. 792-825, June 1974

Saudi Arabia: Beyond the Sands of Mecca. By Thomas J. Abercrombie. 1-53, Jan. 1966

The Sword and the Sermon. By Thomas J. Abercrombie. 3-45, July 1972
    Included: Mecca; Medina

Troubled Waters East of Suez. By Ernest M. Eller. 483-522, Apr. 1954

SAVANNAH, N.S.:

Aboard the N.S. *Savannah:* World's First Nuclear Merchantman. By Alan Villiers. Photos by John E. Fletcher. 280-298, Aug. 1962

SAVE-THE-REDWOODS League. 682, May 1951; 510, Oct. 1957; 658, Nov. 1963; 15, 28, 44, July 1964; 60, 63, 67, July 1966

SAVING Brazil's Stone Age Tribes From Extinction. By Orlando and Claudio Villas Boas. Photos by W. Jesco von Puttkamer. 424-444, Sept. 1968

SAVING Earth's Oldest Living Things. By Andrew H. Brown. Photos by Raymond Moulin and author. 679-695, May 1951

SAVING Man's Wildlife Heritage. By John H. Baker. Photos by Robert F. Sisson. 581-620, Nov. 1954

SAVING the Ancient Temples at Abu Simbel. By Georg Gerster. Paintings by Robert W. Nicholson. 694-742, May 1966

SAVING the Nene, World's Rarest Goose. By S. Dillon Ripley. Photos by Jerry Chong. 745-754, Nov. 1965

SCALLOPS:

The Magic Lure of Sea Shells. By Paul A. Zahl. Photos by Victor R. Boswell, Jr. and author. 386-429, Mar. 1969

Shells Take You Over World Horizons. By Rutherford Platt. 33-84, July 1949

SCAMMON LAGOON, Baja California, Mexico:

The California Gray Whale Comes Back. By Theodore J. Walker. 394-415, Mar. 1971

Hunting the Heartbeat of a Whale. By Paul Dudley White and Samuel W. Matthews. 49-64, July 1956

SCANDINAVIA:

Friendly Flight to Northern Europe. By Lyndon B. Johnson. Photos by Volkmar Wentzel. 268-293, Feb. 1964

Northern Europe, map supplement. Aug. 1954

Scandinavia, Atlas series supplement. Apr. 1963

See also Denmark; Finland; Iceland; Norway; Sweden

SCAPEGOAT WILDERNESS, Montana:

Studying Grizzly Habitat by Satellite. By John Craighead. 148-158, July 1976

SCARLET IBIS:

New Scarlet Bird in Florida Skies. By Paul A. Zahl. 874-882, Dec. 1967

Search for the Scarlet Ibis in Venezuela. By Paul A. Zahl. 633-661, May 1950

SCENES of Postwar Finland. By La Verne Bradley. Photos by Jerry Waller. 233-264, Aug. 1947

SCHALLER, GEORGE B.: Author-Photographer:

Imperiled Phantom of Asian Peaks: First Photographs of Snow Leopards in the Wild. 702-707, Nov. 1971

Life with the King of Beasts. 494-519, Apr. 1969

SCHEFFER, VICTOR B.: Author:

Exploring the Lives of Whales. 752-767, Dec. 1976

Author-Photographer

The Fur Seal Herd Comes of Age. By Victor B. Scheffer and Karl W. Kenyon. 491-512, Apr. 1952

SCHELLBACH, LOUIS: Author:

Grand Canyon: Nature's Story of Creation. Photos by Justin Locke. 589-629, May 1955

SCHERSCHEL, JOSEPH J.: Photographer:

Ancient Shipwreck Yields New Facts — and a

SCHERSCHEL, JOSEPH J.: Photographer — *Continued*

Strange Cargo. By Peter Throckmorton. Photos by Kim Hart and Joseph J. Scherschel. 282-300, Feb. 1969

Andalusia, the Spirit of Spain. By Howard La Fay. 833-857, June 1975

Freedom's Progress South of the Sahara. By Howard La Fay. 603-637, Nov. 1962

Guatemala, Maya and Modern. By Louis de la Haba. 661-689, Nov. 1974

Hungary: Changing Homeland of a Tough, Romantic People. By Bart McDowell. Photos by Albert Moldvay and Joseph J. Scherschel. 443-483, Apr. 1971

Illinois: The City and the Plain. By Robert Paul Jordan. Photos by James L. Stanfield and Joseph J. Scherschel. 745-797, June 1967

Inside Europe Aboard *Yankee.* By Irving and Electa Johnson. 157-195, Aug. 1964

Lombardy's Lakes, Blue Jewels in Italy's Crown. By Franc Shor. 58-99, July 1968

Macao Clings to the Bamboo Curtain. By Jules B. Billard. 521-539, Apr. 1969

Mobile, Alabama's City in Motion. By William Graves. Photos by Joseph J. Scherschel and Robert W. Madden. 368-397, Mar. 1968

Preserving the Treasures of Olduvai Gorge. By Melvin M. Payne. 701-709, Nov. 1966

South Australia, Gateway to the Great Outback. By Howell Walker. 441-481, Apr. 1970

Sunny Corsica: French Morsel in the Mediterranean. By Robert Cairns. 401-423, Sept. 1973

Yankee Cruises Turkey's History-haunted Coast. By Irving and Electa Johnson. 798-845, Dec. 1969

SCHIRRA, WALTER M., Jr.:

Space Rendezvous, Milestone on the Way to the Moon. By Kenneth F. Weaver. 539-553, Apr. 1966

SCHMIDT, BERNHARD:

Mapping the Unknown Universe. By F. Barrows Colton. 401-420, Sept. 1950
   Note: Bernhard Schmidt invented the "Big Schmidt" telescope.

SCHMITT, HARRISON H.: Author-Photographer:

Exploring Taurus-Littrow. 290-307, Sept. 1973

Photographer

"The Earth From Space," photo supplement. Painting on reverse. Sept. 1973

SCHNEEBERGER, JON: Author-Photographer:

Escalante Canyon — Wilderness at the Crossroads. 270-285, Aug. 1972

SCHOOL BULLETIN, NGS:

The *School Bulletin* is retired after 56 years; replaced by *WORLD.* 299, Sept. 1975

SCHOOL for Space Monkeys. 725-729, May 1961

SCHOOL for Survival. By Curtis E. LeMay. 565-602, May 1953

SCHOOLS:

The DAR Story. By Lonnelle Aikman. Photos by B. Anthony Stewart and John E. Fletcher. 565-598, Nov. 1951
   Note: DAR partially supports a dozen schools and

SCHOOLS—*Continued*

colleges in this country, maintains a large student-loan fund, presents annual awards for high standing in certain subjects, and operates two schools of its own, the Kate Duncan Smith School, Grant, Alabama, and Tamassee School, South Carolina.

Round the World School (International School of America). By Paul Antze. Photos by William Eppridge. 96-127, July 1962

We Build a School for Sherpa Children. By Sir Edmund Hillary. 548-551, Oct. 1962

Zoo Animals Go to School. By Marion P. McCrane. Photos by W. E. Garrett. 694-706, Nov. 1956

See also Deaf, Institutes for teaching the; National Outdoor Leadership School; Outward Bound School; U. S. Air Force Academy; U. S. Merchant Marine Academy; U. S. Military Academy; Universities and Colleges

SCHOONERS. *See* Fishing (Industry); *Georg Stage; Portuguese Fishing Fleet; Vaitere*

SCHREIBER, RALPH W.: Author-Photographer:

Bad Days for the Brown Pelican. Photos by William R. Curtsinger and author. 111-123, Jan. 1975

SCHREIDER, HELEN and FRANK:

Author-Photographers

East From Bali by Seagoing Jeep to Timor. 236-279, Aug. 1962

From the Hair of Siva (Ganges River, India). 445-503, Oct. 1960

In the Footsteps of Alexander the Great. Paintings by Tom Lovell. 1-65, Jan. 1968

Indonesia, the Young and Troubled Island Nation. 579-625, May 1961

Journey Into the Great Rift: the Northern Half. 254-290, Aug. 1965

Taiwan: The Watchful Dragon. 1-45, Jan. 1969

SCHROEDER, ROBERT E.: Author-Photographer:

Photographing the Night Creatures of Alligator Reef (Florida). Photos by author and Walter A. Starck II. 128-154, Jan. 1964

Photographer

Imperiled Gift of the Sea: Caribbean Green Turtle. By Archie Carr. 876-890, June 1967

SCHULKE, FLIP: Photographer:

My Neighbors Hold to Mountain Ways (Blue Ridge, North Carolina). By Malcolm Ross. 856-880, June 1958

Titicaca, Abode of the Sun. By Luis Marden. 272-294, Feb. 1971

SCHULMAN, EDMUND: Author:

Bristlecone Pine, Oldest Known Living Thing. Photos by W. Robert Moore. 355-372, Mar. 1958

SCHULTZ, HARALD: Author-Photographer:

Blue-eyed Indian. 65-89, July 1961

Brazil's Big-lipped Indians. 118-133, Jan. 1962

Children of the Sun and Moon (Kraho Indians). Translated from German by Curtis T. Everett. 340-363, Mar. 1959

Indians of the Amazon Darkness. 737-758, May 1964

Tukuna Maidens Come of Age. 629-649, Nov. 1959

The Waurá: Brazilian Indians of the Hidden Xingu. 130-152, Jan. 1966

SCHULTZ, JOHN E.: Author:

Sea Fever. 237-268, Feb. 1949

SCIENCE Finds New Clues to Our Climate in Alaska's Mighty Rivers of Ice. By Maynard M. Miller. Photos by Christopher G. Knight. 194-217, Feb. 1967

SCIENCE'S Window on the Sea. By John G. VanDerwalker. Photos by Bates Littlehales. 256-289, Aug. 1971

SCIENTIST Studies Japan's Fantastic Long-tailed Fowl. By Frank X. Ogasawara. Photos by Eiji Miyazawa. 845-855, Dec. 1970

A **SCIENTIST** Visits Some of the World's Oldest People. By Alexander Leaf. Photos by John Launois. 93-119, Jan. 1973

SCIENTISTS Drill at Sea to Pierce Earth's Crust. By Samuel W. Matthews. Photos by J. Baylor Roberts. 686-697, Nov. 1961

SCIENTISTS Ride Ice Islands on Arctic Odysseys. By Lowell Thomas, Jr. Photos by Ted Spiegel. 670-691, Nov. 1965

SCILLY, Isles of, England:

England's Scillies, the Flowering Isles. By Alan Villiers. Photos by Bates Littlehales. 126-145, July 1967

SCINTILLATING Siam. By W. Robert Moore. 173-200, Feb. 1947

SCOFIELD, JOHN:

Editor, Associate. 698, Nov. 1970; 73, Jan. 1971; 546, Oct. 1974; 584, Nov. 1975; 658, Nov. 1976

Author

Character Marks the Coast of Maine. Photos by B. Anthony Stewart. 798-843, June 1968

Christopher Columbus and the New World He Found. Photos by Adam Woolfitt. 584-625, Nov. 1975

The Friendly Irish. Photos by James A. Sugar. 354-391, Sept. 1969

Israel: Land of Promise. Photos by B. Anthony Stewart. 395-434, Mar. 1965

Jerusalem, the Divided City. Photos by Brian Brake. 492-531, Apr. 1959

The Lower Keys, Florida's "Out Islands." Photos by Emory Kristof and Bates Littlehales. 72-93, Jan. 1971

A New Volcano Bursts from the Atlantic (Ilha Nova). Photos by Robert F. Sisson. 735-757, June 1958

Virgin Islands: Tropical Playland, U.S.A. Photos by Charles Allmon. 201-232, Feb. 1956

Author-Photographer

Australian New Guinea. 604-637, May 1962

Bhutan Crowns a New Dragon King. 546-571, Oct. 1974

Easter Week in Indian Guatemala. 406-417, Mar. 1960

Freedom Speaks French in Ouagadougou. 153-203, Aug. 1966

Gangtok, Cloud-wreathed Himalayan Capital. 698-713, Nov. 1970

Haiti—West Africa in the West Indies. 226-259, Feb. 1961

Hashemite Jordan, Arab Heartland. 841-856, Dec. 1952

SCOFIELD, JOHN: Author-Photographer — *Continued*

Hong Kong Has Many Faces. 1-41, Jan. 1962

India in Crisis. 599-661, May 1963

Life Slowly Changes in Remote Bhutan. 658-683, Nov. 1976

Netherlands New Guinea. 584-603, May 1962

Photographer

Venice, City of Twilight Splendor. By Joe Alex Morris. 543-569, Apr. 1961

SCORPIONFISH:

Something's Fishy About That Fin! (Decoy Fish). Photos by Robert J. Shallenberger and William D. Madden. 224-227, Aug. 1974

SCORPIONS: Living Fossils of the Sands. By Paul A. Zahl. 436-442, Mar. 1968

SCOTLAND:

The Britain That Shakespeare Knew. By Louis B. Wright. Photos by Dean Conger. 613-665, May 1964

British Castles, History in Stone. By Norman Wilkinson. 111-129, July 1947

British Isles, Atlas series supplement. July 1958

The British Isles, map supplement. Apr. 1949

The British Way. By Sir Evelyn Wrench. 421-541, Apr. 1949
Included: James I; James Watt

The Highlands, Stronghold of Scottish Gaeldom. By Kenneth MacLeish. Photos by Winfield Parks. 398-435, Mar. 1968

Midshipmen's Cruise. By William J. Aston and Alexander G. B. Grosvenor. 711-754, June 1948

Playing 3,000 Golf Courses in Fourteen Lands. By Ralph A. Kennedy. 113-132, July 1952

Poets' Voices Linger in Scottish Shrines. By Isobel Wylie Hutchison. Photos by Kathleen Revis. 437-488, Oct. 1957

Rhododendron Glories of Southwest Scotland. By David S. Boyer. Photos by B. Anthony Stewart and author. 641-664, May 1954

Scotland From Her Lovely Lochs and Seas. By Alan Villiers. Photos by Robert F. Sisson. 492-541, Apr. 1961

Scotland's Golden Eagles at Home. By C. Eric Palmar. 273-286, Feb. 1954

A Stroll to John o'Groat's. By Isobel Wylie Hutchison. 1-48, July 1956

A Stroll to London. By Isobel Wylie Hutchison. Photos by B. Anthony Stewart. 171-204, Aug. 1950

A Traveler's Map of the British Isles, map supplement. Text on reverse. Apr. 1974

See also Arran, Island of; Edinburgh; Hebrides; Orkney Islands; Shetland Islands

SCOTT, DAVID R.:

Apollo 15 Explores the Mountains of the Moon. By Kenneth F. Weaver. Photos from NASA. 233-265, Feb. 1972

Author

What Is It Like to Walk on the Moon? 326-331, Sept. 1973

SCOTT, DOUGLAS: Photographer:

High Adventure in the Himalayas. By Thomas Weir. 193-234, Aug. 1952

SCOTT, ROBERT F.:

All-out Assault on Antarctica. By Richard E. Byrd. 141-180, Aug. 1956

The British Way. By Sir Evelyn Wrench. 421-541, Apr. 1949

Our Navy Explores Antarctica. By Richard E. Byrd. U. S. Navy official photos. 429-522, Oct. 1947

SCOTT, SIR WALTER:

The British Way. By Sir Evelyn Wrench. 421-541, Apr. 1949

Poets' Voices Linger in Scottish Shrines. By Isobel Wylie Hutchison. Photos by Kathleen Revis. 437-488, Oct. 1957

A Stroll to London. By Isobel Wylie Hutchison. Photos by B. Anthony Stewart. 171-204, Aug. 1950

SCOTT EXPEDITION:

The British Way. By Sir Evelyn Wrench. 421-541, Apr. 1949
A Very Gallant Gentleman — Lawrence Edward Grace Oates (1880-1912)

See also Scott, Robert F.

SCOTTISH TRANS-GREENLAND EXPEDITION:

First Woman Across Greenland's Ice. By Myrtle Simpson. Photos by Hugh Simpson. 264-279, Aug. 1967

SCOUGALL, IRENE. *See* Burdett-Scougall, Irene

SCOUTS AND SCOUTING. *See* Boy Scouts

SCRIPPS INSTITUTION OF OCEANOGRAPHY:

Expeditions. *See* Deep Sea Drilling Project

La Jolla, a Gem of the California Coast. By Deena Clark. Photos by J. Baylor Roberts. 755-782, Dec. 1952

SCROLLS. *See* Dead Sea Scrolls

SCULPTURE:

Ancient Aphrodisias and Its Marble Treasures. By Kenan T. Erim. Photos by Jonathan S. Blair. 280-294, Aug. 1967

Aphrodisias, Awakened City of Ancient Art. By Kenan T. Erim. Photos by Jonathan S. Blair. 766-791, June 1972

The British Way. By Sir Evelyn Wrench. 421-541, Apr. 1949
Included: Landseer Lions

The Caves of the Thousand Buddhas (Tunhwang, China). By Franc and Jean Shor. 383-415, Mar. 1951

China Unveils Her Newest Treasures. Photos by Robert W. Madden. 848-857, Dec. 1974

Darius Carved History on Ageless Rock. By George G. Cameron. 825-844, Dec. 1950

India's Sculptured Temple Caves. By Volkmar Wentzel. 665-678, May 1953

Lascaux Cave, Cradle of World Art (France). By Norbert Casteret. Photos by Maynard Owen Williams. 771-794, Dec. 1948
Included: Clay statues of the Old Stone Age

The Louvre, France's Palace of the Arts. By Hereward Lester Cooke, Jr. 796-831, June 1971

The Maya. 729-811, Dec. 1975
I. Children of Time. By Howard La Fay. Photos by David Alan Harvey. 729-767

SCULPTURE — *Continued*

    II. Riddle of the Glyphs. By George E. Stuart. Photos by Otis Imboden. 768-791

    III. Resurrecting the Grandeur of Tikal. By William R. Coe. 792-798

    Petra, Rose-red Citadel of Biblical Edom. By David S. Boyer. 853-870, Dec. 1955

    Searching Out Medieval Churches in Ethiopia's Wilds. By Georg Gerster. 856-884, Dec. 1970

    See also Afo-A-Kom; Akhenaten Temple Project; Dreyfus Collection (Renaissance Bronzes); War Memorials; *and* Abu Simbel; Athens; Florence; Rome; Tuscany; Washington, D. C.; *and* Goldsmithing; Wood Carving

SCULPTURE, Gravel. *See* Gravel Pictographs

SCULPTURE, Ice:

    Snow Festival in Japan's Far North. By Eiji Miyazawa. 824-833, Dec. 1968

SEA AND SPACE RESEARCH PROJECT. *See* Tektite II

SEA ANEMONES:

    Camera Under the Sea. By Luis Marden. 162-200, Feb. 1956

    Oregon's Sidewalk on the Sea. By Paul A. Zahl. 708-734, Nov. 1961

SEA BIRDS:

    Peru Profits from Sea Fowl. By Robert Cushman Murphy. Photos by author and Grace E. Barstow Murphy. 395-413, Mar. 1959

    Sea Bird Cities Off Audubon's Labrador. By Arthur A. Allen. 755-774, June 1948

    Sea Birds of Isla Raza. By Lewis Wayne Walker. 239-248, Feb. 1951

    See also Albatrosses; Brown Pelican; Puffins; Terns

SEA-CORE DATING:

    What's Happening to Our Climate? By Samuel W. Matthews. 576-615, Nov. 1976

SEA COWS. *See* Manatees

SEA *DIVER* (Research Vessel):

    The Deepest Days. By Robert Sténuit. 534-547, Apr. 1965

    The Long, Deep Dive. By Lord Kilbracken. Photos by Bates Littlehales. 718-731, May 1963

    Our Man-in-Sea Project. By Edwin A. Link. 713-717, May 1963

    Outpost Under the Ocean. By Edwin A. Link. Photos by Bates Littlehales. 530-533, Apr. 1965

    A Taxi for the Deep Frontier. By Kenneth MacLeish. Photos by Bates Littlehales. 139-150, Jan. 1968

    Tomorrow on the Deep Frontier. By Edwin A. Link. 778-801, June 1964

SEA DYAKS (Tribespeople). *See* Iban

SEA ELEPHANTS:

    Off Santa Barbara: California's Ranches in the Sea. By Earl Warren, Jr. Photos by Bates Littlehales. 257-283, Aug. 1958

SEA Fever. By John E. Schultz. 237-268, Feb. 1949

SEA GYPSIES of the Philippines. By Anne de Henning Singh. Photos by Raghubir Singh. 659-677, May 1976

SEA HORSES:

    Little Horses of the Sea. By Paul A. Zahl. 131-153, Jan. 1959

SEA ISLANDS: Adventuring Along the South's Surprising Coast. By James Cerruti. Photos by Thomas Nebbia and James L. Amos. 366-393, Mar. 1971

    Included: Blackbeard, Cumberland, Jekyll, Ossabaw, St. Catherines, St. Simons, Sapelo, Sea Island, Wassaw, in Georgia; Daufuskie, Hilton Head, Johns, Port Royal Sound, in South Carolina

SEA LAMPREYS:

    New Era on the Great Lakes. By Nathaniel T. Kenney. 439-490, Apr. 1959

SEA LIONS:

    The Galapagos, Eerie Cradle of New Species. By Roger Tory Peterson. Photos by Alan and Joan Root. 541-585, Apr. 1967

    Lost World of the Galapagos. By Irving and Electa Johnson. 681-703, May 1959

    Where Two Worlds Meet (Patagonia). Photos by Des and Jen Bartlett. 298-321, Mar. 1976

SEA Nymphs of Japan. By Luis Marden. 122-135, July 1971

SEA OTTERS:

    Return of the Sea Otter. By Karl W. Kenyon. Photos by James A. Mattison, Jr. 520-539, Oct. 1971

SEA *ROBIN* (Submarine):

    'Round the Horn by Submarine. By Paul C. Stimson. 129-144, Jan. 1948

SEA SHELLS. *See* Shells

SEA SLUGS. *See* Nudibranchs

SEA SNAKES:

    Diving With Sea Snakes. By Kenneth MacLeish. Photos by Ben Cropp. 565-578, Apr. 1972

SEA to Lakes on the St. Lawrence. By George W. Long. Photos by B. Anthony Stewart and John E. Fletcher. 323-366, Sept. 1950

SEA URCHINS:

    Giant Kelp, Sequoias of the Sea. By Wheeler J. North. Photos by Bates Littlehales. 251-269, Aug. 1972

    Included: Destruction of kelp by sea urchins

SEAFOOD INDUSTRY:

    Cajunland, Louisiana's French-speaking Coast. By Bern Keating. Photos by Charles Harbutt and Franke Keating. 353-391, Mar. 1966

    Chesapeake Country. By Nathaniel T. Kenney. Photos by Bates Littlehales. 370-411, Sept. 1964

    "Delmarva," Gift of the Sea. By Catherine Bell Palmer. 367-399, Sept. 1950

    The Sailing Oystermen of Chesapeake Bay. By Luis Marden. 798-819, Dec. 1967

    See also Crabs; Lobsters; Shrimp Fishing

SEAGO, EDWARD: Artist:

    Off the Beaten Track of Empire (Prince Philip's Tour). By Beverley M. Bowie. Photos by Michael Parker. 584-626, Nov. 1957

SEALING:

    Cliff Dwellers of the Bering Sea. By Juan Muñoz. 129-146, Jan. 1954

SEALING — *Continued*

Life or Death for the Harp Seal. By David M. Lavigne. Photos by William R. Curtsinger. 129-142, Jan. 1976

Seal Hunting Off Jan Mayen. By Ole Friele Backer. 57-72, Jan. 1948

SEALS:

The Fur Seal Herd Comes of Age. By Victor B. Scheffer and Karl W. Kenyon. 491-512, Apr. 1952

A Naturalist in Penguin Land. By Niall Rankin. 93-116, Jan. 1955
    Included: Atlantic, crabeater, elephant, leopard, and Weddell seals

Nature's Clown, the Penguin. By David Hellyer and Malcolm Davis. 405-428, Sept. 1952
    Included: Elephant seal, fur seal, and sea leopard

Our Friend From the Sea. By Robert and Nina Horstman. Photos by Robert F. Sisson. 728-736, Nov. 1968

The Romance of American Furs. By Wanda Burnett. 379-402, Mar. 1948

Seal Hunting Off Jan Mayen. By Ole Friele Backer. 57-72, Jan. 1948
    Contents: Harp (Greenland) seal, hooded seal ("Blueback")

Stalking Seals Under Antarctic Ice. By Carleton Ray. 54-65, Jan. 1966

See also Harp Seals; Sea Elephants; Sea Lions

SEAMANS, ROBERT C., Jr.:

Board of Trustees, member. 860, June 1970; 289, Mar. 1976

The **SEARCH** for Life on Mars. By Kenneth F. Weaver. 264-265, Feb. 1973

SEARCH for the Oldest People. By Alexander Leaf. Photos by John Launois. 93-119, Jan. 1973

SEARCH for the Scarlet Ibis in Venezuela. By Paul A. Zahl. 633-661, May 1950

The **SEARCH** for Tomorrow's Power. By Kenneth F. Weaver. Photos by Emory Kristof. 650-681, Nov. 1972

SEARCHING for Cliff Dwellers' Secrets. By Carroll A. Burroughs. 619-625, Nov. 1959

SEARCHING Out Medieval Churches in Ethiopia's Wilds. By Georg Gerster. 856-884, Dec. 1970

SEASHORE:

The Living Sand. By William H. Amos. 820-833, June 1965

Oregon's Sidewalk on the Sea. By Paul A. Zahl. 708-734, Nov. 1961

Our Changing Atlantic Coastline (U. S.). By Nathaniel T. Kenney. Photos by B. Anthony Stewart. 860-887, Dec. 1962

Seashore Summer. By Arline Strong. 436-444, Sept. 1960

See also Cape Cod; Outer Banks

SEATTLE, Washington:

Making Friends With a Killer Whale. By Edward I. Griffin. 418-446, Mar. 1966

Seattle, City of Two Voices. By Anne Grosvenor Robinson. Photos by B. Anthony Stewart. 494-513, Apr. 1960

Seattle Fair Looks to the 21st Century. By Carolyn

SEATTLE, Washington — *Continued*

Bennett Patterson. Photos by Thomas Nebbia. 402-427, Sept. 1962

SEAWEED:

Algae: the Life-givers. By Paul A. Zahl. 361-377, Mar. 1974

See also Giant Kelp; Sargassum

SECRET of the Discus Fish. By Gene Wolfsheimer. 675-681, May 1960

The **SECRETS** of Nature's Night Lights. By Paul A. Zahl. 45-69, July 1971

SEED INDUSTRY. *See* Floriculture (Flower Seed Growers)

SEEING Birds as Real Personalities. By Hance Roy Ivor. 523-530, Apr. 1954

SEEING-EYE DOGS:

Dogs Work for Man. By Edward J. Linehan. Paintings by Edward Megargee and R. E. Lougheed. 190-233, Aug. 1958

SEEING the Earth from 80 Miles Up. By Clyde T. Holliday. 511-528, Oct. 1950

SEEKING Mindanao's Strangest Creatures. By Charles Heizer Wharton. 389-408, Sept. 1948

SEEKING the Secret of the Giants. By Frank M. Setzler. Photos by Richard H. Stewart. 390-404, Sept. 1952

SEEKING the Truth About the Feared Piranha. By Paul A. Zahl. 715-733, Nov. 1970

SEIDLER, NED: Artist:

A Continent's Living Treasure. 164-167, Feb. 1972

India's Wildlife Vanishes As Man Alters the Land. 307-309, Sept. 1976

The Lost Empire of the Incas. By Loren McIntyre. Art by Ned and Rosalie Seidler. 729-787, Dec. 1973

Seven Giants Who Led the Way. Text by Rick Gore. 401-407, Sept. 1976

SEIDLER, ROSALIE: Artist:

The Lost Empire of the Incas. By Loren McIntyre. Art by Ned and Rosalie Seidler. 729-787, Dec. 1973

SEINE FISHING:

Golden Beaches of Portugal. By Alan Villiers. 673-696, Nov. 1954

Menhaden — Uncle Sam's Top Commercial Fish. By Leonard C. Roy. Photos by Robert F. Sisson. 813-823, June 1949

Scenes of Postwar Finland. By La Verne Bradley. Photos by Jerry Waller. 233-264, Aug. 1947

SEISMIC SEA WAVES. *See* Tsunamis

SEISMOLOGY:

First Explorers on the Moon: The Incredible Story of Apollo 11. 735-797, Dec. 1969

Have We Solved the Mysteries of the Moon? By Kenneth F. Weaver. Paintings by William H. Bond. 309-325, Sept. 1973

See also Earthquakes

SEMINOLES (Indians):

Florida's Emerging Seminoles. By Louis Capron. Photos by Otis Imboden. 716-734, Nov. 1969

SEMINOLES (Indians)—*Continued*

Florida's "Wild" Indians, the Seminole. By Louis Capron. Photos by Willard R. Culver. 819-840, Dec. 1956

Haunting Heart of the Everglades. By Andrew H. Brown. Photos by author and Willard R. Culver. 145-173, Feb. 1948

SENEGAL:

Freedom Speaks French in Ouagadougou. By John Scofield. 153-203, Aug. 1966

SENGSENG (People):

Blowgun Hunters of the South Pacific. By Jane C. Goodale. Photos by Ann Chowning. 793-817, June 1966

SENNETT, TOMAS: Photographer:

North for Oil: *Manhattan* Makes the Historic Northwest Passage. By Bern Keating. 374-391, Mar. 1970

SENTINEL RANGE, Antarctica:

First Conquest of Antarctica's Highest Peaks. By Nicholas B. Clinch. 836-863, June 1967

SENTINELESE (Negrito Tribe):

The Last Andaman Islanders. By Raghubir Singh. 66-91, July 1975

SEOUL, South Korea:

Roaming Korea South of the Iron Curtain. By Enzo de Chetelat. 777-808, June 1950

South Korea: Success Story in Asia. By Howard Sochurek. 301-345, Mar. 1969

South Korea: What Next? By Peter T. White. Photos by H. Edward Kim. 394-427, Sept. 1975

With the U. S. Army in Korea. By John R. Hodge. 829-840, June 1947

SEPIK RIVER, and Region, New Guinea:

Change Ripples New Guinea's Sepik River. By Malcolm S. Kirk. 354-381, Sept. 1973

To the Land of the Head-hunters. By E. Thomas Gilliard. 437-486, Oct. 1955

SEQUOIA GIGANTEA:

The General Sherman: Earth's Biggest Living Thing. 605-608, May 1958

SEQUOIA NATIONAL PARK, California:

Giant Sequoias Draw Millions to California Parks. By John Michael Kauffmann. Photos by B. Anthony Stewart. 147-187, Aug. 1959

Saving Earth's Oldest Living Things. By Andrew H. Brown. Photos by Raymond Moulin and author. 679-695, May 1951

SEQUOIA SEMPERVIRENS. See Redwoods

SEQUOIAS of the Sea: Giant Kelp. By Wheeler J. North. Photos by Bates Littlehales. 251-269, Aug. 1972

SERBIA (Republic), Yugoslavia:

Yugoslavia: Six Republics in One. By Robert Paul Jordan. Photos by James P. Blair. 589-633, May 1970

SERENGETI NATIONAL PARK, Tanzania:

African Wildlife: Man's Threatened Legacy. By Allan C. Fisher, Jr. Photos by Thomas Nebbia. Paintings by Ned Seidler. 147-187, Feb. 1972

Hyenas, the Hunters Nobody Knows. By Hans

SERENGETI NATIONAL PARK, Tanzania—*Continued*

Kruuk. Photos by Baron Hugo van Lawick. 44-57, July 1968

Life With the King of Beasts. By George B. Schaller. 494-519, Apr. 1969

Man of the Serengeti (Television film). 179A-179B, Feb. 1972

Tool-using Bird: The Egyptian Vulture. By Baroness Jane van Lawick-Goodall. Photos by Baron Hugo van Lawick. 631-641, May 1968

SERTÃO (Brazilian Backland):

Drought Bedevils Brazil's Sertão. By John Wilson. Photos by Gordon W. Gahan. 704-723, Nov. 1972

SETO NAIKAI. *See* Inland Sea, Japan

SETTON, KENNETH M.: Author:

A New Look at Medieval Europe. Paintings by Andre Durenceau and Birney Lettick. 799-859, Dec. 1962

900 Years Ago: the Norman Conquest. Photos by George F. Mobley. 206-251, Aug. 1966

SETÚBAL CANYON, Atlantic Ocean:

Four Years of Diving to the Bottom of the Sea. By Georges S. Houot. 715-731, May 1958

SETZLER, FRANK M.: Author:

Seeking the Secret of the Giants (Gravel Figures). Photos by Richard H. Stewart. 390-404, Sept. 1952

SEVEN Giants Who Led the Way. Paintings by Ned Seidler. Text by Rick Gore. 401-407, Sept. 1976

SEVEN Men Who Solved Riddles of the Cosmos. Paintings by Jean-Leon Huens. Text by Thomas Y. Canby. 627-633, May 1974

SEVENTH FLEET, U. S.:

Our Navy in the Far East. By Arthur W. Radford. Photos by J. Baylor Roberts. 537-577, Oct. 1953

Pacific Fleet: Force for Peace. By Franc Shor. Photos by W. E. Garrett. 283-335, Sept. 1959

Patrolling Troubled Formosa Strait. 573-588, Apr. 1955

75 YEARS Exploring Earth, Sea, and Sky: National Geographic Society Observes Its Diamond Anniversary. By Melvin M. Payne. 1-43, Jan. 1963

SEVERY, MERLE: Author:

Northwest Wonderland: Washington State. Photos by B. Anthony Stewart. 445-493, Apr. 1960

SEVILLA, Spain:

Andalusia, the Spirit of Spain. By Howard La Fay. Photos by Joseph J. Scherschel. 833-857, June 1975

Holy Week and the Fair in Sevilla. By Luis Marden. 499-530, Apr. 1951

SEYCHELLES, Tropic Isles of Eden. By Quentin Keynes. 670-695, Nov. 1959

'S GRAVENHAGE (The Hague), Netherlands:

Mid-century Holland Builds Her Future. By Sydney Clark. 747-778, Dec. 1950

The Netherlands: Nation at War With the Sea. By Alan Villiers. Photos by Adam Woolfitt. 530-571, Apr. 1968

SHA'AB RŪMI (Reef), Red Sea:
At Home in the Sea. By Jacques-Yves Cousteau. 465-507, Apr. 1964

SHACKLETON, SIR ERNEST H.:
Our Navy Explores Antarctica. By Richard E. Byrd. U. S. Navy official photos. 429-522, Oct. 1947

SHAD in the Shadow of Skyscrapers. By Dudley B. Martin. Photos by Luis Marden. 359-376, Mar. 1947

SHADBOLT, MAURICE: Author:
In Storied Lands of Malaysia. Photos by Winfield Parks. 734-783, Nov. 1963
New Zealand: Gift of the Sea. Photos by Brian Brake. 465-511, Apr. 1962
New Zealand's Cook Islands: Paradise in Search of a Future. Photos by William Albert Allard. 203-231, Aug. 1967
Western Samoa, the Pacific's Newest Nation. Photos by Robert B. Goodman. 573-602, Oct. 1962

The SHADOWY World of Salamanders. By Paul A. Zahl. 104-117, July 1972

SHAKERS (Religious Sect):
Home to the Enduring Berkshires. By Charles McCarry. Photos by Jonathan S. Blair. 196-221, Aug. 1970

SHAKESPEARE, WILLIAM:
The Britain That Shakespeare Knew. By Louis B. Wright. Photos by Dean Conger. 613-665, May 1964
The British Way. By Sir Evelyn Wrench. 421-541, Apr. 1949
Founders of Virginia. By Sir Evelyn Wrench. Photos by B. Anthony Stewart. 433-462, Apr. 1948
Included: Stratford on Avon and *The Tempest*
Shakespeare's Britain, map supplement. May 1964
A Stroll to London. By Isobel Wylie Hutchison. Photos by B. Anthony Stewart. 171-204, Aug. 1950
The World of Elizabeth I. By Louis B. Wright. 668-709, Nov. 1968
See also Folger (Library); Henry E. Huntington Library and Art Gallery

SHALLENBERGER, ROBERT J.: Photographer:
Something's Fishy About That Fin! Photos by Robert J. Shallenberger and William D. Madden. 224-227, Aug. 1974

SHAN STATE, Burma. *See* Inle (Lake)

SHANGHAI, China:
Along the Yangtze, Main Street of China. By W. Robert Moore. 325-356, Mar. 1948
Eyes on the China Coast. By George W. Long. 505-512, Apr. 1953
This Is the China I Saw. By Jørgen Bisch. 591-639, Nov. 1964

SHARING the Lives of Wild Golden Eagles. By John Craighead. Photos by Charles and Derek Craighead. 420-439, Sept. 1967

SHARKS:
Calypso Explores for Underwater Oil. By Jacques-Yves Cousteau. 155-184, Aug. 1955
Included: Aqualung divers' war on sharks in the Indian Ocean

SHARKS — *Continued*
Fish Men Explore a New World Undersea. By Jacques-Yves Cousteau. 431-472, Oct. 1952
Into the Lairs of "Sleeping" Sharks. By Eugenie Clark. Photos by David Doubilet. 570-584, Apr. 1975
Marineland, Florida's Giant Fish Bowl. By Gilbert Grosvenor La Gorce. Photos by Luis Marden. 679-694, Nov. 1952
The Red Sea's Sharkproof Fish. By Eugenie Clark. Photos by David Doubilet. 718-727, Nov. 1974
Sharks: Wolves of the Sea. By Nathaniel T. Kenney. 222-257, Feb. 1968

SHAWNEETOWN Forsakes the Ohio. By William H. Nicholas. Photos by J. Baylor Roberts. 273-288, Feb. 1948

SHEATS, DOROTHEA: Author-Photographer:
I Walked Some Irish Miles. 653-678, May 1951
See also Jones, Dorothea

SHEEP AND SHEEP RAISING:
America's "Meat on the Hoof." By William H. Nicholas. 33-72, Jan. 1952
Better Days for the Navajos. By Jack Breed. Photos by Charles W. Herbert. 809-847, Dec. 1958
Housewife at the End of the World. By Rae Natalie P. Goodall. Photos by James L. Stanfield. 130-150, Jan. 1971
Land of the Ancient Basques. By Robert Laxalt. Photos by William Albert Allard. 240-277, Aug. 1968
Lonely Sentinels of the American West: Basque Sheepherders. By Robert Laxalt. Photos by William Belknap, Jr. 870-888, June 1966
The Navajos. By Ralph Looney. Photos by Bruce Dale. 740-781, Dec. 1972
New South Wales, the State That Cradled Australia. By Howell Walker. Photos by David Moore. 591-635, Nov. 1967
New Zealand: Gift of the Sea. By Maurice Shadbolt. Photos by Brian Brake. 465-511, Apr. 1962
New Zealand's Bountiful South Island. By Peter Benchley. Photos by James L. Amos. 93-123, Jan. 1972
New Zealand's North Island: The Contented Land. By Charles McCarry. Photos by Bates Littlehales. 190-213, Aug. 1974
People and Penguins of the Faraway Falklands. By Olin Sewall Pettingill, Jr. 387-416, Mar. 1956
Scotland's Inner Hebrides: Isles of the Western Sea. By Kenneth MacLeish. Photos by R. Stephen Uzzell III. 690-717, Nov. 1974
Sheep Airlift in New Guinea. Photos by Ned Blood. 831-844, Dec. 1949
Winter Caravan to the Roof of the World. By Sabrina and Roland Michaud. 435-465, Apr. 1972
Yugoslavia: Six Republics in One. By Robert Paul Jordan. Photos by James P. Blair. 589-633, May 1970
See also Bighorn Sheep

SHEEP TREK:
Arizona Sheep Trek. By Francis R. Line. 457-478, Apr. 1950
Sheep Trek in the French Alps. By Maurice Moyal. Photos by Marcel Coen. 545-564, Apr. 1952

SHELLFISH. *See* Crustaceans; Mollusks

SHELLS (Mollusks):

Little Horses of the Sea. By Paul A. Zahl. 131-153, Jan. 1959
> Note: Sanibel Island, Florida, is one of the most famous shelling centers in the world.

The Magic Lure of Sea Shells. By Paul A. Zahl. Photos by Victor R. Boswell, Jr. and author. 386-429, Mar. 1969
> Contents: More than 100 kinds of shells

On Australia's Coral Ramparts. By Paul A. Zahl. 1-48, Jan. 1957

Shells Take You Over World Horizons. By Rutherford Platt. 33-84, July 1949
> Contents: *Conus, Helicostyla, Liguus, Murex, Patella, Pecten, Pelecypoda, Tellina, Terebra, Thais, Tridacna, Trochus, Voluta*

X-Rays Reveal the Inner Beauty of Shells. By Hilary B. Moore. 427-434, Mar. 1955

See also Abalone; Mother-of-Pearl; Nautilus, Chambered

SHENANDOAH NATIONAL PARK, Virginia:

Skyline Trail from Maine to Georgia. By Andrew H. Brown. Photos by Robert F. Sisson. 219-251, Aug. 1949

SHENANDOAH VALLEY, Virginia-West Virginia:

Appalachian Valley Pilgrimage. By Catherine Bell Palmer. Photos by Justin Locke. 1-32, July 1949

Shenandoah, I Long to Hear You. By Mike W. Edwards. Photos by Thomas Anthony DeFeo. 554-588, Apr. 1970

SHENYANG (Mukden), Manchuria:

In Manchuria Now. By W. Robert Moore. 389-414, Mar. 1947

SHEPARD, ALAN B., Jr.:

The Flight of *Freedom 7.* By Carmault B. Jackson, Jr. 416-431, Sept. 1961
> Author

The Pilot's Story. Photos by Dean Conger. 432-444, Sept. 1961
> Photographer

The Climb Up Cone Crater. By Alice J. Hall. Photos by Edgar D. Mitchell and Alan B. Shepard, Jr. 136-148, July 1971

SHERPAS:

Sherpaland, My Shangri-La. By Desmond Doig. 545-577, Oct. 1966

We Build a School for Sherpa Children. By Sir Edmund Hillary. 548-551, Oct. 1962

See also American Mount Everest Expedition; British Mount Everest Expedition

SHERWOOD GARDENS, Baltimore, Maryland:

Maytime Miracle in Sherwood Gardens. By Nathaniel T. Kenney. 700-709, May 1956

SHETLAND ISLANDS, Scotland:

Shetland and Orkney, Britain's Far North. By Isobel Wylie Hutchison. 519-536, Oct. 1953

Viking Festival in the Shetlands. Photos by Karl W. Gullers. 853-862, Dec. 1954

SHINTOISM:

Cruising Japan's Inland Sea. By Willard Price. 619-650, Nov. 1953

SHINTOISM—*Continued*

Kayak Odyssey: From the Inland Sea to Tokyo. By Dan Dimancescu. Photos by Christopher G. Knight. 295-337, Sept. 1967

See also Kansai; Kyoto

SHIPBUILDING:

Ships Through the Ages: A Saga of the Sea. By Alan Villiers. 494-545, Apr. 1963

See also Kyrenia Ship; *Mayflower II;* Vikings

SHIPLIFT:

Passage to Freedom in Viet Nam. By Gertrude Samuels. 858-874, June 1955

SHIPPING:

The Coming Revolution in Transportation. By Fredric C. Appel. Photos by Dean Conger. 301-341, Sept. 1969
> Included: Containerized cargo, Hovercraft, hydrofoils, supertankers

Here's New York Harbor. By Stuart E. Jones. Photos by Robert F. Sisson and David S. Boyer. 773-813, Dec. 1954

Louisiana Trades with the World. By Frederick Simpich. Photos by J. Baylor Roberts. 705-738, Dec. 1947

New Era on the Great Lakes. By Nathaniel T. Kenney. 439-490, Apr. 1959

New Orleans: Jambalaya on the Levee. By Harnett T. Kane. Photos by Justin Locke. 143-184, Feb. 1953

Norway, Land of the Generous Sea. By Edward J. Linehan. Photos by George F. Mobley. 1-43, July 1971

Portsmouth, Britannia's Sally Port. By Thomas Garner James. Photos by B. Anthony Stewart. 513-544, Apr. 1952

Work-hard, Play-hard Michigan. By Andrew H. Brown. 279-320, Mar. 1952

See also Tankers; U. S. Merchant Marine Academy; *and* Panama Canal; St. Lawrence Seaway; Suez Canal

SHIPS:

The Marvelous Maldive Islands. By Alan Villiers. 829-849, June 1957
> Included: Indian and Maldivian *baggalas*

Men, Ships, and the Sea. Book announced. 552-555, Oct. 1962

Milestones in My Arctic Journeys. By Willie Knutsen. 543-570, Oct. 1949
> Included: *Effie M. Morrissey, Endurance, Northland, Polarbjörn, Quest, Ringsel (En Avant)*

Ships Through the Ages: A Saga of the Sea. By Alan Villiers. 494-545, Apr. 1963

The Yankee Sailor Who Opened Japan. By Ferdinand Kuhn. 85-102, July 1953

See also Dhows; Galleons; Junks; Longships; Mohole, Project; Research Vessels; Sailing Vessels; Shipping; Shipwrecks; Submarines; Tall-Ships Race; U. S. Coast Guard; U. S. Navy; listing under Yachts; *and Af Chapman; Amphitrite; Beagle,* H.M.S.; *Bounty; Endeavour; J. W. Westcott; Mayflower II; Ra II; Savannah,* N.S.

SHIPWORMS, Saboteurs of the Sea. By F. G. Walton Smith. 559-566, Oct. 1956

SHIPWRECKS:

Ancient Shipwreck Yields New Facts—and a

SHIPWRECKS — *Continued*

Strange Cargo. By Peter Throckmorton. Photos by Kim Hart and Joseph J. Scherschel. 282-300, Feb. 1969

Atocha, Tragic Treasure Galleon of the Florida Keys. By Eugene Lyon. 787-809, June 1976
Included: *Santa Margarita* wreck

Bermuda — Balmy, British, and Beautiful. By Peter Benchley. Photos by Emory Kristof. 93-121, July 1971

Drowned Galleons Yield Spanish Gold. By Kip Wagner. Photos by Otis Imboden. 1-37, Jan. 1965

England's Scillies, the Flowering Isles. By Alan Villiers. Photos by Bates Littlehales. 126-145, July 1967

Fish Men Discover a 2,200-year-old Greek Ship. By Jacques-Yves Cousteau. 1-36, Jan. 1954

Life Springs From Death in Truk Lagoon. By Sylvia A. Earle. Photos by Al Giddings. 578-613, May 1976

Lonely Cape Hatteras, Besieged by the Sea. By William S. Ellis. Photos by Emory Kristof. 393-421, Sept. 1969
Included: Map, Ghost Fleet of the Outer Banks

The Lower Keys, Florida's "Out Islands." By John Scofield. Photos by Emory Kristof and Bates Littlehales. 72-93, Jan. 1971

New Tools for Undersea Archeology. By George F. Bass. Photos by Charles R. Nicklin, Jr. 403-423, Sept. 1968

Oldest Known Shipwreck Yields Bronze Age Cargo. By Peter Throckmorton. 697-711, May 1962

Priceless Relics of the Spanish Armada. By Robert Sténuit. Photos by Bates Littlehales. 745-777, June 1969

Safe Landing on Sable, Isle of 500 Shipwrecks. By Melville Bell Grosvenor. 398-431, Sept. 1965

That Dammed Missouri River. By Gordon Young. Photos by David Hiser. 374-413, Sept. 1971

Thirty-three Centuries Under the Sea. By Peter Throckmorton. 682-703, May 1960

Treasure! (Television film). 575, Nov. 1976; cover, Dec. 1976

Underwater Archeology: Key to History's Warehouse. By George F. Bass. Photos by Thomas J. Abercrombie and Robert B. Goodman. 138-156, July 1963

White Mist Cruises to Wreck-haunted St. Pierre and Miquelon. By Melville Bell Grosvenor. 378-419, Sept. 1967

See also Kyrenia Ship; *Monitor; Slot ter Hooge; Thresher; Vasa*

SHIRALA, Maharashtra (State), India:

The Cobra, India's "Good Snake." By Harry Miller. Photos by author and Naresh and Rajesh Bedi. 393-409, Sept. 1970

SHOEMAKER, EUGENE M.: Author:

The Moon Close Up. Photos by Ranger 7. 690-707, Nov. 1964

SHOOTING Rapids in Dinosaur Country. By Jack Breed. Photos by author and Justin Locke. 363-390, Mar. 1954

SHOOTING Rapids in Reverse! By William Belknap, Jr. 552-565, Apr. 1962

SHOR, DONNA HAMILTON: Author:

San Marino, Little Land of Liberty. Photos by Ted H. Funk. 233-251, Aug. 1967

SHOR, FRANC:

Editor, Associate. 583, Oct. 1967; 299, Mar. 1968; 309, Sept. 1968

Editor, Senior Assistant. 864, Dec. 1959; 193, Aug. 1960; 890, Dec. 1962; 857, Dec. 1963

Executive Editorial Council meeting. 586-587, Oct. 1967

Author

Boom on San Francisco Bay. Photos by David S. Boyer. 181-226, Aug. 1956

The City They Call Red China's Showcase. Photos by Brian Brake. 193-223, Aug. 1960

Crusader Road to Jerusalem. Photos by Thomas Nebbia. 797-855, Dec. 1963
I. Desert Ordeal of the Knights. 797-837
II. Conquest of the Holy City. 839-855

Cyprus, Geography's Stepchild. 873-884, June 1956

In the Crusaders' Footsteps. Photos by Thomas Nebbia and James P. Blair. 731-789, June 1962

Iran's Shah Crowns Himself and His Empress. Photos by James L. Stanfield and Winfield Parks. 301-321, Mar. 1968

Japan, the Exquisite Enigma. Photos by John Launois. 733-777, Dec. 1960

Life under Shellfire on Quemoy. Photos by Wilbur E. Garrett. 415-438, Mar. 1959

Lombardy's Lakes, Blue Jewels in Italy's Crown. Photos by Joseph J. Scherschel. 58-99, July 1968

Pacific Fleet: Force for Peace. Photos by W. E. Garrett. 283-335, Sept. 1959

Paris Flea Market. Photos by Alexander Taylor. 318-326, Mar. 1957

Author-Photographer

Argentina: Young Giant of the Far South. By Jean and Franc Shor. 297-352, Mar. 1958

At World's End in Hunza. By Jean and Franc Shor. 485-518, Oct. 1953

Athens to Istanbul. By Jean and Franc Shor. 37-76, Jan. 1956

The Balearics Are Booming. By Jean and Franc Shor. 621-660, May 1957

The Caves of the Thousand Buddhas. By Franc and Jean Shor. 383-415, Mar. 1951

Coal Makes the Saar a Prize. 561-576, Apr. 1954

Cyprus, Idyllic Island in a Troubled Sea. By Jean and Franc Shor. 627-664, May 1952

East Pakistan Drives Back the Jungle. By Jean and Franc Shor. 399-426, Mar. 1955

From Sea to Sahara in French Morocco. By Jean and Franc Shor. 147-188, Feb. 1955

Iraq — Where Oil and Water Mix. By Jean and Franc Shor. 443-489, Oct. 1958

North with Finland's Lapps. By Jean and Franc Shor. 249-280, Aug. 1954

On the Winds of the Dodecanese. By Jean and Franc Shor. 351-390, Mar. 1953

Pakistan, New Nation in an Old Land. By Jean and Franc Shor. 637-678, Nov. 1952

Robert College, Turkish Gateway to the Future. 399-418, Sept. 1957

Spain's "Fortunate Isles," the Canaries. By Jean and Franc Shor. 485-522, Apr. 1955

Surprising Switzerland. By Jean and Franc Shor. 427-478, Oct. 1956

Switzerland's Once-in-a-generation Festival (Vevey). By Jean and Franc Shor. 563-571, Oct. 1958

SHOR, FRANC: Author-Photographer—*Continued*

We Dwelt in Kashgai Tents (Iran). By Jean and Franc Shor. 805-832, June 1952

We Took the Highroad in Afghanistan. By Jean and Franc Shor. 673-706, Nov. 1950

Photographer

The Camargue, Land of Cowboys and Gypsies. By Eugene L. Kammerman. 667-699, May 1956

SHOR, JEAN: Author-Photographer:

Argentina: Young Giant of the Far South. By Jean and Franc Shor. 297-352, Mar. 1958

At World's End in Hunza. By Jean and Franc Shor. 485-518, Oct. 1953

Athens to Istanbul. By Jean and Franc Shor. 37-76, Jan. 1956

The Balearics Are Booming. By Jean and Franc Shor. 621-660, May 1957

The Caves of the Thousand Buddhas. By Franc and Jean Shor. 383-415, Mar. 1951

Cyprus, Idyllic Island in a Troubled Sea. By Jean and Franc Shor. 627-664, May 1952

East Pakistan Drives Back the Jungle. By Jean and Franc Shor. 399-426, Mar. 1955

From Sea to Sahara in French Morocco. By Jean and Franc Shor. 147-188, Feb. 1955

Iraq—Where Oil and Water Mix. By Jean and Franc Shor. 443-489, Oct. 1958

North with Finland's Lapps. By Jean and Franc Shor. 249-280, Aug. 1954

On the Winds of the Dodecanese. By Jean and Franc Shor. 351-390, Mar. 1953

Pakistan, New Nation in an Old Land. By Jean and Franc Shor. 637-678, Nov. 1952

Spain's "Fortunate Isles," the Canaries. By Jean and Franc Shor. 485-522, Apr. 1955

Surprising Switzerland. By Jean and Franc Shor. 427-478, Oct. 1956

Switzerland's Once-in-a-generation Festival (Vevey). By Jean and Franc Shor. 563-571, Oct. 1958

We Dwelt in Kashgai Tents (Iran). By Jean and Franc Shor. 805-832, June 1952

We Took the Highroad in Afghanistan. By Jean and Franc Shor. 673-706, Nov. 1950

Photographer

The Camargue, Land of Cowboys and Gypsies. By Eugene L. Kammerman. 667-699, May 1956

SHORES and Sails in the South Seas. By Charles Allmon. 73-104, Jan. 1950

SHOSHONEAN LINGUISTIC STOCK:

Indians of the Far West (United States). By Matthew W. Stirling. Paintings by W. Langdon Kihn. 175-200, Feb. 1948

SHOSHONI INDIANS:

Following the Trail of Lewis and Clark. By Ralph Gray. 707-750, June 1953

SHOULD They Build a Fence Around Montana? By Mike W. Edwards. Photos by Nicholas deVore III. 614-649, May 1976

SHOWCASE of Red China (Peking). By Franc Shor. Photos by Brian Brake. 193-223, Aug. 1960

SHREWS. *See* Tree Shrews

SHRIMP:

Life in a "Dead" Sea—Great Salt Lake. By Paul A. Zahl. 252-263, Aug. 1967
Included: Brine shrimp

Miracle of the Potholes. By Rowe Findley. Photos by Robert F. Sisson. 570-579, Oct. 1975

Night Life in the Gulf Stream. By Paul A. Zahl. 391-418, Mar. 1954

Shrimp Nursery: Science Explores New Ways to Farm the Sea. By Clarence P. Idyll. Photos by Robert F. Sisson. 636-659, May 1965

SHRIMP FISHING:

Greenland's "Place by the Icebergs." By Mogens Bloch Poulsen. Photos by Thomas Nebbia. 849-869, Dec. 1973

Shrimpers Strike Gold in the Gulf. By Clarence P. Idyll. Photos by Robert F. Sisson. 699-707, May 1957

SHRINES, Historic:

Across the Potomac from Washington. By Albert W. Atwood. 1-33, Jan. 1953

America's Historylands, Landmarks of Liberty. Book announced. 360-363, Mar. 1962

Dog Mart Day in Fredericksburg (Virginia). By Frederick G. Vosburgh. 817-832, June 1951
Included: Kenmore, Mary Washington House, Ferry Farm, James Monroe Law Office, the John Paul Jones house, and Civil War battlesites

Founders of Virginia. By Sir Evelyn Wrench. Photos by B. Anthony Stewart. 433-462, Apr. 1948
Included: Historic and hallowed places in England

Shrines of Each Patriot's Devotion (United States). By Frederick G. Vosburgh. 51-82, Jan. 1949

Vacation Tour Through Lincoln Land. By Ralph Gray. 141-184, Feb. 1952

See also Arlington National Cemetery, Virginia; Harpers Ferry, West Virginia; Missions; Monticello, Virginia; Monuments and Memorials; Mount Vernon, Virginia

SHRIVER, SARGENT: Author:

Ambassadors of Good Will: The Peace Corps. By Sargent Shriver and Peace Corps Volunteers. 297-345, Sept. 1964

The SHY and Spectacular Kingfisher. Photos by Carl-Johan Junge and Emil Lütken. 413-419, Sept. 1974

SHY Monster, the Octopus. By Gilbert L. Voss. Photos by Robert F. Sisson. 776-799, Dec. 1971

SIAM. *See* Thailand

SIBERIA (Region), U.S.S.R.:

Eastern Soviet Union, Atlas series supplement. Mar. 1967

Siberia: Russia's Frozen Frontier. By Dean Conger. 297-345, Mar. 1967

Siberia: The Endless Horizon (Television film). 734A-734B, Nov. 1969

Siberia's Empire Road, the River Ob. By Robert Paul Jordan. Photos by Dean Conger. 145-181, Feb. 1976

SICILY (Island), Italy:

Fishing in the Whirlpool of Charybdis. By Paul A. Zahl. 579-618, Nov. 1953

Roman Life in 1,600-year-old Color Pictures (Mosaics). By Gino Vinicio Gentili. Photos by Duncan Edwards. 211-229, Feb. 1957

SICILY (Island), Italy—*Continued*

Sicily, Where All the Songs Are Sad. By Howard La Fay. Photos by Jonathan Blair. 407-436, Mar. 1976

Sicily the Three-cornered. By Luis Marden. 1-48, Jan. 1955

SICKLES, NOEL: Artist:

Alone to Antarctica. By David Lewis. 808-821, Dec. 1973

SIDEWHEELER. *See Rhode Island*

SIEMEL, SASHA: Author-Photographer:

The Jungle Was My Home. 695-712, Nov. 1952

SIENA, Italy:

The Palio of Siena. By Edgar Erskine Hume. 231-244, Aug. 1951

The Renaissance Lives On in Tuscany. By Luis Marden. Photos by Albert Moldvay. 626-659, Nov. 1974
    Included: The Palio

SIERRA LEONE. *See* Freetown

SIERRA MADRE OCCIDENTAL (Mountain Range), Mexico:

Found at Last: the Monarch's Winter Home. By Fred A. Urquhart. Photos by Bianca Lavies. 161-173, Aug. 1976

The Tarahumaras: Mexico's Long Distance Runners. By James Norman. Photos by David Hiser. 702-718, May 1976

SIERRA NEVADA (Mountains), California:

The Fabulous Sierra Nevada. By J. R. Challacombe. 825-843, June 1954

Golden Ghosts of the Lost Sierra. By Robert Laxalt. Photos by David Hiser. 332-353, Sept. 1973

John Muir's Wild America. By Harvey Arden. Photos by Dewitt Jones. 433-461, Apr. 1973

Mexico to Canada on the Pacific Crest Trail. By Mike W. Edwards. Photos by David Hiser. 741-779, June 1971

School for Survival. By Curtis E. LeMay. 565-602, May 1953

Sierra High Trip. By David R. Brower. 844-868, June 1954

See also Kings Canyon National Park; Yosemite National Park

SIFFRE, MICHEL: Author-Photographer:

Six Months Alone in a Cave (Biorhythm Research). 426-435, Mar. 1975

SIKANG (Former Chinese Province):

Adventures in Lololand. By Rennold L. Lowy. 105-118, Jan. 1947

A SIKH Discovers America. By Joginder Singh Rekhi. 558-590, Oct. 1964

SIKHS:

India's Energetic Sikhs. By John E. Frazer. Photos by James P. Blair. 528-541, Oct. 1972

SIKKIM:

Gangtok, Cloud-wreathed Himalayan Capital. By John Scofield. 698-713, Nov. 1970

Sikkim. By Desmond Doig. 398-429, Mar. 1963

Wedding of Two Worlds. By Lee E. Battaglia. 708-727, Nov. 1963

SILK:

A Lady From China's Past. Photos from *China Pictorial*. Text by Alice J. Hall. 660-681, May 1974

Thailand Bolsters Its Freedom. By W. Robert Moore. 811-849, June 1961

SILKWORMS:

Silkworms in England Spin for the Queen. By John E. H. Nolan. 689-704, May 1953

Spain's Silkworm Gut. By Luis Marden. 100-108, July 1951

This Is the China I Saw. By Jørgen Bisch. 591-639, Nov. 1964

SILVER. *See Slot ter Hooge;* Spanish Treasure

SILVER DART I and II (Airplanes):

Canada's Winged Victory: the *Silver Dart*. By Gilbert M. Grosvenor. 254-267, Aug. 1959

SILVERSMITHS:

Better Days for the Navajos. By Jack Breed. Photos by Charles W. Herbert. 809-847, Dec. 1958

SILVERSTONE, MARILYN: Photographer:

Royal Wedding at Jaisalmer. 66-79, Jan. 1965

SIMLA, Trinidad:

Keeping House for Tropical Butterflies. By Jocelyn Crane. Photos by M. Woodbridge Williams. 193-217, Aug. 1957

SIMONS, VERA: Author:

Laboratory in a Dirty Sky. By Rudolf J. Engelmann and Vera Simons. 616-621, Nov. 1976

SIMPICH, FREDERICK: Author:

Around the "Great Lakes of the South." Photos by J. Baylor Roberts. 463-491, Apr. 1948

California, Horn of Plenty. Photos by Willard R. Culver. 553-594, May 1949

4-H Boys and Girls Grow More Food. 551-582, Nov. 1948

From Indian Canoes to Submarines at Key West. Photos by J. Baylor Roberts. 41-72, Jan. 1950

Here Come the Marines. 647-672, Nov. 1950

Louisiana Trades with the World. Photos by J. Baylor Roberts. 705-738, Dec. 1947

Mapping the Nation's Breadbasket. 831-849, June 1948

So Much Happens Along the Ohio River. Photos by Justin Locke. 177-212, Feb. 1950

South Dakota Keeps Its West Wild. 555-588, May 1947

Uncle Sam Bends a Twig in Germany. Photos by J. Baylor Roberts. 529-550, Oct. 1948

With Uncle Sam and John Bull in Germany. 117-140, Jan. 1949

SIMPICH, FREDERICK, Jr.: Author:

Because It Rains on Hawaii. 571-610, Nov. 1949

Changing Formosa, Green Island of Refuge. Photos by Horace Bristol. 327-364, Mar. 1957

Fountain of Fire in Hawaii. Photos by Robert B. Goodman and Robert Wenkam. 303-327, Mar. 1960

Hawaii, U.S.A. Photos by Thomas Nebbia. 1-45, July 1960

Honolulu, Mid-ocean Capital. Photos by B. Anthony Stewart. 577-624, May 1954

SIMPSON, HUGH: Photographer:
First Woman Across Greenland's Ice. By Myrtle Simpson. 264-279, Aug. 1967

SIMPSON, MYRTLE: Author:
First Woman Across Greenland's Ice. Photos by Hugh Simpson. 264-279, Aug. 1967

SINAI, Mount, and Peninsula, Egypt:
In Search of Moses. By Harvey Arden. Photos by Nathan Benn. 2-37, Jan. 1976

Island of Faith in the Sinai Wilderness (St. Catherine's Monastery). By George H. Forsyth. Photos by Robert F. Sisson. 82-106, Jan. 1964

Mount Sinai's Holy Treasures (St. Catherine's Monastery). By Kurt Weitzmann. Photos by Fred Anderegg. 109-127, Jan. 1964

New Life for the Troubled Suez Canal. By William Graves. Photos by Jonathan Blair. 792-817, June 1975

Sinai Sheds New Light on the Bible. By Henry Field. Photos by William B. and Gladys Terry. 795-815, Dec. 1948

See also Ras Muhammad

SING-SING (Fair):
Australian New Guinea. By John Scofield. 604-637, May 1962

Blowgun Hunters of the South Pacific. By Jane C. Goodale. Photos by Ann Chowning. 793-817, June 1966

New Guinea Festival of Faces. By Malcolm S. Kirk. 148-156, July 1969

New Guinea's Rare Birds and Stone Age Men. By E. Thomas Gilliard. 421-488, Apr. 1953

To the Land of the Head-hunters. By E. Thomas Gilliard. 437-486, Oct. 1955

SINGAPORE:
In Storied Lands of Malaysia. By Maurice Shadbolt. Photos by Winfield Parks. 734-783, Nov. 1963

Malaya Meets Its Emergency. By George W. Long. Photos by J. Baylor Roberts and author. 185-228, Feb. 1953

Singapore, Reluctant Nation. By Kenneth MacLeish. Photos by Winfield Parks. 269-300, Aug. 1966

SINGH, ANNE DE HENNING: Author:
Sea Gypsies of the Philippines. Photos by Raghubir Singh. 659-677, May 1976

SINGH, RAGHUBIR: Author-Photographer:
The Last Andaman Islanders. 66-91, July 1975
Photographer
Calcutta, India's Maligned Metropolis. By Peter T. White. 534-563, Apr. 1973

The Ganges, River of Faith. By John J. Putman. 445-483, Oct. 1971

Sea Gypsies of the Philippines. By Anne de Henning Singh. 659-677, May 1976

SINKIANG:
The Caves of the Thousand Buddhas. By Franc and Jean Shor. 383-415, Mar. 1951
Included: Urumchi, Turfan, and Qomul (Hami), visited on way to the caves in Kansu Province

How the Kazakhs Fled to Freedom. By Milton J. Clark. 621-644, Nov. 1954

SINT EUSTATIUS (Island), Netherlands Antilles:
A Fresh Breeze Stirs the Leewards. By Carleton Mitchell. Photos by Winfield Parks. 488-537, Oct. 1966

The Netherlands Antilles: Holland in the Caribbean. By James Cerruti. Photos by Emory Kristof. 115-146, Jan. 1970

SINT MAARTEN (Island), Netherlands Antilles:
The Netherlands Antilles: Holland in the Caribbean. By James Cerruti. Photos by Emory Kristof. 115-146, Jan. 1970

SIOUX FALLS, South Dakota:
Satellites Gave Warning of Midwest Floods. By Peter T. White. Photos by Thomas A. DeFeo. 574-592, Oct. 1969

SIOUX INDIANS:
Back to the Historic Black Hills. By Leland D. Case. Photos by Bates Littlehales. 479-509, Oct. 1956

South Dakota Keeps Its West Wild. By Frederick Simpich. 555-588, May 1947

SIPLE, GREG and JUNE:
Bikepacking Across Alaska and Canada. By Dan Burden. 682-695, May 1973

SIPLE, PAUL A.:
All-out Assault on Antarctica. By Richard E. Byrd. 141-180, Aug. 1956

Antarctic Scientist Honored by the Society. 792-793, June 1958

Our Navy Explores Antarctica. By Richard E. Byrd. U. S. Navy official photos. 429-522, Oct. 1947

To the Men at South Pole Station. By Richard E. Byrd. 1-4, July 1957
Author
Man's First Winter at the South Pole. 439-478, Apr. 1958

We Are Living at the South Pole. Photos by David S. Boyer. 5-35, July 1957

SIR FRANCIS DRAKE. By Alan Villiers. Photos by Gordon W. Gahan. 216-253, Feb. 1975

SISSON, ROBERT F.:
Octopus-training experiments. 788-789, 792, 794-795, Dec. 1971

Photographic feats. 880, Dec. 1961; 901, Dec. 1962; 107, Jan. 1970; 692, Nov. 1970; 265, 266, Feb. 1971; 727, 748, June 1973
Author-Photographer
Aha! It Really Works! 143-147, Jan. 1974

At Home With the Bulldog Ant. 62-75, July 1974
Face-to-Face With a World of Ants. 72-75

Frost, Nature's Icing. 398-405, Mar. 1976

Life Cycle of a Coral. 780-793, June 1973

Snowflakes to Keep. 104-111, Jan. 1970

The Spider That Lives Under Water. 694-701, May 1972

The Wasp That Plays Cupid to a Fig. 690-697, Nov. 1970

The World of My Apple Tree. 836-847, June 1972
Photographer
Adrift on a Raft of Sargassum. 188-199, Feb. 1976

Algeria: France's Stepchild, Problem and Promise. By Howard La Fay. 768-795, June 1960

SISSON, ROBERT F.: Photographer — *Continued*

Arizona: Booming Youngster of the West. By Robert de Roos. 299-343, Mar. 1963

Behind New York's Window on Nature: The American Museum of Natural History. By James A. Oliver. 220-259, Feb. 1963

The Crab That Shakes Hands. By Clarence P. Idyll. 254-271, Feb. 1971

"Delmarva," Gift of the Sea. By Catherine Bell Palmer. 367-399, Sept. 1950

Disaster in Paradise (Bali). By Windsor P. Booth and Samuel W. Matthews. 436-458, Sept. 1963

Eastman of Rochester: Photographic Pioneer. By Allan C. Fisher, Jr. 423-438, Sept. 1954

Exploring 1,750,000 Years Into Man's Past. By L. S. B. Leakey. 564-589, Oct. 1961

The FBI: Public Friend Number One. By Jacob Hay. 860-886, June 1961

Following the Ladybug Home. By Kenneth S. Hagen. 543-553, Apr. 1970

4-H Boys and Girls Grow More Food. By Frederick Simpich. 551-582, Nov. 1948

Freedom Flight from Hungary. 424-436, Mar. 1957

Friendless Squatters of the Sea (Barnacles). By Ethel A. Starbird. 623-633, Nov. 1973

The Goats of Thunder Hill. By Elizabeth Nicholds. 625-640, May 1954

Grunion, the Fish That Spawns on Land. By Clarence P. Idyll. 714-723, May 1969

Here's New York Harbor. By Stuart E. Jones. Photos by Robert F. Sisson and David S. Boyer. 773-813, Dec. 1954

The Incredible Salmon. By Clarence P. Idyll. Paintings by Walter A. Weber. 195-219, Aug. 1968

Island of Faith in the Sinai Wilderness. By George H. Forsyth. 82-106, Jan. 1964

Lake Sunapee's Golden Trout. 529-536, Oct. 1950

Land of the Pilgrims' Pride. By George W. Long. 193-219, Aug. 1947

The Magic Road Round Ireland. By H. V. Morton. 293-333, Mar. 1961

Mardi Gras in New Orleans. By Carolyn Bennett Patterson. Photos by Robert F. Sisson and John E. Fletcher. 726-732, Nov. 1960

MATS: America's Long Arm of the Air. By Beverley M. Bowie. 283-317, Mar. 1957

Menhaden — Uncle Sam's Top Commercial Fish. By Leonard C. Roy. 813-823, June 1949

Miracle of the Potholes. By Rowe Findley. 570-579, Oct. 1975

Mountains Top Off New England. By F. Barrows Colton. 563-602, May 1951

Nature's Toy Train, the Railroad Worm. By Darwin L. Tiemann. 56-67, July 1970

New Discoveries on the Mid-Atlantic Ridge. By Maurice Ewing. 611-640, Nov. 1949

New Florida Resident, the Walking Catfish. By Clarence P. Idyll. 847-851, June 1969

New Tricks Outwit Our Insect Enemies. By Hal Higdon. Photos by Robert F. Sisson and Emory Kristof. 380-399, Sept. 1972

A New Volcano Bursts from the Atlantic (Ilha Nova). By John Scofield. 735-757, June 1958

New York State's New Main Street. By Matt C. McDade. 567-618, Nov. 1956

Newfoundland, Canada's New Province. By Andrew H. Brown. 777-812, June 1949

SISSON, ROBERT F.: Photographer — *Continued*

Nomad Sails Long Island Sound. By Thomas Horgan. 295-338, Sept. 1957

Our Friend From the Sea (Seal). By Robert and Nina Horstman. 728-736, Nov. 1968

Pack Trip Through the Smokies. By Val Hart. 473-502, Oct. 1952

Saving Man's Wildlife Heritage. By John H. Baker. 581-620, Nov. 1954

Science Explores the Monsoon Sea. By Samuel W. Matthews. 554-575, Oct. 1967

Scotland From Her Lovely Lochs and Seas. By Alan Villiers. 492-541, Apr. 1961

Shipworms, Saboteurs of the Sea. By F. G. Walton Smith. 559-566, Oct. 1956

Shrimp Nursery: Science Explores New Ways to Farm the Sea. By Clarence P. Idyll. 636-659, May 1965

Shrimpers Strike Gold in the Gulf (Gulf of Mexico). By Clarence P. Idyll. 699-707, May 1957

Shy Monster, the Octopus. By Gilbert L. Voss. 776-799, Dec. 1971

Skyline Trail from Maine to Georgia. By Andrew H. Brown. 219-251, Aug. 1949

South Carolina Rediscovered. By Herbert Ravenel Sass. 281-321, Mar. 1953

Squids: Jet-powered Torpedoes of the Deep. By Gilbert L. Voss. 386-411, Mar. 1967

Stately Homes of Old Virginia. By Albert W. Atwood. 787-802, June 1953

Sugar Weather in the Green Mountains. By Stephen Greene. 471-482, Apr. 1954

The Thames Mirrors England's Varied Life. By Willard Price. 45-93, July 1958

Today on the Delaware, Penn's Glorious River. By Albert W. Atwood. 1-40, July 1952

Tracking America's Man in Orbit. By Kenneth F. Weaver. 184-217, Feb. 1962

The Upper Mississippi. By Willard Price. 651-699, Nov. 1958

Westminster, World Series of Dogdom. By John W. Cross, Jr. 91-116, Jan. 1954

The Wild Animals in My Life. By William M. Mann. 497-524, Apr. 1957

Windjamming Around New England. By Tom Horgan. 141-169, Aug. 1950

SISTINE CHAPEL, Vatican City:

When in Rome. . . . By Stuart E. Jones. Photos by Winfield Parks. 741-789, June 1970

SIX Months Alone in a Cave. By Michel Siffre. 426-435, Mar. 1975

SIX to the Summit (Everest). By Norman G. Dyhrenfurth. Photos by Barry C. Bishop. 460-473, Oct. 1963

SKAGWAY, Alaska:

Along the Yukon Trail. By Amos Burg. 395-416, Sept. 1953

SKATE (Nuclear-powered Submarine):

The Arctic as a Sea Route of the Future. By William R. Anderson. 21-24, Jan. 1959

Up Through the Ice of the North Pole. By James F. Calvert. 1-41, July 1959

SKATES (Fish):

Miracle of the Mermaid's Purse. By Ernest L. Libby. 413-420, Sept. 1959

SKIING:

First Woman Across Greenland's Ice. By Myrtle Simpson. Photos by Hugh Simpson. 264-279, Aug. 1967

Golden Ghosts of the Lost Sierra. By Robert Laxalt. Photos by David Hiser. 332-353, Sept. 1973
Included: Long-board skiing

North Toward the Pole on Skis. By Bjørn O. Staib. 254-281, Feb. 1965

Rafting Down the Yukon. By Keith Tryck. Photos by Robert Clark. 830-861, Dec. 1975
Note: Three of the four men finished the trek on skis along 150 miles of the frozen Yukon to the Bering Sea.

Skiing in the United States. By Kathleen Revis. 216-254, Feb. 1959

Soaring on Skis in the Swiss Alps. By Carolyn Bennett Patterson. Photos by Kathleen Revis. 94-121, Jan. 1961

A Town . . . a Mountain . . . a Way of Life (Aspen, Colorado). By Jill Durrance and Dick Durrance II. 788-807, Dec. 1973

Yosemite National Park. 491-498, Apr. 1951

SKINGLE, DEREK:

Journey Into Stone Age New Guinea. By Malcolm S. Kirk. 568-592, Apr. 1969

SKOMER (Island), Wales:

The Solemn, Sociable Puffins. By R. M. Lockley. 414-422, Sept. 1954

SKOPJE, Yugoslavia:

Yugoslavia: Six Republics in One. By Robert Paul Jordan. Photos by James P. Blair. 589-633, May 1970
Included: Earthquake, 1963

SKULL 1470. By Richard E. Leakey. Photos by Bob Campbell. 819-829, June 1973

"SKUNK" (Train):

The Friendly Train Called Skunk. By Dean Jennings. Photos by B. Anthony Stewart. 720-734, May 1959

SKUNKS Want Peace—or Else! By Melvin R. Ellis. Photos by Charles Philip Fox. 279-294, Aug. 1955

SKY-HIGH Bolivia. 481-496, Oct. 1950

"SKY PEOPLE." *See* Ainu

SKY Road East. By Tay and Lowell Thomas, Jr. 71-112, Jan. 1960

SKY SURVEY:

Completing the Atlas of the Universe (National Geographic Society-Palomar Observatory Sky Survey). By Ira Sprague Bowen. 185-190, Aug. 1955
Sky Survey Plates Unlock Secrets of the Stars. 186-187

Current Scientific Projects of the National Geographic Society. 143-144, July 1953

Exploring the Farthest Reaches of Space. By George O. Abell. 782-790, Dec. 1956

Mapping the Unknown Universe. By F. Barrows Colton. 401-420, Sept. 1950

Our Universe Unfolds New Wonders (National Geographic-Palomar Sky Survey). By Albert G. Wilson. 245-260, Feb. 1952

Sky Survey Charts the Universe. By Ira Sprague Bowen. 780-781, Dec. 1956

SKY SURVEY—*Continued*

Twelve National Geographic Society Scientific Projects Under Way. 869-870, June 1954

SKYE, Isle of, Inner Hebrides:

Over the Sea to Scotland's Skye. By Robert J. Reynolds. 87-112, July 1952

SKYLAB MISSIONS:

Skylab. Photos by the nine mission astronauts. 441-503, Oct. 1974
I. Outpost in Space. By Thomas Y. Canby. 441-469
II. Its View of Earth. 471-493
III. The Sun Unveiled. By Edward G. Gibson. 494-503

SKYLINE Trail from Maine to Georgia. By Andrew H. Brown. Photos by Robert F. Sisson. 219-251, Aug. 1949

SKYSCRAPERS:

The Mohawks Scrape the Sky. By Robert L. Conly. Photos by B. Anthony Stewart. 133-142, July 1952

SKYWAY Below the Clouds. By Carl R. Markwith. Photos by Ernest J. Cottrell. 85-108, July 1949
Contents: Skyway 1 (Wright Way), a route planned and marked especially for the use of private flyers

SLADEN, WILLIAM J. L.: Author:

Tireless Voyager, the Whistling Swan. Photos by Bianca Lavies. 134-147, July 1975

SLAYTON, DONALD K.:

Apollo-Soyuz: Handclasp in Space. By Thomas Y. Canby. 183-187, Feb. 1976

SLED DOGS:

Trek Across Arctic America. By Colin Irwin. 295-321, Mar. 1974

SLIPHER, E. C.: Author:

New Light on the Changing Face of Mars. 427-436, Sept. 1955

SLOT TER HOOGE (Dutch East Indiaman):

The Treasure of Porto Santo. By Robert Sténuit. Photos by author and William R. Curtsinger. 260-275, Aug. 1975

SLOVENIA (Republic), Yugoslavia:

Yugoslavia: Six Republics in One. By Robert Paul Jordan. Photos by James P. Blair. 589-633, May 1970

SLOW Boat to Florida. By Dorothea and Stuart E. Jones. 1-65, Jan. 1958

SLOW Death Threatens Man in the Thin Air of 19,000 Feet. 530-531, Oct. 1962

SLOW Train Through Viet Nam's War. By Howard Sochurek. 412-444, Sept. 1964

SMALL NAMBAS (People):

Taboos and Magic Rule Namba Lives. By Kal Muller. 57-83, Jan. 1972

SMALL Service With a Big Mission: The Coast Guard. By William S. Ellis. 113-139, July 1974

SMALL WORLD (Balloon):

Braving the Atlantic by Balloon. By Arnold Eiloart. 123-146, July 1959

SMART, MAXWELL:

Journey Into Stone Age New Guinea. By Malcolm S. Kirk. 568-592, Apr. 1969

SMITH, BRADFORD: Author:

Captain Smith of Jamestown. 581-620, May 1957

SMITH, F. G. WALTON: Author:

Shipworms, Saboteurs of the Sea. 559-566, Oct. 1956

SMITH, HERVEY GARRETT: Artist:

"Mayflower II," painting supplement. Nov. 1957

Ships Through the Ages: A Saga of the Sea. By Alan Villiers. 494-545, Apr. 1963

SMITH, JANE M., AWARD: Recipients:

Ingram, Sir Bruce. 474, Apr. 1961

Johnson, Lyndon B. 906, Dec. 1962; 113, Jan. 1966; 468, Oct. 1966

See also list preceding this index

SMITH, JOHN:

Capt. John Smith's Map of Virginia.—Captain Smith's New England . . . and the Pilgrims' Cape Cod. 760, 765, June 1953

Captain Smith of Jamestown. By Bradford Smith. 581-620, May 1957

Founders of Virginia. By Sir Evelyn Wrench. Photos by B. Anthony Stewart. 433-462, Apr. 1948

SMITH, L. H.: Author-Photographer:

Lyrebird, Australia's Meistersinger. 849-857, June 1955

SMITH, R. V. FRANCIS: Author:

Finding an "Extinct" New Zealand Bird (Takahe). 393-401, Mar. 1952

SMITH, RAY WINFIELD: Author:

Computer Helps Scholars Re-create an Egyptian Temple. Photos by Emory Kristof. 634-655, Nov. 1970

History Revealed in Ancient Glass. Photos by B. Anthony Stewart and Lee E. Battaglia. 346-369, Sept. 1964

SMITHSON, JAMES:

The Smithsonian, Magnet on the Mall. By Leonard Carmichael. Photos by Volkmar Wentzel. 796-845, June 1960

The Smithsonian Institution. By Thomas R. Henry. 325-348, Sept. 1948

SMITHSONIAN ASTROPHYSICAL OBSERVATORY:

Cambridge, Massachusetts. 190, Feb. 1962; 808, 812, Dec. 1966; Ikeya-Seki comet. 260, 261, Feb. 1966; Kohoutek comet. 148, Jan. 1974

Solar Eclipse, Nature's Super Spectacular. By Donald H. Menzel and Jay M. Pasachoff. 222-233, Aug. 1970

Solar studies. 334, 343, 344, 346, Sept. 1948

SMITHSONIAN INSTITUTION:

Air and Space Museum. 533, Apr. 1976; National Air Museum. 798, 805, 838, June 1960; 152, Feb. 1962

Bureau of American Ethnology. 339, 341, Sept. 1948; 798, 827-829, June 1960

American Indians: Bering Sea Expedition, 1936. 339, Sept. 1948; Broken Bow, Oklahoma. 189, Aug. 1971; Fort Berthold, North Dakota. 721, 731, June 1953; Gravel pictographs. 389-404, Sept. 1952; Lindenmeier valley site, Colo-

SMITHSONIAN INSTITUTION—*Continued*

rado. 340, Sept. 1948, 793, Dec. 1955; Missouri River, North Dakota: Indian villages submerged in 1946. 385, 387, Sept. 1971; Olmec culture: Mexico. 137-172, Feb. 1947, 736, June 1947, 117, Jan. 1948, 341, Sept. 1948, 807, Dec. 1950, 816, Dec. 1951, 420, Mar. 1953, 367-375, Sept. 1956, 505, 521, Oct. 1968; Panama. 373-399, Mar. 1949, 227-246, Feb. 1950, 420, Mar. 1953, 143, 144, July 1953, 271-290, Aug. 1953; Pueblo Bonito, Chaco Canyon, New Mexico. 340-341, Sept. 1948, 785, Dec. 1950, 34-35, 36, Jan. 1963, 332, Sept. 1970; Russell Cave, Alabama. 542-558, Oct. 1956, 427-438, Mar. 1958, 614, May 1958, 34-36, Jan. 1963, 440, Sept. 1967

Eskimos: Sadlermiut. 669, 672, Nov. 1956; Sadlermiut and Dorset. 870, June 1954; Thule and Dorset. 562, Apr. 1955

Canal Zone Biological Area: Sea level canal study. 772, Dec. 1970; Tropical Research Institute. 417, 440, Mar. 1970; 575, Apr. 1972

Center for Short-Lived Phenomena, Cambridge, Massachusetts. 286B, Feb. 1973

Chesapeake Bay Center for Environmental Studies: Whistling swan. 140, 141, 144, July 1975

"Contributions to Knowledge" (1848): Indian mounds. 106, Jan. 1948

Expeditions and research. 328, Sept. 1948; 13-16, 34-35, 36, 37, 38, Jan. 1963

Akhenaten Temple Project, Egypt. 636, 637, Nov. 1970

Arnhem Land, Australia: Aborigines. 430, Mar. 1948, 637, May 1949, 417-430, Sept. 1949, 745-782, Dec. 1949, 870, June 1954, 828, June 1960, 37, Jan. 1963; Cattle egret. 292, Aug. 1954

"Around the World for Animals" (1937). 497, 504, 505, 516, Apr. 1957

British Guiana: Hoatzin. 825, June 1960, 391-401, Sept. 1962, 42, Jan. 1963; Wai Wai Indians. 329-346, Mar. 1955

Glomar Challenger: Ocean samples. 597, May 1975

Kalahari Desert, Africa: Bushmen. 877, June 1963

Lake Champlain, New York: Search for Benedict Arnold's fleet. 72, Jan. 1969

Marine biology: Mollusks. 397, Mar. 1969; Shark-attack file. 224, 256, Feb. 1968

Nanmatol, Ponape: Archeology. 735, May 1967

Nicaragua: Cerro Negro 1968 volcanic eruption. 497, Oct. 1969

Port Royal, Jamaica. 151-183, Feb. 1960; 871, Dec. 1967

Powell Grand Canyon Expedition, 1869. 686, May 1969

Red Sea. 727, Nov. 1972

Spiny babbler: Nepal. 1-40, Jan. 1950

Stone spheres: Costa Rica. 142, 144, July 1965; Mexico. 300, Aug. 1969

Sudan: Giraffes. 725, June 1947

Tecumseh, U.S.S. 380, 382, Mar. 1968

Veracruz, Mexico: New birds discovered. 344, Sept. 1948

Virú Valley, Peru: Archeology. 454, 464, Apr. 1947

Freer Gallery of Art. 348, Sept. 1948; 798, 805, 832-833, 838, June 1960; 363, Sept. 1964

SMITHSONIAN INSTITUTION — *Continued*

Hall of Gems and Minerals. 568, 575, 579, 584, Apr. 1958; 835-839, 852-853, 858-863, Dec. 1971

International Exchange Service. 798, 816, June 1960

Museum of History and Technology. 741, 743, Dec. 1964; 873, 874, Dec. 1973; 95-97, 99, July 1975

National Collection of Fine Arts. 798, 831, 838, June 1960; 508, 511, Apr. 1967

National Herbarium. 477, Oct. 1950

Natural History Museum. 874, Dec. 1973
Ice Age "Mummy." 297, Mar. 1972
Mural. 294-295, Mar. 1972

"Science City," Maui. 515, 527, Apr. 1971

Science Information Exchange. 614, Nov. 1970

The Smithsonian, Magnet on the Mall. By Leonard Carmichael. Photos by Volkmar Wentzel. 796-845, June 1960

The Smithsonian Institution. By Thomas R. Henry. 325-348, Sept. 1948

U. S. National Museum. 792, 798, 800, 803, 805, 806, Dec. 1950; 367, Mar. 1954; 90, Jan. 1956; 264, Feb. 1956; 276, Aug. 1956; 829, 832, Dec. 1956
First Lady exhibit. 328, 347, Sept. 1948; 90, Jan. 1957
Fossil collection. 363, 365, 376, 379, 381, Mar. 1956
Mineral collection. 631, 638-641, Nov. 1951
Shell collection. 39, 68, 71, July 1949

See also National Gallery of Art; National Zoological Park, Washington, D. C.; Smithsonian Astrophysical Observatory

SMOKEJUMPING. *See* Forest Fire

SMOKY MOUNTAINS. *See* Great Smoky Mountains

SNAILS:

Blue-water Plankton: Ghosts of the Gulf Stream. By William M. Hamner. 530-545, Oct. 1974
Included: Planktonic snails

Shells Take You Over World Horizons. By Rutherford Platt. 33-84, July 1949
Included: Land, marine, and tree snails

See also Giant African Land Snails; Tree Snails

SNAKE (River), Wyoming-Idaho-Washington:

A Map Maker Looks at the United States. By Newman Bumstead. 705-748, June 1951

Wildlife Adventuring in Jackson Hole. By Frank and John Craighead. 1-36, Jan. 1956

SNAKES:

The Lure of the Changing Desert. 817-824, June 1954

Our Snake Friends and Foes. By Doris M. Cochran. Paintings by Walter A. Weber. 334-364, Sept. 1954

The People of Cumberland Gap. By John Fetterman. Photos by Bruce Dale. 591-621, Nov. 1971
Included: Snake hunting

Wildlife of Everglades National Park. By Daniel B. Beard. Paintings by Walter A. Weber. 83-116, Jan. 1949
Included: Indigo snake, rattlesnake, water snake

Zoo Animals Go to School. By Marion P. McCrane. Photos by W. E. Garrett. 694-706, Nov. 1956

SNAKES — *Continued*

See also Cobras; Garter Snakes; Sea Snakes

SNAKETOWN (Excavation Site), Arizona:

The Hohokam: First Masters of the American Desert. By Emil W. Haury. Photos by Helga Teiwes. 670-695, May 1967

Magnetic Clues Help Date the Past. By Kenneth F. Weaver. 696-701, May 1967

SNO-CATS Mechanize Oregon Snow Survey. By Andrew H. Brown. Photos by John E. Fletcher. 691-710, Nov. 1949

SNOW FESTIVAL in Japan's Far North. By Eiji Miyazawa. 824-833, Dec. 1968

SNOW GEESE:

Beyond the North Wind With the Snow Goose. By Des and Jen Bartlett. 822-843, Dec. 1973

SNOW LEOPARDS:

Imperiled Phantom of Asian Peaks: First Photographs of Snow Leopards in the Wild. By George B. Schaller. 702-707, Nov. 1971

SNOW-MANTLED Stehekin: Where Solitude Is in Season. Photos by Bruce Dale. Text by Pat Hutson. 572-588, Apr. 1974

SNOW SURVEY:

Sno-Cats Mechanize Oregon Snow Survey. By Andrew H. Brown. Photos by John E. Fletcher. 691-710, Nov. 1949

SNOWFLAKE (White Gorilla):

Growing Up With Snowflake. By Arthur J. Riopelle. Photos by Michael Kuh. 491-503, Oct. 1970

"Snowflake," the World's First White Gorilla. By Arthur J. Riopelle. Photos by Paul A. Zahl. 443-448, Mar. 1967

SNOWFLAKES to Keep. By Robert F. Sisson. 104-111, Jan. 1970

SNYDER, HELEN: Photographer:

Can the Cooper's Hawk Survive? By Noel Snyder. Photos by author and Helen Snyder. 433-442, Mar. 1974

SNYDER, NOEL: Author-Photographer:

Can the Cooper's Hawk Survive? Photos by author and Helen Snyder. 433-442, Mar. 1974

SO Long, St. Louis, We're Heading West. By William C. Everhart. 643-669, Nov. 1965

SO Much Happens Along the Ohio River. By Frederick Simpich. Photos by Justin Locke. 177-212, Feb. 1950

SOARING:

Happy Birthday, Otto Lilienthal! By Russell Hawkes. Photos by James Collison. 286-292, Feb. 1972

Sailors of the Sky. By Gordon Young. Photos by Emory Kristof and Jack Fields. Paintings by Davis Meltzer. 49-73, Jan. 1967

SOARING on Skis in the Swiss Alps. By Carolyn Bennett Patterson. Photos by Kathleen Revis. 94-121, Jan. 1961

SOBHUZA II, King (Swaziland):

Swaziland Tries Independence. By Volkmar Wentzel. 266-293, Aug. 1969

SOC (Sub-ice Observation Chamber):

Stalking Seals Under Antarctic Ice. By Carleton Ray. 54-65, Jan. 1966

SOCHUREK, HOWARD: Author-Photographer:

Air Rescue Behind Enemy Lines (North Viet Nam). 346-369, Sept. 1968

American Special Forces in Action in Viet Nam. 38-65, Jan. 1965

Berlin, on Both Sides of the Wall. 1-47, Jan. 1970

Slow Train Through Viet Nam's War. 412-444, Sept. 1964

South Korea: Success Story in Asia. 301-345, Mar. 1969

Viet Nam's Montagnards. 443-487, Apr. 1968

The Volga, Russia's Mighty River Road. 579-613, May 1973

Photographer

The Laser's Bright Magic. By Thomas Meloy. 858-881, Dec. 1966

World War I Aircraft Fly Again in Rhinebeck's Rickety Rendezvous. By Harvey Arden. 578-587, Oct. 1970

SOCIETY Honors the Conquerors of Antarctica. 589-590, Apr. 1959

SOCIETY ISLANDS, South Pacific Ocean:

The *Yankee*'s Wander-world. By Irving and Electa Johnson. 1-50, Jan. 1949

See also Tahiti

The SOCIETY Reports to Its Members on Russia Today. The Editor. 351, Sept. 1959

The SOCIETY'S Great 75th Anniversary Issue. Introduction by Melville Bell Grosvenor. 459, Oct. 1963

The SOCIETY'S Hubbard Medal Awarded to Commander MacMillan. 563-564, Apr. 1953

SOCKEYE SALMON:

The Incredible Salmon. By Clarence P. Idyll. Photos by Robert F. Sisson. Paintings by Walter A. Weber. 195-219, Aug. 1968

SOIL EROSION:

Erosion, Trojan Horse of Greece. By F. G. Renner. 793-812, Dec. 1947

This Land of Ours—How Are We Using It? By Peter T. White. Photos by Emory Kristof. 20-67, July 1976

Water for the World's Growing Needs. By Herbert B. Nichols and F. Barrows Colton. 269-286, Aug. 1952

See also Forests and Reforestation; U. S. Soil Conservation Service

SOLAR ECLIPSE, Nature's Super Spectacular. By Donald H. Menzel and Jay M. Pasachoff. 222-233, Aug. 1970

The SOLAR ECLIPSE From a Jet. By Wolfgang B. Klemperer. 785-796, Nov. 1963

SOLAR ENERGY:

The Next Frontier? By Isaac Asimov. Paintings by Pierre Mion. 76-89, July 1976

The Search for Tomorrow's Power. By Kenneth F. Weaver. Photos by Emory Kristof. 650-681, Nov. 1972

SOLAR ENERGY—*Continued*

Solar Energy, the Ultimate Powerhouse. By John L. Wilhelm. Photos by Emory Kristof. 381-397, Mar. 1976

The Sun. By Herbert Friedman. 713-743, Nov. 1965

What's Happening to Our Climate? By Samuel W. Matthews. 576-615, Nov. 1976

SOLAR SYSTEM. *See* Comets; Moon; Planets; Sun

SOLE:

The Red Sea's Sharkproof Fish. By Eugenie Clark. Photos by David Doubilet. 718-727, Nov. 1974

The SOLEMN, Sociable Puffins. By R. M. Lockley. 414-422, Sept. 1954

SOLHEIM, WILHELM G., II: Author:

New Light on a Forgotten Past. 330-339, Mar. 1971

SOLOMON ISLANDS, South Pacific Ocean:

A Teen-ager Sails the World Alone. By Robin Lee Graham. 445-491, Oct. 1968

Yankee Roams the Orient. By Irving and Electa Johnson. 327-370, Mar. 1951

See also Florida Island

SOLVING Life Secrets of the Sailfish. By Gilbert Voss. Photos by B. Anthony Stewart. Paintings by Craig Phillips. 859-872, June 1956

SOLVING the Mystery of Mexico's Great Stone Spheres. By Matthew W. Stirling. Photos by David F. Cupp. 295-300, Aug. 1969

SOLVING the Riddle of Chubb Crater. By V. Ben Meen. Photos by Richard H. Stewart. 1-32, Jan. 1952

SOLVING the Riddles of Wetherill Mesa. By Douglas Osborne. Paintings by Peter V. Bianchi. 155-195, Feb. 1964

SOMETHING'S Fishy About That Fin! Photos by Robert J. Shallenberger and William D. Madden. 224-227, Aug. 1974

SONAKUL, D.: Author:

Pageantry of the Siamese Stage. Photos by W. Robert Moore. 201-212, Feb. 1947

SONAR (Sound Navigation and Ranging):

Down to *Thresher* by Bathyscaph. By Donald L. Keach. 764-777, June 1964

From Indian Canoes to Submarines at Key West. By Frederick Simpich. Photos by J. Baylor Roberts. 41-72, Jan. 1950

Our Navy's Long Submarine Arm. By Allan C. Fisher, Jr. 613-636, Nov. 1952

SONAR ABILITY. *See* Bats; Killer Whales; Oilbirds; Porpoises; Weddell Seals

SONGHAIS (Tribespeople):

The Niger: River of Sorrow, River of Hope. By Georg Gerster. 152-189, Aug. 1975

SONGS:

Hunting Folk Songs in the Hebrides. By Margaret Shaw Campbell. 249-272, Feb. 1947

Hunting Musical Game in West Africa. By Arthur S. Alberts. 262-282, Aug. 1951

SONOMA VALLEY, California. *See* Valley of the Moon

SONORA (State), Mexico:

From Sun-clad Sea to Shining Mountains. By Ralph Gray. Photos by James P. Blair. 542-589, Apr. 1964

Sonora Is Jumping. By Mason Sutherland. 215-246, Feb. 1955

SONORAN DESERT, Arizona-Mexico:

Abundant Life in a Desert Land. By Walter Meayers Edwards. 424-436, Sept. 1973

SORCERY:

American Special Forces in Action in Viet Nam. By Howard Sochurek. 38-65, Jan. 1965
Included: Rhadé tribe sorcerers

Journey Into Stone Age New Guinea. By Malcolm S. Kirk. 568-592, Apr. 1969
Included: Sorcerers of Nomad River, and Oksapmin

Viet Nam's Montagnards. By Howard Sochurek. 443-487, Apr. 1968
Included: Mnong tribe sorcerers

See also Voodooism

The **SOUL** of a Tribe Returns to Africa. By William S. Ellis. Photos by James P. Blair. 141-148, July 1974

SOULEN, HENRY J.: Artist:

Bringing Old Testament Times to Life. By G. Ernest Wright. 833-864, Dec. 1957

The Last Thousand Years Before Christ. By G. Ernest Wright. Paintings by H. J. Soulen and Peter V. Bianchi. 812-853, Dec. 1960

SOURIAL, GEORGES: Photographer:

The Voyage of *Ra II*. By Thor Heyerdahl. Photos by Carlo Mauri and Georges Sourial. 44-71, Jan. 1971

SOUTH (Region), U. S.:

Around the "Great Lakes of the South." By Frederick Simpich. Photos by J. Baylor Roberts. 463-491, Apr. 1948

Beauty and Bounty of Southern State Trees. By William A. Dayton. Paintings by Walter A. Weber. 508-552, Oct. 1957

Close-up: U.S.A., The South Central States, map supplement. Text on reverse. Oct. 1974

Close-up: U.S.A., The Southeast, map supplement. Text on reverse. Oct. 1975

Dixie Spins the Wheel of Industry. By William H. Nicholas. Photos by J. Baylor Roberts. 281-324, Mar. 1949

Sea Islands: Adventuring Along the South's Surprising Coast. By James Cerruti. Photos by Thomas Nebbia and James L. Amos. 366-393, Mar. 1971

South Central United States, Atlas series supplement. Feb. 1961

South Central United States, map supplement. Dec. 1947

Southeastern United States, Atlas series supplement. Jan. 1958

Southeastern United States, map supplement. Feb. 1947

Timber: How Much Is Enough? By John J. Putman. Photos by Bruce Dale. 485-511, Apr. 1974

See also Intracoastal Waterway; *and* names of individual states

SOUTH AFRICA, Republic of:

Adventures With South Africa's Black Eagles. By

SOUTH AFRICA, Republic of—*Continued*

Jeanne Cowden. Photos by author and Arthur Bowland. 533-543, Oct. 1969

Africa: The Winds of Freedom Stir a Continent. By Nathaniel T. Kenney. Photos by W. D. Vaughn. 303-359, Sept. 1960

First Flight Across the Bottom of the World. By James R. Reedy. Photos by Otis Imboden. 454-464, Mar. 1964

Freedom's Progress South of the Sahara. By Howard La Fay. Photos by Joseph J. Scherschel. 603-637, Nov. 1962

Gold, the Eternal Treasure. By Peter T. White. Photos by James L. Stanfield. 1-51, Jan. 1974

The Many-sided Diamond. By George Switzer. 568-586, Apr. 1958

New Light on the Changing Face of Mars. By E. C. Slipher. 427-436, Sept. 1955
Included: The Lamont-Hussey Observatory

Questing for Gems. By George S. Switzer. 835-863, Dec. 1971

Roaming Africa's Unfenced Zoos. By W. Robert Moore. 353-380, Mar. 1950
Included: Hluhluwe, Kruger, and Umfolozi reserves

Safari Through Changing Africa. By Elsie May Bell Grosvenor. Photos by Gilbert Grosvenor. 145-198, Aug. 1953

South Africa Close-up. By Kip Ross. 641-681, Nov. 1962

World-roaming Teen-ager Sails On. By Robin Lee Graham. 449-493, Apr. 1969

The Zulus: Black Nation in a Land of Apartheid. By Joseph Judge. Photos by Dick Durrance II. 738-775, Dec. 1971

See also Dassen Island; Good Hope, Cape of

SOUTH AMERICA:

The Amazon. Photos by Loren McIntyre. 445-455, Oct. 1972

Amazon—The River Sea. By Loren McIntyre. 456-495, Oct. 1972

Ambassadors of Good Will: The Peace Corps. By Sargent Shriver and Peace Corps Volunteers. 297-345, Sept. 1964
Included: Bolivia; Ecuador

Birds That "See" in the Dark With Their Ears. By Edward S. Ross. 282-290, Feb. 1965

Eastern South America, Atlas series supplement. Sept. 1962

Eastern South America, map supplement. Mar. 1955

Flags of the Americas. By Elizabeth W. King. 633-657, May 1949
Included: Argentina; Bolivia; Brazil; Chile; Colombia; Ecuador; Paraguay; Peru; Uruguay; Venezuela

Gold, the Eternal Treasure. By Peter T. White. Photos by James L. Stanfield. 1-51, Jan. 1974

How Fruit Came to America. By J. R. Magness. Paintings by Else Bostelmann. 325-377, Sept. 1951

In the Wake of Darwin's *Beagle*. By Alan Villiers. Photos by James L. Stanfield. 449-495, Oct. 1969
Included: Argentina; Brazil; Chile; Peru; Uruguay

Jungle Jaunt on Amazon Headwaters. By Bernice M. Goetz. 371-388, Sept. 1952

Magellan: First Voyage Around the World. By Alan Villiers. Photos by Bruce Dale. 721-753, June 1976

Northwestern South America, Atlas series supplement. Feb. 1964

SOUTH AMERICA—*Continued*

Our Vegetable Travelers. By Victor R. Boswell. Paintings by Else Bostelmann. 145-217, Aug. 1949

Pan American Highway system in southern South America, map. 665, Nov. 1967

Parks, Plans, and People: How South America Guards Her Green Legacy. By Mary and Laurance Rockefeller. Photos by George F. Mobley. 74-119, Jan. 1967

Playing 3,000 Golf Courses in Fourteen Lands. By Ralph A. Kennedy. 113-132, July 1952

Sea Fever. By John E. Schultz. 237-268, Feb. 1949
    Contents: The author's 6,000-mile trip from Quito, Ecuador, to Miami, Florida, by way of the Napo and Amazon Rivers and the West Indies

Sir Francis Drake. By Alan Villiers. 216-253, Feb. 1975

South America, Atlas series supplement. Feb. 1960

South America, map supplement. Oct. 1950

South America, map supplement. Text on reverse. Oct. 1972

Southern South America, Atlas series supplement. Mar. 1958

Theodore Roosevelt: a Centennial Tribute. By Bart McDowell. 572-590, Oct. 1958
    Included: Travels in South America

The World in Your Garden (Flowers). By W. H. Camp. Paintings by Else Bostelmann. 1-65, July 1947

See also individual countries; *and* Drugs; Indians of South America

SOUTH AUSTRALIA (State), Australia:

South Australia, Gateway to the Great Outback. By Howell Walker. Photos by Joseph J. Scherschel. 441-481, Apr. 1970

See also Coober Pedy

SOUTH CALAVERAS GROVE, California:

Saving Earth's Oldest Living Things (Sequoias). By Andrew H. Brown. Photos by Raymond Moulin and author. 679-695, May 1951

SOUTH CAROLINA:

Dixie Spins the Wheel of Industry. By William H. Nicholas. Photos by J. Baylor Roberts. 281-324, Mar. 1949

Here Come the Marines. By Frederick Simpich. 647-672, Nov. 1950
    Included: Parris Island

Sea Islands: Adventuring Along the South's Surprising Coast. By James Cerruti. Photos by Thomas Nebbia and James L. Amos. 366-393, Mar. 1971

South Carolina Rediscovered. By Herbert Ravenel Sass. Photos by Robert F. Sisson. 281-321, Mar. 1953

See also Charleston

SOUTH CENTRAL STATES:

Close-up: U.S.A., The South Central States, map supplement. Text on reverse. Oct. 1974

South Central United States, Atlas series supplement. Feb. 1961

South Central United States, map supplement. Dec. 1947

See also names of individual states

SOUTH DAKOTA:

Back to the Historic Black Hills. By Leland D.

SOUTH DAKOTA—*Continued*

Case. Photos by Bates Littlehales. 479-509, Oct. 1956

Big Game Hunting in the Land of Long Ago. By Joseph P. Connolly and James D. Bump. 589-605, May 1947

Following the Trail of Lewis and Clark. By Ralph Gray. 707-750, June 1953

South Dakota Keeps Its West Wild. By Frederick Simpich. 555-588, May 1947
    Over Plains and Hills of South Dakota. Photos by J. Baylor Roberts. 563-586

See also Sioux Falls; *Strato-Lab* (Balloon)

SOUTH GEORGIA ISLAND, South Atlantic Ocean:

A Naturalist in Penguin Land. By Niall Rankin. 93-116, Jan. 1955

SOUTH in the Sudan. By Harry Hoogstraal. 249-272, Feb. 1953

SOUTH ISLAND, New Zealand:

New Zealand's Bountiful South Island. By Peter Benchley. Photos by James L. Amos. 93-123, Jan. 1972

SOUTH KOREA. *See* Korea, South

SOUTH POLE:

All-out Assault on Antarctica. By Richard E. Byrd. 141-180, Aug. 1956

Antarctica: Icy Testing Ground for Space. By Samuel W. Matthews. Photos by Robert W. Madden. 569-592, Oct. 1968

The Crossing of Antarctica. By Sir Vivian Fuchs. Photos by George Lowe. 25-47, Jan. 1959

Man's First Winter at the South Pole. By Paul A. Siple. 439-478, Apr. 1958

Our Navy Explores Antarctica. By Richard E. Byrd. U. S. Navy official photos. 429-522, Oct. 1947

To the Men at South Pole Station. By Richard E. Byrd. 1-4, July 1957

We Are Living at the South Pole. By Paul A. Siple. Photos by David S. Boyer. 5-35, July 1957

What We've Accomplished in Antarctica. By George J. Dufek. 527-557, Oct. 1959

Year of Discovery Opens in Antarctica. By David S. Boyer. 339-381, Sept. 1957

SOUTH SEA ISLANDS:

Adventures with the Survey Navy. By Irving Johnson. 131-148, July 1947
    Contents: The surveying and charting of Deboyne Lagoon, Louisiade Archipelago; Florida Island and Guadalcanal, Solomon Islands; Funafuti and Nukufetau, Ellice Islands; Kwajalein, Marshall Islands; Tarawa, Gilbert Islands; Ulithi, Caroline Islands; Uvéa, Wallis Islands

Pacific Wards of Uncle Sam. By W. Robert Moore. 73-104, July 1948
    Contents: The United States Trust Territory of Pacific Islands comprising the Carolines with Palau, the Marshalls, and the Marianas

A Teen-ager Sails the World Alone. By Robin Lee Graham. 445-491, Oct. 1968
    Included: Fiji Islands; Samoa Islands; Solomon Islands; Tonga

The *Yankee's* Wander-world. By Irving and Electa Johnson. 1-50, Jan. 1949
    Included: Ahé; Bora Bora; Easter Island; Mooréa; Pitcairn; Raïvavaé; Rapa; Tahiti

SOUTH SEA ISLANDS—*Continued*
See also Melanesia; Micronesia; Polynesia

SOUTH SHETLAND ISLANDS, Antarctica. *See* Deception Island

SOUTH to Mexico City. By W. E. Garrett. 145-193, Aug. 1968

SOUTH UIST (Island), Scotland:
Isles on the Edge of the Sea: Scotland's Outer Hebrides. By Kenneth MacLeish. Photos by Thomas Nebbia. 676-711, May 1970

SOUTH VIET NAM. *See* Viet Nam, South

SOUTHAMPTON, THIRD EARL OF (Henry Wriothesley):
Founders of Virginia. By Sir Evelyn Wrench. Photos by B. Anthony Stewart. 433-462, Apr. 1948

SOUTHAMPTON ISLAND, Northwest Territories, Canada:
Twelve National Geographic Society Scientific Projects Under Way. 869-870, June 1954
Vanished Mystery Men of Hudson Bay. By Henry B. Collins. 669-687, Nov. 1956

SOUTHEAST (Region), U. S.:
Close-up: U.S.A., The Southeast, map supplement. Text on reverse. Oct. 1975
Southeastern United States, Atlas series supplement. Jan. 1958
Southeastern United States, map supplement. Feb. 1947
See also names of individual states

SOUTHEAST ASIA:
The Lands and Peoples of Southeast Asia. 295-365, Mar. 1971
1. Mosaic of Cultures. By Peter T. White. Photos by W. E. Garrett. 296-329
2. New Light on a Forgotten Past. By Wilhelm G. Solheim II. 330-339
3. Pagan, on the Road to Mandalay. By W. E. Garrett. 343-365
The Mekong, River of Terror and Hope. By Peter T. White. Photos by W. E. Garrett. 737-787, Dec. 1968
The Peoples of Mainland Southeast Asia, double-sided map supplement. Mar. 1971
Southeast Asia, Atlas series supplement. May 1961
Southeast Asia, map supplement. Sept. 1955
Southeast Asia, map supplement. Dec. 1968
Viet Nam, Cambodia, Laos, and Eastern Thailand, map supplement. Text on reverse. Jan. 1965
Viet Nam, Cambodia, Laos, and Thailand, map supplement. Feb. 1967
See also Burma; Cambodia; Hong Kong; Indochina; Indonesia; Laos; Macao; Malaysia; Philippines; Singapore; Taiwan; Thailand; Viet Nam

SOUTHERN California's Trial by Mud and Water. By Nathaniel T. Kenney. Photos by Bruce Dale. 552-573, Oct. 1969

SOUTHERN RAILWAY SYSTEM:
Dixie Spins the Wheel of Industry. By William H. Nicholas. Photos by J. Baylor Roberts. 281-324, Mar. 1949

SOUTHWEST (Region), U. S.:
Southwestern United States, Atlas series supplement. Nov. 1959

SOUTHWEST (Region), U. S.—*Continued*
Southwestern United States, map supplement. Dec. 1948
Two Wheels Along the Mexican Border. By William Albert Allard. 591-635, May 1971
See also names of individual states; *and* Colorado (River); Four Corners Country; *and* Pre-Columbian Civilization

SOUTHWEST AUSTRALIA'S Wild Gardens: Bizarre and Beautiful. By Paul A. Zahl. 858-868, Dec. 1976

SOYUZ-APOLLO MISSION:
Apollo-Soyuz: Handclasp in Space. By Thomas Y. Canby. 183-187, Feb. 1976

SPACE COLONIES:
The Next Frontier? By Isaac Asimov. Paintings by Pierre Mion. 76-89, July 1976

SPACE FLIGHTS AND RESEARCH:
Awesome Views of the Forbidding Moonscape. 233-239, Feb. 1969
Behold the Computer Revolution. By Peter T. White. Photos by Bruce Dale and Emory Kristof. 593-633, Nov. 1970
The Long, Lonely Leap. By Joseph W. Kittinger, Jr. Photos by Volkmar Wentzel. 854-873, Dec. 1960
Man's Conquest of Space. Special Publication announced. 844-849, June 1968
The Sun. By Herbert Friedman. 713-743, Nov. 1965
Included: U. S. Naval Research Laboratory studies
We Saw the World From the Edge of Space. By Malcolm D. Ross. Ground photos by Walter Meayers Edwards. 671-685, Nov. 1961
See also Apollo Missions; Gemini Missions; Mariner Missions; Mercury Missions; Pioneer Probes; Ranger Spacecraft; Rockets; Satellites; Skylab Missions; Surveyor Spacecraft; Viking Lander; Voyager; X-15

SPACE MEDICINE:
Aviation Medicine on the Threshold of Space. By Allan C. Fisher, Jr. Photos by Luis Marden. 241-278, Aug. 1955
The Flight of *Freedom 7.* By Carmault B. Jackson, Jr. 416-431, Sept. 1961
The Making of an Astronaut. By Robert R. Gilruth. 122-144, Jan. 1965
School for Space Monkeys. 725-729, May 1961
Skylab, Outpost on the Frontier of Space. By Thomas Y. Canby. Photos by the nine mission astronauts. 441-469, Oct. 1974
We Saw the World From the Edge of Space. By Malcolm D. Ross. Ground photos by Walter Meayers Edwards. 671-685, Nov. 1961
See also Biorhythm Research; Tektite II

SPACE PIONEERS of NASA Journey Into Tomorrow. By Allan C. Fisher, Jr. Photos by Dean Conger. 48-89, July 1960

SPACE RENDEZVOUS, Milestone on the Way to the Moon. By Kenneth F. Weaver. 539-553, Apr. 1966

SPACE SATELLITES. *See* Satellites

SPACE STATIONS:
The Next Frontier? By Isaac Asimov. Paintings by Pierre Mion. 76-89, July 1976

SPACE STATIONS — *Continued*

Solar Energy, the Ultimate Powerhouse. By John L. Wilhelm. Photos by Emory Kristof. 381-397, Mar. 1976

See also Skylab Missions

SPACE WALK:

America's 6,000-mile Walk in Space. 440-447, Sept. 1965

SPACECRAFT. *See* DODGE Satellite; Nimbus I; Ranger Spacecraft; Surveyor Spacecraft; Telstar; *Tiros I;* Viking Lander; Voyager; *and* Space Flights and Research

SPAFFORD MEMORIAL CHILDREN'S HOSPITAL, Jerusalem:

Jerusalem, My Home. By Bertha Spafford Vester. 826-847, Dec. 1964

SPAIN:

"Around the World in Eighty Days." By Newman Bumstead. 705-750, Dec. 1951
  Included: Barcelona; Cape Creus; Madrid

The Changing Face of Old Spain. By Bart McDowell. Photos by Albert Moldvay. 291-339, Mar. 1965
  Included: Barcelona; Madrid; Pamplona; Segovia; Seville; Toledo; Valencia

Christopher Columbus and the New World He Found. By John Scofield. Photos by Adam Woolfitt. 584-625, Nov. 1975

Spain and Portugal, Atlas series supplement. Mar. 1965

Spain's Silkworm Gut. By Luis Marden. 100-108, July 1951

Speaking of Spain. By Luis Marden. 415-456, Apr. 1950

The Sword and the Sermon (Islam). By Thomas J. Abercrombie. 3-45, July 1972

When the President Goes Abroad (Eisenhower Tour). By Gilbert M. Grosvenor. 588-649, May 1960

See also Andalusia; Córdoba; Marismas; Pyrenees; Santander; Sevilla; *and* Balearic Islands; Canary Islands

SPANISH-AMERICAN WAR:

Guantánamo: Keystone in the Caribbean. By Jules B. Billard. Photos by W. E. Garrett and Thomas Nebbia. 420-436, Mar. 1961

SPANISH ARMADA:

Priceless Relics of the Spanish Armada. By Robert Sténuit. Photos by Bates Littlehales. 745-777, June 1969

Sir Francis Drake. By Alan Villiers. Photos by Gordon W. Gahan. 216-253, Feb. 1975

SPANISH RIDING SCHOOL, Vienna, Austria:

The White Horses of Vienna. By Beverley M. Bowie. Photos by Volkmar Wentzel. 401-419, Sept. 1958

SPANISH SAHARA:

Dry-land Fleet Sails the Sahara. By Jean du Boucher. Photos by Jonathan S. Blair. 696-725, Nov. 1967

SPANISH TREASURE:

Atocha, Tragic Treasure Galleon of the Florida Keys. By Eugene Lyon. 787-809, June 1976

Drowned Galleons Yield Spanish Gold. By Kip

SPANISH TREASURE — *Continued*

Wagner. Photos by Otis Imboden. 1-37, Jan. 1965

Priceless Relics of the Spanish Armada. By Robert Sténuit. Photos by Bates Littlehales. 745-777, June 1969

Treasure! (Television film). 575, Nov. 1976; cover announcement. Dec. 1976

SPARROWS POINT, Maryland:

Man's Mightiest Ally (Steel). Photos by Willard R. Culver. 432-450, Apr. 1947

SPAWNING. *See* Grunion; Salmon

SPEAKING of Spain. By Luis Marden. 415-456, Apr. 1950

SPEARING Lions with Africa's Masai. By Edgar Monsanto Queeny. 487-517, Oct. 1954

SPEARS, JOSEPH F.: Author:

The Flying Telegraph. Official U. S. Army Signal Corps photos. 531-554, Apr. 1947

SPECIAL FORCES, U. S. Army. *See* U. S. Army Special Forces

SPECIAL GOLD MEDAL, NGS:

Designs by: Peter V. Bianchi. 146, July 1961; Felix W. deWeldon. 868, Dec. 1957; Laura Gardin Fraser. 45, July 1957

Recipients

Amundsen, Roald:
Received Special Gold Medal for discovery of the South Pole; presentation by Robert E. Peary. 65F, July 1954

Bennett, Floyd:
Awarded Gold Medal; presentation by President Coolidge. 868, Dec. 1957

Byrd, Richard E.:
Awarded Society's Special Medal of Honor; presentation by President Hoover. 38, 45, July 1957; 868, Dec. 1957; 574, 576, Apr. 1962

Cousteau, Jacques-Yves:
Jacques-Yves Cousteau Receives National Geographic Society Medal at White House; presentation by President Kennedy. 146-147, July 1961

Earhart, Amelia:
Awarded Gold Medal; presentation by President Hoover in 1932. 566, Nov. 1951; 868, Dec. 1957; 571, 582, Oct. 1963; 619, Nov. 1966

Goethals, George W.:
Awarded Gold Medal; presentation by President Wilson in 1914. 868, Dec. 1957; 585, Oct. 1963

Peary, Robert E.:
Awarded the Society's Special Gold Medal for being the first to reach the North Pole. 18, Jan. 1963; Medal in the Smithsonian Institution. 347, Sept. 1948

Peary, Mrs. Robert E.:
Gold Medal Awarded to Mrs. Robert E. Peary. 148, Jan. 1956

Philip, Prince:
President Eisenhower Presents to Prince Philip the National Geographic Society's Medal. 865-868, Dec. 1957

Poulter, Thomas C.:
Awarded Special Gold Medal for Antarctic research from 1933-1935. 205, Feb. 1967

The **SPECTACULAR** North Cascades: New National Park Proposed. By Nathaniel T. Kenney. Photos by James P. Blair. 642-667, May 1968

SPECTACULAR Rio de Janeiro. By Hernane Tavares de Sá. Photos by Charles Allmon. 289-328, Mar. 1955

SPECTACULAR Treasures From a Chinese Tomb. Photos from *China Pictorial*. Text by Alice J. Hall. 660-681, May 1974

SPEISER, E. A.: Author:
Ancient Mesopotamia: A Light That Did Not Fail. Paintings by H. M. Herget. 41-105, Jan. 1951

SPELEOLOGY:
Exploring America Underground. By Charles E. Mohr. 803-837, June 1964
Probing Ice Caves of the Pyrenees. By Norbert Casteret. 391-404, Mar. 1953

SPENCER, DONALD A.: Author-Photographer:
Porcupines, Rambling Pincushions. 247-264, Aug. 1950

SPICE ISLANDS. *See* Moluccas

SPICES:
Clove-scented Zanzibar. By W. Robert Moore. 261-278, Feb. 1952
Spices, the Essence of Geography. By Stuart E. Jones. 401-420, Mar. 1949

SPID (Submersible Portable Inflatable Dwelling):
The Deepest Days. By Robert Sténuit. 534-547, Apr. 1965
Outpost Under the Ocean. By Edwin A. Link. Photos by Bates Littlehales. 530-533, Apr. 1965

SPIDERS:
The Spider That Lives Under Water. By Robert F. Sisson. 694-701, May 1972
Spiders. Children's book announced. 728-730, Nov. 1974
What's So Special About Spiders? By Paul A. Zahl. 190-219, Aug. 1971

SPIEGEL, TED: Photographer:
Canada's Window on the Pacific: The British Columbia Coast. By Jules B. Billard. 338-375, Mar. 1972
George Washington: The Man Behind the Myths. By Howard La Fay. 90-111, July 1976
Kansas City, Heartland U.S.A. By Rowe Findley. 112-139, July 1976
The Loyalists. By Kent Britt. 510-539, Apr. 1975
The Philippines, Freedom's Pacific Frontier. By Robert de Roos. 301-351, Sept. 1966
Reunited Jerusalem Faces Its Problems. By Kenneth MacLeish. 835-871, Dec. 1968
Scientists Ride Ice Islands on Arctic Odysseys. By Lowell Thomas, Jr. 670-691, Nov. 1965
Those Proper and Other Bostonians. By Joseph Judge. 352-381, Sept. 1974
The Vikings. By Howard La Fay. 492-541, Apr. 1970
The World of Elizabeth I. By Louis B. Wright. 668-709, Nov. 1968

SPIER, PETER: Artist:
A Traveler's Tale of Ancient Tikal. Text by Alice J. Hall. 799-811, Dec. 1975

SPINY BABBLER (Bird):
Peerless Nepal — A Naturalist's Paradise. By S. Dillon Ripley. Photos by Volkmar Wentzel. 1-40, Jan. 1950

SPINY LOBSTERS:
New Life for the "Loneliest Isle" (Tristan da Cunha). By Lewis Lewis. 105-116, Jan. 1950
Strange March of the Spiny Lobster. By William F. Herrnkind. Photos by Rick Frehsee and Bruce Mounier. 819-831, June 1975
Tektite II: Science's Window on the Sea. By John G. VanDerwalker. Photos by Bates Littlehales. 256-289, Aug. 1971

SPIRITS of Change Capture the Karens. By Peter Kunstadter. 267-285, Feb. 1972

SPITSBERGEN Mines Coal Again. 113-120, July 1948

SPLIT, Yugoslavia:
Yugoslavia, Between East and West. By George W. Long. Photos by Volkmar Wentzel. 141-172, Feb. 1951
Yugoslavia's Window on the Adriatic. By Gilbert M. Grosvenor. 219-247, Feb. 1962

SPLIT-SECOND Time Runs Today's World. By F. Barrows Colton and Catherine Bell Palmer. 399-428, Sept. 1947

SPLIT Seconds in the Lives of Birds. By Arthur A. Allen. 681-706, May 1954

SPONGE-FISHING INDUSTRY:
On the Winds of the Dodecanese. By Jean and Franc Shor. 351-390, Mar. 1953
Sponge Fishermen of Tarpon Springs. By Jennie E. Harris. 119-136, Jan. 1947

SPOONBILLS. *See* Roseate Spoonbills

SPORTS:
Around the "Great Lakes of the South." By Frederick Simpich. Photos by J. Baylor Roberts. 463-491, Apr. 1948
Included: Boating, Fishing, Horseback riding, Swimming
Long Island Outgrows the Country. By Howell Walker. Photos by B. Anthony Stewart. 279-326, Mar. 1951
Included: Baseball, Fishing, Golf, Lawn bowling, Sailing, Swimming, Tennis
Mexico's Booming Capital. By Mason Sutherland. Photos by Justin Locke. 785-824, Dec. 1951
Included: Baseball, Bowling, Bullfighting, Football, Swimming
See also Olympic Games; *and* names of individual sports

SPORTS-MINDED Melbourne, Host to the Olympics. 688-693, Nov. 1956

The **SPOTLIGHT** Swings to Suez. By W. Robert Moore. 105-115, Jan. 1952

SPRING, BOB and IRA: Photographers:
Climbing Our Northwest Glaciers. 103-114, July 1953

SPRING CREEK HUTTERITE COLONY, Montana:
The Hutterites, Plain People of the West. By William Albert Allard. 98-125, July 1970

SPRINGFIELD, Illinois:
Illinois — Healthy Heart of the Nation. By Leo A.

SPRINGFIELD, Illinois — *Continued*
Borah. Photos by B. Anthony Stewart and Willard R. Culver. 781-820, Dec. 1953

Vacation Tour Through Lincoln Land. By Ralph Gray. 141-184, Feb. 1952

SPRINGTIME Comes to Yellowstone National Park. By Paul A. Zahl. 761-779, Dec. 1956

SPRINGTIME of Hope in Poland. By Peter T. White. Photos by James P. Blair. 467-501, Apr. 1972

SPRUNT, ALEXANDER, Jr.: Author:
Blizzard of Birds: The Tortugas Terns. 213-230, Feb. 1947

SQUARE-RIGGERS:
By Square-rigger from Baltic to Bicentennial. By Kenneth Garrett. 824-857, Dec. 1976
Included: *Amerigo Vespucci, Christian Radich, Danmark, Dar Pomorza, Eagle, Esmeralda, Gazela Primeiro, Gloria, Gorch Fock, Juan Sebastián de Elcano, Kruzenshtern, Libertad, Mircea, Nippon Maru, Sagres II, Tovarishch*
Windjamming Around New England. By Tom Horgan. Photos by Robert F. Sisson. 141-169, Aug. 1950
See also Charles W. Morgan; Eagle; Georg Stage; Joseph Conrad; Pamir; Yankee (Brigantine)

SQUAWS Along the Yukon. By Ginny Hill Wood. 245-265, Aug. 1957

SQUIDS:
Nature's Night Lights: Probing the Secrets of Bioluminescence. By Paul A. Zahl. 45-69, July 1971
Squids: Jet-powered Torpedoes of the Deep. By Gilbert L. Voss. Photos by Robert F. Sisson. 386-411, Mar. 1967

SQUIRRELS, Flying:
"Flying" Squirrels, Nature's Gliders. By Ernest P. Walker. 663-674, May 1947

SRI LANKA. *See* former name, Ceylon

SRINAGAR, Kashmir:
The Idyllic Vale of Kashmir. By Volkmar Wentzel. 523-550, Apr. 1948

STAFFORD, MARIE PEARY:
Gold Medal Awarded to Mrs. Robert E. Peary. 148, Jan. 1956
Note: Mrs. Stafford accepted the Special Gold Medal on behalf of her mother.
Author
The Peary Flag Comes to Rest. 519-532, Oct. 1954

STAFFORD, THOMAS P.:
Apollo-Soyuz: Handclasp in Space. By Thomas Y. Canby. 183-187, Feb. 1976
Space Rendezvous, Milestone on the Way to the Moon. By Kenneth F. Weaver. 539-553, Apr. 1966

STAIB, BJØRN O.: Author:
North Toward the Pole on Skis. 254-281, Feb. 1965

STAINED GLASS:
Chartres: Legacy From the Age of Faith. By Kenneth MacLeish. Photos by Dean Conger. 857-882, Dec. 1969

STALINGRAD, U.S.S.R. *See* Volgograd

STALKING Central Africa's Wildlife. By T. Donald Carter. Paintings by Walter A. Weber. 264-286, Aug. 1956

STALKING Seals Under Antarctic Ice. By Carleton Ray. 54-65, Jan. 1966

STALKING the Great Indian Rhino. By Lee Merriam Talbot. 389-398, Mar. 1957

STALKING the Mountain Lion — to Save Him. By Maurice G. Hornocker. 638-655, Nov. 1969

STALKING the West's Wild Foods. By Euell Gibbons. Photos by David Hiser. 186-199, Aug. 1973

STALKING Wild Foods on a Desert Isle. By Euell Gibbons. Photos by David Hiser. 47-63, July 1972

STAMPS, Postage:
Everyone's Servant, the Post Office. By Allan C. Fisher, Jr. Photos by Volkmar Wentzel. 121-152, July 1954
Liechtenstein Thrives on Stamps. By Ronald W. Clark. 105-112, July 1948

STANDARD OIL COMPANY OF CALIFORNIA:
Barehanded Battle to Cleanse the Bay. By Peter T. White. Photos by Jonathan S. Blair. 866-881, June 1971

STANDARD WEIGHTS AND MEASURES:
Uncle Sam's House of 1,000 Wonders (U. S. Bureau of Standards). By Lyman J. Briggs and F. Barrows Colton. 755-784, Dec. 1951

STANFIELD, JAMES L.: Photographer:
Big Bend: Jewel in the Texas Desert. By Nathaniel T. Kenney. 104-133, Jan. 1968
Canadian Rockies, Lords of a Beckoning Land. By Alan Phillips. 353-393, Sept. 1966
Gold, the Eternal Treasure. By Peter T. White. 1-51, Jan. 1974
Golden Masterpieces. 29-39
Housewife at the End of the World. By Rae Natalie P. Goodall. 130-150, Jan. 1971
Human Treasures of Japan. By William Graves. 370-379, Sept. 1972
Illinois: The City and the Plain. By Robert Paul Jordan. Photos by James L. Stanfield and Joseph J. Scherschel. 745-797, June 1967
In the Wake of Darwin's *Beagle*. By Alan Villiers. 449-495, Oct. 1969
The Investiture of Great Britain's Prince of Wales. By Allan C. Fisher, Jr. Photos by James L. Stanfield and Adam Woolfitt. 698-715, Nov. 1969
Iran's Shah Crowns Himself and His Empress. By Franc Shor. Photos by James L. Stanfield and Winfield Parks. 301-321, Mar. 1968
Life's Tempo on Nantucket. By Peter Benchley. 810-839, June 1970
Living in a Japanese Village. By William Graves. 668-693, May 1972
Mark Twain: Mirror of America. By Noel Grove. 300-337, Sept. 1975
More of Sea Than of Land: The Bahamas. By Carleton Mitchell. 218-267, Feb. 1967
The Nation's River. By Allan C. Fisher, Jr. 432-469, Oct. 1976
A Good Life on the Potomac. 470-479
New Orleans and Her River. By Joseph Judge. 151-187, Feb. 1971

STANFIELD, JAMES L.: Photographer — *Continued*

Our Virgin Islands, 50 Years Under the Flag. By Carleton Mitchell. 67-103, Jan. 1968

Quebec: French City in an Anglo-Saxon World. By Kenneth MacLeish. Photos by James L. Stanfield and Declan Haun. 416-442, Mar. 1971

The Red Sea's Gardens of Eels. By Eugenie Clark. Photos by James L. Stanfield and David Doublet. 724-735, Nov. 1972

San Francisco Bay, the Westward Gate. By William Graves. 593-637, Nov. 1969

Western Australia, the Big Country. By Kenneth MacLeish. 150-187, Feb. 1975

STAR CHARTS:

Star charts, supplement. *A Map of the Heavens.* Dec. 1957

Star charts, supplement. *Map of the Heavens.* Aug. 1970

"STAR OF GLADNESS." *See Hokule'a*

STARBIRD, ETHEL A.: Author:

Friendless Squatters of the Sea. Photos by Robert F. Sisson. 623-633, Nov. 1973

From Sword to Scythe in Champlain Country. Photos by B. Anthony Stewart and Emory Kristof. 153-201, Aug. 1967

A River Restored: Oregon's Willamette. Photos by Lowell J. Georgia. 816-835, June 1972

Spain's Sun-blest Pleasure Isles. Photos by James A. Sugar. 679-701, May 1976

Toronto: Canada's Dowager Learns to Swing. Photos by Robert W. Madden. 190-215, Aug. 1975

Vermont — a State of Mind and Mountains. Photos by Nathan Benn. 28-61, July 1974

STARCK, JO D.: Author-Photographer:

Probing the Deep Reefs' Hidden Realm. By Walter A. Starck II and Jo D. Starck. 867-886, Dec. 1972

STARCK, WALTER A., II: Author-Photographer:

Marvels of a Coral Realm. 710-738, Nov. 1966

Probing the Deep Reefs' Hidden Realm. By Walter A. Starck II and Jo D. Starck. 867-886, Dec. 1972

Photographer

Photographing the Night Creatures of Alligator Reef. By Robert E. Schroeder. Photos by author and Walter A. Starck II. 128-154, Jan. 1964

STARFISH:

Starfish (Crown-of-thorns) Threaten Pacific Reefs. By James A. Sugar. 340-353, Mar. 1970

STARFISH HOUSE (Conshelf Two):

At Home in the Sea. By Jacques-Yves Cousteau. 465-507, Apr. 1964

STARLING, GUY W.: Photographer:

Eclipse Hunting in Brazil's Ranchland. By F. Barrows Colton. Photos by Richard H. Stewart and Guy W. Starling. 285-324, Sept. 1947

STARS:

The Incredible Universe. By Kenneth F. Weaver. Photos by James P. Blair. 589-625, May 1974

Wind, Wave, Star, and Bird. By David Lewis. Photos by Nicholas deVore III. 747-781, Dec. 1974
Included: Navigating by the stars

See also Star Charts; Sun

STATE HERMITAGE MUSEUM: Leningrad, U.S.S.R. *See* Hermitage

STATE PARKS:

Finding the Mt. Everest of All Living Things (Redwood Tree). By Paul A. Zahl. 10-51, July 1964
Included: California state parks: Del Norte Coast State Park; Humboldt Redwoods State Park; Jedediah Smith Redwoods State Park; Prairie Creek Redwoods State Park; Richardson Grove State Park

Mexico to Canada on the Pacific Crest Trail. By Mike W. Edwards. Photos by David Hiser. 741-779, June 1971

The Parks in Your Backyard. By Conrad L. Wirth. 647-707, Nov. 1963
The East. 675-689
The Midlands. 691-697
The West. 699-707

Vacationlands of the United States and Southern Canada, map supplement. Text on reverse. July 1966

See also Adirondack Mountains, for Adirondack State Park; Calaveras Big Trees State Park; John Pennekamp Coral Reef State Park; Palisades Interstate Park; Valley Forge

STATELY Homes of Old Virginia. By Albert W. Atwood. 787-802, June 1953

STATEN ISLAND FERRY, New York's Seagoing Bus. By John T. Cunningham and Jay Johnston. Photos by W. D. Vaughn. 833-843, June 1959

STATIA (Island). *See* Sint Eustatius

STATION WAGON Odyssey: Baghdad to Istanbul. By William O. Douglas. 48-87, Jan. 1959

STATUES:

The Nation Honors Admiral Richard E. Byrd. 567-578, Apr. 1962

See also Blessing of the Fleet, for Our Lady of Good Voyage; Buddhism, for Buddhas; Sculpture; War Memorials; *and* Abu Simbel; Aegean Islands; Aphrodisias; Athens; Easter Island; Florence; Rome; Scotland (Poets' Voices)

STAVANGER, Norway:

Norway Cracks Her Mountain Shell. By Sydney Clark. Photos by Gilbert H. Grosvenor and Ole Friele Backer. 171-211, Aug. 1948

Stop-and-Go Sail Around South Norway. By Edmond J. Moran. Photos by Randi Kjekstad Bull and Andrew H. Brown. 153-192, Aug. 1954

STEAD AIR FORCE BASE, Nevada:

School for Survival. By Curtis E. LeMay. 565-602, May 1953

STEAMBOATS:

Henry Hudson's River. By Willard Price. Photos by Wayne Miller. 364-403, Mar. 1962

Mark Twain: Mirror of America. By Noel Grove. Photos by James L. Stanfield. 300-337, Sept. 1975

The Mighty Hudson. By Albert W. Atwood. Photos by B. Anthony Stewart. 1-36, July 1948

Ships Through the Ages: A Saga of the Sea. By Alan Villiers. 494-545, Apr. 1963

Squaws Along the Yukon. By Ginny Hill Wood. 245-265, Aug. 1957

That Dammed Missouri River. By Gordon Young.

STEAMBOATS — *Continued*

Photos by David Hiser. 374-413, Sept. 1971
Included: The discovery of sunken steamer, *Bertrand*

Tom Sawyer's Town. By Jerry Allen. 121-140, July 1956

The Upper Mississippi. By Willard Price. 651-699, Nov. 1958

See also Rhode Island; and Magdalena (River), Colombia

STEEL BANDS:

Carnival in Trinidad. By Howard La Fay. Photos by Winfield Parks. 693-701, Nov. 1971

"The Music of Trinidad." NGS recording announced. 701, Nov. 1971

STEEL INDUSTRY:

Coal Makes the Saar a Prize. By Franc Shor. 561-576, Apr. 1954

Luxembourg, the Quiet Fortress. By Robert Leslie Conly. Photos by Ted H. Funk. 69-97, July 1970

Ohio Makes Its Own Prosperity. By Leo A. Borah. Photos by B. Anthony Stewart. 435-484, Apr. 1955

Pittsburgh, Pattern for Progress. By William J. Gill. Photos by Clyde Hare. 342-371, Mar. 1965

Pittsburgh: Workshop of the Titans. By Albert W. Atwood. 117-144, July 1949

Steel: Master of Them All. By Albert W. Atwood. 415-452, Apr. 1947
Man's Mightiest Ally. Photos by Willard R. Culver. 423-450

Today on the Delaware, Penn's Glorious River. By Albert W. Atwood. Photos by Robert F. Sisson. 1-40, July 1952

STEHEKIN, Washington:

Snow-mantled Stehekin: Where Solitude Is in Season. Photos by Bruce Dale. Text by Pat Hutson. 572-588, Apr. 1974

STEINEMANN, PAUL: Photographer:

Jambo — First Gorilla Raised by Its Mother in Captivity. By Ernst M. Lang. 446-453, Mar. 1964

STÉNUIT, ROBERT:

The Long, Deep Dive. By Lord Kilbracken. Photos by Bates Littlehales. 718-731, May 1963

Outpost Under the Ocean. By Edwin A. Link. Photos by Bates Littlehales. 530-533, Apr. 1965

Author

The Deepest Days. 534-547, Apr. 1965

Priceless Relics of the Spanish Armada. Photos by Bates Littlehales. 745-777, June 1969

Author-Photographer

The Treasure of Porto Santo. Photos by author and William R. Curtsinger. 260-275, Aug. 1975

STEVENSON, ADLAI E.: Author:

The United Nations: Capital of the Family of Man. Photos by B. Anthony Stewart and John E. Fletcher. 297-303, Sept. 1961

STEVENSON, ROBERT LOUIS:

Poets' Voices Linger in Scottish Shrines. By Isobel Wylie Hutchison. Photos by Kathleen Revis. 437-488, Oct. 1957

STEWART, B. ANTHONY:

National Geographic Photographers Win Top Magazine Awards. 830-831, June 1959

STEWART, B. ANTHONY — *Continued*
Author-Photographer

Focusing on the Tournament of Roses. By B. Anthony Stewart and J. Baylor Roberts. 805-816, June 1954

Photographer

Across the Potomac from Washington. By Albert W. Atwood. 1-33, Jan. 1953

The Bahamas, Isles of the Blue-green Sea. By Carleton Mitchell. 147-203, Feb. 1958

Ballerinas in Pink. By Carleton Mitchell. 553-571, Oct. 1957

California's Wonderful One (State Highway No. 1). By Frank Cameron. 571-617, Nov. 1959

Captain Smith of Jamestown. By Bradford Smith. 581-620, May 1957

Character Marks the Coast of Maine. By John Scofield. 798-843, June 1968

Christmas in Cookie Tree Land. By Louise Parker La Gorce. 844-851, Dec. 1955

The DAR Story. By Lonnelle Aikman. Photos by B. Anthony Stewart and John E. Fletcher. 565-598, Nov. 1951

Date Line: United Nations, New York. By Carolyn Bennett Patterson. Photos by B. Anthony Stewart and John E. Fletcher. 305-331, Sept. 1961

Dog Mart Day in Fredericksburg. By Frederick G. Vosburgh. 817-832, June 1951

Drums to Dynamos on the Mohawk. By Frederick G. Vosburgh. 67-110, July 1947

Easter Egg Chickens. By Frederick G. Vosburgh. 377-387, Sept. 1948

The Fabulous State of Texas. By Stanley Walker. Photos by B. Anthony Stewart and Thomas Nebbia. 149-195, Feb. 1961

Folger: Biggest Little Library in the World. By Joseph T. Foster. Photos by B. Anthony Stewart and John E. Fletcher. 411-424, Sept. 1951

Fossils Lift the Veil of Time. By Harry S. Ladd and Roland W. Brown. 363-386, Mar. 1956

Founders of New England. By Sir Evelyn Wrench. 803-838, June 1953

Founders of Virginia. By Sir Evelyn Wrench. 433-462, Apr. 1948

The Friendly Train Called Skunk. By Dean Jennings. 720-734, May 1959

From Sword to Scythe in Champlain Country. By Ethel A. Starbird. Photos by B. Anthony Stewart and Emory Kristof. 153-201, Aug. 1967

Giant Sequoias Draw Millions to California Parks. By John Michael Kauffmann. 147-187, Aug. 1959

The Greener Fields of Georgia. By Howell Walker. Photos by author and B. Anthony Stewart. 287-330, Mar. 1954

History Revealed in Ancient Glass. By Ray Winfield Smith. Photos by B. Anthony Stewart and Lee E. Battaglia. 346-369, Sept. 1964

Honolulu, Mid-ocean Capital. By Frederick Simpich, Jr. 577-624, May 1954

Illinois — Healthy Heart of the Nation. By Leo A. Borah. Photos by B. Anthony Stewart and Willard R. Culver. 781-820, Dec. 1953

Incredible Andorra. By Lawrence L. Klingman. 262-290, Aug. 1949

Inside the White House. By Lonnelle Aikman. Photos by B. Anthony Stewart and Thomas Nebbia. 3-43, Jan. 1961

STEWART, B. ANTHONY: Photographer—*Continued*

Israel: Land of Promise. By John Scofield. 395-434, Mar. 1965

Kew: The Commoners' Royal Garden. By Thomas Garner James. 479-506, Apr. 1950

The Land of Galilee. By Kenneth MacLeish. 832-865, Dec. 1965

Literary Landmarks of Massachusetts. By William H. Nicholas. Photos by B. Anthony Stewart and John E. Fletcher. 279-310, Mar. 1950

London's Zoo of Zoos. By Thomas Garner James. 771-786, June 1953

Long Island Outgrows the Country. By Howell Walker. 279-326, Mar. 1951

The Making of a West Pointer. By Howell Walker. 597-626, May 1952

Massachusetts Builds for Tomorrow. By Robert de Roos. 790-843, Dec. 1966

The Merrimack: River of Industry and Romance. By Albert W. Atwood. 106-140, Jan. 1951

Mexico's Window on the Past (National Museum). By Bart McDowell. 492-519, Oct. 1968

Midshipmen's Cruise. By William J. Aston and Alexander G. B. Grosvenor. 711-754, June 1948

The Mighty Hudson. By Albert W. Atwood. 1-36, July 1948

Minnesota Makes Ideas Pay. By Frederick G. Vosburgh. Photos by John E. Fletcher and B. Anthony Stewart. 291-336, Sept. 1949

Mr. Jefferson's Charlottesville. By Anne Revis. 553-592, May 1950

The Mohawks Scrape the Sky. By Robert L. Conly. 133-142, July 1952

Nautical Norfolk Turns to Azaleas. By William H. Nicholas. 606-614, May 1947

New England, a Modern Pilgrim's Pride. By Beverley M. Bowie. 733-796, June 1955

New Rush to Golden California. By George W. Long. 723-802, June 1954

New York State's New Main Street. By Matt C. McDade. 567-618, Nov. 1956

North Carolina, Dixie Dynamo. By Malcolm Ross. 141-183, Feb. 1962

Northwest Wonderland: Washington State. By Merle Severy. 445-493, Apr. 1960

Ohio Makes Its Own Prosperity. By Leo A. Borah. 435-484, Apr. 1955

Ontario, Pivot of Canada's Power. By Andrew H. Brown. Photos by B. Anthony Stewart and Bates Littlehales. 823-852, Dec. 1953

Our Changing Atlantic Coastline. By Nathaniel T. Kenney. 860-887, Dec. 1962

Our Magnificent Capital City. 715-738, June 1947

Pittsburgh: Workshop of the Titans. By Albert W. Atwood. 117-144, July 1949

Portsmouth, Britannia's Sally Port. By Thomas Garner James. 513-544, Apr. 1952

Portugal's Gem of the Ocean: Madeira. By David S. Boyer. 364-394, Mar. 1959

The Post Road Today. 206-233, Aug. 1962

Puerto Rico's Seven-league Bootstraps. By Bart McDowell. 755-793, Dec. 1962

Rhododendron Glories of Southwest Scotland. By David S. Boyer. Photos by B. Anthony Stewart and author. 641-664, May 1954

Rome: Eternal City with a Modern Air. By Harnett

STEWART, B. ANTHONY: Photographer—*Continued*

T. Kane. 437-491, Apr. 1957

Roving Maryland's Cavalier Country. By William A. Kinney. 431-470, Apr. 1954

Russia as I Saw It. By Richard M. Nixon. 715-750, Dec. 1959

Sea to Lakes on the St. Lawrence. By George W. Long. Photos by B. Anthony Stewart and John E. Fletcher. 323-366, Sept. 1950

Seattle, City of Two Voices. By Anne Grosvenor Robinson. 494-513, Apr. 1960

Solving Life Secrets of the Sailfish. By Gilbert Voss. Paintings by Craig Phillips. 859-872, June 1956

A Stroll to John o'Groat's. By Isobel Wylie Hutchison. 1-48, July 1956

A Stroll to London. By Isobel Wylie Hutchison. 171-204, Aug. 1950

Trieste—Side Door to Europe. By Harnett T. Kane. 824-857, June 1956

The United Nations: Capital of the Family of Man. By Adlai E. Stevenson. Photos by B. Anthony Stewart and John E. Fletcher. 297-303, Sept. 1961

Vacation Tour Through Lincoln Land. By Ralph Gray. 141-184, Feb. 1952

Washington's Historic Georgetown. By William A. Kinney. 513-544, Apr. 1953

We're Coming Over on the *Mayflower*. By Alan Villiers. 708-728, May 1957

Williamsburg: Its College and Its Cinderella City. By Beverley M. Bowie. 439-486, Oct. 1954

Wonderland in Longwood Gardens (Du Pont Estate). By Edward C. Ferriday, Jr. 45-64, July 1951

You and the Obedient Atom. By Allan C. Fisher, Jr. 303-353, Sept. 1958

STEWART, RICHARD H.: Photographer:

Eclipse Hunting in Brazil's Ranchland. By F. Barrows Colton. Photos by Richard H. Stewart and Guy W. Starling. 285-324, Sept. 1947

Exploring Ancient Panama by Helicopter. By Matthew W. Stirling. 227-246, Feb. 1950

Exploring the Past in Panama. By Matthew W. Stirling. 373-399, Mar. 1949

Hunting Prehistory in Panama Jungles. By Matthew W. Stirling. 271-290, Aug. 1953

On the Trail of La Venta Man. By Matthew W. Stirling. 137-172, Feb. 1947
    Hunting Mexico's Buried Temples. 145-168

Seeking the Secret of the Giants (Gravel Figures). By Frank M. Setzler. 390-404, Sept. 1952

Solving the Riddle of Chubb Crater (Quebec). By V. Ben Meen. 1-32, Jan. 1952

STILTS (Birds):

The Dauntless Little Stilt. By Frederick Kent Truslow. 241-245, Aug. 1960

STIMSON, PAUL C.: Author:

'Round the Horn by Submarine. 129-144, Jan. 1948

STIRLING, MATTHEW W.: Author:

Exploring Ancient Panama by Helicopter. Photos by Richard H. Stewart. 227-246, Feb. 1950

Exploring the Past in Panama. Photos by Richard H. Stewart. 373-399, Mar. 1949

Hunting Prehistory in Panama Jungles. Photos by

STIRLING, MATTHEW W.: Author—*Continued*

Richard H. Stewart. 271-290, Aug. 1953

Indians of the Far West (United States). Paintings by W. Langdon Kihn. 175-200, Feb. 1948

Nomads of the Far North. Paintings by W. Langdon Kihn. 471-504, Oct. 1949

On the Trail of La Venta Man. Photos by Richard H. Stewart. 137-172, Feb. 1947

Solving the Mystery of Mexico's Great Stone Spheres. Photos by David F. Cupp. 295-300, Aug. 1969

STOCKHOLM, Sweden:

Baltic Cruise of the *Caribbee.* By Carleton Mitchell. 605-646, Nov. 1950

Stockholm, Where "Kvalitet" Is a Way of Life. By James Cerruti. Photos by Albert Moldvay and Jonathan Blair. 43-69, Jan. 1976

Sweden, Quiet Workshop for the World. By Andrew H. Brown. 451-491, Apr. 1963

Thumbs Up Round the North Sea's Rim. By Frances James. Photos by Erica Koch. 685-704, May 1952

See also Vasa

STONE. *See* Marble; Rocks

STONE AGE. *See* Eskimos (Vanished Mystery Men); Ice Age Man; Russell Cave, Alabama

STONE AGE PEOPLES of Today. *See* Arnhem Land; Cinta Larga Indians; Kreen-Akarores; Negritos; New Guinea; Tasaday Tribe; Xingu National Park

STONE SPHERES:

Solving the Mystery of Mexico's Great Stone Spheres. By Matthew W. Stirling. Photos by David F. Cupp. 295-300, Aug. 1969

STONEHENGE—New Light on an Old Riddle. By Harold E. Edgerton. Paintings by Brian Hope-Taylor. 846-866, June 1960

STONES, Precious and Semiprecious. *See* Gems

STONEY INDIANS:

On the Ridgepole of the Rockies. By Walter Meayers Edwards. 745-780, June 1947

STOP-AND-GO Sail Around South Norway. By Edmond J. Moran. Photos by Randi Kjekstad Bull and Andrew H. Brown. 153-192, Aug. 1954

STORES. *See* Markets and Stores; *and* names of cities

STORIED Lands of Malaysia. By Maurice Shadbolt. Photos by Winfield Parks. 734-783, Nov. 1963

STORKS:

Our Only Native Stork, the Wood Ibis. By Robert Porter Allen. Photos by Frederick Kent Truslow. 294-306, Feb. 1964

White Storks, Vanishing Sentinels of the Rooftops. By Roger Tory Peterson. 838-853, June 1962

STORMS:

Our Changing Atlantic Coastline (U. S.). By Nathaniel T. Kenney. Photos by B. Anthony Stewart. 860-887, Dec. 1962

We're Doing Something About the Weather! By Walter Orr Roberts. 518-555, Apr. 1972

See also Hurricanes; Monsoons; *and* Okinawa, for typhoons

STRACHAN, ROBIN: Author:

With the Nuba Hillmen of Kordofan. 249-278, Feb. 1951

STRANGE Animals of Australia. By David Fleay. Photos by Stanley Breeden. 388-411, Sept. 1963

STRANGE Babies of the Sea. By Hilary B. Moore. Paintings by Craig Phillips and Jacqueline Hutton. 41-56, July 1952

STRANGE Courtship of Birds of Paradise. By S. Dillon Ripley. Paintings by Walter A. Weber. 247-278, Feb. 1950

STRANGE Courtship of the Cock-of-the-Rock. By E. Thomas Gilliard. 134-140, Jan. 1962

STRANGE Little World of the Hoatzin. By J. Lear Grimmer. Photos by M. Woodbridge Williams. 391-401, Sept. 1962

STRANGE March of the Spiny Lobster. By William F. Herrnkind. Photos by Rick Frehsee and Bruce Mounier. 819-831, June 1975

The STRANGEST Sea. By Eugenie Clark. Photos by David Doubilet. 338-343, Sept. 1975

STRASBOURG, France:

The Rhine: Europe's River of Legend. By William Graves. Photos by Bruce Dale. 449-499, Apr. 1967

STRATEGIC AIR COMMAND (SAC):

Of Planes and Men (U. S. Air Force). By Kenneth F. Weaver. Photos by Emory Kristof and Albert Moldvay. 298-349, Sept. 1965

School for Survival. By Curtis E. LeMay. 565-602, May 1953

See also DEW Line

STRATFORD-UPON-AVON, England:

The Britain That Shakespeare Knew. By Louis B. Wright. Photos by Dean Conger. 613-665, May 1964

STRATOBOWL, South Dakota. *See Explorer II; Strato-Lab* (To 76,000 Feet)

STRATO-LAB (Balloon):

To 76,000 Feet by *Strato-Lab* Balloon. By Malcolm D. Ross and M. Lee Lewis. 269-282, Feb. 1957

We Saw the World From the Edge of Space. By Malcolm D. Ross. Ground photos by Walter Meayers Edwards. 671-685, Nov. 1961

STRIFE-TORN Indochina. By W. Robert Moore. 499-510, Oct. 1950

STRIP MINING:

Illinois—Healthy Heart of the Nation. By Leo A. Borah. Photos by B. Anthony Stewart and Willard R. Culver. 781-820, Dec. 1953

The People of Cumberland Gap. By John Fetterman. Photos by Bruce Dale. 591-621, Nov. 1971

Should They Build a Fence Around Montana? By Mike W. Edwards. Photos by Nicholas deVore III. 614-649, May 1976

This Land of Ours—How Are We Using It? By Peter T. White. Photos by Emory Kristof. 20-67, July 1976

Will Coal Be Tomorrow's "Black Gold"? By Gordon Young. Photos by James P. Blair. 234-259, Aug. 1975

A **STROLL** to John o' Groat's. By Isobel Wylie Hutchison. 1-48, July 1956

A **STROLL** to London. By Isobel Wylie Hutchison. Photos by B. Anthony Stewart. 171-204, Aug. 1950

A **STROLL** to Venice. By Isobel Wylie Hutchison. 378-410, Sept. 1951
    Note: The author trekked from Innsbruck, Austria, through the Tyrol and Dolomites, to Venice, Italy.

STRONG, ARLINE: Author-Photographer:
Seashore Summer. 436-444, Sept. 1960

STRONG, WILLIAM DUNCAN: Author:
Finding the Tomb of a Warrior-God. Photos by Clifford Evans, Jr. 453-482, Apr. 1947

STROUD, W. G.: Author:
Our Earth as a Satellite Sees It. 293-302, Aug. 1960

STRUM, SHIRLEY C.: Author:
Life with the "Pumphouse Gang": New Insights Into Baboon Behavior. Photos by Timothy W. Ransom. 672-691, May 1975

STRUTT, JOHN WILLIAM (Third Baron Rayleigh):
The British Way. By Sir Evelyn Wrench. 421-541, Apr. 1949

STUART, GEORGE E.: Author:
The Maya: Riddle of the Glyphs. Photos by Otis Imboden. 768-791, Dec. 1975

Who Were the "Mound Builders"? 783-801, Dec. 1972

STUBENRAUCH, ROBERT: Photographer:
Okinawa, Pacific Outpost. 538-552, Apr. 1950

STUDENTS:
Helping Holland Rebuild Her Land. By Gilbert M. Grosvenor and Charles Neave. 365-413, Sept. 1954

Norway Cracks Her Mountain Shell. By Sydney Clark. Photos by Gilbert H. Grosvenor and Ole Friele Backer. 171-211, Aug. 1948
See also Experiment in International Living; Schools; Universities and Colleges; YWCA

STUDYING Grizzly Habitat by Satellite. By John Craighead. 148-158, July 1976

STUDYING Wildlife by Satellite. By Frank Craighead, Jr. and John Craighead. 120-123, Jan. 1973

SUB-IGLOO (Underwater Workshop):
Diving Beneath Arctic Ice. By Joseph B. MacInnis. Photos by William R. Curtsinger. 248-267, Aug. 1973

SUBMARINES:
From Indian Canoes to Submarines at Key West. By Frederick Simpich. Photos by J. Baylor Roberts. 41-72, Jan. 1950

Our Navy's Long Submarine Arm. By Allan C. Fisher, Jr. 613-636, Nov. 1952

Pacific Fleet: Force for Peace. By Franc Shor. Photos by W. E. Garrett. 283-335, Sept. 1959
    Included: *Grayback, Gudgeon, Sterlet*
See also Sea Robin; and Submarines

SUBMARINES, Nuclear-powered:
Four-ocean Navy in the Nuclear Age. By Thomas

SUBMARINES, Nuclear-powered—*Continued*
W. McKnew. 145-187, Feb. 1965
    Included: *Nautilus, Shark, Skate, Triton*

Man's New Servant, the Friendly Atom. By F. Barrows Colton. Photos by Volkmar Wentzel. 71-90, Jan. 1954
    Included: *Nautilus, Seawolf*

Our Nuclear Navy. By George W. Anderson, Jr. 449-450, Mar. 1963

You and the Obedient Atom. By Allan C. Fisher, Jr. 303-353, Sept. 1958
    Included: *Nautilus, Seawolf*
See also Nautilus; Skate; Thresher; Triton

SUBMERSIBLES:
Diving Saucer *(Denise)* Takes to the Deep. By Jacques-Yves Cousteau. 571-586, Apr. 1960

Project FAMOUS. 586-615, May 1975
    I. Where the Earth Turns Inside Out. By J. R. Heirtzler. Photos by Emory Kristof. 586-603
    II. Dive Into the Great Rift. By Robert D. Ballard. Photos by Emory Kristof. 604-615
    Included: *Alvin, Archimède, Cyana*

Window on Earth's Interior. By Robert D. Ballard. Photos by Emory Kristof. 228-249, Aug. 1976
See also Asherah; Bathyscaphs; DS-2; Deep Diver; Deepstar; Denise; Submarines

SUDAN:
Africa: Countries of the Nile, Atlas series supplement. Oct. 1963

Journey Into the Great Rift: the Northern Half. By Helen and Frank Schreider. 254-290, Aug. 1965

Kayaks Down the Nile. By John M. Goddard. 697-732, May 1955

Locusts: "Teeth of the Wind." By Robert A. M. Conley. Photos by Gianni Tortoli. 202-227, Aug. 1969

Proud Primitives, the Nuba People. By Oskar Luz. Photos by Horst Luz. 673-699, Nov. 1966

Safari from Congo to Cairo. By Elsie May Bell Grosvenor. Photos by Gilbert Grosvenor. 721-771, Dec. 1954

South in the Sudan. By Harry Hoogstraal. 249-272, Feb. 1953
See also Kordofan; Nubia (Region)

SUEHSDORF, ADOLPH: Author:
The Cats in Our Lives. Photos by Walter Chandoha. 508-541, Apr. 1964

SUEZ CANAL:
An Engineer's View of the Suez Canal. By Glen E. Edgerton. 123-140, Jan. 1957

New Life for the Troubled Suez Canal. By William Graves. Photos by Jonathan Blair. 792-817, June 1975

The Spotlight Swings to Suez. By W. Robert Moore. 105-115, Jan. 1952

SUGAR, JAMES A.: Author-Photographer:
The Family Farm Ain't What It Used to Be. 391-411, Sept. 1974

Starfish Threaten Pacific Reefs. 340-353, Mar. 1970

Trucks Race the Clock From Coast to Coast. 226-243, Feb. 1974
                    Photographer
Easter Greetings From the Ukrainians. By Robert Paul Jordan. 556-563, Apr. 1972

SUGAR, JAMES A.: Photographer—*Continued*

Ethiopia's Artful Weavers. By Judith Olmstead. 125-141, Jan. 1973

Florida's Manatees, Mermaids in Peril. By Daniel S. Hartman. 342-353, Sept. 1969

The Friendly Irish. By John Scofield. 354-391, Sept. 1969

North With the Wheat Cutters. By Noel Grove. 194-217, Aug. 1972

Provence, Empire of the Sun. By William Davenport. 692-715, May 1975

Sailing Iceland's Rugged Coasts. By Wright Britton. 228-265, Aug. 1969

Spain's Sun-blest Pleasure Isles. By Ethel A. Starbird. 679-701, May 1976

SUGAR INDUSTRY:

Barbados, Outrider of the Antilles. By Charles Allmon. 363-392, Mar. 1952

Because It Rains on Hawaii. By Frederick Simpich, Jr. 571-610, Nov. 1949

Cuba—American Sugar Bowl. By Melville Bell Grosvenor. 1-56, Jan. 1947

Growing Pains Beset Puerto Rico. By William H. Nicholas. Photos by Justin Locke. 419-460, Apr. 1951

Hawaii, U.S.A. By Frederick Simpich, Jr. Photos by Thomas Nebbia. 1-45, July 1960

Land of Louisiana Sugar Kings. By Harnett T. Kane. Photos by Willard R. Culver. 531-567, Apr. 1958

Mauritius, Island of the Dodo. By Quentin Keynes. 77-104, Jan. 1956

Puerto Rico's Seven-league Bootstraps. By Bart McDowell. Photos by B. Anthony Stewart. 755-793, Dec. 1962

See also Maple Sugar and Syrup

SUGAR Weather in the Green Mountains. By Stephen Greene. Photos by Robert F. Sisson. 471-482, Apr. 1954

SULAWESI (Island), Indonesia:

Life and Death in Tana Toradja. By Pamela and Alfred Meyer. 793-815, June 1972

SULLIVAN, SIR ARTHUR:

The British Way. By Sir Evelyn Wrench. 421-541, Apr. 1949

SULU ARCHIPELAGO, Philippines:

Sea Gypsies of the Philippines. By Anne de Henning Singh. Photos by Raghubir Singh. 659-677, May 1976

SUMATRA (Island), Indonesia:

Indonesia, the Young and Troubled Island Nation. By Helen and Frank Schreider. 579-625, May 1961

Republican Indonesia Tries Its Wings. By W. Robert Moore. 1-40, Jan. 1951

This Young Giant, Indonesia. By Beverley M. Bowie. Photos by J. Baylor Roberts. 351-392, Sept. 1955

SUMERIANS (People):

Ancient Mesopotamia: A Light That Did Not Fail. By E. A. Speiser. Paintings by H. M. Herget. 41-105, Jan. 1951

SUMMER INSTITUTE OF GLACIOLOGICAL AND ARCTIC SCIENCES, Alaska:

Alaska's Mighty Rivers of Ice. By Maynard M. Miller. Photos by Christopher G. Knight. 194-217, Feb. 1967

SUMNER, U.S.S. (Survey Ship):

Adventures with the Survey Navy. By Irving Johnson. 131-148, July 1947

SUN:

The Incredible Universe. By Kenneth F. Weaver. Photos by James P. Blair. 589-625, May 1974

Skylab, Outpost on the Frontier of Space. By Thomas Y. Canby. 441-469, Oct. 1974

Solar Eclipse, Nature's Super Spectacular. By Donald H. Menzel and Jay M. Pasachoff. 222-233, Aug. 1970

The Sun. By Herbert Friedman. 713-743, Nov. 1965

The Sun As Never Seen Before. By Edward G. Gibson. 494-503, Oct. 1974

Unlocking Secrets of the Northern Lights. By Carl W. Gartlein. Paintings by William Crowder. 673-704, Nov. 1947

See also Eclipses; Photosynthesis; Solar Energy

SUNAPEE LAKE, New Hampshire:

Lake Sunapee's Golden Trout. Photos by Robert F. Sisson. 529-536, Oct. 1950

A SUNKEN Japanese Fleet Becomes a Scientific Laboratory: Truk Lagoon. By Sylvia A. Earle. Photos by Al Giddings. 578-613, May 1976

SUNNY Corsica: French Morsel in the Mediterranean. By Robert Cairns. Photos by Joseph J. Scherschel. 401-423, Sept. 1973

SUPERFORTRESSES:

Flying in the "Blowtorch" Era. By Frederick G. Vosburgh. 281-322, Sept. 1950
Included: B-29; B-50

Operation Eclipse: 1948. By William A. Kinney. 325-372, Mar. 1949

SUPERIOR, Lake, Canada-U. S.:

The Great Lakes: Is It Too Late? By Gordon Young. Photos by James L. Amos and Martin Rogers. 147-185, Aug. 1973

Work-hard, Play-hard Michigan. By Andrew H. Brown. 279-320, Mar. 1952

SUPERPORTS, Tanker:

Nova Scotia, the Magnificent Anchorage. By Charles McCarry. Photos by Gordon W. Gahan. 334-363, Mar. 1975
Included: Gulf Oil deepwater port

Oil, the Dwindling Treasure. By Noel Grove. Photos by Emory Kristof. 792-825, June 1974
Included: Plans for superports in Alabama, Louisiana, Texas

SUPPLEMENTS. *See* Map Supplements; Painting Supplements; Photo Supplements

SURINAM:

World-roaming Teen-ager Sails On. By Robin Lee Graham. 449-493, Apr. 1969

SURPRISE CREEK HUTTERITE COLONY, Montana:

The Hutterites, Plain People of the West. By William Albert Allard. 98-125, July 1970

SURPRISING Switzerland. By Jean and Franc Shor. 427-478, Oct. 1956

SURTSEY (Island), North Atlantic Ocean:
Surtsey: Island Born of Fire. By Sigurdur Thorarinsson. 713-726, May 1965

"SURVEY NAVY":
Adventures with the Survey Navy. By Irving Johnson. 131-148, July 1947

SURVEY SHIP, U. S. See Sumner, U.S.S.

SURVEYOR SPACECRAFT:
Surveyor: Candid Camera on the Moon. By Homer E. Newell. 578-592, Oct. 1966
That Orbèd Maiden . . . the Moon. By Kenneth F. Weaver. 207-230, Feb. 1969

SURVIVAL TRAINING:
Journey to the Outer Limits (Television film). 150A-150B, Jan. 1974
    Contents: Outward Bound School
The Making of an Astronaut. By Robert R. Gilruth. 122-144, Jan. 1965
Nevada Learns to Live with the Atom. By Samuel W. Matthews. 839-850, June 1953
Philmont Scout Ranch Helps Boys Grow Up. By Andrew H. Brown. 399-416, Sept. 1956
School for Survival. By Curtis E. LeMay. 565-602, May 1953
We Survive on a Pacific Atoll. By John and Frank Craighead. 73-94, Jan. 1948
Wind River Range: Many-treasured Splendor. By Joseph Judge. 198-205, Feb. 1974
See also Wild Foods

SUSQUEHANNA (River), New York-Pennsylvania-Maryland:
Down the Susquehanna by Canoe. By Ralph Gray. Photos by Walter Meayers Edwards. 73-120, July 1950

SUTHERLAND, MASON: Author:
Adobe New Mexico. Photos by Justin Locke. 783-830, Dec. 1949
Californians Escape to the Desert. Photos by Charles W. Herbert. 675-724, Nov. 1957
Carlsbad Caverns in Color. Photos by E. "Tex" Helm. 433-468, Oct. 1953
Carnival in San Antonio. Photos by J. Baylor Roberts. 813-844, Dec. 1947
From Tucson to Tombstone (Arizona). 343-384, Sept. 1953
Mexico's Booming Capital. Photos by Justin Locke. 785-824, Dec. 1951
Sonora (Mexico) Is Jumping. 215-246, Feb. 1955

SUYÁ INDIANS:
Brazil's Big-lipped Indians. By Harald Schultz. 118-133, Jan. 1962

SVALBARD (Archipelago), Arctic Ocean:
Polar Bear: Lonely Nomad of the North. By Thor Larsen. 574-590, Apr. 1971
Spitsbergen Mines Coal Again. 113-120, July 1948

The SWALLOW-TAILED KITE: Graceful Aerialist of the Everglades. 496-505, Oct. 1972

SWAMPS. See Big Cypress Swamp; Northern Territory, Australia; Okefenokee; Pine Barrens

SWANS:
The Swans of Abbotsbury (England). By Michael Moynihan. Photos by Barnet Saidman. 563-570, Oct. 1959
See also Trumpeter Swans; Whistling Swans

SWAT (State), Pakistan:
Pakistan, New Nation in an Old Land. By Jean and Franc Shor. 637-678, Nov. 1952

SWATEK, PHILLIP M.: Author:
Rugged Is the Word for Bravo. 829-843, Dec. 1955

SWAZILAND Tries Independence. By Volkmar Wentzel. 266-293, Aug. 1969

SWEDEN:
Baltic Cruise of the Caribbee. By Carleton Mitchell. 605-646, Nov. 1950
Friendly Flight to Northern Europe. By Lyndon B. Johnson. Photos by Volkmar Wentzel. 268-293, Feb. 1964
Ghost From the Depths: the Warship Vasa. By Anders Franzén. 42-57, Jan. 1962
Sweden, Quiet Workshop for the World. By Andrew H. Brown. 451-491, Apr. 1963
Thumbs Up Round the North Sea's Rim. By Frances James. Photos by Erica Koch. 685-704, May 1952
The Vikings. By Howard La Fay. Photos by Ted Spiegel. 492-541, Apr. 1970
See also Gotland; Stockholm

SWEET, O. C.: Photographer:
Busy Fairbanks Sets Alaska's Pace. By Bruce A. Wilson. 505-523, Oct. 1949

SWIMMING With Patagonia's Right Whales. By Roger Payne. Photos by William R. Curtsinger and Charles R. Nicklin, Jr. 576-587, Oct. 1972

SWINE. See Hogs and Hog Raising

SWISS COLONISTS: United States:
Deep in the Heart of "Swissconsin." By William H. Nicholas. Photos by J. Baylor Roberts. 781-800, June 1947

SWITZER, GEORGE S.: Author:
The Many-sided Diamond. 568-586, Apr. 1958
Questing for Gems. 835-863, Dec. 1971
"Rockhounds" Uncover Earth's Mineral Beauty. 631-660, Nov. 1951

SWITZERLAND:
Across the Alps in a Wicker Basket (Bernina). By Phil Walker. 117-131, Jan. 1963
The Alps: Man's Own Mountains. By Ralph Gray. Photos by Walter Meayers Edwards and William Eppridge. 350-395, Sept. 1965
"Around the World in Eighty Days." By Newman Bumstead. 705-750, Dec. 1951
    Included: Geneva; Jungfraujoch, in the Alps
Children's Village in Switzerland, Pestalozzi. Photos by Alfred Lammer. 268-282, Aug. 1959
Europe Via the Hostel Route. By Joseph Nettis. 124-154, July 1955
The Great St. Bernard Hospice Today. By George Pickow. 49-62, Jan. 1957
Little Tibet in Switzerland. By Laura Pilarski. Photos by Fred Mayer. 711-727, Nov. 1968
The Rhine: Europe's River of Legend. By William

SWITZERLAND — *Continued*

Graves. Photos by Bruce Dale. 449-499, Apr. 1967

Soaring on Skis in the Swiss Alps. By Carolyn Bennett Patterson. Photos by Kathleen Revis. 94-121, Jan. 1961

Surprising Switzerland. By Jean and Franc Shor. 427-478, Oct. 1956

Switzerland, Austria, and Northern Italy, double-sided Atlas series supplement. Sept. 1965

Switzerland, Europe's High-rise Republic. By Thomas J. Abercrombie. 68-113, July 1969

Switzerland Guards the Roof of Europe. By William H. Nicholas. Photos by Willard R. Culver. 205-246, Aug. 1950

Switzerland's Enchanted Val d'Hérens. By Georgia Engelhard Cromwell. 825-848, June 1955

Switzerland's Once-in-a-generation Festival (Vevey). By Jean and Franc Shor. 563-571, Oct. 1958

The **SWORD** and the Sermon. By Thomas J. Abercrombie. 3-45, July 1972

SYDNEY, Australia:

Australia. By Alan Villiers. 309-385, Sept. 1963

The Making of a New Australia. By Howell Walker. 233-259, Feb. 1956

New South Wales, the State That Cradled Australia. By Howell Walker. Photos by David Moore. 591-635, Nov. 1967

SYRIA:

Abraham, the Friend of God. By Kenneth MacLeish. Photos by Dean Conger. 739-789, Dec. 1966

The Arab World. 712-732, Nov. 1958

Damascus, Syria's Uneasy Eden. By Robert Azzi. 512-535, Apr. 1974

Journey Into the Great Rift: the Northern Half. By Helen and Frank Schreider. 254-290, Aug. 1965

SZECHWAN (Province), China:

Adventures in Lololand. By Rennold L. Lowy. 105-118, Jan. 1947

See also Yangtze (River and Basin)

T

T-3 (Fletcher's Ice Island), Arctic Region:

Scientists Ride Ice Islands on Arctic Odysseys. By Lowell Thomas, Jr. Photos by Ted Spiegel. 670-691, Nov. 1965

Three Months on an Arctic Ice Island. By Joseph O. Fletcher. 489-504, Apr. 1953

We Followed Peary to the Pole. By Gilbert Grosvenor and Thomas W. McKnew. 469-484, Oct. 1953

TABOOS and Magic Rule Namba Lives. By Kal Muller. 57-83, Jan. 1972

TACTICAL AIR COMMAND (TAC):

Of Planes and Men. By Kenneth F. Weaver. Photos by Emory Kristof and Albert Moldvay. 298-349, Sept. 1965

TAFT, WILLIAM HOWARD:

Profiles of the Presidents: IV. America Enters the Modern Era. By Frank Freidel. 537-577, Oct. 1965

TAHITI (Island), Society Islands:

Captain Cook: The Man Who Mapped the Pacific. By Alan Villiers. Photos by Gordon W. Gahan. 297-349, Sept. 1971

Huzza for Otaheite! By Luis Marden. 435-459, Apr. 1962

In the Wake of Darwin's *Beagle.* By Alan Villiers. Photos by James L. Stanfield. 449-495, Oct. 1969

Tahiti, "Finest Island in the World." By Luis Marden. 1-47, July 1962

The *Yankee's* Wander-world. By Irving and Electa Johnson. 1-50, Jan. 1949

TAIF, Saudi Arabia:

Saudi Arabia, Oil Kingdom. Photos by Maynard Owen Williams. 497-512, Apr. 1948

TAIPEI, Taiwan:

Taiwan: The Watchful Dragon. By Helen and Frank Schreider. 1-45, Jan. 1969

TAIWAN (Formosa):

Changing Formosa, Green Island of Refuge. By Frederick Simpich, Jr. Photos by Horace Bristol. 327-364, Mar. 1957

China, Atlas series supplement. Nov. 1964

Eyes on the China Coast. By George W. Long. 505-512, Apr. 1953

Formosa — Hot Spot of the East. By Frederick G. Vosburgh. Photos by J. Baylor Roberts. 139-176, Feb. 1950

Our Navy in the Far East. By Arthur W. Radford. Photos by J. Baylor Roberts. 537-577, Oct. 1953

Taiwan: The Watchful Dragon. By Helen and Frank Schreider. 1-45, Jan. 1969

See also Formosa Strait; Pescadores

TAIYALS (Aborigines):

Formosa — Hot Spot of the East. By Frederick G. Vosburgh. Photos by J. Baylor Roberts. 139-176, Feb. 1950

TA'IZZ, Yemen:

Behind the Veil of Troubled Yemen. By Thomas J. Abercrombie. 403-445, Mar. 1964

TAJ MAHAL, Agra, India:

Around the World and the Calendar with the Geographic: The President's Annual Message. By Melville Bell Grosvenor. 832-866, Dec. 1959

"Around the World in Eighty Days." By Newman Bumstead. 705-750, Dec. 1951

From the Hair of Siva (Ganges River). By Helen and Frank Schreider. 445-503, Oct. 1960

India in Crisis. By John Scofield. 599-661, May 1963

When the President Goes Abroad (Eisenhower Tour). By Gilbert M. Grosvenor. 588-649, May 1960

TAKAHE:

Finding an "Extinct" New Zealand Bird. By R. V. Francis Smith. 393-401, Mar. 1952

TAKAROA (Atoll), Tuamotu Archipelago:

Twenty Fathoms Down for Mother-of-Pearl. By Winston Williams. Photos by Bates Littlehales. 512-529, Apr. 1962

TALBOT, LEE MERRIAM: Author-Photographer:

Stalking the Great Indian Rhino. 389-398, Mar. 1957

TALBOT, PHILLIPS: Author:

Delhi, Capital of a New Dominion. 597-630, Nov. 1947

TALL-SHIPS RACE:

By Square-rigger from Baltic to Bicentennial. By Kenneth Garrett. 824-857, Dec. 1976
    Included: Training ships from Argentina, Chile, Colombia, Denmark, England, Italy, Japan, Norway, Poland, Portugal, Romania, Spain, Union of Soviet Socialist Republics, United States, West Germany

TAMPA, Florida:

America Goes to the Fair. By Samuel W. Matthews. 293-333, Sept. 1954
    Included: Florida State Fair, Gasparilla Celebration

TAMPA BAY, Gulf of Mexico:

Cruising Florida's Western Waterways. By Rube Allyn. Photos by Bates Littlehales. 49-76, Jan. 1955

TANA TORADJA (Region), Sulawesi:

Life and Death in Tana Toradja. By Pamela and Alfred Meyer. 793-815, June 1972

TANGANYIKA:

Ambassadors of Goodwill: The Peace Corps. By Sargent Shriver and Peace Corps Volunteers. 297-345, Sept. 1964
    Tanganyika. By Ruth E. Dygert. 321-323
Britain Tackles the East African Bush. By W. Robert Moore. 311-352, Mar. 1950
The Last Great Animal Kingdom. 390-409, Sept. 1960
Roaming Africa's Unfenced Zoos. By W. Robert Moore. 353-380, Mar. 1950
Spearing Lions with Africa's Masai. By Edgar Monsanto Queeny. 487-517, Oct. 1954
Weighing the Aga Khan in Diamonds. Photos by David J. Carnegie. 317-324, Mar. 1947
See also Tanzania

TANGIER ISLAND, Virginia:

This Is My Island, Tangier. By Harold G. Wheatley. Photos by David Alan Harvey. 700-725, Nov. 1973

TANJUNG PUTING RESERVE, Indonesia:

Orangutans, Indonesia's "People of the Forest." By Biruté Galdikas-Brindamour. Photos by Rod Brindamour. 444-473, Oct. 1975

TANKERS, Oil:

Oil, the Dwindling Treasure. By Noel Grove. Photos by Emory Kristof. 792-825, June 1974
See also Manhattan, S.S.; Oil Spills

TANNA (Island), New Hebrides:

Tanna Awaits the Coming of John Frum. By Kal Muller. 706-715, May 1974

TANZANIA, United Republic of:

Tanzania Marches to Its Own Drum. By Peter T. White. Photos by Emory Kristof. 474-509, Apr. 1975
See also Gombe Stream Game Reserve; Natron, Lake; Ngorongoro Crater; Olduvai Gorge; Serengeti National Park; Tanganyika; Zanzibar

TAOIST SHRINES:

Kunming Pilgrimage. 213-226, Feb. 1950

TAPESTRIES. *See* Bayeux Tapestry

TARAHUMARA INDIANS:

South to Mexico City. By W. E. Garrett. 145-193, Aug. 1968
The Tarahumaras: Mexico's Long Distance Runners. By James Norman. Photos by David Hiser. 702-718, May 1976

TARANTO, Gulf of, Italy:

Ancient Shipwreck Yields New Facts—and a Strange Cargo. By Peter Throckmorton. Photos by Kim Hart and Joseph J. Scherschel. 282-300, Feb. 1969

TARANTULAS:

What's So Special About Spiders? By Paul A. Zahl. 190-219, Aug. 1971

TARASCANS (Indians):

Lost Kingdom in Indian Mexico. By Justin Locke. 517-546, Oct. 1952
South to Mexico City. By W. E. Garrett. 145-193, Aug. 1968

TARAWA (Atoll), Gilbert Islands:

Adventures with the Survey Navy. By Irving Johnson. 131-148, July 1947

TARPON KEY, Florida:

Bad Days for the Brown Pelican. By Ralph W. Schreiber. Photos by William R. Curtsinger and author. 111-123, Jan. 1975

TARPON SPRINGS, Florida:

Sponge Fishermen of Tarpon Springs. By Jennie E. Harris. 119-136, Jan. 1947

TARSIERS:

Seeking Mindanao's Strangest Creatures. By Charles Heizer Wharton. 389-408, Sept. 1948

TASADAY TRIBE:

First Glimpse of a Stone Age Tribe. 881-882, Dec. 1971
The Last Tribes of Mindanao (Television film). 882A-882B, Dec. 1971; 227, Aug. 1972
The Tasadays, Stone Age Cavemen of Mindanao. By Kenneth MacLeish. Photos by John Launois. 219-249, Aug. 1972

TASMANIA, Australia's Island State. By Howell Walker. 791-818, Dec. 1956

TAUFAʻAHAU TUPOU IV, King (Tonga):

South Seas' Tonga Hails a King. By Melville Bell Grosvenor. Photos by Edwin Stuart Grosvenor. 322-343, Mar. 1968

TAURUS-LITTROW (Valley), Moon:

Exploring Taurus-Littrow. By Harrison H. Schmitt. 290-307, Sept. 1973

A TAXI for the Deep Frontier. By Kenneth MacLeish. Photos by Bates Littlehales. 139-150, Jan. 1968

TAYLOR, ALEXANDER: Author-Photographer:

Chessmen Come to Life in Marostica. 658-668, Nov. 1956

Photographer

By Full-rigged Ship to Denmark's Fairyland. By Alan Villiers. Photos by Alexander Taylor and author. 809-828, Dec. 1955
Paris Flea Market. By Franc Shor. 318-326, Mar. 1957

TAYLOR, VALERIE and RON: Photographers:

Australia's Great Barrier Reef. 728-741, June 1973

Exploring Australia's Coral Jungle. By Kenneth MacLeish. 743-779, June 1973

TAYLOR, ZACHARY:

Profiles of the Presidents: II. A Restless Nation Moves West. By Frank Freidel. 80-121, Jan. 1965

T'BOLI TRIBE:

Help for Philippine Tribes in Trouble. By Kenneth MacLeish. Photos by Dean Conger. 220-255, Aug. 1971

The Last Tribes of Mindanao (Television film). 882A-882B, Dec. 1971

TCHIKAO INDIANS:

Saving Brazil's Stone Age Tribes From Extinction. By Orlando and Claudio Villas Boas. Photos by W. Jesco von Puttkamer. 424-444, Sept. 1968

TE ANAU (Lake), New Zealand:

Finding an "Extinct" New Zealand Bird. By R. V. Francis Smith. 393-401, Mar. 1952

TEAL, JOHN J., Jr.: Author:

Domesticating the Wild and Woolly Musk Ox. Photos by Robert W. Madden. 862-879, June 1970

TECHNOLOGY:

Behold the Computer Revolution. By Peter T. White. Photos by Bruce Dale and Emory Kristof. 593-633, Nov. 1970

Can We Harness the Wind? By Roger Hamilton. Photos by Emory Kristof. 812-829, Dec. 1975

Crystals, Magical Servants of the Space Age. By Kenneth F. Weaver. Photos by James P. Blair. 278-296, Aug. 1968

Five Noted Thinkers Explore the Future. 68-75, July 1976

> Included: Isaac Asimov, Richard F. Babcock, Edmund N. Bacon, Buckminster Fuller, Gerard Piel

Landsat. 140-158, July 1976

I. Landsat Looks at Hometown Earth. By Barry C. Bishop. 140-147

> Contents: How the satellite photomosaic, *Portrait U.S.A.*, was made

II. Studying Grizzly Habitat by Satellite. By John Craighead. 148-158

Remote Sensing: New Eyes to See the World. By Kenneth F. Weaver. 46-73, Jan. 1969

The Revolution in American Agriculture. By Jules B. Billard. Photos by James P. Blair. 147-185, Feb. 1970

Solar Energy, the Ultimate Powerhouse. By John L. Wilhelm. Photos by Emory Kristof. 381-397, Mar. 1976

What's Happening to Our Climate? By Samuel W. Matthews. 576-615, Nov. 1976

> Included: The application of the research tools of the 1970's: advanced satellites, computers, and microscopes; laser; spectrometer

See also names of specific applied sciences; *and* Energy Sources; Space Flights and Research

TECTONA (Ketch):

Channel Cruise to Glorious Devon (England). By Alan Villiers. Photos by Bates Littlehales. 208-259, Aug. 1963

TEEMING Life of a Pond. By William H. Amos. 274-298, Aug. 1970

A **TEEN-AGER** Sails the World Alone. By Robin Lee Graham. 445-491, Oct. 1968

TEGRE PROVINCE, Ethiopia:

Searching Out Medieval Churches in Ethiopia's Wilds. By Georg Gerster. 856-884, Dec. 1970

TEHRAN, Iran:

Beside the Persian Gulf. Photos by Maynard Owen Williams. 341-356, Mar. 1947

Iran: Desert Miracle. By William Graves. Photos by James P. Blair. 2-47, Jan. 1975

Iran's Shah Crowns Himself and His Empress. By Franc Shor. Photos by James L. Stanfield and Winfield Parks. 301-321, Mar. 1968

Journey Into Troubled Iran. By George W. Long. Photos by J. Baylor Roberts. 425-464, Oct. 1951

Old-New Iran, Next Door to Russia. By Edward J. Linehan. Photos by Thomas J. Abercrombie. 44-85, Jan. 1961

We Lived in Turbulent Tehran. By Rebecca Shannon Cresson. 707-720, Nov. 1953

TEIWES, HELGA: Photographer:

The Hohokam: First Masters of the American Desert. By Emil W. Haury. 670-695, May 1967

TEKTITE II (Sea and Space Research Project):

Tektite II. 256-296, Aug. 1971

I. Science's Window on the Sea. By John G. VanDerwalker. Photos by Bates Littlehales. 256-289

II. All-girl Team Tests the Habitat. By Sylvia A. Earle. Paintings by Pierre Mion. 291-296

TEL AVIV-JAFFA, Israel:

Eyewitness to War in the Holy Land. By Charles Harbutt. 782-795, Dec. 1967

Home to the Holy Land. By Maynard Owen Williams. 707-746, Dec. 1950

Israel: Land of Promise. By John Scofield. Photos by B. Anthony Stewart. 395-434, Mar. 1965

Israel — The Seventh Day. By Joseph Judge. Photos by Gordon W. Gahan. 816-855, Dec. 1972

TELEPHONE:

Miracle Men of the Telephone. By F. Barrows Colton. 273-316, Mar. 1947

> Birthplace of Telephone Magic. Photos by Willard R. Culver. 289-312

New Miracles of the Telephone Age. By Robert Leslie Conly. 87-120, July 1954

TELEPHONE a Star: the Story of Communications Satellites. By Rowe Findley. 638-651, May 1962

TELESCOPES:

First Photographs of Planets and Moon Taken with Palomar's 200-inch Telescope. By Milton L. Humason. 125-130, Jan. 1953

The Incredible Universe. By Kenneth F. Weaver. Photos by James P. Blair. 589-625, May 1974

Mapping the Unknown Universe. By F. Barrows Colton. 401-420, Sept. 1950

> Included: "Big Schmidt" and the 200-inch Hale telescope or "Big Eye"

Pioneers in Man's Search for the Universe. Paintings by Jean-Leon Huens. Text by Thomas Y. Canby. 627-633, May 1974

See also Sky Survey; Skylab Missions

TELEVISION:

Fish Men Discover a 2,200-year-old Greek Ship. By

TELEVISION—*Continued*

Jacques-Yves Cousteau. 1-36, Jan. 1954

New Miracles of the Telephone Age. By Robert Leslie Conly. 87-120, July 1954

Your Society Observes Eclipse in Brazil. 661, May 1947

TELEVISION FILMS, NGS:

National Geographic's Newest Adventure: a Color Television Series. By Melville Bell Grosvenor. 448-452, Sept. 1965
Note: The first program was "Americans on Everest."

Announcements

Alaska! 215A-215B, Feb. 1967

Amazon. 295A-295B, Feb. 1968

Americans on Everest. 448-452, Sept. 1965; 575, Nov. 1976

America's Wonderlands: The National Parks. 549A-549B, Oct. 1968

The Animals Nobody Loved. cover, Feb. 1976

Australia: The Timeless Land. 300A-300B, Feb. 1969

The Big Cats. 442A-442B, Mar. 1974

Bushmen of the Kalahari. 578A-578B, Apr. 1973; 732A-732B, May 1974

Dr. Leakey and the Dawn of Man. 703A-703B, Nov. 1966

Ethiopia: The Hidden Empire. 884A-884B, Dec. 1970

The Great Mojave Desert. 294A-294B, Feb. 1971

Grizzly! 639A-639B, Nov. 1967

The Hidden World. 853A-853B, Dec. 1966

Holland Against the Sea. 588A-588B, Apr. 1970

The Incredible Machine. 299, Sept. 1975; cover, Oct. 1975; 583, Nov. 1975; 575, Nov. 1976

Journey to the High Arctic. 590A-590B, Apr. 1971

Journey to the Outer Limits. 150A-150B, Jan. 1974

The Last Tribes of Mindanao. 882A-882B, Dec. 1971; 227, Aug. 1972

The Last Vikings. 434A-434B, Mar. 1972

The Lonely Dorymen. 579A-579B, Apr. 1968

Man of the Serengeti. 179A-179B, Feb. 1972

Miss Goodall and the Wild Chimpanzees. 831A-831B, Dec. 1965

Monkeys, Apes, and Man. 585A-585B, Oct. 1971

The Mystery of Animal Behavior. 592A-592B, Oct. 1969

The New Indians. 575, Nov. 1976

Polynesian Adventure. 592A-592B, Apr. 1969

Reptiles and Amphibians. 875A-875B, Dec. 1968

Search for the Great Apes. cover, Jan. 1976

Siberia: The Endless Horizon. 734A-734B, Nov. 1969

Strange Creatures of the Night. 144A-144B, Jan. 1973

This Britain. 583, Nov. 1975; cover, Dec. 1975

Treasure! 575, Nov. 1976; cover, Dec. 1976

The Violent Earth. 286A-286B, Feb. 1973

The Volga. 575, Nov. 1976

The Voyage of the Brigantine *Yankee*. 265A-265B, Feb. 1966

Voyage of the *Hokule'a*. 575, Nov. 1976

Wild River. 239A-239B, Feb. 1970

Wind Raiders of the Sahara. 436A-436B, Sept. 1973

TELEVISION FILMS, NGS—*Continued*

Winged World. 877A-877B, Dec. 1967

The World of Jacques-Yves Cousteau. 529A-529B, Apr. 1966

Yankee Sails Across Europe. 469A-469B, Apr. 1967

Zoos of the World. 503A-503B, Oct. 1970

TELL EL MUTASALLIM, Israel. *See* Megiddo

TELSTAR:

Telephone a Star: the Story of Communications Satellites. By Rowe Findley. 638-651, May 1962

TEMPLE CAVES:

The Caves of the Thousand Buddhas. By Franc and Jean Shor. 383-415, Mar. 1951

India's Sculptured Temple Caves. By Volkmar Wentzel. 665-678, May 1953

See also Amarnath Cave

TEMPLES:

Computer Helps Scholars Re-create an Egyptian Temple. By Ray Winfield Smith. Photos by Emory Kristof. 634-655, Nov. 1970

Kyoto and Nara: Keepers of Japan's Past. By Charles McCarry. Photos by George F. Mobley. 836-859, June 1976
Kyoto Says Happy New Year. 852-859
Included: Chion-in, Daisen-in, Daitoku-ji, Gyo-kurin-in, Heian Shrine, Jinko-in, Todai-ji, To-ji

"Pyramids" of the New World. By Neil Merton Judd. 105-128, Jan. 1948

Republican Indonesia Tries Its Wings. By W. Robert Moore. 1-40, Jan. 1951
Included: Borobudur, Prambanan, Temple of Agriculture, and Temple of Irrigation

Thailand Bolsters Its Freedom. By W. Robert Moore. 811-849, June 1961

See also Abu Simbel; Pagodas

TENNESSEE:

Around the "Great Lakes of the South." By Frederick Simpich. Photos by J. Baylor Roberts. 463-491, Apr. 1948

Dixie Spins the Wheel of Industry. By William H. Nicholas. Photos by J. Baylor Roberts. 281-324, Mar. 1949

The Lower Mississippi. By Willard Price. Photos by W. D. Vaughn. 681-725, Nov. 1960

Pack Trip Through the Smokies. By Val Hart. Photos by Robert F. Sisson. 473-502, Oct. 1952

Skyline Trail from Maine to Georgia. By Andrew H. Brown. Photos by Robert F. Sisson. 219-251, Aug. 1949

Today Along the Natchez Trace, Pathway Through History. By Bern Keating. Photos by Charles Harbutt. 641-667, Nov. 1968

Whatever Happened to TVA? By Gordon Young. Photos by Emory Kristof. 830-863, June 1973

See also Cades Cove; Oak Ridge; Roan Mountain

TENNESSEE VALLEY AUTHORITY:

Around the "Great Lakes of the South." By Frederick Simpich. Photos by J. Baylor Roberts. 463-491, Apr. 1948

Whatever Happened to TVA? By Gordon Young. Photos by Emory Kristof. 830-863, June 1973

TENOC (Ten-year Oceanographic Program). *See* National Oceanographic Program

TENZING NORGAY:

President Eisenhower Presents the Hubbard Medal to Everest's Conquerors. 64, July 1954

Triumph on Everest. 1-63, July 1954
I. Siege and Assault. By Sir John Hunt. 1-43
II. The Conquest of the Summit. By Sir Edmund Hillary. 45-63

TEOTIHUACÁN, Mexico:

Mexico's Booming Capital. By Mason Sutherland. Photos by Justin Locke. 785-824, Dec. 1951

"Pyramids" of the New World. By Neil Merton Judd. 105-128, Jan. 1948

South to Mexico City. By W. E. Garrett. 145-193, Aug. 1968

TEPE GAWRA (Archeological Site), Iraq:

Ancient Mesopotamia: A Light That Did Not Fail. By E. A. Speiser. Paintings by H. M. Herget. 41-105, Jan. 1951

TEREDOS. See Shipworms

TERNATE (Island), Moluccas, Indonesia:

Yankee Roams the Orient. By Irving and Electa Johnson. 327-370, Mar. 1951

TERNS:

Blizzard of Birds: The Tortugas Terns. By Alexander Sprunt, Jr. 213-230, Feb. 1947
Included: Noddy Terns; Sooty Terns

Friend of the Wind: The Common Tern. By Ian Nisbet. Photos by Hope Alexander. 234-247, Aug. 1973

Sea Birds of Isla Raza. By Lewis Wayne Walker. 239-248, Feb. 1951
Included: Elegant Terns; Royal Terns

What A Place to Lay an Egg! By Thomas R. Howell. 414-419, Sept. 1971
Contents: Fairy Terns

TERRY, WILLIAM B. and GLADYS: Photographers:

Sinai Sheds New Light on the Bible. By Henry Field. 795-815, Dec. 1948

TETON RANGE, Wyoming:

Cloud Gardens in the Tetons. By Frank and John Craighead. 811-830, June 1948

See also Grand Teton National Park

TEXAS:

America Goes to the Fair. By Samuel W. Matthews. 293-333, Sept. 1954
Included: Texas State Fair at Dallas

America's "Meat on the Hoof." By William H. Nicholas. 33-72, Jan. 1952
King Ranch, Cattle Empire in Texas. 41-64

Big Thicket of Texas. By Don Moser. Photos by Blair Pittman. 504-529, Oct. 1974

Boundary changes between Texas and Mexico due to shifting of Rio Grande; El Chamizal restored to Mexico, map. 590, Apr. 1964

The Fabulous State of Texas. By Stanley Walker. Photos by B. Anthony Stewart and Thomas Nebbia. 149-195, Feb. 1961

North With the Wheat Cutters. By Noel Grove. Photos by James A. Sugar. 194-217, Aug. 1972

The Pink Birds of Texas. By Paul A. Zahl. 641-654, Nov. 1949

Roseate Spoonbills, Radiant Birds of the Gulf Coast. By Robert Porter Allen. Photos by Freder-

TEXAS — *Continued*

ick Kent Truslow. 274-288, Feb. 1962

Saving Man's Wildlife Heritage. By John H. Baker. Photos by Robert F. Sisson. 581-620, Nov. 1954
Included: Audubon sanctuaries in Texas

Skyway Below the Clouds. By Carl R. Markwith. Photos by Ernest J. Cottrell. 85-108, July 1949
Included: Abilene; Big Spring; Dallas; El Paso; Fort Worth; Guadalupe Peak; Salt Flat CAA Intermediate Field; Tyler; Wink Municipal Airport

Two Wheels Along the Mexican Border. By William Albert Allard. 591-635, May 1971

We Captured a 'Live' Brontosaur. By Roland T. Bird. 707-722, May 1954

See also Aransas National Wildlife Refuge; Big Bend National Park; Houston; Midnight Cave; San Antonio

TEXTILE INDUSTRY:

Dixie Spins the Wheel of Industry. By William H. Nicholas. Photos by J. Baylor Roberts. 281-324, Mar. 1949

The Merrimack: River of Industry and Romance. By Albert W. Atwood. Photos by B. Anthony Stewart. 106-140, Jan. 1951
Included: Cotton and wool

North Carolina, Dixie Dynamo. By Malcolm Ross. Photos by B. Anthony Stewart. 141-183, Feb. 1962

South Carolina Rediscovered. By Herbert Ravenel Sass. Photos by Robert F. Sisson. 281-321, Mar. 1953

See also Qiviut; Tweed; Weaving

THAILAND:

Around the World and the Calendar with the Geographic: The President's Annual Message. By Melville Bell Grosvenor. 832-866, Dec. 1959

"Around the World in Eighty Days." By Newman Bumstead. 705-750, Dec. 1951

Hopes and Fears in Booming Thailand. By Peter T. White. Photos by Dean Conger. 76-125, July 1967

The Lands and Peoples of Southeast Asia. 295-365, Mar. 1971
I. Mosaic of Cultures. By Peter T. White. Photos by W. E. Garrett. 296-329
II. New Light on a Forgotten Past. By Wilhelm G. Solheim II. 330-339

Living With Thailand's Gentle Lua. By Peter Kunstadter. 122-152, July 1966

The Mekong, River of Terror and Hope. By Peter T. White. Photos by W. E. Garrett. 737-787, Dec. 1968

Operation Eclipse: 1948. By William A. Kinney. 325-372, Mar. 1949

Pageantry of the Siamese Stage. By D. Sonakul. Photos by W. Robert Moore. 201-212, Feb. 1947

The Peoples of Mainland Southeast Asia; Asia, double-sided map supplement. Mar. 1971

Round the World School. By Paul Antze. Photos by William Eppridge. 96-127, July 1962

Scintillating Siam. By W. Robert Moore. 173-200, Feb. 1947

Spirits of Change Capture the Karens. By Peter Kunstadter. 267-285, Feb. 1972

Thailand Bolsters Its Freedom. By W. Robert Moore. 811-849, June 1961

Viet Nam, Cambodia, Laos, and Eastern Thailand, map supplement. Text on reverse. Jan. 1965

THAILAND—*Continued*

Viet Nam, Cambodia, Laos, and Thailand, map supplement. Feb. 1967

War and Quiet on the Laos Frontier. By W. Robert Moore. 665-680, May 1954
Included: Eastern Thailand

YWCA: International Success Story. By Mary French Rockefeller. Photos by Otis Imboden. 904-933, Dec. 1963

Yankee Roams the Orient. By Irving and Electa Johnson. 327-370, Mar. 1951

See also Bangkok

THAMES (River), England:

One Man's London. By Allan C. Fisher, Jr. Photos by James P. Blair. 743-791, June 1966

The Thames Mirrors England's Varied Life. By Willard Price. Photos by Robert F. Sisson. 45-93, July 1958

THARUS (People):

Peerless Nepal—A Naturalist's Paradise. By S. Dillon Ripley. Photos by Volkmar Wentzel. 1-40, Jan. 1950

THAT Dammed Missouri River. By Gordon Young. Photos by David Hiser. 374-413, Sept. 1971

THAT Orbèd Maiden . . . the Moon. By Kenneth F. Weaver. 207-230, Feb. 1969

THEATER:

The Britain That Shakespeare Knew. By Louis B. Wright. Photos by Dean Conger. 613-665, May 1964

The British Way. By Sir Evelyn Wrench. 421-541, Apr. 1949
Included: William Shakespeare; Sir William Gilbert and Sir Arthur Sullivan

Chelsea, London's Haven of Individualists. By James Cerruti. Photos by Adam Woolfitt. 28-55, Jan. 1972
Included: Brendan Behan, Julie Christie, R. J. Minney, Sir Laurence Olivier, John Osborne, Vanessa Redgrave, George Bernard Shaw, Dame Sybil Thorndike, Oscar Wilde

The Lights Are Up at Ford's Theatre. By Lonnelle Aikman. 392-401, Mar. 1970

Miami's Expanding Horizons. By William H. Nicholas. 561-594, Nov. 1950
Included: Barry College Dramatic Department; University of Miami Drama Department

Pageantry of the Siamese Stage. By D. Sonakul. Photos by W. Robert Moore. 201-212, Feb. 1947

Wonderland in Longwood Gardens. By Edward C. Ferriday, Jr. 45-64, July 1951
Included: Indoor and outdoor theaters

See also Folger (Library), for Elizabethan theater; Kabuki

THEBES (Ancient City), Egypt:

Computer Helps Scholars Re-create an Egyptian Temple. By Ray Winfield Smith. Photos by Emory Kristof. 634-655, Nov. 1970

THEODORE ROOSEVELT: a Centennial Tribute. By Bart McDowell. 572-590, Oct. 1958

See also Roosevelt, Theodore

THEODORE ROOSEVELT NATIONAL MEMORIAL PARK, North Dakota:

North Dakota Comes into Its Own. By Leo A.

THEODORE ROOSEVELT NATIONAL MEMORIAL PARK—*Continued*
Borah. Photos by J. Baylor Roberts. 283-322, Sept. 1951

THERA (Island), Aegean Sea:

The Isles of Greece: Aegean Birthplace of Western Culture. By Melville Bell Grosvenor. Photos by Edwin Stuart Grosvenor and Winfield Parks. 147-193, Aug. 1972

Thera, Key to the Riddle of Minos. By Spyridon Marinatos. Photos by Otis Imboden. 702-726, May 1972

THESIGER, WILFRED: Author:

Marsh Dwellers of Southern Iraq. Photos by Gavin Maxwell. 205-239, Feb. 1958

THIELEN, BENEDICT: Author:

Florida Rides a Space-age Boom. Photos by Winfield Parks and James P. Blair. 858-903, Dec. 1963

THIMPHU, Bhutan:

Bhutan Crowns a New Dragon King. Photos by John Scofield. 546-571, Oct. 1974

3RD AEROSPACE RESCUE AND RECOVERY GROUP:

Air Rescue Behind Enemy Lines. By Howard Sochurek. 346-369, Sept. 1968

THIRTY-THREE Centuries Under the Sea. By Peter Throckmorton. 682-703, May 1960

THIS Changing Earth. By Samuel W. Matthews. 1-37, Jan. 1973

THIS Is My Island, Tangier. By Harold G. Wheatley. Photos by David Alan Harvey. 700-725, Nov. 1973

THIS Is the China I Saw. By Jørgen Bisch. 591-639, Nov. 1964

THIS Is the World's Richest Nation—All of It! By Mike Holmes. 344-353, Sept. 1976

"THIS land is your land . . ." (A Portfolio). 2-11, July 1976

THIS Land of Ours (Bicentennial Issue). 1-158, July 1976

THIS Young Giant, Indonesia. By Beverley M. Bowie. Photos by J. Baylor Roberts. 351-392, Sept. 1955

THOM, JAMES ALEXANDER: Author:

Indiana's Self-reliant Uplanders. Photos by J. Bruce Baumann. 341-363, Mar. 1976

THOMAS, ELIZABETH MARSHALL: Author:

Bushmen of the Kalahari. Photos by Laurence K. Marshall and other members of the expeditions. 866-888, June 1963

THOMAS, LOWELL, Jr.: Author:

Scientists Ride Ice Islands on Arctic Odysseys. Photos by Ted Spiegel. 670-691, Nov. 1965
Author-Photographer

Flight to Adventure. By Tay and Lowell Thomas, Jr. 49-112, July 1957

Sky Road East. By Tay and Lowell Thomas, Jr. 71-112, Jan. 1960

THOMAS, MARJORY C.: Author:
Copra-ship Voyage to Fiji's Outlying Islands. 121-140, July 1950

THOMAS, TAY: Author:
An Alaskan Family's Night of Terror (Earthquake). 142-156, July 1964
Author-Photographer
Flight to Adventure. By Tay and Lowell Thomas, Jr. 49-112, July 1957
Sky Road East. By Tay and Lowell Thomas, Jr. 71-112, Jan. 1960

THOMAS, VERONICA: Author:
The Arans, Ireland's Invincible Isles. Photos by Winfield Parks. 545-573, Apr. 1971
Madeira, Like Its Wine, Improves With Age. Photos by Jonathan Blair. 488-513, Apr. 1973
The Manx and Their Isle of Man. Photos by Ted H. Funk. 426-444, Sept. 1972
The Original Boston: St. Botolph's Town (England). Photos by James L. Amos. 382-389, Sept. 1974

THOMAS JEFFERSON: Architect of Freedom. By Mike W. Edwards. Photos by Linda Bartlett. 231-259, Feb. 1976
See also Jefferson, Thomas

THOMPSON, J. CHARLES: Photographer:
Trawling the China Seas. 381-395, Mar. 1950

THOMSON, DONALD F.: Author-Photographer:
An Arnhem Land Adventure. 403-430, Mar. 1948

THOMSON, SIR J. J.:
The British Way. By Sir Evelyn Wrench. 421-541, Apr. 1949

THOR HEYERDAHL'S Own Story of Ra II. Photos by Carlo Mauri and Georges Sourial. 44-71, Jan. 1971

THORARINSSON, SIGURDUR: Author:
Surtsey: Island Born of Fire. 713-726, May 1965

THOREAU, HENRY DAVID:
Literary Landmarks of Massachusetts. By William H. Nicholas. Photos by B. Anthony Stewart and John E. Fletcher. 279-310, Mar. 1950

THOROUGHBREDS:
Heart of the Bluegrass (Kentucky). By Charles McCarry. Photos by J. Bruce Baumann. 634-659, May 1974

THOSE Fiery Brazilian Bees. By Rick Gore. Photos by Bianca Lavies. 491-501, Apr. 1976

THOSE Outlandish Goldfish! By Paul A. Zahl. 514-533, Apr. 1973

THOSE Popular Pandas. By Theodore H. Reed. Photos by Donna K. Grosvenor. 803-815, Dec. 1972

THOSE Proper and Other Bostonians. By Joseph Judge. Photos by Ted Spiegel. 352-381, Sept. 1974

THOSE Successful Japanese. By Bart McDowell. Photos by Fred Ward. 323-359, Mar. 1974

THREATENED Glories of Everglades National Park. By Frederick Kent Truslow and Frederick G. Vosburgh. Photos by Frederick Kent Truslow and Otis Imboden. 508-553, Oct. 1967

THREATENED Treasures of the Nile. By Georg Gerster. 587-621, Oct. 1963

THREE Months on an Arctic Ice Island. By Joseph O. Fletcher. 489-504, Apr. 1953

THREE Roads to Rainbow. By Ralph Gray. 547-561, Apr. 1957

THREE Whales That Flew. By Carleton Ray. Photos by W. Robert Moore. 346-359, Mar. 1962

THRESHER, U.S.S. (Submarine):
Thresher Tragedy Spurs Deep-sea Research. 759-777, June 1964
I. Lesson and Challenge. By James H. Wakelin, Jr. 759-763
II. Down to Thresher by Bathyscaph. By Donald L. Keach. 764-777

THROCKMORTON, PETER: Author:
Ancient Shipwreck Yields New Facts—and a Strange Cargo. Photos by Kim Hart and Joseph J. Scherschel. 282-300, Feb. 1969
Oldest Known Shipwreck Yields Bronze Age Cargo. 697-711, May 1962
Thirty-three Centuries Under the Sea. 682-703, May 1960

THRONE Above the Euphrates. By Theresa Goell. 390-405, Mar. 1961

THROUGH Europe by Trailer Caravan. By Norma Miller. Photos by Ardean R. Miller III. 769-816, June 1957

THROUGH Ozark Hills and Hollows. By Mike W. Edwards. Photos by Bruce Dale. 656-689, Nov. 1970

THROUGH the Northwest Passage for Oil. By Bern Keating. Photos by Tomas Sennett. 374-391, Mar. 1970

The THRUSH on the Island of Barra. By Archibald MacLeish. 692-693, May 1970

THULE AIR BASE, Greenland:
We Followed Peary to the Pole. By Gilbert Grosvenor and Thomas W. McKnew. 469-484, Oct. 1953
Weather from the White North. By Andrew H. Brown. Photos by John E. Fletcher. 543-572, Apr. 1955

THUMBS Up Round the North Sea's Rim. By Frances James. Photos by Erica Koch. 685-704, May 1952

THUNDER HILL GOAT FARM, New York:
The Goats of Thunder Hill. By Elizabeth Nicholds. Photos by Robert F. Sisson. 625-640, May 1954

THURBER, MURIEL: Photographer:
Squaws Along the Yukon. By Ginny Hill Wood. 245-265, Aug. 1957

TIBET:
Caught in the Assam-Tibet Earthquake. By F. Kingdon-Ward. 403-416, Mar. 1952
A Woman Paints the Tibetans. By Lafugie. 659-692, May 1949
See also Lhasa

TIBETANS:
A Journey to "Little Tibet" (Ladakh). By Enakshi Bhavnani. Photos by Volkmar Wentzel. 603-634, May 1951

TIBETANS—*Continued*

Little Tibet in Switzerland. By Laura Pilarski. Photos by Fred Mayer. 711-727, Nov. 1968

A Woman Paints the Tibetans. By Lafugie. 659-692, May 1949

TICONDEROGA, New York:

From Sword to Scythe in Champlain Country. By Ethel A. Starbird. Photos by B. Anthony Stewart and Emory Kristof. 153-201, Aug. 1967

North Through History Aboard *White Mist*. By Melville Bell Grosvenor. Photos by Edwin Stuart Grosvenor. 1-55, July 1970

TIDES AND TIDAL BORES:

Amazon—The River Sea. By Loren McIntyre. 456-495, Oct. 1972
Included: Amazon tidal bore, the *pororoca*

Cruising Japan's Inland Sea. By Willard Price. 619-650, Nov. 1953
Included: The tidal whirlpools of Naruto Strait

The Giant Tides of Fundy. By Paul A. Zahl. 153-192, Aug. 1957

Sea Fever. By John E. Schultz. 237-268, Feb. 1949
Included: Amazon tidal bore, the *pororoca*

Venice Fights for Life. By Joseph Judge. Photos by Albert Moldvay. 591-631, Nov. 1972

See also Blue Holes; Farne Islands; Messina, Strait of; St. Michael's Mount; Wight, Isle of

TIDEWATER AREA. *See* Chesapeake Bay

TIEMANN, DARWIN L.: Author:

Nature's Toy Train, the Railroad Worm. Photos by Robert F. Sisson. 56-67, July 1970

TIERRA DEL FUEGO (Archipelago), South America:

Argentina: Young Giant of the Far South. By Jean and Franc Shor. 297-352, Mar. 1958

Chile, the Long and Narrow Land. By Kip Ross. 185-235, Feb. 1960

Housewife at the End of the World. By Rae Natalie P. Goodall. Photos by James L. Stanfield. 130-150, Jan. 1971

In the Wake of Darwin's *Beagle*. By Alan Villiers. Photos by James L. Stanfield. 449-495, Oct. 1969

TIGERS:

Enchantress! (White Tigress). By Theodore H. Reed. Photos by Thomas J. Abercrombie. 628-641, May 1961

India Struggles to Save Her Wildlife. By John J. Putman. 299-343, Sept. 1976

White Tiger in My House. By Elizabeth C. Reed. Photos by Donna K. Grosvenor. 482-491, Apr. 1970

TIHWA, Sinkiang. *See* Urumchi

TIJUANA, Mexico:

Two Wheels Along the Mexican Border. By William Albert Allard. 591-635, May 1971

TIKAL (Maya Ruin), Guatemala:

Guatemala, Maya and Modern. By Louis de la Haba. Photos by Joseph J. Scherschel. 661-689, Nov. 1974

The Maya. 729-811, Dec. 1975
III. Resurrecting the Grandeur of Tikal. By William R. Coe. 792-798
IV. A Traveler's Tale of Ancient Tikal. Paintings by Peter Spier. Text by Alice J. Hall. 799-811

TIKOPIA (Island), Santa Cruz Islands:

Yankee Roams the Orient. By Irving and Electa Johnson. 327-370, Mar. 1951

TIMBER: How Much Is Enough? By John J. Putman. Photos by Bruce Dale. 485-511, Apr. 1974

TIME Turns Back in Picture-book Portofino. By Carleton Mitchell. Photos by Winfield Parks. 232-253, Feb. 1965

TIMEKEEPING:

Split-second Time Runs Today's World. By F. Barrows Colton and Catherine Bell Palmer. 399-428, Sept. 1947

The Tower of the Winds. By Derek J. de Solla Price. Paintings by Robert C. Magis. 587-596, Apr. 1967

TIMOR (Island), Malay Archipelago:

East From Bali by Seagoing Jeep to Timor. By Helen and Frank Schreider. 236-279, Aug. 1962

TIN AND TIN MINING:

Malaya Meets Its Emergency. By George W. Long. Photos by J. Baylor Roberts. 185-228, Feb. 1953

TIN TRADE. *See* St. Michael's Mount

TINKERS, Irish. *See* Appleby Fair

TINOS (Island), Greece:

The Isles of Greece: Aegean Birthplace of Western Culture. By Melville Bell Grosvenor. Photos by Edwin Stuart Grosvenor and Winfield Parks. 147-193, Aug. 1972

TIRELESS Voyager, the Whistling Swan. By William J. L. Sladen. Photos by Bianca Lavies. 134-147, July 1975

TIROL, Austria's Province in the Clouds. By Peter T. White. Photos by Volkmar Wentzel. 107-141, July 1961
See also Tyrol

TIROS I (Weather Satellite):

Our Earth as a Satellite Sees It. By W. G. Stroud. 293-302, Aug. 1960

TITAN (Rock Spire), Fisher Towers, Utah:

We Climbed Utah's Skyscraper Rock. By Huntley Ingalls. Photos by author and Barry C. Bishop. 705-721, Nov. 1962

TITAN II (Rocket). *See* Gemini Missions

TITICACA, Lake, Bolivia-Peru:

Flamboyant Is the Word for Bolivia. By Loren McIntyre. 153-195, Feb. 1966

The Lost Empire of the Incas. By Loren McIntyre. Art by Ned and Rosalie Seidler. 729-787, Dec. 1973

Sky-high Bolivia. 481-496, Oct. 1950

Titicaca, Abode of the Sun. By Luis Marden. Photos by Flip Schulke. 272-294, Feb. 1971

TITO, JOSIP BROZ:

Yugoslavia: Six Republics in One. By Robert Paul Jordan. Photos by James P. Blair. 589-633, May 1970

Yugoslavia's Window on the Adriatic. By Gilbert M. Grosvenor. 219-247, Feb. 1962

TIVOLI, Copenhagen, Denmark:

Copenhagen, Wedded to the Sea. By Stuart E. Jones. Photos by Gilbert M. Grosvenor. 45-79, Jan. 1963

Denmark, Field of the Danes. By William Graves. Photos by Thomas Nebbia. 245-275, Feb. 1974

TIWI (People):

Expedition to the Land of the Tiwi. By Charles P. Mountford. 417-440, Mar. 1956

TLINGIT INDIANS:

Alaska's Marine Highway: Ferry Route to the North. By W. E. Garrett. 776-819, June 1965

TO Europe with a Racing Start. By Carleton Mitchell. 758-791, June 1958

TO Gilbert Grosvenor: a Monthly Monument 25 Miles High. By Frederick G. Vosburgh and the staff of the National Geographic Society. 445-487, Oct. 1966

TO 76,000 Feet by *Strato-Lab* Balloon. By Malcolm D. Ross and M. Lee Lewis. 269-282, Feb. 1957

TO the Depths of the Sea by Bathyscaphe. By Jacques-Yves Cousteau. 67-79, July 1954

TO the Land of the Head-hunters. By E. Thomas Gilliard. 437-486, Oct. 1955

TO the Memory of Our Beloved President, Friend to All Mankind. 1A-1B, Jan. 1964

TO the Men at South Pole Station. By Richard E. Byrd. 1-4, July 1957

TO the Mountains of the Moon. By Kenneth F. Weaver. Photos from NASA. 233-265, Feb. 1972

TO Torre Egger's Icy Summit. By Jim Donini. 813-823, Dec. 1976

TOADS:

Voices of the Night. By Arthur A. Allen. 507-522, Apr. 1950
Included: Canadian toad, Common toad, Common tree toad, Oak toad, Spadefoot toad, Western toad

TOADSTOOLS:

Bizarre World of the Fungi. By Paul A. Zahl. 502-527, Oct. 1965

TOBACCO GROWING:

Cuba—American Sugar Bowl. By Melville Bell Grosvenor. 1-56, Jan. 1947

Heart of the Bluegrass. By Charles McCarry. Photos by J. Bruce Baumann. 634-659, May 1974

North Carolina, Dixie Dynamo. By Malcolm Ross. Photos by B. Anthony Stewart. 141-183, Feb. 1962

Yesterday Lingers Along the Connecticut. By Charles McCarry. Photos by David L. Arnold. 334-369, Sept. 1972

TOBAGO (Island), West Indies:

Feathered Dancers of Little Tobago. By E. Thomas Gilliard. Photos by Frederick Kent Truslow. 428-440, Sept. 1958

Happy-go-lucky Trinidad and Tobago. By Charles Allmon. 35-75, Jan. 1953

TODAY Along the Natchez Trace, Pathway Through History. By Bern Keating. Photos by Charles Harbutt. 641-667, Nov. 1968

TODAY and Tomorrow in Our National Parks. By Melville Bell Grosvenor. 1-5, July 1966

TODAY on the Delaware, Penn's Glorious River. By Albert W. Atwood. Photos by Robert F. Sisson. 1-40, July 1952

TODD, BURT KERR: Author-Photographer:

Bhutan, Land of the Thunder Dragon. 713-754, Dec. 1952

TOKYO, Japan:

Japan, the Exquisite Enigma. By Franc Shor. 733-777, Dec. 1960

Japan Tries Freedom's Road. By Frederick G. Vosburgh. Photos by J. Baylor Roberts. 593-632, May 1950

Operation Eclipse: 1948. By William A. Kinney. 325-372, Mar. 1949
Note: Tokyo's location error was discovered by expedition scientists.

Those Successful Japanese. By Bart McDowell. Photos by Fred Ward. 323-359, Mar. 1974

Tokyo, the Peaceful Explosion. By William Graves. Photos by Winfield Parks. 445-487, Oct. 1964

TOKYO BAY, Japan:

The Yankee Sailor Who Opened Japan. By Ferdinand Kuhn. 85-102, July 1953

TOLLUND MAN:

Lifelike Man Preserved 2,000 Years in Peat. By P. V. Glob. 419-430, Mar. 1954

TOLTEC CULTURE. *See* Teotihuacán

TOM SAWYER'S Town. By Jerry Allen. 121-140, July 1956

TOMBS:

An Archeologist Looks at Palestine. By Nelson Glueck. 739-752, Dec. 1947

Finding the Tomb of a Warrior-God. By William Duncan Strong. Photos by Clifford Evans, Jr. 453-482, Apr. 1947

Fresh Treasures from Egypt's Ancient Sands. By Jefferson Caffery. Photos by David S. Boyer. 611-650, Nov. 1955

See also Arlington National Cemetery; Etruscans; Han Dynasty Tombs; La Venta; Maya; Petra; Tutankhamun; Ur

TOMBSTONE, Arizona:

From Tucson to Tombstone. By Mason Sutherland. 343-384, Sept. 1953

TOMORROW on the Deep Frontier. By Edwin A. Link. 778-801, June 1964

TONGA:

Coronations a World Apart. By the Editor. 299, Mar. 1968

The Friendly Isles of Tonga. By Luis Marden. 345-367, Mar. 1968

Problems in Paradise. By Mary and Laurance S. Rockefeller. Photos by Thomas Nebbia. 782-793, Dec. 1974

South Seas' Tonga Hails a King. By Melville Bell Grosvenor. Photos by Edwin Stuart Grosvenor. 322-343, Mar. 1968

TONLÉ SAP (Lake and River), Cambodia:

Cambodia: Indochina's "Neutral" Corner. By

TONLÉ SAP (Lake and River), Cambodia—*Continued*
Thomas J. Abercrombie. 514-551, Oct. 1964

TOOL-USING BIRDS:
Aha! It Really Works! By Robert F. Sisson. 143-147, Jan. 1974
Note: A heron fishes with bait.

The Galapagos, Eerie Cradle of New Species. By Roger Tory Peterson. Photos by Alan and Joan Root. 541-585, Apr. 1967
Included: Tool-using finches

Tool-using Bird: The Egyptian Vulture. By Baroness Jane van Lawick-Goodall. Photos by Baron Hugo van Lawick. 631-641, May 1968

TOOL-USING MAMMALS. *See* Chimpanzees; Sea Otters

TOOLS, Primitive:
First Glimpse of a Stone Age Tribe. 881-882, Dec. 1971

The Tasadays, Stone Age Cavemen of Mindanao. By Kenneth MacLeish. Photos by John Launois. 219-249, Aug. 1972

See also Asmat; Cinta Larga Indians; Hoabinhian Culture; Ice Age Man

The **TOP** End of Down Under. By Kenneth MacLeish. Photos by Thomas Nebbia. 145-174, Feb. 1973

TOPPING, AUDREY: Author-Photographer:
Return to Changing China. 801-833, Dec. 1971

TORADJALAND (Region), Sulawesi. *See* Tana Toradja

TORCHBEARERS of the Twilight. By Frederick G. Vosburgh. 697-704, May 1951

TORIES. *See* The Loyalists

TORNADOES:
We're Doing Something About the Weather! By Walter Orr Roberts. 518-555, Apr. 1972

TORONTO, Ontario, Canada:
Canada's Dynamic Heartland, Ontario. By Marjorie Wilkins Campbell. Photos by Winfield Parks. 58-97, July 1963

Ontario, Pivot of Canada's Power. By Andrew H. Brown. Photos by B. Anthony Stewart and Bates Littlehales. 823-852, Dec. 1953

Royal Ontario Museum of Geology and Mineralogy: Expedition. *See* Chubb Crater

Toronto: Canada's Dowager Learns to Swing. By Ethel A. Starbird. Photos by Robert W. Madden. 190-215, Aug. 1975

TORRE EGGER (Mountain), Argentina-Chile:
To Torre Egger's Icy Summit. By Jim Donini. 813-823, Dec. 1976

TORRE SGARRATA EXPEDITION: Italy:
Ancient Shipwreck Yields New Facts—and a Strange Cargo. By Peter Throckmorton. Photos by Kim Hart and Joseph J. Scherschel. 282-300, Feb. 1969

TÓRSHAVN, Faeroe Islands:
The Faeroes, Isles of Maybe. By Ernle Bradford. Photos by Adam Woolfitt. 410-442, Sept. 1970

TORTOISES:
Giant Tortoises: Goliaths of the Galapagos. By

TORTOISES—*Continued*
Craig MacFarland. Photos by author and Jan MacFarland. 632-649, Nov. 1972

TORTOLI, GIANNI: Photographer:
Locusts: "Teeth of the Wind." By Robert A. M. Conley. 202-227, Aug. 1969

TORTUGA II (Amphibious Jeep):
East From Bali by Seagoing Jeep to Timor. By Helen and Frank Schreider. 236-279, Aug. 1962

From the Hair of Siva (Ganges River, India). By Helen and Frank Schreider. 445-503, Oct. 1960

Indonesia, the Young and Troubled Island Nation. By Helen and Frank Schreider. 579-625, May 1961

TORTUGAS (Islands), Florida. *See* Dry Tortugas

TORTUGUERO BEACH, Costa Rica:
Imperiled Gift of the Sea: Caribbean Green Turtle. By Archie Carr. Photos by Robert E. Schroeder. 876-890, June 1967

TOULON CANYON, Mediterranean Sea:
Diving Through an Undersea Avalanche. By Jacques-Yves Cousteau. 538-542, Apr. 1955

To the Depths of the Sea by Bathyscaphe. By Jacques-Yves Cousteau. 67-79, July 1954

TOULOUSE, France:
France's Past Lives in Languedoc. By Walter Meayers Edwards. 1-43, July 1951
Included: Academy of the Floral Games, Canal du Midi, Cathedral of St. Etienne, and St. Sernin

TOURNAMENT OF ROSES: Pasadena, California:
Focusing on the Tournament of Roses. By B. Anthony Stewart and J. Baylor Roberts. 805-816, June 1954

The **TOWER** of the Winds. By Derek J. de Solla Price. Paintings by Robert C. Magis. 587-596, Apr. 1967

TOWERS, Rock. *See* Fisher Towers, Utah

A **TOWN** . . . a Mountain . . . a Way of Life. By Jill Durrance and Dick Durrance II. 788-807, Dec. 1973

TOWNSEND, LLOYD K.: Artist:
Nature's Gifts to Medicine. By Lonnelle Aikman. Paintings by Lloyd K. Townsend and Don Crowley. 420-440, Sept. 1974

TRACKING America's Man in Orbit. By Kenneth F. Weaver. Photos by Robert F. Sisson. 184-217, Feb. 1962

TRACKING Danger With the Ice Patrol. By William S. Ellis. Photos by James R. Holland. 780-793, June 1968

TRADE:
Louisiana Trades with the World. By Frederick Simpich. Photos by J. Baylor Roberts. 705-738, Dec. 1947

Spices, the Essence of Geography. By Stuart E. Jones. 401-420, Mar. 1949

With Uncle Sam and John Bull in Germany. By Frederick Simpich. 117-140, Jan. 1949

See also Shipping

TRADE ROUTES. *See* St. Lawrence Seaway; *and* Phoenicians; Vikings

TRADEWINDS (Ketch):

Slow Boat to Florida. By Dorothea and Stuart E. Jones. 1-65, Jan. 1958

TRAFALGAR, Battle of:

The British Way. By Sir Evelyn Wrench. 421-541, Apr. 1949

Portsmouth, Britannia's Sally Port. By Thomas Garner James. Photos by B. Anthony Stewart. 513-544, Apr. 1952

TRAILING Cosmic Rays in Canada's North. By Martin A. Pomerantz. 99-115, Jan. 1953

TRAILING Yellowstone's Grizzlies by Radio. By Frank Craighead, Jr., and John Craighead. 252-267, Aug. 1966

TRAILS. *See* Appalachian Trail; Great Divide Trail; Lewis and Clark Expedition; Natchez Trace; Outlaw Trail; Pacific Crest Trail; Yukon Territory, for Yukon Trail; *and* Sheep Trek

TRAINING SHIPS:

By Full-rigged Ship to Denmark's Fairyland. By Alan Villiers. Photos by Alexander Taylor and author. 809-828, Dec. 1955
    Included: *Arken, Danmark, Georg Stage, Lilla Dan, Peder Most*

By Square-rigger from Baltic to Bicentennial. By Kenneth Garrett. 824-857, Dec. 1976
    Included: *Amerigo Vespucci, Christian Radich, Danmark, Dar Pomorza, Eagle, Esmeralda, Gazela Primeiro, Gloria, Gorch Fock, Juan Sebastián de Elcano, Kruzenshtern, Libertad, Mircea, Nippon Maru, Sagres II, Tovarishch*

See also Eagle; Midshipmen's Cruise; *and* Portsmouth; *and* listing under Merchant Marine Training Ships

TRAINS:

The Coming Revolution in Transportation. By Fredric C. Appel. Photos by Dean Conger. 301-341, Sept. 1969
    Included: Air-cushion trains, High-speed trains, Pneumatic trains, "Unit trains"

Freedom Train Tours America. 529-542, Oct. 1949

The Friendly Train Called Skunk. By Dean Jennings. Photos by B. Anthony Stewart. 720-734, May 1959

Railroads: The Great American Adventure. Special Publication announced. 860-864, June 1976

Slow Train Through Viet Nam's War. By Howard Sochurek. 412-444, Sept. 1964

See also Southern Railway System

TRANS-ANDEAN PIPELINE:

Colombia, from Amazon to Spanish Main. By Loren McIntyre. 235-273, Aug. 1970

TRANS-DARIÉN EXPEDITION:

We Drove Panama's Darién Gap. By Kip Ross. 368-389, Mar. 1961

TRANSPORTATION:

The Coming Revolution in Transportation. By Fredric C. Appel. Photos by Dean Conger. 301-341, Sept. 1969

See also specific modes of transportation

TRANS-SAHARA SAND AND LAND YACHT RALLY:

Dry-land Fleet Sails the Sahara. By Jean du

TRANS-SAHARA SAND AND LAND YACHT RALLY— *Continued*

Boucher. Photos by Jonathan S. Blair. 696-725, Nov. 1967

A TRAVELER'S Tale of Ancient Tikal. Paintings by Peter Spier. Text by Alice J. Hall. 799-811, Dec. 1975

TRAWLERS. *See* Oyster Fleet; Shrimp Fishing

TRAWLING the China Seas. Photos by J. Charles Thompson. 381-395, Mar. 1950

TREASURE, Sunken:

Bermuda—Balmy, British, and Beautiful. By Peter Benchley. Photos by Emory Kristof. 93-121, July 1971

Treasure! (Television film). 575, Nov. 1976; cover announcement, Dec. 1976

The Treasure of Porto Santo. By Robert Sténuit. Photos by author and William R. Curtsinger. 260-275, Aug. 1975

Treasures in the Sea. Children's book announced. 736-738, Nov. 1972

Undersea Treasures. Special Publication announced. 870-874, June 1974

See also Spanish Treasure

TREE FROGS:

Voices of the Night. By Arthur A. Allen. 507-522, Apr. 1950

TREE-RING DATING:

Bristlecone Pine, Oldest Known Living Thing. By Edmund Schulman. Photos by W. Robert Moore. 355-372, Mar. 1958

What's Happening to Our Climate? By Samuel W. Matthews. 576-615, Nov. 1976

TREE SHREWS:

Seeking Mindanao's Strangest Creatures. By Charles Heizer Wharton. 389-408, Sept. 1948

TREE SNAILS, Gems of the Everglades. By Treat Davidson. 372-387, Mar. 1965

TREES:

Beauty and Bounty of Southern State Trees. By William A. Dayton. Paintings by Walter A. Weber. 508-552, Oct. 1957
    Contents: Cottonwood, Eastern (Kansas); Dogwood (Missouri, Virginia); Live Oak (Georgia); Magnolia (Mississippi); Palmetto, Cabbage (Florida, South Carolina); Paloverde, Blue (Arizona); Pecan (Texas); Pine, Longleaf (Alabama); Pine, Shortleaf (Arkansas); Piñon (New Mexico); Piñon, Singleleaf (Nevada); Redbud, Eastern (Oklahoma); Redwood, Coast (California); Spruce, Blue (Colorado, Utah); Tulip (Indiana, Kentucky, Tennessee); White Oak (Connecticut, Maryland)

A Tree Is an Amazing Mechanism. 672-673, Nov. 1955

Wealth and Wonder of Northern State Trees. By William A. Dayton. Paintings by Walter A. Weber. 651-691, Nov. 1955
    Contents: Birch (New Hampshire); Buckeye (Ohio); Douglas Fir (Oregon); Elm, American (Massachusetts, Nebraska, North Dakota); Hemlock, Eastern (Pennsylvania); Hemlock, Western (Washington); Holly (Delaware); Maple, Red (Rhode Island); Maple, Sugar (New York, Vermont, West Virginia, Wisconsin); Oak, Bur (Illinois); Oak, Northern Red (New Jersey); Pine, Ponderosa (Montana); Pine, Red (Minnesota); Pine, West-

TREES — *Continued*
ern White (Idaho); Pine, White (Maine); Poplar, Balsam (Wyoming); Spruce (South Dakota)

See also Apple Tree; Bristlecone Pine; *Metasequoia;* Redwoods; *Sequoia gigantea; and* Big Cypress Swamp; Sequoia National Park; *and* Forests and Reforestation

TREES, Oldest Known. *See* Bristlecone Pine

TREES, World's Tallest. *See* Redwoods

"TREETOPS" (Game-observing Lodge), Kenya:
A New Look at Kenya's "Treetops." By Quentin Keynes. 536-541, Oct. 1956

TREK Across Arctic America. By Colin Irwin. 295-321, Mar. 1974

TREK by Mule Among Morocco's Berbers. By Victor Englebert. 850-875, June 1968

TREK to Lofty Hunza—and Beyond. By Sabrina and Roland Michaud. 644-669, Nov. 1975

TRENCHES, Undersea. *See* Cayman Trough; Japan Trench; Mariana Trench; Romanche Trench

TRIBAL FAIRS. *See* Sing-Sing

TRIBESPEOPLE. *See* Ethnology

TRIBUTES. *See* Memorial Tributes

TRIESTE—Side Door to Europe. By Harnett T. Kane. 824-857, June 1956

TRIESTE (Bathyscaph):
Down to *Thresher* by Bathyscaph. By Donald L. Keach. 764-777, June 1964
Man's Deepest Dive. By Jacques Piccard. Photos by Thomas J. Abercrombie. 224-239, Aug. 1960

TRINIDAD, Cuba:
Cuba—American Sugar Bowl. By Melville Bell Grosvenor. 1-56, Jan. 1947

TRINIDAD AND TOBAGO, West Indies:
Carib Cruises the West Indies. By Carleton Mitchell. 1-56, Jan. 1948
Carnival in Trinidad. By Howard La Fay. Photos by Winfield Parks. 693-701, Nov. 1971
Feathered Dancers of Little Tobago. By E. Thomas Gilliard. Photos by Frederick Kent Truslow. 428-440, Sept. 1958
Happy-go-lucky Trinidad and Tobago. By Charles Allmon. 35-75, Jan. 1953
The High World of the Rain Forest. By William Beebe. Paintings by Guy Neale. 838-855, June 1958
"The Music of Trinidad." NGS recording announced. 701, Nov. 1971
Sea Fever. By John E. Schultz. 237-268, Feb. 1949
See also Caroni Swamp Sanctuary; Simla

TRIPPE, JUAN T.:
National Geographic Society Honors Air Pioneer Juan Trippe. 584-586, Apr. 1968

TRISTAN DA CUNHA (Island), South Atlantic Ocean:
Death of an Island, Tristan da Cunha. By P. J. F. Wheeler. 678-695, May 1962
Home to Lonely Tristan da Cunha. By James P. Blair. 60-81, Jan. 1964
New Life for the "Loneliest Isle." By Lewis Lewis. 105-116, Jan. 1950

TRITON Follows Magellan's Wake. By Edward L. Beach. Photos by J. Baylor Roberts. 585-615, Nov. 1960

TRIUMPH of the First Crusade to the Holy Land. By Franc Shor. Photos by Thomas Nebbia. 797-855, Dec. 1963

TRIUMPH on Everest. By Sir John Hunt and Sir Edmund Hillary. 1-63, July 1954

TROPICAL Gardens of Key West. By Luis Marden. 116-124, Jan. 1953

The **TROUBLE** With Treasure *(Atocha).* By Eugene Lyon. 787-809, June 1976

TROUBLED Capital of the Arab World: Cairo. By William S. Ellis. Photos by Winfield Parks. 639-667, May 1972

TROUBLED Waters East of Suez. By Ernest M. Eller. 483-522, Apr. 1954

TROUT:
Freezing the Trout's Lightning Leap. By Treat Davidson. 525-530, Apr. 1958
See also Golden Trout

TRUCIAL COAST:
Desert Sheikdoms of Arabia's Pirate Coast. By Ronald Codrai. 65-104, July 1956
Troubled Waters East of Suez. By Ernest M. Eller. 483-522, Apr. 1954
See also United Arab Emirates

TRUCKS AND TRUCKING:
North With the Wheat Cutters. By Noel Grove. Photos by James A. Sugar. 194-217, Aug. 1972
Trucks Race the Clock From Coast to Coast. By James A. Sugar. 226-243, Feb. 1974

"TRUE PEOPLE" of the Jungle (Yanomamo). By Napoleon A. Chagnon. 211-223, Aug. 1976

TRUFFLES:
The Diffident Truffle, France's Gift to Gourmets. 419-426, Sept. 1956

TRUK ISLANDS, Caroline Islands, Pacific Ocean:
Micronesia: The Americanization of Eden. By David S. Boyer. 702-744, May 1967
Pacific Wards of Uncle Sam. By W. Robert Moore. 73-104, July 1948

TRUK LAGOON, Truk Islands, Pacific Ocean:
Life Springs From Death in Truk Lagoon. By Sylvia A. Earle. Photos by Al Giddings. 578-613, May 1976
From Graveyard to Garden. 604-613
Included: Japanese ships sunk in two 1944 attacks by U. S. Navy carrier-launched planes

TRUMAN, HARRY S.:
Inside the White House. By Lonnelle Aikman. Photos by B. Anthony Stewart and Thomas Nebbia. 3-43, Jan. 1961
The Living White House. By Lonnelle Aikman. 593-643, Nov. 1966
Profiles of the Presidents: V. The Atomic Age: Its Problems and Promises. By Frank Freidel. 66-119, Jan. 1966

TRUMPETER SWANS:
Return of the Trumpeter. By Frederick Kent Truslow. 134-150, July 1960

TRUSLOW, FREDERICK KENT:

Author-Photographer

Businessman in the Bush. 634-675, May 1970

The Dauntless Little Stilt. 241-245, Aug. 1960

Eye to Eye With Eagles. 123-148, Jan. 1961

Limpkin, the "Crying Bird" That Haunts Florida Swamps. 114-121, Jan. 1958

Return of the Trumpeter. 134-150, July 1960

Threatened Glories of Everglades National Park. By Frederick Kent Truslow and Frederick G. Vosburgh. Photos by Frederick Kent Truslow and Otis Imboden. 508-553, Oct. 1967

When Disaster Struck a Woodpecker's Home. 882-884, Dec. 1966

Photographer

Feathered Dancers of Little Tobago (Greater Birds of Paradise). By E. Thomas Gilliard. 428-440, Sept. 1958

The Osprey, Endangered World Citizen. By Roger Tory Peterson. 53-67, July 1969

Our Only Native Stork, the Wood Ibis. By Robert Porter Allen. 294-306, Feb. 1964

Roseate Spoonbills, Radiant Birds of the Gulf Coast. By Robert Porter Allen. 274-288, Feb. 1962

Whooping Cranes Fight for Survival. By Robert Porter Allen. 650-669, Nov. 1959

TRUST TERRITORY OF NEW GUINEA. *See* Australian New Guinea; New Britain

TRUST TERRITORY OF THE PACIFIC ISLANDS:

Micronesia: The Americanization of Eden. By David S. Boyer. 702-744, May 1967

Pacific Wards of Uncle Sam. By W. Robert Moore. 73-104, July 1948

See also Ifalik; Kapingamarangi; Kwajalein; Truk Lagoon; Yap Islands

TRYCK, KEITH: Author:

Rafting Down the Yukon. Photos by Robert Clark. 830-861, Dec. 1975

TSAVO NATIONAL PARK, Kenya:

Inside a Hornbill's Walled-up Nest. By Joan and Alan Root. 846-855, Dec. 1969

See also Mzima Springs

TSCHOPIK, HARRY, Jr.: Author-Photographer:

At Home in the High Andes. 133-146, Jan. 1955

TSETSE FLY:

Britain Tackles the East African Bush. By W. Robert Moore. 311-352, Mar. 1950

Safari Through Changing Africa. By Elsie May Bell Grosvenor. Photos by Gilbert H. Grosvenor. 145-198, Aug. 1953

TSUNAMIS:

Earthquake! By William P. E. Graves. 112-139, July 1964

Hawaii, Island of Fire and Flowers. By Gordon Young. Photos by Robert W. Madden. 399-425, Mar. 1975

Thera, Key to the Riddle of Minos. By Spyridon Marinatos. Photos by Otis Imboden. 702-726, May 1972

TUAMOTU ARCHIPELAGO, South Pacific Ocean:

Twenty Fathoms Down for Mother-of-Pearl. By

TUAMOTU ARCHIPELAGO, South Pacific Ocean—

Continued

Winston Williams. Photos by Bates Littlehales. 512-529, Apr. 1962

TUAREG (Tribespeople):

Drought Threatens the Tuareg World. By Victor Englebert. 544-571, Apr. 1974

I Joined a Sahara Salt Caravan. By Victor Englebert. 694-711, Nov. 1965

The Niger: River of Sorrow, River of Hope. By Georg Gerster. 152-189, Aug. 1975

Sand in My Eyes. By Jinx Rodger. 664-705, May 1958

TUCK, JOHN, Jr.:

Man's First Winter at the South Pole. By Paul A. Siple. 439-478, Apr. 1958

We Are Living at the South Pole. By Paul A. Siple. Photos by David S. Boyer. 5-35, July 1957

TUCSON, Arizona:

From Tucson to Tombstone. By Mason Sutherland. 343-384, Sept. 1953

See also Desert Museum

TUKUNA INDIANS:

Tukuna Maidens Come of Age. By Harald Schultz. 629-649, Nov. 1959

TULANE UNIVERSITY:

Delta Regional Primate Research Center. *See* Snowflake (White Gorilla)

Expedition. *See* Dzibilchaltun, Yucatán, Mexico

TULSA, Oklahoma:

Oklahoma, the Adventurous One. By Robert Paul Jordan. Photos by Robert W. Madden. 149-189, Aug. 1971

TUNA:

Golden Beaches of Portugal. By Alan Villiers. 673-696, Nov. 1954

Quicksilver and Slow Death. By John J. Putman. Photos by Robert W. Madden. 507-527, Oct. 1972

Included: Mercury found in tuna

The *Yankee's* Wander-world. By Irving and Electa Johnson. 1-50, Jan. 1949

Included: Portuguese fishermen, out from San Diego, tuna fishing in Tagus Cove, Galapagos Islands

TUNDRA: North America:

Beyond the North Wind With the Snow Goose. By Des and Jen Bartlett. 822-843, Dec. 1973

. . . And Then There Was Fred. . . . 843-847

Caribou: Hardy Nomads of the North. By Jim Rearden. 858-878, Dec. 1974

North to the Tundra. 293-337, Mar. 1972

I. Re-creating a Vanished World. By Russell D. Guthrie. 294-301

"Ice Age Mammals of the Alaskan Tundra." Painting supplement by Jay H. Matternes

II. Portrait of a Fierce and Fragile Land. By Paul A. Zahl. 303-314

III. Plants of the Alaskan Tundra. 315-321

IV. Birds of the Alaskan Tundra. 322-327

V. Mammals of the Alaskan Tundra. 329-337

The Pipeline: Alaska's Troubled Colossus. By Bryan Hodgson. Photos by Steve Raymer. 684-717, Nov. 1976

TUNDRA: North America—*Continued*

Will Oil and Tundra Mix? Alaska's North Slope Hangs in the Balance. By William S. Ellis. Photos by Emory Kristof. 485-517, Oct. 1971

TUNHWANG, Kansu, China:

The Caves of the Thousand Buddhas. By Franc and Jean Shor. 383-415, Mar. 1951

TUNISIA:

When the President Goes Abroad (Eisenhower). By Gilbert M. Grosvenor. 588-649, May 1960

TUNNELS:

The Alps: Man's Own Mountains. By Ralph Gray. Photos by Walter Meayers Edwards and William Eppridge. 350-395, Sept. 1965
Included: Mont Blanc Tunnel

Inside Europe Aboard *Yankee*. By Irving and Electa Johnson. Photos by Joseph J. Scherschel. 157-195, Aug. 1964

See also Chesapeake Bay Bridge-Tunnel; Kitimat

TURKEY:

Ambassadors of Good Will: The Peace Corps. By Sargent Shriver and Peace Corps Volunteers. 297-345, Sept. 1964
Turkey. By Nan and James W. Borton. 331-333

"Around the World in Eighty Days." By Newman Bumstead. 705-750, Dec. 1951
Included: Anatolia; Ankara; The Bosporus; Istanbul; Konya; Rumeli Hissar; Sea of Marmara

In the Footsteps of Alexander the Great. By Helen and Frank Schreider. Paintings by Tom Lovell. 1-65, Jan. 1968

Jerusalem to Rome in the Path of St. Paul. By David S. Boyer. 707-759, Dec. 1956

Oldest Known Shipwreck Yields Bronze Age Cargo. By Peter Throckmorton. 697-711, May 1962

Round the World School. By Paul Antze. Photos by William Eppridge. 96-127, July 1962

Station Wagon Odyssey: Baghdad to Istanbul. By William O. Douglas. 48-87, Jan. 1959

Throne Above the Euphrates. By Theresa Goell. 390-405, Mar. 1961

Turkey Paves the Path of Progress. By Maynard Owen Williams. 141-186, Aug. 1951

When the President Goes Abroad (Eisenhower). By Gilbert M. Grosvenor. 588-649, May 1960

Where Turk and Russian Meet. By Ferdinand Kuhn. 743-766, June 1952

YWCA: International Success Story. By Mary French Rockefeller. Photos by Otis Imboden. 904-933, Dec. 1963

Yankee Cruises Turkey's History-haunted Coast. By Irving and Electa Johnson. Photos by Joseph J. Scherschel. 798-845, Dec. 1969

See also Anatolia; Aphrodisias; Cappadocia; Istanbul; Yassi Ada

TURKEYS, Wild:

The Wichitas: Land of the Living Prairie. By M. Woodbridge Williams. 661-697, May 1957

TURKOMANS:

Bold Horsemen of the Steppes. By Sabrina and Roland Michaud. 634-669, Nov. 1973

TURKS:

Cyprus Under Four Flags: A Struggle for Unity. By

TURKS—*Continued*

Kenneth MacLeish. Photos by Jonathan Blair. 356-383, Mar. 1973

The Isles of Greece: Aegean Birthplace of Western Culture. By Melville Bell Grosvenor. Photos by Edwin Stuart Grosvenor and Winfield Parks. 147-193, Aug. 1972

TURKU ARCHIPELAGO, Finland:

Scenes of Postwar Finland. By La Verne Bradley. Photos by Jerry Waller. 233-264, Aug. 1947

TURNAROUND Time in West Virginia. By Elizabeth A. Moize. Photos by Jodi Cobb. 755-785, June 1976

TURTLE BOGUE. *See* Tortuguero Beach, Costa Rica

TURTLES:

Imperiled Gift of the Sea: Caribbean Green Turtle. By Archie Carr. Photos by Robert E. Schroeder. 876-890, June 1967

In the Wilds of a City Parlor. By Paul A. Zahl. 645-672, Nov. 1954

Nature's Tank, the Turtle. By Doris M. Cochran. Paintings by Walter A. Weber. 665-684, May 1952

One Strange Night on Turtle Beach. By Paul A. Zahl. 570-581, Oct. 1973

See also Tortoises

TUSCANY (Region), Italy:

The Renaissance Lives On in Tuscany. By Luis Marden. Photos by Albert Moldvay. 626-659, Nov. 1974

See also Siena

TUSHINGHAM, A. DOUGLAS: Author:

Jericho Gives Up Its Secrets. By Kathleen M. Kenyon and A. Douglas Tushingham. Photos by Nancy Lord. 853-870, Dec. 1953

The Men Who Hid the Dead Sea Scrolls. Paintings by Peter V. Bianchi. 785-808, Dec. 1958

TUTANKHAMUN:

Golden Masterpieces. 36-39, Jan. 1974

Tutankhamun's Golden Trove. By Christiane Desroches Noblecourt. Photos by F. L. Kenett. 625-646, Oct. 1963

TUVALU. *See* former name, Ellice Islands

TWAIN, MARK:

Mark Twain: Mirror of America. By Noel Grove. Photos by James L. Stanfield. 300-337, Sept. 1975

Tom Sawyer's Town. By Jerry Allen. 121-140, July 1956

The West Through Boston Eyes. By Stewart Anderson. 733-776, June 1949
Included: Today in Mark Twain's Home Town.—Exploring Tom Sawyer's Cave

TWEED:

From Barra to Butt in the Hebrides. By Isobel Wylie Hutchison. 559-580, Oct. 1954

Over the Sea to Scotland's Skye. By Robert J. Reynolds. 87-112, July 1952

TWEEDIE, PENNY: Photographer:

Coober Pedy: Opal Capital of Australia's Outback. By Kenny Moore. 560-571, Oct. 1976

TWELVE National Geographic Society Scientific Projects Under Way. 869-870, June 1954

TWENTIETH Anniversary of the Epoch-making Stratosphere Flight by *Explorer II*. 707, Nov. 1955

20TH-CENTURY Indians Preserve Customs of the Cliff Dwellers. Photos by William Belknap, Jr. 196-211, Feb. 1964

TWENTY Fathoms Down for Mother-of-Pearl. By Winston Williams. Photos by Bates Littlehales. 512-529, Apr. 1962

TWILIGHT Hope for Big Cypress. By Rick Gore. Photos by Patricia Caulfield. 251-273, Aug. 1976

TWILIGHT of the Arab Dhow. By Marion Kaplan. 330-351, Sept. 1974

The TWO Acapulcos. By James Cerruti. Photos by Thomas Nebbia. 848-878, Dec. 1964

TWO and a Half Miles Down. By Georges S. Houot. 80-86, July 1954

2,000 Miles Through Europe's Oldest Kingdom. By Isobel Wylie Hutchison. Photos by Maynard Owen Williams. 141-180, Feb. 1949

2,300-YEAR-OLD Greek Ship Reaches Port at Last. By Susan W. and Michael L. Katzev. 618-625, Nov. 1974

TWO Wheels Along the Mexican Border. By William Albert Allard. 591-635, May 1971

TXUKAHAMEIS (Indians):
Amazon—The River Sea. By Loren McIntyre. 456-495, Oct. 1972
Brazil's Txukahameis: Good-bye to the Stone Age. Photos by W. Jesco von Puttkamer. 270-283, Feb. 1975

TYLER, JOHN:
Profiles of the Presidents: II. A Restless Nation Moves West. By Frank Freidel. 80-121, Jan. 1965

TYREE, DAVID M.: Author:
New Era in the Loneliest Continent (Antarctica). Photos by Albert Moldvay. 260-296, Feb. 1963

TYROL (Region), Austria-Italy:
Occupied Austria, Outpost of Democracy. By George W. Long. Photos by Volkmar Wentzel. 749-790, June 1951
A Stroll to Venice. By Isobel Wylie Hutchison. 378-410, Sept. 1951
Tirol, Austria's Province in the Clouds. By Peter T. White. Photos by Volkmar Wentzel. 107-141, July 1961

TYRRHENIAN SEA:
Fishing in the Whirlpool of Charybdis. By Paul A. Zahl. 579-618, Nov. 1953

TYUMEN OBLAST (Region), U.S.S.R.:
Siberia's Empire Road, the River Ob. By Robert Paul Jordan. Photos by Dean Conger. 145-181, Feb. 1976

U

U.S.S.R. *See* Union of Soviet Socialist Republics

UAUPÉS (River), South America. *See* Vaupés

"UBANGI" (Tribespeople). *See* Sara

UBO TRIBE:
Help for Philippine Tribes in Trouble. By Kenneth MacLeish. Photos by Dean Conger. 220-255, Aug. 1971
The Last Tribes of Mindanao (Television film). 882A-882B, Dec. 1971

UDORN ROYAL THAI AIR FORCE BASE, Thailand:
Air Rescue Behind Enemy Lines. By Howard Sochurek. 346-369, Sept. 1968

UGANDA:
Britain Tackles the East African Bush. By W. Robert Moore. 311-352, Mar. 1950
Kayaks Down the Nile. By John M. Goddard. 697-732, May 1955
Orphans of the Wild. By Bruce G. Kinloch. 683-699, Nov. 1962
Roaming Africa's Unfenced Zoos. By W. Robert Moore. 353-380, Mar. 1950
Safari from Congo to Cairo. By Elsie May Bell Grosvenor. Photos by Gilbert Grosvenor. 721-771, Dec. 1954
Uganda, Africa's Uneasy Heartland. By Howard La Fay. Photos by George F. Mobley. 708-735, Nov. 1971
Where Elephants Have Right of Way. By George and Jinx Rodger. Photos by George Rodger. 363-389, Sept. 1960
See also Ruwenzori; Virunga Mountains

UIST, North, and South Uist (Islands), Scotland:
Isles on the Edge of the Sea: Scotland's Outer Hebrides. By Kenneth MacLeish. Photos by Thomas Nebbia. 676-711, May 1970

UKRAINIANS: United States and Canada:
Easter Greetings From the Ukrainians. By Robert Paul Jordan. Photos by James A. Sugar. 556-563, Apr. 1972

ULITHI (Atoll), Caroline Islands:
Adventures with the Survey Navy. By Irving Johnson. 131-148, July 1947

ULSTER. *See* Ireland, Northern

ULYSSES. *See* Odyssey

UNCLE Sam Bends a Twig in Germany. By Frederick Simpich. Photos by J. Baylor Roberts. 529-550, Oct. 1948

UNCLE Sam's House of 1,000 Wonders. By Lyman J. Briggs and F. Barrows Colton. 755-784, Dec. 1951

UNDER Canvas in the Atomic Age. By Alan Villiers. 49-84, July 1955

UNDER the Dome of Freedom: The United States Capitol. By Lonnelle Aikman. Photos by George F. Mobley. 4-59, Jan. 1964

UNDERWATER Archeology: Key to History's Warehouse. By George F. Bass. Photos by Thomas J. Abercrombie and Robert B. Goodman. 138-156, July 1963
See also Archeology, Underwater

UNDERWATER DEMOLITION TEAMS:

Goggle Fishing in California Waters. By David Hellyer. Photos by Lamar Boren. 615-632, May 1949

New Life for the Troubled Suez Canal. By William Graves. Photos by Jonathan Blair. 792-817, June 1975

UNDERWATER EXPLORATION:

Diving Into the Blue Holes of the Bahamas. By George J. Benjamin. 347-363, Sept. 1970

Project FAMOUS. Photos by Emory Kristof. 586-615, May 1975
  I. Where the Earth Turns Inside Out. By J. R. Heirtzler. 586-603
  II. Dive Into the Great Rift. By Robert D. Ballard. 604-615

Window on Earth's Interior. By Robert D. Ballard. Photos by Emory Kristof. 228-249, Aug. 1976
  Contents: Cayman Trough

See also Archeology, Underwater; Divers and Diving; Treasure, Sunken

UNDERWATER LIVING:

The Deepest Days. By Robert Sténuit. 534-547, Apr. 1965

Diving Beneath Arctic Ice. By Joseph B. MacInnis. Photos by William R. Curtsinger. 248-267, Aug. 1973

Outpost Under the Ocean. By Edwin A. Link. Photos by Bates Littlehales. 530-533, Apr. 1965

Tomorrow on the Deep Frontier. By Edwin A. Link. 778-801, June 1964

See also Conshelf Bases; Tektite II

UNDERWATER PARKS. See Buck Island; John Pennekamp Coral Reef State Park; Ras Muhammad

UNFAMILIAR Glories of the West. 733-791, June 1974

UNGAVA (Region), Quebec, Canada. See Chubb Crater

UNION OF SOUTH AFRICA. See South Africa, Republic of

UNION OF SOVIET SOCIALIST REPUBLICS:

Down the Danube by Canoe. By William Slade Backer. Photos by Richard S. Durrance and Christopher G. Knight. 34-79, July 1965

Eastern Soviet Union, Atlas series supplement. Mar. 1967

Firsthand Look at the Soviet Union. By Thomas T. Hammond. Photos by Erich Lessing. 352-407, Sept. 1959

Questing for Gems. By George S. Switzer. 835-863, Dec. 1971
  Included: The Czarist Crown Jewels

Russia as I Saw It. By Richard M. Nixon. Photos by B. Anthony Stewart. 715-750, Dec. 1959

The Society Reports to Its Members on Russia Today. The Editor. 351, Sept. 1959

Soviet Union; Peoples of the Soviet Union, double-sided map supplement. Feb. 1976

Union of Soviet Socialist Republics, map supplement. Dec. 1960

The Volga, Russia's Mighty River Road. By Howard Sochurek. 579-613, May 1973

Western Soviet Union, Atlas series supplement. Sept. 1959

Where Turk and Russian Meet. By Ferdinand Kuhn. 743-766, June 1952

UNION OF SOVIET SOCIALIST REPUBLICS— Continued

See also Abkhazian A.S.S.R.; Leningrad; Moscow; Siberia; and Soyuz-Apollo Mission

UNITED ARAB EMIRATES:

The Arab World, Inc. By John J. Putman. Photos by Winfield Parks. 494-533, Oct. 1975

The Peoples of the Middle East, map supplement. Text on reverse. July 1972

See also former designation, Trucial Coast

UNITED ARAB REPUBLIC:

Africa: Countries of the Nile, Atlas series supplement. Oct. 1963

See also Egypt; and Syria, a former member

UNITED Italy Marks Its 100th Year. By Nathaniel T. Kenney. 593-647, Nov. 1961

UNITED KINGDOM OF GREAT BRITAIN AND NORTHERN IRELAND. See Great Britain

UNITED NATIONS:

Date Line: United Nations, New York. By Carolyn Bennett Patterson. Photos by B. Anthony Stewart and John E. Fletcher. 305-331, Sept. 1961

Flags of the United Nations (60 Member States). By Elizabeth W. King. 213-238, Feb. 1951

Flags of the United Nations (99 Member States). 332-345, Sept. 1961

The United Nations: Capital of the Family of Man. By Adlai E. Stevenson. Photos by B. Anthony Stewart and John E. Fletcher. 297-303, Sept. 1961

UNITED NATIONS EDUCATIONAL, SCIENTIFIC AND CULTURAL ORGANIZATION (UNESCO). See Abu Simbel

UNITED NATIONS FOOD AND AGRICULTURE ORGANIZATION (FAO):

Can the World Feed Its People? By Thomas Y. Canby. Photos by Steve Raymer. 2-31, July 1975
  Included: World Food Conference, 1974

Locusts: "Teeth of the Wind." By Robert A. M. Conley. Photos by Gianni Tortoli. 202-227, Aug. 1969

UNITED STATES:

America Goes to the Fair. By Samuel W. Matthews. 293-333, Sept. 1954

The American Cowboy in Life and Legend. Special Publication announced. 882-886, June 1971

American Mountain People. Special Publication announced. 865-868, June 1973

American Wild Flower Odyssey. By P. L. Ricker. 603-634, May 1953

America's Inland Waterway. Special Publication announced. 865-868, June 1973

America's "Meat on the Hoof." By William H. Nicholas. 33-72, Jan. 1952

The Appalachian Trail. Special Publication announced. 870-874, June 1972

As We Live and Breathe: The Challenge of Our Environment. Special Publication announced. 882-886, June 1971

Atlas of the Fifty United States: Bringing America Into Your Home. By Melville Bell Grosvenor. 130-133, July 1960

Census 1960: Profile of the Nation. By Albert W. Atwood and Lonnelle Aikman. 697-714, Nov. 1959

UNITED STATES — *Continued*

Close-up: U.S.A. — a Fresh Look at Our Land and Its Heritage. By Gilbert M. Grosvenor. 287-289, Mar. 1973

Close-up: U.S.A., Alaska, map supplement. Text on reverse. June 1975

Close-up: U.S.A., California and Nevada, map supplement. Text on reverse. June 1974

Close-up: U.S.A., Florida, map supplement. Text on reverse. Nov. 1973

Close-up: U.S.A., Hawaii, map supplement. Text on reverse. Apr. 1976

Close-up: U.S.A., Maine, with the Maritime Provinces of Canada, map supplement. Text on reverse. Mar. 1975

Close-up: U.S.A., The Mid-Atlantic States, map supplement. Text on reverse. Oct. 1976

Close-up: U.S.A., The North Central States, map supplement. Text on reverse. Mar. 1974

Close-up: U.S.A., The Northwest, map supplement. Text on reverse. Mar. 1973

Close-up: U.S.A., The South Central States, map supplement. Text on reverse. Oct. 1974

Close-up: U.S.A., The Southeast, map supplement. Text on reverse. Oct. 1975

Close-up: U.S.A., Western New England, map supplement. Text on reverse. July 1975

Close-up: U.S.A., Wisconsin, Michigan, and the Great Lakes, map supplement. Text on reverse. Aug. 1973

The Craftsman in America. Special Publication announced. 870-874, June 1975

Eight Maps of Discovery. 757-769, June 1953

Exploring America Underground. By Charles E. Mohr. 803-837, June 1964

Flags of the Americas. By Elizabeth W. King. 633-657, May 1949
> Included: The Flag of the United States, the President, the Vice President, Executive Agencies and Departments, and the United States Armed Forces

Following the Trail of Lewis and Clark. By Ralph Gray. 707-750, June 1953

4-H Boys and Girls Grow More Food. By Frederick Simpich. 551-582, Nov. 1948

Freedom Train Tours America. 529-542, Oct. 1949

From Sea to Shining Sea. By Ralph Gray. Photos by Dean Conger and author. 1-61, July 1961

From Sun-clad Sea to Shining Mountains (U. S. 89). By Ralph Gray. Photos by James P. Blair. 542-589, Apr. 1964

The Glittering World of Rockhounds. By David S. Boyer. 276-294, Feb. 1974

Great American Deserts. Special Publication announced. 870-874, June 1972

How Fruit Came to America. By J. R. Magness. Paintings by Else Bostelmann. 325-377, Sept. 1951

I See America First. By Lynda Bird Johnson. Photos by William Albert Allard. 874-904, Dec. 1965

John Muir's Wild America. By Harvey Arden. Photos by Dewitt Jones. 433-461, Apr. 1973

John Muir's Wild America. Special Publication announced. 860-864, June 1976

Life in Rural America. Special Publication announced. 870-874, June 1974

A Map Maker Looks at the United States. By Newman Bumstead. 705-748, June 1951

Mapping the Nation's Breadbasket. By Frederick Simpich. 831-849, June 1948

UNITED STATES — *Continued*

Mark Twain: Mirror of America. By Noel Grove. Photos by James L. Stanfield. 300-337, Sept. 1975

Mexico to Canada on the Pacific Crest Trail. By Mike W. Edwards. Photos by David Hiser. 741-779, June 1971

North Central United States, Atlas series supplement. Nov. 1958

North Central United States, map supplement. June 1948

North With the Wheat Cutters. By Noel Grove. Photos by James A. Sugar. 194-217, Aug. 1972

Northeastern United States, including the Great Lakes Region, Atlas series supplement. Apr. 1959

Northwestern United States, Atlas series supplement. Apr. 1960

Northwestern United States and Neighboring Canadian Provinces, map supplement. June 1950

Our Changing Atlantic Coastline. By Nathaniel T. Kenney. Photos by B. Anthony Stewart. 860-887, Dec. 1962

Our Continent: A Natural History of North America. Book announced. 572-574, Oct. 1976

Our Growing Interstate Highway System. By Robert Paul Jordan. 195-219, Feb. 1968

Our Land Through Lincoln's Eyes. By Carolyn Bennett Patterson. Photos by W. D. Vaughn. 243-277, Feb. 1960

The Pacific Crest Trail. Special Publication announced. 870-874, June 1974

The Parks in Your Backyard. By Conrad L. Wirth. 647-707, Nov. 1963
> The East. 675-689
> The Midlands. 691-697
> The West. 699-707

Playing 3,000 Golf Courses in Fourteen Lands. By Ralph A. Kennedy. 113-132, July 1952

Portrait U.S.A., first satellite photomosaic of the contiguous 48 states; *The United States.* Supplement, July 1976

Railroads: The Great American Adventure. Special Publication announced. 860-864, June 1976

The Revolution in American Agriculture. By Jules B. Billard. Photos by James P. Blair. 147-185, Feb. 1970

The Search for Tomorrow's Power. By Kenneth F. Weaver. Photos by Emory Kristof. 650-681, Nov. 1972

A Sikh Discovers America. By Joginder Singh Rekhi. 558-590, Oct. 1964

Skiing in the United States. By Kathleen Revis. 216-254, Feb. 1959

Skyway Below the Clouds. By Carl R. Markwith. Photos by Ernest J. Cottrell. 85-108, July 1949

Solar Energy, the Ultimate Powerhouse. By John L. Wilhelm. Photos by Emory Kristof. 381-397, Mar. 1976
> Included: Map of average annual hours of sunshine

South Central United States, Atlas series supplement. Feb. 1961

South Central United States, map supplement. Dec. 1947

Southeastern United States, Atlas series supplement. Jan. 1958

Southeastern United States, map supplement. Feb. 1947

UNITED STATES — *Continued*

Southwestern United States, Atlas series supplement. Nov. 1959

Southwestern United States, map supplement. Dec. 1948

This Land of Ours (Bicentennial issue). 1-158, July 1976

Those Inventive Americans. Special Publication announced. 880-884, June 1970

Trucks Race the Clock From Coast to Coast. By James A. Sugar. 226-243, Feb. 1974

Two Wheels Along the Mexican Border. By William Albert Allard. 591-635, May 1971

The United States, Atlas series supplement. July 1961

The United States, map supplement. Sept. 1956

The United States, map supplement. Feb. 1968

United States: Washington to Boston, Atlas series supplement. Aug. 1962

The United States of America, map supplement. June 1951

Vacation Tour Through Lincoln Land. By Ralph Gray. 141-184, Feb. 1952

Vacationland U.S.A. Book announced. 734-740, May 1970; 573, Apr. 1973

Vacationlands of the United States and Southern Canada, map supplement. Text on reverse. July 1966

We Americans. Book announced. 580-582, Oct. 1975

The West Through Boston Eyes. By Stewart Anderson. 733-776, June 1949

What's Happening to Our Climate? By Samuel W. Matthews. 576-615, Nov. 1976

Wilderness U.S.A. Book announced. 582-584, Oct. 1973

The World in Your Garden. By W. H. Camp. Paintings by Else Bostelmann. 1-65, July 1947

You Can't Miss America by Bus. By Howell Walker. Paintings by Walter A. Weber. 1-42, July 1950

See also names of individual cities, lakes, mountains, rivers, and states; *and* Great Lakes and Region; History, U. S.; Immigrants; Indians of North America; National Monuments; National Parks; National Wildlife Refuges; Presidents, U. S.; Space Flights and Research; Wildlife

U. S. AGRICULTURAL RESEARCH CENTER. *See* Beltsville, Maryland

U. S. AIR FORCE:

Across the Frozen Desert to Byrd Station. By Paul W. Frazier. Photos by Calvin L. Larsen. 383-398, Sept. 1957

Air Rescue Behind Enemy Lines. By Howard Sochurek. 346-369, Sept. 1968

Airlift to Berlin. 595-614, May 1949

Artists Roam the World of the U. S. Air Force. By Curtis E. LeMay. 650-673, May 1960

Cape Canaveral's 6,000-mile Shooting Gallery. By Allan C. Fisher, Jr. Photos by Luis Marden and Thomas Nebbia. 421-471, Oct. 1959

Fact Finding for Tomorrow's Planes. By Hugh L. Dryden. Photos by Luis Marden. 757-780, Dec. 1953

Flags of the Americas. By Elizabeth W. King. 633-657, May 1949

Fledgling Wings of the Air Force. By Thomas W.

U. S. AIR FORCE — *Continued*

McKnew. 266-271, Aug. 1957

Flying in the "Blowtorch" Era. By Frederick G. Vosburgh. 281-322, Sept. 1950

History Written in the Skies. 273-294, Aug. 1957

The Long, Lonely Leap. By Joseph W. Kittinger, Jr. Photos by Volkmar Wentzel. 854-873, Dec. 1960

A Map Maker Looks at the United States. By Newman Bumstead. 705-748, June 1951

Men Against the Hurricane. By Andrew H. Brown. 537-560, Oct. 1950

Of Planes and Men. By Kenneth F. Weaver. Photos by Emory Kristof and Albert Moldvay. 298-349, Sept. 1965

> Included: Air Defense Command, Military Air Transport Service, Pacific Air Forces, Strategic Air Command, Tactical Air Command, U. S. Air Forces in Europe

Patrolling Troubled Formosa Strait. 573-588, Apr. 1955

Reaching for the Moon. By Allan C. Fisher, Jr. Photos by Luis Marden. 157-171, Feb. 1959

> Included: First lunar probe by U. S. Air Force's rocket, *Pioneer I*

School for Survival. By Curtis E. LeMay. 565-602, May 1953

Three Months on an Arctic Ice Island. By Joseph O. Fletcher. 489-504, Apr. 1953

Uncle Sam Bends a Twig in Germany. By Frederick Simpich. Photos by J. Baylor Roberts. 529-550, Oct. 1948

U. S. Air Force: Power for Peace. By Curtis E. LeMay. 291-297, Sept. 1965

We Are Living at the South Pole. By Paul A. Siple. Photos by David S. Boyer. 5-35, July 1957

Your Society Observes Eclipse in Brazil. 661, May 1947

See also Air Bases; Air Rescue Squadrons; Aviation Medicine; MATS; U. S. Air Force Academy; X-15; *and* former name, U. S. Army Air Forces

U. S. AIR FORCE ACADEMY, Colorado:

Where Falcons Wear Air Force Blue, United States Air Force Academy. By Nathaniel T. Kenney. Photos by William Belknap, Jr. 845-873, June 1959

U. S. ANTARCTIC RESEARCH PROGRAM (USARP):

Antarctica: Icy Testing Ground for Space. By Samuel W. Matthews. Photos by Robert W. Madden. 569-592, Oct. 1968

Antarctica's Nearer Side. By Samuel W. Matthews. Photos by William R. Curtsinger. 622-655, Nov. 1971

First Conquest of Antarctica's Highest Peaks. By Nicholas B. Clinch. 836-863, June 1967

First Flight Across the Bottom of the World. By James R. Reedy. Photos by Otis Imboden. 454-464, Mar. 1964

First La Gorce Medal Honors Antarctic Expedition. 864-867, June 1967

Flight Into Antarctic Darkness. By J. Lloyd Abbot, Jr. Photos by David S. Boyer. 732-738, Nov. 1967

New Era in the Loneliest Continent. By David M. Tyree. Photos by Albert Moldvay. 260-296, Feb. 1963

Stalking Seals Under Antarctic Ice. By Carleton Ray. 54-65, Jan. 1966

U. S. ARMED FORCES:

Flags of the Americas. By Elizabeth W. King. 633-657, May 1949
Included: Flags of the United States Air Force, Army, Coast Guard, Marine Corps, Navy

The Incredible Helicopter. By Peter T. White. 533-557, Apr. 1959

See also Unknown Servicemen; War Memorials; *and* names of individual branches

U. S. ARMY:

Across the Frozen Desert to Byrd Station. By Paul W. Frazier. Photos by Calvin L. Larsen. 383-398, Sept. 1957

The Eisenhower Story. By Howard La Fay. 1-39, July 1969

Flags of the Americas. By Elizabeth W. King. 633-657, May 1949

The GI and the Kids of Korea. By Robert H. Mosier. 635-664, May 1953

Masterpieces on Tour. By Harry A. McBride. 717-750, Dec. 1948

Reaching for the Moon. By Allan C. Fisher, Jr. Photos by Luis Marden. 157-171, Feb. 1959
Included: U. S. Army's first lunar probe *(Pioneer III)*

Uncle Sam Bends a Twig in Germany. By Frederick Simpich. Photos by J. Baylor Roberts. 529-550, Oct. 1948

With the U. S. Army in Korea. By John R. Hodge. 829-840, June 1947

See also Camp Century, Greenland; U. S. Military Academy; Viet Nam, South; War Memorials; *and* Fifth Army; Unknown Servicemen

U. S. ARMY AIR FORCES:

Adventures in Lololand. By Rennold L. Lowy. 105-118, Jan. 1947

Carnival in San Antonio. By Mason Sutherland. Photos by J. Baylor Roberts. 813-844, Dec. 1947
Included: Duncan Field, Fort Sam Houston, Kelly Field, Randolph Field

Eclipse Hunting in Brazil's Ranchland. By F. Barrows Colton. Photos by Richard H. Stewart and Guy W. Starling. 285-324, Sept. 1947

Fun Helped Them Fight. By Stuart E. Jones. 95-104, Jan. 1948

Milestones in My Arctic Journeys. By Willie Knutsen. 543-570, Oct. 1949
Included: The Arctic Search and Rescue section at Frobisher Bay, Baffin Island and at Goose Bay, Labrador

See also U. S. Air Force

U. S. ARMY CORPS OF ENGINEERS:

The Imperiled Everglades. By Fred Ward. 1-27, Jan. 1972

The Lower Mississippi. By Willard Price. Photos by W. D. Vaughn. 681-725, Nov. 1960

Satellites Gave Warning of Midwest Floods. By Peter T. White. Photos by Thomas A. DeFeo. 574-592, Oct. 1969

U. S. ARMY QUARTERMASTER CORPS:

First American Ascent of Mount St. Elias. By Maynard M. Miller. 229-248, Feb. 1948

U. S. ARMY SIGNAL CORPS:

The Flying Telegraph (Pigeons). By Joseph F. Spears. Official U. S. Army Signal Corps photos. 531-554, Apr. 1947

U. S. ARMY SPECIAL FORCES:

American Special Forces in Action in Viet Nam. By

U. S. ARMY SPECIAL FORCES—*Continued*

Howard Sochurek. 38-65, Jan. 1965

Viet Nam's Montagnards. By Howard Sochurek. 443-487, Apr. 1968

UNITED STATES ATLAS. *See* Atlases, NGS

U. S. ATOMIC ENERGY COMMISSION. *See* Atomic Bomb Tests; South Carolina Rediscovered, for H-Bomb Project; Uranium (Hunting)

U. S. BUREAU OF STANDARDS. *See* National Bureau of Standards

U. S. CAPITOL, Washington, D. C.:

The Last Full Measure (Tribute to President Kennedy). By Melville Bell Grosvenor. 307-355, Mar. 1964

The Nation's Capitol Revealed as Never Before. By Carl Hayden. 1-3, Jan. 1964

Under the Dome of Freedom: The United States Capitol. By Lonnelle Aikman. Photos by George F. Mobley. 4-59, Jan. 1964

U. S. Capitol, Citadel of Democracy. By Lonnelle Aikman. 143-192, Aug. 1952

We, the People, Capitol guidebook. Published in cooperation with the United States Capitol Historical Society. 1, 2, Jan. 1964; 411, Mar. 1966; 586, Oct. 1967

U. S. CENSUS BUREAU:

Census 1960: Profile of the Nation. By Albert W. Atwood and Lonnelle Aikman. 697-714, Nov. 1959

U. S. COAST AND GEODETIC SURVEY:

Charting Our Sea and Air Lanes. By Stuart E. Jones. Photos by J. Baylor Roberts. 189-209, Feb. 1957

U. S. COAST GUARD:

The Coast Guard: Small Service With a Big Mission. By William S. Ellis. 113-139, July 1974

Flags of the Americas. By Elizabeth W. King. 633-657, May 1949

Lonely Cape Hatteras, Besieged by the Sea. By William S. Ellis. Photos by Emory Kristof. 393-421, Sept. 1969

Rugged Is the Word for Bravo. By Phillip M. Swatek. 829-843, Dec. 1955

Tracking Danger With the Ice Patrol. By William S. Ellis. Photos by James R. Holland. 780-793, June 1968

Under Canvas in the Atomic Age. By Alan Villiers. 49-84, July 1955
Included: U. S. Coast Guard Academy training ship *Eagle*

U. S. CONGRESS:

Under the Dome of Freedom: The United States Capitol. By Lonnelle Aikman. Photos by George F. Mobley. 4-59, Jan. 1964

U. S. DEPARTMENT OF AGRICULTURE:

How Fruit Came to America. By J. R. Magness. Paintings by Else Bostelmann. 325-377, Sept. 1951

New Tricks Outwit Our Insect Enemies. By Hal Higdon. Photos by Robert F. Sisson and Emory Kristof. 380-399, Sept. 1972

Report from the Locust Wars. By Tony and Dickey Chapelle. 545-562, Apr. 1953
Included: U. S. Department of Agriculture's Bureau of Entomology and Plant Quarantine

U. S. DEPARTMENT OF AGRICULTURE — *Continued*

The Revolution in American Agriculture. By Jules B. Billard. Photos by James P. Blair. 147-185, Feb. 1970

See also Beltsville, Maryland; U. S. Forest Service; U. S. Soil Conservation Service

U. S. DEPARTMENT OF COMMERCE. *See* National Bureau of Standards; National Weather Service; U. S. Census Bureau; U. S. Coast and Geodetic Survey; U. S. Patent Office

U. S. DEPARTMENT OF DEFENSE. *See* Civil Air Patrol; DEW Line; DODGE Satellite; U. S. Armed Forces

U. S. DEPARTMENT OF JUSTICE. *See* Federal Bureau of Investigation

U. S. DEPARTMENT OF STATE. *See* Peace Corps

U. S. DEPARTMENT OF THE INTERIOR:

Expeditions and Research. *See* Starfish; Tektite II

See also National Park Service; U. S. Fish and Wildlife Service

U. S. DEPARTMENT OF TRANSPORTATION:

The Coming Revolution in Transportation. By Fredric C. Appel. Photos by Dean Conger. 301-341, Sept. 1969

See also Interstate Highway System; U. S. Coast Guard

U. S. EXECUTIVE DEPARTMENTS:

Flags of the Americas. By Elizabeth W. King. 633-657, May 1949
Included: Flags of the President of the United States, the Vice President of the United States, Secretary of Agriculture, Secretary of the Air Force, Secretary of the Army, Secretary of Commerce, Secretary of Defense, Secretary of the Interior, Attorney General, Secretary of Labor, Secretary of the Navy, Postmaster General, Secretary of State, Secretary of the Treasury

U. S. FISH AND WILDLIFE SERVICE:

An Exotic New Oriole Settles in Florida. By Charles M. Brookfield and Oliver Griswold. 261-264, Feb. 1956

The Gooney Birds of Midway. By John W. Aldrich. 839-851, June 1964

See also Aransas National Wildlife Refuge; Bear River Migratory Bird Refuge; National Elk Refuge; Wichita Mountains Wildlife Refuge; *and* listing under Woods Hole Oceanographic Institution

U. S. FOOD AND DRUG ADMINISTRATION:

Quicksilver and Slow Death. By John J. Putman. Photos by Robert W. Madden. 507-527, Oct. 1972

U. S. FOREST SERVICE:

Forest Fire: The Devil's Picnic. By Stuart E. Jones and Jay Johnston. 100-127, July 1968
Included: Northern regional headquarters, Missoula, Montana; Smokejumper Center; Northern Forest Fire Laboratory

Mexico to Canada on the Pacific Crest Trail. By Mike W. Edwards. Photos by David Hiser. 741-779, June 1971

Our Green Treasury, the National Forests. By Nathaniel T. Kenney. Photos by J. Baylor Roberts. 287-324, Sept. 1956

Timber: How Much Is Enough? By John J. Put

U. S. FOREST SERVICE — *Continued*

man. Photos by Bruce Dale. 485-511, Apr. 1974

Washington Wilderness, the North Cascades. By Edwards Park. Photos by Kathleen Revis. 335-367, Mar. 1961

U. S. GEOLOGICAL SURVEY:

California's San Andreas Fault. By Thomas Y. Canby. Photos by James P. Blair. 38-53, Jan. 1973

Can We Predict Quakes? By Thomas Y. Canby. 830-835, June 1976

Fountain of Fire in Hawaii. By Frederick Simpich, Jr. Photos by Robert B. Goodman and Robert Wenkam. 303-327, Mar. 1960
Included: The Hawaiian Volcano Observatory

Hunting Uranium Around the World. By Robert D. Nininger. Photos by Volkmar Wentzel. 533-558, Oct. 1954

U. S. GOVERNMENT AGENCIES:

Flags of the Americas. By Elizabeth W. King. 633-657, May 1949
Included: U. S. Coast and Geodetic Survey, U. S. Customs Service, U. S. Fish and Wildlife Service, U. S. Foreign Service, U. S. Geological Survey, U. S. Immigration and Naturalization Service, U. S. Maritime Commission, U. S. Public Health Service, U. S. Yacht Ensign

See also individual Government agencies

U. S. IMMIGRATION AND NATURALIZATION SERVICE:

Immigrants Still Flock to Liberty's Land. By Albert W. Atwood. 708-724, Nov. 1955

U. S. MARINE CORPS:

Behind the Headlines in Viet Nam. By Peter T. White. Photos by Winfield Parks. 149-189, Feb. 1967

Flags of the Americas. By Elizabeth W. King. 633-657, May 1949

Four-ocean Navy in the Nuclear Age. By Thomas W. McKnew. 145-187, Feb. 1965

Freedom Train Tours America. 529-542, Oct. 1949
Included: U. S. Marine Corps guards

The GI and the Kids of Korea. By Robert H. Mosier. 635-664, May 1953

Helicopter War in South Viet Nam. By Dickey Chapelle. 723-754, Nov. 1962

Here Come the Marines. By Frederick Simpich. 647-672, Nov. 1950

The President's Music Men. By Stuart E. Jones. Photos by William W. Campbell III. 752-766, Dec. 1959

See also Unknown Servicemen

U. S. MERCHANT MARINE ACADEMY, Kings Point, New York:

Kings Point: Maker of Mariners. By Nathaniel T. Kenney. Photos by Volkmar Wentzel. 693-706, Nov. 1955

Long Island Outgrows the Country. By Howell Walker. Photos by B. Anthony Stewart. 279-326, Mar. 1951

U. S. MILITARY ACADEMY, West Point, New York:

The Making of a West Pointer. By Howell Walker. 597-626, May 1952

The Mighty Hudson. By Albert W. Atwood. Photos by B. Anthony Stewart. 1-36, July 1948

U.S. NAVAL ACADEMY, Annapolis, Maryland:
Midshipmen's Cruise. By William J. Aston and Alexander G. B. Grosvenor. 711-754, June 1948

U.S. NAVAL AIR STATION, Lakehurst, New Jersey. *See* Parachute Rigger School

U.S. NAVAL OBSERVATORY, Washington, D. C.:
Split-second Time Runs Today's World. By F. Barrows Colton and Catherine Bell Palmer. 399-428, Sept. 1947

U.S. NAVY:
Adventures with the Survey Navy. By Irving Johnson. 131-148, July 1947

Expeditions and Research. *See* American Antarctic Mountaineering Expedition; Operation Deep Freeze; Operation Highjump

First Flight Across the Bottom of the World. By James R. Reedy. Photos by Otis Imboden. 454-464, Mar. 1964

Flags of the Americas. By Elizabeth W. King. 633-657, May 1949

Flying in the "Blowtorch" Era. By Frederick G. Vosburgh. 281-322, Sept. 1950

Four-ocean Navy in the Nuclear Age. By Thomas W. McKnew. 145-187, Feb. 1965

From Indian Canoes to Submarines at Key West. By Frederick Simpich. Photos by J. Baylor Roberts. 41-72, Jan. 1950
Included: U. S. Naval Station Submarine Base, Air Station, and Fleet Sonar School

The Gooney Birds of Midway. By John W. Aldrich. 839-851, June 1964

Medals awarded the Navy:
Replica of first La Gorce Medal for support of American Antarctic Mountaineering Expedition. 865, 867, June 1967
Society Honors the Conquerors of Antarctica (U. S. Navy Antarctic Expeditions, 1955-1959). 589-590, Apr. 1959

Men Against the Hurricane. By Andrew H. Brown. 537-560, Oct. 1950

Midshipmen's Cruise. By William J. Aston and Alexander G. B. Grosvenor. 711-754, June 1948

Our Navy Explores Antarctica. By Richard E. Byrd. U. S. Navy official photos. 429-522, Oct. 1947

Our Navy in the Far East. By Arthur W. Radford. Photos by J. Baylor Roberts. 537-577, Oct. 1953

Our Navy's Long Submarine Arm. By Allan C. Fisher, Jr. 613-636, Nov. 1952

Our Nuclear Navy. By George W. Anderson, Jr. 449-450, Mar. 1963

Pacific Fleet: Force for Peace. By Franc Shor. Photos by W. E. Garrett. 283-335, Sept. 1959

Patrolling Troubled Formosa Strait. 573-588, Apr. 1955

'Round the Horn by Submarine. By Paul C. Stimson. 129-144, Jan. 1948

Sailors in the Sky: Fifty Years of Naval Aviation. By Patrick N. L. Bellinger. 276-296, Aug. 1961

Troubled Waters East of Suez. By Ernest M. Eller. 483-522, Apr. 1954

We Survive on a Pacific Atoll. By John and Frank Craighead. 73-94, Jan. 1948

The Yankee Sailor Who Opened Japan. By Ferdinand Kuhn. 85-102, July 1953

U.S. NAVY—*Continued*
Yemen Opens the Door to Progress. By Harry Hoogstraal. 213-244, Feb. 1952
Included: A United States Navy team of medical research workers

See also Guantánamo; Honolulu, Hawaii, for Pearl Harbor; San Diego, California; *and* Aviation Medicine; *Enterprise;* MATS; Office of Naval Research; Shiplift; *Strato-Lab;* Submarines; *Trieste;* Unknown Servicemen; War Memorials

U.S. PATENT OFFICE:
Patent Plants Enrich Our World. By Orville H. Kneen. 357-378, Mar. 1948

U.S. POSTAL SERVICE:
Everyone's Servant, the Post Office. By Allan C. Fisher, Jr. Photos by Volkmar Wentzel. 121-152, July 1954
See also J. W. Westcott (Mail Boat); Post Roads

U.S. PUBLIC HEALTH SERVICE:
Immigrants Still Flock to Liberty's Land. By Albert W. Atwood. 708-724, Nov. 1955

U.S. ROUTE 40:
From Sea to Shining Sea. By Ralph Gray. Photos by Dean Conger and author. 1-61, July 1961

U.S. ROUTE 89:
From Sun-clad Sea to Shining Mountains. By Ralph Gray. Photos by James P. Blair. 542-589, Apr. 1964

U.S. SOIL CONSERVATION SERVICE:
Sno-Cats Mechanize Oregon Snow Survey. By Andrew H. Brown. Photos by John E. Fletcher. 691-710, Nov. 1949

U.S. SUBMARINE SCHOOL, New London, Connecticut:
Our Navy's Long Submarine Arm. By Allan C. Fisher, Jr. 613-636, Nov. 1952

U.S. TRUST TERRITORY OF THE PACIFIC ISLANDS. *See* Trust Territory of the Pacific Islands

U.S. VIRGIN ISLANDS. *See* Virgin Islands

U.S. WEATHER BUREAU:
Men Against the Hurricane. By Andrew H. Brown. 537-560, Oct. 1950

Milestones in My Arctic Journeys. By Willie Knutsen. 543-570, Oct. 1949

River Forecasting Center. *See* Midwest Flood

Rugged Is the Word for Bravo. By Phillip M. Swatek. 829-843, Dec. 1955

Weather from the White North. By Andrew H. Brown. Photos by John E. Fletcher. 543-572, Apr. 1955

See also National Weather Service

UNIVERSE:
The Amazing Universe. Special Publication announced. 870-874, June 1975

The Incredible Universe. By Kenneth F. Weaver. Photos by James P. Blair. 589-625, May 1974
Pioneers in Man's Search for the Universe. Paintings by Jean-Leon Huens. Text by Thomas Y. Canby. 627-633

UNIVERSITIES AND COLLEGES:
Atlanta, Pacesetter City of the South. By William S.

UNIVERSITIES AND COLLEGES — *Continued*
Ellis. Photos by James L. Amos. 246-281, Feb. 1969
Included: Atlanta University Center (Atlanta University, Clark, Interdenominational Theological Center, Morehouse, Morris Brown, Spelman); Emory University; Georgia Institute of Technology

California, the Golden Magnet. By William Graves. 595-679, May 1966
Included: Stanford University, University of California, University of Southern California

Expeditions and Research. *See* listings under the following: Columbia University; Cornell University; Princeton University; Purdue University; St. Elias, Mount, Expedition (Harvard Mountaineering Club); University of Alaska; University of Alexandria; University of Arizona; University of California; University of Costa Rica; University of Florida; University of Miami; University of Michigan; University of Pennsylvania

Literary Landmarks of Massachusetts. By William H. Nicholas. Photos by B. Anthony Stewart and John E. Fletcher. 279-310, Mar. 1950
Included: Amherst College, Boston College, College of the Holy Cross, Harvard University, Smith College

Pittsburgh, Pattern for Progress. By William J. Gill. Photos by Clyde Hare. 342-371, Mar. 1965
Included: Carnegie Institute of Technology, University of Pittsburgh

Pittsburgh: Workshop of the Titans. By Albert W. Atwood. 117-144, July 1949
Included: Carnegie Institute of Technology, University of Pittsburgh

Robert College, Turkish Gateway to the Future. By Franc Shor. 399-418, Sept. 1957
Included: American College for Girls, Robert Academy

Young-Old Lebanon Lives by Trade. By Thomas J. Abercrombie. 479-523, Apr. 1958
Included: American University of Beirut

See also California Institute of Technology; Cornell University; William and Mary College; *and* Georgetown, for Georgetown University; *and* the following universities

UNIVERSITY OF ALASKA: Arctic Research Laboratory:
Scientists Ride Ice Islands on Arctic Odysseys. By Lowell Thomas, Jr. Photos by Ted Spiegel. 670-691, Nov. 1965

UNIVERSITY OF ALEXANDRIA: Expeditions and Research:
Island of Faith in the Sinai Wilderness. By George H. Forsyth. Photos by Robert F. Sisson. 82-106, Jan. 1964

UNIVERSITY OF ARIZONA-ARIZONA STATE MUSEUM EXPEDITION. *See* Snaketown, Arizona

UNIVERSITY OF CALIFORNIA: Expeditions and Research:
Giant Kelp, Sequoias of the Sea. By Wheeler J. North. Photos by Bates Littlehales. 251-269, Aug. 1972

Gifts for the Jaguar God. By Philip Drucker and Robert F. Heizer. 367-375, Sept. 1956
Contents: Olmec archeological expedition

La Jolla, a Gem of the California Coast. By Deena Clark. Photos by J. Baylor Roberts. 755-782, Dec. 1952
Included: Scripps Institution of Oceanography

Sinai Sheds New Light on the Bible. By Henry

UNIVERSITY OF CALIFORNIA: Expeditions and Research — *Continued*
Field. Photos by William B. and Gladys Terry. 795-815, Dec. 1948

UNIVERSITY OF COSTA RICA: Research:
One Strange Night on Turtle Beach. By Paul A. Zahl. 570-581, Oct. 1973

UNIVERSITY OF FLORIDA: Research:
Imperiled Gift of the Sea: Caribbean Green Turtle. By Archie Carr. Photos by Robert E. Schroeder. 876-890, June 1967

UNIVERSITY OF MIAMI:
Miami's Expanding Horizons. By William H. Nicholas. 561-594, Nov. 1950
Included: College of Arts and Sciences, Drama Department, Food Technology Department, Graduate School, Marine Biology Department, Medical Research Unit, School of Business Administration, School of Education, School of Engineering, School of Law, School of Music

Marine Research

Shrimp Nursery: Science Explores New Ways to Farm the Sea. By Clarence P. Idyll. Photos by Robert F. Sisson. 636-659, May 1965

Shrimpers Strike Gold in the Gulf. By Clarence P. Idyll. Photos by Robert F. Sisson. 699-707, May 1957

Strange Babies of the Sea. By Hilary B. Moore. Paintings by Craig Phillips and Jacqueline Hutton. 41-56, July 1952
Contents: Plankton study and other marine life

See also Catfish (New Florida Resident); Crabs (The Crab That Shakes Hands); Grunion; Man-of-War (The Deadly Fisher); Octopuses (Shy Monster); Sailfish (Solving Life Secrets); Salmon (The Incredible); Shells (X-Rays Reveal); Shipworms (Saboteurs); Squids (Jet-powered)

UNIVERSITY OF MICHIGAN: Expeditions and Research:
Island of Faith in the Sinai Wilderness. By George H. Forsyth. Photos by Robert F. Sisson. 82-106, Jan. 1964

UNIVERSITY OF PENNSYLVANIA: Museum: Expeditions and Research:
Computer Helps Scholars Re-create an Egyptian Temple. By Ray Winfield Smith. Photos by Emory Kristof. 634-655, Nov. 1970

The Maya: Resurrecting the Grandeur of Tikal. By William R. Coe. 792-798, Dec. 1975

Medical Research: Undersea Living (Man-in-Sea Project). 530, 541, Apr. 1965

New Tools for Undersea Archeology. By George F. Bass. Photos by Charles R. Nicklin, Jr. 403-423, Sept. 1968

Oldest Known Shipwreck Yields Bronze Age Cargo. By Peter Throckmorton. 697-711, May 1962

Underwater Archeology: Key to History's Warehouse. By George F. Bass. Photos by Thomas J. Abercrombie and Robert B. Goodman. 138-156, July 1963

UNIVERSITY OF VIRGINIA:
Mr. Jefferson's Charlottesville. By Anne Revis. 553-592, May 1950

Thomas Jefferson: Architect of Freedom. By Mike W. Edwards. Photos by Linda Bartlett. 231-259, Feb. 1976

UNKNOWN FALLS, Upper and Lower, Labrador:
Labrador Canoe Adventure. By Andrew H. Brown and Ralph Gray. 65-99, July 1951

UNKNOWN SERVICEMEN: World War II and Korea: 'Known But to God.' By Beverley M. Bowie. 593-605, Nov. 1958

UNLOCKING Secrets of the Northern Lights. By Carl W. Gartlein. Paintings by William Crowder. 673-704, Nov. 1947

UNOTO (Masai Ceremony):
Spearing Lions with Africa's Masai. By Edgar Monsanto Queeny. 487-517, Oct. 1954

UNSINKABLE Malta. By Ernle Bradford. Photos by Ted H. Funk. 852-879, June 1969

UNSOELD, WILLIAM F.: Author:
The First Traverse. By Thomas F. Hornbein and William F. Unsoeld. 509-513, Oct. 1963
See also American Mount Everest Expedition

UNSUNG Beauties of Hawaii's Coral Reefs. By Paul A. Zahl. 510-525, Oct. 1959

UP HELLY AA (Festival):
Viking Festival in the Shetlands. Photos by Karl W. Gullers. 853-862, Dec. 1954

UP Through the Ice of the North Pole. By James F. Calvert. 1-41, July 1959

The UPPER Mississippi. By Willard Price. 651-699, Nov. 1958

UPPER VOLTA:
Freedom Speaks French in Ouagadougou. By John Scofield. 153-203, Aug. 1966

Al 'UQAYR, Saudi Arabia. See Gerrha

UR (Ancient City):
Abraham, the Friend of God. By Kenneth Mac-Leish. Photos by Dean Conger. 739-789, Dec. 1966

URANIUM:
The Canadian North: Emerging Giant. By David S. Boyer. 1-43, July 1968
    Included: Eldorado Mining and Refining Ltd.'s uranium mine in Saskatchewan
Hunting Uranium Around the World. By Robert D. Nininger. Photos by Volkmar Wentzel. 533-558, Oct. 1954
Man's New Servant, the Friendly Atom. By F. Barrows Colton. Photos by Volkmar Wentzel. 71-90, Jan. 1954
White Magic in the Belgian Congo. By W. Robert Moore. 321-362, Mar. 1952
See also Nuclear Energy

URANUS (Planet):
Voyage to the Planets. By Kenneth F. Weaver. Paintings by Ludek Pesek. 147-193, Aug. 1970

URBAN LIFE:
Five Noted Thinkers Explore the Future. 68-75, July 1976
    Included: Isaac Asimov, Richard F. Babcock, Edmund N. Bacon, Buckminster Fuller, Gerard Piel

URBAN RENEWAL:
Atlanta, Pacesetter City of the South. By William S.

URBAN RENEWAL—Continued
Ellis. Photos by James L. Amos. 246-281, Feb. 1969
Baltimore: The Hidden City. By Fred Kline. Photos by Martin Rogers. 188-215, Feb. 1975
Kansas City, Heartland U.S.A. By Rowe Findley. Photos by Ted Spiegel. 112-139, July 1976
Massachusetts Builds for Tomorrow. By Robert de Roos. Photos by B. Anthony Stewart. 790-843, Dec. 1966
New Grandeur for Flowering Washington. By Joseph Judge. Photos by James P. Blair. 500-539, Apr. 1967
Pittsburgh, Pattern for Progress. By William J. Gill. Photos by Clyde Hare. 342-371, Mar. 1965
St. Louis: New Spirit Soars in Mid-America's Proud Old City. By Robert Paul Jordan. Photos by Bruce Dale. 605-641, Nov. 1965
Stockholm, Where "Kvalitet" Is a Way of Life. By James Cerruti. Photos by Albert Moldvay and Jonathan Blair. 43-69, Jan. 1976
Venice Fights for Life. By Joseph Judge. Photos by Albert Moldvay. 591-631, Nov. 1972
Washington, the City Freedom Built. By William Graves. Photos by Bruce Dale and Thomas Nebbia. 735-781, Dec. 1964

URICK, FRANK, and Family:
Growing Up in Montana. Photos by Nicholas deVore III. 650-657, May 1976

URQUHART, FRED A.: Author:
Found at Last: the Monarch's Winter Home. Photos by Bianca Lavies. 161-173, Aug. 1976

URU INDIANS:
Titicaca, Abode of the Sun. By Luis Marden. Photos by Flip Schulke. 272-294, Feb. 1971

URUGUAY:
Parks, Plans, and People: How South America Guards Her Green Legacy. By Mary and Laurance Rockefeller. Photos by George F. Mobley. 74-119, Jan. 1967
The Purple Land of Uruguay. By Luis Marden. 623-654, Nov. 1948

URUMCHI (Wulumuchi), Sinkiang:
The Caves of the Thousand Buddhas. By Franc and Jean Shor. 383-415, Mar. 1951

UTAH:
From Sun-clad Sea to Shining Mountains. By Ralph Gray. Photos by James P. Blair. 542-589, Apr. 1964
A Map Maker Looks at the United States. By Newman Bumstead. 705-748, June 1951
    Included: Arches National Monument; Bryce Canyon; Price; Provo; Roan (Brown) Cliffs; Salt Lake City
Miracle of the Potholes. By Rowe Findley. Photos by Robert F. Sisson. 570-579, Oct. 1975
Riding the Outlaw Trail. By Robert Redford. Photos by Jonathan Blair. 622-657, Nov. 1976
Skiing in the United States. By Kathleen Revis. 216-254, Feb. 1959
Utah's Shining Oasis. By Charles McCarry. Photos by James L. Amos. 440-473, Apr. 1975
See also Arches National Monument; Bear River Migratory Bird Refuge; Bryce Canyon National Park; Canyonlands National Park; Dinosaur National Monument; Escalante Canyon; Fisher

UTAH—*Continued*

Towers; Great Salt Lake; Powell, Lake; Rainbow Bridge National Monument; San Juan (River); Zion National Park

UVÉA (Island), Wallis Islands, Pacific Ocean:

Adventures with the Survey Navy. By Irving Johnson. 131-148, July 1947

UZZELL, R. STEPHEN, III: Photographer:

Scotland's Inner Hebrides: Isles of the Western Sea. By Kenneth MacLeish. 690-717, Nov. 1974

V

V-2 (Rocket):

Seeing the Earth from 80 Miles Up. By Clyde T. Holliday. 511-528, Oct. 1950

VACATION Tour Through Lincoln Land. By Ralph Gray. 141-184, Feb. 1952

VADUZ, Liechtenstein:

Liechtenstein Thrives on Stamps. By Ronald W. Clark. 105-112, July 1948

VAITERE (Schooner):

Shores and Sails in the South Seas. By Charles Allmon. 73-104, Jan. 1950

VAL D'HÉRENS, Switzerland:

Switzerland's Enchanted Val d'Hérens. By Georgia Engelhard Cromwell. 825-848, June 1955

VALENCIA, Spain:

The Changing Face of Old Spain. By Bart McDowell. Photos by Albert Moldvay. 291-339, Mar. 1965

Speaking of Spain. By Luis Marden. 415-456, Apr. 1950

VALLEY FORGE, Pennsylvania:

Patriots in Petticoats. By Lonnelle Aikman. Paintings by Louis S. Glanzman. 475-493, Oct. 1975

Washington Lives Again at Valley Forge. By Howell Walker. 187-202, Feb. 1954

VALLEY OF TEN THOUSAND SMOKES, Alaska:

Lonely Wonders of Katmai. By Ernest Gruening. Photos by Winfield Parks. 800-831, June 1963

VALLEY OF THE MOON (Sonoma Valley), California:

My Life in the Valley of the Moon. By H. H. Arnold. Photos by Willard R. Culver. 689-716, Dec. 1948

Wildlife In and Near the Valley of the Moon. By H. H. Arnold. Photos by Paul J. Fair. 401-414, Mar. 1950

VALPARAÍSO, Chile:

Chile, the Long and Narrow Land. By Kip Ross. 185-235, Feb. 1960

VAN BIESBROECK, GEORGE:

Burr Prizes Awarded to Dr. Edgerton and Dr. Van Biesbroeck. 705-706, May 1953

Eclipse Hunting in Brazil's Ranchland. By F. Barrows Colton. Photos by Richard H. Stewart and Guy W. Starling. 285-324, Sept. 1947

Operation Eclipse: 1948. By William A. Kinney. 325-372, Mar. 1949

South in the Sudan. By Harry Hoogstraal. 249-272, Feb. 1953

VAN BUREN, MARTIN:

Profiles of the Presidents: II. A Restless Nation Moves West. By Frank Freidel. 80-121, Jan. 1965

VANCOUVER ISLAND, British Columbia, Canada:

British Columbia: Life Begins at 100. By David S. Boyer. 147-189, Aug. 1958

Canada's Window on the Pacific: The British Columbia Coast. By Jules B. Billard. Photos by Ted Spiegel. 338-375, Mar. 1972

VanDERWALKER, JOHN G.: Author:

Tektite II: Science's Window on the Sea. Photos by Bates Littlehales. 256-289, Aug. 1971

VANISHED Mystery Men of Hudson Bay. By Henry B. Collins. 669-687, Nov. 1956

VAN LAWICK, HUGO. *See* Lawick, Hugo van

VAN LAWICK-GOODALL, JANE. *See* Lawick-Goodall, Jane van

VAN RIPER, WALKER: Author-Photographer:

Freezing the Flight of Hummingbirds. By Harold E. Edgerton, R. J. Niedrach, and Walker Van Riper. 245-261, Aug. 1951

VASA (Swedish Warship):

Ghost From the Depths: the Warship *Vasa*. By Anders Franzén. 42-57, Jan. 1962

VATICAN CITY:

Rome: Eternal City with a Modern Air. By Harnett T. Kane. Photos by B. Anthony Stewart. 437-491, Apr. 1957

St. Peter's, Rome's Church of Popes. By Aubrey Menen. Photos by Albert Moldvay. 865-879, Dec. 1971

When in Rome. . . . By Stuart E. Jones. Photos by Winfield Parks. 741-789, June 1970

When the President Goes Abroad (Eisenhower Tour). By Gilbert M. Grosvenor. 588-649, May 1960

VAUGHN, W. D.: Photographer:

Africa: The Winds of Freedom Stir a Continent. By Nathaniel T. Kenney. 303-359, Sept. 1960

Exploring Antarctica's Phantom Coast. By Edwin S. McDonald. 251-273, Feb. 1962

The Lower Mississippi. By Willard Price. 681-725, Nov. 1960

New Era on the Great Lakes. By Nathaniel T. Kenney. 439-490, Apr. 1959

Our Land Through Lincoln's Eyes. By Carolyn Bennett Patterson. 243-277, Feb. 1960

Staten Island Ferry, New York's Seagoing Bus. By John T. Cunningham and Jay Johnston. 833-843, June 1959

VAUPÉS RIVER, Colombia-Brazil:

Jungle Jaunt on Amazon Headwaters. By Bernice M. Goetz. 371-388, Sept. 1952

VEGETABLES:

California, Horn of Plenty. By Frederick Simpich. Photos by Willard R. Culver. 553-594, May 1949

Our Vegetable Travelers. By Victor R. Boswell. Paintings by Else Bostelmann. 145-217, Aug. 1949

Contents: Artichoke, Asparagus, Beans (Great Northern, Kidney, Lima, Marrow, Navy or Pea, Pinto,

VEGETABLES — *Continued*

Stringless or Snap, Yellow), Broccoli, Brussels Sprouts, Cabbage, Cardoon, Carrots, Cauliflower, Celery, Chard, Chinese Cabbage, Collards, Corn, Cowpea, Cucumber, Eggplant, Endive, Kale, Kohlrabi, Lettuce, Muskmelons (Banana Melon, Cantaloupe, Casaba, Honey Dew, Montreal, Santa Claus), Mustard, Okra, Onions (Chive, Garlic, Leek), Parsnip, Peas, Peppers (Garden Pepper, Pimiento), Potato, Radish, Rhubarb, Romaine, Rutabaga, Salsify, Soybeans, Spinach, Squash (Acorn, Boston Marrow, Cocozelle, Crookneck, Cushaw, Cymling, Delicious, Hubbard, Marblehead, Pumpkin, Straightneck, Turks Turban, White Bush Scallop, Zucchini), Sweet Potato, Tomato, Turnip, Watermelon

The World in Your Garden. Book announced. 729-730, May 1957

See also Beltsville, Maryland, for Agricultural Research Center; Potatoes and Potato Growing

VENEZUELA:

Search for the Scarlet Ibis in Venezuela. By Paul A. Zahl. 633-661, May 1950

Venezuela Builds on Oil. By Thomas J. Abercrombie. 344-387, Mar. 1963

Venezuela's Crisis of Wealth. By Noel Grove. Photos by Robert W. Madden. 175-209, Aug. 1976

Yanomamo, the True People. By Napoleon A. Chagnon. 211-223, Aug. 1976

See also Angel Falls

VENICE, Italy:

Italy Smiles Again. By Edgar Erskine Hume. 693-732, June 1949

A Stroll to Venice. By Isobel Wylie Hutchison. 378-410, Sept. 1951

Venice, City of Twilight Splendor. By Joe Alex Morris. Photos by John Scofield. 543-569, Apr. 1961

Venice Fights for Life. By Joseph Judge. Photos by Albert Moldvay. 591-631, Nov. 1972
Venice's Golden Legacy. Photos by Victor R. Boswell, Jr. 609-619

VENUS (Planet):

Mariner Scans a Lifeless Venus. By Frank Sartwell. Paintings by Davis Meltzer. 733-742, May 1963

Mariner Unveils Venus and Mercury. By Kenneth F. Weaver. 858-869, June 1975

Voyage to the Planets. By Kenneth F. Weaver. Paintings by Ludek Pesek. 147-193, Aug. 1970

VENUS FLYTRAP:

Plants That Eat Insects. By Paul A. Zahl. 643-659, May 1961

VERACRUZ (State), Mexico. *See* San Lorenzo

VERAGUAS (Province), Panama. *See* La Pita

VERMONT:

New England, a Modern Pilgrim's Pride. By Beverley M. Bowie. 733-796, June 1955

Robert Frost and New England. By Archibald MacLeish. 438-467, Apr. 1976
Look of a Land Beloved. Photos by Dewitt Jones. 444-467

Skiing in the United States. By Kathleen Revis. 216-254, Feb. 1959

Vermont — a State of Mind and Mountains. By Ethel A. Starbird. Photos by Nathan Benn. 28-61, July 1974

VERMONT — *Continued*

See also Champlain, Lake; Connecticut River; Green Mountains

VERONA, Italy:

Italy Smiles Again. By Edgar Erskine Hume. 693-732, June 1949

VERREAUX'S EAGLES. *See* Black Eagles

VERSATILE Wood Waits on Man. By Andrew H. Brown. 109-140, July 1951

VEST FJORDEN, Norway:

Fishing in the Lofotens. Photos by Lennart Nilsson. 377-388, Mar. 1947

VEST SPITSBERGEN (Island), Svalbard:

Spitsbergen Mines Coal Again. 113-120, July 1948

VESTER, BERTHA SPAFFORD:

Author-Photographer-Artist
Jerusalem, My Home. 826-847, Dec. 1964

VESTMANNAEYJAR, Heimaey, Iceland:

A Village Fights for Its Life. By Noel Grove. 40-67, July 1973

VEVEY, Switzerland:

Switzerland's Once-in-a-generation Festival. By Jean and Franc Shor. 563-571, Oct. 1958

VÉZELAY, Hill of the Pilgrims. By Melvin Hall. 229-247, Feb. 1953

VICKSBURG, Mississippi:

Gettysburg and Vicksburg: the Battle Towns Today. By Robert Paul Jordan. Map notes by Carolyn Bennett Patterson. 4-57, July 1963

VICTOR, PAUL-EMILE: Author:

Wringing Secrets from Greenland's Icecap. 121-147, Jan. 1956

VICTORIA, Queen (Great Britain and Ireland):

The British Way. By Sir Evelyn Wrench. 421-541, Apr. 1949

VICTORIA (State), Australia:

Australia's Pacesetter State, Victoria. By Allan C. Fisher, Jr. Photos by Thomas Nebbia. 218-253, Feb. 1971
See also Melbourne

VICTORIA, British Columbia, Canada:

British Columbia: Life Begins at 100. By David S. Boyer. 147-189, Aug. 1958

Canada's Window on the Pacific: The British Columbia Coast. By Jules B. Billard. Photos by Ted Spiegel. 338-375, Mar. 1972

VICTORIA, Kansas:

Hays, Kansas, at the Nation's Heart. By Margaret M. Detwiler. Photos by John E. Fletcher. 461-490, Apr. 1952

VICTORIA, Lake, Kenya-Tanzania-Uganda:

Adventures in the Search for Man. By Louis S. B. Leakey. Photos by Hugo van Lawick. 132-152, Jan. 1963

Britain Tackles the East African Bush. By W. Robert Moore. 311-353, Mar. 1950

Uganda, Africa's Uneasy Heartland. By Howard La Fay. Photos by George F. Mobley. 708-735, Nov. 1971

VICTORIA FALLS, Rhodesia-Zambia:

Africa: The Winds of Freedom Stir a Continent. By Nathaniel T. Kenney. Photos by W. D. Vaughn. 303-359, Sept. 1960

Rhodesia, a House Divided. By Allan C. Fisher, Jr. Photos by Thomas Nebbia. 641-671, May 1975

VICTORIAN AGE:

The England of Charles Dickens. By Richard W. Long. Photos by Adam Woolfitt. 443-483, Apr. 1974

VICUÑAS:

High, Wild World of the Vicuña. By William L. Franklin. 77-91, Jan. 1973

VIENNA, Austria:

Building a New Austria. By Beverley M. Bowie. Photos by Volkmar Wentzel. 172-213, Feb. 1959

Occupied Austria, Outpost of Democracy. By George W. Long. Photos by Volkmar Wentzel. 749-790, June 1951

Vienna, City of Song. By Peter T. White. Photos by John Launois. 739-779, June 1968

The Vienna Treasures and Their Collectors. By John Walker. 737-776, June 1950
    Included: Kunsthistorisches Museum

What I Saw Across the Rhine. By J. Frank Dobie. 57-86, Jan. 1947

See also Spanish Riding School

VIET NAM:

Indochina Faces the Dragon. By George W. Long. Photos by J. Baylor Roberts. 287-328, Sept. 1952

The Lands and Peoples of Southeast Asia. 295-365, Mar. 1971
    I. Mosaic of Cultures. By Peter T. White. Photos by W. E. Garrett. 296-329
    II. New Light on a Forgotten Past. By Wilhelm G. Solheim II. 330-339

Passage to Freedom in Viet Nam. By Gertrude Samuels. 858-874, June 1955

The Peoples of Mainland Southeast Asia; Asia, double-sided map supplement. Mar. 1971

Portrait of Indochina. By W. Robert Moore and Maynard Owen Williams. Paintings by Jean Despujols. 461-490, Apr. 1951

Strife-torn Indochina. By W. Robert Moore. 499-510, Oct. 1950

Viet Nam, Cambodia, Laos, and Eastern Thailand, map supplement. Text on reverse. Jan. 1965

Viet Nam, Cambodia, Laos, and Thailand, map supplement. Feb. 1967

See also Viet Nam, North; Viet Nam, South

VIET NAM, North:

Air Rescue Behind Enemy Lines. By Howard Sochurek. 346-369, Sept. 1968

VIET NAM, South:

American Special Forces in Action in Viet Nam. By Howard Sochurek. 38-65, Jan. 1965

Behind the Headlines in Viet Nam. By Peter T. White. Photos by Winfield Parks. 149-189, Feb. 1967

Helicopter War in South Viet Nam. By Dickey Chapelle. 723-754, Nov. 1962

The Mekong, River of Terror and Hope. By Peter T. White. Photos by W. E. Garrett. 737-787, Dec. 1968

Of Planes and Men. By Kenneth F. Weaver. Photos

VIET NAM, South—*Continued*

by Emory Kristof and Albert Moldvay. 298-349, Sept. 1965
    Included: Bien Hoa and Tan Son Nhut air bases at Saigon; Da Nang Air Base; and outposts at Khe Sahn and Vinh Long

Slow Train Through Viet Nam's War. By Howard Sochurek. 412-444, Sept. 1968

South Viet Nam Fights the Red Tide. By Peter T. White. Photos by W. E. Garrett. 445-489, Oct. 1961

Viet Nam's Montagnards. By Howard Sochurek. 443-487, Apr. 1968

Water War in Viet Nam. By Dickey Chapelle. 272-296, Feb. 1966

See also Saigon

VIGOROUS Young Nation in the South Sea. By Alan Villiers. 309-385, Sept. 1963

VIKING FESTIVAL in the Shetlands. Photos by Karl W. Gullers. 853-862, Dec. 1954

VIKING LANDER (Spacecraft):

The Search for Life on Mars. By Kenneth F. Weaver. 264-265, Feb. 1973

See also Voyager

VIKINGS:

A New Look at Medieval Europe. By Kenneth M. Setton. Paintings by Andre Durenceau and Birney Lettick. 799-859, Dec. 1962

The Vikings. By Howard La Fay. Photos by Ted Spiegel. 492-541, Apr. 1970

The Vikings. Special Publication announced. 870-874, June 1972

Vinland Ruins Prove Vikings Found the New World. By Helge Ingstad. 708-734, Nov. 1964

VILCABAMBA, Cordillera, Peru:

By Parachute Into Peru's Lost World. By G. Brooks Baekeland. Photos by author and Peter R. Gimbel. 268-296, Aug. 1964

VILCABAMBA, Ecuador:

"Every Day Is a Gift When You Are Over 100." By Alexander Leaf. Photos by John Launois. 93-119, Jan. 1973

A VILLAGE Fights for Its Life. By Noel Grove. 40-67, July 1973

VILLARD, HENRY S.: Author:

Rubber-cushioned Liberia. Photos by Charles W. Allmon. 201-228, Feb. 1948

VILLAS BOAS, CLAUDIO and ORLANDO: Authors:

Saving Brazil's Stone Age Tribes From Extinction. Photos by W. Jesco von Puttkamer. 424-444, Sept. 1968

VILLAVICENCIO, Colombia:

Keeping House for a Biologist in Colombia. By Nancy Bell Fairchild Bates. Photos by Marston Bates. 251-274, Aug. 1948

VILLIERS, ALAN:

Editorial. 149, Feb. 1975
                    Author

Aboard the N.S. *Savannah:* World's First Nuclear Merchantman. Photos by John E. Fletcher. 280-298, Aug. 1962

The Age of Sail Lives On at Mystic. Photos by Wes-

VILLIERS, ALAN: Author—*Continued*

ton Kemp. 220-239, Aug. 1968

"The Alice" in Australia's Wonderland. Photos by Jeff Carter and David Moore. 230-257, Feb. 1966

Australia. 309-385, Sept. 1963

Captain Cook: The Man Who Mapped the Pacific. Photos by Gordon W. Gahan. 297-349, Sept. 1971

Channel Cruise to Glorious Devon. Photos by Bates Littlehales. 208-259, Aug. 1963

Cowes to Cornwall. Photos by Robert B. Goodman. 149-201, Aug. 1961

England's Scillies, the Flowering Isles. Photos by Bates Littlehales. 126-145, July 1967

Fabled Mount of St. Michael. Photos by Bates Littlehales. 880-898, June 1964

In the Wake of Darwin's *Beagle*. Photos by James L. Stanfield. 449-495, Oct. 1969

Last of the Cape Horners. 701-710, May 1948

Magellan: First Voyage Around the World. Photos by Bruce Dale. 721-753, June 1976

The Netherlands: Nation at War With the Sea. Photos by Adam Woolfitt. 530-571, Apr. 1968

Prince Henry, the Explorer Who Stayed Home. Photos by Thomas Nebbia. 616-656, Nov. 1960

Scotland From Her Lovely Lochs and Seas. Photos by Robert F. Sisson. 492-541, Apr. 1961

Ships Through the Ages: A Saga of the Sea. 494-545, Apr. 1963

Sir Francis Drake. Photos by Gordon W. Gahan. 216-253, Feb. 1975

Wales, Land of Bards. Photos by Thomas Nebbia. 727-769, June 1965

We're Coming Over on the *Mayflower*. 708-728, May 1957

Author-Photographer

By Full-rigged Ship to Denmark's Fairyland. Photos by Alexander Taylor and author. 809-828, Dec. 1955

Golden Beaches of Portugal. 673-696, Nov. 1954

How We Sailed the New *Mayflower* to America. 627-672, Nov. 1957

I Sailed with Portugal's Captains Courageous. 565-596, May 1952

The Marvelous Maldive Islands. 829-849, June 1957

Sailing with Sindbad's Sons. 675-688, Nov. 1948

Under Canvas in the Atomic Age. 49-84, July 1955

VINEYARDS. *See* Grapes and Grape Culture

VINLAND Ruins Prove Vikings Found the New World. By Helge Ingstad. 708-734, Nov. 1964

VIRGIN ISLANDS, West Indies:

A Fresh Breeze Stirs the Leewards. By Carleton Mitchell. Photos by Winfield Parks. 488-537, Oct. 1966

Our Virgin Islands, 50 Years Under the Flag. By Carleton Mitchell. Photos by James L. Stanfield. 67-103, Jan. 1968

Virgin Islands: Tropical Playland, U.S.A. By John Scofield. Photos by Charles Allmon. 201-232, Feb. 1956

See also Buck Island Reef National Monument, St. Croix; St. John (Island)

VIRGIN RIVER, Utah-Arizona-Nevada:

Amid the Mighty Walls of Zion. By Lewis F. Clark. 37-70, Jan. 1954

VIRGINIA:

Capt. John Smith's Map of Virginia. — George Washington's Travels, Traced on the Arrowsmith Map. 760, 768, June 1953

Chesapeake Country. By Nathaniel T. Kenney. Photos by Bates Littlehales. 370-411, Sept. 1964

Exploring America's Great Sand Barrier Reef. By Eugene R. Guild. Photos by author and John E. Fletcher. 325-350, Sept. 1947

Firebrands of the Revolution. By Eric F. Goldman. Photos by George F. Mobley. 2-27, July 1974

Founders of Virginia. By Sir Evelyn Wrench. Photos by B. Anthony Stewart. 433-462, Apr. 1948

History Keeps House in Virginia. By Howell Walker. 441-484, Apr. 1956

Indian Life Before the Colonists Came. By Stuart E. Jones. Engravings by Theodore de Bry, 1590. 351-368, Sept. 1947

The Nation's River. By Allan C. Fisher, Jr. Photos by James L. Stanfield. 432-469, Oct. 1976
  A Good Life on the Potomac. 470-479

Over and Under Chesapeake Bay. By David S. Boyer. 593-612, Apr. 1964

A *Pocket Map of Suburban Washington; Central Washington,* double-sided map supplement. Sept. 1948

Round About the Nation's Capital, map supplement. Apr. 1956

Shrines of Each Patriot's Devotion. By Frederick G. Vosburgh. 51-82, Jan. 1949

Stately Homes of Old Virginia. By Albert W. Atwood. 787-802, June 1953

Suburban Washington; Tourist Washington, double-sided Atlas series supplement. Dec. 1964

The Virginians. By Mike W. Edwards. Photos by David Alan Harvey. 588-617, Nov. 1974

Witness to a War: British Correspondent Frank Vizetelly. By Robert T. Cochran, Jr. 453-491, Apr. 1961

See also Appomattox; Arlington County; Arlington National Cemetery; Delmarva Peninsula; Fredericksburg; Harmony Hollow; Jamestown; Monticello; Mount Vernon; Norfolk; Shenandoah National Park; Tangier Island; Williamsburg

VIRÚ VALLEY, Peru:

Finding the Tomb of a Warrior-God. By William Duncan Strong. Photos by Clifford Evans, Jr. 453-482, Apr. 1947

VIRUNGA MOUNTAINS, Rwanda-Uganda-Zaire:

Making Friends With Mountain Gorillas. By Dian Fossey. Photos by Robert M. Campbell. 48-67, Jan. 1970

More Years With Mountain Gorillas. By Dian Fossey. Photos by Robert M. Campbell. 574-585, Oct. 1971

VISBY, Gotland, Sweden:

Gotland: Sweden's Treasure Island. By James Cerruti. Photos by Albert Moldvay. 268-288, Aug. 1973

A VISIT to the Living Ice Age. By Rutherford Platt. 525-545, Apr. 1957

VIZCAYA: An Italian Palazzo in Miami. By William H. Nicholas. Photos by Justin Locke. 595-604, Nov. 1950

VIZETELLY, FRANK:

Witness to a War: British Correspondent Frank Vizetelly. By Robert T. Cochran, Jr. 453-491, Apr. 1961

VOAS, ROBERT B.: Author:

°John Glenn's Three Orbits in *Friendship 7:* A Minute-by-Minute Account of America's First Orbital Space Flight. 792-827, June 1962

VOICES of the Night. By Arthur A. Allen. 507-522, Apr. 1950

VOLCANIC ACTIVITY, Subsea. *See* Ilha Nova; Myojin Island; Surtsey

VOLCANO ISLANDS, Pacific Ocean. *See* Iwo Jima

VOLCANOES:

Death of an Island, Tristan da Cunha. By P. J. F. Wheeler. 678-695, May 1962

Disaster in Paradise. By Windsor P. Booth and Samuel W. Matthews. Photos by Robert F. Sisson. 436-458, Sept. 1963
Contents: The eruption of Mount Agung, Bali

El Sangay, Fire-breathing Giant of the Andes. By G. Edward Lewis. 117-138, Jan. 1950
Contents: El Antisana, El Cayambe, El Chimborazo, El Cotopaxi, El Pichincha, El Sangay, El Tulabug, and Imbabura

Exploring Aleutian Volcanoes. By G. D. Robinson. 509-528, Oct. 1948

Have We Solved the Mysteries of the Moon? By Kenneth F. Weaver. Paintings by William H. Bond. 309-325, Sept. 1973

Hawaii, U.S.A. By Frederick Simpich, Jr. Photos by Thomas Nebbia. 1-45, July 1960
Included: Kilauea; Mauna Loa

Iceland Tapestry. By Deena Clark. 599-630, Nov. 1951
Included: Hekla

Journey to Mars. By Kenneth F. Weaver. Paintings by Ludek Pesek. 231-263, Feb. 1973
Included: Discovery of nineteen volcanic features, the largest being Nix Olympica

Lost Kingdom in Indian Mexico. By Justin Locke. 517-546, Oct. 1952
Included: El Pilon, Parícutin

Our Home-town Planet, Earth. By F. Barrows Colton. 117-139, Jan. 1952

Sicily the Three-cornered. By Luis Marden. 1-48, Jan. 1955
Included: Etna, Stromboli

This Changing Earth. By Samuel W. Matthews. 1-37, Jan. 1973

The Violent Earth (Television film). 286A-286B, Feb. 1973

Volcano and Earthquake Show Nature's Awesome Power. The Editor. 303, Mar. 1960

Volcano Overwhelms an Icelandic Village. By Noel Grove. 40-67, July 1973
Contents: The eruption of Kirkjufell

What's Happening to Our Climate? By Samuel W. Matthews. 576-615, Nov. 1976

See also Crater Lake National Park, Oregon; Craters of the Moon National Monument, Idaho; Deception Island, Antarctica; Haleakala National Park, Hawaii; Ilha Nova, Azores; Irazú, Costa Rica; Katmai National Monument, Alaska; Kilauea Volcano, Hawaii; Lanzarote, Canary Islands; Myojin Island, Pacific Ocean; Pompeii, Italy; Surtsey (Island), North Atlantic Ocean; Thera (Island), Aegean Sea

VOLGA (River), U.S.S.R.:

The Volga (Television film). 575, Nov. 1976

The Volga, Russia's Mighty River Road. By Howard Sochurek. 579-613, May 1973

VOLGOGRAD, U.S.S.R.:

The Volga, Russia's Mighty River Road. By Howard Sochurek. 579-613, May 1973

VOLTA BUREAU, Georgetown, Washington, D. C.:

Washington's Historic Georgetown. By William A. Kinney. 513-544, Apr. 1953

VOODOOISM:

Haiti: Beyond Mountains, More Mountains. By Carolyn Bennett Patterson. Photos by Thomas Nebbia. 70-97, Jan. 1976

Haiti—West Africa in the West Indies. By John Scofield. 226-259, Feb. 1961

VOSBURGH, FREDERICK G.:

Board of Trustees, member. 867, Dec. 1957; 485, Oct. 1966; 589, Oct. 1967; 838, Dec. 1970; 226, Aug. 1976

Editor (1967-1970). 576, 577, 579, 586, 588, Oct. 1967; 861, June 1970; 841, Dec. 1970

Editor, Assistant. 841, Dec. 1970

Editor, Associate. 419, 420, 423, Mar. 1957; 867, Dec. 1957; 834, Dec. 1959; 585, Oct. 1963; 485, Oct. 1966; 579, Oct. 1967; 841, Dec. 1970

Vice President of NGS. 585, Oct. 1963; 485, Oct. 1966; 576, 577, 588, Oct. 1967; 861, June 1970; 838, Dec. 1970

Author

Berlin, Island in a Soviet Sea. Photos by Volkmar Wentzel. 689-704, Nov. 1951

Dog Mart Day in Fredericksburg. 817-832, June 1951

Drums to Dynamos on the Mohawk. Photos by B. Anthony Stewart. 67-110, July 1947

Easter Egg Chickens. Photos by B. Anthony Stewart. 377-387, Sept. 1948

Flying in the "Blowtorch" Era. 281-322, Sept. 1950

Formosa—Hot Spot of the East. Photos by J. Baylor Roberts. 139-176, Feb. 1950

Japan Tries Freedom's Road. Photos by J. Baylor Roberts. 593-632, May 1950

Minnesota Makes Ideas Pay. Photos by John E. Fletcher and B. Anthony Stewart. 291-336, Sept. 1949

Shrines of Each Patriot's Devotion. 51-82, Jan. 1949

Threatened Glories of Everglades National Park. By Frederick Kent Truslow and Frederick G. Vosburgh. Photos by Frederick Kent Truslow and Otis Imboden. 508-553, Oct. 1967

To Gilbert Grosvenor: a Monthly Monument 25 Miles High. By Frederick G. Vosburgh and the staff of the National Geographic Society. 445-487, Oct. 1966

Torchbearers of the Twilight. 697-704, May 1951

VOSS, GILBERT L.: Author:

Shy Monster, the Octopus. Photos by Robert F. Sisson. 776-799, Dec. 1971

Solving Life Secrets of the Sailfish. Photos by B. Anthony Stewart. Paintings by Craig Phillips. 859-872, June 1956

Squids: Jet-powered Torpedoes of the Deep. Photos by Robert F. Sisson. 386-411, Mar. 1967

VOURAIKOS RIVER WATERSHED, Greece:

Erosion, Trojan Horse of Greece. By F. G. Renner. 793-812, Dec. 1947

A **VOYAGE** Into the Unknown Changed Man's Understanding of His World. By Alan Villiers. Photos by Bruce Dale. 721-753, June 1976

The **VOYAGE** of *Ra II.* By Thor Heyerdahl. Photos by Carlo Mauri and Georges Sourial. 44-71, Jan. 1971

VOYAGE to the Planets. By Kenneth F. Weaver. Paintings by Ludek Pesek. 147-193, Aug. 1970

VOYAGE to Venus: The Story of Mariner II. By Frank Sartwell. Paintings by Davis Meltzer. 733-742, May 1963

VOYAGER (Spacecraft):

Mars: A New World to Explore. By Carl Sagan. 821-841, Dec. 1967

VOYAGERS, Solo. *See* Graham, Robin Lee; *Ice Bird,* for David Lewis; Schultz, John E.

VOYAGES. *See* Cruises and Voyages

The **VOYAGES** and Historic Discoveries of Capt. Jas. Cook. By Alan Villiers. Photos by Gordon W. Gahan. 297-349, Sept. 1971

VOYAGEURS:

Relics from the Rapids. By Sigurd F. Olson. Photos by David S. Boyer. 413-435, Sept. 1963

VULTURES. *See* Andean Condors; Egyptian Vulture

W

WAGNER, KIP: Author:

Drowned Galleons Yield Spanish Gold. Photos by Otis Imboden. 1-37, Jan. 1965

WAHGI VALLEY, New Guinea:

New Guinea's Paradise of Birds. By E. Thomas Gilliard. 661-688, Nov. 1951

New Guinea's Rare Birds and Stone Age Men. By E. Thomas Gilliard. 421-488, Apr. 1953

Sheep Airlift in New Guinea. Photos by Ned Blood. 831-844, Dec. 1949

WAI WAI INDIANS:

Life Among the Wai Wai Indians. By Clifford Evans and Betty J. Meggers. 329-346, Mar. 1955

WAITOMO CAVES, New Zealand:

Nature's Night Lights: Probing the Secrets of Bioluminescence. By Paul A. Zahl. 45-69, July 1971

WAKELIN, JAMES H., Jr.: Author:

Thresher: Lesson and Challenge. 759-763, June 1964

WAKHAN (Region), Afghanistan:

Afghanistan: Crossroad of Conquerors. By Thomas J. Abercrombie. 297-345, Sept. 1968

We Took the Highroad in Afghanistan. By Jean and Franc Shor. 673-706, Nov. 1950

Winter Caravan to the Roof of the World. By Sabrina and Roland Michaud. 435-465, Apr. 1972

WAKHI (People):

Winter Caravan to the Roof of the World. By Sabrina and Roland Michaud. 435-465, Apr. 1972

WALES:

British Castles, History in Stone. By Norman Wilkinson. 111-129, July 1947

The Investiture of Great Britain's Prince of Wales. By Allan C. Fisher, Jr. Photos by James L. Stanfield and Adam Woolfitt. 698-715, Nov. 1969
Included: Caernarvon Castle

A Traveler's Map of the British Isles, map supplement. Text on reverse. Apr. 1974

Wales, Land of Bards. By Alan Villiers. Photos by Thomas Nebbia. 727-769, June 1965

See also Caldy; Skomer

A **WALK** Through the Wilderness: Yellowstone at 100. By Karen and Derek Craighead. Photos by Sam Abell. 579-603, May 1972

WALKER, ERNEST P.: Author:

"Flying" Squirrels, Nature's Gliders. 663-674, May 1947

Author-Photographer

Portraits of My Monkey Friends. 105-119, Jan. 1956

Photographer

The Wild Animals in My Life. By William M. Mann. 497-524, Apr. 1957

WALKER, HOWELL: Author:

Italian Riviera, Land That Winter Forgot. 743-789, June 1963

Long Island Outgrows the Country. Photos by B. Anthony Stewart. 279-326, Mar. 1951

The Making of a West Pointer. 597-626, May 1952

The More Paris Changes. . . . Photos by Gordon W. Gahan. 64-103, July 1972

New South Wales, the State That Cradled Australia. Photos by David Moore. 591-635, Nov. 1967

South Australia, Gateway to the Great Outback. Photos by Joseph J. Scherschel. 441-481, Apr. 1970

Washington Lives Again at Valley Forge. 187-202, Feb. 1954

Author-Photographer

Air Age Brings Life to Canton Island. 117-132, Jan. 1955

Aroostook County, Maine, Source of Potatoes. 459-478, Oct. 1948

Belgium Welcomes the World (1958 World's Fair). 795-837, June 1958

Cities Like Worcester Make America. 189-214, Feb. 1955

Cruise to Stone Age Arnhem Land. 417-430, Sept. 1949

France Meets the Sea in Brittany. 470-503, Apr. 1965

From Spear to Hoe on Groote Eylandt. 131-142, Jan. 1953

The Greener Fields of Georgia. Photos by author and B. Anthony Stewart. 287-330, Mar. 1954

Here Rest in Honored Glory . . . (War Memorials). 739-768, June 1957

History Keeps House in Virginia. 441-484, Apr. 1956

Lafayette's Homeland, Auvergne. 419-436, Sept. 1957

The Making of a New Australia. 233-259, Feb. 1956

New Zealand, Pocket Wonder World. 419-460, Apr. 1952

WALKER, HOWELL: Author—*Continued*

Normandy Blossoms Anew. 591-631, May 1959

Tasmania, Australia's Island State. 791-818, Dec. 1956

You Can't Miss America by Bus. Paintings by Walter A. Weber. 1-42, July 1950

Photographer

Exploring Stone Age Arnhem Land. By Charles P. Mountford. 745-782, Dec. 1949

King Ranch, Cattle Empire in Texas. 41-64, Jan. 1952

WALKER, JOHN: Author:

American Masters in the National Gallery. 295-324, Sept. 1948

The National Gallery After a Quarter Century. 348-371, Mar. 1967

The Nation's Newest Old Masters. Paintings from Kress Collection. 619-657, Nov. 1956

The Vienna Treasures and Their Collectors. 737-776, June 1950

Your National Gallery of Art After 10 Years. Paintings from Kress Collection. 73-103, Jan. 1952

WALKER, JOSEPH A.: Author:

I Fly the X-15. Photos by Dean Conger. 428-450, Sept. 1962

WALKER, LEWIS WAYNE: Author-Photographer:

Arizona's Window on Wildlife. 240-250, Feb. 1958

Sea Birds of Isla Raza. 239-248, Feb. 1951

WALKER, PHIL: Author:

Across the Alps in a Wicker Basket *(Bernina)*. 117-131, Jan. 1963

WALKER, STANLEY: Author:

The Fabulous State of Texas. Photos by B. Anthony Stewart and Thomas Nebbia. 149-195, Feb. 1961

WALKER, THEODORE J.: Author:

The California Gray Whale Comes Back. 394-415, Mar. 1971

WALKING CATFISH:

New Florida Resident, the Walking Catfish. By Clarence P. Idyll. Photos by Robert F. Sisson. 847-851, June 1969

WALKING TOURS:

From Barra to Butt in the Hebrides. By Isobel Wylie Hutchison. 559-580, Oct. 1954

I Walked Some Irish Miles. By Dorothea Sheats. 653-678, May 1951

A Stroll to John o'Groat's. By Isobel Wylie Hutchison. 1-48, July 1956

A Stroll to London. By Isobel Wylie Hutchison. Photos by B. Anthony Stewart. 171-204, Aug. 1950

A Stroll to Venice. By Isobel Wylie Hutchison. 378-410, Sept. 1951

See also Hiking; *and* Hostels

WALLER, JERRY: Photographer:

Scenes of Postwar Finland. By La Verne Bradley. 233-264, Aug. 1947

WALLIS ISLANDS, Pacific Ocean. *See* Uvéa

WALLO PROVINCE, Ethiopia. *See* Lalibala

WALRUS HUNTING:

Cliff Dwellers of the Bering Sea. By Juan Muñoz. 129-146, Jan. 1954

Nomad in Alaska's Outback. By Thomas J. Abercrombie. 540-567, Apr. 1969

WALT DISNEY: Genius of Laughter and Learning. By Melville Bell Grosvenor. 157D, Aug. 1963

See also Disney, Walt

WALT DISNEY WORLD, Florida:

Florida's Booming—and Beleaguered—Heartland. By Joseph Judge. Photos by Jonathan Blair. 585-621, Nov. 1973

WANGCHUCK DYNASTY (Bhutan):

Bhutan, Land of the Thunder Dragon. By Burt Kerr Todd. 713-754, Dec. 1952

Bhutan Crowns a New Dragon King. By John Scofield. 546-571, Oct. 1974

Life Slowly Changes in a Remote Himalayan Kingdom. By John Scofield. 658-683, Nov. 1976

WAR and Quiet on the Laos Frontier. By W. Robert Moore. 665-680, May 1954

WAR MEMORIALS:

Gettysburg and Vicksburg: the Battle Towns Today. By Robert Paul Jordan. Map notes by Carolyn Bennett Patterson. 4-57, July 1963

Here Rest in Honored Glory . . . The United States Dedicates Six New Battle Monuments in Europe to Americans Who Gave Their Lives During World War II. By Howell Walker. 739-768, June 1957

Our War Memorials Abroad: A Faith Kept. By George C. Marshall. 731-737, June 1957

See also Arlington National Cemetery, Virginia; Civil War, U. S.

WAR-TORN Greece Looks Ahead. By Maynard Owen Williams. 711-744, Dec. 1949

WARBLERS:

The Bird's Year. By Arthur A. Allen. 791-816, June 1951

Included: Chestnut-sided, Kentucky, Magnolia, Mourning, and Yellow warblers

WARD, FRED: Author-Photographer:

The Changing World of Canada's Crees. 541-569, Apr. 1975

The Imperiled Everglades. 1-27, Jan. 1972

Photographer

New England's "Lively Experiment," Rhode Island. By Robert de Roos. 370-401, Sept. 1968

Those Successful Japanese. By Bart McDowell. 323-359, Mar. 1974

WARNER, CONSTANCE P.: Author-Photographer:

Nature's Alert Eyes. 558-569, Apr. 1959

WARREN, CHARLES: Author:

The Washington National Monument Society. 739-744, June 1947

WARREN, EARL:

Board of Trustees, member. 422, Mar. 1957; 835, Dec. 1959; 880, Dec. 1961; 670, 671, May 1964; 751, Dec. 1964; 485, Oct. 1966; 589, Oct. 1967; 860, June 1970

Hubbard Medal Presentations

Paul A. Siple. 792-793, June 1958; Dr. and Mrs. Louis S. B. Leakey. 903, 905, Dec. 1962; 197,

WARREN, EARL — *Continued*
231, Feb. 1965; Juan Trippe. 584-586, Apr. 1968
La Gorce Medal Presentation
Antarctic Expedition. 864-867, June 1967

WARREN, EARL, Jr.: Author:
Off Santa Barbara: California's Ranches in the Sea.
257-283, Aug. 1958

WARROAD, Minnesota:
Men, Moose, and Mink of Northwest Angle. By
William H. Nicholas. Photos by J. Baylor Roberts. 265-284, Aug. 1947

WARSAW, Poland:
Poland Opens Her Doors. By Delia and Ferdinand
Kuhn. Photos by Erich Lessing. 354-398, Sept.
1958
Springtime of Hope in Poland. By Peter T. White.
Photos by James P. Blair. 467-501, Apr. 1972

WARSHIPS:
Ships Through the Ages: A Saga of the Sea. By Alan
Villiers. 494-545, Apr. 1963
See also Monitor; Spanish Armada; *Vasa; and*
Battleships

WASATCH FRONT (Valleys), Utah:
Utah's Shining Oasis. By Charles McCarry. Photos
by James L. Amos. 440-473, Apr. 1975

WASHBURN, BRADFORD: Author:
Canada's Mount Kennedy: I. The Discovery. 1-3,
July 1965
Author-Photographer
Mount McKinley Conquered by New Route. 219-248, Aug. 1953

WASHINGTON, GEORGE:
Across the Potomac from Washington. By Albert
W. Atwood. 1-33, Jan. 1953
G. Washington — Man and Monument. Published
in cooperation with the Washington National
Monument Association. 586, Oct. 1967
George Washington: The Man Behind the Myths.
By Howard La Fay. Photos by Ted Spiegel. 90-111, July 1976
George Washington's Travels, Traced on the Arrowsmith Map. 768-769, June 1953
The Living White House. By Lonnelle Aikman.
593-643, Nov. 1966
Mount Vernon Lives On. By Lonnelle Aikman.
651-682, Nov. 1953
Profiles of the Presidents: I. The Presidency and
How It Grew. By Frank Freidel. 642-687, Nov.
1964
Shrines of Each Patriot's Devotion. By Frederick
G. Vosburgh. 51-82, Jan. 1949
Included: George Washington Birthplace; Mount
Vernon; Valley Forge Park
Washington Lives Again at Valley Forge. By
Howell Walker. 187-202, Feb. 1954

WASHINGTON, MARTHA:
Patriots in Petticoats. By Lonnelle Aikman. Paintings by Louis S. Glanzman. 475-493, Oct. 1975

WASHINGTON:
Climbing Our Northwest Glaciers. Photos by Bob
and Ira Spring. 103-114, July 1953
Endeavour Sails the Inside Passage. By Amos
Burg. 801-828, June 1947
Following the Trail of Lewis and Clark. By Ralph

WASHINGTON — *Continued*
Gray. 707-750, June 1953
From Sagebrush to Roses on the Columbia. By Leo
A. Borah. 571-611, Nov. 1952
A Map Maker Looks at the United States. By Newman Bumstead. 705-748, June 1951
Included: Aberdeen; Adams, Mount; Blewett; Bremerton; Chelan, Lake; Cle Elum; Cle Elum Lake;
Dosewallips River; Duckabush River; Dungeness Spit;
Ediz Hook; Franklin Delano Roosevelt Lake; Gifford
Pinchot National Forest; Grand Coulee Dam; Greenacres; Hoh River Valley; Hood Canal; Hoquiam; Kachess Lake; Olympic National Park; Olympic Peninsula; Opportunity; Port Angeles; Port Orchard; Port
Townsend; Puget Sound; Rosalia; St. Helens, Mount;
Seattle; Sequim; Snoqualmie Pass; Spokane; Walla Walla; Wenatchee; Wenatchee Mountains; Yakima; Zenith
Mexico to Canada on the Pacific Crest Trail. By
Mike W. Edwards. Photos by David Hiser. 741-779, June 1971
Mount Rainier: Testing Ground for Everest. By
Barry C. Bishop. 688-711, May 1963
New National Park Proposed: The Spectacular
North Cascades. By Nathaniel T. Kenney. Photos by James P. Blair. 642-667, May 1968
Northwest Wonderland: Washington State. By
Merle Severy. Photos by B. Anthony Stewart.
445-493, Apr. 1960
Powerhouse of the Northwest (Columbia River). By
David S. Boyer. 821-847, Dec. 1974
Snow-mantled Stehekin: Where Solitude Is in Season. Photos by Bruce Dale. Text by Pat Hutson.
572-588, Apr. 1974
Timber: How Much Is Enough? By John J. Putman. Photos by Bruce Dale. 485-511, Apr. 1974
Washington Wilderness, the North Cascades. By
Edwards Park. Photos by Kathleen Revis. 335-367, Mar. 1961
See also Olympic National Park; Puget Sound Area;
Seattle

WASHINGTON, D. C.:
Across the Potomac from Washington. By Albert
W. Atwood. 1-33, Jan. 1953
American Processional: History on Canvas. By
John and Blanche Leeper. 173-212, Feb. 1951
The DAR Story. By Lonnelle Aikman. Photos by B.
Anthony Stewart and John E. Fletcher. 565-598,
Nov. 1951
Included: Headquarters of the National Society of
Daughters of the American Revolution
The Last Full Measure (Tribute to President Kennedy). By Melville Bell Grosvenor. 307-355,
Mar. 1964
New Grandeur for Flowering Washington. By Joseph Judge. Photos by James P. Blair. 500-539,
Apr. 1967
Parkscape, U.S.A.: Tomorrow in Our National
Parks. By George B. Hartzog, Jr. 48-93, July
1966
Included: National Capital Parks; Pennsylvania
Avenue
Pennsylvania Avenue, Route of Presidents. By
Dorothea and Stuart E. Jones. Photos by Volkmar Wentzel. 63-95, Jan. 1957
*A Pocket Map of Central Washington; Suburban
Washington,* double-sided map supplement.
Sept. 1948
Round About the Nation's Capital, map supplement. Apr. 1956

WASHINGTON, D.C. — *Continued*

Tourist Washington; Suburban Washington, double-sided U.S. Atlas series supplement. Dec. 1964

Washington: Home of the Nation's Great. By Albert W. Atwood. 699-738, June 1947
   Our Magnificent Capital City. Photos by B. Anthony Stewart. 715-738

Washington: The City Freedom Built. By William Graves. Photos by Bruce Dale and Thomas Nebbia. 735-781, Dec. 1964

Washington's Historic Georgetown. By William A. Kinney. 513-544, Apr. 1953

Waterway to Washington, the C & O Canal. By Jay Johnston. 419-439, Mar. 1960

World's Last Salute to a Great American (Dwight D. Eisenhower). By William Graves and other members of the NGS staff. 40-51, July 1969

See also Folger (Library); Ford's Theatre; Library of Congress; National Bureau of Standards; National Gallery of Art; National Zoological Park; Presidents, U.S.; Smithsonian Institution; U.S. Capitol; Washington Monument; White House; *and* names of U.S. Government departments

WASHINGTON, Mount, New Hampshire:

The Friendly Huts of the White Mountains. By William O. Douglas. Photos by Kathleen Revis. 205-239, Aug. 1961

Mountains Top Off New England. By F. Barrows Colton. Photos by Robert F. Sisson. 563-602, May 1951

Skyline Trail (Appalachian Trail) from Maine to Georgia. By Andrew H. Brown. Photos by Robert F. Sisson. 219-251, Aug. 1949

WASHINGTON MONUMENT, Washington, D.C.:

G. Washington — Man and Monument. Published in cooperation with the Washington National Monument Association. 586, Oct. 1967

The Washington National Monument Society. By Charles Warren. 739-744, June 1947

WASPS:

New Tricks Outwit Our Insect Enemies. By Hal Higdon. Photos by Robert F. Sisson and Emory Kristof. 380-399, Sept. 1972

The Wasp That Plays Cupid to a Fig. By Robert F. Sisson. 690-697, Nov. 1970

WASSAW (Island), Georgia:

Sea Islands: Adventuring Along the South's Surprising Coast. By James Cerruti. Photos by Thomas Nebbia and James L. Amos. 366-393, Mar. 1971

WATCH INDUSTRY:

Switzerland, Europe's High-rise Republic. By Thomas J. Abercrombie. 68-113, July 1969

Switzerland Guards the Roof of Europe. By William H. Nicholas. Photos by Willard R. Culver. 205-246, Aug. 1950

WATCHING a Baby Gorilla Grow Up. By Ernst M. Lang. Photos by Paul Steinemann. 446-453, Mar. 1964

WATER CLOCKS. *See* The Tower of the Winds

WATER Dwellers in a Desert World. By Gavin Young. Photos by Nik Wheeler. 502-523, Apr. 1976

WATER POLLUTION:

Can We Save Our Salt Marshes? By Stephen W.

WATER POLLUTION — *Continued*

Hitchcock. Photos by William R. Curtsinger. 729-765, June 1972

The Great Lakes: Is It Too Late? By Gordon Young. Photos by James L. Amos and Martin Rogers. 147-185, Aug. 1973

North Through History Aboard *White Mist.* By Melville Bell Grosvenor. Photos by Edwin Stuart Grosvenor. 1-55, July 1970
   Included: Champlain Canal; Hudson River

Pollution, Threat to Man's Only Home. By Gordon Young. Photos by James P. Blair. 738-781, Dec. 1970

Quicksilver and Slow Death (Mercury). By John J. Putman. Photos by Robert W. Madden. 507-527, Oct. 1972

A River Restored: Oregon's Willamette. By Ethel A. Starbird. Photos by Lowell J. Georgia. 816-835, June 1972

Yesterday Lingers Along the Connecticut. By Charles McCarry. Photos by David L. Arnold. 334-369, Sept. 1972

See also Oil Spills

WATER POWER. *See* Hydroelectric Power

WATER SKIING:

The Booming Sport of Water Skiing. By Wilbur E. Garrett. 700-711, Nov. 1958

WATER SUPPLY:

Sno-Cats Mechanize Oregon Snow Survey. By Andrew H. Brown. Photos by John E. Fletcher. 691-710, Nov. 1949

Water for the World's Growing Needs. By Herbert B. Nichols and F. Barrows Colton. 269-286, Aug. 1952

See also Dams; Dikes and Levees; Floods and Flood Control; Irrigation; *and* Los Angeles Aqueduct

WATER War in Viet Nam. By Dickey Chapelle. 272-296, Feb. 1966

WATERFALLS:

Labrador Canoe Adventure. By Andrew H. Brown and Ralph Gray. 65-99, July 1951
   Included: Grand Falls of the Hamilton River, Lower Unknown Falls, Upper Unknown Falls

Land of the Havasupai. By Jack Breed. 655-674, May 1948
   Included: Beaver Falls, Fifty-foot Falls, Havasu or Bridal Veil Falls, Mooney Falls, Navajo Falls

See also Angel Falls, Venezuela; Niagara Falls, Canada-U.S.; Victoria Falls, Rhodesia-Zambia

WATERTON-GLACIER INTERNATIONAL PEACE PARK, Canada-U.S.:

Canadian Rockies, Lords of a Beckoning Land. By Alan Phillips. Photos by James L. Stanfield. 353-393, Sept. 1966

Many-splendored Glacierland. By George W. Long. Photos by Kathleen Revis. 589-636, May 1956

WATERWAY to Washington, the C & O Canal. By Jay Johnston. 419-439, Mar. 1960

WATERWAYS. *See* Canals; Great Lakes; Inland Sea, Japan; Inside Passage; Intracoastal Waterway, Atlantic; Rivers and River Trips; St. Lawrence Seaway

WATSON, DON: Author:

Ancient Cliff Dwellers of Mesa Verde. Photos by Willard R. Culver. 349-376, Sept. 1948

WATT, JAMES:

The British Way. By Sir Evelyn Wrench. 421-541, Apr. 1949

WAURÁ (Indians):

Amazon—The River Sea. By Loren McIntyre. 456-495, Oct. 1972

The Waurá: Brazilian Indians of the Hidden Xingu. By Harald Schultz. 130-152, Jan. 1966

WAVES (Women's Reserve of the U. S. Naval Reserve). *See* Parachute Rigger School

WE're Coming Over on the *Mayflower.* By Alan Villiers. 708-728, May 1957

WE're Doing Something About the Weather! By Walter Orr Roberts. 518-555, Apr. 1972

WE Are Living at the South Pole. By Paul A. Siple. Photos by David S. Boyer. 5-35, July 1957

WE Build a School for Sherpa Children. By Sir Edmund Hillary. 548-551, Oct. 1962

WE Captured a 'Live' Brontosaur. By Roland T. Bird. 707-722, May 1954

WE Climbed Utah's Skyscraper Rock. By Huntley Ingalls. Photos by author and Barry C. Bishop. 705-721, Nov. 1962

WE Drove Panama's Darién Gap. By Kip Ross. 368-389, Mar. 1961

WE Dwelt in Kashgai Tents. By Jean and Franc Shor. 805-832, June 1952

WE Followed Peary to the Pole. By Gilbert Grosvenor and Thomas W. McKnew. 469-484, Oct. 1953

WE Lived in Turbulent Tehran. By Rebecca Shannon Cresson. 707-720, Nov. 1953

WE Saw the World From the Edge of Space. By Malcolm D. Ross. Ground photos by Walter Meayers Edwards. 671-685, Nov. 1961

WE Survive on a Pacific Atoll. By John and Frank Craighead. 73-94, Jan. 1948

WE Took the Highroad in Afghanistan. By Jean and Franc Shor. 673-706, Nov. 1950

"WE Who Face Death." By LeRoy Woodson, Jr. 364-387, Mar. 1975

WEALTH and Wonder of Northern State Trees. By William A. Dayton. Paintings by Walter A. Weber. 651-691, Nov. 1955

WEATHER:

Extraordinary Photograph Shows Earth Pole to Pole. Photos by Nimbus I. 190-193, Feb. 1965

Men Against the Hurricane. By Andrew H. Brown. 537-560, Oct. 1950

Our Changing Atlantic Coastline (March 1962 Storm). By Nathaniel T. Kenney. Photos by B. Anthony Stewart. 860-887, Dec. 1962

We're Doing Something About the Weather! By Walter Orr Roberts. 518-555, Apr. 1972

See also Climate; Drought; Lightning; Storms

WEATHER SATELLITES:

The Earth From Orbit. By Paul D. Lowman, Jr. 645-671, Nov. 1966

Extraordinary Photograph Shows Earth Pole to Pole. Photos by Nimbus I. 190-193, Feb. 1965

How Man-made Satellites Can Affect Our Lives.

WEATHER SATELLITES—*Continued*

By Joseph Kaplan. Paintings by Gilbert Emerson. 791-810, Dec. 1957

Our Earth as a Satellite (*Tiros I*) Sees It. By W. G. Stroud. 293-302, Aug. 1960

Satellites Gave Warning of Midwest Floods. By Peter T. White. Photos by Thomas A. DeFeo. 574-592, Oct. 1969

Space Satellites, Tools of Earth Research. By Heinz Haber. Paintings by William N. Palmstrom. 487-509, Apr. 1956

See also Remote Sensing

WEATHER STATIONS AND RESEARCH:

Man's First Winter at the South Pole. By Paul A. Siple. 439-478, Apr. 1958

Men Against the Hurricane. By Andrew H. Brown. 537-560, Oct. 1950
    Included: Joint Hurricane Warning Center, Miami

Milestones in My Arctic Journeys. By Willie Knutsen. 543-570, Oct. 1949
    Included: Weather stations in Arctic Canada

Our Navy Explores Antarctica. By Richard E. Byrd. U. S. Navy official photos. 429-522, Oct. 1947

Rugged Is the Word for Bravo (Weather Patrol). By Phillip M. Swatek. 829-843, Dec. 1955

Three Months on an Arctic Ice Island. By Joseph O. Fletcher. 489-504, Apr. 1953

We Followed Peary to the Pole. By Gilbert Grosvenor and Thomas W. McKnew. 469-484, Oct. 1953

Weather from the White North. By Andrew H. Brown. Photos by John E. Fletcher. 543-572, Apr. 1955

We're Doing Something About the Weather! By Walter Orr Roberts. 518-555, Apr. 1972

Year of Discovery Opens in Antarctica. By David S. Boyer. 339-381, Sept. 1957

WEAVER, KENNETH F.: Author:

And Now to Touch the Moon's Forbidding Face. 633-635, May 1969

Apollo 15 Explores the Mountains of the Moon. Photos from NASA. 233-265, Feb. 1972

Athens: Her Golden Past Still Lights the World. Photos by Phillip Harrington. 100-137, July 1963

Countdown for Space. 702-734, May 1961

Crystals, Magical Servants of the Space Age. Photos by James P. Blair. 278-296, Aug. 1968

The Five Worlds of Peru. Photos by Bates Littlehales. 213-265, Feb. 1964

The Flight of Apollo 11: "One giant leap for mankind." 752-787, Dec. 1969

Giant Comet Grazes the Sun. 259-261, Feb. 1966

Have We Solved the Mysteries of the Moon? Paintings by William H. Bond. 309-325, Sept. 1973

Historic Color Portrait of Earth From Space. Photos by DODGE Satellite. 726-731, Nov. 1967

How Old Is It? By Lyman J. Briggs and Kenneth F. Weaver. 234-255, Aug. 1958

How to Catch a Passing Comet. 148-150, Jan. 1974

The Incredible Universe. Photos by James P. Blair. 589-625, May 1974

Journey to Mars. Paintings by Ludek Pesek. 231-263, Feb. 1973

Magnetic Clues Help Date the Past. 696-701, May 1967

WEAVER, KENNETH F.: Author—*Continued*

Mariner Unveils Venus and Mercury. 858-869, June 1975

Maui, Where Old Hawaii Still Lives. Photos by Gordon W. Gahan. 514-543, Apr. 1971

Mystery Shrouds the Biggest Planet (Jupiter). 285-294, Feb. 1975

Of Planes and Men. Photos by Emory Kristof and Albert Moldvay. 298-349, Sept. 1965

Remote Sensing: New Eyes to See the World. 46-73, Jan. 1969

Rip Van Winkle of the Underground (Cicada). 133-142, July 1953

The Search for Life on Mars. 264-265, Feb. 1973

The Search for Tomorrow's Power. Photos by Emory Kristof. 650-681, Nov. 1972

Space Rendezvous, Milestone on the Way to the Moon. 539-553, Apr. 1966

That Orbèd Maiden . . . the Moon. 207-230, Feb. 1969

Tracking America's Man in Orbit. Photos by Robert F. Sisson. 184-217, Feb. 1962

Voyage to the Planets. Paintings by Ludek Pesek. 147-193, Aug. 1970

What the Moon Rocks Tell Us. 788-791, Dec. 1969

What You Didn't See in Kohoutek. 214-223, Aug. 1974

WEAVER, ROBERT F.: Author:

The Cancer Puzzle. 396-399, Sept. 1976

WEAVING:

Ethiopia's Artful Weavers. By Judith Olmstead. Photos by James A. Sugar. 125-141, Jan. 1973

See also Rugs and Rug Making; Tweed

WEBBER, JOHN:

Captain Cook: The Man Who Mapped the Pacific. By Alan Villiers. Photos by Gordon W. Gahan. 297-349, Sept. 1971
Included: Oil painting of Captain Cook (1776), and sketches by *Resolution* artist John Webber

WEBER, WALTER A.: Artist:

An Artist's Glimpses of Our Roadside Wildlife. 16-32, July 1950

Beauty and Bounty of Southern State Trees. By William A. Dayton. 508-552, Oct. 1957

Born Hunters, the Bird Dogs. By Roland Kilbon. 369-398, Sept. 1947

Honey-Guide: The Bird That Eats Wax. By Herbert Friedmann. 551-560, Apr. 1954

Life Portraits of a Famous Family: Pacific Salmon. 214-216, Aug. 1968

Nature's Tank, the Turtle. By Doris M. Cochran. 665-684, May 1952

Our Snake Friends and Foes. By Doris M. Cochran. 334-364, Sept. 1954

Stalking Central Africa's Wildlife. By T. Donald Carter. 264-286, Aug. 1956

Strange Courtship of Birds of Paradise. By S. Dillon Ripley. 247-278, Feb. 1950

Wealth and Wonder of Northern State Trees. By William A. Dayton. 651-691, Nov. 1955

Wildlife of Everglades National Park. By Daniel B. Beard. 83-116, Jan. 1949

Wildlife of Mount McKinley National Park. By Adolph Murie. 249-270, Aug. 1953

WEBSTER, NOAH:

Literary Landmarks of Massachusetts. By William H. Nicholas. Photos by B. Anthony Stewart and John E. Fletcher. 279-310, Mar. 1950

WEDDELL SEALS:

Stalking Seals Under Antarctic Ice. By Carleton Ray. 54-65, Jan. 1966

WEDDINGS:

Royal Wedding at Jaisalmer. By Marilyn Silverstone. 66-79, Jan. 1965

Wedding of Two Worlds. By Lee E. Battaglia. 708-727, Nov. 1963
Contents: The wedding uniting Hope Cooke of New York and Palden Thondup Namgyal, Crown Prince of Sikkim

WEEDS, Aquatic:

Florida, Noah's Ark for Exotic Newcomers. By Rick Gore. Photos by David Doubilet. 538-559, Oct. 1976

WEEKS EXPEDITION:

Into the Heart of Africa. By Gertrude S. Weeks. 257-263, Aug. 1956

Stalking Central Africa's Wildlife. By T. Donald Carter. Paintings by Walter A. Weber. 264-286, Aug. 1956

WEIGHING the Aga Khan in Diamonds. Photos by David J. Carnegie. 317-324, Mar. 1947

WEIGHTS AND MEASURES. *See* National Bureau of Standards, Washington, D. C.

WEIR, THOMAS: Author:

High Adventure in the Himalayas. 193-234, Aug. 1952

WEITZ, PAUL J.:

Skylab, Outpost on the Frontier of Space. By Thomas Y. Canby. Photos by the nine mission astronauts. 441-469, Oct. 1974

WEITZMANN, KURT: Author:

Mount Sinai's Holy Treasures. Photos by Fred Anderegg. 109-127, Jan. 1964

WELLINGTON, New Zealand:

New Zealand: Gift of the Sea. By Maurice Shadbolt. Photos by Brian Brake. 465-511, Apr. 1962

New Zealand, Pocket Wonder World. By Howell Walker. 419-460, Apr. 1952

New Zealand's North Island: The Contented Land. By Charles McCarry. Photos by Bates Littlehales. 190-213, Aug. 1974

WELLS, MARGARETTA BURR: Author:

The Ape with Friends in Washington. 61-74, July 1953

WELLS, VIRGINIA L.: Author-Photographer:

Photographing Northern Wild Flowers. 809-823, June 1956

WELLS, Natural. *See* Chichén Itzá, Mexico; Dzibilchaltun, Mexico

WENKAM, ROBERT: Photographer:

Fountain of Fire in Hawaii. By Frederick Simpich, Jr. Photos by Robert B. Goodman and Robert Wenkam. 303-327, Mar. 1960

WENTZEL, VOLKMAR: Author-Photographer:

Angola, Unknown Africa. 347-383, Sept. 1961

WENTZEL, VOLKMAR: Author-Photographer — *Continued*

Feudal Splendor Lingers in Rajputana. 411-458, Oct. 1948

History Awakens at Harpers Ferry. 399-416, Mar. 1957

The Idyllic Vale of Kashmir. 523-550, Apr. 1948

India's Sculptured Temple Caves. 665-678, May 1953

Life in Walled-off West Berlin. By Nathaniel T. Kenney and Volkmar Wentzel. 735-767, Dec. 1961

Mozambique: Land of the Good People. 197-231, Aug. 1964

Swaziland Tries Independence. 266-293, Aug. 1969

Photographer

Atlantic Odyssey: Iceland to Antarctica. By Newman Bumstead. 725-780, Dec. 1955

Berlin, Island in a Soviet Sea. By Frederick G. Vosburgh. 689-704, Nov. 1951

Building a New Austria. By Beverley M. Bowie. 172-213, Feb. 1959

Delhi, Capital of a New Dominion. By Phillips Talbot. 597-630, Nov. 1947

Everyone's Servant, the Post Office. By Allan C. Fisher, Jr. 121-152, July 1954

Friendly Flight to Northern Europe. By Lyndon B. Johnson. 268-293, Feb. 1964

Hunting Uranium Around the World. By Robert D. Nininger. 533-558, Oct. 1954

I'm From New Jersey. By John T. Cunningham. 1-45, Jan. 1960

A Journey to "Little Tibet." By Enakshi Bhavnani. 603-634, May 1951

Kings Point: Maker of Mariners. By Nathaniel T. Kenney. 693-706, Nov. 1955

The Long, Lonely Leap (Parachute Jump). By Joseph W. Kittinger, Jr. 854-873, Dec. 1960

Man's New Servant, the Friendly Atom. By F. Barrows Colton. 71-90, Jan. 1954

The Most Mexican City, Guadalajara. By Bart McDowell. 412-441, Mar. 1967

Occupied Austria, Outpost of Democracy. By George W. Long. 749-790, June 1951

Peerless Nepal — A Naturalist's Paradise. By S. Dillon Ripley. 1-40, Jan. 1950

Pennsylvania Avenue, Route of Presidents. By Dorothea and Stuart E. Jones. 63-95, Jan. 1957

Portugal at the Crossroads. By Howard La Fay. 453-501, Oct. 1965

Salzkammergut, Austria's Alpine Playground. By Beverley M. Bowie. 246-275, Aug. 1960

School for Survival. By Curtis E. LeMay. 565-602, May 1953

The Smithsonian, Magnet on the Mall. By Leonard Carmichael. 796-845, June 1960

A Stroll to Venice. By Isobel Wylie Hutchison. 378-410, Sept. 1951

Tirol, Austria's Province in the Clouds. By Peter T. White. 107-141, July 1961

The White Horses of Vienna. By Beverley M. Bowie. 401-419, Sept. 1958

Wisconsin, Land of the Good Life. By Beverley M. Bowie. 141-187, Feb. 1957

Yugoslavia, Between East and West. By George W. Long. 141-172, Feb. 1951

WESLEY, JOHN and CHARLES:

The British Way. By Sir Evelyn Wrench. 421-541, Apr. 1949

WEST (Region), U. S.:

Close-up: U.S.A., California and Nevada, map supplement. Text on reverse. June 1974

Close-up: U.S.A., The Northwest, map supplement. Text on reverse. Mar. 1973

Cowpunching on the Padlock Ranch. By William Albert Allard. 478-499, Oct. 1973

From Sun-clad Sea to Shining Mountains. By Ralph Gray. Photos by James P. Blair. 542-589, Apr. 1964

I See America First. By Lynda Bird Johnson. Photos by William Albert Allard. 874-904, Dec. 1965

Lonely Sentinels of the American West: Basque Sheepherders. By Robert Laxalt. Photos by William Belknap, Jr. 870-888, June 1966

A Map Maker Looks at the United States. By Newman Bumstead. 705-748, June 1951

Included: Bremerton Shipyards; Columbia River; Continental Divide; Denver; Dry Falls; El Morro; Hells Canyon; Los Angeles; Mojave Desert; Mount Shasta; Olympic Peninsula rain forest; Provo; San Francisco; Tetons; Tillamook Burn

Mexico to Canada on the Pacific Crest Trail. By Mike W. Edwards. Photos by David Hiser. 741-779, June 1971

Northwestern United States, Atlas series supplement. Apr. 1960

Northwestern United States and Neighboring Canadian Provinces, map supplement. June 1950

The Opening of the American West: Burr's 1840 Map. 763, June 1953

The Parks in Your Backyard. By Conrad L. Wirth. 647-707, Nov. 1963
   The West. 699-707

Profiles of the Presidents: II. A Restless Nation Moves West. By Frank Freidel. 80-121, Jan. 1965

Riding the Outlaw Trail. By Robert Redford. Photos by Jonathan Blair. 622-657, Nov. 1976

A Sikh Discovers America. By Joginder Singh Rekhi. 558-590, Oct. 1964

So Long, St. Louis, We're Heading West. By William C. Everhart. 643-669, Nov. 1965

Southwestern United States, Atlas series supplement. Nov. 1959

Southwestern United States, map supplement. Dec. 1948

Stalking the West's Wild Foods. By Euell Gibbons. Photos by David Hiser. 186-199, Aug. 1973

Theodore Roosevelt: a Centennial Tribute. By Bart McDowell. 572-590, Oct. 1958

Two Wheels Along the Mexican Border. By William Albert Allard. 591-635, May 1971

The West Through Boston Eyes. By Stewart Anderson. 733-776, June 1949

See also names of western states and rivers

WEST AFRICA:

Freedom Speaks French in Ouagadougou. By John Scofield. 153-203, Aug. 1966

Hunting Musical Game in West Africa. By Arthur S. Alberts. 262-282, Aug. 1951

See also Mali; Mauritania; Niger; *and* Tuareg

WEST from the Khyber Pass. By William O. Douglas. Photos by Mercedes H. Douglas and author. 1-44, July 1958

WEST GERMANY. *See* Germany, Federal Republic of

WEST INDIES:

Cape Canaveral's 6,000-mile Shooting Gallery. By Allan C. Fisher, Jr. Photos by Luis Marden and Thomas Nebbia. 421-471, Oct. 1959
Included: Antigua; Bahama Islands; Dominican Republic; Grand Turk; Puerto Rico; St. Lucia

Carib Cruises the West Indies. By Carleton Mitchell. 1-56, Jan. 1948

Christopher Columbus and the New World He Found. By John Scofield. Photos by Adam Woolfitt. 584-625, Nov. 1975

Countries of the Caribbean, including Mexico, Central America, and the West Indies, map supplement. Oct. 1947

Finisterre Sails the Windward Islands. By Carleton Mitchell. Photos by Winfield Parks. 755-801, Dec. 1965

Flags of the Americas. By Elizabeth W. King. 633-657, May 1949
Included: Cuba; Dominican Republic; Haiti

A Fresh Breeze Stirs the Leewards. By Carleton Mitchell. Photos by Winfield Parks. 488-537, Oct. 1966

How Fruit Came to America. By J. R. Magness. Paintings by Else Bostelmann. 325-377, Sept. 1951

Our Vegetable Travelers. By Victor R. Boswell. Paintings by Else Bostelmann. 145-217, Aug. 1949

Robin Sails Home. By Robin Lee Graham. 504-545, Oct. 1970

Sea Fever. By John E. Schultz. 237-268, Feb. 1949

West Indies, Atlas series supplement. Dec. 1962

West Indies, map supplement. Mar. 1954

West Indies and Central America, map supplement. Jan. 1970

See also Bahama Islands; Barbados; Bimini Islands; Cuba; Haiti; Jamaica; Martinique; Netherlands Antilles; Puerto Rico; Trinidad and Tobago; Virgin Islands

WEST IRIAN: People. *See* Asmat

WEST POINT, New York:

The Making of a West Pointer. By Howell Walker. 597-626, May 1952

The Mighty Hudson (River). By Albert W. Atwood. Photos by B. Anthony Stewart. 1-36, July 1948

WEST VIRGINIA:

Appalachian Valley Pilgrimage. By Catherine Bell Palmer. Photos by Justin Locke. 1-32, July 1949

Down the Potomac by Canoe. By Ralph Gray. Photos by Walter Meayers Edwards. 213-242, Aug. 1948

Mountain Voices, Mountain Days. By Bryan Hodgson. Photos by Linda Bartlett. 118-146, July 1972

The Nation's River. By Allan C. Fisher, Jr. Photos by James L. Stanfield. 432-469, Oct. 1976

Shenandoah, I Long to Hear You. By Mike W. Edwards. Photos by Thomas Anthony DeFeo. 554-588, Apr. 1970

So Much Happens Along the Ohio River. By Fred

WEST VIRGINIA—*Continued*
erick Simpich. Photos by Justin Locke. 177-212, Feb. 1950

Turnaround Time in West Virginia. By Elizabeth A. Moize. Photos by Jodi Cobb. 755-785, June 1976

See also Harpers Ferry

WESTCOTT (Mail Boat). *See J. W. Westcott*

WESTERN AUSTRALIA (State), Australia:

Western Australia, the Big Country. By Kenneth MacLeish. Photos by James L. Stanfield. 150-187, Feb. 1975

WESTERN SAMOA, the Pacific's Newest Nation. By Maurice Shadbolt. Photos by Robert B. Goodman. 573-602, Oct. 1962

WESTMANN ISLANDS, Iceland. *See* Heimaey

WESTMINSTER KENNEL CLUB DOG SHOW, New York City:

Westminster, World Series of Dogdom. By John W. Cross, Jr. 91-116, Jan. 1954

WETHERILL MESA, Colorado:

Searching for Cliff Dwellers' Secrets. By Carroll A. Burroughs. 619-625, Nov. 1959

Solving the Riddles of Wetherill Mesa. By Douglas Osborne. Paintings by Peter V. Bianchi. 155-195, Feb. 1964

20th-century Indians Preserve Customs of the Cliff Dwellers. Photos by William Belknap, Jr. 196-211, Feb. 1964
Included: Artifacts of Mesa Verde

Your Society to Seek New Light on the Cliff Dwellers. 154-156, Jan. 1959

WETLANDS:

Florida's Booming—and Beleaguered—Heartland. By Joseph Judge. Photos by Jonathan Blair. 585-621, Nov. 1973

See also listings under Marshes; Swamps

WETMORE, ALEXANDER:

Board of Trustees, member. 595, May 1947; 344, Sept. 1948; 65A-65B, July 1954; 364, Mar. 1956; 835, Dec. 1959; 883, Dec. 1960; 555, Oct. 1964; 485, Oct. 1966; 839, Dec. 1970; 151, Aug. 1975; 227, Aug. 1976

Committee for Research and Exploration, Vice Chairman. 705, June 1947; 175, Feb. 1960; 532, Oct. 1965; 489, Oct. 1967; 881-882, Dec. 1967

Hubbard Medal recipient (1975). 151, Aug. 1975

Author

Re-creating Madagascar's Giant Extinct Bird. 488-493, Oct. 1967

WHALES:

Calypso Explores for Underwater Oil. By Jacques-Yves Cousteau. Photos by Louis Malle. 155-184, Aug. 1955

Hunting the Heartbeat of a Whale. By Paul Dudley White and Samuel W. Matthews. 49-64, July 1956

Namu. Children's book announced. 726-728, Nov. 1973

Whales of the World. 722-767, Dec. 1976
I. The Imperiled Giants. By William Graves. 722-751
II. Exploring the Lives of Whales. By Victor B. Scheffer. 752-767

WHALES — *Continued*

"Whales of the World." Painting supplement. Map on reverse, *The Great Whales: Migration and Range*. Dec. 1976

See also Belugas; Bowhead Whales; Gray Whales; Killer Whales; Right Whales

WHALING:

The Azores, Nine Islands in Search of a Future. By Don Moser. Photos by O. Louis Mazzatenta. 261-288, Feb. 1976

The Last U. S. Whale Hunters. By Emory Kristof. 346-353, Mar. 1973
"Ocean mammals are to us what the buffalo was to the Plains Indian." By Lael Morgan. 354-355

Martha's Vineyard. By William P. E. Graves. Photos by James P. Blair. 778-809, June 1961

A Naturalist in Penguin Land. By Niall Rankin. 93-116, Jan. 1955

Nomad Sails Long Island Sound. By Thomas Horgan. 295-338, Sept. 1957

Off the Beaten Track of Empire. By Beverley M. Bowie. Photos by Michael Parker. 584-626, Nov. 1957

To Europe with a Racing Start. By Carleton Mitchell. 758-791, June 1958

Whales of the World. 722-767, Dec. 1976

See also Faeroe Islands; Nantucket; Western Australia

WHARTON, CHARLES HEIZER: Author:

Seeking Mindanao's Strangest Creatures. 389-408, Sept. 1948

WHAT a Place to Lay an Egg! By Thomas R. Howell. 414-419, Sept. 1971

WHAT Causes Earthquakes. By Maynard M. Miller. 140-141, July 1964

WHAT I Saw Across the Rhine. By J. Frank Dobie. 57-86, Jan. 1947

WHAT'S Black and White and Loved All Over? By Theodore H. Reed. Photos by Donna K. Grosvenor. 803-815, Dec. 1972

WHAT'S Happening to Our Climate? By Samuel W. Matthews. 576-615, Nov. 1976

WHAT Is It Like to Walk on the Moon? By David R. Scott. 326-331, Sept. 1973

WHAT'S So Special About Spiders? By Paul A. Zahl. 190-219, Aug. 1971

WHAT the Moon Rocks Tell Us. By Kenneth F. Weaver. 788-791, Dec. 1969

WHAT Was a Woman Doing There? By W. E. Garrett. 270-271, Feb. 1966

WHAT We've Accomplished in Antarctica. By George J. Dufek. 527-557, Oct. 1959

WHAT You Didn't See in Kohoutek. By Kenneth F. Weaver. 214-223, Aug. 1974

WHATEVER Happened to TVA? By Gordon Young. Photos by Emory Kristof. 830-863, June 1973

WHEAT AND WHEAT GROWING:

Can the World Feed Its People? By Thomas Y. Canby. Photos by Steve Raymer. 2-31, July 1975

WHEAT AND WHEAT GROWING — *Continued*

Canada's Heartland, the Prairie Provinces. By W. E. Garrett. 443-489, Oct. 1970

North Dakota Comes into Its Own. By Leo A. Borah. Photos by J. Baylor Roberts. 283-322, Sept. 1951

North With the Wheat Cutters. By Noel Grove. Photos by James A. Sugar. 194-217, Aug. 1972

WHEATLEY, HAROLD G.: Author:

This Is My Island, Tangier. Photos by David Alan Harvey. 700-725, Nov. 1973

WHEELER, NIK: Photographer:

Water Dwellers in a Desert World. By Gavin Young. 502-523, Apr. 1976

WHEELER, P. J. F.: Author:

Death of an Island, Tristan da Cunha. 678-695, May 1962

WHEELING, West Virginia:

So Much Happens Along the Ohio River. By Frederick Simpich. Photos by Justin Locke. 177-212, Feb. 1950

WHEN Disaster Struck a Woodpecker's Home. By Frederick Kent Truslow. 882-884, Dec. 1966

WHEN Giant Bears Go Fishing. By Cecil E. Rhode. 195-205, Aug. 1954

WHEN Gypsies Gather at Appleby Fair. Photos by Bruce Dale. 848-869, June 1972

WHEN in Rome. . . . By Stuart E. Jones. Photos by Winfield Parks. 741-789, June 1970

WHEN Mt. Mazama Lost Its Top: The Birth of Crater Lake. By Lyman J. Briggs. 128-133, July 1962

WHEN the President Goes Abroad. By Gilbert M. Grosvenor. 588-649, May 1960

WHERE Elephants Have Right of Way. By George and Jinx Rodger. 363-389, Sept. 1960

WHERE Falcons Wear Air Force Blue, United States Air Force Academy. By Nathaniel T. Kenney. Photos by William Belknap, Jr. 845-873, June 1959

WHERE Jesus Walked. By Howard La Fay. Photos by Charles Harbutt. 739-781, Dec. 1967

WHERE Old Hawaii Still Lives: Maui. By Kenneth F. Weaver. Photos by Gordon W. Gahan. 514-543, Apr. 1971

WHERE Solitude Is in Season: Snow-mantled Stehekin. Photos by Bruce Dale. Text by Pat Hutson. 572-588, Apr. 1974

WHERE the Earth Turns Inside Out. By J. R. Heirtzler. Photos by Emory Kristof. 586-603, May 1975

WHERE Turk and Russian Meet. By Ferdinand Kuhn. 743-766, June 1952

WHERE Two Worlds Meet. Photos by Des and Jen Bartlett. 298-321, Mar. 1976

WHERE Would We Be Without Algae? By Paul A. Zahl. 361-377, Mar. 1974

WHICH Way Now for Argentina? By Loren McIntyre. 296-333, Mar. 1975

WHISTLING SWANS:

Tireless Voyager, the Whistling Swan. By William J. L. Sladen. Photos by Bianca Lavies. 134-147, July 1975

WHITE, EDWARD H.:

America's 6,000-mile Walk in Space. 440-447, Sept. 1965

WHITE, JOHN:

Indian Life Before the Colonists Came. By Stuart E. Jones. Engravings by Theodore de Bry, 1590. 351-368, Sept. 1947

Included: John White, one of Sir Walter Raleigh's colonists on Roanoke Island, 1585, and reproductions of his paintings from De Bry's copper plate engravings

WHITE, PAUL DUDLEY: Author:

Hunting the Heartbeat of a Whale. By Paul Dudley White and Samuel W. Matthews. 49-64, July 1956

WHITE, PETER T.: Author:

Barehanded Battle to Cleanse the Bay. Photos by Jonathan S. Blair. 866-881, June 1971

Behind the Headlines in Viet Nam. Photos by Winfield Parks. 149-189, Feb. 1967

Behold the Computer Revolution. Photos by Bruce Dale and Emory Kristof. 593-633, Nov. 1970

Brazil, Ôba! Photos by Winfield Parks. 299-353, Sept. 1962

Calcutta, India's Maligned Metropolis. Photos by Raghubir Singh. 534-563, Apr. 1973

Gold, the Eternal Treasure. Photos by James L. Stanfield. 1-51, Jan. 1974

Hopes and Fears in Booming Thailand. Photos by Dean Conger. 76-125, July 1967

The Incredible Helicopter. 533-557, Apr. 1959

The Mekong, River of Terror and Hope. Photos by W. E. Garrett. 737-787, Dec. 1968

Mosaic of Cultures (Southeast Asia). Photos by W. E. Garrett. 296-329, Mar. 1971

Report on Laos. Photos by W. E. Garrett. 241-275, Aug. 1961

Saigon: Eye of the Storm. Photos by W. E. Garrett. 834-872, June 1965

Satellites Gave Warning of Midwest Floods. Photos by Thomas A. DeFeo. 574-592, Oct. 1969

South Korea: What Next? Photos by H. Edward Kim. 394-427, Sept. 1975

South Viet Nam Fights the Red Tide. Photos by W. E. Garrett. 445-489, Oct. 1961

Springtime of Hope in Poland. Photos by James P. Blair. 467-501, Apr. 1972

Tanzania Marches to Its Own Drum. Photos by Emory Kristof. 474-509, Apr. 1975

This Land of Ours — How Are We Using It? Photos by Emory Kristof. 20-67, July 1976

Tirol, Austria's Province in the Clouds. Photos by Volkmar Wentzel. 107-141, July 1961

Vienna, City of Song. Photos by John Launois. 739-779, June 1968

The World in New York City. 52-107, July 1964

The **WHITE HORSES** of Vienna. By Beverley M. Bowie. Photos by Volkmar Wentzel. 401-419, Sept. 1958

WHITE HOUSE, Washington, D. C.:

Inside the White House. By Lonnelle Aikman. Pho-

WHITE HOUSE, Washington, D. C. — *Continued*

tos by B. Anthony Stewart and Thomas Nebbia. 3-43, Jan. 1961

The Last Full Measure (Tribute to President Kennedy). By Melville Bell Grosvenor. 307-355, Mar. 1964

The Living White House. By Lonnelle Aikman. 593-643, Nov. 1966

The Living White House. Published in cooperation with the White House Historical Association. 641, Nov. 1966; 586, Oct. 1967

Washington: Home of the Nation's Great. By Albert W. Atwood. 699-738, June 1947

The White House (guidebook). Published in cooperation with the White House Historical Association. 888-893, Dec. 1962

See also Presidents, U. S.

WHITE MAGIC in the Belgian Congo. By W. Robert Moore. 321-362, Mar. 1952

WHITE MIST (Yawl):

Homeward With Ulysses. By Melville Bell Grosvenor. Photos by Edwin Stuart Grosvenor. 1-39, July 1973

The Isles of Greece: Aegean Birthplace of Western Culture. By Melville Bell Grosvenor. Photos by Edwin Stuart Grosvenor and Winfield Parks. 147-193, Aug. 1972

North (U. S. and Canada) Through History Aboard *White Mist.* By Melville Bell Grosvenor. Photos by Edwin Stuart Grosvenor. 1-55, July 1970

Safe Landing on Sable, Isle of 500 Shipwrecks. By Melville Bell Grosvenor. 398-431, Sept. 1965

White Mist Cruises to Wreck-haunted St. Pierre and Miquelon. By Melville Bell Grosvenor. 378-419, Sept. 1967

WHITE MOUNTAINS, California:

Bristlecone Pine, Oldest Known Living Thing. By Edmund Schulman. Photos by W. Robert Moore. 355-372, Mar. 1958

WHITE MOUNTAINS, New Hampshire:

The Friendly Huts of the White Mountains. By William O. Douglas. Photos by Kathleen Revis. 205-239, Aug. 1961

Mountains Top Off New England. By F. Barrows Colton. Photos by Robert F. Sisson. 563-602, May 1951

Skyline Trail (Appalachian Trail) from Maine to Georgia. By Andrew H. Brown. Photos by Robert F. Sisson. 219-251, Aug. 1949

WHITE SANDS NATIONAL MONUMENT, New Mexico:

New Mexico: The Golden Land. By Robert Laxalt. Photos by Adam Woolfitt. 299-345, Sept. 1970

New Mexico's Great White Sands. By William Belknap, Jr. 113-137, July 1957

WHITE SANDS PROVING GROUND, New Mexico:

Seeing the Earth from 80 Miles Up. By Clyde T. Holliday. 511-528, Oct. 1950

WHITE STORKS, Vanishing Sentinels of the Rooftops. By Roger Tory Peterson. 838-853, June 1962

WHITE TIGERS:

Enchantress! By Theodore H. Reed. Photos by Thomas J. Abercrombie. 628-641, May 1961

White Tiger in My House. By Elizabeth C. Reed.

WHITE TIGERS—*Continued*

Photos by Donna K. Grosvenor. 482-491, Apr. 1970

WHITE-WATER Adventure on Wild Rivers of Idaho. By Frank Craighead, Jr. and John Craighead. 213-239, Feb. 1970

WHITE WATER Yields Relics of Canada's Voyageurs. By Sigurd F. Olson. Photos by David S. Boyer. 413-435, Sept. 1963

WHITEFISH. *See* Menhaden

WHITNEY, Mount, California:

Sierra High Trip. By David R. Brower. 844-868, June 1954

WHITTAKER, JAMES W.:

Six to the Summit. By Norman G. Dyhrenfurth. Photos by Barry C. Bishop. 460-473, Oct. 1963
Note: Jim Whittaker was the first American to reach the summit of Everest.

Author

Canada's Mount Kennedy: III. The First Ascent. Photos by William Albert Allard. 11-33, July 1965

See also American Mount Everest Expedition

WHITTIER, JOHN GREENLEAF:

Literary Landmarks of Massachusetts. By William H. Nicholas. Photos by B. Anthony Stewart and John E. Fletcher. 279-310, Mar. 1950

WHO Are Earth's Richest People? By Mike Holmes. 344-353, Sept. 1976

WHO Says Fish Can't Climb Trees? By Ivan Polunin. 85-91, Jan. 1972

WHO Were the "Mound Builders"? By George E. Stuart. 783-801, Dec. 1972

WHOOPING CRANES Fight for Survival. By Robert Porter Allen. Photos by Frederick Kent Truslow. 650-669, Nov. 1959

WHY Is It That Calcutta—the World's Most Maligned Metropolis—Is Where So Many People Want To Be? By Peter T. White. Photos by Raghubir Singh. 534-563, Apr. 1973

WICHITA MOUNTAINS WILDLIFE REFUGE, Oklahoma:

The Wichitas: Land of the Living Prairie. By M. Woodbridge Williams. 661-697, May 1957

WIGHT, Isle of, England:

Portsmouth, Britannia's Sally Port. By Thomas Garner James. Photos by B. Anthony Stewart. 513-544, Apr. 1952

See also Cowes

The WILD ANIMALS in My Life. By William M. Mann. 497-524, Apr. 1957

WILD BUNCH:

Riding the Outlaw Trail. By Robert Redford. Photos by Jonathan Blair. 622-657, Nov. 1976

The WILD BURROS of Death Valley. By Patricia des Roses Moehlman. Photos by Ira S. Lerner and author. 502-517, Apr. 1972

WILD ELEPHANT Roundup in India. By Harry Miller. Photos by author and James P. Blair. 372-385, Mar. 1969

WILD FLOWERS:

American Wild Flower Odyssey. By P. L. Ricker. 603-634, May 1953

Australia's Bizarre Wild Flowers. By Paul A. Zahl. 858-868, Dec. 1976

Cloud Gardens in the Tetons. By Frank and John Craighead. 811-830, June 1948

Eden in the Outback. By Kay and Stanley Breeden. 189-203, Feb. 1973

The Fragile Beauty All About Us. Photos by Harry S. C. Yen. 785-795, Dec. 1970

In the Gardens of Olympus. By Paul A. Zahl. 85-123, July 1955

Photographing Northern Wild Flowers. By Virginia L. Wells. 809-823, June 1956

Plants of the Alaskan Tundra. 315-321, Mar. 1972

Saving Man's Wildlife Heritage. By John H. Baker. Photos by Robert F. Sisson. 581-620, Nov. 1954

A Visit to the Living Ice Age. By Rutherford Platt. 525-545, Apr. 1957

WILD FOODS:

The Making of an Astronaut. By Robert R. Gilruth. 122-144, Jan. 1965

Philmont Scout Ranch Helps Boys Grow Up. By Andrew H. Brown. 399-416, Sept. 1956

Stalking the West's Wild Foods. By Euell Gibbons. Photos by David Hiser. 186-199, Aug. 1973

Stalking Wild Foods on a Desert Isle. By Euell Gibbons. Photos by David Hiser. 47-63, July 1972

We Survive on a Pacific Atoll. By John and Frank Craighead. 73-94, Jan. 1948

WILD RIVERS: Preservation:

White-water Adventure on Wild Rivers of Idaho. By Frank Craighead, Jr. and John Craighead. 213-239, Feb. 1970
Included: Middle Fork Salmon; Salmon; and rivers protected or proposed for protection under the Wild and Scenic Rivers Act of 1968

Wild River (Television film). 239A-239B, Feb. 1970
Included: Middle Fork Salmon; Salmon

See also Allagash Wilderness Waterway

A WILD SHORE Where Two Worlds Meet. Photos by Des and Jen Bartlett. 298-321, Mar. 1976

WILD WEST:

Riding the Outlaw Trail. By Robert Redford. Photos by Jonathan Blair. 622-657, Nov. 1976

WILDERNESS: United States:

Alaskan Family Robinson. By Nancy Robinson. Photos by John Metzger and Peter Robinson. 55-75, Jan. 1973

America's Wilderness: How Much Can We Save? By Gilbert M. Grosvenor, François Leydet, and Joseph Judge. Photos by Farrell Grehan. 151-205, Feb. 1974
Included: Allagash Wilderness Waterway; Mazatzal Wilderness; Okefenokee Swamp; Olympic National Park; Wind River Range

Escalante Canyon—Wilderness at the Crossroads. By Jon Schneeberger. 270-285, Aug. 1972

John Muir's Wild America. By Harvey Arden. Photos by Dewitt Jones. 433-461, Apr. 1973

John Muir's Wild America. Special Publication announced. 860-864, June 1976

WILDERNESS — *Continued*

Mexico to Canada on the Pacific Crest Trail. By Mike W. Edwards. Photos by David Hiser. 741-779, June 1971
    Included: Glacier Peak Wilderness, Washington; Goat Rocks Wilderness, Washington; John Muir Wilderness, California; Mount Jefferson Wilderness, Oregon; Pasayten Wilderness, Washington

New National Park Proposed: The Spectacular North Cascades. By Nathaniel T. Kenney. Photos by James P. Blair. 642-667, May 1968
    Included: Glacier Peak Wilderness, Washington; Pasayten Wilderness, Washington

Preserving America's Last Great Wilderness (Alaska). By David Jeffery. 769-791, June 1975

White-water Adventure on Wild Rivers of Idaho. By Frank Craighead, Jr. and John Craighead. 213-239, Feb. 1970

Wilderness U.S.A. Book announced. 582-584, Oct. 1973

Yellowstone at 100: A Walk Through the Wilderness. By Karen and Derek Craighead. Photos by Sam Abell. 579-603, May 1972

See also Scapegoat Wilderness

WILDLIFE:

Florida, Noah's Ark for Exotic Newcomers. By Rick Gore. Photos by David Doubilet. 538-559, Oct. 1976

Man's Wildlife Heritage Faces Extinction. By H. R. H. The Prince Philip, Duke of Edinburgh. 700-703, Nov. 1962

Studying Wildlife by Satellite. By Frank Craighead, Jr. and John Craighead. 120-123, Jan. 1973

See also Birds; Fishes; Mammals; *and* Eyes

Africa

African Wildlife: Man's Threatened Legacy. By Allan C. Fisher, Jr. Photos by Thomas Nebbia. 147-187, Feb. 1972
    A Continent's Living Treasure. Paintings by Ned Seidler. 164-167

Africa's Uncaged Elephants. Photos by Quentin Keynes. 371-382, Mar. 1951

Animals of East Africa. Special Publication announced. 844-849, June 1968

Hyenas, the Hunters Nobody Knows. By Hans Kruuk. Photos by Baron Hugo van Lawick. 44-57, July 1968
    Included: Lions, Wildebeests, Zebras

The Last Great Animal Kingdom. 390-409, Sept. 1960

Mzima, Kenya's Spring of Life. By Joan and Alan Root. 350-373, Sept. 1971

A New Look at Kenya's "Treetops." By Quentin Keynes. 536-541, Oct. 1956

Orphans of the Wild (Animal Orphanage, Uganda). By Bruce G. Kinloch. 683-699, Nov. 1962

Roaming Africa's Unfenced Zoos. By W. Robert Moore. 353-380, Mar. 1950

Safari from Congo to Cairo. By Elsie May Bell Grosvenor. Photos by Gilbert Grosvenor. 721-771, Dec. 1954

Safari Through Changing Africa. By Elsie May Bell Grosvenor. Photos by Gilbert Grosvenor. 145-198, Aug. 1953

Stalking Central Africa's Wildlife. By T. Donald Carter. Paintings by Walter A. Weber. 264-286, Aug. 1956

WILDLIFE — *Continued*

Tanzania Marches to Its Own Drum. By Peter T. White. Photos by Emory Kristof. 474-509, Apr. 1975

Where Elephants Have Right of Way. By George and Jinx Rodger. 363-389, Sept. 1960
    Included: Buffaloes; Giraffes; Hippopotamuses; Lyrehorned ankoles; Rhinoceroses

See also Baboons; Black Eagles; Cattle Egrets; Chimpanzees; Egyptian Vulture; Flamingos; Gorillas; Honey-Guide; Hornbills; Lions; *and* National Parks (Africa)

Antarctic and Subantarctic

See Penguins; Weddell Seals

Arctic

Journey to the High Arctic (Television film). 590A-590B, Apr. 1971

See also Musk Oxen; Polar Bear; Reindeer; Seals; *and* Ice Ages *(Ice Age Mammals)*

Asia

Bhutan, Land of the Thunder Dragon. By Burt Kerr Todd. 713-754, Dec. 1952

The Elephant and I. By M. D. Chaturvedi. 489-507, Oct. 1957

India Struggles to Save Her Wildlife. By John J. Putman. Paintings by Ned Seidler. 299-343, Sept. 1976

Seeking Mindanao's Strangest Creatures. By Charles Heizer Wharton. 389-408, Sept. 1948

Stalking the Great Indian Rhino. By Lee Merriam Talbot. 389-398, Mar. 1957

Wild Elephant Roundup in India. By Harry Miller. Photos by author and James P. Blair. 372-385, Mar. 1969

See also Cattle Egrets; Komodo Dragons; Orangutans; Pandas; Spiny Babbler; *and* Red Sea

Australia

Eden in the Outback. By Kay and Stanley Breeden. 189-203, Feb. 1973

Strange Animals of Australia. By David Fleay. Photos by Stanley Breeden. 388-411, Sept. 1963

See also Bowerbirds; Kangaroos; Lorikeets; Lyrebird; Platypuses

Europe

Rare Birds Flock to Spain's Marismas. By Roger Tory Peterson. 397-425, Mar. 1958

See also Cattle Egrets; Golden Eagles (Scotland); Kingfishers; Puffins; Reindeer; Swans (England); White Storks; *and* Zoos

Hawaii

See Nene

Midway Islands

See Albatrosses

New Guinea

See Birds of Paradise

New Zealand

See Kiwi; Takahe

North America

Arizona's Window on Wildlife. By Lewis Wayne Walker. 240-250, Feb. 1958

An Artist's Glimpses of Our Roadside Wildlife. Paintings by Walter A. Weber. 16-32, July 1950

Businessman in the Bush. By Frederick Kent Truslow. 634-675, May 1970

Cajunland, Louisiana's French-speaking Coast. By Bern Keating. Photos by Charles Harbutt and

WILDLIFE — *Continued*

Franke Keating. 353-391, Mar. 1966

Can We Save Our Salt Marshes? By Stephen W. Hitchcock. Photos by William R. Curtsinger. 729-765, June 1972

Corkscrew Swamp — Florida's Primeval Show Place. By Melville Bell Grosvenor. 98-113, Jan. 1958

Haunting Heart of the Everglades. By Andrew H. Brown. Photos by author and Willard R. Culver. 145-173, Feb. 1948

Men, Moose, and Mink of Northwest Angle. By William H. Nicholas. Photos by J. Baylor Roberts. 265-284, Aug. 1947

Nature's Year in Pleasant Valley. By Paul A. Zahl. 488-525, Apr. 1968

Preserving America's Last Great Wilderness (Alaska). By David Jeffery. 769-791, June 1975

Saving Man's Wildlife Heritage. By John H. Baker. Photos by Robert F. Sisson. 581-620, Nov. 1954

Springtime Comes to Yellowstone National Park. By Paul A. Zahl. 761-779, Dec. 1956

Threatened Glories of Everglades National Park. By Frederick Kent Truslow and Frederick G. Vosburgh. Photos by Frederick Kent Truslow and Otis Imboden. 508-553, Oct. 1967

Twilight Hope for Big Cypress. By Rick Gore. Photos by Patricia Caulfield. 251-273, Aug. 1976

Vanishing Wildlife of North America. Special Publication announced. 865-868, June 1973

White-water Adventure on Wild Rivers of Idaho. By Frank Craighead, Jr. and John Craighead. 213-239, Feb. 1970

The Wichitas: Land of the Living Prairie. By M. Woodbridge Williams. 661-697, May 1957

Wild Animals of North America. Book announced. 554-557, Oct. 1960

Wildlife Adventuring in Jackson Hole. By Frank and John Craighead. 1-36, Jan. 1956

Wildlife In and Near the Valley of the Moon. By H. H. Arnold. Photos by Paul J. Fair. 401-414, Mar. 1950

Wildlife of Everglades National Park. By Daniel B. Beard. Paintings by Walter A. Weber. 83-116, Jan. 1949

Wildlife of Mount McKinley National Park. By Adolph Murie. Paintings by Walter A. Weber. 249-270, Aug. 1953

Wolves Versus Moose on Isle Royale. By Durward L. Allen and L. David Mech. 200-219, Feb. 1963

Yellowstone at 100: A Walk Through the Wilderness. By Karen and Derek Craighead. Photos by Sam Abell. 579-603, May 1972

Yellowstone Wildlife in Winter. By William Albert Allard. 637-661, Nov. 1967

See also Bird Sanctuaries and Rookeries; National Parks (Canada; U. S.); Tundra

South America

Animal Safari to British Guiana. By David Attenborough. Photos by Charles Lagus and author. 851-874, June 1957

Capturing Strange Creatures in Colombia. By Marte Latham. Photos by Tor Eigeland. 682-693, May 1966

The Galapagos, Eerie Cradle of New Species. By Roger Tory Peterson. Photos by Alan and Joan Root. 541-585, Apr. 1967

The Jungle Was My Home. By Sasha Siemel. 695-712, Nov. 1952

WILDLIFE — *Continued*

Keeping House for a Biologist in Colombia. By Nancy Bell Fairchild Bates. Photos by Marston Bates. 251-274, Aug. 1948

Lost World of the Galapagos. By Irving and Electa Johnson. 681-703, May 1959

Patagonia. 290-339, Mar. 1976

Peru Profits from Sea Fowl. By Robert Cushman Murphy. Photos by author and Grace E. Barstow Murphy. 395-413, Mar. 1959

See also Cock-of-the-Rock; Flamingos; Hoatzin; Hummingbirds (Brazil); Oilbirds; Scarlet Ibis; Tortoises; *and* National Parks (South America); Tierra del Fuego

West Indies

See Flamingos; Greater Birds of Paradise

WILDLIFE MANAGEMENT INSTITUTE: Expeditions and Research. *See* Isle Royale, Michigan

WILDLIFE REFUGES:

Africa. *See* Entebbe Animal Refuge, Uganda; Serengeti National Park, Tanzania

Asia. *See* India (India Struggles to Save Her Wildlife); Kaziranga Wild Life Sanctuary, India; Tanjung Puting Reserve, Indonesia

Australia. *See* Victoria (State)

Caribbean. *See* Little Tobago (Island)

Europe. *See* Abbotsbury Swannery, England; The Camargue, France; Las Marismas, Spain

South America. *See* Pampa Galeras National Vicuña Reserve, Peru

United States. *See* Aransas National Wildlife Refuge, Texas; Bear River Migratory Bird Refuge, Utah; Corkscrew Swamp, Florida; Desert Museum, Arizona; Everglades National Park, Florida; McNeil River State Game Sanctuary, Alaska; National Elk Refuge, Wyoming; Okefenokee Swamp, Georgia; Pribilof Islands, Alaska; Red Rock Lakes National Wildlife Refuge, Montana; Santa Barbara Islands, California; Sapsucker Woods, New York; Wichita Mountains Wildlife Refuge, Oklahoma

See also Bird Sanctuaries and Rookeries; Game Preserves; National Parks

WILES, WILBUR:

Stalking the Mountain Lion — to Save Him. By Maurice G. Hornocker. 638-655, Nov. 1969

WILHELM, JOHN L.: Author:

Solar Energy, the Ultimate Powerhouse. Photos by Emory Kristof. 381-397, Mar. 1976

WILKINSON, NORMAN: Author-Artist:

British Castles, History in Stone. 111-129, July 1947

WILL Brazil's Fiery Bees Reach the U. S.? By Rick Gore. Photos by Bianca Lavies. 491-501, Apr. 1976

WILL Coal Be Tomorrow's "Black Gold"? By Gordon Young. Photos by James P. Blair. 234-259, Aug. 1975

WILL Oil and Tundra Mix? Alaska's North Slope Hangs in the Balance. By William S. Ellis. Photos by Emory Kristof. 485-517, Oct. 1971

WILLAMETTE RIVER AND VALLEY, Oregon:

A River Restored: Oregon's Willamette. By Ethel

WILLAMETTE RIVER AND VALLEY, Oregon—*Continued*

A. Starbird. Photos by Lowell J. Georgia. 816-835, June 1972

WILLCOX, ALEX R.: Photographer:

Africa's Bushman Art Treasures. By Alfred Friendly. 848-865, June 1963

WILLEMSTAD, Curaçao, Netherlands Antilles:

The Netherlands Antilles: Holland in the Caribbean. By James Cerruti. Photos by Emory Kristof. 115-146, Jan. 1970

WILLIAM THE CONQUEROR:

The British Way. By Sir Evelyn Wrench. 421-541, Apr. 1949

A New Look at Medieval Europe. By Kenneth M. Setton. Paintings by Andre Durenceau and Birney Lettick. 799-859, Dec. 1962

900 Years Ago: the Norman Conquest. By Kenneth M. Setton. Photos by George F. Mobley. 206-251, Aug. 1966

WILLIAM AND MARY COLLEGE, Williamsburg, Virginia:

Williamsburg: Its College and Its Cinderella City. By Beverley M. Bowie. 439-486, Oct. 1954

WILLIAMS, JOHN G.: Author:

Freeing Flamingos From Anklets of Death. Photos by Alan Root. 934-944, Dec. 1963

WILLIAMS, M. WOODBRIDGE: Author-Photographer:

The Wichitas: Land of the Living Prairie. 661-697, May 1957

Photographer

History and Beauty Blend in a Concord Iris Garden. By Robert T. Cochran, Jr. 705-719, May 1959

Keeping House for Tropical Butterflies. By Jocelyn Crane. 193-217, Aug. 1957

Strange Little World of the Hoatzin. By J. Lear Grimmer. 391-401, Sept. 1962

WILLIAMS, MAYNARD OWEN:

Chief of the NGS Foreign Staff for 20 years; total service, 34 years. 627, Oct. 1963

Author

Pilgrims Follow the Christmas Star. 831-840, Dec. 1952

Portrait of Indochina. By W. Robert Moore and Maynard Owen Williams. Paintings by Jean Despujols. 461-490, Apr. 1951

Turkey Paves the Path of Progress. 141-186, Aug. 1951

War-torn Greece Looks Ahead. 711-744, Dec. 1949

Author-Photographer

Crete, Cradle of Western Civilization. 693-706, Nov. 1953

Dublin's Historic Horse Show. 115-132, July 1953

Home to the Holy Land. 707-746, Dec. 1950

Oasis-hopping in the Sahara. 209-236, Feb. 1949

Pennsylvania Dutch Folk Festival. 503-516, Oct. 1952

Photographer

Belgium Comes Back. By Harvey Klemmer. 575-614, May 1948

Beside the Persian Gulf. 341-356, Mar. 1947

Lascaux Cave, Cradle of World Art. By Norbert

WILLIAMS, MAYNARD OWEN—*Continued*

Casteret. 771-794, Dec. 1948

Luxembourg, Survivor of Invasions. By Sydney Clark. 791-810, June 1948

Operation Eclipse: 1948. By William A. Kinney. 325-372, Mar. 1949

Saudi Arabia, Oil Kingdom. 497-512, Apr. 1948

2,000 Miles Through Europe's Oldest Kingdom (Denmark). By Isobel Wylie Hutchison. 141-180, Feb. 1949

WILLIAMS, WINSTON: Author:

Twenty Fathoms Down for Mother-of-Pearl. Photos by Bates Littlehales. 512-529, Apr. 1962

WILLIAMSBURG, Brooklyn, New York:

The Pious Ones (Hasidic Jews). By Harvey Arden. Photos by Nathan Benn. 276-298, Aug. 1975

WILLIAMSBURG, Virginia:

Firebrands of the Revolution. By Eric F. Goldman. Photos by George F. Mobley. 2-27, July 1974

Williamsburg, City for All Seasons. By Joseph Judge. Photos by James L. Amos. 790-823, Dec. 1968

Williamsburg: Its College and Its Cinderella City. By Beverley M. Bowie. 439-486, Oct. 1954

WILLM, PIERRE HENRI:

Two and a Half Miles Down. By Georges S. Houot. 80-86, July 1954

WILSON, ALBERT G.: Author:

Our Universe Unfolds New Wonders. 245-260, Feb. 1952

WILSON, BRUCE A.: Author:

Busy Fairbanks Sets Alaska's Pace. 505-523, Oct. 1949

WILSON, JAY: Photographer:

To Torre Egger's Icy Summit. By Jim Donini. 813-823, Dec. 1976

WILSON, JOHN: Author:

Drought Bedevils Brazil's Sertão. Photos by Gordon W. Gahan. 704-723, Nov. 1972

WILSON, PHYLLIS: Author:

Queen of Canada (Elizabeth II). Photos by Kathleen Revis. 825-829, June 1959

WILSON, WOODROW:

Inside the White House. By Lonnelle Aikman. Photos by B. Anthony Stewart and Thomas Nebbia. 3-43, Jan. 1961

The Living White House. By Lonnelle Aikman. 593-643, Nov. 1966

Profiles of the Presidents: IV. America Enters the Modern Era. By Frank Freidel. 537-577, Oct. 1965

WIND, Wave, Star, and Bird. By David Lewis. Photos by Nicholas deVore III. 747-781, Dec. 1974

WIND-POWER RESEARCH:

Can We Harness the Wind? By Roger Hamilton. Photos by Emory Kristof. 812-829, Dec. 1975

WIND RIVER RANGE, Wyoming:

Wind River Range: Many-treasured Splendor. By Joseph Judge. 198-205, Feb. 1974

WINDJAMMING Around New England. By Tom Horgan. Photos by Robert F. Sisson. 141-169, Aug. 1950

WINDMILLS:

Can We Harness the Wind? By Roger Hamilton. Photos by Emory Kristof. 812-829, Dec. 1975

WINDOW on Earth's Interior. By Robert D. Ballard. Photos by Emory Kristof. 228-249, Aug. 1976

WINDOW on Nature: The American Museum of Natural History. By James A. Oliver. Photos by Robert F. Sisson. 220-259, Feb. 1963

The **WINDS** of Freedom Stir a Continent. By Nathaniel T. Kenney. Photos by W. D. Vaughn. 303-359, Sept. 1960

WINDWARD ISLANDS, West Indies:

Carib Cruises the West Indies. By Carleton Mitchell. 1-56, Jan. 1948

Finisterre Sails the Windward Islands. By Carleton Mitchell. Photos by Winfield Parks. 755-801, Dec. 1965

See also Martinique

WINE MAKING:

Italian Riviera, Land That Winter Forgot. By Howell Walker. 743-789, June 1963

Madeira, Like Its Wine, Improves With Age. By Veronica Thomas. Photos by Jonathan Blair. 488-513, Apr. 1973

My Life in the Valley of the Moon (California). By H. H. Arnold. Photos by Willard R. Culver. 689-716, Dec. 1948
    Included: Vineyards and wineries of the Sonoma, Napa, and Petaluma Valleys

Portugal at the Crossroads. By Howard La Fay. Photos by Volkmar Wentzel. 458-501, Oct. 1965

Provence, Empire of the Sun. By William Davenport. Photos by James A. Sugar. 692-715, May 1975

The Renaissance Lives On in Tuscany. By Luis Marden. Photos by Albert Moldvay. 626-659, Nov. 1974

WINEGROWERS' FESTIVAL:

Switzerland's Once-in-a-generation Festival. By Jean and Franc Shor. 563-571, Oct. 1958

WING-BORNE Lamps of the Summer Night. By Paul A. Zahl. 48-59, July 1962

WINNIPESAUKEE, Lake, New Hampshire:

The Merrimack: River of Industry and Romance. By Albert W. Atwood. Photos by B. Anthony Stewart. 106-140, Jan. 1951

WINSTON-SALEM, North Carolina:

Old Salem, Morning Star of Moravian Faith. By Rowe Findley. Photos by Robert W. Madden. 818-837, Dec. 1970

WINTER Caravan to the Roof of the World. By Sabrina and Roland Michaud. 435-465, Apr. 1972

WINTER CARNIVALS:

Snow Festival in Japan's Far North. By Eiji Miyazawa. 824-833, Dec. 1968

Winter Brings Carnival Time to Quebec. By Kathleen Revis. 69-97, Jan. 1958

WINTER in Snowy Stehekin. Photos by Bruce Dale. Text by Pat Hutson. 572-588, Apr. 1974

WINTERING on the Roof of the World. By Barry C. Bishop. 503-547, Oct. 1962

WIRTH, CONRAD L.: Author:

Heritage of Beauty and History (U. S. National Parks). 587-661, May 1958

The Mission Called 66: Today in Our National Parks. 7-47, July 1966

The Parks in Your Backyard. 647-707, Nov. 1963

WISCONSIN:

Close-up: U.S.A., Wisconsin, Michigan, and the Great Lakes, map supplement. Text on reverse. Aug. 1973

Deep in the Heart of "Swissconsin." By William H. Nicholas. Photos by J. Baylor Roberts. 781-800, June 1947

The Great Lakes: Is It Too Late? By Gordon Young. Photos by James L. Amos and Martin Rogers. 147-185, Aug. 1973

In Touch With Nature. By Elizabeth A. Moize. Photos by Steve Raymer. 537-543, Apr. 1974
    Contents: Towering Pines and Woodland Camps, Eagle River

Mapping the Nation's Breadbasket. By Frederick Simpich. 831-849, June 1948

Wisconsin, Land of the Good Life. By Beverley M. Bowie. Photos by Volkmar Wentzel. 141-187, Feb. 1957

Wisconsin's Door Peninsula. By William S. Ellis. Photos by Ted Rozumalski. 347-371, Mar. 1969

Wisconsin's Menominees: Indians on a Seesaw. By Patricia Raymer. Photos by Steve Raymer. 228-251, Aug. 1974

WISCONSIN, U.S.S. *See* Midshipmen's Cruise

WISHERD, EDWIN L.: Photographer:

The Wonder City That Moves by Night. By Francis Beverly Kelley. 289-324, Mar. 1948

WITH the Nuba Hillmen of Kordofan. By Robin Strachan. 249-278, Feb. 1951

WITH the U. S. Army in Korea. By John R. Hodge. 829-840, June 1947

WITH Uncle Sam and John Bull in Germany. By Frederick Simpich. 117-140, Jan. 1949

WITNESS to a War: British Correspondent Frank Vizetelly. By Robert T. Cochran, Jr. 453-491, Apr. 1961

WIZARD ISLAND (Volcano), Oregon:

Crater Lake Summer. By Walter Meayers Edwards. 134-148, July 1962

WOLFE, JAMES:

The British Way. By Sir Evelyn Wrench. 421-541, Apr. 1949

WOLFSHEIMER, GENE: Author-Photographer:

The Discus Fish Yields a Secret. 675-681, May 1960

WOLVES Versus Moose on Isle Royale. By Durward L. Allen and L. David Mech. 200-219, Feb. 1963

A **WOMAN** Paints the Tibetans. By Lafugie. 659-692, May 1949

WOMEN DIVERS:

Ama, Sea Nymphs of Japan. By Luis Marden. 122-135, July 1971

Tektite II. 256-296, Aug. 1971
    II. All-girl Team Tests the Habitat. By Sylvia A. Earle. Paintings by Pierre Mion. 291-296

WOMEN of the Revolution: Patriots in Petticoats. By Lonnelle Aikman. Paintings by Louis S. Glanzman. 475-493, Oct. 1975

WOMEN'S RESERVE OF THE U.S. NAVAL RESERVE (WAVES). *See* Parachute Rigger School

The WONDER City That Moves by Night. By Francis Beverly Kelley. 289-324, Mar. 1948

WONDERLAND in Longwood Gardens. By Edward C. Ferriday, Jr. 45-64, July 1951

WOOD, GINNY HILL: Author:
Squaws Along the Yukon. 245-265, Aug. 1957

WOOD:
Versatile Wood Waits on Man. By Andrew H. Brown. 109-140, July 1951
See also Lumber Industry; Paper and Pulp Industry

WOOD CARVING:
An Ozark Family Carves a Living and a Way of Life. By Bruce Dale. 124-133, July 1975
See also Afo-A-Kom

WOOD IBIS. *See* Wood Storks

WOOD STORKS:
Our Only Native Stork, the Wood Ibis. By Robert Porter Allen. Photos by Frederick Kent Truslow. 294-306, Feb. 1964

WOODLAND PERIOD. *See* Russell Cave, Alabama

WOODPECKERS:
The Bird's Year. By Arthur A. Allen. 791-816, June 1951
Included: Gila, Golden-fronted, Red-bellied woodpeckers
When Disaster Struck a Woodpecker's Home. By Frederick Kent Truslow. 882-884, Dec. 1966

WOODS, Lake of the, Canada-U. S.:
Men, Moose, and Mink of Northwest Angle. By William H. Nicholas. Photos by J. Baylor Roberts. 265-284, Aug. 1947

WOODS HOLE, Massachusetts:
Cape Cod, Where Sea Holds Sway Over Man and Land. By Nathaniel T. Kenney. Photos by Dean Conger. 149-187, Aug. 1962
Windjamming Around New England. By Tom Horgan. Photos by Robert F. Sisson. 141-169, Aug. 1950

WOODS HOLE OCEANOGRAPHIC INSTITUTION:
Expeditions and Research. *See* Mid-Atlantic Ridge; Mid-Atlantic Rift; *and* Weddell Seals

WOODSON, LeROY, Jr.:
Editorial on writer-photographers. 295, Mar. 1975
Author-Photographer
The Kurds of Iraq: "We Who Face Death." 364-387, Mar. 1975

WOOL:
The Cotswolds, "Noicest Parrt o'England." By James Cerruti. Photos by Adam Woolfitt. 846-869, June 1974
High, Wild World of the Vicuña. By William L. Franklin. 77-91, Jan. 1973
See also Qiviut; Tweed

WOOLFITT, ADAM: Photographer:
Amiable Amsterdam. By William Davenport. 683-705, May 1974
Chelsea, London's Haven of Individualists. By James Cerruti. 28-55, Jan. 1972
Christopher Columbus and the New World He Found. By John Scofield. 584-625, Nov. 1975
The Cotswolds, "Noicest Parrt o'England." By James Cerruti. 846-869, June 1974
Edinburgh: Capital in Search of a Country. By James Cerruti. 274-296, Aug. 1976
The England of Charles Dickens. By Richard W. Long. 443-483, Apr. 1974
The Faeroes, Isles of Maybe. By Ernle Bradford. 410-442, Sept. 1970
The Investiture of Great Britain's Prince of Wales. By Allan C. Fisher, Jr. Photos by James L. Stanfield and Adam Woolfitt. 698-715, Nov. 1969
The Netherlands: Nation at War With the Sea. By Alan Villiers. 530-571, Apr. 1968
New Mexico: The Golden Land. By Robert Laxalt. 299-345, Sept. 1970

WORCESTER, Massachusetts:
Cities Like Worcester Make America. By Howell Walker. 189-214, Feb. 1955

WORDEN, ALFRED M.:
Apollo 15 Explores the Mountains of the Moon. By Kenneth F. Weaver. Photos from NASA. 233-265, Feb. 1972

WORDSWORTH, WILLIAM:
The British Way. By Sir Evelyn Wrench. 421-541, Apr. 1949
Lake District, Poets' Corner of England. By H. V. Morton. Photos by David S. Boyer. 511-545, Apr. 1956

WORK-HARD, Play-hard Michigan. By Andrew H. Brown. 279-320, Mar. 1952

WORKING for Weeks on the Sea Floor. By Jacques-Yves Cousteau. Photos by Philippe Cousteau and Bates Littlehales. 498-537, Apr. 1966

WORLD:
The Political World; The Physical World, double-sided map supplement. Nov. 1975
The World, Atlas series supplement. Nov. 1960
The World, map supplement. Mar. 1957; Feb. 1965
The World, map supplement. Painting and text on reverse. Dec. 1970; Dec. 1976
The World Map, supplement. Dec. 1951
See also Earth

WORLD (Magazine for Young Readers):
The *School Bulletin* is retired after 56 years; replaced by *WORLD*. 299, Sept. 1975
Start the World, I Want to Get On! Text announcing National Geographic *WORLD*. 148-150, July 1975

WORLD ATLAS. *See* Atlases, NGS: World

WORLD CRUISES AND VOYAGES:
"Around the World in Eighty Days." By Newman Bumstead. 705-750, Dec. 1951
Captain Cook: The Man Who Mapped the Pacific. By Alan Villiers. Photos by Gordon W. Gahan. 297-349, Sept. 1971

WORLD CRUISES AND VOYAGES — *Continued*

In the Wake of Darwin's *Beagle*. By Alan Villiers. Photos by James L. Stanfield. 449-495, Oct. 1969

Magellan: First Voyage Around the World. By Alan Villiers. Photos by Bruce Dale. 721-753, June 1976

Off the Beaten Track of Empire (Prince Philip's Tour). By Beverley M. Bowie. Photos by Michael Parker. 584-626, Nov. 1957

Robin Sails Home. By Robin Lee Graham. 504-545, Oct. 1970

Saga of a Ship, the *Yankee*. By Luis Marden. 263-269, Feb. 1966

Sir Francis Drake. By Alan Villiers. Photos by Gordon W. Gahan. 216-253, Feb. 1975

A Teen-ager Sails the World Alone. By Robin Lee Graham. 445-491, Oct. 1968

Triton Follows Magellan's Wake. By Edward L. Beach. Photos by J. Baylor Roberts. 585-616, Nov. 1960

The Voyage of the Brigantine *Yankee* (Television film). 265A-265B, Feb. 1966

World-roaming Teen-ager Sails On. By Robin Lee Graham. 449-493, Apr. 1969

The WORLD in Dolls. By Samuel F. Pryor. Photos by Kathleen Revis. 817-831, Dec. 1959

The WORLD in New York City. By Peter T. White. 52-107, July 1964

The WORLD in Your Garden. By W. H. Camp. Paintings by Else Bostelmann. 1-65, July 1947

The WORLD of Elizabeth I. By Louis B. Wright. Photos by Ted Spiegel. 668-709, Nov. 1968

The WORLD of My Apple Tree. By Robert F. Sisson. 836-847, June 1972

The WORLD Pays Final Tribute (Churchill Funeral). Text by Carolyn Bennett Patterson. 199-225, Aug. 1965

WORLD WAR I Aircraft Fly Again in Rhinebeck's Rickety Rendezvous. By Harvey Arden. Photos by Howard Sochurek. 578-587, Oct. 1970

WORLD WAR II:

Adventures with the Survey Navy. By Irving Johnson. 131-148, July 1947

Belgium Comes Back. By Harvey Klemmer. Photos by Maynard Owen Williams. 575-614, May 1948
　　Included: Bastogne; Battle of the Bulge

The Bonins and Iwo Jima Go Back to Japan. By Paul Sampson. Photos by Joe Munroe. 128-144, July 1968

The British Way. By Sir Evelyn Wrench. 421-541, Apr. 1949
　　Included: Sinking of the *Bismarck*, May 27, 1941; Winston Churchill

The Eisenhower Story. By Howard La Fay. 1-39, July 1969

Fun Helped Them Fight. By Stuart E. Jones. 95-104, Jan. 1948
　　Contents: Army Air Forces' informal method of naming and decorating combat aircraft

Here Come the Marines. By Frederick Simpich. 647-672, Nov. 1950

History Written in the Skies (U. S. Air Force). 273-294, Aug. 1957

WORLD WAR II — *Continued*

How One of The Society's Maps (Pacific Ocean) Saved a Precious Cargo. 844, June 1947

Italy Smiles Again. By Edgar Erskine Hume. 693-732, June 1949

Life Springs From Death in Truk Lagoon. By Sylvia A. Earle. Photos by Al Giddings. 578-613, May 1976
　　From Graveyard to Garden. 604-613
　　Included: Japanese ships sunk in two 1944 attacks by U. S. Navy carrier-launched planes

Luxembourg, Survivor of Invasions. By Sydney Clark. Photos by Maynard Owen Williams. 791-810, June 1948

Okinawa, Pacific Outpost. 538-552, Apr. 1950

Sailors in the Sky: Fifty Years of Naval Aviation. By Patrick N. L. Bellinger. 276-296, Aug. 1961

See also Churchill, Sir Winston; Profiles of the Presidents: V; U. S. Army Signal Corps; Unknown Servicemen; War Memorials

WORLD WILDLIFE FUND:

Man's Wildlife Heritage Faces Extinction. By H.R.H. The Prince Philip. 700-703, Nov. 1962

WORLD'S FAIRS:

Belgium Welcomes the World. By Howell Walker. 795-837, June 1958

The Fair Reopens (New York). Photos by James P. Blair. Text by Carolyn Bennett Patterson. 505-529, Apr. 1965

Kansai, Japan's Historic Heartland, Hosts Expo '70. By Thomas J. Abercrombie. 295-339, Mar. 1970

Montreal Greets the World. By Jules B. Billard. 600-621, May 1967

Seattle Fair Looks to the 21st Century. By Carolyn Bennett Patterson. Photos by Thomas Nebbia. 402-427, Sept. 1962

WORLD'S Last Salute to a Great American (Dwight D. Eisenhower). By William Graves and other members of the NGS staff. 40-51, July 1969

WORLD'S Tallest Tree Discovered. By Melville Bell Grosvenor. Photos by George F. Mobley. 1-9, July 1964

WORMS AND WORMLIKE ANIMALS:

Biggest Worm Farm Caters to Platypuses. By W. H. Nicholas. 269-280, Feb. 1949

Capturing Strange Creatures in Colombia. By Marte Latham. Photos by Tor Eigeland. 682-693, May 1966

See also Glowworms; Railroad Worm; Shipworms

WRASSES:

Finned Doctors of the Deep. By Douglas Faulkner. 867-873, Dec. 1965

WREN, CHRISTOPHER:

The British Way. By Sir Evelyn Wrench. 421-541, Apr. 1949

WRENCH, SIR EVELYN: Author:

The British Way. 421-541, Apr. 1949

Founders of New England. Photos by B. Anthony Stewart. 803-838, June 1953

Founders of Virginia. Photos by B. Anthony Stewart. 433-462, Apr. 1948

WRIGHT, BELINDA: Photographer:

India Struggles to Save Her Wildlife. By John J. Putman. 299-343, Sept. 1976

WRIGHT, G. ERNEST: Author:

Bringing Old Testament Times to Life. Paintings by Henry J. Soulen. 833-864, Dec. 1957

The Last Thousand Years Before Christ. Paintings by H. J. Soulen and Peter V. Bianchi. 812-853, Dec. 1960

WRIGHT, JONATHAN: Photographer:

Jackson Hole: Good-bye to the Old Days? By François Leydet. 768-789, Dec. 1976

WRIGHT, LOUIS B.: Author:

The Britain That Shakespeare Knew. Photos by Dean Conger. 613-665, May 1964

The World of Elizabeth I. Photos by Ted Spiegel. 668-709, Nov. 1968

WRIGHT, MYRON H., Jr.: Photographer:

The Swallow-tailed Kite: Graceful Aerialist of the Everglades. 496-505, Oct. 1972

WRIGHT, ORVILLE and WILBUR:

Aviation Looks Ahead on Its 50th Birthday. By Emory S. Land. 721-739, Dec. 1953

Fifty Years of Flight. 740-756, Dec. 1953

Fledgling Wings of the Air Force. By Thomas W. McKnew. 266-271, Aug. 1957

Lonely Cape Hatteras, Besieged by the Sea. By William S. Ellis. Photos by Emory Kristof. 393-421, Sept. 1969

WRIGHT WAY (Skyway 1):

Skyway Below the Clouds. By Carl R. Markwith. Photos by Ernest J. Cottrell. 85-108, July 1949
    Contents: A round-trip flight over Skyway 1, an air-way route planned and marked especially for the use of private flyers

WRINGING Secrets from Greenland's Icecap. By Paul-Emile Victor. 121-147, Jan. 1956

WRIOTHESLEY, HENRY (Third Earl of Southampton):

Founders of Virginia. By Sir Evelyn Wrench. Photos by B. Anthony Stewart. 433-462, Apr. 1948

WRITING:

Ancient Mesopotamia: A Light That Did Not Fail. By E. A. Speiser. Paintings by H. M. Herget. 41-105, Jan. 1951
    Included: How Seal Engraving Led to the Invention of Writing

The Phoenicians, Sea Lords of Antiquity. By Samuel W. Matthews. Photos by Winfield Parks. Paintings by Robert C. Magis. 149-189, Aug. 1974

See also Cuneiform Script; Glyphs

WULUMUCHI, Sinkiang. *See* Urumchi

WYOMING:

Beavers, Nature's Aquatic Engineers. By Des and Jen Bartlett. 716-732, May 1974
    Included: Granite Creek in Teton National Forest

Cloud Gardens in the Tetons. By Frank and John Craighead. 811-830, June 1948

From Sun-clad Sea to Shining Mountains. By Ralph Gray. Photos by James P. Blair. 542-589, Apr. 1964

A Map Maker Looks at the United States. By Newman Bumstead. 705-748, June 1951
    Included: Grand Teton National Park, Jackson, Jackson Hole, Jackson Lake, Jenny Lake, Teton Range

WYOMING — *Continued*

Riding the Outlaw Trail. By Robert Redford. Photos by Jonathan Blair. 622-657, Nov. 1976

Wyoming: High, Wide, and Windy. By David S. Boyer. 554-594, Apr. 1966

Wyoming Muck Tells of Battle: Ice Age Man vs. Mammoth. By Cynthia Irwin, Henry Irwin, and George Agogino. 828-837, June 1962

See also Grand Teton National Park; Jackson Hole; Padlock Ranch; Pryor Mountain Wild Horse Range; Wind River Range; Yellowstone National Park

X

X-1:

Flying in the "Blowtorch" Era. By Frederick G. Vosburgh. 281-322, Sept. 1950

X-15:

I Fly the X-15. By Joseph A. Walker. Photos by Dean Conger. 428-450, Sept. 1962

X RAYS:

The Incredible Universe. By Kenneth F. Weaver. Photos by James P. Blair. 589-625, May 1974

Rockets Explore the Air Above Us. By Newman Bumstead. 562-580, Apr. 1957

The Sun. By Herbert Friedman. 713-743, Nov. 1965

The Sun As Never Seen Before. By Edward G. Gibson. 494-503, Oct. 1974

See also Photography, X-Ray

XINGU NATIONAL PARK, Brazil:

Amazon — The River Sea. By Loren McIntyre. 456-495, Oct. 1972

Brazil's Txukahameis: Good-bye to the Stone Age. Photos by W. Jesco von Puttkamer. 270-283, Feb. 1975

Saving Brazil's Stone Age Tribes From Extinction. By Orlando and Claudio Villas Boas. Photos by W. Jesco von Puttkamer. 424-444, Sept. 1968

The Waurá: Brazilian Indians of the Hidden Xingu. By Harald Schultz. 130-152, Jan. 1966

Y

YWCA: International Success Story. By Mary French Rockefeller. Photos by Otis Imboden. 904-933, Dec. 1963

See also Young Women's Christian Association

YACHTING:

Baltic Cruise of the *Caribbee*. By Carleton Mitchell. 605-646, Nov. 1950
    Included: Sandhamn Regatta Week

The British Way. By Sir Evelyn Wrench. 421-541, Apr. 1949
    Included: Cowes: Cradle of Yachting

"Delmarva," Gift of the Sea. By Catherine Bell Palmer. 367-399, Sept. 1950
    Included: Cambridge Yacht Club's championship races for Hampton-class sloops; and log canoe, *Jay Dee*, racing on the Choptank

Down East Cruise. By Tom Horgan. Photos by Luis Marden. 329-369, Sept. 1952

Down East to Nova Scotia. By Winfield Parks. 853-879, June 1964
    Included: Marblehead-Halifax race, Bras d'Or

YACHTING — *Continued*

McCurdy Cup race, Jones Trophy

Inside Europe Aboard *Yankee*. By Irving and Electa Johnson. Photos by Joseph J. Scherschel. 157-195, Aug. 1964
Included: Fastnet race

More of Sea Than of Land: The Bahamas. By Carleton Mitchell. Photos by James L. Stanfield. 218-267, Feb. 1967
Included: Out-Island Regatta

To Europe with a Racing Start. By Carleton Mitchell. 758-791, June 1958
Included: Newport-to-Bermuda race

Windjamming Around New England. By Tom Horgan. Photos by Robert F. Sisson. 141-169, Aug. 1950
Contents: Weekly regattas of Cape Cod in the summer, the annual Provincetown-Wellfleet competition, Squam Day Regatta on Ipswich Bay, and Race Week at Marblehead

YACHTS. *See Argyll; Betelgeuse; Britannia; Carib; Caribbee; Delight; Elsie; Finisterre; Great Britain II; Mah Jong; Nomad; Tectona; Tradewinds; White Mist; Yankee* (Brigantine); *Yankee* (Ketch)

YACHTS, Sand. *See Sand Yachts*

YAMPA (River), Colorado:

Shooting Rapids in Dinosaur Country. By Jack Breed. Photos by author and Justin Locke. 363-390, Mar. 1954

YANGTZE (River and Basin), China:

Along the Yangtze, Main Street of China. By W. Robert Moore. 325-356, Mar. 1948

YANKEE (Brigantine):

Lost World of the Galapagos. By Irving and Electa Johnson. 681-703, May 1959

New Guinea to Bali in *Yankee*. By Irving and Electa Johnson. 767-815, Dec. 1959

Saga of a Ship, the *Yankee*. By Luis Marden. 263-269, Feb. 1966

The Voyage of the Brigantine *Yankee* (Television film). 265A-265B, Feb. 1966

Yankee Roams the Orient. By Irving and Electa Johnson. 327-370, Mar. 1951

The *Yankee*'s Wander-world. By Irving and Electa Johnson. 1-50, Jan. 1949

YANKEE (Ketch):

Inside Europe Aboard *Yankee*. By Irving and Electa Johnson. Photos by Joseph J. Scherschel. 157-195, Aug. 1964

Yankee Cruises the Storied Nile. By Irving and Electa Johnson. Photos by Winfield Parks. 583-633, May 1965

Yankee Cruises Turkey's History-haunted Coast. By Irving and Electa Johnson. Photos by Joseph J. Scherschel. 798-845, Dec. 1969

Yankee Sails Across Europe (Television film). 469A-469B, Apr. 1967

The **YANKEE** Sailor Who Opened Japan: Commodore Perry. By Ferdinand Kuhn. 85-102, July 1953

YANOMAMO, the True People. By Napoleon A. Chagnon. 211-223, Aug. 1976

YAP ISLANDS, Caroline Islands, Pacific Ocean:

Grass-skirted Yap. By W. Robert Moore. 805-830, Dec. 1952

YAP ISLANDS, Caroline Islands, Pacific Ocean — *Continued*

Micronesia: The Americanization of Eden. By David S. Boyer. 702-744, May 1967

Pacific Wards of Uncle Sam. By W. Robert Moore. 73-104, July 1948

YASSI ADA (Island), Turkey:

New Tools for Undersea Archeology. By George F. Bass. Photos by Charles R. Nicklin, Jr. 403-423, Sept. 1968

Thirty-three Centuries Under the Sea. By Peter Throckmorton. 682-703, May 1960

Underwater Archeology: Key to History's Warehouse. By George F. Bass. Photos by Thomas J. Abercrombie and Robert B. Goodman. 138-156, July 1963

YAWLS. *See Argyll; Caribbee; Delight; Elsie; Finisterre; Mah Jong; White Mist*

YEAR of Discovery Opens in Antarctica. By David S. Boyer. 339-381, Sept. 1957

A **YEAR** of Widening Horizons: The President's Message to Members. By Melville Bell Grosvenor. 888-906, Dec. 1962

YELLOW FEVER:

Exploring Ancient Panama by Helicopter. By Matthew W. Stirling. Photos by Richard H. Stewart. 227-246, Feb. 1950

Keeping House for a Biologist in Colombia. By Nancy Bell Fairchild Bates. Photos by Marston Bates. 251-274, Aug. 1948

YELLOWSTONE NATIONAL PARK, U. S.:

Grizzly! (Television film). 639A-639B, Nov. 1967

Knocking Out Grizzly Bears for Their Own Good. By Frank and John Craighead. 276-291, Aug. 1960

The "Lone" Coyote Likes Family Life. By Hope Ryden. Photos by author and David Hiser. 278-294, Aug. 1974

The Night the Mountains Moved. By Samuel W. Matthews. Photos by J. Baylor Roberts. 329-359, Mar. 1960

Springtime Comes to Yellowstone National Park. By Paul A. Zahl. 761-779, Dec. 1956

Studying Wildlife by Satellite. By Frank Craighead, Jr. and John Craighead. 120-123, Jan. 1973

Trailing Yellowstone's Grizzlies by Radio. By Frank Craighead, Jr. and John Craighead. 252-267, Aug. 1966

The West Through Boston Eyes. By Stewart Anderson. 733-776, June 1949

Wyoming: High, Wide, and Windy. By David S. Boyer. 554-594, Apr. 1966

Yellowstone Wildlife in Winter. By William Albert Allard. 637-661, Nov. 1967

Yellowstone's Hundredth Birthday: A Four-part Report. 579-637, May 1972
I. A Walk Through the Wilderness. By Karen and Derek Craighead. Photos by Sam Abell. 579-603
II. Ageless Splendors of Our Oldest Park. 604-615
III. The Pitfalls of Success. By William S. Ellis. Photos by Jonathan Blair. 616-631
IV. The Next 100 Years: A Master Plan for Yellowstone. By George B. Hartzog, Jr. 632-637

YEMEN:

Behind the Veil of Troubled Yemen. By Thomas J. Abercrombie. 403-445, Mar. 1964

Yemen—Southern Arabia's Mountain Wonderland. By Harlan B. Clark. 631-672, Nov. 1947
Ancient "Skyscrapers" of the Yemen. Photos by Richard H. Sanger. 645-668

Yemen Opens the Door to Progress. By Harry Hoogstraal. 213-244, Feb. 1952

YEMEN, Democratic. *See* former name, Aden

YEN, HARRY S. C.: Photographer:

The Fragile Beauty All About Us. 785-795, Dec. 1970

YESTERDAY Lingers Along the Connecticut. By Charles McCarry. Photos by David L. Arnold. 334-369, Sept. 1972

YESTERDAY'S Congo, Today's Zaire. By John J. Putman. Photos by Eliot Elisofon. 398-432, Mar. 1973

YLLA (Camilla Koffler): Photographer:

Mysore Celebrates the Death of a Demon. By Luc Bouchage. 706-711, May 1958

YOGYAKARTA, Java. *See* Djokjakarta

YOHO NATIONAL PARK, British Columbia, Canada. *See* Great Divide Trail

YOSEMITE NATIONAL PARK, California:

Climbing Half Dome the Hard Way. By Galen Rowell. 782-791, June 1974

John Muir's Wild America. By Harvey Arden. Photos by Dewitt Jones. 433-461, Apr. 1973

New Rush to Golden California. By George W. Long. 723-802, June 1954

The Other Yosemite. By Nathaniel T. Kenney. Photos by Dean Conger. 762-781, June 1974

Yosemite National Park. 491-498, Apr. 1951

YOU and the Obedient Atom. By Allan C. Fisher, Jr. 303-353, Sept. 1958

YOU Can't Miss America by Bus. By Howell Walker. Paintings by Walter A. Weber. 1-42, July 1950

YOUNG, GAVIN: Author:

Water Dwellers in a Desert World. Photos by Nik Wheeler. 502-523, Apr. 1976

YOUNG, GORDON: Author:

Chile, Republic on a Shoestring. Photos by George F. Mobley. 437-477, Oct. 1973

The Great Lakes: Is It Too Late? Photos by James L. Amos and Martin Rogers. 147-185, Aug. 1973

Great Smokies National Park: Solitude for Millions. Photos by James L. Amos. 522-549, Oct. 1968

Hawaii, Island of Fire and Flowers. Photos by Robert W. Madden. 399-425, Mar. 1975

"How Man Pollutes His World," painting supplement. Map on reverse. Dec. 1970

Pollution, Threat to Man's Only Home. Photos by James P. Blair. 738-781, Dec. 1970

Sailors of the Sky. Photos by Emory Kristof and Jack Fields. Paintings by Davis Meltzer. 49-73, Jan. 1967

That Dammed Missouri River. Photos by David Hiser. 374-413, Sept. 1971

YOUNG, GORDON: Author—*Continued*

Whatever Happened to TVA? Photos by Emory Kristof. 830-863, June 1973

Will Coal Be Tomorrow's "Black Gold"? Photos by James P. Blair. 234-259, Aug. 1975

YOUNG-OLD Lebanon Lives by Trade. By Thomas J. Abercrombie. 479-523, Apr. 1958

YOUNG WOMEN'S CHRISTIAN ASSOCIATION (YWCA):

Parks, Plans, and People: How South America Guards Her Green Legacy. By Mary and Laurance Rockefeller. Photos by George F. Mobley. 74-119, Jan. 1967

YWCA: International Success Story. By Mary French Rockefeller. Photos by Otis Imboden. 904-933, Dec. 1963

YOUR National Gallery of Art After 10 Years. By John Walker. Paintings from Kress Collection. 73-103, Jan. 1952

YOUR Society Observes Eclipse in Brazil. 661, May 1947

YOUR Society Takes Giant New Steps: The President's Annual Message to Members. By Melville Bell Grosvenor. 874-886, Dec. 1961

YOUR Society to Seek New Light on the Cliff Dwellers. 154-156, Jan. 1959

YOUR Society's President Reports: A Year of Widening Horizons. By Melville Bell Grosvenor. 888-906, Dec. 1962

YOUTH. *See* Boy Scouts; 4-H Clubs; Hostels; Peace Corps; Students; Young Women's Christian Association

YUCATÁN PENINSULA, Mexico:

The Maya. 729-811, Dec. 1975
I. Children of Time. By Howard La Fay. Photos by David Alan Harvey. 729-767
Included: Archeological sites: Becan, Chichén Itzá, Dzibilchaltun, Jaina Island, Tancah, Tulum, Uxmal; present-day Maya of Xcobenhaltun and elsewhere
II. Riddle of the Glyphs. By George E. Stuart. Photos by Otis Imboden. 768-791
Included: Cobá; Kohunlich; Tancah
See also Chichén Itzá; Dzibilchaltun; Mujeres, Isla; "Pyramids" of the New World

YUGOSLAVIA:

The Balkans, Atlas series supplement. Feb. 1962

Down the Danube by Canoe. By William Slade Backer. Photos by Richard S. Durrance and Christopher G. Knight. 34-79, July 1965

Yugoslavia, Between East and West. By George W. Long. Photos by Volkmar Wentzel. 141-172, Feb. 1951

Yugoslavia: Six Republics in One. By Robert Paul Jordan. Photos by James P. Blair. 589-633, May 1970
Contents: Bosnia-Hercegovina; Croatia; Macedonia; Montenegro; Serbia; Slovenia

Yugoslavia's Window on the Adriatic. By Gilbert M. Grosvenor. 219-247, Feb. 1962

See also Trieste

YUKON (River), Canada-Alaska:

Rafting Down the Yukon. By Keith Tryck. Photos by Robert Clark. 830-861, Dec. 1975

YUKON (River), Canada-Alaska—*Continued*
Squaws Along the Yukon. By Ginny Hill Wood. 245-265, Aug. 1957

YUKON TERRITORY, Canada:
Along the Yukon Trail. By Amos Burg. 395-416, Sept. 1953
The Canadian North: Emerging Giant. By David S. Boyer. 1-43, July 1968
Rafting Down the Yukon. By Keith Tryck. Photos by Robert Clark. 830-861, Dec. 1975
Squaws Along the Yukon. By Ginny Hill Wood. 245-265, Aug. 1957
See also Kennedy, Mount; St. Elias, Mount

YUNGKI (Kirin), China. *See* Chilin

YUNNAN (Province), China. *See* Kunming

Z

ZAGREB, Yugoslavia:
Yugoslavia, Between East and West. By George W. Long. Photos by Volkmar Wentzel. 141-172, Feb. 1951
Yugoslavia: Six Republics in One. By Robert Paul Jordan. Photos by James P. Blair. 589-633, May 1970

ZAHL, PAUL A.: Author-Photographer:
Algae: the Life-givers. 361-377, Mar. 1974
Australia's Bizarre Wild Flowers. 858-868, Dec. 1976
Back-yard Monsters in Color. 235-260, Aug. 1952
Bizarre World of the Fungi. 502-527, Oct. 1965
Exotic Birds in Manhattan's Bowery. 77-98, Jan. 1953
Face to Face With Gorillas in Central Africa. 114-137, Jan. 1960
Finding the Mt. Everest of All Living Things. 10-51, July 1964
Fishing in the Whirlpool of Charybdis. 579-618, Nov. 1953
Flamingos' Last Stand on Andros Island. 635-652, May 1951
Fluorescent Gems From Davy Jones's Locker. 260-271, Aug. 1963
Giant Insects of the Amazon. 632-669, May 1959
The Giant Tides of Fundy. 153-192, Aug. 1957
Glass Menageries of the Sea. 797-822, June 1955
Hatchetfish, Torchbearers of the Deep. 713-714, May 1958
Hidden Worlds in the Heart of a Plant. 389-397, Mar. 1975
Honey Eaters of Currumbin. 510-519, Oct. 1956
How the Sun Gives Life to the Sea. 199-225, Feb. 1961
In Quest of the World's Largest Frog. 146-152, July 1967
In the Gardens of Olympus. 85-123, July 1955
In the Wilds of a City Parlor. 645-672, Nov. 1954
Life in a "Dead" Sea—Great Salt Lake. 252-263, Aug. 1967
Little Horses of the Sea. 131-153, Jan. 1959
The Magic Lure of Sea Shells. Photos by Victor R. Boswell, Jr. and author. 386-429, Mar. 1969
Malaysia's Giant Flowers and Insect-trapping Plants. 680-701, May 1964

ZAHL, PAUL A.: Author-Photographer—*Continued*
Man-of-war Fleet Attacks Bimini. 185-212, Feb. 1952
Mountains of the Moon. 412-434, Mar. 1962
Mystery of the Monarch Butterfly. 588-598, Apr. 1963
Nature's Living, Jumping Jewels. 130-146, July 1973
Nature's Night Lights: Probing the Secrets of Bioluminescence. 45-69, July 1971
Nature's Year in Pleasant Valley. 488-525, Apr. 1968
New Scarlet Bird in Florida Skies. 874-882, Dec. 1967
Night Life in the Gulf Stream. 391-418, Mar. 1954
On Australia's Coral Ramparts. 1-48, Jan. 1957
One Strange Night on Turtle Beach. 570-581, Oct. 1973
Oregon's Sidewalk on the Sea. 708-734, Nov. 1961
The Pink Birds of Texas. 641-654, Nov. 1949
Plants That Eat Insects. 643-659, May 1961
Portrait of a Fierce and Fragile Land. 303-314, Mar. 1972
Sailing a Sea of Fire. 120-129, July 1960
Scorpions: Living Fossils of the Sands. 436-442, Mar. 1968
Search for the Scarlet Ibis in Venezuela. 633-661, May 1950
Seeking the Truth About the Feared Piranha. 715-733, Nov. 1970
The Shadowy World of Salamanders. 104-117, July 1972
Springtime Comes to Yellowstone National Park. 761-779, Dec. 1956
Those Outlandish Goldfish! 514-533, Apr. 1973
Unsung Beauties of Hawaii's Coral Reefs. 510-525, Oct. 1959
Volcanic Fires of the 50th State: Hawaii National Park. 793-823, June 1959
What's So Special About Spiders? 190-219, Aug. 1971
Wing-borne Lamps of the Summer Night. 48-59, July 1962

Photographer
"Snowflake," the World's First White Gorilla. By Arthur J. Riopelle. 443-448, Mar. 1967

ZAIRE, Republic of:
Yesterday's Congo, Today's Zaire. By John J. Putman. Photos by Eliot Elisofon. 398-432, Mar. 1973
See also Virunga Mountains; *and* former name, Congo, Democratic Republic of the

ZANTE (Island), Greece:
Homeward With Ulysses. By Melville Bell Grosvenor. Photos by Edwin Stuart Grosvenor. 1-39, July 1973

ZANZIBAR:
Clove-scented Zanzibar. By W. Robert Moore. 261-278, Feb. 1952
Safari from Congo to Cairo. By Elsie May Bell Grosvenor. Photos by Gilbert Grosvenor. 721-771, Dec. 1954
Tanzania Marches to Its Own Drum. By Peter T. White. Photos by Emory Kristof. 474-509, Apr. 1975

ZANZIBAR—*Continued*

Yankee Roams the Orient. By Irving and Electa Johnson. 327-370, Mar. 1951

ZEN BUDDHISM:

Kyoto and Nara: Keepers of Japan's Past. By Charles McCarry. Photos by George F. Mobley. 836-859, June 1976
Kyoto Says Happy New Year. 852-859

ZIMBABWE, Rhodesia:

Safari Through Changing Africa. By Elsie May Bell Grosvenor. Photos by Gilbert Grosvenor. 145-198, Aug. 1953

ZINJANTHROPUS (Near-man):

Finding the World's Earliest Man. By L. S. B. Leakey. Photos by Des Bartlett. 420-435, Sept. 1960
Preserving the Treasures of Olduvai Gorge. By Melvin M. Payne. Photos by Joseph J. Scherschel. 701-709, Nov. 1966
See also Australopithecus

ZION NATIONAL PARK, Utah:

Amid the Mighty Walls of Zion. By Lewis F. Clark. 37-70, Jan. 1954

ZOOS:

Jambo—First Gorilla Raised by Its Mother in Captivity. By Ernst M. Lang. Photos by Paul Steinemann. 446-453, Mar. 1964
Included: The Zoological Gardens of Basel, Switzerland

ZOOS—*Continued*

London's Zoo of Zoos. By Thomas Garner James. 771-786, June 1953
Included: Regent's Park; Whipsnade

Zoo Animals Go to School. By Marion P. McCrane. Photos by W. E. Garrett. 694-706, Nov. 1956
Contents: Animals from New York Zoological Park (Bronx Zoo)

Zoos of the World (Television film). 503A-503B, Oct. 1970

See also Barcelona Zoo; Central Park, New York; National Zoological Park, Washington, D. C.; New York Zoological Park; *and* Animal Orphanage; Animal Safari

ZULULAND (Region), South Africa:

Safari Through Changing Africa. By Elsie May Bell Grosvenor. Photos by Gilbert Grosvenor. 145-198, Aug. 1953
The Zulus: Black Nation in a Land of Apartheid. By Joseph Judge. Photos by Dick Durrance II. 738-775, Dec. 1971
See also Hluhluwe Game Reserve

ZUMBACH, EARL:

The Family Farm Ain't What It Used to Be. By James A. Sugar. 391-411, Sept. 1974

ZÜRICH, Switzerland:

Switzerland, Europe's High-rise Republic. By Thomas J. Abercrombie. 68-113, July 1969